KU-480-738

Other Microsoft .NET resources from O'Reilly

Related titles

Excel 2003 Programming: A Developer's Notebook

Excel Hacks™

Excel Annoyances™

Excel: The Missing Manual

Integrating Excel and Access

Analyzing Business Data with Excel

VB and VBA in a Nutshell: The Language

Excel 2003 Personal Trainer

Excel Scientific and Engineering Cookbook™

Writing Excel Macros with VBA

Office 2003 XML

.NET Books Resource Center

dotnet.oreilly.com is a complete catalog of O'Reilly's books on .NET and related technologies, including sample chapters and code examples.

ONDotnet.com provides independent coverage of fundamental, interoperable, and emerging Microsoft .NET programming and web services technologies.

Conferences

O'Reilly brings diverse innovators together to nurture the ideas that spark revolutionary industries. We specialize in documenting the latest tools and systems, translating the innovator's knowledge into useful skills for those in the trenches. Visit *conferences.oreilly.com* for our upcoming events.

Safari Bookshelf (*safari.oreilly.com*) is the premier online reference library for programmers and IT professionals. Conduct searches across more than 1,000 books. Subscribers can zero in on answers to time-critical questions in a matter of seconds. Read the books on your Bookshelf from cover to cover or simply flip to the page you need. Try it today for free.

Programming Excel with VBA and .NET

Programming Excel with VBA and .NET

Jeff Webb and Steve Saunders

O'REILLY®

Beijing · Cambridge · Farnham · Köln · Paris · Sebastopol · Taipei · Tokyo

Programming Excel with VBA and .NET
by Jeff Webb and Steve Saunders

Copyright © 2006 O'Reilly Media, Inc. All rights reserved.
Printed in the United States of America.

Published by O'Reilly Media, Inc., 1005 Gravenstein Highway North, Sebastopol, CA 95472.

O'Reilly books may be purchased for educational, business, or sales promotional use. Online editions are also available for most titles (*safari.oreilly.com*). For more information, contact our corporate/institutional sales department: (800) 998-9938 or *corporate@oreilly.com*.

Editors: Simon St.Laurent, John Osborn	**Cover Designer:** Karen Montgomery
Production Editor: Sanders Kleinfeld	**Interior Designer:** David Futato
Copyeditor: Norma Emory	**Illustrators:** Robert Romano, Jessamyn Read,
Indexer: Ellen Troutman-Zaig	and Lesley Borash

Printing History:

April 2006:	First Edition.

ISBN: 0-596-00766-3
[M]

Table of Contents

Part I.   Learning VBA

Preface

I was lucky enough to be at Microsoft when Visual Basic was added to Excel. I had just wrapped up working on OLE Automation—the technology used to make Excel objects programmable—and I remember that meetings with the Excel group were, at times, difficult. Why should a premier Microsoft product like Excel put so much effort into adding a low-profit item like Visual Basic when it already had a macro language?

"Because BillG said so" takes you only so far, even at Microsoft. The facts are that programmability doesn't sell products the way some other whizbang feature might, it adds risk to delivering the product bug-free and on time, and (we found out) it poses a security hazard.

What programmability *does* do is make your product a platform for others. Today, Excel is the foundation for probably millions of small spreadsheet-based software solutions and is used by certainly thousands of very large and sophisticated applications. *That* sells products.

It also makes the skill of programming Excel extremely valuable. The community of Excel programmers is large, knowledgeable, and (I hope) well paid.

Learn by Doing

There are always new Excel programmers joining our ranks. If you are new to Excel or new to programming, I welcome you. This book isn't a beginner series, but if you read the early chapters and are motivated, I think you'll find this book a great way to learn a lot very quickly.

If you are an experienced Excel user or a Visual Basic programmer, howdy! I've got a lot to show you.

Don't Force It

If you get stuck, there are a number of ways to resume your progress:

- Try turning on macro recording (Tools → Macros → Record a New Macro), performing the task in Excel, and then turning off recording and examining the code that Excel generates.
- Search MSDN (*http://www.microsoft.com/msdn*) to see if Microsoft has addressed your problem.
- Search newsgroups (*http://groups.google.com/groups*) to see if someone else has solved your problem.
- And of course, you can always check *http://excelworkshop.com* to see if I've solved the problem!

If something still seems too difficult, examine your approach. I generally go fishing in that situation and come back to the problem later. If you don't live somewhere with good fishing, I guess you're just stuck.

Excel Versions

This book was developed with Excel 2003 Professional Edition and is designed to be compatible with Excel 2000 and later. If a feature is not available in Excel 2000, I make an effort to note that, but if you are developing for a specific version of Excel, please check Appendix B for specific version compatibility and read Chapter 6 for information on developing design requirements and testing for compatibility.

If you are developing with .NET, I strongly recommend that you target Excel 2003 or later. The code shown in this book is written in the Visual Basic Applications Edition, but parallel .NET samples are provided online (see the next section).

Get the Samples

The samples for this book are available at *http://excelworkshop.com*. You'll need them, so go get them now. The examples come in a Windows compressed folder (*.zip*) that you'll need to expand on your computer.

The samples are organized by chapter, and each chapter has parallel samples written as Visual Studio .NET projects. Each chapter uses one main workbook (*ch01.xls*, *ch02.xls*, etc.) as a starting point to provide instructions and navigation.

What's in This Book

Chapters in this book are organized by programming task. I cover the most common tasks for each subject within a chapter. Subjects usually correspond to one or more

Excel objects, and I include important reference information for those objects within each chapter, rather than pushing that information to the back of the book.

 I don't expect this book will be your only resource, and I try not to duplicate stuff you already have (like online Help), so I include cross-references to other sources. I've also included those resources as hyperlinks in the sample workbooks (see the Resources sheet). Mostly, those links deal with much more specific issues related to the topic, but they also include links to toolkits and other software you may need.

Here is a brief overview of each chapter:

- Chapter 1, *Becoming an Excel Programmer*, is meant for those new to Excel programming. It covers how to record, change, run, and debug code in the Excel Visual Basic Editor. Experienced Excel programmers can skip this chapter, although they may want to read the section "Write Bug-Free Code."

- Chapter 2, *Knowing the Basics*, explains the parts of a program: classes, modules, procedures, properties, events, variables, constants, and all the other programming fundamentals. Experienced programmers might want to skip right to "Objects" and "Exceptions" in this chapter.

- Chapter 3, *Tasks in Visual Basic*, teaches how to use core Visual Basic features to display simple dialog boxes, perform calculations, work with text, read and write files, check results, and run other applications. Experienced readers will be most interested in the section "Compare Bits."

- Chapter 4, *Using Excel Objects*, shows you how objects work and helps you find the right object for any given task in Excel. The object diagrams in this chapter are a road map to the many objects that Excel provides. This is the first place to look when searching for the appropriate object for a particular task.

- Chapter 5, *Creating Your Own Objects*, goes in-depth about object-oriented programming (OOP). You'll learn how to construct classes, methods, properties, collections, and events. I also explain why it is important to destroy your creations once you are done using them.

- Chapter 6, *Writing Code for Use by Others*, is about taking your skills to the next level. I cover the types of applications you can create, explain the development process, and show how to properly deploy a completed application.

- Chapter 7, *Controlling Excel*, begins the task-specific part of this book. It shows how to use the top-level Application object to open and close Excel windows, display dialogs, and get references to other Excel objects.

- Chapter 8, *Opening, Saving, and Sharing Workbooks*, teaches you how to work with Excel document files (workbooks). As a bonus, I cover how to work with XML and use SharePoint workspaces from Excel.

- Chapter 9, *Working with Worksheets and Ranges*, covers the two most-used objects in Excel. Almost everything you do in Excel involves worksheets and ranges in some way.

- Chapter 10, *Linking and Embedding*, discusses how to add comments, hyperlinks, and objects from other applications to a worksheet. I also show how to make Excel speak out loud—weird but true!

- Chapter 11, *Printing and Publishing*, is about sending output to the printer or the Web. I show how to control paging, change printer settings, filter output, preview results, and publish ranges to a web page.

- Chapter 12, *Loading and Manipulating Data*, is all about connecting to databases. I show how to use Query Tables and use the ADO and DAO object models.

- Chapter 13, *Analyzing Data with Pivot Tables*, shows how to program with one of Excel's most celebrated features. I show how to reorganize data from a wide variety of data sources, including OLAP data cubes.

- Chapter 14, *Sharing Data Using Lists*, goes into detail on one of Excel's newest features: data lists. I show how to use them to sort, filter, and even share lists across the network through SharePoint.

- Chapter 15, *Working with XML*, is also a ground-breaker, by showing how to convert XML datafiles into Excel workbooks and vice versa. I provide a brief introduction to XML and XSL, then dive to the heart of how to import XML data to lists through XML maps.

- Chapter 16, *Charting*, covers how to create different types of charts and control the main parts of a chart. Charting is a large and complex topic in Excel, so I also include a road map to the chart objects.

- Chapter 17, *Formatting Charts*, explains how to control the fonts, backgrounds, and 3-D effects used on a chart. It is the companion to Chapter 16.

- Chapter 18, *Drawing Graphics*, is really just for fun. Excel's drawing tools let you create diagrams and other graphics from data, but you need to know about a couple gotchas. I cover those here.

- Chapter 19, *Adding Menus and Toolbars*, helps you hook your application into the Excel user interface. I also show how to distribute the menus and toolbars with your code.

- Chapter 20, *Building Dialog Boxes*, is about creating data entry and User Forms to get input or display results to users. I cover the controls included in the Microsoft Forms libraries here.

- Chapter 21, *Sending and Receiving Workbooks*, shows all the ways to send email from Excel.

- Chapter 22, *Building Add-Ins*, covers how to create and distribute your program as an Excel Add-In. This chapter begins the advanced programming material.

- Chapter 23, *Integrating DLLs and COM*, shows how to use code from Windows itself or other applications within your Excel programs.

- Chapter 24, *Getting Data From the Web*, explains how to scrape data from web pages using web queries and how to execute web services to perform tasks remotely across a network.

- Chapter 25, *Programming Excel with .NET*, teaches how to use .NET code from within Excel, use Excel code from .NET, or integrate between Excel and .NET using Visual Studio Tools for Office (VSTO).

- Chapter 26, *Exploring Security in Depth*, discusses Windows security, encryption, passwords, protection, and Information Rights Management (IRM) within Excel. I also show how well (or poorly) certain security features perform.

Font Conventions

This book follows certain conventions for font usage. Understanding these conventions up front makes it easier to use this book.

Italic is used for:

- Pathnames, filenames, program names, compilers, options, and commands
- New terms where they are defined
- Internet addresses, such as domain names and URLs

`Constant width` is used for:

- Anything that appears literally in a Visual Basic program, including keywords, data types, constants, method names, variables, class names, and interface names
- Command lines and options that should be typed verbatim on the screen
- All code listings
- HTML documents, tags, and attributes

`Constant width italic` is used for:

- General placeholders that indicate that an item is replaced by some actual value in your own program

`Constant width bold` is used for:

- Text in code examples that is typed by the user
- Highlighting code additions or changes that should be noted by the reader

This icon designates a note, which is an important aside to the nearby text.

This icon designates a warning relating to the nearby text.

Syntax Conventions

Books about computer languages require a way to express the kinds of information you need to provide on one or more lines as you type. That is called the syntax of the language and Backus-Naur Form (BNF) is the format used in this book and most others. In BNF notation, the following conventions apply:

Example	Meaning
Keyword	Roman (non-italic) words are keywords that must be typed exactly as shown.
Argument	Italics indicate an item you must provide, such as an object variable a setting.
[ ]	Square brackets indicate an optional item.
*choice1	choice2*	A straight bar indicates a choice between two or more items.
{*choice1	choice2*}	Braces indicate that you must choose one of the indicated settings.
[*choice1	choice2*]	Square brackets indicate that the choice is optional.

These conventions are used in headings within the reference sections of this book and also within the text sometimes. You'll also see them in the online help from Microsoft.

Using Code Examples

This book is here to help you get your job done. In general, you may use the code in this book in your programs and documentation. You do not need to contact us for permission unless you're reproducing a significant portion of the code. For example, writing a program that uses several chunks of code from this book does not require permission. Selling or distributing a CD-ROM of examples from O'Reilly books *does* require permission. Answering a question by citing this book and quoting example code does not require permission. Incorporating a significant amount of example code from this book into your product's documentation *does* require permission.

We appreciate, but do not require, attribution. An attribution usually includes the title, author, publisher, and ISBN. For example: "*Programming Excel with VBA and .NET*, by Jeff Webb and Steve Saunders. Copyright 2006 O'Reilly Media, Inc., 0-596-00766-3."

If you feel your use of code examples falls outside fair use or the permission given above, feel free to contact us at *permissions@oreilly.com*.

Safari® Enabled

 When you see a Safari® Enabled icon on the cover of your favorite technology book, that means the book is available online through the O'Reilly Network Safari Bookshelf.

Safari offers a solution that's better than e-books. It's a virtual library that lets you easily search thousands of top tech books, cut and paste code samples, download chapters, and find quick answers when you need the most accurate, current information. Try it for free at *http://safari.oreilly.com*.

How to Contact Us

Please address comments and questions concerning this book to the publisher:

> O'Reilly Media, Inc.
> 1005 Gravenstein Highway North
> Sebastopol, CA 95472
> (800) 998-9938 (in the United States or Canada)
> (707) 829-0515 (international or local)
> (707) 829-0104 (fax)

We have a web page for this book, where we list errata, examples, or any additional information. You can access this page at:

> *http://www.oreilly.com/catalog/progexcel/*

To comment or ask technical questions about this book, send email to:

> *bookquestions@oreilly.com*

For more information about our books, conferences, Resource Centers, and the O'Reilly Network, see our web site at:

> *http://www.oreilly.com/*

Acknowledgments

It takes a long time and a great deal of help to write a book this big. I would like to thank Steve Saunders for joining the effort and contributing Chapters 9 and 12. Steve and I go back a very long way, through years at Microsoft and Digital Equipment Corp. Steve's an Access expert and a great writer, and he sings well, too.

I'd also like to thank Simon St.Laurent for his work throughout the project. We've done four books together now—that's close to 2000 pages. Finishing this together is like climbing a mountain: his company improved the ascent and it's great to stand with him here at the summit. Nice view.

Learning VBA

These chapters teach you how to write professional-quality code using Excel Visual Basic (VBA). This is more than an entry-level tutorial to a macro language: it's a full set of lessons for readers who are serious about programming. Once you've finished these chapters, you'll be ready to program Excel, Word, or any other application that exposes objects to Visual Basic.

Becoming an Excel Programmer

How do you become an excellent Excel programmer? The first step for most folks is to buy a book. I'm glad you bought this one. Next, you've got to learn the programming tools that Excel provides. Visual Basic is ideally suited as a learning tool because it lets you get started without a lot of pedagogical preparation. That's an alliterative way of saying that you can learn the rules as you go.

So let's go!

 Code used in this chapter and additional samples are available in *ch01.xls*.

Why Program?

Excel is a mature product with every imaginable feature—doesn't it do everything it needs to already? Excel *is* amazingly complete, but programming Excel isn't really about adding new features as much as it is about combining existing features to solve specific problems.

Excel is a platform for solving complex calculations and presenting results. Programming transforms that general platform into a task-specific piece of software. The phrase *task-specific piece of software* is kind of a mouthful, and most folks use the word *solution* instead. In my opinion, that's awfully vague but probably better than a new acronym.

The reason to program Excel is to make some task easier or more reliable. Programming languages make things easier because they are great at performing repetitive operations and following a logical path without getting tired or bored. They make things more reliable because they slavishly follow your directions and never, ever get creative.

Having such a devoted servant comes with a lot of responsibility, however. For instance, if you tell Excel to "lather, rinse, repeat" like it says on the back of a shampoo bottle, it's liable to scrub the hair right off your head since you never told it when to stop repeating. (Hint: if that ever happens to you, press Ctrl-Break and step out of the shower.)

You need to understand the basic rules common to all programming languages before you can write real programs in Excel (see Chapter 2). That's kind of dry stuff, though, so right now I'm going to jump ahead to something more fun.

Record and Read Code

The best way to learn about Excel objects, properties, and methods is by recording code. It's even better than online Help. Recording will almost always tell you what you need to know *if* you know how to use it. When Excel records code, it translates your actions into Visual Basic code. This lets you reverse-engineer recorded actions or simply cut and paste recorded actions into other procedures.

For example, suppose that you have a workbook containing multiple sheets of sales data as shown in Figure 1-1. You want to format the data on each of the sheets and add a chart comparing units sold and revenue. This is a great opportunity to record some code.

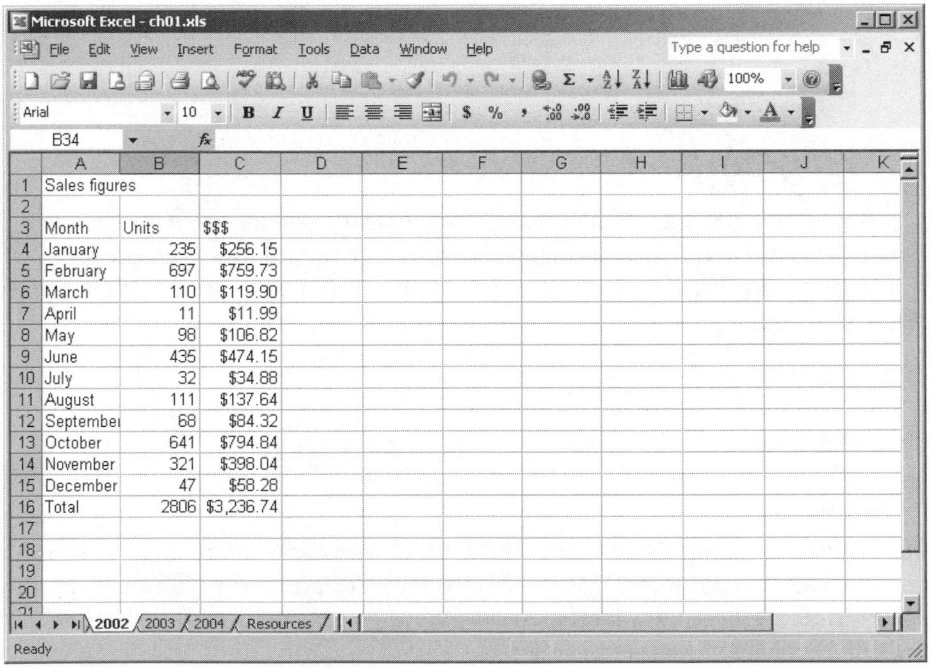

Figure 1-1. An example for recording code

To record your code:

1. Choose Tools → Macros → Record New Macro. Excel displays the Record Macro dialog (Figure 1-2).

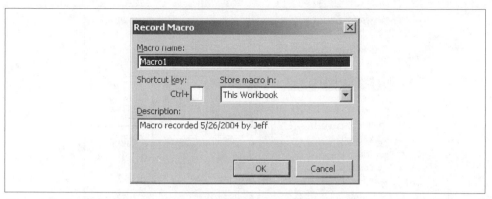

Figure 1-2. Step 1

2. Select the range A1:C16 and choose Format → AutoFormat. Excel displays the AutoFormat dialog (Figure 1-3).

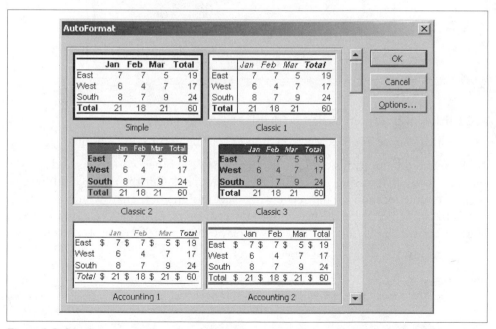

Figure 1-3. Step 2

3. Select the Simple format and click OK. Excel formats the range.

4. Press Shift-Up to deselect the Total row and then choose Insert → Chart. Excel displays the Chart Wizard (Figure 1-4).

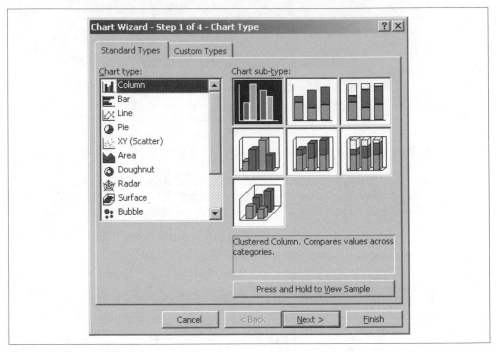

Figure 1-4. Step 4

5. Click Finish to insert a chart on the sheet as shown in Figure 1-5.

6. Finally, choose Tools → Macro → Stop Recording to turn off recording.

Now you could repeat this task by selecting one of the other worksheets and run the recorded code by pressing Alt-F8 and running Macro1, but the data would have to be in the same location on the active worksheet and the new chart would appear on the 2002 worksheet, not the active one. Instead, press Alt-F8 and click Edit. Excel starts the Visual Basic Editor (VBE) and displays your recorded code, as shown here:

```
Sub Macro1()      '<---------- Name of procedure.
'
' Macro1 Macro   <----------- Comments describing procedure.
' Macro recorded 5/26/2004 by Jeff
'


'
    Range("A1:C16").Select    '<---- Following lines record what you did.
    Selection.AutoFormat Format:=xlRangeAutoFormatSimple, Number:=True, Font _
        :=True, Alignment:=True, Border:=True, Pattern:=True, Width:=True
    Range("A1:C15").Select
```

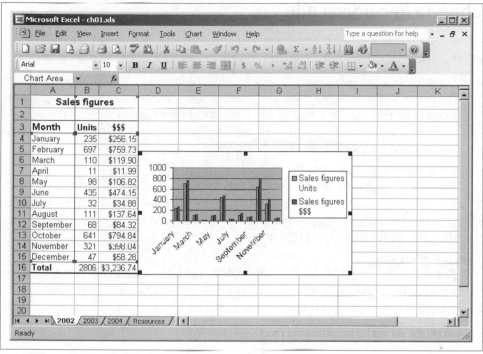

Figure 1-5. Step 5

```
        Charts.Add
        ActiveChart.ChartType = xlColumnClustered
        ActiveChart.SetSourceData Source:=Sheets("2002").Range("A1:C15"), PlotBy:= _
            xlColumns        ' Long lines are continued using an underscore ---------^
        ActiveChart.Location Where:=xlLocationAsObject, Name:="2002"
    End Sub                  '<---------- End of procedure.
```

I added some labels in the recorded code to identify its parts:

- Each procedure in a workbook has a unique name. Excel assigns the names Macro1, Macro2, and so on to recorded code.

- Anything that appears after ' is a comment. *Comments* are descriptive text that don't run as code.

- Lines of text that aren't comments are executable statements. *Statements* tell Visual Basic what to do in Excel.

- Lines that are longer than about 80 characters are continued on the next line using the _ character. Excel does that for readability. Actually, Visual Basic allows lines of code to be much longer if you don't mind horizontal scrolling.

- Procedures always include an End statement to tell Visual Basic where to stop.

So now that you've recorded code, what can you do with it? That's up next.

Change Recorded Code

Recorded code is a great way to learn, but it's not really a program. Real programs are much more flexible, and recorded code always has the following limitations:

Follows a linear path
> Excel can't infer logic from the user's actions—even if the user repeats an action, Excel only records the action twice. It doesn't know how to record "repeat until end" or "do this task if..." Excel can "replace all" and perform other global actions, but that's still linear logic.

Actions apply to the active item
> Excel bases recorded actions on whatever worksheet, range, or chart is currently selected by the user. If you want your code to work with other sheets or ranges, you need to either change the active selection or add object references that tell the code which items to work with.

Uses cell addresses
> For example, Range("A1:C16"). Although Excel keeps references on worksheets up-to-date, Excel can't update addresses in code. That means if your data is moved on the worksheet, the code won't work correctly. To fix this, use Excel range properties or named ranges instead of addresses in code.

Methods include all the default arguments
> That means lines of code are sometimes longer and more complicated than they really need to be. You can often simplify recording by removing unneeded default arguments.

Doesn't use variables
> Most programs create names to identify things that can change as the code executes. These names are called *variables*. Recorded code doesn't use variables because the logic is always linear—variables are required only if the code repeats or makes decisions.

So if you want the code you just recorded to repeat the formatting and charting tasks for all worksheets in your workbook, you'll need to make a few changes. I'll do that in a number of steps so it's clearer. First, add the logic to repeat the formatting for each worksheet:

```
Sub Macro1()
'
' Macro1 Macro
' Macro recorded 5/26/2004 by Jeff
'

    '
    For Each ws In Worksheets '<--- Added to repeat actions for each worksheet.
        Range("A1:C16").Select
        Selection.AutoFormat Format:=xlRangeAutoFormatSimple, Number:=True, Font _
            :=True, Alignment:=True, Border:=True, Pattern:=True, Width:=True
```

```
        Range("A1:C15").Select
        Charts.Add
        ActiveChart.ChartType = xlColumnClustered
        ActiveChart.SetSourceData Source:=ws.Range("A1:C15"), PlotBy:= _
            xlColumns
        ActiveChart.Location Where:=xlLocationAsObject, Name:=ws.Name '"2002"
        ' Change Name to match the worksheet's name ----------^
    Next     '<--- End of actions to repeat.
End Sub
```

The preceding For Each statement tells Excel to repeat the following task for every
worksheet in the workbook. The Next statement ends the set of tasks to repeat. In
programming, this kind of logic is called a *loop* because the flow of execution runs
around and around in a circle until told to stop. In this case, the loop stops after it
reaches the last worksheet in the workbook.

There's something subtle about the previous code: the For Each statement gets a reference for each worksheet as it loops and stores it using the name ws. We need to use
that name (called a *variable*) to get the location where Excel should insert the chart.
Thus, ws replaces Sheets("2002"), so each time Excel creates a chart, it inserts it on
the right worksheet. Remember to search for literal references like this and replace
them with variables any time you are adding logic to recorded code.

That was step 1, adding logic. If you run the code now, Excel will repeat the task for
each worksheet in your workbook and it will work correctly as long as each worksheet has its sales figures in the range A1:C16. If that's not the case, the code won't
format or chart the right range. To handle data in other locations, change Range("A1:
C16") to use Excel's UsedRange property as shown here:

```
Sub Macro1b( )
'
' Macro1b Macro
' Change absolute ranges to relative ones.
'


    For Each ws In Worksheets
        'Range("A1:C16").Select
        Set rng = ws.UsedRange '<-- Get all the cells with data.
        'Selection.AutoFormat Format:=xlRangeAutoFormatSimple, Number:=True, Font _
        '    :=True, Alignment:=True, Border:=True, Pattern:=True, Width:=True
        ' Use reference (below) rather than Selection (above).
        rng.AutoFormat Format:=xlRangeAutoFormatSimple, Number:=True, Font _
            :=True, Alignment:=True, Border:=True, Pattern:=True, Width:=True
        'Range("A1:C15").Select
        ' Remove the last row (Total) from the range.
        Set rng = ws.Range(ws.Cells(rng.Row, rng.Column), _
          rng.SpecialCells(xlCellTypeLastCell).Offset(-1, 0))
        Charts.Add
        ActiveChart.ChartType = xlColumnClustered
        'ActiveChart.SetSourceData Source:=Sheets("2002").Range("A1:C15"), PlotBy:= _
        '    xlColumns
```

```
        ActiveChart.SetSourceData Source:=rng, PlotBy:=xlColumns
        ' Use the range reference here ----^
        ActiveChart.Location Where:=xlLocationAsObject, Name:=ws.Name
    Next
End Sub
```

 UsedRange was introduced in Excel 97, and it is one of those incredibly useful properties that you'll be seeing over and over again.

The preceding changes use the UsedRange property to get all the cells on the worksheet that contain data. The hard part comes with the second change that removes the Total row from the range to chart:

```
Set rng = ws.Range(ws.Cells(rng.Row, rng.Column), _
    rng.SpecialCells(xlCellTypeLastCell).Offset(-1, 0))
```

Wow, that's complicated! To break it down a bit, ws.Cells (rng.Row, rng.Column) gets the first cell in the range, and rng.SpecialCells(xlCellTypeLastCell).Offset(-1, 0) gets the last cell minus one row (omitting the Total row). The enclosing ws.Range(...) method combines those start and end points into a rectangular block of cells. Don't worry if you don't completely understand at this point; you'll find much more material on working with ranges of cells in later chapters.

Finally, I changed the chart's Source argument to use this new range. Now if you run the code, Excel will format and chart sales data on each of the worksheets regardless of where the data is on each worksheet. The code is still a bit rough, though, because it doesn't declare the variables it uses, it includes some arguments that aren't really needed, and it is still named Macro1, which isn't descriptive at all. Here's a cleaned-up version with all the fixes:

```
Sub FormatAndChart( )
' AutoFormats and Charts all of the worksheets in a workbook.
' Designed to work with Sales Data tables.
' 5/28/04 by Jeff Webb
'
    Dim rng As Range, ws As Worksheet
    ' Repeats actions for all Worksheets in the workbook.
    For Each ws In Worksheets
        ' Get the cells with data in them.
        Set rng = ws.UsedRange
        ' Apply AutoFormat
        rng.AutoFormat Format:=xlRangeAutoFormatSimple
        ' Omit the Total row from the range.
        Set rng = ws.Range(ws.Cells(rng.Row, rng.Column), _
            rng.SpecialCells(xlCellTypeLastCell).Offset(-1, 0))
        ' Create a chart.
        Charts.Add
        ' Set chart properties.
        ActiveChart.ChartType = xlColumnClustered
        ActiveChart.SetSourceData Source:=rng, PlotBy:=xlColumns
```

```
        ' Insert the chart on the worksheet.
            ActiveChart.Location Where:=xlLocationAsObject, Name:=ws.Name
        Next
    End Sub
```

 Declaring the variables enables handy Visual Basic features like Auto Complete (I discuss that later).

You might notice that I also rewrote the comments in this final version. It's always a good idea to write out in words what your code is doing. Even if the code is only for your personal use, it's surprising how easy it is to forget what you did.

Fix Misteakes

Mistakes are a fact of life, and Visual Basic is fairly intolerant of them. If you followed along with the preceding lab, you probably already encountered that fact. Sometimes it's pretty easy to tell what you've done wrong, and sometimes it's almost impossible—even for experienced programmers! What marks the difference between beginning and expert programmers is how they go about solving those problems.

To help you understand fixing mistakes, you need to know that there are four different kinds of errors that are generally identified by where or why they happen:

Syntax errors
> Occur when you mistype a statement, such as omitting a closing parenthesis or omitting some part of the statement that is required. Visual Basic detects these errors right away and highlights them in red as soon as you move to the next line of code.

Semantic errors
> Are also often the result of a typo, but they *appear* valid to Visual Basic as you type. Examples of this kind of error include misspelling a method or property name or using a variable or procedure name that isn't defined yet. Visual Basic checks for these errors the moment you run your code (for instance, when you press F5). At that point, Visual Basic converts your code into a form that Excel understands (this is called *compiling*), and if any of the names you used aren't found, compiling stops and Visual Basic highlights the error. Semantic errors are sometimes called *compile-time errors* for that reason.

Logic errors
> Can be the hardest to detect. These errors occur when your code simply doesn't do what you expected it to do. Infinite loops (lather, rinse, repeat...) are an example, as are unexpected results such as formatting code that doesn't format everything it should. Logic errors can sometimes halt your code while it is running, and for that reason they are often called *runtime errors*.

Expected errors

Aren't your fault, but you need to deal with them all the same. These are another type of runtime error, and they are usually the result of using resources outside of Excel, such as trying to get a file from disk or trying to connect to a database somewhere. In those cases, you need to anticipate the possibility of a problem using a technique called exception handling (which I cover in Chapter 2).

The real name for expected errors is *exceptions*. (Since you expect them, they aren't really errors, are they?)

For now, let's look at fixing the errors that *are* your fault.

Fix Syntax Errors

Visual Basic can detect many kinds of typos as you move from line to line in the code window. This is the most common type of error you'll make as you learn programming. Fortunately, Visual Basic can generally tell what you did wrong, as shown in Figure 1-6.

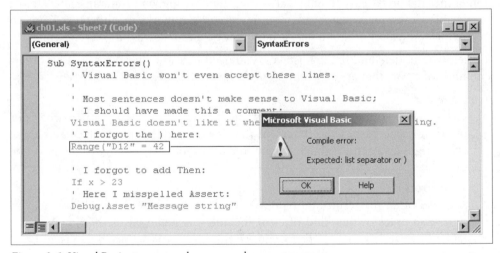

Figure 1-6. Visual Basic stops you when you make a syntax error

If you click OK but don't fix the error, Visual Basic leaves the line colored red as a reminder that you should fix it. If you look at the SyntaxErrors sample, you'll see that it looks like a Christmas tree with all the green comments and red errors that I've deliberately included to illustrate the different ways errors in syntax can occur.

If you don't understand the error dialog box Visual Basic displays, you can either click Help to get more information about the error or click OK, select the item you have a question about, and press F1 as shown in Figure 1-7.

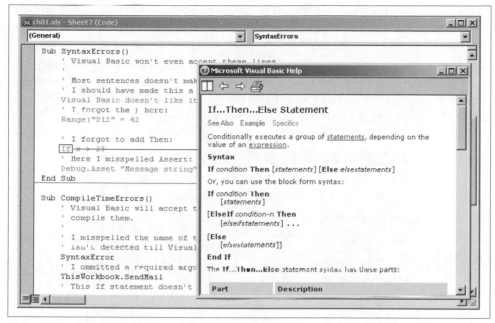

Figure 1-7. Select If and press F1 to find out about it

Help often tells you what you need to know about a specific Visual Basic statement. Sometimes it's less helpful about Excel methods, but it's always a good first place to look since it's only a key press away. Another good, easy way to figure things out is by using Visual Basic's Auto Complete feature. By default, Visual Basic displays lists of items that could complete statements as you type, as shown in Figure 1-8.

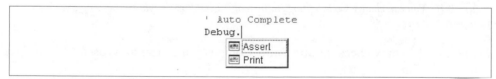

Figure 1-8. Visual Basic lists items that could complete a statement as you type it

To insert one of the items from the list, use the arrow keys or mouse to select the item and press the spacebar to insert the item in your code. A similar thing happens when you add a statement that takes arguments, as shown in Figure 1-9. (*Arguments* are additional pieces of information that a statement needs to accomplish its task.)

```
' More Auto Complete:
Charts.Add
        Add([Before], [After], [Count], [Type]) As Object
```

Figure 1-9. Visual Basic also lists the arguments that a statement takes

In this case, the arguments are shown in italics with the current one shown in bold. Arguments are always separated by commas and once you type a comma, the next argument becomes bold. Square brackets mean that an argument can be omitted.

Visual Basic's automatic syntax checking and Auto Complete features can help you learn the language, but some programmers find the error dialogs and pop-up text annoying in some situations. Visual Basic lets you turn off these features by choosing Tools → Options and selecting the Editor tab as shown in Figure 1-10.

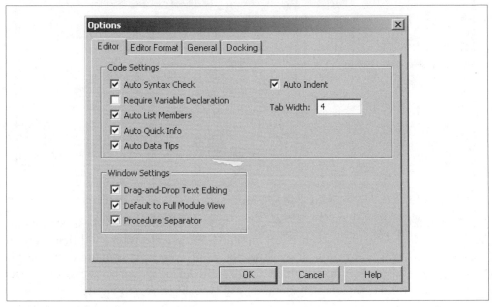

Figure 1-10. You can change Code Settings to turn off Visual Basic's syntax checking and Auto Complete features

Don't do it! Syntax checking and Auto Complete are incredibly useful if you are learning the language.

Fix Compile-Time Errors

In some cases, statements look correct to Visual Basic as you are writing them, but they don't make sense when Visual Basic tries to compile them into a program. This occurs because there are some things Visual Basic has to ignore as you are writing the code but can't ignore when you try to run it.

A simple example is when your code calls a procedure that you haven't written yet. Visual Basic doesn't flag that statement as a syntax error, because it assumes you'll get around to writing the procedure. If you forget to do that, Visual Basic reminds you when you try to run the code (Figure 1-11).

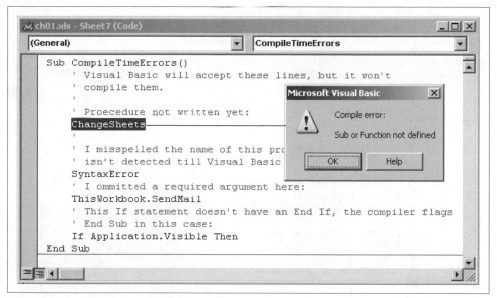

Figure 1-11. Visual Basic couldn't find ChangeSheets, so it displays an error during compilation

Visual Basic alerts you to compile-time errors one at a time, so if you fix the one shown in Figure 1-11 and then try to run again, another error will pop up on the SyntaxError line—that's a case of a simple misspelling, it should be SyntaxErrors.

 Visual Basic is strict about spelling and doesn't guess at what you meant to write. It would be cool if it were that intuitive, but it would cause bigger problems if it guessed wrong!

Sometimes compile-time errors are similar to syntax errors, such as when you omit a required argument or don't terminate a statement that spans multiple lines, such as a loop or a decision statement. In those cases, Visual Basic flags the End Sub or End Function statement because it searched to the end of the procedure without finding the end of the previous block (Figure 1-12).

The missing End If is pretty obvious in Figure 1-12 because the procedure is not very long, but it can be much harder to locate where the End If should go in longer passages of code. For that reason, programmers usually indent blocks of code that are logically related, for example:

```
' Activate the next worksheet or chart, depending on
' what type of sheet is currently active. Return to
' first sheet when the end is reached.
Sub ChangeSheets( )
    Select Case TypeName(ActiveSheet)
    Case "Worksheet"
        If ActiveSheet.Index < Worksheets.Count Then
            Worksheets(ActiveSheet.Index + 1).Activate
```

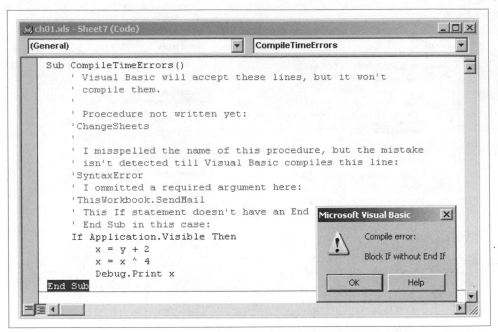

```
Sub CompileTimeErrors()
    ' Visual Basic will accept these lines, but it won't
    ' compile them.
    '
    ' Proecedure not written yet:
    'ChangeSheets
    '
    ' I misspelled the name of this procedure, but the mistake
    ' isn't detected till Visual Basic compiles this line:
    'SyntaxError
    ' I ommitted a required argument here:
    'ThisWorkbook.SendMail
    ' This If statement doesn't have an End
    ' End Sub in this case:
    If Application.Visible Then
        x = y + 2
        x = x ^ 4
        Debug.Print x
End Sub
```

Microsoft Visual Basic

Compile error:

Block If without End If

OK   Help

Figure 1-12. Visual Basic flags End Sub because it couldn't find End If before it

```
        Else
            Worksheets(1).Activate
        End If
    Case "Chart"
        If ActiveSheet.Index < Charts.Count Then
            Charts(ActiveSheet.Index + 1).Activate
        Else
            Charts(1).Activate
        End If
    Case Else
        Debug.Print TypeName(ActiveSheet), ActiveSheet.Name
    End Select
End Sub
```

In this case, indents make it easier for you to match the begin and end statements for various blocks of code (seen here with all the details removed):

```
Sub
    Select Case
    Case
        If
            ' task
        Else
            ' task
        End If
    Case
        If
            ' task
```

```
            Else
                ' task
            End If
        Case Else
            ' task
        End Select
    End Sub
```

Indenting is a standard practice that helps you avoid errors by making it easier to read and interpret logically related pieces of your code. It is not required by Visual Basic, and adding or omitting indents does not affect how your code runs.

Fix Runtime Errors

Boy, it seems like a lot of things can go wrong! However, most of these problems are pretty obvious and easy to fix. That's not so true for errors that occur when your program is running. Unlike other types of errors, Visual Basic can't detect these until the program actually tries to execute the statement. That makes it harder to tell where the error occurred and why it happened. For example, Figure 1-13 shows a procedure with a runtime error.

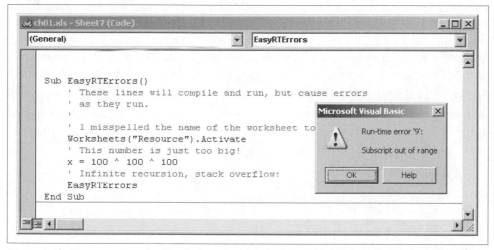

Figure 1-13. Runtime error displayed after pressing F5; doesn't highlight the line where the error occurred

You don't know which line the error occurred on, although you might guess it was the Worksheets("Resource").Activate statement because I said so in my comments. If you want to confirm that's the error, press F8 instead of F5 to step through the procedure (Figure 1-14).

In this case, you have to ask yourself why Excel couldn't find the Resource worksheet. Well, it's because the worksheet is actually named Resource**s**. I don't mean to beat you over the head with this, but spelling is important!

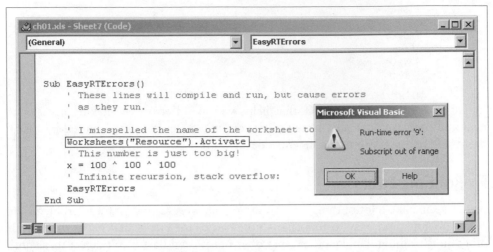

```
ch01.xls - Sheet7 (Code)
(General)                                    EasyRTErrors

Sub EasyRTErrors()
    ' These lines will compile and run, but cause errors
    ' as they run.
    '
    ' I misspelled the name of the worksheet to
    Worksheets("Resource").Activate
    ' This number is just too big!
    x = 100 ^ 100 ^ 100
    ' Infinite recursion, stack overflow:
    EasyRTErrors
End Sub
```

Microsoft Visual Basic

Run-time error '9':

Subscript out of range

OK   Help

Figure 1-14. Press F8 to run the procedure one line at a time to locate runtime errors

Runtime errors occur for a variety of reasons. For instance, there is a limit to how big a number can be in Visual Basic and 100 ^ 100 ^ 100 exceeds that limit (Visual Basic calls that an overflow). Other errors are harder to find with F8, for example the EasyRTErrors statement calls itself over and over again indefinitely. That's similar to an infinite loop, but since it's calling itself, it's referred to as *infinite recursion* instead. If you try F8 on that line, you'll see that you can execute it more than 5000 times without an error. In that case, you just need to remember that an Out of stack space error usually means you've got an infinite recursion.

Another type of runtime error that's very common but difficult to find is misspelled variable names. For example, the following code displays a dialog box, but never says "Howdy" no matter what the user clicks:

```
Sub SubtleRTErrors()
    ' I misspelled answer, you never hear Howdy:
    answer = MsgBox("Click OK to hear Howdy.")
    If aswer = vbOK Then Application.Speech.Speak "Howdy"
End Sub
```

 The Speech object was added to Excel in 2002. If you have an earlier version, use MsgBox instead of Application.Speech.Speak for this sample.

There's nothing technically wrong with the code, other than the fact that it doesn't work! This problem occurs because Visual Basic lets you create variables without ever declaring them. That makes life easier in the beginning (about 30 minutes) but adds a tremendous burden later on trying to locate and fix this type of subtle error. Fortunately, there's a fix: turn off automatic variables by choosing Tools → Options and selecting the Editor tab, then selecting Require Variable Declaration as shown in Figure 1-15.

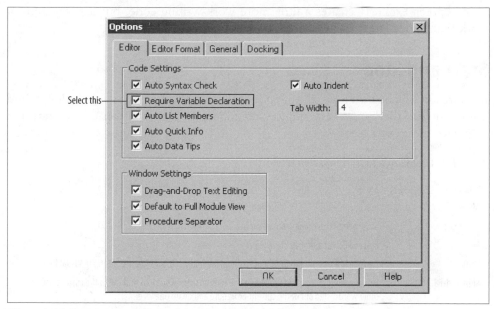

Figure 1-15. Require Variable Declaration will avoid subtle runtime errors

When you select Require Variable Declaration, Visual Basic adds an `Option Explicit` statement any time it creates a new class or module. If you wrote code before changing that option, you need to add `Option Explicit` yourself. The `Option Explicit` statement causes a compile-time error whenever it encounters an undefined variable, as shown in Figure 1-16.

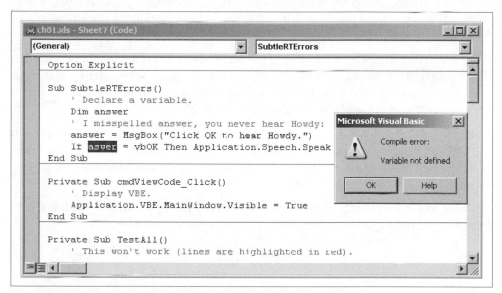

Figure 1-16. Option Explicit helps identify misspelled variable names

Using `Option Explicit` creates a little more work writing code, but it saves a lot of work fixing code later.

Start and Stop

I've already touched on how to run code from Excel or Visual Basic a little bit, and Table 1-1 lists the handy keys and key combinations that you can use to start and stop code in Excel.

Table 1-1. Useful keys to start and stop code

Press	To
Alt-F8	Run or edit a Visual Basic procedure from an Excel workbook.
Esc or Ctrl-Break	Stop code that is running out of control.
F8	Run one line at a time in Visual Basic.
Shift-F8	Run one line as a single statement (without stepping in to another procedure) in Visual Basic.
Shift-Ctrl-F8	Finish running the current procedure and return to the procedure that called the current one. In other words, step out of the current procedure and go up one level.
Ctrl-F8	Run all the code from the beginning of a procedure to the current cursor position in Visual Basic.
F5	Run a procedure from beginning to end in Visual Basic.
F9	Set or remove a stopping point (called a *breakpoint*) in code.
Ctrl-Shift-F9	Remove all breakpoints from all classes and modules.

Of these, F9 to add a breakpoint combined with F5 and F8 are perhaps the most useful combinations to help solve runtime errors or just to help figure out how the code works. When you set a breakpoint in code, Visual Basic highlights the whole line by making its background red (Figure 1-17).

Now if you run the code, it will stop if the active sheet is not a worksheet or a chart (for instance, it might be an old-style dialog sheet). Breakpoints change the focus from Excel to Visual Basic, so they are a great way to step in to a procedure that is triggered by Excel in some way (for example, through an event).

Basically, any time you have a question about what code is doing, set a breakpoint somewhere before the point that you have a question about, then run the code. When Visual Basic hits the breakpoint, it will stop and you can press F8 to step through the code one line at a time.

Running to a breakpoint puts the code in context by filling in variables with live data from Excel. Looking at the values Excel fills in is what I cover next.

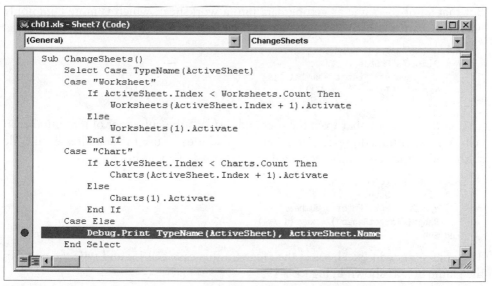

```
ch01.xls - Sheet7 (Code)                                          _ □ ×
(General)                              ▼    ChangeSheets              ▼
    Sub ChangeSheets()
        Select Case TypeName(ActiveSheet)
        Case "Worksheet"
            If ActiveSheet.Index < Worksheets.Count Then
                Worksheets(ActiveSheet.Index + 1).Activate
            Else
                Worksheets(1).Activate
            End If
        Case "Chart"
            If ActiveSheet.Index < Charts.Count Then
                Charts(ActiveSheet.Index + 1).Activate
            Else
                Charts(1).Activate
            End If
        Case Else
            Debug.Print TypeName(ActiveSheet), ActiveSheet.Name
        End Select
    End Select
```

Figure 1-17. You can also set/clear a breakpoint by clicking to the left of the line of code (where the dot is)

View Results

There are a number of ways to display results from code in Excel. One common way that is used a lot in Help is to display a message box:

```
Sub ShowMessage()
    Dim x As Integer
    x = Sheets.Count
    MsgBox "This workbook contains " & x & " sheets."
End Sub
```

This code displays the number of sheets in the workbook using a simple dialog box as shown in Figure 1-18.

Figure 1-18. It's easy to display results using MsgBox

But that's not the same as getting data into a worksheet, which is more commonly what you want to do. To do that, you set the value of a Range object. For example:

```
Sub ChangeRange( )
    Dim x As Double
    x = InputBox("Enter a number.")
    Range("J5") = x ^ (1 / 3)
End Sub
```

That code gets a number from the user and displays the cube root of that number in cell J5. As mentioned previously, it's not a good idea to use range addresses in code so the following version uses a named range instead of an address:

```
Sub ChangeRange( )
    Dim x As Double
    x = InputBox("Enter a number.")
    Range("targetRange") = x ^ (1 / 3)
End Sub
```

To name a range in Excel, select the range (in this case cell J5) and type the name in the Name box as shown in Figure 1-19.

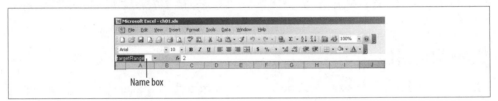

Figure 1-19. It's better to use named ranges in code

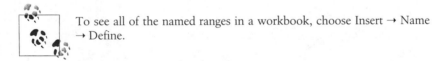 To see all of the named ranges in a workbook, choose Insert → Name → Define.

You can even display results in a range using the formula bar if your procedure returns a value. The following code shows changes to make to repackage the cube root calculation for use in a formula:

```
Public Function CubeRoot(x As Double) As Double
    CubeRoot = x ^ (1 / 3)
End Function
```

In order to use a procedure in a formula, the procedure must:

- Not be Private (the Private keyword hides functions from the formula bar).
- Return a value (that is, it must be a Function)
- Be part of a module, not a class

If the procedure follows those rules, you can enter its name in the formula bar as shown in Figure 1-20.

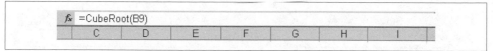

Figure 1-20. You can use public functions in formulas

 Visual Basic procedures that can be used in the formula bar are sometimes called *user-defined functions*, or *UDFs* for short.

In other cases, you might want to view a result, but not show that result to users. A
good example of this is when you're developing your code or when you're making
sure it works correctly. In that situation, you usually set a breakpoint in your code,
then view the values in variables using *watches*. There are three kinds of watches in
Visual Basic, and none of them go ticktock:

Automatic watches
> Display the value of a simple variable or property when you move the cursor
> over the item after stopping at a breakpoint.

Quick watches
> Display the value of a variable or property when you select the item and press Shift-
> F9. Quick watches can display returned values, such as `TypeName(ActiveSheet)`,
> which automatic watches can't.

Watch points
> Display the value of a variable or property in the Watch window. Watch points
> can also stop code if an item reaches a certain value. In that way, they function
> as conditional breakpoints.

Figures 1-21 through 1-23 show the different types of watches in action.

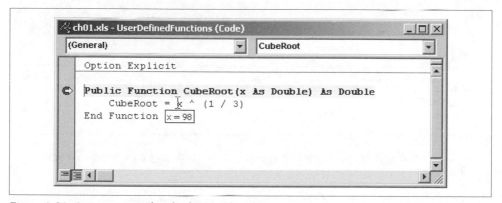

Figure 1-21. Automatic watches display simple values

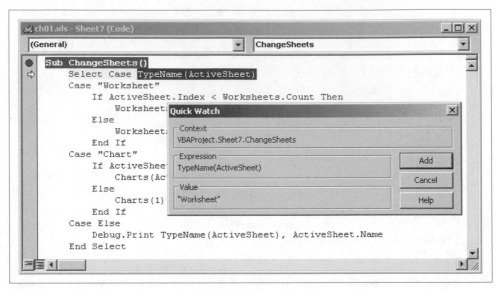

Figure 1-22. Select an item and press Shift-F9 to see a quick watch

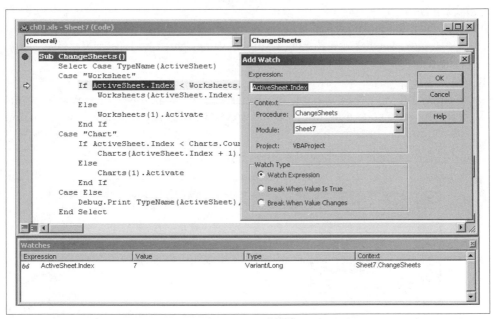

Figure 1-23. Select an item and choose Debug → Add Watch to display the value of that item in the watch window

Watches are the best way to look at a value at one point in time, but when you need to track how a value changes, they are kind of limited. In those situations, it's often best to display your results in the Immediate window using the Debug.Print statement. An easy way to illustrate this is to go back to the runtime error sample we showed earlier that causes an infinite recursion. I've made some changes (in **bold**) to show how to track how many levels deep the recursion goes before failing:

```
Sub EasyRTErrors()
    ' Previous code deleted for this example.
    Static i
    i = i + 1
    ' Show how many times recusion will run before error.
    Debug.Print i
    ' Infinite recursion, stack overflow:
    EasyRTErrors
End Sub
```

Now, if you run this code, a stream of numbers will display in the Immediate window (Figure 1-24). If you don't see the Immediate window in VBE, press Ctrl-G to redisplay it.

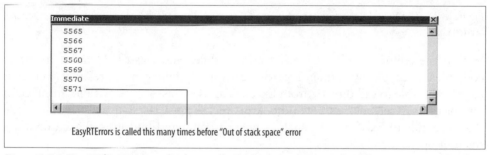

Figure 1-24. Use Debug.Print to display results in the Immediate window

You can also use the Immediate window to run procedures and perform quick calculations. In effect, it functions as a single-line Visual Basic interpreter as shown in Figure 1-25.

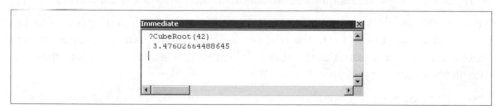

Figure 1-25. Type statements in the Immediate window to see their result, err...immediately

 The ? character is a shortcut for Print in Visual Basic.

Where's My Code?

Excel stores Visual Basic code in the workbook (*.xls*), template (*.xlt*), or add-in (*.xla*) file when you save it. File formats other than those omit the Visual Basic code the same way that special formatting is lost when you save a workbook as a text (*.txt*) or comma-delimited file (*.csv*).

You can view the code in a currently open Excel file by pressing Alt-F11, by choosing Tools → Macro → Visual Basic Editor or by clicking the Visual Basic Editor button on the Visual Basic toolbar (Figure 1-26).

Figure 1-26. The Visual Basic toolbar lets you edit, run, or stop code; create controls; and set macro security

Within the editor, code is organized into modules and classes. *Modules* are static code files that typically contain recorded code and public procedures that you want users to be able to call directly from Excel. *Classes* are associated with an instance of an object in Excel, such as a workbook or worksheet. Classes usually contain code that responds to Excel events, such as when a command button is clicked or when the user opens the workbook.

Excel creates a new module called Module1 when you first record code as shown earlier in this chapter. Excel provides a class for each new sheet you add to a workbook. Similarly, Excel deletes that sheet's class when you delete the sheet from the workbook, so be careful when deleting sheets while programming! You can see a workbook's classes and modules in the editor's Project window (Figure 1-27).

You can also use the Project window to export classes or modules to text files and to import code stored as text into the workbook. Unfortunately, there's no easy way to store code separately from the workbook (which would be nice when more than one person is working on code).

Visual Basic displays information about each class or module in the Properties window below the Project window, as shown in Figure 1-28. As you select a different item in the Project window, the item displayed in the Properties window changes.

You can use the Properties window to rename modules or classes or to control various aspects of a class. For example, to rename Module1 something descriptive, like RecordedCode, select Module1 in the Project window and type RecordedCode in the (Name) property of the Properties window. You can also use the Properties window to hide sheets by setting the class's Visible property.

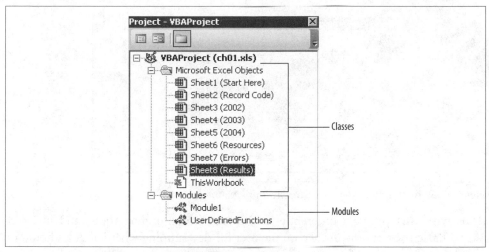

Figure 1-27. Double-click on a class or module to open it in a code window

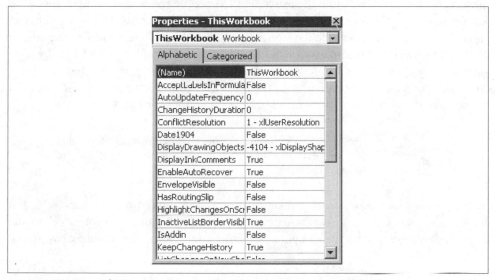

Figure 1-28. Select ThisWorkbook in the Project window to see the workbook's properties

Macros and Security

When you open a workbook that contains code, Excel displays a security warning suggesting you might want to disable the code, as shown in Figure 1-29.

Microsoft included this warning because, once a user enables the macros in a workbook, that code has full access to the user's system and can do some pretty nasty things (such as changing or deleting files) without the user knowing it. Microsoft

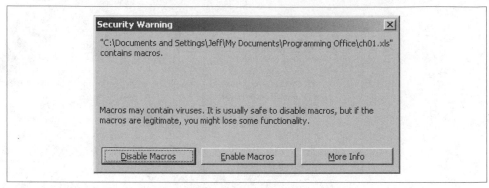

Figure 1-29. Excel's macro security warning is pretty dire

deals with this problem differently in different programming tools, and in Excel Visual Basic they put the burden on the user for determining whether code should or should not be trusted.

Unfortunately, users are often the least-qualified people to make this judgment. Who knows where *ch01.xls* came from or what it will do if I open it? The way to answer those questions is to add a digital signature. A *digital signature* identifies the author of the content or the macros contained in a workbook, template, or add-in. By digitally signing a workbook's code, you add a unique identifier that says the code came from you (or your organization) and thus the user may have more confidence that the workbook won't insert the word *Wazoo* in all your correspondence.

 I once received a work-for-hire contract from Microsoft legal that occasionally declared *Wazoo!* I thought they were just checking to make sure I read the thing....

There's a lot more information on security and digital signatures in Chapter 26, but for now I'll tell you how to eliminate the warning in Figure 1-29 for Excel Visual Basic code you create and use on your own computer. Doing that involves two major steps:

1. Create a personal digital signature for signing your workbooks.
2. Sign your workbooks with that certificate.

These steps are detailed in the following procedures.

To create a personal digital signature:

1. From the Windows Programs menu, choose Microsoft Office → Microsoft Office Tools → Digital Certificate for VBA Projects. Windows runs *SelfCert.exe* and displays the Create Digital Certificate dialog box (Figure 1-30).
2. Type the name you want displayed within the signature and click OK. *SelfCert.exe* creates a local certificate and displays a success message.

Figure 1-30. Creating a personal digital signature

 SelfCert.exe is provided with Office 2000 and later. If it is not installed on your system, run Office Setup and install Office Tools → Digital Signature for VBA Projects.

This certificate is valid on only the machine on which you created it. Therefore, its use is really limited to signing macros on your own machine to avoid the security prompt you get each time you open a workbook containing macros you've written.

To sign a Visual Basic project in a workbook, follow these steps:

1. From within the workbook, open the Visual Basic Editor.
2. Choose Tools → Digital Signature. Visual Basic displays the Digital Signature dialog box (Figure 1-31).
3. Click Choose. Visual Basic displays a dialog box containing all the digital signatures installed on your system (Figure 1-32).
4. Select the certificate to use, and click OK. Then click OK again to close the Digital Signature dialog box.

Once the code is signed, you may see the security warning in Figure 1-33 when you open a workbook, template, or add-in containing the code you just signed.

If you select the option to "Always trust macros from this publisher" and click Enable Macros, you won't see this warning every time you open your own signed workbooks.

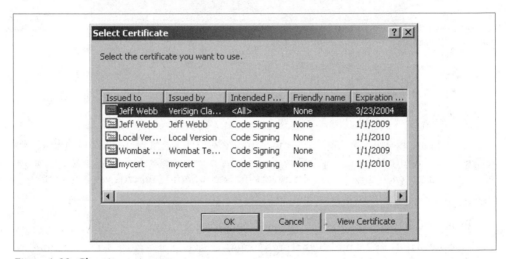

Figure 1-31. Signing a Visual Basic project

Figure 1-32. Choosing a signature

Write Bug-Free Code

I encourage a guided, trial-and-error approach to learning how to program. This is mainly because I don't think anyone can remember all the facts and information you need to know without having some way to apply that information in a practical way. Also, I think most of us are impatient by nature and want to get started as soon as possible.

However, I don't want you to confuse this approach with disorganization or sloppiness. Either of those bad habits will make your programming experience difficult and frustrating. The following list is a collection of *good habits* that will pay off as you learn and develop your career:

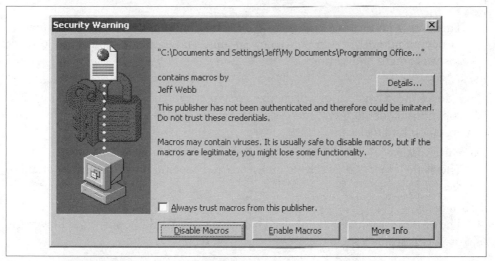

Figure 1-33. Your digital signature now appears in the macro security warning

Declare all your variables

Adding `Option Explicit` to the top of each class or module helps make sure you don't accidentally misspell a variable name and cause a subtle error that can be hard to locate.

Type carefully

Many names in Excel, such as worksheet names or named ranges, can't be checked through `Option Explicit` and misspelling one of those in code can lead to similarly hard-to-locate errors.

Use short, descriptive names

There are different conventions for naming variables and procedures but the crux of all of them is to be short and descriptive. Be careful not to be too descriptive though. I try to keep variable names down to a few characters and I tend to use whole words when naming procedures.

Avoid `ActiveSheet` and `Selection`

I know Excel records code this way, but it is much better to get a worksheet or range by name if possible. Relying on which worksheet or range is selected makes it harder to debug and reuse your code. The exception to this guideline is when you really want to act on the `ActiveSheet` or `Selection`, such as when you are creating general tools that work on any worksheet or range.

Try to think clearly

For complicated tasks, it can help to write out what you want to do on a pad of paper, then try to do those steps in Excel with macro recording on. Often it helps to break a task up into several different steps and make those steps procedures that you can call from one central procedure.

Rely on friends

There are a lot of programmers in the Excel community and they communicate through a number of very active newsgroups. Those are great places to look for answers and to find samples.

Copy others

I don't mean you should plagiarize copyright-protected work, but it's OK to copy most code snippets, and it's good practice to follow the coding style of others if you find it elegant.

Share with others

This is the other side of relying on friends and copying others. Don't be afraid of feedback, either.

Take a break

The best programmers I know lead balanced lives. You'll be surprised how many problems seem to solve themselves once you relax.

Navigate Samples and Help

I've organized my samples by chapter, so the samples for this chapter are in *ch01.xls*, the next chapter is *ch02.xls*, and so on. Within each sample, I include a Start Here sheet that provides general instructions on using the samples, a Resources sheet that includes links to other sources of information, and in between I include sheets related to the specific topics covered in the chapter (Figure 1-34).

Figure 1-34. Chapter samples are stored in a workbook; topics are covered on individual sheets

In some cases, a chapter's samples may include other files or folders, but in all cases, links to those locations are found in the main chapter sample.

In other words, I've tried to organize stuff as simply as possible.

Excel's Visual Basic Help is also organized fairly simply, however there are a couple gotchas:

• Make sure that you have installed Visual Basic Help for Excel. Earlier versions of Excel did not install Help for Visual Basic by default. If you press F1 in Visual Basic and Help is not displayed, you probably need to run the Excel Setup program to update your installation so it includes Visual Basic Help.

• If you are using Excel 2003 you may want to start Help by opening the Help file directly rather than through pressing F1. Excel 2003 provides navigation tools in a Help task pane rather than in the Help window (Figure 1-35 versus Figure 1-36), and it's harder to navigate that way!

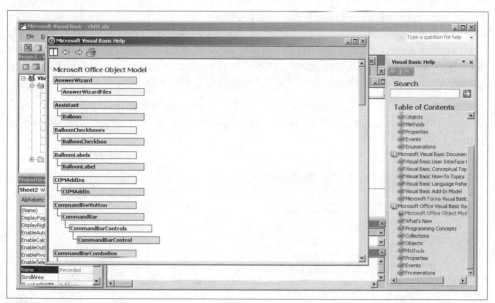

Figure 1-35. Excel 2003 navigates Help from the task pane on the right

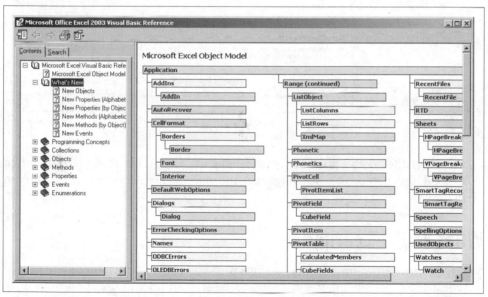

Figure 1-36. Earlier Excel versions, or opening the file directly, provides navigation as part of the Help window, on the left

To open the Excel 2003 Help file directly, either click on the link on the Resources sheet or double-click on the Help file in Windows Explorer. The Excel 2003 Help file is stored at *C:\Program Files\Microsoft Office\OFFICE11\1033\VBAXL10.CHM* by default. The Visual Basic language reference is stored at *C:\Program Files\Common Files\Microsoft Shared\Vba\Vba6\1033\VBLr6.chm* by default.

The graphic in Figure 1-36 shows how the Excel objects are organized. If you click on one of the boxes, you'll get more information about that object, as shown in Figure 1-37.

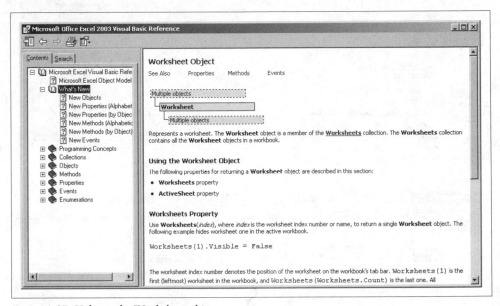

Figure 1-37. Help on the Worksheet object

Excel's Help often does a good job of explaining *what* a specific object is, but it often lacks good direction on *why* you might use the object. Those are the blanks I'll try to fill in for you.

What You've Learned

So far, you've learned how to record a macro from Excel and then modify that code to repeat the task globally. In the process, you learned how to use the Visual Basic Editor to step through code, fix errors, and get online Help.

You should have turned on Option Explicit for all your code and created a digital signature that you can use to avoid the macro security warning when working on your code.

Come back to this chapter later if you need help finding and fixing errors or using the Visual Basic Editor.

CHAPTER 2

Knowing the Basics

Visual Basic comes from a long line of Basics. In fact, BASIC was Microsoft's first product. Bill Gates and Paul Allen developed a BASIC interpreter for use on the Altair personal computer in their Harvard dorm rooms many years ago.

Back at Microsoft, I got to play a small role in the evolution of computer languages. I was the guy who changed BASIC to Basic. Death to acronyms!

The Visual Basic language is distinct from the objects, properties, and methods that Excel provides. If you know Visual Basic, you can program Word or PowerPoint, or even Windows. I'll teach you the fundamental elements of the language here.

Code used in this chapter and additional samples are available in *ch02.xls*.

Parts of a Program

A program is made up of the basic parts shown in Figure 2-1.

Project
> Is the workbook where the program is stored. Each workbook has one Visual Basic project.

Classes and modules
> Store the code associated with the workbook and the sheets the workbook contains. Classes and modules help organize the procedures in your program.

Procedures
> Perform the program's work. You can't do anything in Visual Basic without creating at least one procedure.

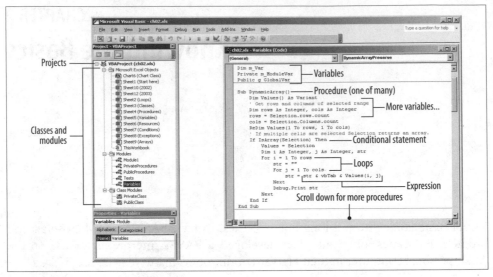

Figure 2-1. The main parts of a program

Variables

> Store values used by your program.

Conditional statements

> Make decisions within procedures.

Loops

> Repeat actions. Together, conditional statements and loops form the logic that your procedure uses to accomplish its task.

Expressions

> Evaluate a combination of items to return a single result. Expressions are the smallest unit of work in a program and they usually involve operators such as +, -, *, or & (combine strings).

The following sections describe these parts in detail. If you are new to programming, I recommend that you follow along with the samples carefully. I take a top-down approach and I've tried to be clear about how, when, and why you use each part.

If you're an experienced programmer, the top-down organization of this chapter should work well for you as a reference. If you think you know this already, I recommend that you read the sections "Classes and Modules," "Events," and "Exceptions" just to make sure.

Classes and Modules

Excel stores recorded code in modules and stores code associated with workbooks and worksheets in classes. Here's why:

Modules are static

> That is, they exist without having to be created in memory at runtime. That means the code in modules is always available to Excel; however, it limits what type of code they can contain. Specifically, modules can't contain event procedures.

Classes are dynamic

> They must be *instantiated* at runtime (that means an instance of an object must be created from the class at runtime). Classes can contain event procedures because of this relationship with an object.

Workbook, chart, and worksheet classes are automatically instantiated by Excel because those classes are associated with visible Excel objects: the current workbook and each of the sheets it contains. Because of that relationship, Visual Basic shows those classes as Microsoft Excel Objects in the Project window (Figure 2-2).

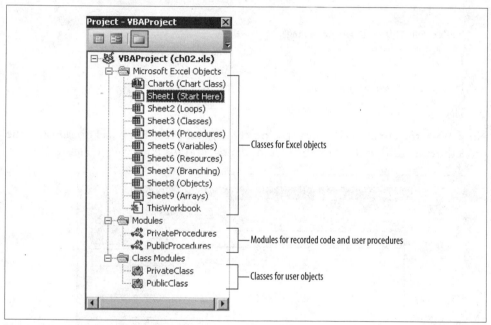

Figure 2-2. Excel Visual Basic projects store code in three different folders

Because Excel instantiates classes automatically, how you create objects from classes is mostly hidden and therefore often not completely understood. To see how creating an object from a class works, create a new workbook in Excel, start the Visual Basic Editor, and follow these steps:

1. Choose Insert → Class Module. Visual Basic creates a new class and adds it to the Class Modules folder of the Project window.

2. Select the Properties window and rename the class PublicClass and set the Instancing property to 2 - PublicNotCreatable, as shown in Figure 2-3.

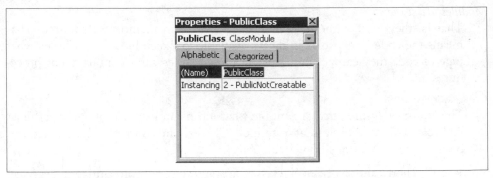

Figure 2-3. Create a user class

Click on the class's Code window and type the following code:

```
' From PublicClass class
Dim m_name As String

Public Sub SetName(name As String)
    m_name = name
End Sub

Public Sub ShowName( )
    Debug.Print m_name
End Sub
```

Now move the cursor to the ShowName procedure and press F5. Excel doesn't run the procedure; instead, it displays the Macros dialog, and it's empty! (See Figure 2-4.)

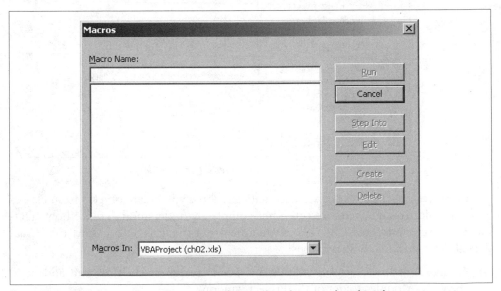

Figure 2-4. Procedures in user classes don't show up here because they don't have an instance

In order to run the ShowName procedure, you need to choose Insert → Module and add the following code:

```
' From Tests module.
Sub TestUserClass()
    Dim obj As New PublicClass
    obj.SetName ("New object")
    obj.ShowName
End Sub
```

TestUserClass creates an instance of PublicClass as a new object named obj, then calls the SetName and ShowName methods of that object. In short, you can't do anything with a class until you create an object from it. Why is that useful? Because each object has its own storage. For example, you can create three different objects from the same class if you like:

```
' From Tests module.
Sub MultipleObjects()
    Dim obj1 As New PublicClass, obj2 As New PublicClass, obj3 As New PublicClass
    obj1.SetName ("First object")
    obj2.SetName ("Second object")
    obj3.SetName ("Third object")
    obj1.ShowName
    obj2.ShowName
    obj3.ShowName
End Sub
```

The preceding code displays each object's name in the Immediate window:

```
First object
Second object
Third object
```

You can't do that with code stored in a module because the m_name variable changes each time you call SetName. With modules, you have only one instance, and you can't create that instance:

```
' From Tests module.
Sub MultipleModules()
    ' Code in modules is static, there's no such thing as:
    'Dim mod As New PublicProcedures
    PublicProcedures.SetName ("First object")
    PublicProcedures.SetName ("Second object")
    PublicProcedures.SetName ("Third object")
    ' All display "Third object"
    PublicProcedures.ShowName
    PublicProcedures.ShowName
    PublicProcedures.ShowName
End Sub
```

 Most programmers omit the module name when calling procedures from a module, but you *can* include it if you like, as shown by this example. The module name is required only if there is a procedure with the same name in two or more modules.

The classes that Excel provides for sheets and workbooks are *single-instance classes*. That means they follow some special rules that are different from user classes. You can create multiple variables that refer to a single-instance class, but all those variables refer to the same object. For example, the following code creates object variables that refer to the same worksheet:

```
' From Tests module
Sub TestSheetClass()
    Dim obj1 As New Sheet1, obj2 As New Sheet1
    obj1.Name = "New name"
    Debug.Print obj2.Name
End Sub
```

When you run the preceding code, Debug.Print displays New Name in the Immediate window! This limitation comes from Excel—you can't have two sheets with the same name in a single Excel workbook, and you can't have two workbooks with the same name open at the same time in Excel.

Since Excel handles the creation of workbook and sheet classes, the New keyword in the preceding code is misleading: you can't really create new instances of those classes. However, you can create new instances of generic versions of those objects using Excel's Add method:

```
' Creates a new, blank worksheet
Sub NewWorksheet()
    Dim ws As Worksheet
    Set ws = Worksheets.Add
    ws.Name = "New sheet"
End Sub
```

One other quirk of workbook and sheet classes is that you can run their procedures from the Code window by pressing F5. You don't need to first create an instance of those classes—Excel's already done it.

Procedures

Procedures are named blocks of code that perform a task. I've shown a lot of procedures already and I feel a little bad about waiting this long to define that term. Procedures can have *arguments*, which let you pass values in to the procedure from somewhere, and they may *return values* through their name. Figure 2-5 illustrates these parts using the CubeRoot example from Chapter 1.

Visual Basic has four kinds of procedures:

Sub procedures
> Perform a task but don't have return values.

Function procedures
> Perform a task and return a value as their result.

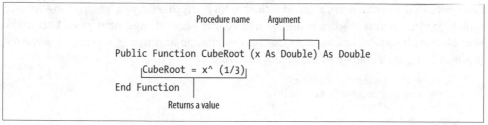

Figure 2-5. Parts of a procedure

Property procedures

Get or set a value in an object or module.

Event procedures

A special kind of Sub procedure that respond to events that occur in Excel. Only classes can contain event procedures.

The following sections explain these different types of procedures and how you use them.

Arguments and Results

I've heard some people say "Sub procedures don't return a value; Function procedures do." I may have said that myself once or twice, but it's not exactly true. Actually Sub and Function procedures can both return values through their arguments. Only Function procedures return a value as their result. In other words, only Function procedures can be used on the righthand side of the equals sign (=).

For example, the CubeRoot procedure in Figure 2-5 can return a result and store that result in a variable as shown here:

```
x = CubeRoot(42)
```

You couldn't do that if it were a Sub procedure. But what if it were? Here's what CubeRoot might look like if it were rewritten as a Sub (changes are in **bold**):

```
Public Sub CubeRoot2(x As Double, result As Double)
    result = x ^ (1 / 3)
End Sub
```

This Sub just returns the result as an argument rather than through the function name. Using the CubeRoot2 procedure is a lot more awkward than using CubeRoot, however:

```
' Use the CubeRoot2 Sub
Sub TestCubeRoot2()
    Dim res As Double
    CubeRoot2 42, res
    Debug.Print res
End Sub
```

One problem is that it isn't always clear which argument you are passing in and which argument returns the result—I named the second argument result to make that clearer. It's more common to use Subs to change arguments when you want the input argument to change to the result, like this:

```
' Change the passed-in argument
Public Sub GetCubeRoot(x As Double)
    x = x ^ (1 / 3)
End Sub
```

Now the Sub changes the value of whatever argument you pass in:

```
Sub TestGetCubeRoot()
    Dim x As Double
    x = 42
    GetCubeRoot x
    Debug.Print x
End Sub
```

This works because Visual Basic passes arguments *by reference*. That means the argument x is not really 42; it's actually an address in memory that contains the value 42. You can change this by declaring the argument as ByVal:

```
' Doesn't change the passed-in argument
Public Sub GetCubeRoot2(ByVal x As Double)
    x = x ^ (1 / 3)
End Sub
```

The preceding code doesn't change the argument since it is passed *by value*. To confirm that it doesn't change, try this:

```
Sub TestGetCubeRoot2()
    Dim x As Double
    x = 42
    GetCubeRoot2 x
    Debug.Print x
End Sub
```

The preceding code displays 42, not the result you probably want. The default is to pass arguments by reference, and you can include the optional ByRef keyword if you want to be absolutely clear what you are doing:

```
Public Sub CubeRoot2(ByVal x As Double, ByRef result As Double)
    result = x ^ (1 / 3)
End Sub
```

Now, it is clearer which argument is for input (x) and which is for output (result).

Optional Arguments

Sometimes you can avoid having an argument. The Optional keyword tells Visual Basic than an argument can be omitted. The following code shows changes to the ChangeSheets procedure from Chapter 1 to add an optional argument:

```
Sub ChangeSheets2(Optional index As Integer = 1)
    Select Case TypeName(ActiveSheet)
    Case "Worksheet"
        If ActiveSheet.index < Worksheets.Count Then
            Worksheets(ActiveSheet.index + index).Activate
        Else
            Worksheets(1).Activate
        End If
    Case "Chart"
        If ActiveSheet.index < Charts.Count Then
            Charts(ActiveSheet.index + index).Activate
        Else
            Charts(1).Activate
        End If
    Case Else
        Debug.Print TypeName(ActiveSheet), ActiveSheet.Name
    End Select
End Sub
```

Now, you can call the procedure with or without an index argument:

```
Sub TestChangeSheets2()
    ' Activates the sheet three sheets away.
    ChangeSheets2 3
    ' Activates the next sheet (omits argument)
    ChangeSheets2
End Sub
```

Visual Basic illustrates the optional argument and its default as you type, using the autocompletion feature as shown in Figure 2-6.

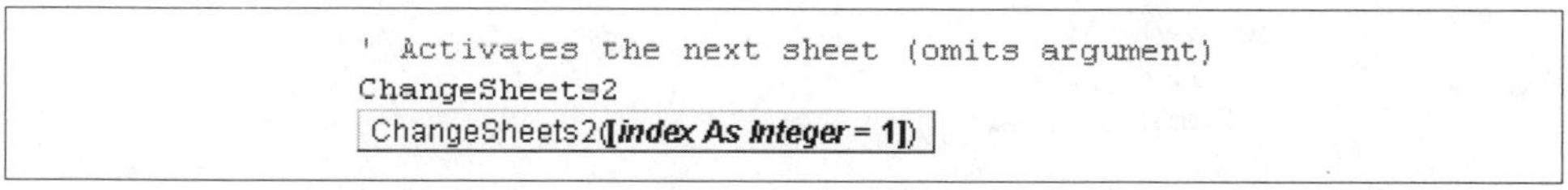

```
' Activates the next sheet (omits argument)
ChangeSheets2
ChangeSheets2(index As Integer = 1)
```

Figure 2-6. Optional arguments are shown with their default values

In some cases, you might want to fill in the default value of an optional argument with a value that is available only while the code is running instead of using a fixed setting. To do that, omit the default setting and test to see if the argument is Nothing in code. For example, the following procedure automatically formats the active worksheet if the ws argument is omitted:

```
Public Sub Reformat(Optional ws As Worksheet)
    ' Check if argument was omitted.
    If TypeName(ws) = "Nothing" Then
        ' Check the type of the active sheet.
        If TypeName(ActiveSheet) = "Worksheet" Then
            ' Format the active worksheet.
            Set ws = ActiveSheet
        Else
            ' You can't reformat nonworksheets.
            MsgBox "Select a worksheet and try again."
```

```
            Exit Sub
        End If
    End If
    Dim rng As Range
    ' Get the cells with data in them.
    Set rng = ws.UsedRange
    ' Apply AutoFormat
    rng.AutoFormat xlRangeAutoFormatSimple
End Sub
```

Most of the preceding code is devoted to checking whether the argument is missing and whether the active sheet is a worksheet. That is usually the case in this situation; you need to be careful to make sure the selected item will work with the rest of your code when filling in a default value this way.

In a few rare cases, you might want to write a procedure that takes any number of similar arguments. In that situation, declare the argument as a `ParamArray` as shown here:

```
Public Sub Reformat2(ParamArray sheets( ) As Variant)
    ' If argument is ommitted, call Reformat
    If IsMissing(sheets) Then
        Reformat
        Exit Sub
    End If
    ' Otherwise, go through each argument in the array.
    Dim var As Variant, ws As Worksheet
    For Each var In sheets
        If TypeName(var) = "Worksheet" Then
            ' Convert the type to Worksheet.
            Set ws = var
            ' Call Reformat.
            Reformat ws
        End If
    Next
End Sub
```

The `Reformat2` procedure can have any number of arguments, including none: the `IsMissing` function checks for that case. `ParamArray` arguments can only be `Variant`s, so you need to check each argument as shown in the `For Each` loop to make sure it's the right type. `Reformat2` simply reuses the `Reformat` procedure I created earlier to do the real work. Reusing existing code is always a good idea.

 The keyword `ParamArray` points up a terminology detail I'd rather ignore: the names used between parentheses in a procedure definition are called *arguments*; the variables passed in when the procedure is called are referred to as *parameters*. Confused? That's why I just call them all arguments.

To see how `ParamArray` works, call `Reformat2` as shown here:

```
Sub TestReformat2( )
    ' Format two worksheets
```

```
    Reformat2 Worksheets("2002"), Worksheets("2003")
    ' Format the active worksheet
    Reformat2
End Sub
```

Named Arguments

Visual Basic lets you include the name of arguments when you call a procedure. This is most obvious in recorded code:

```
Selection.AutoFormat Format:=xlRangeAutoFormatSimple, Number:=True, Font _
    :=True, Alignment:=True, Border:=True, Pattern:=True, Width:=True
```

The name before the := is the name of the argument and the item after it is the value of that argument. This is handy if you want to use mostly default values; for instance, the following code reformats a selection without adding borders or changing column widths:

```
Selection.AutoFormat Format:=xlRangeAutoFormatSimple, Border:=False, Width:=False
```

You can do the same thing without names by relying on the positions of the arguments instead. The following line does exactly the same thing as the preceding one:

```
Selection.AutoFormat xlRangeAutoFormatSimple, , , , False, , False
```

 I tend to omit named arguments because I feel they are often too verbose and because the next generation of Visual Basic (Visual Basic .NET) doesn't use them. Feel free to disagree with me on this one, though.

An approach that works better than named arguments in my opinion is using Visual Basic's Auto Complete feature. That feature doesn't work with generic types of objects like Selection and ActiveSheet, so you must first get the specific type of object as shown in Figure 2-7.

```
Dim rng As Range          ]— Get a specific type of object
Set rng = Selection       ]
rng.AutoFormat xlRangeAutoFormatSimple, , , , False
    AutoFormat([Format As XlRangeAutoFormat = xlRangeAutoFormatClassic1], [Number], [Font], [Alignment],
    [Border], [Pattern], [Width])

    Auto complete highlights the current argument
    each time you type a comma
```

Figure 2-7. Auto Complete makes named arguments unnecessary in my opinion

Properties

Function procedures return a result and so can be used on the righthand side of an assignment:

```
x = CubeRoot(42)
```

But what if you want to put a procedure name on the lefthand side? That's what properties do. *Property procedures* can be assigned to or assigned from—they can appear on *either* side of =. For example, the following code defines a Name property for a module:

```
' Code in PublicProcedures module
Dim m_name As String

' Assign the name.
Public Property Let Name(arg As String)
    m_name = arg
End Property

' Return the name
Public Property Get Name() As String
    Name = m_name
End Property
```

Code outside the module can set or return the value from m_name by calling the Name property:

```
Sub TestProperties()
    PublicProcedures.Name = "Module name"
    Debug.Print PublicProcedures.Name
End Sub
```

You could do something similar by just making m_name a public variable, but properties allow you special control that you don't get with that technique. For example, the following code makes sure that Name is set only once:

```
Public Property Let Name(arg As String)
    If arg <> "" And m_name = "" Then
        m_name = arg
    Else
        MsgBox "Name is already set to: " & m_name
    End If
End Property
```

You can make a property read-only by not defining a Let procedure:

```
Const m_date = #6/5/2004#

' Read-only property (no Let procedure)
Public Property Get Created()
    Created = m_date
End Property
```

Properties can represent objects if they use Set instead of Let. For example, the following read/write property keeps track of a range of cells currently in use by the module:

```
' Object property (uses Set instead of Let)
Public Property Set CurrentRange(arg As Range)
    Set m_range = arg
End Property
```

```
Public Property Get CurrentRange() As Range
    Set CurrentRange = m_range
End Property
```

You can use an object property as part of a Set statement as shown here:

```
Set PublicProcedures.CurrentRange = Selection
Debug.Print PublicProcedures.CurrentRange.Address
```

All of the property samples I show here are part of a module. It is more common to find properties defined in classes. In those cases, you must first create an instance of an object from the class before using the property. For example, if you created the preceding properties in a class module named PublicClass, you'd use the following code to test them:

```
Sub TestObjectProperties()
    Dim obj As New PublicClass
    ' Read-write property.
    obj.Name = "Module name"
    Debug.Print obj.Name
    ' Read-only property
    Debug.Print obj.Created
    ' Object property
    Set obj.CurrentRange = Selection
    Debug.Print obj.CurrentRange.Address
End Sub
```

Events

The last kind of procedure is special type of Sub called an event procedure. *Event procedures* are where you write code that responds to things that happen in Excel, such as the user opening a workbook, clicking on a button, or changing a selection.

Events can exist only in classes, so it's easiest to see them by looking somewhere like the ThisWorkbook class shown in Figure 2-8.

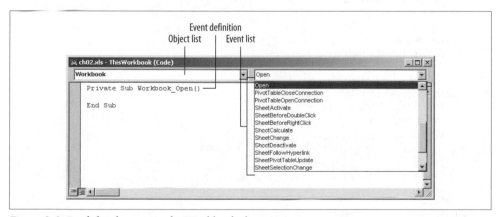

Figure 2-8. Predefined events in the Workbook class

To view the events that Excel defines for a class:

1. Open the class module in a Code window.
2. Select an object from the Code window's object list.
3. Select an event from the Code window's event list. Visual Basic inserts the event definition for the selected event in the Code window.

The event definition is a Sub procedure that matches to the event's name and argument list. Some events, such as Open, don't have any arguments; others, such as SheetSelectionChange, have several. Any code you add to an event definition is run whenever that event occurs in Excel. You can see how this works by adding the following event procedure to the ThisWorkbook class:

```
Private Sub Workbook_SheetSelectionChange(ByVal Sh As Object, _
  ByVal Target As Range)
    MsgBox "Sheet: " & Sh.Name & " " & " Selected range: " & Target.Address
End Sub
```

The preceding code displays the sheet name and range address any time you click on a new cell in the Excel workbook. There's more on Excel's built-in events later in this book. Right now, I'd like to tell you how to create your own events.

There are two phases to creating your own events in a class:

1. Declare the event using the Event keyword.
2. Trigger the event using the RaiseEvent keyword.

Go back to the PublicClass example I've been using, and add the following lines shown in **bold**:

```
' Code in PublicClass class

' Class-level variables used by properties
Dim m_name As String
Const m_date = "6/5/2004"
Dim m_range As range

' Event declaration
Public Event RangeChange(rng As range)

' Assign the Name property
Public Property Let Name(arg As String)
    If arg <> "" And m_name = "" Then
        m_name = arg
    Else
        MsgBox "Name is already set to: " & m_name
    End If
End Property

' Return the Name property
Public Property Get Name() As String
    Name = m_name
```

```
    End Property

    ' Read-only property (no Let procedure)
    Public Property Get Created()
        Created = CDate(m_date)
    End Property

    ' Object property (uses Set instead of Let)
    Public Property Set CurrentRange(arg As range)
        Set m_range = arg
        ' Trigger the event
        RaiseEvent RangeChange(m_range)
    End Property

    Public Property Get CurrentRange() As range
        Set CurrentRange = m_range
    End Property
```

Now objects created from PublicClass will include a RangeChange event that occurs whenever the class's CurrentRange property is set. To use this event from another class, such as ThisWorkbook, you must:

1. Declare an object using the WithEvents keyword. That adds the object to the Code window's events list.

2. Create an instance of the object.

3. Add an event definition for the event.

4. Do something to trigger the event.

To see the new event at work, open the ThisWorkbook class in a Code window and make the following changes:

```
' Code in ThisWorkbook class
Dim WithEvents obj As PublicClass

' Respond to the RangeChange event.
Private Sub obj_RangeChange(rng As range)
    ' Display the new current range.
    MsgBox "Current range: " & rng.Address
End Sub

Private Sub Workbook_SheetSelectionChange(ByVal Sh As Object, _
    ByVal Target As range)
    'MsgBox "Sheet: " & Sh.Name & " " & " Selected range: " & Target.Address
    ' Create object if it has not already been created.
    If TypeName(obj) = "Nothing" Then Set obj = New PublicClass
    ' Set the object's current range to trigger the event.
    Set obj.CurrentRange = Target
End Sub
```

Now when you click on cells in the workbook, your code changes the CurrentRange property which triggers the RangeChange event and displays a message box with the current setting. It might be useful to set a breakpoint in Workbook_SheetSelectionChange and step through the code to see how the code executes.

 If an event procedure takes arguments, you can't run it by pressing F5. Instead, you have to set a breakpoint and then trigger the event in Excel.

Variables

Variables are names that your code uses to refer to pieces of information. I've already shown lots of variables in code and used the word many times—you can't say much about programming without doing that and fortunately variables aren't a difficult concept to grasp, but there's a lot of details to know about them.

The following sections tell you all you need to know (possibly all there is to know) about variables in Visual Basic.

Names

Anything that you name in Visual Basic (variables, procedures, classes, etc.) has to follow certain rules. For example, if you try to name module 1off, you'll get an error (Figure 2-9).

Figure 2-9. Not all names are allowed in Visual Basic

To be valid in Visual Basic, a name must:

- Start with a letter (*A–Z*)
- Not include any of the restricted characters listed in Table 2-1
- Not be one of the Visual Basic restricted words listed in Table 2-1
- Be less than 256 characters long
- Be unique within its scope (more on scope later)

Table 2-1. Characters you can't use in Visual Basic names

(space)	~	`	'
"	.	^	*
(	)	-	+

Table 2-1. Characters you can't use in Visual Basic names (continued)

=	<	>	?
/	\	[	]
{	}	|	:
;	:	**%**	**!**
&	**$**	**#**	**@**

The last seven characters in Table 2-1 (in bold) are allowed if used as the last character in a name—in that case, they identify the data type of the variable. That is a holdover from older versions of Basic and it's not a good idea to use that practice in modern programs.

The words listed in Table 2-2 are restricted because Visual Basic couldn't determine the meaning of certain statements if they were allowed as variable or procedure names. In some cases, the word is no longer commonly used in Visual Basic programs (Rem, GoSub), but the restriction remains for compatibility with earlier versions.

Table 2-2. Words that can't be used as names in Visual Basic

AddressOf	And	Any	As	Boolean
ByRef	Byte	ByVal	Call	Case
CBool	CByte	CCur	CDate	CDbl
CInt	CLng	Close	Const	CSng
CStr	Currency	CVar	CVErr	Date
Debug	Declare	DefBool	DefByte	DefCur
DefDate	DefDbl	DefInt	DefLng	DefObj
DefSng	DefStr	DefVar	Dim	Do
Double	Each	Else	Empty	End
Enum	Eqv	Erase	Event	Exit
False	For	Friend	Function	Get
Global	GoSub	GoTo	If	Imp
Implements	In	Input	Integer	Is
LBound	Len	Let	Like	Lock
Long	Loop	LSet	Me	Mod
New	Next	Not	Nothing	Null
On	Open	Option	Optional	Or
ParamArray	Preserve	Print	Private	Public
Put	RaiseEvent	ReDim	Rem	Resume
Return	RSet	Seek	Select	Set
Single	Spc	Static	Stop	String
Sub	Tab	Then	To	True

Table 2-2. Words that can't be used as names in Visual Basic (continued)

AddressOf	And	Any	As	Boolean
Type	UBound	Unlock	Variant	Wend
While	With	WithEvents	Write	Xor

Declarations

Visual Basic has *automatic variables* by default. That means a new variable is created the first time you use it. This makes life somewhat easier for beginning programmers, but it makes things harder when writing and maintaining complex programs. For that reason, most experts recommend that you require variable declarations by adding Option Explicit to the beginning of each class or module.

Option Explicit turns off Visual Basic's automatic variables and thus requires that you declare each variable before you use it. To declare a variable, use the Dim statement:

```
Dim x As Integer
```

The preceding code declares that the name x is a variable that can contain an integer. The 12 different types of variables in Visual Basic are listed in Table 2-3.

Table 2-3. Data types for variables in Visual Basic

Type	Kind of data	Size	Values
Boolean	True/false choices	2 bytes	True (0), False (-1)
Byte	Binary data	1 byte	0–255
Currency	Monetary values	8 bytes	-922,337,203,685,477.5808 to 922,337,203,685,477.5807
Date	A date or time	8 bytes	1 January 100 to 31 December 9999
Double	Large decimal numbers	8 bytes	1.79769313486231E308 to -4.94065645841247E-324 for negative values and from 4.94065645841247E-324 to 1.79769313486232E308 for positive values
Integer	Whole numbers	2 bytes	-32,768 to 32,767
Long	Large whole numbers	4 bytes	-2,147,483,648 to 2,147,483,647
Object	An instance of a class	4 bytes	Address of the object in memory
Single	Decimal values	4 bytes	3.402823E38 to -1.401298E-45 for negative values and from 1.401298E-45 to 3.402823E38 for positive values
String	Text values	4 bytes	0 to approximately 2 billion (2^{31}) characters
String (fixed)	Fixed-length text values	1 byte per character	1 to 10,000 characters
Variant	Data that might be any type	4 bytes	Same as numeric and String types

If you don't specify a type when declaring a variable, Visual Basic makes it a Variant by default.

You can use any of the types listed in Table 2-3 as part of a `Dim` statement. For example, the following line declares integer, single, and string variables:

```
Dim i as Integer, s As Single, str As String
```

Most of the types in Table 2-3 are *value types*. Those types are stored as real values in an area of memory called the stack. The *stack* is a place that Visual Basic can access very quickly, but it has a limited size and can accommodate only variables that have fixed lengths. Some types, such as `Object`, `String`, and `Variant` don't have fixed lengths and so Visual Basic handles those as reference types. *Reference types* store a 4-byte number on the stack that resolves to the address where the data is actually stored.

String variables are kind of a special case because they can be value types or reference types depending on whether or not they have a fixed length. Most strings have a variable length—that is, they can grow or shrink as needed to fix the data they are assigned. However, you can define the length of a string if you like:

```
Dim fs As String * 12
```

The preceding line declares a fixed-length string 12 characters long. Visual Basic stores `fs` as a value type on the stack, but it truncates any strings that are more than 12 characters:

```
fs = "This is way too long for a 12-character string."
```

Becomes `This is way`. Fixed-length strings are mainly used in combination with advanced programming techniques such as reading binary files.

Modern computers come with lots of memory, and you're not likely to run out while programming in Excel. So why show size in Table 2-3? A few reasons:

- The size of a variable helps you understand its limits. For example, `Integers` are 2 bytes (which is 16 bits) and so have 65,536 (2^{16}) possible values. When you divide that between negative and positive numbers, you get a range of -32,768 to 32,767. Numbers outside that range result in an overflow error if assigned to an `Integer` variable.

- Size matters when converting from one data type to another. Larger types can cause overflow errors when converted to smaller types.

- You need to know the size of data types when creating user-defined types, reading binary data, or performing bitwise operations.

Conversions

Visual Basic automatically converts between data types during assignment. If one variable doesn't exactly match the type of another, Basic changes the value to fit. You can see this easily if you perform the following assignments:

```
Sub Conversions()
    Dim d As Double, s As Single, i As Integer
```

```
      d = WorksheetFunction.Pi
      s = d
      i = d
      Debug.Print d, s, i
   End Sub
```

The preceding code displays the following output in the Immediate window:

```
3.14159265358979           3.141593      3
```

 You need to be aware of automatic conversion, because it can result in the unintended loss of precision.

Here the conversion is done by rounding the number up or down to reflect the precision of the variable receiving the assignment. Not all conversion can be done by rounding. For example, the following lines convert pi to a string:

```
Dim str As String
str = WorksheetFunction.Pi
```

Warning: not all conversions succeed. The following line causes a type mismatch error because d is a numeric variable and the "Pi" can't be converted to a number:

```
d = "Pi"
```

Conversions may also fail if the assignment exceeds the limit of the target variable. For example, the following lines result in an overflow error since the positive limit for Integers is 32,627:

```
Dim l As Long
l = 32768
i = l
```

You can explicitly perform any of these automatic conversions using the Visual Basic conversion functions listed in Table 2-4.

Table 2-4. Visual Basic type conversion functions

CBool	CByte	CCur	CDate	CDbl
CDec	CInt	CLng	CSng	CStr
CVar				

It would be nice if you could turn off Visual Basic's automatic conversions and use the explicit conversion functions shown in Table 2-4 only when needed. But you can't. In addition to the conversion functions, Visual Basic provides other keywords that are useful when working with types; they are listed in Table 2-5.

Table 2-5. Visual Basic keywords for working with types

Keyword	Use to
IsDate	Return True if the variable is a date
IsEmpty	Return True if the variable hasn't been initialized
IsNull	Return True if a Variant variable does not contain valid data
IsNumeric	Return True if the variable can be converted to a numeric value
IsObject	Return True if the variable is a reference to an object
TypeName	Return the name of the variable's type as a string
TypeOf	Determine the type of an object variable within an If statement

Scope and Lifetime

Dim is not the only way to declare a variable. The full list of declaration keywords is shown in Table 2-6.

Table 2-6. Visual Basic declaration statements

Statement	Use to declare	Available
Dim	A variable with the default scope	Inside or outside a procedure
Public	A variable or procedure that is available from other modules or classes	Outside a procedure only
Private	A variable or procedure that is not available from other modules or classes	Outside a procedure only
Static	A variable that retains its value between procedure calls	Inside a procedure only

Which statement you use to declare a variable and where you declare it determines the scope and lifetime of that variable. *Scope* is the range of places from which a name is visible. Dim, Public, and Private are statements that specify scope. *Lifetime* is how long Visual Basic retains the value of a variable; Static specifies lifetime.

There are three levels of scope in a Visual Basic project:

- Local variables are declared with Dim inside a procedure and are visible only from within that procedure.
- Module-level variables are declared outside of a procedure with Dim or Private and are visible only from all procedures within that module or class.
- Global variables are declared outside of a procedure with Public and are visible from all procedures in all modules and classes within the project.

Figure 2-10 illustrates the different levels of scope within a Visual Basic project.

 It's a common practice to prefix global variables with g_ and module-level variable names with m_ as shown in Figure 2-10.

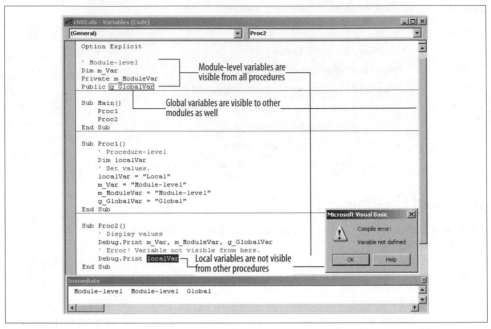

Figure 2-10. If Option Explicit is specified, you get an error when a variable is not visible

A variable defined at one level of scope can be shadowed by another defined at a lower level of scope. *Shadowing* hides the higher-level variable from the local use. For example, Proc1 in Figure 2-10 could shadow m_Var by declaring it at the procedure level as shown here in **bold**:

```
Sub Proc1( )
    ' Procedure-level
    Dim localVar
    ' Shadow module-level variable.
    Dim m_Var
    ' Set values.
    m_Var = "Private module-level"
    m_PublicVar = "Public module-level"
    m_PrivateVar = "Private module-level"
    localVar = "Procedure-level"
End Sub
```

In this case, Proc1 creates a new, local version of m_Var and sets its value. Proc2 can't see that value but it can still see the module-level version of m_Var, which doesn't contain a value. If you run Main, the output is this (note the blank space where m_Var should be):

```
Public module-level     Private module-level
```

Shadowing is often a mistake, rather than an intentional technique. Using a scope prefix like g_ or m_ for global and module-level variables helps to avoid this problem.

Declaring a local variable as Static tells Visual Basic to retain the variable's value between procedure calls. Ordinarily, local variables are created when a procedure is called, then destroyed when the procedure ends. This means local variables have a very short lifetime. Static tells Visual Basic to keep the variable alive as long as the program is running—for Excel Visual Basic projects, that lifetime begins when the user opens the workbook and ends when he closes it.

As a practical matter, you can do much the same thing with global and module-level variables since they are also created when Excel opens the workbook and destroyed when the workbook closes. The difference is scope; Static variables are local and so can't be changed outside of the procedure where they are declared. The following example demonstrates using a Static variable:

```
Sub StaticVariable()
    ' Static variables are local.
    Static staticVar As Integer
    staticVar = staticVar + 1
    ' This variable is global.
    g_GlobalVar = g_GlobalVar + 1
    ' They both retain their value.
    Debug.Print staticVar, g_GlobalVar
End Sub
```

Both staticVar and g_GlobalVar display the same value. If you run StaticVariable repeatedly, you'll see their values increment. The difference is that other procedures can see (and change) the value of g_GlobalVar.

Why is this important? Because restricting the scope of variables is one of the keys to preventing accidental errors in your code. The more global variables you have, the more likely you are to have adverse interactions between procedures.

Keep variables as private as possible. Use arguments to pass values between procedures. Use module-level or global variables for values that need to be shared by most or all procedures.

Scope for Procedures

You may have guessed that procedures have levels of scope, too. In fact, Visual Basic uses the same keywords (plus one) to define the scope of a procedure. The following procedure declarations show the scope and lifetime keywords in use (in **bold**):

```
Private Sub Proc1()
    ' Private procedures are local to the module or class.
End Sub

Public Sub Proc2()
    ' Public procedures are global to all open projects.
End Sub

Friend Sub Proc3()
```

```
    ' Friend procedures are public to the project that contains them.
    ' This is available only in classes.
End Sub

Private Static Sub Proc3()
    ' In Static procedures, all local variables are Static.
    ' Static procedures may be Private, Public, or Friend.
End Sub
```

The default scope for procedures is public, so omitting the scope keyword is the same as declaring the procedure as `Public`. Most of the procedures you create will probably be public. Use `Private` or `Friend` when you want to restrict how others use a procedure. For example, declaring a function in a module as `Private` prevents users from using it as a user-defined function in an Excel formula.

Constants and Enumerations

Constants are names that have fixed values. Visual Basic and Excel each defines many constants that are used to identify commonly used settings and values. For example, the constant `vbCrLf` is used to start new paragraphs within strings:

```
Debug.Print "This" & vbCrLf & "and that"
```

To declare your own constants, use the `Const` statement:

```
' Module level
Const AUTHOR = "Jeff Webb"
Const VERSION = 1.1
Const CHANGED = #6/5/2004#
```

 It's a common practice to capitalize constant names in code. It's also common to avoid using local (procedure-level) constants since they may shadow global or module-level constants.

Constant have global (`Public`), module-level (`Private`), or local scope and they can be shadowed. However, you can't assign to a constant after it is declared. That is what distinguishes constants from variables! The following code demonstrates using the preceding module-level constants in a procedure:

```
Sub Constants()
    ' Constants can be shadowed.
    Const AUTHOR = "Joey"
    Debug.Print AUTHOR, VERSION, "Days since changed: " & Round(Now - CHANGED)
End Sub
```

If you run the code, you'll see the following output in the Immediate window:

```
Joey           1.1         Days since changed: 4
```

You don't specify a type when declaring constants, but Visual Basic assigns one based on the value you set. The # signs in the preceding declarations identify the value as a date, so Visual Basic can use those values to evaluate how much time has passed since the last change. You can use the other type-declaration characters if you want to use a special data type for the constant, such as Currency (@):

```
Public Const PRICE = 24.95@
```

Enumerations are a special type of constant that organizes a group of values by name. There are all sorts of enumerations used in Visual Basic itself; a good example is the VbMsgBoxResult enumeration:

```
Sub GetResponse( )
    ' Declare variable as an enumerated value
    Dim res As VbMsgBoxResult
    ' Get the response.
    res = MsgBox("What's your response?", vbYesNoCancel)
    ' Test the response against possible values.
    Debug.Print "Response is:", Switch(res = vbYes, "Yes", _
        res = vbNo, "No", res = vbCancel, "Cancel")
End Sub
```

In the preceding code, the variable res can contain any of the possible message box results. The Switch function compares the variable to each of the possible responses to display an appropriate string in the Immediate window.

These enumerations are handy in part because they enable Auto Complete for the variable in the Visual Basic code window. If you type res = or VbMsgBoxResult, you'll automatically see the possible settings for the variable—that really helps you remember the Visual Basic constant names, which are sometimes very long.

You can create your own enumerations by using the Enum keyword. Enum is kind of like a block Const statement:

```
Enum Numbers
    One = 1
    Two = 2
    Three = 3
End Enum
```

You can use the Numbers enumeration in code, just as you would any Visual Basic enumeration:

```
Sub DemoEnum( )
    ' Declare a variable as a user-defined enumerated value.
    Dim res As Numbers
    ' Set the value of the variable.
    res = One
    ' Display its value.
    Debug.Print res
End Sub
```

Arrays

Arrays are variables that identify a set of values. That set has one or more *dimensions*, and each item within the set is identified by an *index* within that dimension, as illustrated in Figures 2-11 and 2-12.

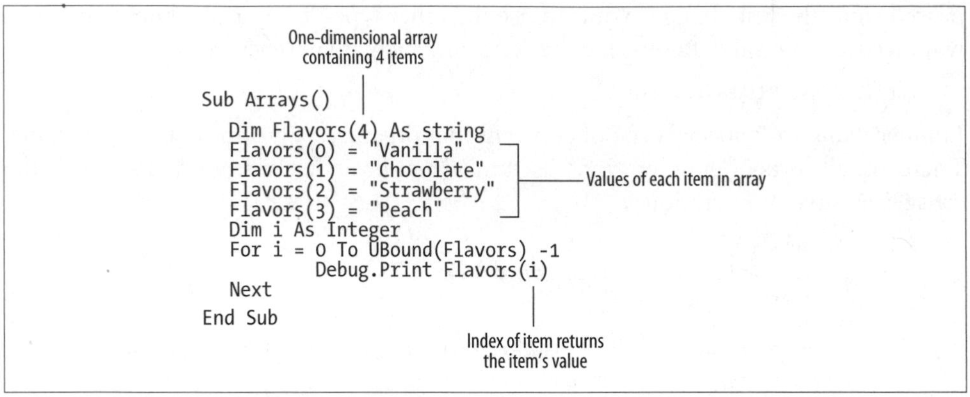

```
                    One-dimensional array
                    containing 4 items
                         |
Sub Arrays()             |

    Dim Flavors(4) As string
    Flavors(0) = "Vanilla"
    Flavors(1) = "Chocolate"
    Flavors(2) = "Strawberry"        Values of each item in array
    Flavors(3) = "Peach"
    Dim i As Integer
    For i = 0 To UBound(Flavors) -1
            Debug.Print Flavors(i)

    Next
End Sub                          |
                     Index of item returns
                       the item's value
```

Figure 2-11. One-dimensional arrays are simply lists

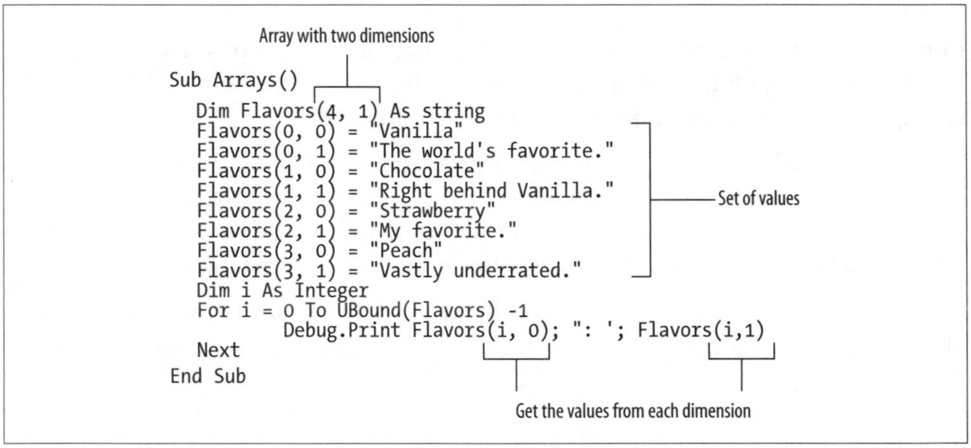

```
                    Array with two dimensions
                            |
Sub Arrays()          |_____|_____|

    Dim Flavors(4, 1) As string
    Flavors(0, 0) = "Vanilla"
    Flavors(0, 1) = "The world's favorite."
    Flavors(1, 0) = "Chocolate"
    Flavors(1, 1) = "Right behind Vanilla."
    Flavors(2, 0) = "Strawberry"               Set of values
    Flavors(2, 1) = "My favorite."
    Flavors(3, 0) = "Peach"
    Flavors(3, 1) = "Vastly underrated."
    Dim i As Integer
    For i = 0 To UBound(Flavors) -1
            Debug.Print Flavors(i, 0); ": "; Flavors(i,1)
    Next
End Sub
                            Get the values from each dimension
```

Figure 2-12. Arrays with two dimensions are tables

Arrays can have more than two dimensions, but that starts to get hard to illustrate on paper. One- and two-dimensional arrays are by far the most common. You use arrays whenever you have a set of data that you want to work with as a unit—lists and tables are typical examples of when to use an array.

The items in an array must all have the same data type, but that's not very restrictive considering that you can have arrays of Variants, which can assume any other type. For example, the following array contains the names of products and their prices. To prove that the stored prices are numbers, I calculate the tax on each price before displaying the table in the Immediate window:

```
Sub ShowVariantArray()
    Const RATE = 0.06
    Dim PriceChart(4, 1) As Variant
    PriceChart(0, 0) = "Grudgeon"
    PriceChart(0, 1) = 24.95@
    PriceChart(1, 0) = "Pintle"
```

```
        PriceChart(1, 1) = 11.15@
        PriceChart(2, 0) = "Tiller"
        PriceChart(2, 1) = 93.75@
        PriceChart(3, 0) = "Rudder"
        PriceChart(3, 1) = 42.49@
        Dim i As Integer
        Debug.Print "Item", "Price", "Tax"
        For i = 0 To UBound(PriceChart) - 1
            Debug.Print PriceChart(i, 0), PriceChart(i, 1), _
                Round(PriceChart(i, 1) * RATE, 2)
        Next
    End Sub
```

The preceding arrays have a fixed number of items, set when the array was declared. That's realistic if you know that the number of items won't change frequently, but it's much more handy to be able to change the number of items dynamically at run-time. To create a dynamic array, declare the array with an empty number of dimensions, then use ReDim to declare the bounds. For example, the following code declares an array named Values, resizes the array to fit the number of cells selected in Excel, then copies the values from the selected range of cells into that array (key items in **bold**):

```
Sub DynamicArray()
    Dim Values() As Variant
    ' Get rows and columns of selected range
    Dim rows As Integer, cols As Integer
    rows = Selection.rows.count
    cols = Selection.Columns.count
    ReDim Values(1 To rows, 1 To cols)
    ' If multiple cells are selected, Selection returns an array.
    If IsArray(Selection) Then
        Values = Selection
        Dim i As Integer, j As Integer, str As String
        For i = 1 To rows
            str = ""
            For j = 1 To cols
                str = str & vbTab & Values(i, j)
            Next
            Debug.Print str
        Next
    End If
End Sub
```

 By default, arrays' bounds start at 0, but you can change that as shown by ReDim Values(1 To rows, 1 To cols). I do that so the Values array matches the bounds used by the array returned by Excel's Selection method. Arrays returned by Excel always start at 1.

Dynamic arrays are usually cleared any time you call ReDim. The exception to that rule occurs if you are using a one-dimensional array (a list) and you qualify ReDim with Preserve to save the existing data in the array. Here's our Flavors array again, but this time you can add items:

```
Sub DynamicArrayPreserve()
    Dim Flavors() As String
    ' Set the inital size of the array.
    ReDim Flavors(4)
    ' Set some values.
    Flavors(0) = "Vanilla"
    Flavors(1) = "Chocolate"
    Flavors(2) = "Strawberry"
    Flavors(3) = "Peach"
    ' Add items to the list, enlarging it as needed.
    Dim str As String, count As Integer
    Do
        ' Get the count of items in list.
        count = UBound(Flavors)
        str = InputBox("Enter a flavor.")
        ' Exit if nothing entered.
        If str = "" Then Exit Do
        ' Make the array bigger.
        ReDim Preserve Flavors(count + 1)
        ' Set the value of the new item
        Flavors(count) = str
    Loop
    ' Display the items
    Dim i As Integer
    For i = 0 To UBound(Flavors) - 1
        Debug.Print Flavors(i)
    Next
End Sub
```

Visual Basic can make arrays larger at runtime because all arrays are reference types. The value represented by the array name in Visual Basic is the address of where the array starts. Table 2-7 lists the keywords that Visual Basic provides for working with arrays.

Table 2-7. Visual Basic array keywords

Keyword	Use to
Array	Create an array from a list of values.
Erase	Clear the values in an array.
IsArray	Determine whether or not a variable is an array.
LBound	Get the lower bound of an array dimension.
Option Base	Change the default lower bound of arrays. (This is not generally a good practice and is mainly provided for compatibility with earlier Basics.)
UBound	Get the upper bound of an array dimension.

User-Defined Types

You can create your own composite types out of the existing Visual Basic types. These composite types are called *user-defined types* in Visual Basic and they are used primarily for advanced tasks such as reading and writing binary files or working with Windows API functions.

Use the Type statement to define a user-defined type:

```
' Code in Variables module
Private Type POINTAPI
    x As Long
    y As Long
End Type

Private Declare Function GetCursorPos _
    Lib "user32" (lp As POINTAPI) As Long
```

The preceding module-level definition creates a type named POINTAPI that contains two Long types. This definition matches the argument returned by the GetCursorPos Windows API function, and it enables you to get at the values returned by that function in code. For example, the following procedure displays the location of the cursor:

```
Sub ShowCursorPosition()
    Dim point As POINTAPI
    GetCursorPos point
    MsgBox point.x & " " & point.y
End Sub
```

The preceding code declares the point variable using the POINTAPI type defined earlier; then it calls the Windows GetCursorPos function to fill in the value of point. It is common for Windows API functions to return values through user-defined types in this way (Windows calls user-defined types *structures*). Variables with user-defined types use the period to get items from within the type. Thus, point.x gets the value of the x-coordinate in the preceding example.

Objects

Object is the general term for an instance of a class. Visual Basic has an Object type that you can use to create variables that reference any generic object; however, you usually want to create variables of a specific class of object. Objects are a special kind of variable because you can control when they are created. Other types of variables in Visual Basic are initialized whenever they are declared, but that's not true with objects.

The easiest way to create an object variable is to include the New keyword in the variable declaration. For example, the following line creates a new object variable from the PublicClass class definition:

```
Dim obj As New PublicClass
```

Once created, you can use that object's properties and methods to do whatever it is you want to do. New is an executable statement; if you use it at the module level, the actual creation of the object is delayed till the first time the object is referenced within a procedure—a confusing situation that is best to avoid. If you declare an object variable at the module level, omit New, then create the object within a procedure explicitly. For example, the following code creates a global object variable and creates the object the first time UseObject runs:

```
' Global object variable
Public g_obj As PublicClass

Sub UseObject( )
    ' Create global object variable
    If g_obj Is "Nothing" Then Set g_obj = New PublicClass
    ' Show that the object exists
    Debug.Print g_obj.CREATED
End Sub
```

There are a few significant things to point out about the preceding code:

- The module-level declaration uses a specific class type. That makes the class's methods and properties available to Visual Basic's Auto Complete feature as you write code.

- TypeName(g_obj) = "Nothing" is True if the object has not been created. In that case, the Set statement creates a new instance of the object.

- Visual Basic also provides an IsEmpty function to check if an object has been created, but that works only with the generic Object type—it doesn't work with specific classes.

To destroy an object, set the object variable to Nothing:

```
Set g_obj = Nothing
```

This is not necessary when the object is a local variable, since those are automatically destroyed when the procedure ends. However, global, module-level, and Static variables exist as long as the workbook is open unless you explicitly destroy them.

Excel provides many objects that you can use from Visual Basic, but they can be created only through other Excel objects. For example, the following two statements are equivalent, and neither one creates a new worksheet!

```
Dim ws1 As Worksheet
Dim ws2 As New Worksheet
```

To create an object from Excel, you usually use the Add method of the object's collection class:

```
Sub CreateExcelObject( )
    ' Declare a Worksheet object variable
    Dim ws As Worksheet
    ' Create the Worksheet
    Set ws = Worksheets.Add
End Sub
```

Since Excel controls the creation of its objects, it also controls their destruction. Setting ws to Nothing just destroys the object reference; it doesn't remove the worksheet. To destroy an Excel object, you usually use the object's Delete method as shown here:

```
ws.Delete
```

Visual Basic includes the keyword With to create blocks of code that work *with* a specific object. The With statement creates a shorthand for repeatedly referring to the same object, and you will frequently see it in recorded code. For example, the following code creates a new worksheet and sets the object's properties using With:

```
Sub UseWith( )
    ' Create a new worksheet in a With statement
    With Worksheets.Add
        .Name = "New Worksheet"
        .Range("A1") = "Some new data..."
        ActiveWindow.DisplayGridlines = False
    End With
End Sub
```

The Worksheets.Add method returns a reference to the worksheet object that is then used by the subsequent properties. Each property begins with a period inside of the With block. Statements that don't refer to the object, such as ActiveWindow, simply omit the period.

> There's nothing wrong with using With, but I prefer to use the variable name explicitly. That's just my style.

Conditional Statements

One of the fundamental elements of programming is making decisions based on inputs. Visual Basic provides the If statement for making either/or decisions and the Select statement for making multiple-choice decisions. These two statements form the core of any logic your program uses to adjust to different conditions, and for that reason they are called *conditional statements*.

The If statement has several different forms:

- A very simple one-line form:

```
If IsArray(Selection) Then MsgBox "Multiple cells selected."
```

- A block form that can contain multiple lines and alternative actions:

```
Dim str As String
If IsArray(Selection) Then
    str = "Grand total: " &
        WorksheetFunction.Sum(Selection)
Else
    str = "Please select more than one cell"
End If
MsgBox str
```

- A block form with multiple conditions and alternate actions:

```
If IsArray(Selection) Then
    str = "Grand total: " & _
      WorksheetFunction.Sum(Selection)
ElseIf TypeName(ActiveSheet) = "Worksheet" Then
    str = "Worksheet total: " & _
      WorksheetFunction.Sum(ActiveSheet.UsedRange)
Else
    str = "Please select a worksheet"
End If
MsgBox str
```

You can have multiple `ElseIf` statements within an `If` block as shown by the following general form:

```
If condition Then
    ' Do something
[ElseIf condition Then
    ' Do something else]
[ElseIf condition Then
    ' Can repeat ElseIf]
[Else
    ' Do something else]
End If
```

For more complex logic, you can include `If` statements within an enclosing `If` statement, or you can use the `Select Case` statement. The following `Select Case` statement compares the current time against a list of literal times to determine which message to display:

```
Dim str As String
Select Case Time
    Case Is > #10:00:00 PM#
        str = "Bed time!"
    Case Is > #7:00:00 PM#
        str = "Time to relax."
    Case Is > #6:00:00 PM#
        str = "Dinner time!"
    Case Is > #5:00:00 PM#
        str = "Drive time."
    Case Is > #1:00:00 PM#
        str = "Work time."
    Case Is > #12:00:00 PM#
        str = "Lunch time!"
    Case Is > #8:00:00 AM#
        str = "Work time."
    Case Is > #7:00:00 AM#
        str = "Breakfast time!"
    Case Else
        str = "Too early!"
End Select
MsgBox str
```

Select statements are evaluated from the top down. Select exits after the first match, so only one of the messages is set.

Visual Basic provides one more conditional statement, though it is not commonly used. The Switch statement is similar to Select, but rather than executing statements, Switch returns a value based on different conditions. The following code is equivalent to the preceding example, except it uses Switch rather than Select:

```
Dim str As String
str = Switch(Time > #10:00:00 PM#, "Bed time!", _
    Time > #7:00:00 PM#, "Time to relax.", _
    Time > #6:00:00 PM#, "Dinner time!", _
    Time > #5:00:00 PM#, "Drive time.", _
    Time > #1:00:00 PM#, "Work time.", _
    Time > #12:00:00 PM#, "Lunch time!", _
    Time > #8:00:00 AM#, "Work time.", _
    Time > #7:00:00 AM#, "Breakfast time!", _
    Time >= #12:00:00 AM#, "Too early!")
MsgBox str
```

Perhaps the reason Switch isn't used more often is because it results in long statements that must be broken over multiple lines to be readable in the Code window.

Loops

The other fundamental part of programming logic is the ability to repeat a set of actions until some condition is met. This type of logic is called *looping*. I talked a little about loops in Chapter 1; here I'll show you the different types of loops Visual Basic provides. Table 2-8 lists the looping statements in Visual Basic.

Table 2-8. Visual Basic statements for repeating actions

Statement	Use to
Do...Loop or While...Wend	Repeat a set of actions until a condition is met
For...Next	Repeat a set of actions a number of times using a counter
For Each	Repeat as set of actions for each item in a collection

Do...Loop and While...Wend are similar, but Do...Loop is more flexible so most programmers simply ignore While...Wend. I'm going to follow their lead—if you're interested, you can read about While...Wend in Help.

The Do...Loop statement repeats a set of actions until a condition is met; you can include the condition at the beginning or the end of the loop. For example, the following code speaks any words you type in an input box and exits if you don't type anything:

```
Sub RepeatAfterMe( )
    Dim str As String
    Do
```

```
        str = InputBox("Enter something to say.", "Repeat after me...")
        Application.Speech.Speak str
    Loop While str <> ""
End Sub
```

The preceding code executes the Speak method one time more than it really needs to —after the user cancels the input. This isn't a big problem, but you can avoid it by using an Exit Do statement instead of testing the condition at the end of the loop (change shown in **bold**):

```
Sub RepeatAfterMe( )
    Dim str As String
    Do
        str = InputBox("Enter something to say.", "Repeat after me...")
        If str = "" Then Exit Do
        Application.Speech.Speak str
    Loop
End Sub
```

It's not good style to use Exit Do within long, complicated loops. In those situations, it's important to be able to easily locate the exit condition, and burying it within the body of the loop makes it harder to find. If the unneeded Speak method still bothers you, just change the loop as shown here:

```
Sub RepeatAfterMe( )
    Dim str As String
    Do
        str = InputBox("Enter something to say.", "Repeat after me...")
        If str <> "" Then _
            Application.Speech.Speak str
    Loop While str <> ""
End Sub
```

Now the loop executes no unneeded statements. There's one last step in this example: the Speech object was introduced in Excel 2002. If you want the preceding code to work with previous versions of Excel, you need to add some conditional logic as shown here:

```
Sub RepeatAfterMe( )
    Dim str As String
    Do
        str = InputBox("Enter something to say.", "Repeat after me...")
        ' Speech was added in Excel 10
        If Application.VERSION >= 10 And str <> "" Then
            Application.Speech.Speak str
        ' This is boring, but it works with all versions!
        ElseIf str <> "" Then
            MsgBox str, , "Repeat after me."
        End If
    Loop While str <> ""
End Sub
```

This example shows how loops and conditional statements are often used together. Together they form the logical path that your program follows.

Placing the condition first in a Do...Loop prevents the loop from running unless the condition is true to start with. You can choose between While and Until when testing a condition; they are inverses of each other so While str <> "" is the same as Until str = "". The basic form of a Do...Loop is as follows:

```
Do [While condition | Until condition]
    ' action
    [If condition Then Exit Do]
Loop [While condition | Until condition]
```

For...Next statements perform an action a set number of times as determined by a variable used as a counter. In many situations, you know how many times you want to repeat an action, but the most common is probably when working with lists or tables of items from an array. In that case, you know the start point (the lower bound of the array) and the end point (the upper bound of the array), as shown by this code from an earlier sample:

```
' Display the items in the Flavors array
Dim i As Integer
For i = 0 To UBound(Flavors) - 1
    Debug.Print Flavors(i)
Next
```

By default, For...Next increments the counter (i) by one each time the loop executes. Thus, Flavors(i) gets each element of the array from 0 to one less than the upper bound. That last bit might seem a little odd, but UBound returns the number of elements in the array, not the maximum index of the array; in this case, the array starts at 0, so the maximum index is one less than the upper bound. If the lower bound is 1 (as it is for arrays returned by Excel methods), then the For...Next loop looks like this:

```
Sub ForNextLoop()
    If Not IsArray(Selection.Value) Then Exit Sub
    Dim i As Integer, j As Integer, str As String
    For i = 1 To UBound(Selection.Value, 1)
        str = ""
        For j = 1 To UBound(Selection.Value, 2)
            str = str & vbTab & Selection(i, j)
        Next
        Debug.Print str
    Next
End Sub
```

In the preceding code, `Selection.Value` returns an array if more than one cell is selected. Since Excel arrays start at 1, the count of elements in the array is the same as the array's upper bound.

You can change the increment used by `For...Next` by using the `Step` keyword as shown by the following general version of the `For...Next` statement:

```
For counter = start To stop [Step increment]
    ' action
    [If condition Then Exit For]
Next [counter]
```

Use a negative number for *increment* to count backward. For example, the following code performs a 10-second countdown:

```
Sub CountDown( )
    Dim i As Integer
    For i = 10 To 1 Step -1
        Debug.Print i
        Application.Wait Now + #12:00:01 AM#
    Next
    Debug.Print "Blast off!"
End Sub
```

In some cases, it is more convenient to perform an action on each item in a group, rather than relying on the number of items in the group. For those situations, Visual Basic provides the `For Each` statement. The following code displays a list of the workbook's worksheets in the Immediate window:

```
Dim ws As Worksheet
For Each ws In Worksheets
    Debug.Print ws.Name
Next
```

`For Each` works only with *collections*, which are a special type of object that contains a group of other objects. All collections have a special, hidden property called an *enumerator* that allows them to work with `For Each`. Collections also usually have an `Add` method and a `Count` property and are usually named using the plural form of the name of the object they contain. Thus the `Worksheets` collection contains `Worksheet` objects.

> Excel doesn't always follow these rules for collections. That's why I say *usually* here.

`For Each` sets the object variable to the next object in the collection each time the loop executes and automatically ends after it reaches the last object. There's no `Step` keyword to skip objects or count backward; the general form of the statement looks like this:

```
For Each object In collection
    ' action
    [If condition Then Exit For]
Next [object]
```

The type of *object* must be the same as the type of objects in *collection*. Some collections, such as the collection returned by the Excel Sheets method, can contain objects of more than one type. Therefore, the following code would cause a type-mismatch error if a workbook contains a Chart sheet:

```
Sub ForEachLoop()
    Dim ws As Worksheet
    For Each ws In Sheets ' Possible error!
        Debug.Print ws.Name
    Next
End Sub
```

If you want to work with a mixed collection like Sheets, use a generic object as shown here:

```
Sub ForEachLoop()
    Dim obj As Object
    For Each obj In Sheets
        Debug.Print obj.Name, TypeName(obj)
    Next
End Sub
```

Now the code displays a list of all the sheets in the workbook, along with their type.

Expressions

In programming languages, *expressions* are anything that produces a result. You use expressions to evaluate something, such as a math calculation or a true/false condition. In Visual Basic, the Immediate window functions as an expression evaluator, so it's a good place to try out different expressions, as shown in Figure 2-13.

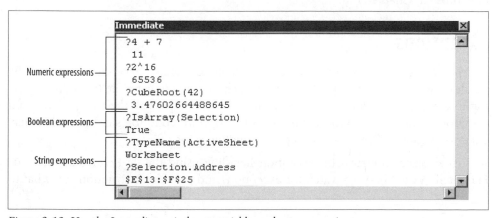

Figure 2-13. Use the Immediate window to quickly evaluate expressions

Expressions can return values of any type, including arrays or references to objects. The Immediate window can't display those types, however. Within a program, expressions are usually found to the right of the equals sign:

```
res = CubeRoot(42)
```

But they can also be used as part of any statement that takes a value:

```
If IsArray(Selection) Then MsgBox("You selected multiple cells.")
```

Simple expressions can be combined to form complex ones using *operators*. Visual Basic provides different sets of operators depending on the type of the expression, as listed in Table 2-9.

Table 2-9. Visual Basic operators

Numeric operators	Comparison operators (return Boolean values)	Logical operators	String operators	Object operators
^	=	And	&	Is
-	<>	Eqv	Like	Set (assign)
*	<	Imp	= (assign)	
/	>	Not		
\	<=	Or		
Mod	>=	Xor		
+				
= (assign)				

The Like and Is operators in Table 2-9 return Boolean values, but I group them with the String and Object types because they operate on those types exclusively.

Expressions are often the result of a function call. There are many built-in functions for working with numbers, dates, times, strings, and objects in Visual Basic. I discuss those in Chapter 3.

Exceptions

Exceptions are runtime errors that you anticipate. Generally, exceptions occur as the result of using resources outside of Excel, such as trying to get a file from disk or trying to connect to a database. It's very difficult to anticipate all the things that could go wrong and unnecessarily complex to try to write code for situations that may occur only rarely. That's what exception handling is for.

In Visual Basic, you turn on exception handling using the On Error statement. On Error tells Visual Basic to watch for exceptions and provides instructions on what to do if one happens. For example, the following code starts Notepad from Excel; if Notepad isn't installed or can't be found, Excel displays a warning message:

```
Sub ShowNotepad( )
    On Error Resume Next
    Shell "notepad.exe", vbNormalFocus
    If Err Then MsgBox "Notepad could not be found.", , "Warning"
End Sub
```

This style of exception handling is called *inline* because On Error Resume Next tells Visual Basic to execute the rest of the procedure one line at a time even if a problem occurs. With this technique you typically test the value of Err after each line that you think might cause an exception.

Err returns an Error object if an error occurred. The Error object's default property is the error code number, and the preceding code simply tests if that value is not zero (False). In some cases you may want to test the value within a Select Case statement. On Error provides an alternate syntax that causes any error to jump to a generalized exception-handling routine, as shown here:

```
Sub GetFile( )
    Dim str As String
    On Error GoTo errGetFile
    ' Open a file
    Open "a:\datafile.txt" For Input As #1
    Exit Sub
' Handle possible exceptions
errGetFile:
    Select Case Err
        Case 53
            str = "File not found. Insert data disk in drive A."
        Case 55
            str = "File in use by another application. " & _
                "Close the file and retry."
        Case 71
            str = "Insert disk in drive A."
        Case Else
            str = Err.Description
    End Select
    MsgBox str, , "Error"
End Sub
```

If an exception occurs in the preceding code, execution jumps to the errGetFile label and the Select statement sets the message to display based on the error code. You must include an Exit statement before the label to prevent the procedure from displaying a message if no exception occurs.

This style of exception handling allows you provide specific responses to different types of exceptions, but as a practical matter it isn't as useful as inline exception handling since knowing the line where an exception occurred is usually more informative than the error code.

 It can be difficult to debug procedures when exception handling is turned on, since exceptions don't immediately stop the code and display a message.

To turn off exception handling within a procedure, use this statement:

```
On Error Goto 0
```

You should turn off exception handling after you've completed the statements you think might cause an exception. Visual Basic automatically turns off exception handling after the procedure completes, so you need to worry about this only if your procedure calls other procedures or if you have a very long procedure.

What You've Learned

In this chapter you learned how Visual Basic programs are constructed. You should be able to create procedures that use arguments and variables and to call one procedure from another.

You should be comfortable using the sample code, creating conditional statements and loops, using arrays, and creating expressions that use the Visual Basic operators.

Come back here later if you need help with optional arguments, properties, events, data types, or exceptions.

Tasks in Visual Basic

Once you're comfortable recording and changing code in Excel and you're familiar with the structure of a Visual Basic program, you can focus your effort on doing real work with your programs. By real work, I mean: performing calculations, composing text, comparing dates and times, and accomplishing the other tasks provided by the Visual Basic language.

As with Chapter 2, most of the tasks I cover here are not unique to Excel, and if you learn them well, you can use these skills to program Word, PowerPoint, or even Windows itself. This chapter is the companion to Chapter 2; between the two chapters you'll learn most of what you need to know about the Visual Basic programming language.

 Code used in this chapter and additional samples are available in *ch03.xls*.

Types of Tasks

You can perform several broad categories of tasks with the Visual Basic language. Since we're talking about Visual Basic (not Excel), these tasks tend to be very general. More specific tasks are usually handled through Excel objects.

I've organized this chapter so the simplest tasks are first. By the end, things get pretty advanced, so if you feel overwhelmed at any point, feel free to come back later—you may just need some time to digest these concepts. Table 3-1 organizes the sections in this chapter to give you a bit of an overview.

Table 3-1. An overview of Visual Basic programming tasks

Category	Section	Overview
Users	Interact with Users	Use simple dialog boxes to get or display information.
Data	Do Math	Perform calculations.
	Work with Text	Compose and modify strings of text.
	Get Dates and Times	Get current dates and times and perform calculations on dates and times.
Storage	Read and Write Files	Open, read, write, and close files stored on disk.
Expressions	Check Results	Find what kind of data was returned by an operation.
	Find Truth	Combine expressions to create complex conditions.
	Compare Bits	Get multiple pieces of information from a single value.
Interoperate	Run Other Applications	Exchange data with other Windows applications.
Compiler	Control the Compiler	Create debug and release versions of code within the same source file.

Interact with Users

Visual Basic provides two simple ways to interact with users:

- Use InputBox to get text input.
- Use MsgBox to display short messages and get button-click responses.

I've already used InputBox and MsgBox a number of times in previous examples, but one more sample won't hurt:

```
Sub MsgBoxInputBox( )
    Dim str As String, val As VbMsgBoxResult
    ' InputBox gets simple text input.
    str = InputBox("Enter some text.", "Chapter 3", "Some text")
    ' Use If to test if a value was entered.
    If str <> "" Then
        ' You can combine style constants in MsgBox.
        val = MsgBox(str, vbQuestion + vbOKCancel, "Chapter 3")
        ' Return value indicates which button was clicked.
        If val = vbOK Then Debug.Print "OK" Else Debug.Print "Cancel"
    End If
End Sub
```

The preceding code displays a simple dialog box to get text, then displays the text in another simple dialog box, as shown in Figure 3-1.

The MsgBox function can display many different styles and buttons, depending on the Button argument setting. All of the VbMsgBoxStyle settings are listed in Table 3-2.

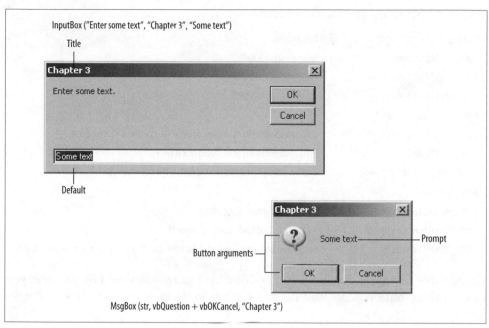

InputBox ("Enter some text", "Chapter 3", "Some text")

Title

Chapter 3

Enter some text.

OK

Cancel

Some text

Default

Chapter 3

Some text — Prompt

Button arguments

OK   Cancel

MsgBox (str, vbQuestion + vbOKCancel, "Chapter 3")

Figure 3-1. InputBox and MsgBox functions display simple dialog boxes

Table 3-2. VbMsgBoxStyle settings

Setting	Description
Button	
vbOKOnly	Displays OK button.
vbOKCancel	Displays OK, Cancel buttons.
vbAbortRetryIgnore	Displays Abort, Retry, Ignore buttons.
vbYesNoCancel	Displays Yes, No, Cancel buttons.
vbYesNo	Displays Yes, No buttons.
vbRetryCancel	Displays Retry, Cancel buttons.
Icon	
vbCritical	Adds Critical icon (red x).
vbQuestion	Adds Question icon (?).
vbExclamation	Adds Exclamation icon (!).
vbInformation	Adds Information icon (i).
Default setting	
vbDefaultButton1	First button is default.

Table 3-2. VbMsgBoxStyle settings (continued)

Setting	Description
vbDefaultButton2	Second button is default.
vbDefaultButton3	Third button is default.
vbDefaultButton4	Fourth button is default.
Focus	
vbApplicationModal	Halts workbook until dialog box is closed (this is the default in Excel).
vbSystemModal	Halts all applications until dialog box is closed.
vbMsgBoxSetForeground	Displays dialog in the foreground (this is the default in Excel).
Miscellaneous	
vbMsgBoxHelpButton	Adds a Help button to the dialog.
vbMsgBoxRight	Right-aligns text (default is left-aligned).
vbMsgBoxRtlReading	Swaps icon and button positions for right-to-left reading languages such as Arabic.

Compatible settings in Table 3-2 can be combined using addition. For instance, you can combine button, icon, and default settings in a single message box as shown here:

```
val = MsgBox("Unable to continue.", _
    vbCritical + vbAbortRetryIgnore + vbDefaultButton2, "Error")
```

The value returned by MsgBox is a VbMsgBoxResult constant that indicates which button the user clicked. Typically, you compare that result to the button constants listed in Table 3-2 in an If or Select statement:

```
If val = VbMsgBoxResult.vbAbort Then ...
```

If you are displaying a dialog with only a single OK button, you probably don't care about the value returned by MsgBox. In that case, you can omit the parentheses:

```
MsgBox "The answer is " & val, , "Chapter 3"
```

In addition to Visual Basic's built-in InputBox and MsgBox functions, there are several other ways to display much more complex dialog boxes and data-entry forms from Excel (see Table 3-3).

Table 3-3. Ways to display complex data-entry forms and dialog boxes

Technique	Use to	See
User forms	Create custom dialog boxes or data-entry forms for display from Visual Basic	Chapter 20
Excel's built-in dialogs	Display the standard Excel dialog boxes to get filenames, printer settings, or other common tasks	Chapter 7
InfoPath forms	Collect data in XML format	Chapter 26

Do Math

Visual Basic provides built-in operators and functions that perform many of the same calculations that you are used to using from Excel formulas. If you are new to programming, the way you write mathematical formulas in Visual Basic may seem backward:

```
x = 43 + 37 / 2  ' Not 43 + 37 / 2 = x
```

That's because the equals sign (=) performs an operation called *assignment*. The result of the preceding calculation is assigned to the variable x. In Visual Basic, the assignment operation is always performed last, after all other operations. Other operators are evaluated in the sequence shown in Table 3-4.

Table 3-4. Visual Basic mathematical operators' order of precedence (left to right)

( ) group	^ exponent	- negation	* multiply	/ divide
\ integer divide	Mod modulus	+ add	- subtract	= assign

Most of these operators are self-explanatory, but there are two exceptions:

- Use \ to divide two numbers and ignore the remainder.
- Use Mod to divide two numbers and return only the remainder.

For example, the following simple function divides two numbers and returns the result as a string:

```
Function IntegerMath(numerator As Integer, denominator As Integer) As String
    Dim quotient As Integer, remainder As Integer
    ' Find the quotient.
    quotient = numerator \ denominator
    ' Find the remainder
    remainder = numerator Mod denominator
    ' Return the result
    IntegerMath = "Result is " & quotient & " remainder " & denominator
End Function
```

Mod is frequently used in loops to perform some task once every *N* number of times. For example, the following code fragment builds a single string out of an array of words and adds a paragraph break every five words:

```
For i = 0 To UBound(words) - 1
    str = str & words(i) & " "
    If i <> 0 And i Mod 5 = 0 Then _
        str = str & vbCrLf
Next
```

Visual Basic also provides a set of math functions to perform some common tasks. Since these functions are built in to the language, they are called *intrinsic functions*. Excel provides equivalent worksheet functions for the intrinsic trigonometric and financial functions listed in Table 3-5. That duplication reflects the fact that Visual Basic is a general programming language used by many different applications.

Table 3-5. Visual Basic math functions

General				
Abs	Exp	Fix	Int	Log
Rnd	Sgn	Sqr		
Trigonometric				
Atn	Cos	Sin	Tan	
Financial				
DDB	FV	IPmt	IRR	MIRR
NPer	NPV	Pmt	PPmt	PV
Rate	SLN	SYD		

As with the operators, most of the functions in Table 3-5 are self-explanatory with a couple of exceptions:

- Use the Fix or Int function to get the whole-number portion of a decimal number.
- Use Rnd to generate random numbers.

The Rnd function returns a random number between 0 and 1. To generate a random integer between two numbers, use the following formula:

```
' Returns a random integer that is > min and < max.
Function Random(min As Integer, max As Integer) As Integer
    ' Initialize the random-number generator.
    Randomize
    ' Calculate a random integer.
    Random = Int((max - min + 1) * Rnd + min)
End Function
```

The Randomize statement initializes the random-number generator. You can repeat sequences of the generated numbers by calling Randomize with a negative number, for example Randomize -1.

You can derive complex functions from Visual Basic's intrinsic functions using the formulas shown in Table 3-6. These functions are also provided in the sample workbook and there are some worksheet function equivalents as well.

Table 3-6. Derived math functions

Function	Formula
Secant (Sec)	1 / Cos(x)
Cosecant (Cosec)	1 / Sin(x)
Cotangent (Cotan)	1 / Tan(x)

Table 3-6. Derived math functions (continued)

Function	Formula
Inverse Sine (Arcsin)	Atn(x / Sqr(-x * x + 1))
Inverse Cosine (Arccos)	Atn(-x / Sqr(-x * x + 1)) + 2 * Atn(1)
Inverse Secant (Arcsec)	Atn(x / Sqr(x * x - 1)) + Sgn((x) - 1) * (2 * Atn(1))
Inverse Cosecant (Arccosec)	Atn(Sgn(x) / Sqr(x * x 1))
Inverse Cotangent (Arccotan)	2 * Atn(1) - Atn(x)
Hyperbolic Sine (HSin)	(Exp(x) - Exp(-x)) / 2
Hyperbolic Cosine (HCos)	(Exp(x) + Exp(-x)) / 2
Hyperbolic Tangent (HTan)	(Exp(x) - Exp(-x)) / (Exp(x) + Exp(-x))
Hyperbolic Secant (HSec)	2 / (Exp(x) + Exp(-x))
Hyperbolic Cosecant (HCosec)	2 / (Exp(x) - Exp(-x))
Hyperbolic Cotangent (HCotan)	(Exp(x) + Exp(-x)) / (Exp(x) - Exp(-x))
Inverse Hyperbolic Sine (HArcsin)	Log(x + Sqr(x * x + 1))
Inverse Hyperbolic Cosine (HArccos)	Log(x + Sqr(x * x - 1))
Inverse Hyperbolic Tangent (HArctan)	Log((1 + x) / (1 x)) / 2
Inverse Hyperbolic Secant (HArcsec)	Log((Sqr(-x * x + 1) + 1) / x)
Inverse Hyperbolic Cosecant (HArccosec)	Log((Sgn(x) * Sqr(x * x + 1) + 1) / x)
Inverse Hyperbolic Cotangent (HArccotan)	Log(x + Sqr(x * x - 1))
Logarithm to base N (LogN)	Log(x) / Log(n)

Table 3-5 lists Visual Basic's financial functions. Excel provides its own (larger) set of financial functions, which are covered in Chapter 4.

Work with Text

Working with text is probably just as common as working with numbers in most programs. Visual Basic refers to text data as *strings* and it provides a set of string operators and functions just as it does for math. Since strings and numbers are very different types of data, the nature of operators and functions are very different, as shown by Tables 3-7 and 3-8.

Table 3-7. Visual Basic string operators

& (join)	Like (compare)	= (assign)

Table 3-8. Visual Basic string functions

Task	Function	Use to
Compare	Option Compare	Change the string comparison rules
	Instr	Find one string inside of another
	StrComp	Compare one string to another

Table 3-8. Visual Basic string functions (continued)

Task	Function	Use to
Convert	Asc	Convert a character to its numeric ANSI value
	Chr	Convert a numeric ANSI value to a character
	Format	Convert a number or a date to a string using a specific format
	LCase	Make a string lowercase
	UCase	Make a string uppercase
	StrConv	Change the capitalization, locale, or encoding of a string
	Val	Get the numeric value of a string
Arrays	Split	Convert a string to a one-dimensional array
	Join	Convert a one-dimensional array to a string
Change	Left	Get a number of characters from the left side of the string
	Len	Get the length of a string
	LTrim	Remove spaces from the left side of a string
	LSet	Copy one string to another, left-aligning the result
	Mid	Get a specified number of characters from within as string
	Replace	Search and replace words or characters in a string
	Right	Get a number of characters from the right side of a string
	RSet	Copy one string to another, right-aligning the result
	RTrim	Remove spaces from the right side of a string
	Trim	Remove spaces from the right and left sides of a string
Repeat	Space	Create a string containing a number of spaces
	String	Create a string containing a repeating character

The following sections explain how to use the string functions to perform the major tasks listed in Table 3-8.

Compare Strings

By default, Visual Basic compares strings in a case-sensitive way. That means "Jeff" and "jeff" are not considered the same. You can change that by adding an Option Compare Text statement at the beginning of a module or class, as shown here:

```
' Ignore case when comparing strings.
Option Compare Text

Sub CompareStrings()
    ' Displays True if Option Compare is Text.
    Debug.Print "Jeff" = "jeff"
End Sub
```

Option Compare applies to all the ways to compare string (=, Like, StrComp) through-out the module or class. You can achieve a similar result on a smaller scale by tempo-rarily converting the strings to upper- or lowercase before comparing them:

```
Debug.Print LCase("Jeff") = LCase("jeff")
```

That approach is actually more common than changing Option Compare since it allows you to use both case-sensitive and case-insensitive comparisons within a class or module.

The Like operator is similar to = in Visual Basic, except it also allows you to match patterns of characters using the comparison characters listed in Table 3-9.

Table 3-9. Pattern-matching characters

Use	To match
?	Any single character
*	Zero or more characters
#	Any single digit
[list]	Any single character in list
[!list]	Any single character not in list

For example, the following function returns True if a passed-in argument is format-ted as a Social Security number:

```
Function IsSSN(ssn As String) As Boolean
    If ssn Like "###-##-####" Then
        IsSSN = True
    Else
        IsSSN = False
    End If
End Function
```

The Instr function returns the location of one string within another string. This is one of the most-used functions in Visual Basic, since it allows you to break up strings and to do all sorts of search-and-replace tasks.

The StrComp function compares two strings for sorting. If the first string sorts before the second string, StrComp returns -1; if they sort the same, it returns 0; and if the first string sorts after the second string, StrComp returns 1. The following example demon-strates how to use StrComp to sort an array:

```
Sub SortArray(arr As Variant, _
    Optional compare As VbCompareMethod = vbBinaryCompare)
        Dim lb As Integer, ub As Integer, i As Integer, str As String
        Dim j As Integer
        ' If argument is not an array, then exit.
        If Not IsArray(arr) Then Exit Sub
        lb = LBound(arr)
```

```
        ub = UBound(arr)
        ' If only one element, then exit.
        If lb = ub Then Exit Sub
        For i = lb To ub
            str = arr(i)
            For j = lb To ub
                ' Swap  values if out of order.
                If StrComp(str, arr(j), compare) = -1 Then
                    str = arr(j)
                    arr(j) = arr(i)
                    arr(i) = str
                End If
            Next
        Next
    End Sub
```

 There are more efficient sorting routines than the one shown here. I chose this one for its simplicity.

The SortArray procedure lets you specify whether or not to ignore the case of characters when sorting. The default is to use vbBinaryCompare for case-sensitive sorting. You can use the SortArray function to create a function that sorts strings:

```
Function SortString(str As String, Optional ignorecase = False)
    Dim arr As Variant
    ' Covert the string to an array.
    arr = Split(str, " ")
    ' Sort the array case-sensitive or case-insensitive.
    If ignorecase Then
        SortArray arr, vbTextCompare
    Else
        SortArray arr, vbBinaryCompare
    End If
    ' Convert the array back to a string and return it.
    SortString = Join(arr, " ")
End Function
```

To see how these functions work together, step through the following code in the sample worksheet:

```
Sub DemoSort( )
    Dim str As String, arr As Variant
    str = "Q z v w p x f g J l h r y D k i e T s u o n M a c b"
    ' Show case-sensitive sort.
    Debug.Print SortString(str, False)
    ' Show case-insensitive sort.
    Debug.Print SortString(str, True)
End Sub
```

I have an ulterior motive for showing you these procedures: I'm often asked how you break tasks into procedures and I think this set of procedures illustrates the logical division of tasks very well. SortString and SortArray both make sense as a stand-alone procedure because they might be reused any number of ways elsewhere in the program. Writing effective, reusable procedures is one of the key skills that identify you as an excellent programmer. The best way to learn that skill is by studying good examples and then practicing on your own!

Convert Strings

I touched on two very common conversion functions already: LCase and UCase convert a string to lower- or uppercase, usually because you want to ignore case while comparing strings. Your computer can perform these conversions and comparisons because it actually stores strings as numbers using something called *ANSI character codes*.

The Asc function converts characters to their numeric ANSI character codes; Chr converts those numeric codes back to characters. The following code displays the ANSI character codes in the Immediate window (Figure 3-2):

```
Sub ShowAnsiCodes()
    Dim i As Integer, str As String
    For i = 0 To 255
        str = str & i & ": " & Chr(i) & vbTab
        If i Mod 10 = 0 Then
            Debug.Print str
            str = ""
        End If
    Next
End Sub
```

 Not all character codes have an appearance. Chr(0), Chr(9), Chr(10), and Chr(13) represent the null, tab, line-feed, and carriage-return characters respectively.

Looking at Figure 3-2, you can see that you can convert individual characters from upper- to lowercase by adding 32 or from lower- to uppercase by subtracting 32. UCase and LCase just make those conversions easier.

The StrConv function is related to UCase and LCase. It can perform the same conversions, plus it can convert the words in a string to use initial capitalization as is used in proper names:

```
' Displays St. Thomas Aquinas
Debug.Print StrConv("st. thomas aquinas", vbProperCase)
```

 StrConv also converts strings to or from other encodings or locales. Those are pretty advanced topics and I'm just going to skip them here.

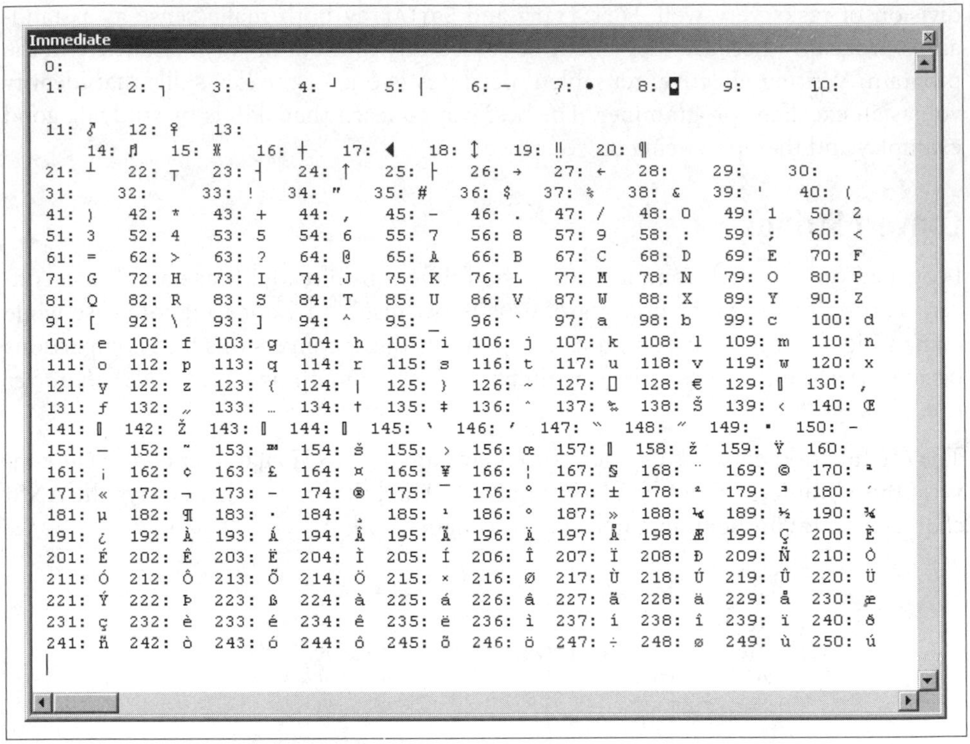

```
Immediate
0:
1: ⌐   2: ¬   3: ∟   4: ⌐   5: |    6: ─    7: •    8: ▪   9:        10:

11: ♪  12: ♀  13:
     14: ♫   15: ☼   16: ►   17: ◄   18: ↕   19: ‼   20: ¶
21: ⊥  22: ┬   23: ┤   24: ↑   25: ┣   26: →   27: ←   28:       29:       30:
31:      32:       33: !   34: "   35: #   36: $   37: %   38: &   39: '    40: (
41: )  42: *   43: +   44: ,   45: -   46: .   47: /   48: 0   49: 1    50: 2
51: 3  52: 4   53: 5   54: 6   55: 7   56: 8   57: 9   58: :   59: ;    60: <
61: =  62: >   63: ?   64: @   65: A   66: B   67: C   68: D   69: E    70: F
71: G  72: H   73: I   74: J   75: K   76: L   77: M   78: N   79: O    80: P
81: Q  82: R   83: S   84: T   85: U   86: V   87: W   88: X   89: Y    90: Z
91: [  92: \   93: ]   94: ^   95: _   96: `   97: a   98: b   99: c    100: d
101: e 102: f  103: g  104: h  105: i  106: j  107: k  108: l  109: m  110: n
111: o 112: p  113: q  114: r  115: s  116: t  117: u  118: v  119: w  120: x
121: y 122: z  123: {  124: |  125: }  126: ~  127: ⌂  128: €  129: ▯  130: ,
131: ƒ 132: „  133: …  134: †  135: ‡  136: ^  137: ‰  138: Š  139: ‹  140: Œ
141: ▯ 142: Ž  143: ▯  144: ▯  145: '  146: '  147: "  148: "  149: •  150: –
151: — 152: ˜  153: ™  154: š  155: ›  156: œ  157: ▯  158: ž  159: Ÿ  160:
161: ¡ 162: ¢  163: £  164: ¤  165: ¥  166: ¦  167: §  168: ¨  169: ©  170: ª
171: « 172: ¬  173: -  174: ®  175: ¯  176: °  177: ±  178: ²  179: ³  180: ´
181: µ 182: ¶  183: ·  184: ¸  185: ¹  186: º  187: »  188: ¼  189: ½  190: ¾
191: ¿ 192: À  193: Á  194: Â  195: Ã  196: Ä  197: Å  198: Æ  199: Ç  200: È
201: É 202: Ê  203: Ë  204: Ì  205: Í  206: Î  207: Ï  208: Ð  209: Ñ  210: Ò
211: Ó 212: Ô  213: Õ  214: Ö  215: ×  216: Ø  217: Ù  218: Ú  219: Û  220: Ü
221: Ý 222: Þ  223: ß  224: à  225: á  226: â  227: ã  228: å  229: å  230: æ
231: ç 232: è  233: é  234: ê  235: ë  236: ì  237: í  238: î  239: ï  240: ð
241: ñ 242: ò  243: ó  244: ô  245: õ  246: ö  247: ÷  248: ø  249: ù  250: ú
|
```

Figure 3-2. ANSI character codes

The Format function converts various types of data into strings using predefined or custom formats. The Val function converts strings containing numeric data back into numeric data types. This simple example illustrates how these functions work:

```
Sub ShowFormatVal( )
    Dim num As Double, str As String
    str = Format(Now, "Short Time")
    num = Val(str)
    ' If the time is 4:31 PM, displays: 16:31     16
    Debug.Print str, num
End Sub
```

You might notice that Val doesn't do anything fancy—it just gets the first part of the string that is numeric and returns it as a number. Val can recognize a few special strings as numbers. For instance, it interprets &HFF as the hexadecimal (base 16) number 255 and &o77 as the octal (base 8) number 63. Format is really more interesting, since it provides useful built-in formats as listed in Table 3-10.

Table 3-10. The Format function's built-in formats

Category	Named format	Converts
Numeric	General Number	Number to string without thousands separator. This is the default.
	Currency	Number to string using the decimal, separator, and currency characters that are appropriate for the locale. Negative values are enclosed in parentheses.
	Fixed	Number to string with at least one digit to the left of the decimal and two digits to the right of the decimal.
	Standard	Same as Fixed but includes a thousands separator.
	Percent	Multiplies number by 100 and includes at least two digits to the right of the decimal.
	Scientific	Number to string using standard scientific notation.
	Yes/No	Zero to No, nonzero to Yes.
	True/False	Zero to False, nonzero to True.
	On/Off	Zero to Off, nonzero to On.
Date/Time	General Date	Number or date to string using MM/DD/YY HH:MM:SS format. Omits time if number is a whole number.
	Long Date	Number or date to string using your system's long date format.
	Medium Date	Number or date to string using your system's medium date format.
	Short Date	Number or date to string using your system's short date format.
	Long Time	Number or date to string using your system's long time format. Includes hours, minutes, and seconds.
	Medium Time	Number or date to string in 12-hour time format. Includes hours, minutes, and AM/PM designator.
	Short Time	Number or date to string in 24-hour time format. Includes hours and minutes.

If the built-in formats don't give you what you need, you can build your own format strings using the Format function's formatting codes listed in Table 3-11.

Table 3-11. The Format function's formatting codes

Category	Code	Use to
String	@	Include a character or space if there is no character in this position (creates fill spaces for columns).
	&	Include a character (no fill).
	<	Force lowercase.
	>	Force uppercase.
	!	Right-align string (default is left-align).
	\	Include characters that otherwise have special meaning in the format string (e.g., use \@ to include the @ character).

Table 3-11. The Format function's formatting codes (continued)

Category	Code	Use to
	`""literal""`	Include literal characters in a format string.
Numeric	`None`	Include number with no special formatting.
	`0`	Include a digit or zero if there is no digit in this position (creates zero fill).
	`#`	Include a digit (no fill).
	`.`	Include decimal placeholder.
	`%`	Convert number to percentage and include % sign.
	`,`	Include a thousands separator.
	`E,-E+, e-,e+`	Convert to scientific notation.
	`-, +, $, ( )`	Include these literal characters (no double quotes or \ is required to include these characters in numeric strings).
Date/Time	`:`	Include time separator.
	`/`	Include date separator.
	`c`	Same as General Date.
	`d, dd`	Include day of month as digit.
	`ddd`	Include day of week as an abbreviation.
	`dddd`	Include full day of week.
	`ddddd`	Same as Short Date.
	`dddddd`	Same as Long Date.
	`aaaa`	Include localized name of the weekday.
	`w`	Include day of week as a number (1 to 7).
	`ww`	Include week or year as number.
	`m, mm`	Include month as number. (Exception: includes minutes if it follows the hour, e.g., `hh:mm`.)
	`mmm`	Include month as an abbreviation.
	`mmmm`	Include full month name.
	`oooo`	Include full, localized month name.
	`q`	Include quarter of year (1 to 4).
	`y`	Include day of year (1 to 366).
	`yy, yyyy`	Include year as digit.
	`h, hh`	Include hour.
	`n, nn`	Include minute (or you can use `m, mm` if following hour).
	`s, ss`	Include second.
	`ttttt`	Same as Long Time.
	`AM/PM, am/pm, A/P, a/p`	Use 12-hour time and include the specified meridian designator.
	`AMPM, ampm`	Use 12-hour time and include the system meridian designator.

Some of the format codes in Tables 3-10 and 3-11 refer to system or localized settings. Those codes allow you to use the calendar and time features from the user's system, rather than using the default Visual Basic settings, which are based on the Julian calendar and English month and weekday names. It's important to be aware of those settings if your program is for use outside of the English-speaking world.

You can combine formatting code to produce quite sophisticated results. For example:

```
Debug.Print Format(Now, """Today is ""dddd, mmmm d, yyyy" & _
    """ the ""y""th day of the year. The time is now"" ttttt.")
```

displays this result:

```
Today is Thursday, June 17, 2004 the 169th day of the year. The time is now
10:28:22 AM.
```

Change Strings

A lot of programming tasks involve getting or changing parts of a string. For simple replacement tasks, use the Replace method as shown here:

```
Sub DemoSearchAndReplace()
    Dim str As String
    str = "this is some text and some more text"
    str = Replace(str, "some", "different")
    Debug.Print str
End Sub
```

The preceding code replaces all instances of *some* with *different* in a case-sensitive way. Replace also provides option for replacing a certain number of occurrences, starting at a specific position within the string and doing case-insensitive searches. Replace also replaces one string with another regardless of their length. If the strings are the same length, you could use the Mid statement to change the source string, instead:

```
Mid(str, InStr(1, str, "text")) = "word"
Debug.Print str
' Displays: this is different word and different more text
```

The Mid statement is unusual in that it receives an assignment—in this case the replacement string "word". Since Mid can't make strings longer or shorter, it is mainly useful for modifying string data that is in a fixed-width format or for replacing single characters, such as punctuation.

Visual Basic also provides a set of functions to remove leading, trailing, or leading *and* trailing whitespace characters from a string: LTrim, RTrim, and Trim. Excel does Visual Basic one better by adding the Trim worksheet function, which removes repeated internal spaces as well. The following code demonstrates each of the different trim functions:

```
Sub DemoTrims()
    Dim str As String
    str = "  this is    a string    to trim.           "
```

```
        Debug.Print "LTrim:", ">"; LTrim(str); "<"
        Debug.Print "RTrim:", ">"; RTrim(str); "<"
        Debug.Print "Trim:", ">"; Trim(str); "<"
        Debug.Print "Excel Trim:", ">"; _
            WorksheetFunction.Trim(str); "<"
    End Sub
```

The preceding code produces the following output in the Immediate window:

```
LTrim:        >this is      a string    to trim.              <
RTrim:        > this is     a string   to trim.<
Trim:         >this is      a string    to trim.<
Excel Trim:   >this is a string to trim.<
```

Repeat Characters

Finally, Visual Basic includes a couple of simple functions that create strings of repeated characters. The Space function returns a string containing spaces, and the String function returns a string containing a repeated character. Those functions are sometimes used in combination with Chr when creating reports or drawing text borders as shown here:

```
' Draws a little box in the Immediate window.
Sub DrawBox( )
    Debug.Print Chr(1) & String(20, Chr(6)) & Chr(2)
    Debug.Print Chr(5) & Space(20) & Chr(5)
    Debug.Print Chr(5) & Space(20) & Chr(5)
    Debug.Print Chr(5) & Space(20) & Chr(5)
    Debug.Print Chr(3) & String(20, Chr(6)) & Chr(4)
End Sub
```

Get Dates and Times

Visual Basic stores dates and times as decimal numbers. The digits to the left of the decimal represent the number of days since December 30, 1899, and the digits to the right of the decimal represent the fraction of the day that has passed (for instance, 0.5 = noon).

This means that dates and times use the same operators as numeric types. For example, the following expression shows yesterday's date:

```
Debug.Print Date - 1
```

This also means that you can use date or time literals to work with dates. For example, if you type #0.0# in the Code window, Visual Basic automatically changes what you typed into the time literal for midnight shown here:

```
dt = #12:00:00 AM#
```

You can edit that literal to add a certain number of seconds, minutes, or hours to the time. For example, the following code pauses Excel for five seconds:

```
Sub TakeFive( )
    Dim dt As Date
    ' Five seconds.
    dt = #12:00:05 AM#
    Debug.Print "Paused..."
    ' Wait till five seconds from now.
    Application.Wait Now + dt
    Debug.Print "Resumed."
End Sub
```

Visual Basic provides a whole set of functions for working with dates and times, as listed in Table 3-12.

Table 3-12. *Visual Basic functions for working with date and time*

Category	Function	Use to
Current	Date	Get or set the system date
	Now	Get the current date and time
	Time	Get or set the system time
	Timer	Get the number of seconds since midnight (often used to measure performance)
Date	DateSerial	Convert year, month, and day numbers into a date
	DateValue	Convert a string into a date
	Day	Get the day of the month from a date
	Month	Get the month of the year from a date
	Weekday	Get the weekday from a date (1 to 7)
	Year	Get the year from a date
Time	Hour	Get the hour from a time
	Minute	Get the minute from a time
	Second	Get the second from a time
	TimeSerial	Convert hour, minute, and second numbers into a time
	TimeValue	Convert a string into a time

For most conversions, the Format function works better than the functions listed in Table 3-12. The date/time functions are mainly used for simple operations, such as getting the current year:

```
Debug.Print Year(Now)
```

The Timer function is very handy when developing programs since it lets you see how long your code takes to run. When developing large or complex programs, it is pretty common to record the Timer value at the start of the process, then display the difference between that value and the current Timer when the task completes, as shown by the following changes to DemoSort:

```
Sub DemoSort( )
    Dim str As String, arr As Variant, d As Double
    ' Time this operation.
    d = Timer
```

```
                str = "Q z v w p x f g J l h r y D k i e T s u o n M a c b"
                ' Show case-sensitive sort.
                Debug.Print SortString(str, False)
                ' Show case-insensitive sort.
                Debug.Print SortString(str, True)
                ' Display how long the task took.
                Debug.Print Timer - d
        End Sub
```

You should use the Double data type when measuring performance since many tasks take only a fraction of a second. On my computer, DemoSort takes only about 0.00128 seconds.

Read and Write Files

There are a number of different ways to read and write files in Visual Basic, and which you choose depends on what you are trying to do, as described in Table 3-13.

Table 3-13. File-access techniques in Excel Visual Basic

Technique	Use to	Look here
Intrinsic functions	Read or write simple datafiles	This section
FileSystemObject	Create files, folders, and control file attributes	Chapter 6
Workbooks, Workbook objects	Create, open, and save Excel workbook files; import datafiles into workbooks	Chapter 8
XMLMap object	Import or export XML datafiles from a workbook	Chapter 15

In short, you shouldn't assume the Visual Basic intrinsic functions are the best way to read and write files in all situations. Actually, I prefer the FileSystemObject for most general file-access tasks, but it's important to be thorough, so I'll cover the intrinsic file-access functions here (Table 3-14).

Table 3-14. Visual Basic's intrinsic file-access functions

Category	Function	Use to
Access	Close	Close an open file
	FileCopy	Copy a file
	FreeFile	Get a file number for Open
	Lock...Unlock	Prevent others from accessing all or part of a file
	LOF	Get the length of an open file in bytes
	Open	Open a file
	Reset	Close all open files
Attributes	FileAttr	Get the attributes of an open file
	FileDateTime	Get the date that a file was created or changed

Table 3-14. Visual Basic's intrinsic file-access functions (continued)

Category	Function	Use to
	FileLen	Get the length of a file in bytes before opening it
	GetAttr	Get the attributes of a file, folder, or volume label
	SetAttr	Change the attributes of a file, folder, or volume label
Drives	ChDir	Set the current folder
	ChDrive	Set the current drive
	CurDir	Get the current folder
	MkDir	Create a new folder
	RmDir	Delete an empty folder
Manage	Dir	List files in a folder
	Kill	Delete a file
	Name	Rename a file
Read	Get	Read data from an open binary or random-access file
	EOF	Test you have reached the end of the file
	Input #	Read records from an open sequential file
	Line Input #	Read a line from an open sequential file
	Loc	Return the current position within a file
	Seek	Get or set the current position within a file
Write	Print #	Write a line to an open sequential file
	Put	Write data to an open binary or random-access file
	Spc	Insert blank spaces in a sequential file
	Tab	Insert tab characters in a sequential file
	Width #	Set the width of a sequential file
	Write #	Write records to a sequential file

The functions in Table 3-14 reflect the fact that there are three different types of file access in Visual Basic:

Sequential access
> Reads files one line at a time

Random access
> Reads files as a collection of fixed-length records

Binary access
> Reads files as an arbitrary number of bytes

All of these types of access follow the same pattern, which is based on a very old programming concept called *file handles*:

1. Use FreeFile to get a number that is available for use as a file handle.
2. Open the file using that number and the chosen file-access method.

3. Read data from the file using `Input #` (sequential access) or `Get` (random or binary access), or write data using `Print #`, `Write #` (sequential), or `Put` (random or binary).

4. Close the file handle.

 The modern approach, such as that used by the `FileSystemObject`, is to use object references rather than numeric file handles.

Of the three types of file access, binary is the most useful in today's world because it allows you to read an entire file into a variable with a single statement. It is by far the fastest way to get the contents of a file. The following `QuickRead` function opens and reads a file and returns the data it contains as a string variable:

```
' Reads a file into a string.
Function QuickRead(fname As String) As String
    Dim i As Integer, res As String, l As Long
    ' Get a free file handle.
    i = FreeFile
    ' Get the length of the file
    l = FileLen(fname)
    ' Create a string to contain the data.
    res = Space(l)
    ' Open the file.
    Open fname For Binary Access Read As #i
    ' Read the whole file into res.
    Get #i, , res
    ' Close the file
    Close i
    ' Return the string.
    QuickRead = res
End Function
```

How big of a file can you read this way? Pretty big! I had no problem loading an 8.4 MB art file using this technique. String variables can be *very* large in Visual Basic. Similarly, you can write files very quickly with binary access. The following `QuickWrite` function saves a string as a file and returns True if it succeeded:

```
' Writes data to a file.
Function QuickWrite(data As String, fname As String, _
    Optional overwrite As Boolean = False) As Boolean
    Dim i As Integer, l As Long
    ' If file exists and overwrite is True, then
    If Dir(fname) <> "" Then
        If overwrite Then
            ' delete the file.
            Kill fname
        Else
            ' else, return False and exit.
            QuickWrite = False
            Exit Function
```

```
        End If
    End If
    ' Get a free file handle.
    i = FreeFile
    ' Get the length of the file
    l = Len(data)
    ' Open the file.
    Open fname For Binary Access Write As #i Len = l
    ' Write the string to the file.
    Put #i, , data
    ' Close the file
    Close i
    ' Return True.
    QuickWrite = True
End Function
```

This approach was first pointed out to me by Mark Chase, senior developer on Basic at Microsoft. He deserves credit for clear thinking and also for being a darn nice guy. You can test that these functions work by running the following code from the sample workbook:

```
Sub DemoQuickReadWrite()
    Dim pth As String, data As String
    ' Get the folder that this workbook is in.
    pth = ThisWorkbook.Path
    ' Read the ReadMe.txt file.
    data = QuickRead(pth & "\in.txt")
    ' Display the file
    Debug.Print data
    ' Change the file.
    data = Replace(data, "text", "data")
    ' Save the file.
    Debug.Print QuickWrite(data, pth & "\out.txt", True)
End Sub
```

Sequential Access

Sequential access reads and writes files one line at a time. In the past, sequential access was often used to write reports or other data to human-readable files. For example, the following WriteArray function writes a two-dimensional array to disk as a comma-delimited file using sequential access:

```
' Writes a two-dimensional array to a comma-delimited file.
' (Use to create CSV file out of a selected range.)
Function WriteArray(arr As Variant, fname As String, _
    Optional overwrite As Boolean = False) As Boolean
    Dim lb1 As Long, lb2 As Long, ub1 As Long, ub2 As Long
    Dim i As Integer, rows As Long, cols As Long, rec As String
    ' If arr isn't an array, return False and exit.
    If Not IsArray(arr) Then WriteArray = False: Exit Function
    ' Get bounds for For loops.
    lb1 = LBound(arr, 1)
    lb2 = LBound(arr, 2)
```

```
        ub1 = UBound(arr, 1)
        ub2 = UBound(arr, 2)
        ' If file exists and overwrite is True, then
        If Dir(fname) <> "" Then
            If overwrite Then
                ' delete the file.
                Kill fname
            Else
                ' else, return False and exit.
                WriteArray = False
                Exit Function
            End If
        End If
        ' Get a free file handle.
        i = FreeFile
        ' Open the file.
        Open fname For Append As #i
        ' For each row in the array.
        For rows = lb1 To ub1
            ' For each column in the array.
            For cols = lb2 To ub2
                rec = rec & arr(rows, cols) & ", "
            Next
            ' Remove the last ", " from rec.
            rec = Left(rec, Len(rec) - 2)
            ' Write rec to the file.
            Print #i, rec
            ' Clear rec
            rec = ""
        Next
        ' Close the file
        Close i
        ' Return True.
        WriteArray = True
    End Function
```

That looks complicated, but the actual file-access code (in **bold**) is really very simple and follows the pattern described previously: get a file handle, open the file, read or write to the file, close the file. Sequential access is suited to this task since you are building the string data one line at a time as you loop over the rows in the array.

Perhaps a better approach to this task would be to build a string from the array in one procedure and then save that string using the QuickWrite function. That approach would *isolate* file access in one place (QuickWrite) instead of *integrating* it into the task of converting the array into a string. The following code shows that alternate approach:

```
' Better approach -- don't integrate file access within
' array conversion task.
Function TableToCSV(arr As Variant) As String
    Dim lb1 As Long, lb2 As Long, ub1 As Long, ub2 As Long
    Dim rows As Long, cols As Long, rec As String
```

```
    ' If arr is not an array, return "" and exit.
    If Not IsArray(arr) Then TableToCSV = "": Exit Function
    ' Get bounds for For loops.
    lb1 = LBound(arr, 1)
    lb2 = LBound(arr, 2)
    ub1 = UBound(arr, 1)
    ub2 = UBound(arr, 2)
    For rows = lb1 To ub1
        For cols = lb2 To ub2
            rec = rec & arr(rows, cols) & ", "
        Next
        ' Remove last ", " and add carriage return/line feed.
        rec = Left(rec, Len(rec) - 2) & vbCrLf
    Next
    TableToCSV = rec
End Function
```

Using `TableToCSV` instead of `WriteArray` involves the extra step of calling `QuickWrite`, but the logic is still very clear:

```
Sub DemoTableToCSV()
    Dim arr As Variant, data As String, pth As String
    pth = ThisWorkbook.Path
    ' Get cells from the active worksheet.
    arr = ActiveSheet.UsedRange.Value
    ' If the range contains cells.
    If IsArray(arr) Then
        ' Convert array to CSV.
        data = TableToCSV(arr)
        If data <> "" Then
            ' Save the result
            QuickWrite data, pth & "\selection.csv", True
            ' Display the result
            Debug.Print data
        End If
    End If
End Sub
```

Random Access

Random-access files are read or written one record at a time. In this case, *record* usually means a fixed-size data structure identified by a user-defined type. Because Visual Basic knows the length of each record, you can jump to any record in the file using the Seek statement (that's what makes the access *random*).

In order to use random access, you must first define the structure of your record with a Type statement. You then declare a variable with that type and use it to read and/or write records to the file. I'm not going to show you how to do all that, because XML files and databases both provide a much better approach for storing and retrieving structured data. I cover those topics in Chapters 12 and 15.

Why is random access not such a great approach? A few reasons:

- The records are fixed-length by definition, which means names, addresses, and other variable-length data must be stored in fixed-length strings. You have to correctly guess the maximum size of those items during design.

- Changes to your data structure, such as adding a field, means you have to convert all of your existing datafiles. You have to write code to open, convert, and save files using the new structure. (In programming circles this is called tying your data structure to your implementation, and it's a bad thing.)

- You're programming in Excel! You already have better tools for doing these types of tasks.

Common Tasks

In addition to reading and writing files, you also often need to manage the files on a computer. The most common tasks are listed in Table 3-15.

Table 3-15. Common tasks for Visual Basic's intrinsic file functions

Task	Function	Comments
Check if file exists	Dir	Also used to list files in a folder.
Delete a file	Kill	Deletes a file if it is not locked or read-only.
Get the current folder	CurDir	Excel may change the current folder when a workbook is saved or opened by the user.
Change current folder	ChDir	You can use characters like .. to move up one folder.
Change current drive	ChDrive	Only the first letter from the argument is used.
Create a folder	MkDir	May include path specifiers like . (current folder) or .. (up one folder). Does not change the current folder.
Delete a folder	RmDir	Folder must be empty before it can be deleted.
Get/change file attributes	FileAttr	File attributes include hidden, read-only, archive.
Make a backup copy	FileCopy	Copies an existing file to a new filename.
Rename a file	Name	Changes a filename.

In general, it is not a good idea to get the current folder (CurDir) or change the current folder (ChDir) from Visual Basic when working with Excel because saving or opening a file from the Excel user interface may subsequently change the current folder. It is a better practice to use the path properties provided by Excel objects when working with folders in Excel.

For example, the following code displays the paths available for various Excel objects:

```
Sub ShowPaths( )
    Dim wbPth As String, appPth As String, stPth As String, _
        altPth As String, tpPth As String, adPth As String
```

```
        wbPth = ThisWorkbook.Path
        appPth = Application.Path
        stPth = Application.StartupPath
        altPth = Application.AltStartupPath
        tpPth = Application.TemplatesPath
        adPth = Application.AddIns(1).Path
        Debug.Print "Workbook path:", wbPth
        Debug.Print "Application path:", appPth
        Debug.Print "Startup path: ", stPth
        Debug.Print "All startup path:", altPth
        Debug.Print "Template path:", tpPth
        Debug.Print "Add-in path:    ", adPth
    End Sub
```

I often use `ThisWorkbook.Path` within my samples to get or save files associated with the current workbook. That strategy keeps all of the related files in the same folder, so it is easier to copy the samples to a new location or to install them on your computer. Alternately, you may choose to create a fixed folder location for use in your code such as shown here:

```
    ' A fixed path.
    Const SAMPLEPTH = "\Excel\Samples"

    ' Run once to create folder.
    Sub CreateSamplesFolder()
        ' Create the SAMPLEPTH folder
        On Error Resume Next
        MkDir "\Excel"
        MkDir "\Excel\Samples"
        If Err Then _
            MsgBox ("Couldn't create folder. It may already exist.")
    End Sub
```

Using a fixed location for your files poses the problem illustrated by the preceding exception handling: the folder may already exist! That's another reason to use the `ThisWorkbook.Path` approach.

You can use the `Dir` function to check whether a file exists in a folder or to get a list of all of the files in a folder. When getting a list of files, `Dir` acts a little strangely. The first time you call it, specify the folder you want to search; then call `Dir` without an argument to get the next file in the folder, as shown here:

```
    Function GetFiles(filepath As String) As Variant
        Dim arr() As String, fname As String, count As Integer
        ' Get the first file.
        fname = Dir(filepath & "\*")
        Do Until fname = ""
            count = count + 1
            ReDim Preserve arr(count)
            arr(count - 1) = fname
            ' Get next file.
            fname = Dir()
        Loop
```

```
    ' Return the array
    GetFiles = arr
End Function
```

Dir does not order the files it returns alphabetically, so you may need to sort the list before displaying it. For example, the following code uses the GetFiles function to list the files in the current workbook's folder:

```
Sub DemoGetFiles()
    Dim flist As Variant, str As String
    flist = GetFiles(ThisWorkbook.Path)
    ' Sort the file list
    Text.SortArray (flist)
    str = Join(flist, vbCrLf)
    Debug.Print str
End Sub
```

The FileSystemObject provides more extensive methods for working with files, folders, and drives. See Chapters 6 and 23 for information on performing these tasks using the FileSystemObject rather than Visual Basic's intrinsic functions.

Check Results

In many situations, you need to check the result of an operation to tell if it succeeded. The result-checking functions in Visual Basic let you test results before you take actions that might otherwise cause an error. Table 3-16 lists the result-checking functions.

Table 3-16. Visual Basic result-checking functions

Category	Function	Use to
Boolean tests	IsArray	Tell if a variable is an array
	IsDate	Tell if a variable contains data that can be converted to a Date
	IsEmpty	Tell if a variable has not yet been initialized
	IsError	Tell if a variable contains an Error object
	IsMissing	Tell if a ParamArray argument was omitted
	IsNull	Tell if a variable contains no valid data
	IsNumeric	Tell if a variable contains a value that can be converted to a number
	IsObject	Tell if a variable is a reference to a valid object
Type tests	TypeName	Get the name of the variable's type as a string
	TypeOf	Test the type of a variable within an If block
	VarType	Get the variable's type as a VbVarType constant

Most of these tests are used with variables that were declared as Variant or Object data types. Those types of variables can contain many different kinds of data, so it is often necessary to test what the variable contains before proceeding in code.

There are several common uses of this in Excel. The first is ActiveSheet.*property*, which may refer to a Worksheet, Chart, or other object:

```
Sub ChangeSheets()
    Select Case TypeName(ActiveSheet)
    Case "Worksheet"
        If ActiveSheet.Index < Worksheets.Count Then
            Worksheets(ActiveSheet.Index + 1).Activate
        Else
            Worksheets(1).Activate
        End If
    Case "Chart"
        If ActiveSheet.Index < Charts.Count Then
            Charts(ActiveSheet.Index + 1).Activate
        Else
            Charts(1).Activate
        End If
    Case Else
        Debug.Print TypeName(ActiveSheet), ActiveSheet.Name
    End Select
End Sub
```

The preceding code uses a Select statement to perform different actions based on the TypeName of the active sheet. You usually combine TypeName with Select when there are more than two possibilities as shown in the preceding block. TypeName is also handy for checking whether or not an optional argument has been omitted:

```
Public Sub Reformat(Optional ws As Worksheet)
    ' Check if argument was omitted.
    If TypeName(ws) = "Nothing" Then
        ' Check the type of the active sheet.
        If TypeName(ActiveSheet) = "Worksheet" Then
            ' Format the active worksheet.
            Set ws = ActiveSheet
        Else
            ' You can't reformat nonworksheets.
            MsgBox "Select a worksheet and try again."
            Exit Sub
        End If
    End If
    Dim rng As Range
    ' Get the cells with data in them.
    Set rng = ws.UsedRange
    ' Apply AutoFormat
    rng.AutoFormat xlRangeAutoFormatSimple
End Sub
```

In the preceding code, the choices are either/or: if the argument is omitted, check the active sheet; if that sheet is a worksheet, use it. Alternately, you can use the TypeOf keyword within an If statement; however, TypeOf can't test if the variable is Nothing.

To do that, you need to use either TypeName or the Is operator, as shown by this different version of the preceding code:

```
Public Sub Reformat2(Optional ws As Worksheet)
    ' Check if argument was omitted.
    If ws Is Nothing Then
        ' Check the type of the active sheet.
        If TypeOf ActiveSheet Is Worksheet Then
            ' Format the active worksheet.
            Set ws = ActiveSheet
        Else
            ' You can't reformat nonworksheets.
            MsgBox "Select a worksheet and try again."
            Exit Sub
        End If
    End If
    Dim rng As Range
    ' Get the cells with data in them.
    Set rng = ws.UsedRange
    ' Apply AutoFormat
    rng.AutoFormat xlRangeAutoFormatSimple
End Sub
```

Reformat and Reformat2 are equivalent. I tend to use the TypeName test rather than TypeOf or Is because it lets me use a consistent test for all types of objects, but that's really just a personal preference.

The IsNumeric and IsDate functions are useful when receiving data from a user. Rather than returning specific information about the type of the variable, they let you know if the data in the variable can be converted to those types. For instance, the following code checks the value entered in an InputBox to determine the type of entry the user made:

```
Sub CheckEntry()
    Dim var As String, msg As String
    var = InputBox("Enter a number, word, or date.")
    ' Use Boolean tests to check an entry.
    If IsNumeric(var) Then
        msg = "number."
    ElseIf IsDate(var) Then
        msg = "date."
    ElseIf var = "" Then
        msg = "empty."
    Else
        msg = "string."
    End If
    Debug.Print "Entry is a " & msg
End Sub
```

IsNumeric and IsDate are a good way to check values before calling conversion functions like CDate or CDouble.

Find Truth

If statements and Do loops rely on Boolean expressions to control what they do. Those Boolean expressions are usually shown as a *condition* placeholder in the statement's syntax:

```
If condition Then ...
```

and:

```
Do While condition ...
```

A *Boolean expression* is simply an item that Visual Basic can determine to be either True or False. Mostly those expressions are very obvious. The fragment If str = "" Then says "if the variable str is an empty string, then execute the following lines of code." In this case, the equal sign (=) works as a comparison operator, not an assignment operator. Visual Basic can use the operator both ways because it understands that the context of an If statement is different from the standalone statement:

```
str = ""
```

That line performs an assignment, not a comparison! This type of dual use is called *overloading*. If you hear someone say "operators are overloaded in Visual Basic," they are just stating that = can be used two different ways.

There's something else you need to know about Boolean expressions, though. In Visual Basic, *any* nonzero value is considered to be True. I know that's weird, but it's important because it means the following two fragments are equivalent:

```
If str = "" Then ...
```

```
If Len(str) Then ...
```

The second form literally says "if the length of str, then…" which doesn't make any sense unless you know that 0 equals False and any other value equals True. This second form used to be a common optimization technique because Visual Basic returns the length of a string very quickly. These types of optimizations are less popular today, because the clarity of code is now considered more important than saving a few processor cycles.

Table 3-17 lists the Visual Basic operators that are used to perform comparisons that result in Boolean expressions.

Table 3-17. Visual Basic comparison operators

Operator	Comparison	Operator	Comparison
=	Equal to	<>	Not equal to
<	Less than	>	Greater than
<=	Less than or equal to	>=	Greater than or equal to
Like	Pattern match (strings)	Is	Exact match (objects)

Expressions can also be combined to form compound Boolean expressions using the operators listed in Table 3-18.

Table 3-18. Visual Basic Boolean operators truth table

exp1	Operator	exp2	= Result
True	And	True	True
True	Or	False	True
False	Or	True	True
—	Not	False	True
True	Eqv	True	True
False	Eqv	False	True
True	Imp	True	True
False	Imp	True	True
False	Imp	False	True
True	XOR	False	True
False	XOR	True	True

The most-used Boolean operators are And, Or, and Not.

Compare Bits

Computers use binary numbers internally. That's because they don't have 10 fingers to count on; they have only 2: on and off, which represent 1 and 0, respectively. Knowing that helps you understand another use for the operators in Table 3-18—Boolean operators can also be used in mathematical operations to change the individual bits that make up a number, as illustrated by the following code:

```
Sub ToBorNotToB( )
    Dim b As Byte
    b = 93
    Debug.Print b, Not b, b Or Not b
    ' Displays: 93        162        255
End Sub
```

In the preceding code, Not and Or have a mathematical effect on b. Specifically, Not returns the bits that are 0 (255 − b) and Or combines the bits in b and Not b (93 + 162). These are called *bitwise* operations and they make more sense if you look at b as a binary number (Figure 3-3).

Bitwise operations are used to determine if a number contains one or more bit flags. *Bit flags* are numeric constants that can be combined in a single number without interfering with each other, as shown in Figure 3-4.

Figure 3-4 illustrates that the result of the VarType function can contain both the vbArray flag and any of the other type flags. For instance, vbArray And vbVariant

Expression	Binary	Decimal
b	01011101	93
Not b	10100010	162
b Or Not b	11111111	255

Figure 3-3. Evaluating bitwise operations

Constant	Bits	Value
VbVarType.vbEmpty	0000000000000000	0
VbVarType.vbNull	0000000000000001	1
VbVarType.vbInteger	0000000000000010	2
VbVarType.vbLong	0000000000000011	3
VbVarType.vbSingle	0000000000000100	4
VbVarType.vbDouble	0000000000000101	5
VbVarType.vbCurrency	0000000000000110	6
VbVarType.vbDate	0000000000000111	7
VbVarType.vbString	0000000000001000	8
VbVarType.vbObject	0000000000001001	9
VbVarType.vbError	0000000000001010	10
VbVarType.vbBoolean	0000000000001011	11
VbVarType.vbVariant	0000000000001100	12
VbVarType.vbDataObject	0000000000001101	13
VbVarType.vbDecimal	0000000000001110	14
VbVarType.vbByte	0000000000010001	17
VbVarType.vbUserDefinedType	0000000000100100	36
VbVarType.vbArray	0010000000000000	8192

Won't interfere
with other bits

Figure 3-4. VbVarType constants are bit flags

indicates an array of variants. You can test if a variable contains an array of variants by combining the type flags with the Or operator:

```
Sub TestArrayType( )
    Dim arr, vt As VbVarType
    arr = Array(1, 2, 3, 4, 5)
    vt = VarType(arr)
    If vt And (vbArray Or vbVariant) Then _
        MsgBox "Variable arr is an array of variants."
End Sub
```

If the bit pattern of vt and vbArray Or vbVariant match, the expression is True and the message is displayed. That kind of test is sometimes called a *bit mask*. Bit masking is also used to extract parts of a variable. For instance, the Excel Color property returns a Long integer value that contains three byte values indicating the red, green, and blue components of the color as shown by the following code:

```
Sub ShowColors( )
    Dim i As Integer, rng As Range, rgb As Long
    Set rng = Range("ColorTable")
    For i = 1 To 56
      rng.Offset(i, 0).Interior.ColorIndex = i
      rgb = rng.Offset(i, 0).Interior.Color
      rng.Offset(i, 1).Value = rgb And &HFF
      rng.Offset(i, 2).Value = rgb \ &H100 And &HFF
```

```
      rng.Offset(i, 3).Value = rgb \ &H10000 And &HFF
    Next
End Sub
```

The expression `rgb And &HFF` returns any of the bits in the first byte of `rgb` that are 1. The subsequent expressions use integer division to shift to the next byte, getting the second and third bytes from `rgb`, which are then masked. It often helps to see the bits in a variable when working with bitwise operators, so I wrote the following functions to convert numbers into strings that represent the bit values:

```
Function ByteToBin(byt As Byte) As String
    Dim i As Integer, bin As String
    For i = 0 To 7
        If byt And 2 ^ i Then
            bin = "1" & bin
        Else
            bin = "0" & bin
        End If
    Next
    ByteToBin = bin
End Function

Function IntToBin(itg As Integer) As String
    Dim i As Integer, bin As String
    For i = 0 To 15
        If itg And 2 ^ i Then
            bin = "1" & bin
        Else
            bin = "0" & bin
        End If
    Next
    IntToBin = bin
End Function

Function LngToBin(lng As Long) As String
    Dim i As Integer, bin As String
    ' Note that this omits 2 ^ 31 because of overflow.
    For i = 0 To 30
        If lng And 2 ^ i Then
            bin = "1" & bin
        Else
            bin = "0" & bin
        End If
    Next
    LngToBin = bin
End Function
```

Run Other Applications

Being able to start one application from another is one of the significant advantages of Windows. Within Visual Basic you may want to start another application to load data from Excel, to display a web page, to edit text files, or to perform some other task not easily done in Excel itself. Visual Basic provides the functions shown in Table 3-19 to run other applications.

Table 3-19. Visual Basic functions for running other applications

Function	Use to
AppActivate	Switch focus to a running application
CreateObject	Start an ActiveX application and get an object reference to that application
GetObject	Get a running ActiveX application and get an object reference to that application
SendKeys	Send keystrokes to a running Windows application
Shell	Start an application using its file (*.exe*) name

CreateObject and GetObject work only with Windows applications that have support for ActiveX automation built in to them. Most Microsoft products and many other Windows products support that type of automation, which is sometimes also called *OLE automation*.

ActiveX or OLE automation allows you to use the internal objects, properties, and methods of the application in the same way that you control Excel from Visual Basic. For example, the following code starts Microsoft Word from Excel, creates a new document, inserts some text, and saves the file:

```
Sub UseWord( )
    Dim word As Object, doc As Object
    Set word = CreateObject("Word.Application")
    ' Show Word (otherwise it's invisible).
    word.Visible = True
    ' Create document.
    Set doc = word.Documents.Add
    ' Insert some text
    doc.Range.InsertAfter "Some text to insert."
    ' Save the file
    doc.SaveAs ThisWorkbook.Path & "\StartWord.doc"
End Sub
```

You can use GetObject to get a running instance of an application. For example, the following code uses a running instance of Word to open the document created by the preceding code:

```
Sub GetWord( )
    Dim word As Object, doc As Object
    ' Get a running instance of Word.
    Set word = GetObject(, "Word.Application")
    ' Open a document.
    Set doc = word.documents.Open(ThisWorkbook.Path & "\StartWord.doc")
    word.Visible = True
End Sub
```

In the preceding code, GetObject fails if Word is not already running. You can use GetObject with a filename to start the application associated with the file if it is not already running, as shown here:

```
Sub GetDocument( )
    Dim word As Object, doc As Object
    ' Get the demo document whether or not is it open.
    Set doc = GetObject(ThisWorkbook.Path & "\StartWord.doc")
    ' Show the document.
    doc.Application.Visible = True
End Sub
```

In this case, GetObject starts Word if it is not already running and loads the document. If Word is running or if the document is already open, the code just returns a reference to that object without starting a new instance.

Both CreateObject and GetObject do something called late binding. *Late binding* means that the type of the object is not checked until the application is running. It's often better to use *early binding*, since that allows Visual Basic to check that types match when the code is compiled, which helps correct type-mismatch errors.

Early binding requires that you add a reference to the library for the application you want to use from Excel. To add a reference to an application in Visual Basic:

1. Select Tools → References. Visual Basic displays the References dialog box, shown in Figure 3-5.

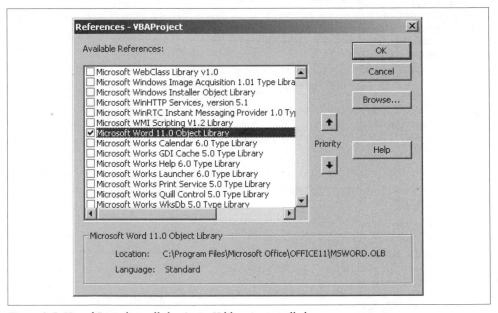

Figure 3-5. Visual Basic lists all the ActiveX libraries installed on your computer

2. Scroll down the list of applications installed on your system and select the ones you want by clicking the box next to the application's name.

3. Click OK when done.

There may be quite a few libraries installed on your computer, and sometimes it is difficult to find the one you want. Microsoft groups most of its libraries under the company name so they sort together, and most other companies do the same.

 If you distribute your Visual Basic code to others, any applications you use must also be installed on their computer, otherwise the code will fail.

Once you have added a reference to another application, you can use objects from that application in the same way that you use Excel objects. For example, the following code creates a new document in Word and inserts some text:

```
' Requires reference to Microsoft Word object library.
Sub EarlyBinding( )
    Dim doc As New Word.Document
    doc.Range.InsertAfter "This is early-bound."
    doc.Application.Visible = True
End Sub
```

One of the key advantages of using explicit types, such as Word.Document, is that it enables Visual Basic's Auto Complete features to help you navigate through the various objects, properties, and methods that an application provides. Figure 3-6 shows the Auto Complete feature in action for the Word objects.

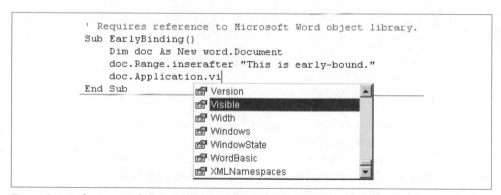

Figure 3-6. References and explicit types enable Auto Complete

Table 3-20 lists some common applications that provide ActiveX objects you can use from Visual Basic. Be aware that most of these applications provide a very complex set of objects that may be organized differently from Excel's objects. Using the objects from other applications often requires a good deal of research and learning.

Table 3-20. Some applications that you can automate from Visual Basic

Application name	Library name (for References dialog)	Programmatic IDs (for CreateObject/GetObject)
Microsoft Word	Microsoft Word 11.0 Object Library	Word.Application Word.Document
Microsoft PowerPoint	Microsoft PowerPoint 11.0 Object Library	PowerPoint.Application PowerPoint.Show PowerPoint.Slide
Microsoft Access	Microsoft Access 11.0 Object Library	Access.Application Access.Workgroup Access.Project
Microsoft Excel	Microsoft Excel 11.0 Object Library	Excel.Application Excel.Sheet Excel.Chart
Microsoft Graph	Microsoft Graph 11.0 Object Library	MSGraph.Application MSGraph.Chart
Microsoft Outlook	Microsoft Outlook 11.0 Object Library	Outlook.Application
Microsoft Internet Explorer	Microsoft Internet Controls	InternetExplorer.Application

Not all applications support ActiveX, however. Some of the simple (and common) applications can be started only with the Shell function. Shell runs the application using its filename and returns a nonzero number if the application started successfully. You can combine Shell with SendKeys to automate applications in a simple way:

```
Sub StartNotepad()
    Dim id As Integer
    id = Shell("notepad.exe", vbNormalFocus)
    ' If id is not zero, then Shell worked. This is some text to insert
    If id Then
        SendKeys "This is some text to insert", True
        SendKeys "^s", True
        SendKeys ThisWorkbook.Path & "\StartNote.txt", True
        SendKeys "~", True
    End If
End Sub
```

The preceding code starts Notepad, inserts some text, and saves the file. You can send keystrokes to only the application that currently has focus in Windows. If the user changes the focus while your code is running, the keystrokes may go to the wrong application. This makes debugging the preceding code very difficult. If you try to step through the code, the keystrokes are sent to the Code window, rather than to Notepad!

You can switch the focus to another application using the AppActivate function. AppActivate uses the text displayed in the window's titlebar to select the window to grant focus. If you run the preceding code, the Notepad window will contain the text "StartNote.txt -- Notepad", so the following code will switch focus to that window to make some changes:

```
Sub GetNotepad( )
    Dim id As Integer
    On Error Resume Next
    AppActivate "StartNote.txt - Notepad", True
    If Err Then MsgBox ("StartNote.txt is not open."): Exit Sub
    SendKeys "{end}", True
    SendKeys ". Some more text to insert.", True
    SendKeys "^s", True
End Sub
```

You can also use the ID returned by the Shell function with AppActivate to activate a running application. SendKeys uses the predefined codes listed in Table 3-21 to send special keys, such as Enter or Page Up, to an application.

Table 3-21. SendKeys codes

Key	Code	Key	Code
Shift	+	Ctrl	^
Alt	%	Backspace	{BACKSPACE}, {BS}, or {BKSP}
Break	{BREAK}	Caps Lock	{CAPSLOCK}
Del or Delete	{DELETE} or {DEL}	Down Arrow	{DOWN}
End	{END}	Enter	{ENTER} or ~
Esc	{ESC}	Help	{HELP}
Home	{HOME}	Ins or Insert	{INSERT} or {INS}
Left Arrow	{LEFT}	Num Lock	{NUMLOCK}
Page Down	{PGDN}	Page Up	{PGUP}
Print Screen	{PRTSC}	Right Arrow	{RIGHT}
Scroll Lock	{SCROLLLOCK}	Tab	{TAB}
Up Arrow	{UP}	F1–F16	{F1}–{F16}

I should point out here that Excel provides methods for running two of the most commonly used applications. Use the FollowHyperlink method to display a web page in the default browser or to create a new email message. Use the SendMail method to send a workbook as an attachment. The following code demonstrates these different approaches:

```
Sub BrowserAndMail( )
    ' Starts browser and displays page.
    ThisWorkbook.FollowHyperlink "http://www.mstrainingkits.com"
    ' Creates a new, blank mail message
    ThisWorkbook.FollowHyperlink "mailto:exceldemo@hotmail.com"
    ' Sends the workbook as an attachment without displaying message.
    ThisWorkbook.SendMail "exceldemo@hotmail.com"
End Sub
```

Control the Compiler

Visual Basic includes two instructions that tell the compiler to take special actions, as listed in Table 3-22.

Table 3-22. Visual Basic compiler directives

Directive	Use to
#Const	Define a literal constant. The compiler replaces these constants will their literal value in the compiled code.
#If...Then...#End If	Conditionally compile code based on a literal constant.

These directives are commonly used to switch between debug and release versions of code. Often, debug versions include extra statements that display output in the Immediate window. That makes it easier to locate problems while debugging, however you might *not* want that code to run in the released version. Rather than remove the statements manually, you can simply turn them off by changing a global setting, as shown here:

```
#Const ISDEBUG = True

Sub DemoDirectives()
    #If ISDEBUG Then
        MsgBox "Running in Debug mode."
    #Else
        MsgBox "Running in Release mode."
    #End If
End Sub
```

Changing the value of ISDEBUG changes which code runs—in fact, Visual Basic actually omits the unused code in its internal compiled version (the source code isn't affected, however). The constant ISDEBUG isn't really a symbol: you can't see its value with a watch. Instead, it's a literal value that the compiler replaces throughout your code.

Not Covered Here

Chapters 2 and 3 give you a lot to think about. Still, there are a few things about Visual Basic I haven't touched on. The two reasons I haven't covered everything yet:

- Some functions are obsolete or not particularly useful from Excel.
- Other Visual Basic keywords are very advanced.

Table 3-23 lists the Visual Basic functions that are obsolete or aren't often used in Excel. Table 3-24 lists advanced keywords.

Table 3-23. *Obsolete or obscure Visual Basic functions*

Function	Use to
Beep	Play a beep through the computer's speaker.
Environ	Get strings from the operating system's environment string table. For instance, Environ("path") returns the MS-DOS PATH environment variable.
Command	Get command-line arguments. Excel applications don't use command-line arguments.

Table 3-24. *Advanced Visual Basic keywords*

Category	Keyword
System registry	DeleteSetting
	GetSetting
	GetAllSettings
	SaveSetting
Windows APIs	Declare
	AddressOf

What You've Learned

This chapter taught you about the core language of Visual Basic—that is, all the statements and functions that perform general programming tasks. At this point in the book, you've covered all the Visual Basic fundamentals: using the editor, constructing a program, and performing tasks. Congratulations!

You should now be comfortable displaying simple dialogs and working with numbers, strings, and arrays, and you should know something about working with files.

Don't worry if you're not an expert at working with dates, comparing bits, or running other applications. You can always come back later for a refresher on those topics.

CHAPTER 4

Using Excel Objects

Programming Excel is all about objects. In Chapter 2, I defined what objects are and showed you a little about how they work. In this chapter, I'll take a closer look at the Excel object library and give you the tools you need to find the right Excel object for any task you want to perform.

Code used in this chapter and additional samples are available in *ch04.xls*.

Objects and Their Members

The most obvious difference between objects and other parts of the Visual Basic language is the *dot notation*. Objects use the period (or *dot*) to separate the object name from the member name as shown in Figure 4-1.

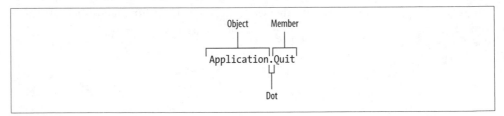

Figure 4-1. The dot separates the object from the member

Member is the general term for a property, method, enumeration, or constant that belongs to the object. Objects help organize members by grouping them into functional units. Objects are used throughout Visual Basic to organize things. In fact, if you type VBA. in the Code window, you'll see a list of the functions that are part of the Visual Basic language (Figure 4-2).

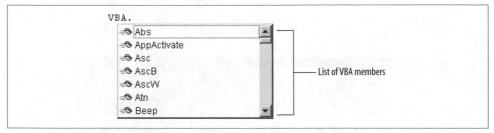

Figure 4-2. Visual Basic uses objects to organize its members

The VBA object library even uses dot syntax to organize other objects. For example, type `VBA.Strings.` and you'll see a list of the string functions. The symbols in the Auto Complete list identify the type of member, as shown in Figure 4-3.

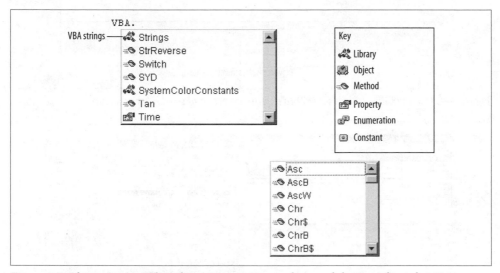

Figure 4-3. Objects can use other objects to organize members, and the type of member is illustrated by an icon

In Figure 4-3, the Library symbol identifies a grouping of related members; the Enumeration symbol identifies a grouping of related constants. Visual Basic uses these same icons in the Object Browser—a tool that lets you explore the objects contained in any of the object libraries (Figure 4-4). To see the Object Browser, press F2.

The Object Browser lists only the object libraries that you have established references to. That means the libraries listed in the Object Brower's drop-down list match the checkboxes selected in the Visual Basic References dialog box (Figure 4-5).

You may notice that not all of the Visual Basic language is listed in the VBA object library. Keywords like `If`, `Sub`, `Function`, and `End` are structural components and so aren't part of the library. I covered those keywords (sometimes called *reserved words*) in Chapter 2, and I covered the members of the VBA object library in Chapter 3.

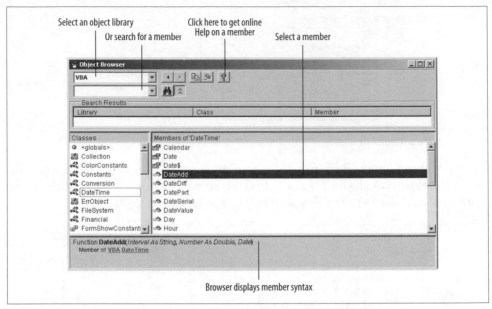

Figure 4-4. Use the Object Browser (F2) to explore objects and search for members

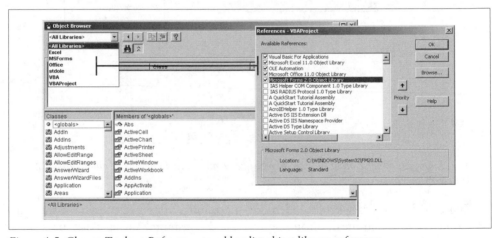

Figure 4-5. Choose Tools → References to add or list object library references

You need to know about two other icons in the Object Browser (see Figure 4-6):

Global members

Members for which you can omit the object name. In the case of the VBA object library, all members are global so you never have to type `VBA.`. In the case of the Excel object library, the global members are often synonymous with the `Application` object. That means that `Application.ActiveSheet` and `ActiveSheet` are equivalent expressions.

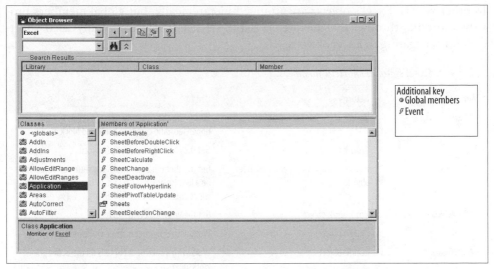

Figure 4-6. Listing global members and events

Events

Procedures that execute automatically when something happens in Excel. They take the form *objectname_eventname* in Visual Basic.

Get Excel Objects

In Excel, you always get one object from another, and everything starts with the Application object. So, if you want to change the font of cell C2 to bold, you would simply type:

```
Application.ActiveWorkbook.ActiveSheet.Range("C2").Font.Bold = True
```

Not really! Application, ActiveWorkbook, and ActiveSheet are all global members in Excel, so you can shorten your code to:

```
ActiveWorkbook.ActiveSheet.Range("C2").Font.Bold = True
```

or:

```
ActiveSheet.Range("C2").Font.Bold = True
```

or more likely:

```
Range("C2").Font.Bold = True
```

Each of the members in the original line of code returns an object reference that navigates from the top-level object (the Excel Application object) to the low-level object (a Font object) for which you want to set the Bold property. The order of objects looks like this:

```
Application → Workbook → Worksheet → Range → Font (set Bold property)
```

In other words, Excel's objects are arranged hierarchically, but global members provide shortcuts through that hierarchy. Table 4-1 lists some commonly used shortcuts for navigating to Excel objects.

Table 4-1. Excel's global shortcut members

Member	Returns	Use to
ActiveCell	Range object containing a single cell	Work with the currently selected cell or get the upper-lefthand corner of a selected block of cells.
ActiveChart	Chart object	Get the chart that currently has focus.
ActiveSheet	Worksheet, Chart, or other sheet object.	Get the sheet that has focus. The returned object may be a Worksheet, a Chart, or one of the obsolete sheet types.
ActiveWorkbook	Workbook object	Get the workbook that has focus.
Cells	Range object	Work with cells on the active worksheet.
Range	Range object	Work with a specific set of cells on the active worksheet.
Selection	Varies	Get the selected object. That may be a range of cells, a chart, or some other object.
Sheets	Collection of Worksheet, Chart, or other sheet objects	Get a sheet by its numeric index or name.
ThisWorkbook	Workbook object	Get the workbook that contains the current Visual Basic project. This contrasts with ActiveWorkbook, which may be different from ThisWorkbook if the user has switched focus.
UsedRange	Range object	Get the block of cells on the active worksheet that contains data.
Workbooks	Collection of Workbook objects	Get a workbook by its numeric index or name.
Worksheets	Collection of Worksheet objects	Get a worksheet by its numeric index or name.

In general, the members that return only one type of object are easier to work with than members that can return various types. This is probably best demonstrated by contrasting the Sheets and Worksheets methods. Sheets can return several different types of objects: Worksheet, Chart, DialogSheet (which is obsolete), and so on. Worksheets returns only Worksheet objects. That means Visual Basic knows the object type when you are working with Worksheets, but not when working with Sheets. You can tell that because Auto Complete doesn't work with Sheets. It also means you have to be careful what methods you call objects returned by Sheets, since trying to use a Worksheet method, like Range, will fail if the object is a Chart.

Therefore, if you want to do something to all worksheets in a workbook, you use the Worksheets method:

```
Sub UseWorksheets( )
    Dim ws As Worksheet
```

```
        For Each ws In Worksheets
            ' Do some task
        Next
    End Sub
```

If you want to do something to all of the sheets in workbook, use the Sheets method as shown here:

```
Sub UseSheets( )
    Dim obj As Object, ws As Worksheet, chrt As Chart
    For Each obj In Sheets
        Select Case Typename(obj)
            Case "Worksheet"
                ' OK to use Worksheet methods.
                Set ws = obj
            Case "Chart"
                ' OK to use Chart methods.
                Set chrt = obj
            Case Else
                ' An obsolete sheet type.
        End Select
    Next
End Sub
```

In the preceding code, I set the generic object returned by Sheets to a specific Worksheet or Chart type so that I could make sure I wasn't using any members that weren't allowed for the object. If I were doing a task that is common to all objects, such as setting the Name property, I could avoid that step and just use the returned obj variable.

This points up a problem for Excel programmers: there is no ActiveWorksheet property. The ActiveSheet property returns a generic object type—that might be a Worksheet, a Chart, or something else. Sometimes you definitely know that the sheet that has focus is a Worksheet—for example, when you create a new worksheet in code. In this case, you can safely use the Worksheet members. Otherwise, you need to test if the object is a worksheet before proceeding as shown here:

```
If TypeName(ActiveSheet) = "Worksheet" Then
    ' OK to use Worksheet members on ActiveSheet
End If
```

This isn't really an oversight by the Excel team. If they did provide an ActiveWorksheet property, it would return Nothing if a chart sheet had focus. You'd still have to write similar code to test for that condition!

 Checking and working with specific types of objects, rather than using the generic Object type, is sometimes called *type-safe programming*, and it's a good technique to help prevent errors in your code.

Get Objects from Collections

Excel members like Workbooks, Worksheets, Charts, Sheets, and Range return groups of objects called *collections*. Collections are special because they provide a hidden enumerator method that lets you use them with the For Each statement as well as Item and Count methods that let you get specific objects from the group.

In Excel, collections are usually (but not always) named as the plural form of the objects they contain: so the Workbooks collection contains Workbook objects, the Worksheets collection contains Worksheet objects, and so on. There are some obvious exceptions: Sheets contains various types of sheet objects, and Range contains other Range objects, each of which contains a single cell. The Range collection is definitely weird, but Excel has no Cell object so that's just the way things work!

In Excel, you get collections using a property from the collection's parent object. The property usually has the same name as the returned collection, which can make using Help a little frustrating (Figure 4-7).

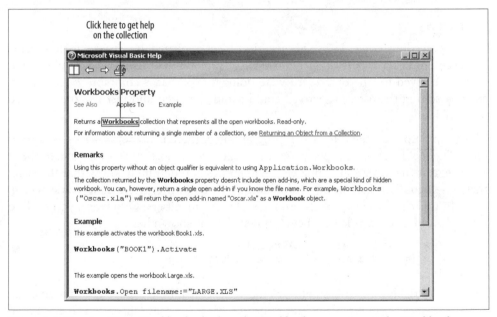

Figure 4-7. Pressing F1 on Workbooks displays the Workbooks property, not the Workbooks collection you might expect!

To see Help on the collection, including a list of its members, click the link for the collection object on the property Help topic. Figure 4-8 shows the Help for the Workbooks collection object.

The graphic in Figure 4-8 shows how you navigate from the Application object to the Workbook object. You can interpret that graphic as saying "Use the Application

---

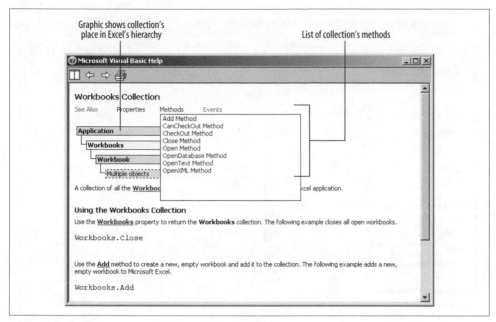

Figure 4-8. It takes an extra click to get Help on collections

object's Workbooks property to get the Workbooks collection, which contains Workbook objects, from which you can use other properties to get other objects." You can see why they used a graphic instead of words! If you click on any of the boxes in the graphic, you'll get Help on that object. If you click on the Multiple Objects box, you'll see a list of the objects you can get from the Workbook object (Figure 4-9).

You often need to use Help to figure out how to navigate to the object you need. Excel's object library is complicated, as shown by Figure 4-10. Knowing how to navigate it is one of the key skills you must develop as an Excel programmer.

In fact, Figure 4-10 cheats by using shortcut methods like Application.Range to simplify the hierarchy. The real hierarchy is Application → Workbooks → Workbook → Worksheets → Worksheet → Range, but that *really* wouldn't fit!

You get specific objects from a collection using the collection's Item property:

```
' Show the name of the first worksheet.
Debug.Print Application.Workbooks.Item(1).Worksheets.Item(1).Name
```

Wait! That's not the way it's usually shown. You can omit Item because it is the default property of the collection. You can also omit Application.Workbooks since Worksheets is a global method. The way you'd usually write that code is this:

```
' Show the name of the first worksheet (simplified)
Debug.Print Worksheets(1).Name
```

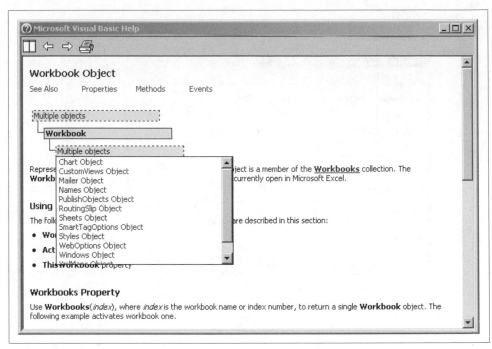

Figure 4-9. Click on the graphic to navigate to other objects in Help

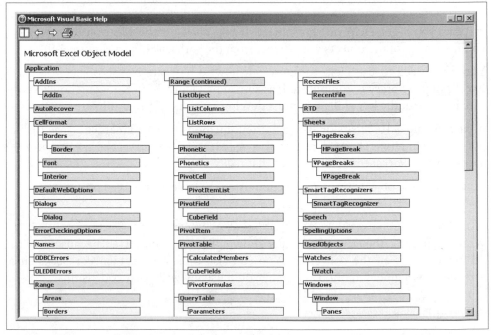

Figure 4-10. Excel's object hierarchy doesn't fit on one Help screen (look at the scrollbar)

Or you can use the collection with For Each to show a list of all worksheets:

```
Dim ws As Worksheet
' Show names of all worksheets.
For Each ws In Worksheets
    Debug.Print ws.Name
Next
```

 Most collections have two types of indexes. The first type is numeric (Worksheets(1)), and the second type uses the item's name (Worksheets("Sheet1")).

Collections are also usually the way you create new objects in Excel—most collections provide an Add method for creating new instances of objects and adding them to the collection. Interestingly, you usually delete items from Excel collections using the individual object's Delete method. The following code illustrates adding and deleting a worksheet:

```
' Create a new workhseet
Set ws = Worksheets.Add
' Delete that sheet
ws.Delete
```

Table 4-2 lists the members that are common to most collections.

Table 4-2. Common members for collection objects

Member	Use to	Example
Add	Create a new object and add it to the collection.	`Workbooks.Add`

Count	Get the number of objects in the collection.	`' Alternative to For Each`
		`For i = 1 to Sheets.Count`
		`    Debug.Print Sheets(i).Name`
		`Next`

Item	Get an object from the collection. This member name is usually omitted since it is the default member.	`Worksheets("Objects").UsedRange.` `AutoFormat`

About Me and the Active Object

The Visual Basic Me keyword provides a way to refer to an instance of the object created by the current class. I know that's a little confusing; here's how it works: if you write code in the ThisWorkbook class, Me is the same as ThisWorkbook, as shown by Figure 4-11.

If you write that same code for one of the Worksheet classes, you get a different result as shown by the following code:

```
' In Objects sheet class.
Sub AboutMe( )
    Debug.Print Me.Name              ' Displays:
    Debug.Print ThisWorkbook.Name    '   Objects
                                     '   ch04.xls
```

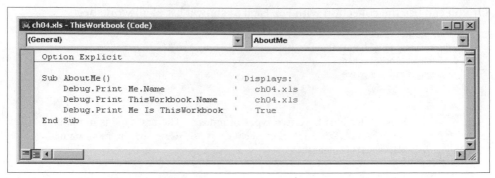

```
ch04.xls - ThisWorkbook (Code)                              _ |□| x|
(General)                              ▼   AboutMe                 ▼
    Option Explicit

    Sub AboutMe()                       ' Displays:
        Debug.Print Me.Name             '   ch04.xls
        Debug.Print ThisWorkbook.Name   '   ch04.xls
        Debug.Print Me Is ThisWorkbook  '   True
    End Sub
```

Figure 4-11. ThisWorkbook and Me are the same here

```
        Debug.Print Me Is Sheets("Objects") '    True
    End Sub
```

That's because Excel creates an object out of the class at runtime, and Me refers to
that object. You can use Me to refer to members of the class using the dot notation:

```
Sub DemoMe( )
    Me.AboutMe     ' Calls preceding AboutMe procedure.
End Sub
```

You can't use Me in a Module. It's valid only in classes since it refers to the instance of
the object created from the class and modules don't have instances—modules are
static code.

Excel provides a number of properties that return objects that currently have focus in
the Excel interface. Some of these properties were included in the list of shortcuts
shown in Table 4-1, but they bear repeating in Table 4-3.

Table 4-3. Active object properties

Property	Returns
ActiveCell	Range containing the cell that currently has focus for input
ActiveChart	Chart that has focus
ActiveMenuBar	MenuBar currently displayed in Excel
ActivePane	Pane within the active window
ActivePrinter	Name of the default printer in Excel (not an object)
ActiveSheet	Worksheet, Chart, or other sheet type that has focus
ActiveWindow	Window that has focus
ActiveWorkbook	Workbook that has focus
Selection	Selected item (may be a Range, Chart, drawing object, or other object)

These properties are very useful in code because they tell you what the user is looking at. Often you'll want your code to affect that item—for example, you might want
to display a result in the active cell. Normally, the user can change the active object

in Excel by clicking on a worksheet tab, switching to a new window, and the like, but she can't do that while a Visual Basic procedure is running, as shown in Figure 4-12.

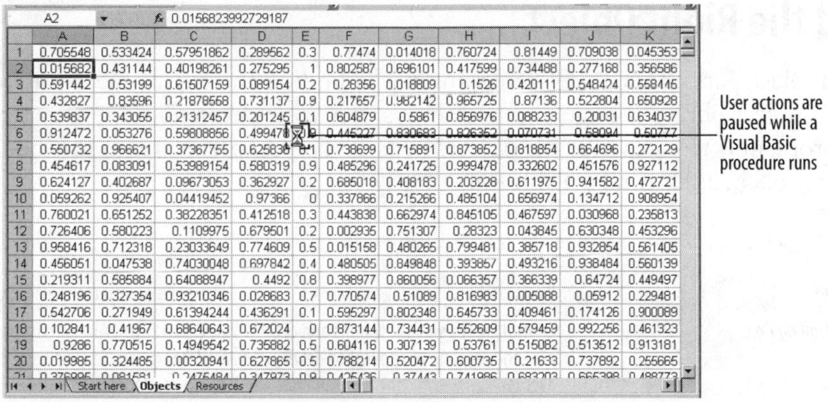

User actions are paused while a Visual Basic procedure runs

Figure 4-12. The user can't change the active object while a procedure runs

Code can change the active object, however. Many objects provide Activate methods that switch focus within Excel, and some objects, such as Window, provide ActivateNext and ActivatePrevious methods as well. If you rely on active objects, you need to be careful about changing the active object in code.

Many Excel programmers rely on activation a little too much in my opinion, as shown here:

```
Sub DemoActivation1( )
    Dim cel As range
    ' Make sure a range is selected.
    If TypeName(Selection) <> "Range" Then Exit Sub
    For Each cel In Selection
        ' Activate the cell.
        cel.Activate
        ' Insert a random value
        ActiveCell.Value = Rnd
    Next
End Sub
```

In reality, there's no good reason to do this since you've got a perfectly good object reference (cel) that you can use instead:

```
Sub DemoActivation2( )
    ' Make sure a range is selected.
    If TypeName(Selection) <> "Range" Then Exit Sub
    Dim cel As range
    For Each cel In Selection
        ' Insert a random value
        cel.Value = Rnd
    Next
End Sub
```

`DemoActivation2` runs faster because it avoids an unneeded `Activate` step in the `For Each` loop. There's nothing wrong with using the active object when you need it; I just see it overused a lot.

Find the Right Object

The hardest part about Excel programming is finding the right object for the job. Excel's object library is huge and not always easy to understand. One way to tackle that problem is to categorize the objects by task. The chapters later in this book take that approach, as shown by Table 4-4.

Table 4-4. How this book organizes Excel objects by task

Chapter	Description	Covers these objects
7, *Controlling Excel*	Control Excel's general options and display and respond to application-level events	`Application`, `AutoCorrect`, `AutoRecover`, `ErrorChecking`, `Windows`, and `Panes`
8, *Opening, Saving, and Sharing Workbooks*	Access workbooks and their properties and respond to workbook events	`Workbook` and `RecentFile`
9, *Working with Worksheets and Ranges*	Perform general tasks on ranges of cells including inserting values, search and replace, and formatting and respond to worksheet events	`Worksheet` and `Range`
10, *Linking and Embedding*	Add comments, hyperlinks, and various OLE objects to worksheets	`Comment`, `Hyperlink`, `OLEObject`, `Speech`, and `UsedObjects`
11, *Printing and Publishing*	Create hardcopy and online output from workbooks	`AutoFilter`, `Filter`, `HPageBreak`, `VPageBreak`, `PageSetup`, `Graphic`, `PublishObject`, `DefaultWebOptions`, and `WebOptions`
12, *Loading and Manipulating Data*	Bring data into a workbook from a database or other data source	`Parameter` and `QueryTable` ADO objects: `Command`, `Connection`, `Field`, `Parameter`, and `RecordSet` DAO objects: `Database`, `DbEngine`, `Document`, `QueryDef`, and `Recordset`
13, *Analyzing Data with Pivot Tables*	Organize, sort, and filter data through pivot tables	`CalculatedField`, `CalculatedMember`, `CubeField`, `PivotCache`, `PivotCell`, `PivotField`, `PivotFormula`, `PivotItem`, `PivotItemList`, `PivotLayout`, and `PivotTable`

Table 4-4. How this book organizes Excel objects by task (continued)

Chapter	Description	Covers these objects
14, *Sharing Data Using Lists*	Use lists for data entry, filtering, sorting, and sharing data	`ListObject`, `ListRow`, `ListColumn`, and `ListDataFormat`
15, *Working with XML*	Import XML data into Excel and export data from workbooks in XML format	`XmlMap`, `XmlDataBinding`, `XmlNamespace`, `XmlSchema`, and `XPath`
16, *Charting*	Display numeric data graphically	`Axis`, `Chart`, `ChartGroup`, `ChartObject`, `DataTable`, `Point`, `Series`, and `SeriesLines`
17, *Formatting Charts*	Change low-level aspects of the chart	`ChartArea`, `ChartColorFormat`, `ChartFillFormat`, `Corners`, `DataLabel`, `DownBars`, `DropLines`, `ErrorBars`, `Floor`, `Gridlines`, `HiLoLines`, `LeaderLines`, `Legend`, `LegendEntry`, `LegendKey`, `PlotArea`, `TickLabels`, `Trendline`, `Trendlines`, `UpBars`, and `Walls`
18, *Drawing Graphics*	Create graphics on Excel worksheets	`Adjustments`, `CalloutFormat`, `ColorFormat`, `ConnectorFormat`, `ControlFormat`, `FillFormat`, `FreeFormBuilder`, `GroupShapes`, `LineFormat`, `LinkFormat`, `PictureFormat`, `ShadowFormat`, `Shape`, `ShapeNode`, `ShapeRange`, `TextEffectFormat`, `TextFrame`, and `ThreeDFormat`
19, *Adding Menus and Toolbars*	Add items to the Excel user interface	`CommandBar`, `CommandBarButton`, `CommandBarComboBox`, and `CommandBarPopup`
20, *Building Dialog Boxes*	Create forms and use controls in Excel	Forms 2.0 objects: `UserForm`, `CheckBox`, `ComboBox`, `CommandButton`, `Control`, `Frame`, `Image`, `Label`, `ListBox`, `MultiPage`, `OptionButton`, `RefEdit`, `ScrollBar`, `SpinButton`, `TabStrip`, and `ToggleButton`
21, *Sending and Receiving Workbooks*	Send mail from Excel	`MsoEnvelope`, `MailItem`, and `RoutingSlip`

Table 4-4. How this book organizes Excel objects by task (continued)

Chapter	Description	Covers these objects
22, *Building Add-ins*	Load and use add-ins as well as create and distribute new ones	`AddIn`
26, *Exploring Security in Depth*	Limit edits to sheets and ranges of cells	`AllowEditRange`, `Protection`, `Permission`, `UserAccess`, `UserAccessList`

To give you an overview of how the Excel object library is organized, the following sections break the Excel object library into parts and illustrate how the objects are organized graphically. These illustrations are similar to those found in online Help as shown in Figure 4-10 earlier but are a little more complete (and I think more accurate) than Excel's Help.

Top-Level Objects

Excel's top-level objects control Excel's application options, such as automatic correction, and provide ways to navigate to lower-level objects, such as workbooks. Figure 4-13 shows the objects you can get directly from the `Application` object with the most significant ones shown in **bold**. You can also use the `Application` object's `ActiveSheet`, `ActiveCell`, `ActiveChart`, and other methods to get lower-level objects directly (see Table 4-1).

Workbook Objects

Excel files are called workbooks and Excel controls its files through the `Workbook` object. This object is the next major object in the Excel object library, right after the `Application` object, as shown in Figure 4-14. You use the `Workbook` objects to share, email, and publish workbooks as well as to get to the contents of the workbook through lower-level `Worksheet` and `Chart` objects.

Worksheet and Range Objects

You use the `Worksheet` and `Range` objects to control the contents of a workbook. These are perhaps the two most-important objects in the Excel object library because they let you get at cell values and objects displayed on worksheets, as shown in Figure 4-15.

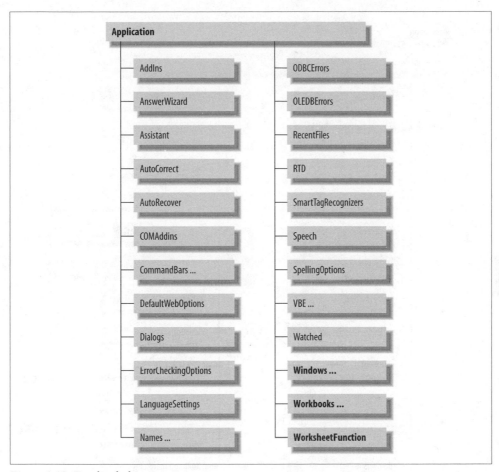

Application	
AddIns	ODBCErrors
AnswerWizard	OLEDBErrors
Assistant	RecentFiles
AutoCorrect	RTD
AutoRecover	SmartTagRecognizers
COMAddins	Speech
CommandBars ...	SpellingOptions
DefaultWebOptions	VBE ...
Dialogs	Watched
ErrorCheckingOptions	**Windows ...**
LanguageSettings	**Workbooks ...**
Names ...	**WorksheetFunction**

Figure 4-13. Top-level objects

Chart Objects

You use the Chart objects to display data graphically. Excel charts may exist on their own sheets or be embedded on a worksheet, so you can get at Excel charts through the Charts collection (for chart sheets) or the ChartObjects collection (for embedded charts), as shown in Figure 4-16. This part of the Excel object library is many levels deep, because it provides control over every graphic object on a chart...right down to the individual points in a series.

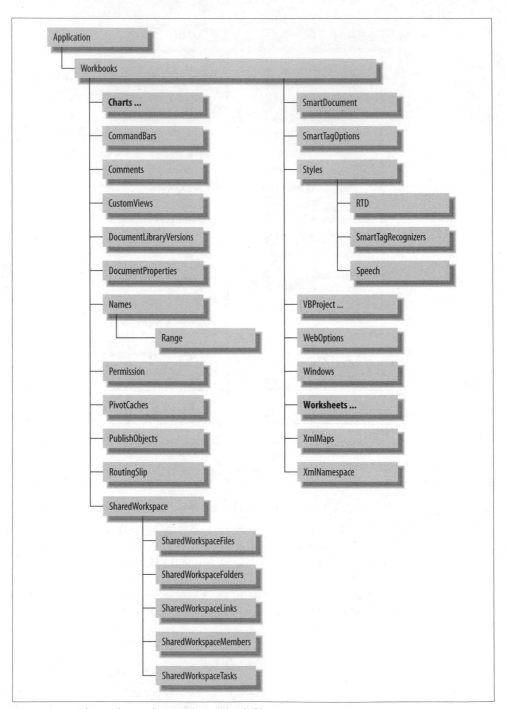

Figure 4-14. Objects for working with workbook files

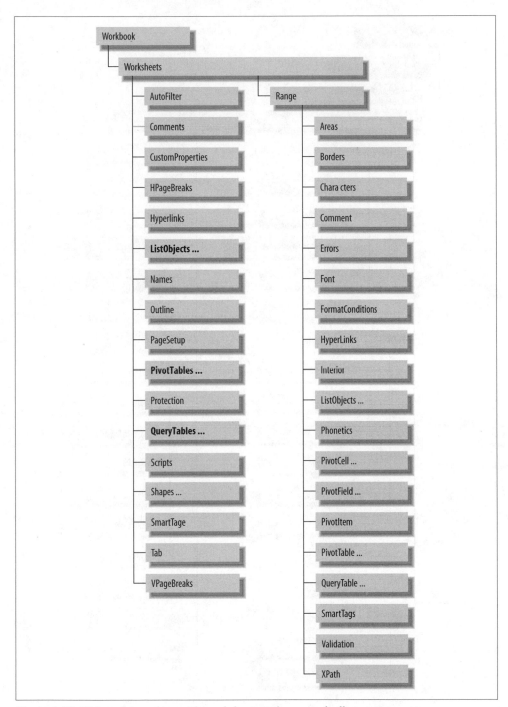

Figure 4-15. Objects for working with worksheets and ranges of cells

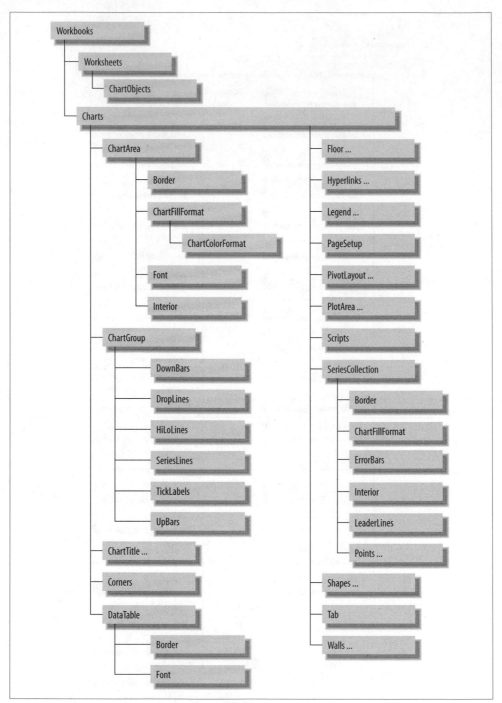

Figure 4-16. Objects for charting and formatting charts

Data List and XML Objects

Data lists are new in Excel 2003 and are closely related to Excel's new XML features. That's why I show them together in Figure 4-17. Excel controls data lists through the `ListObjects` collection and can import or export XML data using the `XmlMaps` collection.

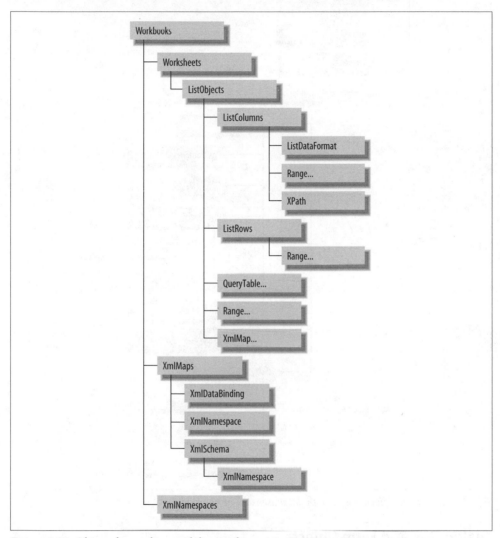

Figure 4-17. Objects for working with lists and importing/exporting XML

Database Objects

Excel interacts with databases through `PivotTable` and `QueryTable` objects, as shown in Figure 4-18. There are also a couple of special-purpose objects at the application level for getting data-access errors and for interacting with real-time data servers (RTD).

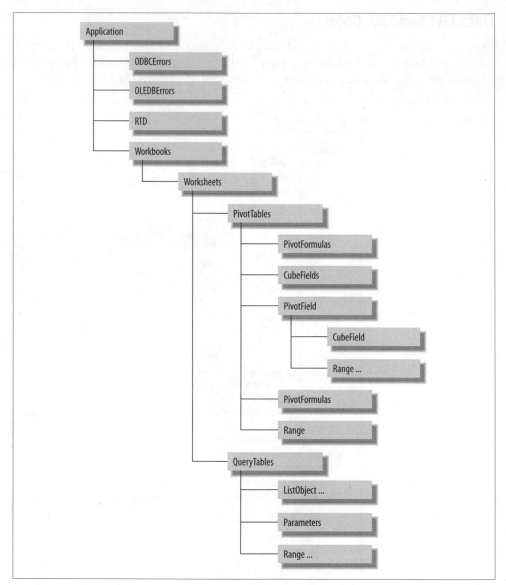

Figure 4-18. Objects for working with databases and pivot tables

Dialog Box and Form Objects

Excel's `Dialogs` collection lets you display any of the application's built-in dialog boxes or get information from one of Excel's file dialog boxes. However, you display custom dialog boxes using the Microsoft Forms object library—*not* the Excel object library. Figure 4-19 shows the dialog box objects from both object libraries.

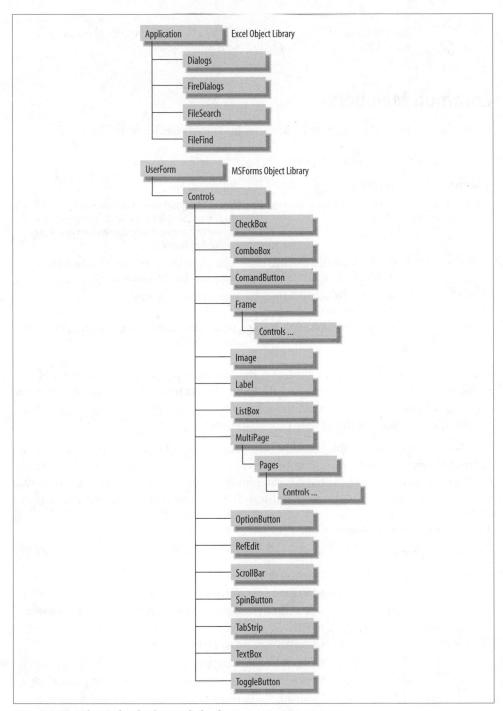

Figure 4-19. Objects for displaying dialog boxes

Early versions of Excel used the DialogSheets collection to display custom dialog boxes, but that technique is now obsolete.

Common Members

Most objects in Excel have several members in common as listed in Table 4-5.

Table 4-5. Common Excel object members

Member	Description	Use to
Application	Returns the Excel Application object	This isn't really useful from within Excel since the Application object is readily available anyway. It's somewhat useful when programming Excel from other applications, however.
Creator	Returns a numeric code identifying the application that created the object	Again, this isn't really useful from within Excel. You can pretty much ignore this property.
Parent	Returns the next-higher object in Excel's object hierarchy	Map Excel's object hierarchy.
Name	Returns a string describing the object	Display information about an object or get a specific object from a collection.

You might be able to tell from Table 4-5 that the Name property is the most useful of the common members. Most (but not all) Excel objects have a Name property that identifies the object within its containing collection. For example, Worksheets("Sheet1") returns the worksheet with the Name property Sheet1.

That's not true for all objects, however. The Range object, for instance, has an Address property instead of a Name property. Other objects, such as Window, use the Caption property, instead. Table 4-6 categorizes some of the common members that aren't as universal as those listed in Table 4-5, but are actually more useful to know.

Table 4-6. Other useful, common members by category

Category	Member	Use to
General	Activate	Set focus on an object.
	Caption	Set or return the text that appears in an object's titlebar.
	Value	Set or return the value displayed by an object. This is often the default property of an object.
Collections	Add	Create a new object and add it to the collection.
	Count	Get the number of objects in a collection.
	Index	Get the position of an object within a collection (use on the object, not the collection).
	Item( )	Get an object by name or index from a collection. This is the default property of most collections.

Table 4-6. Other useful, common members by category (continued)

Category	Member	Use to
	Delete	Remove an object from a collection (use on the object, not the collection).
Appearance	Height	Set or return the height of an object in points. (There are 72 points in an inch.)
	Left	Set or return the horizontal position of an object in points.
	Top	Set or return the vertical position of an object in points.
	Visible	Show or hide an object (True/False).
	Width	Set or return the width of an object in points.
Printing	PrintOut	Print an object.
	PrintPreview	View the object before printing.

The following sections explain using these common members.

Activate Objects: Get Names and Values

You can use the `Activate` method to set focus on the following objects:

```
Chart
ChartObject
OLEObject
Pane
Range
Window
Workbook
Worksheet
```

Usually, you'll use `Activate` in combination with one of the collection methods to set focus on a member of the collection. For example, the following line sets focus on the first sheet in a workbook:

```
Sheets(1).Activate
```

Similarly, the following line sets focus on the last sheet:

```
Sheets(Sheets.Count).Activate
```

As mentioned previously, not all objects have a `Name` property. In those cases, the `Caption` or `Address` property is sometimes equivalent. The following procedure uses exception handling to return the name of an object of any type:

```
Function GetName(obj) As String
    Dim res As String
    ' Use exception handling in case object
    ' doesn't support Name property.
    On Error Resume Next
    res = obj.Name
    If Err Then res = obj.Address
    If Err Then res = obj.Caption
```

```
            If Err Then res = obj.Index
            If Err Then res = "no name"
            On Error GoTo 0
            GetName = res
    End Function
```

Some objects (such as points within a chart series) don't have any identifiers. In that case, GetName returns no name. The Range and Hyperlink objects use the Address property, and the following objects have Caption properties:

Application	AxisTitle	Characters
ChartTitle	CheckBox[1]	CommandButton[1]
DataLabel	Frame[1]	Label[1]
OptionButton[1]	Menu	MenuBar
MenuItem	Page[1]	Tab[1]
ToggleButton[1]	UserForm[1]	

[1] These objects are part of the Microsoft Forms object library that ships with Excel.

In some cases, objects may have both a Name and a Caption property. For example, the following code changes the text displayed in the Excel titlebar:

```
    Application.Caption = "Programming Excel Rules!"
```

Many objects also have a Value property. This is usually the default property of an object, so you don't often see Value in code. Usually it looks like this:

```
    Range("A2") = 42
```

Sometimes Value is synonymous with the Name property. For example, both of the following lines display "Microsoft Excel":

```
    Debug.Print Application.Value    ' Displays Microsoft Excel
    Debug.Print Application.Name     ' Displays Microsoft Excel
```

Why did Microsoft do this? I have no idea. The main thing you need to know is that the following objects all have Value properties:

Application	Borders	CheckBox[1]
ComboBox[1]	CommandButton[1]	ControlFormat
CubeField	CustomProperty	Error
ListBox[1]	MultiPage[1]	Name
OptionButton[1]	PivotField	PivotItem
PivotTable	Range	ScrollBar[1]
SpinButton[1]	Style	TextBox[1]
ToggleButton[1]	Validation	XmlNamespaces
XPath		

[1] These objects are part of the Microsoft Forms object library that ships with Excel.

Add or Delete Objects Through Collections

I already showed how to get objects from a collection and how collections help organize the Excel object library. Here, I would like to emphasize that you create new objects in Excel using the collection's Add method and that you can usually delete objects using the individual object's Delete method.

For example, the following code creates a new chart from a selected range and adds it to the active worksheet:

```
Sub AddChart( )
    Dim sel
    Set sel = Selection
    If TypeName(sel) = "Range" Then
        Charts.Add
        ActiveChart.Location xlLocationAsObject, sel.Parent.name
    End If
End Sub
```

Run the preceding code a number of times, and you'll wind up with numerous charts on the worksheet. To clean that up, use this code:

```
Sub RemoveChart( )
    Dim chrt As ChartObject, ans As VbMsgBoxResult
    For Each chrt In ActiveSheet.ChartObjects
        chrt.Activate
        ans = MsgBox("Delete " & chrt.name & "?", vbYesNo)
        If ans = vbYes Then _
           chrt.Delete
    Next
End Sub
```

OK, these two procedures are a little tricky. The AddChart actually creates the chart as a separate sheet, but then moves it onto the active worksheet as a Chart object using the Location method. RemoveChart then uses the worksheet's ChartObjects collection to selectively delete charts from the worksheet. It would be easier to create the chart as a separate chart sheet, then delete it as shown here:

```
' Not as much fun...
Sub SimpleAddDelete( )
    Dim chrt As Chart
    If TypeName(Selection) = "Range" Then
        Set chrt = Charts.Add
        ' Wait five seconds.
        Application.Wait Now + #12:00:05 AM#
        ' Delete the chart
        chrt.Delete
    End If
End Sub
```

Notice that the Add method returns the object that was created. The line Set chrt = Charts.Add gets a reference to the new chart, which is later used to delete the chart. But you could just as easily use that reference to set the formatting, title, or other attributes of the chart.

Not all collections provide an Add method, however. For example, there is no Range.Add. There is, however, an Insert method for the Columns and Rows collections:

```
Sub InsertRows()
    ' Insert rows at top of sheet. Shift other rows down.
    Range("1:1").Rows.Insert True
End Sub

Sub InsertColumns()
    ' Insert columns at beginning of sheet. Shift columns right.
    Range("A:A").Columns.Insert True
End Sub
```

In other words, Excel collections are not always consistent. This is further illustrated by the fact that the Rows and Columns collections provide a Delete method:

```
Sub DeleteRows()
    ' Insert rows at top of sheet. Shift other rows down.
    Range("1:1").Rows.Delete True
End Sub

Sub DeleteColumns()
    ' Insert columns at beginning of sheet. Shift columns right.
    Range("A:A").Columns.Delete True
End Sub
```

Change Size and Position of Objects

The following objects have Left, Top, Height, and Width properties that control their size and position:

Application	Axis	AxisTitle
ChartArea	ChartObject	ChartObjects
ChartTitle	DataLabel	DisplayUnitLabel
Legend	LegendEntry	LegendKey
MS Form controls	OLEObject	OLEObjects
PlotArea	Range	Shape
ShapeRange	Window	

Excel measures objects in points. A *point* is a typographical measure equal to $1/72$nd of an inch, but since the size and resolution of monitors varies, these units aren't useful as an absolute measure. Instead, they are used to size and position objects relative to one another.

For example, the following code resizes Excel to half of the screen height and width and centers the window onscreen:

```
Sub ResizeExcel()
    Dim maxHeight As Double, maxWidth As Double
    ' Maximize window to get the full height/width
    Application.WindowState = xlMaximized
    maxHeight = Application.Height
    maxWidth = Application.Width
    ' Set the window style back to normal.
    Application.WindowState = xlNormal
    ' Resize the application window.
    Application.Height = maxHeight / 2
    Application.Width = maxWidth / 2
    ' Reposition the application window
    Application.Top = maxHeight / 2 - Application.Height / 2
    Application.Left = maxWidth / 2 - Application.Width / 2
End Sub
```

In addition, most of the preceding objects also have a Visible property that you can use to hide or show the object. The Visible property is mainly useful for hiding worksheets or form controls. For example, the following code hides the Objects worksheet:

```
Worksheets("Objects").Visible = False
```

To hide columns or rows on a worksheet, use the Hidden property instead:

```
Columns("C:C").Hidden = True
```

You can also use the Visible property to hide the Excel application, but that's a little risky since hiding Excel prevents the user from closing the application other than by pressing Ctrl-Alt-Delete. Just to show how this works, the following code hides Excel for five seconds:

```
Sub HideExcel()
    Application.Visible = False
    Application.Wait Now + #12:00:05 AM#
    Application.Visible = True
End Sub
```

Print Objects

These objects provide PrintOut and PrintPreview methods:

```
Chart
Charts
Range
Sheets
Window
Workbook
Worksheet
Worksheets
```

For example, the following code prints the currently selected range:

```
If TypeName(Selection) = "Range" Then Selection.PrintOut
```

Interestingly, the UserForm object in the Microsoft Forms object library uses the PrintForm method rather than PrintOut.

Respond to Events in Excel

Chapter 2 discussed events in a general way and showed you how to create your own events. Excel introduced real events to its object library in 1997, and they are one of the key improvements that allow Excel applications to be truly interactive with users.

The most obvious events occur for the Workbook, Worksheet, and Chart objects since those objects include accompanying classes that you can view in the Visual Basic Editor (Figure 4-20).

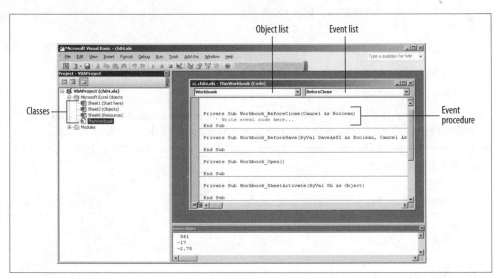

Figure 4-20. Finding events in the Visual Basic Editor

You can list the events for Workbook, Worksheet, or Chart objects by clicking on the object and event listboxes in the Code window, or you can refer to Table 4-7.

Table 4-7. Events available from Excel objects

Object	Event
Application	NewWorkbook
	SheetActivate
	SheetBeforeDoubleClick
	SheetBeforeRightClick
	SheetCalculate

Table 4-7. Events available from Excel objects (continued)

Object	Event
	SheetChange
	SheetDeactivate
	SheetFollowHyperlink
	SheetPivotTableUpdate
	SheetSelectionChange
	WindowActivate
	WindowDeactivate
	WindowResize
	WorkbookActivate
	WorkbookAddinInstall
	WorkbookAddinUninstall
	WorkbookAfterXmlExport
	WorkbookAfterXmlImport
	WorkbookBeforeClose
	WorkbookBeforePrint
	WorkbookBeforeSave
	WorkbookBeforeXmlExport
	WorkbookBeforeXmlImport
	WorkbookDeactivate
	WorkbookNewSheet
	WorkbookOpen
	WorkbookPivotTableCloseConnection
	WorkbookPivotTableOpenConnection
	WorkbookSync
Chart	Activate
	BeforeDoubleClick
	BeforeRightClick
	Calculate
	Deactivate
	DragOver
	DragPlot
	MouseDown
	MouseMove
	MouseUp
	Resize
	Select

Table 4-7. Events available from Excel objects (continued)

Object	Event
	SeriesChange
QueryTable	AfterRefresh
	BeforeRefresh
Workbook	Activate
	AddinInstall
	AddinUninstall
	AfterXmlExport
	AfterXmlImport
	BeforeClose
	BeforePrint
	BeforeSave
	BeforeXmlExport
	BeforeXmlImport
	Deactivate
	NewSheet
	Open
	PivotTableCloseConnection
	PivotTableOpenConnection
	SheetActivate
	SheetBeforeDoubleClick
	SheetBeforeRightClick
	SheetCalculate
	SheetChange
	SheetDeactivate
	SheetFollowHyperlink
	SheetPivotTableUpdate
	SheetSelectionChange
	Sync
	WindowActivate
	WindowDeactivate
Worksheet	Activate
	BeforeDoubleClick
	BeforeRightClick
	Calculate
	Change
	Deactivate
	FollowHyperlink

Table 4-7. Events available from Excel objects (continued)

Object	Event
	PivotTableUpdate
	SelectionChange

You'll notice that some of the same events occur for a number of objects. For example, the SheetActivate event occurs for the Application, Workbook, Worksheet, and Chart objects (for Worksheet and Chart, it's simply called the Activate event). In this case, the Application-level event is the most general event handler since it receives SheetActivate events from all sheets in all open workbooks; the Workbook-level event is next, receiving SheetActivate events only from sheets in the open workbook; and the Worksheet- or Chart-level events are the most specific, receiving the Activate event only from that specific Worksheet or Chart object.

Events occur at the most specific level first; then move up to more general levels. So, if the SheetActivate event is handled at all three levels, the Worksheet-level event procedure runs first, then the Workbook-level event procedure, and finally the Application-level procedure.

The object and event lists are built in to the Code window for Workbook and Worksheet objects (Figure 4-20), but how do you use events for other objects, like Application? To do so:

1. Declare a variable for the object using the WithEvents keyword.
2. Initialize that object in code.
3. Visual Basic adds the object variable to the Code window's object and event lists, which you can then use to add event procedures.

For example, the following code from the Workbook class creates an object variable m_app for the Application object, initializes that object in the Workbook_Activate event, then uses an Application-level event:

```
Dim WithEvents m_app As Application              ' (1)

Private Sub Workbook_SheetActivate(ByVal Sh As Object)
    ' Initialize the object variable if it was not already.
    If m_app Is Nothing Then _
        Set m_app = Application                  ' (2)
    ' Indicate the Workbook-level event occurred.
    MsgBox "Workbook-level event"
End Sub

Private Sub m_app_SheetActivate(ByVal Sh As Object)  ' (3)
    ' Indicate the Application-level event occurred.
    MsgBox "App-level event"
End Sub
```

The initialization step (previous) occurs in a Workbook event so that it happens automatically. I could have placed it in the Workbook_Open event, but that would have required me to close and reopen the workbook to see the code work. It's easier to place the initialization step in an event that happens more frequently (such as SheetActivate) and test if the variable has already been initialized with the If m_app Is Nothing conditional statement.

Another interesting aspect of Excel events are the Before events, like BeforeRightClick. It would be pretty neat if Excel really did know what the user was about to do, but that's not quite how it works. Instead, the Before events are simply processed after the user action, but before Excel does anything with them. That lets you intercept and (optionally) cancel Excel's default action for those events. To see how this works, add the following code to the ThisWorkbook class:

```
Private Sub Workbook_SheetBeforeRightClick(ByVal Sh As Object, _
  ByVal Target As Range, Cancel As Boolean)
    Dim ans As VbMsgBoxResult
    ans = MsgBox("Excel is about to process right-click, proceed?", vbYesNo)
    ' If no, then cancel the action.
    If ans = vbNo Then Cancel = True
End Sub
```

Now, when you right-click on a sheet, you'll see a message asking if the action should be processed. If you select Yes, Excel displays the sheet's pop-up menu (that's the default action for a right-click). If you select no, the menu is not displayed.

That's a simple example that doesn't do much, but Before events are really pretty handy—for example, you can require that a user saves a workbook as shown by the following code:

```
Private Sub Workbook_BeforeClose(Cancel As Boolean)
    ' Require the user to save.
    If Not ThisWorkbook.Saved Then
        MsgBox "You must save this workbook before closing."
        Cancel = True
    End If
End Sub
```

Try it!

Finally, you can turn Excel's event processing off and on using the Application object's EnableEvents property. Setting EnableEvents to False tells Excel to ignore any event procedures you've written in Visual Basic—the events still occur in Excel (so choosing File → Save saves the file, for instance) but none of your event procedures are run.

EnableEvents affects only Excel events, so controls from the Microsoft Forms object library will still respond to events. You can see this by adding a checkbox to a worksheet and then writing the following code:

```
Private Sub chkEvents_Click()
    ' Turn off Excel events if checkbox cleared.
    Application.EnableEvents = chkEvents.Value
End Sub
```

The Global Object

As mentioned earlier in this chapter, Excel provides shortcuts into its object hierarchy through properties like `ActiveCell` and the `Sheets` collection. Those shortcuts are actually members of the `Global` object, which is a sort of default object that Excel uses if you omit an object name. This allows you to write code like:

```
ActiveCell = 42
```

rather than:

```
Application.ActiveCell = 42
```

The `Global` object includes many of the same members as the `Application` object, as shown in this list:

ActiveCell	ActiveChart	ActiveDialog
ActiveMenuBar	ActivePrinter	ActiveSheet
ActiveWindow	ActiveWorkbook	AddIns
Application	Assistant	Calculate
Cells	Charts	Columns
CommandBars	Creator	DDEAppReturnCode
DDEExecute	DDEInitiate	DDEPoke
DDERequest	DDETerminate	DialogSheets
Equals	Evaluate	Excel4IntlMacroSheets
Excel4MacroSheets	ExecuteExcel4Macro	Intersect
MenuBars	Modules	Names
Parent	Range	Rows
Run	Selection	SendKeys
Sheets	ShortcutMenus	ThisWorkbook
Toolbars	Union	Windows
Workbooks	WorksheetFunction	Worksheets

Many of these members return objects or collections, so they look like absolute references. In reality, they are all members of the `Global` object (even `Application` is a property of the `Global` object). In short, the `Global` object is the granddaddy of all the Excel objects.

You don't *have to* understand the `Global` object to use Excel's object library, but knowing something about it helps explain why the same objects turn up at various levels in the Excel object hierarchy. It also helps to explain how the Excel team implemented their objects, which is useful for advanced tasks, such as using the Excel object library from other programming languages, like Visual Basic .NET and C#.

The WorksheetFunction Object

Another useful top-level object to know about is the `WorksheetFunction` object. That object provides the functions from the Excel formula bar to your Visual Basic code.

Some of these members are redundant with those provided by the VBA object library, however, others provide very useful (and advanced) analytical and statistical functions, as described in Table 4-8.

Table 4-8. Members of the WorksheetFunction object

Member	Description
Acos	Returns the arccosine, or inverse cosine, of a number. The arccosine is the angle whose cosine is a number. The returned angle is given in radians in the range 0 to π.
Acosh	Returns the inverse hyperbolic cosine of a number.
And	The same as the Visual Basic And operator.
Asc	Converts double-byte characters to single-byte characters.
Asin	Returns the arcsine, or inverse sine, of a number. The arcsine is the angle whose sine is the given number. The returned angle is given in radians in the range $-\pi/2$ to $\pi/2$.
Asinh	Returns the inverse hyperbolic sine of a number.
Atan2	Returns the arctangent, or inverse tangent, of the specified x- and y-coordinates.
Atanh	Returns the inverse hyperbolic tangent of a number.
AveDev	Returns the average of the absolute deviations of data points from their mean. AveDev is a measure of the variability in a data set.
Average	Returns the average (arithmetic mean) of the arguments.
BetaDist	Returns the beta cumulative distribution function.
BetaInv	Returns the inverse of the cumulative distribution function for a specified beta distribution.
BinomDist	Returns the individual term binomial distribution probability.
Ceiling	Returns a number rounded up, away from 0, to the nearest multiple of significance.
ChiDist	Returns the one-tailed probability of the chi-squared distribution.
ChiInv	Returns the inverse of the one-tailed probability of the chi-squared distribution.
ChiTest	Returns the test for independence. Determines whether hypothesized results are verified by an experiment.
Choose	Uses an index to return a value from the list of value arguments.
Clean	Removes all nonprintable characters from text.
Combin	Returns the number of combinations for a given number of items.
Confidence	Returns a value that you can use to construct a confidence interval for a population mean.
Correl	Returns the correlation coefficient of two cell ranges.
Cosh	Returns the hyperbolic cosine of a number.
Count	Counts the number of cells that contain numbers and also numbers within the list of arguments.
CountA	Counts the number of cells that are not empty and the values within the list of arguments.
CountBlank	Counts empty cells in a specified range of cells.
CountIf	Counts the number of cells within a range that meet the given criteria.
Covar	Returns covariance, the average of the products of deviations for each data point pair.
CritBinom	Returns the smallest value for which the cumulative binomial distribution is greater than or equal to a criterion value.
DAverage	Averages the values in a column of a list or database that match conditions you specify.

Table 4-8. Members of the WorksheetFunction object (continued)

Member	Description
Days360	Returns the number of days between two dates based on a 360-day year (12 30-day months), which is used in some accounting calculations.
Db	Returns the depreciation of an asset for a specified period using the fixed-declining-balance method.
DCount	Counts the cells that contain numbers in a column of a list or database that match conditions you specify.
DCountA	Counts the nonblank cells in a column of a list or database that match specified conditions.
Ddb	Returns the depreciation of an asset for a specified period using the double-declining-balance method or some other method you specify.
Degrees	Converts radians into degrees.
DevSq	Returns the sum of squares of deviations of data points from their sample mean.
DGet	Extracts a single value from a column of a list or database that matches specified conditions.
DMax	Returns the largest number in a column of a list or database that matches specified conditions.
DMin	Returns the smallest number in a column of a list or database that matches specified conditions.
Dollar	Formats a number as currency using the local currency symbol.
DProduct	Multiplies the values in a column of a list or database that match conditions you specify.
DStDev	Estimates the standard deviation of a population based on a sample by using the numbers in a column of a list or database that match specified conditions.
DStDevP	Calculates the standard deviation of a population based on the entire population, using the numbers in a column of a list or database that match specified conditions.
DSum	Adds the numbers in a column of a list or database that match specified conditions.
DVar	Estimates the variance of a population based on a sample by using the numbers in a column of a list or database that match conditions you specify.
DVarP	Calculates the variance of a population based on the entire population by using the numbers in a column of a list or database that match specified conditions.
Even	Returns a number rounded up to the nearest even integer.
ExponDist	Returns the exponential distribution.
Fact	Returns the factorial of a number.
FDist	Returns the F probability distribution.
Find	Finds the location of one string within another (similar to `Instr`).
FindB	Finds the location of one double-byte string within another (similar to `Instr`).
FInv	Returns the inverse of the F probability distribution.
Fisher	Returns the Fisher transformation at x. This transformation produces a function that is normally distributed rather than skewed.
FisherInv	Returns the inverse of the Fisher transformation. Use this transformation when analyzing correlations between ranges or arrays of data.
Fixed	Rounds a number to the specified number of decimals, formats the number in decimal format using a period and commas, and returns the result as text.
Floor	Rounds a number down, toward 0, to the nearest multiple of significance.
Forecast	Calculates, or predicts, a future value by using existing values.
Frequency	Calculates how often values occur within a range of values and then returns a vertical array of numbers.

Table 4-8. Members of the WorksheetFunction object (continued)

Member	Description
FTest	Returns the result of an F-test. An F-test returns the one-tailed probability that the variances in *array1* and *array2* are not significantly different.
Fv	Returns the future value of an investment based on periodic, constant payments and a constant interest rate.
GammaDist	Returns the gamma distribution. You can use this function to study variables that may have a skewed distribution. The gamma distribution is commonly used in queuing analysis.
GammaInv	Returns the inverse of the gamma cumulative distribution.
GammaLn	Returns the natural logarithm of the gamma function (x).
GeoMean	Returns the geometric mean of an array or range of positive data. For example, you can use GeoMean to calculate average growth rate given compound interest with variable rates.
Growth	Calculates predicted exponential growth by using existing data.
HarMean	Returns the harmonic mean of a data set. The harmonic mean is the reciprocal of the arithmetic mean of reciprocals.
HLookup	Searches for a value in the top row of a table or an array of values and then returns a value in the same column from a row you specify in the table or array.
HypGeomDist	Returns the hypergeometric distribution. Hypergeometric distribution is the probability of a given number of sample successes, given the sample size, population successes, and population size.
Intercept	Calculates the point at which a line will intersect the y-axis by using existing x-values and y-values. The intercept point is based on a best-fit regression line plotted through the known x-values and known y-values.
Ipmt	Returns the interest payment for a given period for an investment based on periodic, constant payments and a constant interest rate.
Irr	Returns the internal rate of return for a series of cash flows represented by the numbers in values.
IsErr	Returns True if a cell contains an error other than #N/A.
IsError	Returns True if a cell contains an error.
IsLogical	Returns True if a cell contains a Boolean value.
IsNA	Returns True if a cell contains the #N/A error value.
IsNonText	Returns True if a cell does not contain text.
IsNumber	Returns True if a cell contains a numeric value.
Ispmt	Calculates the interest paid during a specific period of an investment.
IsText	Returns True if a cell contains a string.
Kurt	Returns the kurtosis of a data set. Kurtosis characterizes the relative peakedness or flatness of a distribution compared with the normal distribution.
Large	Returns the kth largest value in a data set. You can use this function to select a value based on its relative standing.
LinEst	Calculates the statistics for a line by using the least-squares method to calculate a straight line that best fits your data, and returns an array that describes the line.
Ln	Returns the natural logarithm of a number.
Log	Returns the logarithm of a number to the specified base.
Log10	Returns the base-10 logarithm of a number.

Table 4-8. Members of the WorksheetFunction object (continued)

Member	Description
LogEst	Calculates an exponential curve that fits your data and returns an array of values that describes the curve. Returns an array of values.
LogInv	Returns the inverse of the lognormal cumulative distribution function of x, where $\ln(x)$ is normally distributed with parameters mean and standard_dev.
LogNormDist	Returns the cumulative lognormal distribution of x, where $\ln(x)$ is normally distributed with parameters mean and standard_dev.
Lookup	Finds a value in an array and returns that value. For two-dimensional arrays, it is better to use HLookup or VLookup.
Match	Returns the relative position of an item in an array that matches a specified value in a specified order.
Max	Returns the largest value in a set of values.
MDeterm	Returns the matrix determinant of an array.
Median	Returns the median of the given numbers.
Min	Returns the smallest number in a set of values.
MInverse	Returns the inverse matrix for the matrix stored in an array.
MIrr	Returns the modified internal rate of return for a series of periodic cash flows.
MMult	Returns the matrix product of two arrays. The result is an array with the same number of rows as *array1* and the same number of columns as *array2*.
Mode	Returns the most frequently occurring, or repetitive, value in an array or range of data.
NegBinomDist	Returns the negative binomial distribution. NegBinomDist returns the probability that there will be *number_f* failures before the *number_s*th success, when the constant probability of a success is *probability_s*.
NormDist	Returns the normal distribution for the specified mean and standard deviation. This function has a wide range of applications in statistics, including hypothesis testing.
NormInv	Returns the inverse of the normal cumulative distribution for the specified mean and standard deviation.
NormSDist	Returns the standard normal cumulative distribution function. The distribution has a mean of 0 and a standard deviation of 1. Use this function in place of a table of standard normal curve areas.
NormSInv	Returns the inverse of the standard normal cumulative distribution. The distribution has a mean of 0 and a standard deviation of 1.
NPer	Returns the number of periods for an investment based on periodic, constant payments and a constant interest rate.
Npv	Calculates the net present value of an investment by using a discount rate and a series of future payments (negative values) and income (positive values).
Odd	Returns a number rounded up to the nearest odd integer.
Or	The same as the Visual Basic Or operator.
Parent	Returns the parent object for the specified object.
Pearson	Returns the Pearson product moment correlation coefficient, r, a dimensionless index that ranges from -1.0 to 1.0 inclusive and reflects the extent of a linear relationship between two data sets.
Percentile	Returns the kth percentile of values in a range. You can use this function to establish a threshold of acceptance. For example, you can decide to examine candidates who score above the 90th percentile.
PercentRank	Returns the rank of a value in a data set as a percentage of the data set.

Table 4-8. Members of the WorksheetFunction object (continued)

Member	Description
Permut	Returns the number of permutations for a given number of objects that can be selected from number objects. A permutation is any set or subset of objects or events in which internal order is significant.
Phonetic	Extracts the phonetic (furigana) characters from a text string.
Pi	Returns the number 3.14159265358979, the mathematical constant π, accurate to 15 digits.
Pmt	Calculates the payment for a loan based on constant payments and a constant interest rate.
Poisson	Returns the Poisson distribution. A common application of the Poisson distribution is predicting the number of events over a specific time, such as the number of cars arriving at a toll plaza in one minute.
Power	Returns the result of a number raised to a power.
Ppmt	Returns the payment on the principal for a given period for an investment based on periodic, constant payments and a constant interest rate.
Prob	Returns the probability that values in a range are between two limits. If upper_limit is not supplied, returns the probability that values in x_range are equal to lower_limit.
Product	Multiplies all the numbers given as arguments and returns the product.
Proper	Capitalizes the first letter in a text string and any other letters in text that follow any character other than a letter. Converts all other letters to lowercase letters.
Pv	Returns the present value of an investment. The present value is the total amount that a series of future payments is worth now. For example, when you borrow money, the loan amount is the present value to the lender.
Quartile	Returns the quartile of a data set. Quartiles often are used in sales and survey data to divide populations into groups.
Radians	Converts degrees to radians.
Rank	Returns the rank of a number in a list of numbers. If you sort a list, the rank of the number is its position in the list.
Rate	Returns the interest rate per period of an annuity.
Replace	Replaces part of one string with another.
ReplaceB	Replaces part of one double-byte string with another.
Rept	Repeats text a given number of times.
Roman	Formats an Arabic numeral as a Roman numeral.
Round	Rounds a number to a specified number of digits.
RoundDown	Rounds a number down, toward 0.
RoundUp	Rounds a number up, away from 0.
RSq	Returns the square of the Pearson product moment correlation coefficient through data points in *known_y's* and *known_x's*.
RTD	Retrieves real-time data from a program that supports automation.
Search	Finds the location of one string within another (similar to Instr).
SearchB	Finds the location of one double-byte string within another (similar to Instr).
Sinh	Returns the hyperbolic sine of a number.
Skew	Returns the skewness of a distribution. Skewness characterizes the degree of asymmetry of a distribution around its mean.

Table 4-8. Members of the WorksheetFunction object (continued)

Member	Description
Sln	Returns the straight-line depreciation of an asset for one period.
Slope	Returns the slope of the linear regression line through data points in *known_y's* and *known_x's*. The slope is the vertical distance divided by the horizontal distance between any two points on the line, which is the rate of change along the regression line.
Small	Returns the kth smallest value in a data set. Use this function to return values with a particular relative standing in a data set.
Standardize	Returns a normalized value from a distribution characterized by mean and standard deviation.
StDev	Estimates standard deviation based on a sample. The standard deviation is a measure of how widely values are dispersed from the average value (the mean).
StDevP	Calculates standard deviation based on the entire population given as arguments. The standard deviation is a measure of how widely values are dispersed from the average value (the mean).
StEyx	Returns the standard error of the predicted y-value for each x in the regression. The standard error is a measure of the amount of error in the prediction of y for an individual x.
Substitute	Substitutes *new_text* for *old_text* in a text string.
Subtotal	Returns a subtotal in a list or database.
Sum	Adds all the numbers in a range of cells.
SumIf	Adds cells that meet specified criteria.
SumProduct	Multiplies corresponding components in the given arrays and returns the sum of those products.
SumSq	Returns the sum of the squares of the arguments.
SumX2MY2	Returns the sum of the difference of squares of corresponding values in two arrays.
SumX2PY2	Returns the sum of the sum of squares of corresponding values in two arrays. The sum of the sum of squares is a common term in many statistical calculations.
SumXMY2	Returns the sum of squares of differences of corresponding values in two arrays.
Syd	Returns the sum-of-years digits depreciation of an asset for a specified period.
Tanh	Returns the hyperbolic tangent of a number.
TDist	Returns the percentage points (probability) for the student t-distribution where a numeric value (x) is a calculated value of t for which the percentage points are to be computed. The t-distribution is used in the hypothesis testing of small sample data sets.
Text	Converts a value to text in a specific number format.
TInv	Returns the t-value of the student t-distribution as a function of the probability and the degrees of freedom.
Transpose	Returns a vertical range of cells as a horizontal range or vice versa.
Trend	Returns values along a linear trend. Fits a straight line (using the method of least squares) to the arrays *known_y's* and *known_x's*. Returns the y-values along that line for the array of *new_x's* that you specify.
Trim	Removes all spaces from text except for single spaces between words.
TrimMean	Returns the mean of the interior of a data set. TrimMean calculates the mean taken by excluding a percentage of data points from the top and bottom tails of a data set. You can use this function when you wish to exclude outlying data from your analysis.

Table 4-8. Members of the WorksheetFunction object (continued)

Member	Description
TTest	Returns the probability associated with a student t-test. Use TTest to determine whether two samples are likely to have come from the same two underlying populations that have the same mean.
USDollar	Formats a number as U.S. currency.
Var	Estimates variance based on a sample.
VarP	Calculates variance based on the entire population.
Vdb	Returns the depreciation of an asset for any period you specify, including partial periods, using the double-declining-balance method or some other method you specify. VDB stands for variable declining balance.
VLookup	Searches for a value in the leftmost column of a table and then returns a value in the same row from a column you specify in the table.
Weekday	Returns the day of the week corresponding to a date. The day is given as an integer, ranging from 1 (Sunday) to 7 (Saturday), by default.
Weibull	Returns the Weibull distribution. Use this distribution in reliability analysis, such as calculating a device's mean time to failure.
ZTest	Returns the one-tailed probability-value of a z-test. For a given hypothesized population mean, that is, the observed sample mean.

There is no Help for members in Table 4-8 from Visual Basic, but you can look up these functions in the Excel Help file as shown in Figure 4-21.

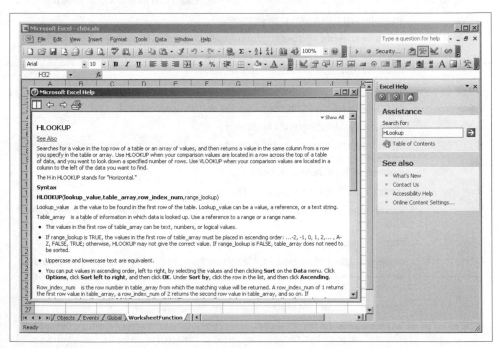

Figure 4-21. Use Excel Help to find information on the WorksheetFunction members

What You've Learned

By now you should have a pretty good grasp on how to get around in the Excel object library, find the object you need for a task, and do some simple things like switch focus to an object, get its value or name, and so on. You should also understand how to respond to events that occur in Excel so that your code runs automatically in response to user actions.

The Excel object library is extremely large and complex, however, so don't worry if you're a little confused about which object to use for a specific task—that's really what the later chapters are about.

CHAPTER 5

Creating Your Own Objects

Chapter 4 showed you how to use Excel's objects; now you get to create your own. This chapter shows you how to define custom classes and instantiate objects from those classes to create in-memory representations of visual or functional elements.

In the process, I try to explain why you'd use classes and how you perform specific tasks that are unique to object-oriented programming. You'll also learn how to send mail from Excel, which is kind of handy.

 Code used in this chapter and additional samples are available in *ch05.xls*.

Modules Versus Classes

The main difference between the modules and classes is how you use them:

- Code contained in modules can be used from formulas entered in cells.
- Code stored in a class can respond to events that occur in Excel.

That distinction determines where you put your code—whether you create it in a module or a class. In general, put your code in a module if it performs a general-purpose task that you plan on reusing many different places. Put your code in a class if it responds to events or represents a visual component.

Those are just guidelines. The following two sections illustrate the differences more fully.

Modules

For example, to create a module containing new mathematical functions, you can use in-cell formulas:

1. In Excel, open a workbook and choose Tools → Macro → Visual Basic Editor to start programming.

2. In the Visual Basic Editor, choose Insert → Module. Visual Basic adds a new module to the Project window and displays the new, empty module in an Edit window.

3. Select Name in the module's Properties window and type Math to rename the module.

4. Add the following code by typing in the module's Edit window:

```
' Math module.
Public Function Inverse(x As Double) As Double
    If x = 0 Then Inverse = 0 Else Inverse = 1 / x
End Function

Public Function CubeRoot(x As Double) As Double
    If x < 0 Then CubeRoot = 0 Else CubeRoot = x ^ (1 / 3)
End Function
```

To use these new functions from Excel, include them in a formula as shown in Figure 5-1.

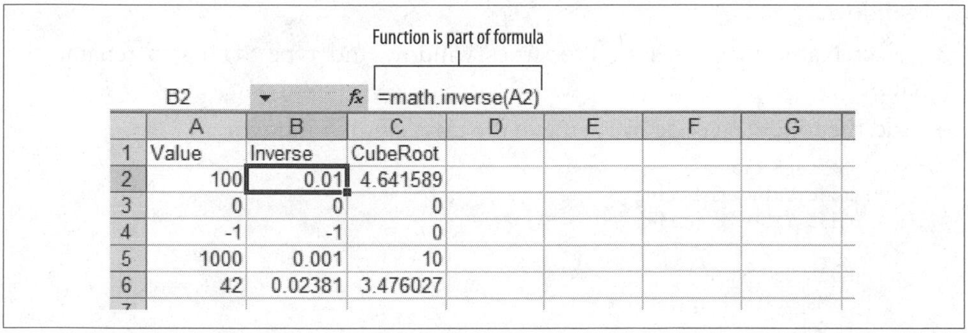

Figure 5-1. Use modules to create user-defined functions

To use these functions from Visual Basic, include them in an expression as shown here:

```
Sub TestMathFunctions()
    Dim result As Double, value As Double, str As String
    value = 42
    result = Inverse(value)
    str = "The inverse of " & value & " is " & result
    result = CubeRoot(value)
    str = str & " and the cube root is " & result
    MsgBox str, , "Test Math Functions"
End Sub
```

Here, result = Inverse(value) calculates the inverse and assigns that number to result. Alternately, I could write that as Math.Inverse(value); including the module name is optional and it's a good idea if it makes the code clearer or if you reuse the procedure name in another project.

Classes

Excel provides built-in classes for each workbook and sheet. You can add code directly to those classes to respond to events on those objects as described in Chapter 4. You can also create your own custom classes that you can use elsewhere in code.

Custom classes need to be instantiated as objects before they can be used. This allows you to create multiple instances of the code, each running at the same time and acting independently of one another.

To create a new class:

1. In Excel, open a workbook and choose Tools → Macro → Visual Basic Editor to start programming.
2. In the Visual Basic Editor, choose Insert → Class Module. Visual Basic adds a new class to the Project window and displays the new, empty class in an Edit window.
3. Select Name in the class's Properties window and type `String` to rename the class.
4. Add the following code by typing in the class's Edit window:
   ```
   ' Message class
   Public Value As String
   Public Title As String

   Public Sub Show( )
       MsgBox value, , title
   End Sub
   ```

You can't run this class just by pressing F5; instead, you must first create an instance of the class from a module, then use the class in some way as shown here:

```
' TestMessage module
Sub TestMessageClass( )
    Dim msg1 As New Message, msg2 As New Message
    msg1.Title = "Msg1 Object"
    msg1.Value = "This message brought to you by Msg1."
    msg2.Title = "Msg2 Object"
    msg2.Value = "This message brought to you by Msg2."
    msg1.Show
    msg2.Show
End Sub
```

The preceding code creates two objects from the `Message` class, `msg1` and `msg2`, to demonstrate that each has different `value` and `title` settings. This independence is sometimes called *encapsulation*, because outside forces can't change the object without having a direct reference to it. That allows objects to represent a visual element, such as a worksheet or a message box, and respond to events on that particular object as illustrated in Figure 5-2.

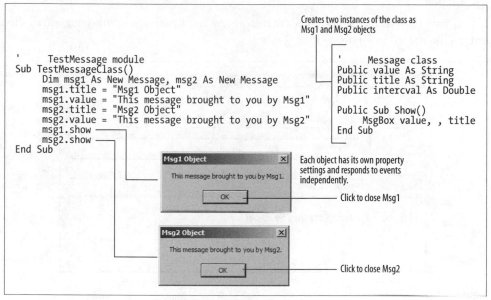

Figure 5-2. Using classes to create multiple objects

You can't do that with modules! You can have only one, fixed instance of any given module, and variables within that module aren't encapsulated.

Add Methods

Methods are Sub or Function procedures within a class. You use methods to define actions within a class, such as calculating a result. For example, the following addition to the Message class sends the message via email:

```
' Send method: sends the message via email.
Public Sub Send(ToAddress As String)
    Dim msgToSend As String, result As Double
    msgToSend = "mailto:" & ToAddress
    msgToSend = msgToSend & "?SUBJECT=" & Title
    msgToSend = msgToSend & "&BODY=" & Value
    ThisWorkbook.FollowHyperlink msgToSend, , True
End Sub
```

To use this method from code, create an object and call Send with the email address of the recipient:

```
' TestMessage module
Sub TestMessageSend()
```

```
        Dim msg1 As New Message
        msg1.Title = "Message to Send"
        msg1.Value = "This message brought to you by Excel."
        msg1.Send ("ExcelDemo@hotmail.com")
    End Sub
```

If you run TestMessageSend, Excel creates a new mail message using your email client, as illustrated in Figure 5-3.

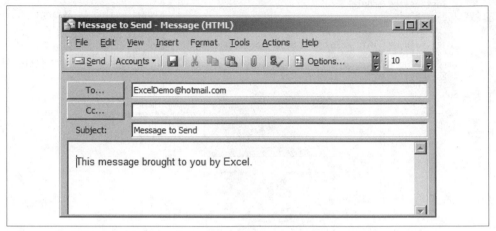

Figure 5-3. Sending mail from Excel

Create Properties

Properties are values stored by a class. Simple properties, often called *fields*, may just be public variables within the class, as shown by the Title and Value properties of the Message class earlier. More complex properties are created using Property procedures.

Why would a property need to be complex? Several possible reasons:

- Most often, properties are complex if they represent a value that is calculated in some way, such as the count of a list of items.
- In other cases, a property may represent information that can be read, but not changed. These are called *read-only* properties.
- Less often, a property may represent information that can be set only once, but never changed. These are called *write-once* properties.
- Finally, a property may represent a value that can be set but never read. You almost never need to do that, but if you do, you'd call it a *write-only* property.

Let's continue on with the Message class example a bit to create two new properties that extend its email capabilities. The Recipients property that follows is another simple property that accepts a list of email addresses to send the message to:

```
' Message class
Public Recipients As String
```

To use this property from the Send method, we make these changes shown in **bold**:

```
Public Sub Send(Optional ToAddress As String)
    Dim msgToSend As String, result As Double
    If (ToAddress = "") Then ToAddress = Recipients
    msgToSend = "mailto:" & ToAddress
    msgToSend = msgToSend & "?SUBJECT=" & Title
    msgToSend = msgToSend & "&BODY=" & Value
    ThisWorkbook.FollowHyperlink msgToSend, , True
End Sub
```

Now, you can add Recipients as a list of email addresses separated by semicolons, just as they would be in a regular email message. Send no longer requires a ToAddress; if omitted, it uses the Recipients property. For example, this code sends a message to two recipients:

```
' TestMessage module
Sub TestMessageRecipients1()
    Dim msg1 As New Message
    msg1.Title = "Message to Send"
    msg1.Recipients = "ExcelDemo@hotmail.com;BeigeBond@hotmail.com"
    msg1.value = "This message brought to you by Excel."
    msg1.Send
End Sub
```

That was a pretty easy, but what if the addresses come from a range of cells? It would be nice if the class were smart enough to convert those settings. To do that, you need to add Property procedures that convert values from a range of cells into a string of email addresses. You'd want Recipients to accept string values as well, so you need to create three different types of Property procedures: a Set procedure to accept the range setting, a Let procedure to accept a string setting, and a Get procedure to return the setting as a string. The following sample shows those additions to the Message class:

```
' Message class
Private m_Recipients As String

' Accept Range settings.
Property Set Recipients(value As Range)
    Dim cel As Range
    m_Recipients = ""
    For Each cel In value
        m_Recipients = m_Recipients & cel.value & ";"
    Next
End Property

' Accept String settings as well.
Property Let Recipients(value As String)
    ' Set the internal variable.
    m_Recipients = value
    ' Exit if ""
    If value = "" Then Exit Property
    ' Make sure last character is ;
```

```
        If Mid(value, Len(value) - 1, 1) = ";" Then
            m_Recipients = value
        Else
            m_Recipients = value & ";"
        End If
    End Property

    ' Return the internal string variable.
    Property Get Recipients() As String
        Recipients = m_Recipients
    End Property
```

Notice that I used a private variable, m_Recipients, to store the property setting within the class. That's a common practice with Property procedures—the Set, Let, and Get procedures control access to that internal variable. In programming circles, those procedures are called *accessor functions*; often, you use accessors to validate a setting. For example, you might want to check whether email addresses are valid before allowing the property to be set.

To test the new Recipients property, enter some email addresses in A1:A3 and run the following code:

```
' TestMessage module
Sub TestMessageRecipients2()
    Dim msg1 As New Message
    msg1.Title = "Message to Send"
    msg1.value = "Some message text."
    ' Set the property as a range.
    Set msg1.Recipients = [a1:a3]
    ' Show the addresses (gets property as string).
    MsgBox "About to send to: " & msg1.Recipients
    ' Create message.
    msg1.Send
End Sub
```

Read-Only Properties

Recipients is a read/write property. To create a read-only property, omit the Let and Set procedures. For example, the following code creates a RecipientCount property that returns the number of people set to receive a message:

```
' Read-only property to get the number of recipients.
Property Get RecipientCount() As Integer
    Dim value As Integer
    If m_Recipients <> "" Then
        value = UBound(Me.AddressArray)
    Else
        value = 0
    End If
    RecipientCount = value
End Property

' Read-only property to get an array of recipients.
```

```
Property Get AddressArray() As String()
    Dim value() As String
    If m_Recipients <> "" Then
        ' This is why m_Recipients must end with ;
        value = VBA.Split(m_Recipients, ";")
    End If
    AddressArray = value
End Property
```

OK, I got a little tricky there and created two read-only properties. `RecipientCount` uses `AddressArray` to convert the string of recipients into an array, and then it counts the number of items in the array. There are other ways to get the count, but this way demonstrates using `Me` to call a property from within the class itself. Besides, `AddressArray` might come in handy later on...

Write-Once/Write-Only Properties

These types of properties are rarely needed and I thought about omitting them, but in the interest of being thorough, I decided to include some discussion here. It's easy to create a write-only property—just omit the `Get` procedure—but it's hard to even *think* of a situation in which that's useful to anyone...maybe setting a password or something:

```
Private m_Password As String

' Write-only property, rarely used.
Property Let Password(value As String)
    m_Password = value
End Property
```

Because there is only a `Let` procedure and `m_Password` is `Private`, users can set the `Password` property but they can't get it. That might also be useful for database connection strings that can include username and password information that you should keep secure.

Write-once properties are somewhat more useful because they can represent information used to initialize an object. Once they are initialized, you usually don't want those settings to change, so a write-once property makes sense.

Write-once properties check to see if they have been previously set, and if they have, they raise an error:

```
Private m_Connection As String

' Write-once property, use to initialize object settings.
Property Let ConnectionString(value As String)
    If m_Connection <> "" Then
        Err.Raise 2001, "ConnectionString", "Property already set"
    Else
        m_Connection = value
    End If
End Property
```

In this case, ConnectionString is both write-once and write-only since I don't want others to see the setting once it is established. If the connection needs to change, the only way to do it is to create a new object with a new ConnectionString.

 Anything you can do with write-only properties can be done equally well using methods. Defining Password or ConnectionString as Sub procedures, rather than as Property Let procedures, results in equivalent code.

Define Enumerations

Enumerations are a handy way to publish the possible settings for a property. For example, the following addition to the Message class allows users to set the icon that appears on the message when it is shown:

```
Public Icon As IconType

Enum IconType
    None
    Critical = VbMsgBoxStyle.vbCritical
    Warning = VbMsgBoxStyle.vbExclamation
    Question = VbMsgBoxStyle.vbQuestion
    Information = VbMsgBoxStyle.vbInformation
End Enum

' Show method: displays the message.
Public Sub Show( )
    MsgBox value, Me.Icon, Title
End Sub
```

I added Me.Icon to the Show method to display the appropriate icon in the MsgBox. The point of using an enumeration is that the available settings are now automatically listed when you set the property, as shown in Figure 5-4.

You can use enumerations within methods as well. For example, the following changes allow the Show method to accept an icon setting:

```
Public Sub Show(Optional icon As IconType = -1)
    If (icon = -1) Then icon = Me.icon
    MsgBox value, icon, Title
End Sub
```

In the preceding code, I made icon an optional argument with a default setting outside of the possible IconType values so I can tell whether or not the argument was set. If icon is omitted, I use the setting from the Icon property instead. In this case, the icon argument overrides the Icon property.

When you use Show, Visual Basic displays the possible settings for the icon argument, as shown in Figure 5-5.

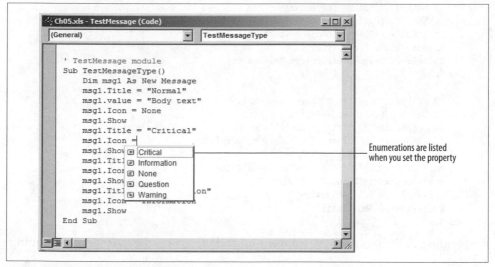

Figure 5-4. Use enumerations to publish available settings

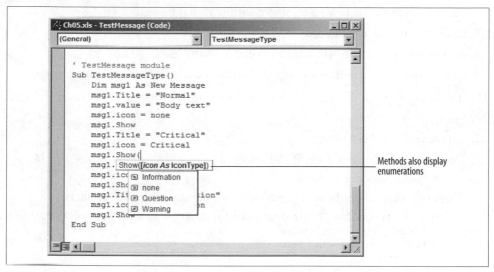

Figure 5-5. Enumerations are handy in methods as well

Raise Events

I mentioned earlier that, unlike modules, classes can include events. Classes define events using an Event statement and then raise those events using RaiseEvent. For example, the following additions (in **bold**) create an event that occurs whenever a message is shown or sent using the Message class:

```
' Message class
Public Event OnShow(arg As MessageType)
```

```
' Show method: displays the message.
Public Sub Show(Optional icon As IconType = -1)
    If (icon = -1) Then icon = Me.icon
    MsgBox value, icon, Title
    RaiseEvent OnShow(MessageType.MessageBox)
End Sub

' Send method: sends the message via email.
Public Sub Send(Optional ToAddress As String)
    Dim msgToSend As String, result As Double
    If ToAddress = "" Then ToAddress = m_Recipients
    msgToSend = "mailto:" & ToAddress
    msgToSend = msgToSend & "?SUBJECT=" & Title
    msgToSend = msgToSend & " &BODY=" & value
    ThisWorkbook.FollowHyperlink msgToSend, , True
    RaiseEvent OnShow(Email)
End Sub
```

Responding to the OnShow event from within code that uses the Message class requires a few steps:

1. Write your code in a class—you can't intercept events from a module. For example, write your code in a Sheet object within Visual Basic.

2. Declare the object at the class level using WithEvents.

3. Initialize that object by creating an instance of the class.

4. Create an event procedure to respond to the event.

The following sample illustrates the steps to using the OnShow event from a Sheet object:

1. Create code in Sheet object.

2. Declare Message object using WithEvents:

   ```
   Dim WithEvents msg As Message
   ```

   This code runs when the user double-clicks a certain range on the sheet:

   ```
   Private Sub Worksheet_BeforeDoubleClick(ByVal Target As Range, Cancel As Boolean)
       Select Case Target.address
       Case [ShowPreview].address
           CreateMsg
           msg.Show (Information)
       Case [SendMail].address
           CreateMsg
           msg.Send
       Case Else
           ' Do nothing
       End Select
   End Sub
   ```

3. Initialize the Message class:

   ```
   Sub CreateMsg( )
       Set msg = New Message
       Set msg.Recipients = [Addresses]
   ```

```
        msg.Title = "Values from Class worksheet"
        msg.value = RangeToString([SendRange])
    End Sub

    Function RangeToString(rng As Range) As String
        Dim cel As Range, result As String
        For Each cel In rng
            result = result & cel.value & ", "
        Next
        RangeToString = result
    End Function
```

4. Respond to the event:

```
    Private Sub msg_OnShow(arg As MessageType)
        Select Case arg
        Case MessageType.Email
            Application.StatusBar = "Sending message..."
        Case MessageType.MessageBox
            Application.StatusBar = "Preview complete."
        End Select
    End Sub
```

When you declare an object WithEvents at the class level, Visual Basic adds the events for that object to the object list as shown in Figure 5-6.

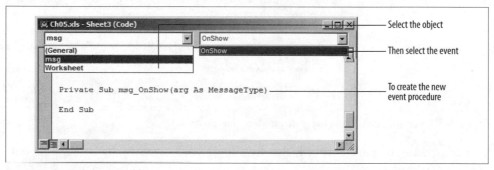

Figure 5-6. WithEvents adds events to the event list

The object is declared at the class level, but it must be initialized within a procedure. In the preceding example, that occurs in CreateObject, which is called by the Sheet object's Worksheet_BeforeDoubleClick event. If you are working within the ThisWorkbook object, you should initialize your objects in the Workbook_Open event so that the objects are created once at start-up. Unfortunately, the Sheet object doesn't have an equivalent event.

If you run the preceding example, you'll notice that the OnShow event occurs after the Message class displays a message box, but before the email message is displayed. There's a good reason for that: the message box runs within the Excel application, whereas the email message is displayed by your email application (e.g., Outlook). When working within Excel, Visual Basic waits for statements to complete before it continues. When working outside of Excel, it doesn't wait.

Collect Objects

Earlier I included a small procedure that converts values from a Range to a String:

```
Function RangeToString(rng As Range) As String
    Dim cel As Range, result As String
    For Each cel In rng
        result = result & cel.value & ", "
    Next
    RangeToString = result
End Function
```

The For Each loop in that code works because Range is a collection. A *collection* is a special type of object that includes a way to enumerate items contained by the object. Excel uses collections to organize its objects into a hierarchy, which is sometimes called the Excel *object model*. Figure 5-7 shows how collections are used to organize part of the Excel object model.

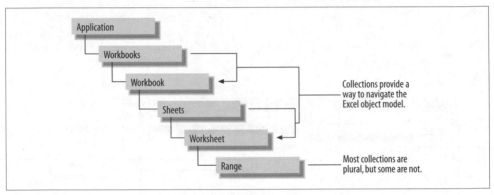

Figure 5-7. Excel uses collections to create an object hierarchy

You can create the same sort of hierarchy among your own objects by defining collections. To create a collection:

1. Create a new class that provides at least one method that returns a Collection object.

2. Provide a method in the class that allows others to add items to that collection.

3. Optionally, provide methods to remove and count items in the collection.

Most collections provide the following methods: Items, Item, Add, Remove, and Count. It's a good idea to follow that convention unless there's a specific reason *not* to enable one of those tasks. The following code shows the Messages collection, which, as the name suggests, provides a collection of Message objects:

```
' Messages class.
' Internal variable to contain the collection.
Private m_col As Collection
```

```
' Standard members provided by most collections:
' Items, Item, Add, Remove, Count.
Public Function Items() As Collection
    Set Items = m_col
End Function

Public Function Item(index) As Message
    Set Item = m_col(index)
End Function

Public Sub Add(msg As Message)
    ' Initialize the collection on first Add.
    If m_col Is Nothing Then _
      Set m_col = New Collection
    m_col.Add msg
End Sub

Public Sub Remove(index)
    m_col.Remove index
End Sub
```

You can use the preceding code as a template for any collection you need to create. Just change the data types of the `Item` method and the `msg` argument in the `Add` method to match the class of your collected object.

To use this collection in code, create new `Message` objects and add them to the collection. The following code shows a simple demo of the `Messages` collection. The first procedure creates three new `Message` objects and adds them to the collection. The second procedure displays each of the `Messages` from the collection:

```
' TestMessage module
Dim m_Messages As Messages

Sub TestInitializeCollection()
    ' Intialize the Messages collection.
    Set colMessages = New Messages
    ' Create some messages
    Dim msg1 As New Message
    msg1.Title = "Msg1"
    msg1.Value = "From collection."
    msg1.icon = Information
    m_Messages.Add msg1
    Dim msg2 As New Message
    msg2.Title = "Msg2"
    msg2.Value = "From collection."
    msg2.icon = Warning
    m_Messages.Add msg2
    Dim msg3 As New Message
    msg3.Title = "Msg3"
    msg3.Value = "From collection."
    msg3.icon = Critical
    m_Messages.Add msg3
End Sub
```

```
Sub TestCollection()
    Dim msg As Message
    For Each msg In m_Messages.Items
        msg.Show
    Next
End Sub
```

In the real world, you would probably initialize the collection in the `ThisWorkbook` class's `Workbook_Open` event procedure so that the collection is created automatically on start-up.

The previous `TestCollection` procedure shows one key difference between custom collections and Excel's built-in collections: custom collections don't have a default property. In other words, you must write `For Each msg in m_Message.Items`, whereas Excel collections can omit the `Items` property.

Excel's Visual Basic doesn't provide a way to designate a default property for a class. That's probably a good thing though, because default properties go away entirely in the .NET Framework.

Expose Objects

The objects you create within a workbook are usually private to that workbook. That means outside applications can't see them or use them in their code. In some rare cases, you may want to expose a custom object so that other applications can use it. To do so:

1. Declare the object as `Public`.

2. Initialize the object. Usually you do that on start-up when the workbook loads.

3. Change the class's `Instancing` property to `2 - Public not creatable`.

To see how this works, select the `Messages` class in the Visual Basic Project window and change the Instancing property as shown in Figure 5-8.

Repeat that for the `Message` class, and then add the following code to the `ThisWorkbook` object:

```
' ThisWorkbook object.
Public g_Messages As Messages

Private Sub Workbook_Open()
    ' Intialize the Messages collection.
    Set g_Messages = New Messages
    ' Create some messages
    Dim msg1 As New Message
    msg1.Title = "Msg1"
    msg1.Value = "From collection."
    msg1.icon = Information
    g_Messages.Add msg1
    Dim msg2 As New Message
```

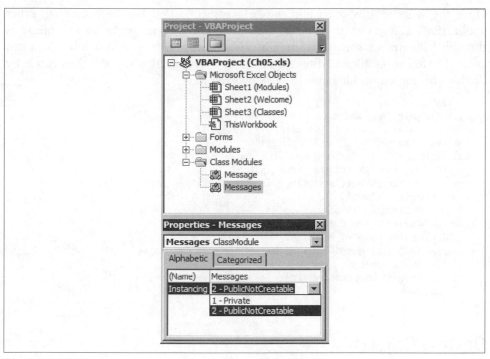

Figure 5-8. The Instancing property exposes objects outside Excel

```
        msg2.Title = "Msg2"
        msg2.Value = "From collection."
        msg2.icon = Warning
        g_Messages.Add msg2
    End Sub
```

The preceding code creates two `Message` objects and adds them to the `Messages` collection. That collection is then exposed through the `g_Messages` collection.

Save and close the workbook, and then reopen it to run the `Workbook_Open` procedure. If you forgot to set the `Instancing` property of the `Message` class, you'll see the error message in Figure 5-9.

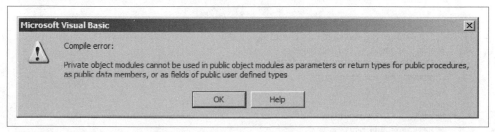

Figure 5-9. This error occurs if you try to expose an object without setting its Instancing property

Once the workbook is open and the Messages collection has been created, other applications can get at the object. One common way to get at these objects is through VBScript—a sort of lightweight Visual Basic built-in to Windows. You can create the following file in Notepad, save it as *TestCollection.vbs* and then run it by double-clicking on the file name in Windows Explorer:

```
' TestCollection.vbs
dim xl, path, fso, wb, msg
' Start Excel and make it visible.
set xl = CreateObject("Excel.Application")
xl.Visible = True
' Use this object to get the current path.
set fso = CreateObject("Scripting.FileSystemObject")
path = fso.getfolder(".")
' Open the sample workbook.
set wb = xl.Workbooks.Open(path & "\ch05.xls")
' Display the number of messages.
MsgBox "Ch05.xls exposes " & wb.g_Messages.Count & " messages."
' Show each message.
For each msg in wb.g_Messages.Items
    msg.Show
Next
```

Destroy Objects

In Visual Basic, objects remain in memory as long as there is a reference to them *in scope*. What's that mean? Scope is determined by where the variable is declared. So, a Message declared within a procedure is in scope while that procedure executes. When the procedure ends, the Message goes out of scope and it is removed from memory (some people say it gets *destroyed*).

At that point, the object is no longer available and any property settings it contained are lost. A way to prevent that is to make a reference at another level of scope. For instance, the following m_Messages variable keeps the Message collection around after TestInitializeCollection ends:

```
' TestMessage module
Public m_Messages As Messages

Sub TestInitializeCollection( )
    ' Intialize the Messages collection.
    Set m_Messages = New Messages
    ' Create some messages
    Dim msg1 As New Message
    msg1.Title = "Msg1"
    msg1.Value = "From collection."
    msg1.icon = Information
    m_Messages.Add msg1
    ' and so on...
End Sub
```

The trick here is that the msg1 object is also preserved, even though it is declared within the procedure that just ended. In this case, the collection holds a reference to that Message object, which keeps it in memory until the workbook closes or the object is explicitly destroyed. There are several ways to explicitly destroy the Message object:

- Remove it from the collection.
- Set the collection to Nothing.
- Set the m_Messages variable to a new Messages collection.

This code illustrates each technique:

```
' You must run TestInitializeCollection
' before running this one.
Sub TestDestroyObject()
    ' Remove a single object.
    m_Messages.Remove (1)
    ' Destroy the whole collection.
    Set m_Messages = Nothing
    ' Create a new collection (destroys prior one)
    Set m_Messages = New Messages
End Sub
```

The concept of references is important in Excel because it is possible to leave large, invisible objects in memory inadvertently. As long as someone holds a reference to an object, it is kept alive. Accidental references like that can result in *memory leaks*—a situation in which unused objects take up memory and slow your computer down unnecessarily.

To see how bad that can be, run this code:

```
Public m_xl As New Collection

Sub DemoMemoryLeak()
    Dim i As Integer
    For i = 1 To 10
        m_xl.Add (CreateObject("Excel.application"))
    Next
End Sub
```

If you switch to the Windows Task Manager (Figure 5-10), you'll see that there are now 11 instances of Excel loaded on your computer even though you can see only one of them.

Don't panic! You can make the hidden instances go way by setting m_xl to Nothing in the Immediate window as shown here:

```
Set m_xl = Nothing
```

My point is simple: be very careful when creating large objects that the user can't see. Watch out for module-level and class-level object variables—especially collections—and remember to set them to Nothing when you are done.

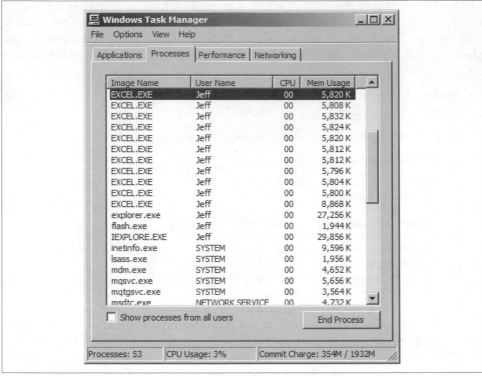

Figure 5-10. Yow, 11 instances of Excel! That can't be good.

The system of keeping track of objects as described here is called *reference counting*, and it's used by all Microsoft Office applications. The .NET Framework uses a more reliable system that periodically checks whether or not objects are still in use. That approach is called *garbage collection*.

Things You Can't Do

If you are familiar with an object-oriented programming language such as Java or Visual Basic .NET you might be waiting for me to discuss constructors, inheritance, and overloading. You'll have a long wait, because Excel's Visual Basic can't do any of those. There are also some limits on things you might assume you can do from looking at the Excel objects. For instance, you can't create default properties. Table 5-1 lists these language limitations and provides some detail.

Table 5-1. *Object-oriented features not available in Excel*

Feature	Limitation and workaround
Constructors	Only a default constructor is available. If you want to initialize an object, you must implement an `Initialize` method or something similar.
Destructors	Only a default destructor is available. If you want to free nonmemory resources used by an object, you must implement a separate `Dispose` method or something similar.
Collection types	There is only one collection type: `Collection`. To implement a collection, create a class that "wraps" that type as shown earlier in "Collect Objects."
Default properties	Not available in custom classes. Properties must be called by name.
Inheritance	Not available. You can't base one class on another.
Interfaces	Not available. You can't create a prototype for a class.
Overloaded methods	Not available. Use the `Optional` keyword to create methods that accept different sets of arguments.

I include Table 5-1 because it's hard to know what's missing simply by omission. It's not meant to denigrate Excel or to make you feel limited—you can still do a lot.

What You've Learned

Congratulations, you are now an object-oriented programmer (OOP). You've learned most of the key terms that relate to objects and should have an inkling of how to use them to impress your friends.

I hope you remember that classes allow you to create events and that a single class can be used to create multiple instances of an object in memory. Don't worry if you still feel a bit at sea regarding collections and exposing objects to other applications.

CHAPTER 6

Writing Code for Use by Others

Programming Excel for personal use is very common and it's how most of us get started. But what happens when you graduate to creating code for others? Once your audience expands from just yourself to your friends, your coworkers, or even the world, you'll find that expectations change—it's no longer OK if a procedure occasionally fails or that you have to know where to copy files to make them work. In short, programming for a wide audience requires a new set of skills.

This chapter walks you through the process of developing and distributing Excel Visual Basic code as workbooks, templates, and add-ins. I include information about testing your code because that's probably the most important (and most overlooked) aspect of Visual Basic programming.

 Code used in this chapter and additional samples are available in *ch06.xls*, *ch06.xlt*, *ch06.xla*, *ch06TemplateSetup.vbs*, *ch06AddinSetup. vbs*, and *ch06AddinRemove.vbs*.

Types of Applications

You can create three different types of applications from within Excel. Which type you choose determines how the application is used and distributed:

Workbooks
> Package code as part of a unique document. The code is stored with the workbook file (*.xls*) and is available whenever the user opens that file in Excel. If the user copies the file, the code is copied along with the rest of the workbook.

Templates
> Include code as part of a template for new Excel workbooks. When a user creates a new workbook file (*.xls*) from the template (*.xlt*), the code contained in the template is available in that new workbook though the code is not actually copied to the workbook.

Add-ins

> Include code as a file that can be loaded into the Excel application. If a user loads an add-in file (*.xla*), code from that add-in is available for any workbook a user opens.

Table 6-1 describes the relative advantages of these different types of applications.

Table 6-1. Ways to distribute code in Excel

Code stored in	Available to	Advantage	Disadvantage
Workbook (*.xls*)	Currently loaded workbooks	No installation required; easy to distribute.	Updates are difficult because the workbooks may be copied/renamed and there's no way to merge new code.
Template (*.xlt*)	Workbooks based on the template	Single file; code applies to specific type of workbook.	Templates must be installed.
Add-in (*.xla*)	All workbooks	Single file; code most widely available.	Add-ins must be installed; don't include worksheets.

One of the major differences between templates and add-ins is that templates include worksheets, charts, and document-based elements from Excel. Add-ins don't automatically include those visual elements.

You develop each of these application types starting from a workbook (*.xls*), then you save that workbook as the appropriate type, as shown in Figure 6-1.

After you save the workbook in the target format, you can still open it for editing in Excel, but you may have to look for the file in a different location. Excel stores templates in the *C:\Documents and Settings\user\Application Data\Microsoft\Templates* folder, and it stores add-ins in *C:\Documents and Settings\user\Application Data\ Microsoft\AddIns*. You can save to any location; these are just the defaults.

Understanding these different application types is important before you begin the development process. The rest of this chapter describes that process as it applies to Excel. Most of that information applies to other types of programming as well, though it is hardly the final word. See "Resources" at the end of this chapter for further reading on how to develop software professionally.

The Development Process

A friend of mine jokes that developing software is like constructing a house: the first step is to build the roof. His point is that nobody thinks you're crazy if you start implementing the user interface before you've thought through the design, organized your tools, and built a foundation.

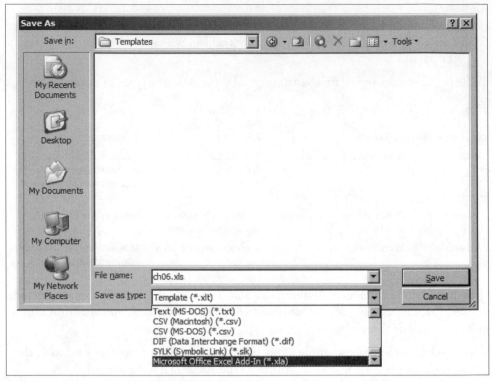

Figure 6-1. Saving a workbook as a template or add-in

The purpose of having a development process is to avoid that upside-down approach. Following a process helps you:

- Detect problems as early as possible
- Create reproducible results
- Know when you're done

Much has been written on the development process; I won't try to cover all the approaches or explain their differences here. Instead, I'll give you some practical tips specifically oriented toward working with Excel.

In my experience, the best advice is to use a test-driven approach and to get feedback as early as possible by following these general steps:

1. Determine requirements.
2. Create an initial design.
3. Implement features and unit tests.
4. Integrate features and test their interaction.
5. Test on target platforms.

6. Document the software and create training materials for users.

7. Deploy the software.

8. Archive what was deployed and get ready for the next version.

Each of these steps includes an implicit "Gather feedback and revise" step before proceeding to the next. How you gather and manage feedback must be tailored to your situation—your process may include formal approvals and management sign-off, or it may be as simple as a series of email messages. My point is that you need some series of steps to know where to start and how to proceed. The following sections describe these steps in greater detail.

Determine Requirements

Requirements may be clearly laid out by your manager, or you may be completely responsible for determining them yourself. In either case, it is helpful to test assumptions at this point and get direct feedback from those who will use the product to make sure the requirements are realistic and that nothing was omitted.

It's important to understand the difference between requirements and design: *Requirements* define what the product does; *design* determines how the product does it. In other words, it is a requirement that users log on before using the product, but determining how the username and password are validated is a design issue.

Requirements answer specific questions that help later with design, testing, and documentation. Table 6-2 categorizes some of the common questions.

Table 6-2. Common requirements questions

Category	Question
Function	What tasks does the product perform?
Audience	What level of experience do the users have with the tasks and with Excel in general?
Compatibility	What version or versions of Excel must the product work with?
	Do users have PCs, Macs, or both?
Deployment	Will the product be distributed on disk or from a network share or downloaded over the Internet?
Dependencies	Are there other components that must be installed for the product to work?
	Will this product be used by other products as a component?
	Does the product use external data, and if so what is the data source?

Obviously, these general questions may need to be followed up on for more detail. The purpose of the requirements is to state clearly what is expected and to create an understanding between those who will use the product and those who are building it.

Design

Design creates a framework for the product based upon requirements. Design documents usually include the following:

- General description of how the product performs the tasks described in the requirements
- Lists of menus presented to the user
- Sketches of screens that the product displays
- Conventions used in menus and screens
- Descriptions of data sources used by the product
- Details about any components used
- Special considerations, such as how platform differences are handled

A good design document tells programmers *what* they need to do but not *how* to do it. Designs are subject to change, so it is best if they aren't so complex that they are difficult to read or revise.

It is easiest to make changes during design, and it's important to take time to think things through. However, it's unrealistic to think a design is ever perfect. Devote a reasonable amount of time to the initial design, then plan on making updates along the way.

Implement and Test

Finally, you get to write some code! But since this code is going out to a wide audience, you need to do some extra work to make sure it functions correctly. In short, you need to test *as* you implement your code.

Each procedure that you write should have a unit test written to test it. Unit tests are procedures that call the functional procedures to make sure they work correctly. I use unit tests in all of the sample workbooks; for example, the TestMathFunctions unit test from *ch05.xls* tests the Inverse and CubeRoot procedures:

```
' Unit test
Sub TestMathFunctions( )
    Dim result As Double, Value As Double, str As String
    Value = 42
    result = Inverse(Value)
    str = "The inverse of " & Value & " is " & result
    result = CubeRoot(Value)
    str = str & " and the cube root is " & result
    MsgBox str, , "Test Math Functions"
End Sub

' Functional code
Public Function Inverse(x As Double) As Double
```

```
        If x = 0 Then Inverse = 0 Else Inverse = 1 / x
    End Function

    ' Functional code
    Public Function CubeRoot(x As Double) As Double
        If x < 0 Then CubeRoot = 0 Else CubeRoot = x ^ (1 / 3)
    End Function
```

I prefix the names of unit tests and the modules that contain them with Test to make their purpose clear. You'll see that again and again throughout this book.

Unit testing is not the same as stepping through the functional procedures manually. Manual testing, sometimes called ad hoc testing, is an important way to find errors during development but it does not create a reproducible result. Unit tests can be run repeatedly, and the result should always be the same. This allows you to automate the testing process as described in the next section.

Integrate

The TestMathFunctions unit test in the preceding section is a bit of a cheat because it combines the tests for two procedures: Inverse and CubeRoot. In general, unit tests and procedures have a one-to-one correspondence to make it easier to locate problems when they occur. Also, unit tests are easier to use if they don't display message boxes, because that requires you to manually click through the test.

For those reasons, I generally follow these conventions when writing unit tests:

- Return a string indicating pass/fail from each test.
- Where the results aren't pass/fail, return the result of the operation.
- Call the unit tests from a TestxxxMain procedure and display the results in the Immediate window using Debug.Print.

The following code shows unit tests for the QuickRead and QuickWrite procedures from Chapter 3 written with those conventions in mind:

```
    Const fpathtest = "c:\temp.txt"

    Sub TestFilesMain( )
        Debug.Print TestQuickWrite
        Debug.Print TestQuickRead
    End Sub

    Private Function TestQuickWrite( ) As String
        Dim s As String
        Dim result As String
        result - "failed"
        s = "This is some sample text."
        If Files.QuickWrite(s, fpathtest, True) Then result = "passed"
        TestQuickWrite = "TestQuickWrite " & result
    End Function
```

```
Private Function TestQuickRead() As String
    Dim s1 As String, s2 As String
    Dim result As String
    result = "failed"
    s1 = "This is some sample text."
    s2 = Files.QuickRead(fpathtest)
    If s1 = s2 Then result = "passed"
    TestQuickRead = "TestQuickRead " & result
End Function
```

These tests create a new text file, *c:\temp.txt*, then open that file and check its contents. When run within the Visual Basic Editor, the results appear in the Immediate window as shown in Figure 6-2.

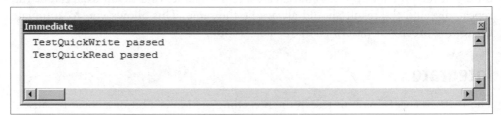

Figure 6-2. Unit tests write output to the Immediate window

Because these two unit tests are interdependent, the combined test checks their integration as well. Furthermore, if there are any changes to QuickRead or QuickWrite, you can rerun the test to check for regressions. Finally, you can run all of the tests of each of the different target platforms to check for compatibility problems. Table 6-3 describes each of these different types of tests.

Table 6-3. Types of tests

Test type	Verifies that
Unit test	The individual pieces work correctly.
Integration tests	The pieces work together.
Regression test	Changes to pieces don't break existing features.
Platform tests	The product works correctly on various operating systems and hardware configurations.

These different tests are used together during the development process as illustrated in Figure 6-3.

In the preceding example, TestQuickRead and TestQuickWrite are the unit tests and TestFilesMain is the integration test. After any changes, you rerun TestFilesMain as a regression test. And at the end of the cycle you run it again on each different set of hardware as a platform test.

If a problem is reported after deployment, you can create a new unit test to help you identify and fix the bug. That new test then becomes part of the testing cycle in Figure 6-3 to ensure the quality of future releases.

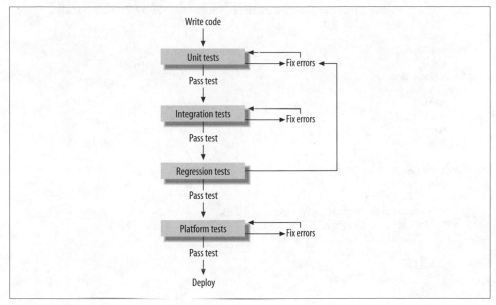

Figure 6-3. Testing is integral to the development process

Test Platforms

Although Excel runs on both PCs and Macs, there are quite a few differences between the objects Excel provides for each of those operating systems. Also, code written for the PC often relies on external components that are not available on the Mac or on early versions of Windows. In other words, it is very difficult to get the same code to work correctly on multiple operating systems.

The easiest solution to this problem is to require a specific operating system. The second easiest solution is to pick one operating system as your primary target and provide a reduced feature set on the others.

You can tell which operating system is in use by checking `Application.OperatingSystem`. The following code checks the operating system when the workbook loads and warns the user if it is not the primary target:

```
' ThisWorkbook class
Private Sub Workbook_Open()
    Select Case GetOS
        Case OS.Win32
            ' Full features, no message.
        Case OS.Mac
            ' Reduced features, display a warning.
            MsgBox "Running in compatibilty mode. "& _
                "Some features are disabled.", vbExclamation
        Case OS.Win16
            ' Not supported at all!
```

```
            MsgBox "This application requires Windows NT or XP.", vbCritical
            Application.Quit
    End Select
End Sub

' Platform module
Enum OS
    Win16
    Win32
    Mac
End Enum

Function GetOS( ) As OS
    Dim result As OS
    Dim s As String
    s = Application.OperatingSystem
    If InStr(1, s, "Windows") Then
        If InStr(1, s, "32-bit") Then
            result = Win32
        Else
            result = Win16
        End If
    Else
        result = Mac
    End If
    GetOS = result
End Function
```

Similarly, different versions of Excel can pose problems since early versions support fewer features than later ones. If your requirements specify a particular version of Excel, it is best to do all your development using that version. Then, compatibility with later versions is (almost) guaranteed.

 What! Later versions of Excel don't always include all of the previous versions' features? No, Excel is not always forward-compatible. In particular, Windows and Mac versions are out of sync, so code written for Excel 2003 (Windows) may not run on Excel 2004 (Mac).

If your requirements don't specify an Excel version, it's important to determine the version compatibility of your code before you deploy it. The easiest way to do that is to run the integration tests under different versions of Excel. For instance, you may develop a workbook using Excel 2003, then open the workbook in Excel 2000 and run the integration test to verify compatibility. If the test passes, you can assume compatibility; otherwise, you may need to test for the version at start-up as shown here:

```
' ThisWorkbook class
Private Sub Workbook_Open( )
    TestVersion
End Sub
```

```
Sub TestVersion( )
    If Application.Version < 10 Then
        MsgBox "This application requires Excel 2002 or later.", _
            vbCritical
        Application.Quit
    End If
End Sub
```

Hardware issues such as screen size, processor speed, and peripheral devices such as printers can also pose problems. It is best to try to detect those problems before you deploy and set some minimum requirements. It may not be necessary to test for those requirements thoroughly on start-up; it's often sufficient just to specify them in a *Readme.txt* file or some other documentation.

A final word of advice: don't try to write code that dynamically adjusts features for different platforms unless you've got a really good reason to do so. That approach requires a lot of effort in both development and testing and usually just confuses users. Instead, code for a specific set of minimum requirements, such as "Windows Excel 2000 or later." If you need to support two platforms, consider creating a separate version specifically for the secondary platform after completing the primary one.

Document

Documentation has evolved over the last several years to the point where most Help is provided over the Internet. That makes updating content easier, allows feedback, and probably most importantly maintains contact with customers.

You can create HTML documentation for your application using Word, FrontPage, or another editing tool—I wind up using Notepad more than I'd expect. HTML documents can be posted to a web server or they can be copied to the user's machine along with the application.

Then, you simply link items to help pages using hyperlinks on the worksheets or by using the Application.Help or Workbook.FollowHyperlink method in code:

```
Sub TestShowHelp( )
    Dim result As VbMsgBoxResult
    result = MsgBox("An error occured. Click OK to show help.", _
        vbOKCancel, "Error")
    If result = vbOK Then
        ' Display Help in Help window.
        Application.Help ("http://excelworkshop.com/Help/error51.htm")
        ' Alternate approach: display Help in browser.
        'ThisWorkbook.FollowHyperlink _
        '   ("http://excelworkshop.com/Help/error51.htm")
    End If
End Sub
```

The Help method displays the page in Excel's Help window. The FollowHyperlink method displays the page in the browser. Using the browser provides better navigation tools, but the Help window shares the screen with Excel a little better.

You can also add links to Help from menu items in Excel. To do so:

1. Choose Tools → Customize → Commands and select the Window and Help category.

2. Drag Contact Us from the Commands list to the Help menu as shown in Figure 6-4.

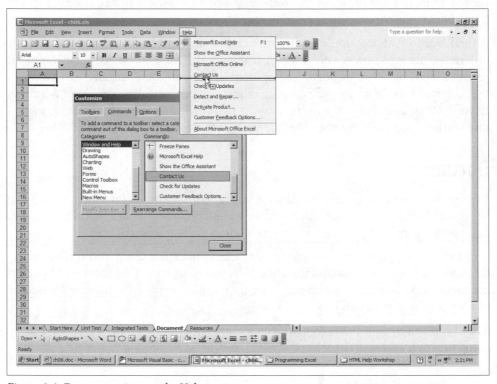

Figure 6-4. Drag a new item to the Help menu

3. Expand the Help menu and right-click on the Contact Us item you just added. This puts that item in edit mode, which is available only when the Customize dialog box is displayed.

4. Rename the menu item by typing in the Name property as shown in Figure 6-5.

5. Choose Assign Hyperlink → Open to set the address of the page to display when the user selects the menu item.

6. When finished, choose Close in the Customize dialog box.

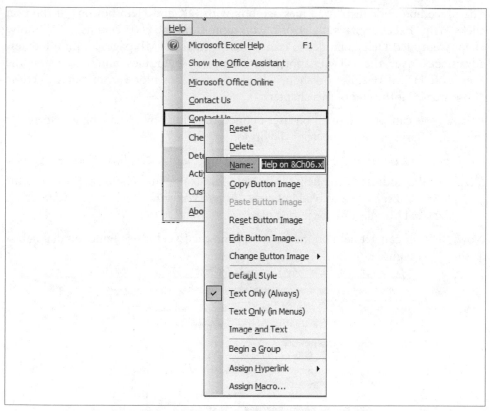

Figure 6-5. Rename and assign a hyperlink to the new menu item

Linking an application directly to HTML pages in this way is a little different than using some of Excel's built-in help features. For example, the MsgBox function allows you to link a Help button to a compiled help file (*.chm*) or a local HTML file, but not one located on the Web:

```
Sub TestContextHelp( )
    Dim path As String
    path = ThisWorkbook.path
    ' This works:
    MsgBox "An unexpected error occurred.", vbMsgBoxHelpButton, , _
      path & "/ch06.chm::Error51.htm", 0
    ' And so does this:
    'MsgBox "An unexpected error occurred.", vbMsgBoxHelpButton, , _
    '  path & "/error51.htm", 0
    ' But this doesn't work:
    'MsgBox "An unexpected error occurred.", vbMsgBoxHelpButton, , _
    '  "http://www.excelworkshop.com/Help/ch06.htm", 0
End Sub
```

The preceding code displays a message box with OK and Help buttons. If the user clicks Help, Excel displays the *error51.htm* topic from the *ch05.chm* using Windows Help. Compiled Help is harder to create than regular HTML pages and it offers few advantages over the HTML approach. Compiled help files are built using the Microsoft HTML Help Workshop, which is a free download from Microsoft (see "Resources," at the end of this chapter).

Finally, you can provide help on user-defined functions by specifying a help file in the Visual Basic project properties. To do so:

1. Right-click on the Project window in Visual Basic and select VBA Project Properties.

2. Enter the address of the help file in Help File Name and choose OK to close the dialog. You can use a web address (e.g., *http://excelworkshop.com/help/Ch06.htm*), a local HTML file, or a local *.chm* file.

Now, the user can get help on the function from the Excel Insert Function dialog box as shown in Figure 6-6.

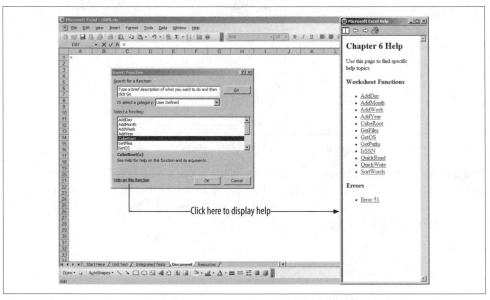

Figure 6-6. Set VBA Project Properties to specify a help file for user-defined functions

Since not all users have Internet access, you may want to combine approaches and install a help file locally that links to the Web for more detailed help and updates.

Deploy

Excel Visual Basic applications aren't compiled in the conventional sense. Instead, the code is saved in the file and it is interpreted at runtime. In the old days, before viruses and security concerns, you could just save an Excel workbook and then distribute it to your users without a second thought. Now, you need to take additional steps to make sure your users will be able to trust the code you send them:

1. Protect your code to prevent users from seeing or changing it.

2. Digitally sign the files and provide instructions on setting macro security to allow the application to run.

3. Create an installation program to copy the files to the user's system.

The following sections describe these steps in more detail.

Protect Code

To protect your Visual Basic code from changes:

1. Right-click on the Project window in Visual Basic and choose VBA Project Properties.

2. Choose the Protection tab, select Lock Project for Viewing and enter a password as shown in Figure 6-7.

3. Choose OK to close the dialog box. The changes take effect after you close and reopen the workbook.

Figure 6-7. Protect your Visual Basic code

Sign Files

Any files that contain code for use by others should be signed with a digital signature. Chapter 1 showed you how to self-sign macros so that the code you create for your own use can run without a security warning. If others try to run code that you signed in that way, they will see a warning that the certificate can't be verified (Figure 6-8).

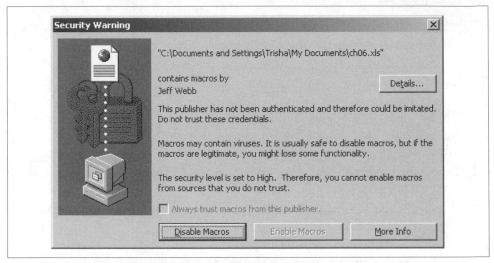

Figure 6-8. Self-signed macros aren't trusted on other users' machines

Other users can't choose to trust macros that you've self-signed because they can't be authenticated through a certificate authority.

To create code that others can choose to trust:

1. Get a digital signature from a certificate authority, such as Verisign, Inc., or *CAcert.org*.

2. In Visual Basic, sign your code with that digital signature (Tools → Digital Signature → Choose).

3. Save and close the file.

There are several types of digital signatures, which are also called *digital IDs* or *certificates*. You'll need one that permits code signing. Other types are used to sign email messages or to identify web servers online. Licenses for digital signatures used to be very cheap, but they've gone up to several hundred dollars a year—which is a significant expense for an individual. For a company with multiple developers, this expense is less significant since a company generally uses the same digital signature to sign all of its published code, which distributes the cost.

Lower-cost digital signatures are available from the nonprofit certificate authority CAcert. Digital signatures from CAcert support code signing. See "Resources," at the end of this chapter, for links to more information.

Digital signatures may also be generated internally by your company if your company has a server with the certificate authority service installed. If you think this is the case for your company, you should contact your IT department for more information.

Once you've signed your code with a digital signature from a certificate authority (CA), the new signature appears when users open your workbook. Because the signature can be authenticated from the CA, users can add it to their list of trusted publishers so they will not be prompted each time they open a file from you. Figure 6-9 shows opening a workbook that uses a signature from CAcert.

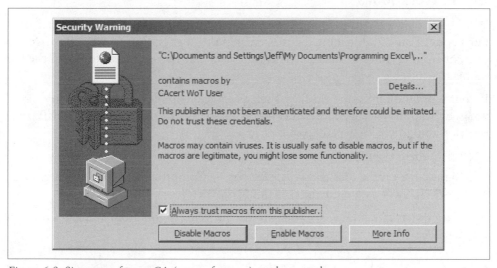

Figure 6-9. Signatures from a CA (even a free one) can be trusted

When Signatures Expire

Digital signatures have expiration dates to help ensure their authenticity. When a user opens a signed Excel file after the signature's expiration date, she sees a security warning saying that the signature has expired. To avoid this problem, you can timestamp signatures so that Excel compares the signature expiration to the timestamp rather than the current date.

Unfortunately, timestamps aren't automatic in Excel. In order to get it working, you need to edit your system registry to use a timestamp service provided by your certificate authority. For example, the following registry entries configure your system to use Verisign's timestamp service (*timestamp.reg*):

```
Windows Registry Editor Version 5.00
[HKEY_CURRENT_USER\Software\Microsoft\VBA\Security]
[HKEY_CURRENT_USER\Software\Microsoft\VBA\Security\TimeStampRetryCount]
@="10"
[HKEY_CURRENT_USER\Software\Microsoft\VBA\Security\TimeStampRetryDelay]
```

```
@="10"
[HKEY_CURRENT_USER\Software\Microsoft\VBA\Security\TimpeStampURL]
@="http://timestamp.verisign.com/scripts/timstamp.dll"
```

To merge these entries into your system registry, double-click on the sample file *timestamp.reg* in Windows Explorer. Before you rely on timestamps, you should test this procedure on your machine by signing code in an Excel file, closing it, changing your system date, then reopening the file in Excel. Please contact your certificate authority if you have problems.

Install Workbooks

Workbooks are easy to distribute since they are usually just a single file that contains code. You can distribute them as email attachments, from a network share, by disk, or from an Internet address. Then, the user can choose where to install the file on his machine.

If your workbook uses support files, such as a local help file or database query (*.iqy*), you may want to package files as a compressed folder. To use the Windows XP compression tool to package a group of files:

1. Select the files in Windows Explorer.
2. Right-click on the files and select Send to → Compressed (zipped) Folder. Windows creates a single *.zip* file containing the files.

If you don't have Windows XP, you can use the WinZip tool from WinZip Computing, Inc. (see "Resources," at the end of this chapter).

Install Templates and Add-ins

Templates and add-ins must be installed at specific locations on the user's machine in order to appear automatically in Excel. Where you install the file determines whether it is available only to the current user or to all users. Table 6-4 lists the various locations used by Excel for templates and add-ins.

Table 6-4. Install locations for workbooks, templates, and add-ins

Name	Location	Comments
Startup	*%ProgramFiles%\Microsoft Office\ OFFICE11\XLSTART*	Excel loads workbooks in this folder on startup. Excel includes templates in this folder on the General page of the Templates dialog.
Alt startup	Configured by the user on the General page of the Options dialog.	Workbooks and templates copied to this folder are loaded automatically on start-up in the same way as *\XLSTART*.

Table 6-4. Install locations for workbooks, templates, and add-ins (continued)

Name	Location	Comments
Network templates	If the user specified a shared network folder in Alt startup before, Excel loads templates from that location.	If set, this folder is returned as the `Application` object's `NetworkTemplatesPath` property.
Add-ins library	*%ProgramFiles%\Microsoft Office\ OFFICE11\Library*	Add-ins copied to this folder appear in the Available Add-Ins list of the Add-Ins dialog.
Spreadsheet solutions library	*%ProgramFiles%\Microsoft Office\ Templates\1033*	Displays templates in the Spreadsheet Solutions page of the Templates dialog.
User add-ins	*%UserProfile%\Application Data\ Microsoft\AddIns*	This is the default location when the user saves a file as an add-in. Add-ins copied to this folder appear in the Available Add-Ins list of the Add-Ins dialog.
User templates	*%UserProfile%\Application Data\ Microsoft\Templates*	This is the default location when a user saves a file as a template. Templates copied to this folder appear on the General page of Templates dialog.

For earlier versions of Windows, the locations vary depending on whether user profiles are enabled. Table 6-5 lists the folders used by earlier versions of Windows.

Table 6-5. Install locations for Windows NT and earlier

Name	User profiles disabled	User profiles enabled
User templates	*%windir%\Application Data\Microsoft\ Templates*	*%UserProfiles%\Application Data\Microsoft\ Templates*
User add-ins	*%windir%\Application Data\Microsoft\AddIns*	*%UserProfiles%\Application Data\Microsoft\AddIns*

> The values `%ProgramFiles%`, `%UserProfile%`, and `%windir%` are environment variables that map to special folders on your system. For example, `%ProgramFiles%` is usually *C:\Program Files*.

There are many ways to create installation programs that install templates or add-ins to these locations. Perhaps the simplest way is to use the WinZip self-extractor to create a compressed folder that runs a simple installation script when finished.

See "Resources," at the end of this chapter, for information on where to get the WinZip self-extractor. That tool includes information on how to run installation scripts after the extraction completes. You can write the installation script as a batch file, but I prefer to use VBScript since it leverages what we already know about Visual Basic and Excel.

Templates are simply copied to one of the template locations that Excel uses. For example, this VBScript installs the template *ch06.xlt* so that it shows up when the user chooses to look for templates "installed on my computer":

```
' Ch06TemplateSetup.vbs
' Get the objects used by this script.
Dim oXL, fso
Set oXL = CreateObject("Excel.Application")
Set fso = CreateObject("Scripting.FileSystemObject")
' Make Excel visible (always a good idea)
oXL.Visible = True
' Get the current folder (must add "\")
srcpath = fso.GetFolder(".").Path & "\"
' Get the Excel template folder
destpath = oXL.TemplatesPath
' Copy the file to the template folder.
fso.CopyFile srcpath & "ch06.xlt", destpath & "ch06.xlt"
' Close Excel
oXL.Quit
Set oXL = Nothing
```

Add-ins can be installed from any location, but it is a good idea to copy them to one of the standard folders listed in Table 6-4 so that users can find them easily. Add-ins also have an Installed property that loads them in Excel. For example, the following VBscript installs the add-in *ch06.xla*:

```
' Ch06AddinSetup.vbs
' Get the objects used by this script.
Dim oXL, oAddin, fso, wsh, srcPath, destPath
Set oXL = CreateObject("Excel.Application")
Set fso = CreateObject("Scripting.FileSystemObject")
Set wsh = WScript.CreateObject("WScript.Shell")
' Make Excel visible in case something goes wrong.
oXL.Visible = True
' Create a temporary workbook (required to access add-ins)
oXL.Workbooks.Add
' Get the current folder.
srcpath = fso.GetFolder(".")
destPath = wsh.Environment("PROCESS")("HOMEDRIVE") & _
    wsh.Environment("PROCESS")("HOMEPATH") & _
    "\Application Data\Microsoft\Addins"
' Copy the file to the template folder.
fso.CopyFile srcpath & "\ch06.xla", destpath & "\ch06.xla"
' Add the add-in to Excel.
Set oAddin = oXL.AddIns.Add(destpath & "\ch06.xla", true)
' Mark the add-in as installed so Excel loads it.
oAddin.Installed = True
' Close Excel.
oXL.Quit
Set oXL = Nothing
```

The preceding script copies *ch06.xla* to the user's add-ins folder, then marks the add-in as installed in Excel so the code is available immediately.

You remove templates and add-ins by deleting them from the folder where they were copied. For add-ins, it is a good idea to set their Installed property to False before deleting so Excel does not display an error when it no longer finds the deleted add-in. The following script shows how to remove *ch06.xla* after it is installed:

```
' Ch06AddinRemove.vbs
' Get the objects used by this script.
Dim oXL, oAddin, fso, wsh, srcPath, destPath
Set oXL = CreateObject("Excel.Application")
Set fso = CreateObject("Scripting.FileSystemObject")
Set wsh = WScript.CreateObject("WScript.Shell")
' Make Excel visible in case something goes wrong.
oXL.Visible = True
' Create a temporary workbook (required to access add-ins)
oXL.Workbooks.Add
' Mark the add-in as not installed.
oXL.AddIns("ch06").Installed - False
' Get the add-ins folder.
destPath = wsh.Environment("PROCESS")("HOMEDRIVE") & _
    wsh.Environment("PROCESS")("HOMEPATH") & _
    "\Application Data\Microsoft\Addins"
' Delete the file.
fso.GetFile(destpath & "\ch06.xla").Delete
' Close Excel.
oXL.Quit
Set oXL = Nothing
```

See "Resources" for links to information on VBScript, the FileSystemObject, and WScript.Shell.

What You've Learned

By now, you should understand what it takes to deliver professional-quality code to the world. Understanding is different from being able to accomplish something, however. It takes a great deal of practice to develop the skills you are ready to acquire.

Be patient and develop experience with the Excel objects described in the rest of this book. As you program, look for ways to integrate testing into your process.

Resources

For information on	Look here
The development process	*Extreme Programming Explained: Embrace Change* (Addison-Wesley)
Purchasing digital signatures	*http://www.verisign.com*
Learning about nonprofit digital signatures	*http://www.cacert.org*
Adding timestamps to digital signatures	*http://searchsupport.verisign.com/content/kb/vs5069.html*
Configuring a server to provide digital certificates	Search the Windows 2003 Server Help for "Installing and configuring a certification authority"
Digital signatures for normal people	*https://www.cacert.org/help.php?id=2*
Compiled help files	Search *http://www.microsoft.com/downloads* for "Help Workshop"
WinZip and WinZip self-extractor	*http://www.winzip.com*
VBScript	*http://msdn.microsoft.com/library/en-us/script56/html/vtoriVBScript.asp*
`FileSystemObject`	*http://msdn.microsoft.com/library/en-us/script56/html/fsooriScriptingRun-TimeReference.asp*
`WScript.Shell`	*http://msdn.microsoft.com/library/en-us/script56/html/wsObjWshShell.asp*

PART II

Excel Objects

These chapters provide a comprehensive guide to using the Excel objects to perform specific tasks. Each chapter in this part combines how-to sections and extensive examples with reference sections for the objects used to perform the tasks. This combined approach helps you navigate the vast set of objects, properties, and methods that Excel provides.

Controlling Excel

I talked a little about the `Application` object back in Chapter 4. `Application` is where everything starts in Excel: it's the grandma of all the other objects. You use the `Application` object to:

- Perform top-level actions, such as quitting Excel, showing dialog boxes, or recalculating all workbooks
- Control the Excel options, such as the settings on the Tools → Options dialog box
- Get references to the other objects in Excel

In this chapter, you will learn about those tasks in detail. This chapter includes task-oriented reference information for the following objects: `Application`, `AutoCorrect`, `AutoRecover`, `ErrorChecking`, `Windows`, and `Panes`.

    Code used in this chapter and additional samples are available in *ch07.xls*.

Perform Tasks

Use `Application` object to perform top-level tasks in Excel. The following sections describe how to:

- Quit the Excel application from code
- Turn user interaction and screen updates off and on
- Open, close, and arrange Excel windows
- Display Excel dialog boxes

These are the most common tasks for the `Application` object.

Quit Excel

Use the Quit method to quit Excel. If there are any workbooks with unsaved changes, Excel displays a dialog box asking the user if those changes should be saved. There are several ways to change that behavior:

- Save all workbooks before quitting.
- Set the all workbooks Saved property to True.
- Set DisplayAlerts to False.

The following code shows how to save all open workbooks before closing without prompting the user:

```
Sub QuitSaveAll( )
    Dim wb As Workbook
    For Each wb In Workbooks
        wb.Save
    Next
    Application.Quit
End Sub
```

Conversely, this code quits Excel without saving any of the workbooks:

```
Sub QuitSaveNone( )
    Dim wb As Workbook
    For Each wb In Workbooks
        ' Mark workbook as saved.
        wb.Saved = True
    Next
    Application.Quit
End Sub
```

Setting the Saved property fools Excel into thinking that it doesn't need to save changes and they are lost when Excel quits.

There's one other handy member to know about when quitting Excel: the SaveWorkspace method lets you save an *.xlw* file that you can use to restore the workbooks and windows currently in use. The following code saves those settings as *Resume.xlw*:

```
Sub QuitWithResume( )
    Application.SaveWorkspace "Resume.xlw"
    Application.Quit
End Sub
```

Lock Out User Actions

Sometimes you want to prevent users from interrupting Excel while you perform some time-consuming task in code. The Application object provides these ways to limit user interaction:

- Set DisplayAlerts to False to hide standard Excel dialogs while code runs

---

- Set Interactive to False to lock users out of Excel completely
- Set ScreenUpdating to False to hide changes as they are made by code

Each of these approaches should include some code at the end of the procedure to change the settings back to their defaults when your code finishes. Otherwise, you might lock a user out permanently!

The following code demonstrates how to lock out user actions temporarily while a long task executes:

```
Sub LockOutUser()
    Dim cel As Range
    ' Show the hourglass cursor.
    Application.Cursor = xlWait
    ' Turn off user interaction, screen updates.
    Application.Interactive = False
    Application.ScreenUpdating = False
    ' Simulate a long task.
    For Each cel In [a1:iv999]
        cel.Select
    Next
    ' Restore default settings.
    Application.Interactive = True
    Application.ScreenUpdating = True
    Application.Cursor = xlDefault
    [a1].Select
End Sub
```

One of the side benefits of setting ScreenUpdating to False is that the preceding code executes more quickly since Excel doesn't have to update the screen or scroll the worksheet as cells are selected. Again, just be sure to turn screen updates back on when done.

Open and Close Excel Windows

The Application object provides a Windows collection that lets you open, arrange, resize, and close Excel's child windows. For example, the following code opens a new child window and then cascades the open windows for the active workbook:

```
Sub OpenCascadeWindows()
    ActiveWindow.NewWindow
    Application.Windows.Arrange xlArrangeStyleCascade, True
End Sub
```

You close and maximize child windows using methods on the Window object. For example, the following code closes the window opened in the preceding code and restores the original window to a maximized state in Excel:

```
Sub CloseMaximize()
    ActiveWindow.Close
    ActiveWindow.WindowState = xlMaximized
End Sub
```

Closing the last child window for a workbook also closes the workbook.

Finally, you can control the Excel parent window using the `Application` object's `WindowState` and `DisplayFullScreen` properties:

```
Sub ChangeExcelWindowState()
    Application.WindowState = xlMaximized
    API.Sleep 1000
    Application.WindowState = xlMinimized
    API.Sleep 1000
    Application.WindowState = xlNormal
    API.Sleep 1000
    Application.DisplayFullScreen = True
    API.Sleep 1000
    Application.DisplayFullScreen = False
End Sub
```

Display Dialogs

The three different sorts of dialog boxes in Excel are built-in dialogs that perform actions, built-in dialogs that return information, and custom dialogs you build from Visual Basic forms. The `Application` object gives you several ways to display the first two types:

- Use the `FindFile` method to let the user select a file to open in Excel.
- Use the `Dialogs` collection to display Excel's other built-in dialog boxes to perform those specific actions.
- Use `FileDialog` method to get file and folder names from the user.
- Use the `InputBox` method to get ranges or formulas.

For example, the following code displays Excel's built-in Open dialog box and then opens the file selected by the user:

```
Sub OpenFile1()
    On Error Resume Next
    Application.FindFile
    If Err Then Debug.Print "User cancelled import."
End Sub
```

You can do the same thing using the `Dialogs` collection:

```
Sub OpenFile2()
    On Error Resume Next
    Application.Dialogs(XlBuiltInDialog.xlDialogOpen).Show
    If Err Then Debug.Print "User cancelled import."
End Sub
```

Both of the preceding samples display the Open dialog box and open the file in Excel. You have to include error-handling statements in case the user chooses a non-Excel file then cancels importing the file—otherwise that action halts your code with an application error.

The Dialogs collection can display any of the Excel dialog boxes. See Appendix A for a list of those dialogs—about 250 of them! Displaying a dialog that way is just like displaying it through the user interface: Excel uses its current settings and takes whatever actions the user chooses from the dialog.

Sometimes you *don't* want Excel to perform its standard action after the user closes the dialog; instead, you'd rather get the information from the dialog and take your own actions in code. The most common example of this is when you want to get a file or folder name. In that case, use the FileDialog method.

FileDialog displays the built-in Excel Open dialog box, but doesn't open the file. You can change the caption, file filter, and other settings as well. The following code uses the FileDialog to open a web file in the browser:

```
Sub OpenWebFile()
    With Application.FileDialog(msoFileDialogFilePicker)
        ' Set dialog box options
        .Title = "Show web file"
        .Filters.Add "Web files (*.htm)", "*.htm;*.html;*.xml", 1
        .FilterIndex = 1
        .AllowMultiSelect = False
        ' If the user chose a file, open it in the browser.
        If .Show = True Then _
          ThisWorkbook.FollowHyperlink .SelectedItems(1)
    End With
End Sub
```

Finally, the Application object's InputBox method lets you get Excel ranges and formulas from the user. This method is otherwise identical to the Visual Basic InputBox. Figure 7-1 shows the Excel InputBox in action.

The *Type* argument of InputBox determines the kind of data the user can enter. The most common settings are 0 for a formula, 1 for a number, or 8 for a range. The following code displays the input box shown in Figure 7-1:

```
Sub GetRange()
    Dim rng As Range
    Set rng = Application.InputBox("Select a range", _
      "Application InputBox", , , , , , 8)
    rng.Select
End Sub
```

Control Excel Options

All of the Excel settings and options can be controlled in code through Application object properties. Quite a few of the Application properties are devoted to Excel settings and options, but you only occasionally need to change these settings in code—it is usually a better idea to let the users maintain their own settings.

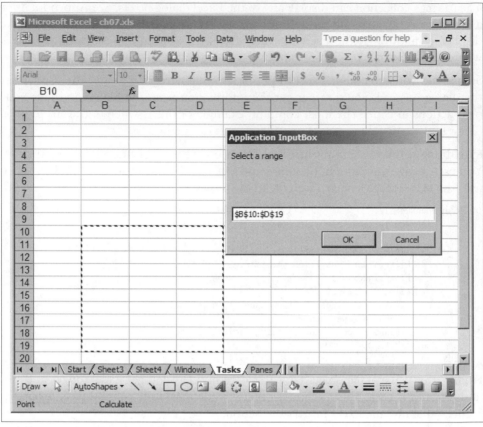

Figure 7-1. Use Application.InputBox to get ranges and formulas

If you do change Excel options in code, it is polite to restore the user's settings when you are done. To do that, save the original setting in a module-level variable and restore that setting before exiting.

Set Startup Paths

Excel uses several predefined folders to load workbooks, add-ins, and templates. You can get or set these folders from code using the properties in Table 7-1.

Table 7-1. Application properties for predefined folders

Property	Use to
AltStartupPath	Get or set the user folder used to load add-ins and workbooks automatically
DefaultFilePath	Get or set the default folder to which workbooks are saved
LibraryPath	Get the built-in Excel add-in library folder
NetworkTemplatesPath	Get the AltStartupPath if it is a network share

Table 7-1. Application properties for predefined folders (continued)

Property	Use to
Path	Get the folder where Excel is installed
StartupPath	Get the built-in folder Excel uses to load add-ins and workbooks automatically (*XLSTART*)
TemplatesPath	Get the user folder Excel from which loads templates

You use these properties when installing templates and add-ins, as covered in Chapter 6, and when your code relies on specific locations. For example you might want to change the DefaultFilePath to a specific folder while your application runs:

```
Dim m_originalPath As String
Const APP_PATH = "c:\ExcelDocs"

Sub SetPath( )
    ' Store the user settng.
    m_oringalPath = Application.DefaultFilePath
    ' Use this setting while application runs.
    Application.DefaultFilePath = APP_PATH
End Sub

Sub RestorePath( )
    ' Restore the user setting before exit.
    Application.DefaultFilePath = m_originalPath
End Sub
```

View System Settings

There are a great many other settings and options in Excel. Chapter 6 showed how to find operating system and version information from the Application object. You can also get and set the options set through the Excel Options dialog box (Figure 7-2) using individual Application properties.

For example, to select the R1C1 reference style in Figure 7-2, use this code:

```
Sub SetReferenceStyle( )
    Application.ReferenceStyle = xlR1C1
End Sub
```

Get References

As the top-level object in Excel, Application is the source of all other object references. However, the object name Application isn't always used in code because Excel includes shortcuts (called *global members*) that let you omit it. For instance, the following two lines are equivalent:

```
Application.Selection.Clear ' Clear selected cells.
Selection.Clear            ' Same thing!
```

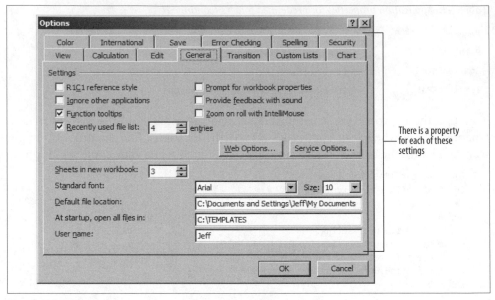

There is a property for each of these settings

Figure 7-2. Use Application properties to get or set these options

In this case, Selection returns the selected cells on the active worksheet as a Range object. Table 7-2 lists the Application members that return references to other objects.

Table 7-2. Application object members that return object references

ActiveCell	ActiveChart	ActivePrinter
ActiveSheet	ActiveWindow	ActiveWorkbook
AddIns	Assistant	AutoCorrect
AutoRecover	Cells	Charts
Columns	COMAddIns	CommandBars
Dialogs	ErrorCheckingOptions	FileDialog
FileFind	FileSearch	FindFile
FindFormat	International	Intersect
LanguageSettings	Names	NewWorkbook
ODBCErrors	OLEDBErrors	PreviousSelections
Range	RecentFiles	Rows
RTD	Selection	Sheets
SmartTagRecognizers	Speech	SpellingOptions
ThisCell	ThisWorkbook	Union
UsedObjects	Watches	Windows
Workbooks	WorksheetFunction	Worksheets

Most of the names of the members in Table 7-2 are descriptive of the objects they return. The exceptions to that rule are the members that can return a mixed collection of objects, such as Selection, and members that return Range objects: ActiveCell, Cells, Columns, Range, Rows, and ThisCell.

Application Members

The Application object has the following members. Key members (shown in **bold**) are covered in the following reference section:

ActivateMicrosoftApp	ActiveCell	ActiveChart
ActivePrinter	ActiveSheet	ActiveWindow
ActiveWorkbook	**AddChartAutoFormat**	**AddCustomList**
AddIns	**AlertBeforeOverwriting**	**AltStartupPath**
Application	**ArbitraryXMLSupportAvailable**	AskToUpdateLinks
Assistant	**AutoCorrect**	**AutoFormatAsYouType** ReplaceHyperlinks
AutomationSecurity	**AutoPercentEntry**	**AutoRecover**
Build	**Calculate**	**CalculateBeforeSave**
CalculateFull	**CalculateFullRebuild**	**Calculation**
CalculationInterruptKey	**CalculationState**	**CalculationVersion**
Caller	CanPlaySounds	CanRecordSounds
Caption	**CellDragAndDrop**	**Cells**
CentimetersToPoints	**Charts**	**CheckAbort**
CheckSpelling	**ClipboardFormats**	ColorButtons
Columns	**COMAddIns**	**CommandBars**
CommandUnderlines	**ConstrainNumeric**	**ControlCharacters**
ConvertFormula	**CopyObjectsWithCells**	Creator
Cursor	**CursorMovement**	**CustomListCount**
CutCopyMode	**DataEntryMode**	**DecimalSeparator**
DefaultFilePath	**DefaultSaveFormat**	**DefaultSheetDirection**
DefaultWebOptions	**DeleteChartAutoFormat**	**DeleteCustomList**
Dialogs	**DisplayAlerts**	**DisplayClipboardWindow**
DisplayCommentIndicator	**DisplayDocumentActionTaskPane**	**DisplayExcel4Menus**
DisplayFormulaBar	**DisplayFullScreen**	**DisplayFunctionToolTips**
DisplayInsertOptions	**DisplayNoteIndicator**	**DisplayPasteOptions**
DisplayRecentFiles	**DisplayScrollBars**	**DisplayStatusBar**
DisplayXMLSourcePane	**DoubleClick**	**EditDirectlyInCell**
EnableAnimations	**EnableAutoComplete**	**EnableCancelKey**
EnableEvents	**EnableSound**	**ErrorCheckingOptions**
Evaluate	**ExtendList**	**FeatureInstall**
FileConverters	**FileDialog**	**FileFind**
FileSearch	**FindFile**	**FindFormat**
FixedDecimal	**FixedDecimalPlaces**	**GenerateGetPivotData**
GetCustomListContents	**GetCustomListNum**	**GetOpenFilename**
GetPhonetic	**GetSaveAsFilename**	**Goto**
Height	**Help**	**Hinstance**
Hwnd	**InchesToPoints**	**InputBox**
Interactive	**International**	**Intersect**

Iteration	LanguageSettings	LargeButtons
Left	LibraryPath	MacroOptions
MailLogoff	MailLogon	MailSession
MailSystem	MapPaperSize	MaxChange
MaxIterations	MoveAfterReturn	MoveAfterReturnDirection
Name	Names	NetworkTemplatesPath
NewWorkbook	NextLetter	ODBCErrors
ODBCTimeout	OLEDBErrors	OnKey
OnRepeat	OnTime	OnUndo
OnWindow	OperatingSystem	OrganizationName
Parent	Path	PathSeparator
PivotTableSelection	PreviousSelections	ProductCode
PromptForSummaryInfo	Quit	Range
Ready	RecentFiles	RecordMacro
RecordRelative	ReferenceStyle	RegisteredFunctions
RegisterXLL	Repeat	ReplaceFormat
RollZoom	Rows	RTD
Run	SaveWorkspace	ScreenUpdating
Selection	SendKeys	SetDefaultChart
Sheets	SheetsInNewWorkbook	ShowChartTipNames
ShowChartTipValues	ShowStartupDialog	ShowToolTips
ShowWindowsInTaskbar	SmartTagRecognizers	Speech
SpellingOptions	StandardFont	StandardFontSize
StartupPath	StatusBar	TemplatesPath
ThisCell	ThisWorkbook	ThousandsSeparator
Top	TransitionMenuKey	TransitionMenuKeyAction
TransitionNavigKeys	Undo	Union
UsableHeight	UsableWidth	UsedObjects
UserControl	UserLibraryPath	UserName
UseSystemSeparators	Value	VBE
Version	Visible	Volatile
Wait	Watches	Width
Windows	WindowsForPens	WindowState
Workbooks	WorksheetFunction	Worksheets

[Application.]ActivateMicrosoftApp(*XlMSApplication*)

Starts or activates another Microsoft Office application. XlMSApplication can be one of the following settings:

xlMicrosoftWord

xlMicrosoftPowerPoint

xlMicrosoftMail

xlMicrosoftAccess

xlMicrosoftFoxPro

xlMicrosoftProject

xlMicrosoftSchedulePlus

This method causes an error if the requested application is not installed. xlMicrosoftMail activates the user's default mail application.

[Application.]ActivePrinter [= *setting*]

Sets or returns the printer that Excel will use. When setting this property, the printer name must include the port number, for example:

```
Sub SetPrinter( )
    ActivePrinter = "\\wombat2\Lexmark Z52 Color Jetprinter on Ne04:"
End Sub
```

The preceding code tells Excel to use a shared printer over the network. The port number used by Excel is Ne*nn*: for virtual ports but is LPT*n*: or COM*n*: for physical ports. The following code gets an array of the available printers in a format that can be used by Excel:

```
Function GetPrinters() As String()
    ' Use a suitably large array (supports up to 100 printers).
    ReDim result(100) As String
    Dim wshNetwork As Object, oPrinters As Object, temp As String
    ' Get the network object
    Set wshNetwork = CreateObject("WScript.Network")
    Set oPrinters = wshNetwork.EnumPrinterConnections
    ' Get the current active printer
    temp = ActivePrinter
    ' Printers collection has two elements for each printer.
    For i = 0 To oPrinters.Count - 1 Step 2
        ' Set the default printer.
        wshNetwork.SetDefaultPrinter oPrinters.Item(i + 1)
        ' Get what Excel sees.
        result(i \ 2) = ActivePrinter
        ' For debug purposes, show printer.
        Debug.Print ActivePrinter
    Next
    ' Trim empty elements off the array.
    ReDim Preserve result(i \ 2)
    ' Change back to original printer
    ActivePrinter = temp
    ' Return the result.
    GetPrinters = result
End Function
```

Application.AddChartAutoFormat(*Chart, Name, [Description]*)

Creates a new chart type based on an existing chart.

Argument	Setting
Chart	A chart object to get formatting from
Name	The name to add to the chart autoformat list
Description	A description of the chart type

The following code adds a custom chart type to Excel based on an existing chart in the current workbook:

```
Sub TestAddChartType( )
    Application.AddChartAutoFormat Charts(1), _
        "new custom", "my description"
End Sub
```

To see the new chart type, select some data on a worksheet and choose Insert → Chart → Custom Types → User Defined.

Application.AddCustomList(*ListArray*, [*ByRow*])

Creates a new automatic list based on an array or a range of cells.

Argument	Setting
ListArray	The array or range of cells containing the items for the list.
ByRow	True creates the list from rows in a range; False creates the list from columns in the range. Ignored if ListArray is a single row or column. Causes an error if ListArray is not a range.

The first item in each list must be unique. An error occurs if a list with an identical first item already exists. The following code creates a new custom list from a range on the active worksheet:

```
Sub TestCustomList( )
    Application.AddCustomList [a1:a10]
End Sub
```

To see the new list, choose Tools → Options → Custom Lists.

Application.AlertBeforeOverwriting [= *setting*]

True displays an alert if a drag-and-drop changes cells that contain data; False does not. The default is True.

Application.AltStartupPath

Sets or returns the folder from which to automatically load templates and add-ins.

Application.ArbitraryXMLSupportAvailable

Returns True if Excel accepts custom XML schemas. This property is available only in Excel 2003.

Application.AskToUpdateLinks [= *setting*]

True asks prompts before updating external links when a workbook is opened; False does not prompt before updating. The default is True.

Application.Assistant

Returns a reference to the annoying Office Assistant character. For example, the following code displays the assistant and then animates its departure:

```
Sub TestAssistant( )
    Application.Assistant.Visible = True
    With Application.Assistant.NewBalloon
        .Text = "Ciao for now!"
        .Show
    End With
    Application.Assistant.Animation = msoAnimationGetArtsy
    Application.Assistant.Animation = msoAnimationGoodbye
End Sub
```

As of Office 2003, the assistant is no longer installed by default.

Application.AutoCorrect

Returns a reference to the AutoCorrect object. That object determines how Excel makes automatic corrections to user data entry.

Application.AutoFormatAsYouTypeReplaceHyperlinks [= *setting*]

True automatically reformats entries that begin with http://, ftp://, mailto:, and other protocols as hyperlinks; False does not. The default is True.

Application.AutomationSecurity [=*MsoAutomationSecurity*]

Set or returns the macro security setting used when opening Office documents in code. Possible settings are:

msoAutomationSecurityLow
    Enable all macros. This is the default.

msoAutomationSecurityByUI
    Use the security setting specified in the Security dialog box.

msoAutomationSecurityForceDisable
    Disable all without showing any security alerts.

These settings apply only to files opened in code. Files opened by the user apply the settings in the Security dialog box.

The default setting for this property is a security hole created to provide backward compatibility with multifile macros written for earlier versions of Excel. You should close this hole in your own code by setting the property to msoAutomationSecurityByUI before opening files, as shown here:

```
Sub TestMacroSecurity( )
    ' Enable macro security on file to open
    Application.AutomationSecurity = msoAutomationSecurityByUI
    With Application.FileDialog(msoFileDialogOpen)
```

```
          .AllowMultiSelect = False
          ' Get a file
          .Show
          ' Open it.
          Application.Workbooks.Open .SelectedItems(1)
     End With
End Sub
```

Application.AutoPercentEntry [= *setting*]

True multiplies values formatted as percentage by 100 when displayed (e.g., entering 99 displays 9900%); False does not. Default is True.

Application.AutoRecover

Returns the AutoRecover object, which controls Excel's automatic file recovery features.

Application.Build

Returns the Excel build number. The following code displays Excel's version, build number, and calculation engine version:

```
Sub ShowVersion( )
    Debug.Print Application.Version; Application.Build; _
      Application.CalculationVersion
End Sub
```

[Application.]Calculate( )

Recalculates the formulas in all open workbooks.

Application.CalculateBeforeSave [= *setting*]

True recalculates workbooks before they are saved; False does not. Default is True.

Application.CalculateFull( )

Forces a full recalculation of all formulas in all workbooks.

Application.CalculateFullRebuild( )

Forces a full recalculation of all formulas and rebuilds dependencies in all workbooks.

Application.Calculation [= *XlCalculation*]

Sets or returns the calculation mode. Can be one of the following settings:

xlCalculationAutomatic
 Recalculates cells as data is entered (default)

xlCalculationManual
 Recalculates only when the user chooses Calculate Now (F9)

xlCalculationSemiautomatic
 Recalculates all cells except data tables automatically

Application.CalculationInterruptKey [= *XlCalculationInterruptKey*]

Sets or returns which key halts recalculation. Can be one of the following settings:

 xlAnyKey (default)
 xlEscKey
 xlNoKey

Application.CalculationState

Sets or returns a constant indicating the state of all open workbooks. Can be one of the following:

 xlCalculating
 xlDone
 xlPending

Application.CalculationVersion

Returns the version number of the calculation engine.

Application.Caller

Returns information about how the macro was called, as described in the following table:

When called from	Returns
A formula entered in a cell	A Range object for the cell
An array formula in a range of cells	A Range object for the range of cells
VBA code, the Run Macro dialog box, or anywhere else	Error 2023
An Auto_Open, Auto_Close, Auto_Activate, or Auto_Deactivate macro	The name of the workbook (Obsolete)
A macro set by the OnDoubleClick or OnEntry property	The name of the chart or cell to which the macro applies (Obsolete)

Application.Caption [= *setting*]

Sets or returns the text displayed in the Excel titlebar. For example, the following code replaces "Microsoft Excel" with "Funky Monkey" in the titlebar:

```
Sub TestCaption( )
    Application.Caption = "Funky Monkey"
End Sub
```

Application.CellDragAndDrop [= *setting*]

True enables drag-and-drop; False disables. Default is true.

[Application.]Cells[(*row, column*)]

Returns a range of cells on the active worksheet. For example, the following code selects cell B1 on the active worksheet:

```
Sub TestCells( )
    Cells(1, 2).Select
End Sub
```

Application.CentimetersToPoints(*Centimeters*)

Converts centimeters to points. This is the same as multiplying by 0.035.

[Application.]Charts([*index*])

Returns a reference to the Charts collection.

Application.CheckAbort([*KeepAbort*])

Aborts recalculation. The argument *KeepAbort* accepts a Range object to continue recalculating. This lets you stop recalculation for all but a specific range of cells.

Application.CheckSpelling(*Word*, [*CustomDictionary*], [*IgnoreUppercase*])

Returns True if *Word* is spelled correctly; False if it is not.

Argument	Setting
Word	The word to spellcheck.
CustomDictionary	The filename of the custom dictionary to use if the word isn't found in the main dictionary. Defaults to the user setting.
IgnoreUppercase	True excludes words that are all uppercase; False includes them. Defaults to the user setting.

Application.ClipboardFormats

Returns an array of XlClipboardFormat constants indicating the types of data currently on the clipboard. Possible array values are:

xlClipboardFormatBIFF	xlClipboardFormatBIFF2
xlClipboardFormatBIFF3	xlClipboardFormatBIFF4
xlClipboardFormatBinary	xlClipboardFormatBitmap
xlClipboardFormatCGM	xlClipboardFormatCSV
xlClipboardFormatDIF	xlClipboardFormatDspText
xlClipboardFormatEmbeddedObject	xlClipboardFormatEmbedSource
xlClipboardFormatLink	xlClipboardFormatLinkSource
xlClipboardFormatLinkSourceDesc	xlClipboardFormatMovie
xlClipboardFormatNative	xlClipboardFormatObjectDesc
xlClipboardFormatObjectLink	xlClipboardFormatOwnerLink
xlClipboardFormatPICT	xlClipboardFormatPrintPICT
xlClipboardFormatRTF	xlClipboardFormatScreenPICT
xlClipboardFormatStandardFont	xlClipboardFormatStandardScale
xlClipboardFormatSYLK	xlClipboardFormatTable
xlClipboardFormatText	xlClipboardFormatToolFace
xlClipboardFormatToolFacePICT	xlClipboardFormatVALU
xlClipboardFormatWK1	

Use ClipboardFormats to determine the type of data available on the clipboard before taking other actions, such as Paste. For example, this code copies a chart into the clipboard, then pastes it into Paint:

```
Declare Sub Sleep Lib "kernel32" (ByVal dwMilliseconds As Long)

Sub TestClipBoardFormats()
    Dim fmt, chrt As Chart
    ' Copy a chart image into the clipboard.
    Set chrt = Charts(1)
    chrt.CopyPicture xlScreen, xlBitmap
    For Each fmt In Application.ClipboardFormats
        ' If the bitmap is in the clipboard
        If fmt = xlClipboardFormatBitmap Then
        ' Start Paint
        Shell "mspaint.exe", vbNormalFocus
        ' Wait a half second to catch up.
        Sleep 500
        ' and paste the Chart image.
        SendKeys "%EP", True
        Exit For
        End If
    Next
End SubEnd Sub
```

The Sleep API shown in the preceding code is required to wait for focus to change to the newly opened Paint application.

[Application].Columns([*index*])

Returns one or more columns on the active worksheet as a Range object. For example, the following code selects column C on the active worksheet:

```
Sub TestColumns( )
    Columns(3).Select
End Sub
```

Application.COMAddIns([*index*])

Returns a collection of the installed COM add-ins. If there are no COM add-ins installed, causes an error. The following code lists the COM add-ins:

```
Sub TestCOMAddins( )
    Dim c  As COMAddIn
    On Error Resume Next
    For Each c In Application.COMAddIns
        If Err Then Debug.Print "No COM addins."
        Debug.Print Join(Array(c.Description, c.progID, c.Application, _
            c.Connect), ", ")
    Next
End Sub
```

Application.CommandBars([*index*])

Returns one or more command bars. The following code displays a list of the command bars with their status:

```
Sub TestCommandbars( )
    Dim cb As CommandBar
    Debug.Print "Name", "Visible?", "BuiltIn?"
    For Each cb In Application.CommandBars
        Debug.Print cb.Name, cb.Visible, cb.BuiltIn
    Next
End Sub
```

Application.CommandUnderlines [= *xlCommandUnderlines*]

(Macintosh only.) Sets or returns how commands are highlighted. Can be one of the following settings:

xlCommandUnderlinesOn

xlCommandUnderlinesOff

xlCommandUnderlinesAutomatic

For Windows, CommandUnderlines always returns xlCommandUnderlinesOn and cannot be set.

Application.ConstrainNumeric [= *setting*]

(Windows for Pen only.) True restricts handwriting recognition to numbers and punctuation; False allows the full alphabet.

Application.ControlCharacters [= *setting*]

(Right-to-left language display only.) True displays control characters for right-to-left languages; False hides the characters.

Application.ConvertFormula(Formula, FromReferenceStyle, [ToReferenceStyle], [ToAbsolute], [RelativeTo])

Converts cell references in a formula between the A1 and R1C1 reference styles, between relative and absolute references, or both.

Argument	Description	Settings
Formula	The formula you want to convert.	Must be a valid formula beginning with an equals sign
FromReferenceStyle	The XlReferenceStyle of the formula.	xlA1 xlR1C1
ToReferenceStyle	The XlReferenceStyle style you want returned. If this argument is omitted, the reference style isn't changed; the formula stays in the style specified by *FromReferenceStyle*.	xlA1 xlR1C1
ToAbsolute	The converted XlReferenceStyle. If omitted, the reference type isn't changed. Defaults to xlRelative.	xlAbsolute xlAbsRowRelColumn xlRelRowAbsColumn xlRelative
RelativeTo	The cell that references are relative to. Defaults to active cell.	Range object

The following code converts a formula to R1C1 style relative to cell A1:

```
Sub TestConvertFormula( )
    Dim str As String
    str = "=Sum(A1:A20)"
    Debug.Print Application.ConvertFormula(str, xlA1, xlR1C1, _
        xlRelative, [a1])
End Sub
```

Application.CopyObjectsWithCells [= *setting*]

True copies objects, such as buttons, with selected cells; False omits objects. Default is True.

Application.Cursor [= XlMousePointer]

Sets or returns the mouse pointer image. Can be one of these settings:

```
xlDefault
xlIBeam
xlNorthwestArrow
xlWait
```

Application.CursorMovement [= setting]

Sets or returns whether a visual cursor or a logical cursor is used. Can be one of these settings:

```
xlVisualCursor
xlLogicalCursor
```

Application.CustomListCount

Returns the number of custom lists. To view custom lists, select Tools → Options → Custom Lists.

Application.CutCopyMode [= setting]

Sets or returns whether or not the user is currently cutting or copying cells. Return settings are:

```
False, Excel is not in either mode
xlCopy
xlCut
```

Setting CutCopyMode to True or False cancels the current mode.

Application.DataEntryMode [= setting]

Sets or returns whether or not Excel is in data-entry mode. Can be one of these settings:

```
xlOn
xlOff
xlStrict, prevents the user from exiting the mode by pressing Esc
```

Data-entry mode restricts users to unlocked cells. By default, cell protection is set to Locked, so you must unlock a range to demonstrate this feature. The following code restricts data entry to range A1:D4; the user can return to regular mode by pressing Esc, as shown by the following code:

```
Sub TestDataEntryMode( )
    Range("a1:d4").Locked = False
    Application.DataEntryMode = xlOn
End Sub
```

Application.DecimalSeparator [= *setting*]

Sets or returns the character used as the decimal separator.

Application.DefaultFilePath [= *setting*]

Sets or returns the path Excel uses by default when opening files.

Application.DefaultSaveFormat [= *XlFileFormat*]

Sets or returns the file format used by Excel when saving. Can be one of these settings:

xlAddIn	xlCSV	xlCSVMac
xlCSVMSDOS	xlCSVWindows	xlCurrentPlatformText
xlDBF2	xlDBF3	xlDBF4
xlDIF	xlExcel2	xlExcel2FarEast
xlExcel3	xlExcel4	xlExcel4Workbook
xlExcel5	xlExcel7	xlExcel9795
xlHtml	xlIntlAddIn	xlIntlMacro
xlSYLK	xlTemplate	xlTextMac
xlTextMSDOS	xlTextPrinter	xlTextWindows
xlUnicodeText	xlWebArchive	xlWJ2WD1
xlWJ3	xlWJ3FJ3	xlWK1
xlWK1ALL	xlWK1FMT	xlWK3
xlWK3FM3	xlWK4	xlWKS
xlWorkbookNormal	xlWorks2FarEast	xlWQ1
xlXMLSpreadsheet		

Application.DefaultSheetDirection [= *setting*]

Sets or returns the default reading direction. Can be one of these settings:

xlRTL
xlLTR

Application.DefaultWebOptions

Returns a `DefaultWebOptions` object that determines how Excel saves workbooks as web pages.

Application.DeleteChartAutoFormat(*Name*)

Removes a custom chart type. The following code removes the custom chart type created earlier in AddChartAutoFormat:

```
Sub TestDeleteChartType( )
    Application.DeleteChartAutoFormat "new custom"
End Sub
```

[Application.]DeleteCustomList(ListNum)

Removes a custom list. The following code removes the list created earlier in AddCustomList:

```
Sub TestDeleteCustomList( )
    ' Delete the last list.
    Application.DeleteCustomList Application.CustomListCount
End Sub
```

Application.Dialogs(*XlBuiltInDialog*)

Returns the collection of Excel's dialog boxes. Use `Dialogs` to display any of the Excel dialog boxes from code. The following code displays the Activate Workbook dialog box:

```
Sub TestDialogs( )
    Application.Dialogs(XlBuiltInDialog.xlDialogActivate).Show
End Sub
```

Excel has hundreds of dialog boxes. See Appendix A for a list of them.

Application.DisplayAlerts [= *setting*]

True displays standard Excel dialogs while a macro runs; False hides those dialogs and automatically uses the default response for each. Default is True.

Set this property to False for batch operations in which you don't want user intervention; be sure to reset the property to True when done. For example, the following code closes all workbooks but the current one without saving or prompting the user:

```
Sub CloseAllNoSave( )
    Dim wb As Workbook
    ' Turn off warnings.
    Application.DisplayAlerts = False
    For Each wb In Workbooks
        ' Close all workbooks but this one.
        If Not (wb Is ThisWorkbook) Then _
            wb.Close
```

```
    Next
    ' Turn warnings back on.
    Application.DisplayAlerts = True
End Sub
```

Application.DisplayClipboardWindow [= *setting*]

True displays the Clipboard window; False hides it. For example, the following code copies
a chart and displays the Clipboard window:

```
Sub TestClipBoardWindow( )
    Dim chrt As Chart
    ' Copy a Chart image into the Clipboard.
    Set chrt = Charts(1)
    chrt.CopyPicture xlScreen, xlBitmap
    Application.DisplayClipboardWindow = True
End Sub
```

Application.DisplayCommentIndicator [=*XlCommentDisplayMode*]

Sets or returns the icon displayed for comments. Can be one of the following settings:

```
xlNoIndicator
xlCommentIndicatorOnly (default)
xlCommentAndIndicator
```

Application.DisplayDocumentActionTaskPane [= *setting*]

For Smart documents, True displays the Document Action task pane, and False hides it.
Setting this property causes an error if the workbook is not a Smart document.

Application.DisplayExcel4Menus [= *setting*]

True uses Excel Version 4.0 menus; False uses the current version menus. Default is False.

Application.DisplayFormulaBar [= *setting*]

True displays the Formula bar; False hides it. Default is True.

Application.DisplayFullScreen [= *setting*]

True displays Excel in full-screen mode; False uses the standard window mode. Default is
False.

Application.DisplayFunctionToolTips [= *setting*]

True displays the function tool tips; False does not. Default is True.

Application.DisplayInsertOptions [= *setting*]

True displays a dialog with special options, such as Clear Formatting, when inserting cells; False does not display the dialog. Default is True.

Application.DisplayNoteIndicator [= *setting*]

True displays an icon indicating cells with notes; False hides the icon. Default is True.

Application.DisplayPasteOptions [= *setting*]

True displays a dialog with special options when pasting cells; False does not display the dialog. Default is True.

Application.DisplayRecentFiles [= *setting*]

True displays a list of recently opened files on the File menu; False does not. Default is True.

Application.DisplayScrollBars [= *setting*]

True displays scrollbars for workbooks; False does not. Default is True.

Application.DisplayStatusBar [= *setting*]

True displays application status bar; False does not. Default is True.

Application.DisplayXMLSourcePane([*XmlMap*])

(Excel 2003 Professional Edition only.) Displays the XML Source task pane.

Argument	Setting
XmlMap	The XmlMap object to display in the task pane

Application.DoubleClick( )

Double-clicks the active cell. This method emulates the user action.

Application.EditDirectlyInCell [= *setting*]

True allows editing in cells; False requires edits to be made in the Formula bar. Default is True.

Application.EnableAnimations [= *setting*]

True animates insertions and deletions; False does not animate those operations. Default is True.

[Application.]EnableAutoComplete [= *setting*]

True automatically completes words; False does not. Default is True.

Application.EnableCancelKey [= *XlEnableCancelKey*]

Sets or returns how Excel handles the Esc, Ctrl-Break, and Command-Period (Macintosh) keys. Can be one of these settings:

xlDisabled
    Cancel key trapping disabled.

xlErrorHandler
    Cancel key causes error 18, which can be trapped by an On Error statement.

xlInterrupt
    Cancel interrupts the current procedure, and the user can debug or end it (default).

Application.EnableEvents [= *setting*]

True turns on Excel events; False turns off Excel events. Default is True. Setting this property to False prevents code written for Workbook, Worksheet, and other object events from running.

Application.EnableSound [= *setting*]

True allows Excel to play sounds; False disables sounds. Default is True.

Application.ErrorCheckingOptions

Returns the ErrorCheckingOptions object, which controls Excel's settings for automatic error checking.

[Application.]Evaluate(*Name*)

Evaluates an expression and returns the result. Evaluate is equivalent to enclosing the expression in square brackets ([ ]).

Argument	Setting
Name	A range address, a named range, or a formula

It is common to use the bracket notation for the Evaluate method since it is shorter. The following code displays various values from the active sheet:

```
Sub TestEvaluate()
    ' Show value of cell A1.
    Debug.Print [a1]
    ' Show total of A1:A3.
    Debug.Print [sum(a1:a3)]
    ' Show table of named ranges
    Dim n As Name, str As String
    Debug.Print "Name", "# w/data", "Address"
    For Each n In Names
        str = "Count(" & n.Name & ")"
        Debug.Print n.Name, Evaluate(str), [n]
    Next
End Sub
```

Using the bracket notation with a Name object returns the address of the name.

Application.ExtendList [= *setting*]

True extends formatting and formulas to new data added to a custom list; False does not. Default is True.

Application.FeatureInstall [= *MsoFeatureInstall*]

Determines how to handle calls to methods and properties that require features that aren't yet installed. Can be one of these settings:

msoFeatureInstallNone
   Doesn't install; causes an error when uninstalled features is called (default)

msoFeatureInstallOnDemand
   Prompts the user to install feature

msoFeatureInstallOnDemandWithU
   Automatically installs the feature; doesn't prompt the user

Application.FileConverters[(*Index1*, *Index2*)]

Returns an array of installed file converters.

Argument	Setting
Index1	The full name of the converter including file type
Index2	The path of the converter's DLL

If arguments are omitted, FileConverters returns Null if there are no converters or a two-dimensional array containing the name, DLL path, and extension for each converter. The following code displays a table of the installed converters:

```
Sub TestFileConverters()
    Dim cnv As Variant, i As Integer
    cnv = Application.FileConverters
    ' Display table columns
    Debug.Print "Name", "DLL", "Extension"
    ' Check if converters are installed
    If Not IsNull(cnv) Then
        For i = 1 To UBound(cnv, 1)
            Debug.Print cnv(i, 1), cnv(i, 2), cnv(i, 3)
        Next
    Else
        Debug.Print "No converters installed."
    End If
End Sub
```

Application.FileDialog (*MsoFileDialogType*)

Returns the FileDialog object.

Argument	Description	Settings
MsoFileDialogType	Determines which Excel dialog to return	msoFileDialogFilePicker msoFileDialogFolderPicker msoFileDialogOpen msoFileDialogSaveAs

The following code displays the file picker dialog box and lets the user select a text file to open in Notepad:

```
Sub TestFileDialog()
    Dim fname As String
    With Application.FileDialog(msoFileDialogFilePicker)
        .AllowMultiSelect = False
        .Filters.Add "Text files (*.txt)", "*.txt", 1
        .FilterIndex = 1
        .Title = "Open text file"
        If .Show = True Then _
            Shell "notepad.exe " & .SelectedItems(1)
    End With
End Sub
```

Application.FileFind

(Macintosh only.) Returns the `FileFind` object. The following code displays all of the files by Jeff:

```
Sub TestFind( ) ' Macintosh only
    Dim s
    With Application.FileFind
        .Author = "Jeff"
        .Execute
        For Each s In .Results
            Debug.Print s
        Next
    End With
End Sub
```

Application.FileSearch

(Windows only.) Returns the `FileSearch` object. The following code displays all of the text files in the current folder:

```
Sub TestSearch( ) ' Windows only
    Dim s
    With Application.FileSearch
        .LookIn = ThisWorkbook.Path
        .Filename = ".txt"
        .Execute
        For Each s In .FoundFiles
            Debug.Print s
        Next
    End With
End Sub
```

Application.FindFile( )

Displays the Open File dialog box and opens the selected file in Excel.

Application.FindFormat

Returns the `CellFormat` object used by the `Find` method. For example, the following code selects the first bold cell on the active worksheet:

```
Sub TestFindFormat( )
    With Application.FindFormat
        .Font.Bold = True
    End With
    Cells.Find("", , , , , , , , True).Select
End Sub
```

Application.FixedDecimal [= *setting*]

True assumes a fixed decimal place for data entries; False assumes each entry has a variable decimal place. Default is False.

Application.FixedDecimalPlaces [= *setting*]

Sets the placement of the decimal assumed during data entry. Default is 2. The following code configures Excel to treat the entry 1000 as 0.1, 45000 as 4.5, and so on:

```
Sub TestDecimal()
    ' Turn on fixed decimal.
    Application.FixedDecimal = True
    ' Set the decimal place.
    Application.FixedDecimalPlaces = 4
End Sub
```

Application.GenerateGetPivotData [= *setting*]

True turns the GenerateGetPivotData command on; False turns the command off. The GenerateGetPivotData command substitutes cell references for GETPIVOTDATA worksheet functions in formulas.

Application.GetCustomListContents

Returns an array of items from a custom list. For example, the following code displays all of the items in each of the custom lists:

```
Sub TestListContent()
    Dim i As Integer, lst(), str As String, num As Integer
    Debug.Print "List Number", "Contents"
    For i = 1 To Application.CustomListCount
        lst = Application.GetCustomListContents(i)
        str = Join(lst, ", ")
        num = Application.GetCustomListNum(lst)
        Debug.Print num, str
    Next
End Sub
```

Application.GetCustomListNum(*ListArray*)

Returns the index of a custom list.

Argument	Setting
ListArray	The array of custom list items to look up.

Application.GetOpenFilename([*FileFilter*], [*FilterIndex*], [*Title*], [*ButtonText*], [*MultiSelect*])

Displays the Open File dialog box and returns a filename or False if no file is selected. Does not open the file.

Argument	Setting
FileFilter	A filter to use in the drop-down list on the dialog box. Each filter is a pair separated by a comma: *DisplayString*, *Type*. See the following example.
FilterIndex	The index of the filter to display initially.
Title	The caption for the dialog box. Default is Open.
ButtonText	(Macintosh only.) The caption to show on the action button. Default is Open.
MultiSelect	True allows the user to select multiple files.

The following code displays the File Open dialog box for web file types; if the user selects a file, the code opens the file in Notepad:

```
Sub TestGetOpen( )
    Dim fname As String, fltr As String
    fltr = "Web page (*.htm),*.htm,XML data (*.xml),*.xml," & _
      "XML Style Sheet (*.xsl),*.xsl"
    fname = Application.GetOpenFilename(fltr, _
      1, "Open web file", , False)
    If fname <> "False" Then _
        Shell "Notepad.exe " & fname
End Sub
```

Application.GetPhonetic([*Text*])

Returns the Japanese phonetic text of a string. Available only with Japanese language support.

Application.GetSaveAsFilename([*InitialFilename*], [*FileFilter*], [*FilterIndex*], [*Title*], [*ButtonText*])

Displays the Save File As dialog box and returns a filename or False if no file is selected. Does not save the file.

Argument	Setting
InitialFileName	The name to display in the File text box
Other arguments	See "Application.GetOpenFilename"

The following code saves the active workbook as a web page, closes the newly saved file, and reopens the original workbook in XLS format:

```
Sub TestGetSaveAs( )
    Dim fname1 As String, fname2 As String, fname3 As String
```

```
    Dim fltr As String
    ' Save changes
    ActiveWorkbook.Save
    ' Get current filename.
    fname1 = ActiveWorkbook.Name
    ' Get filename for web page.
    fname2 = Replace(fname1, "xls", "htm")
    fltr = "Web page (*.htm),*.htm,XML data (*.xml),*.xml," & _
      "XML Style Sheet (*.xsl),*.xsl"
    ' Show the Save As dialog.
    fname3 = Application.GetSaveAsFilename(fname2, fltr, _
      1, "Export to web")
    ' If not cancelled, save the file as a web page.
    If fname3 <> "False" Then _
        ActiveWorkbook.SaveAs fname3, xlHtml
    ' Reopen the original file.
    Workbooks.Open fname1
    ' Close the web page file.
    Workbooks(fname2).Close
End Sub
```

Application.Goto([*Reference*], [*Scroll*])

Selects a range of cells and activates the sheet containing the cells.

Argument	Setting
Reference	A range, named range, or string that evaluates to one of those.
Scroll	True scrolls the sheet so that the selection is in the upper-left corner.

Goto is similar to Select, except Select does not activate the sheet.

Application.Height

Returns the height of the Excel window in pixels. Use the WindowState property to maximize window or minimize Excel.

Application.Help([*HelpFile*], [*HelpContextID*])

Displays a help topic in Excel's Help window.

Argument	Setting
HelpFile	The file to display. Can be compiled Help (*.chm* or *.hlp*) or a web page (*.htm*). Defaults to the Excel help file.
HelpContextID	For compiled help files, the numeric ID of the topic to display. Ignored for web pages.

See Chapter 6 for details on creating and displaying Help. The following code displays an error message help page in the Help window:

```
Sub TestApplicationHelp( )
    ' Display Help in Help window.
    Application.Help ("http://excelworkshop.com/Help/error51.htm")
End Sub
```

Application.Hinstance

Returns a handle to the Excel application instance.

Application.Hwnd

Returns a handle to the top-level Excel window. You use handles with the Windows API to do low-level tasks not available through Excel objects. For example, the following code displays the Excel always on top of all other windows, even if Excel doesn't have focus:

```
Declare Function SetWindowPos Lib "user32" (ByVal hwnd As Long, _
    ByVal hWndInsertAfter As Long, ByVal x As Long, ByVal y As Long, _
    ByVal cx As Long, ByVal cy As Long, ByVal wFlags As Long) As Long
Const SWP_NOSIZE = &H1
Const SWP_NOMOVE = &H2
Const HWND_TOPMOST = -1
Const HWND_NOTOPMOST = -2

Sub TestShowXLOnTop( )
    ' Change to False to return to normal.
    ShowXLOnTop True
End Sub

Public Function ShowXLOnTop(ontop As Boolean)
    Dim hXl As Long, setting As Long
    If ontop Then setting = HWND_TOPMOST _
      Else setting = HWND_NOTOPMOST
    hXl = Application.hwnd
    SetWindowPos hXl, setting, 0, 0, _
      0, 0, SWP_NOSIZE Or SWP_NOMOVE
End Sub
```

Application.InchesToPoints(*Inches*)

Converts a measurement from inches to points. This is the same a multiplying the value by 72.

[Application.]InputBox(*Prompt*, [*Title*], [*Default*], [*Left*], [*Top*], [*HelpFile*], [*HelpContextID*], [*Type*])

This is the same as the Visual Basic InputBox method with one addition: Application.InputBox allows you to get a selected range using the *Type* argument which accepts the settings in the following table:

Setting	Input is
0	A formula
1	A number
2	Text (a string)
4	A logical value (True or False)
8	A cell reference, as a Range object
16	An error value, such as #N/A
64	An array of values

The following code demonstrates getting a range using InputBox:

```
Sub TestInputBox()
    Dim rng As Range
    On Error Resume Next
    Set rng = Application.InputBox( _
      "Select a cell", , , , , , , 8)
    If Not (rng Is Nothing) Then
        Debug.Print rng.Count & " cells selected."
    Else
        Debug.Print "Input cancelled."
    End If
End Sub
```

See Chapter 3 for details on the Visual Basic InputBox method.

Application.Interactive [= *setting*]

True allows users to interact with Excel; False prevents user actions. Set the Interactive property to False to prevent user actions while performing time-consuming operations in code. Be sure to set Interactive back to True when done.

Application.International(*XlApplicationInternational*)

Returns an array of locale settings. XlApplicationInternational can be one of the settings from the following table:

Category	Setting	Returns
Cell references	xlLeftBrace	Character used instead of the left brace ({) in array literals.
	xlLeftBracket	Character used instead of the left bracket ([) in R1C1-style relative references.
	xlLowerCaseColumnLetter	Lowercase column letter.
	xlLowerCaseRowLetter	Lowercase row letter.
	xlRightBrace	Character used instead of the right brace (}) in array literals.
	xlRightBracket	Character used instead of the right bracket (]) in R1C1-style references.

Category	Setting	Returns
	xlUpperCaseColumnLetter	Uppercase column letter.
	xlUpperCaseRowLetter	Uppercase row letter (for R1C1-style references).
Country/Region	xlCountryCode	Excel country/region version setting.
	xlCountrySetting	Windows country/region setting.
	xlGeneralFormatName	Name of the General number format.
Currency	xlCurrencyBefore	True if the currency symbol precedes the currency values; False if it follows them.
	xlCurrencyCode	Currency symbol.
	xlCurrencyDigits	Number of decimal digits to be used in currency formats.
	xlCurrencyLeadingZeros	True if leading zeros are displayed for zero currency values.
	xlCurrencyMinusSign	True if a minus sign indicates negative numbers; False if using parentheses.
	xlCurrencyNegative	Currency format for negative currency values: • 0, parentheses, ($nnn) or (nnn$) • 1, minus before, -$nnn or -nnn$ • 2, minus mid, $-nnn or nnn-$ • 3, minus after, $nnn- or nnn$-
	xlCurrencySpaceBefore	True adds a space before the currency symbol.
	xlCurrencyTrailingZeros	True displays trailing zeros for zero currency values.
	xlNoncurrencyDigits	Number of decimal digits to be used in noncurrency formats.
Date and Time	xl24HourClock	True uses 24-hour time; False uses 12-hour time.
	xl4DigitYears	True uses four-digit years; False uses two-digit years.
	xlDateOrder	Order of date elements: • 0, month-day-year • 1, day-month-year • 2, year-month-day
	xlDateSeparator	Date separator (/).
	xlDayCode	Day symbol (d).
	xlDayLeadingZero	True includes leading zero in days.
	xlHourCode	Hour symbol (h).
	xlMDY	True orders dates month-day-year in the long form; False orders dates day-month-year.
	xlMinuteCode	Minute symbol (m).
	xlMonthCode	Month symbol (m).
	xlMonthLeadingZero	True includes leading zero in months displayed as numbers.
	xlMonthNameChars	Obsolete, always returns 3.
	xlSecondCode	Second symbol (s).
	xlTimeLeadingZero	True includes leading zero in times.

Category	Setting	Returns
	xlTimeSeparator	Time separator (:)
	xlWeekdayNameChars	Obsolete, always returns 3.
	xlYearCode	Year symbol in number formats (y).
Measurement	xlMetric	True is metric system in use; False if the English measurement system is in use.
	xlNonEnglishFunctions	True if functions are not displayed in English.
Separators	xlAlternateArraySeparator	Alternate array item separator to be used if the current array separator is the same as the decimal separator.
	xlColumnSeparator	Character used to separate columns in array literals.
	xlDecimalSeparator	Decimal separator.
	xlListSeparator	List separator.
	xlRowSeparator	Character used to separate rows in array literals.
	xlThousandsSeparator	Zero or thousands separator.

[Application.]Intersect(*Arg1*, *Arg2*, [*Argn*], ...)

Returns the Range object containing the overlapping region of the ranges *Arg1* through *Argn*.

Argument	Setting
Arg1	The first Range object to intersect
Arg2	The second Range object to intersect
Argn	Any number of additional Range objects to intersect

Application.Iteration [= *setting*]

True uses iteration to calculate formulas that refer to themselves (this is called a *circular reference*); False causes an error for circular references. Default is False. Use the MaxChange and MaxIterations properties to control how many calculations are performed during iteration.

Application.LanguageSettings

Returns a LanguageSettings object containing information about the user's locale.

Application.LargeButtons [= *setting*]

True displays large toolbar buttons; False displays regular-size buttons. Default is False.

Application.Left [= *setting*]

Sets or returns the distance between the left edge of the screen and the left edge of the Excel window in pixels.

Application.LibraryPath

Returns the path to the Excel add-in library, for example *C:\Program Files\Microsoft Office\ OFFICE11\LIBRARY*.

Application.MacroOptions([Macro], [Description], [HasMenu], [MenuText], [HasShortcutKey], [ShortcutKey], [Category], [StatusBar], [HelpContextId], [HelpFile])

Sets the description and help files displayed for a macro or user-defined function.

Argument	Setting
Macro	The name of the macro to set.
Description	A description that appears in the Macro or Formula dialog box.
HasMenu	Ignored.
MenuText	Ignored.
HasShortcutKey	True assigns a shortcut key to the macro.
ShortcutKey	The shortcut key to assign.
Category	The name of a category for the user-defined function. Default is User Defined.
StatusBar	Ignored.
HelpContextId	The context ID for the help topic within the compiled help file. Ignored for other help file types.
HelpFile	The name of the help file to display for user-defined functions.

The usable arguments are different for macros (Subs) and user-defined functions (Functions). The Macro dialog box doesn't use *Category*, *HelpContextId*, or *HelpFile* arguments. The Insert Function dialog box doesn't use *HasShortcutKey* or *ShortcutKey* arguments.

The following code sets the options for the ShowXlOnTop user-defined function:

```
Sub TestMacroOptions()
    Application.MacroOptions "ShowXlOnTop", _
      "Set Excel as the top-most window.", , , , , _
      "Windows", "Excel On Top", , _
      "http:\\excelworkshop.com\Help\ch07.htm"
End Sub
```

After this code runs, Excel displays the options on the Insert Function dialog as shown in Figure 7-3.

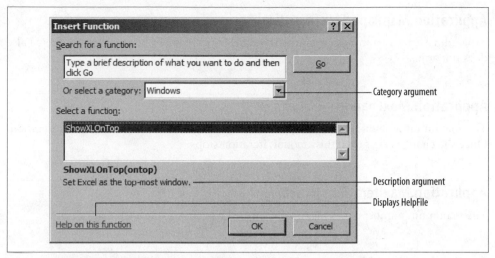

Figure 7-3. How Excel displays macro options for user-defined functions

Application.MailLogoff( )

Ends a MAPI mail session.

Application.MailLogon([*Name*], [*Password*], [*DownloadNewMail*])

Closes any existing MAPI sessions and creates a new one, starting the Microsoft Mail spooler. Returns True if Mail is started successfully, False if not.

Argument	Setting
Name	The username for the mail session.
Password	User password.
DownloadNewMail	True downloads new mail immediately. Default is False.

Application.MailSession

Returns the MAPI session number begun by Excel. Returns Null if there is no session.

Application.MailSystem

Returns the XlMailSystem setting indicating the users installed mail system. Can be one of these settings:

    xlMAPI
    xlNoMailSystem
    xlPowerTalk

Application.MapPaperSize [= *setting*]

True adjusts printing to map from the standard paper size of one locale to another; False does not adjust.

Application.MaxChange [= *setting*]

The maximum amount of change allowed in resolving circular references using iteration. Once the change is less than this amount, iteration stops.

Application.MaxIterations [= *setting*]

The maximum number of calculations performed when resolving a circular reference.

Application.MoveAfterReturn [= *setting*]

True activates the next cell after the user presses Enter; False keeps the current cell active. Default is True.

Application.MoveAfterReturnDirection [=*XlDirection*]

Sets or returns which cell is activated after the user presses Enter. Can be one of these settings:

    xlDown (default)
    xlToLeft
    xlToRight
    xlUp

Application.Names([*index*])

Returns the collection of named ranges in the active workbook. The following code displays a table of named ranges:

```
Sub TestNames( )
    Dim n As Name
    Debug.Print "Name", "Address"
    For Each n In Names
        Debug.Print n.Name, n.RefersTo
    Next
End Sub
```

Application.NetworkTemplatesPath

Returns the AltStartupPath property if that setting is a network share. Otherwise, returns an empty string.

Application.NewWorkbook

Returns an Office `NewFile` object that represents an item on the New Workbook task pane. You can use this object to add or remove items from the task pane. For example, the following code adds the Invoice template and displays the task pane:

```
Sub TestNewWorkbook( )
    With Application.NewWorkbook
      .Add "Invoice.xlt", _
        MsoFileNewSection.msoNewfromTemplate, _
        "New Invoice", MsoFileNewAction.msoCreateNewFile
    End With
    Application.CommandBars("Task Pane").Visible = True
End Sub
```

See the Office VBA help file (*VBAOF11.CHM*) for information about the `NewFile` object.

Application.NextLetter( )

(Macintosh with PowerTalk mail only.) Opens the next unread mail message in the In Tray.

Application.ODBCErrors

Returns the `ODBCErrors` collection generated by the most recent query table or PivotTable report.

Application.ODBCTimeout [= *setting*]

Sets or returns the time limit for ODBC queries. Default is 45 seconds.

Application.OLEDBErrors

Returns the `OLEDBErrors` collection generated by the most recent OLE DB query.

Application.OnKey(*Key*, [*Procedure*])

Assigns a macro to run when a key is pressed. Can also be used to disable built-in Excel key combinations.

Argument	Setting
Key	The key combination to assign. The character codes are the same as for `SendKeys`. See Chapter 3 for the `SendKeys` codes.
Procedure	The name of the macro to run. Setting to "" disables any built-in action for those keys; omitting this argument restores the built-in action.

The following code demonstrates how to reassign, disable, and restore a built-in key assignment:

```
Sub TestOnKey()
    ' Reassign Ctrl+C
    Application.OnKey "^c", "CopyMsg"
    ' Disable Ctrl+C
    'Application.OnKey "^c", ""
    ' Restore Ctrl+C
    ' Application.OnKey "^c"
End Sub

Sub CopyMsg()
    MsgBox "You can't copy right now."
End Sub
```

Application.OnRepeat(*Text, Procedure*)

Reassigns the Repeat item on the Edit menu (Ctrl-Y).

Argument	Setting
Text	The text to display instead of Repeat…
Procedure	The procedure to run when the user chooses Edit → Repeat or presses Ctrl-Y.

The following code replaces the Repeat item on the Edit menu with the item Do Over and runs the DoOver procedure with the user selects the item:

```
Sub TestOnRepeat()
    Application.OnRepeat "Do over", "DoOver"
End Sub
```

Application.OnTime(*EarliestTime, Procedure, [LatestTime], [Schedule]*)

Sets the name of a procedure to run at a specified time.

Argument	Setting
EarliestTime	The earliest time you want to run the procedure.
Procedure	The name of the procedure to run.
LatestTime	The latest time you want to run the procedure. Default is no limit.
Schedule	True schedules the procedure to run; False removes the procedure from the schedule to run. Default is True.

Application.OnUndo(*Text, Procedure*)

Reassigns the Undo item on the Edit menu (Ctrl-Z). The arguments are the same as for OnRepeat.

Application.OnWindow [= *setting*]

Sets or returns a procedure to run when a window is activated.

Application.OperatingSystem

Returns the name, version, and address model of the operating system. For example, "Windows (32-bit) NT 5.01" indicates Windows XP Professional.

Application.OrganizationName

Returns the name of the user's organization as entered during installation.

Application.Path

Returns the path to the folder where Excel is installed.

Application.PathSeparator

Returns "\" in Windows and ":" on the Macintosh.

Application.PivotTableSelection [= *setting*]

True enables structured selection PivotTable reports; False disables. Default is False.

Application.PreviousSelections([*index*])

Returns one of the four last-selected ranges entered in the Go To dialog box.

Application.ProductCode

Returns the programmatic ID (ProgId) of Excel. This value is a globally unique identifier (GUID) used in Windows programming.

Application.PromptForSummaryInfo [= *setting*]

True prompts the user for the workbook properties when files are first saved; False does not prompt. Default is False.

Application.Quit( )

Exits Excel. Excel prompts to save changes before closing unless `DisplayAlerts` is set to False or the workbook's Saved property is set to True.

[Application.]Range([*cell1*],[*cell2*])

Returns a range of cells.

Argument	Setting
cell1	The upper-left corner of the range
cell2	The lower-right corner of the range

The three ways to specify the Range method are cell references, strings, or brackets. The following three lines all select the same range:

```
Range(Cells(1, 1), Cells(3, 3)).Select
Range("A1", "C3").Select
[A1:C3].Select
```

Application.Ready

Returns True if Excel is ready for input, False otherwise. Excel is not "ready" while a user is editing a cell (edit mode) or when a dialog box is displayed. In those situations, macros must wait to run.

Application.RecentFiles([*index*])

Returns the RecentFiles collection. RecentFiles represents the list of recently used files displayed at the bottom of the File menu. For example, the following code displays the path- and filenames for each file in the Recent Files list:

```
Sub TestRecentFiles( )
    Dim f As RecentFile
    For Each f In Application.RecentFiles
        Debug.Print f.Path
    Next
End Sub
```

Application.RecordMacro([*BasicCode*], [*XlmCode*])

Sets the code for Excel to record if the user selects Tools → Macro → Record New Macro and then performs a task that runs this macro.

Argument	Setting
BasicCode	The string to record in place of the default
XlmCode	Obsolete

By default, Excel records `Application.Run` "*workbook!macro*" whenever a user runs a macro while recording. To prevent recording, set *BasicCode* to "" for the macro:

```
Sub SecretMacro( )
    ' Don't record this!
    Application.RecordMacro ""
    ' Secret stuff...
End Sub
```

Application.RecordRelative [= *setting*]

True uses relative references when recording; False uses absolute references. Default is False.

Application.ReferenceStyle [=*XlReferenceStyle*]

Sets or returns the style Excel uses to refer to cells. Can be one of these settings:

```
xlA1
xlR1C1
```

Application.RegisteredFunctions

Returns an array of DLL functions registered with Excel. The following code displays a list of the registered functions:

```
Sub TestRegisteredFunctions( )
    Dim i As Integer, func
    func = Application.RegisteredFunctions
    Debug.Print "DLL", "Function", "Arguments/Return type"
    If Not IsNull(func) Then
        For i = 1 To UBound(func, 1)
          Debug.Print func(i, 1), func(i, 2), func(i, 3)
        Next
    Else
     Debug.Print "No functions registered."
    End If
End Sub
```

Application.RegisterXLL(*Filename*)

Loads an Excel DLL (XLL) and registers it.

Argument	Setting
Filename	The name of the file to register

Application.Repeat( )

Repeats the last user action.

Application.ReplaceFormat [= *setting*]

Sets or returns the CellFormat object used when reformatting during search and replace. For example, the following code replaces all bold with italic:

```
Sub TestReplaceFormat( )
    Dim fBold As CellFormat, fItal As CellFormat
    Set fBold = Application.FindFormat
    Set fItal = Application.ReplaceFormat
    fBold.Font.Bold = True
    fItal.Font.Bold = False
    fItal.Font.Italic = True
    Cells.Replace "", "", , , , , True, True
End Sub
```

Application.RollZoom [= *setting*]

True sets the IntelliMouse wheel to zoom the display rather than scroll it; False sets the wheel to scroll. Default is False.

[Application.]Rows([*index*])

Returns a range containing the cells in a row on the active worksheet. For example, the following code selects row 3:

```
Rows(3).Select
```

Application.RTD

Returns a real-time data object.

Application.Run([*Macro*], [*Args*])

Runs a macro.

Argument	Setting
Macro	The name of the macro to run
Args	Arguments for the macro

This method is mainly used by Excel itself when recording user actions that run macros. However, you can also use it to run automated tests during development.

Application.SaveWorkspace([*Filename*])

Saves the current settings as an Excel workspace file.

Argument	Setting
Filename	The name of the file to save. Default is *RESUME.XLW*.

Excel workspace files include the open documents, window placement, and other settings that are restored when the user opens the file. Don't confuse this with shared workspaces, which is a way to share a workbook with others through SharePoint.

Application.ScreenUpdating [= *setting*]

True updates the Excel display as tasks are performed; False hides updates. Default is True. Setting ScreenUpdating to False speeds up lengthy operations, such as changing all the cells on a worksheet. Be sure to set this property back to True when done.

Application.Selection

Returns the currently selected objects on the active worksheet. Returns Nothing if no objects are selected. Use the Select method to set the selection, and use TypeName to discover the kind of object that is selected. The following code displays information about the current selection:

```
Sub TestSelection( )
    Dim str As String
    Select Case TypeName(Selection)
    Case "Nothing"
        str = "Please select something."
    Case "Range"
        str = "You selected the range: " & Selection.Address
    Case "Picture"
        str = "You selected a picture."
    Case Else
        str = "You selected a " & TypeName(Selection) & "."
    End Select
    MsgBox str
End Sub
```

Application.SendKeys(*Keys*, [*Wait*])

This method is the same as the Visual Basic SendKeys method. See Chapter 3 for details.

Application.SetDefaultChart([*FormatName*], [*Gallery*])

Sets the default chart type used by Excel.

Argument	Setting
FormatName	Can be one of the XlChartType constants, xlBuiltIn, or the name of a custom chart type
Gallery	Not used

For example, the following code sets the default chart type to a 3-D style:

```
Sub TestSetChartType( )
    Application.SetDefaultChart XlChartType.xl3DArea
End Sub
```

[Application.]Sheets([index])

Returns the Worksheet and Chart objects in the active workbook. Sheets is a mixed collection, so you can't count on every item being a specific type. Instead, you must test check the TypeName before calling methods on the object, as shown by the following code:

```
Sub TestSheet( )
    Dim itm As Object, ws As Worksheet, ct As Chart
    For Each itm In Sheets
        Select Case TypeName(itm)
            Case "Worksheet"
                Set ws = itm
                Debug.Print ws.UsedRange.Address
            Case "Chart"
                Set ct = itm
                If ct.HasTitle Then _
                    Debug.Print ct.ChartTitle
            Case Else
                Debug.Print TypeName(itm)
        End Select
    Next
End Sub
```

Use the Worksheets or Charts method to get those specific object types.

Application.SheetsInNewWorkbook [= *setting*]

Gets or sets the number of worksheets automatically included in new workbooks. Default is 3.

Application.ShowChartTipNames [= *setting*]

True shows the names of items on a chart as tool tips; False hides the names. Default is True.

Application.ShowChartTipValues [= *setting*]

True includes the values of series points in the tool tips displayed on a chart; False hides the values. Default is True.

Application.ShowStartupDialog [= *setting*]

True displays the New Workbook task pane when the user chooses File → New; False creates the workbook without displaying the task pane. Default is True.

Application.ShowToolTips [= *setting*]

True displays pop-up tool tips when the mouse pointer pauses over a toolbar button; False does not display tool tips. Default is True.

Application.ShowWindowsInTaskbar [= *setting*]

True displays each open workbook as a separate instance of Excel with its own item on the Windows task bar; False collects all workbooks into a single instance of Excel with only one task bar item. Default is True.

ShowWindowsInTaskbar affects only how Excel appears in Windows. It doesn't affect how much memory it uses or the number of processes running for Excel.

Application.SmartTagRecognizers

Returns a collection of SmartTagRecognizer objects.

Application.Speech

Returns a Speech object that can be used to say words. Using Speech causes an error if the feature is not installed. The following code tries to say "Hazelnootpasta":

```
Sub TestSpeech( )
    On Error Resume Next
    Application.Speech.Speak "Hazelnootpasta"
    If Err Then MsgBox "Speech not installed."
End Sub
```

Application.SpellingOptions

Returns a SpellingOptions object that you can use to control how Excel performs spellchecking. The following code displays the main spelling option settings:

```
Sub TestSpellingOptions( )
    With Application.SpellingOptions
        Debug.Print .DictLang
        Debug.Print .IgnoreCaps
        Debug.Print .IgnoreMixedDigits
        Debug.Print .IgnoreFileNames
        Debug.Print .SuggestMainOnly
    End With
End Sub
```

Application.StandardFont [= *setting*]

Sets or returns the standard font name. For Windows, the default is Arial.

Application.StandardFontSize [= *setting*]

Sets or returns the standard font point size. For Windows, the default is 10.

Application.StartupPath

Returns the path to the XLSTART directory.

Application.StatusBar [= *setting*]

Sets or returns the text in the Excel status bar.

Application.TemplatesPath

Returns the path to the user's Templates folder.

Application.ThisCell

Returns the Range object of the cell calling the current user-defined function.

Application.ThisWorkbook

Returns the Workbook object of the Excel file that contains the current procedure. ThisWorkbook is different from ActiveWorkbook in that ActiveWorkbook changes based on the current selection, whereas ThisWorkbook always refers to the file that contains the running code.

Application.ThousandsSeparator [= *setting*]

Sets or returns the character used to separate thousands.

Application.Top [= *setting*]

Sets or returns the distance between the top of the Excel window and the top of the screen.

Application.Undo( )

Cancels the last user action.

[Application.]Union(*Arg1*, *Arg2*, [*Argn*])

Joins two or more Range objects into a single Range.

Argument	Setting
Arg1	The first Range object to join
Arg2	The second Range object to join
Argn	Any number of additional Range objects to join

Application.UsableHeight

Returns the maximum height of the usable area of Excel in points. This is the Height minus the title, menu, tool, status bars, and column header.

Application.UsableWidth

Returns the maximum width of the usable area of Excel in points. This is the Width minus the scrollbar and row header.

Application.UsedObjects

Returns a collection of all the objects used in Excel. This code displays the names and types of all the objects currently in use by Excel:

```
Sub TestUsedObjects()
    Dim o, name As String
    On Error Resume Next
    Debug.Print "Type", "Name"
    For Each o In Application.UsedObjects
        name = o.name
        Debug.Print TypeName(o), name
    Next
End Sub
```

Application.UserControl

Returns True if Excel is visible, False if Excel was started programmatically and is not visible. When UserControl is False, Excel quits if there are no references to it.

Application.UserLibraryPath

Returns the path to the user's Addins folder.

Application.UserName [= *setting*]

Sets or returns the user's name.

Application.UseSystemSeparators [= *setting*]

True uses the operating system settings for thousands and decimal separators; False uses the Excel settings. Default is True.

Application.VBE

Returns the VBE object that represents the Visual Basic Editor. The following code displays the Visual Basic Editor:

```
Private Sub cmdViewCode_Click( )
    On Error Resume Next
    Application.VBE.MainWindow.Visible = True
    ' An error occurs if security settings prohibit this.
    If Err Then
        MsgBox "You must change Macro security options " & _
            "before you can view code in this way. " & _
            "Choose Tools>Macro>Security>Trusted Publishers and " & _
            "select Trust access to Visual Basic Project."
    End If
End Sub
```

Application.Version

Returns the Excel version number. For example, Excel 2003 returns 11.0.

Application.Visible [= *setting*]

True if the Excel window is visible; False if it is hidden. When Excel is not visible, it doesn't appear on the task bar, and the only way to close the application may be to use the Task Manager (Ctrl-Delete) in Windows.

Application.Volatile([*Volatile*])

Marks a user-defined function for recalculation whenever any cells on the worksheet are recalculated.

Argument	Setting
Volatile	True causes the function to recalculate when any cell on the worksheet is recalculated; False recalculates only when the input values change. Default is True.

Application.Wait(*Time*)

Pauses Excel.

Argument	Setting
Time	The time to resume Excel

You can specify an interval of time to wait by incrementing Now. The following code uses that technique to create a procedure that pauses for an interval specified in milliseconds (the same as the Windows API Sleep function):

```
Sub TestSleep()
    ' Wait 5 seconds.
    Sleep 5000
    MsgBox "Time's up!"
End Sub

Sub Sleep(milsecs As Long)
    Dim dt As Date
    ' 0.00001 = 1 second in the Date type.
    dt = Now + (milsecs / 100000000)
    Application.Wait (dt)
End Sub
```

Application.Watches([*index*])

Returns a collection of Watch objects that represent items in a Watch window.

Application.Width [= *setting*]

Sets or returns the width of the Excel window in pixels.

Application.Windows([*index*])

Returns a collection of Window objects that represent the windows displayed by Excel.

Application.WindowsForPens

Returns True if Excel is running under Windows for Pen Computing, False otherwise.

Application.WindowState [= *XlWindowState*]

Sets or returns the state of the Excel window. Can be one of these settings:

```
xlMaximized
xlNormal
xlMinimized
```

[Application.]Workbooks([*index*])

Returns a collection of Workbook objects that represent workbooks that are currently open in Excel.

[Application.]WorksheetFunction

Returns the WorksheetFunction object, which is used to access Excel's built-in functions. See Chapter 4 for a description of the available functions.

[Application.]Worksheets([*index*])

Returns a collection containing the Worksheet objects in the active workbook. This is different from the Sheets collection, which returns Worksheet, Chart, and other types of sheet objects.

AutoCorrect Members

The AutoCorrect object has the following members. Key members (shown in **bold**) are covered in the following reference section:

AddReplacement	Application
AutoExpandListRange	CapitalizeNamesOfDays
CorrectCapsLock	CorrectSentenceCap
Creator	**DeleteReplacement**
DisplayAutoCorrectOptions	Parent
ReplacementList	ReplaceText
TwoInitialCapitals	

The AutoCorrect object provides a set of properties that determine how Excel handles automatic correction. Most of the AutoCorrect members are True/False properties that enable or disable specific Auto Correct options. The following code displays a list of the current Auto Correct settings in Excel:

```
Sub ShowAutoCorrectSettings( )
    With Application.AutoCorrect
        Debug.Print .AutoExpandListRange
        Debug.Print .CapitalizeNamesOfDays
        Debug.Print .CorrectCapsLock
        Debug.Print .CorrectSentenceCap
        Debug.Print .DisplayAutoCorrectOptions
        Debug.Print .ReplaceText
        Debug.Print .TwoInitialCapitals
    End With
End Sub
```

These properties correspond to the settings on the AutoCorrect dialog box (Figure 7-4). To see that dialog, choose Tools → AutoCorrect Options.

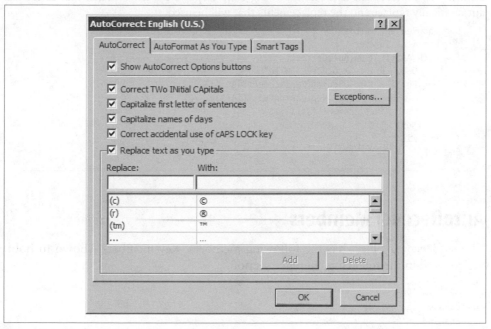

Figure 7-4. Displaying the AutoCorrect options

AutoCorrect.AddReplacement(*What, Replacement*)

Adds an item to the replacement list shown at the bottom of Figure 7-4.

Argument	Setting
What	The typed sequence to automatically correct
Replacement	The correction to use

AutoCorrect.DeleteReplacement(*What*)

Deletes an item from the replacement list.

Argument	Setting
What	The typed sequence to delete from the replacement list

AutoCorrect.ReplacementList

Returns the replacement list. The following code displays the list of items that Excel will automatically replace and the replacements that will be used:

```
Sub ShowReplacementList()
    Dim i As Integer
    With Application.AutoCorrect
        Debug.Print "Replace", "With"
        For i = 1 To UBound(.ReplacementList, 1)
            Debug.Print .ReplacementList(i)(1), _
                .ReplacementList(i)(2)
        Next
    End With
End Sub
```

AutoRecover Members

The AutoRecover object has the following members. Key members (shown in **bold**) are covered in the following reference section:

```
Application
Creator
```
Enabled
```
Parent
```
Path
Time

AutoRecover.Enabled [= *setting*]

True enables automatic recovery; False disables it.

AutoRecover.Path [= *setting*]

Sets or returns the path where Excel stores the files used by automatic recovery.

AutoRecover.Time [= *setting*]

Sets or returns the number of minutes between when automatic recovery files are saved. Must be between 1 and 120. Default is 10.

ErrorChecking Members

The ErrorChecking object has the following members:

Application	BackgroundChecking
Creator	EmptyCellReferences
EvaluateToError	InconsistentFormula
IndicatorColorIndex	ListDataValidation
NumberAsText	OmittedCells
Parent	TextDate
UnlockedFormulaCells	

Most of the ErrorChecking members are True/False properties that enable or disable specific error-checking options. The following code displays a list of the current error-checking settings in Excel:

```
Sub ShowErrorCheckingSettings( )
    With Application.ErrorCheckingOptions
        Debug.Print .BackgroundChecking
        Debug.Print .EmptyCellReferences
        Debug.Print .EvaluateToError
        Debug.Print .InconsistentFormula
        Debug.Print .IndicatorColorIndex
        Debug.Print .ListDataValidation
        Debug.Print .NumberAsText
        Debug.Print .OmittedCells
        Debug.Print .TextDate
        Debug.Print .UnlockedFormulaCells
    End With
End Sub
```

These properties correspond to the settings on the Error Checking dialog box shown in Figure 7-5. To see the dialog, choose Tools → Error Checking → Options.

SpellingOptions Members

The SpellingOptions object has the following members:

ArabicModes	DictLang
GermanPostReform	HebrewModes
IgnoreCaps	IgnoreFileNames
IgnoreMixedDigits	KoreanCombineAux
KoreanProcessCompound	KoreanUseAutoChangeList
SuggestMainOnly	UserDict

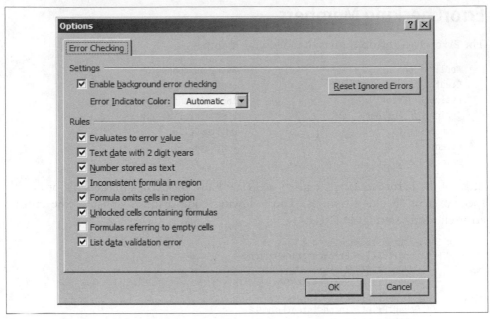

Figure 7-5. Displaying error-checking options

The `SpellingOptions` object provides a set of properties that determine how Excel handles spellchecking. All of the `Spelling` members are read/write properties that enable or disable specific options. The following code displays a list of the current spell-checking settings in Excel:

```
Sub ShowSpellCheckSettings( )
    With Application.SpellingOptions
        Debug.Print .DictLang
        Debug.Print .IgnoreCaps
        Debug.Print .IgnoreMixedDigits
        Debug.Print .SuggestMainOnly
        Debug.Print .UserDict
    End With
End Sub
```

These properties correspond to the settings on the Spelling tab of the Options dialog box (Figure 7-6). To see that dialog, choose Tools → Options → Spelling.

 Language-specific settings in Figure 7-6 are disabled because my selected language is English (U.S.). You must install those language versions of Excel to use those settings.

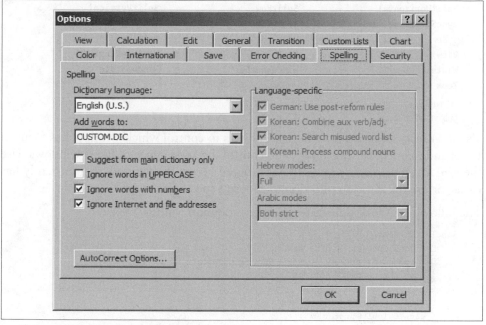

Figure 7-6. Displaying the spellchecking options

Window and Windows Members

The Window object and Windows collection have the following members. Key members (shown in **bold**) are covered in the following reference section:

Activate	**ActivateNext**	**ActivatePrevious**
ActiveCell	ActiveChart	ActivePane
ActiveSheet	Application[2]	**Arrange**[1]
BreakSideBySide[1]	Caption	**Close**
CompareSideBySideWith[1]	Count[1]	Creator[2]
DisplayFormulas	**DisplayGridlines**	**DisplayHeadings**
DisplayHorizontalScrollBar	**DisplayOutline**	**DisplayRightToLeft**
DisplayVerticalScrollBar	**DisplayWorkbookTabs**	**DisplayZeros**
EnableResize	**FreezePanes**	**GridlineColor**
GridlineColorIndex	Height	Index
LargeScroll	Left	Panes
Parent[1]	**PointsToScreenPixelsX**	**PointsToScreenPixelsY**
RangeFromPoint	**RangeSelection**	**ResetPositionsSideBySide**[1]
ScrollColumn	**ScrollIntoView**	**ScrollRow**
ScrollWorkbookTabs	**SelectedSheets**	**Selection**
SmallScroll	**Split**	**SplitColumn**

SplitHorizontal	SplitRow	SplitVertical
SyncScrollingSideBySide[1]	TabRatio	Top
Type	UsableHeight	UsableWidth
View	Visible	**VisibleRange**
Width	**WindowNumber**	**WindowState**
Zoom		

[1] Collection only
[2] Object and collection

Use the Windows collection and Window objects to control which window has focus in Excel and to open, close, arrange, and control the appearance of Excel windows. Use the Application object's ActiveWindow property to get the window that currently has focus, or use the Windows collection to choose a specific window.

The following code demonstrates the most common window tasks:

```
Sub TestWindows()
    Dim i As Integer, wnd As Window
    Dim curWnd As Window, curState As XlWindowState
    ' Save the current settings
    Set curWnd = ActiveWindow
    curState = curWnd.WindowState
    ' Create four new windows.
    For i = 1 To 4
        Set wnd = curWnd.NewWindow
        wnd.Caption = "New Window: " & i
    Next
    ' Cascade the windows.
    Application.Windows.Arrange (xlArrangeStyleCascade)
    ' Activate each in turn.
    For Each wnd In Application.Windows
        wnd.Activate
        ' Wait 1 second.
        API.Sleep (1000)
    Next
    ' Close created windows
    For Each wnd In Application.Windows
        If wnd.Caption Like "New Window: ?" Then wnd.Close
    Next
    ' Restore original window and state.
    curWnd.Activate
    curWnd.WindowState = curState
End Sub
```

window.Activate( )

Sets focus on the window, bringing it to the top.

window.**ActivateNext( )**

Sets focus to the next window in the Excel windows list.

window.**ActivatePrevious( )**

Sets focus to the previous window in the Excel windows list.

windows.**Arrange([*ArrangeStyle*], [*ActiveWorkbook*], [*SyncHorizontal*], [*SyncVertical*])**

Arranges the Excel windows.

Argument	Setting
ArrangeStyle	Can be one of these XlArrangeStyle settings: xlArrangeStyleCascade, xlArrangeStyleTiled (default), xlArrangeStyleHorizontal, xlArrangeStyleVertical.
ActiveWorkbook	True arranges only the windows of the active workbook; False arranges all workbooks. Default is False.
SyncHorizontal	True links the windows so that they scroll together horizontally; False allows independent scrolling. Default is False. Ignored if ActiveWorkbook is not True.
SyncVertical	True links the windows so that they scroll together vertically; False allows independent scrolling. Default is False. Ignored if ActiveWorkbook is not True.

windows.**BreakSideBySide( )**

Ends the side-by-side comparison of two workbooks. See CompareSideBySideWith for details.

window.**Close([*SaveChanges*], [*Filename*], [*RouteWorkbook*])**

Close the window. Closing the last open window for a workbook closes the workbook, so Close has these arguments in the following table that determine what to do in that case:

Argument	Setting
SaveChanges	True saves changes to the workbook; False abandons changes. Prompts the user if omitted.
Filename	The name of the file to save the workbook as; default is the current filename.
RouteWorkbook	If the workbook has a routing slip attached, True routes the workbook to the next recipient; False does not route. Prompts the user if omitted.

windows.CompareSideBySideWith(*WindowName*)

Starts side-by-side comparison between the active window and another window. Side-by-side comparison links the scrolling of the two windows so that you can more easily compare different versions of a workbook. Use BreakSideBySide to turn off this comparison.

The following code demonstrates turning side-by-side comparison on and off. Ordinarily, you would open two existing versions of a workbook, but I create the second version here so that the demonstration is self-contained:

```
Sub TestBeginSideBySide( )
    Dim fpath As String, wnd As Window
    ' Get the window for active workbook.
    Set wnd = Application.ActiveWindow
    ' Get the workbook's full filename.
    fname = ActiveWorkbook.Path & "\" & ActiveWorkbook.name
    ' Change it to a new filename.
    fname = VBA.Replace(fname, ".xls", "_v2.xls")
    ' Save a copy of the workbook.
    ActiveWorkbook.SaveCopyAs fpath
    ' Open the copy (makes the copy the active window).
    Application.Workbooks.Open fname
    ' Turn on side-by-side comparision.
    Application.Windows.CompareSideBySideWith wnd.Caption
End Sub

Sub TestEndSideBySide( )
    ' Turn off side-by-side comparision.
    Application.Windows.BreakSideBySide
End Sub
```

window.DisplayFormulas [= *setting*]

True displays formulas in cells; False displays result of formulas (values). Default is False.

window.DisplayGridlines [= *setting*]

True displays gridlines showing cell boundaries; False hides gridlines. Default is True.

window.DisplayHeadings [= *setting*]

True displays column headings (A, B, C, ...); False hides headings. Default is True.

window.DisplayHorizontalScrollBar [= *setting*]

True displays the horizontal scrollbar; False hides it. Default is True.

window.DisplayOutline [= *setting*]

True displays outlining symbols; False hides them. Default is True. To outline a work-sheet, choose Data → Group and Outline → Auto Outline. The outlining symbols appear to the left of the row numbers.

window.DisplayRightToLeft [= *setting*]

True displays Excel in right-to-left fashion; False displays Excel left-to-right. DisplayRightToLeft is used for locales with left-to-right languages, such as Saudi Arabia.

window.DisplayVerticalScrollBar [= *setting*]

True displays the vertical scrollbar; False hides it. Default is True.

window.DisplayWorkbookTabs [= *setting*]

True displays the sheet tabs at the bottom of the workbook; False hides them. Default is True.

window.DisplayZeros [= *setting*]

True displays zero values as 0 in cells; False hides zero values. Default is True.

window.EnableResize [= *setting*]

True allows the user to resize the window; False prohibits resizing. Default is True. Accessing this property causes an error if WindowState is not xlNormal. The following code prevents the user from changing the active window's size:

```
Sub TestDisableResize()
    If ActiveWindow.WindowState = xlNormal Then _
        ActiveWindow.EnableResize = False
End Sub
```

window.FreezePanes [= *setting*]

True locks panes to prevent horizontal and vertical scrolling; False allows panes to scroll. Default is False.

window.GridlineColor [= *setting*]

Sets or returns the color of gridlines as an RGB color. RGB colors are long integers that you can create using the RGB function or (commonly) by specifying a value in hexadecimal. The following code changes the grid color to red, green, blue, and back to normal:

```
Sub TestGridlineColor()
    ' Change grid color using hexidecimal values.
    ActiveWindow.GridlineColor = &HFF      ' Red
    ' Wait 1 second.
    API.Sleep (1000)
    ActiveWindow.GridlineColor = &HFF00   ' Green
    API.Sleep (1000)
    ActiveWindow.GridlineColor = &HFF0000 ' Blue
    API.Sleep (1000)
    ' Restore the default.
    ActiveWindow.GridlineColorIndex = xlColorIndexAutomatic
End Sub
```

window.GridlineColorIndex [=*xlColorIndexAutomatic*]

Sets or returns the color of the gridlines based on the index into the color palette. Default is xlColorIndexAutomatic.

window.LargeScroll([*Down*], [*Up*], [*ToRight*], [*ToLeft*])

Scrolls the window a number of pages in a given direction. You can combine arguments to scroll diagonally.

Argument	Setting
Down	Number of pages to scroll down
Up	Number of pages to scroll up
ToRight	Number of pages to scroll right
ToLeft	Number of pages to scroll left

window.Panes

Returns the collection of Panes objects for the window. Windows that are not split return one pane.

window.PointsToScreenPixelsX(*Points*)

Converts an application width measurement of points to a screen measurement in pixels. The following code displays the screen dimensions in pixels:

```
Sub TestPointsToPixels()
    Application.DisplayFullScreen = True
```

```
        Debug.Print Application.Windows(1).PointsToScreenPixelsX(Application.Width)
        Debug.Print Application.Windows(1).PointsToScreenPixelsX(Application.Height)
        Application.DisplayFullScreen = False
    End Sub
```

window.PointsToScreenPixelsY(*Points*)

Converts the application height measurement of points to a screen measurement in pixels.

window.RangeFromPoint(*x, y*)

Returns the Range object at the specified *x* and *y* coordinates. Coordinates are in pixels, not points.

window.RangeSelection

Returns a Range object containing the selected cells on the window. RangeSelection is slightly different from Selection, since Selection can include drawing objects as well as ranges.

windows.ResetPositionsSideBySide( )

Restores the side-by-side comparison display after one of the windows is maximized or minimized while the user is doing a comparison.

window.ScrollColumn [= *setting*]

Sets or returns the column number displayed in the leftmost side of the Excel window.

window.ScrollIntoView(*Left, Top, Width, Height,* [*Start*])

Scrolls the window to a rectangular region on the worksheet.

Argument	Setting
Left	The left edge of the rectangle in points.
Top	The top edge of the rectangle in points.
Width	The width of the rectangle in points.
Height	The height of the rectangle in points.
Start	True scrolls the upper-left corner of the rectangle to the upper-left corner of the window; False scrolls the lower-right corner of the rectangle to the lower-right corner of the window. Default value is True.

window.ScrollRow [= setting]

Sets or returns the row number displayed at the top of the Excel window.

window.ScrollWorkbookTabs([Sheets], [Position])

Scrolls the worksheet tabs displayed at the bottom of a workbook.

Argument	Setting
Sheets	The number of tabs to scroll in either direction. Positive values scroll to the right; negative values scroll left.
Position	Can be one of the following settings: xlFirst, xlLast.

window.SelectedSheets

Returns the collection of worksheets and charts selected in the window. More than one sheet can be selected by multiselecting the sheet tabs at the bottom of the window.

window.Selection

Returns the objects selected on the window.

window.SmallScroll([Down], [Up], [ToRight], [ToLeft])

Scrolls the window a number of rows or columns in a given direction. You can combine arguments to scroll diagonally.

Argument	Setting
Down	Number of rows to scroll down
Up	Number of rows to scroll up
ToRight	Number of columns to scroll right
ToLeft	Number of columns to scroll left

window.Split [= setting]

True splits the window into panes; False displays the window as a single pane. Default is False. Use Split in combination with the following properties to divide a window into panes. For example, the following code splits the active window vertically at column C:

```
Sub TestSplitVertically()
    With ActiveWindow
        .SplitColumn = 3
        .SplitRow = 0
        .Split = True
    End With
End Sub
```

window.SplitColumn [= setting]

Sets or returns the column number at which to split a window vertically.

window.SplitHorizontal [= setting]

Sets or returns the location in points at which to split a window horizontally.

window.SplitRow [= setting]

Sets or returns the row number at which to split a window horizontally.

window.SplitVertical [= setting]

Sets or returns the location in points at which to split a window vertically.

windows.SyncScrollingSideBySide [= setting]

True synchronizes the two windows displayed during side-by-side comparison so that scrolling one window scrolls the other window an equal amount; False allows the windows to scroll independently.

window.TabRatio [= setting]

Sets or returns the ratio between the width of the tab area and the width of the window's horizontal scrollbar. Default is 0.6.

window.View [= XlWindowView]

Sets or returns whether page breaks are displayed. Can be one of these settings:

    xlNormalView
    xlPageBreakView

window.VisibleRange

Returns the Range object that is visible on the window.

window.WindowNumber [= setting]

Returns the number portion of the window caption. For example, the window captioned ch07.xls:2 returns 2.

window.WindowState [= XlWindowState]

Sets or returns the state of the window. Can be one of these settings:

```
xlMaximized
xlNormal
xlMinimized
```

window.Zoom [= setting]

Sets or returns a percentage by which to magnify the window.

Pane and Panes Members

The Pane object and Panes collection have the following members. These members are the same as the Window members of the same name.

Activate	Application[2]
Count[1]	Creator[2]
Index	LargeScroll
Parent[2]	ScrollColumn
ScrollIntoView	ScrollRow
SmallScroll	VisibleRange

[1] Collection only
[2] Object and collection

Pane objects represent the regions of a window. By default, Excel windows have one pane; additional panes are created when the user or code splits the window into two or four regions.

The following code demonstrates splitting the active window into four panes, then scrolling each of those panes:

```
Sub TestPanes()
    Dim pn As Pane, down As Integer, right As Integer
    Dim i As Integer
    With ActiveWindow
        ' Set the location for the split.
        .SplitColumn = 10
        .SplitRow = 16
        ' Split into four panes.
        .Split = True
        For i = 1 To .Panes.Count
            down = i * 2
            right = i + 3
```

```
                    ' Scroll each pane.
                    .Panes(i).SmallScroll down, , right
            Next
        End With
End Sub
```

The preceding code demonstrates two key things:

- The Panes collection can't be used in a For Each statement. Instead, you must use For Next.

- Scrolling is cumulative for pairs of panes. In other words, the horizontal pairs of panes are always on the same row and the vertical pairs are always on the same column.

To close panes, set the Window object's Split property to False:

```
Sub TestClosePanes()
    ActiveWindow.Split = False
End Sub
```

CHAPTER 8

Opening, Saving, and Sharing Workbooks

Workbooks represent documents in Excel. Use the Workbooks collection to create new documents, to open existing ones, or to perform operations on all open documents. Use the Workbook object to add worksheets and to save or otherwise change a single, open document.

The Workbook object is one of the central objects in Excel and most of the code you write will use Workbook in some way. Partly because of this, the Workbook object is also complex, providing more than 150 different properties and methods as well as two dozen or so events. I've tried to lay out the most common tasks in this chapter first, before delving into those details.

In this chapter, I show how to:

- Create new workbooks and open existing ones
- Save changes to a workbook and close without saving
- Base a new workbook on a template
- Create workbooks from text files
- Create workbooks from XML data
- Share a single workbook among multiple users
- Use a workbook as part of a shared workspace through a SharePoint server
- Respond to events that occur within a workbook

This chapter includes task-oriented reference information for the following objects and their related collections: Workbook and RecentFile.

 Code used in this chapter and additional samples are available in *ch08.xls*.

Add, Open, Save, and Close

Use Workbook objects to open, save, and control files in Excel. To create a new, empty file in Excel, use the Add method on the Workbooks collection:

```
Dim wb As Workbook
Set wb = Application.Workbooks.Add
```

Use the Workbook object's Save or SaveAs method to name the workbook and save the file to disk. The default save location in Excel is set in the Application object's DefaultFilePath property, which is usually My Documents. For example, the following line saves the workbook created before as *NewWorkbook.xls* in My Documents:

```
wb.SaveAs "NewWorkbook"
```

The Save method is similar to SaveAs, except it uses the default filename (*Bookn.xls*) the first time a file is saved. Use SaveAs the first time you save a file or to save an existing workbook in a new file; use Save when you want to keep the workbook's current name.

Use the Close method to close an open workbook. Closing does not automatically save changes to the workbook, but if there are any changes, Excel displays a Save Changes dialog box before closing. You must close a workbook before it can be deleted. Excel doesn't provide objects to delete workbooks since they are simply files stored on disk. Instead, you use the Kill method or a similar technique to delete a workbook. The following code closes the workbook created previously and deletes it:

```
wb.Close
VBA.Kill "NewWorkbook.xls"
```

If you want to open an existing workbook, use the Open method:

```
Set wb = Application.Workbooks.Open("MyBook.xls")
```

As with Save, Excel looks first in the current default directory, which may or may not be where the workbook is located. In this book, I often use the Workbook's Path property to tell Excel to look in the same folder that the current workbook resides in:

```
Set wb = Application.Workbooks.Open(ThisWorkbook.Path & "\MyBook.xls")
```

This works well for me because I've structured my samples so that related ones are all in the same folder. Also, I don't know where that folder might be installed on your machine—I just assume they'll be kept together in the same folder.

Templates

The way Excel comes from Microsoft, new workbooks contain three worksheets and no charts or other sheets. You can change this by setting Excel's Options (Tools →

Options → General tab), but sometimes you just want to create a workbook with one worksheet in code, leaving the Option settings alone. There's an easy way to do this:

```
Set wb = Workbooks.Add(XlWBATemplate.xlWBATWorksheet)
```

The preceding line creates a new workbook containing one worksheet. You can use a similar line to create a workbook containing one chart:

```
Set wb = Workbooks.Add(XlWBATemplate.xlWBATChart)
```

Of course, you can also use the Add method to create a new workbook based on a template, as shown here:

```
Set wb = Workbooks.Add("C:\Program Files\Microsoft
Office\Templates\1033\timecard.xlt")
```

Open as Read-Only or with Passwords

The Open method is actually quite complex. If you type Workbooks.Open in the Code window, Visual Basic displays a dizzying array of possible arguments (Figure 8-1).

```
Sub TestOpen()
    workbooks.Open
End Sub        Open(Filename As String, [UpdateLinks], [ReadOnly], [Format], [Password], [WriteResPassword],
               [IgnoreReadOnlyRecommended], [Origin], [Delimiter], [Editable], [Notify], [Converter], [AddToMru], [Local],
               [CorruptLoad]) As Workbook
```

Figure 8-1. The Open method can be complex

Thankfully, only *Filename* is required! Most of these are pretty special-purpose (you can read about them later); the most important ones are *ReadOnly*, *Password*, and *Format*. Opening a file as read-only is handy if a workbook is stored at a network location and might be open by another user—in that case you can open the file only as read-only:

```
Set wb = Workbooks.Open("//wombat1/public/copy of files.xls", , True)
```

If you try to open a workbook that has a password in code, Excel will prompt the user for that password. You can avoid this by putting the password in code:

```
Set wb = Workbooks.Open(ThisWorkbook.Path & "/security.xls", , , , "Excel2003")
```

Of course, that's a *spectacularly bad idea* if you are at all concerned about security: never write passwords, usernames, email addresses, or other sensitive data in code. The only reason to use this approach is if your passwords are merely intended to prevent accidental access—the analogy would be closing your front door rather than locking it, locking it and setting the alarm, or locking it, setting the alarm, and releasing ravening hounds; you get the idea.

Finally, the *Format* argument lets you open text files as Excel workbooks. If *Format* is 1, Excel interprets tab characters in the file as new columns. Each line in the file is a new row. For example, a text file that looks like Figure 8-2 can be opened as a workbook using this code:

```
Set wb = Workbooks.Open(ThisWorkbook.Path & "/data.txt", , , 1)
```

resulting in a workbook that looks like Figure 8-3.

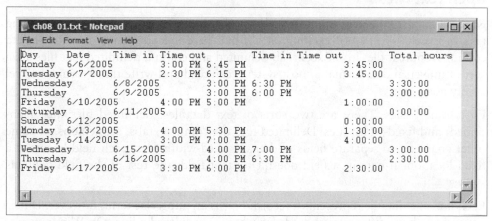

Figure 8-2. A tabbed text file

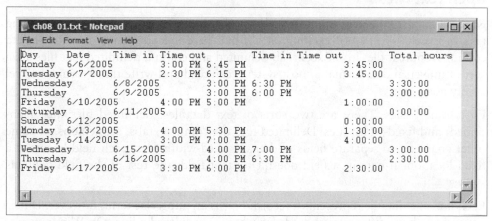

Figure 8-3. The tabbed file open in Excel

That said, the *Format* argument is a bit obsolete. Instead, you can use the OpenText method to do the same task and have much more control over how the text file is interpreted. The next section discusses that technique.

Open Text Files

Reading data from text files into Excel is probably the most common programming task in Excel. No, it's not exciting (at all) but there is a surprising amount of data coming from text files into Excel. Tab-delimited and comma-delimited text files are a sort of universal data format—most systems can read and write those formats. Excel is very good at it.

First some basics. There are two sorts of text datafiles: delimited files (just mentioned) and fixed-width files. Delimited files use commas, tabs, semicolons, or some other character to separate fields of data. In fixed-width files, each field begins at a fixed location. If data in a field doesn't fill that field, the rest of the field contains spaces.

Each line in a datafile represents a record. *Line* is an imprecise term, however. Different systems have different standards for what is considered a line. On Windows systems, a newline is indicated by the carriage-return and line-feed characters (Chr(13) and Chr(10) or vbCrLf in Visual Basic). On Macintosh and Linux systems, it's just line feed (Chr(10)).

When Excel opens a text file, it needs to know how the fields and records are identified. Once it has that information, it can read the text file, place fields into columns, and create a new row for each record. Excel can guess at a lot of that—for example, it just assumes that the file was created by the operating system that Excel is currently running under—and you can see these assumptions by choosing File → Open → *txtfile* to run the Excel Text Import Wizard (Figure 8-4).

You can choose Tools → Macro → Record Macro before running the Text Import Wizard to generate the code needed to import a particular text file. For example, the following code was recorded when I imported my sample text file in Excel:

```
' Recorded code.
Sub Macro1()
    Workbooks.OpenText Filename:= _
        "C:\Documents and Settings\Jeff\My Documents\Programming Excel\products.txt"_
        , Origin:=xlWindows, StartRow:=1, DataType:=xlDelimited, TextQualifier _
        :=xlDoubleQuote, ConsecutiveDelimiter:=False, Tab:=False, Semicolon:= _
        False, Comma:=True, Space:=False, Other:=False, FieldInfo:=Array(Array( _
        1, 9), Array(2, 1), Array(3, 9), Array(4, 9), Array(5, 1), _
        Array(6, 1), Array(7, 1), Array(8, 9), Array(9, 9), Array(10, 9)), _
        TrailingMinusNumbers:=True
End Sub
```

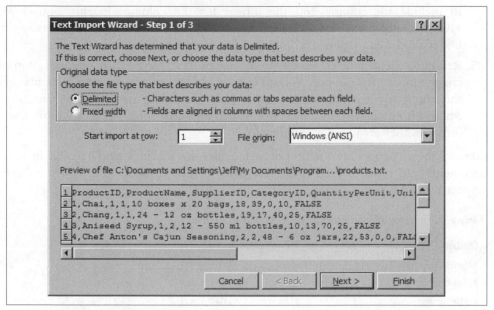

Figure 8-4. Excel's Text Import Wizard

The key parts of this code are the *Filename*, *StartRow*, *DataType*, *Comma* (delimiter), and *FieldInfo*. If you are going to reuse this code, it makes sense to reorganize it a bit, as shown here:

```
' Modifications to recorded code.
Sub TestOpenTextModifiedCode()
  Dim fld, fil As String
  ' Filename to open (look in this workbook's folder)
  fil = ThisWorkbook.Path & "\products.txt"
  ' Array describing how to format or omit columns.
  fld = Array(Array(1, xlSkipColumn), Array(2, xlGeneralFormat), _
    Array(3, xlSkipColumn), Array(4, xlSkipColumn), _
    Array(5, xlGeneralFormat), Array(6, xlGeneralFormat), _
    Array(7, xlGeneralFormat), Array(8, xlSkipColumn), _
    Array(9, xlSkipColumn), Array(10, xlSkipColumn))
  ' Create a workbook and load the text file.
  Workbooks.OpenText fil, , 1, xlDelimited, , , , , True, , , , fld
End Sub
```

The changes to the recorded code are spelled out here:

1. Replaced the absolute path- and filenames with a variable using the current workbook's path. This makes it easier to adapt the code for other files in the future.

2. Rewrote the *FieldInfo* arrays to use the Excel constants. The first element of each array is the column number; the second element describes whether or not

to include the column and the format for the column. In this case, 1 = xlGeneralFormat and 9 = xlSkipColumn. Using the constants makes it easier to understand what is going on. Table 8-1 lists these constants for your reference.

3. Removed the default arguments from the OpenText method. Items that I didn't change in the Text Import Wizard can simply be omitted. In code, this makes the important items stand out more. I also removed the argument names—Microsoft eliminated the concept of named arguments in .NET and I think that indicates they aren't really very helpful.

Some of these changes are a matter of preference—for instance, you may *like* named arguments and want to keep them. My point here is to show you how the Text Import Wizard can help you tackle the multifaceted OpenText method.

Table 8-1. FieldInfo xlColumnDataType constants and values

Constant	Value	Constant	Value
xlGeneralFormat	1	xlMYDFormat	6
xlTextFormat	2	xlDYMFormat	7
xlMDYFormat	3	xlYDMFormat	8
xlDMYFormat	4	xlSkipColumn	9
xlYMDFormat	5	xlEMDFormat	10

Open XML Files

 Important XML features are part of Excel 2003 Professional and standalone versions for Windows. Earlier and Macintosh versions of Excel support only limited access to XML files.

Text files may be the universal data format of today, but the future belongs to XML. XML is actually a type of text file, since XML files are stored as text. But unlike delimited text files, they are *self-describing*. That means Excel doesn't have to guess where a field or record starts; the information is right there in the file:

```
<?xml version="1.0" encoding="UTF-8" standalone="yes"?>
<Order>
    <ID>2002</ID>
    <BillTo>
        <Address>
            <Name>Biege Bond</Name>
            <Street1>55 Lost Lane</Street1>
            <City>Anywhere</City>
            <State>AR</State>
            <Zip>67832</Zip>
        </Address>
    </BillTo>
    <Line>
```

```
        <Number>10</Number>
        <Description>Qt Microballoons</Description>
        <Quantity>1</Quantity>
        <UnitPrice>95</UnitPrice>
        <Taxible>No</Taxible>
        <Total>95</Total>
      </Line>
    </Order>
```

In the preceding XML, items surrounded by brackets identify the data, <*tag*> and
</*tag*> notation shows where a data item starts and ends, and the fact that some
tags contain others establishes the relationships between items. You'll notice that
this is not a strict row/column relationship—not all data is grid oriented! This
means that Excel often has to be told where to put XML items on a worksheet.

The easiest way to see how this works is to follow these steps:

1. Open an XML file in Excel. Choose File → Open, select an XML file, and click
   OK. Excel displays a dialog box asking how you want to open the file
   (Figure 8-5).

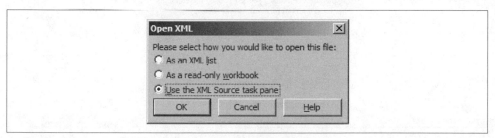

Figure 8-5. You can open XML files in several different modes

2. Select "Use the XML Source task pane" and click OK. Excel may tell you that
   the file doesn't contain a schema; if this happens, click OK. Excel creates a new
   workbook and displays the structure of the XML file in the righthand task pane
   as shown in Figure 8-6.

3. Drag items from the task pane to cells on the worksheet. Nonrepeating items,
   such as Address, create nonrepeating cells; repeating items, such as Line, create
   lists of data.

4. Click Refresh XML Data (Data → XML → Refresh XML Data) to import the data
   from the XML file (Figure 8-7).

I need to explain a few key concepts here:

- Excel interprets XML through an *XML map*. That's the thing you created in Step
  2. The XML map is displayed in the XML Source task pane.

- Dragging items from the XML Source task pane creates a data binding between
  items on a worksheet and the XML map.

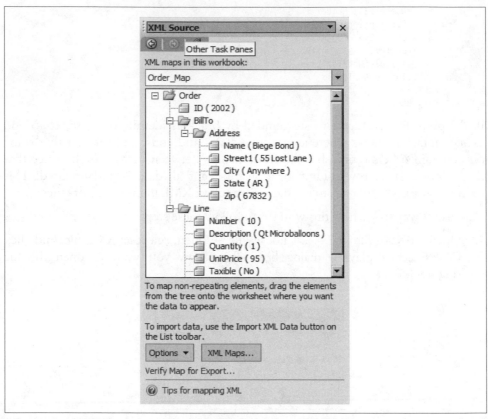

Figure 8-6. The Source task pane lets you map XML items to cells or ranges

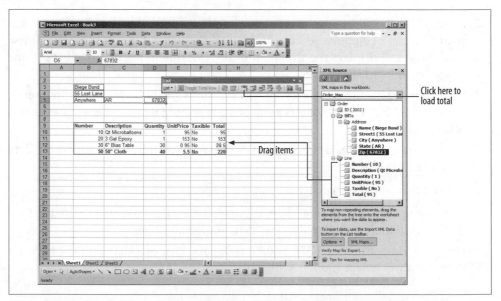

Figure 8-7. Drag items to create a mapping, then click Refresh XML Data to display the data

- Refreshing loads the XML data through the XML map and then updates the data bindings.

If you record the preceding steps, you'll get code that looks like this:

```
Sub Macro2( )
    Workbooks.OpenXML Filename:= _
        "C:\Documents and Settings\Jeff\My Documents\Programming Office\ch08_2002.xml" _
        , LoadOption:=xlXmlLoadMapXml
    ActiveWorkbook.XmlMaps("Order_Map").DataBinding.Refresh
End Sub
```

The first line (OpenXML) handles the first two steps. The last line (DataBinding.Refresh) handles Step 4. Step 3 is simply missing—Excel can't record your drag actions—and if you run the recorded code, you'll get an error. Although you can establish these data bindings in code, it is laborious and (really) unnecessary.

Instead, set up your XML the way you want it displayed, then save the workbook as an Excel template. Then you can create new workbooks based on that template and import XML using the ImportXML method as shown here:

```
Sub TestImportToXMLTemplate( )
    Dim xmap As XmlMap, wb As Workbook
    ' Create a workbook using the Order template.
    Set wb = Workbooks.Open(ThisWorkbook.Path & "\ch08_order.xlt")
    ' Get the XML Map.
    Set xmap = wb.XmlMaps("Order_Map")
    ' Import the data.
    wb.XmlImport ThisWorkbook.Path & "\ch08_2002.xml", xmap
End Sub
```

This approach takes advantage of the fact that the format of XML doesn't change as often as the content does. By using a template, you automatically get the XML map you need to interpret data from similar XML files. Of course, if the XML format changes (items are added, moved, or deleted), you'll need to create a new template containing a revised XML map.

Close Workbooks

If you close a workbook that has unsaved changes, Excel prompts whether you want to save before closing. This works the same way whether you close a workbook through the user interface or through code. You can turn off the prompt in code by setting the SaveChanges argument, however:

```
ThisWorkbook.Close True
```

The preceding code saves the current file, then closes it. You can just as easily discard changes by setting SaveChanges to False:

```
ThisWorkbook.Close False
```

In either case, Excel closes the workbook without displaying any prompts. You can even use Close to save a workbook to a new file, as shown here:

```
ThisWorkbook.Close True, "Copy of " & ThisWorkbook.Name
```

That's a little unusual, but it comes in handy if you are creating workbooks from some other source, such as text or XML data, as shown by the following **bold** additions to the previous example:

```
Sub TestImportToXMLTemplate( )
    Dim xmap As XmlMap, wb As Workbook
    ' Create a workbook using the Order template.
    Set wb = Workbooks.Open(ThisWorkbook.Path & "\ch08_order.xlt")
    ' Get the XML Map.
    Set xmap = wb.XmlMaps("Order_Map")
    ' Import the data.
    wb.XmlImport ThisWorkbook.Path & "\ch08_2002.xml", xmap
    ' Save the file in Excel format and close.
    wb.Close True, wb.Name
End Sub
```

In this case, Excel creates a new workbook, imports XML data, then saves and closes the workbook. You can work through a long list of XML files this way converting them to workbooks for later use.

If you use the Close method on the Workbooks collection, Excel closes all open workbooks. This version of Close doesn't accept arguments so Excel always prompts whether there are unsaved changes:

```
Sub TestCloseAll( )
    Workbooks.Close
End Sub
```

What's interesting about this is that Excel closes all open workbooks, but doesn't close itself. In this way, Workbooks.Close is different from Application.Quit.

Share Workbooks

Excel lets teams collaborate on workbooks through two main approaches:

Shared workbooks
> Allow multiple users to edit a single workbook file stored in a public location. The history of changes to the workbook can be stored with the file, and edits can be rolled back or accepted by date, user, or range of cells.

Shared workspaces
> Manage collaboration through SharePoint Services, allowing users to open, check out, view revision history, and manage contributors from a central web site.

These two approaches provide many of the same features through very different means. The most obvious difference is that shared workspaces require Windows

Server 2003 with SharePoint Services installed to be available somewhere on the user's network, whereas shared workbooks require only read and write access to a public network address.

To create a shared workbook:

1. Choose Tools → Shared Workbook. Excel displays the Share Workbook dialog box (Figure 8-8).
2. Select "Allow changes by more than one user at the same time" and click OK. Excel saves the workbook and enables it for shared access.

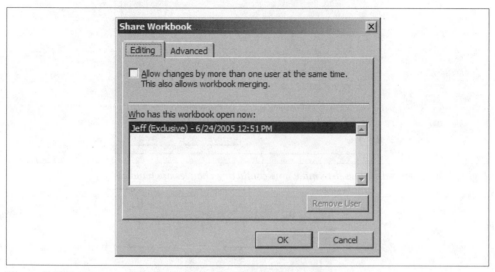

Figure 8-8. Sharing a workbook

Once a workbook is shared, multiple users can open the file from a public network address and save the file back to that address. Excel maintains a change history and merges changes automatically where it can. How conflicting changes are resolved is determined by the share settings on the Advanced tab of the Share Workbook dialog (Figure 8-9).

Shared workspaces are created differently. To create a shared workspace:

1. Choose Tools → Shared Workspace. Excel displays the Shared Workspace pane in the Task window (Figure 8-10).
2. Type the address of your SharePoint site in the Location for New Workspace text box and click Create to save the document to the SharePoint site and create a document workspace for it there.

Once a shared workspace is created, users can get updates, receive alerts, check out, edit, and view revision history for the document through the Shared Workspace pane

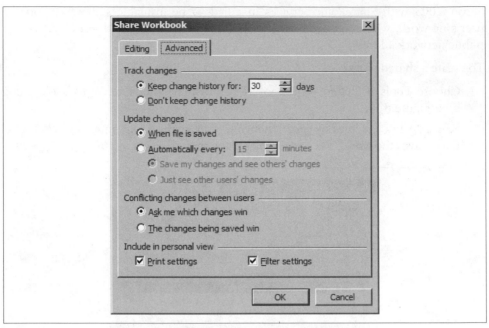

Figure 8-9. Advanced settings determine how conflicting changes are handled

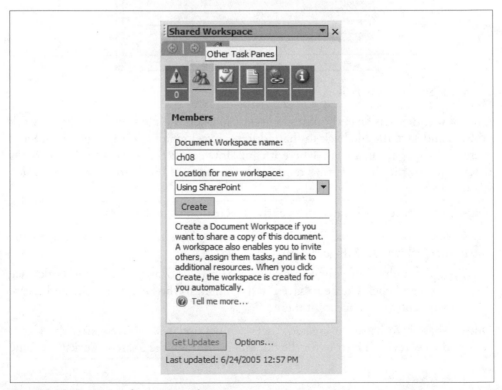

Figure 8-10. Creating a document workspace

of the Task window. How automatic updates and alerts are handled is determined by clicking Options at the bottom of the Shared Workspace pane, which displays the Service Options dialog (Figure 8-11).

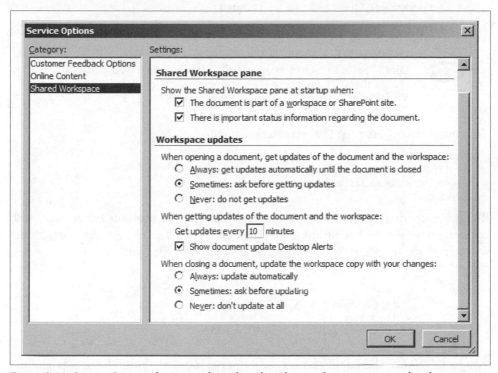

Figure 8-11. Service Options determines how shared workspace documents are updated

Whether you choose to collaborate through shared workbooks or shared workspaces will probably depend on whether you have access to a SharePoint server. Shared workspaces provide a more complete solution for collaborating, including the ability to check workbooks out while editing, notify teammates of changes, and request online meetings to discuss changes. Still, shared workbooks do provide a practical solution for sharing work among small teams and are the only approach supported for versions of Excel prior to 2003.

Program with Shared Workbooks

Once you share a workbook, any Visual Basic project it contains is no longer accessible. Excel can't deal with multiple users editing the same macros, so it simply prevents changes to those macros. You can't record new macros, either. However, you can run macros from shared workbooks.

Use the SaveAs method to share a workbook from within code. For example, the following code saves the active workbook for sharing:

```
Sub SaveAsShared()
    ActiveWorkbook.SaveAs , , , , , , xlShared
End Sub
```

 Once you share a workbook, you can no longer edit the macros it contains. The macros still exist and they can still run; you just can't change them. That's because Excel doesn't support shared editing in Visual Basic. To edit the macros, remove sharing.

To remove sharing, use the ExclusiveAccess method:

```
Sub RemoveSharing()
    If ThisWorkbook.MultiUserEditing Then _
        ThisWorkbook.ExclusiveAccess
End Sub
```

Removing sharing in this way erases change history and prevents other users who currently have the file open from saving their changes to the file. An alternate, kinder way to remove sharing is to save the workbook as a new file with the xlExclusive setting as shown here:

```
Sub SaveCopyAs()
    fil = ThisWorkbook.Path & "\" & "Copy of " & _
        ThisWorkbook.Name
    ThisWorkbook.SaveAs fil, , , , , , xlExclusive
End Sub
```

You can't remove sharing in this way without renaming the file. The SaveAs method doesn't change the access mode if you don't specify a new filename.

When you save a shared workbook, your changes to the file are synchronized with any changes that have been saved by others while you have been editing. If both you and another user happened to change the same item (such as the value of a cell), Excel displays the Resolve Conflicts dialog box during your save as shown in Figure 8-12.

If edits from other users don't conflict with any changes you've made, those edits automatically update your workbook when you save. This is a slightly curious situation, because the act of saving changes the workbook you are working on. To help avoid confusion about this, Excel displays a notice telling you what has happened.

You can determine whether a workbook is shared by checking its MultiUserEditing property. It is important to check MultiUserEditing before calling other sharing-related methods because many of them cause runtime errors if the workbook is *not* shared. For example, the following code verifies that a workbook is shared before accepting changes made by others:

```
If ThisWorkbook.MultiUserEditing Then _
    ThisWorkbook.AcceptAllChanges
```

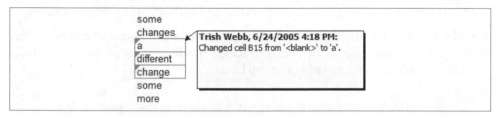

Figure 8-12. Excel lets you resolve conflicting changes to shared workbooks

The AcceptAllChanges and RejectAllChanges methods let you specify a date, user list, or range of cells that you want to accept or reject changes from. It's important to remember that these methods affect the underlying server-side copy of the shared workbook, not just the local copy you are working on. Multiuser editing may cause the user who made those changes some confusion—hey, where'd my work go? Excel adds a note to items that changed another user's edits (Figure 8-13).

Figure 8-13. Edits from other users can change your workbook when you save

Any user who has access to the network address where the workbook is saved can open the workbook and make changes. You can restrict access to the workbook by restricting the users who are allowed to view or open files at the network address and/or by specifying a password for the workbook. You can view information about users who have the workbook open using the UserStatus property. For example, the following code displays the names, time opened, and access mode for all current users of a shared workbook:

```
Sub TestUserStatus
    Dim usr(), msg As String, i As Integer
    usr = ThisWorkbook.UserStatus
    For i = 1 To UBound(usr)
        msg = msg & usr(i, 1) & " Opened: " & _
            usr(i, 2) & " Shared? " & _
            (usr(i, 3) = 2) & vbCrLf
    Next
    MsgBox msg
End Sub
```

Finally, you can change the workbook's sharing options using the following properties:

AutoUpdateFrequency
    Sets the number of minutes between automatically checking for updates

AutoUpdateSave
    Determines whether current changes are sent to other users when the workbook
    is automatically updated

PersonalViewListSettings
    Determines whether sorting and filter settings are shared with other users

PersonalViewPrintSettings
    Determines whether print settings are shared with other users

These properties correspond to items on the Advanced tab of the Share Workbook
dialog box.

Program with Shared Workspaces

Shared workbooks provide no infrastructure for managing users and very little ability to administer changes to a workbook. Shared workspaces address those shortcomings by allowing users to check out files before making edits, automatically notify others when changes occur, assign tasks, and add or remove team members.

Workbooks included in a shared workspace don't lock out changes to macros or prevent macro recording since the change-tracking mechanism is provided externally through SharePoint Services rather than by Excel.

 Don't confuse shared workspaces with Excel workspace files (*.xlw*).
Excel workspace files save the state of Excel's windows and open files
so you can easily return to some point in your work.

Use the Workbook object's SharedWorkspace property to share the workbook, update the workbook, and navigate among other elements in the shared workspace. For example, use the SharedWorkspace object's CreateNew method to create a new shared workspace and add a workbook to it:

```
Sub CreateWorkspace()
    ThisWorkbook.Save
    ThisWorkbook.SharedWorkspace.CreateNew "http://wombat2/", _
        "Team Wombat"
End Sub
```

You must save the workbook before adding it to a shared workspace; otherwise, the CreateNew method fails. The preceding code adds the current workbook to the SharePoint site on the Wombat2 server. If you click on Open Site in Browser in the Excel Shared Workspace pane, Excel displays the new workspace site created at *http://wombat2/Team%20Wombat*, as shown in Figure 8-14.

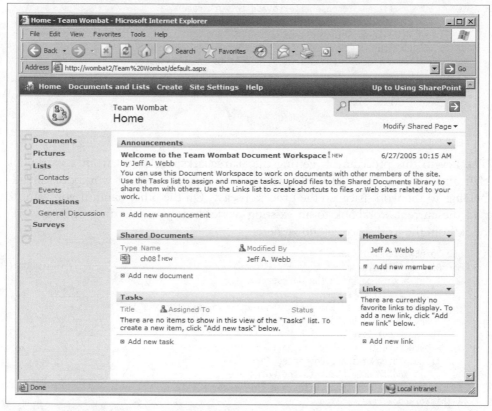

Figure 8-14. Excel creates a new SharePoint site when you call the CreateNew method

If you call CreateNew from another workbook using the same workspace name, Excel creates another, new SharePoint site and increments the site name to *http://wombat2/ Team%20Wombat(1)*. To add a workbook to an existing SharePoint site instead of creating a new site, follow these steps:

1. Open an existing document from the SharePoint site.

2. Get a reference to that document's SharedWorkspace object.

3. Add workbooks to the SharedWorkspace object's Files collection.

The following code demonstrates how to add files to the current workbook's workspace:

```
' Run to add a file to workspace
Sub AddFile()
    Dim fname As String
    ' Check to make sure this workbook is shared.
    If ThisWorkbook.SharedWorkspace.Connected Then
        ' Show file dialog box
        With Application.FileDialog(msoFileDialogFilePicker)
            .AllowMultiSelect = False
```

```
            .Title = "Choose file to add to workspace"
            .Show
            fname = .SelectedItems(1)
        End With
        ' If a filename was selected, add it to the workspace.
        If fname <> "" Then
            ThisWorkbook.SharedWorkspace.Files.Add fname, , _
                True, True
        End If
    End If
End Sub
```

The key to this procedure is getting the SharedWorkspace object from a workbook that already belongs to the workspace. In this case, the current workbook already belongs to the workspace, so the process is easy. On the other hand, if you want to add the current workbook to an existing workspace, you must first open a workbook from the workspace, as shown here:

```
Sub JoinExistingWorkspace()
    Dim wb As Workbook
    ' Get a workbook from the workspace.
    Set wb = Workbooks.Open _
        ("http://wombat2/Team Wombat/Shared Documents/ch08.xls")
    ' Save this workbook.
    ThisWorkbook.Save
    ' Make sure the workbook is part of the workspace.
    If wb.SharedWorkspace.Connected Then
        ' Add this workbook to the workspace.
        wb.SharedWorkspace.Files.Add ThisWorkbook.Path & "\" _
& ThisWorkbook.Name, , True
    End If
    ' Close the workbook.
    wb.Close
End Sub
```

Even though you have added the workbook file to the workspace, the currently open workbook is the local version, not the shared version. You can't close the current workbook from code and then open it from the SharePoint site for two reasons:

- The code stops running the moment you close the current workbook.

- You can't have two workbooks with the same name open at one time.

The easiest way to work around this is to display the SharePoint site and allow the user to reopen the shared workbook from there. The following code demonstrates that last approach:

```
Sub OpenWorkbookFromWorkspace()
    Dim wb As Workbook
    Set wb = Application.Workbooks.Open _
        ("http://wombat2/Team Wombat/Shared Documents/Ch08.xls")
    If MsgBox("Click Yes to close this workbook " & _
        "and then open the workbook from the SharePoint site.", vbYesNo, _
        "Workbook added to shared workspace.") = vbYes Then
```

```
            ' Open the SharePoint site in IE.
            ThisWorkbook.FollowHyperlink wb.SharedWorkspace.url, , True
            ' Close the temporary workbook.
            wb.Close
            ' Close this workbook.
            ThisWorkbook.Close
        End If
End Sub
```

Now, if the user clicks Yes, Excel displays the SharePoint web site and closes the current and temporary workbooks.

 You can tell if a workbook belongs to a shared workspace by checking the `Connected` property. Make sure the `Connected` property is True before using `SharedWorkspace` methods, otherwise an error may occur.

Open Workbooks from a Shared Workspace

If you double-click on a workbook in the workspace, Excel opens the workbook as read-only. To open the workbook for editing, select Edit in Microsoft Office Excel from the pop-up menu on the site as shown in Figure 8-15.

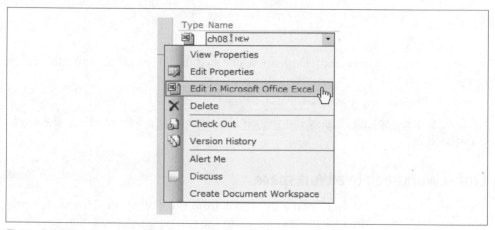

Figure 8-15. Opening a workbook from a shared workspace

To open a workbook from a shared workspace in code, simply use the `Open` method with the address of the workbook from the workspace. For example, the following code opens a workbook from *http://wombat2/Team Wombat*:

```
Workbooks.Open "http//wombat2/Team Wombat/Shared Documents/ch08.xls"
```

If you want exclusive access to a file, you can choose Check Out from the pop-up menu before opening the workbook for editing—*checking out* doesn't open the file; it just reserves it so other users can't make changes. You won't be able to check the workbook out if other users have the file open, however.

To check a file out from code, use the `Workbook` object's `CanCheckOut` property and the `CheckOut` method. For example, the following code attempts to check out a file, and if it is successful, it opens the file in Excel:

```
Sub CheckOut()
    fil = " http//wombat2/Team Wombat/Shared Documents/ch08.xls"
    If Application.Workbooks.CanCheckOut(fil) Then
        Application.Workbooks.CheckOut fil
        Set wb = Application.Workbooks.Open(fil)
        MsgBox wb.Name & " is check out to you."
    End If
End Sub
```

The `CheckOut` method doesn't open the workbook, so you need to add the `Open` method as shown in the preceding code. Checking a file in automatically closes the file as shown here:

```
Sub CheckIn()
    Set wb = Application.Workbooks("ch08.xls")
    If wb.CanCheckIn Then
        ' CheckIn closes the file.
        wb.CheckIn True, "Minor change"
        MsgBox "File was checked in."
    Else
        MsgBox wb.Name & " could not be checked in."
    End If
End Sub
```

In some cases, a file may not be able to be checked in. For instance, you can't check in the current workbook from within its own code:

```
If ThisWorbook.CanCheckIn Then ' Always False!
```

In those cases, you can display the workspace to provide a way to check the workbook back in.

Link a Workbook to a Workspace

Only one user at a time may open a workbook from the workspace. However, workbooks may also be stored locally and linked to the workspace copy. To create a local copy of the workbook that is linked to the workspace:

1. Open the workbook from the workspace.

2. Save the workbook to your computer.

3. Excel displays a prompt (Figure 8-16) asking if you want to link the local copy to the workspace. Choose Yes.

Once you've linked a workbook to the workspace, changes you make are synchronized with changes from other users. If changes conflict, you resolve them using the Document Updates task pane (Figure 8-17).

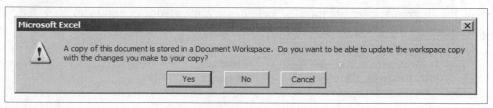

Figure 8-16. Linking a local copy to the workspace

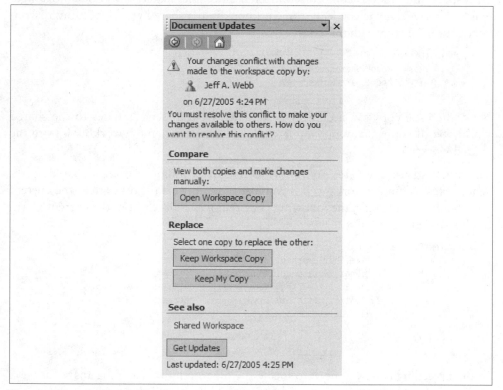

Figure 8-17. Resolving conflicting changes with linked files

Remove Sharing

There are two levels of removing sharing from a workbook stored in a shared workspace. You can:

- Delete the file from the workspace. This breaks the connection that other users share.
- Disconnect the file from the workspace. This breaks the connection only between the local copy of the workbook and the shared workbook.

Use the `RemoveDocument` method to delete the current document from the shared workspace as shown by the following code:

```
Sub TestRemove( )
    If ThisWorkbook.SharedWorkspace.Connected Then _
        ThisWorkbook.SharedWorkspace.RemoveDocument
End Sub
```

The preceding code leaves local copies that users have downloaded from the shared workspace, but they become disconnected since the shared workbook no longer exists. Alternately, you can leave the workbook in the shared workspace, but disconnect your local copy with this code:

```
Sub TestDisconnect( )
    If ThisWorkbook.SharedWorkspace.Connected Then _
        ThisWorkbook.SharedWorkspace.Disconnect
End Sub
```

Now, the local copy can no longer be updated from or send updates to the shared workbook. If you want an updatable copy, you must reopen the workbook from the shared workspace.

You can also use the `Files` collection to remove workbooks from a shared workspace. This technique works well if you want to remove a file other than the current workbook. For example, the following code removes *ch08.xls* from the current workbook's shared workspace:

```
Sub TestRemoveFile( )
    Dim file As Office.SharedWorkspaceFile
    If ThisWorkbook.SharedWorkspace.Connected Then
        For Each file In ThisWorkbook.SharedWorkspace.Files
                If InStr(1, file.urlThisWorkbook, "ch08.xls") Then _
                    file.Delete
        Next
    End If
End Sub
```

In the preceding case, you need to locate the file to remove using the `Instr` function —the `Files` collection doesn't provide a way to locate the file by name.

Respond to Actions

The `Workbook` object provides events you can use to respond to user actions. In order to use these events, write your code in the `ThisWorkbook` module of the workbook (in the Visual Basic Editor, double-click on `ThisWorkbook` in the Project window). Visual Basic displays the `Workbook` events in the event list at the top of the Code window as shown in Figure 8-18.

Selecting an event from the event list inserts a template for the event in the Code window, as shown here:

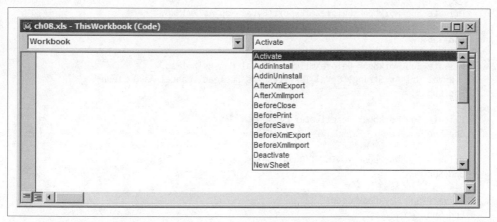

Figure 8-18. Select Workbook events from the Code window events list

```
Private Sub Workbook_Activate( )

End Sub
```

Any code you add to this procedure executes when the event occurs—in this case when the workbook receives focus. This event doesn't just occur when the user activates the workbook, it also occurs when code activates the workbook.

The names of most events are pretty self-explanatory and I won't bore you with circular definitions. Instead, here is the list of events that the Workbook object provides:

```
Private Sub Workbook_Activate( )
End Sub

Private Sub Workbook_AddinInstall( )
End Sub

Private Sub Workbook_AddinUninstall( )
End Sub

Private Sub Workbook_AfterXmlExport(ByVal Map As XmlMap, _
  ByVal Url As String, ByVal Result As XlXmlExportResult)
End Sub

Private Sub Workbook_AfterXmlImport(ByVal Map As XmlMap, _
  ByVal IsRefresh As Boolean, ByVal Result As XlXmlImportResult)
End Sub

Private Sub Workbook_BeforeClose(Cancel As Boolean)
End Sub

Private Sub Workbook_BeforePrint(Cancel As Boolean)
End Sub

Private Sub Workbook_BeforeSave(ByVal SaveAsUI As Boolean, _
  Cancel As Boolean)
End Sub
```

```
Private Sub Workbook_BeforeXmlExport(ByVal Map As XmlMap, _
  ByVal Url As String, Cancel As Boolean)
End Sub

Private Sub Workbook_BeforeXmlImport(ByVal Map As XmlMap, _
  ByVal Url As String, ByVal IsRefresh As Boolean, Cancel As Boolean)
End Sub

Private Sub Workbook_Deactivate()
End Sub

Private Sub Workbook_NewSheet(ByVal Sh As Object)
End Sub

Private Sub Workbook_Open()
End Sub

Private Sub Workbook_PivotTableCloseConnection( _
  ByVal Target As PivotTable)
End Sub

Private Sub Workbook_PivotTableOpenConnection( _
  ByVal Target As PivotTable)
End Sub

Private Sub Workbook_SheetActivate(ByVal Sh As Object)
End Sub

Private Sub Workbook_SheetBeforeDoubleClick(ByVal Sh As Object, _
  ByVal Target As Range, Cancel As Boolean)
End Sub

Private Sub Workbook_SheetBeforeRightClick(ByVal Sh As Object, _
  ByVal Target As Range, Cancel As Boolean)
End Sub

Private Sub Workbook_SheetCalculate(ByVal Sh As Object)
End Sub

Private Sub Workbook_SheetChange(ByVal Sh As Object, _
  ByVal Target As Range)
End Sub

Private Sub Workbook_SheetDeactivate(ByVal Sh As Object)
End Sub

Private Sub Workbook_SheetFollowHyperlink(ByVal Sh As Object, _
  ByVal Target As Hyperlink)
End Sub

Private Sub Workbook_SheetPivotTableUpdate(ByVal Sh As Object, _
  ByVal Target As PivotTable)
End Sub
```

```
Private Sub Workbook_SheetSelectionChange(ByVal Sh As Object, _
  ByVal Target As Range)
End Sub

Private Sub Workbook_Sync( _
   ByVal SyncEventType As Office.MsoSyncEventType)
End Sub

Private Sub Workbook_WindowActivate(ByVal Wn As Window)
End Sub

Private Sub Workbook_WindowDeactivate(ByVal Wn As Window)
End Sub

Private Sub Workbook_WindowResize(ByVal Wn As Window)
End Sub
```

As you can see, some events come in pairs that occur before and after user actions take place. The word *before* isn't quite right; Excel doesn't anticipate user actions. In this case, *before* means after the user does something but before Excel acts on it.

Before events usually include a Cancel argument that lets you prevent Excel from acting on the user action. For instance, this simple event procedure prevents the user from closing the workbook without saving it first:

```
Private Sub Workbook_BeforeClose(Cancel As Boolean)
    If Not ThisWorkbook.Saved Then Cancel = True
End Sub
```

Pretty handy! You can use the Before events' Cancel argument any time you want to prevent something. Just set Cancel to False and Excel throws away the action.

Some of the Workbook events echo events from other Excel objects. For example, both the Worksheet and Workbook objects have events that respond to the selected cell changing (Worksheet_SelectionChange and Workbook_SheetSelectionChange). If there is code written for both event procedures, Excel processes the worksheet-level event first; then it processes the workbook-level event.

Sometimes this is explained as events "bubbling up" through the object hierarchy. My point is simply that an event may be handled in more than one place—they don't just stop the first time they are handled (even if Cancel is set to True).

Handling a single event multiple places isn't common, but it's important to know that high-level objects like Application and Workbook can provide general handlers for events that may also occur on lower-level objects, such as Worksheets. So, for instance, if you want some code to run every time a selection changes on any worksheet, put the code in the Workbook_SheetSelectionChange event. If you want the code to run only when the selection changes on a single worksheet, put the code in the Worksheet_SelectionChange event.

Finally, the ThisWorkbook class isn't the only place that Workbook events are available. You can hook in to Workbook events in any class module by declaring a class-level Workbook variable WithEvents, then initializing that variable with the workbook. For example, the following code declares a Workbook object variable in a Worksheet class; Worksheet_Activate hooks the events up to the m_wb variable, and m_wb_SheetChange responds to worksheet change events for all worksheets in the workbook:

```
Dim WithEvents m_wb As Workbook

' Initialize Workbook object if it wasn't already
Private Sub Worksheet_Activate()
    If TypeName(m_wb) = "Nothing" Then Set m_wb = ThisWorkbook
End Sub

' Workbook-level handler for Sheet change events.
Private Sub m_wb_SheetChange(ByVal Sh As Object, ByVal Target As Range)
    If Target.Address = "$A$1" Then _
        Sh.[a2] = Sh.[a1] ^ 2
End Sub
```

Whenever you declare an object variable WithEvents at the class level, Visual Basic adds that object's events to the event list Code window. You can write code for those events, but that code won't execute unless the class-level object variable is initialized as shown earlier in the Worksheet_Activate procedure. It's easy to forget that step. It's also important to know that you can "unhook" the events by setting the object variable to Nothing:

```
' Unhook Workbook events.
Private Sub Worksheet_Deactivate()
    Set m_wb = Nothing
End Sub
```

Workbook and Workbooks Members

Use the Workbooks collection to create new and open existing workbooks in Excel. Use the Application object's Workbooks method to get a reference to this collection. Use the Workbook object to save and control individual workbooks. The Workbooks collection and Workbook object have the following members. Key members (shown in **bold**) are covered in the following reference section:

 Password and protection members are covered in Chapter 26.

AcceptAllChanges	**AcceptLabelsInFormulas**	**Activate**
ActiveChart	**ActiveSheet**	**Add**[1]
AddToFavorites	Application[2]	**Author**
AutoUpdateFrequency	**AutoUpdateSaveChanges**	**BreakLink**

BuiltinDocumentProperties
CanCheckOut[1]
ChangeLink
CheckOut[1]
Colors
ConflictResolution
CreateBackup
CustomViews
DialogSheets (obsolete)
DocumentLibraryVersions
EnvelopeVisible
ExclusiveAccess
ForwardMailer
HasMailer
HighlightChangesOnScreen
InactiveListBorderVisible
Item[1]
LinkInfo
Mailer
MultiUserEditing
NewWindow
OnSheetDeactivate (obsolete)
OpenLinks
Parent[2]
PasswordEncryptionFile
    Properties
Path
PersonalViewPrintSettings
Post
PrintPreview
ProtectStructure
PurgeChangeHistoryNow
RecheckSmartTags
ReloadAs
Reply
ResetColors
Routed
Save
SaveCopyAs
SendFaxOverInternet
SendMailer
SharedWorkspace
ShowPivotTableFieldList
Styles
Title
UnprotectSharing
UpdateLinks

CalculationVersion
ChangeFileAccess
Charts
Close[2]
CommandBars
Container (obsolete)
Creator[2]
Date1904
DisplayDrawingObjects
EnableAutoRecover
Excel4IntlMacroSheets
FileFormat
FullName
HasPassword
HighlightChangesOptions
IsAddin
KeepChangeHistory
LinkSources
MergeWorkbook
Name
OnSave (obsolete)
Open[1]
OpenText[1]
Password
PasswordEncryptionKeyLength
Permission
PivotCaches
PrecisionAsDisplayed
Protect
ProtectWindows
ReadOnly
RefreshAll
RemovePersonalInformation
ReplyAll
RevisionNumber
RoutingSlip
SaveAs
Saved
SendForReview
SetLinkOnData
Sheets
SmartDocument
Subject
ToggleFormsDesign
UpdateFromFile
UpdateRemoteReferences

CanCheckIn
ChangeHistoryDuration
CheckIn
CodeName
Comments
Count[1]
CustomDocumentProperties
DeleteNumberFormat
DisplayInkComments
EndReview
Excel4MacroSheets
FollowHyperlink
FullNameURLEncoded
HasRoutingSlip
HTMLProject
IsInplace
Keywords
ListChangesOnNewSheet
Modules (obsolete)
Names
OnSheetActivate (obsolete)
OpenDatabase[1]
OpenXML[1]
PasswordEncryptionAlgorith
PasswordEncryptionProvider
PersonalViewListSettings
PivotTableWizard
PrintOut
ProtectSharing
PublishObjects
ReadOnlyRecommended
RejectAllChanges
RemoveUser
ReplyWithChanges
Route
RunAutoMacros
SaveAsXMLData
SaveLinkValues
SendMail
SetPasswordEncryptionOptions
ShowConflictHistory
SmartTagOptions
TemplateRemoveExtData
Unprotect
UpdateLink
UserStatus

VBASigned	VBProject	WebOptions
WebPagePreview	Windows	Worksheets
WritePassword	WriteReserved	WriteReservedBy
Xmlimport	XmlImportXml	XmlMaps
XmlNamespaces		

[1] Collection only
[2] Object and collection

workbook.**AcceptAllChanges**([*When*], [*Who*], [*Where*])

For shared workbooks, commits the changes to the workbook.

Argument	Settings
When	A string indicating the time after which to accept changes
Who	A string indicating the user from which to accept changes
Where	A string indicating a range of cells for which to accept changes

It's easiest to see the effect of AcceptAllChanges when you combine it with RejectAllChanges. For example, the following code accepts all of the changes made to the range A2:D4, but rejects changes to other cells if they were made within the last minute:

```
If ThisWorkbook.MultiUserEditing Then
    [a1] = "Value rejected": [b2] = "Value kept"
    ThisWorkbook.AcceptAllChanges , , "$A$2:$D$4"
    ' Reject other changes made in the last minute.
    ThisWorkbook.RejectAllChanges CStr(Now - 0.001)
End If
```

workbook.**AcceptLabelsInFormulas** [= *setting*]

True allows formulas to include range labels as if they were named ranges; False disables the use of labels in formulas. Default is True.

The following code creates some column headings and then makes those headings usable as labels in formulas that display the sum of each column:

```
' Create two column headings.
[a1] = "col1": [b1] = "col2"
' Add some data.
[a2] = 2: [a3] = 10: [a4] = 12: [a5] = 5
[b2] = 9: [a3] = 17: [b4] = 2: [b5] = 13: [b6] = 29
' Allow labels in formulas.
ThisWorkbook.AcceptLabelsInFormulas = True
' Create labels out of the column headings.
[a1:b1].FormulaLabel = xlColumnLabels
' Use the labels in formulas
[c1] = "=sum(col1)"
[c2] = "=sum(col2)"
```

If you set AcceptLabelsInFormulas to False in the preceding code, C1 and C2 display an error.

workbook.Activate( )

Activates the workbook giving it focus in Excel and making it the ActiveWorkbook. For example, the following code opens a new workbook, then returns the focus to the current workbook:

```
Workbooks.Open (ThisWorkbook.Path & "\blank.xls")
ThisWorkbook.Activate
```

workbook.ActiveChart

Returns a reference to the Chart object that currently has focus in Excel. If some other type of object has focus, returns Nothing. The following code captures a bitmap of the active chart and pastes the image into Microsoft Paint:

```
If Not (ActiveChart Is Nothing) Then
    ActiveChart.CopyPicture xlScreen, xlBitmap, xlScreen
    Shell "mspaint.exe", vbNormalFocus
    DoEvents
    AppActivate "Untitled - Paint", True
    SendKeys "^v", True
End If
```

workbook.ActiveSheet

Returns a reference to the worksheet, chart sheet, Excel 4.0 macro sheet, or Excel 5.0 dialog sheet that currently has focus. In most cases, ActiveSheet returns a reference to the active worksheet, but it is important to make sure that it is a worksheet before proceeding in code. For example, the following code checks whether ActiveSheet is a worksheet before performing some task:

```
Dim ws As Worksheet
If TypeName(ActiveSheet) = "Worksheet" Then
    Set ws = ActiveSheet
    ws.Cells(1, 1) = 42
    ' Some other code...
Else
    MsgBox "Please activate a worksheet."
End If
```

workbooks.Add([*Template*])

Creates a new workbook and opens it in Excel.

Argument	Settings
Template	The filename of a template to base the new workbook on. Alternately, this argument may be one of the following XlWBATemplate settings: xlWBATChart, xlWBATExcel4IntlMacroSheet, xlWBATExcel4MacroSheet, or xlWBATWorksheet. In those cases, the new workbook contains a single sheet of the specified type.

After calling Add, the new workbook becomes the ActiveWorkbook in Excel. The following line creates a workbook and returns a reference to the new Workbook object:

```
Set wb = Application.Workbooks.Add
```

workbook.AddToFavorites

Adds a link to the workbook in the Internet Explorer Favorites menu. The link appears on the Favorites menu in this form: *filename*.xls#[*filename*.xls]*sheetname*.

workbook.Author [= *setting*]

Sets or returns the name of the author displayed in the workbook's properties.

workbook.AutoUpdateFrequency [= *setting*]

For shared workbooks, sets or returns the number of minutes before the workbook is automatically refreshed.

workbook.AutoUpdateSaveChanges [= *setting*]

For shared workbooks, True saves changes to the current workbook back to the shared version when the workbook is automatically refreshed; False does not send those changes on during automatic refresh. The default is True.

workbook.BreakLink(*Name, Type*)

Breaks links to other workbooks or OLE objects. When a link is broken, the data is retained at the site of the link, but the ability to refresh the data from its source is lost.

Argument	Settings
Name	The name of the link to break. Link names are returned by the LinkSources method.
Type	Use xlLinkTypeExcelLinks to break a link to a Microsoft Excel source; use xlLinkTypeOLELinks to break a link to an OLE source.

For example, the following code iterates through the Excel links in a workbook and asks the user whether each link should be broken:

```
Dim link, linkSources
linkSources = ThisWorkbook.linkSources(xlLinkTypeExcelLinks)
If IsArray(linkSources) Then
    For Each link In linkSources
        If MsgBox("Break link to " & link) = vbOK Then _
            ThisWorkbook.BreakLink link, xlLinkTypeExcelLinks
    Next
End If
```

workbook.BuiltinDocumentProperties

Returns the collection of Excel's built-in document properties. In some cases, properties may not be initialized, so you must use error handling when getting their values. The following code displays the names and settings of all of a workbook's built-in properties:

```
Dim prop As DocumentProperty
On Error Resume Next
For Each prop In ActiveWorkbook.BuiltinDocumentProperties
    Debug.Print prop.Name, prop.Value
    If Err Then Debug.Print prop.Name, "Not set."
    Err.Clear
Next
On Error GoTo 0
```

workbook.CalculationVersion

Returns a number representing the major and minor versions of Excel last used to recalculate the workbook. For example, the following code displays "114210" on my machine, where "11" is the major version of Excel (2003 is Version 11) and "4210" is the minor, or build version:

```
Debug.Print ThisWorkbook.CalculationVersion
```

workbook.CanCheckIn

For workbooks belonging to shared workspaces, returns True if the workbook has been checked out from the workspace and can be checked in; returns False if the workbook cannot be checked in. Use CanCheckIn before calling CheckIn.

workbooks.CanCheckOut(*Filename*)

For workbooks that are part of a shared workspace, verifies that the workbook is available to be checked out. Use CanCheckOut to verify that the file is available before calling the CheckOut method.

Argument	Settings
Filename	The address of the file on the SharePoint server for which to verify the status

Returns True if the current user can check out a shared workbook from the SharePoint server. Returns False if the workbook cannot be checked out. Causes an error if the SharePoint server or file can't be found.

The following code checks out a file from a SharePoint server, first verifying that it is available:

```
fil = "//wombat2/Team Wombat/Shared Documents/ch08.xls"
If Application.Workbooks.CanCheckOut(fil) Then
    Application.Workbooks.CheckOut (fil)
```

```
        Set wb = Application.Workbooks.Open(fil)
        If wb.SharedWorkspace.Connected Then _
            msg = "ch08.xls is check out to you."
    Else
        msg = "ch08.xls could not be checked out."
    End If
    MsgBox msg
```

workbook.ChangeFileAccess(*Mode*, [*WritePassword*], [*Notify*])

Changes a workbook to read-only or read/write access.

Argument	Settings
Mode	xlReadOnly changes the access to read-only; xlReadWrite changes access to read/write.
WritePassword	The password required for write access if the workbook is write-protected.
Notify	True displays a message if the file is not available for read/write access, perhaps because it is open for another user; False does not notify. Default is True.

Switching a read-only workbook to read/write may reload the file in Excel. The following code demonstrates changing file-access modes on the current workbook:

```
    ' Save changes.
    ThisWorkbook.Save
    ' Change to read-only.
    ThisWorkbook.ChangeFileAccess xlReadOnly
    ' Change back. (May reload file.)
    ThisWorkbook.ChangeFileAccess xlReadWrite
```

workbook.ChangeHistoryDuration [= *setting*]

For shared workbooks, sets or returns the number of days changes are tracked. The KeepChangeHistory property must be True for this property to have an effect. The following code tracks changes for seven days if the workbook is shared:

```
    If ThisWorkbook.MultiUserEditing Then
        ThisWorkbook.KeepChangeHistory = True
        ThisWorkbook.ChangeHistoryDuration = 7
    End If
```

workbook.ChangeLink(*Name, NewName,* [*Type*])

Changes the source of a link.

Argument	Settings
Name	The name of the link to change. Link names are returned by the LinkSources method.
NewName	The source of the new link.
Type	Use xlLinkTypeExcelLinks to change a link from a Microsoft Excel source; use xlLinkTypeOLELinks for an OLE source.

For example, the following code iterates through the Excel links in a workbook and changes links from the *test1.xls* file to *test2.xls*:

```
Dim link, linkSources, newLink As String
newLink = ThisWorkbook.Path & "\test2.xls"
linkSources = ThisWorkbook.linkSources(xlLinkTypeExcelLinks)
If IsArray(linkSources) Then
    For Each link In linkSources
        If InStr(link, "test1.xls") Then _
            ThisWorkbook.ChangeLink link, newLink, xlLinkTypeExcelLinks
    Next
End If
```

workbook.Charts

Returns a collection of chart sheets as Chart objects. Does not return charts that are embedded in worksheets. The following code saves each of the chart sheets as JPEG files:

```
For Each chrt In ThisWorkbook.Charts
    chrt.Export ThisWorkbook.Path & "/" & _
        chrt.Name & ".jpg", "jpeg"
Next
```

workbook.CheckIn([*SaveChanges*], [*Comments*], [*MakePublic*])

For workbooks that are part of a shared workspace, checks the workbook back in to the SharePoint server and closes the workbook.

Argument	Settings
SaveChanges	True saves current changes back to the server before checking the workbook in; False does not save current changes to the server.
Comments	Comments to save with changes.
MakePublic	True allows all users of the shared workspace to read the workbook; False denies read-only users access to the workbook.

The following code saves changes and checks a workbook back into the shared workspace:

```
Set wb = ThisWorkbook
If wb.SharedWorkspace.Connected And wb.CanCheckIn Then
    ThisWorkbook.CheckIn True, "Minor change"
    MsgBox ThisWorkbook.Name & " is checked in."
Else
    MsgBox "Could not check in " & ThisWorkbook.Name
End If
```

workbooks.CheckOut(*Filename*)

For workbooks that are part of a shared workspace, checks out a workbook from the SharePoint server. Excel returns an error if the workbook could not be checked out, so use the CanCheckOut method before calling CheckOut.

Argument	Settings
Filename	The address of the file on the SharePoint server to check out

The CheckOut method doesn't open the file or download it from the SharePoint server. Use the Open method to open the file after checking it out, as shown here:

```
fil = "//wombat1/Team Wombat/Shared Documents/blank.xls"
If Application.Workbooks.CanCheckOut(fil) Then
    Application.Workbooks.CheckOut fil
    Application.Workbooks.Open fil
End If
```

workbook.Close([*SaveChanges*], [*Filename*], [*RouteWorkbook*])

Closes an open workbook and optionally saves changes or distributes that workbook to a routing list. When used with the Workbooks collection, closes all open workbooks in the current instance of Excel. The following arguments apply to closing a single workbook.

Argument	Settings
SaveChanges	True saves current changes; False does not save changes. The default is to prompt the user.
Filename	If *SaveChanges* is True, the filename with which to save the workbook. The default is to prompt for the filename.
RouteWorkbook	If the workbook has a routing list, True routes the workbook; False does not route. The default is to prompt.

The Close method does not run Auto_Close macros, but it does trigger the Before_Close event.

The following code closes all open workbooks. If any of the workbooks has unsaved changes, the user is prompted whether they should be saved:

```
Workbooks.Close
```

workbook.CodeName

Returns *ThisWorkbook* for workbook objects.

workbook.Colors [= setting]

Returns the collection of RGB colors in the workbook's color palette. Workbooks have 56 colors that can be used. The following code displays the RGB value for each of a workbook's colors in hexadecimal:

```
For Each clr In ThisWorkbook.Colors
    Debug.Print Hex(clr)
Next
```

RGB values are often expressed in hexadecimal. For example, &hff0000 is red, &hff00 is green, &hff is blue, &hffffff is white, and &h0 is black.

workbook.CommandBars

Returns a collection containing the command bars associated with a workbook. Returns Nothing if the workbook has no command bars. The following code displays the name of visible workbook-level command bars:

```
If Not (ThisWorkbook.CommandBars Is Nothing) Then
    For Each bar In ThisWorkbook.CommandBars
        If bar.Visible Then _
            Debug.Print bar.Name
    Next
Else
    Debug.Print "No workbook-level command bars."
End If
```

workbook.Comments [= setting]

Sets or returns the comments property for the workbook. Comments are displayed in the workbook's Properties dialog box.

workbook.ConflictResolution [= setting]

For shared workbooks, determines how conflicting changes are handled. Setting may be one of the following values:

xlLocalSessionChanges
    Local changes overwrite changes from other users.

xlOtherSessionChanges
    Changes from other users overwrite local changes.

xlUserResolution
    Displays a dialog box to resolve the conflict.

workbook.Container

For workbooks contained in Office Binder documents, returns the containing binder object.

workbook.CreateBackup [= *setting*]

True creates a backup copy of the workbook when the workbook is saved; False does not create a backup. Default is False.

workbook.CustomDocumentProperties

Returns a collection of custom document properties. The following code displays the settings of a workbook's custom properties:

```
For Each prop In ActiveWorkbook.CustomDocumentProperties
    Debug.Print prop.Name, prop.Value
Next
```

workbook.CustomViews

Returns a collection containing the custom views of a workbook. Use the CustomViews collection's Add method to create new views.

workbook.DeleteNumberFormat(NumberFormat)

Removes a custom number format from a workbook.

workbook.DisplayDrawingObjects [= *setting*]

Sets or returns how drawing objects are displayed. Possible settings are:

xlDisplayShapes
    Shows shapes (default)

xlPlaceholders
    Shows placeholders

xlHide
    Hides shapes

workbook.DisplayInkComments [= *setting*]

True displays comments entered using digital ink; False hides those comments. Default is True.

workbook.DocumentLibraryVersions

For workbooks that are part of a shared workspace, returns a collection containing the revision history for the workbook. For example, the following code displays revisions tracked for a workbook in a shared workspace:

```
Dim ver As DocumentLibraryVersion
If ThisWorkbook.SharedWorkspace.Connected Then
    For Each ver In ThisWorkbook.DocumentLibraryVersions
        Debug.Print ver.ModifiedBy, ver.Modified, ver.Comments
    Next
End If
```

workbook.EnableAutoRecover [= *setting*]

True enables Excel to automatically recover files if an error or hardware problem closes Excel unexpectedly; False disables Auto Recover. Default is True.

workbook.EndReview

Ends the review of a workbook distributed for review by the SendForReview method. After you use this method on the source workbook, you will not be able to automatically merge comments from reviewers.

workbook.EnvelopeVisible [= *setting*]

True displays the email composition header and the envelope toolbar; False hides those items.

workbook.ExclusiveAccess

For shared workbooks, removes sharing and grants the current user exclusive access to the workbook. The following code removes sharing from a workbook:

```
If ThisWorkbook.MultiUserEditing Then
    ThisWorkbook.ExclusiveAccess
End If
```

workbook.FileFormat

Returns a constant indicating the file format of the workbook. May be one of the following:

xlAddIn	xlCSV	xlCSVMac
xlCSVMSDOS	xlCSVWindows	xlCurrentPlatformText
xlDBF2	xlDBF3	xlDBF4
xlDIF	xlExcel2	xlExcel2FarEast

xlExcel3	xlExcel4	xlExcel4Workbook
xlExcel5	xlExcel7	xlExcel9795
xlHtml	xlIntlAddIn	xlIntlMacro
xlSYLK	xlTemplate	xlTextMac
xlTextMSDOS	xlTextPrinter	xlTextWindows
xlUnicodeText	xlWebArchive	xlWJ2WD1
xlWJ3	xlWJ3FJ3	xlWK1
xlWK1ALL	xlWK1FMT	xlWK3
xlWK3FM3	xlWK4	xlWKS
xlWorkbookNormal	xlWorks2FarEast	xlWQ1
xlXMLSpreadsheet		

workbook.FollowHyperlink(*Address*, [*SubAddress*], [*NewWindow*], [*AddHistory*], [*ExtraInfo*], [*Method*], [*HeaderInfo*])

Displays a web page in the default browser.

Argument	Settings
Address	The address of the web page to display.
SubAddress	A target within the requested web page.
NewWindow	True displays the browser window; False maximizes the browser window. Default is False.
AddHistory	Not used.
ExtraInfo	A string or byte array that specifies additional information for HTTP to use to resolve the hyperlink.
Method	msoMethodGet sends the request as an HTTP GET method; *ExtraInfo* is sent as a string appended to the address. msoMethodPost sends the request as an HTTP POST method; *ExtraInfo* is posted as a string or byte array.
HeaderInfo	A string specifying the HTTP header to be sent with the request.

For example, the following code displays my web site in a new, maximized browser window:

```
ThisWorkbook.FollowHyperlink "http://www.excelworkshop.com", , False
```

workbook.ForwardMailer( )

For Macintosh users with PowerTalk mail systems, creates a mailer used to forward the workbook after it has been received from another user. ForwardMailer creates the mailer; use SendMailer to send the workbook.

workbook.FullName

Returns the full name of the workbook file, including path and filename extension.

workbook.FullNameURLEncoded

Returns the full name of the workbook file, including path and filename extension. If the file was opened from a web address, this method returns the name as it is encoded. For example, spaces are replaced with %20.

workbook.HasMailer

For Macintosh users with PowerTalk mail systems; returns True if the workbook has a mailer, False otherwise.

workbook.HasPassword

Returns True if the workbook has a password, False otherwise.

workbook.HasRoutingSlip [= *setting*]

Returns True if the workbook has a routing slip, False otherwise. Setting this property to True creates a routing slip.

workbook.HighlightChangesOnScreen [= *setting*]

For shared workbooks, True highlights changes from other users; False does not. Default is False.

workbook.HighlightChangesOptions([When], [Who], [Where])

For shared workbooks, controls which changes are highlighted.

Argument	Settings
When	One of the following constants: xlSinceMyLastSave, xlAllChanges, or xlNotYetReviewed.
Who	A string indicating the user from which to accept changes. Can be "Everyone," "Everyone but Me," or the name of one of the users of the shared workbook.
Where	A string indicating a range of cells for which to accept changes.

The following code turns on change highlighting, makes some changes to highlight, then accepts those changes:

```
If ThisWorkbook.MultiUserEditing Then
    ThisWorkbook.HighlightChangesOnScreen = True
    ThisWorkbook.HighlightChangesOptions xlSinceMyLastSave
    [b2] = "Value kept"
    MsgBox "Pause: Highlighted changes"
    ThisWorkbook.AcceptAllChanges
    MsgBox "Pause: Changes accepted"
End If
```

workbook.HTMLProject

Returns a reference to the workbook's HTMLProject object. For example, the following code opens the current workbook as HTML in the Microsoft Script Editor:

```
ThisWorkbook.HTMLProject.Open
```

workbook.InactiveListBorderVisible [= setting]

True displays borders around lists even if they do not have focus; False displays a border only if the list has focus. Default is True.

workbook.IsAddin [= setting]

Setting IsAddin to True causes Excel to treat the workbook as an add-in; False treats the workbook as a regular workbook. In Excel, add-ins hide any macros or worksheets they contain. To see how this works, step through the following code in a workbook:

```
ThisWorkbook.IsAddin = True
ThisWorkbook.IsAddin = False
```

When the first line runs, all worksheets are hidden and macros no longer appear in the Run Macros dialog box. When the second line runs, the workbook returns to its normal state.

workbook.IsInplace

True if the workbook is embedded as an OLE object and is being edited in place in another document; False if the workbook is being edited in Excel.

workbook.KeepChangeHistory [= setting]

For shared workbooks, True tracks changes; False does not track changes. Use in combination with the ChangeHistoryDuration property.

workbook.Keywords [= setting]

Sets or returns keywords from the workbook's Properties dialog box.

workbook.LinkInfo(Name, LinkInfo, [Type], [EditionRef])

Returns information about a link. The information returned depends on the type of link.

Argument	Settings
Name	The name of the link.
LinkInfo	Determines the type of information to return. Possible settings are xlEditionDate, xlLinkInfoStatus.

Argument	Settings
Type	The type of link to get information about. Possible settings are `xlLinkInfoOLELinks`, `xlLinkInfoPublishers`, `xlLinkInfoSubscribers`.
EditionRef	If the link is an edition, *EditionRef* specifies the edition reference. Required if there's more than one publisher or subscriber with the same name in the workbook.

For example, the following code displays a message telling the user to update Excel links that are out-of-date:

```
linkSources = ThisWorkbook.linkSources(xlLinkTypeExcelLinks)
If IsArray(linkSources) Then
    For Each link In linkSources
        If ThisWorkbook.LinkInfo(link, xlLinkInfoStatus, _
            xlLinkTypeExcelLinks) = XlLinkStatus.xlLinkStatusOld Then
            MsgBox "Update link: " & link
        End If
    Next
End If
```

workbook.LinkSources([*Type*])

Returns an array containing the links in a workbook.

Argument	Settings
Type	The type of links to return. Possible settings are `xlExcelLinks` (default), `xlOLELinks`, `xlPublishers`, `xlSubscribers`.

The following code displays the Excel links in a workbook:

```
linkSources = ThisWorkbook.linkSources(xlOLELinks)
If IsArray(linkSources) Then
    For Each link In linkSources
        Debug.Print link
    Next
End If
```

workbook.ListChangesOnNewSheet [*— setting*]

For shared workbooks, True displays changes from other users on a new worksheet; False displays changes on the existing worksheet.

workbook.Mailer

For Macintosh users with PowerTalk mail systems; returns the `Mailer` object attached to a workbook.

workbook.MergeWorkbook(*Filename*)

Merges one workbook with another. For example, the following code merges the current workbook with *Test2.xls*:

```
ThisWorkbook.MergeWorkbook ThisWorkbook.Path & "\Test2.xls"
```

workbook.MultiUserEditing

True if the workbook is shared; False if the workbook is not shared. Use this method to test if the workbook is a shared workbook before calling sharing-related methods. For example:

```
If ThisWorkbook.MultiUserEditing Then
    ThisWorkbook.KeepChangeHistory = True
End If
```

workbook.Names

Returns the Names collection containing all the names in the workbook. For example, the following code displays all of the names in a workbook, allowing you to delete them individually:

```
Dim nm As Name
For Each nm In ThisWorkbook.Names
    If MsgBox("Delete " & nm.Name & "?", vbYesNo) = vbYes Then _
      nm.Delete
Next
```

workbook.NewWindow

Displays a new window for the workbook.

workbooks.Open(*Filename*, [*UpdateLinks*], [*ReadOnly*], [*Format*], [*Password*], [*WriteResPassword*], [*IgnoreReadOnlyRecommended*], [*Origin*], [*Delimiter*], [*Editable*], [*Notify*], [*Converter*], [*AddToMru*], [*Local*], [*CorruptLoad*])

Opens an existing workbook and adds it to the Workbooks collection. Returns a reference to the workbook that was opened.

Argument	Settings
Filename	The file to open.
UpdateLinks	One of these settings: 0, don't update; 1, update external links but not remote links; 2, update remote links but not external links; 3, update all links. The default is to prompt the user.
ReadOnly	True opens the workbook as read-only; False opens as read/write. Default is False.

Argument	Settings
Format	When opening a text file, this argument specifies the column separator character as follows: 1, tab; 2, comma; 3, space; 4, semicolon; 5, no separator; 6, character specified in Delimiter argument. Default is 1.
Password	If the workbook requires a password, this is the password to open the file. The default is to prompt the user.
WriteResPassword	If the workbook has a password for write access, this is the password to write to the file. The default is to prompt the user.
IgnoreReadOnlyRecommended	True does not display Excel's Read Only Recommended dialog if the file was saved with that option; False displays the prompt. Default is False.
Origin	Indicates the operating system that created the file. One of the following xlPlatform settings: xlWindows, xlMSDOS, xlMacintosh. The default is the current platform.
Delimiter	When opening text files with the Format argument set to 6, this is the delimiter character used to identify new columns.
Editable	For workbook templates (.xlt): True opens the template for editing; False creates a new workbook based on the template. Default is False.
	For Excel 4.0 add-ins: True displays the add-in in a window and does not run Auto_Open macros; False hides the add-in. Default is False.
Notify	For shared workbooks, True opens the workbook read-only if it is not available for read/write and notifies the user when it becomes available for read/write; False causes Open to fail if the file is not available for the requested access type. Default is False.
Converter	The index of the converter to try first when opening the file. If the file does not match the file type, other converters are tried in turn. This index corresponds to the first-dimension index in the array returned by Application.FileConverters.
AddToMru	True adds the workbook to Excel's list of recently used files; False does not. Default is False.
Local	True sets the save language for the workbook to the local language; False sets it to the Visual Basic language (usually English). Default is False.
CorruptLoad	Indicates how to handle workbooks that may be corrupted. One of the following xlCorruptLoad settings: xlNormalLoad, xlRepairFile, xlExtractData.

The following code opens a workbook and returns a reference to the Workbook object:

```
Dim wb As Workbook
Set wb = Workbooks.Open("new.xls")
```

If the workbook does not exist, Open causes an error.

workbooks.OpenDatabase(*Filename*, [*CommandText*], [*CommandType*], [*BackgroundQuery*], [*ImportDataAs*])

Creates a new workbook and imports data from a database into it. Returns a reference to the new workbook.

Argument	Settings
Filename	The database file to open, or an Office Data Connection (*.odc*) file specifying the data source.
CommandText	A command to execute on the database. Typically, this is a SQL command.
CommandType	The type of command to execute. This seems to be ignored, but you can specify "SQL", "Table", or "Default" if you like.
BackgroundQuery	True retrieves the data asynchronously in the background; False retrieves the data synchronously. Default is False.
ImportDataAs	It is not clear how this argument is used.

When working with file-based databases, such as from Microsoft Access, you can specify the filename to use as the data source as shown here:

```
cnn = "C:\Program Files\Microsoft Office\OFFICE11" & _
    "\SAMPLES\Northwind.mdb"
sql = "SELECT * FROM Employees"
Set wb = Application.Workbooks.OpenDatabase(cnn, sql, , False)
```

The preceding code creates a new workbook and imports the Employees table from the Northwind Access database.

When working with server-based databases, such as from Microsoft SQL, you must specify the connection information in an Office Data Connection file (*.odc*). For example, the following code creates a new workbook and imports invoice information from the Northwind SQL database:

```
Dim wb As Workbook, cnn As String, sql As String
cnn = ThisWorkbook.Path & "\NWindInvoices.odc"
Set wb = Application.Workbooks.OpenDatabase(cnn, , , True)
MsgBox "Performing query..."
```

The preceding code also demonstrates *asynchronous* access. In this case, the message box is displayed before the query is complete.

workbook.OpenLinks(*Name*, [*ReadOnly*], [*Type*])

Opens the source document from a link.

Argument	Settings
Name	The name of the link.
ReadOnly	True opens the source document as read-only; False opens the document as read/write.
Type	The type of link to get information about. Possible settings are xlExcelLinks, xlOLELinks, xlPublishers, xlSubscribers.

For example, the following code opens the sources of each of the Excel links in a workbook:

```
linkSources = ThisWorkbook.linkSources(xlLinkTypeExcelLinks)
If IsArray(linkSources) Then
    For Each link In linkSources
        ThisWorkbook.OpenLinks (link)
    Next
End If
```

workbooks.OpenText(*Filename*, [*Origin*], [*StartRow*], [*DataType*], [*TextQualifier*], [*ConsecutiveDelimiter*], [*Tab*], [*Semicolon*], [*Comma*], [*Space*], [*Other*], [*OtherChar*], [*FieldInfo*], [*TextVisualLayout*], [*DecimalSeparator*], [*ThousandsSeparator*], [*TrailingMinusNumbers*], [*Local*]**)**

Opens a text file and interprets it as a workbook. How OpenText interprets the text file is determined by the method's many arguments.

Argument	Settings
Filename	The text file to open.
Origin	The platform to create the text file; can be one of the following xlPlatform settings: xlWindows, xlMSDOS, xlMacintosh. The default is the current platform.
StartRow	The row within the file at which to start parsing. Default is 1 for the first row.
DataType	Determines how the columns are delimited; can be one of the following xlTextParsingType settings: xlDelimited or xlFixedWidth. If omitted, Excel tries to determine the correct setting.
TextQualifier	Determines how text values are identified; can be one of the following xlTextQualifier settings: xlTextQualifierDoubleQuote (default), xlTextQualifierNone, xlTextQualifierSingleQuote.
ConsecutiveDelimiter	True parses consecutive delimiters as indicating a single column; False parses consecutive delimiters as multiple, empty columns. Default is False.
Tab	True parses the tab character as the column delimiter; False does not.
Semicolon	True parses the semicolon as the column delimiter; False does not.
Comma	True parses the comma as the column delimiter; False does not.
Space	True parses the space character as the column delimiter; False does not.
Other	True uses the character specified in OtherChar as the column delimiter; False does not.
OtherChar	If Other is True, the character to use as the column delimiter.
FieldInfo	A two-dimensional array containing the Excel number format to use for each column.
TextVisualLayout	One of the following xlTextVisualLayoutType settings: xlTextVisualLTR (default) or xlTextVisualRTL.
DecimalSeparator	The character used as the decimal separator in the text file. Default is the system decimal separator (for example, "." in the U.S.; "," in most of Europe).
ThousandsSeparator	The character used as the thousands separator in the text file. Default is the system decimal separator (for example, "," in the U.S.; "." in most of Europe).
TrailingMinusNumbers	True interprets hyphens after numbers as negative numbers; False does not.
Local	True sets the save language for the workbook to the local language; False sets it to the Visual Basic language (usually English). Default is False.

By default, Excel makes a best guess as to how to interpret data from a text file. It will use commas or tabs as the column delimiter, depending on which is found first. For example, the following code loads a simple comma-delimited text file as a single worksheet in a new workbook:

```
Workbooks.OpenText "data.csv"
```

This is similar to using the Open method with the *Format* argument set to 2. The advantage of using OpenText is the level of control you have over how the text file is parsed. For example, you can use the *FieldInfo* array to interpret columns of data as specific data types:

```
fld = Array(Array(1, xlGeneralFormat), Array(2, xlMDYFormat), _
Array(4, xlSkipColumn), Array(5, xlSkipColumn), Array(6, xlSkipColumn), _
Array(7, xlSkipColumn), Array(8, xlSkipColumn), Array(9, xlSkipColumn), _
Array(10, xlSkipColumn), Array(11, xlSkipColumn), Array(12, xlSkipColumn), _
Array(13, xlSkipColumn), Array(14, xlSkipColumn), Array(15, xlGeneral))
Workbooks.OpenText "data.txt", , 2, , , , True, , , , , , fld
```

In these cases, it is usually easiest to record the code generated by the Text Import Wizard and then modify it to get the results you want.

workbooks.OpenXML(*Filename*, [*Stylesheets*], [*LoadOption*])

Creates a new workbook and loads an XML file into it. Returns a reference to the new workbook.

Argument	Settings
Filename	The name of the XML file to load.
Stylesheets	A number or an array of numbers indicating the XML Style Sheet (XSL) instructions to execute.
LoadOption	Determines how the XML file is interpreted or loaded; may be one of the following xlXMLLoadOption settings: xlXmlLoadImportToList, xlXmlLoadMapXml, xlXmlLoadOpenXml, xlXmlLoadPromptUser.

The idea of executing a limited number of XSL processing instructions seems strange and there are no examples of this provided in Help. Excel ignores the argument if there are no processing instructions in the XML file.

Use the LoadOption argument to control how Excel loads the XML. For example, complex XML files are "flattened" by default, which often isn't what you want. By using the *LoadOption* xmlLoadMapXml, you can load the XML as an XML map and allow the user to choose the items to import into the worksheets as lists. The following code imports an XML file as an XML map:

```
Set wb = Workbooks.OpenXML( _
    "http://www.mstrainingkits.com/excel/excelobjects.xml", , _
    XlXmlLoadOption.xlXmlLoadMapXml)
```

workbook.Path

Returns the path of the workbook. This property is useful for locating other files in the workbook's folder. For example, the following code lists all the workbooks in the current workbook's folder:

```
fname = Dir(ThisWorkbook.Path & "\*.xls")
Do While fname <> ""
    Debug.Print fname
    fname = Dir( )
Loop
```

workbook.PersonalViewListSettings [= *setting*]

For shared workbooks, True saves sort and filter settings in the user's personal view of the workbook; False does not save those settings. Default is True.

workbook.PersonalViewPrintSettings [= *setting*]

For shared workbooks, True saves print settings in the user's personal view of the workbook; False does not save those settings. Default is True.

workbook.PivotCaches

Returns the collection of PivotCache objects contained in a workbook. Pivot caches are the in-memory data sets used by pivot tables. See Chapter 13 for examples of working with pivot caches.

workbook.PivotTableWizard([*SourceType*], [*SourceData*], [*TableDestination*], [*TableName*], [*RowGrand*], [*ColumnGrand*], [*SaveData*], [*HasAutoFormat*], [*AutoPage*], [*Reserved*], [*BackgroundQuery*], [*OptimizeCache*], [*PageFieldOrder*], [*PageFieldWrapCount*], [*ReadData*], [*Connection*])

Creates a pivot table in the workbook.

Argument	Settings
SourceType	One of these settings: xlConsolidation, xlDatabase (default), xlExternal, xlPivotTable.
SourceData	Any of a number of possible sources, such as a Range object, an array of ranges, the name of another pivot table, or an array of strings containing the SQL query string.
TableDestination	A Range object indicating where to place the pivot table. The default is the active range.
TableName	A name for the pivot table.
RowGrand	True displays grand totals for rows; False does not.
ColumnGrand	True displays grand totals for columns; False does not.
SaveData	True saves the data with the pivot table; False saves only the pivot table definition.
HasAutoFormat	True applies automatic formatting to the pivot table; False does not.
AutoPage	If *SourceType* is xlConsolidation, True automatically creates page field; False does not.
Reserved	Not used.
BackgroundQuery	True performs the query asynchronously in the background; False performs the query synchronously.
OptimizeCache	True optimizes the pivot cache; False does not (default).
PageFieldOrder	One of these settings: xlDownThenOver or xlOverThenDown (default).
PageFieldWrapCount	The number of page fields in each column or row. Default is 0.

Argument	Settings
ReadData	True reads all data into the pivot cache; False allows data to be read into the pivot cache by page. Use False for queries that return large amounts of data.
Connection	The ODBC connection string for the query that creates the pivot cache.

workbook.Post([*DestName*])

For Microsoft Exchange clients, posts a workbook to a Microsoft Exchange server. The *DestName* argument is ignored.

workbook.PrecisionAsDisplayed [= *setting*]

True calculates results using the displayed precision of numbers; False uses full precision. Default is False.

workbook.PrintOut([*From*], [*To*], [*Copies*], [*Preview*], [*ActivePrinter*], [*PrintToFile*], [*Collate*], [*PrToFileName*])

Prints the workbook.

Argument	Settings
From	The starting page number to print.
To	The ending page number to print.
Copies	The number of copies to print.
Preview	True previews the workbook before printing; False does not (default).
ActivePrinter	The name of the printer to use.
PrintToFile	True sends output to a file; False sends output to the printer (default).
Collate	True prints in collated order; False prints from first page to last (default).
PrToFileName	If PrintToFile is True, the name of the file to create; Excel prompts for a filename if PrintToFile is True and this argument is omitted.

The following code prints the first page of the current workbook:

```
ThisWorkbook.PrintOut 1, 1
```

workbook.PrintPreview([*EnableChanges*])

Displays the workbook in Print Preview mode.

Argument	Settings
EnableChanges	True allows the user to change margins from the print preview before printing; False does not allow changes. Default is True.

workbook.PublishObjects

Returns the PublishObjects collection for the workbook. A PublishObject represents an item that has been saved to a web page and can be refreshed from its source in Excel.

workbook.PurgeChangeHistoryNow(*Days*, [*SharingPassword*])

For a shared workbook, removes change history for a workbook.

Argument	Settings
Days	The number of days of history to keep
SharingPassword	The password for the workbook if the workbook has one

workbook.ReadOnly

True if the workbook is open for read-only access; False if the workbook is read/write.

workbook.ReadOnlyRecommended

True if the workbook is read-only recommended; False if the workbook is read-only or read/write.

workbook.RecheckSmartTags

Forces Excel to scan the workbook for items that SmartTags may apply to. Generally, SmartTags are applied as the user enters data; however, they may not be applied if data is imported through code.

workbook.RefreshAll

Refreshes external data ranges and pivot tables in the workbook.

workbook.RejectAllChanges([When], [Who], [Where])

For shared workbooks, rolls back changes made by others. RejectAllChanges can remove changes that are in the workbook's change history that have not yet been committed by an AcceptAllChanges method.

Argument	Settings
When	A string indicating the time after which to reject changes.
Who	A string indicating the user from which to reject changes. Can be "Everyone", "Everyone but Me", or the name of one of the users of the shared workbook.
Where	A string indicating a range of cells for which to reject changes.

For example, the following code rejects all of the changes made within the last 24 hours:

```
If ThisWorkbook.MultiUserEditing Then
    ThisWorkbook.RejectAllChanges CStr(Now - 1)
End If
```

workbook.ReloadAs(*Encoding*)

Reloads a workbook that was based on an HTML document.

Argument	Settings
Encoding	An MsoEncoding constant that indicates the character encoding to use when interpreting the HTML

For example, this line reloads a workbook using the UTF8 (Unicode) character encoding:

```
ThisWorkbook.ReloadAs (MsoEncoding.msoEncodingUTF8)
```

workbook.RemovePersonalInformation [= *setting*]

True removes personal information, such as author name, from a workbook when it is saved; False retains that information (default). The following code saves the workbook, omitting personal information:

```
ThisWorkbook.RemovePersonalInformation = True
ThisWorkbook.Save
```

The user receives a security warning if the workbook contains macros, since they may contain personal information that Excel can't remove.

workbook.RemoveUser(*Index*)

For shared workbooks, disconnects a user from editing the workbook.

Argument	Settings
Index	The index of the user to disconnect

Use the UserStatus method to get an array containing the users editing a shared workbook. The following code allows you to disconnect users from a shared workbook:

```
If ThisWorkbook.MultiUserEditing Then
    Dim usr(), msg As String
    usr = ThisWorkbook.UserStatus
    For i = 1 To UBound(usr)
        msg = "Disconnect user " & usr(i, 1) & "?"
        If MsgBox(msg, vbYesNo) = vbYes Then _
            ThisWorkbook.RemoveUser (i)
    Next
End If
```

workbook.Reply

For Macintosh users with PowerTalk mail systems, creates a copy of the workbook and attaches it as a reply to the person who sent the workbook.

workbook.ReplyAll

For Macintosh users with PowerTalk mail systems, creates a copy of the workbook and attaches it as a reply to the sender and recipients of the workbook.

workbook.ReplyWithChanges([*ShowMessage*])

For workbooks that have been distributed using the `SendForReview` method, this method sends notification to the original sender letting him know that the review is complete.

Argument	Settings
ShowMessage	True displays the email message before sending; False does not display the message first. Default is True.

workbook.ResetColors

Resets the workbook's color palette to the Excel defaults.

workbook.RevisionNumber

For shared workbooks, returns the number of times the workbook has been saved locally.

workbook.Route

Sends the workbook using the workbook's routing slip.

workbook.Routed

True if the workbook has been sent to the next recipient in the workbook's routing slip; False if the workbook has not yet been sent.

workbook.RoutingSlip

Returns the workbook's `RoutingSlip` object. Use `HasRoutingSlip` to create a routing slip and to determine if a workbook has a routing slip. The following code creates a routing slip and routes a workbook:

```
ThisWorkbook.HasRoutingSlip = True
With ThisWorkbook.RoutingSlip
```

```
      .Recipients = Array("Beige Bond", "Jeff Webb")
      .Message = "For your review"
      .Subject = "New budget"
      .Delivery = xlOneAfterAnother
   End With
   ThisWorkbook.Route
```

workbook.RunAutoMacros(*Which*)

Runs a workbook's automacros. This method is provided for compatibility with versions of Excel that did not support events.

Argument	Settings
Which	One of these settings: xlAutoActivate, xlAutoClose, xlAutoDeactivate, or xlAutoOpen

workbook.Save

Saves the workbook.

workbook.SaveAs([*Filename*], [*FileFormat*], [*Password*], [*WriteResPassword*], [*ReadOnlyRecommended*], [*CreateBackup*], [*AccessMode*], [*ConflictResolution*], [*AddToMru*], [*TextCodepage*], [*TextVisualLayout*], [*Local*])

Saves the workbook and sets the workbook's file properties.

Argument	Settings
Filename	The name of the file to save. Default is current filename.
FileFormat	One of the following xlFileFormat settings: xlCS, xlCSVMSDOS, xlCurrentPlatformText, xlDBF3, xlDIF, xlExcel2FarEast, xlExcel4, xlAddIn, xlCSVMac, xlCSVWindows, xlDBF2, xlDBF4, xlExcel2, xlExcel3, xlExcel4Workbook, xlExcel5, xlExcel7, xlExcel9795, xlHtml, xlIntlAddIn, xlIntlMacro, xlSYLK, xlTemplate, xlTextMac, xlTextMSDOS, xlTextPrinter, xlTextWindows, xlUnicodeText, xlWebArchive, xlWJ2WD1, xlWJ3, xlWJ3FJ3, xlWK1, xlWK1ALL, xlWK1FMT, xlWK3, xlWK3FM3, xlWK4, xlWKS, xlWorkbookNormal, xlWorks2FarEast, xlWQ1, xlXMLSpreadsheet.
Password	A password the user must enter to open the file.
WriteResPassword	A password the user must enter to open the file for read/write access.
ReadOnlyRecommended	True causes Excel to display a dialog box recommending the file be opened for read-only access when the user opens the file; False does not display the dialog box. Default is False.
CreateBackup	True creates a backup version of the file when the file is saved; False does not create a backup. Default is False.
AccessMode	One of the following xlSaveAccessMode settings: xlExclusive, xlNoChange (default), xlShared. Use xlShared to share a workbook, xlExclusive to remove sharing.

Argument	Settings
ConflictResolution	For shared workbooks, one of the following xlSaveConflictResolution settings: xlUserResolution (default), xlLocalSessionChanges, xlOtherSessionChanges.
AddToMru	True adds this workbook to Excel's most recently used file list on the File menu; False omits this workbook from the list. Default is False.
TextCodepage	For foreign-language versions of Excel only, the code page to save the workbook with.
TextVisualLayout	For foreign-language versions of Excel only, orientation to use when presenting data.
Local	True saves the workbook against the local user language; False saves the workbook against the language used in Visual Basic (typically, English).

The following code saves the workbook for single-user access using a new filename:

```
fil = ThisWorkbook.Path & "\Copy of " & ThisWorkbook.Name
ThisWorkbook.SaveAs fil, , , , , , xlExclusive
```

This code saves the workbook as an XML spreadsheet using the current filename (note that warnings are displayed if the file contains macros or drawing objects):

```
ThisWorkbook.SaveAs , xlXMLSpreadsheet
```

workbook.SaveAsXMLData(*Filename, Map*)

Exports a workbook to an XML datafile through an XML map contained in the workbook.

Argument	Settings
Filename	The name of the XML datafile to create when the export is complete
Map	A reference to an XMLMap object contained in the workbook

Use the XMLMap object's IsExportable property to test if data can be exported through the map before calling SaveAsXMLData. In some cases, data loaded through an XML map cannot be exported through the same map.

The following code gets a reference to an XML map, checks if the workbook's data can be exported, then exports the data to a new XML file:

```
Set xmap = ThisWorkbook.XmlMaps("Order_Map")
If xmap.IsExportable Then
    ThisWorkbook.SaveAsXMLData ThisWorkbook.Path & "\data.xml", xmap
Else
    MsgBox "XML data could not be exported."
End If
```

workbook.SaveCopyAs([*Filename*])

Saves a copy of the workbook without changing the name of the open workbook.

Argument	Settings
Filename	The filename with which to save the copy

Although *Filename* is optional, CopyAs may fail if it tries to use the current filename to save to the current folder since the source workbook may be open. It is a good idea to supply a filename to avoid this problem.

The following code saves a copy of the current workbook, giving it a new name without changing the name of the current workbook:

```
ThisWorkbook.SaveCopyAs "Copy of " & ThisWorkbook.Name
```

workbook.Saved [= *setting*]

True indicates there are no unsaved changes to the workbook; False indicates that changes have not been saved. Setting Saved to True allows you to close a workbook without being prompted to save changes, discarding any changes since the last save.

workbook.SaveLinkValues [= *setting*]

True saves the values of external links with the workbook; False saves the link but not the data, refreshing the data when the workbook is opened. Default is True.

workbook.SendFaxOverInternet([*Recipients*], [*Subject*], [*ShowMessage*])

Sends a fax over the Internet using a fax service provider. If no fax service provider is configured for your system, Excel displays a prompt directing you to providers.

Argument	Settings
Recipients	The email names or phone numbers of fax recipients.
Subject	A subject line to include with the fax.
ShowMessage	True displays the fax before sending; False does not.

The following code sends the current workbook as a fax:

```
ThisWorkbook.SendFaxOverInternet "ExcelDemo@Hotmail.com", _
    "Workbook Samples"
```

workbook.SendForReview([*Recipients*], [*Subject*], [*ShowMessage*], [*IncludeAttachment*])

Sends a workbook via email, beginning the review process. In order to track reviewers' comments, the workbook must be shared.

Argument	Settings
Recipients	The email names or aliases of the reviewers.
Subject	A subject line to include with the email.
ShowMessage	True displays the email message before sending; False does not. Default is True.

Argument	Settings
IncludeAttachment	True includes the workbook as a file attachment; False includes a link to the workbook (file must be saved at a network address). Default is True.

The following code sends a workbook for review, previewing the message before sending. If the workbook is not already shared, Excel displays a prompt asking if you would like to save it as a shared workbook before sending:

```
ThisWorkbook.SendForReview "ExcelDemo@Hotmail.com", "Workbook samples"
```

Use the EndReview method to end the review process.

workbook.SendMail(*Recipients*, [*Subject*], [*ReturnReceipt*])

Sends a workbook via email as an attachment.

Argument	Settings
Recipients	The email names or aliases of the recipients.
Subject	A subject line to include with the email.
ReturnReceipt	True notifies the sender when the recipient receives the mail; False does not (default).

The following line sends the current workbook as an email:

```
ThisWorkbook.SendMail "ExcelDemo@Hotmail.com", "Workbook samples"
```

workbook.SendMailer([*FileFormat*], [*Priority*])

For Macintosh users with PowerTalk mail systems, sends a workbook as a PowerTalk email message.

Argument	Settings
FileFormat	An xlFileFormat setting that determines the format of the file to send.
Priority	An xlPriority setting determining the priority of the email. Default is xlPriorityNormal.

workbook.SetLinkOnData(*Name*, [*Procedure*])

Sets a procedure to run whenever a DDE link is updated.

Argument	Settings
Name	The name of the OLE or DDE link as returned by the LinkSources property
Procedure	The name of a procedure to run when the link is updated

The following code sets the OnUpate procedure to run whenever a DDE link is updated within the workbook:

```
linkSources = ThisWorkbook.linkSources(xlOLELinks)
If IsArray(linkSources) Then
```

```
    For Each link In linkSources
        If InStr(1, link, "DDE") Then _
            ThisWorkbook.SetLinkOnData link, "OnUpdate( )"
    Next
End If
```

workbook.SharedWorkspace

For workbooks that are part of a shared workspace, returns the SharedWorkspace object used to connect to and maintain the workbook through the SharePoint server. The SharedWorkspace object exists even if the workbook is not shared via SharePoint Services. You can tell whether or not a workbook is part of a shared workspace by checking the object's Connected property. For example, the following code checks if a workbook is part of a shared workspace before adding another workbook to the shared workspace:

```
Dim sw As Office.SharedWorkspace
Set sw = ThisWorkbook.SharedWorkspace
If sw.Connected Then
    sw.Files.Add ThisWorkbook.Path & "\" & "new.xls"
End If
```

workbook.Sheets

Returns a collection of all the sheets in a workbook. There is no "Sheet" object type, so the Sheets collection returns a varied collection of objects that may include Worksheet, Chart, and DialogSheet objects.

DialogSheet objects are now considered obsolete by Microsoft and are no longer documented. The same applies to the xlExcel4MacroSheet and xlExcel4IntlMacroSheet subtypes of the Worksheet object. However, Excel still supports their creation and you may encounter them when working with the Sheets collection.

In general, it is a good idea to use specific types for objects if at all possible. For instance, the Worksheets collection returns the collection of Worksheet objects in the workbook, and the Charts collection returns the collection of Chart sheet objects in the workbook.

The Sheets collection is most useful when you want to work with general aspects that apply to all sheets, such as their order in a workbook. For instance, this code moves the currently active sheet to be the first one in the active workbook:

```
ActiveSheet.Move Sheets(1)
```

In the preceding case, it doesn't matter what type of sheet it is—the workbook is reordered.

workbook.ShowConflictHistory [= setting]

For shared workbooks, True displays the conflict history worksheet; False does not. Default is False.

workbook.ShowPivotTableFieldList [= setting]

True displays pivot table field lists; False does not. Default is True.

workbook.SmartDocument

Returns a reference to the workbook's SmartDocument object.

workbook.SmartTagOptions

Returns a reference to the workbook's SmartTagOptions object. The SmartTagOptions object controls how SmartTags are displayed. For example, the following code displays the SmartTag button, omitting the SmartTag indicator in cells:

```
ThisWorkbook.SmartTagOptions.DisplaySmartTags = xlButtonOnly
```

By default, Excel displays both the SmartTag indicator and button.

workbook.Styles [= setting]

Returns the collection of Style objects in the workbook. The following code displays information about each style in the current workbook:

```
Dim sty As Style
For Each sty In ThisWorkbook.Styles
    Debug.Print sty.Name, sty.NumberFormat, sty.Font.Name
Next
```

workbook.Subject [= setting]

Sets or returns the Subject item in the workbook's Properties page.

workbook.TemplateRemoveExtData [= setting]

True removes references to external data if the workbook is saved as a template; False does not remove references. Default is False.

workbook.Title [= setting]

Sets or returns the Title item in the workbook's Properties page.

workbook.ToggleFormsDesign [= setting]

This method is undocumented. It seems to turn on and off the ability to edit Visual Basic Forms, but it is not clear how that is useful.

workbook.UpdateFromFile

For workbooks opened as read-only, updates the open workbook with the most recent version saved to disk. Causes an error if the workbook is not read-only. The following code updates a read-only workbook:

```
If ThisWorkbook.ReadOnly Then _
    ThisWorkbook.UpdateFromFile
```

workbook.UpdateLink([*Name*], [*Type*])

Updates a link in a workbook.

Argument	Settings
Name	The name of the link to update as returned by the LinkSources property.
Type	The xlLinkType of the link; possible settings are xlLinkTypeExcelLinks (default) or xlLinkTypeOLELinks.

The following code updates each of the Excel links in a workbook:

```
Dim link, linkSources
linkSources = ThisWorkbook.linkSources(xlExcelLinks)
If IsArray(linkSources) Then
    For Each link In linkSources
        ThisWorkbook.UpdateLink Name, XlLinkType.xlLinkTypeExcelLinks
    Next
End If
```

workbook.UpdateLinks [= *setting*]

Changes the way OLE links are updated when the workbook is opened. Possible xlUpdateLink settings are:

xlUpdateLinksAlways
  Updates links when the workbook is opened, does not alert the user

xlUpdateLinksNever
  Does not update links when the workbook is opened or alert the user

xlUpdateLinksUserSetting
  Alerts the user if the workbook contains links when the workbook is opened and asks if those links should be updated (default)

workbook.UpdateRemoteReferences [= *setting*]

True updates remote references in the workbook; False does not update. Default is True.

workbook.UserStatus

Returns an array containing information about each user who is currently connected to a workbook. This property is primarily used for listing the users of a shared workbook. The following code displays a list of the users for the current workbook:

```
Dim usr( ), msg As String
usr = ThisWorkbook.UserStatus
For i = 1 To UBound(usr)
    msg = msg & usr(i, 1) & " Opened: " & _
        usr(i, 2) & " Shared? " & _
        (usr(i, 3) = 2) & vbCrLf
Next
MsgBox msg
```

workbook.VBASigned

Returns True if the Visual Basic project contained in the workbook was digitally signed, otherwise, returns False.

workbook.VBProject

Returns a reference to the Visual Basic project that the workbook contains.

workbook.WebOptions

Returns the WebOptions object for a workbook. Use the WebOptions object to determine how a workbook is saved as a web page. The following code sets the workbook's web options to support Internet Explorer, Version 3.0, then saves the workbook as a web page:

```
Dim wo As WebOptions
Set wo = ThisWorkbook.WebOptions
wo.TargetBrowser = msoTargetBrowserV3
ThisWorkbook.SaveAs ThisWorkbook.Path & "\new.HTML", XlFileFormat.xlHtml
```

 Excel's web file format features don't work well with non-Microsoft browsers.

workbook.WebPagePreview

Previews a workbook in the default web browser.

workbook.Windows [= setting]

Returns the collection of Excel windows in which the workbook is displayed. Use the NewWindow method to open new windows, the Window Close method to close existing windows, and the `Windows Arrange` method to arrange open windows. If you close the last window displaying a workbook, Excel prompts the user to save any changes before closing.

The following code opens two new windows for the current workbook, arranges them, then closes the three new windows:

```
ThisWorkbook.NewWindow
ThisWorkbook.NewWindow
ThisWorkbook.Windows.Arrange
If MsgBox("Click OK to close new windows.", vbOKCancel) Then
    ThisWorkbook.Windows(3).Close
    ThisWorkbook.Windows(2).Close
End If
ThisWorkbook.Windows.Arrange
```

workbook.Worksheets

Returns a collection containing all the worksheets in a workbook. Use the `Worksheets` collection to get a specific worksheet from a workbook. For example, the following code gets a reference to the General worksheet and assigns it to an object variable:

```
Dim ws As Worksheet
Set ws = ThisWorkbook.Worksheets("General")
```

workbook.XmlImport(*Url, ImportMap, [Overwrite], [Destination]*)

Imports an XML file into a list in the workbook. Returns an `xlXMLImportResult` value indicating whether the import succeeded.

Argument	Settings
Url	The address of the XML file to import. The file may be stored on the local machine or at a network address.
ImportMap	An XMLMap object from the workbook to use to interpret the XML. If omitted, Excel creates an XML map for the XML data.
Overwrite	True overwrites any data previously imported through the XML map; False appends data. Default is True.
Destination	A Range object identifying the upper-left corner of the destination for the imported data.

The `ImportMap` argument is required, but it doesn't have to be initialized, since `XmlImport` creates the XML map if none exists. For example, the following code imports an XML file into a new worksheet and creates the XML map based on the XML source file:

```
Dim ws As Worksheet, xmap As XmlMap, msg As String
' Create a new worksheet for the imported data.
Set ws = ThisWorkbook.Worksheets.Add
ret = ThisWorkbook.XmlImport( _
  "http://www.mstrainingkits.com/excel/ExcelObjects.xml", _
  xmap, , ws.Range("A1"))
Select Case ret
    Case XlXmlImportResult.xlXmlImportElementsTruncated
        msg = "Data was truncated."
    Case XlXmlImportResult.xlXmlImportSuccess
```

```
            msg = "XML data imported successfully."
        Case XlXmlImportResult.xlXmlImportValidationFailed
            msg = "XML was not valid."
    End Select
    MsgBox msg
```

The return value of XmlImport indicates one of three possible conditions:

xlXmlImportSuccess
: The data was successfully imported.

xlXmlImportElementsTruncated
: The entire XML file could not be downloaded for some reason, perhaps because there were more elements than would fit on a spreadsheet.

xlXmlImportValidationFailed
: The XML either wasn't valid according to the XML map's schema, or the XML simply wasn't valid XML.

workbook.XmlImportXml(*Data, ImportMap,* [*Overwrite*], [*Destination*])

Imports XML data into a list in the workbook. Returns an xlXMLImportResult value indicating whether the import succeeded.

This method is identical to XmlImport, however, it accepts a string argument containing the XML data, rather than the address of an XML file. This allows you to use XML data returned from web services and to perform XSL transformations before displaying XML data in Excel.

The following code performs an XSL transformation to limit the data displayed when importing XML data to a new worksheet:

```
' Requires reference to Microsoft XML
Dim ws As Worksheet, xmap As XmlMap
Dim msg As String, xml As String
Dim xdoc As New DOMDocument, xstyle As New DOMDocument
' Create a new worksheet for the data.
Set ws = ThisWorkbook.Worksheets.Add
' Load XML.
If Not xdoc.Load("http://www.mstrainingkits.com/excel/ExcelObjects.xml") Then _
    MsgBox "Error loading XML source."
' Load XSL transform.
If Not xstyle.Load("http://www.mstrainingkits.com/excel/ObjByDate.xslt") Then _
    MsgBox "Error loading XSL transform."
' Transform XML.
xml = xdoc.transformNode(xstyle)
' Display results.
ret = ThisWorkbook.XmlImportXml(xml, xmap, , ws.Range("A1"))
Select Case ret
    Case XlXmlImportResult.xlXmlImportElementsTruncated
        msg = "Data was truncated."
    Case XlXmlImportResult.xlXmlImportSuccess
        msg = "XML data imported successfully."
    Case XlXmlImportResult.xlXmlImportValidationFailed
        msg = "XML was not valid."
End Select
MsgBox msg
```

workbook.XmlMaps

Returns the collection of XML maps in a workbook. Use this collection to select an existing XML map to use for importing data or when refreshing XML data displayed in a list. The following code uses the XmlMaps collection to get the ExcelObjects map and then refreshes the data displayed through that map:

```
Dim xmap As XmlMap
Set xmap = ThisWorkbook.XmlMaps("ExcelObjects")
xmap.DataBinding.Refresh
```

workbook.XmlNamespaces

Returns the collection of XmlNamespace objects in a workbook. The XmlNamespaces collection is primarily used to install and manage XML expansion packs that provide SmartDocument features in Excel.

For example, the following code installs one of the sample expansion packs from the Smart Document SDK for all users:

```
sdoc = "C:\Program Files\Microsoft Office 2003 Developer Resources" & _
    "\Microsoft Office 2003 Smart Document SDK\Samples\SimpleSample" & _
    "\SourceFiles\manifest.xml"
ThisWorkbook.XmlNamespaces.InstallManifest sdoc, True
```

RecentFile and RecentFiles Members

Use the RecentFiles collection to get the list of recently opened files from the Excel File menu. Use the Application object's RecentFiles method to get a reference to this collection. Use the RecentFile object to open or remove files from this list. The RecentFiles collection and RececentFile object have the following members. Key members (shown in **bold**) are covered in the following reference section:

Add[2]	Application[2]
Count[1]	Creator[2]
Delete	Index
Item[1]	**Maximum**[1]
Name	**Open**
Parent[2]	**Path**

[1] Collection only
[2] Object and collection

By default, Excel doesn't add files opened programmatically to the recent file list. To add those files, use the Open method with the AddToMRU argument set to True or use the RecentFiles collection's Add method.

recentfiles.Add(*Name*)

Adds a file to the recent-files list. If the file already appears in the recent-files list, the list does not change.

Argument	Settings
Name	The path and name of the file to add to the list. Excel does not check that the file exists before it is added to the list.

The following code updates the recent-files list to make sure all currently open files are included:

```
Sub UpdateRecentFiles( )
    Dim wb As Workbook
    For Each wb In Application.Workbooks
        Application.RecentFiles.Add wb.FullName
    Next
End Sub
```

 Use the Workbook's FullName property when adding workbooks to the list so that Excel can set the recent file's Path property correctly.

recentfile.Delete( )

Removes a file from the recent files list.

recentfiles.Maximum [= *setting*]

Sets or returns the number of files allowed in the recent-files list. Once this maximum is met, least-recent files are removed as new files are added. Must be between 0 and 9.

recentfile.Name

Returns the name of the file as it appears in the recent-files list.

recentfile.Open

Attempts to open the recent file in Excel. This method may fail if the file has been deleted or moved.

recentfile.Path

Returns the full filename and path of the recent file if it is available.

CHAPTER 9
Working with Worksheets and Ranges

If workbooks are the documents of Excel, then worksheets and ranges are the chapters and paragraphs, and individual cells are the words. Most of the work you do takes place on a worksheet and involves manipulating ranges of cells or individual cells. From a programmer's perspective, you are most often working with Worksheet and Range objects, although of course you use other objects to accomplish specific tasks.

One concept that any beginning Excel programmer encounters is that, within the world of Excel objects, a cell is not a Cell object—it is a single-cell Range object. So you will often use a Range object to manipulate individual cells. You use a Worksheet object to control what happens at the worksheet level, and you use a Range object whenever you work with a cell or cells.

In this chapter, I show how to:

- Work with worksheets
- Get cells in a worksheet
- Work with the Sheets collection
- Work with outlines
- Work with ranges
- Find and replace text in a range
- Use named ranges
- Format and change text
- Work with scenarios

This chapter includes task-oriented reference information for the following objects and their related collections: Worksheet, Outline, Range, and Scenario.

 Code used in this chapter and additional samples are available in *ch09.xls*.

Work with Worksheet Objects

Worksheets are the workhorses of Excel. Most of the time when you program Excel, you are doing something with a worksheet, either with the active sheet or some other sheet that you specify. Use the `Worksheets` collection to create new worksheets or to refer to a specific worksheet. For example, to create a new, empty worksheet in Excel, use the `Add` method on the `Sheets` or `Worksheets` collection:

```
Dim ws1 As Worksheet
Dim ws2 As Sheet

Set ws1 = Worksheets.Add
Set ws2 = Sheets.Add
```

Once you've declared a worksheet variable and assigned it a reference to a `Worksheet` object, as in the previous code for creating a new worksheet, you can use the variable to refer to the worksheet's properties and methods. You can also use the `ActiveSheet` method to refer directly to the worksheet that currently has the focus, or refer to a specific worksheet as a member of the `Worksheets` collection.

For example, to set the text for all cells in the current worksheet to bold, you can use either of the variables in the preceding example to return an object that represents all the cells in the worksheet:

```
ws1.Cells.Font.Bold = True
```

You could accomplish the same task for the current worksheet by using the `ActiveSheet` property, which represents the active worksheet. This is the most common way to refer to the properties and methods of the currently active worksheet:

```
ActiveSheet.Cells.Font.Bold = True
```

You can also refer to a specific worksheet as a member of the `Worksheets` collection:

```
Worksheets("WombatBattingAverages").Cells.Font.Bold = True
```

Get Cells in a Worksheet

As you saw in the previous examples, you can use the `Cells` property of a worksheet to work with all the cells on a worksheet as a group. Two other ways you can work with ranges of cells in a worksheet are to:

- Use the `Range` property to work with a specific range of cells
- Use the `UsedRange` property to work with only cells that have data

For example, you could use the `Range` property to set the text of cells in the range C5:D10 on the active worksheet to bold type:

```
ActiveSheet.Range("C5:D10").Font.Bold = True
```

The Range property may be the most commonly used property in Excel programming. You will use it a lot!

The `UsedRange` property returns the rectangular block of cells that contain values. The upper-left corner of the block is the first cell that contains a value, and the lower-right corner of the block is the last cell that contains a value. In between there may or may not be empty cells—the range is contiguous. It's more efficient to work with `UsedRange` than the `Cells` property because it returns a smaller, more specific range of cells. For example, the following code selects all of the cells that have negative values on the active worksheet:

```
Sub DemoUsedRange( )
    Dim cel As Range, str As String
    For Each cel In ActiveSheet.UsedRange
        If cel.Value < 0 Then str = str & cel.Address & ","
    Next
    If str <> "" Then _
        ActiveSheet.Range(Left(str, Len(str) - 1)).Select
End Sub
```

Worksheets and Worksheet Members

Use the `Worksheets` collection to create new and get existing worksheets in Excel. Use the `Workbook` object's `Worksheets` method to get a reference to this collection. Use the `Worksheet` object to activate and work with ranges on individual worksheets. The `Worksheets` collection and `Worksheet` object have the following members. Key members (shown in **bold**) are covered in the following reference section:

Activate	**Add**[1]	Application[2]
AutoFilter	AutoFilterMode	**Calculate**
Cells	ChartObjects	**CheckSpelling**
CircleInvalid	CircularReference	ClearArrows
ClearCircles	CodeName	**Columns**
Comments	ConsolidationFunction	ConsolidationOptions
ConsolidationSources	**Copy**[2]	Count[1]
Creator[2]	CustomProperties	Delete
DisplayPageBreaks	DisplayRightToLeft	EnableAutoFilter
EnableCalculation	**EnableOutlining**	**EnablePivotTable**
EnableSelection	Evaluate	FillAcrossSheets[1]
FilterMode	HPageBreaks[2]	**Hyperlinks**
Index	Item	ListObjects
MailEnvelope	**Move**[2]	Name
Names	Next	OLEObjects
Outline	**PageSetup**	Parent[2]
Paste	**PasteSpecial**	PivotTables
PivotTableWizard	Previous	PrintOut[2]
PrintPreview[2]	**Protect**	**ProtectContents**
ProtectDrawingObjects	Protection	**ProtectionMode**
ProtectScenarios	**QueryTables**	**Range**
ResetAllPageBreaks	Rows	SaveAs

Scenarios	Scripts	**ScrollArea**
Select[2]	**SetBackgroundPicture**	**Shapes**
ShowAllData	ShowDataForm	SmartTags
StandardHeight	**StandardWidth**	Tab
TransitionExpEval	TransitionFormEntry	**Type**
Unprotect	**UsedRange**	Visible[2]
VPageBreaks[2]	XmlDataQuery	XmlMapQuery

[1] Collection only
[2] Object and collection

worksheet.Activate( )

Activates the specified worksheet giving it focus. For example, the following code activates the WombatBattingAverages worksheet:

```
Worksheets("WombatBattingAverages").Activate
```

worksheets.Add(*Before, After, Count, Type*)

Creates one or more worksheets. If you create a single worksheet, it is the active sheet. If you create more than one worksheet, the last sheet created is the active sheet.

Argument	Settings
Before	Specifies an existing worksheet if you want to place the new worksheet before that sheet.
After	Specifies an existing worksheet if you want to place the new worksheet after that sheet.
Count	Specifies the number of sheets to be added if you want to create more than one sheet.
Type	Use xlChart to insert a chart, xlExcel4MacroSheet to insert a macro sheet, or the path to a template if you are inserting a sheet based on an existing template.

The following code creates two worksheets after the WombatBattingAverages worksheet:

```
ActiveWorkbook.Sheets.Add After:=Worksheets("WombatBattingAverages"), Count:=2
```

worksheet.Calculate( )

Calculates the formulas on the specified worksheet. For example, the following code calculates the formulas for the batting averages of a renowned softball team:

```
Worksheets("WombatBattingAverages").Calculate
```

worksheet.Cells

Returns a Range object that represents cells on the worksheet. The syntax shows the Cells property without arguments, which returns all the cells in a worksheet as a Range object. However, you can also enter the specific range you want to return as if you were using the syntax for a Range object.

The following code sets the font size to 12 for every cell in the WombatBattingAverages worksheet so the athletes can easily read them:

```
Worksheets("WombatBattingAverages").Cells.Font.Size = 12
```

The following code highlights batting averages .300 and over:

```
Dim rwIndex As Integer
For rwIndex = 1 To 3
    With Worksheets("WombatBattingAverages").Cells(rwIndex, 2)
        If .Value >= 0.3 Then
            .Font.Color = RGB(255, 0, 0)
        End If
    End With
Next rwIndex
```

worksheet.CheckSpelling(*CustomDictionary, IgnoreUppercase, AlwaysSuggest, SpellLang*)

Checks the spelling of text on the specified worksheet and displays the Spelling dialog box.

The following code checks the spelling of text in the cells of the WombatBattingAverages worksheet:

```
Worksheets("WombatBattingAverages").CheckSpelling
```

worksheet.Columns([*Index*])

Returns a Range object that represents the column specified by *Index* or all the columns in a worksheet.

The following code selects the second column (column B) in the active worksheet:

```
ActiveSheet.Columns(2).Select
```

worksheet.Comments

Returns the collection of comments on a worksheet.

The following code deletes comments by Jeff Webb:

```
Dim cmt As Comment
For Each cmnt in ActiveSheet.Comments
    If cmnt.Author = "Jeff Webb" Then cmnt.Delete
Next
```

worksheet.Copy(*Before, After*)

Copies the specified sheet to another location in the workbook.

Argument	Settings
Before	Specifies an existing worksheet if you want to place the copied worksheet before that sheet
After	Specifies an existing worksheet if you want to place the copied worksheet after that sheet

The following code copies the KarmaFactor worksheet after the WombatBattingAverages worksheet:

```
ActiveWorkbook.Worksheets("KarmaFactor").Copy
After:=Worksheets("WombatBattingAverages")
```

worksheet.DisplayPageBreaks

Set this property to True to display page breaks for the worksheet.

worksheet.EnableCalculation [= *setting*]

True allows calculations on the worksheet; False disables calculations. Default is True.

worksheet.EnableOutlining [= *setting*]

Set this property to True to automatically enable outlining symbols on the worksheet.

worksheet.EnablePivotTable [= *setting*]

Set this property to True to automatically enable PivotTable controls and actions on the worksheet.

worksheet.EnableSelection [= *setting*]

Set this property to:

xlNoSelection
     To prevent any selection on the worksheet

xlNoRestrictions
     To allow any cell to be selected

xlUnlockedCells
     To allow selection of only unlocked cells

worksheet.Hyperlinks

Returns the collection of hyperlinks on a worksheet.

The following code updates the names of the hyperlinks on a worksheet from one year to another:

```
For Each hlink in Worksheets("WombatBattingAverages").Hyperlinks
     If hlink.Name = "2005Stats" Then hlink.Name = "2006Stats"
Next
```

worksheet.Move(*Before, After*)

Moves the specified sheet to another location in the workbook.

Argument	Settings
Before	Specifies an existing worksheet if you want to place the worksheet before that sheet
After	Specifies an existing worksheet if you want to place the worksheet after that sheet

The following code moves the KarmaFactor worksheet after the WombatBattingAverages worksheet:

```
ActiveWorkbook.Worksheets("KarmaFactor").Move
After:=Worksheets("WombatBattingAverages")
```

worksheet.Outline

Returns an Outline object that represents the outline of a worksheet.

The following code enables automatic outlining for the active worksheet and then shows the top-level view of the outline:

```
ActiveSheet.Cells.AutoOutline
ActiveSheet.Outline.ShowLevels 1, 1
```

worksheet.PageSetup

Returns a PageSetup object that represents the page setup attributes for the worksheet.

The following code sets the page orientation of the WombatBattingAverages worksheet to landscape:

```
With Worksheets("WombatBattingAverages")
    .PageSetup.Orientation = xlLandscape
End With
```

worksheet.Paste([*Destination*], [*Link*])

Pastes the contents of the clipboard onto the specified worksheet.

Argument	Settings
Destination	A Range object that specifies where the clipboard contents are pasted
Link	True to establish a link between the pasted clipboard contents and their source

The following code copies the range of cells B1:B3 to the range E1:E3:

```
Worksheets("WombatBattingAverages ").Range("B1:B3").Copy
ActiveSheet.Paste Destination:=Worksheets("WombatBattingAverages ").Range("E1:E3")
```

worksheet.PasteSpecial([*Format*], [*Link*], [*DisplayAsIcon*], [*IconFileName*], [*IconIndex*], [*IconLabel*], [*NoHTMLFormatting*])

Pastes the contents of the clipboard, including formatting, onto the specified worksheet.

Argument	Settings
Format	The format of the clipboard contents to paste, using one of the strings specified in the As list box of the Paste Special dialog box
Link	True to establish a link between the pasted clipboard contents and their source
DisplayAsIcon	True to display the pasted clipboard contents as an icon
IconFileName	The name of the file containing the icon to display
IconIndex	The numeric index of the icon within the icon file
IconLabel	The label to display with the icon
NoHTMLFormatting	True to remove all HTML formatting from the clipboard contents

The following code pastes the contents of the clipboard into cell D2 as a hyperlink:

```
Worksheets("WombatBattingAverages ").Range("D2").Select
ActiveSheet.PasteSpecial Format:= "Hyperlink"
```

worksheet.Protect([*Password*], [*DrawingObjects*], [*Contents*], [*Scenarios*], [*UserInterfaceOnly*], [*AllowFormattingCells*], [*AllowFormattingColumns*], [*AllowFormattingRows*], [*AllowInsertingColumns*], [*AllowInsertingRows*], [*AllowInsertingHyperlinks*], [*AllowDeletingColumns*], [*AllowDeletingRows*], [*AllowSorting*], [*AllowFiltering*], [*AllowUsingPivotTables*])

Prevents changes to a worksheet.

Argument	Settings
Password	A case-sensitive password string.
DrawingObjects	True prevents changes to shapes.
Contents	True prevents changes to the contents of cells.
Scenarios	True prevents changes to scenarios.
UserInterfaceOnly	True prevents changes to the user interface, but not macros.
AllowFormattingCells	True allows formatting changes to cells.
AllowFormattingColumns	True allows formatting changes to columns.
AllowFormattingRows	True allows formatting changes to rows.
AllowInsertingColumns	True allows inserting of columns.
AllowInsertingRows	True allows inserting of rows.
AllowInsertingHyperlinks	True allows inserting of hyperlinks.
AllowDeletingColumns	True allows deleting of columns.

Argument	Settings
AllowDeletingRows	True allows deleting of rows.
AllowSorting	True allows sorting on the worksheet.
AllowFiltering	True allows filtering on the worksheet.
AllowUsingPivotTables	True allows pivot tables on the worksheet.

worksheet.ProtectContents

Set this property to True to prevent changes to a worksheet.

worksheet.ProtectDrawingObjects

Set this property to True to prevent changes to shapes.

worksheet.Protection

Returns a Protection object that represents the protection attributes of the worksheet.

The following code displays a message if you can't delete rows in a worksheet:

```
If ActiveSheet.Protection.AllowDeletingRows = False Then
    MsgBox "Sorry, you can't delete this row."
End If
```

worksheet.ProtectionMode

Returns True if the user interface is protected. To protect the user interface, use the Protect method with the *UserInterfaceOnly* argument set to True.

worksheet.ProtectScenarios

Returns True if scenarios are protected.

worksheet.QueryTables

Returns the QueryTables collection of the worksheet's query tables.

worksheet.Range([*Cell1*], [*Cell2*])

Returns a Range object that represents a range of cells.

The following code highlights batting averages .300 and over:

```
For Each c in Worksheets("WombatBattingAverages").Range("B1:B10")
    If c.Value >= 0.3 Then
```

```
        .Font.Color = RGB(255, 0, 0)
    End If
Next c
```

worksheet.Rows([*Index*])

Returns a Range object that represents the row specified by *Index* or all the rows in a worksheet.

The following code selects the second row in the active worksheet:

```
ActiveSheet.Rows(2).Select
```

worksheet.Scenarios([*Index*])

Returns a Scenario object that represents the scenario specified by *Index* or all the scenarios in a worksheet.

worksheet.ScrollArea

Sets the cell range where scrolling is allowed.

The following code sets the scroll area for the WombatBattingAverages worksheet:

```
Worksheets("WombatBattingAverages").ScrollArea = "B1:B10"
```

worksheet.SetBackgroundPicture([*Filename*])

Displays the specified graphic as the background for the worksheet.

worksheet.Shapes

Returns the collection of the Shape objects in the worksheet's drawing layer, such as the AutoShapes, freeforms, OLE objects, or pictures.

worksheet.StandardHeight

Returns the default height of rows, in points.

worksheet.StandardWidth

Returns the default width of columns, in normal font character widths or the width of the zero character (0) for proportional fonts.

worksheet.Type [= *setting*]

Returns or sets the type of worksheet: xlChart, xlDialogSheet, xlExcel4IntlMacroSheet, xlExcel4MacroSheet, or xlWorksheet.

worksheet.Unprotect([*Password*])

Allows changes to a worksheet.

Argument	Settings
Password	A case-sensitive password string

worksheet.UsedRange

Returns a Range object that represents the cell range that contains data.

The following code returns the cell range on the WombatBattingAverages worksheet that contains the worksheet's data.

```
Worksheets("WombatBattingAverages").UsedRange.Address
```

Sheets Members

Use the Sheets collection to access all the sheets in the active workbook, including both Chart and Worksheet objects. For example, the following code inserts a worksheet after the first sheet in the active workbook and then inserts a chart after the new worksheet:

```
Sheets.Add type:=xlWorksheet, after:=Sheets(1)
Sheets.Add type:=xlChart, after:=Sheets(2)
```

The Sheets collection has the following members. Key members (shown in **bold**) are covered in the following reference section:

Add	**Copy**
Count	Delete
FillAcrossSheets	HPageBreaks
Item	**Move**
PrintOut	PrintPreview
Select	Visible
VPageBreaks	

Sheets.Copy(*Before, After*)

Copies the specified sheet to another location in the workbook.

Argument	Settings
Before	Specifies an existing worksheet if you want to place the copied worksheet before that sheet
After	Specifies an existing worksheet if you want to place the copied worksheet after that sheet

Sheets.FillAcrossSheets(*Range, Type*)

Copies the specified range to the same location on all the worksheets in the workbook.

Argument	Settings
Range	Specifies a Range object representing the range to copy to the worksheets
Type	Specifies how to copy the range: xlFillWithAll, xlFillWithContents, or xlFillWithFormats

Sheets.Move(*Before, After*)

Moves the specified sheet to another location in the workbook.

Argument	Settings
Before	Specifies an existing worksheet if you want to place the worksheet before that sheet
After	Specifies an existing worksheet if you want to place the worksheet after that sheet

Work with Outlines

Outlining lets you quickly switch between the big picture and the details of a summary worksheet. In Figure 9-1, you can see the detail view of a summary worksheet, and in Figure 9-2 you can see the corresponding big picture.

You can control outlining programmatically by using the Outline property of a Worksheet object to return an Outline object. You can use the properties and methods of the Outline object to control how the outline is displayed and how levels are assigned.

The following code creates an AutoOutline and displays the outline levels:

```
ActiveSheet.UsedRange.AutoOutline
ActiveSheet.Outline.AutomaticStyles = True
ActiveSheet.Outline.ShowLevels 1, 1
```

If you have an outline with many levels, the following code displays all levels. An outline can have up to eight levels:

```
ActiveSheet.Outline.ShowLevels 8,8
```

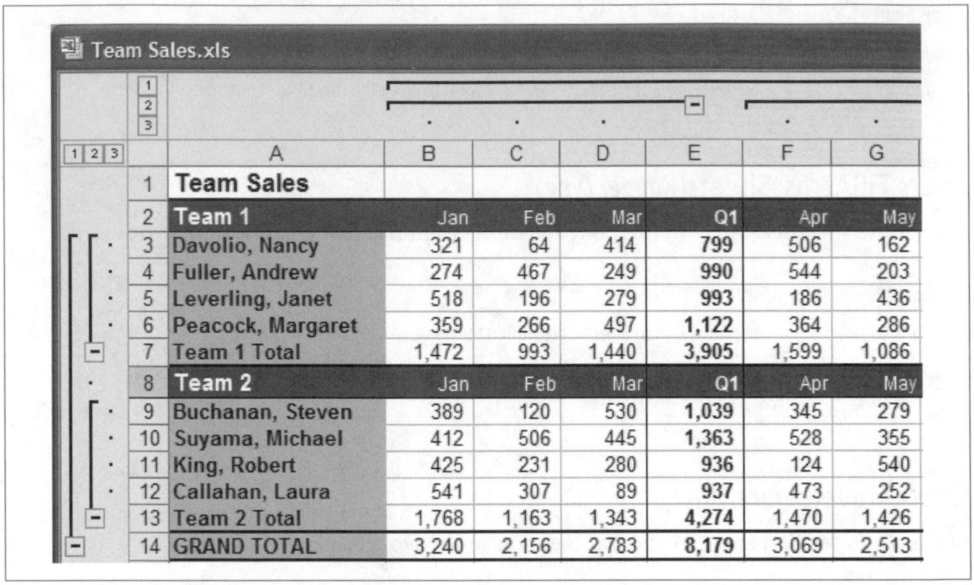

	A	B	C	D	E	F	G
1	Team Sales						
2	Team 1	Jan	Feb	Mar	Q1	Apr	May
3	Davolio, Nancy	321	64	414	799	506	162
4	Fuller, Andrew	274	467	249	990	544	203
5	Leverling, Janet	518	196	279	993	186	436
6	Peacock, Margaret	359	266	497	1,122	364	286
7	Team 1 Total	1,472	993	1,440	3,905	1,599	1,086
8	Team 2	Jan	Feb	Mar	Q1	Apr	May
9	Buchanan, Steven	389	120	530	1,039	345	279
10	Suyama, Michael	412	506	445	1,363	528	355
11	King, Robert	425	231	280	936	124	540
12	Callahan, Laura	541	307	89	937	473	252
13	Team 2 Total	1,768	1,163	1,343	4,274	1,470	1,426
14	GRAND TOTAL	3,240	2,156	2,783	8,179	3,069	2,513

Figure 9-1. A detail view of team sales

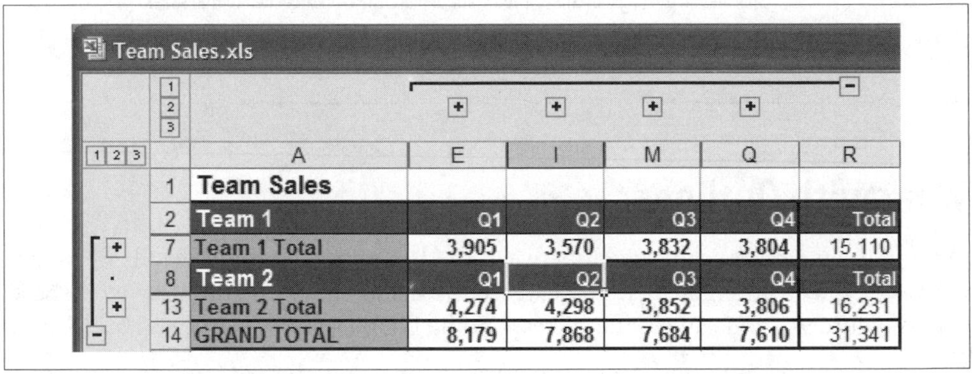

	A	E	I	M	Q	R
1	Team Sales					
2	Team 1	Q1	Q2	Q3	Q4	Total
7	Team 1 Total	3,905	3,570	3,832	3,804	15,110
8	Team 2	Q1	Q2	Q3	Q4	Total
13	Team 2 Total	4,274	4,298	3,852	3,806	16,231
14	GRAND TOTAL	8,179	7,868	7,684	7,610	31,341

Figure 9-2. The corresponding big picture

Outline Members

Use the `Outline` object to control the level of summary displayed for an outlined range. Use the `Worksheet` object's `Outline` property to get a reference to this object. The `Outline` object has the following members. Key members (shown in **bold**) are covered in the following reference section:

`Application`	**`AutomaticStyles`**
`Creator`	`Parent`
`ShowLevels`	**`SummaryColumn`**
`SummaryRow`	

outline.AutomaticStyles

True if the outline uses automatic styles.

outline.ShowLevels(*RowLevels, ColumnLevels*)

Displays a specified number of row and column levels for the outline.

Argument	Settings
RowLevels	The number of row levels to display
ColumnLevels	The number of column levels to display

outline.SummaryColumn

Sets or returns the location of the outline's summary columns, either xlSummaryOnRight to position the summary column to the right of the detail columns or xlSummaryOnLeft to position the summary columns to the left of the detail columns.

outline.SummaryRow

Sets or returns the location of the outline's summary rows, either xlSummaryBelow to position the summary column below the detail rows or xlSummaryAbove to position the summary columns above the detail rows.

Work with Ranges

When you want to do just about anything in code with a cell or group of cells in a worksheet, you do it using a Range object. It is the most frequently used object in Excel programming.

It can also be confusing. You can return a Range object in many ways in your code, and it can represent both individual cells and groups of cells, depending on the circumstances. Compounding the confusion, the Excel programming reference topics do not document Range as an object, even though Range objects are referred to frequently throughout the reference documentation, and you often declare variables of type Range. Once you become familiar with Range objects, however, they are not difficult to use.

The most common way to return a Range object is using the Range property, which lets you specify a single cell or a range of cells. The following code returns the value of cell A9 on the currently active worksheet:

```
ActiveSheet.Range("A9")
```

The following code selects all the cells in the range A1:A9:

```
ActiveSheet.Range("A1:A9").Select
```

Another common way to return a Range object is to use the Cells property to return an individual cell based on its row and column position in a worksheet. For example, the following code sets the value of cell F4 (the cell in the fourth row and sixth column) to 12:

```
ActiveSheet.Cells(4, 6)=12
```

The advantage of using the Cells property to return a range is that you can use variables to represent the row or column values. For example, the following code uses the variable rwIndex to iterate through rows of a worksheet:

```
Dim r As Range
Dim rwIndex As Integer

For rwIndex = 1 To 3
    Set r = ActiveSheet.Cells(rwIndex, 2)
    With r
        If .Value >= 0.3 Then
            .Font.Bold = True
        End If
    End With
Next rwIndex
```

Other common ways to return a Range object are:

The Columns property
    Returns all the cells in a specified worksheet column

The Rows property
    Returns all the cells in a specified worksheet row

The UsedRange property
    Returns all the cells in a worksheet that contain data

There are other ways to return a Range object, but those are the techniques you will likely use most often.

Find and Replace Text in a Range

Finding and replacing text is a familiar operation to anyone who has spent quality time with a word processing program such as Microsoft Word, or even good old Notepad. It's a pretty common operation in many other applications as well, including Excel.

You would think, then, that performing an Excel find and replace operation in code would be a pretty straightforward thing. Unfortunately, it can be a little quirky.

As you might expect, you use the Find method and its close relatives, the FindNext and FindPrevious methods, to find text, numbers, or cell formatting in a worksheet.

You use the `Replace` method to replace what you found. Here are a couple of things that you might not expect:

- If you specify a range in which to perform the `Find` operation, the first cell in the range is, by default, the current cell. So even if that first cell contains what you are looking for, the `Find` operation will move to the next occurrence in the range if one exists, rather than keeping the focus on the first cell.

- If the search is not successful and your code then uses the `Select` method to attempt to select the result, it will return an error.

The following code finds the first occurrence of the string "Ichiro" in the specified range:

```
Dim myrange As Range
Dim foundcell As Range
Dim strSearch As String

Set myrange = ActiveSheet.Range("A1:A7")
strSearch = "Ichiro"
' Check the first cell in the range.
If myrange(1).Value = strSearch Then
    myrange(1).Select
Else
    Set foundcell = myrange.Find(strSearch, LookIn:=xlValues)
    ' Check to see if the string is found before selecting the cell.
    If Not foundcell Is Nothing Then
        foundcell.Select
    Else
        MsgBox "String not found."
    End If
End If
```

Note that if the first cell in the range contains the string, it will be selected. If you do not explicitly check to see if the first cell contains what you are looking for, the code will move to the next occurrence of the search string. Note also that the code checks to see whether the string is found before selecting the cell.

The following code uses the `FindNext` method to find the next occurrence of the current search string:

```
Dim curCell As Range
Dim foundcell As Range

Set curCell = ActiveCell
Set foundcell = ActiveSheet.Range("A1:A7").FindNext(curCell)
foundcell.Select
```

The following code uses the `Replace` method to replace all occurrences of the string "Ichiro" in the specified range with the string "Suzuki":

```
Dim r As Range

Set r = ActiveSheet.Range("A1:A7")
r.Replace "Ichiro", "Suzuki"
```

Use Named Ranges

Sometimes it is easier and clearer to refer to a particular range of cells by name than by notation, particularly if you plan to refer to that range frequently. For example, if the range of cells between A1 and F10 contains monthly sales information, you could refer to it by the name "MonthlySales" rather than `Range("A1:F10")`.

You create a named range by defining the range that it applies to and then adding the name to the `Names` collection for the workbook. For example, the following code establishes the name "MonthlySales" for the range of cells between A1 and F10 on Sheet1:

```
Names.Add "MonthlySales", "=Sheet1!$A$1:$F$10"
```

You can use the `ListNames` method to display a list of all the named ranges in a workbook. The following code pastes a list of the current named ranges into cell A1 on Sheet 2:

```
Worksheets("Sheet2").Range("A1").ListNames
```

Once you have defined a named range, you can use the name rather than specifying the beginning and ending of the range when you want to change attributes of the range. For example, the following code changes the font of all the cells in the specified named range to bold type:

```
Range("MonthlySales").Font.Bold = True
```

You can use the `GoTo` method to select the cells in the specified named range:

```
Application.GoTo "MonthlySales"
```

If you need to refer to a named range in a worksheet other than the current worksheet, you must include the name of the worksheet when you specify the named range. For example, if the current worksheet is Sheet1, the following code selects the MonthlySales named range on Sheet2:

```
Application.GoTo "Sheet2!MonthlySales"
```

Format and Change Text

Changing the appearance of text in cells is one of the most common operations when you are working with a worksheet. You can spend hours getting your worksheet to look just the way you like.

When you want to use code to set or change the format of text in a cell, you have two choices:

- Use the `Font` property to return a `Font` object, which lets you set or change the format of the entire cell.
- Use the `Characters` collection to set or change the format of individual characters within a cell.

The following code uses the Font property to format the cells in the specified range in bold type:

```
ActiveSheet.Range("A1:A7").Font.Bold = True
```

The following code uses the Characters collection to change the font to bold type for the first six characters in cell A7. For example, if the first word in the cell is "urgent," the following code displays only that word in bold type:

```
ActiveSheet.Range("A9").Characters(1, 6).Font.Bold = True
```

Range Members

Use the Range collection to work with cells on a worksheet. Use the Worksheet object's Cells, Range, UsedRange, Columns, or Rows method to get a reference to this object. The Range collection has the following members. Key members (shown in **bold**) are covered in the following reference section:

Activate	**AddComment**	**AddIndent**
Address	AddressLocal	AdvancedFilter
AllowEdit	Application	ApplyNames
ApplyOutlineStyles	Areas	AutoComplete
AutoFill	AutoFilter	AutoFit
AutoFormat	AutoOutline	**BorderAround**
Borders	**Calculate**	Cells
Characters	**CheckSpelling**	**Clear**
ClearComments	**ClearContents**	**ClearFormats**
ClearNotes	ClearOutline	**Column**
ColumnDifferences	**Columns**	**ColumnWidth**
Comment	Consolidate	**Copy**
CopyFromRecordset	CopyPicture	Count
CreateNames	CreatePublisher	Creator
CurrentArray	CurrentRegion	**Cut**
DataSeries	**Delete**	**Dependents**
DialogBox	**DirectDependents**	**DirectPrecedents**
Dirty	**End**	**EntireColumn**
EntireRow	Errors	**FillDown**
FillLeft	**FillRight**	**FillUp**
Find	**FindNext**	**FindPrevious**
Font	FormatConditions	**Formula**
FormulaArray	FormulaHidden	FormulaLabel
FormulaLocal	**FormulaR1C1**	FormulaR1C1Local
FunctionWizard	GoalSeek	Group
HasArray	HasFormula	Height
Hidden	**HorizontalAlignment**	**Hyperlinks**
ID	IndentLevel	**Insert**
InsertIndent	Interior	**Item**
Justify	Left	ListHeaderRows

ListNames	ListObject	LocationInTable
Locked	**Merge**	**MergeArea**
MergeCells	Name	NavigateArrow
Next	**NoteText**	**NumberFormat**
NumberFormatLocal	**Offset**	Orientation
OutlineLevel	**PageBreak**	Parent
Parse	**PasteSpecial**	Phonetic
Phonetics	PivotCell	PivotField
PivotItem	PivotTable	**Precedents**
PrefixCharacter	**Previous**	**PrintOut**
PrintPreview	QueryTable	Range
ReadingOrder	RemoveSubtotal	**Replace**
Resize	**Row**	**RowDifferences**
RowHeight	**Rows**	Run
Select	SetPhonetic	**Show**
ShowDependents	**ShowDetail**	**ShowErrors**
ShowPrecedents	**ShrinkToFit**	SmartTags
Sort	SortSpecial	Speak
SpecialCells	**Style**	SubscribeTo
Subtotal	Summary	**Table**
Text	**TextToColumns**	Top
Ungroup	**UnMerge**	**UseStandardHeight**
UseStandardWidth	Validation	**Value**
Value2	**VerticalAlignment**	Width
Worksheet	**WrapText**	XPath

range.Activate( )

Activates the specified cell, giving it focus. The following code activates cell B2 on the current worksheet:

```
ActiveSheet.Range("B2").Activate
```

range.AddComment( )

Adds a comment to the specified range. The following code adds a comment to cells with batting averages .300 and over:

```
Dim r As Range
Dim rwIndex As Integer

For rwIndex = 1 To 3
    Set r = Worksheets("WombatBattingAverages").Cells(rwIndex, 2)
    With r
        If .Value >= 0.3 Then
            .AddComment "All Star!"
        End If
    End With
Next rwIndex
```

range.AddIndent[= setting]

Set this property to True to automatically indent text cells that have distributed alignment. Use the HorizontalAlignment and VerticalAlignment properties to set distributed alignment.

range.Address([RowAbsolute], [ColumnAbsolute], [ReferenceStyle], [External], [RelativeTo])

Returns the range reference for the specified range.

Argument	Settings
RowAbsolute	True (default) returns the row reference as an absolute reference.
ColumnAbsolute	True (default) returns the column reference as an absolute reference.
ReferenceStyle	xlA1 (default) returns an A1-style reference. Use xlR1C1 to return an R1C1 reference.
External	False (default) returns a local reference, without including a workbook and worksheet reference.
RelativeTo	The Range object that defines the starting point for a relative range. Use this argument if RowAbsolute and ColumnAbsolute are False, and ReferenceStyle is R1C1.

range.AllowEdit

True if the specified range on a protected worksheet can be edited.

range.Areas([Index])

Returns a collection of Range objects representing the ranges in a multiple-area selection or the range in the area specified by Index. The following code displays the range references for each range in a multiple-area selection:

```
Dim r As Range

For each r in Selection.Areas
    MsgBox r.Address
Next r
```

range.AutoFill(Destination, [Type])

Automatically fills in the cells in a specified destination range based on the specified source range.

Argument	Settings
Destination	The cells to be filled, including the source range.
Type	The default value is xlFillDefault, which attempts to select the most appropriate fill type based on the source range. You can also explicitly specify the type using one of the following constants: xlFillDays, xlFillFormats, xlFillSeries, xlFillWeekdays, xlGrowthTrend, xlFillCopy, xlFillMonths, xlFillValues, xlFillYears, xlLinearTrend.

If the value of cell A1 is 1, the following code automatically fills in the remaining cells in the range A1:A5 with the values 2 through 5:

```
Dim srcRange As Range
Dim destRange As Range

Set srcRange = ActiveSheet.Range("A1")
Set destRange = ActiveSheet.Range("A1:A5")
srcRange.AutoFill destRange, xlFillSeries
```

*range.*AutoFit

Sizes the height and width of the cells in the specified range to fit their contents.

*range.*BorderAround([*LineStyle*], [*Weight*], [*ColorIndex*], [*Color*])

Adds a border around the specified range of cells.

Argument	Settings
LineStyle	The line style of the border. The default value is xlContinuous, which uses a continuous line. You can also explicitly specify the line style using one of the following constants: xlDash, xlDashDot, xlDashDotDot, xlDot, xlDouble, xlLineStyleNone, xlSlantDashDot, xlLineStyleNone.
Weight	The thickness of the border line. The default value is xlThin, which uses a thin line. You can also explicitly specify the weight style using one of the following constants: xlHairline, xlMedium, xlThick.
ColorIndex	The border color, as an index of the color in the current color palette or as one of the following constants: xlColorIndexAutomatic (default) and xlColorIndexNone.
Color	The border color as an RGB value.

*range.*Borders([*Index*])

Returns the collection of Border objects representing the borders of the specified range or a Border object representing a border specified by one of the following constants: xlDiagonalDown, xlDiagonalUp, xlEdgeBottom, xlEdgeLeft, xlEdgeRight, xlEdgeTop, xlInsideHorizontal, or xlInsideVertical.

The following code adds a border around the specified range:

```
With ActiveSheet.Range("B2:B5")
    .Borders(xlEdgeBottom).LineStyle = xlContinuous
    .Borders(xlEdgeLeft).LineStyle = xlContinuous
    .Borders(xlEdgeRight).LineStyle = xlContinuous
    .Borders(xlEdgeTop).LineStyle = xlContinuous
End With
```

range.**Calculate( )**

Calculates the formulas in the specified range.

range.**Cells([*RowIndex*], [*ColumnIndex*])**

Returns a Range object representing all the cells in the specified range or a subset indexed by row number and/or column number.

Argument	Settings
RowIndex	The row number of the cells to return
ColumnIndex	The column number of the cells to return

The following code changes the font to bold type for cells in the specified range with batting averages over .300:

```
Dim r As Range
Dim rwIndex As Integer

Set r = Worksheets("WombatBattingAverages").Range("B1:B3")

For rwIndex = 1 To 3
    With r.Cells(rwIndex)
        If .Value >= 0.3 Then
            .Font.Bold = True
        End If
    End With
Next rwIndex
```

range.**Characters([*Start*], [*Length*])**

Returns a Characters object representing all the characters in a text cell or a specified string within the text.

Argument	Settings
Start	The position of the first character in the string. The default is the first character.
Length	The number of characters in the string. The default is the remaining characters in the cell.

The following code changes the font to bold type for the first six characters in cell A9. For example, if the first word in the cell is "urgent," the following code displays only that word in bold type:

```
ActiveSheet.Range("A9").Characters(1, 6).Font.Bold = True
```

range.**CheckSpelling([***CustomDictionary***], [***IgnoreUppercase***], [***AlwaysSuggest***], [***SpellLang***])**

Checks the spelling of the words in the specified range.

Argument	Settings
CustomDictionary	The filename of a custom dictionary. The custom dictionary is checked if a word isn't found in the main dictionary.
IgnoreUppercase	True ignores uppercase words.
AlwaysSuggest	True displays suggested alternate spellings.
SpellLang	An msoLanguageID constant specifying the Language ID used for the spellcheck.

range.**Clear( )**

Clears the cells in the specified range.

range.**ClearContents( )**

Clears the cells in the specified range but preserves formatting.

range.**ClearFormats( )**

Clears the formatting of cells in the specified range.

range.**Column**

Returns the number of the first column in the specified range. For example, column A is 1, column B is 2, and so on. The following code returns 2:

```
ActiveSheet. Range("B3").Column
```

range.**Columns([***Index***])**

Returns a Range object that represents the columns in the specified range or the column specified by *Index*. The following code changes the font in column A of the specified range to bold type:

```
ActiveSheet.Range("A1:B4").Columns(1).Font.Bold = True
```

range.**ColumnWidth**

Sets the width of columns in the specified range. If all the columns have the same width, returns the width; otherwise, returns Null.

range.Copy([*Destination*])

Copies the specified range to the specified destination range or to the clipboard.

Argument	Settings
Destination	Specifies the destination range. If this argument is omitted, the range is copied to the clipboard.

range.CopyFromRecordset([*Data, MaxRows, MaxColumns*])

Copies the contents of a Recordset object into the specified range.

Argument	Settings
Data	The Recordset object to copy.
MaxRows	If you do not want to copy all records, this argument specifies the maximum number of records to copy.
MaxColumns	If you do not want to copy all fields, this argument specifies the maximum number of fields to copy.

range.Cut([*Destination*])

Cuts the specified range to the specified destination range or to the clipboard.

Argument	Settings
Destination	Specifies the destination range. If this argument is omitted, the range is copied to the clipboard.

range.Delete([*Shift*])

Deletes the specified range and shifts the cells based on the shape of the specified range or the specified *Shift* argument.

Argument	Settings
Shift	Specifies whether cells are shifted up (xlShiftUp) or to the left (xlShiftToLeft) when the specified range of cells is deleted. If you don't supply a *Shift* argument, the cells are shifted according to the shape of the range.

range.Dependents

Returns a Range object that represents the cell or cells whose values depend directly or indirectly on cells in the specified range. If cell F2 contains a formula that uses cell B2, and cell G2 contains a formula that uses cell F2, the following code selects both cell F2 and cell G2:

```
Dim r As Range

Set r = ActiveSheet.Range("B2")
r.Dependents.Select
```

range.**DirectDependents**

Returns a Range object that represents the cell or cells whose values depend directly on cells in the specified range. If cell F2 contains a formula that uses cell B2, and cell G2 contains a formula that uses cell F2, the following code selects only cell F2:

```
Dim r As Range

Set r = ActiveSheet.Range("B2")
r.DirectDependents.Select
```

range.**DirectPrecedents**

Returns a Range object that represents the cell or cells that directly use the cells in the specified range. If cell F2 contains a formula that uses cell B2, and cell G2 contains a formula that uses cell F2, the following code selects only cell F2:

```
Dim r As Range

Set r = ActiveSheet.Range("G2")
r.DirectPrecedents.Select
```

range.**End([*Direction*])**

Returns a Range object that represents the cell at the end a region of cells containing the specified range, in the specified direction. The following code selects the cell at the bottom end of the region containing cell A2:

```
Dim r As Range

Set r = ActiveSheet.Range("A2")
r.End(xlDown).Select
```

range.**EntireColumn**

Returns a Range object that represents the entire column or columns containing the specified range.

range.**EntireRow**

Returns a Range object that represents the entire row or rows containing the specified range.

range.**FillDown**

Fills the contents and formatting of the top cell or cells in the specified range to all cells in the range in the downward direction.

range.FillLeft

Fills the contents and formatting of the right cell or cells in the specified range to all cells in the range to the left.

range.FillRight

Fills the contents and formatting of the left cell or cells in the specified range to all cells in the range to the right.

range.FillUp

Fills the contents and formatting of the bottom cell in the specified range to all cells in the range in the upward direction.

range.Find(*What*, [*After*], [*LookIn*], [*LookAt*]), [*SearchOrder*], [*SearchDirection*], [*MatchCase*], [*MatchByte*], [*SearchFormat*])

Returns a Range object representing the cell containing the first occurrence of the specified item within the specified range.

Argument	Settings
What	The item to search for. Can be a string or Excel data type.
After	The cell after which the search begins.
LookIn	Specify xlFormulas, xlValues, or xlNotes to limit the search to those types of information.
LookAt	xlPart (default) searches within the cell contents; xlWhole searches whole cells.
SearchOrder	xlByRows (default) searches one row at a time; xlByColumns searches one column at a time.
SearchDirection	xlNext (default) searches down and to the right; xlPrevious searches up and to the left.
MatchCase	False (default) ignores case; True performs a case-sensitive search.
MatchByte	If double-byte language support is enabled: • True matches double-byte characters. • False matches double-byte characters to their single-byte equivalents.
SearchFormat	True uses the FindFormat property setting to find cells with specific formatting; False ignores the FindFormat property. Default is False.

The following code selects the first cell in row A that contains the string "Ichiro". Note that the code checks whether the Find method returns Nothing. If you don't check for Nothing and the Find item isn't found, the Select method returns an error.

```
Dim r As Range
Dim foundCell As Range

Set r = ActiveSheet.Range("A1:A6")
Set foundCell = r.Find("Ichiro", LookIn:=xlValues)
```

```
If Not foundCell Is Nothing Then
    foundCell.Select
Else
    MsgBox "String not found."
End If
```

range.FindNext([*After*])

Repeats the last Find operation and returns a Range object representing the cell containing the next occurrence of the specified item within the specified range.

Argument	Settings
After	The cell after which the search begins

range.FindPrevious([*After*])

Repeats the last Find operation and returns a Range object representing the cell containing the previous occurrence of the specified item within the specified range.

Argument	Settings
After	The cell after which the search begins

range.Font

Returns a Font object that lets you set Font properties for the specified range. The following code formats the cells in the specified range in bold type:

```
ActiveSheet.Range("A1:A5").Font.Bold = True
```

range.Formula

Sets or returns a formula for the specified cell or range in A1-style notation. The following code sets a formula for cell E1:

```
ActiveSheet.Range("E1").Formula = "=B1*C1"
```

range.FormulaR1C1

Sets or returns a formula for the specified cell or range in R1C1-style notation. It is easier to work with formulas in code using this notation. The following code sets a formula for cell E1:

```
ActiveSheet.Range("E1").FormulaR1C1 = "=Sum(R2C:R[-1]C)"
```

range.Hidden

True if the specified row or column is hidden. The following code hides column D:

```
Dim r As Range

Set r = ActiveSheet.Columns("D")
r.Hidden = True
```

range.HorizontalAlignment

Sets or returns the horizontal alignment for the specified range. xlGeneral (default) left-aligns text and right-aligns numbers; xlLeft left-aligns values; xlRight right-aligns values; xlCenter centers values within each cell; xlCenterAcrossSelection centers values across the range; xlJustify and xlDistributed justify wrapped text within cells; xlFill repeats values to fill each cell.

range.Hyperlinks

Returns a Hyperlinks collection that represents the hyperlinks in the specified range. The following code changes the address of hyperlinks in the specified range that have the address "\\koala\bear":

```
Dim r As Range
Dim h As Hyperlink

Set r = ActiveSheet.Range("D1:D7")
For Each h In r.Hyperlinks
    If h.Address = "\\koala\bear" Then
        h.Address = "\\wombat\mojo"
    End If
Next
```

range.Insert([Shift])

Inserts the current cut or copied range into the specified range and shifts the cells based on the shape of the specified range or the specified *Shift* argument.

Argument	Settings
Shift	Specifies whether cells are shifted to the right (xlShiftToRight) or down (xlShiftDown) when the specified range of cells is inserted. If you don't supply a *Shift* argument, the cells are shifted according to the shape of the range.

range.Interior

Returns an Interior object that represents the interior of the range. The following code changes the color of the specified range to red:

```
ActiveSheet.Range("A1:A5").Interior.ColorIndex = 3
```

range.Item(RowIndex, [ColumnIndex])

Returns a Range object representing a cell within the specified range.

Argument	Settings
RowIndex	The row index of the row to return, relative to the first cell of the range
ColumnIndex	The column index of the column to return, relative to the first cell of the range

The following code changes the color of the cell in the second row and column of the range to green:

```
Dim r As Range

Set r = ActiveSheet.Range("A1:B5")
r.Item(2, 2).Interior.ColorIndex = 4
```

range.Justify

Justifies text within cells in the range.

range.Locked

If the worksheet is protected, True prevents changes to the cells in the range, and False enables changes to the cells.

range.Merge([Across])

Merges the cells of the range.

Argument	Settings
Across	True merges cells in each row as separate merged cells.

range.MergeArea

Returns a Range object that represents the merged range containing the specified cell.

range.MergeCells

True if the range contains merged cells.

range.Next

Returns a Range object that represents the next cell on the worksheet if the specified range is a single cell. If the range contains multiple cells, returns the next cell starting with the first cell in the range.

range.NoteText([*Text*], [*Start*], [*Length*])

Sets or returns the text of the note for the first cell in the specified range.

Argument	Settings
Text	The text of the note
Start	The position of the first character within the note to set or return
Length	The number or characters to set or return

The following code adds a note if the specified cell is greater than the specified value:

```
With ActiveSheet.Range("B3")
    If .Value >= 0.3 Then
        .NoteText "All Star!"
    End If
End With
```

range.NumberFormat

Sets or returns the number formatting for the specified range. Returns Null if the range has mixed formats. The format code corresponds to the Format Codes option in the Format Cells dialog box. The following code changes the color of the specified range to red:

```
Dim w As Worksheet

Set w = Worksheets("WombatBattingAverages")
w.Range("B1:B5").NumberFormat = "#.000"
```

range.NumberFormatLocal

Sets or returns the number formatting for the specified range based on the language in the current system settings.

range.Offset([*RowOffset*], [*ColumnOffset*])

Returns a Range object representing a range of cells offset from the specified range by a specified number of rows or columns.

Argument	Settings
RowOffset	The number of rows by which the range should be offset. A negative value offsets the rows upward.
ColumnOffset	The number of columns by which the range should be offset.

The following code activates a range one row down and one column to the right of the specified range:

```
Dim r As Range

Set r = ActiveSheet.Range("A1:B5")
r.Offset(1, 1).Activate
```

range.PageBreak

Sets or returns the location of a page break. The following code sets a page break at row 40:

```
ActiveSheet.Row(40).PageBreak = xlManual
```

range.PasteSpecial([Paste], [Operation], [SkipBlanks], [Transpose])

Inserts the contents of the clipboard to the specified range.

Argument	Settings
Paste	An xlPasteType constant indicating the part of the range to be pasted. The default is xlAll, which pastes all cell values and attributes.
Operation	xlNone (default) replaces the contents of the range; xlAdd adds the pasted values to the range; xlSubtract subtracts the pasted values; xlMultiply multiplies values; xlDivide divides the current values by the pasted ones.
SkipBlanks	True ignores blank cells on the clipboard so existing cells aren't replaced with blank ones.
Transpose	True transposes rows and columns on the clipboard.

range.Precedents

Returns a Range object that represents the cell or cells whose values are used directly or indirectly to calculate the values of the specified range. If cell E1 contains a formula that uses cells B1 and C1, the following code selects cells B1 and C1:

```
Activesheet.Range("E1").Precedents.Select
```

range.Previous

Returns a Range object that represents the previous cell on the worksheet if the specified range is a single cell. If the range contains multiple cells, returns the cell previous to the first cell in the range.

range.PrintOut([From], [To], [Copies], [Preview], [ActivePrinter], [PrintToFile], [Collate], [PrToFileName])

Prints the specified range.

Argument	Settings
From	The number of the first page to print.
To	The number of the last page to print.
Copies	The number of copies to print.
Preview	True to display Print Preview.
ActivePrinter	The name of the active printer.

Argument	Settings
PrintToFile	True prints to a file.
Collate	True to collate multiple copies.
PrToFileName	If PrintToFile is True, specifies the name of a file to print to.

range.PrintPreview

Displays Print Preview for the specified range.

range.Replace(*What, Replacement, [LookAt]), [SearchOrder], [MatchCase], [MatchByte], [SearchFormat], [ReplaceFormat]*)

Replaces text within the cells in the specified range.

Argument	Settings
What	The string to search for.
Replacement	The replacement string.
LookAt	xlPart (default) searches within the cell contents; xlWhole searches whole cells.
SearchOrder	xlByRows (default) searches one row at a time; xlByColumns searches one column at a time.
MatchCase	False (default) ignores case; True performs a case-sensitive search.
MatchByte	If double-byte language support is enabled: • True matches double-byte characters. • False matches double-byte characters to their single-byte equivalents.
SearchFormat	The search format.
ReplaceFormat	The replace format.

The following code replaces all occurrences of the string "Ichiro" in the specified range with the string "Suzuki":

```
Dim r As Range

Set r = ActiveSheet.Range("A1:A6")
r.Replace "Ichiro", "Suzuki"
```

range.Resize([*RowSize*]), [*ColumnSize*])

Resizes the specified range.

Argument	Settings
RowSize	The number of rows in the resized range
ColumnSize	The number of columns in the resized range

range.Row

Returns the row number of the first cell in the specified range.

range.RowDifferences(*Comparison*)

Returns a Range object that represents all the cells whose contents are different from those of the specified comparison cell in each row.

Argument	Settings
Comparison	A cell whose value should be compared to the cell values in the specified range

range.RowHeight

Sets or returns the height of rows in the specified range, measured in points. Returns Null if all rows are not the same height.

range.Rows([*Index*])

Returns a Range object that represents the row specified by *Index* in the specified range or all the rows in the range.

The following code selects the second row in the range:

```
Dim r As Range

Set r = ActiveSheet.Range("A1:A6")
r.Rows(2).Select
```

range.Select

Selects the specified range of cells.

range.Show

If the specified range is a single cell and not currently displayed, scrolls the worksheet to display it. The following code displays cell F216:

```
Dim r As Range

Set r = ActiveSheet.Range("F216")
r.Show
```

range.ShowDependents([*Remove*])

Shows or removes the tracer arrows between a range and its dependents.

range.**ShowDetail** [= *setting*]

True displays rows or columns that are part of an outline. False hides them.

range.**ShowErrors( )**

Draws tracer arrows to the cell that is the source of the error.

range.**ShowPrecedents([*Remove*])**

Shows or removes the tracer arrows between a range and its precedents.

range.**ShrinkToFit** [= *setting*]

True displays if text shrinks to fit the column width.

range.**Sort([*Key1*]), [*Order1*], [*Key2*], [*Type*], [*Order2*], [*Key3*], [*Order3*], [*Header*], [*OrderCustom*], [*MatchCase*], [*Orientation*], [*SortMethod*], [*DataOption1*], [*DataOption2*], [*DataOption3*])**

Sorts the current active region or a specific range of cells using the specified range, which must be a single cell.

Argument	Settings
Key1	The first row or column to sort. Can be either a single cell range or heading text.
Order1	xlAscending (default) sorts in ascending order; xlDescending sorts in descending order.
Key2	The second row or column to sort.
Type	Specifies which elements should be sorted if you are sorting a PivotTable report.
Order2	Same as Order1.
Key3	The third row or column to sort.
Order3	Same as Order1.
Header	Specifies whether the first row or column contains header information. xlNo (default) sorts the entire row or column; xlYes does not include the first row or column in the sort; xlGuess lets Excel determine if there is a header.
OrderCustom	The index of a custom sort order from the Sort Options dialog box.
MatchCase	True to perform a case-sensitive search.
Orientation	xlSortRows sorts by row; xlSortColumns sorts by column.
SortMethod	For non-English sorts, xlStroke sorts by the quantity of strokes in each character; xlPinYin (default) uses phonetic Chinese sort order.
DataOption1	xlSortTextAsNumber treats text as numeric data for the sort for Key1.
DataOption2	xlSortTextAsNumber treats text as numeric data for the sort for Key2.
DataOption3	xlSortTextAsNumber treats text as numeric data for the sort for Key3.

The following code sorts column G:

```
Dim r As Range

Set r = ActiveSheet.Range("G1")
r.Sort ActiveSheet.Range("G1")
```

range.SpecialCells(*Type*, [*Value*])

Returns a Range object representing cells of the specified type.

Argument	Settings
Type	xlCellTypeAllFormatConditions returns cells of any format; xlCellTypeAllValidation returns cells having validation criteria; xlCellTypeBlanks returns empty cells; xlCellTypeComments returns cells containing notes; xlCellTypeConstants returns cells containing constants; xlCellTypeFormulas returns cells containing formulas; xlCellTypeLastCell returns the last cell in the used range; xlCellTypeSameFormatConditions returns cells having the same format; xlCellTypeSameValidation returns cells having the same validation criteria; xlCellTypeVisible returns all visible cells.
Value	It *Type* is xlConstants or xlFormulas, xlNumbers returns cells containing numbers; xlTextValues returns cells containing text; xlLogical returns cells containing logical values; and xlErrors returns cells containing error values.

range.Style

Returns a Style object representing the style of cells in the specified range or Null if the range contains a mix of styles.

range.Table([*RowInput*], [*ColumnInput*])

Creates a data table based on input values and formulas defined on a worksheet.

Argument	Settings
RowInput	A cell to use as the basis for row values of the data table
ColumnInput	A cell to use as the basis for column values of the data table

range.Text

Returns the text in cells in the specified range if all the cells contain the same value or Null if the cells do not all contain the same value.

range.TextToColumns([*Destination*]), [*DataType*], [*TextQualifier*], [*ConsecutiveDelimiter*], [*Tab*], [*Semicolon*], [*Comma*], [*Space*], [*Other*], [*OtherChar*], [*FieldInfo*], [*DecimalSeparator*], [*ThousandsSeparator*], [*TrailingMinusNumbers*])

Breaks a column containing text into several columns.

Argument	Settings
Destination	A Range object specifying the cell where the columns should be placed.
DataType	xlDelimited (default) if the text is delimited; xlFixed if it has a fixed length.
TextQualifier	xlDoubleQuote (default) uses double quotes to indicate text; xlSingleQuote uses single quotes; xlNone evaluates fields to see if they are text or numbers.
ConsecutiveDelimiter	True inteprets consecutive delimiters as a single delimiter.
Tab	True uses tabs as the delimiter.
Semicolon	True uses semicolons as the delimiter.
Comma	True uses commas as the delimiter.
Space	True uses spaces as the delimiter.
Other	True uses OtherChar as the delimiter.
OtherChar	Specifies a character to use as a delimiter.
FieldInfo	An array that describes the data types of fields in the text.
DecimalSeparator	The decimal separator to use when recognizing numbers.
ThousandsSeparator	The thousands separator to use when recognizing numbers.
TrailingMinusNumbers	True interprets numbers followed by - as being negative; False interprets numbers followed by - as a string. Default is False.

The following code breaks the specified column containing semicolon-delimited text into two columns beginning at cell J3:

```
Dim r As Range

Set r = ActiveSheet.Range("I1:I5")
r.TextToColumns Destination:=ActiveSheet.Range("J3"), Semicolon:=True
```

range.UnMerge

Returns a merged area of cells to separate cells. The following code returns a merged area containing cell C3 to separate cells:

```
ActiveSheet.Range("C3").UnMerge
```

range.UseStandardHeight [= *setting*]

Returns True if all cells in the specified range are the standard height or Null if they aren't.

range.UseStandardWidth [= *setting*]

Returns True if all cells in the specified range are the standard width or Null if they aren't.

range.Value([*RangeValueDataType*]) [= *setting*]

Sets or returns the value of the specified range.

Argument	Settings
RangeValueDataType	xlRangeValueDefault returns Empty if the specified range is empty or an array of values if the range contains more than one cell; xlRangeValueMSPersistXML returns the recordset representation of the range in XML format; xlRangeValueXMLSpreadsheet returns the values, formatting, formulas, and names of the specified range in XML spreadsheet format.

The following code returns the values of the specified range in XML format:

```
ActiveSheet.Range("G1:G5").Value(xlRangeValueMSPersistXML)
```

range.VerticalAlignment

Sets or returns the vertical alignment for the specified range.

range.Worksheet

Returns the Worksheet object that contains the specified range.

range.WrapText[= *setting*]

True wraps text in cells within the specified range.

Work with Scenario Objects

When you need to look at the possible consequences of applying different sets of values to your worksheet calculations, it can be useful to define scenarios for each possibility. You can do this in code by creating a scenario and adding it to the Scenarios collection, which contains all the scenarios for the specified worksheet. For example, you can create one scenario that uses conservative sales results and another that is more optimistic, and then compare what happens to your bottom line.

The following code adds a formula to a worksheet cell to show the sum of a set of values and then creates a scenario for a set of values that is very conservative:

```
With ActiveSheet
    ' Set cell A6 as the sum of cells A1 through A5.
```

```
        .Range("A6") = "=Sum(A1:A5)"
        ' Create a low-value scenario.
        .Scenarios.Add "Low", .Range("A1:A5"), Array(10, 20, 30, 40, 50)
        .Scenarios("Low").Show
    End With
```

The following code creates a second scenario with a set of values that is more optimistic:

```
    With ActiveSheet
        ' Create a high-value scenario.
        .Scenarios.add "High", .Range("A1:A5"), Array(100, 200, 300, 400, 500)
        .Scenarios("High").Show
    End With
```

If you want to change the values in a particular scenario, you can use the ChangeScenario method. The following code upgrades the values in the "Low" scenario:

```
    With ActiveSheet.Scenarios("Low")
        ' Change the values of the low value scenario.
        .ChangeScenario ChangingCells:=ActiveSheet.Range("A1:A5"), Values:-Array(15,
    25, 35, 45, 55)
        .Show
    End With
```

If you want to view a summary of your current scenarios, you can use the CreateSummary method. The following code summarizes the results of the current scenarios:

```
    ActiveSheet.Scenarios.CreateSummary
```

Scenario and Scenarios Members

Use the Scenarios collection to create new scenarios. Use the Worksheet object's Scenarios method to get a reference to this collection. Use the Scenario object to set the criteria of the scenario. The Scenarios collection and Scenario object have the following members. Key members (shown in **bold**) are covered in the following reference section:

Add[1]	Application[2]
ChangeScenario	**ChangingCells**
Comment	Count[1]
Creator[2]	CreateSummary[1]
Delete	**Hidden**
Index	Item[1]
Locked	Merge[1]
Name	Parent[2]
Show	**Values**

[1] Collection only
[2] Object and collection

scenario.**ChangeScenario(***ChangingCells*, [*Values*]**)**

Resets the scenario to a new set of changing cells and values.

Argument	Settings
ChangingCells	A Range object that specifies a new set of changing cells
Values	An optional array of new values

scenario.**ChangingCells**

Returns a Range object that specifies a new set of changing cells. This is equivalent to the ChangingCells argument of the ChangeScenario method.

scenario.**Comment** [= *setting*]

Sets or returns a comment associated with the scenario.

scenario.**Hidden** [= *setting*]

True if the scenario is hidden.

scenario.**Locked** [= *setting*]

True if the scenario is locked.

scenario.**Show**

Inserts the scenario values on the active worksheet.

scenario.**Values**

Returns an array containing the values of the scenario's changing cells.

Resources

Additional information about the topics in this section is available from the following online source:

Topic	Source
Smart Document SDK	*http://msdn.microsoft.com/library/en-us/sdsdk/html/sdconGettingStartedAbout.asp*

CHAPTER 10

Linking and Embedding

Linking and embedding are ways to include information other than numbers and formulas on a worksheet. There are quite a few different types of information you might want to include: text comments, links to web pages, controls, or even whole documents from other applications.

In this chapter, I show how to include the most common types of information through the Excel user interface, and I show how to create and control those items through code. I also cover how to make Excel read aloud—I didn't know where else to put that!

This chapter includes task-oriented reference information for the following objects and their collections: Comment, Hyperlink, OLEObject, Speech, and UsedObjects.

 Code used in this chapter and additional samples are available in *ch10.xls*.

Add Comments

Comments are a way to annotate cells on a worksheet with descriptive text. To add a comment in Excel:

1. Right-click the cell.
2. Choose Insert Comment from the pop-up menu.
3. Type your comment in the Edit region.

Cells with comments have a comment indicator in their upper-right corner. When the cursor pauses over the cell, the comment pops up as shown in Figure 10-1.

Each comment is anchored to a specific cell, so you create comments in code using the Range object's AddComment method. Once a worksheet contains comments, you can get at them through the Worksheet object's Comments collection or through the Next and Previous methods of the Comment object. This is a little different from the

Figure 10-1. Use comments to annotate cells

way most collections work: there is no `Add` method for the `Comments` collection. The following code adds a comment to each cell on a worksheet that contains a non-numeric value:

```
Sub AddAuditComments( )
    Dim cel As Range, cmt As Comment
    For Each cel In ActiveSheet.UsedRange
        If Not IsNumeric(cel.Value) Then
            cel.AddComment.Text "Audit:" & vbLf & "Should be a number?"
        End If
    Next
End Sub
```

You remove comments using the `Delete` method. For example, the following code removes the audit comments inserted by the preceding code:

```
Sub RemoveAuditComments( )
    Dim cmt As Comment
    For Each cmt In ActiveSheet.Comments
        If InStr(1, cmt.Text, "Audit:") Then cmt.Delete
    Next
End Sub
```

You *can't* set a comment's `Author` property from code. Comments inserted from code have a null `Author` property. The preceding samples work around that by adding `Audit: & vbLf` to the comment text and then checking for that string before deleting.

Use Hyperlinks

Most of us think of hyperlinks as links that take you to a web page when you click them; Excel uses a broader definition. Yes, Excel hyperlinks can take you to a web page, but they can also:

- Create a new document or open an existing one for editing
- Take you to a reference in an Excel workbook
- Compose an email

To create a hyperlink in Excel:

1. Right-click a cell.
2. Choose Hyperlink from the pop-up menu.
3. Choose the type of link and set the link properties in the Edit Hyperlink dialog box (Figure 10-2).

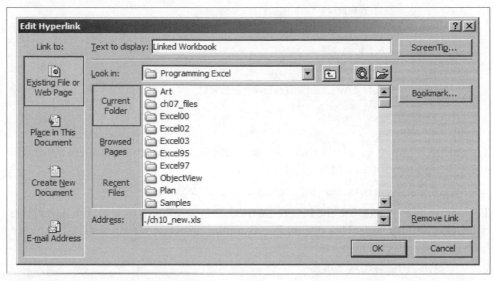

Figure 10-2. Creating a hyperlink in Excel

To create a hyperlink in code, use the `Hyperlinks` collection's `Add` method. Like comments, hyperlinks are anchored to a cell address that you specify in `Add`. For example, the following code adds a link at cell A3 to my web site:

```
ActiveSheet.Hyperlinks.Add [a3], "http:\\excelworkshop.com\", _
    , "Go to Jeff's site.", "Excel Workshop"
```

To link to a location on a worksheet, set the `Add` method's *Address* argument to `""` and the *SubAddress* argument to the target location. *SubAddress* has this format:

sheetName!targetAddress

However, the *targetAddress* part can't include dollar signs, like normal Excel addresses. To use normal Excel addresses, you must strip out the dollar signs using `VBA.Replace`. For instance, the following code adds hyperlinks that link to the first and last cells of a worksheet; the `ConvertAddress` helper function reformats the target Range to the correct form for the `Add` method:

```
' Adds links to beginning and end of worksheet.
Sub AddLinkToLocation( )
    Dim ws As Worksheet, celEnd As Range
    Set ws = ActiveSheet
    ' Get the last cell in column A.
    Set celEnd = ws.Cells(ws.UsedRange.Rows.Count, 1)
    ' Add a link to the last cell.
    ws.Hyperlinks.Add [a5], "", ConvertAddress(celEnd), , _
        "Go to end"
    ' Add a link back to the first cell.
    ws.Hyperlinks.Add celEnd, "", ConvertAddress(ws.[a1]), , _
        "Go to start"
End Sub
```

```
' Converts a cell reference to a Hyperlink address.
Function ConvertAddress(cel As Range) As String
    Dim result As String
    ' Start with the worksheet name.
    result = cel.Worksheet.Name & "!"
    ' Add the address, but remove "$"
    result = result & VBA.Replace(cel.Address, "$", "")
    ' Return result
    ConvertAddress = result
End Function
```

To link to a range in another workbook, include the workbook's filename in the Address argument of the Add method:

```
ActiveSheet.Hyperlinks.Add [a7], "ch08.xls", , , "Go to Ch08.xls"
```

To remove hyperlinks, use the Delete method. Delete applies to both the Hyperlinks collection and the Hyperlink object. For example, this code removes all of the hyperlinks on the active worksheet:

```
ActiveSheet.Hyperlinks.Delete
```

Link and Embed Objects

You can include objects created by other applications in an Excel worksheet by linking or embedding the object:

Linked objects
    Display a bitmap image of the object that opens the object's file in its source application when the user edits the object.

Embedded objects
    Also display a bitmap image, but the data for the object is stored within the workbook. Editing the object opens the object in place so Excel still appears to have focus and changes don't affect the original source file, only the embedded copy.

This feature was originally called OLE, for Object Linking and Embedding, but Microsoft later renamed it ActiveX and now sometimes calls it COM, for Component Object Model. All those names basically refer to the same thing when dealing with Excel.

Any Windows application can provide these objects, but it is up to the developers of that source application to do it correctly—sometimes that is a tall order. Crashes, printing problems, and quirky displays are hallmarks of many linked or embedded objects. However, Microsoft has invested a great deal of effort to make OLE work within the Microsoft Office product suite, and linked and embedded objects usually work correctly within that family of products.

In general, it is a good idea to use linking and embedding only among Office or other well-tested applications and to be *very* careful when using it with workbooks you plan on distributing to others. That is because all users must have the source application to edit linked or embedded objects. Different platforms, configurations, or even application versions can cause significant hurdles to using a workbook that contains embedded objects from other applications.

So should you just avoid OLE altogether? No, in fact that's not even likely given the level of integration with Excel. Form controls, charts, and other objects are all embedded as OLE objects when they appear on a worksheet. Here are some considerations for making OLE objects trouble-free:

- You can assume that objects provided with Excel work correctly; that includes form controls.
- Check whether other objects are installed before using them.
- Test the object before you distribute your workbook. If the source application is not part of the Office suite, make sure the linked or embedded object displays correctly, can be opened for editing, and prints correctly.

The following sections discuss the most common OLE object tasks.

Embed Controls

Embedded form controls let you get input from the user through standard controls like text boxes, command buttons, listboxes, and so on. They are handy for collecting values that populate ranges of cells or to simply get and display values in something other than a grid.

To embed a control on a worksheet:

1. Choose View → Toolbars → Control Toolbox to display the Controls Toolbox.
2. Click the control to add and then click and drag on the worksheet to draw the control as shown in Figure 10-3.
3. Excel embeds the control on the worksheet.
4. Click the Properties button to edit the control's appearance.
5. Click the Code button to add an event procedure for the control.
6. Click the Design button when finished to switch out of design mode.

You can link embedded controls to values entered in cells. For example, to link the text box in Figure 10-3 to cell A3, set its LinkCell property to $A$3. Now changes to the TextBox update cell A3 and vice versa (Figure 10-4).

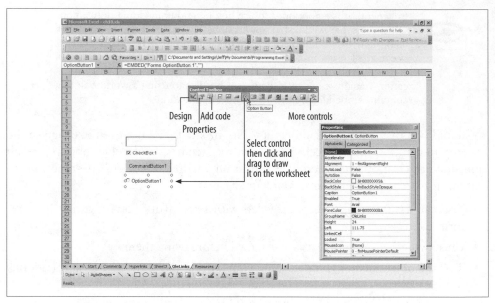

Figure 10-3. Adding form controls to a worksheet

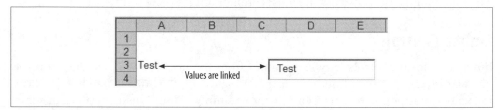

Figure 10-4. Linking cells to controls through the LinkedCell property

To create an event procedure for a control so it responds to user actions:

1. Click the Design button to enter design mode.
2. Select the control.
3. Click the View Code button. Excel opens the Visual Basic Editor and creates an event procedure in the worksheet object's class.

You can also select events from the list in the Code window to add event procedures as shown in Figure 10-5.

Excel puts event procedures in the worksheet class because only classes can respond to events. This is one of the key differences between controls created using the Controls Toolbox and those created using the older Forms toolbar (Figure 10-6). Controls from the Forms toolbar don't have these events and instead run a single macro from a module in response to their default action.

Controls from the Forms toolbar still work, but they provide fewer properties, can't link to cells, and are now hidden in the Help and object model. I think that's a tip-off

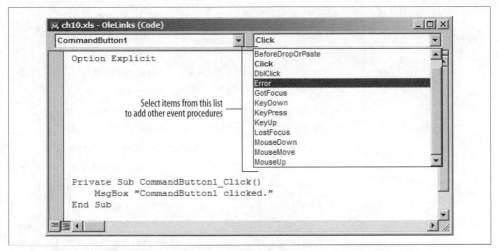

Figure 10-5. Adding event procedures for embedded controls

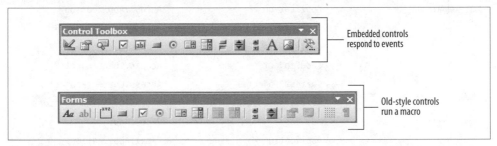

Figure 10-6. Control Toolbox versus Forms toolbars

from Microsoft that they are included only for compatibility with earlier versions and that you should now avoid them.

Use OleObjects in Code

You can create new linked and embedded objects dynamically by using the OleObjects Add method. For embedded objects, the Add method requires that you know the programmatic ID (progID) of the object you are creating. For linked objects, you can simply provide the source file name. Table 10-1 lists the progIDs of the most common objects.

Table 10-1. ProgIDs of common Office objects

Application	Object	ProgID
Controls	CheckBox	Forms.CheckBox.1
	ComboBox	Forms.ComboBox.1
	CommandButton	Forms.CommandButton.1

Table 10-1. ProgIDs of common Office objects (continued)

Application	Object	ProgID
	Frame	Forms.Frame.1
	Image	Forms.Image.1
	Label	Forms.Label.1
	ListBox	Forms.ListBox.1
	MultiPage	Forms.MultiPage.1
	OptionButton	Forms.OptionButton.1
	ScrollBar	Forms.ScrollBar.1
	SpinButton	Forms.SpinButton.1
	TabStrip	Forms.TabStrip.1
	TextBox	Forms.TextBox.1
	ToggleButton	Forms.ToggleButton.1
	Calendar	MSCal.Calendar
Microsoft Access	Application	Access.Application
	CodeData	Access.CodeData
	CurrentData	Access.CurrentData
	CodeProject	Access.CodeProject
	CurrentProject	Access.CurrentProject
	DefaultWebOptions	Access.DefaultWebOptions
Microsoft Excel	Add-in	Excel.AddIn
	Application	Excel.Application
	Chart	Excel.Chart
	Worksheet	Excel.Sheet
Microsoft Graph	Application	MSGraph.Application
	Chart	MSGraph.Chart
Microsoft Office Web Components	ChartSpace	OWC.Chart
	DataSourceControl	OWC.DataSourceControl
	ExpandControl	OWC.ExpandControl
	PivotTable	OWC.PivotTable
	RecordNavigationControl	OWC.RecordNavigationControl
	Spreadsheet	OWC.Spreadsheet
Microsoft Outlook	Application	Outlook.Application
Microsoft PowerPoint	Application	PowerPoint.Application
Microsoft Word	Application	Word.Application
	Document	Word.Document
	Global	Word.Global
	Template	Word.Template

Not all of the objects listed in Table 10-1 can be embedded in a worksheet. For example, the `Application` objects are used to access specific applications programmatically—not to embed one application inside of another. You can use the progIDs of those objects with `CreateObject` to create an instance of those objects for use within Excel.

Before using an external application in code, you should make sure the application is installed on the user's system. The following helper function allows you to test a progID to make sure it is installed:

```
' Checks the registry to see if a given progID is installed.
Function IsInstalled(progID As String) As Boolean
    Dim wsh As Object, result As Boolean, key As String
    result = False
    Set wsh = CreateObject("WScript.Shell")
    On Error Resume Next
    key = wsh.RegRead("HKEY_CLASSES_ROOT\" & progID & "\CLSID\")
    If Not Err And key <> "" Then _
      result = True
    IsInstalled = result
End Function
```

After you've checked for the application, you can create new objects in code. For example, the following code embeds a Word document in an Excel worksheet:

```
Sub EmbedWordObject()
    Dim ws As Worksheet, ole As OleObject, progID As String
    progID = "Word.Document"
    ' Make sure Word is installed.
    If IsInstalled(progID) Then
        Set ws = ActiveSheet
        ' Create the object.
        Set ole = ws.OleObjects.Add(progID, , , , , , , 60, 60, 200, 400)
        ' Name the object so you can get it later.
        ole.Name = "WordDocument"
        ' Activate the object for editing.
        ole.Activate
    End If
End Sub
```

 Set the object's `Name` property so you can get it from the `OleObjects` collection easily.

Use the `Object` property to get the underlying programmable object from an `OleObject`. For example, the following code gets the Word `Document` object from the embedded document created by `EmbedWordObject`, then uses that object's methods to insert some text:

```
' Assumes AddWordObject has run.
Sub EditWordObject()
```

```
        Dim ws As Worksheet, ole As OleObject
        Set ws = ActiveSheet
        ' Get the object by name and insert some text.
        ws.OleObjects("WordDocument").Object.Range.InsertAfter "Some text."
    End Sub
```

That technique is useful when working with embedded controls. For example, the following code creates a new text box, sets the value of its Text property, and links that control to a cell:

```
    Sub CreateTextBox()
        Dim ws As Worksheet, ole As OleObject
        Set ws = ActiveSheet
        ' Create a new text box.
        Set ole = ws.OleObjects.Add("Forms.TextBox.1")
        ' Name the object.
        ole.Name = "TextBox"
        ' Set the text.
        ole.Object.text = "Some text"
        ' Link the control to a cell.
        ole.LinkedCell = "$a$3"
    End Sub
```

Notice that you need to use the Object property to get to the control's underlying Text property, but not to get to LinkedCell. That's because LinkedCell is provided by OleObject, not the text box.

Speak

Speech is fun to demo, but it's not really a mainstream feature. Most often it is used to enable people with disabilities to read spreadsheets, but you can use it to read any text. For example, the following code reads comments aloud whenever a cell with a comment receives focus:

```
    ' ThisWorkbook object
    Dim WithEvents g_app As Application

    ' Hook up the global Application object handler when this
    ' workbook opens.
    Private Sub Workbook_Open()
        If Not (g_app Is Nothing) Then _
            Set g_app = Application
    End Sub

    ' Read comments aloud when cell is selected.
    Private Sub g_app_SheetSelectionChange(ByVal Sh As Object, _
      ByVal Target As Range)
        ' If the cell has a comment.
        If Not (Target.Comment Is Nothing) Then
            On Error Resume Next
            ' Read the comment text aloud.
            Application.Speech.Speak Target.Comment.Text
```

```
    End If
End Sub

' Unhook handler
Private Sub Workbook_BeforeClose(Cancel As Boolean)
    Set g_app = Nothing
End Sub
```

It is important to turn on error handling in case speech is not installed on the user's system.

Comment and Comments Members

Use the Range object's AddComment method to create comments. Use the Comment object to get the author of a comment, get or set comment text, and delete comments. The Comments collection and Comment object have the following members. Key members (shown in **bold**) are covered in the following reference section:

Application[2]	**Author**
Count[1]	Creator[2]
Delete	Item[1]
Next	Parent[2]
Previous	**Shape**
Text	Visible

[1] Collection only
[2] Object and collection

---

comment.Author

Returns the name of the comment's author.

---

comment.Delete

Deletes a comment. The following code deletes all of the comments on the active sheet:

```
Sub DeleteComments( )
    Dim cmt As Comment
    For Each cmt In ActiveSheet.Comments
        cmt.Delete
    Next
End Sub
```

---

comment.Shape

Returns the Shape object that represents the comment. The appearance of comments is built in to Excel and can't be changed by setting Shape object properties.

comment.Text([*Text*], [*Start*], [*Overwrite*])

Gets or sets the text displayed in a comment.

Argument	Settings
Text	The text to display in the comment.
Start	The character position at which to insert the text. If omitted, any existing comment is overwritten.
Overwrite	True replaces the existing comment; False appends. Default is False.

The following code creates four new comments on the active worksheet:

```
Sub CreateComments()
    Dim cel As Range
    For Each cel In [a1:b2]
        cel.AddComment "Comment for " & cel.Address
    Next
End Sub
```

The Text method also returns the text of the comment. For example, the following code lists all of the comments on the active sheet:

```
Sub ShowComments()
    Dim cmt As Comment
    Debug.Print "Author", "Text"
    For Each cmt In ActiveSheet.Comments
        Debug.Print cmt.Author, cmt.Text
    Next
End Sub
```

Hyperlink and Hyperlinks Members

Use the Hyperlinks collection to add hyperlinks. Use the Worksheet or Chart object's Hyperlinks method to get a reference to this collection. Use the Hyperlink object to follow the hyperlink. The Hyperlinks collection and Hyperlink object have the following members. Key members (shown in **bold**) are covered in the following reference section:

Add	**Address**
AddToFavorites	Application[1]
Count[1]	**CreateNewDocument**
Creator[1]	Delete[2]
EmailSubject	**Follow**
Item[1]	Name
Parent[1]	**Range**
ScreenTip	**Shape**
SubAddress	**TextToDisplay**
Type	

[1] Collection only
[2] Object and collection

hyperlinks.**Add**(*Anchor, Address,* [*SubAddress*], [*ScreenTip*], [*TextToDisplay*])

Adds a hyperlink.

Argument	Settings
Anchor	A Range or Shape object to set as the location of the hyperlink.
Address	The URL to navigate to when the hyperlink is clicked.
SubAddress	A location on the page. SubAddress is appended to Address and preceded by #.
ScreenTip	A tool tip to display when the mouse pointer pauses over the hyperlink.
TextToDisplay	The text to show on screen in place of the hyperlink.

For example, the following code adds a hyperlink to range A1:

```
Sub AddHyperlink( )
    Dim ws As Worksheet
    Set ws = ActiveSheet
    ws.Hyperlinks.Add [a1], "http:\\excelworkshop.com\", _
        , "Go to Jeff's site.", "Excel Workshop"
End Sub
```

hyperlink.**Address** [= *setting*]

Sets or returns the URL of the hyperlink.

hyperlink.**AddToFavorites**( )

Adds the URL to the user's Favorites folder in Internet Explorer.

hyperlink.**CreateNewDocument**(*Filename, EditNow, Overwrite*)

Sets the hyperlink to create a new file when clicked.

Argument	Settings
Filename	The name of the file to create.
EditNow	True opens the file for editing when the method runs; False waits until the user clicks the hyperlink to edit the document.
Overwrite	True replaces any existing file of the same name with a new, blank file when the method runs; False causes an error if the file already exists.

 Excel may lock up if *EditNow* is True and *Filename* is a workbook (*.xls*).

Excel opens the file in the user's default editor for the given file type. For example, the following code creates a new text file and opens it for editing in Notepad:

```
Sub CreateLinkedFile()
    Dim ws As Worksheet, hyp As Hyperlink, path As String
    Set ws = ActiveSheet
    path = ThisWorkbook.path
    Set hyp = ws.Hyperlinks.Add([a3], path & "\ch10_Readme.txt", _
        , "Click to edit the text file.", "Application Notes")
    hyp.CreateNewDocument path & "\ch10_Readme.txt", True, True
End Sub
```

hyperlink.EmailSubject [= *setting*]

Gets or sets the subject line of a `mailto:` link. This property overrides the subject setting included in the URL. For example, the following code creates an email link with a subject, but then changes the subject line:

```
Sub CreateMailLink()
    Dim ws As Worksheet, hyp As Hyperlink
    Set ws = ActiveSheet
    ' Create an email link.
    Set hyp = ws.Hyperlinks.Add([a3], _
        "mailto:someone@microsoft.com&subject=Help on Excel", _
        , "Click to send mail.", "Contact Microsoft")
    ' Change the subject...
    hyp.EmailSubject = "Different subject"
End Sub
```

hyperlink.Follow([*NewWindow*], [*AddHistory*], [*ExtraInfo*], [*Method*], [*HeaderInfo*])

Navigates to the URL of the hyperlink. This is the same as clicking on the link.

Argument	Settings
NewWindow	This argument is ignored when used with a link that appears on a worksheet. Links always appear in a new browser window.
AddHistory	This argument is ignored.
ExtraInfo	A string or array of bytes that includes information passed to the URL.
Method	The way to send *ExtraInfo* to the URL. Possible settings are msoMethodGet or msoMethodPost.
HeaderInfo	Header information to send with the HTTP request.

The following code navigates to each of the links on the page:

```
Sub TestLinks()
    Dim hyp As Hyperlink
    For Each hyp In ActiveSheet.Hyperlinks
        hyp.Follow
    Next
End Sub
```

hyperlink.Range

Returns the link's location on the worksheet as a Range object.

hyperlink.ScreenTip [= *setting*]

Sets or returns a pop-up tool tip to display when the mouse pointer pauses over the link.

hyperlink.Shape

If the link is anchored to a shape, returns the link's location as a Shape object.

hyperlink.SubAddress [= *setting*]

Sets or returns the location within the URL for the link. The URL is composed of the Address and SubAddress properties as follows:

> *Address#SubAddress*

hyperlink.TextToDisplay [= *setting*]

Sets or returns the text to show on the worksheet as the link.

hyperlink.Type

Not used; always returns 0.

OleObject and OleObjects Members

Use the OleObjects collection to add linked or embedded objects. Use the Worksheet object's OleObjects method to get a reference to this collection. Use the OleObject object to control the location and appearance of a linked or embedded object. The OleObjects collection and OleObject object have the following members. Key members (shown in **bold**) are covered in the following reference section:

Activate	**Add**[1]	Application[2]
AutoLoad[2]	**AutoUpdate**	Border[2]
BottomRightCell	**BringToFront**[2]	**Copy**[2]
CopyPicture[2]	Count[1]	Creator[2]
Cut[2]	Delete[2]	**Duplicate**[2]
Enabled[2]	**Group**[1]	Height[2]
Index	Interior[2]	Item[1]

Left[2]	LinkedCell	ListFillRange
Locked[2]	Name	**Object**
OLEType	**OnAction**[2]	Parent[2]
Placement[2]	PrintObject[2]	**progID**
Select[2]	SendToBack[2]	**Shadow**[2]
ShapeRange[2]	**SourceName**[2]	Top[2]
TopLeftCell	**Update**	**Verb**
Visible[2]	Width[2]	ZOrder[2]

[1] Collection only
[2] Object and collection

oleobject.Add([*ClassType*], [*Filename*], [*Link*], [*DisplayAsIcon*], [*IconFileName*], [*IconIndex*], [*IconLabel*], [*Left*], [*Top*], [*Width*], [*Height*])

Creates a new OLE object on a sheet.

Argument	Settings
ClassType	The programmatic ID of the object to create. For example "Word.Document" or "MSGraph.Chart".
Filename	The filename of the object to create. You must specify *ClassType* or *Filename*.
Link	True links the object to *Filename*; False makes a copy of *Filename* to store in the workbook.
DisplayAsIcon	True displays the object as an icon or a picture; False renders the object in the worksheet.
IconFileName	If *DisplayAsIcon* is True, specifies a file containing the icon to display.
IconIndex	If *DisplayAsIcon* is True, specifies the index of the icon within the icon file. Default is the first icon in the file.
IconLabel	If *DisplayAsIcon* is True, specifies the text to display beneath the icon.
Left	The distance between cell A1 and the left edge of the object in point.
Top	The distance between cell A1 and the top edge of the object in point.
Width	The width of the object in points.
Height	The height of the object in points.

 The *Width* and *Height* arguments aren't absolute. Their actual result depends on the OLE object being created.

The following code creates a new embedded Word document on the active worksheet:

```
Sub AddObject( )
    Dim ws As Worksheet, ole
    Set ws = ActiveSheet
    ' Create the object.
    Set ole = ws.OleObjects.Add("Word.Document", , , , , , , 60, 60, 200, 400)
    ' Activate the object for editing.
    ole.Activate
End Sub
```

If you run the preceding code, the initial height of the object is set to fit the text you enter in the object.

oleobject.AutoLoad [= *setting*]

True reloads and rerenders the object when the workbook is opened; False does not rerender the object and instead uses the image stored when the workbook is saved. Default is False. Setting AutoLoad to True can cause significant delays when opening a workbook.

oleobject.AutoUpdate [= *setting*]

For objects with OleType of xlLink, True updates the object when the source changes; False does not automatically update the object.

oleobject.BottomRightCell

Returns the Range object for the cell that is under the lower-right corner of the object.

oleobject.BringToFront( )

Displays the object on top of all others.

oleobject.Copy( )

Copies the object to the clipboard.

oleobject.CopyPicture([*Appearance*], [*Format*])

Copies an image of the object to the clipboard.

Argument	Settings
Appearance	Specifies the resolution of the image. Can be one of these settings: xlPrinter, xlScreen. Default is xlScreen.
Format	Specifies the image format. Can be one of these settings: xlBitmap, xlPicture. Default is xlPicture.

oleobject.Duplicate( )

Creates a copy of the object and returns a reference to the copy. The following code creates a copy of an object and moves it beneath the original:

```
Sub CopyObject( )
    Dim ole1 As OleObject, ole2 As OleObject
```

```
        ' Get the object.
        Set ole1 = ActiveSheet.OleObjects(1)
        ' Create a copy.
        Set ole2 = ole1.Duplicate
        ' Move copy under first object.
        ole2.Top = ole1.Top + ole1.Height
    End Sub
```

oleobjects.**Group( )**

Groups the objects on a worksheet so they can be selected, moved, or deleted as a single item together.

oleobject.**LinkedCell**

For embedded controls linked to the value of a cell, returns the address of that cell.

oleobject.**ListFillRange** [= *setting*]

For an ActiveX list control linked to a range of cells, returns the address of that range.

oleObject.**Object**

Returns the underlying object. Use the Object property to get at the properties of embedded controls and to programmatically control objects from other applications such as Word.

oleobject.**OLEType**

Returns xlOLELink if the object is linked to a source file, xlOLEEmbed if the object is embedded in the worksheet.

oleobject.**OnAction** [= *setting*]

Sets or returns the name of a macro to run when the object is clicked.

oleobject.**Placement** [= *xlPlacement*]

Sets or returns how the OLE object is moved or sized in relation to its underlying cells. Can be one of these settings:

    xlMove (default)
    xlMoveAndSize
    xlFreefloating

Set to xlFreefloating to prevent the object from moving when the cells beneath it are moved.

oleobject.progID [= *setting*]

Returns the programmatic identifier (progID) for the object. progIDs identify the source application and type of the object.

oleobject.Shadow [= *setting*]

True displays a shadow with the object; False does not. Default is False.

oleobject.ShapeRange

Returns a ShapeRange object for the OLE object. ShapeRange is used to control the appearance of graphic objects on a worksheet. OLE objects don't support some of the changes you can make through ShapeRange. See Chapter 18 for more information about the ShapeRange object.

oleobject.SourceName

For objects with OleType of xlLink, returns the name of the source document.

oleobject.Update( )

For objects with OleType of xlLink, updates the link and rerenders the object.

oleobject.Verb([*Verb*])

Opens or performs the default verb on the object. The default verb is usually to edit the object.

Argument	Settings
Verb	Can be one of these settings: xlOpen, xlPrimary. Default is xlPrimary.

oleobject.ZOrder

Returns the z-order of the object. Z-order determines which objects appear on top of others: a z-order of 1 indicates the topmost object.

OLEFormat Members

Use the OLEFormat object to get an OleObject from a Shape object. The OLEFormat object has the following members:

    Activate
    Application
    Creator
    Object
    Parent
    progID
    Verb

The following code demonstrates getting OLE objects from the Shapes collection rather than the OleObjects collection:

```
Sub GetOleObjectFromShapes()
    Dim shp As Shape, ole As OleObject
    ' Get the object.
    For Each shp In ActiveSheet.Shapes
        If shp.Type = msoEmbeddedOleObject Then
            ' Get the OleObject
            Set ole = shp.OLEFormat.Object
            ' Display some information.
            Debug.Print ole.progID
        End If
    Next
End Sub
```

Speech Members

Use the Speech object to read words or ranges aloud. To get the Speech object, use the Application object's Speech property. The Speech object has the following members. Key members (shown in **bold**) are covered in the following reference section:

    Direction
    Speak
    SpeakCellOnEnter

speech.Direction [*= XlSpeakDirection*]

Sets or returns the direction in which cells are read out loud. Possible settings are:

    xlSpeakByColumns
    xlSpeakByRows

speech.**Speak(***Text**, [SpeakAsync], [SpeakXML], [Purge]*)

Reads text out loud.

Argument	Settings
Text	The text to read out loud.
SpeakAsync	True executes the next statement without waiting for the reading to complete; False pauses code until *Text* has been completely read. Default is False.
SpeakXML	True interprets *Text* as XML or HTML, skipping tags; False reads all text. Default is False.
Purge	True stops the current text being read and starts reading the new text immediately; False waits for current text to complete before reading new text. Default is False.

The following code reads a short poem:

```
Sub ReadPoem( )
    Dim spch As Speech, poem As String
    Set spch = Application.Speech
    poem = "Some men lead lives of quiet desperation. " & _
      "Our Joey lays in silent anticipation, " & _
      "of morsels dropped from Sophie's eating station."
    spch.Speak poem
End Sub
```

speech.**SpeakCellOnEnter** [= *setting*]

True reads the contents of a cell aloud when the user selects it; False does not read the cell aloud. Default is False.

UsedObjects Members

Use the UsedObjects collection to get a mixed collection of all of the objects currently loaded in Excel. The UsedObjects collection has the following members:

```
Application
Count
Creator
Item
Parent
```

The following code displays a list of all the objects loaded in Excel. The code uses error handling to skip over properties not available for the different types of objects included in the UsedObjects collection:

```
Sub ShowObjects()
    Dim obj As Object, str As String
    On Error Resume Next
    Debug.Print "Type", "Name", "ProgID"
    For Each obj In Application.UsedObjects
        str = TypeName(obj)
        str = str & vbTab & obj.Name
        str = str & vbTab & obj.progID
        Debug.Print str
    Next
End Sub
```

Printing and Publishing

Excel provides objects and methods for printing and previewing workbooks, worksheets, ranges, and other objects. It also allows you to publish those objects to the Web as an interactive alternative to printing and distributing hardcopies. This chapter explains how you print and publish objects from Visual Basic for Applications (VBA) as well as how to control the various aspects of printing such as printer settings, page breaks, and views. Some general features such as autofilters and default web options are most closely related to printing and publish, so they are covered here as well.

This chapter includes task-oriented reference information for the following objects and their related collections: `AutoFilter`, `Filter`, `CustomView`, `HPageBreak`, `VPageBreak`, `PageSetup`, `Graphic`, `PublishObject`, `DefaultWebOptions`, and `WebOptions`.

 Code used in this chapter and additional samples are available in *ch11.xls*.

Print and Preview

Use the `PrintOut` or `PrintPreview` method to print or preview objects from code. These objects can print:

- `Charts`, `Chart`
- `Range`
- `Sheets`, `Worksheets`, `Worksheet`
- `Window`
- `Workbook`

The syntax and arguments for `PrintOut` and `PrintPreview` are the same for all objects, so see the `Workbook` object reference section in Chapter 8 for that information. These

methods also apply to the current selection; for instance, the following code previews and prints the selected range:

```
Sub PrintSelection( )
    ' Print with preview
    Selection.PrintOut , , , True
End Sub
```

 In my sample code, I set the *Preview* argument to True so you can see
what will print without wasting paper. Simply click Close on the preview window to cancel printing.

You can turn printing on or off for some objects embedded on a worksheet using the
PrintObject property. The following code prints a worksheet but omits any embedded controls or other OLE objects:

```
Sub PrintWithOutObjects( )
    Dim ws As Worksheet
    Set ws = ActiveSheet
    ' Prevent printing of controls.
    ws.OLEObjects.PrintObject = False
    ' Print with preview.
    ws.PrintOut , , , True
    ' Restore printing for controls.
    ws.OLEObjects.PrintObject = True
End Sub
```

You can further control printing through the Workbook object's BeforePrint event.
For instance, this code prevents the user from printing any part of the workbook:

```
' ThisWorkbook module

' Cancel print jobs before they are processed.
Private Sub Workbook_BeforePrint(Cancel As Boolean)
    Cancel = True
    ' Display a message
    MsgBox "Printing is disabled for this workbook."
End Sub
```

That's a neat trick, but it works only if macros are enabled for the workbook. If macros are disabled because of security settings, the user can still print.

Control Paging

Use the HPageBreaks and VPageBreaks collections to add manual page breaks to a
worksheet in code. For example, this code adds horizontal page breaks to a worksheet every specified number of rows:

```
Sub AddHBreaks(rows As Integer)
    Dim ws As Worksheet, hpb As HPageBreak, i As Integer
    Set ws = ActiveSheet
```

```
        For i = rows To ws.UsedRange.rows.Count Step rows
            ws.HPageBreaks.Add ws.rows(i)
        Next
    End Sub
```

Use the `HPageBreak` and `VPageBreak` objects' `Delete` method to remove individual page breaks or use the `Worksheet` object's `ResetAllPageBreaks` method to remove all manual page breaks as shown here:

```
Sub RemoveBreaks()
    ActiveSheet.ResetAllPageBreaks
End Sub
```

The page break collections contain only manual page breaks. Even though there is a `Type` property that suggests you might be able to get automatic page breaks, you can't. That means the `Count` properties of the collections return only the number of manual page breaks. For example, this code displays the page count of a worksheet that contains only manual page breaks:

```
Sub ShowPageCount()
    Dim ws As Worksheet, hb As Integer, vb As Integer
    Set ws = ActiveSheet
    hb = ws.HPageBreaks.Count + 1
    vb - ws.VPageBreaks.Count
    If vb = 0 Then vb = 1
    MsgBox "This worksheet has " & hb * vb & " pages."
End Sub
```

The only way to control automatic page breaks is to change the page margins using the `PageSettings` object.

Change Printer Settings

Use the `Worksheet` or `Chart` objects' `PageSettings` property to get or set the printer settings before printing. The `PageSettings` object provides a set of read/write properties that correspond to the Page Setup dialog box (Figure 11-1).

For example, this procedure displays common printer settings in some named ranges on a worksheet:

```
Sub GetProperties()
    Dim ws As Worksheet, ps As PageSetup
    Set ws = ActiveSheet
    Set ps = ws.PageSetup
    [BlackAndWhite] = ps.BlackAndWhite
    [Draft] = ps.Draft
    [BottomMargin] = ps.BottomMargin
    [TopMargin] = ps.TopMargin
    [RightMargin] = ps.RightMargin
    [LeftMargin] = ps.LeftMargin
    [Zoom] = ps.Zoom
End Sub
```

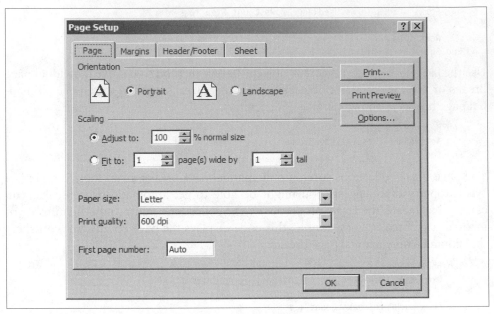

Figure 11-1. The PageSettings object provides properties that control these settings

This procedure changes the print settings by applying the settings from the named ranges back to the PageSettings object:

```
Sub SetProperties()
    Dim ws As Worksheet, ps As PageSetup
    Set ws = ActiveSheet
    Set ps = ws.PageSetup
    ps.BlackAndWhite = [BlackAndWhite]
    ps.Draft = [Draft]
    ps.BottomMargin = [BottomMargin]
    ps.TopMargin = [TopMargin]
    ps.RightMargin = [RightMargin]
    ps.LeftMargin = [LeftMargin]
    ps.Zoom = [Zoom].Value
End Sub
```

You have to use the Value property of the named range when setting Zoom in the preceding code because the Zoom property is a Variant type. Variants accept objects, so Visual Basic doesn't automatically call the default property of the range; you have to call Value explicitly.

You can see the effects of the changes by running PrintPreview:

```
Sub PrintPreview()
    Dim ws As Worksheet, ps As PageSetup
    Set ws = ActiveSheet
    ws.PrintOut , , , True
End Sub
```

The print settings are stored with the worksheet or chart. When you create a new worksheet, that object uses the default settings. Therefore, you can restore the defaults by creating a temporary worksheet, getting its PageSettings object, and assigning the property values from that object, as shown here:

```
Sub RestoreDefaultPageSetup()
    Dim ps As PageSetup
    ' Get the default settings (creates a temporary worksheet).
    Set ps = DefaultPageSetup
    ' Restore the active sheet's settings.
    With ActiveSheet.PageSetup
        .BlackAndWhite = ps.BlackAndWhite
        .Draft = ps.Draft
        .BottomMargin = ps.BottomMargin
        .TopMargin = ps.TopMargin
        .RightMargin = ps.RightMargin
        .LeftMargin = ps.LeftMargin
        .Zoom = ps.Zoom
    End With
    ' Silently delete the temporary worksheet.
    Application.DisplayAlerts = False
    ps.Parent.Delete
    Application.DisplayAlerts = True
End Sub

Function DefaultPageSetup() As PageSetup
    Dim ws As Worksheet, result As PageSetup
    Set ws = ThisWorkbook.Worksheets.Add()
    Set result = ws.PageSetup
    Set DefaultPageSetup = result
End Function
```

You can't assign one PageSetting object to another. The worksheet and chart object's PageSettings property is read-only.

Filter Ranges

Filters work by hiding rows that don't meet certain criteria. Filter criteria are selected from drop-down lists in a column's heading. You can select built-in criteria, such as Top 10, or enter your own custom criteria. To create a filter in Excel:

1. Select the header row of the rows you want to filter.

2. Choose Data → Filter → AutoFilter. Excel adds a filter drop-down list to each of the selected columns.

> Lists provide a more powerful and flexible tool for filtering ranges. Lists are available only in Excel 2003, however.

To apply the filter, select the criteria from one of the drop-down lists as shown in Figure 11-2. Excel hides the rows below that don't match the criteria. You can apply filters for more than one column to further narrow the range of displayed rows.

Date ▾	Open ▾	High ▾	Low ▾	Close ▾	Volume ▾	Adj. ▾
Jun-23-05	25.17	25.62	25.15	25	Sort Ascending	25.31
Apr-15-05	24.58	24.9	24.41	24	Sort Descending	24.38
Mar-22-05	24.19	24.27	23.96	23	(All)	23.91
Mar-18-05	24.53	24.91	24.28	24	(Top 10...)	24.23
Jan-28-05	26.54	26.65	25.96	26	(Custom...)	26.02
Jan-04-05	26.87	27.1	26.66	26	24,398,700	26.67
					27,212,500	
Dec-17-04	27	27.32	26.8	26	35,749,000	26.79
Dec-15-04	27.22	27.4	27.07	27	38,401,500	26.94
Dec-14-04	27.05	27.33	27.04	27	39,459,800	27.06
					39,668,000	
Dec-07-04	27.26	27.38	27	27	39,983,200	26.9
Nov-15-04	27.34	27.5	27.2	27	40,756,900	27.22
Nov-12-04	30.16	30.2	29.8	29	41,548,700	26.72
					44,243,300	
Nov-09-04	29.43	29.89	29.35	29	44,691,000	26.54
Nov-08-04	29.18	29.48	29.13	29	44,749,200	26.11
					45,369,700	
Oct-22-04	28.3	28.34	27.58	27	46,131,100	24.73

Only rows that meet the criteria are shown

Drop down the header row and choose a criteria to filter the range

Figure 11-2. Applying a filter to a stock price history table

To create a filter in code, use the Range object's AutoFilter method without arguments. To apply a filter, call AutoFilter again with the column to filter and the criteria as arguments. The following ApplyFilter procedure creates a filter and applies a filter to display 10 days with the most volume (column 6 in Figure 11-2):

```
Sub ApplyFilter( )
    Dim header As Range
    Set header = [e21:k21]
    ' Create filter
    header.AutoFilter
    ' Apply filter to show top 10 volume days.
    header.AutoFilter 6, "10", XlAutoFilterOperator.xlTop10Items
End Sub
```

You've got to call AutoFilter twice: once to create the filter and once to apply a filter. If you try to create and apply a filter in a single statement, you'll get an error.

To remove filtering, call AutoFilter again without arguments. Because AutoFilter toggles filtering on and off, you need to check the worksheet's AutoFilter property to make sure the filter exists before removing it. The following code removes filtering from the table in Figure 11-2:

```
' If worksheet is filtered, remove the filter.
Sub RemoveFilter( )
    Dim header As Range, ws As Worksheet
    Set ws = ActiveSheet
```

```
        Set header = [e21:k21]
        If ws.AutoFilterMode Then _
            header.AutoFilter
    End Sub
```

The Worksheet object also has an AutoFilter member, but it's a property that returns a reference to autofilters on the worksheet, which in turn provides a collection of read-only Filter objects that represent each of the filtered columns. You can't change or apply filters through the Filters collection; you can only read the settings and then only if the filter is on. That's not too useful, but I illustrate it later in this chapter in "AutoFilter Members" in case you're curious.

The Range object's AdvancedFilter method lets you hide blocks of cells or copy those blocks to a new location. The AdvancedFilter method is the code equivalent of choosing Data → Filter → Advanced Filter and it doesn't add dropdowns to the column headings as does autofilter. For example, the following code displays the first five rows from the table in Figure 11-2:

```
Sub AdvancedFilter()
    ' Show first five rows.
    [d21:k224].AdvancedFilter xlFilterInPlace, [d21:d26], False
End Sub
```

AdvancedFilter removes the autofilter if there is one. AdvancedFilter provides a quick way to hide duplicate rows (including empty rows), as shown here:

```
Sub HideDuplicates()
    Dim ws As Worksheet
    Set ws = ActiveSheet
    ' Hide nonunique rows
    ws.UsedRange.AdvancedFilter xlFilterInPlace, ws.UsedRange, False, True
End Sub
```

Finally, the Worksheet object's ShowAllData method turns off all of the filters on a worksheet and redisplays any hidden rows:

```
Sub ShowAll()
    Dim ws As Worksheet
    Set ws = ActiveSheet
    ' Turn off all filters.
    ws.ShowAllData
End Sub
```

Save and Display Views

Views store printer and hidden range settings for a workbook. For example, you might create two views for a complex worksheet: one named Summary that hides detail rows and one named Detail that hides no rows. Users can then switch between those views easily. Similarly, you can use views to store printer settings to make switching between portrait and landscape modes more convenient.

To use views in Excel, start with the default settings you want to use and then follow these steps:

1. Choose Views → Custom Views → Add. Excel displays the Add View dialog.

2. Enter a name for the default view and click OK.

3. Select rows or columns to hide in the new view and choose Format → Row/Column → Hide.

4. Choose File → Print → Properties and set the printer properties to use in the view.

5. Repeat Step 1 and name the new view.

To switch between views in Excel:

1. Choose Views → Custom Views. Excel displays the Custom Views dialog.

2. Select the view to display and click Show.

 Since autofilters work by selectively hiding rows, views can be used to store filter criteria. You can then quickly switch between criteria using the views.

To create a view in code, use the Add method of the CustomViews collection. For example, the following code creates Summary and Detail views for a worksheet:

```
Sub CreateViews()
    Dim ws As Worksheet, wb As Workbook
    Set ws = ActiveSheet
    Set wb = ThisWorkbook
    ' Create Detail view
    ' Show all cells.
    ws.UsedRange.EntireRow.Hidden = False
    ' Hide an unneeded header from the web query.
    ws.Rows("10:20").EntireRow.Hidden = True
    ' Create the view.
    wb.CustomViews.Add "Detail", False, True
    ' Hide price history detail.
    [PriceHistory].EntireRow.Hidden = True
    ' Create summary view
    wb.CustomViews.Add "Summary", False, True
End Sub
```

Use the Show method to switch between views. For example, the following command button code switches between the Summary and Detail views created in the preceding code:

```
Private Sub cmdSwitchView_Click()
    Static view As String
    ' Toggle setting.
    If view = "" Or view = "Summary" Then
        view = "Detail"
    Else
```

```
            view = "Summary"
        End If
        ' Activate the view.
        ThisWorkbook.CustomViews(view).Show
    End Sub
```

Publish to the Web

Publishing items to the Web is an alternative to printing and distributing workbooks or worksheets manually. Unlike printed copies, published items may be interactive and can update automatically when you save changes to a workbook. To use these features you must have Excel 2000 or later and have write access to a web site or a network share. SharePoint document libraries support Excel publishing features, so I'll use the document library *http://www.excelworkshop.com/Ch11Sample/* as the publishing location throughout this chapter.

To publish an item from Excel:

1. Select the item to publish and choose File → Save, then select "Web Page (*.htm; *.html)" from the "Save as Type" listbox. Excel displays the publish options on the Save As dialog box (Figure 11-3).

2. Choose a public location such as a network share, FTP address, or URL to save the web page to and click Publish. Excel displays the Publish as Web Page dialog box (Figure 11-4).

3. Choose additional publishing options and click Publish to save the item as a web page.

If you select Add Interactivity With in Figure 11-4, Excel adds the following ActiveX control to the web page:

```
<object id="ch11_publish_Spreadsheet"
 classid="CLSID:0002E559-0000-0000-C000-000000000046">
 <param name=DisplayTitleBar value=false>
 <param name=Autofit value=true>
 <param name=DataType value=XMLData>
 <param name=XMLData value="...">
 <p style='margin-top:100;font-family:Arial;font-size:8.0pt'>To use this Web
 page interactively, you must have Microsoft!!R!! Internet Explorer 5.01 Service
 Pack 2 (SP2) or later and the Microsoft Office 2003 Web Components.</p>
 <p style='margin-top:100;font-family:Arial;font-size:8.0pt'>See the <a
 href="http://r.office.microsoft.com/r/rlidmsowcpub?clid=1033&amp;p1=Excel">Microsoft
 Office Web site</a> for more information.</p>
</object>
```

This ActiveX control runs only if you:

- Have the Office Web Components installed. Search *http://www.microsoft.com/ downloads* for "Office Web Components" to download.

- Are browsing with Internet Explorer (IE) 5.01 SP2 or later.

Figure 11-3. Use Save As to publish a workbook or a selected item

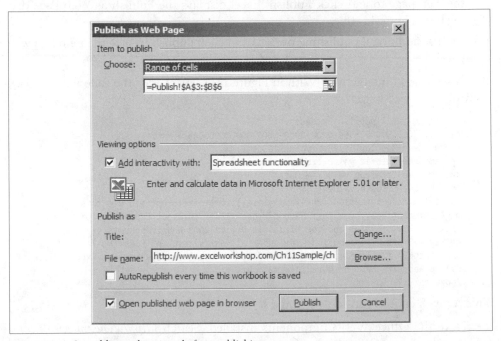

Figure 11-4. Set additional options before publishing

- Are viewing the page from an intranet or trusted Internet site or have set your IE security settings to a low level (*not* a good idea).

 Non-Microsoft browsers don't support ActiveX controls. In fact, ActiveX controls pose a significant security risk, so it is important to run them only if they are from trusted vendors or from trusted locations.

If you meet those conditions, you can enter values in cells on the interactive web page and see results as shown in Figure 11-5.

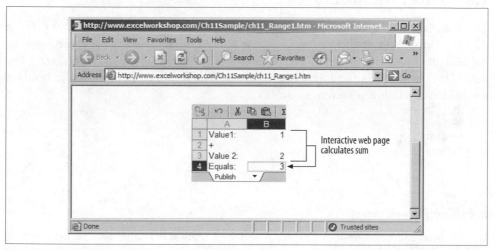

Figure 11-5. A published, interactive range

To publish objects from code, use the `PublishObjects` collection's `Add` method to create a `PublishObject`, then call the `Publish` method to publish the object. You get the `PublishObjects` collection from the `Workbook` object; the following code demonstrates publishing a workbook to a web site:

```
Sub PublishWorkbook()
    Dim wb As Workbook, po As PublishObject
    Set wb = ActiveWorkbook
    ' Create a publish object .
    Set po = wb.PublishObjects.Add(XlSourceType.xlSourceWorkbook, _
        "http://www.excelworkshop.com/Ch11Sample/Ch11_WB1.htm", _
        , , XlHtmlType.xlHtmlCalc)
    ' Publish the worksheet.
    po.Publish True
End Sub
```

The `PublishObject` is saved with the workbook; you can retrieve the object from its collection to republish it or to change its properties as shown here:

```
Sub RepublishAll()
    Dim po As PublishObject
    For Each po In ActiveWorkbook.PublishObjects
```

```
            ' Show  properties in the Immediate window.
            Debug.Print po.Source, po.Filename, po.Title
            ' Republish.
            po.Publish True
        Next
    End Sub
```

Alternately, you can set the AutoRepublish property to republish the web pages every time the workbook is saved.

AutoFilter Members

Use the AutoFilter object to get the Filter object for a column. Use the Range object's AutoFilter method to create a new filtered range. Use the Worksheet object's AutoFilter property to get a reference to the autofilters on a worksheet. The AutoFilter object has the following members. The key member (shown in **bold**) is covered in the following reference section:

```
Application
Creator
Filters
Parent
```

autofilter.Filters(*index*)

The Filters collection returns a Filter object with read-only properties that list the state and criteria for each filtered column on the worksheet. You can't change or apply filters through the Filters collection; you can only read the settings and then only if the filter is on as shown here:

```
Sub ShowFilters()
    Dim ws As Worksheet, flt As Filter, i As Integer
    Set ws = ActiveSheet
    ' If there are filters
    If ws.AutoFilterMode Then
        ' Get each Filter object
        For i = 1 To ws.AutoFilter.Filters.Count
            Set flt = ws.AutoFilter.Filters(i)
            '  And if the filter is on, show its criterion.
            If flt.On Then
                Debug.Print "Column " & i & ": " & flt.Criteria1
            End If
        Next
    End If
End Sub
```

 Use the Range object's AutoFilter method to set Filter properties and apply filters.

Filter and Filters Members

Use the Filters collection to get the state and settings of autofilters on a worksheet. Use the AutoFilter object's Filters property to get a reference to this collection. The Filters collection, and Filter object have the following members. Key members (shown in **bold**) are covered in the following reference section:

Application[2]
Count[1]
Creator[2]
Criteria[1]
Criteria[2]
Item[1]
On
Operator
Parent[2]

[1] Collection only
[2] Object and collection

filter.Criteria1

Returns the first criterion for a filter as a string.

filter.Criteria2

Returns the second criterion for a filter as a string.

filter.On

Returns True if the filter is applied to the range, False if not. The other Filter properties return values only if On is True; otherwise they return Nothing.

filter.Operator

Returns an xlAutoFilterOperator constant indicating the filter's operator. Possible settings are:

xlAnd
xlBottom10Percent
xlTop10Items
xlBottom10Items
xlOr
xlTop10Percent

CustomView and CustomViews Members

Use the CustomViews collection to save print settings and hidden cells as a special view of a workbook. Use the Workbook object's CustomViews property to get a reference to this collection. Use the CustomView object's Show method to display the view. The CustomViews collection and CustomView object have the following members. Key members (shown in **bold**) are covered in the following reference section:

Add[1]	Application[2]
Count[1]	Creator[2]
Delete	Item[1]
Name	Parent[2]
PrintSettings	**RowColSettings**
Show	

[1] Collection only
[2] Object and collection

---

customviews.Add(ViewName, [PrintSettings], [RowColSettings])

Creates a new view for the workbook.

Argument	Settings
ViewName	The name of the view to create.
PrintSettings	True saves printer settings with the view; False omits them. Default is True.
RowColSettings	True saves hidden cell settings with the view; False omits them. Default is True.

For example, the following code creates a new view that prints all worksheets in landscape orientation. The code also restores the original view:

```
Sub CreateLandscapeView( )
    Dim ws As Worksheet, vw As CustomView, wb As Workbook
    Set ws = ActiveSheet
    Set wb = ThisWorkbook
    ' Save current settings.
    wb.CustomViews.Add ("Default")
    ' Set worksheets to print landscape.
    For Each ws In wb.Worksheets
        ws.PageSetup.Orientation = xlLandscape
    Next
    ' Save print settings as a view.
    wb.CustomViews.Add "Landscape", True, False
    ' Restore the previous settings.
    wb.CustomViews("Default").Show
End Sub
```

customview.PrintSettings

Returns True if printer settings are stored with the view, False otherwise.

customview.RowColSettings

Returns True if filters and hidden ranges are included with the view, False otherwise.

customview.Show

Makes a view active. This may or may not change the display. For example, the following code switches to the Landscape view created earlier, prints the workbook, then restores the default view. Because the Landscape view includes only print settings, the appearance of the worksheets does not change.

```
Sub PrintLandscape()
    Dim wb As Workbook
    Set wb = ThisWorkbook
    ' Set landscape view.
    wb.CustomViews("Landscape").Show
    wb.PrintOut , , , True
End Sub
```

HPageBreak, HPageBreaks, VPageBreak, VPageBreaks Members

Use the HPageBreaks and VPageBreaks collections to add manual page breaks to a worksheet. Use the Worksheet object's HPageBreaks and VPageBreaks properties to get a reference to those collections. Use the HPageBreak and VPageBreak objects to remove manual page breaks. The HPageBreaks, HPageBreak, VPageBreak, and VPageBreaks objects have the following members. Key members (shown in **bold**) are covered in the following reference section:

Add[1]	Application[2]
Count[1]	Creator[2]
Delete	**DragOff**
Extent	Item[1]
Location	Parent[2]
Type	

[1] Collection only
[2] Object and collection

pagebreaks.Add(*Before*)

Adds a manual page break to a worksheet.

Argument	Settings
Before	A Range object indicating the location of the page break. Breaks are inserted above or to the left of this location.

pagebreak.DragOff(*Direction, RegionIndex*)

Used to record deleting a page break during macro recording. Use Delete instead in code.

pagebreak.Extent

Returns xlPageBreakFull if the break is full-screen, xlPageBreakPartial if the break is only within the print area.

pagebreak.Location

Returns the Range object indicating the location of the break. The following code displays the locations of manual page breaks in the Immediate window:

```
Sub ShowBreakLocations( )
    Dim ws As Worksheet, hpb As HPageBreak
    Set ws = ActiveSheet
    For Each hpb In ws.HPageBreaks
        Debug.Print hpb.Location.Address
    Next
End Sub
```

pagebreak.Type

Returns xlPageBreakManual (2).

PageSetup Members

Use the PageSetup object to control the printer settings for a worksheet or chart. Use the Worksheet and Chart objects' PageSetup property to get a reference to this object. The PageSetup object has the following members. Key members (shown in **bold**) are covered in the following reference section:

Application	**BlackAndWhite**	BottomMargin
CenterFooter	CenterFooterPicture	CenterHeader
CenterHeaderPicture	CenterHorizontally	CenterVertically

ChartSize	Creator	Draft
FirstPageNumber	FitToPagesTall	FitToPagesWide
FooterMargin	HeaderMargin	LeftFooter
LeftFooterPicture	LeftHeader	LeftHeaderPicture
LeftMargin	Order	Orientation
PaperSize	Parent	PrintArea
PrintComments	PrintErrors	PrintGridlines
PrintHeadings	PrintNotes	PrintQuality
PrintTitleColumns	PrintTitleRows	RightFooter
RightFooterPicture	RightHeader	RightHeaderPicture
RightMargin	TopMargin	Zoom

pagesetup.BlackAndWhite [= *setting*]

True prints in black and white; False prints in color if it is available.

pagesetup.BottomMargin [= *setting*]

Sets or returns the bottom margin in points.

pagesetup.CenterFooter [= *setting*]

Sets or returns a string to print in the center footer region.

pagesetup.CenterFooterPicture

Returns the Graphic object to print in the center footer region.

pagesetup.CenterHeader [= *setting*]

Sets or returns a string to print in the center header region.

pagesetup.CenterHeaderPicture

Returns the Graphic object to print in the center header region.

pagesetup.CenterHorizontally [= *setting*]

True centers the worksheet or chart horizontally on the page when printing; False aligns the page to the top margin.

pagesetup.**CenterVertically** [= *setting*]

True centers the worksheet or chart vertically on the page when printing; False aligns the page to the lefthand margin.

pagesetup.**ChartSize** [= *setting*]

Sets or returns an `xlObjectSize` constant that determines how a chart is sized; causes an error for worksheet objects. Can be one of the following settings:

`xlFitToPage`
  Prints the chart as large as possible, while retaining the chart's height-to-width ratio.

`xlFullPage`
  Prints the chart to fit the page, adjusting the height-to-width ratio (this is the default).

`xlScreenSize`
  Prints the chart the same size as it appears on the screen.

pagesetup.**Draft** [= *setting*]

True omits graphics when printing; False includes graphics.

pagesetup.**FirstPageNumber** [= *setting*]

Sets or returns the starting number used for page numbering. Default is `xlAutomatic`.

pagesetup.**FitToPagesTall** [= *setting*]

For worksheets, specifies the number of worksheet pages to include vertically on a single print page. Ignored if the Zoom property is True; causes an error for charts.

pagesetup.**FitToPagesWide** [= *setting*]

For worksheets, specifies the number of worksheet pages to include horizontally on a single print page. Ignored if the Zoom property is True; causes an error for charts.

pagesetup.**FooterMargin** [= *setting*]

Sets or returns the distance from the bottom of the page to the footer in points.

pagesetup.**HeaderMargin** [= *setting*]

Sets or returns the distance from the top of the page to the header in points.

pagesetup.**LeftFooter** [= *setting*]

Sets or returns a string to print in the left footer region.

pagesetup.**LeftFooterPicture**

Returns the Graphic object to print in the left footer region.

pagesetup.**LeftHeader** [= *setting*]

Sets or returns a string to print in the left header region.

pagesetup.**LeftHeaderPicture**

Returns the Graphic object to print in the left header region.

pagesetup.**LeftMargin** [= *setting*]

Sets or returns the size of the left margin in points.

pagesetup.**Order** [= *setting*]

Sets or returns an XlOrder constant that determines how multiple pages are printed. Possible settings are:

> xlDownThenOver (default)
> xlOverThenDown

pagesetup.**Orientation** [= *setting*]

Sets or returns an XlPageOrientation constant that determines whether the page prints in portrait or landscape mode. Possible settings are:

> xlPortrait (default)
> xlLandscape

pagesetup.**PaperSize** [= *setting*]

Sets or returns an XlPaperSize constant that determines the paper size used by the printer. Possible settings are:

xlPaper10x14	xlPaper11x1
xlPaperA3 (297 mm × 420 mm)	xlPaperA4 (210 mm × 297 mm)
xlPaperA4Small (210 mm × 297 mm)	xlPaperA5 (148 mm × 210 mm)

xlPaperB4 (250 mm × 354 mm)   xlPaperB5 (148 mm × 210 mm)

xlPaperCsheet   xlPaperDsheet

xlPaperEnvelope9 (3 $7/8$ in. × 8 $7/8$ in.)   xlPaperEnvelope10 (4 $1/8$ in. × 9 $1/2$ in.)

xlPaperEnvelope11 (4 $1/2$ in. × 10 $3/8$ in.)   xlPaperEnvelope12 (4 $1/2$ in. × 11 in.)

xlPaperEnvelope14 (5 in. × 11 $1/2$ in.)   xlPaperEnvelopeB4 (250 mm × 353 mm)

xlPaperEnvelopeB5 (176 mm × 250 mm)   xlPaperEnvelopeB6 (176 mm × 125 mm)

xlPaperEnvelopeC3 (324 mm × 458 mm)   xlPaperEnvelopeC4 (229 mm × 324 mm)

xlPaperEnvelopeC5 (162 mm × 229 mm)   xlPaperEnvelopeC6 (114 mm × 162 mm)

xlPaperEnvelopeC65 (114 mm × 229 mm)   xlPaperEnvelopeDL (110 mm × 220 mm)

xlPaperEnvelopeItaly (110 mm × 230 mm)   xlPaperEnvelopeMonarch (3 $7/8$ in. × 7 $1/2$ in.)

xlPaperEnvelopePersonal (3 $5/8$ in. × 6 $1/2$ in.)   xlPaperEsheet

xlPaperExecutive (7 $1/2$ in. × 10 $1/2$ in.)   xlPaperFanfoldLegalGerman (8 $1/2$ in. × 13 in.)

xlPaperFanfoldStdGerman (8 $1/2$ in. × 13 in.)   xlPaperFanfoldUS U.S. (14 $7/8$ in. × 11 in.)

xlPaperFolio (8 $1/2$ in. × 13 in.)   xlPaperLedger (17 in. × 11 in.)

xlPaperLegal (8 $1/2$ in. × 14 in.)   xlPaperLetter (8 $1/2$ in. × 11 in.)

xlPaperLetterSmall (8 $1/2$ in. × 11 in.)   xlPaperNote (8 $1/2$ in. × 11 in.)

xlPaperQuarto (215 mm × 275 mm)   xlPaperStatement (5 $1/2$ in. × 8 $1/2$ in.)

xlPaperTabloid (11 in. × 17 in.)   xlPaperUser (User-defined)

pagesetup.PrintArea [= *setting*]

Sets or returns the address of the range to be printed as a string using A1-style references. Causes an error for charts.

pagesetup.PrintComments [= *setting*]

Sets or returns an XlPrintLocation constant that determines how comments are printed. Possible settings are:

    xlPrintInPlace
    xlPrintNoComments (default)
    xlPrintSheetEnd

pagesetup.PrintErrors [= *setting*]

Sets or returns an XlPrintErrors constant that determines how error values are printed. Possible settings are:

    xlPrintErrorsBlank
    xlPrintErrorsDash
    xlPrintErrorsDisplayed (default)
    xlPrintErrorsNA

pagesetup.**PrintGridlines** [= *setting*]

True prints gridlines; False hides them. Default is False. Causes an error for charts.

pagesetup.**PrintHeadings** [= *setting*]

True prints row numbers and column letters with the worksheet; False does not print those headings. Default is False. Causes an error for charts.

pagesetup.**PrintNotes** [= *setting*]

True prints cell notes at the end of the worksheet; False does not print notes. Default is False. Causes an error for charts.

pagesetup.**PrintQuality**(*index*) [= *setting*]

Sets or returns the horizontal and vertical print resolution as a two-element array. Some printers do not support multiple resolutions, and setting `PrintQuality` causes an error if the setting is not available or if the object is a chart. The following code displays the printer resolution settings:

```
Sub ShowResolution()
    Dim ws As Worksheet, x As Integer, y As Integer
    Set ws = ActiveSheet
    x = ws.PageSetup.PrintQuality(1)
    y = ws.PageSetup.PrintQuality(2)
    MsgBox "Printer resolution is " & x & "x" & y
End Sub
```

pagesetup.**PrintTitleColumns** [= *setting*]

Sets or returns the address of a column to repeat at the top of each printed page as column headings. The address is specified as a string.

pagesetup.**PrintTitleRows** [= *setting*]

Sets or returns the address of a row to repeat at the left of each printed page as row headings. The address is specified as a string.

pagesetup.**RightFooter** [= *setting*]

Sets or returns a string to print in the right footer region.

pagesetup.**RightFooterPicture**

Returns the Graphic object to print in the right footer region.

pagesetup.**RightHeader** [= *setting*]

Sets or returns a string to print in the right header region.

pagesetup.**RightHeaderPicture**

Returns the Graphic object to print in the right header region.

pagesetup.**RightMargin** [= *setting*]

Sets or returns the size of the right margin in points.

pagesetup.**TopMargin** [= *setting*]

Sets or returns the size of the top margin in points.

pagesetup.**Zoom** [= *setting*]

Sets or returns a percentage between 10 and 400 percent to scale the worksheet by when printing. Default is 100. Causes an error for charts.

Graphic Members

Use the Graphic object to add pictures to headers and footers through the PageSetup object. Use the PageSetup object's CenterFooterPicture, CenterHeaderPicture, LeftFooterPicture, LeftHeaderPicture, RightFooterPicture, or RightHeaderPicture methods to get a reference to this object. The Graphic object has the following members, most of which are shared by the PictureFormat object. Unique, key members (shown in **bold**) are covered in the following reference section:

Application	Brightness
ColorType	Contrast
Creator	CropBottom
CropLeft	CropRight
CropTop	**Filename**
Height	**LockAspectRatio**
Parent	Width

To add a graphic to a header or footer in code:

1. Use one of the `PageSetup` object's header or footer picture methods to get a reference to the `Graphic` object.

2. Set the `Filename` property of the `Graphic` object.

3. Set the `PageSetup` object's corresponding header or footer property to &G.

The following code demonstrates adding a bitmap to the center footer of the active worksheet and previews the result before printing:

```
Sub AddFooterGraphic()
    Dim ws As Worksheet, ps As PageSetup
    Set ws = ActiveSheet
    Set ps = ws.PageSetup
    ps.CenterFooterPicture.Filename = _
      ThisWorkbook.Path & "\wombatright.bmp"
    ps.CenterFooter = "&G"
    ws.PrintOut , , , True
End Sub
```

To remove the graphic from the header or footer, remove the &G from the header or footer as shown here:

```
Sub RemoveFooterGraphic()
    Dim ws As Worksheet
    Set ws = ActiveSheet
    ws.PageSetup.CenterFooter = ""
End Sub
```

---

graphic.**Filename** [= *setting*]

Sets or returns the name of the graphic file to include in the header or footer.

---

graphic.**LockAspectRatio** [= *setting*]

True retains the aspect ratio when the height or width is set; False stretches or squashes the image to match the height or width settings. The following code demonstrates the result of both settings; notice that the image filename must be reset to restore the original proportions after resizing the image:

```
Sub GraphicAspectRatio()
    Dim gr As Graphic
    ' Add the footer image.
    ActiveSheet.PageSetup.CenterFooterPicture.Filename = _
      ThisWorkbook.Path & "\wombatright.bmp"
    ActiveSheet.PageSetup.CenterFooter = "&G"
    ' Get the graphic object.
    Set gr = ActiveSheet.PageSetup.CenterFooterPicture
    ' Squash the image (height stays the same)
    gr.LockAspectRatio = False
    gr.Height = 20
```

```
      ActiveSheet.PrintOut , , , True
      ' Restore the footer image.
      ActiveSheet.PageSetup.CenterFooterPicture.Filename = _
        ThisWorkbook.Path & "\wombatright.bmp"
      ' Scale image to this width
      gr.LockAspectRatio = True
      gr.Height = 20
      ActiveSheet.PrintOut , , , True
  End Sub
```

PublishObject and PublishObjects Members

Use the PublishObjects collection to publish items from a workbook to the Web. Use the Workbook object's PublishObjects property to get a reference to this collection. Use the PublishObject object to save the item as a web page and to control the appearance of that web page. The PublishObjects collection and PublishObject object have the following members. Key members (shown in **bold**) are covered in the following reference section:

Add[1]	Application[2]
AutoRepublish	Count[1]
Creator[2]	Delete[2]
DivID	**Filename**
HtmlType	Item[1]
Parent[2]	**Publish**[2]
Sheet	**Source**
SourceType	**Title**

[1] Collection only
[2] Object and collection

publishobjects.Add(SourceType, Filename, [Sheet], [Source], [HtmlType], [DivID], [Title])

Creates an object that can be published from the workbook as a web page.

Argument	Settings
SourceType	An XlSourceType constant identifying the type of object to publish. Can be one of these settings: xlSourceAutoFilter xlSourceChart xlSourcePivotTable xlSourcePrintArea xlSourceQuery xlSourceRange xlSourceSheet xlSourceWorkbook

Argument	Settings
Filename	The full URL of the web page to create.
Sheet	If *SourceType* is xlSourceSheet or xlSourcePrintArea, this is the name of the worksheet to publish.
Source	If *SourceType* is xlSourceAutofilter or xlSourceRange, this argument is the address of the range, or the name of the range to publish entered as a string. If *SourceType* is xlSourceChart, xlSourcePivotTable, or xlSourceQuery, this argument is the name of the chart, pivot table, or query to publish.
HtmlType	An XlHTMLType constant identifying whether the published object is interactive. Can be one of these settings: xlHtmlCalc (interactive range) xlHtmlChart (interactive chart) xlHtmlList (interactive list) xlHtmlStatic (noninteractive)
DivID	The ID attribute of a <DIV> element in the target web page to replace. This argument allows you to replace part of a web page with the published item.
Title	A title to include in the <Title> element on the web page.

The arguments used by Add are complicated and their meanings vary based on the published source and target. It is easiest to turn on macro recording, publish the item, turn off recording, then use the generated Add method as a starting point for writing your code.

publishobject.AutoRepublish [= *setting*]

True automatically republishes the item when the workbook is saved; False does not automatically republish. Default is False.

publishobject.DivID

Returns the ID attribute of the <DIV> element on the web page to be replaced when the item is published. This property is set by the Add method.

publishobject.Filename [= *setting*]

The URL of the web page to publish.

publishobject.HtmlType [= *setting*]

Sets or returns an XlHTMLType constant identifying whether the published object is interactive. See the Add method *HtmlType* argument for a list of settings.

publishobjects.Publish([*Create*])

Publishes the item by saving it as a web page.

Argument	Settings
Create	True replaces an existing file with a new file; False appends the item to the file if it already exists. In either case, the file is created if it does not already exist.

publishobject.Sheet

Returns the name of the sheet being published. Use the Add method's *Sheet* argument to set this property.

publishobject.Source

Returns the address or name of the item being published. Use the Add method's *Source* argument to set this property.

publishobject.SourceType

Returns the type of item being published. Use the Add method's *SourceType* argument to set this property.

publishobject.Title [= *setting*]

Sets or returns the title included in the <Title> element of the published web page.

WebOptions and DefaultWebOptions Members

Use the WebOptions and DefaultWebOptions objects to set the default web publishing options at the application or workbook levels. Use the Application object's DefaultWebOptions property or the Workbook object's WebOptions property to get a reference to these objects. The WebOptions and DefaultWebOptions objects have the following members. Key members (shown in **bold**) are covered in the following reference section:

AllowPNG	AlwaysSaveInDefaultEncoding[1]
Application	**CheckIfOfficeIsHTMLEditor**[1]
Creator	**DownloadComponents**
Encoding	**FolderSuffix**
Fonts[1]	**LoadPictures**[1]
LocationOfComponents	**OrganizeInFolder**

Parent	PixelsPerInch
RelyOnCSS	RelyOnVML
SaveHiddenData[1]	SaveNewWebPagesAsWebArchives[1]
ScreenSize	TargetBrowser
UpdateLinksOnSave	UseLongFileNames

[1] The DefaultWebOptions members are a superset of the WebOptions members. These members apply to DefaultWebOptions only.

 Excel saves graphics with only noninteractive web pages. Interactive web pages automatically omit pictures, controls, and other Shape objects, and image-related web options have no effect.

options.AllowPNG [= *setting*]

True allows web page graphics to be saved in Portable Network Graphics (PNG) format, which can improve the resolution and performance of the graphic. Not all browsers support PNG, however, so the default is False.

defaultweboptions.AlwaysSaveInDefaultEncoding [= *setting*]

True uses the Encoding property when updating existing web pages, overriding the file settings. Default is False.

defaultweboptions.CheckIfOfficeIsHTMLEditor [= *setting*]

True causes Excel to check if Microsoft Office is the default HTML editor whenever Excel starts. Default is True.

options.DownloadComponents [= *setting*]

True automatically downloads the Office Web Components from the URL in LocationOfComponents if the user does not have those components installed before viewing the web page. The user must have Microsoft Office 2000 or later installed, however. Default is False.

options.Encoding [= *msoEncoding*]

Sets or returns the msoEncoding constant for the code page or character set to use on the web page. The default is the system code page.

options.FolderSuffix

Returns the folder suffix used if `UseLongFileNames` and `OrganizeInFolder` are set to True. By default, the name of the supporting folder is the name of the web page—plus an underscore (_), a period (.), or a hyphen (-)—and the word `files`.

defaultweboptions.Fonts

Returns a `WebPageFonts` collection that represents the fonts Excel uses when saving a web page. Changing the font name or size properties of the returned `WebPageFont` objects does not seem to have an effect on web pages published from Excel:

```
Sub WebFonts( )
    Dim fnt As WebPageFont
    Set fnt = _
      Application.DefaultWebOptions.Fonts _
      (msoCharacterSetEnglishWesternEuropeanOtherLatinScript)
    ' Show the current settings.
    Debug.Print fnt.FixedWidthFont
    Debug.Print fnt.FixedWidthFontSize
    Debug.Print fnt.ProportionalFont
    Debug.Print fnt.ProportionalFontSize
End Sub
```

defaultweboptions.LoadPictures [= *setting*]

True loads images when an Excel file is opened for a web address; False if the images are not loaded. Default is True.

options.LocationOfComponents [= *setting*]

Sets or returns the URL from which to download the Office Web Components (*owc10.exe* or *owc11.exe*) if they are not installed on the user's machine. The default is the drive from which Office was originally installed (usually the CD drive).

You can copy the Office Web Components to a folder on your web server, then set this property to ensure the components will be installed automatically if needed, as shown here:

```
Sub SetDownload( )
    Dim wo As DefaultWebOptions
    Set wo = Application.DefaultWebOptions
    wo.LocationOfComponents = _
      "http://www.excelworkshop.com/Ch11Sample/owc11.exe"
    wo.DownloadComponents = True
End Sub
```

options.**OrganizeInFolder** [= *setting*]

True saves supporting files such as graphics in a subfolder created at the location of the web page; False saves supporting files in the same folder as the web page. Default is True.

options.**RelyOnCSS** [= *setting*]

True creates a cascading stylesheet (CSS) file and saves it with the supporting files for formatting set through Excel styles; False saves the formatting information in the web page. Default is True.

options.**RelyOnVML** [= *setting*]

True does not render Vector Markup Language (VML) graphics as image files when saving; not all browsers support VML, so the default is False.

defaultweboptions.**SaveHiddenData** [= *setting*]

True saves values that lie outside of the published range but that are referenced within the published range with the web page; False converts those references to static values. Default is True.

defaultweboptions.**SaveNewWebPagesAsWebArchives** [= *setting*]

True allows web pages to be saved in Multipurpose Internet Mail Extension HTML (MHTML) format, which includes graphics and embedded contents in a single file. Default is True.

options.**ScreenSize** [= *msoScreenSize*]

Sets or returns the `msoScreenSize` constant that determines the target screen size for the web page. Possible settings are:

msoScreenSize1152x882	msoScreenSize1280x1024
msoScreenSize1800x1440	msoScreenSize544x376
msoScreenSize720x512	msoScreenSize1024x768
msoScreenSize1152x900	msoScreenSize1600x1200
msoScreenSize1920x1200	msoScreenSize640x480
msoScreenSize800x600	

options.TargetBrowser [= *msoTargetBrowser*]

Sets or returns the `msoTargetBrowser` constant that determines browser capabilities to target when generating the web page. Possible settings are:

```
msoTargetBrowserIE4
msoTargetBrowserIE5
msoTargetBrowserIE6
msoTargetBrowserV3
msoTargetBrowserV4
```

defaultweboptions.UpdateLinksOnSave [= *setting*]

True updates linked values before saving as a web page; False does not automatically update links. Default is True.

options.UseLongFileNames [= *setting*]

True allows long filenames when saving web pages; False uses the DOS filename format (8.3).

CHAPTER 12

Loading and Manipulating Data

A lot of data is managed in and never leaves an Excel worksheet. But much of the data that Excel users work with comes from external databases such as SQL Server, Oracle, or Microsoft Access. You can work with data in various ways in Excel, usually by importing an entire table of data from a database or by using a query to import data that meets specific criteria. From a developer's perspective, you also have great programmatic control over the data you expose to users.

The Excel object model lets you create and manipulate queries from a variety of sources using the QueryTable object. If you want more programmatic control over your data, you have a choice of two programming interfaces. The ActiveX Data Objects (ADO) interface gives you access to data from a variety of data sources. The Data Access Objects (DAO) interface, which is native to Access databases, provides an easy-to-use interface for working with Access data.

In this chapter, I show how to:

- Work with QueryTable objects
- Work with Parameter objects
- Work with the ADO and DAO database programming interfaces

This chapter contains reference information for the following objects and their related collections: QueryTable, Parameter, ADO.Command, ADO.Connection, ADO.Field, ADO.Parameter, ADO.Record, ADO.RecordSet, DAO.Database, DAO.DbEngine, DAO.Document, DAO.QueryDef, and DAO.Recordset.

 Code used in this chapter and additional samples are available in *ch12.xls*.

Working with QueryTable Objects

The QueryTable object gives you programmatic access to the database queries that are native to Excel. These database queries let you retrieve data from a variety of data sources and insert the data into your worksheets. In the Excel interface, you create a database query by clicking Import External Data, New Database Query on the Data menu.

In code, you create a database query by adding a QueryTable object to the QueryTables collection. When you do this, you supply a connection string to your data source as well as a destination on your worksheet where you want the results of the query to be inserted. For example, the following code inserts information for a specific product from the Products table of the Northwind Traders sample database into the current worksheet, starting with the first cell of the worksheet:

```
Dim strConn As String
Dim strSQL As String
Dim qt As QueryTable

strConn = "ODBC;DSN=MS Access Database;" & _
    "DBQ=C:\Program Files\Microsoft Office\OFFICE11\SAMPLES\Northwind.mdb;"

Set qt = ActiveSheet.QueryTables.Add(Connection:=strConn, _
    Destination:=ActiveSheet.Range("A1"))
qt.CommandText = "SELECT * FROM Products WHERE (Products.ProductID=10)"
qt.Refresh
```

You can also use the ADO or DAO programming interfaces to create a recordset, and use the resulting Recordset object as your data source. To use either of these programming interfaces in Excel, you need to add a reference to the appropriate object library. On the Tools menu in the VBA programming environment, select References, then select the appropriate object library from the list. For example, the following code creates a query table using the Employees table in the Northwind Traders sample database and inserts the recordset name and data in the active worksheet:

```
Dim strDbPath As String
Dim db As DAO.Database
Dim rs As DAO.Recordset
Dim qt As QueryTable

strDbPath = "C:\Program Files\Microsoft Office\" & _
    "OFFICE11\SAMPLES\Northwind.mdb"

Set db = OpenDatabase(strDbPath)
Set rs = db.OpenRecordset("Employees")

Set qt = ActiveSheet.QueryTables.Add(Connection:=rs, _
    Destination:=ActiveSheet.Range("A3"))
```

```
ActiveSheet.Range("A1") = qt.Recordset.Name & " table:"

qt.Refresh
```

The ADO and DAO programming interfaces are discussed later in this chapter.

QueryTable and QueryTables Members

Use the QueryTables collection to create new query tables and add them to a worksheet. Use the Worksheet object's QueryTables property to get a reference to this collection. Use the QueryTable object to refresh the data in the query table and to control other aspects of the query. The QueryTables and QueryTable objects have the following members. Key members (shown in **bold**) are covered in the following reference section:

 Web query members are covered in Chapter 24.

Add[1]	**AdjustColumnWidth**
AfterRefresh	Application[2]
BackgroundQuery	BeforeRefresh
CancelRefresh	**CommandText**
CommandType	**Connection**
Count[1]	Creator[2]
Delete	**Destination**
EditWebPage	**EnableEditing**
EnableRefresh	**FetchedRowOverflow**
FieldNames	**FillAdjacentFormulas**
Item[1]	ListObject
MaintainConnection	Name
Parameters	Parent[2]
PostText	**PreserveColumnInfo**
PreserveFormatting	**QueryType**
Recordset	**Refresh**
Refreshing	**RefreshOnFileOpen**
RefreshPeriod	**RefreshStyle**
ResetTimer	**ResultRange**
RobustConnect	**RowNumbers**
SaveAsODC	SaveData
SavePassword	SourceConnectionFile
SourceDataFile	**TextFileColumnDataTypes**
TextFileCommaDelimiter	**TextFileConsecutiveDelimiter**
TextFileDecimalSeparator	**TextFileFixedColumnWidths**
TextFileOtherDelimiter	**TextFileParseType**
TextFilePlatform	**TextFilePromptOnRefresh**

TextFileSemicolonDelimiter	TextFileSpaceDelimiter
TextFileStartRow	TextFileTabDelimiter
TextFileTextQualifier	TextFileThousandsSeparator
TextFileTrailingMinusNumbers	TextFileVisualLayout
WebConsecutiveDelimitersAsOne	WebDisableDateRecognition
WebDisableRedirections	WebFormatting
WebPreFormattedTextToColumns	WebSelectionType
WebSingleBlockTextImport	WebTables

[1] Collection only
[2] Object and collection

querytables.Add(*Connection, Destination, [Sql]*)

Creates a new query table and adds it to the worksheet. Returns a QueryTable object.

Argument	Description
Connection	A string or object reference identifying the source of the data.
Destination	A Range object identifying the upper-lefthand corner of the destination of the query table.
Sql	If the Connection argument is an ODBC data source, this argument is a string containing the SQL query to perform. Otherwise, including this argument either causes an error or is ignored.

querytable.AdjustColumnWidth [= *setting*]

Set this property to False to disable the automatic adjustment for the best fit for columns in the specified query table.

querytable.BackgroundQuery [= *setting*]

True refreshes data in the query table asynchronously. False refreshes data synchronously. Default is True.

The BeforeRefresh and AfterRefresh events occur whether or not the query is refreshed synchronously or asynchronously. When synchronous, both events occur before the Refresh method completes. When asynchronous, only the BeforeRefresh event occurs before the Refresh method completes, then program flow continues.

querytable.CancelRefresh

Cancels an asynchronous query. You can't refresh or delete a query while that query has refresh pending. When working with asynchronous queries, you should check the query table's Refreshing property and (possibly) cancel the pending refresh before deleting or refreshing that query again.

The following code cancels any pending refreshes before refreshing a query:

```
If qt.Refreshing Then qt.CancelRefresh
qt.Refresh
```

*querytable.*CommandText [= *setting*]

Sets or returns the command string for the specified query table. The following code returns the results of a query with the specified command string:

```
Dim strConn As String
Dim strSQL As String
Dim qt As QueryTable

strConn = "ODBC;DSN=MS Access Database;" & _
    "DBQ=C:\Program Files\Microsoft Office\OFFICE11\SAMPLES\Northwind.mdb;"
Set qt = ActiveSheet.QueryTables.Add(Connection:=strConn, _
    Destination:=ActiveSheet.Range("A1"))

qt.CommandText = "SELECT * FROM Products WHERE (Products.ProductID=10)"
qt.Refresh
```

*querytable.*CommandType [= *setting*]

Sets or returns the type of command string used by the specified query table. The type can be xlCmdSQL, a SQL string (default); xlCmdCub, a cube name for an online analytical processing (OLAP) data source; xlCmdDefault, command text that the OLE DB provider understands; or xlCmdTable, a table name for accessing OLE DB data sources.

*querytable.*Connection [= *setting*]

Sets or returns the connection string for the specified query table. The following code creates a query table, returns its results, and displays the connection string in cell A6:

```
Dim strConn As String
Dim strSQL As String
Dim qt As QueryTable

strConn - "ODBC;DSN=MS Access Database;" & _
    "DBQ=C:\Program Files\Microsoft Office\OFFICE11\SAMPLES\Northwind.mdb;"

Set qt = ActiveSheet.QueryTables.Add(Connection:=strConn, _
    Destination:=ActiveSheet.Range("A1"))
qt.CommandText = "SELECT * FROM Products WHERE (Products.ProductID=10)"
qt.Refresh
ActiveSheet.Range("A6") = qt.Connection
```

*querytable.*Delete

Deletes a query table. If the query table is refreshing asynchronously, Delete causes an error. Deleting a query table docs not remove data from cells on a worksheet—it just removes the ability to refresh those cells from their data source.

The following code deletes all of the query tables on the active worksheet and clears their data:

```
Dim qt As QueryTable
For Each qt In ActiveSheet.QueryTables
    If qt.Refreshing Then qt.CancelRefresh
    qt.Delete
Next
ActiveSheet.UsedRange.Clear
```

*querytable.*Destination

Returns a Range object containing the cell in the upper-lefthand corner of the query table.

The following code selects the first cell of a query table on the active worksheet and asks if the user wants to delete it:

```
For Each qt In ActiveSheet.QueryTables
    qt.Destination.Select
    If MsgBox("Delete query table?", vbYesNo) = vbYes Then
        If qt.Refreshing Then qt.CancelRefresh
        qt.ResultRange.Clear
        qt.Delete
    End If
Next
```

*querytable.*EnableEditing [= *setting*]

True allows the user to change the query definition through the Data menu's Import External Data submenu. False disables the Import External Data menu items. Default is True.

*querytable.*EnableRefresh [= *setting*]

True allows the user to refresh the query through the Data menu's Refresh Data item. False disables the Refresh Data menu item. Default is True.

*querytable.*FetchedRowOverflow [= *setting*]

True if the number of rows returned by the last refresh of the specified query table is greater than the available number of rows.

*querytable.*FieldNames [= *setting*]

True if field names from the data source are displayed as column headings for the returned data. The following code specifies that field names will not be displayed in the query table:

```
ActiveSheet.QueryTables(1).FieldNames = False
```

*querytable.*FillAdjacentFormulas [= *setting*]

True causes calculated cells to the right of the query table to be repeated for each row when the query table is refreshed. False does not repeat adjacent formulas. Default is False.

Set FillAdjacentFormulas to True in order to create row totals, or other calculations, for each row in the query table automatically. To use this feature, create a query table, add a formula for the first row in the query table, set FillAdjacentFormulas to True, then refresh the data. For more information, see Chapter 24.

*querytable.*MaintainConnection [= *setting*]

This property returns True if the connection to the specified query table's data source is maintained after a refresh operation. You can set this property for queries to OLEDB sources only.

*querytable.*Parameters

Returns a Parameters collection object that represents the parameters of the specified query table. Working with Parameter objects is covered later in this chapter.

*querytable.*PreserveColumnInfo [= *setting*]

True preserves the column sorting, filtering, and layout information when the specified query table is refreshed. False does not preserve formatting. Default is False.

*querytable.*PreserveFormatting [= *setting*]

True preserves the cell formatting of the query table when data is refreshed. False does not preserve formatting. Default is False.

If PreserveFormatting is True and a refresh imports new rows of data, formatting common to the first five rows of the query table is automatically applied to the new rows.

*querytable.*QueryType [= *setting*]

Returns a value identifying the type of data source used by the query table. Possible values are:

```
xlTextImport
xlOLEDBQuery
xlWebQuery
xlADORecordset
xlDAORecordSet
xlODBCQuery
```

*querytable.*Recordset [= *setting*]

Sets or returns a Recordset object that serves as the data source for the specified query table. The following code creates a query table using the Employees table in the North-wind Traders sample database as the recordset and inserts the name of the recordset as well as the recordset data in the active worksheet:

```
Dim strDbPath As String
Dim db As DAO.Database
Dim rs As DAO.Recordset
Dim qt As QueryTable

strDbPath = "C:\Program Files\Microsoft Office\" & _
    "OFFICE11\SAMPLES\Northwind.mdb"

Set db = OpenDatabase(strDbPath)
Set rs = db.OpenRecordset("Employees")

Set qt = ActiveSheet.QueryTables.Add(Connection:=rs, _
    Destination:=ActiveSheet.Range("A3"))

ActiveSheet.Range("A1") = qt.Recordset.Name & " table:"

qt.Refresh
```

*querytable.*Refresh([*BackgroundQuery*])

Refreshes a query table from its data source. Returns True if the refresh was submitted successfully, False if the user canceled the refresh.

Argument	Description
BackgroundQuery	True refreshes the data asynchronously; False refreshes the data synchronously. Default is True.

Most types of query table store connection and data source information that is used by Refresh. The exception is recordset queries—you must set a new recordset before calling Refresh for query tables based on recordsets. See the Recordset property for an example.

When refreshing asynchronously, check the Refreshing property before calling Refresh. Otherwise, pending refreshes will cause an error. The following code cancels any pending asynchronous refresh before refreshing a query table:

```
If qt.Refreshing Then qt.CancelRefresh
qt.Refresh
```

*querytable.*Refreshing

Returns True if an asynchronous refresh is pending for this query table, False if no refresh is pending.

querytable.RefreshOnFileOpen [= setting]

True refreshes the query table when the workbook is opened; False does not refresh on open. Default is False.

querytable.RefreshPeriod [= setting]

Sets or returns the number of minutes between automatic refreshes. The default is 0, for no automatic refreshing. You can set automatic refreshing on synchronous or asynchronous queries. RefreshPeriod is ignored for query tables created from recordsets.

The following code creates a query table from an ODBC data source and sets the query table to refresh once a minute:

```
Dim strConn As String
Dim strSQL As String
Dim qt As QueryTable

strConn="ODBC;DRIVER=SQL Server;SERVER=.;UID=Jeff;APP=Microsoft Office "& _
"XP;WSID=WOMBAT2;DATABASE=pubs;Trusted_Connection=Yes"
strSQL = "SELECT titles.title, titles.price, titles.pubdate, titles.ytd_sales
FROM pubs.dbo.titles titles"
Set qt = ActiveSheet.QueryTables.Add(strConn, [QueryDestination], strSQL)
qt.RefreshPeriod = 1
qt.Refresh
```

querytable.RefreshStyle [= setting]

Determines how the query affects surrounding items on the worksheet when the query table is refreshed.

Setting	Description
xlInsertDeleteCells	Inserts or deletes new rows and columns created by the query, moving surrounding items up or down and to the right or left as needed (default).
xlOverwriteCells	No new rows or columns are added to the worksheet. Surrounding items are overwritten as needed.
xlInsertEntireRows	Inserts a new row for each record returned by the query. Shifts existing items down as needed to accommodate the number of records returned.

The following code modifies an existing query table to insert new rows on the worksheet as needed, shifting existing items on the worksheet down:

```
Set qt = ActiveSheet.QueryTables(1)
qt.RefreshStyle = xlInsertEntireRows
qt.Refresh
```

If a subsequent query reduces the number of records returned, the contents of the query table are replaced, but the rows that were previously shifted down are not shifted back up again as they would be if RefreshStyle was set to xlInsertDeleteCells.

querytable.ResetTimer

Resets the timer used for periodic queries, in effect delaying when a query occurs. Use the RefreshPeriod property to automatically refresh a query periodically.

querytable.ResultRange

Returns the range containing the results of the query. For example, the following code clears the results from a query table on the active worksheet:

```
ActiveSheet.QueryTables(1).ResultRange.Clear
```

If a query table has been created but not yet refreshed, accessing ResultRange causes an error. There's no direct way to test whether a query table has been refreshed. One solution to this problem is to write a helper function similar to the following to check if a query table has a result before accessing ResultRange elsewhere in code:

```
Public Function HasResult(qt As QueryTable) As Boolean
    Dim ret As Boolean
    On Error Resume Next
    Debug.Print qt.ResultRange.Address
    If Err Then ret = False Else ret = True
    On Error GoTo 0
    HasResult = ret
End Function
```

Now, you can easily test if a query table has a result before clearing the result range or performing other tasks as shown here:

```
Set qt = ActiveSheet.QueryTables(1)
If HasResult(qt) Then qt.ResultRange.Clear
```

querytable.RowNumbers [= setting]

Set this property to True to display row numbers in the first column of the specified query table. The numbers do not display until the query table is refreshed. They will be reset each time the query table is refreshed. The following code adds row numbers to the first query table on the active worksheet:

```
With ActiveSheet.QueryTables(1)
    .RowNumbers = True
    .Refresh
End With
```

querytable.SavePassword [= setting]

Set this property to True to save password information in an ODBC connection string with the specified query table.

*querytable.***TextFileColumnDataTypes** [= *setting*]

Sets or returns an array of constants specifying the data types applied to a text file being imported into the specified query table.

*querytable.***TextFileCommaDelimiter** [= *setting*]

True if you are using a comma delimiter when you are importing a text file into the specified query table.

*querytable.***TextFileConsecutiveDelimiter** [= *setting*]

True if consecutive delimiters are treated as a single delimiter when you are importing a text file into the specified query table.

*querytable.***TextFileDecimalSeparator** [= *setting*]

Sets or returns the decimal separator used when you are importing a text file into the specified query table.

*querytable.***TextFileFixedColumnWidths** [= *setting*]

Sets or returns an array of integers that correspond to the widths of the columns in the text file that you are importing into the specified query table. The following code imports text from a sample file and places the characters in each row of the active worksheet as follows:

- The first five characters are placed in the first column.
- The next four characters are placed in the second column.
- The remaining characters are placed in the third column:

```
Dim strCnn As String
Dim qt As QueryTable

strCnn = "TEXT;C:\My Documents\qtsample.txt"
Set qt = ActiveSheet.QueryTables.Add(Connection:=strCnn,& _
    Destination:=ActiveSheet.Range("A1"))
With qt
    .TextFileParseType = xlFixedWidth
    .TextFileFixedColumnWidths = Array(5, 4)
    .Refresh
End With
```

*querytable.***TextFileOtherDelimiter** [= *setting*]

Sets or returns the character used as a delimiter when you are importing a text file into the specified query table.

querytable.TextFileParseType [= setting]

Set this property to xlFixedWidth if the column data in the text file you are importing into the specified query table has a fixed width. Set this property to xlDelimited (default) if the column data in the text file is separated by a delimiter character.

querytable.TextFilePlatform [= setting]

Set this property to xlMacintosh if the text file you are importing into the specified query table originated on the Macintosh operating system. Set this property to xlMSDOS if the text file originated on the MS-DOS operating system. Set this property to xlWindows if the text file originated on the Windows operating system.

querytable.TextFilePromptOnRefresh [= setting]

True if you want to be prompted for the name of the text being imported into the specified query table each time the query table is refreshed.

querytable.TextFileSemicolonDelimiter [= setting]

True if you are using a semicolon delimiter when you are importing a text file into the specified query table.

querytable.TextFileSpaceDelimiter [= setting]

True if you are using a space character delimiter when you are importing a text file into the specified query table.

querytable.TextFileTabDelimiter [= setting]

True if you are using a tab character delimiter when you are importing a text file into the specified query table.

querytable.TextFileTextQualifier [= setting]

Set this property to xlTextQualifierSingleQuote if the text file you are importing into the specified query table uses single quotes rather than double quotes to indicate what is enclosed between the quotes is text. Set this property to xlTextQualifierNone if the file does not use quotes to indicate a text string. Set this property to xlTextQualifierDoubleQuote (default) if the file uses double quotes as a text qualifier.

*querytable.*TextFileThousandsSeparator [= *setting*]

Sets or returns the thousands separator used when you are importing a text file into the specified query table.

*querytable.*TextFileTrailingMinusNumbers [= *setting*]

True if numbers imported into the specified query table that begin with the hyphen character (-) are treated as negative numbers. False if they are treated as text.

*querytable.*TextFileVisualLayout [= *setting*]

Sets or returns the left-to-right layout of text for text imported into the specified query table. When the property is set to 1, layout is left-to-right. When the property is set to 2, the layout is right-to-left.

Working with Parameter Objects

The `Parameter` object lets you supply parameter criteria to limit the data returned by a query. This is useful if you want to create a query that returns a general set of data but you want to work with different subsets of that data or different individual records. You can supply different parameters rather than creating a new query for each subset or record.

You create a parameter by adding a `Parameter` object to the `Parameters` collection of a `QueryTable` object. You can then supply a specific parameter value or use a value in a cell on your worksheet. For example, the following code creates a query table that uses the value in cell A1 as the parameter:

```
Dim strConn As String
Dim strSQL As String
Dim qt As QueryTable
Dim param As Parameter

strConn = "ODBC;DSN=MS Access Database;" & _
    "DBQ=C:\Program Files\Microsoft Office\OFFICE11\SAMPLES\Northwind.mdb;"

Set qt = ActiveSheet.QueryTables.Add(Connection:=strConn, _
    Destination:=ActiveSheet.Range("C1"))
qt.CommandText = "SELECT * FROM Products WHERE (Products.ProductID=?)"
Set param = qt.Parameters.Add("ProductsParam")
param.SetParam xlRange, Range("A1")
qt.Refresh
```

Parameter Members

Use the Parameters collection to add parameters to the SQL query used by a query table. Use the QueryTable object's Parameters property to get a reference to this collection. Use the Parameter object to set the contents of the parameter. The Parameters collection and Parameter object have the following members. Key members (shown in **bold**) are covered in the following reference section:

Add[1]	Application[2]
Count[1]	Creator[2]
DataType	**Delete**
Item[1]	Name
Parent[2]	**PromptString**
RefreshOnChange	**SetParam**
SourceRange	**Type**
Value	

[1] Collection only
[2] Object and collection

parameters.Add(Name, [iDataType])

Creates a new query parameter. Returns a Parameter object.

Argument	Description
Name	A string that identifies the parameter.
iDataType	If you want to specify a data type for the parameter, use one of the following constants:
	xlParamTypeBigInt
	xlParamTypeBinary
	xlParamTypeBit
	xlParamTypeChar
	xlParamTypeDate
	xlParamTypeDecimal
	xlParamTypeDouble
	xlParamTypeFloat
	xlParamTypeInteger
	xlParamTypeLongVarBinary
	xlParamTypeWChar
	xlParamTypeNumeric
	xlParamTypeLongVarChar
	xlParamTypeReal
	xlParamTypeSmallInt
	xlParamTypeTime
	xlParamTypeTimeStamp
	xlParamTypeTinyInt
	xlParamTypeUnknown
	xlParamTypeVarBinary
	xlParamTypeVarChar

The following code creates a query table that uses a parameter to supply the product ID to the underlying query. The ? character is a placeholder for the query value, which in this case is the value 10 for the ProductID:

```
Dim strConn As String
Dim qt As QueryTable
Dim param As Parameter

strConn = "ODBC;DSN=MS Access Database;" & _
    "DBQ=C:\Program Files\Microsoft Office\OFFICE11\SAMPLES\Northwind.mdb;"

Set qt = ActiveSheet.QueryTables.Add(Connection:=strConn, _
    Destination:=ActiveSheet.Range("A1"))
qt.CommandText = "SELECT * FROM Products WHERE (Products.ProductID=?)"
Set param = qt.Parameters.Add("ProductsParam")
param.SetParam xlConstant, 10
qt.Refresh
```

parameter.DataType [= setting]

Sets or returns the data type of the specified parameter. See the Add method for a list of possible values.

parameter.Delete

Deletes the specified parameter.

parameter.PromptString [= setting]

If the specified parameter uses a prompt string, this property returns the prompt string. The following code creates two parameter query tables on the active worksheet and uses the same prompt string for both:

```
Dim strConn As String
Dim qt As QueryTable
Dim param As Parameter

strConn = "ODBC;DSN=MS Access Database;" & _
    "DBQ=C:\Program Files\Microsoft Office\OFFICE11\SAMPLES\Northwind.mdb;"

Set qt1 = ActiveSheet.QueryTables.Add(Connection:=strConn, _
    Destination:=ActiveSheet.Range("A1"))
qt1.CommandText = "SELECT * FROM Products WHERE (Products.ProductID=?)"
Set param1 = qt1.Parameters.Add("ProductsParam1")
param1.SetParam xlPrompt, "Please enter a Product ID."

Set qt2 = ActiveSheet.QueryTables.Add(Connection:=strConn, _
Destination:=ActiveSheet.Range("A5"))
qt2.CommandText = "SELECT * FROM Products WHERE (Products.ProductID=?)"
Set param2 = qt2.Parameters.Add("ProductsParam2")
```

```
param2.SetParam xlPrompt, param1.PromptString

qt1.Refresh
qt2.Refresh
```

*parameter.***RefreshOnChange** [= *setting*]

If the specified parameter uses a single-cell range as a parameter value, this property refreshes the query table whenever the cell value changes.

*parameter.***SetParam** [= *setting*]

Defines the specified parameter. The following code creates a query table that uses the value in cell A1 as the parameter:

```
Dim strConn As String
Dim strSQL As String
Dim qt As QueryTable
Dim param As Parameter

strConn = "ODBC;DSN=MS Access Database;" & _
    "DBQ=C:\Program Files\Microsoft Office\OFFICE11\SAMPLES\Northwind.mdb;"

Set qt = ActiveSheet.QueryTables.Add(Connection:=strConn, _
    Destination:=ActiveSheet.Range("C1"))
qt.CommandText = "SELECT * FROM Products WHERE (Products.ProductID=?)"
Set param = qt.Parameters.Add("ProductsParam")
param.SetParam xlRange, Range("A1")
qt.Refresh
```

*parameter.***SourceRange** [= *setting*]

If the specified parameter uses a single-cell range as its parameter, returns the corresponding Range object.

*parameter.***Type** [= *setting*]

Sets or returns the type of the specified parameter, either xlConstant if the parameter is a constant, xlPrompt if it is a prompt string, or xlRange if it is a single-cell range.

*parameter.***Value** [= *setting*]

Sets or returns the value of the specified parameter, either a constant, a prompt string, or a single-cell Range object.

Working with ADO and DAO

If you want to be able to manage all the details of working with data in your worksheets, you can manipulate data programmatically using one of the two programming interfaces: ActiveX Data Objects (ADO) and Data Access Objects (DAO).

DAO came first. It was developed in conjunction with Microsoft Access and is the native programming interface for the Jet database engine, the built-in data engine for Access. ADO came later, incorporating some of the database cursor optimization that came with Microsoft's acquisition of FoxPro. It is more flexible, better suited for high-performance applications, and designed to be more neutral in dealing with different data sources. But, truth be told, many experienced and respected Access developers still do most of their work in DAO.

To use either of these programming interfaces in Excel, you need to add a reference to the appropriate object library. On the Tools menu in the VBA programming environment, select References, then select the appropriate object library from the list.

A full discussion of ADO and DAO is beyond the scope of this book, but we will touch on some of the key objects and members of each interface.

ADO Objects and Members

The ADO object model includes the key objects listed in the following table. There are additional objects, but these cover the fundamentals of working with ADO. For information about the additional objects, see the ADO Help.

Object	Description
Command	Defines a specific command—such as a SQL statement, table name, or stored procedure—that returns data from a data source.
Connection	Represents a connection to a data source.
Field	Represents a field of data from a data source.
Parameter	Represents a parameter associated with a specific command.
Record	Represents a single record in a recordset.
Recordset	Represents a set of records from a table or command.

Descriptions of the members of these objects follow. Key members (shown in **bold**) are covered in the following reference sections.

ADO.Command Members

ActiveConnection	Cancel
CommandStream	**CommandText**
CommandTimeout	**CommandType**

CreateParameer	Dialect
Execute	Name
Prepared	Properties
State	

---

command.ActiveConnection [= setting]

Sets or returns the connection used by the specified command. The following code returns a record by executing a SQL command using the active connection:

```
Dim cnn As ADODB.Connection
Dim cmd As ADODB.Command
Dim rs As ADODB.Recordset
Dim strDbPath As String

Set cnn = New ADODB.Connection
Set cmd = New ADODB.Command
Set rs = New ADODB.Recordset
strDbPath = "C:\Program Files\Microsoft Office\OFFICE11\SAMPLES\Northwind.mdb"
cnn.ConnectionString = "Provider=Microsoft.Jet.OLEDB.4.0;" _
    & "Data Source=" & strDbPath
cnn.Open
Set cmd.ActiveConnection = cnn
cmd.CommandText = "SELECT * FROM Employees Where EmployeeID = 9;"
Set rs = cmd.Execute

Set qt = ActiveSheet.QueryTables.Add(Connection:=rs, _
    Destination:=ActiveSheet.Range("A3"))
qt.Refresh

ActiveSheet.Range("A1") = qt.Recordset.Source
rs.Close
cnn.Close
Set rs = Nothing
Set cnn = Nothing
```

---

command.CommandText [= setting]

Sets or returns the command text used by the specified command. See the ActiveConnection code example for an example of using CommandText.

---

command.CommandType [= setting]

Sets or returns the type of the specified command: adCmdUnspecified, adCmdText, adCmdTable, adCmdStoredProc, adCmdUnknown, adCmdFile, or adCmdTableDirect.

---

command.CreateParameter

Creates a new parameter for the specified command.

---

*command.*Execute

Executes the specified command. See the ActiveConnection code example for an example of using Execute.

*command.*Name [= *setting*]

Sets or returns the name of the specified command.

ADO.Connection Members

Attributes	**BeginTrans**
Cancel	Close
CommandTimeout	**CommitTrans**
ConnectionString	**ConnectionTimeout**
CursorLocation	DefaultDatabase
Execute	IsolationLevel
Mode	**Open**
OpenSchema	Provider
RollbackTrans	State
Version	

*connection.*BeginTrans

Begins a transaction—a series of operations performed as a whole (committed) or canceled (rolled back). The following code wraps the code example used for the Command object's ActiveConnection method around a transaction so that it can be committed or rolled back:

```
Dim cnn As ADODB.Connection
Dim cmd As ADODB.Command
Dim rs As ADODB.Recordset
Dim strDbPath As String

Set cnn = New ADODB.Connection
Set cmd = New ADODB.Command
Set rs = New ADODB.Recordset
strDbPath = "C:\Program Files\Microsoft Office\OFFICE11\SAMPLES\Northwind.mdb"
cnn.ConnectionString = "Provider=Microsoft.Jet.OLEDB.4.0;" _
    & "Data Source=" & strDbPath
cnn.Open
Set cmd.ActiveConnection = cnn
cnn.BeginTrans

cmd.CommandText = "SELECT * FROM Employees Where EmployeeID = 9;"
Set rs = cmd.Execute

' Prompt user to commit all changes made
```

```
If MsgBox("Save all changes?", vbYesNo) = vbYes Then
    cnn.CommitTrans
    Set qt = ActiveSheet.QueryTables.Add(Connection:=rs, _
    Destination:=ActiveSheet.Range("A3"))
    qt.Refresh
    ActiveSheet.Range("A1") = qt.Recordset.Source
Else
    cnn.RollbackTrans
End If

rs.Close
cnn.Close
Set rs = Nothing
Set cnn = Nothing
```

connection.Cancel

Cancels the specified connection object's last Execute or Open operation.

connection.CommandTimeout [= setting]

Specifies the time to wait, in seconds, while executing a command on the specified connection before terminating it.

connection.CommitTrans

Saves any changes made during a transaction. See the BeginTrans code example for an example of using CommitTrans.

connection.ConnectionString [= setting]

Specifies the connection string used to connect to a data source. See the BeginTrans code example for an example of using ConnectionString.

connection.ConnectionTimeout [= setting]

Specifies the time to wait, in seconds, while establishing a connection before terminating it.

connection.Open

Opens the specified connection. See the BeginTrans code example for an example of using Open.

connection.RollbackTrans

Cancels any changes made during a transaction. See the BeginTrans code example for an example of using RollbackTrans.

connection.Version [= setting]

Returns the ADO version number.

ADO.Field and ADO.Fields Members

ActualSize	Append[1]
AppendChunk	Attributes
CancelUpdate[1]	Count[1]
DefinedSize	Delete[1]
GetChunk	Item[1]
Name	NumericScale
OriginalValue	Precision
Refresh[1]	Resync[1]
Status	Type
UnderlyingValue	Update[1]
Value	

[1] Collection only

field.ActualSize [= setting]

Returns the actual size of the data in a field. Use the DefinedSize property to return the size of data that the field is capable of holding.

field.AppendChunk

Appends data to a large text or binary field.

fields.CancelUpdate

Cancels any updates made to the specified Fields collection.

field.DefinedSize [= setting]

Returns the size of data that the field is capable of holding. Use the ActualSize property to return the actual size of the data in a field.

field.GetChunk(*Size*)

Returns all or a specified portion of a large text or binary file.

Argument	Description
Size	The number of bytes or characters that you want to return

field.NumericScale [= *setting*]

Sets or returns the number of decimal places to use for numeric values.

field.OriginalValue [= *setting*]

Returns the value of a field before any changes were made. Use this property with the UnderlyingValue property in a multiuser environment when you want to make sure that you are using the most current data.

field.UnderlyingValue [= *setting*]

Returns the current value of a field. Use this property with the OriginalValue property in a multiuser environment when you want to make sure that you are using the most current data.

field.Value [= *setting*]

Sets or returns the value of data stored in the specified field.

ADO.Parameter and ADO.Parameters Members

Append[1]	**AppendChunk**
Attributes	Count[1]
Delete[1]	Direction
Item[1]	**Name**
NumericScale	**Precision**
Properties	Refresh[1]
Size	Type
Value	

[1] Collection only

*Parameter.*AppendChunk

Appends data to a large text or binary field.

*Parameter.*Name [= *setting*]

Sets or returns the name of the specified parameter.

*Parameter.*NumericScale [= *setting*]

Sets or returns the number of numeric decimal places in the specified parameter.

*Parameter.*Precision [= *setting*]

Sets or returns the maximum number of digits in a numeric parameter value.

*parameter.*Size [= *setting*]

Sets or returns the maximum size of the specified parameter, in bytes or characters.

*parameter.*Value [= *setting*]

Sets or returns the parameter's value.

ADO.Record Members

ActiveConnection	Cancel
Close	CopyRecord
DeleteRecord	**GetChildren**
Mode	MoveRecord
Open	ParentURL
Properties	**RecordType**
Source	**State**

*record.*ActiveConnection [= *setting*]

Sets or returns the connection used by the specified record.

record.Cancel

Cancels a pending CopyRecord, DeleteRecord, MoveRecord, or Open operation.

record.GetChildren

Returns a Recordset object whose rows are children of the specified record in a parent-child relationship.

record.Open([Source], [ActiveConnection], [Mode]), [CreateOptions], [Options], [UserName], [Password])

Opens the record.

Argument	Description
Source	If the record source has not already been specified, you can specify a Command, Record, or Recordset object; table; or SQL statement as the source.
ActiveConnection	If the connection has not already been specified, you can specify a Connection object or connect stiring.
Mode	If the mode has not already been specified, you can specify a ConnectModeEnum constant value that specifies the access mode. The value can be adModeRead, adModeReadWrite, adModeRecursive, adModeShareDenyNone, adModeShareDenyRead, adModeShareDenyWrite, adModeShareExclusive, adModeUnknown, adModeWrite.
CreateOptions	Lets you specify whether an existing file or directory should be opened or a new file or directory should be created.
Options	Lets you specify options for opening the record. The value can be adDelayFetchFields, adDelayFetchStream, adOpenAsync, adOpenExecuteCommand, adOpenRecordUnspecified, or adOpenOutput.
UserName	Lets you specify a username granting access to Source.
Password	Lets you specify a password for the username.

record.RecordType

Returns the Record object type, either adSimpleRecord, adCollectionRecord, adRecordUnknown, or adStructDoc.

record.Source [= setting]

Sets or returns the data source for the record.

record.State

Returns the state of the record, either adStateClosed, adStateOpen, adStateConnecting, adStateExecuting, or adStateFetching.

ADO.Recordset Members

AbsolutePage	**AbsolutePosition**
ActiveCommand	**ActiveConnection**
AddNew	**BOF**
Bookmark	CacheSize
Cancel	CancelBatch
CancelUpdate	Clone
Close	CompareBookmarks
CursorLocation	CursorType
DataMember	DataSource
Delete	EditMode
EOF	**Filter**
Find	GetRows
GetString	Index
LockType	MarshalOptions
MaxRecords	Move
MoveFirst	**MoveLast**
MoveNext	**MovePrevious**
NextRecordset	**Open**
PageCount	PageSize
RecordCount	**Requery**
Resync	Save
Seek	Sort
Source	State
Status	StayInSync
Supports	**Update**
UpdateBatch	

recordset.AbsolutePosition [= setting]

Sets or returns the ordinal position of the current record in the recordset.

. recordset.ActiveCommand [= setting]

Returns the Command object used to create the recordset.

recordset.**ActiveConnection** [= *setting*]

Sets or returns the connection string or Connection object used by the recordset.

recordset.**AddNew**([*FieldList*], [*Values*])

Creates a new record.

Argument	Description
FieldList	A single field name or an array of names or ordinal numbers specifying the fields in the new record
Values	A single field value or an array of values for the fields

The following code adds a new record to the Employees table in the Northwind Traders sample database using cell values on the current worksheet:

```
Dim cnn As ADODB.Connection
Dim cmd As ADODB.Command
Dim rs As ADODB.Recordset
Dim strDbPath As String
Dim strConnect As String

Set cnn = New ADODB.Connection
Set cmd = New ADODB.Command
Set rs = New ADODB.Recordset
strDbPath = "C:\Program Files\Microsoft Office\OFFICE11\SAMPLES\Northwind.mdb"
cnn.ConnectionString = "Provider=Microsoft.Jet.OLEDB.4.0;" _
    & "Data Source=" & strDbPath

cnn.Open
rs.Open "Employees", cnn, adOpenDynamic, adLockOptimistic, adCmdTable

rs.AddNew
rs!LastName = ActiveSheet.Range("B4")
rs!FirstName = ActiveSheet.Range("C4")
rs.Update

rs.Close
cnn.Close
Set rs = Nothing
Set cnn = Nothing
```

recordset.**BOF** [= *setting*]

True if the current record position is before the first record in the recordset.

recordset.**Cancel**

Cancels the last Open operation for the recordset.

*recordset.*CancelUpdate

Cancels any pending changes for the current record.

*recordset.*Delete([*AffectRecords*])

Deletes the current record or a group of records.

Argument	Description
AffectRecords	A constant that specifies the records affected by the delete operation, either adAffectAll, adAffectAllChapters, adAffectCurrent, or adAffectGroup.

*recordset.*EOF [= *setting*]

True if the current record position is after the last record in the recordset. The following code uses the EOF property to test for the end of the recordset, adding names from the Employees table in the Northwind Traders sample database to the first column of the current worksheet:

```
Dim cnn As ADODB.Connection
Dim cmd As ADODB.Command
Dim rs As ADODB.Recordset
Dim strDbPath As String
Dim intIdx As Integer

Set cnn = New ADODB.Connection
Set cmd = New ADODB.Command
Set rs = New ADODB.Recordset
strDbPath = "C:\Program Files\Microsoft Office\OFFICE11\SAMPLES\Northwind.mdb"
cnn.ConnectionString = "Provider=Microsoft.Jet.OLEDB.4.0;" _
    & "Data Source=" & strDbPath

cnn.Open
rs.Open "Employees", cnn, adOpenStatic, adLockReadOnly, adCmdTable

rs.MoveFirst
intIdx = 1
Do Until rs.EOF
    strName = rs!FirstName & " " & rs!LastName
    ActiveSheet.Cells(intIdx, 1) = strName
    rs.MoveNext
    intIdx = intIdx + 1
Loop

rs.Close
cnn.Close
Set rs = Nothing
Set cnn = Nothing
```

*recordset.*Filter [= *setting*]

Sets or returns a filter for the recordset. You can use filters to work with different sets of data in a table without having to open separate recordsets. The following code adds product names for all beverages from the Products table in the Northwind Traders sample database to the first column of the current worksheet:

```
Dim cnn As ADODB.Connection
Dim cmd As ADODB.Command
Dim rs As ADODB.Recordset
Dim strDbPath As String
Dim intIdx As Integer

Set cnn = New ADODB.Connection
Set cmd = New ADODB.Command
Set rs = New ADODB.Recordset
strDbPath = "C:\Program Files\Microsoft Office\OFFICE11\SAMPLES\Northwind.mdb"
cnn.ConnectionString = "Provider=Microsoft.Jet.OLEDB.4.0;" _
    & "Data Source=" & strDbPath

cnn.Open
rs.Open "Products", cnn, adOpenStatic, adLockReadOnly, adCmdTable
rs.Filter = "CategoryID = 1"

rs.MoveFirst
intIdx = 1
Do Until rs.EOF
    strName = rs!ProductName
    ActiveSheet.Cells(intIdx, 1) = strName
    rs.MoveNext
    intIdx = intIdx + 1
Loop

rs.Close
cnn.Close
Set rs = Nothing
Set cnn = Nothing
```

*recordset.*MoveFirst

Moves to the first record in the recordset.

*recordset.*MoveLast

Moves to the last record in the recordset.

*recordset.*MoveNext

Moves to the next record in the recordset. See the EOF and Filter code examples for examples of using MoveNext.

---

*recordset.***MovePrevious**

Moves to the previous record in the recordset.

*recordset.***Open(**[*Source*], [*ActiveConnection*], [*CursorType*] , [*LockType*] , [*Options*]**)**

Opens the recordset for database operations.

Argument	Description
Source	The source of the recordset. The source can be a Command object, an SQL statement, a table name, a stored procedure call, a URL, or the name of a file or Stream object.
ActiveConnection	A Connection object or connection string.
CursorType	The type of database cursor to use for the recordset. The cursor can be adOpenDynamic, adOpenForwardOnly (default), adOpenKeyset, adOpenStatic, or adOpenUnspecified.
LockType	The type of locking to use for the recordset. The cursor can be adLockBatchOptimistic, adLockOptimistic, adLockPessimistic, adLockReadOnly, or adLockUnspecified.
Options	A constant specifying how a command source should be interpreted or executed.

*recordset.***RecordCount** [= *setting*]

Returns the number of records in the recordset.

*recordset.***Requery**

Updates the recordset by running the query on which it is based.

*recordset.***Source** [= *setting*]

Returns a string or Command object indicating the source of the recordset.

*recordset.***Update(**[*Fields*], [*Value*]**)**

Saves changes made to the current record.

Argument	Description
Fields	The name of the field being updated or an array of names or ordinal positions if you are updating multiple fields
Value	The updated value of the field or an array of values if you are updating multiple fields

See the AddNew code example for an example of using Update.

DAO Objects and Members

The DAO object model includes the key objects listed in the following table. There are additional objects, but these cover the fundamentals of working with DAO. For information about the additional objects, see the DAO Help.

Object	Description
Database/Databases	The Database object represents an open database. The Databases collection contains all open databases.
DbEngine	Represents the Jet database engine. It is the top-level object in the DAO object model.
Document/Documents	The Document object represents information about an instance of a Microsoft Access object, such as a form or report. The Documents collection contains all the Document objects of the same type.
QueryDef/QueryDefs	The QueryDef object represents a Microsoft Access query. The QueryDefs collection contains all the queries in a database.
Recordset/Recordsets	The Recordset object represents a set of records from a table or query. The Recordsets collection contains all open recordsets in a database.

Descriptions of the members of these objects follow. Key members (shown in **bold**) are covered in the following reference sections.

DAO.Database and DAO.Databases Members

Close	CollatingOrder
Connect	**Connection**
Containers	Count[1]
CreateProperty	CreateQueryDef
CreateRelation	CreateTableDef
DesignMasterID	**Execute**
MakeReplica	Name
NewPassword	**OpenRecordset**
PopulatePartial	Properties
QueryTimeout	RecordsAffected
Refresh[1]	Relations
ReplicaID	Synchronize
Transactions	Updatable
Version	

[1] Collection only

database.Connection

Returns the Connection object for the database.

database.**Execute(***Source*, [*Options*]**)**

Executes an action query or SQL statement.

Argument	Description
Source	An SQL statement or the name of a query.
Options	A combination of constants that specify characteristics of the recordset. See DAO Help for more information about these options.

database.**OpenRecordset(***Source*, [*Type*], [*Options*]**), [***LockEdits***])**

Opens the record.

Argument	Description
Source	The source of the recordset: a table name, query name, or SQL statement.
Type	The type of recordset to open: dbOpenTable, dbOpenDynamic, dbOpenDynaset, dbOpenSnapshot, or dbOpenForwardOnly.
Options	A combination of constants that specify characteristics of the recordset. See DAO Help for more information about these options.
LockEdits	The locking used by the recordset: dbReadOnly, dbPessimistic, dbOptimistic, dbOptimisticValue, or dbOptimisticBatch.

The following code example opens the Employees table in the Northwind Traders sample database as a recordset and displays its contents on the active sheet:

```
Dim strDbPath As String
Dim db As DAO.Database
Dim rs As DAO.Recordset
Dim qt As QueryTable

strDbPath = "C:\Program Files\Microsoft Office\" & _
    OFFICE11\SAMPLES\Northwind.mdb"

Set db = OpenDatabase(strDbPath)
Set rs = db.OpenRecordset("Employees")

Set qt = ActiveSheet.QueryTables.Add(Connection:=rs, _
    Destination:=ActiveSheet.Range("A3"))

ActiveSheet.Range("A1") = qt.Recordset.Name & " table:"

qt.Refresh
```

DAO.DbEngine Members

BeginTrans	CommitTrans
CompactDatabase	CreateDatabase
CreateWorkspace	DefaultPassword
DefaultType	DefaultUser
Errors	Idle
IniPath	LoginTimeout
OpenConnection	**OpenDatabase**
Properties	RegisterDatabase
Rollback	SetOption
SystemDB	Version
Workspaces	

dbengine.**CompactDatabase**(*olddb*, *newdb*, [*locale*]), [*options*] , [*password*])

Copies and compacts a database. The database must be closed.

Argument	Description
olddb	The name and path of the existing database file.
newdb	The name and path of the compacted database file.
locale	An optional collating order used in creating the compacted database file. See DAO Help for more information about collating order settings.
options	A combination of constants that specify characteristics of the recordset. See DAO Help for more information about these options.
password	An optional password string.

dbengine.**OpenDatabase**(*dbname*, [*options*], [*read-only*], [*connect*])

Copies and compacts a database. The database must be closed.

Argument	Description
dbname	The name and path of the existing database file.
options	A combination of constants that specify characteristics of the recordset. See DAO Help for more information about these options.
read-only	Use True if you want to open the database for read-only access.
connect	A connection string.

See the Database.OpenRecordset method for an example of using OpenDatabase. Note that you use the OpenDatabase method without explicitly specifying the DbEngine object.

DAO.Document and DAO.Documents Members

AllPermissions	**Container**
Count[1]	CreateProperty
DateCreated	LastUpdated
Name	Owner
Permissions	Properties
Refresh[1]	UserName

[1] Collection only

Document.Container

Returns the name of the container to which the document belongs.

Document.Name

Returns the name of the specified table, query, form, or report. The following code example displays the names of all the reports in the Northwind Traders sample database in the first column of the active worksheet:

```
Dim strDbPath As String
Dim db As DAO.Database
Dim docRpt As DAO.Document
Dim intIdx As Integer

strDbPath = "C:\Program Files\Microsoft Office\OFFICE11\SAMPLES\Northwind.mdb"

Set db = OpenDatabase(strDbPath)
intIdx = 0
With db.Containers!Reports
    For Each docRpt In .Documents
        ActiveSheet.Cells(intIdx + 1, 1) = .Documents(intIdx).Name
        intIdx = intIdx + 1
    Next docRpt


End With
```

DAO.QueryDef and DAO.QueryDefs Members

Append[1]	CacheSize
Cancel	Close
Connect	Count[1]
CreateProperty	DateCreated
Delete[1]	**Execute**

LastUpdated	**MaxRecords**
Name	ODBCTimeout
OpenRecordset	Prepare
RecordsAffected	Refresh[1]
ReturnsRecords	**SQL**
StillExecuting	Type
Updatable	

[1] Collection only

querydef.**Execute**([*Options*])

Executes the specified action query.

Argument	Description
Options	A combination of constants that specify characteristics of the recordset. See DAO Help for more information about these options.

querydef.**MaxRecords** [= *setting*]

For and ODBC data source, returns the maximum number of records to return from the query.

querydef.**OpenRecordset**([*Type*], [*Options*]), [*LockEdits*])

Opens the record.

Argument	Description
Type	The type of recordset to open: dbOpenTable, dbOpenDynamic, dbOpenDynaset, dbOpenSnapshot, or dbOpenForwardOnly.
Options	A combination of constants that specify characteristics of the recordset. See DAO Help for more information about these options.
LockEdits	The locking used by the recordset: dbReadOnly, dbPessimistic, dbOptimistic, dbOptimisticValue, or dbOptimisticBatch.

The following code example displays the contents of the recordset produced by the Invoices query in the Northwind Traders sample database on the active sheet:

```
Dim strDbPath As String
Dim db As DAO.Database
Dim qry As DAO.QueryDef
Dim rs As DAO.Recordset
Dim qt As QueryTable

strDbPath = "C:\Program Files\Microsoft Office\OFFICE11\SAMPLES\Northwind.mdb"

Set db = OpenDatabase(strDbPath)
```

```
Set qry = db.QueryDefs("Invoices")
Set rs = qry.OpenRecordset

Set qt = ActiveSheet.QueryTables.Add(Connection:=rs, _
    Destination:=ActiveSheet.Range("A1"))

qt.Refresh
```

querydef.SQL [= *setting*]

Sets or returns the query's SQL string.

DAO.Recordset and DAO.Recordsets Members

AbsolutePosition	**AddNew**	BatchCollisionCount
BatchCollisions	BatchSize	**BOF**
Bookmark	Bookmarkable	CacheSize
CacheStart	Cancel	CancelUpdate
Clone	Close	Connection
CopyQueryDef	Count[1]	DateCreated
Delete	Edit	EditMode
EOF	FillCache	Filter
FindFirst	FindLast	FindNext
FindPrevious	GetRows	Index
LastModified	LastUpdated	LockEdits
Move	**MoveFirst**	**MoveLast**
MoveNext	**MovePrevious**	Name
NextRecordset	NoMatch	OpenRecordset
PercentPosition	RecordCount	RecordStatus
Refresh[1]	Requery	Restartable
Seek	Sort	StillExecuting
Transactions	Type	Updatable
Update	UpdateOptions	ValidationRule
ValidationText		

[1] Collection only

recordset.AddNew

Adds a new record to the recordset. The following code adds a new record to the Employees table in the Northwind Traders sample database using cell values on the current worksheet:

```
Dim strDbPath As String
Dim db As DAO.Database
Dim rs As DAO.Recordset
```

```
strDbPath = "C:\Program Files\Microsoft Office\OFFICE11\SAMPLES\Northwind.mdb"

Set db = OpenDatabase(strDbPath)
Set rs = db.OpenRecordset("Employees")

rs.AddNew
rs!LastName = ActiveSheet.Range("B4")
rs!FirstName = ActiveSheet.Range("C4")
rs.Update
```

*recordset.*BOF [= *setting*]

True if the current record position is before the first record in the recordset.

*recordset.*EOF [= *setting*]

True if the current record position is after the last record in the recordset. The following code uses the EOF property to test for the end of the recordset, adding names from the Employees table in the Northwind Traders sample database to the first column of the current worksheet:

```
recordset.MoveFirst Dim strDbPath As String
Dim db As DAO.Database
Dim rs As DAO.Recordset

strDbPath = "C:\Program Files\Microsoft Office\OFFICE11\SAMPLES\Northwind.mdb"
Set db = OpenDatabase(strDbPath)
Set rs = db.OpenRecordset("Employees")

rs.MoveFirst
intIdx = 1
Do Until rs.EOF
    strName = rs!FirstName & " " & rs!LastName
    ActiveSheet.Cells(intIdx, 1) = strName
    rs.MoveNext
    intIdx = intIdx + 1
Loop
```

*recordset.*MoveFirst

Moves to the first record in the recordset.

*recordset.*MoveLast

Moves to the last record in the recordset.

*recordset.*MoveNext

Moves to the next record in the recordset. See the EOF code example for an example of using MoveNext.

*recordset.*MovePrevious

Moves to the previous record in the recordset.

CHAPTER 13

Analyzing Data with Pivot Tables

When you create a spreadsheet, you have to be careful how you organize the columns and rows because that affects how you can sort, filter, or chart the data later. When you import data from an external source, such as a database, web query, SharePoint list, or CSV file, you usually don't have a choice how the spreadsheet is organized—the data just comes in the way it was in the source.

Pivot tables let you reorganize data by dragging and dropping the columns from a data source to different locations on a target worksheet. You can then sort, filter, or chart the results as you like. That makes pivot tables Excel's key data analysis tool.

This chapter includes task-oriented reference information for the following objects and their related collections: `CalculatedField`, `CalculatedMember`, `CubeField`, `PivotCache`, `PivotCell`, `PivotField`, `PivotFormula`, `PivotItem`, `PivotItemList`, `PivotLayout`, and `PivotTable`.

 Code used in this chapter and additional samples are available in *ch13.xls*.

Quick Guide to Pivot Tables

Not everyone is familiar with pivot tables, and they can seem confusing at first. The easiest way to explain them is a quick tutorial to demonstrate how they are useful. Use these general steps to create a pivot table:

1. Create the table using the PivotTable Wizard.

2. Format the table to make it readable.

3. Change field properties such as how totals are calculated.

4. Chart the results (optional).

The following sections walk you through these steps using data that accompanies this chapter's sample workbook.

Create a Pivot Table

Pivot tables are commonly used to plot multiple data values over time. For example, the worksheet in Figure 13-1 contains the sales ranks of books collected from *Amazon.com*.

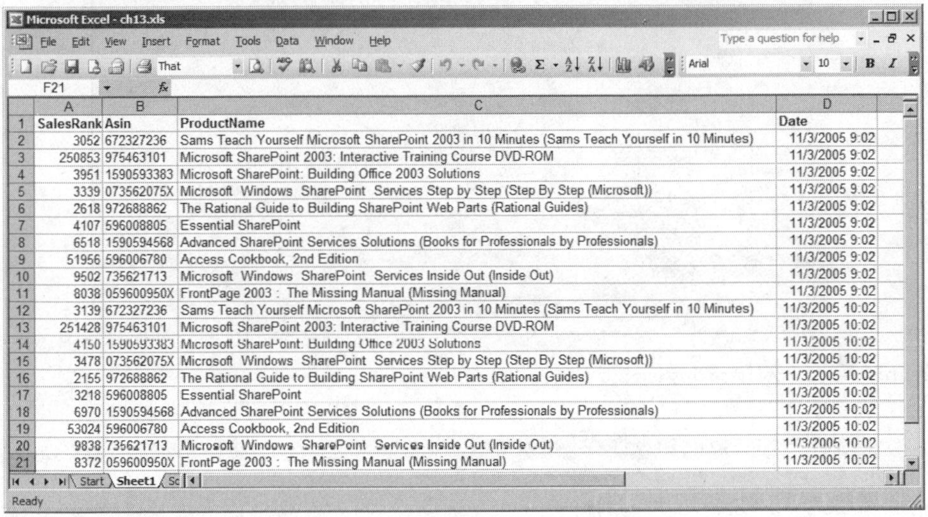

	A	B	C	D
1	SalesRank	Asin	ProductName	Date
2	3052	672327236	Sams Teach Yourself Microsoft SharePoint 2003 in 10 Minutes (Sams Teach Yourself in 10 Minutes)	11/3/2005 9:02
3	250853	975463101	Microsoft SharePoint 2003: Interactive Training Course DVD-ROM	11/3/2005 9:02
4	3951	1590593383	Microsoft SharePoint: Building Office 2003 Solutions	11/3/2005 9:02
5	3339	073562075X	Microsoft Windows SharePoint Services Step by Step (Step By Step (Microsoft))	11/3/2005 9:02
6	2618	972688862	The Rational Guide to Building SharePoint Web Parts (Rational Guides)	11/3/2005 9:02
7	4107	596008805	Essential SharePoint	11/3/2005 9:02
8	6518	1590594568	Advanced SharePoint Services Solutions (Books for Professionals by Professionals)	11/3/2005 9:02
9	51956	596006780	Access Cookbook, 2nd Edition	11/3/2005 9:02
10	9502	735621713	Microsoft Windows SharePoint Services Inside Out (Inside Out)	11/3/2005 9:02
11	8038	059600950X	FrontPage 2003 : The Missing Manual (Missing Manual)	11/3/2005 9:02
12	3139	672327236	Sams Teach Yourself Microsoft SharePoint 2003 in 10 Minutes (Sams Teach Yourself in 10 Minutes)	11/3/2005 10:02
13	251428	975463101	Microsoft SharePoint 2003: Interactive Training Course DVD-ROM	11/3/2005 10:02
14	4150	1590593383	Microsoft SharePoint: Building Office 2003 Solutions	11/3/2005 10:02
15	3478	073562075X	Microsoft Windows SharePoint Services Step by Step (Step By Step (Microsoft))	11/3/2005 10:02
16	2155	972688862	The Rational Guide to Building SharePoint Web Parts (Rational Guides)	11/3/2005 10:02
17	3218	596008805	Essential SharePoint	11/3/2005 10:02
18	6970	1590594568	Advanced SharePoint Services Solutions (Books for Professionals by Professionals)	11/3/2005 10:02
19	53024	596006780	Access Cookbook, 2nd Edition	11/3/2005 10:02
20	9838	735621713	Microsoft Windows SharePoint Services Inside Out (Inside Out)	11/3/2005 10:02
21	8372	059600950X	FrontPage 2003 : The Missing Manual (Missing Manual)	11/3/2005 10:02

Figure 13-1. In source data, rows have mixed content

I'd like to compare each book's sales rank over time, but there's no way to chart that using the worksheet in Figure 13-1 because the rows contain multiple product names. Ideally, each row should reflect a date, each column should be a product name, and each cell should be the sales rank. You can make those changes by creating a pivot table from the source worksheet.

To create a pivot table in Excel:

1. Select the columns to include in the pivot table (A$:D$ in Figure 13-1) and choose Data → Pivot Table and Pivot Chart Report. Excel starts the PivotTable Wizard (Figure 13-2).
2. Click Finish to create the pivot table on a new worksheet or click Next to walk through the pivot table options using the wizard. Excel creates a new pivot table.
3. Drag ProductName from the PivotTable Field List to the column area, drag Date to the row area, and drag SalesRank to the data items area as shown in Figure 13-3.
4. The default formula for data fields is Count, which is always 1 in this case, so right-click on the data field in the upper-left corner of the pivot table, select Field Settings and change the formula to Sum, as shown in Figure 13-4.
5. Pivot tables do not automatically update, so if the source worksheet changes, click Refresh Data on the Pivot Table toolbar to update the table, as shown in Figure 13-5.

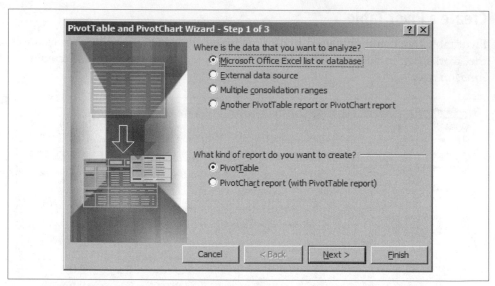

Figure 13-2. Step 1: use this wizard to create the pivot table

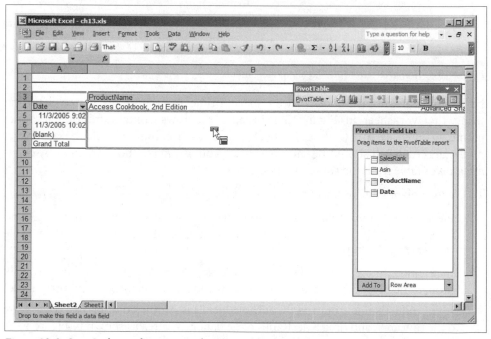

Figure 13-3. Step 3: drag columns onto the pivot table

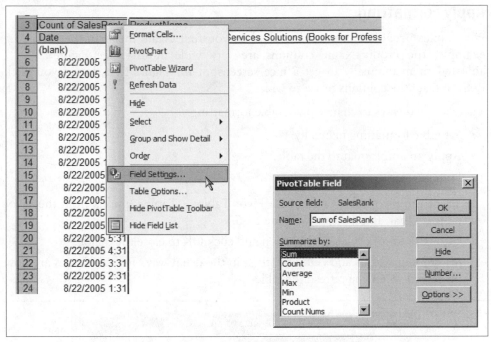

Figure 13-4. Step 4: change the data field formula from Count to Sum

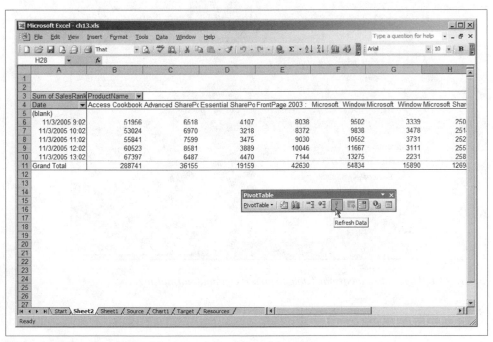

Figure 13-5. Step 5: refresh table to get changes from data source

Apply Formatting

Pivot tables usually look pretty awful when you first create them. In the preceding example, the ProductName columns are very wide at first (see Figure 13-3). I adjusted them manually to get a nice screenshot for Figure 13-5, but if you click Refresh Data the columns revert to wide.

There are two ways to change pivot table formatting:

- Set table formatting manually.
- Apply an autoformat to the table.

To set the formatting manually:

1. Select the pivot table and choose Pivot Table → Table Options from the pivot table toolbar. Excel displays Figure 13-6.
2. Clear the AutoFormat Table option and click OK to close the dialog.
3. Set column widths and cell formatting in the usual way. Those changes are now preserved when you refresh the table.

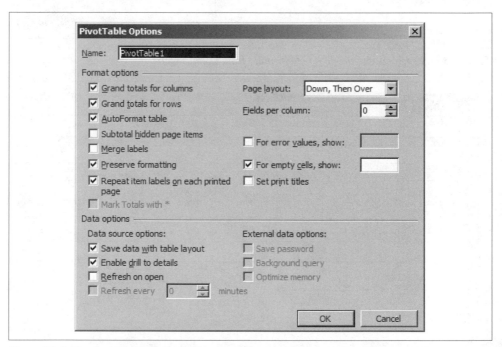

Figure 13-6. Deselect AutoFormat Table to preserve manual formatting

The Preserve Formatting option in Figure 13-6 preserves cell formatting, such as fonts and colors. That option is on by default, so you don't have to change it.

Even with reasonable column widths, the pivot table in Figure 13-5 isn't as readable as it could be. To autoformat the table:

1. Select the pivot table and click the Format Report button on the PivotTable toolbar. Excel displays the AutoFormat dialog box.

2. Choose a format and click OK to apply it to the table. Figure 13-7 shows the result.

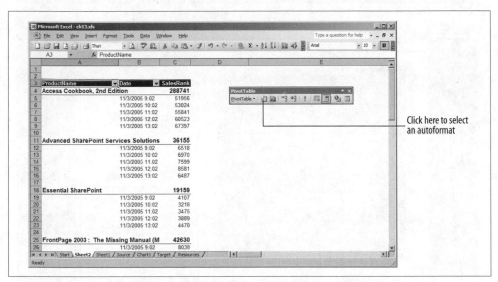

Figure 13-7. Apply an autoformat to create a nice-looking report

Change Totals

The totals shown in Figure 13-7 are the sums of the sales rank for each book. It makes more sense to display the average sales rank. To change the total:

1. Right-click on the total field and choose Field Settings. Excel displays the PivotTable Field dialog for the total (similar to Figure 13-4).

2. Select Average and click OK. Excel changes the total formula from Sum to Average.

It doesn't matter which ProductName total you select in Step 1. Changing the formula for one total changes all of the equivalent total fields in the table.

Chart the Data

The final step is to display the data graphically using a chart. To chart the data from a pivot table:

1. Select the pivot table and click the Chart Wizard button on the PivotTable tool-bar. Excel creates a default pivot chart.

2. Select the chart area and change the chart type to a line chart.

3. Drag the ProductName field to the chart legend. Figure 13-8 shows the result of these changes.

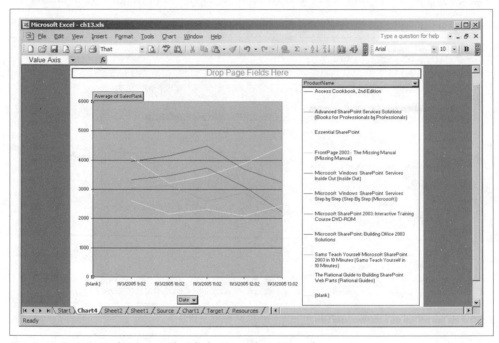

Figure 13-8. A pivot chart created with the PivotChart Wizard

That last step illustrates how pivot charts are different from ordinary Excel charts: you can reposition the fields to get different views of the data. Changing the field lay-out on the chart also changes the layout on the original pivot table. If you want to preserve the pivot table layout, create a new pivot chart based on the original source data.

To create an independent pivot chart:

1. Select the columns to chart on the source worksheet (Figure 13-1).

2. Choose Data → Pivot Table and Pivot Chart Report; select "PivotChart report" on the wizard (Figure 13-2) and click Next to follow the wizard steps or just

click Finish to create the chart quickly. Excel creates a new pivot table and pivot chart based on the original source data.

3. Drag fields from the Field List onto the chart, select the chart type, and format the chart as you would normally.

Each pivot chart must have an underlying pivot table. If you click Next in Step 2, Excel asks if you want to base your new pivot table on the existing pivot table, as shown in Figure 13-9. If you choose Yes, Excel uses the same pivot cache for both the original pivot table and the new one that will be used by the chart.

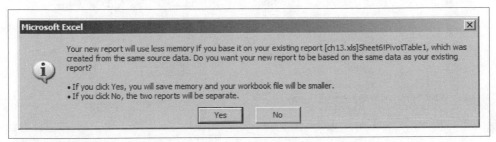

Figure 13-9. Excel asks if you want to share the pivot cache

The *pivot cache* is a hidden data store used to refresh each pivot table. There are several advantages to sharing the pivot cache among pivot tables:

- Refreshing a pivot table refreshes the pivot cache, so other tables that share that pivot cache are also automatically refreshed.

- The layout of each pivot table or pivot chart can be unique, even though they share the same source. That lets you move the fields on a pivot chart without changing the layout of your pivot report.

- The amount of memory required by the workbook and the size of the workbook on disk are reduced.

Don't use a shared pivot cache if you want to refresh pivot tables independently. Also, you can't use a shared pivot cache if the pivot tables don't use the same source. Pivot tables based on worksheets must use exactly the same range in order to share a pivot cache.

Change the Layout

The process of dragging fields from the Field List onto the pivot table as shown in Figure 13-3 is called setting the pivot table layout. You can change that layout by dragging fields to different locations on the pivot table. Figure 13-10 shows the areas to which you can drag fields.

 Excel doesn't call these parts of the pivot table *areas*. It just refers to fields in those locations as *page fields*, *column fields*, *row fields*, or *data fields*.

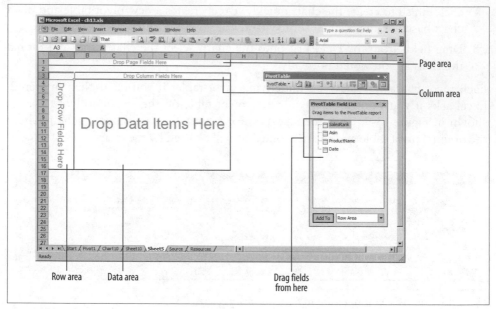

Figure 13-10. Setting pivot table layout

Each of the fields in the PivotTable Field List corresponds to a column in the data source. It's difficult to discuss the effect of dragging fields to the different areas of a pivot table; it is easier to just show you as I did earlier. However, I left out one area: use the page area to create individual views for each item in a field.

For example, if you drag ProductName in Figure 13-7 to the page area, you get a report for a single book, as shown in Figure 13-11.

If you drag ProductName from the legend of the pivot chart in Figure 13-8 to the page area, Excel charts each book separately. Use page fields to summarize large amounts of data—they are kind of overkill for this example, however.

Connect to an External Data Source

Pivot tables based on worksheet data are handy, but it is probably more common to use pivot tables with external data sources such as databases. To get pivot data from a database:

1. Create a new worksheet and choose Data → Pivot Table and Pivot Chart Report. Excel starts the PivotTable Wizard (Figure 13-2).

2. Select External Data Source, click Next, and then click Get Data. Excel displays the Choose Data Source dialog (Figure 13-12).

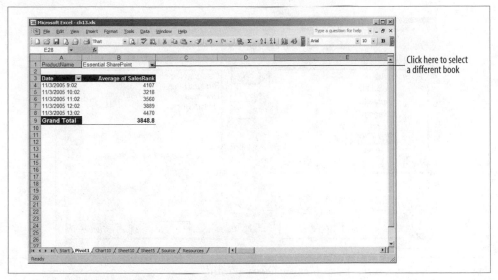

Click here to select a different book

Figure 13-11. Use page fields to view individual items

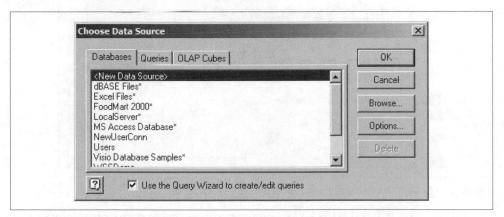

Figure 13-12. Use the Query Wizard to connect to an external data source

3. Follow the Query Wizard steps to connect to the data source. The information required and steps displayed vary based on the type of database. After you connect, the Query Wizard allows you to compose a query to retrieve data from the database as shown in Figure 13-13.

4. Click Next and follow the Query Wizard steps to complete the query. When done, Excel displays Figure 13-14.

5. Choose Return Data to Microsoft Office Excel and click Finish. Excel returns you to the PivotTable Wizard.

6. Click Finish to create the pivot table.

The completed pivot table appears like any other pivot table. You can drag fields from the PivotTable Field List onto the pivot areas, add formatting, and chart the

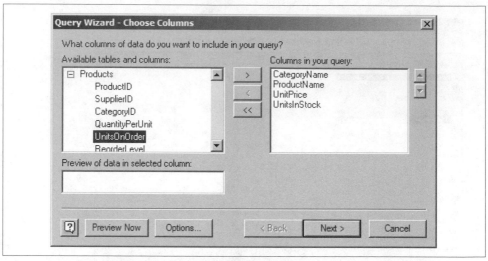

Figure 13-13. Compose the query using the Query Wizard

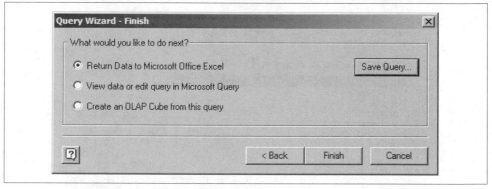

Figure 13-14. Complete the query and return the data to Excel

data as you like. Figure 13-15 shows a completed pivot table created from the North-wind sample SQL Server database.

Unlike the pivot table in Figure 13-7, the pivot table in Figure 13-15 doesn't have an underlying worksheet. Instead, the data is retrieved using a database query file (.dqy). Excel stores .dqy files in the C:\Documents and Settings\user\Application Data\ Microsoft\Queries folder. You can open those files in Notepad to view or modify the query directly. Figure 13-16 shows the query for the preceding pivot table with a description of its parts.

 You can compose a query using the Query Wizard, then open it in Notepad to get the ODBC connection string or SQL query to use in code.

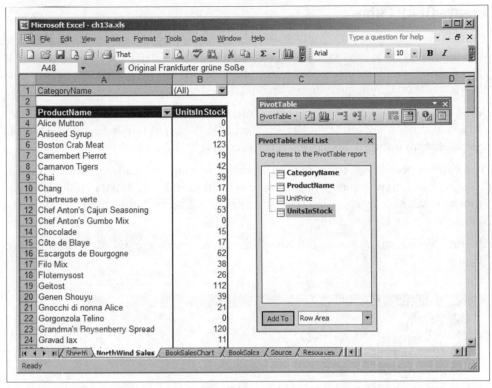

Figure 13-15. A pivot table based on Northwind product inventory

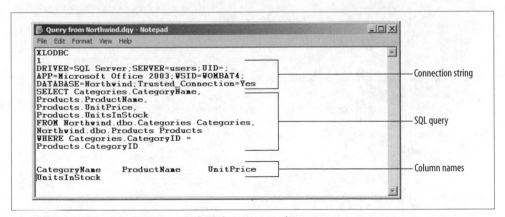

Figure 13-16. You can edit the query directly in Notepad

Create OLAP Cubes

Online analytical processing (OLAP) is a data analysis layer that optimizes database queries. OLAP providers take a snapshot of a relational database and restructure it into a *data cube*, which provides faster query results for multidimensional analysis than a traditional SQL query to the original data source.

Most database vendors, including Microsoft, Oracle, IBM, and SAP, offer OLAP providers. Microsoft's OLAP provider is called SQL Server Analysis Services, which is installed as an optional component with Microsoft SQL Server.

You can connect to one of those OLAP providers using the steps described earlier in "Connect to External Data" or you can create an offline OLAP data cube file (*.cub*) from any database by choosing "Create an OLAP Cube from this query" in Step 5 of that section (see Figure 13-14).

If you choose to create an OLAP cube, Excel starts the OLAP Cube Wizard (Figure 13-17).

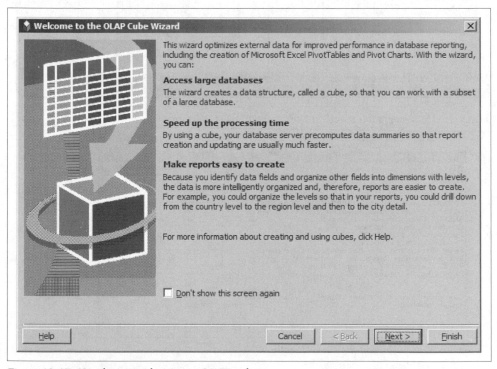

Figure 13-17. Use this wizard to create OLAP cubes

 Creating an offline OLAP cube file is usually the best approach, since changes to the pivot table in Excel often requery the OLAP data source. Using an offline cube file yields the best performance.

There is quite a lot to learn about OLAP, and not enough space here to cover that topic. A web search on "OLAP" will turn up some useful introductions, however.

Program Pivot Tables

You can navigate to pivot table objects from the Workbook, Chart, Worksheet, or Range objects as shown in Figure 13-18.

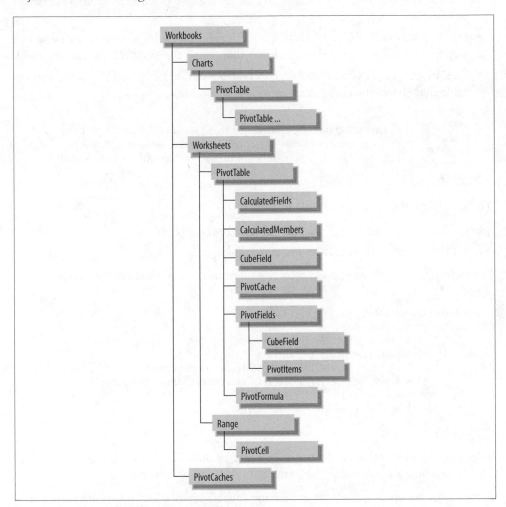

Figure 13-18. Navigating the pivot table objects

Although pivot tables expose a full set of objects, the most common set of programming tasks deal with this narrow set of problems:

- Create a pivot table.
- Refresh a pivot table automatically when the source data changes.

- Build a pivot table from an external data source.

The following sections explain how to program those tasks.

Create Pivot Tables

There are several ways to create a pivot table in code:

- Use the `PivotTableWizard` method to quickly create a pivot table from a `Worksheet` or `PivotTable` object.
- Use the `Workbook` object's `PivotCache` collection to create a new pivot table one step at a time. This is sometimes clearer than using the `PivotTableWizard` method.
- Use an existing `PivotCache` object's `CreatePivotTable` method to create a pivot table that shares the cache of an existing pivot table.

 If you are programming for multiple Excel versions, be sure to test any code using the `PivotCache` object on the earliest version of Excel you plan to support. A large number of that object's members were added in 2002.

To quickly create a new pivot table in code:

1. Call the `Worksheet` object's `CreatePivotTableWizard` method.
2. Set the layout of the fields on the pivot table.

For example, the following code creates a pivot table from data on the current worksheet:

```
Sub QuickPivotTable( )
    Dim pt As PivotTable
    ' Exit if active sheet is not a worksheet
    If TypeName(ActiveSheet) <> "Worksheet" Then Exit Sub
    ' Use pivot table wizard to create table on new worksheet.
    Set pt = ActiveSheet.PivotTableWizard(xlDatabase, ActiveSheet.UsedRange, _
        Worksheets.Add.[a3], "QuickPivot")
    ' Select the table so user can set layout.
    pt.TableRange1.Select
End Sub
```

Selecting the pivot table range in the last line of code displays the PivotTable Field List from which the user can drag items onto the new pivot table.

Pivot tables are created from an underlying `PivotCache` object, so it is often clearer to create that object first, then use the `PivotCache` object to create the pivot table. To use that approach, follow these general steps:

1. Create a new `PivotCache` using the `PivotCache` collection's `Add` method.
2. Create a new worksheet on which to place the pivot table.

3. Use the `PivotCache` object's `CreatePivotTable` method to create the pivot table.

4. Use the `PivotTable` object's `AddFields` method to set the pivot table layout.

5. Use the `AddDataField` method to add the data field and set its formula.

6. Optionally use the `Charts` collection's `Add` method to chart the pivot table.

The following code creates a new pivot table and pivot chart from the currently active worksheet:

```
Sub CreatePivotTable()
    Dim pc As PivotCache, pt As PivotTable, ws As Worksheet
    ' Get the active sheet.
    Set ws = ActiveSheet
    ' 1) Create a new pivot cache.
    Set pc = ActiveWorkbook.PivotCaches.Add(xlDatabase, ws.UsedRange)
    ' 2) Create a new worksheet for the pivot table.
    Set ws = ActiveWorkbook.Worksheets.Add()
    ' 3) Create a pivot table on the worksheet.
    Set pt = pc.CreatePivotTable(ws.[a3], "BookSales")
    ' 4) Set the layout: add the column and row fields.
    pt.AddFields pt.PivotFields(4).Name, pt.PivotFields(3).Name
    ' 5) Add the data field and set its formula.
    pt.AddDataField pt.PivotFields(1), , xlSum
    ' 6) Create a line chart.
    Charts.Add().ChartType = xlLine
End Sub
```

The preceding code sets the pivot table layout using the positions of the fields from the source data range. If the selected worksheet contains fewer than four columns of data, an error occurs. You can use the field positions or the field names to set the layout; however, you must know the contents of each source column. In other words, your data source must have a fixed format. This is often the case when using an SQL query as the data source since the SELECT statement can define the field names and field order. If you don't know the contents of the columns beforehand, you should omit the layout step and let the user perform that task.

Create a pivot table from an existing pivot cache to generate a new view of an existing pivot table. This approach shares the pivot cache between both pivot tables, which keeps the two tables in sync. See "Chart the Data," earlier in this chapter, for an explanation of shared pivot caches.

To create a new pivot table from an existing pivot cache, follow the same steps as the preceding procedure but replace Step 1 with this step:

1. Use the existing `PivotTable` object's `PivotCache` property to get the existing `PivotCache` object.

The following code creates a pivot table that shares the `PivotCache` of the pivot table on the active worksheet:

```
Sub CreateSharedCachePivotTable()
    Dim pc As PivotCache
```

```
        ' Exit if pivot table doesn't exist.
        If ActiveSheet.PivotTables.Count < 1 Then Exit Sub
        ' Get pivot cache.
        Set pc = ActiveSheet.PivotTables(1).PivotCache
        ' Create new pivot table.
        pc.CreatePivotTable Worksheets.Add().[a3], "SharedCachePivot"
        ' Select the pivot table.
        ActiveSheet.PivotTables(1).TableRange1.Select
    End Sub
```

I didn't set the layout in the preceding code, since the main point of creating the new table is to use a different layout than the prior table.

Refresh Pivot Tables and Charts

You can get pivot tables to refresh automatically when the workbook opens by selecting Refresh on Open in the PivotTable Options dialog (Figure 13-6). That option is off by default because refreshing a pivot table may take a long time, depending on the size of the pivot table data.

If the pivot table is based on an external data source, you can also select periodic updates on the PivotTable Options dialog. That option isn't available for pivot tables based on worksheet data and, as mentioned earlier, pivot tables don't automatically refresh when the source data changes.

To implement automatic refresh for pivot tables based on worksheets, add the following code to the workbook's class module:

```
    ' ThisWorkbook class
    Private Sub Workbook_SheetDeactivate(ByVal Sh As Object)
        Dim pc As PivotCache
        ' Get each of the pivot caches.
        For Each pc In ThisWorkbook.PivotCaches
            ' If cache is based on a worksheet.
            If pc.SourceType = xlDatabase Then
                ' Update the cache based on the deactivated worksheet.
                If InStr(1, pc.SourceData, Sh.Name) Then _
                    pc.Refresh
            End If
        Next
    End Sub
```

The preceding code checks whether the deactivated worksheet is the source of PivotCache objects. If it is, the code refreshes that pivot cache, which updates any pivot tables or charts based on the cache. This approach is more efficient than using the PivotTable object because more than one pivot table may share the same cache.

You could make the code even more efficient by checking if any source data had changed before refreshing, but the benefit is incremental and the change adds complexity.

Connect to External Data

To connect a pivot table to an external data source in code, set the `PivotCache` object's `Connection` and `CommandText` properties. The `PivotTableWizard` method sets those properties automatically from a passed-in array argument. The following code creates a new pivot table from a SQL Server database using `PivotTableWizard`:

```
Sub QuickDBPivotTable( )
    Dim ws As Worksheet, pt As PivotTable
    ' Get the active worksheet.
    Set ws = ActiveSheet
    ' Use pivot table wizard to create table on new worksheet.
    Set pt = ws.PivotTableWizard(xlExternal, _
      Array("SELECT Date, SalesRank, ProductName FROM Amazon"), _
      Worksheets.Add.[a1], "QuickDBPivot", , , , , , , , , , , , _
      "ODBC;DRIVER=SQL Server;SERVER=USERS;" & _
      "UID=;APP=Microsoft Office 2003;WSID=WOMBAT4;" & _
      "DATABASE=Sales;Trusted_Connection=True")
    ' Set layout
    pt.AddFields "Date", "ProductName"
    pt.AddDataField pt.PivotFields("SalesRank"), , xlAverage
End Sub
```

If you have trouble composing the connection string, create a connection to the database using the Query Wizard; then use the connection string that the wizard generates in the *.dqy* file as described earlier in this chapter in "Connect to an External Data Source." Prefix that connection string with `ODBC;` as shown in the preceding code.

The `Trusted_Connection=True` element in the connection string tells Excel to use Windows integrated security when connecting to the data source. That approach uses the user's network identity when connecting to the data source rather than a database user ID and password. Integrated security requires a domain-based network, but it is a much more secure approach than hardcoding usernames and passwords in to connection strings.

OLAP Data Cubes

Two pivot table objects apply only to OLAP: `CubeField` and `CalculatedMember`. In addition, many of the other pivot table members are not available for OLAP pivot tables. Those items are noted in the following reference sections.

Finally, OLAP field names include square brackets and use dot notation to indicate hierarchy—for example, [Customers].[Country].

The following code demonstrates how to create an OLAP pivot table from an external OLAP provider, in this case Microsoft SQL Server Analysis Services:

```
Sub CreateOLAPPivotTable( )
    Dim pc As PivotCache, pt As PivotTable, pf As PivotField, _
      ws As Worksheet
```

```
' Create a new pivot cache for database query.
Set pc = ActiveWorkbook.PivotCaches.Add(xlExternal)
' Create a connection string and SQL query.
pc.Connection = "OLEDB;Provider=MSOLAP.2;Data Source=users;" & _
   "Initial Catalog=FoodMart 2000;Client Cache Size=25;Auto Synch Period=10000"
pc.CommandType = xlCmdCube
pc.CommandText = Array("Sales")
pc.MaintainConnection = False
' Create a new worksheet for the pivot table.
Set ws = ActiveWorkbook.Worksheets.Add()
' Create a pivot table.
Set pt = ws.PivotTables.Add(pc, ws.[a3], "FoodMart Sales", False)
' Set the layout: add the column and row fields.
pt.CubeFields("[Customers]").Orientation = xlRowField
pt.CubeFields("[Product]").Orientation = xlColumnField
' Add the data field.
pt.CubeFields("[Measures].[Unit Sales]").Orientation = xlDataField
pt.CubeFields("[Measures].[Sales Average]").Orientation = xlDataField
' Update the pivot table
pc.Refresh
' Rename the sheet to match the table
On Error Resume Next
Worksheets(pt.name).Delete
On Error GoTo 0
ws.name = pt.name
End Sub
```

PivotTable and PivotTables Members

Use the PivotTables collection to get existing pivot tables. Use the Worksheet object's PivotTables property to get a reference to this collection. Use the PivotTable object to set the pivot table layout and options. The PivotTables collection and PivotTable object have the following members. Key members (shown in **bold**) are covered in the following reference section:

Add[2]	**AddDataField**	**AddFields**
Application[2]	**CacheIndex**	**CalculatedFields**
CalculatedMembers	**ColumnFields**	**ColumnGrand**
ColumnRange	Count[1]	**CreateCubeFile**
Creator[2]	**CubeFields**	**DataBodyRange**
DataFields	**DataLabelRange**	**DataPivotField**
DisplayEmptyColumn	**DisplayEmptyRow**	**DisplayErrorString**
DisplayImmediateItems	**DisplayNullString**	**EnableDataValueEditing**
EnableDrilldown	**EnableFieldDialog**	**EnableFieldList**
EnableWizard	**ErrorString**	Format
GetData	**GetPivotData**	**GrandTotalName**
HasAutoFormat	**HiddenFields**	**InnerDetail**
Item[1]	**ListFormulas**	**ManualUpdate**
MDX	**MergeLabels**	Name

NullString	PageFieldOrder	PageFields
PageFieldStyle	PageFieldWrapCount	PageRange
PageRangeCells	Parent[2]	PivotCache
PivotFields	PivotFormulas	PivotSelect
PivotSelection	PivotSelectionStandard	PivotTableWizard
PreserveFormatting	PrintTitles	RefreshDate
RefreshName	RefreshTable	RepeatItemsOnEachPrintedPage
RowFields	RowGrand	RowRange
SaveData	SelectionMode	ShowCellBackgroundFromOLAP
ShowPageMultipleItemLabel	ShowPages	SmallGrid
SourceData	SubtotalHiddenPageItems	TableRange[1]
TableRange[2]	TableStyle	Tag
TotalsAnnotation	Update	VacatedStyle
Value	Version	ViewCalculatedMembers
VisibleFields	VisualTotals	

[1] Collection only
[2] Object and collection

---

pivottables.Add(*PivotCache*, *TableDestination*, [*TableName*], [*ReadData*], [*DefaultVersion*])

Creates a new pivot table from an existing pivot cache and returns the created PivotTable object.

Argument	Settings
PivotCache	The PivotCache object to use as the data source for the pivot table.
TableDestination	The Range object indicating the location of the upper-left corner for the pivot table.
TableName	A name to assign to the pivot table. Default is PivotTable*n*.
ReadData	For database queries, True reads all of the fields from the data source; False delays retrieving the data until the pivot cache is refreshed. Default is True.
DefaultVersion	The Excel version assigned to pivot table. Can be xlPivotTableVersion10, xlPivotTableVersion2000, or xlPivotTableVersionCurrent.

This method is equivalent to the PivotCache object's CreatePivotTable method. The following code creates a pivot cache from a database query and then uses that pivot cache to create a pivot table:

```
Sub CreateSalesThisWeekPT()
    Dim pc As PivotCache, pt As PivotTable, pf As PivotField, _
      ws As Worksheet
    ' Create a new pivot cache for database query.
    Set pc = ActiveWorkbook.PivotCaches.Add(xlExternal)
    ' Create a connection string and SQL query.
    pc.Connection = "ODBC;DRIVER=SQL Server;SERVER=USERS;" & _
      "UID=jeff;APP=Microsoft Office 2003;WSID=WOMBAT4;" & _
```

```
        "DATABASE=Sales;Trusted_Connection=True"
    pc.CommandType = xlCmdSql
    pc.CommandText = "SELECT SalesRank, ProductName, Date FROM Amazon " & _
        "WHERE Date > GetDate() - 7"
    pc.MaintainConnection = False
    ' Create a new worksheet for the pivot table.
    Set ws = ActiveWorkbook.Worksheets.Add()
    ' Create a pivot table.
    Set pt = ws.PivotTables.Add(pc, ws.[a3], "SalesThisWeek", False)
    ' Set the layout: add the column and row fields.
    pt.AddFields "Date", "ProductName"
    ' Add the data field and set its formula.
    Set pf = pt.AddDataField(pt.PivotFields("SalesRank"), , xlAverage)
    ' Update the pivot table
    pc.Refresh
End Sub
```

*pivottable.*AddDataField(*Field*, [*Caption*], [*Function*])

Adds a field to the data area of a pivot table.

Argument	Settings
Field	The PivotField to add to the data area.
Caption	A name to display for the field.
Function	An xlConsolidationFunction constant indicating the type of calculation to perform on the data field items. Can be one of these settings: xlAverage, xlCountNums, xlMin, xlStDev, xlSum, xlVar, xlCount, xlMax, xlProduct, xlStDevP, or xlVarP.

See the preceding topic for an example of how to add a data field.

*pivottable.*AddFields([*RowFields*], [*ColumnFields*], [*PageFields*], [*AddToTable*])

Adds fields to the row, column, or page areas of a pivot table.

Argument	Settings
RowFields	The PivotField objects to add to the row area.
ColumnFields	The PivotField objects to add to the column area.
PageFields	The PivotField objects to add to the page area.
AddToTable	True appends the fields to any existing fields in the table; False replaces any existing fields in the table with the new ones.

To add multiple fields to an area, use an array of PivotField objects for the *RowFields*, *ColumnFields*, or *PageFields* arguments.

pivottable.CacheIndex [= setting]

Sets or returns the index of the pivot cache used by the pivot table. Changing the CacheIndex assigns a different pivot cache to the pivot table, changing the fields and data included in the table.

pivottable.CalculatedFields( )

Returns a collection of PivotField objects that are calculated from other fields.

pivottable.CalculatedMembers

For OLAP pivot tables, returns a collection of CalculatedMember objects containing all the calculated members and calculated measures in the OLAP data cube.

pivottable.ColumnFields

Returns a collection of PivotField objects that are in the column area of the pivot table.

pivottable.ColumnGrand [= setting]

True displays grand totals for column fields; False omits grand totals. Default is true. The following code turns column grand totals on and off:

```
Sub ToggleColumnTotals( )
    ' Ignore error if sheet doesn't have a pivot table.
    On Error Resume Next
    ' Turn totals on/off.
    ActiveSheet.PivotTables(1).ColumnGrand = _
      Not ActiveSheet.PivotTables(1).ColumnGrand
    On Error GoTo 0
End Sub
```

pivottable.ColumnRange

Returns the Range object for the column area of the pivot table.

pivottable.CreateCubeFile(File, [Measures], [Levels], [Members], [Properties])

For OLAP pivot tables, saves the table as a view of the OLAP data cube.

Argument	Settings
File	The name of the file to create.
Measures	An array of names of the OLAP measures to include in the file.

Argument	Settings
Levels	An array of names of the OLAP level names to include in the file.
Members	An array of the names of top-level members in the dimension to include in the file.
Properties	True includes member property settings in the file; False omits properties. Default is True.

The following code saves an OLAP pivot table as a local cube file:

```
Sub SaveOLAPCube( )
    Dim pt As PivotTable
    ' Run CreateOLAPPivotTable to create this pivot table.
    Set pt = Worksheets("FoodMart Sales").PivotTables(1)
    ' Save table as a local cube file.
    pt.CreateCubeFile ThisWorkbook.Path & "\" & pt.Name & ".cub"
End Sub
```

pivottable. CubeFields

For OLAP pivot tables, returns a collection of CubeField objects from the pivot table.

pivottable. DataBodyRange

Returns the Range object for the data area of the pivot table.

pivottable. DataFields

Returns a collection of PivotField objects that are in the data area of the pivot table.

pivottable. DataLabelRange

Returns the Range object for the cells containing the labels for the data fields on the pivot table.

pivottable. DataPivotField

Returns the PivotField object that represents all the fields in the pivot table's data area. This property is similar to the DataFields property, only DataFields returns a collection and DataPivotField combines multiple fields into a single PivotField object.

pivottable. DisplayEmptyColumn [= *setting*]

For OLAP pivot tables, True displays fields containing no data and False hides fields with no data. For other types of pivot tables, causes an error.

pivottable.DisplayEmptyRow [= setting]

For OLAP pivot tables, True displays records containing no data and False hides records with no data. For other types of pivot tables, causes an error.

pivottable.DisplayErrorString [= setting]

True displays a custom error when pivot table cells contain errors; False displays the standard error. Default is False.

Set this property to True and ErrorString to "" to turn off error messages, such as #DIV/0!, in the data area of a pivot table. The following code switches error messages on and off for a pivot table on the active worksheet:

```
Sub ToggleDataFieldErrors()
    Dim pt As PivotTable
    ' Run CreateOLAPPivotTable to create this pivot table.
    Set pt = ActiveSheet.PivotTables(1)
    ' Turn error messages on/off.
    pt.DisplayErrorString = Not pt.DisplayErrorString
    pt.ErrorString = ""
End Sub
```

pivottable.DisplayImmediateItems [= setting]

True displays row and column fields even when the data area of a pivot table is empty; False hides row and column fields when the data area is empty. Default is True.

pivottable.DisplayNullString [= setting]

True displays the value of the NullString property for data field values of ""; False displays 0 for null strings. Default is True.

The NullString property is empty by default, so the default behavior is to display nothing for null strings.

pivottable.EnableDataValueEditing [= setting]

True allows users to change values in the data area of a pivot table; False prohibits changes and displays an alert if the user attempts to change a value. Default is False.

pivottable.EnableDrilldown [= setting]

True allows users to get additional detail about a data field item from the data source by clicking the Show Detail button; False disables getting additional detail. Default is True. For OLAP pivot tables, this property can't be set to False.

*pivottable.*EnableFieldDialog [= *setting*]

True displays the PivotTable Field dialog box (see Figure 13-4) when the user double-clicks a field label; False does not display the dialog. Default is true.

*pivottable.*EnableFieldList [= *setting*]

True displays the PivotTable Field List (see Figure 13-10) when the pivot table is selected; False hides the PivotTable Field List.

*pivottable.*EnableWizard [= *setting*]

True allows users to create pivot tables using the PivotTable Wizard (see Figure 13-2); False disables the wizard. Default is True.

*pivottable.*ErrorString [= *setting*]

Sets or returns a custom error string to display when calculation errors occur in data field items. This string replaces the built-in Excel error message if `DisplayErrorString` is set to True.

*pivottable.*Format(*Format*)

Applies an autoformat to the pivot table.

Argument	Settings
Format	An `xlPivotFormatType` constant indicating the autoformat to apply. Can be one of these settings: `xlPTNone`, `xlPTClassic`, `xlReport1` to `xlReport10`, `xlTable1` to `xlTable10`.

The following code applies an autoformat to a pivot table on the active worksheet:

```
Sub ApplyAutoFormat( )
    Dim pt As PivotTable
    ' Run CreateOLAPPivotTable to create this pivot table.
    Set pt = ActiveSheet.PivotTables(1)
    ' Apply format
     pt.Format xlReport1
End Sub
```

*pivottable.*GetData(*Name*)

Retrieves a value from the pivot table's data area.

Argument	Settings
Name	The column and row names that describe the data item to return

The following code returns the average sales rank from the pivot table created earlier (see Figure 13-7 for an illustration of the pivot table):

```
Sub GetPivotTableData1( )
    Dim pt As PivotTable
    ' Run CreatePivotTable to create this pivot table.
    Set pt = ActiveSheet.PivotTables(1)
     ' Display data in Immediate window.
     Debug.Print pt.GetData(" 'Essential SharePoint' 'Average of SalesRank'")
End Sub
```

pivottable.GetPivotData([*DataField*], [*Field1*], [*Item1*], [*Fieldn*], [*Itemn*])

Returns the Range object containing the items described by the method arguments.

Argument	Settings
DataField	The name of the data field within which to get the range
Field1	The name of the page, row, or column field within which to get the range
Item1	The value to look up within the page, column, or row specified by Field1
Fieldn, Itemn	Additional field and value pairs that define the data value range to retrieve

If you omit all arguments, GetPivotData returns the Range object for the cell containing the grand total for the pivot table. If GetPivotData can't find the item using the criteria in the arguments, an error occurs.

The following code gets a value from the pivot table created earlier (see Figure 13-7 for an illustration of the pivot table):

```
Sub GetPivotTableData2( )
    Dim pt As PivotTable
    ' Run CreatePivotTable to create this pivot table.
    Set pt = ActiveSheet.PivotTables(1)
     ' Display data in Immediate window.
     Debug.Print pt.GetPivotData("SalesRank", "ProductName", _
        "Essential SharePoint", _
        "Date", #11/3/2005 9:02:56 AM#).Value
End Sub
```

pivottable.GrandTotalName [= *setting*]

Sets or returns the label displayed for the pivot table's grand total. Default is "Grand Total".

pivottable.HasAutoFormat [= *setting*]

True automatically adjusts column widths when the pivot table is refreshed; False preserves column widths when the table is refreshed. Setting this property to False also removes any autoformat that was applied to the table.

*pivottable.*HiddenFields

Returns a collection of `PivotField` objects that are in the PivotTable Field List but do not appear on the pivot table.

*pivottable.*InnerDetail [= *setting*]

Sets or returns the name of the field to show when the user selects a pivot data item and then clicks Show Detail. Cannot be set for OLAP pivot tables.

*pivottable.*ListFormulas( )

Creates a new worksheet containing a summary of the formulas used for calculated fields and calculated items on a pivot table.

*pivottable.*ManualUpdate [= *setting*]

True causes `RefreshTable` to clear data from the pivot table, rather than refreshing it; False allows `RefreshTable` to work normally. Default is False. This property is reset to False automatically after the calling procedure ends.

*pivottable.*MDX

For OLAP pivot tables, returns the Multidimensional Expression (MDX) query used to populate the data cube used by the pivot table. MDX is a SQL-like query language.

*pivottable.*MergeLabels [= *setting*]

True merges the pivot table's outer row item, column items, subtotal, and grand total labels with their rows or columns; False uses unmerged cells for the labels. Default is False. Use the following code to see the effect of merged versus unmerged labels:

```
Sub ToggleMergedLabels( )
    Dim pt As PivotTable
    ' Active worksheet must contain a pivot table.
    Set pt = ActiveSheet.PivotTables(1)
    ' Switch merged labels on/off.
     pt.MergeLabels = Not pt.MergeLabels
End Sub
```

*pivottable.*NullString [= *setting*]

Sets or returns the value to display for data field values of "" (null value). Default is "".

pivottable.PageFieldOrder [= xlOrder]

Sets or returns the order in which page fields are added to the page area of the pivot table. Can be xlDownThenOver (default) or xlOverThenDown.

pivottable.PageFields

Returns a collection of PivotField objects that are in the page area of the pivot table.

pivottable.PageFieldWrapCount [= setting]

Sets or returns the number of page fields per column in the page area of the pivot table.

pivottable.PageRange

Returns the Range object for the page area of the pivot table.

pivottable.PageRangeCells

Returns the Range object for the page area of the pivot table.

pivottable.PivotCache( )

Returns the PivotCache object used by the pivot table.

pivottable.PivotFields

Returns a collection of PivotField objects containing all the pivot fields in the pivot table.

pivottable.PivotFormulas

Returns a collection of PivotFormula objects containing all of the formulas used in the pivot table.

pivottable.PivotSelect(Name, [Mode], [UseStandardName])

Selects part of a pivot table.

Argument	Settings
Name	The name of the field or item to select.
Mode	An xlPTSelectionMode constant indicating the item within Name to select. Can be xlBlanks, xlButton, xlDataAndLabel (default), xlDataOnly, xlFirstRow, xlLabelOnly, or xlOrigin.

Argument	Settings
UseStandardName	True uses U.S. English formats for numbers, currency, dates, and times within the *Name* argument; False uses localized formats.

The following code selects the rows for Essential SharePoint from the pivot table created earlier (see Figure 13-7 for an illustration of the pivot table):

```
Sub SelectPivotItem( )
    Dim pt As PivotTable
    ' Run CreatePivotTable to create this pivot table.
    Set pt = ActiveSheet.PivotTables(1)
    ' Select one item.
    pt.PivotSelect "ProductName[Essential SharePoint]"
    ' This line is equivalent to preceding line:
    'pt.PivotSelection = "ProductName[Essential SharePoint]"
End Sub
```

pivottable.PivotSelection [= *setting*]

Sets or returns the selected item in the pivot table. Setting this property is equivalent to calling PivotSelect without optional arguments.

pivottable.PivotSelectionStandard [= *setting*]

Same as PivotSelection, only uses U.S. English formats for numbers, currency, dates, and times.

pivottable.PivotTableWizard([*SourceType*], [*SourceData*], [*TableDestination*], [*TableName*], [*RowGrand*], [*ColumnGrand*], [*SaveData*], [*HasAutoFormat*], [*AutoPage*], [*Reserved*], [*BackgroundQuery*], [*OptimizeCache*], [*PageFieldOrder*], [*PageFieldWrapCount*], [*ReadData*], [*Connection*])

Quickly creates a pivot table and returns a reference to the created PivotTable object.

Argument	Settings
SourceType	An xlPivotTableSourceType constant indicating the source of the data to use in the pivot table. Can be xlConsolidation, xlDatabase, xlExternal, or xlPivotTable.
SourceData	If *SourceType* is xlConsolidation, xlDatabase, or xlPivotTable, a Range object containing the source for the pivot table. If *SourceType* is xlExternal, an array containing the SQL query string used to retrieve the data for the pivot table.
TableDestination	The Range object indicating the location of the upper-left corner for the new pivot table.
TableName	A name to assign to the pivot table. Default is PivotTable*n*.
RowGrand	True displays grand totals for rows; False omits row totals. Default is True.
ColumnGrand	True displays grand totals for columns; False omits column totals. Default is True.

Argument	Settings
SaveData	If *SourceType* is xlExternal, True reads all of the fields from the data source and False delays retrieving the data until the pivot cache is refreshed. Default is True.
HasAutoFormat	True automatically adjusts column widths when the pivot table is refreshed; False preserves column widths when the table is refreshed. Default is True.
AutoPage	If *SourceType* is xlConsolidation, True automatically creates a page field for the consolidation.
Reserved	Do not use this argument.
BackgroundQuery	If *SourceType* is xlExternal, True queries the data source asynchronously when refreshing the pivot table; False performs synchronous queries. Default is False.
OptimizeCache	True optimizes the pivot cache; False does not optimize. Default is False.
PageFieldOrder	The order in which page fields are added to the page area of the pivot table. Can be xlDownThenOver (default) or xlOverThenDown.
PageFieldWrapCount	The number of page fields per column in the page area of the pivot table.
ReadData	If *SourceType* is xlExternal, True reads all of the fields from the data source; False delays retrieving the data until the pivot cache is refreshed. Default is True.
Connection	If *SourceType* is xlExternal, the ODBC connection string used to connect to the external data source.

Use *SourceType* xlDatabase if the pivot table's data source is a worksheet. The following code creates a quick pivot table from the active worksheet:

```
Sub QuickPivotable()
    Dim ws As Worksheet, pt As PivotTable
    ' Get the active worksheet.
    Set ws = ActiveSheet
    ' Use pivot table wizard to create table on new worksheet.
    Set pt = ws.PivotTableWizard(xlDatabase, ws.UsedRange, _
      Worksheets.Add.[a1], "Quick Pivot")
    ' Set layout
    pt.AddDataField pt.PivotFields(1), , xlAverage
    pt.AddFields pt.PivotFields(4).Name, pt.PivotFields(3).Name
End Sub
```

Use *SourceType* xlExternal if the pivot table's data source is a database. The following code creates a quick pivot table using a query to a Microsoft SQL Server database:

```
Sub QuickDBPivotTable()
    Dim ws As Worksheet, pt As PivotTable
    ' Get the active worksheet.
    Set ws = ActiveSheet
    ' Use pivot table wizard to create table on new worksheet.
    Set pt = ws.PivotTableWizard(xlExternal, Array("SELECT * FROM Amazon"), _
      Worksheets.Add.[a1], "QuickDBPivot", , , , , , , , , , , _
      "ODBC;DRIVER=SQL Server;SERVER=USERS;" & _
      "UID=;APP=Microsoft Office 2003;WSID=WOMBAT4;" & _
      "DATABASE-Sales;Trusted_Connection=True")
    ' Set layout
    pt.AddFields pt.PivotFields(4).Name, pt.PivotFields(3).Name
    pt.AddDataField pt.PivotFields(1), , xlAverage
End Sub
```

PivotTableWizard doesn't display the PivotTable Wizard dialog. To do so, use this line of code:

```
Application.Dialogs(xlDialogPivotTableWizard).Show
```

pivottable.PreserveFormatting [= setting]

True preserves cell formatting when the pivot table is refreshed; False removes cell formatting when the pivot table is refreshed. Default is True.

pivottable.PrintTitles [= setting]

True uses print titles from the pivot table; False uses print titles from the worksheet. Default is False. The following code demonstrates the effect of PrintTitles by using print preview:

```
Sub PivotPrintPreview( )
    Dim pt As PivotTable
    ' Run CreatePivotTable to create this pivot table.
    Set pt = ActiveSheet.PivotTables(1)
    ' Change property settings.
    pt.PrintTitles = True
    pt.RepeatItemsOnEachPrintedPage = True
    ' Print preview
    pt.Parent.PrintOut , , , True
End Sub
```

pivottable.RefreshDate

Returns the date and time when the pivot table was last refreshed.

pivottable.RefreshName

Returns the name of the user who last refreshed the pivot table.

pivottable.RefreshTable( )

Refreshes the pivot table's PivotCache object and updates the table.

pivottable.RepeatItemsOnEachPrintedPage [= setting]

True repeats item labels on each printed page; False does not repeat labels. Default is True.

pivottable.RowFields

Returns a collection of PivotField objects that are in the row area of the pivot table.

*pivottable.*RowGrand [= *setting*]

True displays grand totals for row fields; False omits grand totals. Default is True.

*pivottable.*RowRange

Returns the Range object for the row area of the pivot table.

*pivottable.*SaveData [= *setting*]

True saves the pivot cache data with the workbook; False omits the data when saving. For OLAP pivot tables, this property can't be set to True.

*pivottable.*SelectionMode [= *xlPTSelectionMode*]

Sets or returns the pivot table's structured selection mode. Can be one of these settings:

```
xlBlanks                  xlButton
xlDataAndLabel (default)  xlDataOnly
xlFirstRow                xlLabelOnly
xlOrigin
```

*pivottable.*ShowCellBackgroundFromOLAP [= *setting*]

For OLAP pivot tables, True sets cell BackColor properties to match the formatting specified by the OLAP MDX query and False omits formatting. Default is False.

*pivottable.*ShowPageMultipleItemLabel [= *setting*]

True displays "(Multiple Items)" when more than one item is selected within a page field; False displays the first item selected. Default is True.

*pivottable.*ShowPages([*PageField*])

Creates a new pivot table for each item in the page field. Each pivot table appears on a new worksheet.

Argument	Settings
PageField	The name of the page field to split into separate pivot tables

This method is not available for OLAP pivot tables.

*pivottable.*SourceData

Returns the data source for the pivot table. The information returned depends on the *SourceType* set when the pivot table was created, as described in the following table.

SourceType	SourceData returns
xlDatabase	The address of the source range.
xlExternal	An array containing the database connection string and SQL query string divided into 255-character elements.
xlConsolidation	A two-dimensional array. Each row consists of a reference and its associated page field items.
xlPivotTable	One of the preceding kinds of information.

You can find a pivot table's *SourceType* by checking the SourceType property of the underlying PivotCache object.

*pivottable.*SubtotalHiddenPageItems [= *setting*]

True includes hidden page fields in totals; False omits them. Default is False.

*pivottable.*TableRange1

Returns a Range object containing the pivot table minus the page area.

*pivottable.*TableRange2

Returns a Range object containing the pivot table including the page area.

*pivottable.*TableStyle [= *setting*]

Sets or returns the style name to apply to the pivot table. Choose Format → Style to see a list of available styles in Excel.

*pivottable.*TotalsAnnotation [= *setting*]

For OLAP pivot tables, True displays an asterisk on totals, indicating that hidden items are included in the total; False omits the asterisk. Default is True.

*pivottable.*Update( )

Refreshes the pivot table's PivotCache object and updates the table.

*pivottable.*VacatedStyle [= *setting*]

Sets or returns the style name to apply to pivot table cells in that are cleared when the pivot table is refreshed. Choose Format → Style to see a list of available styles in Excel.

*pivottable.*Value [= *setting*]

Sets or returns the name of the pivot table.

*pivottable.*Version

Returns the Excel version used to create the pivot table. Can be xlPivotTableVersion10, xlPivotTableVersion2000, or xlPivotTableVersionCurrent.

*pivottable.*ViewCalculatedMembers [= *setting*]

For OLAP pivot tables, True displays calculated members and False hides calculated members. Default is True.

*pivottable.*VisibleFields

Returns the collection of PivotField objects that are included in the page, column, row, or data areas of the pivot table.

*pivottable.*VisualTotals [= *setting*]

For OLAP pivot tables, True recalculates totals when items are hidden on the pivot table and False does not recalculate totals when items are hidden. Default is False, which includes hidden items in the totals.

PivotCache and PivotCaches Members

Use the PivotCache collection to create new pivot caches. Use the Workbook object's PivotCaches property to get a reference to this collection. Use the PivotCache object to create new pivot tables from the cache, to set the data source, and to refresh the cache. The PivotCaches collection and PivotCache object have the following members. Key members (shown in **bold**) are covered in the following reference section:

Add[1]	**ADOConnection**
Application[2]	**BackgroundQuery**
CommandText	**CommandType**

Connection	Count[1]
CreatePivotTable	Creator[2]
EnableRefresh	Index
IsConnected	Item[1]
LocalConnection	MaintainConnection
MakeConnection	MemoryUsed
MissingItemsLimit	OLAP
OptimizeCache	Parent[2]
QueryType	RecordCount
Recordset	Refresh
RefreshDate	RefreshName
RefreshOnFileOpen	RefreshPeriod
ResetTimer	RobustConnect
SaveAsODC	SavePassword
SourceConnectionFile	SourceData
SourceDataFile	SourceType
Sql	UseLocalConnection

[1] Collection only
[2] Object and collection

pivotcaches.Add(*SourceType*, [*SourceData*])

Creates a new pivot cache and returns a PivotCache object.

Argument	Settings
SourceType	An xlPivotTableSourceType constant indicating the source of the data to use in the pivot table. Can be xlConsolidation, xlDatabase, xlExternal, or xlPivotTable.
SourceData	If *SourceType* is xlConsolidation, xlDatabase, or xlPivotTable, a Range object containing the source for the pivot table. If *SourceType* is xlExternal, use the Connection and CommandText property to set the data source.

To create a pivot cache from a worksheet, use *SourceType* xlDatabase as shown here:

```
Sub CreateWSPivotTable( )
    Dim pc As PivotCache, pt As PivotTable, rng As Range
    ' Create a new pivot cache (assumes active sheet is a worksheet).
    Set pc = ActiveWorkbook.PivotCaches.Add(xlDatabase, ActiveSheet.UsedRange)
    ' Create a pivot table.
    Set pt = pc.CreatePivotTable(Worksheets.Add( ).[a3])
    ' Set the layout: add the column and row fields.
    pt.AddFields pt.PivotFields(4).Name, pt.PivotFields(3).Name
    ' Add the data field and set its formula.
    pt.AddDataField pt.PivotFields(1), , xlSum
End Sub
```

To create a pivot cache from a database query, use *SourceType* xlExternal and then set the Connection and CommandText properties. The following code creates a pivot cache and pivot table from an SQL query to the Northwind SQL Server database:

```
Sub CreateNwindPivotCache( )
    Dim pc As PivotCache, pt As PivotTable, rng As Range
    ' Create a new pivot cache.
    Set pc = ActiveWorkbook.PivotCaches.Add(xlExternal)
    ' Set database connection.
    pc.Connection = "ODBC;DRIVER=SQL Server;SERVER=USERS;" & _
        "UID=;APP=Microsoft Office 2003;WSID=WOMBAT4;" & _
        "DATABASE=Northwind;Trusted_Connection=True"
    ' Create SQL query.
    pc.CommandText = "SELECT CategoryID, ProductName, UnitsInStock, " & _
        "UnitPrice FROM Products"
    ' Create a pivot table.
    Set pt = pc.CreatePivotTable(Worksheets.Add( ).[a3])
    ' Set the layout: add the column and row fields.
    pt.AddFields "ProductName", , "CategoryID"
    ' Add the data field and set its formula.
    pt.AddDataField pt.PivotFields("UnitsInStock"), , xlSum
End Sub
```

pivotcache.ADOConnection

For pivot caches based on ADO database connections, returns the ADO Connection object used by the pivot cache.

pivotcache.BackgroundQuery [= *setting*]

For pivot caches based on database queries, True refreshes the cache asynchronously and False refreshes synchronously. This property is always False for other types of pivot caches, including OLAP caches.

pivotcache.CommandText [= *setting*]

For pivot caches based on database queries, sets or returns the command used to generate the cache. The form of this command depends on the CommandType property.

pivotcache.CommandType [= *xlCmdType*]

For pivot caches based on database queries, sets or returns the type of command used in CommandText as described in the following table.

Setting	CommandText is
xlCmdCube	The name of the OLAP cube
xlCmdDefault	A query string defined by the OLE DB provider
xlCmdSql	A SQL SELECT command
xlCmdTable	A table name from the data source

You can set CommandType only if QueryType is xlOLEDBQuery.

*pivotcache.*Connection [= *setting*]

For pivot caches based on database queries, sets or returns the connection string used to connect to the data source.

*pivotcache.*CreatePivotTable(*TableDestination*, [*TableName*], [*ReadData*], [*DefaultVersion*])

Creates a pivot table from the pivot cache and returns the created PivotTable object.

Argument	Settings
TableDestination	The Range object indicating the location of the upper-left corner for the new pivot table.
TableName	A name to assign to the pivot table. Default is PivotTable*n*.
ReadData	If *SourceType* is xlExternal, True reads all of the fields from the data source and False delays retrieving the data until the pivot cache is refreshed. Default is True.
DefaultVersion	The Excel version assigned to pivot table. Can be xlPivotTableVersion10, xlPivotTableVersion2000, or xlPivotTableVersionCurrent.

The following code creates a new pivot table from an existing pivot cache:

```
Sub CreatePivotTableFromExistingCache( )
    Dim pc As PivotCache, pt As PivotTable
    ' Get an existing pivot cache.
    Set pc = ActiveWorkbook.PivotCaches(1)
    ' Create a new pivot table (shares cache).
    Set pt = pc.CreatePivotTable(Worksheets.Add( ).[a3], "NewPivotTable")
    ' Select the pivot table.
    pt.TableRange2.Select
End Sub
```

*pivotcache.*EnableRefresh [= *setting*]

True allows the user to refresh the pivot cache; False disables refreshes.

*pivotcache.*IsConnected

For pivot caches based on OLE DB database queries, returns True if the cache currently holds an open database connection and False if the database connection is closed.

*pivotcache.*LocalConnection [= *setting*]

For OLAP pivot caches, True uses a local cube file and False uses a remote OLAP provider. Default is False. The following code saves an OLAP pivot table as a local cube file, then uses that data source offline:

```
Sub UseOLAPOffline( )
    Dim pc As PivotCache, pt As PivotTable, fname As String
```

```
      ' Run earlier example to create pivot table.
      CreateOLAPPivotTable
      ' Get pivot table.
      Set pt = ActiveSheet.PivotTables(1)
      ' Get the pivot cache.
      Set pc = pt.PivotCache
      ' Save local cube file.
      fname = ActiveWorkbook.Path & "\" & pt.Name & ".cub"
      pt.CreateCubeFile fname
      ' Take cache offline.
      pc.LocalConnection = "OLEDB;Provider=MSOLAP;Data Source=" & fname
      pc.UseLocalConnection = True
  End Sub
```

pivotcache.MaintainConnection [= *setting*]

For pivot caches based on OLE DB database queries, True keeps the database connection open between refreshes and False closes the connection after refreshing.

pivotcache.MakeConnection( )

For pivot caches based on OLE DB database queries, opens database connection before refreshing.

pivotcache.MemoryUsed

Returns the amount of memory used by the pivot cache in bytes. The following code displays the total memory used by pivot caches in the Immediate window:

```
  Sub CountCache( )
      Dim pc As PivotCache, mem As Long
      For Each pc In ActiveWorkbook.PivotCaches
          mem = mem + pc.MemoryUsed
      Next
      Debug.Print "#PivotCaches", "Mem Used"
      Debug.Print ActiveWorkbook.PivotCaches.Count, mem \ 1024 & "K"
  End Sub
```

pivotcache.MissingItemsLimit [= *setting*]

Sets or returns the maximum number of items per field that are retained even when they have no data in the cache. Must be between -1 (default) and 32,500. This property can't be set for OLAP pivot caches.

pivotcache.OLAP

Returns True if the pivot cache is from an OLAP data source, otherwise returns False.

pivotcache.OptimizeCache [= *setting*]

For pivot caches based on database queries to non-OLE DB data sources, True optimizes the pivot cache when the initial query occurs and False does not optimize the query. Default is False. Optimizing degrades initial cache creation but improves subsequent refreshes.

pivotcache.QueryType

For pivot caches based on database queries, returns the type of query used to create the pivot cache. Can be one of these xlQueryType constants:

```
xlOLEDBQuery
xlADORecordset
xlODBCQuery
```

pivotcache.RecordCount

Returns the number of records in the pivot cache.

pivotcache.Recordset [= *setting*]

Sets or returns the ADO RecordSet object used to create the pivot cache. The following code demonstrates how to use an ADO recordset created from a SQL Server database query to create a pivot cache and pivot table:

```
' Requires reference to Microsoft ActiveX Data Object library
Sub CreateADOPivotCache3( )
    Dim pc As PivotCache, pt As PivotTable
    Dim cnn As New ADODB.Connection, cmd As New ADODB.Command, _
      rs As New ADODB.Recordset

    ' Create ADO recordset.
    cnn.ConnectionString = "Provider=sqloledb;data source=USERS;" & _
      "initial catalog=Northwind;Integrated Security=SSPI;" & _
      "persist security info=True;packet size=4096;Trusted_Connection=True"
    cmd.CommandText = "SELECT CategoryName, ProductName, UnitsInStock, " & _
      "UnitPrice FROM Products, Categories"
    cnn.Open
    Set cmd.ActiveConnection = cnn
    Set rs = cmd.Execute

    ' Create a new pivot cache.
    Set pc = ActiveWorkbook.PivotCaches.Add(xlExternal)
    ' Use the ADO recordset as the data source.
    Set pc.Recordset = rs

    ' Create a pivot table based on the new pivot cache.
    Set pt = pc.CreatePivotTable(Worksheets.Add( ).[A3])
```

```
' Set the layout: add the column and row fields.
pt.AddFields "ProductName", , "CategoryName"
' Add the data field and set its formula.
pt.AddDataField pt.PivotFields("UnitsInStock"), , xlSum

' Close the recordset and database connection.
rs.Close
cnn.Close
End Sub
```

*pivotcache.*Refresh( )

Refreshes the pivot cache data from the data source.

*pivotcache.*RefreshOnFileOpen [= *setting*]

True automatically refreshes the pivot cache when the workbook is opened; False does not refresh on open. Default is False.

*pivotcache.*RefreshPeriod [= *setting*]

For pivot caches based on database queries other than OLAP data sources, sets or returns the number of minutes between automatic refreshes of the pivot cache. Default is 0, which turns automatic refreshes off.

*pivotcache.*ResetTimer( )

Resets the timer used for the RefreshPeriod property.

*pivotcache.*RobustConnect [= *xlRobustConnect*]

For pivot caches based on database queries, sets or returns how the pivot cache reconnects to its data source when the cache is refreshed. Can be one of the settings described in the following table:

Setting	Use this property to connect to data source
xlAlways	SourceConnectionFile or SourceDataFile
xlAsRequired	*Connection*
xlNever	Does not reconnect

*pivotcache.*SaveAsODC(*ODCFileName*, [*Description*], [*Keywords*])

For pivot caches based on ODBC database queries, saves the connection and query information as a Microsoft Office Data Connection (*.odc*) file.

Argument	Settings
ODCFileName	The name of the file to create
Description	A description included in the connection file
Keywords	Keywords included in the connection file

Excel saves .odc files to C:\Documents and Settings\user\My Documents\My Data Sources by default.

pivotcache.SavePassword [= setting]

For pivot caches based on ODBC database queries, True saves password information in the .odc file when SaveAsODC is called and False omits the password. Default is False.

pivotcache.SourceConnectionFile [= setting]

For pivot caches based on ODBC database queries, the Microsoft Office Data Connection (.odc) file used to establish the database connection.

pivotcache.SourceDataFile

For pivot caches based on file-based databases, such as Access, returns the filename of the data source.

pivotcache.SourceType

Returns an xlPivotTableSourceType constant indicating the source of the cache data. Can be one of these settings:

```
xlConsolidation
xlDatabase
xlExternal
xlPivotTable
xlScenario
```

pivotcache.Sql [= setting]

For pivot caches based on database queries, returns the SQL query used to create the cache.

pivotcache.UseLocalConnection [= setting]

True uses the LocalConnection property to connect to the data source; False uses the Connection property to connect.

PivotField and PivotFields Members

Use the `PivotFields` collection to get fields from a pivot table. Use the `PivotTable` object's `PivotFields`, `PageFields`, `ColumnFields`, `RowFields`, `DataFields`, or `HiddenFields` properties to get a reference to this collection. Use the `PivotField` object to set the layout of a pivot table, to filter and sort items, and to get the items in a field. The `PivotFields` collection and `PivotField` object have the following members. Key members (shown in **bold**) are covered in the following reference section:

AddPageItem	Application[2]	**AutoShow**
AutoShowCount	**AutoShowField**	**AutoShowRange**
AutoShowType	**AutoSort**	**AutoSortField**
AutoSortOrder	**BaseField**	**BaseItem**
CalculatedItems	**Calculation**	**Caption**
ChildField	**ChildItems**	Count[1]
Creator[2]	**CubeField**	**CurrentPage**
CurrentPageList	**CurrentPageName**	**DatabaseSort**
DataRange	**DataType**	**Delete**
DragToColumn	**DragToData**	**DragToHide**
DragToPage	**DragToRow**	**DrilledDown**
EnableItemSelection	**Formula**	**Function**
GroupLevel	**HiddenItems**	**HiddenItemsList**
IsCalculated	**IsMemberProperty**	Item[1]
LabelRange	**LayoutBlankLine**	**LayoutForm**
LayoutPageBreak	**LayoutSubtotalLocation**	MemoryUsed
Name	**NumberFormat**	**Orientation**
Parent[2]	**ParentField**	ParentItems
PivotItems	**Position**	**PropertyOrder**
PropertyParentField	**ServerBased**	**ShowAllItems**
SourceName	**StandardFormula**	**SubtotalName**
Subtotals	**TotalLevels**	Value
VisibleItems		

[1] Collection only
[2] Object and collection

---

pivotfield.**AddPageItem**(*Item*, [*ClearList*])

For OLAP pivot tables, selects an item in a page field.

Argument	Settings
Item	The name of the pivot item to select.
ClearList	True deselects all items from the page field before selecting the new one; False retains the current list of items.

To be able to select individual items in an OLAP page field, you must first select Select Multiple Items as shown in Figure 13-19. Use the CubeField object's EnableMultiplePageItems property to select or deselect this option in code.

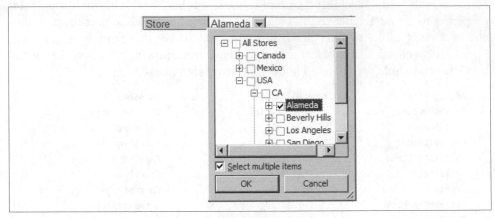

Figure 13-19. Enabling multiselect in OLAP page fields

The following code selects a single item from the FoodMart Sales OLAP pivot table created in an earlier example:

```
Sub ViewSingleStore()
    Dim pt As PivotTable, cf As CubeField
    ' Uncomment this line to create OLAP pivot table.
    'CreateOLAPPivotTable
    ' Get OLAP pivot table.
    Set pt = Worksheets("FoodMart Sales").PivotTables(1)
    ' Get cube field
    Set cf = pt.CubeFields(pt.PageFields(1).Name)
    ' Enable multiselect.
    cf.EnableMultiplePageItems = True
    ' Select one store.
    pt.PageFields(1).AddPageItem "[Store].[All Stores].[USA].[CA].[Alameda]", True
End Sub
```

pivotfield.AutoShow(*Type, Range, Count, Field*)

Applies a filter to a pivot field.

Argument	Settings
Type	The setting xlAutomatic applies the filter; xlManual removes the filter.
Range	The setting xlTop shows the top *Count* of records; xlBottom shows the bottom *Count* of records.
Count	The number of records to show.
Field	The data field to use as the criterion of the filter.

These settings are equivalent to the Top 10 AutoShow options on the PivotTable Field Advanced Options dialog box, shown in Figure 13-20.

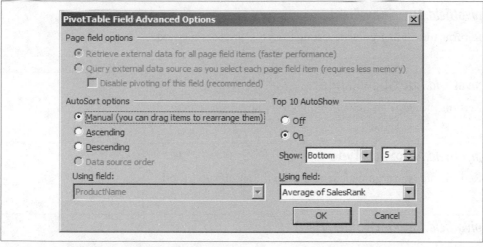

Figure 13-20. Setting advanced field options

The following code shows the bottom ProductName item based on the data field (sales rank, lower is better):

```
Sub ShowBestSeller()
    Dim pt As PivotTable, pf As PivotField
    ' Uncomment next line to create pivot table.
    'CreatePivotTable
    ' Get pivot table.
    Set pt = Worksheets("BookSales").PivotTables(1)
    ' Get pivot field.
    Set pf = pt.PivotFields("ProductName")
    ' Set autoshow.
    pf.AutoShow xlAutomatic, xlBottom, 1, pt.DataFields(1).name
End Sub
```

pivotfield.AutoShowCount

Sets or returns the *Count* argument setting from the AutoShow method. Since all the AutoShow arguments are required, you must use the Auto*xxx* properties to remove filtering from a pivot field, as shown here:

```
Sub ResetAutoShowAutoSort()
    Dim pt As PivotTable, pf As PivotField
    ' Get pivot table.
    Set pt = Worksheets("BookSales").PivotTables(1)
    ' Get pivot fields
    For Each pf In pt.PivotFields
        pf.AutoShow xlManual, pf.AutoShowRange, _
            pf.AutoShowCount, pf.AutoShowField
        pf.AutoSort xlManual, pf.AutoSortField
    Next
End Sub
```

*pivotfield.*AutoShowField

Returns the *Field* argument setting from the AutoShow method.

*pivotfield.*AutoShowRange

Returns the *Range* argument setting from the AutoShow method.

*pivotfield.*AutoShowType

Returns the *Type* argument setting from the AutoShow method.

*pivotfield.*AutoSort(*Order, Field*)

Sort items in a pivot field

Argument	Settings
Order	Can be xlAscending, xlDescending, or xlManual (unsorted)
Field	The data field to sort

These settings are equivalent to the AutoSort Options on the PivotTable Field Advanced Options dialog box shown in Figure 13-20.

The following code sorts items in the ProductName field by sales rank:

```
Sub SortBySalesRank( )
    Dim pt As PivotTable, pf As PivotField
    ' Uncomment this line to create pivot table.
    'CreatePivotTable
    ' Get pivot table.
    Set pt = Worksheets("BookSales").PivotTables(1)
    ' Get pivot field.
    Set pf = pt.PivotFields("ProductName")
    ' Sort items
    pf.AutoSort xlAscending, pt.DataFields(1).name
End Sub
```

*pivotfield.*AutoSortField

Returns the *Field* argument setting from the AutoSort method.

*pivotfield.*AutoSortOrder

Returns the *Order* argument setting from the AutoSort method.

*pivotfield.*BaseField [= *setting*]

Sets or returns the base field name used for a custom calculation. Not available for OLAP pivot fields.

*pivotfield.*BaseItem [= *setting*]

Sets or returns the base item value used for a custom calculation. Not available for OLAP pivot fields.

*pivotfield.*CalculatedItems( )

Returns a collection of `PivotItem` objects containing the items in the pivot field that are calculated.

*pivotfield.*Calculation [= *xlPivotFieldCalculation*]

Sets or returns the calculation used for items in this field. Can be one of these settings:

xlDifferenceFrom	xlIndex
xlNoAdditionalCalculation	xlPercentDifferenceFrom
xlPercentOf	xlPercentOfColumn
xlPercentOfRow	xlPercentOfTotal
xlRunningTotal	

OLAP pivot fields are always xlNoAdditionalCalculation.

*pivotfield.*Caption [= *setting*]

Sets or returns the caption displayed for the field.

*pivotfield.*ChildField

For grouped fields, returns a collection of child `PivotItems` for the field. Not available for OLAP pivot fields.

*pivotfield.*ChildItems

For grouped fields, returns a collection of child `PivotItems` for the field. Not available for OLAP pivot fields.

*pivotfield.*CubeField

For OLAP pivot fields, returns the CubeField object for the pivot field.

*pivotfield.*CurrentPage [= *setting*]

For page fields, sets or returns the currently selected item. The following code displays ProductName as a page field, then selects one book from the list:

```
Sub ViewBook()
    Dim pt As PivotTable, pf As PivotField
    ' Uncomment this line to create pivot table.
    'CreatePivotTable
    ' Get pivot table.
    Set pt = Worksheets("BookSales").PivotTables(1)
    ' Get pivot field.
    Set pf = pt.PivotFields("ProductName")
    ' Make it a page field.
    pf.Orientation = xlPageField
    ' Select my book.
    pf.CurrentPage = "Essential SharePoint"
End Sub
```

*pivotfield.*CurrentPageList [= *setting*]

For OLAP page fields with EnableMultiplePageItems set to True, sets or returns an array of names of selected items in the page field.

*pivotfield.*CurrentPageName [= *setting*]

For OLAP page fields with EnableMultiplePageItems set to False, sets or returns the name of the selected item in the page field. For example, the following code selects a single store in the FoodMart Sales pivot table:

```
Sub ViewSingleStore2()
    Dim pt As PivotTable, pf As PivotField
    ' Uncomment this line to create pivot table.
    'CreateOLAPPivotTable
    ' Get pivot table.
    Set pt = Worksheets("Foodmart Sales").PivotTables(1)
    ' Get pivot field.
    Set pf = pt.PivotFields("[Store]")
    ' Disable multiselect.
    pf.CubeField.EnableMultiplePageItems = False
    ' Select single store.
    pf.CurrentPageName = "[Store].[All Stores].[USA].[CA].[Alameda]"
End Sub
```

pivotfield.DatabaseSort [= setting]

For OLAP row or column fields, returns True if field items are ordered as they were retrieved from the database; False if the items have been reordered. Setting this property to False allows items to be reordered by dragging. Setting this property to True also restores the order from the database.

pivotfield.DataRange

Returns a Range object of the cells that contain the pivot field.

pivotfield.DataType

Returns an xlPivotFieldDataType constant indicating the type of data in the field. Can be xlDate, xlNumber, or xlText.

pivotfield.Delete( )

For calculated fields, deletes the field. This method is not available for other types of fields.

pivotfield.DragToColumn [= setting]

True if the field can be placed in the column area, False otherwise.

pivotfield.DragToData [= setting]

True if the field can be placed in the data area, False otherwise.

pivotfield.DragToHide [= setting]

True if the field can be removed from the pivot table, False otherwise.

pivotfield.DragToPage [= setting]

True if the field can be placed in the page area, False otherwise.

pivotfield.DragToRow [= setting]

True if the field can be placed in the row area, False otherwise.

*pivotfield.*DrilledDown [= *setting*]

For OLAP pivot fields, True views the detail for the field and False hides the detail.

*pivotfield.*EnableItemSelection [= *setting*]

True enables the field drop-down selection box, False disables the dropdown. Default is True. Figure 13-19 shows the drop-down selection box for a page field.

*pivotfield.*Formula [= *setting*]

For calculated fields, set or returns the localized formula used to generate the field values. Use StandardFormula to get the nonlocalized formula. Check the IsCalculated property before using this property. For example:

```
If pf.IsCalculated Then Debug.Print pf.Formula
```

*pivotfield.*Function [= *xlConsolidationFunction*]

For data fields, sets or returns the function used to calculate the value displayed in the data area. Can be one of these settings:

xlAverage	xlCount
xlCountNums	xlMax
xlMin	xlProduct
xlStDev	xlStDevP
xlSum	xlUnknown
xlVar	xlVarP

*pivotfield.*GroupLevel

Returns the placement of a field within a group of fields. For ungrouped fields, returns 1. Not available for OLAP fields.

*pivotfield.*HiddenItems

Returns a collection of PivotItems that are not currently displayed for the pivot field. Not available for OLAP fields.

pivotfield.**HiddenItemsList** [= *setting*]

For OLAP fields, sets or returns an array of strings containing the items not currently displayed for the pivot field.

pivotfield.**IsCalculated**

Returns True if the pivot field is calculated and has a formula, False otherwise.

pivotfield.**IsMemberProperty**

For OLAP fields, returns True if the pivot field contains member properties and False otherwise.

pivotfield.**LabelRange**

Returns the Range object for the cells containing the pivot field's label.

pivotfield.**LayoutBlankLine** [= *setting*]

For row fields, True inserts a blank line after the field when the field detail is collapsed and False does not insert a blank line. Default is False.

pivotfield.**LayoutForm** [= *xlLayoutFormType*]

Sets or returns whether gridlines appear within the pivot table. Can be xlTabular (default, with gridlines) or xlOutline (no gridlines).

pivotfield.**LayoutPageBreak** [= *setting*]

For row fields, True inserts a page break after each row and False breaks pages normally. Default is False. The page breaks appear only if the pivot field isn't the innermost (lowest-level) row field.

pivotfield.**LayoutSubtotalLocation** [= *XlSubtototalLocationType*]

Sets or returns the location for field totals. Can be xlAtTop or xlAtBottom (default).

pivotfield.NumberFormat [= setting]

For data fields, sets or returns the Excel number format string used to format values displayed in the data area.

pivotfield.Orientation [= xlPivotFieldOrientation]

Sets or returns the layout of the pivot field on the pivot table. Can be one of these settings, which correspond to the pivot table layout areas:

```
xlColumnField
xlDataField
xlHidden
xlPageField
xlRowField
```

pivotfield.ParentField

For grouped fields, returns the pivot field's parent.

pivotfield.PivotItems([Index])

Returns the collection of PivotItems for the field. The following code displays the pivot fields and items from a pivot table in the Immediate window:

```
Sub ShowPivotTableValues()
    Dim pt As PivotTable, pf As PivotField, pi As PivotItem
    ' Exit if pivot table doesn't exist.
    If ActiveSheet.PivotTables.Count < 1 Then Exit Sub
    ' Get pivot table.
    Set pt = ActiveSheet.PivotTables(1)
    ' Get pivot fields
    For Each pf In pt.PivotFields
        ' Display pivot fields and items in outline form.
        Debug.Print pf.name
        For Each pi In pf.PivotItems
            Debug.Print , pi.Value
        Next
    Next
End Sub
```

pivotfield.Position [= setting]

Sets or returns the position of the field within its page, column, row, or data area on the pivot table.

*pivotfield.*PropertyOrder [= *setting*]

For OLAP member property fields, sets or returns the order of the field within the field's parent. Check the IsMemberProperty before using this property.

*pivotfield.*PropertyParentField

For OLAP member property fields, returns the field's parent. Check the IsMemberProperty before using this property.

*pivotfield.*ServerBased [= *setting*]

For pivot tables based on non-OLAP database queries, True retrieves values only for the current page field when the pivot table is refreshed, and False retrieves all values.

*pivotfield.*ShowAllItems [= *setting*]

True displays all items in the field, even if they don't contain data; False hides empty items. Default is False. This property is not available for OLAP pivot fields.

*pivotfield.*SourceName

Returns the name of the pivot field as it appears in the original data souce.

*pivotfield.*StandardFormula [= *setting*]

Sets or returns the U.S. English version of the Formula property.

*pivotfield.*SubtotalName [= *setting*]

Sets or returns the label displays for the field total.

*pivotfield.*Subtotals [= *setting*]

Sets or returns an array of values that determine which totals are displayed for a field. Set items in the array to True to add that item to the list of totals. The following table lists the array indexes and their meaning:

Index	Meaning
1	Automatic
2	Sum
3	Count

Index	Meaning
4	Average
5	Max
6	Min
7	Product
8	Count Nums
9	StdDev
10	StdDevp
11	Var
12	Varp

For OLAP fields, only the first item in the array can be set.

*pivotfield.***TotalLevels**

For grouped fields, returns the number of levels in the group. For ungrouped fields, returns 1.

*pivotfield.***VisibleItems**

Returns a collection of `PivotItem` objects that are visible for the pivot field. Returns True for OLAP pivot fields.

CalculatedFields Members

Use the `CalcualtedFields` collection to add new calculated fields to the pivot fields list. Use the `PivotTable` object's `CalculatedFields` property to get a reference to this collection. The `CalculatedFields` collection has the following members. The key member (shown in **bold**) is covered in the following reference section:

```
Add
Application
Count
Creator
Item
Parent
```

*calculatedfields.***Add(***Name, Formula, [UseStandardFormula]***)**

Adds a calculated pivot field to the pivot table's fields list and returns the `PivotField` object.

Argument	Settings
Name	The name of the pivot field to create.
Formula	The Excel formula for the calculation.
UseStandardFormula	True evaluates field names using U.S. English settings; False evaluates names using the user's locale settings. Default is False.

The *Formula* argument omits the equals sign (=) and can't include cell references. The lack of cell references means you have to calculate relative values in code if you want to use them in a calculated field. The following code finds the minimum value of SalesRank and then uses that value to create a RelativeRank calculated field:

```
Sub NewCalcField()
    Dim pt As PivotTable, pfProduct As PivotField, _
      pfCalc As PivotField, min As Single
    ' Uncomment this line to create pivot table.
    'CreatePivotTable
    ' Get pivot table.
    Set pt = Worksheets("BookSales").PivotTables(1)
    ' Show detail for Product name field.
    Set pfProduct = pt.PivotFields("ProductName")
    pfProduct.Orientation = xlRowField
    pfProduct.LabelRange.ShowDetail = True
    ' Find the minimum sales rank.
    min = WorksheetFunction.min(pt.DataFields(1).DataRange)
    'Debug.Print "Min rank: " & min
    ' Delete field if it exists, ignore error if it doesn't.
    On Error Resume Next
    pt.PivotFields("RelativeRank").Delete
    On Error GoTo 0
    ' Create calculated pivot field.
    Set pfCalc = pt.CalculatedFields.Add("RelativeRank", _
      "Round(SalesRank / " & min & ", 1)", True)
    ' Add to data area.
    pfCalc.Orientation = xlDataField
    ' Hide detail.
    pfProduct.LabelRange.ShowDetail = False
End Sub
```

The Delete method in the preceding code removes the calculated field if it already exists. That allows you to rerun NewCalcField to update the calculation as needed. Also, you must show detail before calculating min because only visible items are included; later, you can hide the detail as shown in the code.

CalculatedItems Members

Use the CalculatedItems collection to add calculated items to a pivot field. Use the PivotField object's CalculatedItems property to get a reference to this collection.

The CalculatedItems collection has the following members. The key member (shown in **bold**) is covered in the following reference section:

Add
Application
Count
Creator
Item
Parent

pivotitem.Add(*Name, Formula,* [*UseStandardFormula*])

Adds a calculated pivot item to the pivot field list and returns the created PivotItem object.

Argument	Settings
Name	The name of the pivot item to create.
Formula	The Excel formula for the calculation.
UseStandardFormula	True evaluates field names using U.S. English settings; False evaluates names using the user's locale settings. Default is False.

You can't add calculated items if a pivot table contains a custom subtotal such as Average or StdDev. The following code creates a new calculated item and then displays the pivot table calculations on a new worksheet as shown in Figure 13-21:

```
Sub NewCalcItem( )
    Dim pt As PivotTable, pf As PivotField, pi As PivotItem, min As Integer
    ' Uncomment this line to create pivot table.
    'CreatePivotTable
    ' Get pivot table.
    Set pt = Worksheets("BookSales").PivotTables(1)
    ' Get pivot field
    Set pf = pt.PivotFields("SalesRank")
    ' Delete field if it exists, ignore error if it doesn't.
    On Error Resume Next
    pf.PivotItems("MinRank").Delete
    On Error GoTo 0
    ' Turn off custom subtotals.
    pt.RowFields(1).Subtotals = Array(True, False, False, False, _
      False, False, False, False, False, False, False, False)
    ' Find the minimum sales rank.
    min = WorksheetFunction.min(pt.DataFields(1).DataRange)
    ' Create calculated pivot item.
    Set pi = pf.CalculatedItems.Add("MinRank", min, True)
    ' Show formulas on a worksheet.
    pt.ListFormulas
End Sub
```

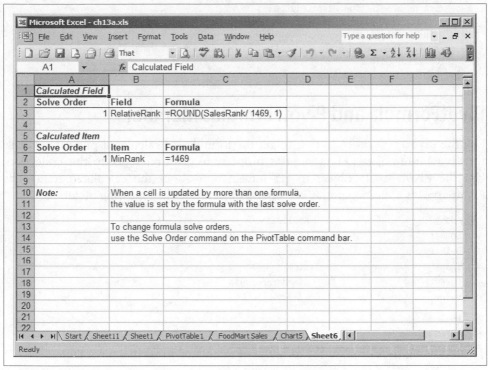

Figure 13-21. Viewing calculated fields and items from a pivot table

PivotCell Members

Use the `PivotCell` object to get pivot table information from a `Range` object. Use the `Range` object's `PivotCell` property to get a reference to this object. The `PivotCell` object has the following members:

Application	ColumnItems
Creator	CustomSubtotalFunction
DataField	Parent
PivotCellType	PivotField
PivotItem	PivotTable
Range	RowItems

Use `PivotCell` when working with user selections to find information about the selected cells. The following code displays pivot table information about the currently selected range:

```
Sub GetPivotCell()
    Dim pc As PivotCell
    On Error Resume Next
    ' Get the pivot cell
```

```
        Set pc = Selection.PivotCell
        Debug.Print pc.PivotCellType, _
          pc.PivotField.name, pc.PivotTable.name
        If Err Then Debug.Print "Selection is not in a pivot range."
        On Error GoTo 0
    End Sub
```

PivotFormula and PivotFormulas Members

Use the PivotFormulas collection to get the formulas of calculated pivot items. Use
the PivotTable object's PivotFormulas property to get a reference to this collection.
Use the PivotFormula object to get information about the calculated item. The
PivotFormulas collection and PivotFormula object have the following members:

Add[1]	Application[2]
Count[1]	Creator[2]
Delete	Formula
Index	Item[1]
Parent[2]	StandardFormula
Value	

[1] Collection only
[2] Object and collection

The following code displays the formulas of calculated items in a pivot table:

```
    Sub GetPivotFormula()
        Dim pt As PivotTable, pfa As PivotFormula
        ' Uncomment next line to add a calculated pivot item.
        'NewCalcItem
        ' Get pivot table.
        Set pt = Worksheets("BookSales").PivotTables(1)
        ' Show formulas for calculated items.
        For Each pfa In pt.PivotFormulas
            Debug.Print pfa.Value
        Next
    End Sub
```

The PivotFormulas collection doesn't include formulas from calculated pivot fields.
Use the CalculatedFields collection to get those formulas.

PivotItem and PivotItems Members

Use the PivotItems collection to get the items in a pivot field. Use the PivotField
object's PivotItems property to get a reference to this collection. Use the PivotItem
object to get information about an item. The PivotItems collection and PivotItem
object have the following members:

Add[1]	Application[2]
Caption	ChildItems
Count[1]	Creator[2]

DataRange	Delete
DrilledDown	Formula
IsCalculated	Item[1]
LabelRange	Name
Parent[2]	ParentItem
ParentShowDetail	Position
RecordCount	ShowDetail
SourceName	SourceNameStandard
StandardFormula	Value
Visible	

[1] Collection only
[2] Object and collection

PivotItem objects represent the individual values stored in each pivot field. The following code displays a pivot table's data hierarchically in the Immediate window:

```
Sub ListAllItems( )
    Dim pt As PivotTable, pf As PivotField, _
      pi1 As PivotItem, pi2 As PivotItem
    ' Get pivot table.
    Set pt = Worksheets("BookSales").PivotTables(1)
    ' Show table name.
    Debug.Print pt.name
    For Each pf In pt.PivotFields
        ' Show each field name.
        Debug.Print , pf.name
        For Each pi1 In pf.PivotItems
            ' Show each item value.
            Debug.Print , , pi1.name
            For Each pi2 In pi1.ChildItems
                ' Show subitems (not available for OLAP).
                Debug.Print , , , pi2.name
            Next
        Next
    Next
End Sub
```

PivotItemList Members

Use the PivotItemList collection to find the row and column of a PivotCell. Use the PivotCell object's RowItems and ColumnItems properties to get a reference to this collection. The PivotItemList collection has the following members:

Application
Count
Creator
Item
Parent

The following code displays the row and column of a selected cell in a pivot table's data area:

```
Sub GetRowAndColumn()
    Dim pc As PivotCell, pi As PivotItem
    On Error Resume Next
    ' Get the pivot cell
    Set pc = Selection.PivotCell
    ' Show the row this item belongs to.
    For Each pi In pc.RowItems
        Debug.Print "Row: " & pi.Value
    Next
    ' Show the column this item belongs to.
    For Each pi In pc.ColumnItems
        Debug.Print "Column: " & pi.Value
    Next
    If Err Then Debug.Print "Selection is not in the data area."
    On Error GoTo 0
End Sub
```

PivotLayout Members

Use the PivotLayout object to access the pivot table of a pivot chart. Use the Chart object's PivotLayout property to get a reference to this object. The PivotLayout object has the following members:

AddFields	Application
ColumnFields	Creator
CubeFields	DataFields
HiddenFields	InnerDetail
PageFields	Parent
PivotCache	PivotFields
PivotTable	RowFields
VisibleFields	

If the active worksheet contains a pivot table and you call Charts.Add, Excel automatically creates a pivot chart for the pivot table. You can then use the chart's PivotLayout property to navigate back to the underlying pivot table to set the pivot chart layout or change other elements. For example, the following code creates a new pivot chart then changes the layout of the pivot chart:

```
Sub ChangeChartLayout()
    Dim chrt As Chart, pt As PivotTable, pf As PivotField
    ' Activate a pivot table.
    Sheets("BookSales").Activate
    ' Create a pivot chart
    Set chrt = Charts.Add
    ' Set chart properties.
    chrt.ChartType = xlLine
    chrt.Axes(xlCategory).TickLabelPosition = xlNone
    ' Get the pivot table.
```

```
        Set pt = chrt.PivotLayout.PivotTable
        ' Change layout
        pt.PivotFields("ProductName").Orientation = xlPageField
        ' Clear data fields (ignore errors).
        On Error Resume Next
        pt.DataPivotField.Orientation = xlHidden
        pt.PivotFields("RelativeRank").Orientation = xlDataField
        pt.PivotFields("SalesRank").Orientation = xlHidden
        On Error GoTo 0
        ' Select a page field
        pt.PageFields("ProductName").CurrentPage = "Essential SharePoint"
        ' Rename the chart sheet.
        RenameChart chrt, pt.name & "Chart"
    End Sub
```

CubeField and CubeFields Members

Use the CubeFields collection to get pivot fields from an OLAP pivot table. Use the PivotTable object's CubeFields property to get a reference to this collection. Use the CubeField object to set the layout and change other properties of fields on an OLAP pivot table. The CubeFields collection and CubeField object provide a subset of the PivotField members; unique members (shown in **bold**) are covered in the following reference section:

   CubeFields and CubeField apply only to OLAP pivot tables.

AddMemberPropertyField	**AddSet**[2]
Application[2]	Caption
Count[1]	Creator[2]
CubeFieldType	Delete
DragToColumn	DragToData
DragToHide	DragToPage
DragToRow	**EnableMultiplePageItems**
HasMemberProperties	**HiddenLevels**
Item[1]	LayoutForm
LayoutSubtotalLocation	Name
Orientation	Parent[2]
PivotFields	Position
ShowInFieldList	**TreeviewControl**
Value	

[1] Collection only
[2] Object and collection

cubefield.AddMemberPropertyField(*Property*, [*PropertyOrder*])

Adds a member property field from the fields list to the cube field.

Argument	Settings
Property	The name of the member property to add.
PropertyOrder	The index of the property within the property list. The default is to append the property to the end of the list.

cubefields.AddSet(*Name*, *Caption*)

Creates a new CubeField and returns the created object.

Argument	Settings
Name	A name of an existing calculated member
Caption	The caption to display for the field in the pivot table

cubefield.CubeFieldType

Returns an xlCubeFieldType constant identifying the type of the cube field. Can be xlHierarchy, xlMeasure, or xlSet.

cubefield.EnableMultiplePageItems [= *setting*]

For page fields, True enables multiple selection and False disables multiple selection. The property reflects the setting on the page field drop-down box (Figure 13-19).

cubefield.HasMemberProperties

Returns True if the cube field contains member properties, False if not.

cubefield.HiddenLevels [= *setting*]

For cube fields with CubeFieldType of xlHierarchy, sets or returns the number of levels that are hidden. Default is 0, for no hidden levels.

cubefield.ShowInFieldList [= *setting*]

True displays the cube field in the PivotTable Fields List; False hides the field. Default is True.

*cubefield.*TreeviewControl

This property is used for macro recording. It is not intended for other uses.

CalculatedMember and CalculatedMembers Members

Use the `CalculatedMembers` collection to add new calculated members to an OLAP pivot table. Use the `PivotTable` object's `CalculatedMembers` property to get a reference to this collection. Use the `CalculatedMember` object to get the member's formula and to delete calculated members. The `CalculatedMembers` collection and `CalculatedMember` object have the following members. The key member (shown in **bold**) is covered in the following reference section:

 `CalculatedMembers` and `CalculatedMember` apply only to OLAP pivot tables.

Add[1]	Application[2]
Count[1]	Creator[2]
Delete	Formula
IsValid	Item[1]
Name	Parent[2]
SolveOrder	SourceName
Type	

[1] Collection only
[2] Object and collection

*calculatedmembers.*Add(*Name, Formula, [SolveOrder], [Type]*)

Adds a new calculated member to the OLAP pivot table and returns the created `CalculatedMember` object.

Argument	Settings
Name	The name of the pivot item to create.
Formula	The MDX expression to evaluate.
SolveOrder	A number indicating the solve order of this calculation when refreshing the pivot table. Default is 0.
Type	An `xlCalculatedMemberType` constant. Can be `xlCalculatedMember` or `xlCalculatedSet`.

See the MDX sample application that ships with Microsoft SQL Analysis Services for help creating MDX expressions. That sample also includes Help on the MDX language.

CHAPTER 14
Sharing Data Using Lists

In Microsoft Excel 2003, *lists* are ranges of cells that can easily be sorted, filtered, or shared. Lists are a little different from the AutoFilter feature available in earlier versions of Excel, in that lists are treated as a single entity, rather than just a range of cells. This unity is illustrated by a blue border that Excel draws around the cells in a list, as shown in Figure 14-1.

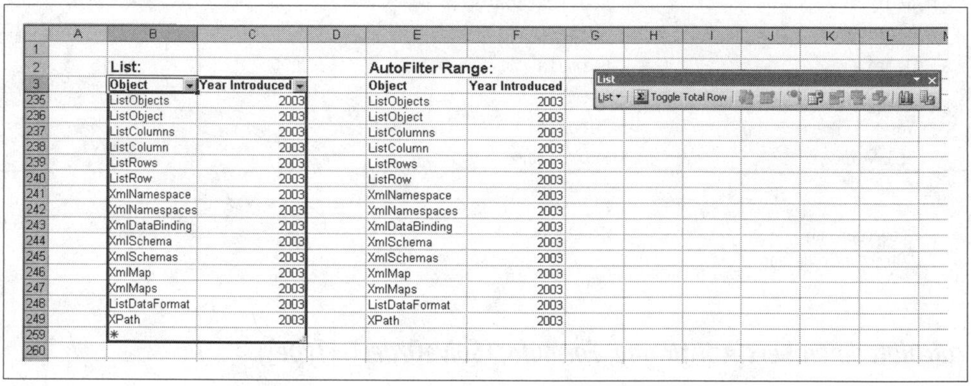

Figure 14-1. A list (left) and an AutoFilter range (right)

Lists have other nice-to-have advantages over AutoFilter ranges:

- Lists automatically add column headers to the range.
- Lists display a handy list toolbar when selected.
- It is easy to total the items in a list by clicking the Toggle Total button.
- XML data can be imported directly into a list.
- Excel automatically checks the data type of list entries as they are made.
- Lists can be shared and synchronized with teammates via Microsoft SharePoint Services.

That last item is the key advantage of lists—really, lists are just a way to share information that fits into columns and rows.

This chapter contains reference information for the following objects and their related collections: ListObject, ListRow, ListColumn, ListDataFormat, and the SharePoint Lists Web Service.

Code used in this chapter and additional samples are available in *ch14.xls*.

Use Lists

Lists reflect a range of cells within a workbook, rather than the entire workbook file itself. By sharing only the germane range of cells, you avoid publishing the underlying data and macros, which protects the original. The shared list can then be included in different workbooks used by others.

The main limitation of lists is that they can be shared only through Windows Server 2003 running SharePoint Services. That's because the sharing and maintenance of lists is provided through the ASP.NET Active Server Pages and Web Services that SharePoint provides. Other types of network shares are simply not supported. Another less important hitch is that you can't include a shared list in a shared workbook. If you want to add a list to a shared workbook, you first need to convert the workbook to single-user.

If you don't have a Windows 2003 server at your site, you can try out SharePoint Services through a hosting provider, such as Apptix or Verio. Check out *http://www. sharepointtrial.com* for a free trial.

When a list is published, SharePoint Services creates an Active Server Page that teammates can use to view or modify the list's data, as shown in Figure 14-2.

SharePoint Services stores lists as XML files. Each list has two different sorts of XML: XML that describes the list and provides its user interface and XML that contains the list data. You can edit or link to a list through its ASPX page, or you can use the SharePoint Lists Web Service to access the list directly through code.

Supported Data Types

Excel lists can contain only data that can be easily represented as XML. Objects such as charts, diagrams, and OLE objects cannot be included in lists. Excel formulas are evaluated and converted to a numeric value when a list is synchronized.

For numeric data, leading and trailing zeros are omitted and positive values are displayed without a plus sign (+) regardless of whether or not it was entered. Excel provides up to 15 significant digits of precision.

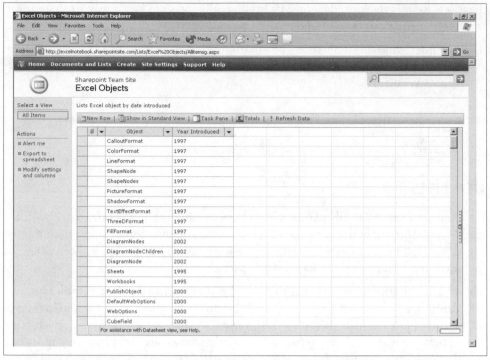

Figure 14-2. SharePoint Services provides an ASPX page to view and manage a list

Finally, the following Excel date/time formats are not directly supported and are converted to text once a list is synchronized:

> $hh:mm:ssZ$
> $Hh:mm:ss.f\text{-}f$
> $yyyy\text{-}mm\text{-}ddThh:mm:ssZ$
> $yyyy\text{-}mm\text{-}ddThh:mm:ss+/\text{-}hh:mm$
> $yyyy\text{-}mm\text{-}ddThh:mm:ss.f\text{-}f$
> $yyyy\text{-}mm\text{-}ddZ$
> $yyyy\text{-}mm\text{-}dd+/\text{-}hh:mm$
> $yyyy+/\text{-}hh:mm$
> $yyyy\text{-}mm+/\text{-}hh:mm$

Resolve Conflicts

Since lists can't include formulas or objects, they are best suited to sharing two classes of information from Excel:

- Results of calculated or summarized information
- Detail information for summary or calculation on clients

In the first case, an author may collect information, generate some results, then share those results for review by others. Alternately, a list may consist of raw data with one or more authors contributing items. Those authors and additional users may read the list and summarize or filter the list in many different workbooks.

In a many-to-many relationship, more than one author may change a particular cell. When this occurs, the second author to synchronize her list sees the Resolve Conflicts and Errors dialog, shown in Figure 14-3.

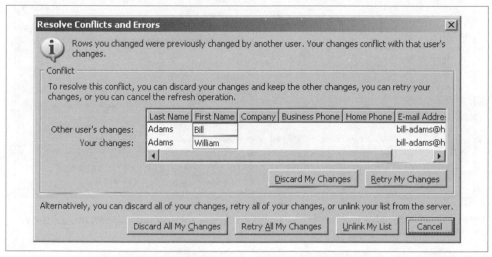

Figure 14-3. When two authors change the same cell, the second author to synchronize must decide what to do

Authorization and Authentication in Shared Lists

In order to share a list through SharePoint Services, an author must have privileges on the SharePoint server. SharePoint provides an easy-to-use interface for adding users and maintaining their passwords, shown in Figure 14-4.

When a user shares a list from Excel, SharePoint authenticates the user with the Connect dialog box, shown in Figure 14-5.

Once the user is authenticated, Excel maintains a session for the user for a period of time determined by the SharePoint settings so that the user doesn't have to sign in again every time he accesses a shared list. When the user closes Excel, his SharePoint session is ended and he will be reauthenticated if he starts Excel and accesses a shared list again.

These same rules apply whether the user is accessing a shared list through the Excel user interface or through Visual Basic code.

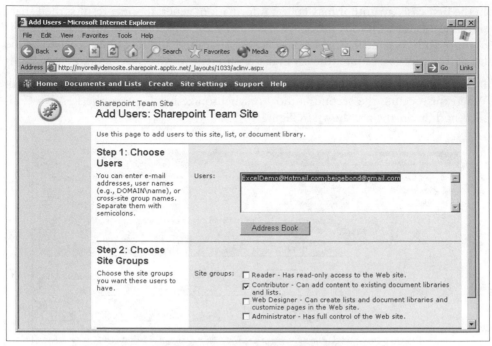

Figure 14-4. Use the SharePoint Add Users page to add new user accounts and set user privileges

Figure 14-5. SharePoint authenticates users before connecting to a shared list

Create a List in Code

Use the Add method of the ListObjects collection to create a list in code. The ListObjects collection is exposed as a property of the Worksheet object. The following code creates a new list for all the contiguous data starting with the active cell:

```
ActiveWorksheet.ListObjects.Add
```

Use the Add method's arguments to create a list out of a specific range of cells. For example, the following code creates a list out of the range A2:D5:

```
Sub CreateList1()
    Dim ws As Worksheet, rng As Range
    Set ws = ActiveSheet
    Set rng = ws.Range("A2:D5")
    ws.ListObjects.Add xlSrcRange, rng
End Sub
```

When Excel creates the preceding list, it automatically adds column headings to the list either by converting the first row into column headings or by adding a new row and shifting the subsequent data rows down. It's hard to know exactly what will happen because Excel evaluates how the first row is intended. You can avoid this assumption by supplying the *HasHeaders* argument, as shown here:

```
ws.ListObjects.Add xlSrcRange, rng, , xlNo
```

Now, the preceding code adds headers to row 2 and shifts the range down one row.

Lists always include column headers. To avoid shifting the range down one row each time you create a list, include a blank row at the top of the source range and specify xlYes for *HasHeaders* as shown here:

```
Sub CreateList2()
    Dim ws As Worksheet, rng As Range
    Set ws = ActiveSheet
    Set rng = ws.Range("A1:D5")
    ' Use first row as headers.
    ws.ListObjects.Add xlSrcRange, rng, , xlYes
End Sub
```

Since column headers and new rows added to a list cause the subsequent rows to shift down, it is a good idea to avoid placing data or other items in the rows below a list. If you do place items there, you receive a warning any time the list expands.

When creating lists in code, it is also a good idea to name the list so that subsequent references to the list can use its name rather than its index on the worksheet. To name a list, set the Name property of the ListObject:

```
Sub CreateList3()
    Dim ws As Worksheet, rng As Range, lst As ListObject
    Set ws = ActiveSheet
    Set rng = ws.Range("A1:D5")
    ' Use first row as headers.
    Set lst = ws.ListObjects.Add(xlSrcRange, rng, , xlYes)
    ' Name list
    lst.Name = "Test List"
End Sub
```

Now, you can get a reference to the named list using the Worksheet object's ListObjects property:

```
Sub ToggleTotals()
    Dim ws As Worksheet, lst As ListObject
```

```
    Set ws = ActiveSheet
    ' Get named list.
    Set lst = ws.ListObjects("Test List")
    ' Turn totals on/off.
    lst.ShowTotals = Not lst.ShowTotals
End Sub
```

Share a List

Once a list exists on a worksheet, you can share that list using the Publish method. The first argument of the Publish method is a three-element string array containing the address of the SharePoint server, a unique name for the list, and an optional description of the list. For example, the following code publishes the list created in the preceding section:

```
Sub ShareList()
    Dim ws As Worksheet, lst As ListObject
    Dim str As String, dest(2) As Variant
    Set ws = ActiveSheet
    Set lst = ws.ListObjects("Test List")
    dest(0) = "http://www.excelworkshop.com"
    dest(1) = "Test List"
    dest(2) = "A description goes here..."
    str = lst.Publish(dest, True)
    MsgBox "Your list has been shared. You can view it at: " & str
End Sub
```

The Publish method returns a string containing the address of the published list. The preceding code displays that address in a message box, but you may want to navigate to that address or include a link to it somewhere on the sheet. To add a hyperlink to the list on the SharePoint server, add a hyperlink to a range as shown here:

```
' Add link instead of showing message box.
Dim lnk As Hyperlink
Set lnk = ws.Hyperlinks.Add([F1], str)
```

After adding the hyperlink, you can display the web page for the list by using the Follow method as shown here:

```
' Display the shared list in the browser.
lnk.Follow
```

To navigate to the list without adding a hyperlink, use the Workbook object's FollowHyperlink method:

```
' Or use the FollowHyperlink method.
ThisWorkbook.FollowHyperlink str
```

The ListObject's SharePointURL property returns the address of the list, so it is easy to get the address of the shared list after it has been created, as shown here:

```
Sub AddLink()
    Dim ws As Worksheet, str As String, lnk As Hyperlink
    Set ws = ActiveSheet
    str = ws.ListObjects("Test List").SharePointURL
```

```
    Set lnk = ws.Hyperlinks.Add([F1], str, , _
        "Click to display list site.", "View")
End Sub
```

Insert a Shared List

Once a list is published on a SharePoint site, you can insert that list into other work-sheets using the ListObject's Add method and the *SourceType* argument xlSrcExternal:

```
Sub InsertSharedList()
    Dim ws As Worksheet, src(1) As Variant
    Set ws = ThisWorkbook.Worksheets.Add(, ActiveSheet)
    ws.Name = "Insert List"
    src(0) = "http://www.excelworkshop.com/_vti_bin"
    src(1) = "Test List"
    ws.ListObjects.Add xlSrcExternal, src, True, xlYes, ws.Range("A1")
End Sub
```

When *SourceType* is xlSrcExternal, the Source argument is a two-element array containing this information:

Element	Data
0	List address. This is the SharePoint address plus the folder name /_vti_bin.
1	The name or GUID of the list. A GUID is a 32-digit numeric string that identifies the list on the server.

To find the GUID of a list, view the list on the SharePoint server and choose Modify Columns and Settings on the list's web page. SharePoint displays the GUID for the list in the browser's Address text box as shown in Figure 14-6.

 Inserting a list manually from a SharePoint site into an existing work-book deletes all of the Visual Basic code contained in the workbook. Inserting a list from code does not delete a workbook's code, however.

Refresh and Update

Use the ListObject's Refresh method to discard changes to the list on the worksheet and refresh it with data from the SharePoint server as shown here:

```
lst.Refresh
```

Use the UpdateChanges method to send data from the worksheet list, to the SharePoint server and retrieve new and changed data from the SharePoint server as shown here:

```
lst.UpdateChanges xlListConflictDialog
```

As mentioned earlier, if two authors modify the same item in a list, a conflict will occur when the second author updates her list. The *iConflictType* argument deter-mines what happens when a conflict occurs. Possible settings are:

xlListConflictDialog (the default)
    Conflict displays dialog.

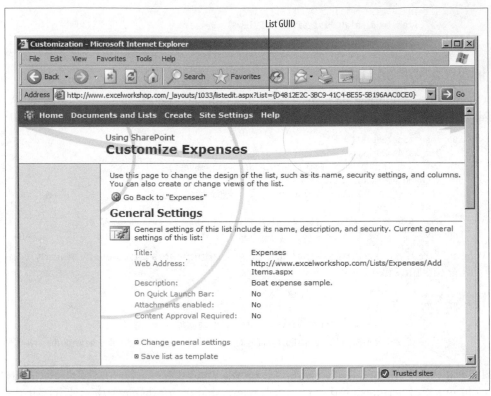

List GUID

Figure 14-6. Find a list's GUID from the SharePoint server

`xlListConflictRetryAllConflicts`
    Worksheet data wins conflict.

`xlListConflictDiscardAllConflicts`
    Server data wins conflict.

`xlListConflictError`
    Conflict causes error.

Unlink, Unlist, and Delete

Use these `ListObject` methods to unlink, unlist, or delete a list:

Method	Use to
Unlink	Remove the link between the worksheet list and the SharePoint list.
Unlist	Convert the worksheet list to a range, preserving the list's data.
Delete	Delete the worksheet list and all its data.

Once you have unlinked a list, you can't relink it. To re-establish the link, you must delete the list and insert it back onto the worksheet from the SharePoint list.

The following sections describe Excel's list objects in greater detail providing the syntax, return values, and details on the properties and methods each object provides.

ListObject and ListObjects Members

The ListObjects collection and ListObject object have the following members. Key members (shown in **bold**) are covered in the following reference section:

Active	**Add**[1]
Application[2]	Count[1]
Creator[2]	**DataBodyRange**
Delete	DisplayRightToLeft
HeaderRowRange	InsertRowRange
Item[1]	ListColumns
ListRows	Name
Parent[2]	**Publish**
QueryTable	Range
Refresh	Resize
SharePointURL	ShowAutoFilter
ShowTotals	SourceType
TotalsRowRange	**Unlink**
Unlist	**UpdateChanges**
XmlMap	

[1] Collection only
[2] Object and collection

---

listobjects.**Add**(*[SourceType]*, *[Source]*, *[LinkSource]*, *[XlListObjectHasHeaders]*, *[Destination]*)

Creates a new list and adds it to a worksheet. The Add method returns a reference to the LinkObject that was created.

Argument	Settings
SourceType	xlSrcRange creates the list from a range of cells. xlSrcExternal inserts a list from a SharePoint server. xlSrcXml is an invalid setting and causes an error when used with the Add method.
Source	If *SourceType* is xlSrcRange, this argument is a range of cells to convert to a list. If *SourceType* is xlSrcExternal, this argument is an array identifying the source of the list.
LinkSource	True links the list to the SharePoint list if *Source* is xlSrcExternal; False omits the link. Must be omitted if *Source* is xlSrcRange.

Argument	Settings
XlListObject HasHeaders	xlYes converts the first row of the list to text headers. xlNo Adds a new row for headers and shifts the range of cells in the list down one row. xlYesNoGuess causes Excel to evaluate whether the first row contains text headers and adds a header row if it does not seem to exist.
Destination	If *Source* is xlSrcExternal, *Destination* must be a single cell that indicates the upper-left corner of the list to create.

The data you include in the *Source* array argument depends on whether you are creating a list from a range of cells or inserting a list from a SharePoint server.

Create a list from a range

When creating a list from a range, use the *Source* argument to identify the range of cells to convert to a list. If *Source* contains only one cell, Excel creates a list out of the range of contiguous cells that contain data. For example, the following code creates a list out of all ranges of contiguous cells containing data that surround the cell C4:

```
Sub ListFromAdjoiningCells()
    Dim ws As Worksheet
    Set ws = ActiveSheet
    ' Create a list from cells adjoining C4.
    ws.ListObjects.Add xlSrcRange, ws.Range("C4"), , xlYes
End Sub
```

The preceding code creates the list and uses the top row of the range as the column headings for the list.

Insert a shared list

When inserting an existing list onto a worksheet from a SharePoint server, use the *Source* array argument to specify the location of the list and the name or GUID of the list on the server. Although it is easier to know the name of a list, that name can be changed by editing the list's General Settings in SharePoint. It is more reliable to use the GUID, since that unique identifier doesn't change over the life of the list.

To find the GUID of a list, view the list on the SharePoint server and choose Modify Columns and Settings on the list's web page. SharePoint displays the GUID for the list in the browser's Address text box after the List= query string.

The following code demonstrates using a GUID to insert a shared list on a new worksheet:

```
Sub InsertListFromGUID()
    Dim ws As Worksheet, src(1) As Variant
    Set ws = ThisWorkbook.Worksheets.Add(, ActiveSheet)
    ws.Name = "Insert List GUID"
    src(0) = "http://www.excelworkshop.com/_vti_bin"
    src(1) = "{4B929DF0-F6C1-4230-A0E6-6AA18D668B15}"
    ws.ListObjects.Add xlSrcExternal, src, True, xlYes, ws.Range("A1")
End Sub
```

listobject.DataBodyRange

Returns the range of cells in the list that contain data. The returned range omits column headers and total rows. You can use DataBodyRange to format or select all of the items in a list, as shown here:

```
Sub FormatList()
    Dim ws As Worksheet, lst As ListObject
    Set ws = ActiveSheet
    Set lst = ws.ListObjects(1)
    lst.DataBodyRange.Style.Font.Bold = True
    lst.DataBodyRange.Activate
End Sub
```

You can also use DataBodyRange to position other items relative to the list using the Range object's End and Offset methods as shown in the SharePointURL example.

listobject.Delete()

Deletes the ListObject and all of the data it contains. Delete does not shift surrounding cells up or to the right.

listobject.Publish(*Target, LinkSource*)

Shares a worksheet list on a SharePoint server. Returns a string containing the address of the list on the Web.

Argument	Settings
Target	The full address of the SharePoint server to share the list on. Includes the http: protocol identifier and the name of any subwebs.
LinkSource	True links the contents of the worksheet list to the SharePoint list for synchronization. False copies the list to the SharePoint server, but does not link the contents.

The following code shares a list on a worksheet and displays the location of the list once it is shared:

```
Sub ShareList()
    Dim ws As Worksheet, lst As ListObject
    Dim str As String, dest(2) As Variant
    Set ws = ActiveSheet
    Set lst = ws.ListObjects("Test List")
    dest(0) = "http://www.excelworkshop.com"
    dest(1) = "Test List"
    dest(2) = "A description goes here..."
    str = lst.Publish(dest, True)
    ' Display the shared list in the browser.
    ThisWorkbook.FollowHyperlink str
End Sub
```

The name of the list (Test List in preceding code) must be unique within the SharePoint site. If a list with that name already exists, an error occurs and the list is not shared.

listobject.SharePointURL

Returns the full address of the default view of a shared list on the SharePoint server. Causes an error if the list has not been shared. The following code adds a hyperlink to display the web page for a shared list:

```
Sub AddLink2( )
    Dim ws As Worksheet, rng As Range
    Dim lst As ListObject, str As String
    Set ws = ActiveSheet
    Set lst = ws.ListObjects(1)
    Set rng = lst.DataBodyRange.End(xlToRight).Offset(-1, 1)
    ws.Hyperlinks.Add rng, str, , _
      "Click to display list site.", "View list..."
End Sub
```

The preceding code uses the Range object's End and Offset methods to locate the new hyperlink at the top and to the right of the list on the worksheet.

listobject.ShowTotals [= *setting*]

Sets or returns a value indicating whether a totals row is displayed on the list. True displays the totals; False hides the totals.

listobject.Unlink( )

Removes the link between the data in the list on a worksheet and the data in the list on a SharePoint server. This link allows the worksheet list to synchronize with the SharePoint list. The following code removes the link from a list:

```
Sub UnlinkList( )
    Dim ws As Worksheet, lst As ListObject
    Set ws = ActiveSheet
    Set lst = ws.ListObjects(1)
    lst.Unlink
End Sub
```

No error occurs if the list was not previously shared.

Once the link is removed, the worksheet list can't be relinked to the SharePoint list. To re-establish a link, you must delete the list on the worksheet, then insert the shared list from the SharePoint server onto the worksheet.

listobject.Unlist( )

Converts a list to a normal range of cells. If the list displays a totals row, that row becomes part of the range. The following code hides the totals row and then converts a list to a range:

```
Sub ConverToRange( )
    Dim ws As Worksheet, lst As ListObject
    Set ws = ActiveSheet
    ' Get the first list on the worksheet.
    Set lst = ws.ListObjects(1)
    ' Convert it to a range.
    lst.Unlist
End Sub
```

listobject.UpdateChanges([*iConflictType*])

Synchronizes the shared list on a worksheet with the list on the SharePoint server. The setting of *iConflictType* determines how list items with changes on both the worksheet and SharePoint server are handled.

Setting	Description
xlListConflictDialog	Displays the Resolve Conflicts and Errors dialog box to resolve the conflict (this is the default).
xlListConflictRetryAllConflicts	Replaces conflicting data on the SharePoint server with data from the worksheet.
xlListConflictDiscardAllConflicts	Replaces conflicting data on the worksheet with updates from the SharePoint server.
xlListConflictError	Updates the items that do not conflict and generates an error, "Cannot update the list to Windows SharePoint Services," leaving the conflicting items unchanged.

If the worksheet list is not shared, UpdateChanges causes an error.

The following code synchronizes a list and overwrites conflicting items with the worksheet version of the item (local version wins):

```
Sub SyncLocalWins( )
    Dim ws As Worksheet, lst As ListObject
    Set ws = ActiveSheet
    Set lst = ws.ListObjects("Test List")
    lst.UpdateChanges xlListConflictRetryAllConflicts
End Sub
```

The following code synchronizes a list and overwrites conflicting items with the Share-Point version of the item (server version wins):

```
Sub SyncServerWins( )
    Dim ws As Worksheet, lst As ListObject
    Set ws = ActiveSheet
    Set lst = ws.ListObjects("Test List")
    lst.UpdateChanges xlListConflictDiscardAllConflicts
End Sub
```

listobject.XMLMap

If the contents of the list were originally imported from XML, then XMLMap returns a reference to an XMLMap object that can be used to import or export XML data into or out of the list. See Chapter 15 for more information on the XMLMap object.

ListRow and ListRows Members

The ListRows collection and ListRow object have the following members. Key members (shown in **bold**) are covered in the following reference section:

Add[1]	Application[2]
Count[1]	Creator[2]
Delete	Index
InvalidData	Item[1]
Parent[2]	**Range**

[1] Collection only
[2] Object and collection

listrows.Add([*Position*])

Inserts a new, blank row into the list, shifting subsequent rows down. The *Position* argument indicates where to insert the row. For example, the following code creates a new, blank row at the second row in the list:

```
Sub InsertRow( )
    Dim ws As Worksheet, lst As ListObject
    Set ws = ActiveSheet
    Set lst = ws.ListObjects("Test List")
    lst.ListRows.Add (2)
End Sub
```

If *Position* is omitted, the new row is inserted at the end of the list.

Each row in a shared list has a unique ID assigned to it. When you create a new shared list, row IDs are created sequentially from top to bottom. As you add and delete rows within a list, new row IDs are created and existing IDs are deleted, so the sequential order of IDs is not preserved.

listrow.Delete

Removes a row from a list, deleting the data it contains and shifting rows up. The Add method acts on the ListRows collection, whereas the Delete method acts on the ListRow object.

Use the `ListObjects Item` method to get the row to delete. For example, the following code deletes the second row of a list (undoing the code shown for the previous `Add` method):

```
Sub DeleteRow()
    Dim ws As Worksheet, lst As ListObject
    Set ws = ActiveSheet
    Set lst = ws.ListObjects("Test List")
    lst.ListRows(2).Delete
End Sub
```

listrow.InvalidData

Returns True if the row contains data that is not valid as per the list schema. Returns False if the row contains only valid data. The following code highlights rows in lists that contain invalid data:

```
Sub HighlightInvalidRows()
    Dim ws As Worksheet, lst As ListObject, row As ListRow
    Set ws = ActiveSheet
    Set lst = ws.ListObjects("Test list")
    For Each row In lst.ListRows
        If row.InvalidData Then
            row.Range.Font.Color = RGB(255, 0, 0)
        Else
            row.Range.Font.Color = RGB(0, 0, 0)
        End If
    Next
End Sub
```

Excel validates list entries as the user enters data, so it is unlikely that invalid data is the result of user edits. However, entries made by code are not automatically validated.

listrow.Range

Returns a reference to the Range object for a row in the list. Use the Range property to get the values and address of items in a list. For example, the following code creates a new row and sets the values of the second, third, and fourth items in the row:

```
Sub SetValues()
    Dim ws As Worksheet, lst As ListObject, row As ListRow
    Set ws = ActiveSheet
    Set lst = ws.ListObjects("Test List")
    lst.ListRows.Add (2)
    lst.ListRows(2).Range.Cells(1, 2).Value = "a"
    lst.ListRows(2).Range.Cells(1, 3).Value = "b"
    lst.ListRows(2).Range.Cells(1, 4).Value = "c"
    lst.ListRows(2).Range.Cells(1, 5).Value = "d"
End Sub
```

ListColumn and ListColumns Members

The `ListColumns` collection and `ListColumn` object have the following members. Key members (shown in **bold**) are covered in the following reference section:

Add[1]	Application[2]
Count[1]	Creator[2]
Delete	Index
Item[1]	**ListDataFormat**
Name	Parent[2]
Range	**SharePointFormula**
TotalsCalculation	**XPath**

[1] Collection only
[2] Object and collection

listcolumn.**ListDataFormat**

Returns a reference to the `ListDataFormat` object for the list column. Use the `ListDataFormat` object to get information about the type of data that the column contains. For example, the following code highlights the required columns in a list:

```
Sub HighlightRequired( )
    Dim ws As Worksheet, lst As ListObject, col As ListColumn
    Set ws = ActiveSheet
    Set lst = ws.ListObjects("Test List")
    For Each col In lst.ListColumns
        If col.ListDataFormat.Required Then
            col.Range.Font.Color = RGB(0, 0, 255)
        End If
    Next
End Sub
```

listcolumn.**SharePointFormula**

For shared lists, returns a string representation of the formula that SharePoint uses to calculate a column. If the column is not calculated by SharePoint, returns an empty string. The following code displays the formula for calculated columns in a list:

```
Sub ShowForumulas( )
    Dim ws As Worksheet, lst As ListObject, col As ListColumn
    Set ws = ActiveSheet
    Set lst = ws.ListObjects("Test List")
    For Each col In lst.ListColumns
        If col.SharePointFormula <> "" Then
            MsgBox "Column: " & col.Name & _
                " Formula: " & col.SharePointFormula
        End If
    Next
End Sub
```

listcolumn.TotalsCalculation [= setting]

Sets or returns the type of calculation used to figure the total for this column. Possible settings are:

xlTotalsCalculationNone   xlTotalsCalculationSum
xlTotalsCalculationAverage   xlTotalsCalculationCount
xlTotalsCalculationCountNums   xlTotalsCalculationMin
xlTotalsCalculationStdDev   xlTotalsCalculationVar
xlTotalsCalculationMax

The following code changes the Total Price column to a sum of its values:

```
Sub ChangeTotal( )
    Dim ws As Worksheet, lst As ListObject, col As ListColumn
    Set ws = ActiveSheet
    Set lst = ws.ListObjects("Test List")
    lst.ListColumns("Total Price").TotalsCalculation = xlTotalsCalculationSum
End Sub
```

listcolumn.XPath

If a list has been created from imported XML data, returns a reference to the column's XPath object. If the list was not created from XML data, returns Nothing. For example, the following code displays the XPath of each column in the Immediate window:

```
Set ws = ThisWorkbook.Worksheets("Sheet1")
Set lst = ws.ListObjects("XML List")
For Each col In lst.ListColumns
    Debug.Print col.XPath.Value
Next
```

For more information on the XPath object, see Chapter 15.

ListDataFormat Members

The ListDataFormat object has the following members. Key members (shown in **bold**) are covered in the following reference section:

AllowFillIn	Application
Choices	Creator
DecimalPlaces	**DefaultValue**
lcid	**IsPercent**
MaxCharacters	**MaxNumber**
MinNumber	Parent
ReadOnly	**Required**
Type	

The ListDataFormat object provides a set of read-only properties that return information about the data format of the list column as set on the SharePoint server. To set these properties:

1. Open the list on the SharePoint site.

2. Choose Modify Setting and Columns.

3. Select a column to modify. SharePoint displays the Change Column web page as shown in Figure 14-7. When you are done, click OK to make the changes.

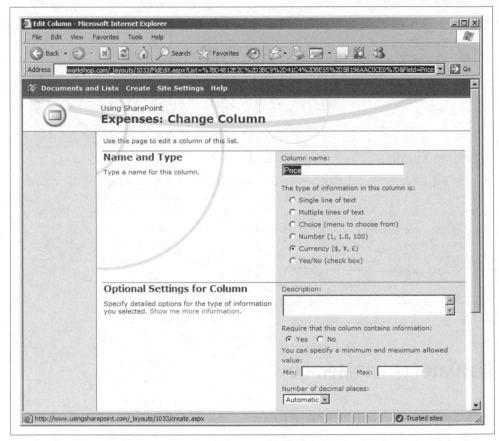

Figure 14-7. SharePoint Optional Settings for Column which correspond to the ListDataFormat properties

The following code displays a report on the data format of each column in a list in the Immediate window:

```
Sub ShowListDataFormat()
    Dim lst As ListObject, col As ListColumn
    Set lst = Worksheets("Lists").ListObjects("Test List")
    For Each col In lst.ListColumns
        Debug.Print "Column: " & col.Name & vbCrLf & _
```

```
         "  Can edit choice? " & col.ListDataFormat.AllowFillIn & vbCrLf & _
         "  Choices: " & col.ListDataFormat.Choices & vbCrLf & _
         "  Decimal places: " & col.ListDataFormat.DecimalPlaces & vbCrLf & _
         "  Default: " & col.ListDataFormat.DefaultValue & vbCrLf & _
         "  Percent? " & col.ListDataFormat.IsPercent & vbCrLf & _
         "  Max char: " & col.ListDataFormat.MaxCharacters & vbCrLf & _
         "  Max #: " & col.ListDataFormat.MaxNumber & vbCrLf & _
         "  Min #: " & col.ListDataFormat.MinNumber & vbCrLf & _
         "  Read only? " & col.ListDataFormat.ReadOnly & vbCrLf & _
         "  Required? " & col.ListDataFormat.Required & vbCrLf & _
         "  Type code: " & col.ListDataFormat.Type & vbCrLf
      Next
   End Sub
```

listdataformat.AllowFillIn

If the values in the column reflect a set of choices and the user can supply an alternate value, returns True. Otherwise, returns False.

listdataformat.Choices

If the values in the column reflect a set of choices, returns an array containing those choices. Otherwise, returns Nothing.

listdataformat.DecimalPlaces

If the column is numeric and the decimal place is assigned automatically, returns xlAutomatic (-4105). If the column has a fixed decimal place, returns the place number of the decimal. Otherwise, returns 0.

listdataformat.DefaultValue

If the column has a default value, returns that value. Otherwise, returns Nothing.

listdataformat.IsPercent

Returns True if the value in the column reflects a percentage; returns False if not.

listdataformat.lcid

Returns the locale ID of the column. In Excel locale determines the symbol used when displaying currency values. Returns 0 if the column has a neutral locale—in which case the currency symbol is determined by the user's system settings.

listdataformat.MaxCharacters

If the column has a maximum length, returns that length in characters. Otherwise, returns -1.

listdataformat.MaxNumber

If the column has a maximum value, returns that value. Otherwise, returns `Nothing`.

listdataformat.MinNumber

If the column has a minimum value, returns that value. Otherwise, returns `Nothing`.

listdataformat.ReadOnly

Returns True if the value in the column is a read-only; returns False if the value is not read-only.

listdataformat.Required

Returns True if the value in the column is a required field; returns False if the value is not required.

listdataformat.Type

Returns one of the following constant values indicating the type of data that the column reflects:

xlListDataTypeCheckbox	xlListDataTypeChoice
xlListDataTypeChoiceMulti	xlListDataTypeCounter
xlListDataTypeCurrency	xlListDataTypeDateTime
xlListDataTypeHyperLink	xlListDataTypeListLookup
xlListDataTypeMultiLineRichText	xlListDataTypeMultiLineText
xlListDataTypeNone	xlListDataTypeNumber
xlListDataTypeText	

Use the Lists Web Service

SharePoint Services includes the Lists Web Service for getting at shared lists and their data directly. The Lists Web Service lets you perform tasks on the server that you cannot otherwise perform through Excel objects; you can use it to:

- Add an attachment to a row in a list
- Retrieve an attachment from a row in a list
- Delete an attachment
- Delete a list from a SharePoint server
- Look up a list GUID
- Perform queries directly on the shared list

To use a web service from Visual Basic:

1. Install the web Services Toolkit from Microsoft at *www.microsoft.com/downloads*.
2. Close and restart Excel.
3. Open the Visual Basic Editor and select Web References from the Tools menu. Visual Basic displays the Microsoft Office 2003 Web Services Toolkit dialog (Figure 14-8).

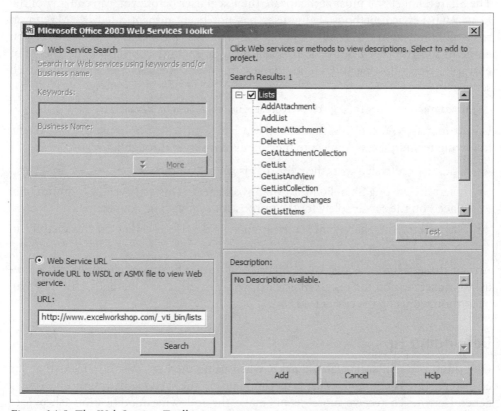

Figure 14-8. The Web Services Toolkit in action

The SharePoint Web Services reside in the *_vti_bin* folder of the SharePoint site. To use the Lists Web Service:

1. Display the Microsoft Office 2003 Web Services Toolkit as described earlier.

2. Select the Web Service URL option button and type the address of the address using this form: *http://sharepointURL/_vti_bin/lists.asmx*.

3. Click Search. The toolkit should find the Lists Web Service and display it in the Search Results list.

4. Select the checkbox beside Lists in Search Results and click Add.

5. The toolkit generates a proxy class named `clsws_Lists` and adds it to the current project.

Authentication and Authorization

The SharePoint server must authenticate the Excel user before you can call any of the Lists Web Service methods. If the user has not been authenticated, a "Maximum retry on connection exceeded" error occurs. In Visual Basic .NET or C# .NET, you authenticate the user from code by creating a `Credentials` object for the user. For example, the following .NET code passes the user's default credentials to a web service:

```
wsAdapter.Credentials = System.Net.CredentialCache.DefaultCredentials
```

Unfortunately, you can't do that directly in Excel. Instead, you must use one of the following techniques to connect to the SharePoint server through Excel:

- Update or refresh a worksheet list that is shared on the server.

- Insert an existing SharePoint list on a worksheet. This can even be a dummy list placed on the server solely for the purpose of establishing connections.

- Navigate to the SharePoint server in code as described earlier in this chapter in "Share a List."

Any of these techniques displays a SharePoint authentication dialog box and establishes a user session for Excel. Afterward, you can call `Lists` methods and they will be authorized using the current session.

Debugging Tip

One thing you will notice fairly quickly when using the Lists Web Service is that the error reporting is minimal. When a method fails on the server side, you receive only a general error. To receive more detail, make the following modification (shown in **bold**) to the `clsws_Lists ListsErrorHander` procedure:

```
Private Sub ListsErrorHandler(str_Function As String)
    If sc_Lists.FaultCode <> "" Then
```

```
        Err.Raise vbObjectError, str_Function, sc_Lists.FaultString & _
            vbCrLf & sc_Lists.Detail
    'Non SOAP Error
    Else
        Err.Raise Err.Number, str_Function, Err.Description
    End If
End Sub
```

Now errors will be reported with details from the server.

Add Attachments to a List

Excel does not directly support attachments to lists; however, you can use the Lists
Web Service AddAttachment method to add a file attachment to a row in a list, then
use GetAttachmentCollection to retrieve attachments from within Excel.

For example, the following code attaches bitmaps of a pintle and a gudgeon to the
Test List created earlier:

```
Sub AddAttachments()
    Dim ws As Worksheet, src As String, dest As String
    Dim lws As New clsws_Lists
    Set ws = ActiveSheet
    ' Requires web reference to SharePoint Lists.asmx
    src = ThisWorkbook.Path & "\pintle.bmp"
    dest = lws.wsm_AddAttachment("Test List", "1", "pintle.bmp", FileToByte(src))
    src = ThisWorkbook.Path & "\gudgeon.bmp"
    dest = lws.wsm_AddAttachment("Test List", "2", "gudgeon.bmp", FileToByte(src))
End Sub
```

The AddAttachment method's last argument is an array of bytes containing the data to
attach. To convert the image file to an array of bytes, the preceding code uses the following helper function:

```
Function FileToByte(fname As String) As Byte()
    Dim fnum As Integer
    fnum = FreeFile
    On Error GoTo FileErr
    Open fname For Binary Access Read As fnum
    On Error GoTo 0
    Dim byt() As Byte
    ReDim byt(LOF(fnum) - 1)
    byt = InputB(LOF(fnum), 1)
    Close fnum
    FileToByte = byt
    Exit Function
FileErr:
    MsgBox "File error: " & Err.Description
End Function
```

Retrieve Attachments

Use the Lists Web Service `GetAttachmentCollection` method to retrieve an attachment from a list. The `GetAttachmentCollection` method returns an XML node list that contains information about each attachment for the row. The following code displays the gudgeon bitmap attached in the previous section:

```
Sub GetAttachment()
    ' Requires web reference to SharePoint Lists.asmx
    Dim lws As New clsws_Lists
    Dim xn As IXMLDOMNodeList  ' Requires reference to Microsoft XML
    Set xn = lws.wsm_GetAttachmentCollection("Test List", "2")
    ThisWorkbook.FollowHyperlink xn.Item(0).Text
End Sub
```

Notice that the returned XML node list is a collection since rows can have multiple attachments. Since the preceding example attached only one file, this sample simply retrieves the first item from the node list. The `Text` property of this item is the address of the attachment on the SharePoint server.

Delete Attachments

Finally, it is very simple to delete an attachment using the `DeleteAttachment` method:

```
Sub DeleteAttachment()
    ' Requires web reference to SharePoint Lists.asmx
    Dim lws As New clsws_Lists
    lws.wsm_DeleteAttachment "Test List", "2", _
      "http://www.excelworkshop.com/Lists/Test List/Attachments/2/gudgeon.bmp"
End Sub
```

Since `DeleteAttachment` requires the fully qualified address of the attachment, it is useful to save the address of each attachment somewhere on the worksheet or to create a helper function to retrieve the address from the SharePoint server as shown here:

```
Function FindAttachment(ListName As String, ID As String) As String
    Dim lws As New clsws_Lists ' Requires Web reference to to SharePoint Lists.asmx
    Dim xn As IXMLDOMNodeList  ' Requires reference to Microsoft XML
    Set xn = lws.wsm_GetAttachmentCollection(ListName, ID)
    FindAttachment = xn.Item(0).Text
End Function
```

Delete a SharePoint List

When you delete a shared list on an Excel worksheet, the SharePoint list remains on the server. To delete the SharePoint list from Excel, use the `DeleteList` method as shown here:

```
Sub DeleteSharedList()
    ' Requires web reference to SharePoint Lists.asmx
```

```
      Dim lws As New clsws_Lists
      lws.wsm_DeleteList ("Test List")
   End Sub
```

If you delete a SharePoint list but not the worksheet list that shares it, you will get an error when you attempt to refresh or update the worksheet list. You can avoid this by unlinking the worksheet list after deleting the list from the server.

Look Up a List GUID

The ListObjects Add method uses a GUID when inserting an existing SharePoint list into a worksheet. You can find this GUID manually by looking on the SharePoint site, or you can use the GetListCollection method to look up the GUID by name as shown here:

```
Function GetListGUID(listName As String) As String
   ' Requires web reference to SharePoint Lists.asmx
   Dim lws As New clsws_Lists
   Dim xn As IXMLDOMNodeList  ' Requires reference to Microsoft XML
   Dim root As IXMLDOMElement
   Dim ele As IXMLDOMElement
   Set xn = lws.wsm_GetListCollection
   Set root = xn.Item(0)
   For Each ele In root.childNodes
       If LCase(ele.getAttribute("Title")) = LCase(listName) Then
           GetListGUID = ele.getAttribute("Name")
           Exit Function
       End If
   Next
   GetListGUID = ""  ' Return empty string if not found.
End Function
```

Looking at the preceding code, it may occur to you that you need to know a lot about the structure of the XML that the Lists Web Service uses before you can accomplish much. It's easy to view an IXMLDOMElement during debugging by printing it to the Immediate window as shown here:

```
Debug.Print root.xml
```

Unfortunately, what you get is a mass of text with no whitespace. To see the structure a little more clearly, you have to use XML reader and writer objects to format the output. The following helper function does just that:

```
Function PrettyPrint(xml As String) As String
   Dim rdr As New SAXXMLReader ' Requires reference to Microsoft XML
   Dim wrt As New MXXMLWriter  ' Requires reference to Microsoft XML
   Set rdr.contentHandler = wrt
   wrt.indent = True
   rdr.Parse (xml)
   PrettyPrint = wrt.output
End Function
```

Now, to display the root element of the Lists collection, run the following line of code:

```
Debug.Print PrettyPrint(root.xml)
```

The output appears as shown in Figure 14-9.

```
Immediate                                                                    X
<?xml version="1.0" encoding="UTF-16" standalone="no"?>
<Lists xmlns="http://schemas.microsoft.com/sharepoint/soap/">
    <List DocTemplateUrl="" DefaultViewUrl="/Lists/Announcements/AllItems.aspx" ID="{59!
    <List DocTemplateUrl="" DefaultViewUrl="/Lists/Books/AllItems.aspx" ID="{99E454F5-2!
    <List DocTemplateUrl="" DefaultViewUrl="/Lists/Businesses/Boxed.aspx" ID="{B95C8144-
    <List DocTemplateUrl="" DefaultViewUrl="/Ch11/Forms/AllItems.aspx" ID="{FB0BABBB-A5(
    <List DocTemplateUrl="" DefaultViewUrl="/Ch11Sample/Forms/AllItems.aspx" ID="{D5E80'
    <List DocTemplateUrl="" DefaultViewUrl="/Lists/Consultants/Boxed.aspx" ID="{453D0EC(
    <List DocTemplateUrl="" DefaultViewUrl="/Lists/Costs/Full list.aspx" ID="{BCBD98B5-!
    <List DocTemplateUrl="" DefaultViewUrl="/Covers/Forms/AllItems.aspx" ID="{BABCAAC0-
    <List DocTemplateUrl="/MSTrainingkits/Forms/_basicpage.htm" DefaultViewUrl="/MSTrair
    <List DocTemplateUrl="" DefaultViewUrl="/Lists/Expenses/Add Items.aspx" ID="{D4812E:
    <List DocTemplateUrl="" DefaultViewUrl="/Lists/foo/AllItems.aspx" ID="{5E991E24-6AB!
    <List DocTemplateUrl="/Handoff/Forms/template.doc" DefaultViewUrl="/Handoff/Forms/A!
    <List DocTemplateUrl="/Help/Forms/_webpartpage.htm" DefaultViewUrl="/Help/Forms/All!
    <List DocTemplateUrl="" DefaultViewUrl="/Lists/issues/AllItems.aspx" ID="{A2205B70-(
    <List DocTemplateUrl="" DefaultViewUrl="/_catalogs/lt/Forms/AllItems.aspx" ID="{D39:
    <List DocTemplateUrl="" DefaultViewUrl="/SPArticle/Forms/AllItems.aspx" ID="{B8A3C7:
    <List DocTemplateUrl="" DefaultViewUrl="/Lists/Projects/Summary.aspx" ID="{B1B6613E-
    <List DocTemplateUrl="" DefaultViewUrl="/RTIDocs/Forms/AllItems.aspx" ID="{DE40D748-
    <List DocTemplateUrl="/SPTraining/Forms/_basicpage.htm" DefaultViewUrl="/SPTraining,
    <List DocTemplateUrl="" DefaultViewUrl="/_catalogs/wt/Forms/Common.aspx" ID="{95C99:
    <List DocTemplateUrl="" DefaultViewUrl="/Temp1/Forms/AllItems.aspx" ID="{7EC59252-4!
    <List DocTemplateUrl="/Travel/Forms/template.htm" DefaultViewUrl="/Travel/Forms/All!
    <List DocTemplateUrl="" DefaultViewUrl="/Lists/TreeView/AllItems.aspx" ID="{73139A9(
    <List DocTemplateUrl="/VB 60 Developers Workshop/Forms/_basicpage.htm" DefaultViewU:
    <List DocTemplateUrl="" DefaultViewUrl="/_catalogs/wp/Forms/AllItems.aspx" ID="{F43:
</Lists>
```

Figure 14-9. Formatted XML is much easier to read than XML without whitespace

Perform Queries

In general, you don't need to perform queries through the Lists Web Service. Most of the operations you want to perform on the list data are handled through the Excel interface or through the Excel list objects as described previously.

However, advanced applications—or especially ambitious programmers—may use the Lists Web Service to exchange XML data directly with the SharePoint server. For instance, you may want to retrieve a limited number of rows from a very large shared list. In this case, you can perform a query directly on the SharePoint list using the GetListItems method. For example, the following code gets the first 100 rows from a shared list:

```
Sub QueryList()
    Dim lws As New clsws_Lists  ' Requires web reference to SharePoint Lists.asmx
    Dim xn As IXMLDOMNodeList  ' Requires reference to Microsoft XML
    Dim query As IXMLDOMNodeList
    Dim viewFields As IXMLDOMNodeList
```

```
        Dim rowLimit As String
        Dim queryOptions As IXMLDOMNodeList
        rowLimit = "100"
        Dim xdoc As New DOMDocument
        xdoc.LoadXml ("<Document><Query /><ViewFields />" & _
            "<QueryOptions /></Document>")
        Set query = xdoc.getElementsByTagName("Query")
        Set viewFields = xdoc.getElementsByTagName("Fields")
        Set queryOptions = xdoc.getElementsByTagName("QueryOptions")
        Set xn = lws.wsm_GetListItems("Test List", "", query, _
            viewFields, rowLimit, queryOptions)
    End Sub
```

The results are returned as XML. To see them, you can simply display the root node of the returned object as shown here:

```
    Debug.Print xn.Item(0).xml
```

The key to the preceding query is the XML supplied by the LoadXml method. You create conditional queries using the Query element and determine the columns included in the results using the ViewFields element. Perhaps the simplest way to create these queries is to write them as a text file in an XML editor (or Notepad), then load them from that file using the Load method shown here:

```
    xdoc.Load ("query.xml")
```

The query file takes this form:

```
<Document>
<Query>
    <OrderBy>
        <FieldRef Name="ID" Asending="FALSE"/>
    </OrderBy>
    <Where>
        <Eq>
            <FieldRef Name="Type" />
            <Value Type="Value">Wood</Value>
        </Eq>
    </Where>
</Query>
<ViewFields>
        <FieldRef Name="ID" />
        <FieldRef Name="Unit Price" />
        <FieldRef Name="Qty" />
</ViewFields>
<QueryOptions>
    <DateInUtc>FALSE</DateInUtc>
    <Folder />
    <Paging />
    <IncludeMandatoryColumns>FALSE</IncludeMandatoryColumns>
    <MeetingInstanceId />
    <ViewAttributes Scope="Recursive" />
    <RecurrenceOrderBy />
    <RowLimit />
    <ViewAttributes />
```

```
    <ViewXml />
  </QueryOptions>
  </Document>
```

The `FieldRef` elements sometimes use the internal SharePoint names to identify columns—lists don't always use the titles displayed in the columns as column names. You can get the internal column names by examining the list's XML. To see the list's XML, use the `GetList` method as shown here:

```
Sub ShowListXML( )
    Dim lws As New clsws_Lists
    Dim xn As IXMLDOMNodeList '
    Set xn = lws.wsm_GetList("Test List")
    Debug.Print PrettyPrint(xn(0).xml)
End Sub
```

More information about the `Query`, `ViewFields`, and `QueryOptions` elements is available in the Microsoft SharePoint SDK. See the links at the end of this chapter for specific addresses.

The following sections describe the Lists Web Service methods in greater detail, providing syntax, return values, and details for each method.

Lists Web Service Members

The Lists Web Service provides the following key members, covered in the following reference section:

AddAttachment	AddList
DeleteAttachment	DeleteList
GetAttachmentCollection	GetList
GetListAndView	GetListCollection
GetListItemChanges	GetListItems
UpdateList	UpdateListItems

wslists.AddAttachment *(listName, listItemID, fileName, attachment)*

Adds a file attachment to a row in a SharePoint list. Returns the address of the attachment.

Argument	Data type	Settings
listName	String	The name or GUID of the list.
listItemID	String	The ID of the row to attach the file to.
fileName	String	The name of the file to attach. This name is used to identify the attachment on the server.
attachment	Byte( )	A byte array containing the file to attach. Uses base-64 encoding.

The ID of a row is not the same as the index of the row within the list. SharePoint assigns a unique ID to each row as it is added. Since rows can be added and deleted throughout the life of the list, IDs may not be contiguous.

wslists.AddList (*listName, description, templateID*)

Creates a list on a SharePoint site. Returns an IXMLDOMNodeList object that contains a description of the list.

Argument	Data type	Settings
listName	String	The name of the list to create
description	String	A description of the list
templateID	Integer	A number identifying a list template to use (see following list)

SharePoint provides the following predefined templates:

Announcements 104	Contacts 105
Custom List 100	Custom List in Datasheet View 120
DataSources 110	Discussion Board 108
Document Library 101	Events 106
Form Library 115	Issues 1100
Links 103	Picture Library 109
Survey 102	Tasks 107

wslists.DeleteAttachment (*listName, listItemID, url*)

Deletes an attachment from a list row.

Argument	Data type	Settings
listName	String	The name or GUID of the list
listItemID	String	The ID of the row for which to delete the attachment
url	String	The address of the attachment on the SharePoint server

wslists.DeleteList (*listName*)

Deletes a list from the SharePoint server.

Argument	Data type	Settings
listName	String	The name or GUID of the list

wslists.GetAttachmentCollection (*listName, listItemID*)

Gets a list of the attachments for a list row. Returns an IXMLDOMNodeList containing the addresses of the attachments.

Argument	Data type	Settings
listName	String	The name or GUID of the list
listItemID	String	The ID of the row for which to retrieve the attachments

wslists.GetList (*listName*)

Gets a description of the SharePoint list. Returns an IXMLDOMNodeList containing the information SharePoint uses to maintain the list.

Argument	Data type	Settings
listName	String	The name or GUID of the list

wslists.GetListAndView (*listName, viewName*)

Gets a description of the SharePoint list including the view schema. Returns an IXMLDOMNodeList containing the information SharePoint uses to display the list.

Argument	Data type	Settings
listName	String	The name or GUID of the list.
viewName	String	The GUID of the view. If omitted, GetListAndView uses the default view.

wslists.GetListCollection ( )

Gets the names and GUIDs for all the lists on the site. Returns an IXMLDOMNodeList containing elements that describe each list on the SharePoint site.

wslists.GetListItemChanges (*listName, viewFields, since, contains*)

Gets changes made to the list since the specified date and time. Returns an IXMLDOMNodeList containing the results of the query.

Argument	Data type	Settings
listName	String	The name or GUID of the list
viewFields	IXMLDOMNodeList	A list of XML ViewFields elements indicating the columns and order of columns to return from the list

Argument	Data type	Settings
since	String	A Coordinated Universal Time (UTC) indicating the time after which you want to retrieve changes
contains	IXMLDOMNodeList	An XML Contains element indicating a filter criterion to use when retrieving changes

wslists.GetListItems (*listName, viewName, query, viewFields, rowLimit, queryOptions*)

Gets data from the rows in a list. Returns an IXMLDOMNodeList containing the results of the query.

Argument	Data type	Settings
listName	String	The name or GUID of the list.
viewName	String	The GUID of the view to use when retrieving rows. If omitted, uses the default view.
query	IXMLDOMNodeList	An XML Query element indicating a query to use when retrieving rows.
viewFields	IXMLDOMNodeList	A list of XML ViewFields elements indicating the columns and order of columns to return from the list.
rowLimit	String	The maximum number of rows to return.
queryOptions	IXMLDOMNodeList	An XML QueryOptions element containing other elements used to set the properties of the SPQuery object on the SharePoint server.

wslists.UpdateList (*listName, listProperties, newFields, updateFields, deleteFields, listVersion*)

Updates a list based on the specified field definitions and list properties. Returns an IXMLDOMNodeList describing the list after changes are made and containing an element for every new, updated, or deleted row.

Argument	Data type	Settings
listName	String	The name or GUID of the list
listProperties	IXMLDOMNodeList	An XML List element that includes elements for the list properties to update
newFields	IXMLDOMNodeList	An XML Fields element containing a list of the new fields and their properties
updateFields	IXMLDOMNodeList	An XML Fields element containing a list of the changed fields and their changes
deleteFields	IXMLDOMNodeList	An XML Fields element containing a list of the deleted fields
listVersion	IXMLDOMNodeList	An XML Version element containing the version of the list

wslists.**UpdateListItems** (*listName, updates*)

Updates the specified items in a list on the current site.

Argument	Data type	Settings
listName	String	The name or GUID of the list
updates	IXMLDOMNodeList	An XML Batch element containing a description of the rows to update

Resources

To learn about	Look here
In-depth coverage of SharePoint	*Essential SharePoint* (O'Reilly)
Free SharePoint trial site	*http://www.sharepointtrial.com*
Office Web Services Toolkit	Search *http://www.microsoft.com/downloads* for "Office Web Services Toolkit"
Lists Web Service	*http://msdn.microsoft.com/library/en-us/spptsdk/html/soapcLists.asp*
DOMDocument	*http://msdn.microsoft.com/library/en-us/xmlsdk/htm/xml_obj_overview_20ab.asp*
IXMLDOMNodeList	*http://msdn.microsoft.com/library/en-us/xmlsdk30/htm/xmobjxmldomnodelist.asp*
MXXMLWriter and SAXXMLReader	*http://msdn.microsoft.com/library/en-us/xmlsdk/htm/sax_devgd_hdi_usemxxmlwriter_7cdj.asp*
Query element	*http://msdn.microsoft.com/library/en-us/spptsdk/html/tscamlquery.asp*
ViewFields element	*http://msdn.microsoft.com/library/en-us/spptsdk/html/tscamlviewfields.asp*
QueryOptions element	*http://msdn.microsoft.com/library/en-us/spptsdk/html/tscSPQuery.asp*
Batch element	*http://msdn.microsoft.com/library/default.asp?url=/library/en-us/spsdk11/caml_schema/spxmlelbatch.asp*

CHAPTER 15

Working with XML

As you may have realized from the previous chapter, lists are one of the ways Excel handles XML data. Shared lists are stored as XML, SharePoint exchanges updates via XML Web Services, and lists can import and export XML.

The Excel features covered in this chapter apply to Office 2003 for Windows. Earlier versions and Macintosh versions of Office do not support these features, although Office 2002 does support saving workbooks in XML format.

I didn't address XML directly in the preceding chapter because lists are just one of the ways Excel handles XML. In this chapter, I show the different ways you can work with XML in Excel. Specifically, I show you how to:

- Save a workbook as XML
- Transform XML from a workbook into other forms of output
- Transform a non-Excel XML file into an XML spreadsheet
- Import XML to a list
- Export XML from a list
- Respond to XML import and export events
- Program with the XML map objects

This chapter contains reference information for the following objects and their related collections: XmlDataBinding, XmlMap, XmlNamespace, XmlSchema, and XPath.

Code used in this chapter and additional samples are available in *ch15.xls*.

Understand XML

Simply put, XML is a way to store data as plain text. This is useful because it allows all sorts of hardware and software to exchange data and, more importantly, understand that data.

Excel 2003 supports XML at two levels:

- The XML spreadsheet file format lets you save and open Excel workbooks stored as plain text in XML format.
- Lists and XML maps let you import and export XML to a range of cells in a worksheet.

The concept behind XML has been around for a very long time. The core idea is that if you store content in plain text, add descriptive tags to that content, then describe those tags somewhere, you enable that content to be shared across applications, networks, and hardware devices in some very interesting ways.

XML is the standard for tagging content and navigating among those tags. XML has related standards for describing tags and transforming documents. All of these standards are maintained by W3C and are published at *www.W3C.org*. There are quite a few acronyms associated with XML, and the following tables will help you understand them. Table 15-1 lists the XML language standards.

Table 15-1. XML language standards

Acronym	Full name	Use to
XML	Extensible Markup Language	Describe data as plain text documents.
XPath	XML Path Language	Define parts of an XML document and navigate between those parts.
DTD	Document Type Definition	Define the tags used to identify content in an XML document.
XSD	XML Schema Definition	An XML-based version of DTD. XSD is the successor to DTD.
XSL/XSLT	XML Style Sheet Language (Transformation)	Transform XML documents into other documents, such as HTML output.

Table 15-2 describes the various ways you can access XML data from code and transmit XML across networks.

Table 15-2. Supporting standards for XML

Acronym	Full name	Description
DOM	Document Object Model	API for manipulating XML documents
SAX	Simple XML API	Another API for manipulating XML documents
SOAP	Simple Object Access Protocol	Defines the structure of XML data transmitted over a network and how to interpret that structure as it is received
WSDL	Web Service Description Language	Describes services that can be invoked across a network through SOAP

The last two items in Table 15-2 concern web services, which are a way to execute programs over the Internet and to receive responses from those programs.

I don't have space here to provide tutorials on how to use the items listed in the tables, but fortunately there are some very good books and online information available about each. See "Resources" at the end of this chapter for pointers to some excellent sources. Excel programmers have such a wide range of XML experience among Excel programmers that I leave the process of selecting from among these sources to you. However, to get the most out of this chapter, you will need to be familiar with at least XML, XPath, XSL, and XSD.

Save Workbooks as XML

In Excel 2003, you can now save a workbook as an XML spreadsheet or as XML Data from the Save As dialog box (Figure 15-1).

Figure 15-1. Saving a workbook as XML

Choosing the XML Spreadsheet file type saves the workbook in an XML file that uses the Microsoft Office schema. Choosing the XML Data file type saves the workbook file in an XML file that uses a schema you provide through an XML map. Since it's a good idea to start simply, I'll discuss the XML spreadsheet format here and the XML data format later in this chapter in "Use XML Maps."

If you save a workbook as an XML spreadsheet, you can open the file in Notepad, edit it, and still reopen/edit it in Excel later—provided you haven't broken any of the rules in the file's schema. A simple, default workbook includes a lot of items that aren't required by the Office schema and you can simply delete those items to see the simplified "core" of an XML spreadsheet as shown here:

```xml
<?xml version="1.0"?>
<?mso-application progid="Excel.Sheet"?>
<Workbook xmlns="urn:schemas-microsoft-com:office:spreadsheet"
 xmlns:o="urn:schemas-microsoft-com:office:office"
 xmlns:x="urn:schemas-microsoft-com:office:excel"
 xmlns:dt="uuid:C2F41010-65B3-11d1-A29F-00AA00C14882"
 xmlns:ss="urn:schemas-microsoft-com:office:spreadsheet"
 xmlns:html="http://www.w3.org/TR/REC-html40"
 xmlns:x2="http://schemas.microsoft.com/office/excel/2003/xml">
 <Worksheet ss:Name="Sheet1">
  <Table ss:ExpandedColumnCount="5" ss:ExpandedRowCount="2" x:FullColumns="1"
   x:FullRows="1">
   <Column ss:Index="5" ss:AutoFitWidth="0" ss:Width="54.75"/>
   <Row>
    <Cell><Data ss:Type="Number">1</Data></Cell>
    <Cell><Data ss:Type="Number">2</Data></Cell>
    <Cell><Data ss:Type="Number">3</Data></Cell>
   </Row>
   <Row>
    <Cell><Data ss:Type="Number">4</Data></Cell>
    <Cell><Data ss:Type="Number">5</Data></Cell>
    <Cell><Data ss:Type="Number">6</Data></Cell>
   </Row>
  </Table>
 </Worksheet>
</Workbook>
```

The preceding XML has these notable features:

- The mso-application processing instruction tells the Microsoft Office XML Editor (*MsoXmlEd.Exe*) to open the file with Excel.

- Office uses numerous namespace definitions to qualify the names used in its XML documents.

- The path to data on a spreadsheet is Workbook/Worksheet/Table/Row/Cell/Data. The Cell node is used to contain formulas, formatting, and other information as attributes.

- The Column element is not a parent of the Row or Cell elements as you might expect. Instead, it is mainly used to set the width of the columns on the worksheet.

You can experiment with the XML Spreadsheet by making changes in Notepad and seeing the results. For instance if you change the `mso-application` processing instruction to:

```
<?mso-application progid="Word.Document"?>
```

Now, the spreadsheet will open in Word 2003 if you double-click on the file in Solution Explorer. Change the `progid` to `"InternetExplorer.Application"` or delete the processing instruction and Windows will open the file as XML rather than as an Excel spreadsheet in Internet Explorer.

The `mso-application` processing instruction is ignored if you don't have Office 2003 installed. So if you post an XML spreadsheet on a network, clients that don't have Office 2003 will see that file as XML rather than as a spreadsheet.

Data Excel Omits from XML

When Excel saves a workbook as XML, it omits these types of data:

- Charts, shapes, and OLE objects
- Macros

Other types of data (numbers, text, formulas, comments, validation, formatting, sheet layout, window and pane positioning, etc.) are preserved, however. It is best to think of XML spreadsheets as vehicles for data, rather than as full-featured workbooks.

To preserve charts, shapes, OLE objects, or macros, save the workbook file first in Excel workbook format, then in XML spreadsheet format as shown here:

```
ThisWorkbook.SaveAs , xlXMLSpreadsheet
ThisWorkbook.SaveAs , xlWorkbookNormal
```

By saving the file as a normal workbook last, you leave the current file type as *.xls* so if the user clicks Save, the full version of the file is saved. Excel keeps the full workbook in memory even after you save it as an XML spreadsheet, so you don't lose data between the two saves. You are, however, prompted several times—first to overwrite existing files since you are using SaveAs, then to note that XML spreadsheets do not save contained objects. You can eliminate the first prompt by deleting the existing file before each step of the save as shown next. You can eliminate the second prompt only by omitting nonsaved items (such as macros) from the workbook:

```
' Requires reference to Microsoft Scripting Runtime
Dim fso As New FileSystemObject
xlsName = ThisWorkbook.fullname
base = fso.GetBaseName(xlsName)
xmlName = ThisWorkbook.path & "\" & base & ".xml"
fso.DeleteFile (xmlName)
ThisWorkbook.SaveAs xmlName, xlXMLSpreadsheet
fso.DeleteFile (xlsName)
ThisWorkbook.SaveAs xlsName, xlWorkbookNormal
```

The preceding code saves two versions of the workbook: one full version with an *.xls* file type and one XML spreadsheet version with an *.xml* file type.

Transform XML Spreadsheets

XML spreadsheets provide Excel data in a format that can be easily used by other applications or transformed into presentation documents, such as HTML web pages. For either task you often need to modify the content of the XML spreadsheet and the best way to do that is with XSLT.

You can use XSLT to perform a wide variety of transformations, such as:

- Extract specific items from a spreadsheet—such as retrieving only worksheets containing data
- Transform the spreadsheet into HTML
- Make global changes to the spreadsheet
- Highlight significant items, such as high or low outlier numbers

To transform an XML spreadsheet, follow these general steps:

1. Create an XSLT file to perform the transformation using Notepad or some other editor.
2. Perform the transformation in code, from the command line, or by including a processing instruction.
3. Save the result.

Table 15-3 compares the three different ways to perform a transformation. The sections that follow describe each of the techniques in more detail.

Table 15-3. Methods to transform XML spreadsheet

Transformation	Use to	Advantages	Disadvantages
Code	Automatically generate the result from within Visual Basic	Can be performed with a single click by the user or in response to an event.	Requires Excel to be running.
Command line	Perform batch transformations	Transformed file is generally smaller than source file.	Uses command-line interface; utility must be downloaded.
Processing instruction	Dynamically transform the file when it is viewed	Changes to the XSLT are reflected automatically; underlying source is preserved.	File is generally larger and displays more slowly since it is transformed on the client.

Create XSLT for an XML Spreadsheet

XSLT is a simple language containing looping, decision-making, evaluation, branching, and functional statements. It follows the same conventions as XML, and its sole purpose is to interpret and transform valid XML documents into some other text.

Excel qualifies the names of the XML nodes it creates with namespaces from the Microsoft Office schemas. An Excel workbook defines the following namespaces:

```
<Workbook xmlns="urn:schemas-microsoft-com:office:spreadsheet"
 xmlns:o="urn:schemas-microsoft-com:office:office"
 xmlns:x="urn:schemas-microsoft-com:office:excel"
 xmlns:dt="uuid:C2F41010-65B3-11d1-A29F-00AA00C14882"
 xmlns:ss="urn:schemas-microsoft-com:office:spreadsheet"
 xmlns:html="http://www.w3.org/TR/REC-html40"
 xmlns:x2="http://schemas.microsoft.com/office/excel/2003/xml">
```

Notice that the default namespace (xmlns, highlighted in **bold**) is "urn:schemas-microsoft-com:office:spreadsheet". This is the same as the namespace for the ss prefix (xmlns:ss, also in **bold**). You use this ss namespace prefix when referring to workbook nodes in your XSLT file.

Different nodes in the XML spreadsheet use different default namespaces. For instance, the DocumentProperties node uses the following default namespace:

```
<DocumentProperties xmlns="urn:schemas-microsoft-com:office:office">
```

Therefore, when referring to the DocumentProperties node or its children, define a prefix for the namespace urn:schemas-microsoft-com:office:office in your XSLT and use that prefix to refer to those nodes. It is convenient to copy the namespace definitions from the XML spreadsheet worksheet node to your XSLT stylesheet. For instance, the following XSLT example uses the copied ss namespace to locate nodes in an XML spreadsheet:

```
<?xml version="1.0"?>
<!-- Strip.xslt transforms an XML spreadsheet to its bare essentials -->
<xsl:stylesheet version="1.0"
    xmlns="urn:schemas-microsoft-com:office:spreadsheet"
    xmlns:xsl="http://www.w3.org/1999/XSL/Transform"
    xmlns:ss="urn:schemas-microsoft-com:office:spreadsheet">
  <xsl:output method="xml" indent="yes" />
  <xsl:template match="ss:Workbook">
    <xsl:processing-instruction name="mso-application">progid="Excel.Sheet"
</xsl:processing-instruction>
    <xsl:element name="ss:Workbook">
        <xsl:copy-of select="ss:Styles" />
        <xsl:for-each select="ss:Worksheet">
            <xsl:if test="count(ss:Table/ss:Row/ss:Cell/ss:Data) &gt; 0">
                <xsl:copy-of select="." />
```

```
          </xsl:if>
        </xsl:for-each>
      </xsl:element>
    </xsl:template>
  </xsl:stylesheet>
```

The preceding transformation copies worksheets that contain data and formatting styles used by cells in those worksheets into a new XML spreadsheet file. Empty worksheets, document properties, and other items are simply omitted. Excel still recognizes the resulting output as an XML spreadsheet since it conforms to the Excel schema and contains the mso-application processing instruction.

To see how this transformation works:

1. Create a workbook in Excel and enter some data in its worksheets.

2. Save the workbook as an XML spreadsheet named *TestStrip.xml*.

3. Process the XML spreadsheet using the sample file XSLT. Ways to process the XML file are described in the following sections.

4. In Windows Explorer, double-click on the output file. Excel will display the transformed XML as shown in Figure 15-2.

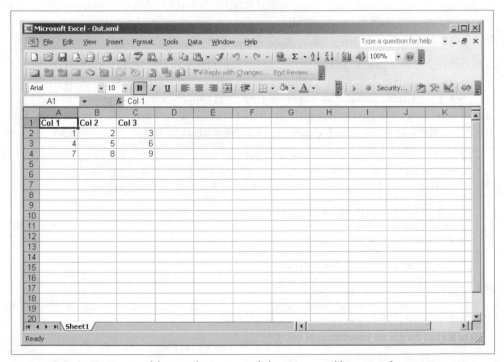

Figure 15-2. An XML spreadsheet with empty worksheets removed by a transformation

Transform in Code

As mentioned previously, there are several ways to transform XML. Transforming XML from Visual Basic code uses the Microsoft XML object library to call the Microsoft XML Parser (*msxml4.dll*). The Microsoft XML object library also provides a means to create new XML files; navigate between nodes; copy, delete, and add nodes; and more.

To perform a transformation in code, follow these steps:

1. In Visual Basic, add a reference to the Microsoft XML object library. The Microsoft XML object library provides the DOMDocument object, which is used to load, transform, and save XML documents.

2. In code, create two instances of DOMDocument objects from the Microsoft XML object library.

3. Load the XML spreadsheet in the first DOMDocument object.

4. Load the XSLT file in the second DOMDocument object.

5. Use the TransformNode method of the first DOMDocument object to perform the transformation.

For example, the following code loads the *TestStrip.xml* XML spreadsheet and *Strip.xslt* transformation, processes the transformation, and saves the result:

```
Sub Strip( )
    ' Requires reference to Microsoft XML
    Dim xdoc As New DOMDocument, xstyle As New DOMDocument
    Dim xml As String
    xdoc.Load (ThisWorkbook.path & "\TestStrip.xml")
    xstyle.Load (ThisWorkbook.path & "\Strip.xslt")
    xml = xdoc.transformNode(xstyle)
    SaveFile xml, "Out.xml"
End Sub

Sub SaveFile(content As String, fileName As String)
    ' Requires reference to Microsoft Scripting Runtime
    Dim fso As New FileSystemObject, strm As TextStream
    fileName = ThisWorkbook.path & "\" & fileName
    If fso.FileExists(fileName) Then fso.DeleteFile (fileName)
    Set strm = fso.CreateTextFile(fileName)
    strm.Write (content)
    strm.Close
End Sub
```

The preceding SaveFile helper procedure is necessary because the transformNode method returns a string containing the XML created by the transformation. Once the XML is saved, you can open the file by double-clicking on it in Windows Explorer or by using the following code:

```
Application.Workbooks.Open ("out.xml")
```

Transform from the Command Line

You can also perform transformations using the command-line transformation utility (*msxsl.exe*). *msxsl.exe* is available from Microsoft for free in the MSDN download area. It is a small shell executable that simply calls the Microsoft XML Parser to perform the transformation.

For example, the following command line transforms the *TestStrip.xml* file using the *Strip.xslt* transformation shown previously and writes the output to *Out.xml*:

```
msxsl TestStrip.xml Strip.xslt -o Out.xml
```

The output is the same as that created by using the `DOMDocument` object's `TransformNode` method shown in the preceding section. The command-line utility allows you to automate transformations using batch files rather than Visual Basic code.

Transform with Processing Instructions

Another way to perform a transformation is to include an `xml-stylesheet` processing instruction in the XML spreadsheet. The `mso-application` instruction supersedes other instructions, so you must replace that processing instruction in order to have a browser perform the translation. The following XML shows the changes you must make to the XML spreadsheet file: deletions are shown in ~~strikethrough~~, and additions are shown in **bold**:

```
<?xml version="1.0"?>
<?xml-stylesheet type="text/xsl" href="worksheet.xslt"?>
<?mso-application progid="Excel.Sheet"?>
<Workbook xmlns="urn:schemas-microsoft-com:office:spreadsheet"
  xmlns:o="urn:schemas-microsoft-com:office:office"
...
```

Now when a user opens the XML file, the file is transformed and displayed in the browser as shown in Figure 15-3.

The transformation shown in Figure 15-3 converts cells in a worksheet to HTML table elements. It also displays document properties of the workbook. The transformation is performed by the following XSLT fragment:

```
<xsl:template match="ss:Workbook">
        <html>
            <body>
            <h1>Display XML Spreadsheets as HTML Tables</h1>
            Author:
<xsl:value-of select="o:DocumentProperties/o:Author" />
<br />
            LastSaved:
<xsl:value-of select="o:DocumentProperties/o:LastSaved" />
<br />
            Number of worksheets:
```

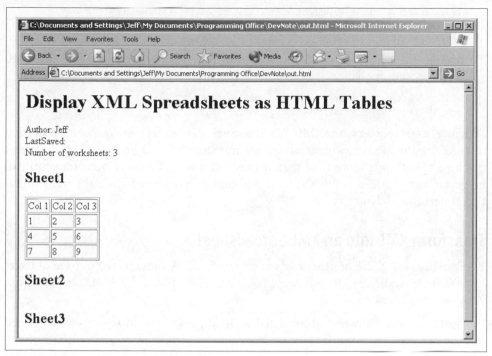

Figure 15-3. Transforming an XML spreadsheet in the browser

```
            <xsl:value-of select="count(ss:Worksheet)" />
        <xsl:for-each select="ss:Worksheet">
            <h2><xsl:value-of select="@ss:Name" /></h2>
            <table border="1" frame="box">
            <xsl:for-each select="ss:Table/ss:Row">
            <tr>
                <xsl:for-each select="ss:Cell/ss:Data">
                    <td><xsl:value-of select="." /></td>
                </xsl:for-each>
            </tr>
            </xsl:for-each>
            </table>
        </xsl:for-each>
        </body>
    </html>
```

The advantage of using a processing instruction to perform the transformation is that you don't alter the underlying content of the spreadsheet. You can switch the file back to an Excel XML spreadsheet simply by removing the xml-stylesheet instruction and replacing the mso-application instruction.

The following XSLT fragment shows a simple transformation that replaces the mso-application instruction with an xml-stylesheet instruction:

```
<xsl:template match="ss:Workbook">
    <xsl:processing-instruction name="xml-stylesheet">
```

```
type="text/xsl" href="Worksheet.xslt"</xsl:processing-instruction>
    <xsl:copy-of select="." />
</xsl:template>
```

To reverse the previous transformation, transforming the file back into an XML spreadsheet, simply change the `xsl:processing-instruction` element as shown here:

```
<xsl:processing-instruction name="mso-application">
progid="Excel.Sheet"</xsl:processing-instruction>
```

When a user requests an XML file that includes an `xml-stylesheet` processing instruction, the file is downloaded and the transformation is processed on the user's machine. That takes more time than if the XML file had already been transformed; however, any changes to the XSLT are automatically reflected since the transformation is performed dynamically.

Transform XML into an XML Spreadsheet

You can also use XSLT or other tools to transform XML files created outside of Excel into XML spreadsheets. In this way, you can create native Excel documents from your own applications.

For instance, the following abbreviated XML represents a customer order created outside of Excel:

```
<?xml version="1.0"?>
<!-- SimpleOrder.xml -->
<Orders>
<Order>
    <ID>1002</ID>
    <BillTo>
        <Address>
            <Name>Joe Magnus</Name>
            <Street1>1234 Made Up Place</Street1>
            <City>Somewhere</City>
            <State>FL</State>
            <Zip>33955</Zip>
        </Address>
    </BillTo>
    <ShipTo>
        <Address>...</Address>
    </ShipTo>
    <Line>
        <Number>20</Number>
        <Description>Mahogany Tiller</Description>
        <Quantity>1</Quantity>
        <UnitPrice>95.00</UnitPrice>
        <Taxible>Yes</Taxible>
        <Total>95.00</Total>
    </Line>
    <Line>...</Line>
```

```
        <Total>
            <SubTotal>540.00</SubTotal>
            <Tax>3.24</Tax>
            <Due>543.24</Due>
        </Total>
    </Order>
</Orders>
```

To convert this XML into an XML spreadsheet, create XSLT that creates the following nodes and processing instruction:

1. The mso-application processing instruction that identifies this file as an XML spreadsheet.

2. A root workbook node that defines the Microsoft Office namespaces.

3. A styles node defining the cell formatting to display in the worksheet. Styles include number formats, such as currency, percentage, or general number.

4. A worksheet node for each order.

5. Column nodes to set the width of the columns on the worksheet.

6. Row, cell, and data nodes for the order items you want to include in the worksheet.

Some of the preceding steps involve extensive XSLT, so it is convenient to break the steps into separate templates that are called or applied by a root template, as shown here:

```
<!-- OrderToExcel.xslt transforms an order XML file into an Excel XML spreadsheet -->
<xsl:template match="/Orders">
    <xsl:processing-instruction name="mso-application">progid="Excel.Sheet"
</xsl:processing-instruction>
    <xsl:element name="Workbook"
namespace="urn:schemas-microsoft-com:office:spreadsheet" >
    <xsl:call-template name="AddStyles" />
        <xsl:for-each select="Order">
            <!-- Create a worksheet for each order -->
            <xsl:element name="Worksheet">
                <!-- Name the worksheet -->
                <xsl:attribute name="ss:Name">
                    <xsl:value-of select="BillTo/Address/Name" />
                    <xsl:value-of select="ID" />
                </xsl:attribute>
                <xsl:element name="Table">
                <xsl:call-template name="AddColumns" />
                <!-- Add bill to headings -->
                <xsl:apply-templates select="BillTo" />
                <!-- Add send to headings -->
                <xsl:apply-templates select="ShipTo" />
                <!-- Add column headings -->
                <xsl:call-template name="AddColumnHeads" />
                    <xsl:for-each select="Line">
```

```
                <xsl:apply-templates select="." />
            </xsl:for-each>
        <xsl:call-template name="AddTotals" />
        </xsl:element>
      </xsl:element>
    </xsl:for-each>
  </xsl:element>
</xsl:template>
```

The preceding template uses `xsl:call-template` to call named templates when the content output does not depend on a specific node. A good example of this is the AddStyles template, which creates the cell formats used in the worksheet:

```
<xsl:template name="AddStyles">
 <Styles xmlns:ss="urn:schemas-microsoft-com:office:spreadsheet">
  <Style ss:ID="ColHead">
    <Alignment ss:Horizontal="Center" ss:Vertical="Bottom"/>
   <Borders>
    <Border ss:Position="Bottom" ss:LineStyle="Continuous" ss:Weight="1"/>
   </Borders>
   <Font ss:Bold="1"/>
  </Style>
  <Style ss:ID="ItemHead">
    <Alignment ss:Horizontal="Right" ss:Vertical="Bottom"/>
   <Font ss:Bold="1"/>
  </Style>
  <Style ss:ID="Currency">
   <NumberFormat ss:Format="Currency"/>
  </Style>
 </Styles>
</xsl:template>
```

Here I just insert the Excel style elements since they are static and it is fairly easy to cut/paste the style elements created by Excel into this template. This is also true for the columns element created by the AddColumns template (not shown).

The main work is performed by the following template, which is applied to each line in order to create the rows in the worksheet:

```
<xsl:template match="Line">
   <xsl:element name="Row">
      <xsl:element name="Cell">
         <xsl:element name="Data">
            <xsl:attribute name="ss:Type">Number</xsl:attribute>
            <xsl:value-of select="Number" />
         </xsl:element>
      </xsl:element>
      <xsl:element name="Cell">
         <xsl:element name="Data">
            <xsl:attribute name="ss:Type">String</xsl:attribute>
            <xsl:value-of select="Description" />
         </xsl:element>
```

```
        </xsl:element>
        <xsl:element name="Cell">
            <xsl:element name="Data">
                <xsl:attribute name="ss:Type">Number</xsl:attribute>
                <xsl:value-of select="Quantity" />
            </xsl:element>
        </xsl:element>
        <xsl:element name="Cell">
            <xsl:attribute name="ss:StyleID">Currency</xsl:attribute>
            <xsl:element name="Data">
                <xsl:attribute name="ss:Type">Number</xsl:attribute>
                <xsl:value-of select="UnitPrice" />
            </xsl:element>
        </xsl:element>
        <xsl:element name="Cell">
            <xsl:attribute name="ss:StyleID">Currency</xsl:attribute>
            <xsl:attribute name="ss:Formula">=RC[-2]*RC[-1]
              </xsl:attribute>
            <xsl:element name="Data">
                <xsl:attribute name="ss:Type">Number</xsl:attribute>
                <xsl:value-of select="Total" />
            </xsl:element>
        </xsl:element>
    </xsl:element>
</xsl:template>
```

The preceding template transforms a line node from an order into a row node in a worksheet. Two important things to note are shown in **bold**:

- First, notice that you format cells using the StyleID attribute of the cell node. This formatting includes aspects programmers sometimes consider data type, such as whether a number is currency, percentage, date, or time. It's easy to confuse this with the type attribute of the data node.

- Second, you include calculations using the Formula attribute of the cell node. The formula shown here uses row/column notation, although you can use absolute or named ranges as well.

Other templates convert the BillTo and ShipTo nodes into rows and add column heads and totals. Rather than reproduce those templates here, please refer to the *OrderToExcel.xslt* sample file. You can use that file as a starting point for converting your own XML files into XML spreadsheets.

Once processed, the transformed orders can be opened in Excel, as shown in Figure 15-4.

One of the beauties of creating your own transformations is that repeating items, such as multiple order nodes, can be mapped to items other than rows. In this sample case, each order becomes a separate worksheet, which then gets a unique name (see the worksheet tabs in Figure 15-4).

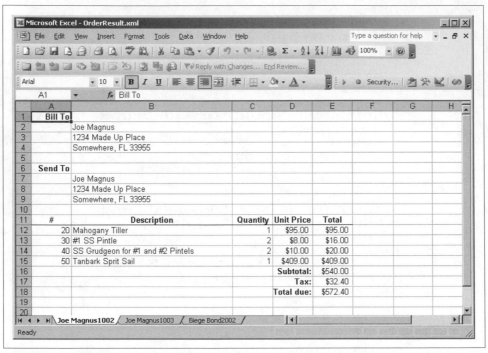

Figure 15-4. XML order information transformed into an XML spreadsheet

Use XML Maps

If all of the XSLT in the preceding sections intimidated you, relax a bit. Excel also provides graphical tools for importing XML into workbooks through XML maps. To see how this works, follow these steps:

1. Open the sample file *SimpleOrder.xml* in Excel using the regular File → Open menu item. Excel displays the Open XML dialog box (Figure 15-5).

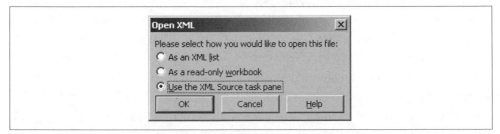

Figure 15-5. Step 1: open the XML file

2. Select the "Use the XML source task pane" option and click OK. Excel creates a new, blank workbook and informs you that the file did not contain a schema, so

Excel will infer one from the XML. Click OK. Excel displays the XML map it created in the task pane (Figure 15-6).

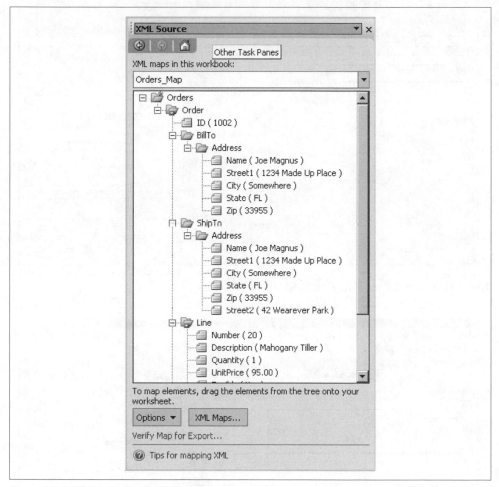

Figure 15-6. Step 2: create an XML map

3. Import XML nodes into a worksheet by selecting the nodes in the XML map and then dragging them onto a worksheet. Excel creates these new items as a list, so use multiselect to include multiple items in one list as shown in Figure 15-7.

4. Click Refresh XML Data to import the data from the XML file into the list as shown in Figure 15-8.

This tutorial works well for the summary information imported here. The order ID, name, subtotal, tax, and due nodes occur once per order. You can sort the list, filter it to see only a specific order ID, and so on. However, if you want to include the detail lines of the order, the list becomes hard to read, as shown in Figure 15-9.

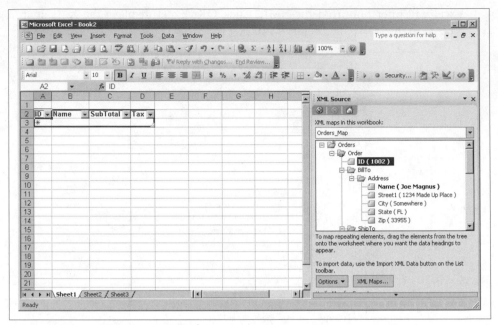

Figure 15-7. Step 3: drag nodes from the XML map to a list

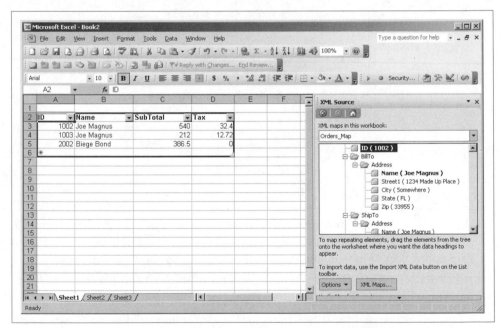

Figure 15-8. Step 4: import data into the list

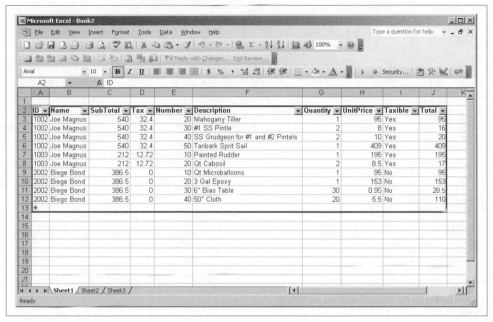

Figure 15-9. Mapped XML with summary and detail combined

Ideally, you should display the line nodes in a separate list linked to each order to create a summary/detail view. To add a detail view to the preceding example, follow these steps:

1. Drag the line node from the XML map to a cell in the same start row but one or more columns away from the summary list. Excel creates a new list for all the items in the line node.

2. Click Refresh XML Data to import the line items onto the worksheet. Excel displays all of the line items in the file.

3. Filter the summary list to display only one order. Excel automatically filters the summary list to display the line items in that order, as shown in Figure 15-10.

Excel links the summary and detail lists only if they start on the same row. Lists that start on different rows are filtered independently. The two lists must be separated by at least one column. If they are adjacent, Excel merges the XML into one list.

Limitations of XML Maps

The preceding tutorial demonstrates a subtle limitation of XML maps—optional nodes, such as Street2 in *SimpleOrder.xml*, are sometimes not imported. This occurs because Excel generates the schema from the first instance of each node it encounters.

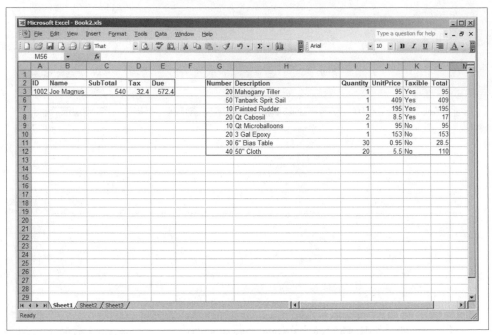

Figure 15-10. Mapped XML with summary/detail lists

To correct this, add an empty Street2 node to the first address node as shown next and open the XML as a new workbook:

```
<Address>
    <Name>Joe Magnus</Name>
    <Street1>1234 Made Up Place</Street1>
    <Street2 />
    <City>Somewhere</City>
    <State>FL</State>
    <Zip>33955</Zip>
</Address>
```

You can't update an existing XML map; you can only create new ones and delete existing ones from within Excel. This means that lists created from XML maps must be re-created any time the source XML schema changes.

Since XML maps are row-based, you can't conditionally omit optional nodes as you can with XSLT. For example, the sample transformation *OrderToExcel.xslt* omits the optional Street2 node if it is empty, using the following xsl:if element:

```
<xsl:if test="./Address/Street2 != ''">
    <xsl:element name="Row">
        <xsl:element name="Cell" />
        <xsl:element name="Cell">
            <xsl:element name="Data">
                <xsl:attribute name="ss:Type">String</xsl:attribute>
                    <xsl:value-of select="Street2" />
```

```
            </xsl:element>
        </xsl:element>
    </xsl:element>
</xsl:if>
```

You can't do that type of conditional processing with XML maps.

Another limitation is that calculated elements, such as total, import from XML as data values rather than as formulas. The sample *OrderToExcel.xslt* creates formulas to calculate line item totals as shown here:

```
<xsl:element name="Cell">
    <xsl:attribute name="ss:StyleID">Currency</xsl:attribute>
    <xsl:attribute name="ss:Formula">=RC[-2]*RC[-1]
    </xsl:attribute>
    <xsl:element name="Data">
        <xsl:attribute name="ss:Type">Number</xsl:attribute>
        <xsl:value-of select="Total" />
    </xsl:element>
</xsl:element>
```

Such calculations must be created manually on the worksheet when using XML maps.

Use Schemas with XML Maps

When Excel imports an XML file that does not reference an XML schema, it *infers* a schema from the nodes in the XML file. The preceding section explains one of the limitations of inferring a schema—optional nodes are sometimes omitted from the resulting XML map.

Another solution to this problem is to include a schema with your XML file. For example, the following XML fragment references a schema for the *SimpleOrder.xml* file:

```
<Orders xmlns="http://www.mstrainingkits.com"
    xmlns:xsi="http://www.w3.org/2001/XMLSchema-instance"
    xsi:schemaLocation="http://www.mstrainingkits.com SimpleOrder.xsd">
```

When Excel imports an XML file that references a schema, it copies that schema into the workbook. If the XML is valid according to that schema, you can drag nodes from the XML map onto the worksheet to create lists and import data as shown previously.

If the XML is not valid for the schema, however, no data will appear in the lists you create. Excel does not automatically validate XML against schemas or display errors if the XML is invalid. To validate XML within Excel:

1. From the Data menu, choose XML then choose XML Map Properties. Excel displays the XML Map Properties dialog box (Figure 15-11).

2. Select "Validate data against schema for import and export" and click OK to close the dialog box.

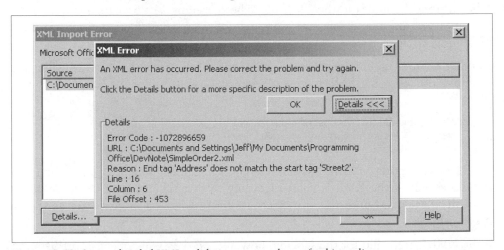

Figure 15-11. Validating XML

Now, Excel will display an error if the XML doesn't conform to the schema. Excel checks the XML against the schema whenever the XML data is imported, exported, or refreshed. You can get detailed information about validation errors by clicking Details on the XML Import Error dialog box as shown in Figure 15-12.

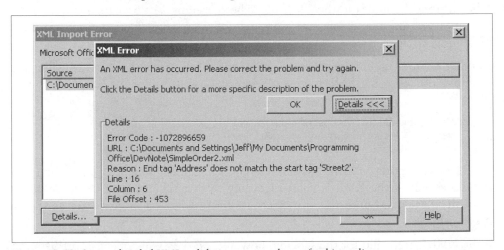

Figure 15-12. Seeing detailed XML validation errors when refreshing a list

Unfortunately, Excel copies the referenced XML schema into the XML map the first time it loads an XML file rather than referencing the schema as an external file. Subsequent changes to the schema do not affect the XML map in the workbook. Again, you can only add or delete XML maps; you can't update them from Excel.

Export XML Data Through XML Maps

Once you have created lists containing XML data, you can export that data to a new XML file from Excel two ways:

- By saving the workbook using the XML Data file type
- By clicking the Export XML toolbar button or selecting Export from the Data menu's XML submenu

In either case, you can export data using only one XML map at a time. If a workbook contains more than one XML map, you are prompted to choose the map to use, as shown in Figure 15-13.

Figure 15-13. Exporting XML uses only one XML Map at a time

When Excel exports a list as XML, it uses the schema stored in the workbook to generate XML that matches the XML source file that the list was created from. However, Excel omits the following items:

- Schema definitions
- Processing instructions
- XML nodes not included in the list

For example, if you create a list from *SimpleOrder.xml* containing only names and totals, only those elements are saved when you export the list as XML (shown here):

```
<Orders>
    <Order>
        <BillTo>
            <Address>
                <Name>Joe Magnus</Name>
            </Address>
        </BillTo>
        <Total>
            <Due>572.4</Due>
        </Total>
    </Order>
    <Order>...</Order>
</Orders>
```

In the preceding XML, the original address and order information is omitted because it wasn't included in the list. From Excel's point of view, the data doesn't exist if it doesn't reside on a worksheet somewhere.

Approaches to Using XML Maps

The limitations that come with XML maps imply a set of approaches when using them with XML. You can't just assume that you will be able to successfully import, edit, and export arbitrary XML data using Excel. XML maps are best suited for XML structured a certain way.

For example, the preceding *SimpleOrder.xml* sample requires some changes if you want to be able to view and edit orders via XML maps. Specifically:

- Each order should be stored in a separate file. XML maps can't export lists of lists, so including multiple orders, each with multiple line items, prevents you from exporting the orders.

- Line items must be presented as a separate list. Simply importing an order as a single list results in denormalized data that can't be exported from the list.

These changes and other recommendations are explained in the following sections.

Avoid lists of lists

Excel can import XML that contains lists of lists, but it can't export it. In XML schema terminology, a *list* is an element with a maxOccurs attribute greater than one. Therefore, XML using the following schema can't be exported from an XML map (significant attributes are in **bold**):

```
<xsd:element minOccurs="0" maxOccurs="unbounded" nillable="true" name="Order"
form="qualified">
    <xsd:complexType>
        <xsd:sequence minOccurs="0"> ... </xsd:sequence>
        <xsd:element minOccurs="0" maxOccurs="unbounded" nillable="true"
        name="Line" form="qualified">
            <xsd:complexType>
                <xsd:sequence minOccurs="0"> ...</xsd:sequence>
            </xsd:complexType>
        </xsd:element>
    </xsd:complexType>
</xsd:element>
```

You can solve this problem by breaking the source XML into smaller pieces. In the case of *SimpleOrder.xml*, this means creating a separate file for each order node. The XML map's root node then becomes Order, as shown in Figure 15-14.

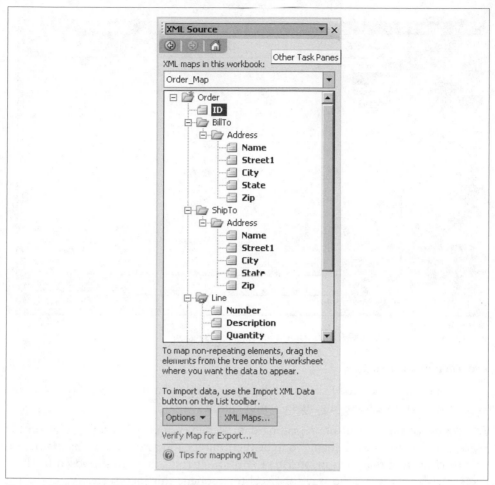

Figure 15-14. Break XML into smaller files to avoid lists of lists

You can organize the new, smaller files into a separate folder or by using a unique file extension, such as ".ord". For example, the following code allows the user to select an order file to open in Excel:

```
Sub cmdOpenOrder( )
    ' Get a filename to open. Use ".ord" extension for orders.
    Dim fname As String
    fname = Application.GetOpenFilename("Orders (*.ord),*.ord", 1, "Open an Order", _
        "Open", False)
    If fname <> "" Then
        ThisWorkbook.XmlMaps("Order_Map").Import (fname)
    End If
End Sub
```

Using the unique *.ord* file extension organizes orders as shown in Figure 15-15. Excel and XML don't care what file extension you use when importing or exporting files.

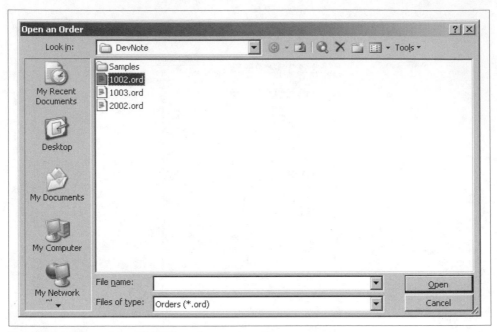

Figure 15-15. Organizing XML files using a unique file extension

Avoid denormalized data

If you drag the order node shown in Figure 15-14 onto a worksheet, you get a list containing denormalized data, as shown in Figure 15-16.

Denormalized means that nonrepeating data elements appear multiple times on the worksheet. A user could change one of the nonrepeating items, such as Name, on one row, making that item inconsistent with other rows that are supposed to show the same data. There is no way for Excel to reconcile this inconsistency, so the list can't be exported.

To avoid this, create nonrepeating and repeating nodes in separate lists, as shown in Figure 15-17.

Create an XML schema

Allowing Excel to infer a schema for an XML map is fine if the nodes don't contain optional items or if the first occurrence of each node contains all of its possible children. Otherwise, Excel may omit items from the schema it creates and some nodes won't appear in the XML map.

You can solve this problem by creating an XML schema and referencing that schema in the XML file you import. Excel copies the referenced XML schema into the XML map when the XML map is created.

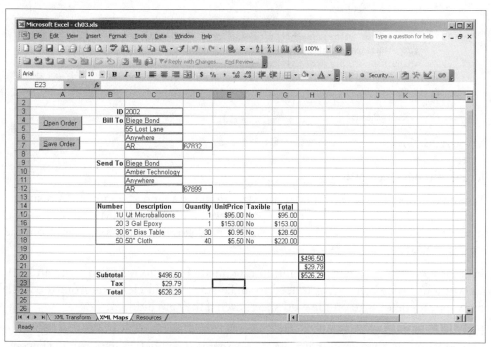

Figure 15-16. A list with denormalized data

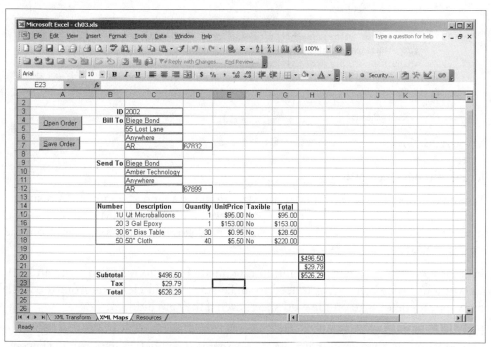

Figure 15-17. Put repeating and nonrepeating data items in separate lists to avoid denormalized data

Having an external XML schema is also useful for making changes to the XML map. As mentioned earlier, you can't update an XML map inside of Excel; you can, however, modify the XML schema stored in the workbook by editing it *outside* of Excel. To edit an XML map schema:

1. In Excel, save the workbook as an XML spreadsheet.
2. Close the workbook in Excel.
3. Open the XML spreadsheet in an XML editor. It is a good idea to use a full-featured XML editor here because the schema generated by Excel does not include whitespace such as tabs and line feeds.
4. Edit the items in the map info/schema node as needed, or simply replace the entire schema node with the contents of your external schema definition file.
5. Save the file.
6. Open the workbook in Excel and click Refresh XML Data to verify that the schema is still valid.

The XML spreadsheet nodes for the schema appear as follows. The nodes to edit or replace are highlighted in **bold**.

```
<x2:MapInfo x2:HideInactiveListBorder="false"
x2:SelectionNamespaces="xmlns:ns1='http://www.mstrainingkits.com'">
<x2:Schema x2:ID="Schema1"
x2:Namespace="http://www.mstrainingkits.com">
        <xsd:schema xmlns:xsd="http://www.w3.org/2001/XMLSchema"
        targetNamespace="http://www.mstrainingkits.com"
        xmlns:ns0="http://www.mstrainingkits.com">
                <xsd:element nillable="true" name="Order">
                ...
                </xsd:element>
        </xsd:schema>
    </x2:Schema>
</x2:MapInfo>
```

Include all nodes if exporting

When you export XML, Excel takes the data found in mapped items on worksheets, applies the XML map, and generates XML nodes defined in the XML map's schema. If some of the XML map's data nodes are not mapped, that data is omitted from the exported XML.

In some cases, this is what you want. But if you are trying to read and write an XML file without losing content, you need to make sure that all elements from the XML map appear somewhere on the worksheet (even if they are hidden).

If a node contains a calculated value, you will need to perform the calculation in a nonmapped cell, then copy that value to the mapped cell before exporting. The Save Order button in Figure 15-17 copies the calculated subtotal, tax, and total values to cells created from the XML map before exporting the XML using the following code:

```
Sub cmdSaveOrder()
    ' Update mapped cells with calculated values.
    Range("XmlSubTotal") = Range("SubTotal")
    Range("XmlTax") = Range("Tax")
    Range("XmlTotal") = Range("Total")
    ' Create filename to save.
    Dim fname As String
    fname = ThisWorkbook.path & "\" & Range("OrderID") & ".ord"
    ' Save the order.
    ThisWorkbook.XmlMaps("Order_Map").Export fname, True
End Sub
```

Other things to avoid

Excel does not support a number of other XML schema constructs when importing XML and a number of schema constructs when exporting XML. These constructs are listed in Tables 15-4 and 15-5, respectively.

Table 15-4. XML schema elements not supported when importing XML

Element	Description
any, anyAttribute	The any and anyAttribute elements allow you to include items that are not declared by the schema. Excel requires imported schemas to be explicit.
Recursive structures	Excel does not support recursive structures that are more than one level deep.
Abstract elements	Abstract elements are meant to be declared in the schema, but never used as elements. Abstract elements depend on other elements being substituted for the abstract element.
Substitution groups	Substitution groups allow an element to be swapped wherever another element is referenced. An element indicates that it's a member of another element's substitution group through the substitutionGroup attribute.
Mixed content	Mixed content is declared using mixed="true" on a complex type definition. Excel does not support the simple content of the complex type, but does support the child tags and attributes defined in that complex type.

Table 15-5. XML schema elements not supported when exporting XML

Item	Description
Lists of lists	Excel can export only repeating items that are one level deep. See the section "Avoid lists of lists," earlier in this chapter.
Denormalized data	See the section "Avoid denormalized data," earlier in this chapter.
Nonrepeating siblings	If nonrepeating items are mapped to lists, they will result in denormalized data.
Repeating elements	If the repetition is not defined by an ancestor, the data relationships can't be preserved.
Child elements from different parents	If children from different XML maps are mapped to the same list, the relationship can't be preserved.
choice	Elements that are part of an XML schema choice construct can't be exported.

Respond to XML Events

The Workbook object provides events that occur before and after data is imported or exported through an XML map. You can use these events to control how the import/export occurs, respond to errors, or cancel the operation.

For example, the following event procedures display information about import and export actions as they occur:

```
Private Sub Workbook_BeforeXmlImport(ByVal Map As XmlMap, _
    ByVal Url As String, ByVal IsRefresh As Boolean, Cancel As Boolean)
        Debug.Print "BeforeImport", Map, Url, IsRefresh, Cancel
End Sub

Private Sub Workbook_BeforeXmlExport(ByVal Map As XmlMap, _
    ByVal Url As String, Cancel As Boolean)
        Debug.Print "BeforeExport", Map, Url, IsRefresh, Cancel
End Sub

Private Sub Workbook_AfterXmlImport(ByVal Map As XmlMap, _
    ByVal IsRefresh As Boolean, ByVal Result As XlXmlImportResult)
        Debug.Print "AfterImport", Map, Url, Result
End Sub

Private Sub Workbook_AfterXmlExport(ByVal Map As XmlMap, _
    ByVal Url As String, ByVal Result As XlXmlExportResult)
        Debug.Print "AfterExport", Map, Url, Result
End Sub
```

To cancel an import or export action, set the event's *Cancel* argument to True. The following code allows the user to cancel refreshing or importing data from the Orders_Map:

```
Private Sub Workbook_BeforeXmlImport(ByVal Map As XmlMap, _
    ByVal Url As String, ByVal IsRefresh As Boolean, Cancel As Boolean)
        If Map.name = "Orders_Map" And Not IsRefresh Then
            res = MsgBox("This action will replace all the data in this list." & _
                "Do you want to continue?", vbYesNo, "Import XML")
            If res = vbNo Then Cancel = True
        End If
End Sub
```

If the import or export action is caused by code, setting *Cancel* to True causes an "Operation cancelled by user" error to occur. You should handle this exception if you allow *Cancel* to be set. For example, the following code handles the potential error when importing data:

```
' If user cancels, handle error.
On Error Resume Next
' Import data.
xmap.Import ThisWorkbook.path & "\SimpleOrder.xml"
If Err = 1004 Then Debug.Print "User cancelled import."
On Error GoTo 0
```

Program with XML Maps

The preceding sections explained how to use the new XML features found in Excel and provided code for saving, transforming, importing, and exporting XML with Excel. Those sections provide a context for Excel's XML features and explain programming tasks that surround those features. The rest of this chapter deals exclusively with the XML objects Excel provides and offers specific examples of programming tasks you can perform with those object, properties, and methods.

Excel's XML object model deals exclusively with XML maps. Opening and saving XML spreadsheets is done through the Workbook object's Open and Save methods. Figure 15-18 illustrates the Excel XML objects hierarchically.

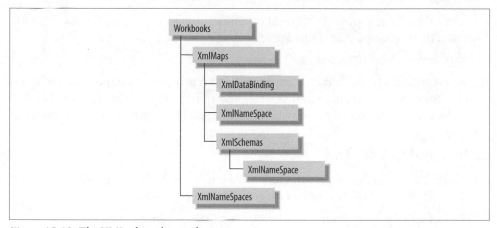

Figure 15-18. The XML object hierarchy

The XmlMap object allows you to perform the following tasks in code:

- Add XML maps to a workbook
- Delete XML maps from a workbook
- Export XML data through an XML map
- Import XML data through an XML map
- Bind an XML map to an XML data source
- Refresh mapped lists and ranges from an XML data source
- View the XML schema used by an XML map

The following sections explain these tasks in greater detail.

Add or Delete XML Maps

Use the XmlMaps collection to add or delete XML maps in a workbook. The Add method takes the location of an XML schema as its first argument, and when Excel adds an XML map to a workbook, it copies the contents of that schema into the workbook. For example, the following line creates a new XML map using the *SimpleOrder.xsd* schema file:

```
ThisWorkbook.XmlMaps.Add (ThisWorkbook.path & "\SimpleOrder.xsd")
```

If you substitute an XML source file for the XML schema, the Add method will infer a schema from the XML source. As noted earlier, inferring a schema can omit some nodes from the resulting XML map.

When Excel creates a new XML map, it names the map using the name of the root node and appending _Map. A number is added to the name if a map with that name already exists. For example, the preceding line of code creates a map named Orders_Map the first time it runs, Orders_Map2 the second time, and so on.

Use the XmlMap object's Delete method to remove a map from a workbook. The following code deletes the map named Orders_Map:

```
ThisWorkbook.XmlMaps("Orders_Map").Delete
```

If you use the Delete method on a map that is currently used to import data to a list, Excel simply deletes the map and disables the refresh XML data task for that list. Excel does not warn you as it does when you delete a map through the user interface.

Export and Import XML

Use the XmlMap object to import or export XML from code. For example, the following line imports an XML file into an existing XML map in a workbook:

```
ThisWorkbook.XmlMaps("Order_Map").Import (ThisWorkbook.Path & "\1002.ord")
```

Similarly, the XmlMap object's Export method exports XML data from a workbook. The following code exports data through an existing XML map:

```
ThisWorkbook.XmlMaps("Order_Map").Export ThisWorkbook.Path & "\1002.ord"
```

Use the ImportXml and ExportXml methods to import or export XML as a string variable rather than as a file. For example, the following code displays the contents of a list mapped using the Order_Map as XML in the Debug window:

```
Dim xmap As XmlMap, xml As String, res As XlXmlExportResult
Set xmap = ThisWorkbook.XmlMaps("Order_Map")
res = xmap.ExportXml(xml)
Debug.Print xml
```

Refresh, Change, or Clear the Data Binding

Use the Databinding object's Refresh method to refresh a list that was linked to XML data through an XML map. The Refresh method is equivalent to clicking the Refresh XML Data button on the List toolbar.

You can use the Databinding object's LoadSettings method to change the data source used by the XML map. When combined, the LoadSettings and Refresh methods are equivalent to calling the XmlMap object's Import method. The advantage of combining LoadSettings and Refresh is that changing the data source and refreshing the list are handled in separate steps, as shown here:

```
Dim xmap As XmlMap, xml As String, res As XlXmlExportResult
Set xmap = ThisWorkbook.XmlMaps("Order_Map")
' Change the data source.
xmap.DataBinding.LoadSettings (ThisWorkbook.path & "\2002.ord")
' Refresh the list from the data source.
res = xmap.DataBinding.Refresh
```

View the Schema

You can get the schema used by an XML map through the Schemas collection. Each XML map has one schema and you can't add or delete schemas through the Schemas collection.

Use the Schema object's Xml method to return the schema used by an XML map. The Xml method returns the schema without whitespace, so you will want to use a formatting helper function such as PrettyPrint when displaying the schema, as shown here:

```
Dim xmap As XmlMap, xsd As String
Set xmap = ThisWorkbook.XmlMaps("Order_Map")
xsd = xmap.Schemas(1).xml
Debug.Print PrettyPrint(xsd)
```

PrettyPrint is defined in Chapter 14 and is provided with the sample files.

XmlMap and XmlMaps Members

The XmlMaps collection and XmlMap object have the following members. Key members (shown in **bold**) are covered in the following reference section:

Add[1]	**AdjustColumnWidth**
AppendOnImport	Application[2]
Count[1]	Creator[2]
DataBinding	**Delete**
Export	**ExportXml**
Import	**ImportXml**
IsExportable	Name
Parent[2]	**PreserveColumnFilter**
PreserveNumberFormatting	**RootElementName**
RootElementNamespace	**SaveDataSourceDefinition**
Schemas	**ShowImportExportValidationErrors**

[1] Collection only
[2] Object and collection

xmlmaps.Add(*Schema*, [*RootElementName*])

Creates a new XML map and adds it to a workbook. Returns the XML map created.

Argument	Settings
Schema	The name of an XML schema file, XML datafile, schema data, or XML data to base the XML map on.
RootElementName	If the schema contains more than one root element, this is the name of the root element to use for the XML map. Otherwise, this argument can be omitted.

Excel names XML maps by appending _Map to the name of the root element of the schema. If an XML map with that name already exists, Excel adds a number to the new name.

The *Schema* argument is very flexible. It can contain a filename as a UNC or URL or it can contain the data for the schema in string format. If the *Schema* argument is XML data, rather than an XML schema, Excel infers a schema from that data. For example, the following code infers a schema from some XML data supplied as a string and creates a new XML map named Numbers_Map:

```
xml = "<Numbers><Number><One /><Two /><Three /></Number>" & _
    "<Number /></Numbers>"
Set xmap = ThisWorkbook.XmlMaps.Add(xml)
```

xmlmap.AdjustColumnWidth [= *setting*]

Sets or returns a value indicating whether to adjust the column width of mapped cells to best fit the imported data when the data is refreshed. Default is True.

xmlmap.AppendOnImport [= *setting*]

Sets or returns a value indicating whether to append data to mapped lists rather than replacing the data in the list. Default is False.

Set the AppendOnImport property to True when you want to append multiple XML data sources to a single XML map. For example, the following code stores three rows of data in a map:

```
Set xmap = ThisWorkbook.XmlMaps("Numbers_Map")
xmap.AppendOnImport = True
xmap.ImportXml ("<Numbers><Number><One>1</One><Two>2</Two>" & _
    "<Three>3</Three></Number></Numbers>")
xmap.ImportXml ("<Numbers><Number><One>4</One><Two>5</Two>" & _
    "<Three>6</Three></Number></Numbers>")
xmap.ImportXml ("<Numbers><Number><One>7</One><Two>8</Two>" & _
    "<Three>9</Three></Number></Numbers>")
```

If you change AppendOnImport to False in the preceding code, only the last row (7, 8, 9) is stored in the map.

xmlmap.DataBinding

Returns an XmlDataBinding object that you can use to refresh the data in the XML map, change the XML data source, or remove the link to an XML data source. See "XmlDataBinding Members," later in this chapter, for more information.

xmlmap.Delete

Deletes an XML map from a workbook. If a list or range uses the XML map, deleting the map removes the link to the data source, but does not remove the data displayed in the list or range. The following code deletes the XML map named Numbers_Map:

```
ThisWorkbook.XmlMaps("Numbers_Map").Delete
```

xmlmap.Export(Url, [Overwrite])

Exports mapped data in an XML map to an XML file. Returns an xlXmlExportResult constant indicating whether the export was successful.

Argument	Settings
Url	The name of the file to create.
Overwrite	True overwrites the file if Url already exists. False does not overwrite the file and triggers an error if the file already exists. Default is False.

Use the IsExportable property to determine if the data can be exported before using the Export method. Excel exports only nodes that have been mapped to a list or range. Unmapped nodes are not exported, although the file still conforms to the XML map's schema.

The following code exports mapped nodes in the XML map named Numbers_Map to create the file *Numbers.xml*:

```
Set xmap = ThisWorkbook.XmlMaps("Numbers_Map")
If xmap.IsExportable Then
    fname = ThisWorkbook.path & "\Numbers.xml"
    res = xmap.Export(fname, True)
End If
```

xmlmap.ExportXml(Data)

Exports mapped data to a string variable. Returns an xlXmlExportResult constant indicating whether the export was successful.

Argument	Settings
Data	The variable in which to store the exported XML data

The `ExportXml` method is equivalent to the Export method except for the target of the data. The following code exports mapped nodes in the XML map named `Numbers_Map` to a variable then display the contents of the variable in the Debug window:

```
Set xmap = ThisWorkbook.XmlMaps("Numbers_Map")
If xmap.IsExportable Then
    res = xmap.ExportXML(xml)
    Debug.Print xml
End If
```

*xmlmap.***Import(***Url, [Overwrite]***)**

Imports data from a file into an XML map. Returns an `xlXmlImportResult` constant indicating whether the export was successful.

Argument	Settings
Url	The name of the file to import.
Overwrite	True replaces the data in the map with the data from the file. False appends the data from the file to the data already in the map. Default is False.

The following code imports the data from *Numbers.xml* and appends the data to the data already in the XML map:

```
Dim xmap As XmlMap, fname As String, res As XlXmlExportResult
Set xmap = ThisWorkbook.XmlMaps("Numbers_Map")
fname = ThisWorkbook.path & "\Numbers.xml"
res = xmap.Import(fname, True)
```

*xmlmap.***ImportXml(***Data, [Overwrite]***)**

Imports data from a string variable into an XML map. Returns an `xlXmlImportResult` constant indicating whether the export was successful.

Argument	Settings
Data	The variable containing the XML data to import.
Overwrite	True replaces the data in the map with the data from the file. False appends the data from the file to the data already in the map. Default is False.

The following code imports three rows of data into the `Numbers_Map`:

```
Set xmap = ThisWorkbook.XmlMaps("Numbers_Map")
res = xmap.ImportXML("<Numbers><Number><One>1</One><Two>2</Two>" & _
    "<Three>3</Three></Number></Numbers>")
res = xmap.ImportXML("<Numbers><Number><One>4</One><Two>5</Two>" & _
    "<Three>6</Three></Number></Numbers>")
res = xmap.ImportXML("<Numbers><Number><One>7</One><Two>8</Two>" & _
    "<Three>9</Three></Number></Numbers>")
```

*xmlmap.*IsExportable

Returns True if the XML map can be exported, False if it cannot. Use the IsExportable property to test if the relationships established in a mapped list or range allow the data contained there to be exported.

Some types of XML data can be imported but not exported, and some lists can create denormalized data that can't be exported. See the earlier section "Approaches to Using XML Maps" for details on what types of data can be exported.

The following code tests if a map can be exported before attempting to export it to a file:

```
Set xmap = ThisWorkbook.XmlMaps("Numbers_Map")
If xmap.IsExportable Then
    res = xmap.Export("Numbers.xml")
End If
```

*xmlmap.*PreserveColumnFilter [= *setting*]

True preserves mapped list column filters when data is refreshed. False resets the filter to show all the data. Default is True.

The following code displays the PreserveColumnFilter and other general property settings for an XML map in the Debug window:

```
Set xmap = ThisWorkbook.XmlMaps("Numbers_Map")
Debug.Print "Preserve column filter? " & xmap.PreserveColumnFilter
Debug.Print "Preserve formatting? " & xmap.PreserveNumberFormatting
Debug.Print "Root node name: " & xmap.RootElementName
Debug.Print "Root namespace: " & xmap.RootElementNamespace
Debug.Print "Save data source definition? " & xmap.SaveDataSourceDefinition
Debug.Print "Show validation errors? " & xmap.ShowImportExportValidationErrors
```

*xmlmap.*PreserveNumberFormatting [= *setting*]

True preserves number formatting in mapped cells when data is refreshed. False resets the number formatting in mapped cells. Default is True.

*xmlmap.*RootElementName

Returns the name of the root node in the XML map.

*xmlmap.*RootElementNamespace

Returns the namespace of the root node in the XML map.

*xmlmap.*SaveDataSourceDefinition [= *setting*]

True saves the name of the XML data source in the workbook. False discards the name of the data source. Default is True.

Use the SaveDataSourceDefinition property to prevent the data in an XML map from being refreshed. For example, the following code imports data from the file *Numbers.xml* but disables the Refresh XML Data button in the user interface:

```
Set xmap = ThisWorkbook.XmlMaps("Numbers_Map")
fname = ThisWorkbook.path & "\Numbers.xml"
res = xmap.Import(fname, True)
xmap.SaveDataSourceDefinition = False
```

*xmlmap.*Schemas

Returns the XmlSchemas collection for the XML map. You can use the XmlSchemas collection to get information about the schema used in the XML map, but you can't change the schema in an XML map. See "XmlSchema and XmlSchemas Members," later in the chapter, for more information.

*xmlmap.*ShowImportExportValidationErrors [= *setting*]

True if Excel displays schema validation errors when an XML map is refreshed or when it imports or exports data. False if Excel does not display validation errors. Default is False.

XmlDataBinding Members

Use the XmlDataBinding object to refresh or change the data source of an XML map. Use the XmlMap object's DataBinding method to get a reference to this object. The XmlDataBinding object has the following members. Key members (shown in **bold**) are covered in the following reference section:

```
Application
ClearSettings
Creator
LoadSettings
Parent
Refresh
SourceUrl
```

xmldatabinding.ClearSettings

Removes the data binding for an XML map, disabling the List toolbar's Refresh XML Data button. Calling the ClearSettings method is equivalent to setting the XmlMap object's SaveDataSourceDefinition property to False.

The following code imports data into an XML map, then removes the map's binding to the source file (*Numbers.xml*):

```
Set xmap = ThisWorkbook.XmlMaps("Numbers_Map")
fname = ThisWorkbook.path & "\Numbers.xml"
res = xmap.Import(fname, True)
xmap.DataBinding.ClearSettings
```

xmldatabinding.LoadSettings(*Url*)

Sets the data source for an XML map.

Argument	Settings
Url	The name of the file or web service to use as a data source. May be a UNC or URL.

The following code sets the data source for an XML map and refreshes the data in that map from the new data source:

```
Set xmap = ThisWorkbook.XmlMaps("Order_Map")
xmap.DataBinding.LoadSettings (ThisWorkbook.path & "\2002.ord")
res = xmap.DataBinding.Refresh
```

xmldatabinding.Refresh

Refreshes the data in an XML map from its data source. The Refresh method is equivalent to clicking the List toolbar's Refresh XML Data button.

xmldatabinding.SourceUrl

Returns the filename or web service name of the data source for an XML map. The following code displays the data source used for an XML map:

```
Set xmap = ThisWorkbook.XmlMaps("Order_Map")
Debug.Print xmap.DataBinding.SourceUrl
```

XmlNamespace and XmlNamespaces Members

Use the Workbook object's XmlNamespaces method to get a reference to the XmlNamespaces collection. Use the XmlDataBinding object's RootElementNamespace method to get a reference to the XmlNamespace object for a specific XML map. The XmlNamespaces collection and XmlNamespace object have the following members. Key members (shown in **bold**) are covered in the following reference section:

```
Application²
Count¹
Creator²
InstallManifest¹
Parent²
Prefix
Uri
Value¹
```

[1] Collection only
[2] Object and collection

XmlNamespace objects are used with both Smart documents and XML maps. Their use with XML maps is informational—you can't add or modify namespaces through the XmlNamespaces collection or XmlNamespace object.

xmlnamespaces.InstallManifest(*Path*, [*InstallForAllUsers*])

Installs an XML expansion pack for use with Smart documents.

Argument	Settings
Path	The name of the file containing the XML expansion pack manifest.
InstallForAllUsers	True registers the XML expansion pack for all users of the computer; False registers for only the current user. Default is False.

The user must have sufficient permissions to install an XML expansion pack. The following code installs one of the sample expansion packs from the Smart Document SDK for all users:

```
sdoc = "C:\Program Files\Microsoft Office 2003 Developer Resources" & _
    "\Microsoft Office 2003 Smart Document SDK\Samples\SimpleSample" & _
    "\SourceFiles\manifest.xml"
ThisWorkbook.XmlNamespaces.InstallManifest sdoc, True
```

xmlnamespace.Prefix

Returns the prefix used with a namespace. The following code displays the prefix and URI for the root namespace used in an XML map:

```
Dim xmap As XmlMap
Set xmap = ThisWorkbook.XmlMaps("Orders_Map")
Debug.Print xmap.RootElementNamespace.Prefix
Debug.Print xmap.RootElementNamespace.Uri
```

xmlnamespace.Uri

Returns the URI for a namespace.

xmlnamespaces.Value

Returns a string containing all the namespaces loaded in a workbook. The following code displays the namespaces from a workbook in the Debug window:

```
Debug.Print ThisWorkbook.XmlNamespaces.Value
```

XmlSchema and XmlSchemas Members

Use the XmlMap object's Schemas method to return the XmlSchemas collection. The XmlSchemas collection and XmlSchema object have the following members. Key members (shown in **bold**) are covered in the following reference section:

Application[2]
Count[1]
Creator[2]
Name
Namespace
Parent[2]
XML

[1] Collection only
[2] Object and collection

Most XML maps contain one schema, so the XmlSchemas collection usually contains only one item.

xmlschema.Namespace

Returns the target namespace used by the schema. The following code displays the target namespace for a schema in the Debug window:

```
Set xmap = ThisWorkbook.XmlMaps("Orders_Map")
Debug.Print xmap.Schemas(1).Namespace
```

xmlschema.XML

Returns the schema definition as a string. Omits whitespace characters such as tabs and line feeds. The following code displays the schema definition for an XML map in the Debug window:

```
Set xmap = ThisWorkbook.XmlMaps("Orders_Map")
xsd = xmap.Schemas(1).xml
Debug.Print PrettyPrint(xsd)
```

The PrettyPrint helper function formats the XML to add tabs and line feeds. PrettyPrint is defined in Chapter 14 and is included with the sample code.

Get an XML Map from a List or Range

Use the XPath object to get or set the XML mapping used by a list column or a range. Figure 15-19 shows the relationship between these objects.

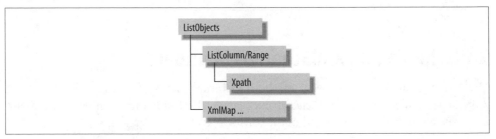

Figure 15-19. Getting an XML map from a list column or range

You can use the XPath object to add or remove mappings to list columns or ranges as described in the following sections.

Map XML to a List Column

Use the XPath object's SetValue method to map data from an XML map to a list column or range. SetValue allows you to dynamically create lists from an XML map. For example, the following code creates a new list, adds three columns to that list, and maps each column to a different node in an XML map:

```
Set ws = ThisWorkbook.Sheets("Sheet1")
Set xmap = ThisWorkbook.XmlMaps("Numbers_Map")
' Create a list object.
Set lo = ws.ListObjects.Add(xlSrcRange, [A1])
' Add a column to the list.
Set lc = lo.ListColumns.Add
' Map the column to an element in an XML map.
lc.XPath.SetValue xmap, "/Numbers/Number/One", , True
' Repeat for two more columns.
Set lc = lo.ListColumns.Add
lc.XPath.SetValue xmap, "/Numbers/Number/Two", , True
Set lc = lo.ListColumns.Add
lc.XPath.SetValue xmap, "/Numbers/Number/Three", , True
```

Remove a Mapping

Use the XPath object's `Clear` method to remove a mapping from a list column or range. For example, the following code removes the mappings from the list created in the preceding section:

```
Set ws = ThisWorkbook.Sheets("Sheet1")
Set lo = ws.ListObjects(1)
For Each lc In lo.ListColumns
    lc.XPath.Clear
Next
```

XPath Members

The XPath object has the following members. Key members (shown in **bold**) are covered in the following reference section:

```
Application
Clear
Creator
Map
Parent
Repeating
SetValue
Value
```

xpath.Clear

Removes an XML mapping from a list column or range. Use this method to remove elements from an XML map. For example, the following code removes the mappings for each of the columns in a list:

```
Set ws = ThisWorkbook.Sheets("Sheet1")
Set lo = ws.ListObjects(1)
For Each lc In lo.ListColumns
    lc.XPath.Clear
Next
```

xpath.Map

Returns the XmlMap object for a mapped range or list column. You can use the returned XmlMap object to refresh data or get information about the mapping. For example, the following code displays a list of each of the mapped cells on a worksheet:

```
Set ws = ThisWorkbook.Sheets("Sheet1")
For Each rng In ws.UsedRange
    If rng.XPath <> "" Then
```

```
         str = rng.Address & "Map : " & rng.XPath.Map.Name
         str = str & " Node: " & rng.XPath
         Debug.Print str
      End If
   Next
```

xpath.Repeating

Returns True if the mapped item is a list column. Returns False if the mapped item is a range containing a single cell.

xpath.SetValue(*Map*, *XPath*, [*SelectionNamespace*], [*Repeating*])

Maps a node from an XML map to a list column or range. Use SetValue when creating new lists or ranges from XML maps.

Argument	Settings
Map	The XmlMap object to use for the mapping.
XPath	A string containing the XPath of the node to map to the list column or range.
SelectionNamespace	A string containing the namespace prefix used in the preceding XPath. The namespace takes the form "xmlns:*prefix*='*namespace*'".
Repeating	True indicates the mapping repeats; False indicates the mapping is to a single cell in a range. Must be True or omitted when mapping to a list column.

The *SelectionNamespace* argument is required only if the specified XPath uses a different namespace from that shown in the XML map. For example, the Orders_Map sample includes the namespace prefix ns1. Since this namespace is defined in the workbook, you can omit the *SelectionNamespace* argument, as shown here:

```
Set xmap = ThisWorkbook.XmlMaps("Orders_Map")
[A10].XPath.SetValue xmap, _
  "/ns1:Orders/ns1:Order/ns1:BillTo/ns1:Address/ns1:Street1"
```

If, however, the XPath uses a different prefix, you must define that new namespace prefix using *SelectionNamespace*, as shown here:

```
[A10].XPath.SetValue xmap, _
  "/ord:Orders/ord:Order/ns1:BillTo/ord:Address/ord:Street1", _
  "xmlns:ord='http://www.mstrainingkits.com'"
```

Use the *Repeating* argument to map a repeating node to a single cell. For example, the preceding code creates a list column at cell A10 since Street1 is a repeating node in the Orders_Map. To map that node to a single cell, specify a *Repeating* argument of False:

```
[A10].XPath.SetValue xmap, _
  "/ns1:Orders/ns1:Order/ns1:BillTo/ns1:Address/ns1:Street1", , False
```

Now, Excel does not create a list column and instead maps the first data item in the source XML to the cell A10.

xpath.Value

Returns the XPath name of the node mapped to a list column or range. For example, the following code displays the XPaths for each of the columns in a mapped list:

```
Set ws = ThisWorkbook.Sheets("Sheet1")
Set lo = ws.ListObjects(1)
For Each lc In lo.ListColumns
    Debug.Print lc.XPath.Value
Next
```

Resources

To learn about	Look here
XML/XSD/XSLT tutorials	*http://www.w3schools.com/*
Office 2003 XML schemas and documentation	*http://www.microsoft.com/office/xml/default.mspx*
Free IE XML validation/XSL transformation viewer	Search for "Validating XSLT" at *http://www.microsoft.com/downloads/*
Free XML/XSL Editor	*http://xmlcooktop.com/*
XML/XSL debugger (free trial)	*http://new.xmlspy.com/products_ide.html*

CHAPTER 16

Charting

Excel is perhaps the preeminent business tool for charting data. It's hard to find a business presentation, technical report, or even a school science project that doesn't chart data, usually through Excel.

In fact, charting is so important that I devote two chapters to it. This chapter covers the primary tasks: how to create different types of charts in code and how to control the main parts of a chart. The following chapter covers the secondary charting tasks.

This chapter includes task-oriented reference information for the following objects and their related collections: Axis, Chart, ChartGroup, ChartObject, DataTable, Point, Series, and SeriesLines.

 Code used in this chapter and additional samples are available in *ch16.xls*.

Navigate Chart Objects

Charting is the most complex part of the Excel object model. To simplify it a bit, I've divided the objects into two chapters. This chapter discusses the core objects used to create charts from data; Chapter 17 covers the lower-level objects used to control the appearance of the parts of a chart. Figure 16-1 illustrates this division of chart objects.

Create Charts Quickly

Use the Chart object's ChartWizard method to create charts quickly in code. ChartWizard is a shortcut through the complex chart object model that lets you chart data in two steps:

1. Create a new Chart object in the workbook.
2. Call the ChartWizard method on that object.

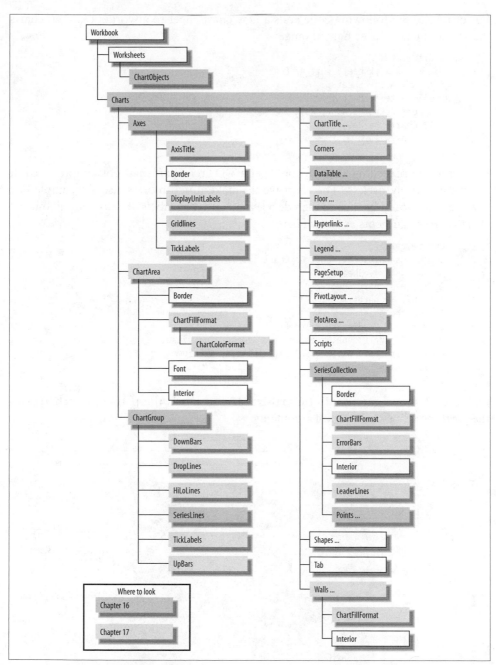

Figure 16-1. *Guide to the chart objects*

For example, the following code adds a new chart sheet to a workbook, then charts data from the HomeSales named range:

```
Sub ChartWizard1()
    Dim ws As Worksheet, chrt As Chart
    Set ws = ActiveSheet
    ' 1) Create a chart sheet.
    Set chrt = Charts.Add(, ws)
    ' 2) Chart the data.
    chrt.ChartWizard ws.[HomeSales]
End Sub
```

If you run the preceding sample, you'll get a 3-D area chart that looks impressive but is almost entirely useless. The chart would make much more sense as a simple line chart, and it would be nice to include a legend and axis labels. To do that, fill out the ChartWizard arguments as shown here:

```
Sub ChartWizard2()
    Dim ws As Worksheet, chrt As Chart
    Set ws = ActiveSheet
    ' Create a chart sheet.
    Set chrt = Charts.Add(, ws)
    ' Name the sheet.
    chrt.Name = "Median FL Prices"
    ' Specify chart type, axis labels, legend, and title.
    chrt.ChartWizard ws.[HomeSales], xlLine, , xlColumns, 1, 1, True, _
        "FL Median Home Prices", "Year", "Price"
End Sub
```

Figure 16-2 shows the result of ChartWizard2 and labels the parts of the chart with the corresponding ChartWizard arguments.

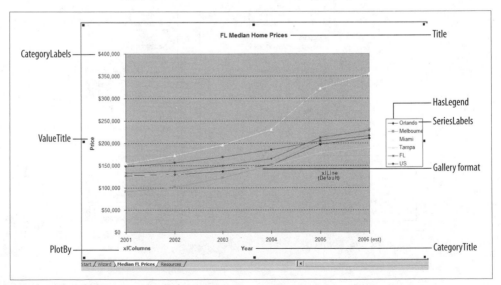

Figure 16-2. Chart parts with corresponding ChartWizard arguments

You can use `ChartWizard` to change existing charts, too. For example, the following code changes the preceding chart's type and title to demonstrate several types of charts:

```
Sub ChangeChart( )
    Dim chrt As Chart
    ' Get the chart sheet.
    Set chrt = Charts("Median FL Prices")
    ' Change the chart type and title.
    chrt.ChartWizard , xlBar, , xlColumns, 1, 1, True, _
        "Bar Chart"
    Application.Wait Now + 0.00003
    chrt.ChartWizard , xlBar, 8, xlColumns, 1, 1, True, _
        "FL Median Home Prices (Bar 8)"
    Application.Wait Now + 0.00003
    chrt.ChartWizard , xlArea, , xlColumns, 1, 1, True, _
        "Area Chart"
    Application.Wait Now + 0.00003
    chrt.ChartWizard , , , xlRows, 1, 1, True, _
        "Area Chart by Row"
    Application.Wait Now + 0.00003
    chrt.ChartWizard , xlLine, 10, xlColumns, 1, 1, True, _
        "FL Median Home Prices (Smooth)"
End Sub
```

`ChangeChart` rotates through different chart types pausing between each. This is a good way to learn about chart settings, and it's fun, too.

Embed Charts

Charts may exist as separate sheets, as shown in the preceding section, or they can be embedded on a worksheet using the `ChartObjects` collection. To embed a chart quickly, use the `Add` method to create a new `ChartObject`, then use that object's `Chart` property to control the underlying chart:

```
Sub EmbedChart( )
    Dim ws As Worksheet, co As ChartObject, chrt As Chart
    Set ws = ActiveSheet
    ' Create an embedded chart object.
    Set co = ws.ChartObjects.Add(40, 160, 400, 200)
    ' Name the ChartObject so it's easy to get later.
    co.Name = "FL Median Home Prices"
    ' Get the underlying Chart object.
    Set chrt = co.Chart
    ' Plot the chart using the ChartWizard method.
    chrt.ChartWizard [HomeSales], xlLine, , xlColumns, 1, 1, True, _
        "FL Median Home Prices"
End Sub
```

The `ChartObject` is simply a container for the chart on the worksheet. You use it to set the size and position of the chart on the worksheet, but for anything else you use the underlying Chart object. For example, the following code gets the Chart object from the embedded chart and rotates through different chart types:

```
Sub ChangeEmbeddedChart( )
    Dim ws As Worksheet, chrt As Chart
    Set ws = ActiveSheet
    ' Get the chart.
    Set chrt = ws.ChartObjects("FL Median Home Prices").Chart
    ' Change the chart type and title.
    chrt.ChartWizard , xlBar, , xlColumns, 1, 1, True, _
      "Bar Chart"
    Application.Wait Now + 0.00003
    chrt.ChartWizard , xlBar, 8, xlColumns, 1, 1, True, _
      "FL Median Home Prices (Bar 8)"
    Application.Wait Now + 0.00003
    chrt.ChartWizard , xlArea, , xlColumns, 1, 1, True, _
      "Area Chart"
    Application.Wait Now + 0.00003
    chrt.ChartWizard , , , xlRows, 1, 1, True, _
      "Area Chart by Row"
    Application.Wait Now + 0.00003
    chrt.ChartWizard , xlLine, 10, xlColumns, 1, 1, True, _
      "FL Median Home Prices (Smooth)"
End Sub
```

ChangeEmbeddedChart does the same thing as ChangeChart, shown earlier; the main difference is how you get the reference to the Chart object.

Create More Complex Charts

You don't have to use the ChartWizard method to plot a chart. If you like, you can use the individual chart members instead. The following code illustrates creating a stock chart without ChartWizard:

```
Sub CreateChart( )
    Dim ws As Worksheet, chrt As Chart
    Set ws = ActiveSheet
    ' Create the chart
    Set chrt = ThisWorkbook.Charts.Add(, ws)
    ' Name the chart sheet.
    chrt.Name = "Stock Price History"
    ' Plot the data in a named range.
    chrt.SetSourceData ws.[HistoryData], xlColumns
    ' Set the chart type to Open, High, Low, Close.
    chrt.ChartType = xlStockOHLC
    ' Dates are in descending order, so reverse the axis.
    chrt.Axes(xlCategory).ReversePlotOrder = True
End Sub
```

The main reason to use this approach rather than the ChartWizard method is that the ChartType property supports the full set of xlChartType constants. ChartWizard supports only a subset. The xlStockOHLC type is one of the types not available through

ChartWizard. Another reason to use this approach is that it doesn't add much complexity if you are already changing other chart settings, such as reversing the plot order as shown earlier.

The disadvantage of this approach is that you have to know what properties and methods control each aspect of the chart. The easiest way to solve this riddle is to turn on Macro Recording, create your chart, format it as you want it to appear, then turn off Macro Recording and examine the generated code.

For example, this code was generated in response to reformatting the chart created by the CreateChart procedure. I added comments to note the steps you can follow to generate the same code:

```
' Recorded code (annotated).
Sub Macro7()
    ' Choose Tools>Chart Options>Title and enter titles.
    With ActiveChart
        .HasTitle = True
        .ChartTitle.Characters.Text = "MSFT"
        .Axes(xlValue, xlPrimary).HasTitle = True
        .Axes(xlValue, xlPrimary).AxisTitle.Characters.Text = "Price"
    End With
    ' Select the Legend tab on Options and clear Show Legend.
    ActiveChart.HasLegend = False
    ' Right-click the plot area, select Format Plot Area,
    ' and set the Area Color to None.
    ActiveChart.PlotArea.Select
    Selection.Interior.ColorIndex = xlNone
    ' Right-click the y-xis, select Format Axis and set the scale.
    ActiveChart.Axes(xlValue).Select
    With ActiveChart.Axes(xlValue)
        .MinimumScale = 20
        .MaximumScale = 30
        .MinorUnitIsAuto = True
        .MajorUnitIsAuto = True
        .Crosses = xlAutomatic
        .ReversePlotOrder = False
        .ScaleType = xlLinear
        .DisplayUnit = xlNone
    End With
End Sub
```

As you can see, Excel records items as they are selected and includes more property settings than I actually changed. You can remove those things to clean the code up a bit:

```
' Based on recorded code.
Sub ChangeChart()
    Dim chrt As Chart
    Set chrt = Charts("Stock Price History")
    With chrt
        ' Change: get title from a named range.
        .HasTitle = True
```

```
        .ChartTitle.Characters.Text = UCase([Symbol])
        ' Note how confusing the Axes collection is!
        .Axes(xlValue, xlPrimary).HasTitle = True
        .Axes(xlValue, xlPrimary).AxisTitle.Characters.Text = "Price"
        .HasLegend = False
        ' ActiveChart.PlotArea.Select returns a PlotArea object.
        .PlotArea.Interior.ColorIndex = xlNone
        ' Change the scale settings for the y-axis.
        .Axes(xlValue).MinimumScale = WorksheetFunction.Min([HistoryData])
        .Axes(xlValue).MaximumScale = WorksheetFunction.Max([HistoryData])
    End With
End Sub
```

Figure 16-3 shows the resulting chart with some of the major objects labeled.

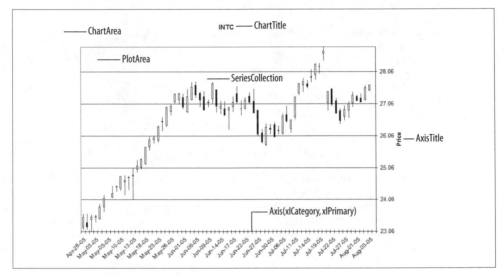

Figure 16-3. Major objects on a chart

Choose Chart Type

The ChartType property controls what type of chart to plot, but not all chart types are compatible with the data you may want to chart. For example, the xlStockOHLC chart plotted in the preceding section requires four series in a particular order: Open, High, Low, and Close prices. To try out different chart types:

1. Select the data to chart, then choose Insert → Chart to start the Chart Wizard.

2. Select a chart type and subtype then click the button below the subtype list to preview the result, as shown in Figure 16-4.

3. If the selected data doesn't match what is required by the chart type, the preview displays a message explaining the problem.

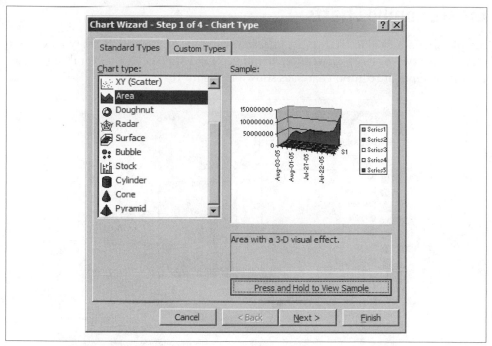

Figure 16-4. Trying out different chart types

Again, you can record your actions to find out the xlChartType constant for the chart type you want.

The DemoChartTypes procedure in the sample workbook cycles through all of the available ChartType settings, pausing after each. You can use that procedure to choose from the many chart types and find the corresponding xlChartType constant. That procedure is too long to reproduce in print, so here is an abridged version:

```
Sub DemoChartTypes()
    Dim chrt As Chart, secs As Double
    secs = 1 / 100000
    Set chrt = Charts("Demo Chart Types")
    chrt.Activate
    chrt.ChartType = xl3DAreaStacked
    chrt.ChartTitle.Caption = "ChartType: xl3DAreaStacked"
    chrt.Refresh
    Application.Wait Now + secs
    ' Repeat for each xlChartType constant (omitted here).
    chrt.ChartType - xlXYScatter
    chrt. ChartTitle.Caption = "ChartType: xlXYScatter"
    chrt.Refresh
End Sub
```

Create Combo Charts

Simple charts have one chart type: line, bar, column, or another chart type. Combo charts have two or more chart types combined for a single chart. Several of the custom chart types are combo charts, as shown in Figure 16-5.

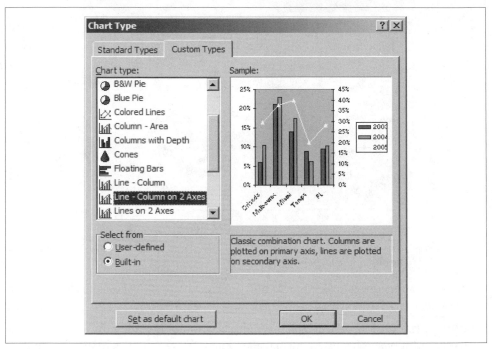

Figure 16-5. Some of the custom charts combine chart types

To create a combo chart in code, use the `ApplyCustomType` method as shown here:

```
Sub CreateComboChart1( )
    Dim chrt As Chart
    ' Create a new chart sheet
    Set chrt = ThisWorkbook.Charts.Add
    ' Name the sheet.
    chrt.Name = "Combo Chart 1"
    ' Plot the data from a named range.
    chrt.SetSourceData [HomeSales], xlColumns
    ' Make the chart a combo chart
    chrt.ApplyCustomType xlBuiltIn, "Line - Column on 2 Axes"
End Sub
```

The custom chart types automatically choose which series to plot with which chart type. In the preceding code, the series is divided equally between column and line chart types. To control that a little more carefully, use the `Series` object's `ChartType` property to create the combo chart instead:

```
Sub CreateComboChart2()
    Dim chrt As Chart, sc As SeriesCollection
    ' Create a new chart sheet
    Set chrt = ThisWorkbook.Charts.Add
    ' Name the sheet.
    chrt.Name = "Combo Chart 2"
    ' Plot the data from a named range.
    chrt.SetSourceData [HomeSales], xlColumns
    ' Set chart type
    chrt.ChartType = xlColumnClustered
    ' Get the series collection
    Set sc = chrt.SeriesCollection
    ' Change the type of the last series
    sc(sc.Count).ChartType = xlLineMarkers
End Sub
```

Now, only the last series is a line chart. You can combine any number of 2-D chart types in this way, but you can't combine 3-D chart types. Setting any series to a 3-D chart type changes the type for the entire chart. In other words, only 2-D charts can be combo charts.

Excel groups series with the same chart type into ChartGroup objects. A chart has one ChartGroup for each different chart type it displays. Simple charts have one ChartGroup; combo charts have two or more.

The ChartGroup object provides access to properties that are specific to the chart type. To get the ChartGroup object, use the Chart object's ChartGroups property or one of the type-specific Chart properties listed here:

Area3DGroup	AreaGroups
Bar3DGroup	BarGroups
Column3DGroup	ColumnGroups
DoughnutGroups	Line3DGroup
LineGroups	Pie3DGroup
PieGroups	RadarGroups
SurfaceGroup	XYGroups

The group properties for 2-D chart types (AreaGroups, BarGroups, etc.) return collections with one item for each subtype of chart. The group properties for 3-D charts (Area3DGroup, Bar3DGroup, etc.) return a single ChartGroup object: 3-D charts have only one chart group.

Add Titles and Labels

The following Chart objects can have captions that serve as titles or labels:

```
AxisTitle
ChartTitle
DataLabel
DisplayUnitLabel
```

To add a caption to one of these objects in code, follow these general steps:

1. Make sure the object exists. For example, to ensure ChartTitle exists, set the HasTitle property to True.

2. Set the Caption property of the title.

3. Refresh the chart to display the changes. This step is not always required, but since charts are not always immediately updated, adding a Refresh statement is good insurance.

 Setting the Caption property and setting Characters.Text (shown earlier) are equivalent. Excel records setting chart titles using Characters.Text, but you can change that to make it shorter.

The following code adds captions to the chart and primary axes:

```
Sub AddTitles()
    Dim chrt As Chart, ax As Axis
    Set chrt = Charts("Demo Chart Types")
    chrt.ChartType = xl3DBarStacked
    chrt.Activate
    ' Make sure ChartTitle exists
    chrt.HasTitle = True
    ' Set caption
    chrt.ChartTitle.Caption = "Total Four-Year Appreciation"
    ' Make sure axis exists
    chrt.HasAxis(xlValue, xlPrimary) = True
    Set ax = chrt.Axes(xlValue, xlPrimary)
    ' Make sure AxisTitle exists
    ax.HasTitle = True
    ' Set caption
    ax.AxisTitle.Caption = "Primary Value Axis"
    ax.AxisTitle.Orientation = xlHorizontal
    chrt.HasAxis(xlValue, xlPrimary) = True
    Set ax = chrt.Axes(xlCategory, xlPrimary)
    ax.HasTitle = True
    ax.AxisTitle.Caption = "Primary Category Axis"
    ax.AxisTitle.Orientation = xlUpward
    ' Update chart to ensure changes are displayed.
    chrt.Refresh
End Sub
```

Adding data label captions is more complex, since they are part of the SeriesCollection hierarchy. The following code turns on data labels for each series and highlights labels that exceed 25 percent by making those captions bold:

```
Sub HightlightDataLabels()
    Dim chrt As Chart, se As Series, dl As DataLabel
    Set chrt = Charts("Demo Chart Types")
    ' Make sure data labels exist
    For Each se In chrt.SeriesCollection
        se.HasDataLabels = True
        For Each dl In se.DataLabels
```

```
                If CInt(VBA.Replace(dl.Caption, "%", "")) > 25 Then
                    dl.Font.Bold = True
                Else
                    dl.Font.Bold = False
                End If
            Next
        Next
        ' Update chart to ensure changes are displayed.
        chrt.Refresh
    End Sub
```

Figure 16-6 shows the result of running the `AddTitles` and `HighlightDataLabels` procedures.

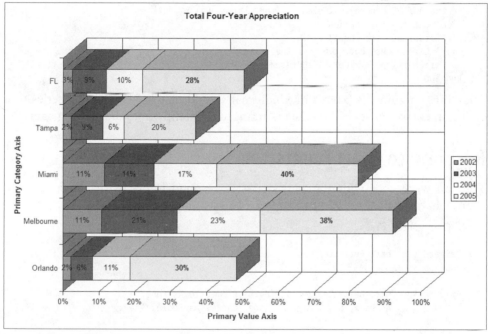

Figure 16-6. Adding chart, axis, and data label captions

Plot a Series

The data plotted on a chart belongs to the chart's `SeriesCollection`. Each column or row of data is represented by a `Series` object and each item in the series is represented by a `Point` object.

You can add series to existing charts by calling the `Add`, `Extend`, or `NewSeries` methods of the `SeriesCollection`. For example, the first of the following procedures creates a new line chart, and the second plots a new series using the column chart type:

```
Sub CreateChart( )
    Dim chrt As Chart
```

```
        Set chrt = Charts.Add(, ActiveSheet)
        chrt.Name = "Plot a Series"
        chrt.SetSourceData [HomeSales], xlColumns
        chrt.ChartType = xlLine
    End Sub

    Sub AddNewSeries()
        Dim chrt As Chart, sc As SeriesCollection, _
          sr As Series
        ' Get the chart.
        Set chrt = Charts("Plot a Series")
        ' Get the series collection.
        Set sc = chrt.SeriesCollection
        ' Add a new series.
        sc.Add [FLGrowth], xlColumns, True, False, False
        ' Get the last series
        Set sr = sc(sc.Count)
        ' Change the chart type for the series.
        sr.ChartType = xlColumnClustered
    End Sub
```

The *PlotBy* arguments (xlRows or xlColumns) should match when adding series to a
chart, unless of course the new data is arranged differently from the existing data.

Respond to Chart Events

You can write code within a chart's class to respond to events that occur on the
chart. Charts provide these events:

```
' Chart sheet class

Private Sub Chart_Activate()
End Sub

Private Sub Chart_BeforeDoubleClick(ByVal ElementID As Long, _
  ByVal Arg1 As Long, ByVal Arg2 As Long, Cancel As Boolean)
End Sub

Private Sub Chart_BeforeRightClick(Cancel As Boolean)
End Sub

Private Sub Chart_Calculate()
End Sub

Private Sub Chart_Deactivate()
End Sub

Private Sub Chart_DragOver()
End Sub

Private Sub Chart_DragPlot()
End Sub
```

```
Private Sub Chart_MouseDown(ByVal Button As Long, ByVal Shift As Long, _
   ByVal x As Long, ByVal y As Long)
End Sub

Private Sub Chart_MouseMove(ByVal Button As Long, _
   ByVal Shift As Long, ByVal x As Long, ByVal y As Long)

End Sub

Private Sub Chart_MouseUp(ByVal Button As Long, _
   ByVal Shift As Long, ByVal x As Long, ByVal y As Long)
End Sub

Private Sub Chart_Resize()
End Sub

Private Sub Chart_Select(ByVal ElementID As Long, _
   ByVal Arg1 As Long, ByVal Arg2 As Long)
End Sub

Private Sub Chart_SeriesChange(ByVal SeriesIndex As Long, _
   ByVal PointIndex As Long)
End Sub
```

The BeforeDoubleClick and Select events return information about the chart item that was clicked. Those arguments are described in Table 16-1 with the GetChartElement topic later.

Chart and Charts Members

Use the Charts collection to add chart sheets to a workbook. Use the Workbook object's Charts property to get a reference to this collection. Use the Chart object to plot numeric data graphically. The Charts collection and Chart object have many of the same members as the Worksheets collection and Worksheet object. Key members that are unique to charts (shown in **bold**) are covered in the following reference section:

Add[1]	Application[2]	**ApplyCustomType**
ApplyDataLabels	**Area3DGroup**	**AreaGroups**
AutoFormat	**AutoScaling**	**Axes**
Bar3DGroup	**BarGroups**	**BarShape**
ChartArea	**ChartGroups**	**ChartObjects**
ChartTitle	**ChartType**	**ChartWizard**
CheckSpelling	**CodeName**	**Column3DGroup**
ColumnGroups	Copy[2]	**CopyPicture**
Corners	Count[1]	**CreatePublisher**
Creator[2]	**DataTable**	Delete[2]
DepthPercent	**Deselect**	**DisplayBlanksAs**
DoughnutGroups	**Elevation**	Evaluate

Export	**Floor**	**GapDepth**
GetChartElement	**HasAxis**	**HasDataTable**
HasLegend	**HasPivotFields**	**HasTitle**
HeightPercent	HPageBreaks[1]	Hyperlinks
Index	Item[1]	**Legend**
Line3DGroup	**LineGroups**	**Location**
MailEnvelope	Move[2]	Name
Next	OLEObjects	PageSetup
Parent[2]	Paste	**Perspective**
Pie3DGroup	**PieGroups**	**PivotLayout**
PlotArea	**PlotBy**	**PlotVisibleOnly**
Previous	PrintOut[2]	PrintPreview[2]
Protect	ProtectContents	ProtectData
ProtectDrawingObjects	ProtectFormatting	ProtectGoalSeek
ProtectionMode	ProtectSelection	RadarGroups
Refresh	**RightAngleAxes**	**Rotation**
SaveAs	Scripts	**Select**[2]
SeriesCollection	**SetBackgroundPicture**	**SetSourceData**
Shapes	**ShowWindow**	**SizeWithWindow**
SurfaceGroup	Tab	Type
Unprotect	Visible[2]	VPageBreaks[1]
Walls	**WallsAndGridlines2D**	**XYGroups**

[1] Collection only
[2] Object and collection

chart.Add([*Before*], [*After*], [*Count*])

Creates one or more chart sheets and returns a reference to the first Chart object created.

Argument	Settings
Before	The sheet in the workbook before which the new chart sheet is placed.
After	The sheet in the workbook after which the new chart sheet is placed.
Count	The number of chart sheets to add. Default is 1.

You can't specify both the *Before* and *After* arguments; you must choose one. The following code creates three new chart sheets at the beginning of a workbook and names the first sheet New Chart:

```
Sub AddCharts( )
    Dim chrt As Chart
    Set chrt = Charts.Add(Sheets(1), , 3)
    chrt.Name = "New Chart"
End Sub
```

The other two charts receive default names (Chart*n*).

*chart.*ApplyCustomType(*ChartType, [TypeName]*)

Applies an autoformat to a chart.

Argument	Settings
ChartType	xlBuiltIn selects from a set of built-in autoformats; xlUserDefined selects from a set of user-defined autoformats.
TypeName	The name of the autoformat to apply.

 If you omit *TypeName*, ApplyCustomType is equivalent to setting the ChartType property and the *ChartType* argument then accepts xlChartType constants.

To see the available autoformats, select a chart, choose Chart → Chart Type, and click the Custom Types tab. The *ChartType* and *TypeName* arguments correspond to items on the Chart Type dialog box as shown in Figure 16-7.

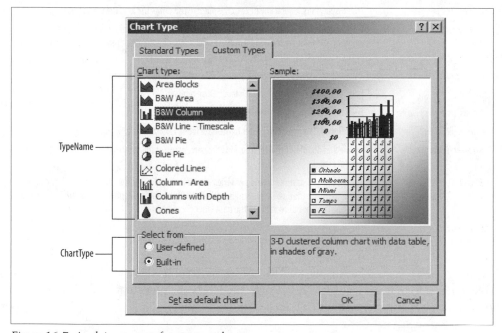

Figure 16-7. Applying an autoformat to a chart

The following code applies the B&W Column autoformat to a chart:

```
Sub ApplyAutoFormat()
    Dim chrt As Chart
    Set chrt = Charts("New Chart")
    chrt.ApplyCustomType xlBuiltIn, "B&W Column"
End Sub
```

chart.ApplyDataLabels([*Type*], [*LegendKey*], [*AutoText*], [*HasLeaderLines*], [*ShowSeriesName*], [*ShowCategoryName*], [*ShowValues*], [*ShowPercentage*], [*ShowBubbleSize*], [*Separator*])

Applies data labels to all of the series on the chart.

Argument	Settings
Type	An xlDataLabelsType constant specifying the type of labels to display. Can be one of the following: xlDataLabelsShowBubbleSizes xlDataLabelsShowLabelAndPercent xlDataLabelsShowPercent xlDataLabelsShowLabel xlDataLabelsShowNone xlDataLabelsShowValue (default) Not all *Type* settings are valid for all types of charts. xlDataLabelsShowPercent and xlDataLabelsShowLabelAndPercent apply to only pie and doughnut chart types. Set *Type* to xlDataLabelsShowNone to remove all data labels from a chart.
LegendKey	True displays the legend key next to the point; False omits the key. Default is False.
AutoText	True automatically generates an appropriate data label based on the type of chart and whether axis titles are included; False uses the *Show* argument settings to determine the label content. Default is True
HasLeaderLines	True displays leader lines for each series; False omits leader lines. Default is False.
ShowSeriesName	True adds the series name to each label; False omits it.
ShowCategoryName	True adds the category axis value to each label; False omits it.
ShowValues	True adds the value of each point to the data label; False omits it.
ShowPercentage	For pie and doughnut charts, True adds the percentage of the total that the value represents to the data label.
ShowBubbleSize	Bubble charts plot three values per series: the first two values determine the x and y position of the item; the third value determines the size of the bubble. Setting *ShowBubbleSize* to True displays that third value in the data label.
Separator	The character used to separate series name, category name, value, and percentage within the data label. Default is comma.

ApplyDataLabels is also available for the Series and Point objects. For example, the following code animates a chart by displaying data labels one point at a time with the series name, then all at once (without the series name):

```
Sub AnimateDataLabels()
    Dim chrt As Chart, sr As Series, pt As Point
    Set chrt = Charts("New Chart")
    ' Use a custom chart type.
    chrt.ApplyCustomType xlBuiltIn, "Smooth Lines"
    For Each sr In chrt.SeriesCollection
        For Each pt In sr.Points
            ' Clear all data labels.
            chrt.ApplyDataLabels xlDataLabelsShowNone
            ' Apply labels to each point in turn.
```

```
            pt.ApplyDataLabels xlDataLabelsShowLabel, , False _
                , , True, False, True
            ' Wait one second.
            Application.Wait Now + 0.00001
        Next
    Next
    ' Show all data labels.
    chrt.ApplyDataLabels xlDataLabelsShowLabel, , False _
        , , False, False, True
End Sub
```

chart.**Area3DGroup**

Returns the ChartGroup object representing the series that are plotted using a 3-D area chart type.

chart.**AreaGroups([***Index***])**

Returns a collection of ChartGroup objects representing series that are plotted using 2-D area chart types.

chart.**AutoFormat(***Gallery*, [*Format*])

This method is now hidden; it is replaced by the ChartType property. It is equivalent to calling the ChartWizard method on an existing chart and omitting the *Source* argument.

chart.**AutoScaling [=** *setting*]

True scales a 3-D chart so that it is closer to the size of an equivalent 2-D chart. Valid only if the RightAngleAxis property is True. Default is True.

chart.**Axes([Type], [AxisGroup])**

Returns one or all of the axes on a chart.

Argument	Settings
Type	For 2-D charts, xlCategory returns the x-axis; xlValue returns the y-axis. For 3-D charts, xlSeries returns the z-axis.
AxisGroup	For 2-D charts, xlPrimary returns primary axis; xlSecondary returns the secondary axis. Default is xlPrimary. Cannot be xlSecondary for 3-D charts.

The following code applies labels to identify the x-, y-, and z-axes of a 3-D chart:

```
Sub LabelAxes()
    Dim chrt As Chart, ax As Axis
    Set chrt = Charts("Demo Chart Types")
```

```
              ' Activate the chart sheet.
              chrt.Activate
              ' Change chart type to 3-D.
              chrt.ApplyCustomType xl3DLine
              ' Get the category axis.
              Set ax = chrt.Axes(xlCategory)
              ' Add a title.
              ax.HasTitle = True
              ' Set the title.
              ax.AxisTitle.Caption = "Category"
              ' Repeat for value axis.
              Set ax = chrt.Axes(xlValue)
              ax.HasTitle = True
              ax.AxisTitle.Caption = "Value"
              ' Repeat for series axis.
              Set ax = chrt.Axes(xlSeries, xlPrimary)
              ax.HasTitle = True
              ax.AxisTitle.Caption = "Series"
          End Sub
```

*chart.*Bar3DGroup

Returns the ChartGroup object representing the series that are plotted using a 3-D bar chart
type.

*chart.*BarGroups([*Index*])

Returns a collection of ChartGroup objects representing series that are plotted using 2-D bar
chart types.

*chart.*BarShape [=*xlBarShape*]

Sets or returns the shape used for bars or columns in a 3-D chart. Can be one of these
settings:

```
xlBox
xlConeToPoint
xlPyramidToMax
xlConeToMax
xlCylinder
xlPyramidToPoint
```

*chart.*ChartArea

Returns the ChartArea object for the chart. Use the ChartArea object to control the appearance of the region outside of the plot area. The following code highlights the chart area:

```
Sub ChangeChartArea( )
    Dim chrt As Chart, ca As ChartArea
    Set chrt = Charts("New Chart")
    Set ca = chrt.ChartArea
     ca.Interior.Pattern = XlPattern.xlPatternGray8
End Sub
```

*chart.*ChartGroups([*Index*])

Returns one or all of the ChartGroup objects in a chart. Each ChartGroup represents one or more series of a particular chart type. Most charts have one chart group; however, combo charts have two or more chart groups. You can't combine 2-D and 3-D chart types, so all of the chart groups are either 2-D or 3-D.

*chart.*ChartObjects([*Index*])

Returns the ChartObjects embedded on a chart sheet. You can embed charts on a chart sheet to plot other data or show other views on the same sheet. The primary chart on a chart sheet is not embedded and is not part of the ChartObject collection.

*chart.*ChartTitle

Returns the ChartTitle object representing the title displayed on the chart. Make sure the HasTitle property is True before using this object. For example, the following code adds a title to a chart:

```
Sub AddTitle( )
    Dim chrt As Chart, ct As ChartTitle
    Set chrt = Charts("New Chart")
    chrt.HasTitle = True
    Set ct = chrt.ChartTitle
    ct.Caption = "New Title"
End Sub
```

*chart.*ChartType [= *xlChartType*]

Sets or returns an xlChartType constant that determines the kind of chart plotted. Can be one of these settings:

xl3DArea	xl3DAreaStacked
xl3DAreaStacked100	xl3DBarClustered
xl3DBarStacked	xl3DBarStacked100
xl3DColumn	xl3DColumnClustered
xl3DColumnStacked	xl3DColumnStacked100
xl3DLine	xl3DPie
xl3DPieExploded	xl3DSurface

xlArea	xlAreaStacked
xlAreaStacked100	xlBarClustered
xlBarOfPie	xlBarStacked
xlBarStacked100	xlBubble
xlBubble3DEffect	xlColumnClustered
xlColumnStacked	xlColumnStacked100
xlConeBarClustered	xlConeBarStacked
xlConeBarStacked100	xlConeCol
xlConeColClustered	xlConeColStacked
xlConeColStacked100	xlCylinderBarClustered
xlCylinderBarStacked	xlCylinderBarStacked100
xlCylinderCol	xlCylinderColClustered
xlCylinderColStacked	xlCylinderColStacked100
xlDefaultAutoFormat	xlDoughnut
xlDoughnutExploded	xlLine
xlLineMarkers	xlLineMarkersStacked
xlLineMarkersStacked100	xlLineStacked
xlLineStacked100	xlPie
xlPieExploded	xlPieOfPie
xlPyramidBarClustered	xlPyramidBarStacked
xlPyramidBarStacked100	xlPyramidCol
xlPyramidColClustered	xlPyramidColStacked
xlPyramidColStacked100	xlRadar
xlRadarFilled	xlRadarMarkers
xlStockHLC	xlStockOHLC
xlStockVHLC	xlStockVOHLC
xlSurface	xlSurfaceTopView
xlSurfaceTopViewWireframe	xlSurfaceWireframe
xlXYScatter	xlXYScatterLines
xlXYScatterLinesNoMarkers	xlXYScatterSmooth
xlXYScatterSmoothNoMarkers	

 Set ChartType to xlDefaultAutoFormat to restore a chart to Excel's default settings.

See the DemoChartTypes procedure in the sample workbook for an animated preview of the available chart types.

chart.ChartWizard([Source], [Gallery], [Format], [PlotBy], [CategoryLabels], [SeriesLabels], [HasLegend], [Title], [CategoryTitle], [ValueTitle], [ExtraTitle])

Quickly creates and formats a chart by setting the most commonly used properties and applying a best guess for omitted settings.

Argument	Settings
Source	The Range object containing the data to chart.
Gallery	A constant indicating the type of chart to create. Can be one of these settings: xl3DArea, xl3DBar, xl3DColumn, xl3DLine, xl3DPie, xl3DSurface, xlArea, xlBar, xlColumn, xlCombination, xlDefaultAutoFormat, xlDoughnut, xlLine, xlPie, xlPie, xlRadar, or xlXYScatter.
Format	A number from 1 to 10 indicating the index of the chart subtype to create from the Chart Type dialog box.
PlotBy	xlRows plots each row as a series; xlColumns plots each column as a series.
CategoryLabels	The number of rows or columns in the source range that contain category labels.
SeriesLabels	The number of rows or columns in the source range that contain series labels.
HasLegend	True creates a legend on the chart; False omits the legend.
Title	The caption to include as the title on the chart. Omitting this argument when creating a chart omits the chart title.
CategoryTitle	The caption to include for the category axis (x-axis) on the chart. Omitting this argument when creating a chart omits the axis title.
ValueTitle	The caption to include for the value axis (y-axis) on the chart. Omitting this argument when creating a chart omits the axis title.
ExtraTitle	The caption to include for the series axis (z-axis) on a 3-D chart. Omitting this argument when creating a chart omits the axis title.

ChartWizard can be used either to plot a new chart or to change an existing chart. When changing a chart, omitted arguments default to the existing chart's settings. When creating a new chart, omitted arguments default to best-guess settings based on the type of data being charted and the type of chart selected.

Settings for the *Gallery* argument are not actually xlChartType constants as the Excel Help says. Some of the possible settings are found in xlChartType, but ChartWizard actually supports a subset of those constants plus a few not found in xlChartType: xl3DBar, xlBar, xlColumn, and xlCombination. Each of those general chart types allows a *Format* argument setting that corresponds to the index of the subtype shown in the Chart Type dialog box (Figure 16-8).

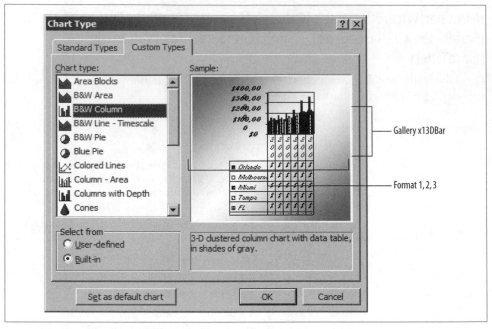

Figure 16-8. How Gallery and Format correspond to chart types

chart.CodeName

Returns the Visual Basic class name of the chart sheet.

chart.Column3DGroup

Returns the ChartGroup object representing the series that are plotted using a 3-D column chart type.

chart.ColumnGroups([Index])

Returns a collection of ChartGroup objects representing series that are plotted using 2-D column chart types.

chart.CopyPicture([Appearance], [Format], [Size])

Copies the image of a chart into the clipboard.

Argument	Settings
Appearance	The resolution of the image. Can be one of these settings: xlPrinter, xlScreen. Default is xlScreen.
Format	The image format. Can be one of these settings: xlBitmap, xlPicture. Default is xlPicture.

Argument	Settings
Size	xlScreen sizes the picture to match the size displayed on screen; xlPrinter sizes the picture to match the printed size.

The following code copies a bitmap of a chart onto the clipboard so that it can be later pasted by the user:

```
Sub DemoCopyPicture( )
    Dim chrt As Chart
    Set chrt = Charts("Demo Chart Types")
    ' Copy a chart image into the clipboard.
    chrt.CopyPicture xlScreen, xlBitmap
End Sub
```

chart.Corners

Returns the Corners object of a 3-D chart.

chart.CreatePublisher([*Edition*], [*Appearance*], [*Size*], [*ContainsPICT*], [*ContainsBIFF*], [*ContainsRTF*], [*ContainsVALU*])

Macintosh only. Creates a publisher for a chart.

Argument	Settings
Edition	The file name of the edition.
Appearance	The resolution. Can be one of these settings: xlPrinter, xlScreen. Default is xlPrinter.
Size	xlScreen sizes the image to match the size displayed on screen; xlPrinter sizes the image to match the printed size.
ContainsPICT	True includes PICT format data. Default is True.
ContainsBIFF	True includes BIFF format data. Default is True.
ContainsRTF	True includes RTF format data. Default is True.
ContainsVALU	True includes VALU format data. Default is True.

chart.DataTable

Returns the DataTable object for the chart. Make sure the HasDataTable property is True before using this object. For example, the following code adds a data table to a chart and makes the table's font italic:

```
Sub GetDataTable( )
    Dim chrt As Chart
    Set chrt = Charts("New Chart")
    chrt.HasDataTable = True
    chrt.DataTable.Font.Italic = True
End Sub
```

*chart.***DepthPercent** [= *setting*]

Sets or returns the depth (z-axis) of a 3-D chart as a percentage of its width. Must be between 20 and 2000. Default is 100.

*chart.***Deselect( )**

Cancels the selection of a chart.

*chart.***DisplayBlanksAs** [= *xlDisplayBlanksAs*]

Sets or returns how omitted values are plotted. Can be one of these settings:

```
xlNotPlotted
xlInterpolated
xlZero
```

*chart.***DoughnutGroups([*Index*])**

Returns a collection of ChartGroup objects representing series that are plotted using doughnut chart types.

*chart.***Elevation** [= *setting*]

Sets or returns the angle at which you view a 3-D chart in degrees. Must be between -90 and 90 for most 3-D chart types and between 0 and 44 for 3-D bar charts.

*chart.***Floor**

Returns the Floor object for a 3-D chart.

*chart.***GapDepth** [= *setting*]

Sets or returns the distance between series on a 3-D chart as a percentage of the marker width. Must be between 0 and 500. Default is 50.

*chart.***GetChartElement(***x, y, ElementID, Arg1, Arg2***)**

Gets information about the chart object at specific screen coordinates.

Argument	Settings
x	The x-coordinate of the object.
y	The y-coordinate of the object.

Argument	Settings
ElementID	An xlChartItem constant identifying the type of object at (x, y). See Table 16-1.
Arg1	Information about the object. See Table 16-1.
Arg2	Information about the object. See Table 16-1.

The *x* and *y* arguments are input arguments; *ElementID*, *Arg1*, and *Arg2* are output arguments. The meaning of the output arguments varies based on the type of object (x, y); Table 16-1 describes those returned values.

Table 16-1. Meaning of GetChartElement output arguments

If ElementID is...	then Arg1 is...	and Arg2 is...
xlAxis, xlAxisTitle, xlDisplayUnitLabel, xlMajorGridlines, or xlMinorGridlines	xlAxisGroup	xlAxisType
xlPivotChartDropZone	xlPivotFieldOrientation	Not set
xlPivotChartFieldButton	xlPivotFieldOrientation	The index of the column in the PivotFields collection of the item
xlDownBars, xlDropLines, xlHiLoLines, xlRadarAxisLabels, xlUpBars	The index of the group within the ChartGroups collection	Not set
xlChartArea, xlChartTitle, xlCorners, xlDataTable, xlFloor, xlLegend, xlNothing, xlPlotArea, or xlWalls	Not set	Not set
xlDataLabel or xlSeries	The index of the series in the SeriesCollection of the chart	The index of the point in the Points collection of the series
xlErrorBars, xlLegendEntry, xlLegendKey, xlXErrorBars, or xlYErrorBars	The index of the series in the SeriesCollection of the chart	Not set
xlShape	The index of the shape in the Shapes collection of the chart	Not set
xlTrendline	The index of the series in the SeriesCollection of the chart	The index of the trendline in the Trendlines collection of the series

The following code displays information about a chart element in the Immediate window when you click on objects in the chart:

```
' Add this code to the Chart sheet class

' Display element info when chart is clicked.
Private Sub Chart_MouseDown(ByVal Button As Long, _
  ByVal Shift As Long, ByVal x As Long, ByVal y As Long)
    Dim chrt As Chart, id As Long, arg1 As Long, arg2 As Long
    Set chrt = Charts("New Chart")
    arg1 = 0: arg2 = 0
```

```
        chrt.GetChartElement x, y, id, arg1, arg2
        Debug.Print id, arg1, arg2
    End Sub
```

chart.**HasAxis(***xlAxisGroup*, *xlAxisType***)** [= *setting*]

True adds an axis to the chart; False removes the axis.

Argument	Settings
xlAxisGroup	The axis to add or remove. Can be one of these settings: xlCategory, xlValue, or xlSeriesAxis (3-D only).
xlAxisType	For 2-D charts can be xlPrimary or xlSecondary. For 3-D charts, can only be xlPrimary.

Charts can have up to four axes, so HasAxis is a 2-D array of True/False values that determines which axes exist on the chart. Be sure to check HasAxis before working with an axis object.

chart.**HasDataTable** [= *setting*]

True adds a data table on the chart; False removes the data table.

chart.**HasLegend** [= *setting*]

True adds a legend to the chart; False removes the legend.

chart.**HasPivotFields** [= *setting*]

For pivot charts, True displays pivot controls and False hides the controls. Default is True for pivot charts, False for other types of charts.

chart.**HasTitle** [= *setting*]

True adds a title to the chart; False removes the title.

chart.**HeightPercent** [= *setting*]

Sets or returns the height (y-axis) of a 3-D chart as a percentage of its width. Must be between 5 and 500. Default is 100.

chart.**Legend**

Returns the Legend object from the chart. Make sure the HasLegend property is True before using this object.

chart.**Line3DGroup**

Returns the ChartGroup object representing the series that are plotted using a 3-D line chart type.

chart.**LineGroups([*Index*])**

Returns a collection of ChartGroup objects representing series that are plotted using 2-D line chart types.

chart.**Location(*Where*, [*Name*])**

Moves the chart to a new worksheet or chart sheet.

Argument	Settings
Where	An xlChartLocation constant that specifies the type of location to move to. Can be one of these settings: xlLocationAsNewSheet, xlLocationAsObject, or xlLocationAutomatic.
Name	The name of the target worksheet or chart sheet.

The Location method removes the chart from its current location and inserts it in the new location. For example, the first procedure in the following code block removes the chart sheet New Chart and inserts the chart as an embedded object on the Start worksheet; the second procedure moves the embedded chart back to a chart sheet:

```
Sub MoveChartToStart()
    Dim chrt As Chart
    Set chrt = Charts("New Chart")
    chrt.Location xlLocationAsObject, "Start"
End Sub

Sub MoveChartBack()
    Dim chrt As Chart
    Set chrt = Worksheets("Start").ChartObjects(1).Chart
    chrt.Location xlLocationAsNewSheet
    ActiveSheet.Name = "New Chart"
End Sub
```

chart.**Perspective [= *setting*]**

Sets or returns the perspective for a 3-D chart. Must be between 0 and 100.

chart.**Pie3DGroup**

Returns the ChartGroup object representing the series that are plotted using a 3-D pie chart type.

*chart.*PieGroups([*Index*])

Returns a collection of ChartGroup objects representing series that are plotted using 2-D pie chart types.

*chart.*PivotLayout

For pivot charts, returns the PivotLayout object from a chart.

*chart.*PlotArea

Returns the PlotArea object of a chart. The PlotArea represents the background on which the chart is plotted. The ChartArea is the larger background surrounding the PlotArea.

*chart.*PlotBy [= *xlRowCol*]

Sets or returns an xlRowCol constant that determines whether series are plotted by row or by column. Can be one of these settings:

```
xlColumns
xlRows
```

*chart.*PlotVisibleOnly [= *setting*]

True plots only rows or columns that are visible in the source range; False plots both visible and hidden data.

Returns a collection of ChartGroup objects representing series that are plotted using 2-D radar chart types.

*chart.*Refresh( )

Refreshes the chart. Charts automatically refresh when their data changes, but Refresh ensures that updates occur immediately.

*chart.*RightAngleAxes [= *setting*]

For 3-D line, bar, and column charts, True places the axes at right angles, ignoring the Perspective settings.

*chart.*Rotation [= *setting*]

For 3-D charts, sets or returns the angle by which the chart is rotated. Must be between 0 and 44 for 3-D bar charts and 0 and 360 for other 3-D types. The following code makes a chart spin around:

```
Sub RotateChart( )
    Dim chrt As Chart, deg As Integer
    Set chrt = Charts("New Chart")
    chrt.ChartType = xl3DArea
    For deg = 15 To 360
        chrt.Rotation = deg
    Next
    chrt.Rotation = 15
End Sub
```

*chart.*Select([*Replace*])

Selects one or all chart sheets in a workbook.

Argument	Settings
Replace	True replaces the current selection with the selected chart or charts; False adds the selection to the current selection. Default is True.

*chart.*SeriesCollection([*Index*])

Returns one or all of the series plotted on the chart. In a line chart, each line is a series and each series represents a row or column of data (depending on the PlotBy property setting).

*chart.*SetBackgroundPicture(*Filename*)

Displays a picture in the chart sheet background.

Argument	Settings
Filename	The file name of the picture to use. The picture is tiled to fill the entire sheet background. Set *Filename* to " " to clear the background picture.

*chart.*SetSourceData(*Source*, [*PlotBy*])

Sets the range to plot in the chart.

Argument	Settings
Source	The Range object to plot.
PlotBy	xlRows plots each row as a series; xlColumns plots each column as a series.

Use SetSourceData to plot new data. This is easier than adding items to the SeriesCollection.

chart.**ShowWindow** [= *setting*]

For embedded charts, copies an image of the chart to its own window in Excel. ShowWindow seems to work only if the embedded chart is activated as shown by this code:

```
Sub ChartWindow( )
    Worksheets("Wizard").Activate
    ActiveSheet.ChartObjects(1).Activate
    ActiveChart.ShowWindow = True
End Sub
```

chart.**SizeWithWindow** [= *setting*]

For chart sheets, True scales the chart to match the size of the Excel window; False does not scale. Default is True.

chart.**SurfaceGroup**

Returns the ChartGroup object representing the series that are plotted using a surface chart type.

chart.**Walls**

For 3-D charts, returns a Walls object representing the vertical visual boundary of the plot area (as opposed to the Floor, which is the other visual boundary).

chart.**WallsAndGridlines2D** [= *setting*]

For 3-D charts, True draws gridlines in 2-D format. Default is False. Any difference in the gridline appearance is minor, as illustrated by the following code:

```
Sub ThreeDGridlines( )
    Dim chrt As Chart
    Set chrt = Charts("New Chart")
    chrt.ChartType = xlSurface
    chrt.WallsAndGridlines2D = True
    chrt.Axes(xlCategory, xlPrimary).HasMajorGridlines = True
    chrt.Axes(xlValue, xlPrimary).HasMajorGridlines = True
    chrt.Axes(xlSeries, xlPrimary).HasMajorGridlines = True
End Sub
```

chart.**XYGroups**([*Index*])

Returns a collection of ChartGroup objects representing series that are plotted using xy scatter chart types.

ChartObject and ChartObjects Members

Use the ChartObjects collection to embed new charts on a worksheet or get existing embedded charts. Use the Worksheet or Chart object's ChartObjects property to get a reference to this collection. Use the individual ChartObject to get a reference to the underlying Chart object for the embedded chart. ChartObjects and ChartObject have the following members. Key members (shown in **bold**) are covered in the following reference section:

Activate	**Add**[1]
Application[2]	Border[2]
BottomRightCell	BringToFront[2]
Chart	Copy[2]
CopyPicture[2]	Count[1]
Creator[2]	Cut[2]
Delete[2]	Duplicate[2]
Enabled[2]	Group[1]
Height[2]	Index
Interior[2]	Item[1]
Left[2]	Locked[2]
Name	Parent[2]
Placement[2]	PrintObject[2]
ProtectChartObject	**RoundedCorners**[2]
Select[2]	SendToBack[2]
Shadow[2]	ShapeRange[2]
Top[2]	**TopLeftCell**
Visible[2]	Width[2]
ZOrder	

[1] Collection only
[2] Object and collection

---

chartobjects.Add(*Left, Top, Width, Height*)

Creates a blank, embedded chart on the worksheet or chart sheet.

Argument	Settings
Left	The distance between the left edge of the sheet and the right edge of the chart in points
Top	The distance between the top of the sheet and the top of the chart in points
Width	The width of the chart in points
Height	The height of the chart in points

Add does not plot the chart, so use the ChartWizard or SetSourceData methods after you create the chart. The following code shows how to quickly create an embedded chart from a selected range of cells:

```
Sub AddEmbeddedChart()
    Dim co As ChartObject
    ' Create the chart object
    Set co = ActiveSheet.ChartObjects.Add(100, 200, 400, 200)
    ' Plot the chart from the selected range.
    co.Chart.ChartWizard Selection, xl3DColumn, , xlRows
End Sub
```

chartobject.BottomRightCell

Returns the Range object for the cell that is under the lower-right corner of the embedded chart.

chartobject.Chart

Returns the Chart object for the embedded chart. You use this object to plot the chart and control the chart's appearance.

chartobjects.RoundedCorners [= *setting*]

True displays the embedded chart with rounded, rather than square, corners. Default is False.

chartobject.TopLeftCell

Returns the Range object for the cell that is under the top left corner of the embedded chart.

ChartGroup and ChartGroups Members

Use the ChartGroups collection to get individual charts from a combo chart. Use the Chart object's ChartGroups property to get a reference to this collection. Use the ChartGroup object to control chart type–specific aspects of a chart. The ChartGroups collection and ChartGroup object have the following members. Key members (shown in **bold**) are covered in the following reference section:

Application[2]	AxisGroup
BubbleScale	Count[1]
Creator[2]	**DoughnutHoleSize**

DownBars	DropLines
FirstSliceAngle	GapWidth
Has3DShading	HasDropLines
HasHiLoLines	HasRadarAxisLabels
HasSeriesLines	HasUpDownBars
HiLoLines	Index
Item[1]	Overlap
Parent[2]	RadarAxisLabels
SecondPlotSize	SeriesCollection
SeriesLines	ShowNegativeBubbles
SizeRepresents	SplitType
SplitValue	SubType
Type	UpBars
VaryByCategories	

[1] Collection only
[2] Object and collection

chartgroup.BubbleScale [= *setting*]

For bubble charts, sets or returns the percentage by which to scale the bubbles up or down. Must be between 1 and 300.

chartgroup.DoughnutHoleSize [= *setting*]

For doughnut charts, sets or returns the size of the hole as a percentage of the chart size. Must be between 10 and 90. Default is 50.

chartgroup.DownBars

For 2-D line charts with HasUpDownBars set to True, returns the UpBars object for the chart. Causes an error for other chart types.

chartgroup.DropLines

For line and area charts with HasDropLines set to True, returns the DropLines object for the chart. Causes an error for other chart types.

chartgroup.FirstSliceAngle [= *setting*]

For pie and doughnut chart types, sets or returns the rotation of the first slice in degrees clockwise from vertical. Default is 0.

chartgroup.GapWidth [= *setting*]

For bar and column chart types, sets or returns the gap between bars/columns as a percentage of the bar/column width. Must be between 0 and 500. Default is 100.

chartgroup.Has3DShading [= *setting*]

For 3D surface charts, True adds shading to the underside of the surface and False does not. Default is False. Causes an error for other chart types.

chartgroup.HasDropLines [= *setting*]

For line and area charts, True adds lines from the series point to the category axis and False omits those lines. Default is False.

chartgroup.HasHiLoLines [= *setting*]

For 2-D line charts, True adds lines between the high and low points for each category and False omits those lines. Default is False.

chartgroup.HasRadarAxisLabels [= *setting*]

For radar charts, True displays labels for the radar axes and False omits the labels. By default, radar charts have one radar axis for each category, and the category names appear as labels outside of each axis.

chartgroup.HasSeriesLines [= *setting*]

For bar and column charts, True adds lines between the each category connecting the bars/columns and False omits the lines. Default is False.

chartgroup.HasUpDownBars [= *setting*]

For 2-D line charts, True displays bars between the high and low points for each category and False does not. Default is False.

chartgroup.HiLoLines

For 2-D line charts with HasHiLoLines set to True, returns the HiLoLines object for the chart. Causes an error for other chart types.

chartgroup.Overlap [= setting]

For bar or column charts, sets the amount of overlap for bars/columns as a percentage of their width. Must be between -100 and 100. Default is 0.

chartgroup.RadarAxisLabels

For radar charts with HasRadarAxisLabels set to True (the default), returns the TickLabels collection for the radar axis.

chartgroup.SecondPlotSize [= setting]

For pie of pie charts and pie of bar charts, sets or returns the size of the secondary chart as a percentage of the size of the primary chart. Must be between 5 and 200. Default is 75.

chartgroup.SeriesLines

For bar and column charts with HasSeriesLines set to True, returns the SeriesLines object for the chart. Causes an error for other chart types.

chartgroup.ShowNegativeBubbles [= setting]

For bubble charts, True plots bubbles that have negative values and False omits them. Default is False.

chartgroup.SizeRepresents [= xlSizeRepresents]

For bubble charts, sets or returns what the size of the bubble represents. Can be one of these settings:

    xlSizeIsArea (default)
    xlSizeIsWidth

chartgroup.SplitType [= xlSplitType]

For pie of pie charts and bar of pie charts, sets or returns how the split between the chart types is displayed. Can be one of these settings:

    xlSplitByCustomSplit
    xlSplitByPercentValue
    xlSplitByPosition (default)
    xlSplitByValue

chartgroup.**SplitValue** [*= setting*]

For pie of pie charts and bar of pie charts with `SplitType` set to `xlSplitByValue` or `xlSplitByPercentValue`, sets or returns the threshold that a category must reach before it is split out of the main pie.

chartgroup.**UpBars**

For 2-D line charts with `HasUpDownBars` set to True, returns the `UpBars` object for the chart. Causes an error for other chart types.

chartgroup.**VaryByCategories** [*= setting*]

For charts containing only one series, True varies the color or pattern of each point in the series; False uses the same color or pattern for each point. Default is True.

SeriesLines Members

Use the `SeriesLines` object to control the appearance of the lines connecting series on 2-D stacked bar and column charts. Use the `ChartGroup` object's `SeriesLines` property to get a reference to this object. The `SeriesLines` object has the following members:

```
Application
Border
Creator
Delete
Name
Parent
Select
```

Set the `HasSeriesLines` property to True before using the `SeriesLines` object. You change the appearance of series lines through the `Border` property, as shown here:

```
Sub ChangeSeriesLines()
    Dim chrt As Chart, cg As ChartGroup, sl As SeriesLines
    ' Get the chart
    Set chrt = ActiveChart
    chrt.ChartType = xlColumnStacked
    ' Get the chart group.
    Set cg = ActiveChart.ChartGroups(1)
    ' Turn on series lines
    cg.HasSeriesLines = True
    Set sl = cg.SeriesLines
```

```
      ' Use dashed line.
      sl.Border.LineStyle = 2
      ' Make the lines bold.
      sl.Border.Weight = 4
  End Sub
```

 Use the Series object to change the lines plotted on a chart. Series lines apply to the lines connecting series on only 2-D column and bar charts.

Axes and Axis Members

Use the Axes collection to get the axes from a chart. Use the Chart object's Axes property to get a reference to this collection. Use the Axis object to control the scale, caption, plot order, and appearance of an axis. The Axes collection and Axis object have the following members. Key members (shown in **bold**) are covered in the following reference section:

Application[2]	**AxisBetweenCategories**
AxisGroup	**AxisTitle**
BaseUnit	**BaseUnitIsAuto**
Border	**CategoryNames**
CategoryType	Count[1]
Creator[2]	**Crosses**
CrossesAt	Delete
DisplayUnit	**DisplayUnitCustom**
DisplayUnitLabel	**HasDisplayUnitLabel**
HasMajorGridlines	**HasMinorGridlines**
HasTitle	Height
Item[1]	Left
MajorGridlines	**MajorTickMark**
MajorUnit	**MajorUnitIsAuto**
MajorUnitScale	**MaximumScale**
MaximumScaleIsAuto	**MinimumScale**
MinimumScaleIsAuto	**MinorGridlines**
MinorTickMark	**MinorUnit**
MinorUnitIsAuto	**MinorUnitScale**
Parent[2]	**ReversePlotOrder**
ScaleType	Select
TickLabelPosition	**TickLabels**
TickLabelSpacing	**TickMarkSpacing**
Top	**Type**
Width	

[1] Collection only
[2] Object and collection

axis.AxisBetweenCategories [= setting]

For category axes, True moves the start point of the category axis away from the value axis so that plotted series move in from the edges of the chart. Default is False. For other axes, causes an error. To see the effect of this property, try the following code on a line chart:

```
Sub MoveCategoryAxis( )
    Dim chrt As Chart, ax As Axis
    Set chrt = ActiveSheet
    Set ax = chrt.Axes(xlCategory, xlPrimary)
    ax.AxisBetweenCategories = True
End Sub
```

axis.AxisGroup

Returns xlPrimary if the object is the primary axis, xlSecondary if it is the secondary axis.

axis.AxisTitle

Returns the AxistTitle object for the axis. Check the HasTitle property before using this object, and use the AxisTitle Caption property to change the title as shown by the following code:

```
Sub ChangeAxisTitle( )
    Dim chrt As Chart, ax As Axis
    Set chrt = ActiveSheet
    Set ax = chrt.Axes(xlCategory, xlPrimary)
    If ax.HasTitle Then _
        ax.AxisTitle.Caption = "New Caption"
End Sub
```

axis.BaseUnit [= setting]

For category axes with CategoryType set to xlTimeScale, sets the unit of time used by the axis. Can be one of the following xlTimeUnit constants:

xlMonths

xlDays

xlYears

This property is ignored if CategoryType is not xlTimeScale; and it causes an error if the axis is not a category axis.

axis.BaseUnitIsAuto [= setting]

For category axes, True selects a BaseUnit automatically. Default is True. Set BaseUnitIsAuto to True to restore the default BaseUnit after changing that property.

axis.CategoryNames [= *setting*]

Sets or returns the array of data used by the category axis. For example, the following code changes the names on the category axis:

```
Sub SetCategoryNames()
    Dim chrt As Chart, ax As Axis
    Set chrt = ActiveSheet
    Set ax = chrt.Axes(xlCategory, xlPrimary)
    ax.CategoryNames = Array("this", "that", "the", "other")
End Sub
```

 Setting an individual element of this array may crash Excel:

```
ax.CategoryNames(1) = "foo"  ' Crash!
```

axis.CategoryType [= *xlCategoryType*]

For category axes, sets or returns the type of scale used. Can be one of these settings:

```
xlAutomaticScale (default)
xlCategoryScale
xlTimeScale
```

axis.Crosses [= *xlAxisCrosses*]

For 2-D charts, sets or returns where the value and category axes meet. Can be one of these settings:

```
xlAxisCrossesAutomatic (default)
xlAxisCrossesCustom
xlMaximum
xlMinimum
```

axis.CrossesAt [= *setting*]

For 2-D charts with Crosses set to xlAxisCrossesCustom, sets or returns the point on the axis where the other axis starts. For example, the following code moves the category axis up to 100,000 on the value axis:

```
Sub MoveCategoryAxisUp()
    Dim chrt As Chart, ax As Axis
    Set chrt = ActiveSheet
    Set ax = chrt.Axes(xlValue, xlPrimary)
    ax.Crosses = xlAxisCrossesCustom
    ax.CrossesAt = 100000
End Sub
```

*axis.*DisplayUnit [= *xlDisplayUnit*]

For value axes, sets or returns the numeric scale used by the axis. Default is xlNone. Can be one of these settings:

xlCustom	xlHundreds
xlHundredMillions	xlHundredThousands
xlMillions	xlMillionMillions
xlNone (default)	xlTenMillions
xlTenThousands	xlThousands
xlThousandMillions	

Setting this property adds a DisplayUnitLabel to the axis. For example, the following code sets the scale of the value axis and changes the display unit caption:

```
Sub SetAxisScale()
    Dim chrt As Chart, ax As Axis
    Set chrt = ActiveSheet
    Set ax = chrt.Axes(xlValue, xlPrimary)
    ax.DisplayUnit = xlThousands
    ax.DisplayUnitLabel.Caption = "(in $K)"
End Sub
```

*axis.*DisplayUnitCustom [= *setting*]

For value axes with DisplayUnit set to xlCustom, sets or returns the unit for the scale. Can be any value between 0 and 1E+308.

*axis.*DisplayUnitLabel

For value axes that have a DisplayUnit setting and HasDisplayUnitLabel set to True, returns the DisplayUnitLabel object. Causes an error in other situations.

*axis.*HasDisplayUnitLabel [= *setting*]

For value axes, True causes any DisplayUnit setting (such as Thousands) to appear next to the axis. Causes an error for other axis types.

*axis.*HasMajorGridlines [= *setting*]

True displays gridlines; False hides them. The following code displays major gridlines on a 3-D chart:

```
Sub SetGridlinesOn()
    Dim chrt As Chart
```

```
        Set chrt = ActiveChart
        chrt.ChartType = xl3DArea
        chrt.Axes(xlCategory, xlPrimary).HasMajorGridlines = True
        chrt.Axes(xlValue, xlPrimary).HasMajorGridlines = True
        chrt.Axes(xlSeries, xlPrimary).HasMajorGridlines = True
    End Sub
```

*axis.*HasMinorGridlines [= *setting*]

True displays minor gridlines; False hides them.

*axis.*HasTitle [= *setting*]

True displays an AxisTitle for the axis; False removes AxisTitle. Make sure to check HasTitle before using the AxisTitle object. Set the AxisTitle object's Caption property to change the text it displays.

axes.[Item](*Type, [AxisGroup]*)

Returns an axis from the Axes collection.

Argument	Settings
Type	The xlAxisType of the axis to return. Can be xlAxisValue, xlAxisCategory, or xlAxisSeries (3-D charts only).
AxisGroup	The xlAxisGroup of the axis to return. Can be xlAxisPrimary or xlAxisSecondary (2-D charts only).

The Axes collection is unique in using a 2-D array to contain its component objects.

*axis.*MajorGridlines

Returns the Gridlines object of the axis. For example, the following code selects the category axis major gridlines if they exist:

```
    Sub SelectGridlines()
        Dim chrt As Chart, gl As Gridlines
        Set chrt = ActiveChart
        chrt.ChartType = xl3DArea
        If chrt.Axes(xlCategory, xlPrimary).HasMajorGridlines Then
            Set gl = chrt.Axes(xlCategory, xlPrimary).MajorGridlines
            gl.Select
        End If
    End Sub
```

axis.MajorTickMark [= *xlTickMark*]

Sets or returns the type of tick mark used on the axis. Can be one of these settings:

```
xlTickMarkCross
xlTickMarkInside
xlTickMarkNonex
lTickMarkOutside (default)
```

axis.MajorUnit [= *setting*]

For the value axis, sets or returns the interval between tick marks. Use the `TickMarkSpacing` property to set this interval on the category axis.

axis.MajorUnitIsAuto [= *setting*]

True causes Excel to calculate `MajorUnit` automatically; False relies on the setting in the `MajorUnit` property. Setting the `MajorUnit` property automatically sets this property to False. Default is True.

axis.MajorUnitScale [= *xlTimeUnit*]

For the category axis when `CategoryType` is `xlTimeScale`, sets or returns the interval between tick marks. Can be one of these settings:

```
xlMonths
xlDays
xlYears
```

axis.MaximumScale [= *setting*]

For value axes, sets or returns the maximum value for the axis. Setting this property automatically sets `MaximumScaleIsAuto` to False. The following code sets the maximum and minimum axis values on a chart to match the maximum and minimum values in the source data range [`PriceHistory`]:

```
Sub ScaleValueAxis()
    Dim chrt As Chart, ax As Axis
    Set chrt = Charts("Stock Price History")
    Set ax = chrt.Axes(xlValue, xlPrimary)
    ax.MaximumScale = WorksheetFunction.Max(Range("PriceHistory"))
    ax.MinimumScale = WorksheetFunction.Min(Range("PriceHistory"))
End Sub
```

axis.MaximumScaleIsAuto [= setting]

For value axes, True causes Excel to calculate the maximum value for the axis based on the source data; False uses the MaximumScale setting instead. Default is True.

axis.MinimumScale [= setting]

For value axes, sets or returns the minimum value for the axis. Setting this property automatically sets MinimumScaleIsAuto to False.

axis.MinimumScaleIsAuto [= setting]

For value axes, True causes Excel to calculate the minimum value for the axis based on the source data and False uses the MinimumScale setting instead. Default is True.

axis.MinorGridlines

For primary axes, returns the Gridlines object representing the minor gridlines of the axis. Be sure to check the HasMinorGridlines property before using this object.

axis.MinorTickMark [= xlTickMark]

Sets or returns how minor tick marks are displayed. Can be one of these settings:

```
xlTickMarkCross
xlTickMarkInside
xlTickMarkNone
xlTickMarkOutside
```

axis.MinorUnit [= setting]

For the value axis, sets or returns the interval between minor tick marks. Use the TickMarkSpacing property to set this interval on the category axis.

axis.MinorUnitIsAuto [= setting]

True causes Excel to calculate MinorUnit automatically; False relies on the setting in the MinorUnit property. Setting the MajorUnit property automatically sets this property to False. Default is True.

axis.MinorUnitScale [= *xlTimeUnit*]

For the category axis when CategoryType is xlTimeScale, sets or returns the interval between minor tick marks. Can be one of these settings:

```
xlMonths
xlDays
xlYears
```

axis.ReversePlotOrder [= *setting*]

True plots data from last to first, reversing the category axis. Default is True.

axis.ScaleType [= *xlScaleType*]

For value axes, sets or returns the type of scale. Can be one of these settings:

```
xlScaleLinear
xlScaleLogarithmic
```

axis.TickLabelPosition [= *xlTickLabelPosition*]

Sets or returns where tick labels are placed. Can be one of these settings:

```
xlTickLabelPositionLow
xlTickLabelPositionHigh
xlTickLabelPositionNextToAxis
xlTickLabelPositionNone
```

axis.TickLabels

Returns the TickLabels object for the axis.

axis.TickLabelSpacing [= *setting*]

For category and series axes, sets or returns the number of categories or series between tick mark labels. Default is 1.

axis.TickMarkSpacing [= *setting*]

For category and series axes, sets or returns the number of categories or series between tick marks. Default is 1. Use the MajorUnit property to set tick mark spacing for value axes.

*axis.*Type

Returns the xlAxisType constant that identifies the type of the axis. Can be one of these settings:

```
xlCategory
xlSeriesAxis
xlValue
```

DataTable Members

Use the DataTable object to control the appearance of a data table on a chart sheet. Use the Chart object's DataTable property to get a reference to this object. The DataTable object has the following members:

Application	AutoScaleFont
Border	Creator
Delete	Font
HasBorderHorizontal	HasBorderOutline
HasBorderVertical	Parent
Select	ShowLegendKey

Most of the DataTable members are True/False properties that enable or disable specific data table items. These properties correspond to the settings on the Format Data Table dialog box (Figure 16-9).

Before you use the DataTable object, make sure to set the chart's HasDataTable property to True—that creates the table if it did not already exist. The following code adds a data table to the active chart and sets some of the table's properties:

```
Sub AddDataTable()
    Dim chrt As Chart, dt As DataTable
    ' Get the chart.
    Set chrt = ActiveChart
    ' Add a data table if it doesn't have one.
    chrt.HasDataTable = True
    ' Get the data table.
    Set dt = chrt.DataTable
    ' Set the data table properties.
    ' These properties are all True by default:
    dt.ShowLegendKey = False
    dt.HasBorderHorizontal = False
    dt.HasBorderOutline = True
    dt.HasBorderVertical = True
End Sub
```

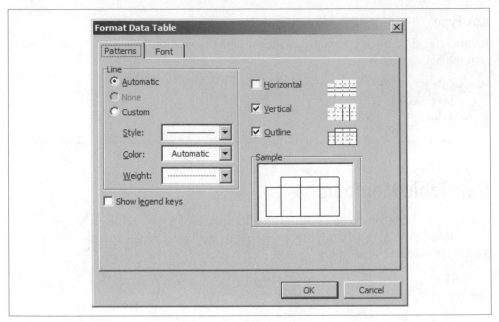

Figure 16-9. Data table properties correspond to these settings

Data tables may appear on chart sheets or on embedded charts, but some chart types, such as xy scatter charts, do not support them; in those cases, trying to set HasDataTable does nothing.

Series and SeriesCollection Members

Use the SeriesCollection to get all of the series plotted on the chart. Use the Chart object's SeriesCollection property to get a reference to this collection. Use the Series object to change an individual series or get the data points that the series plots. The SeriesCollection and Series object have the following members. Key members (shown in **bold**) are covered in the following reference section:

Add[1]	Application[2]
ApplyCustomType	**ApplyDataLabels**
ApplyPictToEnd	**ApplyPictToFront**
ApplyPictToSides	**AxisGroup**
BarShape	Border
BubbleSizes	**ChartType**
ClearFormats	Copy
Count[1]	Creator[2]
DataLabels	Delete
ErrorBar	**ErrorBars**
Explosion	Extend[1]
Fill	Formula
FormulaLocal	**FormulaR1C1**

FormulaR1C1Local	Has3DEffect
HasDataLabels	HasErrorBars
HasLeaderLines	Interior
InvertIfNegative	Item[1]
LeaderLines	MarkerBackgroundColor
MarkerBackgroundColorIndex	MarkerForegroundColor
MarkerForegroundColorIndex	MarkerSize
MarkerStyle	Name
NewSeries[1]	Parent[2]
Paste[2]	PictureType
PictureUnit	PlotOrder
Points	Select
Shadow	Smooth
Trendlines	Type
Values	XValues

[1] Collection only
[2] Object and collection

seriescollection.Add(Source, [Rowcol], [SeriesLabels], [CategoryLabels], [Replace])

Adds a new series and plots it on a chart.

Argument	Settings
Source	The Range object to plot as the new series.
Rowcol	An xlRowCol constant that determines how the series is plotted. Can be xlColumns or xlRows.
SeriesLabels	True interprets the first row or column of Source as a series label; False treats the first row or column as data. Defaults to a best guess based on the source data.
CategoryLabels	True interprets the first row or column of Source as a category label; False treats the first row or column as data. Defaults to a best guess based on the source data.
Replace	If CategoryLabels is True, setting Replace to True replaces matching categories with the new labels; False does not replace the categories.

Use the Chart object's SetSourceData method to replace all of the series on a chart with new data.

series.ApplyCustomType(ChartType)

Applies a chart type to a series. Use this method to create combo charts containing more than one chart type.

Argument	Settings
ChartType	An xlChartType constant. See the reference topic for the Chart object's ChartType property for a list of possible settings.

The following code creates a chart and adds series using the `SeriesCollection` `Add` method; then it changes the chart type of the last series to create a combo chart containing both line and column chart types:

```
Sub AddSeries()
    Dim chrt As Chart, sc As SeriesCollection, _
      sr As Series
    ' Create a line chart.
    Set chrt = Charts.Add
    chrt.ChartType = xlLine
    ' Get the series collection.
    Set sc = chrt.SeriesCollection
    ' Add adds some series (plots data).
    sc.Add Range("GrowthRate"), , True, True
    ' Get the last series.
    Set sr = sc(sc.Count)
    ' Change its chart type.
    sr.ApplyCustomType xlColumnClustered
End Sub
```

series.ApplyDataLabels([*Type*], [*LegendKey*], [*AutoText*], [*HasLeaderLines*], [*ShowSeriesName*], [*ShowCategoryName*], [*ShowValues*], [*ShowPercentage*], [*ShowBubbleSize*], [*Separator*])

Applies data labels to a single series on the chart. The arguments for this method are identical to those for the `Chart` object's `ApplyDataLabels` method. See that reference topic for complete information and an example.

series.ApplyPictToEnd [= *setting*]

For 3-D column and bar charts, True displays the fill picture on the end of the column or bar and False displays the fill color. Default is True if the series has a fill picture. Setting the `ApplyPict` properties causes an error for other chart types.

The following code demonstrates each of the `ApplyPict` properties:

```
Sub ApplyPict()
    Dim chrt As Chart, sc As SeriesCollection, _
      sr As Series
    ' Get a chart.
    Set chrt = ActiveChart
    chrt.ChartType = xl3DColumn
    ' Get the series collection.
    Set sc = chrt.SeriesCollection
    ' Get the first series.
    Set sr = sc(1)
    ' Display a picture on the series column.
    sr.Fill.UserPicture ThisWorkbook.Path & "\small_wombat.GIF"
    sr.Fill.Visible = True
```

```
        ' Show all sides
        Application.Wait Now + 0.00001
        ' Remove picture from end.
        sr.ApplyPictToEnd = False
        Application.Wait Now + 0.00001
        ' Remove picture from all sides.
        sr.ApplyPictToSides = False
        Application.Wait Now + 0.00001
        ' Apply picture to front side.
        sr.ApplyPictToFront = True
    End Sub
```

series.ApplyPictToFront [= setting]

For 3-D column and bar charts, True displays the fill picture on the front of the column or bar.

series.ApplyPictToSides [= setting]

For 3-D column and bar charts, True displays the fill picture on the sides of the column or bar.

series.AxisGroup [= xlAxisGroup]

Sets or returns the axis group that the series belongs to. For 2-D charts, can be xlPrimary or xlSecondary. For 3-D charts, AxisGroup can only be xlPrimary.

series.ChartType [= xlChartType]

Sets or returns the chart type of the series. Changing the chart type of a series makes the chart a combo chart and creates a ChartGroup for the new chart type.

series.ClearFormats( )

Restores the series ChartFillFormat object back to its default. For example, the following code removes the pictures applied in the ApplyPict procedure earlier:

```
    Sub RemovePict( )
        Dim chrt As Chart, sr As Series
        ' Get a chart.
        Set chrt = ActiveChart
        ' Get the first series.
        Set sr = chrt.SeriesCollection(1)
        ' Remove the formatting
        sr.ClearFormats
    End Sub
```

series.DataLabels([*Index*])

Gets one or all of the DataLabel objects for the series. Be sure to set HasDataLabels to True before using this property.

series.ErrorBar(*Direction, Include, Type, [Amount], [MinusValues]*)

For 2-D chart types, adds error bars to the series. Causes an error for 3-D chart types.

Argument	Settings
Direction	An xlErrorBarDirection constant that specifies the axis direction for the bar. Possible settings are xlX or xlY.
Include	An xlErrorBarInclude constant that specifies the type of bar. Possible settings are xlErrorBarIncludeBoth, xlErrorBarIncludeNone, xlErrorBarIncludeMinusValues, or xlErrorBarIncludePlusValues.
Type	An xlErrorBarType constant that specifies the calculation used to size the bar. Possible settings are xlErrorBarTypeCustom, xlErrorBarTypePercent, xlErrorBarTypeStError, xlErrorBarTypeFixedValue, or xlErrorBarTypeStDev.
Amount	If *Type* is xlErrorBarTypeCustom, the positive value of the bar.
MinusValues	If *Type* is xlErrorBarTypeCustom, the negative value of the bar.

The following code adds error bars to the first series of the active chart:

```
Sub AddErrorBars()
    Dim chrt As Chart, sr As Series
    ' Get a chart.
    Set chrt = ActiveChart
    ' Use 2-D chart type.
    chrt.ChartType = xlLineMarkers
    ' Get first series
    Set sr = chrt.SeriesCollection(1)
    ' Add error bars.
    sr.ErrorBar xlY, xlErrorBarIncludeBoth, xlErrorBarTypeStError
End Sub
```

series.ErrorBars

Returns the ErrorBars collection for a series. Use the returned object to remove error bars from a series, as shown by the following code:

```
Sub RemoveErrorBars()
    Dim chrt As Chart, sr As Series
    ' Get a chart.
    Set chrt = ActiveChart
    ' Get first series
    Set sr = chrt.SeriesCollection(1)
    ' Remove the error bars added by AddErrorBars.
    sr.ErrorBars.Delete
End Sub
```

series.Explosion [= *setting*]

For pie and doughnut chart types, sets or returns the amount to move the series out from the center (exploded view) as a percentage of the diameter of the chart. The following code explodes one piece out of a pie chart:

```
Sub ExplodeSlice()
    Dim chrt As Chart, sr As Series
    ' Get a chart.
    Set chrt = ActiveChart
    chrt.ChartType = xlLine
    ' Get first series
    Set sr = chrt.SeriesCollection(1)
    ' Use a pie chart type.
    sr.ChartType = xlPie
    ' Keep pie together
    sr.Explosion = 0
    ' Explode last piece.
    sr.Points(sr.Points.Count).Explosion = 50
End Sub
```

seriescollection.Extend(*Source*, [*Rowcol*], [*CategoryLabels*])

Adds data values to existing series.

Argument	Settings
Source	The Range object containing the data to add to the series.
Rowcol	An xlRowCol constant that determines how the data is plotted. Can be xlColumns or xlRows.
CategoryLabels	True interprets the first row or column of Source as a category label; False treats the first row or column as data. Defaults to a best guess based on the source data.

series.Fill

Returns the ChartFillFormat object for the series. Use this object to change the color, pattern, or picture displayed on the series.

series.Formula [= *setting*]

Gets or sets the formula for a series. This formula uses the Series worksheet function. The Formula properties are the only way to get the source range from the chart. For example, the following code gets the source range from the active chart and then selects that range:

```
Sub TestGetSourceRange()
    Dim chrt As Chart, rng As Range
    ' Get a chart.
    Set chrt = ActiveChart
    Set rng = GetSourceRange(chrt)
    rng.Worksheet.Activate
```

```
        rng.Select
    End Sub

    Function GetSourceRange(chrt As Chart) As Range
        Dim sc As SeriesCollection, sr As Series, _
          result As Range, temp As String, i As Integer, _
          ar() As String, j As Integer
        Set sc = chrt.SeriesCollection
        ' For each of the series.
        For i = 1 To sc.Count
            ' Get the formula.
            temp = sc(i).Formula
            ' Get the address part of the formula.
            temp = Replace(temp, "=SERIES(", "")
            ' Break into an array.
            ar = Split(temp, ",")
            ' Omit the last element, which is the index of the series.
            For j = 0 To UBound(ar) - 1
                ' If the data point is not omitted.
                If ar(j) <> "" Then
                    ' Convert the address to a range.
                    If result Is Nothing Then
                        Set result = Range(ar(j))
                    Else
                        ' Append the range using Union.
                        Set result = Union(result, Range(ar(j)))
                    End If
                End If
            Next
        Next
        ' Return the result.
        Set GetSourceRange = result
```

End Function *series.*FormulaLocal [= *setting*]

Same as the Formula property, only uses the user's language settings rather than English to create the formula.

*series.*FormulaR1C1 [= *setting*]

Same as the Formula property, only uses R1C1 format for the cell references.

*series.*FormulaR1C1Local [= *setting*]

Same as the Formula property, only uses the user's language and R1C1 format for the cell references.

series.Has3DEffect [= *setting*]

For bubble charts, True renders the series with a 3-D look.

series.HasDataLabels [= *setting*]

True adds data labels to the series if they do not already exist; False removes them. Set this property to True before using the DataLabels collection.

series.HasErrorBars [= *setting*]

True adds data error bars to the series if they do not already exist; False removes them. Set this property to True before using the ErrorBars object.

series.HasLeaderLines [= *setting*]

For xy scatter charts, True adds leader lines to the series if they do not already exist; False removes them. Set this property to True before using the LeaderLines object.

series.InvertIfNegative [= *setting*]

True inverts the pattern for the series for negative values; False uses the same pattern as for positive values. Default is False.

series.LeaderLines

For xy scatter charts, returns a LeaderLines object for the series. Be sure to set HasLeaderlines to True before using this object.

series.MarkerBackgroundColor [= *setting*]

For line, xy scatter, and radar charts, sets or returns the background of the point markers as an RGB value.

series.MarkerBackgroundColorIndex [= *setting*]

For line, xy scatter, and radar charts, sets or returns the background of the point markers as the index of the color in the Excel color palette. May also be xlColorIndexAutomatic (default) or xlColorIndexNone.

series.**MarkerForegroundColor** [= *setting*]

For line, xy scatter, and radar charts, sets or returns the foreground of the point markers as an RGB value.

series.**MarkerForegroundColorIndex** [= *setting*]

For line, xy scatter, and radar charts, sets or returns the foreground of the point markers as the index of the color in the Excel color palette. May also be xlColorIndexAutomatic (default) or xlColorIndexNone.

series.**MarkerSize** [= *setting*]

For line, xy scatter, and radar charts, sets or returns the marker size in points.

series.**MarkerStyle** [= *xlMarkerStyle*]

For line, xy scatter, and radar charts, sets or returns the type of marker displayed. Can be one of these settings:

xlMarkerStyleAutomatic (default)	xlMarkerStyleCircle
xlMarkerStyleDash	xlMarkerStyleDiamond
xlMarkerStyleDot	xlMarkerStyleNone
xlMarkerStylePicture	xlMarkerStylePlus
xlMarkerStyleSquare	xlMarkerStyleStar
xlMarkerStyleTriangle	xlMarkerStyleX

seriescollection.**NewSeries( )**

Creates a new, empty series on the chart. For example, the following code creates a new line chart and adds a new series plotted from an array of values:

```
Sub ChartFromArray( )
    Dim chrt As Chart, sr As Series
    ' Create a new chart.
    Set chrt = ThisWorkbook.Charts.Add
    chrt.ChartType = xlLine
    ' Create a new series.
    Set sr = chrt.SeriesCollection.NewSeries
    ' Add some values to the series.
    sr.Values = Array(1, 2, 3, 4)
End Sub
```

seriescollection.Paste([*Rowcol*], [*SeriesLabels*], [*CategoryLabels*], [*Replace*], [*NewSeries*])

Pastes a range from the Clipboard into a chart and plots it as a series.

Argument	Settings
Rowcol	An xlRowCol constant that determines how the series is plotted. Can be xlColumns or xlRows.
SeriesLabels	True interprets the first row or column of *Source* as a series label; False treats the first row or column as data. Defaults to a best guess based on the source data.
CategoryLabels	True interprets the first row or column of *Source* as a category label; False treats the first row or column as data. Defaults to a best guess based on the source data.
Replace	If *CategoryLabels* is True, setting *Replace* to True replaces matching categories with the new labels; False does not replace the categories.
NewSeries	True creates a new series from the data; False appends the data to existing series. Default is True.

series.PictureType [= *xlChartPictureType*]

For column and bar charts, sets or returns how the fill picture is displayed. Can be one of these settings:

    xlStack
    xlStackScale
    xlStretch (default)

series.PictureUnit [= *setting*]

For column and bar charts with PictureType set to xlStackScale, sets or returns the unit value of each fill picture. Default is 1.

series.PlotOrder [= *setting*]

Sets or returns the index of the series in the SeriesCollection. Changing PlotOrder reorders the series on the chart. You can change PlotOrder only for series with the same chart type.

series.Points([*Index*])

Returns one or all of the Point objects contained in a series.

series.**Smooth** [= *setting*]

For line and xy scatter charts, True smooths curves and False does not. Default is False.

series.**Trendlines([*Index*])**

Returns one or all of the Trendline objects for a series. Use the Trendlines collection to add trendlines to a series as shown by the following code:

```
Sub AddTrendline( )
    Dim chrt As Chart, sr As Series, tl As Trendline
    ' Get a chart.
    Set chrt = ActiveChart
    ' Get first series
    Set sr = chrt.SeriesCollection(1)
    ' Add a trendline
    Set tl = sr.Trendlines.Add
    tl.Type = xlMovingAvg
End Sub
```

series.**Values** [= *setting*]

Sets or returns the array of values plotted by the series. For example, this helper function builds an array containing all the values from a chart:

```
' Useful function for getting a chart's source data
' in the form of an array.
Function GetChartData(chrt As Chart) As Variant
    Dim sc As SeriesCollection, i As Integer
    ' Get the series collection.
    Set sc = chrt.SeriesCollection
    ' Size an array to fit all the series.
    ReDim result(1 To sc.Count) As Variant
    ' For each of the series.
    For i = 1 To sc.Count
        ' Add the array of points to the result.
        result(i) = sc(i).Values
    Next
    ' Return the result array.
    GetChartData = result
End Function
```

You can use GetChartData to get values from a chart for use with Excel's WorksheetFunction methods as shown here:

```
Sub TestGetChartData( )
    Dim chrt As Chart, sc As SeriesCollection
    Set chrt = Charts("Stock Price History")
    Debug.Print WorksheetFunction.Min(GetChartData(chrt)), _
        WorksheetFunction.Max(GetChartData(chrt))
End Sub
```

series.XValues [= *setting*]

For xy scatter charts, sets or returns the x values of the series as an array. This property also accepts a Range object when being set. The following code changes the type of a series to xlXYScatter, then sets the x values for the series:

```
Sub SetXYValues( )
    Dim chrt As Chart, sr As Series
    ' Get a chart.
    Set chrt = ActiveChart
    ' Get first series
    Set sr = chrt.SeriesCollection(1)
    ' Set the chart type to xy scatter.
    sr.ChartType = xlXYScatter
    ' Set x values
    sr.XValues = Array(1, 5, 3, 2)
End Sub
```

Point and Points Members

Use the Points collection to get individual data points from a series. Use the Series object's Points property to get a reference to this collection. Use the Point object to change the appearance of a point within a series. The Points collection and Point object have the following members. The key member (shown in **bold**) is covered in the following reference section:

Application[2]	ApplyDataLabels
ApplyPictToEnd	ApplyPictToFront
ApplyPictToSides	Border
ClearFormats	Copy
Count[1]	Creator[2]
DataLabel	Delete
Explosion	Fill
HasDataLabel	Interior
InvertIfNegative	Item[1]
MarkerBackgroundColor	MarkerBackgroundColorIndex
MarkerForegroundColor	MarkerForegroundColorIndex
MarkerSize	MarkerStyle
Parent[2]	Paste
PictureType	PictureUnit
SecondaryPlot	Select
Shadow	

[1] Collection only
[2] Object and collection

Most of the `Point` members are also available on the `Series` object. When those members are applied on the Point object, they affect a single point rather than the entire series. See the `Series` reference topics for complete information and examples of how to use those members.

Only the `SecondaryPlot` property is unique to the `Point` object, so it is covered here.

---

point.**SecondaryPlot** [= *setting*]

For pie of pie charts and pie of bar charts, True displays the point part in the secondary chart; False displays the point in the primary chart.

CHAPTER 17

Formatting Charts

You use Excel's chart format objects to change the fonts, backgrounds, images, and 3-D effects used on a chart. This chapter covers those tasks to take you far beyond the basic chart types and default formatting.

This chapter includes task-oriented reference information for the following objects and their related collections: AxisTitle, ChartArea, ChartColorFormat, ChartFillFormat, ChartTitle, Corners, DataLabel, DisplayUnitLabel, DownBars, DropLines, ErrorBars, Floor, Gridlines, HiLoLines, LeaderLines, Legend, LegendEntry, LegendKey, PlotArea, TickLabels, Trendline, Trendlines, UpBars, and Walls.

 Code used in this chapter and additional samples are available in *ch17.xls*.

Format Titles and Labels

Chapter 16 covered how to add titles and labels to charts, axes, and series using the AxisTitle, ChartTitle, DataLabel, and DisplayUnitLabel objects. This chapter provides a reference for those objects and shows you how to use their members to control the font, color, and orientation of those titles and labels.

All four of those objects provide similar members, but the DataLabel object is a little different since you can format the labels for the entire series through the DataLabels collection or format the label for a single point in the series through the DataLabel object.

Formatting these objects in code involves several steps:

1. Navigate to the parent object (Chart, Axis, or Series) in code.
2. Use the HasTitle, HasDisplayUnitLabel, or HasDataLabel property to make sure the object exists. You can either set this property to True to create the object or use it as part of an If statement to conditionally format the object if it exists.
3. Use the Font, Fill, Orientation, or other property to format the title or label.

The following code illustrates these steps to set the font size and style for each of the titles and labels that can appear on a chart:

```
Sub FormatTitlesAndLabels()
    Dim chrt As Chart, f As Font, ax As Axis, sr As Series
    Set chrt = ActiveChart
    ''''''''''''''''''''''''''''''''''
    ' Format ChartTitle
    ' Make sure chart has title
    chrt.HasTitle = True
    ' Get the font for the chart title.
    Set f = chrt.ChartTitle.Font
    ' Set the size/style
    f.Size = 14
    f.Bold = True
    ''''''''''''''''''''''''''''''''''
    ' Format AxisTitle
    ' Get  each axis
    For Each ax In chrt.Axes
        ' Make sure axis has title.
        ax.HasTitle = True
        ' Get the font.
        Set f = ax.AxisTitle.Font
        ' Set the size/style.
        f.Size = 10
        f.Bold = True
        f.Italic = True
        ''''''''''''''''''''''''''''''''''
        ' Format DisplayUnitLabel
        If ax.Type = xlValue Then
            If ax.HasDisplayUnitLabel Then
                ' Get the font
                Set f = ax.DisplayUnitLabel.Font
                ' Set the size/style.
                f.Size = 10
                f.Bold = True
                f.Italic = True
            End If
        End If
    Next
    ''''''''''''''''''''''''''''''''''
    ' Format DataLabels
    For Each sr In chrt.SeriesCollection
        ' Make sure series has data labels.
        If sr.HasDataLabels Then
            ' Get the font.
            Set f = sr.DataLabels.Font
            ' Set the size/style.
            f.Size = 8
            f.Bold = True
            f.Italic = False
        End If
    Next
End Sub
```

Only the value axis can have a unit label, so you must check the axis type and `HasDisplayUnitLabel` before using that object, as shown in the preceding code.

Setting `Font` properties for the object changes the font for the entire caption. To change part of the caption, use the `Characters` collection as shown here:

```
Sub ChangePartOfCaption( )
    Dim chrt As Chart, t1 As String, t2 As String, cr As Characters
    Set chrt = ActiveChart
    ' Make sure chart has title
    chrt.HasTitle = True
    t1 = "Home Prices"
    t2 = vbLf & "Going Up!"
    ' Set the caption.
    chrt.ChartTitle.Caption = t1 & t2
    ' Get the chartacters for the second line
    Set cr = chrt.ChartTitle.Characters(Len(t1) + 1, Len(t2))
    ' Format them.
    cr.Font.Italic = True ' Italic on.
    cr.Font.Color = &HFF  ' Red text.
End Sub
```

To restore the default formatting, save the caption in a variable, set `HasTitle` to False then back to True, and restore the original caption as shown here:

```
Sub ResetChartTitleFormatting( )
    Dim chrt As Chart, ct As String
    Set chrt = ActiveChart
    ' Save the caption
    ct = chrt.ChartTitle.Caption
    ' Turn the title off/on.
    chrt.HasTitle = False
    chrt.HasTitle = True
    ' Restore text
    chrt.ChartTitle.Caption = ct
End Sub
```

Change Backgrounds and Fonts

Excel provides a large set of built-in gradients and textures that provide visual interest to the chart. You can browse the gradients and fills from the Fill Effects dialog box (Figures 17-1 and 17-2). To see this dialog, right-click the chart area, select Format Chart Area, and click Fill Effects.

Use the `ChartArea` object to apply these gradients or textures to the background for the entire chart. Use the `PlotArea` object to change the background of the area where the series are plotted. Both objects provide a `Fill` property that returns a `ChartFillFormat`

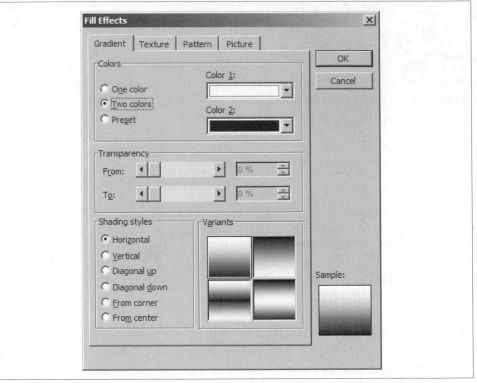

Figure 17-1. Built-in gradients

object you can use to apply gradients, textures, or pictures to the chart background. For example, the following code applies a gradient to the chart background:

```
Sub ApplyGradient()
    Dim chrt As Chart, cf As ChartFillFormat
    ' Get the chart.
    Set chrt = ActiveChart
    ' Get the chart area fill.
    Set cf = chrt.ChartArea.Fill
    ' Make the fill visible.
    cf.Visible = True
    ' Set colors for gradient.
    cf.BackColor.SchemeColor = 17
    cf.ForeColor.SchemeColor = 1
    ' Display a gradient fill.
    cf.TwoColorGradient msoGradientDiagonalUp, 2
End Sub
```

And this code applies a texture to the plot area:

```
Sub ApplyTexture()
    Dim chrt As Chart, cf As ChartFillFormat
    ' Get the chart.
    Set chrt = ActiveChart
```

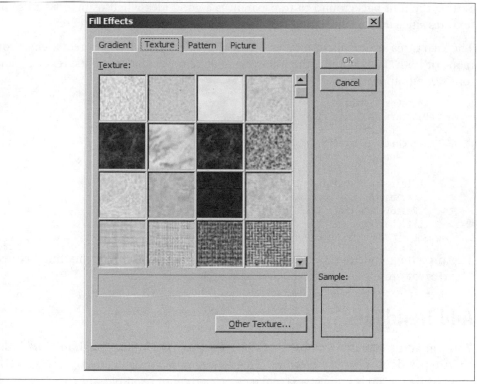

Figure 17-2. Built-in textures

```
        ' Get the plot area fill.
        Set cf = chrt.PlotArea.Fill
        ' Make the fill visible.
        cf.Visible = True
        ' Display a built-in texture.
        cf.PresetTextured msoTextureWhiteMarble
    End Sub
```

The ChartArea object also provides a Font object that you can use to set the default font for the entire chart, as shown here:

```
Sub SetChartFont( )
    Dim chrt As Chart, f As Font
    ' Get the chart.
    Set chrt = ActiveChart
    ' Get the chart area fill.
    Set f = chrt.ChartArea.Font
    ' Change the font.
    f.Name = "Comic Sans MS"
    f.Bold = True
    f.Background = xlBackgroundTransparent
End Sub
```

Setting the font background to transparent is a good idea when using gradients and textures since the default setting creates a block of the color behind the text.

The ChartArea object also provides methods to clear the chart contents, chart formats, or both. For example, the following code removes the gradients, textures, and font settings applied earlier:

```
Sub ResetChartFormats()
    Dim chrt As Chart, ct As XlChartType
    ' Get the chart.
    Set chrt = ActiveChart
    ' Save the chart type
    ct = chrt.ChartType
    ' Clear all formatting
    chrt.ChartArea.ClearFormats
    ' Restore the chart type.
    chrt.ChartType = ct
End Sub
```

The preceding code restores the chart type after removing the formatting because ClearFormats resets the chart type as well as other formatting.

Add Trendlines

You can add trendlines to most types of 2-D charts. 3-D, pie, doughnut, and radar chart types don't permit trendlines. Trendlines apply to a single series, so you add them using the Series object's Trendlines property. For example, the following code adds a trendline to the first series in a chart:

```
Sub AddTrendline()
    Dim chrt As Chart, tl As Trendline, tls As Trendlines
    ' Get the chart.
    Set chrt = ActiveChart
    chrt.ChartType = xlLine
    ' Get a series.
    Set tls = chrt.SeriesCollection(1).Trendlines
    Set tl = tls.Add(xlLogarithmic, , , 10, , , True, True, "Trend1") End Sub
```

 I use variables with explicit types in the preceding code to enable Auto Complete for the Trendlines collection and Trendline object. The expression chrt.SeriesCollection(1).Trendlines doesn't provide member lists or other Auto Complete features.

If a chart has a legend, Excel automatically adds a legend entry for each trendline using the trendline's Name property as the caption. Excel automatically generates that name if you don't provide it as part of the Add method.

You can use the Forward and Backward properties to project a trendline beyond the series in either direction. Excel automatically scales the axis to accommodate the new range. Projecting a trendline in this way is a sort of forecasting.

Add Series Lines and Bars

Series can have a variety of lines and bars attached to them. You can browse these lines and bars from the Format Data Series dialog box (Figures 17-3 and 17-4). To see this dialog, right-click a series and select Format Data Series.

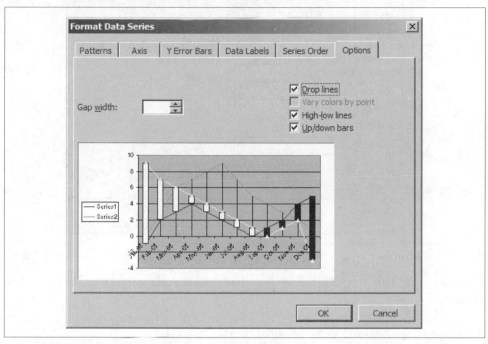

Figure 17-3. Drop lines, high-low lines, and up/down bars

You add drop lines, high-low lines, and up/down bars through the `ChartGroup` object. For example, the following code adds high-low lines to a line chart:

```
Sub AddHiLoLines()
    Dim chrt As Chart, cg As ChartGroup
    ' Get the chart.
    Set chrt = ActiveChart
    ' Make it a line chart
    chrt.ChartType = xlLine
    ' Get the chart group
    Set cg = chrt.LineGroups(1)
    ' Add high-low lines
    cg.HasHiLoLines = True
End Sub
```

Only 2-D line chart types support high-low lines and up/down bars.
Only 2-D line, bar, and column charts support error bars.

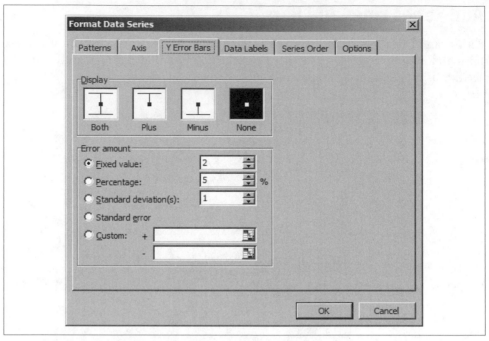

Figure 17-4. Error bars

You add error bars through the Series object. This code adds error bars to a line chart:

```
Sub AddErrorBars( )
    Dim chrt As Chart, sr As Series
    ' Get the chart.
    Set chrt = ActiveChart
    ' Make it a line chart
    chrt.ChartType = xlLineMarkers
    ' Get the chart group
    Set sr = chrt.SeriesCollection(1)
    ' Add error bars.
     sr.ErrorBar xlY, xlErrorBarIncludeBoth, xlErrorBarTypeStError
     ' Format the error bars.
    sr.ErrorBars.EndStyle = xlCap
End Sub
```

ChartTitle, AxisTitle, and DisplayUnitLabel Members

Use the ChartTitle, AxisTitle, and DisplayUnitLabel objects to add and format captions for charts, axes, and unit labels. These objects have the following members. Key members (shown in **bold**) are covered in the following reference section:

Application	AutoScaleFont
Border	**Caption**
Characters	Creator

Delete	**Fill**
Font	**HorizontalAlignment**
Interior	Left
Name	**Orientation**
Parent	**ReadingOrder**
Select	Shadow
Text	Top
VerticalAlignment	

The ChartTitle appears at the top of a chart by default, the AxisTitle appears centered next to each axis, and the DisplayUnitLabel appears next to the value axis indicating the units of the value axis (thousands, millions, etc.). Be sure to check the HasTitle or HasDisplayUnitLabel properties before working with these objects.

The following code adds a chart title, axis title, and display unit label to a chart:

```
Sub AddTitles()
    Dim chrt As Chart, ax As Axis
    Set chrt = ActiveChart
    ' Add a title.
    chrt.HasTitle = True
    ' Set the chart title caption.
    chrt.ChartTitle.Caption = "FL Home Sales"
    ' Add titles to each axis
    For Each ax In chrt.Axes
        ' Add a title.
        ax.HasTitle = True
        ' Set the axis title
        ax.AxisTitle.Caption = "Axis title"
        ' Add a display unit label caption.
        If ax.Type = xlValue Then
            ax.DisplayUnit = xlThousands
            ax.HasDisplayUnitLabel = True
            ax.DisplayUnitLabel.Caption = "In Thousands"
        End If
    Next
End Sub
```

*title.*Caption [*= setting*]

Sets or returns the text displayed in the title.

*title.*Characters

Returns the Characters object used to format the caption. For example, the following code adds a title to a chart and changes the font of the title:

```
Sub AddChartTitle()
    Dim chrt As Chart, ct As ChartTitle
    Set chrt = ActiveChart
    ' Add a title.
```

```
    chrt.HasTitle = True
    ' Get the title
    Set ct = chrt.ChartTitle
    ' Set the text to display.
    ct.Caption = "FL Home Sales"
    ' Format the text.
    ct.Characters.Font.Size = 14
    ct.Characters.Font.Bold = True
End Sub
```

*title.*Fill

Returns the `ChartFillFormat` object for the title. Use this object to change the color or pattern behind the text.

*title.*Font

Returns the `Font` object representing the formatting of the title.

*title.*HorizontalAlignment [= *setting*]

This property has no visible effect on chart, axis, or display unit label captions.

*title.*Orientation [= *setting*]

Sets or returns the angle of rotation for the title in degrees. Must be between -90 and 90. Default is 0.

*title.*ReadingOrder [= *setting*]

Sets or returns the reading order of the title. Can be `xlContext`, `xlLTR`, or `xlRTL`. Setting this property may or may not have an effect, depending on the language support that is installed. For instance, it has no effect in U.S. English (1033).

*title.*VerticalAlignment [= *setting*]

This property has no visible effect on chart, axis, or display unit label captions.

DataLabel and DataLabels Members

Use the `DataLabels` collection to add data labels to series. Use the `Series` object's `DataLabels` property to get a reference to this collection. Use the `DataLabel` object to format individual data labels. The `DataLabels` collection and `DataLabel` object have the following members. Key members (shown in **bold**) are covered in the following reference section:

Application[2]	AutoScaleFont[2]
AutoText[2]	Border[2]
Caption	Characters
Count[1]	Creator[2]
Delete( )[2]	Fill[2]
Font[2]	HorizontalAlignment[2]
Interior[2]	Item[1]
Left	Name[2]
NumberFormat[2]	**NumberFormatLinked**[2]
NumberFormatLocal[2]	Orientation[2]
Parent[2]	**Position**[2]
ReadingOrder[2]	Select[2]
Separator[2]	Shadow[2]
ShowBubbleSize[2]	**ShowCategoryName**[2]
ShowLegendKey[2]	**ShowPercentage**[2]
ShowSeriesName[2]	**ShowValue**[2]
Text	Top
Type[2]	VerticalAlignment[2]

[1] Collection only
[2] Object and collection

datalabel AutoText [*= setting*]

True automatically generates the caption of the data label based on its context; False uses the Caption setting instead. Default is True.

Setting the Caption property automatically sets this property to False. For example, the following code turns off Auto Text by setting the data labels for a series:

```
Sub SetDataLabels( )
    Dim chrt As Chart, sr As Series, dl As DataLabel
    Set chrt = ActiveChart
    chrt.ChartType = xlColumnClustered
    ' Get the first series.
    Set sr = chrt.SeriesCollection(1)
    ' Create data labels.
    sr.HasDataLabels = True
    ' Set data label captions.
    For Each dl In sr.DataLabels
        dl.Caption = sr.Name & ": " & dl.Caption
    Next
End Sub
```

To restore Auto Text, set the AutoText property to True:

```
Sub RestoreAutoDataLabels( )
    Dim chrt As Chart, sr As Series
```

```
        Set chrt = ActiveChart
        chrt.ChartType = xlColumnClustered
        ' Get the first series.
        Set sr = chrt.SeriesCollection(1)
        ' Make sure data labels exist.
        sr.HasDataLabels = True
        ' Restore Auto Text.
        sr.DataLabels.AutoText = True
    End Sub
```

*datalabels.*NumberFormat [= *setting*]

Sets or returns the format string used to display the data label caption. You can see the
available format string settings from the Format Data Labels dialog box (Figure 17-5).

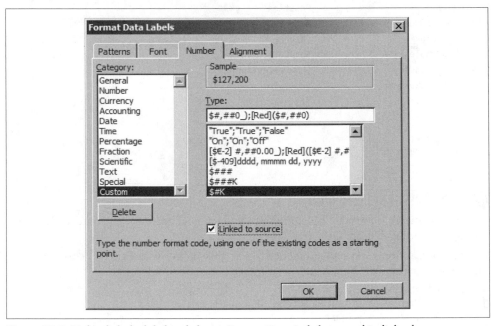

Figure 17-5. Right-click the label and choose Format Data Labels to see this dialog box

The following code sets the scale of the value axis to thousands and then formats the data
labels appropriately:

```
    Sub SetDataLabelNumberFormat()
        Dim chrt As Chart, sr As Series, ds As DataLabels, _
          ax As Axis
        Set chrt = ActiveChart
        ' Get the value axis.
        Set ax = chrt.Axes(xlValue, xlPrimary)
        ' Scale numbers by 1000.
        ax.DisplayUnit = xlThousands
        ' Get the first series.
```

```
    Set sr = chrt.SeriesCollection(1)
    ' Make sure data labels exist.
    sr.HasDataLabels = True
    ' Get the DataLabels collection.
    Set ds = sr.DataLabels
    ' Set the number format (ex. $150K).
    ds.NumberFormat = "$#,###K"
End Sub
```

*datalabel.*NumberFormatLinked [= *setting*]

True uses the number format from the source range; False uses the `NumberFormat` or `NumberFormatLocal` setting. Default is True. Setting either the `NumberFormat` or `NumberFormatLocal` property automatically sets `NumberFormatLinked` to False. Set this property to True to restore the default number format as shown here:

```
Sub RestoreDataLabelNumberFormat( )
    Dim chrt As Chart, sr As Series, ds As DataLabels
    Set chrt = ActiveChart
    ' Get the first series.
    Set sr = chrt.SeriesCollection(1)
    ' Make sure data labels exist.
    sr.HasDataLabels = True
    ' Get the DataLabels collection.
    Set ds = sr.DataLabels
    ' Restore format setting from source range.
    ds.NumberFormatLinked = True
End Sub
```

*datalabel.*NumberFormatLocal [= *setting*]

Sets or returns the format string used to display the data label caption. This property is the same as `NumberFormat` only it uses the localized version of the format strings.

*datalabel.*Position [= *xlDataLabelPosition*]

Sets or returns a constant indicating the placement of the data labels. The default setting depends on the chart type. Can be one of these settings:

xlLabelPositionAbove	xlLabelPositionBelow
xlLabelPositionBestFit	xlLabelPositionCenter
xlLabelPositionCustom	xlLabelPositionInsideBase
xlLabelPositionInsideEnd	xlLabelPositionLeft
xlLabelPositionMixed	xlLabelPositionOutsideEnd
xlLabelPositionRight	

datalabel.Separator [= *setting*]

Sets or returns the character used between the data label and the category name, legend key, or series name if one or more of those are included in the data label. Default is a comma.

The following code demonstrates using the Separator property along with the other data label display items:

```
Sub FullDataLabels()
    Dim chrt As Chart, sr As Series, ds As DataLabels
    Set chrt = ActiveChart
    chrt.ChartType = xlLine
    ' Get the first series.
    Set sr = chrt.SeriesCollection(1)
    ' Make sure data labels exist.
    sr.HasDataLabels = True
    ' Get the DataLabels collection.
    Set ds = sr.DataLabels
    ' Display all of the available info.
    ds.ShowCategoryName = True
    ds.ShowLegendKey = True
    ds.ShowSeriesName = True
    ' Use semicolon between items.
    ds.Separator = ";"
End Sub
```

datalabel.ShowBubbleSize [= *setting*]

For bubble charts, True includes the bubble size in the data label and False does not. Default is False.

datalabel.ShowCategoryName [= *setting*]

True includes the category name in the data label; False does not. Default is False.

datalabel.ShowLegendKey [= *setting*]

True includes the legend key in the data label; False does not. Default is False.

datalabel.ShowPercentage [= *setting*]

For pie and doughnut charts, True adds the percentage of the total that the value represents to the data label. Default is False.

datalabel.**ShowSeriesName** [= *setting*]

True includes the series name in the data label; False does not. Default is False.

datalabel.**ShowValue** [= *setting*]

True adds the value of each point to the data label; False omits it. Default is True.

LeaderLines Members

Use the LeaderLines object to control the appearance of the lines connecting data labels to the data points in a series. LeaderLines are available only for pie chart types. Use the Series object's LeaderLines property to get a reference to this object. LeaderLines has the following members:

```
Application
Border
Creator
Delete
Name
Parent
Select
```

You can select, delete, or change the appearance of LeaderLines in code. The following code adds data labels and leader lines to a pie chart and makes the leader lines bold:

```
Sub LeaderLineMembers()
    Dim chrt As Chart, b As Border
    ' Get the chart.
    Set chrt = ActiveChart
    ' Make it a line chart
    chrt.ChartType = xlPie
    ' Add data labels with leader lines.
    chrt.ApplyDataLabels , , , True
    Set b = chrt.SeriesCollection(1).LeaderLines.Border
    b.Weight = xlThick
End Sub
```

 Leader lines appear only if you drag the data labels away from the pie chart. You may have to manually drag the data labels away from the pie chart in order for the preceding code to work.

ChartArea Members

Use the ChartArea object to format the background of the chart, clear the chart, and set the font for the entire chart. Use the Chart object's ChartArea property to get a reference to this object. The ChartArea object has the following members. Key members (shown in **bold**) are covered in the following reference section:

Application	**AutoScaleFont**
Border	**Clear**
ClearContents	**ClearFormats**
Copy	Creator
Fill	**Font**
Height	**Interior**
Left	Name
Parent	Select
Shadow	Top
Width	

---

chartarea.AutoScaleFont [= *setting*]

For embedded charts, True automatically scales fonts in the chart area up or down when the embedded chart is resized; False does not scale. Default is True. This property has no effect on chart sheets.

---

chartarea.Clear( )

Clears the contents and formatting of the chart area. Clear has the same effect as using ClearContents and ClearFormats in turn. The following code demonstrates the different Clear methods:

```
Sub DemoClearChartArea( )
    Dim chrt As Chart, ca As ChartArea
    ' Copy the chart.
    ActiveChart.Copy , ActiveChart
    ' Get the copy.
    Set chrt = ActiveChart
    Set ca = chrt.ChartArea
    ca.ClearFormats
    ' Wait a sec.
    Application.Wait Now + 0.00001
    ca.ClearContents
    ' Same as.
    'ca.Clear
End Sub
```

---

chartarea.ClearContents( )

Clears the contents of the chart area.

---

chartarea.ClearFormats( )

Clears the formatting from the chart area.

chartarea.Fill

Returns the ChartFillFormat object for the chart area. Use this object to change the color or pattern of the chart area. For example, the following code displays a gradient background on the active chart:

```
Sub ChartAreaFill( )
    Dim chrt As Chart, cf As ChartFillFormat
    ' Get the chart.
    Set chrt = ActiveChart
    ' Get the chart area fill.
    Set cf = chrt.ChartArea.Fill
    ' Make the fill visible.
    cf.Visible = True
    ' Display a gradient fill.
    cf.TwoColorGradient msoGradientDiagonalUp, 2
End Sub
```

chartarea.Font

Returns the Font object representing the formatting of all the text on the chart. For example, the following code makes all of the caption, label, and legend text on the active chart bold:

```
Sub ChartAreaFont( )
    Dim chrt As Chart, f As Font
    ' Get the chart.
    Set chrt = ActiveChart
    ' Get the chart area font.
    Set f = chrt.ChartArea.Font
    f.Bold = True
End Sub
```

chartarea.Interior

Returns the Interior object representing the background of the chart area. For example, the following code changes the color index of the active chart's background:

```
Sub ChartAreaInterior( )
    Dim chrt As Chart, it As Interior
    ' Get the chart.
    Set chrt = ActiveChart
    ' Get the chart area font.
    Set it = chrt.ChartArea.Interior
    it.ColorIndex = 3
End Sub
```

*chartarea.*Shadow [= *setting*]

True adds a shadow border to the chart area; False does not. Default is False.

ChartFillFormat Members

Use the `ChartFillFormat` object to apply colors, gradients, and patterns to objects on a chart. Use the `Fill` property to get a reference to this object. The `ChartFillFormat` object has the following members. Key members (shown in **bold**) are covered in the following reference section:

Application	**BackColor**
Creator	**ForeColor**
GradientColorType	**GradientDegree**
GradientStyle	**GradientVariant**
OneColorGradient	Parent
Pattern	**Patterned**
PresetGradient	**PresetGradientType**
PresetTexture	**PresetTextured**
Solid( )	**TextureName**
TextureType	**TwoColorGradient**
Type	**UserPicture**
UserTextured	Visible

These chart objects all have `Fill` properties, which return a `ChartFillFormat` object:

AxisTitle	ChartArea
ChartTitle	DataLabel
DataLabels	DisplayUnitLabel
DownBars	Floor
Legend	LegendKey
PlotArea	Point
Series	Shape
ShapeRange	UpBars
Walls	

*chartfillformat.*BackColor

Returns a `ChartColorFormat` object you can use to set the background color.

*chartfillformat.*ForeColor

Returns a `ChartColorFormat` object you can use to set the foreground color.

chartfillformat.GradientColorType

Returns an msoGradientColorType constant indicating the type of the gradiant color. Can be one of these settings:

    msoGradientColorMixed
    msoGradientOneColor
    msoGradientPresetColors
    msoGradientTwoColors

chartfillformat.GradientDegree

For one-color gradients, returns the degree of the gradient as a number from 0 (dark) to 1 (light).

chartfillformat.GradientStyle

Returns an msoGradientStyle constant indicating the type of the gradient. Can be one of these settings:

    msoGradientDiagonalDown
    msoGradientDiagonalUp
    msoGradientFromCenter
    msoGradientFromCorner
    msoGradientFromTitle
    msoGradientHorizontal
    msoGradientMixed
    msoGradientVertical

chartfillformat.GradientVariant

Returns the index of the gradient variant selected from the Gradient tab in the Fill Effects dialog box.

chartfillformat.OneColorGradient(*Style, Variant, Degree*)

Applies a one-color gradient.

Argument	Settings
Style	An msoGradientStyle constant indicating the type of the gradient. See the GradientStyle property for a list of settings.
Variant	The index of the gradient variant to use. The variants are listed on the Gradient tab in the Fill Effects dialog box.
Degree	The degree of the gradient as a number from 0 (dark) to 1 (light).

The following code applies a one-color gradient to the chart area:

```
Sub OneColorGradient()
    Dim chrt As Chart, cf As ChartFillFormat
    ' Get the chart.
    Set chrt = ActiveChart
    ' Get the chart area fill.
    Set cf = chrt.ChartArea.Fill
    ' Make the fill visible.
    cf.Visible = True
    ' Display a gradient fill.
    cf.OneColorGradient msoGradientDiagonalUp, 2, 0.9
End Sub
```

chartfillformat.Pattern

Returns the `msoPatternType` constant indicating the pattern used in the fill. Can be one of these settings:

msoPattern5Percent	msoPattern10Percent
msoPattern20Percent	msoPattern25Percent
msoPattern30Percent	msoPattern40Percent
msoPattern50Percent	msoPattern60Percent
msoPattern70Percent	msoPattern75Percent
msoPattern80Percent	msoPattern90Percent
msoPatternDarkDownwardDiagonal	msoPatternDarkHorizontal
msoPatternDarkUpwardDiagonal	msoPatternDarkVertical
msoPatternDashedDownwardDiagonal	msoPatternDashedHorizontal
msoPatternDashedUpwardDiagonal	msoPatternDashedVertical
msoPatternDiagonalBrick	msoPatternDivot
msoPatternDottedDiamond	msoPatternDottedGrid
msoPatternHorizontalBrick	msoPatternLargeCheckerBoard
msoPatternLargeConfetti	msoPatternLargeGrid
msoPatternLightDownwardDiagonal	msoPatternLightHorizontal
msoPatternLightUpwardDiagonal	msoPatternLightVertical
msoPatternMixed	msoPatternNarrowHorizontal
msoPatternNarrowVertical	msoPatternOutlinedDiamond
msoPatternPlaid	msoPatternShingle
msoPatternSmallCheckerBoard	msoPatternSmallConfetti
msoPatternSmallGrid	msoPatternSolidDiamond
msoPatternSphere	msoPatternTrellis
msoPatternWave	msoPatternWeave
msoPatternWideDownwardDiagonal	msoPatternWideUpwardDiagonal
msoPatternZigZag	

chartfillformat.**Patterned(***Pattern***)**

Applies a pattern, replacing any gradients or textures. Can be any of the settings listed for the Pattern property.

chartfillformat.**PresetGradient(***Style, Variant, PresetGradientType***)**

Applies a built-in gradient.

Argument	Settings
Style	An msoGradientStyle constant indicating the type of the gradient. See the GradientStyle property for a list of settings.
Variant	The index of the gradient variant to use. The variants are listed on the Gradient tab in the Fill Effects dialog box.
PresetGradient Type	An msoPresetGradientType constant indicating the built-in gradient to use. See the PresetGradientType property for a list of settings.

The following code applies a built-in gradient to the chart area:

```
Sub BuiltInGradient( )
    Dim chrt As Chart, cf As ChartFillFormat
    ' Get the chart.
    Set chrt = ActiveChart
    ' Get the chart area fill.
    Set cf = chrt.ChartArea.Fill
    ' Make the fill visible.
    cf.Visible = True
    ' Display a built-in gradient.
    cf.PresetGradient msoGradientDiagonalUp, 1, msoGradientBrass
End Sub
```

chartfillformat.**PresetGradientType**

Returns an msoPresetGradientType constant indicating the built-in gradient used in the fill. Can be one of these settings:

msoGradientBrass	msoGradientCalmWater
msoGradientChrome	msoGradientChromeII
msoGradientDaybreak	msoGradientDesert
msoGradientEarlySunset	msoGradientFire
msoGradientFog	msoGradientGold
msoGradientGoldII	msoGradientHorizon
msoGradientLateSunset	msoGradientMahogany
msoGradientMoss	msoGradientNightfall
msoGradientOccan	msoGradientParchment
msoGradientPeacock	msoGradientRainbow

msoGradientRainbowII	msoGradientSapphire
msoGradientSilver	msoGradientWheat
msoPresetGradientMixed	

chartfillformat.**PresetTexture**

Returns an `msoPresetTexture` constant indicating the background's built-in texture used in the fill. Can be one of these settings:

msoPresetTextureMixed	msoTextureBlueTissuePaper
msoTextureBouquet	msoTextureBrownMarble
msoTextureCanvas	msoTextureCork
msoTextureDenim	msoTextureFishFossil
msoTextureGranite	msoTextureGreenMarble
msoTextureMediumWood	msoTextureNewsprint
msoTextureOak	msoTexturePaperBag
msoTexturePapyrus	msoTextureParchment
msoTexturePinkTissuePaper	msoTexturePurpleMesh
msoTextureRecycledPaper	msoTextureSand
msoTextureStationery	msoTextureWalnut
msoTextureWaterDroplets	msoTextureWhiteMarble
msoTextureWovenMat	

chartfillformat.**PresetTextured**(*PresetTexture*)

Applies a built-in texture.

Argument	Settings
PresetTexture	An `msoPresetTexture` constant indicating the built-in texture to use. See the `PresetTexture` property for a list of settings.

The following code applies the white marble texture to a chart area:

```
Sub ApplyTexture( )
    Dim chrt As Chart, cf As ChartFillFormat
    ' Get the chart.
    Set chrt = ActiveChart
    ' Get the chart area fill.
    Set cf = chrt.ChartArea.Fill
    ' Make the fill visible.
    cf.Visible = True
    ' Display a built-in texture.
    cf.PresetTextured msoTextureWhiteMarble
End Sub
```

chartfillformat.Solid( )

Applies a solid color, removing any patterns, textures, or gradients. The following code resets the chart area to solid white:

```
Sub ResetFill( )
    Dim chrt As Chart, cf As ChartFillFormat
    ' Get the chart.
    Set chrt = ActiveChart
    ' Get the chart area fill.
    Set cf = chrt.ChartArea.Fill
    ' Make the fill visible.
    cf.Visible = True
    ' Display a solid color.
    cf.Solid
    ' Set the color to white
    cf.ForeColor.SchemeColor = 2
End Sub
```

chartfillformat.TextureName

For fills with custom textures, returns the name of the texture file. For other types of fills, causes an error.

chartfillformat.TextureType

Returns an msoTextureType constant indicating how the fill's texture was set. Can be one of these settings:

```
msoTexturePreset
msoTextureTypeMixed
msoTextureUserDefined
```

chartfillformat.TwoColorGradient(*Style, Variant*)

Applies a two-color gradient.

Argument	Settings
Style	An msoGradientStyle constant indicating the type of the gradient. See the GradientStyle property for a list of settings.
Variant	The index of the gradient variant to use. The variants are listed on the Gradient tab in the Fill Effects dialog box.

The following code applies a two-color gradient to the chart area:

```
Sub TwoColorGradient( )
    Dim chrt As Chart, cf As ChartFillFormat
    ' Get the chart.
```

```
    Set chrt = ActiveChart
    ' Get the chart area fill.
    Set cf = chrt.ChartArea.Fill
    ' Make the fill visible.
    cf.Visible = True
    ' Set colors for gradient.
    cf.BackColor.SchemeColor = 17
    cf.ForeColor.SchemeColor = 1
    ' Display a gradient fill.
    cf.TwoColorGradient msoGradientDiagonalUp, 2
End Sub
```

chartfillformat.UserPicture(*PictureFile*)

Applies a picture to a fill. Pictures are stretched to fit the fill area.

Argument	Settings
PictureFile	The filename of the picture to apply

 Help specifies additional arguments for this method, but they can't be used with the ChartFillFormat object.

The following code applies a picture to the chart area:

```
Sub UserPictureFill( )
    Dim chrt As Chart, cf As ChartFillFormat
    ' Get the chart.
    Set chrt = ActiveChart
    ' Get the chart area fill.
    Set cf = chrt.ChartArea.Fill
    ' Make the fill visible.
    cf.Visible = True
    ' Display a picture.
    cf.UserPicture ThisWorkbook.Path & "\logo.bmp"
End Sub
```

chartfillformat.UserTextured(*TextureFile*)

Applies a picture file as a texture to the fill. Pictures are tiled to fit the fill area.

Argument	Settings
TextureFile	The filename of the picture to apply

The following code tiles a picture to fill the chart area:

```
Sub UserPictureTexture( )
    Dim chrt As Chart, cf As ChartFillFormat
    ' Get the chart.
    Set chrt = ActiveChart
    ' Get the chart area fill.
    Set cf = chrt.ChartArea.Fill
    ' Make the fill visible.
    cf.Visible = True
    ' Display a picture.
    cf.UserTextured ThisWorkbook.Path & "\logo.bmp"
End Sub
```

ChartColorFormat Members

Use the ChartColorFormat object to change the background or foreground colors using a color index or RGB value. Use the ChartFillFormat object's BackColor or ForeColor property to get a reference to this object. The ChartColorFormat object has the following members:

```
Application
Creator
Parent
RGB
SchemeColor
Type
```

The following code changes the background and foreground colors used in a gradient background for the chart area of the active chart:

```
Sub ChartColorFormat( )
    Dim chrt As Chart, cf As ChartFillFormat
    ' Get the chart.
    Set chrt = ActiveChart
    ' Get the chart area fill.
    Set cf = chrt.ChartArea.Fill
    ' Make the fill visible.
    cf.Visible = True
    ' Display a gradient fill.
    cf.TwoColorGradient msoGradientFromCorner, 2
    ' Set backgroud/foreground colors.
    cf.BackColor.SchemeColor = 17
    cf.ForeColor.SchemeColor = 1
End Sub
```

DropLines and HiLoLines Members

Use the DropLines and HiLoLines objects to control the appearance of those items on a chart. Use the ChartGroup object's DropLines, and HiLoLines properties to get a reference to these objects. These objects have the following members:

```
Application
Border
Creator
Delete
Name
Parent
Select
```

The DropLines and HiLoLines objects provide a small set of programmable features. You can select, delete, or change the appearance these lines. Be sure to check the ChartGroup object's Has*xxx* property before using any of these objects.

The following code uses the Border property to set the weight, color, and style of the drop lines on a line chart:

```
Sub FormatDropLines()
    Dim chrt As Chart, cg As ChartGroup, bd As Border
    ' Get the chart.
    Set chrt = ActiveChart
    ' Set the chart type
    chrt.ChartType = xlLineStacked
    ' Get the chart group.
    Set cg = chrt.LineGroups(1)
    ' Turn on drop lines
    cg.HasDropLines = True
    ' Get the drop line's border
    Set bd = cg.DropLines.Border
    ' Format the lines
    bd.Weight = 4
    bd.Color = &HFF0000
    bd.LineStyle = xlLineStyle.xlDot
End Sub
```

DownBars and UpBars Members

Use the DownBars and UpBars objects to control the appearance of up and down bars on a chart. Use the ChartGroup object's DownBars and UpBars properties to get a reference to these objects. The DownBars and UpBars objects have the following members:

Application	Border
Creator	Delete
Fill	Interior
Name	Parent
Select	

The DownBars and UpBars objects are similar to the DropLines and HiLoLines objects. As with those objects, you can select, delete, or change the appearance of up and down bars. However, up and down bars have an interior region that you can control using two additional members: Fill and Interior. Be sure to check the ChartGroup object's HasUpDownBars property before using these objects. The following code adds up and down bars to a chart and changes their appearance:

```
Sub DownBarsMembers()
    Dim chrt As Chart, cg As ChartGroup
    ' Get the chart.
    Set chrt = ActiveChart
    ' Make it a line chart
    chrt.ChartType = xlLine
    ' Get the chart group.
    Set cg = chrt.LineGroups(1)
    ' Add down bars.
    cg.HasUpDownBars = True
    ' Format the up and down bars.
    On Error Resume Next
    cg.UpBars.Interior.ColorIndex = 1
    cg.DownBars.Interior.ColorIndex = 3
    On Error GoTo 0
End Sub
```

You should include the On Error Resume Next statement when working with up and down bars since the contents of the chart determine whether or not up bars, down bars, or both types of bars exist.

ErrorBars Members

Use the ErrorBars object to control the appearance of error bars on a chart. Use the Series object's ErrorBar method to create error bars, and use the Series object's ErrorBars property to get a reference to this object. The ErrorBars object has the following members. Key members (shown in **bold**) are covered in the following reference section:

Application
Border
ClearFormats
Creator
Delete
EndStyle
Name
Parent
Select

The ErrorBars object is similar to the DropLines, HiLoLines, DownBars, and UpBars objects. As with those objects, you can select, delete, or change the appearance of error bars. However, error bars have two additional members: EndStyle and

ClearFormats. The following code adds error bars to a chart and changes their appearance:

```
Sub ErrorBarsMembers( )
    Dim chrt As Chart, sr As Series, eb As ErrorBars
    ' Get the chart.
    Set chrt = ActiveChart
    ' Make it a line chart
    chrt.ChartType = xlLine
    ' Get a series.
    Set sr = chrt.SeriesCollection(1)
    ' Add error bars.
    sr.ErrorBar xlY, xlErrorBarIncludeBoth, xlErrorBarTypeStError
    ' Format the error bars.
    sr.ErrorBars.EndStyle = xlCap
    sr.ErrorBars.Border.ColorIndex = 3
    ' Remove color
    'sr.ErrorBars.ClearFormats
End Sub
```

---

errorbars.ClearFormats( )

Removes formatting set through the Border object.

---

errorbars.EndStyle [=*xlEndStyleCap*]

Sets or returns the error bar style. Can be xlCap or xlNoCap.

Legend Members

Use the Legend object to format or move a legend or to get the individual entries from the legend. Use the Chart object's Legend property to get a reference to this collection. The Legend object has the following members. Key members (shown in **bold**) are covered in the following reference section:

Application	AutoScaleFont
Border	Clear
Creator	Delete
Fill	Font
Height	Interior
Left	**LegendEntries**
Name	Parent
Position	Select
Shadow	Top
Width	

Be sure to set the Chart object's HasLegend property to True before using this object. The following code moves a chart's legend to the left side and sets its background color:

```
Sub LegendMembers( )
    Dim chrt As Chart, lg As Legend
    ' Get the chart.
    Set chrt = ActiveChart
    ' Make sure chart has a legend.
    chrt.HasLegend = True
    ' Get the legend.
    Set lg = chrt.Legend
    ' Set the position.
    lg.Position = xlLegendPositionLeft
    ' Change the background color.
    lg.Interior.Color = &HFFFF00
End Sub
```

legend.LegendEntries([*Index*])

Returns one or all of the entries in the legend.

legend.Position [= *xlLegendPosition*]

Sets or returns the position of the legend on the chart. Can be one of these settings:

```
xlLegendPositionCorner
xlLegendPositionRight
xlLegendPositionTop
xlLegendPositionBottom
xlLegendPositionLeft
```

LegendEntry and LegendEntries Members

Use the LegendEntries collection to get individual entries from a legend. Use the Legend object's LegendEntries property to get a reference to this collection. The LegendEntries collection and LegendEntry object have the following members. The key member (shown in **bold**) is covered in the following reference section:

Application[2]	AutoScaleFont
Count[1]	Creator[2]
Delete	Font
Height	Index
Item[1]	Left

LegendKey	Parent[2]
Select	Top
Width	

[1] Collection only
[2] Object and collection

Use the LegendEntry object to format, delete, or get the legend key for entries in a chart legend. For example, the following code makes the color of the legend entry text match the color of the legend key:

```
Sub LegendEntryMembers()
    Dim chrt As Chart, lg As Legend, le As LegendEntry
    ' Get the chart.
    Set chrt = ActiveChart
    ' Make sure chart has a legend.
    chrt.HasLegend = True
    ' Get the legend.
    Set lg = chrt.Legend
    For Each le In lg.LegendEntries
        ' Set text color to match series color.
        le.Font.Color = le.LegendKey.Border.Color
    Next
End Sub
```

legendentry.LegendKey

Returns the LegendKey object for the entry.

LegendKey Members

Use the LegendKey object to control the appearance of the series or trendline that corresponds to the legend entry. Use the LegendEntry object's LegendKey property to get a reference to this collection. The LegendKey object has the following members. Key members (shown in **bold**) are covered in the following reference section:

Application	Border
ClearFormats	Creator
Delete	Fill
Height	Interior
InvertIfNegative	Left
MarkerBackgroundColor	**MarkerBackgroundColorIndex**
MarkerForegroundColor	**MarkerForegroundColorIndex**
MarkerSize	**MarkerStyle**
Parent	**PictureType**
PictureUnit	Select
Shadow	**Smooth**
Top	Width

Setting the key properties of the legend key is equivalent to setting them for their corresponding series. LegendKey simply provides an alternate way to get at those settings. See the Series object in Chapter 16 for descriptions of the preceding key members.

The following code shows using the LegendKey to change series markers and also shows the alternate code using the Series object (commented out):

```
Sub LegendKeyMembers()
    Dim chrt As Chart, le As LegendEntry, _
      lk As LegendKey, sr As Series
    ' Get the chart.
    Set chrt = ActiveChart
    chrt.ChartType = xlLineMarkers
    ' Make sure chart has a legend.
    chrt.HasLegend = True
    For Each le In chrt.Legend.LegendEntries
        ' Get the legend key
        Set lk = le.LegendKey
        lk.MarkerStyle = xlMarkerStyleCircle
        lk.MarkerSize = 4
    Next
    ' Equivalent code using the series collection.
    'For Each sr In chrt.SeriesCollection
    '     sr.MarkerStyle = xlMarkerStyleCircle
    '     sr.MarkerSize = 4
    'Next
End Sub
```

LegendKey objects exist only for series that appear in the legend. If a series is omitted from the legend, the preceding commented code is not equivalent.

Use the ClearFormats method to restore the default formats:

```
Sub ResetLegendKeyFormat()
    Dim chrt As Chart, le As LegendEntry, _
      lk As LegendKey, sr As Series
    ' Get the chart.
    Set chrt = ActiveChart
    chrt.ChartType = xlLineMarkers
    ' Make sure chart has a legend.
    chrt.HasLegend = True
    For Each le In chrt.Legend.LegendEntries
        ' Get the legend key
        Set lk = le.LegendKey
        lk.ClearFormats
    Next
End Sub
```

Gridlines Members

Use the Gridlines objects to control the appearance of gridlines on a chart. Use the Axis object's MajorGridlines and MinorGridlines properties to get a reference to this object. The Gridlines object has the following members:

```
Application
Border
Creator
Delete
Name
Parent
Select
```

Use the Axis object's HasMajorGridlines or HasMinorGridlines to make sure these objects exist before using them. For example, the following code changes the appearance of the major gridlines for the value axis:

```
Sub FormatGridLines()
    Dim chrt As Chart, ax As Axis, gl As Gridlines
    ' Get the chart.
    Set chrt = ActiveChart
    ' Get the value axis.
    Set ax = chrt.Axes(xlValue, xlPrimary)
    ' Make sure the gridlines exist.
    ax.HasMajorGridlines = True
    ' Get the gridlines
    Set gl = ax.MajorGridlines
    ' Make them blue.
    gl.Border.Color = &HFF0000
    ' Change the line style.
    gl.Border.LineStyle = XlLineStyle.xlDot
End Sub
```

TickLabels Members

Use the TickLabels object to format the tick labels on an axis. Use the Axis object's TickLabels property to get a reference to this object. The TickLabels object has the following members. Key members (shown in **bold**) are covered in the following reference section:

Alignment	Application
AutoScaleFont	Creator
Delete	**Depth**
Font	Name
NumberFormat	**NumberFormatLinked**
NumberFormatLocal	**Offset**
Orientation	Parent
ReadingOrder	Select

ticklabels.Alignment [= setting]

This property has no apparent effect when used on tick labels. Tick labels are centered by default.

ticklabels.Depth

For tick labels on the category axis, returns the nesting level of the tick labels (usually 1).

ticklabels.Font

Returns a Font object you can use to format tick label text. For example, the following code makes the category axis tick labels italic:

```
Sub FormatTickLabels()
    Dim chrt As Chart, ax As Axis, tl As TickLabels
    ' Get the chart.
    Set chrt = ActiveChart
    ' Get the category axis.
    Set ax = chrt.Axes(xlCategory, xlPrimary)
    ' Get the tick labels.
    Set tl = ax.TickLabels
    ' Format them.
    tl.Font.Italic = True
End Sub
```

ticklabels.NumberFormat [= setting]

Sets or returns the format string used to display the tick label caption. See the DataLabels collection for more information about this property.

ticklabels.NumberFormatLinked [= setting]

True uses the number format from the source range; False uses the NumberFormat or NumberFormatLocal setting. Default is True.

ticklabels.NumberFormatLocal [= setting]

Sets or returns the format string used to display the tick label caption. This property is the same as NumberFormat only it uses the localized version of the format strings.

ticklabels.Offset [= setting]

For 2-D chart types, sets or returns the distance between the tick labels and the axis as a percentage of the default spacing. The default is 100. Must be between 0 and 1000.

ticklabels.Orientation [= *xlTickLabelOrientation*]

Sets or returns the orientation of the tick lable. Can be one of these settings:

xlTickLabelOrientationAutomatic (default)
xlTickLabelOrientationHorizontal
xlTickLabelOrientationVertical
xlTickLabelOrientationDownward
xlTickLabelOrientationUpward

ticklabels.ReadingOrder [= *setting*]

Sets or returns the reading order of the title. Can be xlContext, xlLTR, or xlRTL. Setting this property may or may not have an effect, depending on the language support that is installed. For instance, it has no effect in U.S. English (1033).

Trendline and Trendlines Members

Use the Trendlines collection to add trendlines to a series and to get trendlines from a series. Use the Chart object's Trendlines property to get a reference to this collection. Use the Trendline object to control individual trendlines on the chart. The Trendlines collection and Trendline object have the following members. Key members (shown in **bold**) are covered in the following reference section:

Add[1]	Application[2]
Backward	Border
ClearFormats	Count[1]
Creator[2]	**DataLabel**
Delete	**DisplayEquation**
DisplayRSquared	**Forward**
Index	**Intercept**
InterceptIsAuto	Item[1]
Name	**NameIsAuto**
Order	Parent[2]
Period	Select
Type	

[1] Collection only
[2] Object and collection

Trendline property settings correspond to the settings on the Add Trendline dialog box (Figure 17-6). To see the dialog, right-click a series and select Add Trendline.

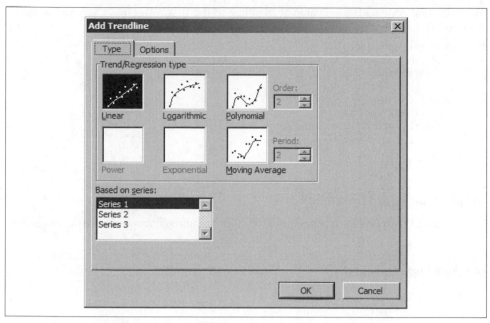

Figure 17-6. Use this dialog to browse trendline settings

---

trendlines.Add([*Type*], [*Order*], [*Period*], [*Forward*], [*Backward*], [*Intercept*], [*DisplayEquation*], [*DisplayRSquared*], [*Name*])

Adds a trendline to a series.

Argument	Settings
Type	An xlTrendlineType constant indicating how the trendline is calculated. Can be one of these settings: xlExponential, xlLinear (default), xlLogarithmic, xlMovingAvg, xlPolynomial, or xlPower.
Order	For polynomial trendlines, the trendline order from 2 to 6.
Period	For moving average trendlines, the number of data points to include in the average.
Forward	The number of periods or units to project the trendline forward beyond the plotted series. Default is 0.
Backward	The number of periods or units to project the trendline backward beyond the plotted series. Default is 0.
Intercept	Where the trendline crosses the x-axis. If this argument is omitted, the intercept is automatically set by the regression.
DisplayEquation	True displays the trendline formula as a data label; False does not. Default is False.
DisplayRSquared	True displays the trendline R-squared value as a data label; False does not. Default is False.
Name	The text to display in the chart legend for the trendline. Default is a brief, generated description of the trendline.

The following code adds a polynomial trendline to the first series in a chart and forecasts the trend three units ahead of the last data point:

```
Sub AddPolyTrendline()
    Dim chrt As Chart, tl As Trendline, tls As Trendlines
    ' Get the chart.
    Set chrt = ActiveChart
    chrt.ChartType = xlLine
    ' Get a series.
    Set tls = chrt.SeriesCollection(1).Trendlines
    Set tl = tls.Add(xlPolynomial, 6, , 3, , , True, , "Trend2")
End Sub
```

trendline.Backward [= setting]

Sets or returns the number of periods to project the trendline backward. The default is 0.

trendline.ClearFormats( )

Clears the formatting from the trendline.

trendline.DataLabel

Returns the DataLabel object for the trendline. Causes an error if DisplayEquation and DisplayRSquared are not True.

trendline.DisplayEquation [= setting]

True adds a data label to the trendline and adds the trendline's formula to the data label caption; False omits the formula. Default is False.

trendline.DisplayRSquared [= setting]

True adds a data label to the trendline and adds the trendline's R-squared value to the data label caption; False omits the value. Default is False.

trendline.Forward [= setting]

Sets or returns the number of periods to project the trendline forward. Default is 0.

trendline.Intercept [= setting]

Sets or returns the point at which the trendline crosses the value axis. Setting this property automatically sets InterceptIsAuto to False.

trendline.**InterceptIsAuto** [= *setting*]

True calculates the point where the trendline crosses the value axis using regression; False uses the Intercept property setting. Default is True.

trendline.**Name** [= *setting*]

Sets or returns the name that appears in the chart legend for the trendline. You can't use this name to retrieve the trendline from the Trendlines collection—Name is used only in the legend. Setting this property automatically sets NameIsAuto to False.

trendline.**NameIsAuto** [= *setting*]

True generates a legend entry for the trendline using the type of trendline and the series name. False uses the Name property setting.

trendline.**Order** [= *setting*]

For polynomial trendlines, sets or returns the trendline order from 2 to 6.

trendline.**Period** [= *setting*]

For moving average trendlines, sets or returns the number of data points to include in the average.

PlotArea Members

Use the PlotArea object to control the appearance of the region behind series on a chart. Use the Chart object's PlotArea property to get a reference to this collection. The PlotArea object has the following members. Key members (shown in **bold**) are covered in the following reference section:

Application	Border
ClearFormats	Creator
Fill	Height
InsideHeight	**InsideLeft**
InsideTop	**InsideWidth**
Interior	Left
Name	Parent
Select	Top
Width	

Plot area property settings correspond to the settings on the Format Plot Area dialog box (Figure 17-7). To see the dialog, right-click the plot area and select Format Plot Area.

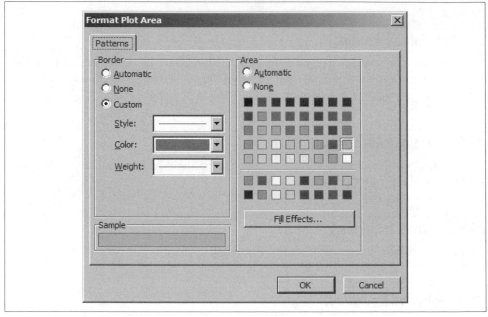

Figure 17-7. Use this dialog to control the appearance of the region behind series

plotarea.ClearFormats( )

Removes formatting from the plot area object. For example, the following code removes the built-in fill applied in ApplyPlotAreaFill:

```
Sub ResetPlotArea( )
    Dim chrt As Chart
    ' Get the chart.
    Set chrt = ActiveChart
    ' Restore default formatting.
    chrt.PlotArea.ClearFormats
End Sub
```

plotarea.Fill

Returns the ChartFillFormat object used to control the background of the plot area. The following code applies a built-in fill to the plot area:

```
Sub ApplyPlotAreaFill()
    Dim chrt As Chart, pa As PlotArea
    ' Get the chart.
    Set chrt = ActiveChart
    ' Make it a line chart
    chrt.ChartType = xlLine
    ' Get the plot area.
    Set pa = chrt.PlotArea
    ' Set a fill texture.
    pa.Fill.Visible = True
    pa.Fill.PresetTextured msoTextureCanvas
End Sub
```

plotarea.InsideHeight

Returns the height of the area on which the series is plotted. The total plot area is larger than the inside dimensions used to plot series, as demonstrated by the following code:

```
Sub CompareDimensions()
    Dim chrt As Chart, pa As PlotArea
    ' Get the chart.
    Set chrt = ActiveChart
    ' Make it a line chart
    chrt.ChartType = xlLine
    ' Get the plot area.
    Set pa = chrt.PlotArea
    ' Show difference between inside and standard dimensions.
    Debug.Print pa.InsideLeft, pa.InsideTop, pa.InsideHeight, pa.InsideWidth
    Debug.Print pa.Left, pa.Top, pa.Height, pa.Width
End Sub
```

plotarea.InsideLeft

Returns the left coordinate of the plot area on which the series is plotted.

plotarea.InsideTop

Returns the top coordinate of the plot area on which the series is plotted.

plotarea.InsideWidth

Returns the width of the plot area on which the series is plotted.

Floor Members

Use the Floor object to format the space beneath series in 3-D charts. Use the Chart object's Floor property to get a reference to this object. The Floor object has the following members:

Application	Border
ClearFormats	Creator
Fill	Interior
Name	Parent
Paste	PictureType
Select	

Only 3-D charts have a Floor object. The following code applies a background picture to the floor of a 3-D chart:

```
Sub FloorMembers()
    Dim chrt As Chart, fr As Floor
    ' Get the chart.
    Set chrt = ActiveChart
    ' Make it a 3-D chart
    chrt.ChartType = xl3DArea
    ' Get the Floor object
    Set fr = chrt.Floor
    ' Stretch the logo to fit.
    fr.Fill.Visible = True
    fr.Fill.UserPicture ThisWorkbook.Path & "\logo.bmp"
    ' Alternate: Tile the logo
    'fr.Fill.UserTextured ThisWorkbook.Path & "\logo.bmp"
End Sub
```

See the ChartFillFormat object for more information about setting fills.

Walls Members

Use the Walls object to format the space behind and to the left of the plot area in 3-D charts. Use the Chart object's Walls property to get a reference to this object. The Walls object has the following members:

Application	Border
ClearFormats	Creator
Fill	Interior
Name	Parent
Paste	PictureType
PictureUnit	Select

Only 3-D charts have a Walls object. The following code applies a background picture to the walls of a chart:

```
Sub FloorMembers()
    Dim chrt As Chart, fr As Floor
    ' Get the chart.
    Set chrt = ActiveChart
    ' Make it a 3-D chart
    chrt.ChartType = xl3DArea
    ' Get the Floor object
    Set fr = chrt.Floor
    ' Stretch the logo to fit.
    fr.Fill.Visible = True
    fr.Fill.UserPicture ThisWorkbook.Path & "\logo.bmp"
    ' Alternate: Tile the logo
    'fr.Fill.UserTextured ThisWorkbook.Path & "\logo.bmp"
End Sub
```

See the `ChartFillFormat` object for more information about setting fills.

Corners Members

Use the `Chart` object's `Corners` property to get a reference to this object. The `Corners` object has the following members:

```
Application
Creator
Name
Parent
Select
```

Only 3-D charts have a `Corners` object, and about the only thing you can do with `Corners` is to select them so the user can click and drag them to rotate the chart, as shown here:

```
Sub SelectCorners ()
    Dim chrt As Chart
    ' Get the chart.
    Set chrt = ActiveChart
    ' Make it a 3-D chart
    chrt.ChartType = xl3DArea
    ' Select the corners.
    chrt.Corners.Select
    ' Now you can drag the corners to rotate the chart...
End Sub
```

CHAPTER 18
Drawing Graphics

I'm pretty sure no one considers Excel his first choice for creating computer graphics, but Excel includes a surprisingly full set of drawing tools. And since those drawing tools are fully programmable, you can render graphics from worksheet data in pretty interesting ways. I'll show you one application of that here by diagramming hierarchical data using Excel shapes and, hopefully, open the doors to your imagination.

This chapter includes task-oriented reference information for the following objects and their related collections: Adjustments, CalloutFormat, ColorFormat, ConnectorFormat, ControlFormat, FillFormat, FreeFormBuilder, GroupShapes, LineFormat, LinkFormat, PictureFormat, ShadowFormat, Shape, ShapeNode, ShapeRange, TextEffectFormat, TextFrame, and ThreeDFormat.

 Code used in this chapter and additional samples are available in *ch18.xls*.

Draw in Excel

To use Excel's drawing tools:

1. Choose View → Toolbars → Drawing. Excel displays the Drawing toolbar (Figure 18-1).
2. Select the toolbar button for the object you want to draw, then click and drag on the worksheet or chart to draw the item.

Figure 18-1 shows a line, oval, rectangle, callout, and an image drawn on a worksheet. All shapes can be moved or resized by selecting and dragging their sizing handles. Shapes also provide a handle at the top that lets you rotate them. Autoshapes include an adjustment handle that is used to change some special aspect of the shape, as shown in Figure 18-2.

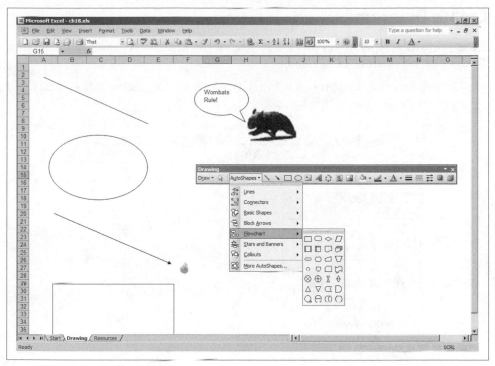

Figure 18-1. Excel's drawing tools

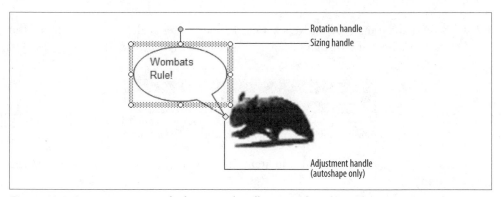

Figure 18-2. Sizing, rotation, and adjustment handles on a selected autoshape

What the adjustment handle does depends on the autoshape. For the Callout autoshape in Figure 18-2, the adjustment handle moves the apparent source of the callout. For Connector autoshapes, it sets the source and destination objects to connect. For most other autoshapes, the adjustment handle changes the aspect ratio between parts of the shape.

Create Diagrams

Excel provides a separate set of tools for creating organization charts and diagrams. To draw an org chart of a diagram in Excel:

1. On the Drawing toolbar, click Insert Diagram or Organizational Chart. Excel displays the Diagram Gallery as shown in Figure 18-3.

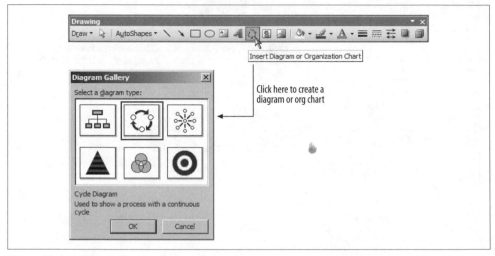

Figure 18-3. Adding a diagram to a worksheet

2. Choose a diagram type and click OK. Excel creates a default diagram on the active worksheet and displays the Diagram toolbar (Figure 18-4).

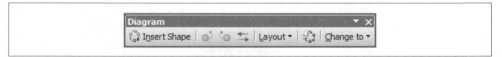

Figure 18-4. Use the Diagram toolbar to add items and control formatting

3. Use the Diagram toolbar to add items to and control the appearance of the diagram.

4. Click on labels in the diagram to add text as shown in Figure 18-5.

Program with Drawing Objects

Any object that can be drawn is considered a Shape object in Excel. You get individual Shape objects from the Worksheet or Chart object's Shapes collection. The Shape

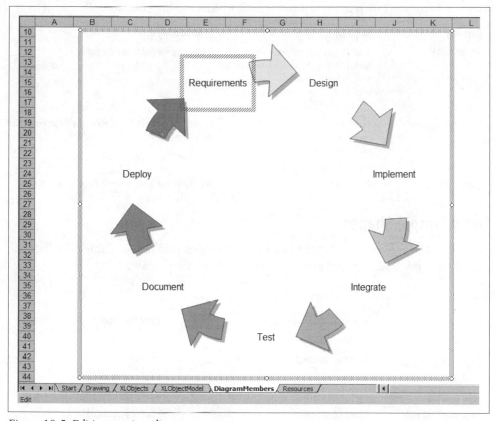

Figure 18-5. Editing text in a diagram

object is unusual because it encapsulates the members from more specific object types. Because of that, any given Shape object may or may not support any given Shape member. For example, the following code flips simple shapes on a worksheet, doesn't affect embedded objects, and causes an error if the worksheet contains a diagram:

```
Sub FlipObjects()
    Dim s As Shape
    For Each s In ActiveSheet.Shapes
        ' Doesn't affect embedded objects. Error on diagrams!
        s.Flip msoFlipHorizontal
    Next
End Sub
```

There are three general categories of Shape objects. You can determine the category of a Shape object by comparing its Type property to those listed in Table 18-1.

Table 18-1. Use the Type property to determine which Shape members are available

Category	Shape Type	Programming notes
Simple shapes	`msoAutoShape, msoFreeForm, msoLine, msoLinkedOLEObject, msoLinkedPicture, msoPicture, msoTextBox, msoTextEffect`	Most Shape members are supported.
Embedded objects	`msoChart, msoComment, msoEmbeddedOLEObject, msoFormControl, msoOLEControlObject`	Convert these objects to a specific type for access to their members.
Diagram shapes	`msoDiagram`	Accessing most Shape members causes an error.

Draw Simple Shapes

Use the Shapes collection Add methods to draw shapes from code. Table 18-2 lists the various Add methods and describes the type of shape they create.

Table 18-2. Shapes collection Add methods

Method	Draws this type of figure	Resulting shape Type
`AddCallout`	Autoshape callout	`msoCallout`
`AddConnector`	Autoshape connector line	`msoAutoShape`
`AddCurve`	Bézier curve	`msoFreeForm`
`AddDiagram`	Diagram or org chart	`msoDiagram`
`AddFormControl`	Forms 1.0 control	`msoFormControl`
`AddLabel`	Text box without a border	`msoTextBox`
`AddLine`	Line	`msoLine`
`AddOLEObject`	Embedded OLE object or Forms 2.0 control (equivalent to the `OLEObjects` collection's Add method)	`msoEmbeddedOLEObject`
`AddPicture`	Image from a file	`msoPicture`
`AddPolyline`	Line with multiple vertices	`msoFreeForm`
`AddShape`	Any autoshape	`msoAutoShape`
`AddTextBox`	Text box with rectangular border	`msoTextBox`
`AddTextEffect`	Embedded WordArt	`msoTextEffect`

Some Add methods create variations of the same type of shape, while others create seldom used or obsolete shapes. The most useful Add methods are:

```
AddConnector
AddPicture
AddShape
```

The `AddShape` method is the most general, and you can use it to create any of the autoshapes. For example, the following code draws a rectangle on the active sheet:

```
Sub DrawRect()
    Dim ws As Worksheet, s As Shape
    Set ws = ActiveSheet
    ' Draw a rectangle.
    Set s = ws.Shapes.AddShape(msoShapeRectangle, 10, 20, 100, 20)
    ' Color it blue
    s.Fill.Visible = True
    s.Fill.ForeColor.SchemeColor = 4
End Sub
```

The `AddShape` method has a long list of possible autoshape types, as shown in Figure 18-6.

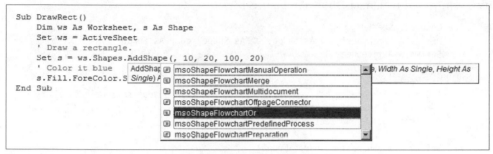

Figure 18-6. Selecting the type of shape to create with AddShape

Add Text

You can add text to any of the autoshapes using the `Shape` object's `TextFrame` property. The `TextFrame` object provides a `Characters` property you can use to set the text displayed on the object, as well as formatting properties, as demonstrated by the following code:

```
Sub DrawText()
    Dim ws As Worksheet, s As Shape
    Set ws = ActiveSheet
    ' Draw a rectangle.
    Set s = ws.Shapes.AddShape(msoShapeRectangle, 10, 20, 100, 20)
    ' Add text.
    s.TextFrame.Characters.text = "Some text to display"
    ' Center the text
    s.TextFrame.HorizontalAlignment = xlHAlignCenter
    s.TextFrame.VerticalAlignment = xlVAlignCenter
    ' Set the font
    s.TextFrame.Characters.Font.Name - "Comic Sans MS"
    s.TextFrame.Characters.Font.Bold = True
    ' Resize to fit text
    s.TextFrame.AutoSize = True
End Sub
```

You could substitute the AddTextBox method for AddShape in the preceding code; however, AddShape is more flexible since you can create any shape—not just rectangles.

Connect Shapes

To draw lines between two shapes:

1. Use the AddConnector method to create a connector shape.

2. Use the connector shape's ConnectorFormat property to establish the connection.

Connectors attach to connection sites on a Shape object and maintain the connection even if you drag the objects to another location. The following code creates the two connected rectangles shown in Figure 18-7:

```
Sub ConnectShapes()
    Dim ws As Worksheet, s1 As Shape, s2 As Shape, conn As Shape
    Set ws = ActiveSheet
    ' Draw rectangle
    DrawRect
    ' Get a reference to new rectangle (last object in Shapes collection)
    Set s1 = ws.Shapes(ws.Shapes.Count)
    ' Repeat for second rectangle.
    DrawRect
    Set s2 = ws.Shapes(ws.Shapes.Count)
    ' Move the second rectangle.
    s2.IncrementLeft 100
    s2.IncrementTop 50
    ' Create a connector (position and size don't matter).
    Set conn = ws.Shapes.AddConnector(msoConnectorCurve, 1, 1, 1, 1)
    ' Connect to each rectangle.
    conn.ConnectorFormat.BeginConnect s1, 3
    conn.ConnectorFormat.EndConnect s2, 2
End Sub
```

 ConnectShapes reuses the DrawRect example shown previously.

The second argument for BeginConnect and EndConnect determines where the connector attaches to the shape. For most shapes, connection sites are numbered counterclockwise on the shape starting at the top, as shown in Figure 18-8.

To establish the shortest path between two objects, call RerouteConnections. That method adjusts the connection to use the two nearest connection sites.

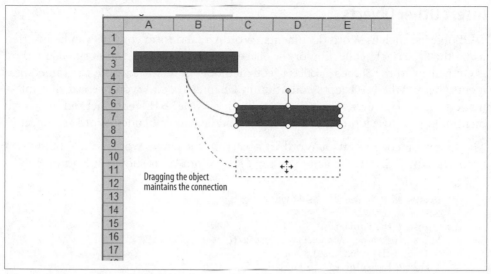

Figure 18-7. Connected shapes stay connected

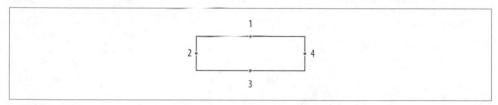

Figure 18-8. Connection site numbering

Insert Pictures

Use the AddPicture method to insert a picture as a shape. Pictures are treated like any other shape, so Shape methods like Flip work fine. In addition, picture shapes have a PictureFormat property that you can use to adjust brightness, transparency, and other attributes of the picture. The following code inserts a logo on the active worksheet, flips it, and makes its background transparent:

```
Sub InsertPicture()
    Dim ws As Worksheet, s As Shape
    Set ws = ActiveSheet
    ' Insert the image.
    Set s = ws.Shapes.AddPicture(ThisWorkbook.Path & "\logo.bmp", _
        False, True, 120, 170, 100, 100)
    ' Flip the image.
    s.Flip msoFlipHorizontal
    ' The picture background is white.
    s.PictureFormat.TransparencyColor = &HFFFFFF
    ' Turn on transparency.
    s.PictureFormat.TransparentBackground = True
End Sub
```

Insert Other Objects

OLE objects, such as Word documents, WordArt, and form controls can be inserted using the OLEObjects collection or the Shapes collection. The OLEObjects.Add method is equivalent to the Shapes.AddOLEObject method—in fact, they take the same arguments. I cover the OLEObjects collection in Chapter 10, so I won't repeat that information here. However, the Shapes collection's AddTextEffect method is worth mentioning because it provides a shortcut to adding an embedded WordArt object.

The following code inserts a WordArt object on the active worksheet, sets the text properties, then displays a picture on top of the WordArt as shown in Figure 18-9:

```
Sub InsertWordArt( )
    Dim ws As Worksheet, s As Shape
    Set ws = ActiveSheet
    ' Insert the WordArt.
    Set s = ws.Shapes.AddTextEffect(msoTextEffect1, "Wombat!", "Arial", 36, _
      True, False, 100, 200)
    ' Change the color of the WordArt
    s.Fill.ForeColor.RGB = &HFF
    ' Display picture using previous example.
    InsertPicture
End Sub
```

Figure 18-9. WordArt combined with a transparent image

Group Shapes

Sometimes you'll want to perform the same operation on more than one shape. The easiest way to do that is to group the shapes using the ShapeRange object, then perform the operation on that object. The following code demonstrates how to group objects as a ShareRange:

```
Sub GroupObjects( )
    Dim ws As Worksheet, s As Shape, sr As ShapeRange
    Set ws = ActiveSheet
    ' Create a ShapeRange containing the last two shapes drawn.
    Set sr = ws.Shapes.Range(Array(ws.Shapes.Count - 1, ws.Shapes.Count))
    ' Flip the objects
    sr.Flip msoFlipHorizontal
    ' Group the objects in the Excel UI.
    sr.Group
End Sub
```

The ShapeRange object's Group method groups the objects so they can be moved, resized, or deleted as a unit by the user. If you run GroupObjects after InsertWordArt, both the wombat and the text are flipped, as shown in Figure 18-10.

Figure 18-10. Grouping objects with ShapeRange

The ShareRange object has almost all of the same members as the Shape object, and as with Shape, some of those members aren't valid for certain types of shapes.

Program Diagrams

Excel diagrams might seem very useful from a programming perspective; however, they have a serious limitation: you can't get or set the text of diagram nodes from code. See *http://support.microsoft.com/default.aspx?scid=kb,en-us;317293* for complete details.

This appears to be a bug in the 2002 and 2003 versions of Excel, so you can assume it will continue into the future. Interestingly, you can use macro recording to record your actions building a diagram in the Excel user interface; however, if you run the macro, you will see the error in Figure 18-11.

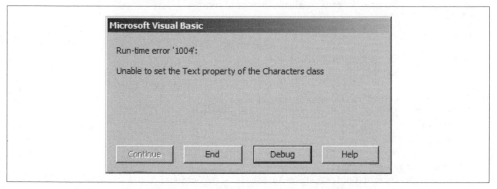

Figure 18-11. Programming diagrams is not well supported in Excel

  Many of the code samples for the Diagram and DiagramNode objects in Help fail if you run them in Excel.

Microsoft suggests using the `Diagram` object in the Word or PowerPoint application as a workaround to this problem, and those applications *do* seem to work. However, I think it's more reliable to use Excel's autoshapes and connectors if you want to diagram data from a worksheet.

The following code draws a hierarchical diagram from items on the active worksheet. Items in the first column are top-level parents and items in subsequent columns are all related as shown in Figure 18-12:

```
' Module-level variable used to set Top property
' of subsequent shapes.
Dim m_lastShape As Shape

Sub DrawDiagram()
    Dim ws1 As Worksheet, ws2 As Worksheet, cel As Range, _
      s As Shape, p() As Shape, top As Single
    ' Get the source worksheet.
    Set ws1 = ActiveSheet
    ' Create a new worksheet for the diagram.
    Set ws2 = Worksheets.Add
    ' Array to keep track parents (for connections).
    ReDim p(1 To ws1.UsedRange.Columns.Count)
    ' For each cell with data.
    For Each cel In ws1.UsedRange
        If cel.Value <> "" Then
            ' Items in the first column are top-level parents.
            If cel.Column = 1 Then
                ' If there's more than one top-level parent, set top.
                If m_lastShape Is Nothing Then top = 5 _
                  Else top = m_lastShape.top
                Set s = DrawParent(5, top, , , ws2)
                ' Track this object as parent (index = column number)
                Set p(cel.Column) = s
            ' Items in other columns are children.
            Else
                Set s = DrawChild(p(cel.Column - 1), ws2)
                ' Keep track of relationships.
                Set p(cel.Column) = s
            End If
            ' Set the text in the Shape object to match cell contents.
            s.TextFrame.Characters.text = cel.Value
        End If
    Next
End Sub

' Draw a top-level Shape.
Function DrawParent(Optional left As Single = 0, Optional top As Single = 0, _
  Optional width As Single = 100, Optional height As Single = 20, _
  Optional ws As Worksheet) As Shape
    Dim res As Shape
    ' Use active sheet if not specified
    If ws Is Nothing Then Set ws = ActiveSheet
    Set res = ws.Shapes.AddShape(msoShapeRoundedRectangle, _
```

```
        left, top, width, height)
    ' Add temporary text (required for alignment properties).
    res.TextFrame.Characters.text = "Parent"
    ' Set formatting.
    res.TextFrame.HorizontalAlignment = xlHAlignCenter
    res.TextFrame.VerticalAlignment = xlVAlignCenter
    Set m_lastShape = res
    ' Return the shape.
    Set DrawParent = res
End Function

Function DrawChild(parent As Shape, Optional ws As Worksheet) As Shape
    Dim res As Shape, conn As Shape, indent As Single
    ' Use active sheet if not specified
    If ws Is Nothing Then Set ws = ActiveSheet
    ' If this is the first child, then parent is source of height.
    If m_lastShape Is Nothing Then Set m_lastShape = parent
    indent = 5
    Set res = ws.Shapes.AddShape(msoShapeRoundedRectangle, _
      parent.left + (parent.width \ 2) + indent, _
      m_lastShape.top + m_lastShape.height + indent, _
      parent.width, parent.height)
    ' Add temporary text (required for alignment properties).
    res.TextFrame.Characters.text = "Child"
    ' Get formatting from parent
    parent.PickUp: res.Apply
    ' Connect the parent and child.
    Set conn = ws.Shapes.AddConnector(msoConnectorElbow, 1, 1, 1, 1)
    conn.ConnectorFormat.BeginConnect parent, 3
    conn.ConnectorFormat.EndConnect res, 2
    ' Save this child for future positioning.
    Set m_lastShape = res
    ' Return the child shape
    Set DrawChild = res
End Function
```

The data must be formatted as shown in Figure 18-12. Feel free to modify this code to use other shapes or layouts. It's harder to create tree-style diagrams than the vertical layout shown here—that might be an interesting way to test your knowledge!

 Never struggle with tools that don't work. For that reason, I've omitted Diagram, DiagramNode, and related members from the reference sections in this chapter. When programming Excel, it is best to simply avoid those objects.

Shape, ShapeRange, and Shapes Members

Use the Shapes collection to draw graphics on a worksheet or chart. Use the Worksheet or Chart object's Shapes property to get a reference to this collection. Use the Shape object to change the appearance of one shape; use ShapeRange to change

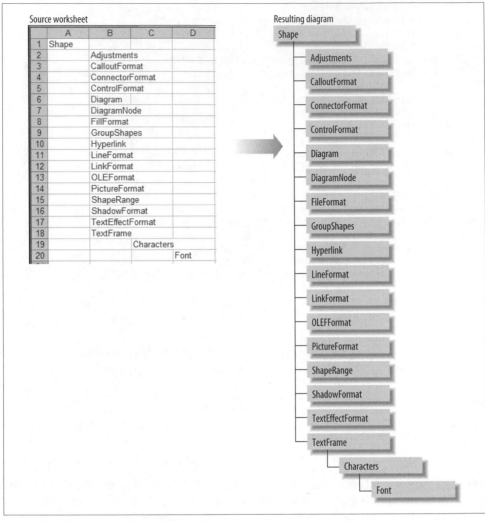

Figure 18-12. Diagramming the Shape object hierarchy

groups of shapes. Shapes, Shape and ShapeRange have the following members. Key
members (shown in **bold**) are covered in the following reference section:

AddCallout[1]	**AddConnector**[1]	**AddCurve**[1]
AddDiagram[2]	AddFormControl[1]	**AddLabel**[1]
AddLine[1]	AddOLEObject[1]	**AddPicture**[1]
AddPolyline[1]	**AddShape**[1]	**AddTextbox**[1]
AddTextEffect[1]	**Adjustments**	**Align**[3]
AlternativeText	Application[2]	**Apply**
AutoShapeType	**BlackWhiteMode**	BottomRightCell
BuildFreeform[1]	**Callout**	Child
ConnectionSiteCount	**Connector**	**ConnectorFormat**
ControlFormat	Copy	CopyPicture

Count[1]	Creator[2]	Cut
Delete	Diagram	DiagramNode
Distribute[3]	**Duplicate**	**Fill**
Flip	FormControlType	**Group[3]**
GroupItems	HasDiagram	HasDiagramNode
Height	**HorizontalFlip**	**Hyperlink**
ID	**IncrementLeft**	**IncrementRotation**
IncrementTop	Item[1]	Left
Line	**LinkFormat**	**LockAspectRatio**
Locked	Name	Nodes
OLEFormat	OnAction	Parent[2]
ParentGroup	**PickUp**	**PictureFormat**
Placement	**Range[1]**	**Regroup[3]**
RerouteConnections	**Rotation**	ScaleHeight
ScaleWidth	Script	Select
SelectAll[1]	**SetShapesDefaultProperties**	**Shadow**
TextEffect	**TextFrame**	**ThreeD**
Top	TopLeftCell	**Type**
Ungroup	**VerticalFlip**	**Vertices**
Visible	Width	ZOrder
ZOrderPosition		

[1] Collection only
[2] Object and collection
[3] ShapeRange only

shapes.AddCallout(*Type, Left, Top, Width, Height*)

Draws a simple callout and returns the callout's Shape object.

Argument	Settings
Type	An msoCalloutType constant indicating the type of callout to draw. Can be msoCalloutOne, msoCalloutTwo, msoCalloutMixed, msoCalloutThree, or msoCalloutFour.
Left	The horizontal position of the shape in points.
Top	The vertical position of the shape in points.
Width	The width of the shape in points.
Height	The height of the shape in points.

shapes.AddConnector(*Type, BeginX, BeginY, EndX, EndY*)

Draws a connector line and returns the connector's Shape object.

Argument	Settings
Type	An msoConnectorType constant. Can be msoConnectorElbow, msoConnectorTypeMixed, msoConnectorCurve, or msoConnectorStraight.
BeginX	The horizontal coordinate of the start of the connector line.

Argument	Settings
BeginY	The vertical coordinate of the start of the connector line.
EndX	The horizontal coordinate of the end of the connector line.
EndY	The vertical coordinate of the end of the connector line.

You can set the begin and end coordinates to an arbitrary value, then use the BeginConnect and EndConnect methods to connect two objects. Using the RerouteConnections method creates the shortest path between the objects. The following code demonstrates using those methods to connect two shapes as shown in Figure 18-13:

```
Sub QuickConnect()
    Dim s1 As Shape, s2 As Shape, conn As Shape
    ' Create a shape
    Set s1 = ActiveSheet.Shapes.AddShape(msoShapeCube, 100, 10, 50, 60)
    ' Create another shape
    Set s2 = ActiveSheet.Shapes.AddShape(msoShapeCan, 50, 100, 50, 60)
    ' Create connector with arbitrary coordinates
    Set conn = ActiveSheet.Shapes.AddConnector(msoConnectorCurve, 1, 1, 1, 1)
    ' Connect shapes
    conn.ConnectorFormat.BeginConnect s1, 1
    conn.ConnectorFormat.EndConnect s2, 1
    ' Connect via shortest path (changes connection sites)
    conn.RerouteConnections
End Sub
```

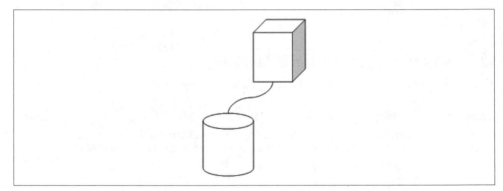

Figure 18-13. Creating a connection

shapes.AddCurve(*SafeArrayOfPoints*)

Draws a Bézier curve from an array of coordinate pairs and returns the curve's Shape object.

Argument	Settings
SafeArrayOfPoints	The 2-D array of points containing the vertices and control points of the curve

The following code draws an S-shaped curve that starts at (80,100) and ends at (110,30):

```
Sub DrawCurve()
    Dim s As Shape, pts() As Single
    ' Array of points.
    ReDim pts(3, 1)
    pts(0, 0) = 80
    pts(0, 1) = 100
    pts(1, 0) = 200
    pts(1, 1) = 150
    pts(2, 0) = 15
    pts(2, 1) = 20
    pts(3, 0) = 110
    pts(3, 1) = 30
    ' Draw a curve
    Set s = ActiveSheet.Shapes.AddCurve(pts)
End Sub
```

shapes.AddLabel(*Orientation, Left, Top, Width, Height*)

Draws a text box without a border and returns the label's Shape object.

Argument	Settings
Orientation	An msoTextOrientation constant. Can be msoTextOrientationDownward, msoTextOrientationHorizontal, msoTextOrientationHorizontalRotatedFarEast, msoTextOrientationMixed, msoTextOrientationUpward, msoTextOrientationVertical, or msoTextOrientationVerticalFarEast.
Left	The horizontal position of the shape in points.
Top	The vertical position of the shape in points.
Width	The width of the shape in points.
Height	The height of the shape in points.

Use the TextFrame property to get or set the text in the label and to set the formatting of the text. The following code draws a label on the active sheet:

```
Sub DrawLabel()
    Dim s As Shape
    ' Create label (height/width will be set automatically).
    Set s = ActiveSheet.Shapes.AddLabel(msoTextOrientationHorizontal, _
        100, 100, 1, 1)
    s.TextFrame.Characters.text = "This is some label text"
End Sub
```

The *Width* and *Height* arguments in the preceding code are required but arbitrary because the TextFrame object's AutoSize property is True by default. The label is automatically resized to fit the text.

shapes.AddLine(*BeginX, BeginY, EndX, EndY*)

Draws a straight line and returns the line's Shape object.

Argument	Settings
BeginX	The horizontal coordinate for the origin of the line
BeginY	The vertical coordinate for the origin of the line
EndX	The horizontal coordinate for the end of the line
EndY	The vertical coordinate for the end of the line

Use the Line property to set the style and formatting used for the line. The following code draws a dashed line with an arrowhead:

```
Sub DrawLine( )
    Dim ws As Worksheet, s As Shape
    Set ws = ActiveSheet
    ' Create label (height/width will be set by AutoSize).
    Set s = ws.Shapes.AddLine(100, 100, 200, 200)
    s.Line.DashStyle = msoLineDash
    s.Line.EndArrowheadStyle = msoArrowheadStealth
End Sub
```

shapes.AddPicture(*Filename, LinkToFile, SaveWithDocument, Left, Top, Width, Height*)

Adds a picture to a worksheet or chart and the picture's Shape object.

Argument	Settings
Filename	The picture file to load.
LinkToFile	True links the shape to the picture file; False copies the image into the file.
SaveWithDocument	True saves the image in the workbook; False saves only link information in the document. If LinkToFile is False, SaveWithDocument must be True.
Left	The horizontal position of the shape in points.
Top	The vertical position of the shape in points.
Width	The width of the shape in points.
Height	The height of the shape in points.

Excel scales the image to fit the *Width* and *Height* arguments. To restore the image's actual height and width, use the ScaleHeight and ScaleWidth methods as shown here:

```
Sub DrawPicture( )
    Dim ws As Worksheet, s As Shape
    Set ws = ActiveSheet
    ' Insert the image.
    Set s = ws.Shapes.AddPicture(ThisWorkbook.Path & "\logo.bmp", _
        False, True, 100, 100, 1, 1)
    ' Use picture's height and width.
```

```
        s.ScaleHeight 1, msoCTrue
        s.ScaleWidth 1, msoCTrue
    End Sub
```

Use the `PictureFormat` property to control a picture's brightness, contrast, and transparency.

shapes.AddPolyline(*SafeArrayOfPoints*)

Draws a segmented line from an array of coordinate pairs and returns the line's `Shape` object.

Argument	Settings
SafeArrayOfPoints	The 2-D array of points containing the vertices of the line

Use the `Line` property to set the style and formatting used for the line. The following code draws a Z-shaped line that starts at (80,100) and ends at (110,30):

```
Sub DrawZ( )
    Dim s As Shape, pts( ) As Single
    ' Array of points.
    ReDim pts(3, 1)
    pts(0, 0) = 80
    pts(0, 1) = 100
    pts(1, 0) = 200
    pts(1, 1) = 150
    pts(2, 0) = 15
    pts(2, 1) = 20
    pts(3, 0) = 110
    pts(3, 1) = 30
    ' Draw a curve
    Set s = ActiveSheet.Shapes.AddPolyline(pts)
End Sub
```

shapes.AddShape(*Type, Left, Top, Width, Height*)

Draws an autoshape and returns the autoshape's `Shape` object.

Argument	Settings
Type	An `msoAutoShapeType` constant. Can be any of the settings listed following this table.
Left	The horizontal position of the shape in points.
Top	The vertical position of the shape in points.
Width	The width of the shape in points.
Height	The height of the shape in points.

The `msoAutoShapeType` constant can be one of:

msoShape4pointStar	msoShape5pointStar
msoShape8pointStar	msoShape16pointStar

```
msoShape24pointStar                       msoShape32pointStar
msoShapeActionButtonBackorPrevious        msoShapeActionButtonBeginning
msoShapeActionButtonCustom                msoShapeActionButtonDocument
msoShapeActionButtonEnd                    msoShapeActionButtonForwardorNext
msoShapeActionButtonHelp                   msoShapeActionButtonHome
msoShapeActionButtonInformation            msoShapeActionButtonMovie
msoShapeActionButtonReturn                 msoShapeActionButtonSound
msoShapeArc                                msoShapeBalloon
msoShapeBentArrow                          msoShapeBentUpArrow
msoShapeBevel                              msoShapeBlockArc
msoShapeCan                                msoShapeChevron
msoShapeCircularArrow                      msoShapeCloudCallout
msoShapeCross                              msoShapeCube
msoShapeCurvedDownArrow                    msoShapeCurvedDownRibbon
msoShapeCurvedLeftArrow                    msoShapeCurvedRightArrow
msoShapeCurvedUpArrow                      msoShapeCurvedUpRibbon
msoShapeDiamond                            msoShapeDonut
msoShapeDoubleBrace                        msoShapeDoubleBracket
msoShapeDoubleWave                         msoShapeDownArrow
msoShapeDownArrowCallout                   msoShapeDownRibbon
msoShapeExplosion1                         msoShapeExplosion2
msoShapeFlowchartAlternateProcess          msoShapeFlowchartCard
msoShapeFlowchartCollate                   msoShapeFlowchartConnector
msoShapeFlowchartData                      msoShapeFlowchartDecision
msoShapeFlowchartDelay                     msoShapeFlowchartDirectAccessStorage
msoShapeFlowchartDisplay                   msoShapeFlowchartDocument
msoShapeFlowchartExtract                   msoShapeFlowchartInternalStorage
msoShapeFlowchartMagneticDisk              msoShapeFlowchartManualInput
msoShapeFlowchartManualOperation           msoShapeFlowchartMerge
msoShapeFlowchartMultidocument             msoShapeFlowchartOffpageConnector
msoShapeFlowchartOr                        msoShapeFlowchartPredefinedProcess
msoShapeFlowchartPreparation               msoShapeFlowchartProcess
msoShapeFlowchartPunchedTape               msoShapeFlowchartSequentialAccessStorage
msoShapeFlowchartSort                      msoShapeFlowchartStoredData
msoShapeFlowchartSummingJunction           msoShapeFlowchartTerminator
msoShapeFoldedCorner                       msoShapeHeart
msoShapeHexagon                            msoShapeHorizontalScroll
msoShapeIsoscelesTriangle                  msoShapeLeftArrow
msoShapeLeftArrowCallout                   msoShapeLeftBrace
msoShapeLeftBracket                        msoShapeLeftRightArrow
msoShapeLeftRightArrowCallout              msoShapeLeftRightUpArrow
```

msoShapeLeftUpArrow	msoShapeLightningBolt
msoShapeLineCallout1	msoShapeLineCallout1AccentBar
msoShapeLineCallout1BorderandAccentBar	msoShapeLineCallout1NoBorder
msoShapeLineCallout2	msoShapeLineCallout2AccentBar
msoShapeLineCallout2BorderandAccentBar	msoShapeLineCallout2NoBorder
msoShapeLineCallout3	msoShapeLineCallout3AccentBar
msoShapeLineCallout3BorderandAccentBar	msoShapeLineCallout3NoBorder
msoShapeLineCallout4	msoShapeLineCallout4AccentBar
msoShapeLineCallout4BorderandAccentBar	msoShapeLineCallout4NoBorder
msoShapeMixed	msoShapeMoon
msoShapeNoSymbol	msoShapeNotchedRightArrow
msoShapeNotPrimitive	msoShapeOctagon
msoShapeOval	msoShapeOvalCallout
msoShapeParallelogram	msoShapePentagon
msoShapePlaque	msoShapeQuadArrow
msoShapeQuadArrowCallout	msoShapeRectangle
msoShapeRectangularCallout	msoShapeRegularPentagon
msoShapeRightArrow	msoShapeRightArrowCallout
msoShapeRightBrace	msoShapeRightBracket
msoShapeRightTriangle	msoShapeRoundedRectangle
msoShapeRoundedRectangularCallout	msoShapeSmileyFace
msoShapeStripedRightArrow	msoShapeSun
msoShapeTrapezoid	msoShapeUpArrow
msoShapeUpArrowCallout	msoShapeUpDownArrow
msoShapeUpDownArrowCallout	msoShapeUpRibbon
msoShapeUTurnArrow	msoShapeVerticalScroll
msoShapeWave	

Use the TextFrame property to add text to an autoshape. Use the AutoShapeType property to convert one autoshape into another.

shapes.AddTextbox(*Orientation, Left, Top, Width, Height*)

Draws a text box surrounded by a rectangular border and returns the text box's Shape object.

Argument	Settings
Orientation	An msoTextOrientation constant. Can be msoTextOrientationDownward, msoTextOrientationHorizontal, msoTextOrientationHorizontalRotatedFarEast, msoTextOrientationMixed, msoTextOrientationUpward, msoTextOrientationVertical, or msoTextOrientationVerticalFarEast.
left	The horizontal position of the shape in points.

Argument	Settings
Top	The vertical position of the shape in points.
Width	The width of the shape in points.
Height	The height of the shape in points.

Use the `TextFrame` property to get or set the text in the shape and to set the formatting of the text. Unlike labels, text boxes do not automatically resize to fit their text. You must set the `AutoSize` property as shown here:

```
Sub DrawTextbox( )
    Dim ws As Worksheet, s As Shape
    Set ws = ActiveSheet
    ' Create label (height/width will be set by AutoSize).
    Set s = ws.Shapes.AddTextbox(msoTextOrientationHorizontal, 100, 100, 1, 1)
    s.TextFrame.Characters.text = "This is some label text"
    ' Resize text box to fit text.
    s.TextFrame.AutoSize = True
End Sub
```

*shapes.*AddTextEffect(*PresetTextEffect, Text, FontName, FontSize, FontBold, FontItalic, Left, Top*)

Adds a WordArt embedded object and returns the Shape object for the embedded object.

Argument	Settings
PresetTextEffect	An `MsoPresetTextEffect` constant. Can be `msoTextEffect1` to `msoTextEffect30`.
Text	The text to embed.
FontName	The name of the font to use.
FontSize	The size of the font in points.
FontBold	True uses bold; False uses the normal weight font.
FontItalic	True uses italic font; False uses roman.
Left	The horizontal position of the shape in points.
Top	The vertical position of the shape in points.

Use the `TextEffect` property, not `TextFrame`, to change the text or appearance of the embedded WordArt object. The following code embeds a WordArt object, then changes its text:

```
Sub EmbedWordArt( )
    Dim ws As Worksheet, s As Shape
    Set ws = ActiveSheet
    ' Create label (height/width will be set by AutoSize).
    Set s = ws.Shapes.AddTextEffect(msoTextEffect19, "Wombat!", "Arial", 36, _
        True, False, 100, 100)
    ' Change text.
    s.TextEffect.text = "New Text"
End Sub
```

shape.**Adjustments**

For an autoshape, connector, or WordArt shape, returns the `Adjustments` collection; for other types of shapes, causes an error. Use `Adjustments` to move the adjustment handles on a shape (the equivalent of clicking and dragging on the adjustment handle). Figure 18-2 illustrates adjustment handles.

shaperange.**Align(***AlignCmd, RelativeTo***)**

Aligns the shapes in a `ShapeRange`.

Argument	Settings
AlignCmd	An `msoAlignCmd` constant. Can be `msoAlignCenters`, `msoAlignMiddles`, `msoAlignTops`, `msoAlignBottoms`, `msoAlignLefts`, or `msoAlignRights`.
RelativeTo	True aligns shapes relative to the Excel window; False aligns shapes relative to the first shape in the `ShapeRange`.

The following code uses previous examples to draw three shapes, adds them to a ShapeRange, then aligns the shapes relative to the first shape drawn:

```
Sub LeftAlign( )
    Dim ws As Worksheet, sr As ShapeRange
    Set ws = ActiveSheet
    ' Draw three objects (call previous examples)
    DrawRect
    DrawLine
    EmbedWordArt
    ' Create a shape range
    Set sr = ws.Shapes.Range(Array(1, 2, 3))
    ' Left-align three shapes
    sr.align msoAlignLefts, False
End Sub
```

shape.**AlternativeText** [= *setting*]

Sets or returns the alternate text used for the shape if the worksheet or chart is saved in HTML format.

shape.**Apply( )**

Applies formatting that was previously picked up from another shape. The `PickUp` and `Apply` methods are used together to copy formatting from one shape to another. For example, the following code copies the formatting from the first shape on a worksheet to all of the others on the same worksheet:

```
Sub FormatSameAsFirst( )
    Dim ws As Worksheet, s As Shape
    Set ws = ActiveSheet
```

```
        For Each s In ws.Shapes
            ' Get formatting from first shape.
            ws.Shapes(1).PickUp
            ' Apply it to each shape.
            s.Apply
        Next
    End Sub
```

Calling Apply clears the formatting being copied, so you must call PickUp before each Apply.

shape.AutoShapeType [= msoAutoShapeType]

Converts one autoshape to another autoshape. Causes an error for connector, line, picture, OLE object, and WordArt shape types. See the list under "*shapes*.AddShape(*Type*, *Left*, *Top*, *Width*, *Height*)," earlier in this chapter, for a list of possible settings.

shape.BlackWhiteMode [= msoBlackWhiteMode]

Sets or returns how the shape appears when viewed in black and white. Can be:

msoBlackWhiteAutomatic	msoBlackWhiteBlack
msoBlackWhiteBlackTextAndLine	msoBlackWhiteDontShow
msoBlackWhiteGrayOutline	msoBlackWhiteGrayScale
msoBlackWhiteHighContrast	msoBlackWhiteInverseGrayScale
msoBlackWhiteLightGrayScale	msoBlackWhiteMixed
msoBlackWhiteWhite	

shapes.BuildFreeform(EditingType, X1, Y1)

Begins drawing freeform line art and returns a FreeformBuilder object used to add elements to the freeform.

Argument	Settings
EditingType	An msoEditingType constant. Can be msoEditingAuto or msoEditingCorner.
X1	The horizontal position of the first element of the shape in points.
Y1	The vertical position of the first element of the shape in points.

Use the ConvertToShape method for drawing the freeform and render it as a shape as shown here:

```
Sub DrawFreeform( )
    Dim ws As Worksheet, s As Shape, fb As FreeformBuilder
    Set ws = ActiveSheet
    ' Create freeform
    Set fb = ws.Shapes.BuildFreeform(msoEditingAuto, 380, 230)
    ' Add segments.
    fb.AddNodes msoSegmentCurve, msoEditingCorner, _
```

```
        380, 230, 400, 250, 450, 300
    fb.AddNodes msoSegmentCurve, msoEditingAuto, 480, 200
    fb.AddNodes msoSegmentLine, msoEditingAuto, 480, 400
    fb.AddNodes msoSegmentLine, msoEditingAuto, 380, 230
    ' Render drawing.
    fb.ConvertToShape
End Sub
```

*shape.*Callout

For callout shapes, returns a `CalloutFormat` object used to format the callout. For other shape types, causes an error.

*shape.*ConnectionSiteCount

Returns the number of connection sites available on the shape.

*shape.*Connector

Returns True if the shape is a connector, False if it is not.

*shape.*ConnectorFormat

For connector shapes, returns a `ConnectorFormat` object. For other shape types, causes an error. The following code changes all of the connections on a worksheet to use the curved connector style:

```
Sub ChangeConnectors()
    Dim ws As Worksheet, s As Shape
    Set ws = ActiveSheet
    For Each s In ws.Shapes
        ' If the shape is a connector, change its style.
        If s.Connector Then _
            s.ConnectorFormat.Type = msoConnectorCurve
    Next
End Sub
```

*shape.*ControlFormat

For Forms 1.0 shapes, returns the `ControlFormat` object used to access the properties and methods of the control. For other shape types, causes an error.

*shaperange.*Distribute(*DistributeCmd, RelativeTo*)

Distributes the shapes in a ShapeRange vertically or horizontally.

Argument	Settings
DistributeCmd	Can be msoDistributeHorizontally or msoDistributeVertically.
RelativeTo	Must be False in Excel.

The following code distributes the shapes on a worksheet vertically; this is the equivalent of selecting Draw → Align or Distribute → Distribute Horizontally on the Drawing toolbar:

```
Sub DistributeVertically( )
    Dim ws As Worksheet, sr As ShapeRange
    Set ws = ActiveSheet
    ' Create a shape range for all shapes on sheet.
    ws.Shapes.SelectAll
    Set sr = Selection.ShapeRange
    ' Distribute shapes
    sr.Distribute msoDistributeVertically, False
End Sub
```

*shape.*Duplicate( )

Copies a shape and returns a reference to the new Shape object. The following code makes a copy of the first shape on a worksheet, then moves the copy to the left:

```
Sub CopyShape( )
    Dim ws As Worksheet, s As Shape
    Set ws = ActiveSheet
    Set s = ws.Shapes(1)
    ' Make copy.
    Set s = s.Duplicate
    ' Move copy.
    s.IncrementLeft 100
End Sub
```

*shape.*Fill

Returns a FillFormat object for the shape.

*shape.*Flip(*FlipCmd*)

Flips the shape vertically or horizontally.

Argument	Settings
FlipCmd	Can be msoFlipHorizontal or msoFlipVertical

Most shapes can be flipped, but OLE objects and form controls cannot.

shape.FormControlType

For Form 1.0 controls, returns an xlFormControl constant indicating the control type. For other shapes, causes an error.

shaperange.Group( )

Groups the shapes in the ShapeRange so that they can be selected, moved, or deleted as a single shape by the user. The following code demonstrates grouping and ungrouping the shapes on a worksheet:

```
Sub GroupUngroup( )
    Dim ws As Worksheet, sr As ShapeRange, s As Shape
    Set ws = ActiveSheet
    Select Case ws.Shapes.Count
        Case Is > 1
            ' Create a shape range for all shapes on sheet.
            ws.Shapes.SelectAll
            Set sr = Selection.ShapeRange
            ' Group all the items
            Set s = sr.Group
            ' Show count of items in group.
            Debug.Print s.GroupItems.Count & " shapes grouped."
        Case 1
            ws.Shapes(1).Ungroup
            Debug.Print "Ungrouped shapes"
        Case 0
            Debug.Print "No shapes to group."
    End Select
End Sub
```

shape.GroupItems

Returns the collection of shapes in a group.

shape.HorizontalFlip

Returns True if the shape has been flipped horizontally, False otherwise.

shape.Hyperlink

Returns a Hyperlink object for the shape. See Chapter 10 for more information on the Hyperlink object.

shape.ID

Returns a numeric identifier for the shape.

shape.**IncrementLeft(***Increment***)**

Moves a shape horizontally.

Argument	Settings
Increment	The number of points to move the shape

shape.**IncrementRotation(***Increment***)**

Rotates a shape.

Argument	Settings
Increment	The number of degrees to rotate the shape

The following code draws and rotates a star:

```
Sub Rotate()
    Dim ws As Worksheet, s As Shape, i As Integer
    Set ws = ActiveSheet
    ' Draw a star.
    Set s = ws.Shapes.AddShape(msoShape5pointStar, 120, 80, 40, 40)
    ' Rotate it.
    For i = 0 To 6
        Application.Wait Now + 0.00001
        s.IncrementRotation 10
    Next
End Sub
```

shape.**IncrementTop(***Increment***)**

Moves a shape vertically.

Argument	Settings
Increment	The number of points to move the shape

shape.**Line**

For line shapes, returns a LineFormat object that controls the appearance of the line. For shape objects with borders, returns a LineFormat object that controls the appearance of the border. For other shape types, causes an error.

shape.**LinkFormat**

For OLE object shapes, returns a LinkFormat object used to update the link. For other shape types, causes an error.

shape.LockAspectRatio [= setting]

This property has no effect in Excel.

shape.Locked [= setting]

If the worksheet is protected, True prevents changes to the shape and False enables changes to the shape.

shape.ParentGroup

For shapes that are grouped, returns the group to which the shape belongs. Causes an error if the shape is not part of a group.

shape.PickUp( )

Copies the formatting from a shape. See the Apply method earlier for a full description and example of copying formatting between shapes.

shape.PictureFormat

For picture and OLE object shapes, returns a PictureFormat object used to control the appearance of the shape. For other shape types, causes an error.

shape.Placement [= xlPlacement]

Sets or returns how the shape is related to the cells underneath it. Can be one of these settings:

> xlFreeFloating (default)
> xlMove
> xlMoveAndSize

shapes.Range(Index)

Returns a ShapeRange object containing a subset of shapes from the Shapes collection.

Argument	Settings
Index	An array containing the names or indexes of the shapes to include in the ShapeRange

Use ShapeRange objects to perform tasks on a group of shapes. Building a ShapeRange from an array of items is complex. It is easier to simply select the items you want in the ShapeRange, then use the Selection.ShapeRange method as shown here:

```
Sub BuildShapeRange()
    Dim ws As Worksheet, s As Shape, sr As ShapeRange, sList As String, arr
    Set ws = ActiveSheet
    ' Clear selection
    [a1].Select
    ' Find each autoshape on the worksheet and build a list.
    For Each s In ws.Shapes
        If s.Type = msoAutoShape Then s.Select False
    Next
    Set sr = Selection.ShapeRange
    ' Move the ShapeRange.
    sr.IncrementLeft 10
End Sub
```

*shaperange.*Regroup( )

For shapes within a ShapeRange that belonged to a group but were ungrouped, Regroup restores those items to their previous group and returns the grouped objects as a single Shape object.

*shape.*RerouteConnections( )

For connector shapes, changes the connection sites so that the connection follows the shortest path. Causes an error for other shape types.

*shape.*Rotation [= *setting*]

Returns the rotation of a shape in degrees.

*shapes.*SelectAll( )

Selects all of the shapes on the worksheet or chart.

*shape.*SetShapesDefaultProperties( )

Makes the shape's formatting the default formatting for all subsequent shapes. Use the PickUp and Apply methods to copy formatting from one shape to another. The following code draws a star, sets its fill, and then makes that formatting the default:

```
Sub Defaults()
    Dim ws As Worksheet, s As Shape
```

```
        Set ws = ActiveSheet
        ' Draw star
        Set s = ws.Shapes.AddShape(msoShape5pointStar, 50, 50, 40, 40)
        ' Set its fill.
        s.Fill.PresetGradient msoGradientDiagonalUp, 1, msoGradientChrome
        ' Make this the default style.
        s.SetShapesDefaultProperties
        ' Draw another star.
        Set s = ws.Shapes.AddShape(msoShape5pointStar, 90, 90, 40, 40)
    End Sub
```

shape.Shadow

Returns a `ShadowFormat` object used to display and set the appearance of a shape's shadow. The following code draws a star with a shadow:

```
Sub DrawShadow( )
    Dim ws As Worksheet, s As Shape
    Set ws = ActiveSheet
    ' Draw star
    Set s = ws.Shapes.AddShape(msoShape5pointStar, 50, 50, 40, 40)
    ' Add a shadow.
    s.Shadow.Type = msoShadow1
End Sub
```

shape.TextEffect

For embedded WordArt shapes, returns a `TextEffectFormat` object used to set the text and change the appearance of the shape. Causes an error for other shape types. Use this property, not `TextFrame`, to change the text displayed in a WordArt shape.

shape.TextFrame

For autoshapes, returns the `TextFrame` object used to set and format text appearing on the shape. Causes an error for most other shape types. The following code draws an oval and adds some text to it:

```
Sub DrawOval( )
    Dim ws As Worksheet, s As Shape
    Set ws = ActiveSheet
    ' Draw a shape
    Set s = ws.Shapes.AddShape(msoShapeOval, 60, 30, 1, 1)
    ' Add text.
    s.TextFrame.Characters.text = "Vigorous writing is concise."
    ' Resize shape to fit text.
    s.TextFrame.AutoSize = True
End Sub
```

*shape.*ThreeD

For autoshapes, returns a ThreeDFormat object used to add a 3-D effect to the shape. The following code draws a wave as a wire-frame 3-D figure:

```
Sub DrawThreeD( )
    Dim ws As Worksheet, s As Shape
    Set ws = ActiveSheet
    ' Draw a shape
    Set s = ws.Shapes.AddShape(msoShapeDoubleWave, 50, 50, 40, 40)
    ' Add 3-D effect.
    s.ThreeD.PresetMaterial = msoMaterialWireFrame
End Sub
```

*shape.*Type

Returns an msoShapeType constant identifying the kind of shape. Can be one of these settings:

msoAutoShape	msoCallout
msoChart	msoComment
msoDiagram	msoEmbeddedOLEObject
msoFormControl	msoFreeform
msoGroup	msoLine
msoLinkedOLEObject	msoLinkedPicture
msoOLEControlObject	msoPicture
msoScriptAnchor	msoShapeTypeMixed
msoTable	msoTextBox
msoTextEffect	

*shape.*Ungroup( )

Separates a previously grouped object into its individual shapes.

*shape.*VerticalFlip

Returns True if the shape has been flipped vertically, False otherwise.

*shape.*Vertices

For a freeform shape, returns a 2-D array containing the coordinate pairs of the shape's vertices.

Adjustments Members

Use the `Adjustments` object to change the adjustment handle values on an autoshape. Use the `Shape` object's `Adjustments` property to get a reference to this object. The `Adjustments` object has the following members:

```
Application
Count
Creator
Item
Parent
```

Adjustment handles change one or more aspects of an autoshape. Usually, they control the relative proportions of parts of the shape, such as the length of an arrowhead or the width of the arrow body.

The `Adjustments` object is a collection of numeric values that correspond to the shapes adjustment handle settings. A shape with a single adjustment handle may have multiple `Adjustments` items, each of which corresponds to dragging the adjustment handle in a different direction.

For example, the following code draws two arrow autoshapes, then changes the adjustment handles on the second shape:

```
Sub UseAdjustments()
    Dim ws As Worksheet, s As Shape
    Set ws = ActiveSheet
    ' Draw an arrow.
    Set s = ws.Shapes.AddShape(msoShapeRightArrow, 20, 120, 100, 20)
    ' Copy the arrow
    Set s = s.Duplicate
    ' Show settings.
    Debug.Print s.Adjustments(1), s.Adjustments(2)
    ' Make adjustments
    s.Adjustments(1) = s.Adjustments(1) + 0.1 ' Shorten arrow head.
    s.Adjustments(2) = s.Adjustments(2) + 0.1  ' Narrow body.
End Sub
```

CalloutFormat Members

Use the `CalloutFormat` object to change the appearance of callout shapes. Use the `Shape` object's `Callout` property to get a reference to this object. The `CalloutFormat` object has the following members. Key members (shown in **bold**) are covered in the following reference section:

Accent	**Angle**
Application	**AutoAttach**
AutoLength	**AutomaticLength**
Border	Creator

CustomDrop	CustomLength
Drop	DropType
Gap	Length
Parent	PresetDrop
Type	

callout.Accent [= setting]

True adds a partial border on the side of the callout's connector; False omits the partial border. Default is False.

callout.Angle [= msoCalloutAngleType]

Sets or returns the angle of the callout's connector line. Can be one of these settings:

    msoCalloutAngle30
    msoCalloutAngle45
    msoCalloutAngle60
    msoCalloutAngle90
    msoCalloutAngleAutomatic (default)
    msoCalloutAngleMixed

callout.AutoAttach [= setting]

Setting this property has no apparent effect in Excel.

callout.AutoLength

Returns True if the callout's length is automatic, False otherwise.

callout.AutomaticLength( )

Sets the length of callout connector lines automatically.

callout.Border [= setting]

True displays a border around the callout text; False omits the border.

callout.CustomDrop(Drop)

Sets the vertical distance between the callout and where connector line is attached to the callout in points.

callout.CustomLength(*Length*)

Sets the length of the first segment of the callout's connector line. Only callout types msoCalloutThree and msoCalloutFour have multiple segments. Use the AutomaticLength method to restore automatic settings.

callout.Drop

Returns the vertical distance between the top of the callout and the connector line.

callout.DropType

Returns an msoCalloutDropType constant indication where the connector attaches to the callout. Can be one of these settings:

    msoCalloutDropCenter (default)
    msoCalloutDropMixed
    msoCalloutDropBottom
    msoCalloutDropCustom
    msoCalloutDropTop

callout.Gap [= *setting*]

Sets or returns the horizontal distance between the callout and the connector line in points.

callout.Length

If CustomLength is set, returns that setting. Otherwise, causes an error.

callout.PresetDrop(*DropType*)

Sets or returns where the connector line attaches to the callout.

Argument	Settings
DropType	An msoCalloutDropType constant. Can be msoCalloutDropBottom, msoCalloutDropCenter, msoCalloutDropMixed, or msoCalloutDropTop.

callout.Type [= *msoCalloutType*]

Sets or returns the kind of callout drawn. Can be msoCalloutOne to msoCalloutFour.

ColorFormat Members

Use the `ColorFormat` object to change the color of a shape's fill. Use the `FillFormat` object's `BackColor` and `ForeColor` properties to get a reference to this object. The `ChartColorFormat` object covered in Chapter 17 is nearly identical to this object, so only the `FillFormat` member with differences (`TintAndShade`) is covered here:

Application
Creator
Parent
RGB
SchemeColor
TintAndShade
Type

---

colorformat.**TintAndShade** [= *setting*]

Sets or returns a value that lightens or darkens a fill. Must be between -1 and 1. Default is 0.

ConnectorFormat Members

Use the `ConnectorFormat` object to attach a connector to other shapes. Use the `Shape` object's `ConnectorFormat` property to get a reference to this object. The `ConnectorFormat` object has the following members. Key members (shown in **bold**) are covered in the following reference section:

Application	**BeginConnect**
BeginConnected	**BeginConnectedShape**
BeginConnectionSite	**BeginDisconnect**
Creator	**EndConnect**
EndConnected	**EndConnectedShape**
EndConnectionSite	**EndDisconnect**
Parent	**Type**

---

connectorformat.**BeginConnect**(*ConnectedShape, ConnectionSite*)

Sets the first shape to connect.

Argument	Settings
ConnectedShape	The first Shape object to connect
ConnectionSite	The index of the connection site on the object

When creating a connection, it is easiest to use arbitrary values for ConnectionSite as well as the size and location of the connector and to call RerouteConnection to establish the shortest path, as shown here:

```
Sub CreateConnection()
    Dim ws As Worksheet, s(1) As Shape, conn As Shape
    Set ws = ActiveSheet
    ' Draw two shapes.
    Set s(0) = ws.Shapes.AddShape(msoShapeCube, 20, 20, 40, 40)
    Set s(1) = ws.Shapes.AddShape(msoShapeCan, 60, 80, 30, 40)
    ' Draw connector.
    Set conn = ws.Shapes.AddConnector(msoConnectorCurve, 1, 1, 1, 1)
    ' Establish connection.
    conn.ConnectorFormat.BeginConnect s(0), 1
    conn.ConnectorFormat.EndConnect s(1), 1
    ' Connect via the shortest path.
    conn.RerouteConnections
End Sub
```

*connectorformat.*BeginConnected

True if the first connection has been established, False otherwise.

*connectorformat.*BeginConnectedShape

Returns the first connected Shape object.

*connectorformat.*BeginConnectionSite

Returns the index of the connection site on the first connected shape.

*connectorformat.*BeginDisconnect( )

Detaches the connector from the first connected shape.

*connectorformat.*EndConnect(*ConnectedShape, ConnectionSite*)

Sets the second shape to connect.

Argument	Settings
ConnectedShape	The second Shape object to connect
ConnectionSite	The index of the connection site on the object

connectorformat.EndConnected

True if the second connection has been established, False otherwise.

connectorformat.EndConnectedShape

Returns the second connected Shape object.

connectorformat.EndConnectionSite

Returns the index of the connection site on the second connected shape.

connectorformat.EndDisconnect( )

Detaches the connector from the second connected shape.

connectorformat.Type [= msoConnectorType]

Sets or returns the kind of connector drawn. Can be one of these settings:

    msoConnectorCurve
    msoConnectorElbow
    msoConnectorStraight

ControlFormat Members

Use the ControlFormat object to get and set the properties on Forms 1.0 controls. Use the Shape object's ControlFormat property to get a reference to this object. The ControlFormat object has the following members:

AddItem	Application
Creator	DropDownLines
Enabled	LargeChange
LinkedCell	List
ListCount	ListFillRange
ListIndex	LockedText
Max	Min
MultiSelect	Parent
PrintObject	RemoveAllItems
RemoveItem	SmallChange
Value	

Forms 1.0 controls are mostly obsolete. The Forms 2.0 controls provide events, properties, and methods that are not available with the Forms 1.0 controls. See Chapter 20 for information on using Forms 2.0 controls on worksheets.

FillFormat Members

Use the `FillFormat` object to apply colors, gradients, and patterns to shapes. Use the `Shape` object's `Fill` property to get a reference to this object. The `ChartFillFormat` covered in Chapter 17 is nearly identical to this object, so only the `FillFormat` members with differences (shown in **bold**) are covered here:

Application	**BackColor**
Background	Creator
ForeColor	GradientColorType
GradientDegree	GradientStyle
GradientVariant	OneColorGradient
Parent	Pattern
Patterned	PresetGradient
PresetGradientType	PresetTexture
PresetTextured	Solid
TextureName	TextureType
Transparency	TwoColorGradient
Type	UserPicture
UserTextured	Visible

fillformat.BackColor

Returns a `ColorFormat` object you can use to set the background color. The following code draws a green tuna can on the active worksheet:

```
Sub FillFormatMembers()
    Dim ws As Worksheet, s As Shape
    Set ws = ActiveSheet
    ' Draw can.
    Set s = ws.Shapes.AddShape(msoShapeCan, 20, 20, 40, 40)
    ' Set green fill.
    s.Fill.ForeColor.RGB = RGB(0, 255, 0)
    s.Fill.Solid
    ' Add label.
    s.TextFrame.Characters.text = "Tuna"
    s.TextFrame.AutoSize = True
End Sub
```

fillformat.ForeColor

Returns a `ColorFormat` object you can use to set the foreground color.

fillformat.Transparency [= setting]

Sets or returns the degree of transparency of solid-color fills. Can be between 0 (opaque) and 1.0 (clear).

FreeFormBuilder

Use the FreeFormBuilder object to draw complex freeform line art. Use the Shapes collection's BuildFreeform method to create a new instance of this object. The FreeFormBuilder object has the following members. Key members (shown in **bold**) are covered in the following reference section:

AddNodes
Application
ConvertToShape
Creator
Parent

freeformbuilder.AddNodes(SegmentType, EditingType, X1, Y1, [X2], [Y2], [X3], [Y3])

Adds a segment to the freeform shape.

Argument	Settings
SegmentType	The type of segment to add. Can be msoSegmentLine or msoSegmentCurve.
EditingType	The editing property of the vertex. Can be msoEditingAuto or msoEditingCorner.
X1, X2, etc.	The horizontal coordinates of the vertices.
Y1, Y2, etc.	The vertical coordinates of the vertices.

The following code creates a freeform, adds segments, and then renders the freeform as a shape on the active worksheet:

```
Sub DrawAndFillFreeForm( )
    Dim ws As Worksheet, fb As FreeformBuilder, s As Shape
    Set ws = ActiveSheet
    ' Create the freeform builder.
    Set fb = ws.Shapes.BuildFreeform(msoEditingCorner, 360, 200)
    ' Add segments.
    fb.AddNodes msoSegmentCurve, msoEditingCorner, _
        380, 230, 400, 250, 450, 300
    fb.AddNodes msoSegmentCurve, msoEditingAuto, 480, 200
    fb.AddNodes msoSegmentLine, msoEditingAuto, 480, 400
```

```
        fb.AddNodes msoSegmentLine, msoEditingAuto, 360, 200
        ' Render the shape.
        Set s = fb.ConvertToShape
        ' Fill the shape.
        s.Fill.ForeColor.RGB = &HFF
        s.Fill.Solid
    End Sub
```

freeformbuilder.ConvertToShape( )

Renders the freeform on the worksheet and returns the created Shape object.

GroupShapes Members

Use the GroupShapes collection to get individual shapes that have been grouped together as a single shape. Use the Shape object's GroupItems property to get a reference to this collection. The GroupShapes collection has the following members:

```
Application
Count
Creator
Item
Parent
Range
```

Use the ShapeRange object's Group method to group multiple shapes so that they can be selected, moved, or deleted as a single shape by the user. The grouped Shape object then has a GroupItems property that you can use to get at the component shapes. The following code draws three stars and groups them:

```
Sub DrawGroup( )
    Dim ws As Worksheet, sr As ShapeRange, s As Shape
    Set ws = ActiveSheet
    ' Draw three stars.
    ws.Shapes.AddShape(msoShape5pointStar, 30, 30, 40, 40).Duplicate.Duplicate
    ' Create a shape range for all shapes on sheet.
    ws.Shapes.SelectAll
    Set sr = Selection.ShapeRange
    ' Group all the items
    Set s = sr.Group
    ' Show count of items in group.
    Debug.Print s.GroupItems.Count & " shapes grouped."
End Sub
```

LineFormat Members

Use the LineFormat object to change the appearance of line shapes. Use the Shape object's Line property to get a reference to this collection. The LineFormat object has the following members:

Application	BackColor
BeginArrowheadLength	BeginArrowheadStyle
BeginArrowheadWidth	Creator
DashStyle	EndArrowheadLength
EndArrowheadStyle	EndArrowheadWidth
ForeColor	Parent
Pattern	Style
Transparency	Visible
Weight	

Use the LineFormat object to add an arrowhead to a line, set the line weight, and set the style as shown by the following code:

```
Sub LineFormatMembers()
    Dim ws As Worksheet, s As Shape
    Set ws = ActiveSheet
    ' Draw a line.
    Set s = ws.Shapes.AddLine(60, 60, 200, 200)
    ' Add an arrowhead.
    s.Line.BeginArrowheadStyle = msoArrowheadOpen
    s.Line.BeginArrowheadLength = msoArrowheadLengthMedium
    s.Line.BeginArrowheadWidth = msoArrowheadWidthMedium
    s.Line.EndArrowheadStyle = msoArrowheadOval
    ' Change line weight (in points)
    s.Line.Weight = 4
    ' Change line style.
    s.Line.DashStyle = msoLineDash
End Sub
```

LinkFormat Members

Use the LinkFormat object to update linked OLE objects. Use the Shape object's LinkFormat property to get a reference to this object. The LinkFormat object has the following members:

Application
AutoUpdate
Creator
Locked
Parent
Update

Make sure the Shape object is a linked object before using the LinkFormat object by testing its Type property as shown here:

```
If s.Type = msoLinkedOLEObject Then
    s.LinkFormat.Update
End If
```

PictureFormat Members

Use the PictureFormat object to change the appearance of picture shapes. Use the Shape object's PictureFormat property to get a reference to this object. The PictureFormat object has the following members. Key members (shown in **bold**) are covered in the following reference section:

Application	**Brightness**
ColorType	**Contrast**
Creator	**CropBottom**
CropLeft	**CropRight**
CropTop	**IncrementBrightness**
IncrementContrast	Parent
TransparencyColor	**TransparentBackground**

*pictureformat.***Brightness** [= *setting*]

Sets or returns the brightness of the picture. Must be between 0 and 1. Default is 0.5.

*pictureformat.***ColorType** [= *msoPictureColorType*]

Sets or returns one of the special color or brightness formats to apply to the picture. Can be one of these settings:

```
msoPictureAutomatic (default)
msoPictureBlackAndWhite
msoPictureGrayscale
msoPictureWatermark
```

*pictureformat.***Contrast** [= *setting*]

Sets or returns the contrast of the picture. Must be between 0 and 1. Default is 0.5.

*pictureformat.***CropBottom** [= *setting*]

Sets or returns the amount cropped off the bottom of the picture, measured in points.

*pictureformat.*CropLeft [= *setting*]

Sets or returns the amount cropped off the left side of the picture, measured in points.

*pictureformat.*CropRight [= *setting*]

Sets or returns the amount cropped off the right side of the picture, measured in points.

*pictureformat.*CropTop [= *setting*]

Sets or returns the amount cropped off the top of the picture, measured in points.

*pictureformat.*IncrementBrightness(*Increment*)

Increases or decreases the brightness of the picture. Must be between -1 and 1.

*pictureformat.*IncrementContrast(*Increment*)

Increases or decreases the contrast of the picture. Must be between -1 and 1.

*pictureformat.*TransparencyColor [= *setting*]

Sets or returns the RGB value of the color made transparent when `TransParentBackground` is set to True.

*pictureformat.*TransparentBackground [= *setting*]

True makes transparent portions of the picture that match `TransparencyColor`; False makes those portions opaque. Default is False.

ShadowFormat

Use the `ShadowFormat` object to add shadows to `Shape` objects. Use the `Shape` object's `Shadow` property to get a reference to this object. The `ShadowFormat` object has the following members:

Application	Creator
ForeColor	IncrementOffsetX
IncrementOffsetY	Obscured
OffsetX	OffsetY
Parent	Transparency
Type	Visible

The ShadowFormat members correspond to the settings on the shadow toolbars shown in Figure 18-14.

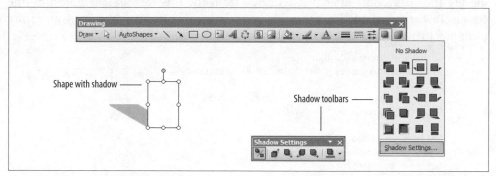

Figure 18-14. Adding shadows

To add a shadow to a shape, simply make the ShadowFormat object visible or set its Type property as shown here:

```
Sub ShadowFormatMembers()
    Dim ws As Worksheet, s As Shape, fil As String
    Set ws = ActiveSheet
    ' Draw a rectangle.
    Set s = ws.Shapes.AddShape(msoShapeRectangle, 50, 50, 40, 60)
    ' Make it solid.
    s.Fill.Solid
    ' Set shadow type.
    s.Shadow.Type = msoShadow3
End Sub
```

If the shape is not solid, the shadow reflects the border of the object.

ShapeNode and ShapeNodes Members

Use the ShapeNodes collection to add or remove segments from a freeform shape. Use the Shape object's Nodes property to get a reference to this collection. Use the Node object to get the coordinates of a specific segment. The ShapeNodes collection and ShapeNode object have the following members:

Application[2]	Count[2]
Creator[2]	Delete[1]
EditingType	Insert[1]
Item[1]	Parent[2]
Points	SegmentType
SetEditingType[1]	SetPosition[1]
SetSegmentType[1]	

[1] Collection only
[2] Object and collection

It's hard to imagine why anyone would need to modify a freeform shape from code within Excel, but if you want to do that, ShapeNodes is the collection to use! You can modify the shape only after it is rendered from the FreeformBuilder object by the ConvertToShape method. The following code draws a freeform shape using an earlier example, then replaces one of the nodes in the shape:

```
Sub ShapeNodesMembers()
    Dim ws As Worksheet, s As Shape, sn As ShapeNodes
    Set ws = ActiveSheet
    ' Use previous example to draw freeform shape.
    DrawAndFillFreeForm
    ' Get the shape
    Set s = ws.Shapes(ws.Shapes.Count)
    ' Get the ShapeNodes
    Set sn = s.Nodes
    ' Delete a node
    sn.Delete (1)
    ' Add a node
    sn.Insert 1, msoSegmentCurve, msoEditingAuto, _
        20, 20, 50, 60, 30, 30
End Sub
```

TextFrame

Use the TextFrame object to add text to a shape and to change the appearance of that text. Use the Shape object's TextFrame property to get a reference to this object. The TextFrame object has the following members. Key members (shown in **bold**) are covered in the following reference section:

Application	**AutoMargins**
AutoSize	**Characters**
Creator	**HorizontalAlignment**
MarginBottom	**MarginLeft**
MarginRight	**MarginTop**
Orientation	Parent
ReadingOrder	**VerticalAlignment**

---

*textframe.*AutoMargins [= *setting*]

True sets margins automatically; False uses margin property settings. Default is True.

---

*textframe.*AutoSize [= *setting*]

True resizes the object to fit the text; False does not resize. Default is False. The following code draws an oval, adds some text, then resizes the shape to fit the text:

```
Sub DrawOval( )
    Dim ws As Worksheet, s As Shape
    Set ws = ActiveSheet
    ' Draw a rectangle.
    Set s = ws.Shapes.AddShape(msoShapeOval, 150, 50, 1, 1)
    ' Add some text
    s.TextFrame.Characters.text = "Vigorous writing is concise."
    ' Resize the object to fit text
    s.TextFrame.AutoSize = True
End Sub
```

textframe.Characters([Start], [Length])

Returns a Characters object representing the text in the text frame.

Argument	Settings
Start	The index of the first character to return
Length	The number of characters to return

The most commonly used properties of the Characters object are Text and Font. I've showed you how to use the Text property many times so far; the following code changes the font for the last word in the DrawOval example:

```
Sub FormatCharacters( )
    Dim ws As Worksheet, s As Shape, fil As String
    Set ws = ActiveSheet
    ' Draw oval using previous example.
    DrawOval
    ' Get the shape object.
    Set s = ws.Shapes(ws.Shapes.Count)
    ' Make last word bold.
    s.TextFrame.Characters(21, 7).Font.Bold = True
End Sub
```

textframe.HorizontalAlignment [= xlHAlign]

Sets or returns the horizontal alignment of the text. Can be one of these settings:

xlHAlignCenter
xlHAlignCenterAcrossSelection
xlHAlignDistributed
xlHAlignFill
xlHAlignGeneral
xlHAlignJustify
xlHAlignLeft (default)
xlHAlignRight

*textframe.*MarginBottom [= *setting*]

Sets or returns the bottom margin of the text frame in points.

*textframe.*MarginLeft [= *setting*]

Sets or returns the left margin of the text frame in points.

*textframe.*MarginRight [= *setting*]

Sets or returns the right margin of the text frame in points.

*textframe.*MarginTop [= *setting*]

Sets or returns the top margin of the text frame in points.

*textframe.*Orientation [= *msoTextOrientation*]

Sets or returns how the text is rotated. Can be one of these settings:

```
msoTextOrientationDownward
msoTextOrientationHorizontal (default)
msoTextOrientationHorizontalRotatedFarEast
msoTextOrientationMixed
msoTextOrientationUpward
msoTextOrientationVertical
msoTextOrientationVerticalFarEast
```

*textframe.*VerticalAlignment [= *xlVAlign*]

Sets or returns the vertical alignment of the text. Can be one of these settings:

```
xlVAlignCenter
xlVAlignJustify
xlVAlignBottom
xlVAlignDistributed
xlVAlignTop (default)
```

TextEffectFormat

Use the TextEffectFormat object to set the text in an embedded WordArt shape. Use the Shape object's TextEffect property to get a reference to this object. The TextEffectFormat object has the following members. Key members (shown in **bold**) are covered in the following reference section:

Alignment	Application
Creator	**FontBold**
FontItalic	**FontName**
FontSize	**KernedPairs**
NormalizedHeight	Parent
PresetShape	**PresetTextEffect**
RotatedChars	**Text**
ToggleVerticalText	**Tracking**

shape.Alignment [= msoTextEffectAlignment]

Sets or returns the alignment of the text in the WordArt shape. Can be one of these settings:

```
msoTextEffectAlignmentCentered (default)
msoTextEffectAlignmentLeft
msoTextEffectAlignmentLetterJustify
msoTextEffectAlignmentMixed
msoTextEffectAlignmentRight
msoTextEffectAlignmentStretchJustify
msoTextEffectAlignmentWordJustify
```

shape.FontBold [= setting]

True applies bold formatting; False removes bold.

shape.FontItalic [= setting]

True applies italic formatting; False removes italics.

shape.FontName [= setting]

Sets or returns the font used in the WordArt shape. If the specified font is not found on the user's system, the property is simply ignored.

*shape.*FontSize [= *setting*]

Returns the size of the font in points. Setting this property has no effect in Excel.

*shape.*KernedPairs [= *setting*]

True decreases spacing between character pairs slightly; False does not decrease spacing. Default is True.

*shape.*NormalizedHeight [= *setting*]

True makes upper- and lowercase letters the same height; False uses different heights. Default is False.

*shape.*PresetShape [= *msoPresetTextEffectShape*]

Sets or returns a shape effect to apply to the text. Can be one of these settings:

msoTextEffectShapeArchDownCurve	msoTextEffectShapeArchDownPour
msoTextEffectShapeArchUpCurve	msoTextEffectShapeArchUpPour
msoTextEffectShapeButtonCurve	msoTextEffectShapeButtonPour
msoTextEffectShapeCanDown	msoTextEffectShapeCanUp
msoTextEffectShapeCascadeDown	msoTextEffectShapeCascadeUp
msoTextEffectShapeChevronDown	msoTextEffectShapeChevronUp
msoTextEffectShapeCircleCurve	msoTextEffectShapeCirclePour
msoTextEffectShapeCurveDown	msoTextEffectShapeCurveUp
msoTextEffectShapeDeflate	msoTextEffectShapeDeflateBottom
msoTextEffectShapeDeflateInflate	msoTextEffectShapeDeflateInflateDeflate
msoTextEffectShapeDeflateTop	msoTextEffectShapeDoubleWave1
msoTextEffectShapeDoubleWave2	msoTextEffectShapeFadeDown
msoTextEffectShapeFadeLeft	msoTextEffectShapeFadeRight
msoTextEffectShapeFadeUp	msoTextEffectShapeInflate
msoTextEffectShapeInflateBottom	msoTextEffectShapeInflateTop
msoTextEffectShapeMixed	msoTextEffectShapePlainText
msoTextEffectShapeRingInside	msoTextEffectShapeRingOutside
msoTextEffectShapeSlantDown	msoTextEffectShapeSlantUp
msoTextEffectShapeStop	msoTextEffectShapeTriangleDown
msoTextEffectShapeTriangleUp	msoTextEffectShapeWave1
msoTextEffectShapeWave2	

shape.PresetTextEffect [= *msoPresetTextEffect*]

Sets or returns the text effect to use from the WordArt Gallery (Figure 18-15). Can be a setting from msoTextEffect1 to msoTextEffect30.

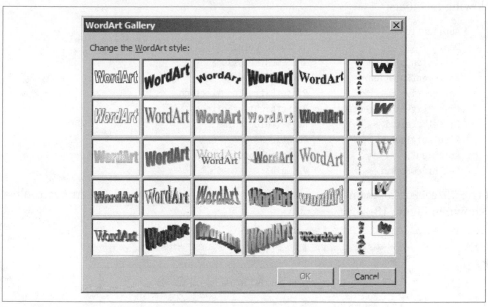

Figure 18-15. View available text effects from the WordArt Gallery

shape.RotatedChars [= *setting*]

True rotates characters in the text 90 degrees; False removes the rotation.

shape.Text [= *setting*]

Sets or returns the text displayed in the WordArt shape.

shape.ToggleVerticalText( )

Switches between horizontal and vertical text.

shape.Tracking [= *setting*]

Sets or returns the ratio of space allotted to each character relative to the width of the actual character. Must be between 0 and 5. Default is 1.

ThreeDFormat

Use the ThreeDFormat object to add a 3-D effect to shapes. Use the Shape object's ThreeD property to get a reference to this object. The ThreeDFormat object has the following members:

Application	Creator
Depth	ExtrusionColor
ExtrusionColorType	IncrementRotationX
IncrementRotationY	Parent
Perspective	PresetExtrusionDirection
PresetLightingDirection	PresetLightingSoftness
PresetMaterial	PresetThreeDFormat
ResetRotation	RotationX
RotationY	SetExtrusionDirection
SetThreeDFormat	Visible

The ThreeDFormat members correspond to the settings on the 3-D Settings toolbar shown in Figure 18-16.

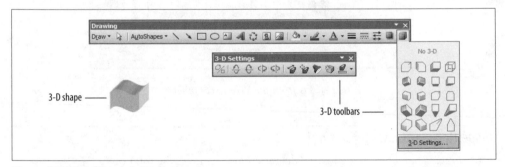

Figure 18-16. Adding a 3-D effect to shapes

Use the SetThreeDFormat method to apply a 3-D effect to a shape. The following code draws the wave shape shown in Figure 18-16 and applies a 3-D effect to it:

```
Sub ThreeDFormatMembers()
    Dim ws As Worksheet, s As Shape, fil As String
    Set ws = ActiveSheet
    ' Insert embedded WordArt.
    Set s = ws.Shapes.AddShape(msoShapeWave, 20, 140, 40, 30)
    s.Fill.Solid
    ' Apply 3-D effect.
    s.ThreeD.SetThreeDFormat msoThreeD1
End Sub
```

CHAPTER 19

Adding Menus and Toolbars

Writing great code doesn't do you much good if users can't easily run it. In this chapter, I show you how to create menus and toolbars that run your code with a single click. These features are actually part of the Office object model, so the skills you learn here apply to Word, PowerPoint, and all of the other Office products.

This chapter includes task-oriented reference information for the following objects and their related collections: CommandBar, CommandBarButton, CommandBarComboBox, CommandBarControl, and CommandBarPopup.

Code used in this chapter and additional samples are available in *ch19.xls*.

About Excel Menus

Excel has two top-level menu bars, and which menu bar is displayed depends on what has focus in Excel. The worksheet menu bar (Figure 19-1) is displayed when Excel first starts up, when a worksheet has focus, and when all workbooks are closed.

Figure 19-1. Worksheet menu bar

The chart menu bar (Figure 19-2) appears when a chart sheet or an embedded chart object has focus.

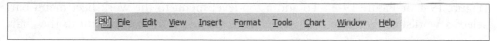

Figure 19-2. Chart menu bar

There are also context menus for just about every item in the Excel interface. *Context menus* pop up when you right-click an item in Excel. For example, Figure 19-3 shows the context menu displayed when you right-click a range of cells.

 Context menus are also sometimes called *shortcut menus*.

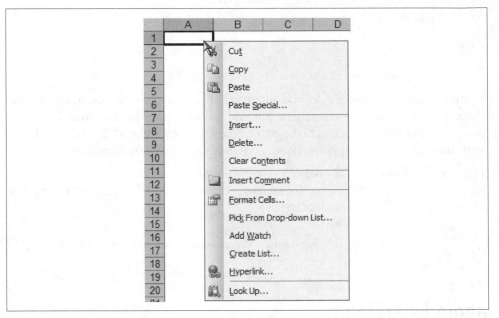

Figure 19-3. The cell context menu

You can change any of these types of menus to:

- Add or delete existing commands
- Create new items that run code
- Build custom menus of items with multiple levels

The following sections detail how to create and modify each of these types of menus.

Build a Top-Level Menu

Top-level menus appear on either the worksheet menu bar or the chart menu bar (Figure 19-1 or Figure 19-2). To add a top-level menu to the worksheet menu bar, select a worksheet before creating the menu. To add a top-level menu to the chart menu bar, select a chart before creating the menu. To add the menu to both menu bars, create the menu twice—once for each menu bar.

To create a new top-level menu on a menu bar in Excel:

1. Choose Tools → Customize → Commands. Excel displays the Commands tab of the Customize dialog box.

2. In the Categories list, choose New Menu. Click New Menu in the Commands list and drag it onto the Excel menu bar as shown in Figure 19-4. Excel adds a new top-level menu to the menu bar.

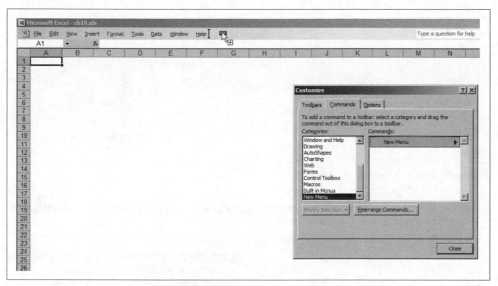

Figure 19-4. Steps 1 and 2: add the top-level menu

3. Right-click on the new menu item and rename it as shown in Figure 19-5.

4. In the Categories list, choose Macros, then click Custom Menu Item from the Commands list and drag it onto the new menu item as shown in Figure 19-6.

5. Right-click the new menu item, rename it, and assign it to run a macro as shown in Figure 19-7.

6. Click Close on the Customize dialog box when you are done adding items and setting menu properties.

> Right-clicking displays the menu properties shown in Figure 19-5 and Figure 19-7 only while the Customize dialog is open.

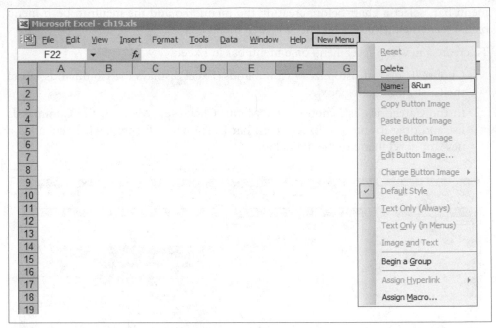

Figure 19-5. Step 3: rename the menu

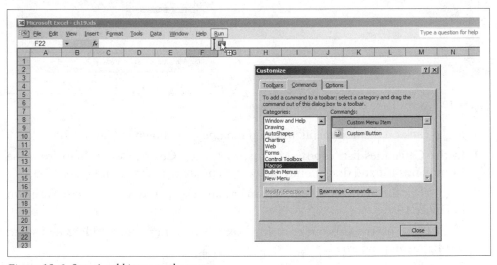

Figure 19-6. Step 4: add items to the menu

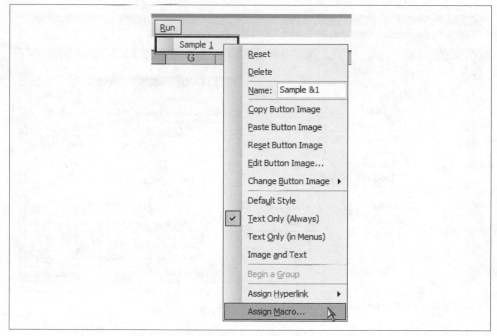

Figure 19-7. Step 5: rename menu item and assign a macro

Change Existing Menus

You can also add built-in commands or create new custom commands on existing Excel menus. To add built-in command to an existing menu:

1. Choose Tools → Customize → Commands. Excel displays the Commands tab of the Customize dialog box.

2. In the Categories list, choose the category of the existing command you want to add. Each category contains a long list of commands, so you may need to check a couple different categories before you find the command you want.

3. Drag the existing command from the Commands list onto the top-level menu you want to add it to. Excel displays the menu once you drag over it and you can drag the command down to the position where you want it to appear on the menu as shown in Figure 19-8.

4. Click Close on the Customize dialog box when you are done adding items and setting menu properties.

To add a new custom command to an existing menu, repeat the preceding procedure, but select Macros from the Categories list and Custom Menu Item from the

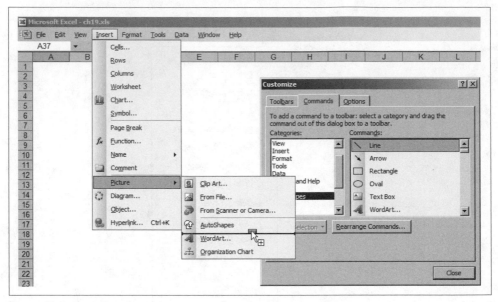

Figure 19-8. Dragging an existing command onto a menu

Commands list in Step 2. You can then rename and assign a macro to the new menu item as shown in Figure 19-7.

Assign Accelerator and Shortcut Keys

It is standard practice to provide keyboard alternatives to using point-and-click menus. There are two ways to do so:

Accelerator keys
Appear underlined in the menu name. They allow you to activate the menu item by pressing Alt-*key*. For example Alt-F-S saves an Excel workbook.

Shortcut keys
Appear next to the menu item. They provide direct access to a task listed on a menu. For example, Ctrl-S saves an Excel workbook—the same as Alt-F-S.

To assign an accelerator key to a menu item, use an ampersand (&) in the menu name before the accelerator key. For example, &Run defines R as the accelerator key for the menu.

To assign a short-cut key to a menu item:

1. Choose Tools → Customize → Commands. Excel displays the Commands tab of the Customize dialog box.

2. Right-click on the new menu item and rename to add the short-cut sequence after the menu item's name. For example, Run &All Ctrl-Shift-R.

3. Close the Customize dialog box.

4. Choose Tools → Macro → Macros to display the Macro dialog box.

5. Select the macro that is assigned to the menu item and click Options.

6. Press the letter to assign as the short-cut. Pressing Shift adds that key to the combination as shown in Figure 19-9.

7. Type a description and press OK twice to close the dialogs.

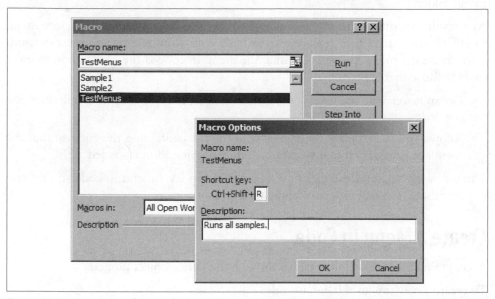

Figure 19-9. Assigning a shortcut key sequence

Menus often group similar items using *separator bars*. To start a new group of items by adding a separator bar:

1. Choose Tools → Customize → Commands. Excel displays the Commands tab of the Customize dialog box.

2. Right-click on the menu item before which to add the separator bar and select Begin a Group.

3. Close the Customize dialog box. Excel adds a separator bar before the item as shown in Figure 19-10.

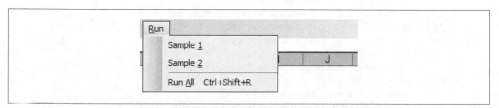

Figure 19-10. Menu items with accelerator and shortcut keys and a separator bar

Save and Distribute Menus

When you close Excel, any menu changes you made are automatically saved in an *.xlb* file. The filename and location varies based on the version of Excel. Versions 2000, XP, and 2003 are *Excel9.xlb*, *Excel10.xlb*, and *Excel11.xlb*, respectively. On Windows XP, the files are stored in the *%UserProfile%\Application Data\Microsoft\ Excel* folder.

As a result, custom menus are user-specific. If you want to distribute a custom menu to others, you must either replace their *.xlb* file with your own or you must dynamically create the menu in code. Creating the menu in code is the best option in most cases because that approach:

- Doesn't overwrite the users' own menu changes, the way that replacing their *.xlb* file does
- Allows you to associate the menus with the file containing the code so that the menus appear only if that workbook, template, or add-in is loaded

The following section describes how to create a top-level menu in code so that you can distribute it as part of a workbook, template, or add-in.

Create a Menu in Code

Access to menus in Excel is provided through the Office object model.

To create a new top-level menu in code:

1. Get a reference to the menu bar on which you want to create the new top-level menu.
2. Add a pop-up menu control to the menu bar and set its Caption and Tag properties.
3. Add button menu controls to the pop-up menu and set the Caption, OnAction, ShortcutText, and other properties.

For example, the following code creates a top-level menu on the worksheet menu bar that is very similar to the menu shown in Figure 19-10:

```
Sub BuildMenu( )
    Dim cb As CommandBar, cpop As CommandBarPopup, cbtn As CommandBarButton
    ' Get the menu bar (CommandBar).
    Set cb = Application.CommandBars("Worksheet Menu Bar")
    ' Add top-level menu item (CommandBarPopup).
    Set cpop = cb.Controls.Add(msoControlPopup, , , , True)
    cpop.Caption = "&Run2"
    ' The Tag property makes it easy to delete this menu later.
    cpop.Tag = "Run2"
    ' Add items to the menu (CommandBarButton).
    Set cbtn = cpop.Controls.Add(msoControlButton, , , , True)
    ' Set menu item properties.
    cbtn.Caption = "Sample &1"
```

```
        cbtn.OnAction = "Sample1"
        ' Add a second item.
        Set cbtn = cpop.Controls.Add(msoControlButton, , , , True)
        cbtn.Caption = "Sample &2"
        cbtn.OnAction = "Sample2"
        ' Add a third item.
        Set cbtn = cpop.Controls.Add(msoControlButton, , , , True)
        cbtn.Caption = "Run &All"
        cbtn.ShortcutText = "Ctrl+Shift+A"
        cbtn.OnAction = "TestMenus"
        ' Add a separator bar before this item.
        cbtn.BeginGroup = True
    End Sub
```

The last argument for each of the preceding Add methods specifies that the new item is temporary—in other words, it won't be saved in the user's *.xlb* file. When the user closes Excel, temporary menus are deleted. You can ensure that this menu appears when the workbook, template, or add-in is loaded by calling BuildMenu from the Workbook_Open event, as shown here:

```
' ThisWorksbook class.
Private Sub Workbook_Open()
    ' Create temporary menus when this workbook opens.
    BuildMenu
End Sub
```

Remove the Menu on Close

Interestingly, temporary menus still persist if the user closes the workbook but not Excel. Therefore, you may want to remove the menu explicitly when the file closes. Why use temporary menus if you are going to delete them anyway? Using a temporary menu ensures that the menu is removed if Excel crashes while the file is open.

The following code removes the top-level menu created by the BuildMenu sample when the workbook closes:

```
Private Sub Workbook_BeforeClose(Cancel As Boolean)
    ' Enable error handling in case menu was deleted earlier somehow.
    On Error Resume Next
    ' Make sure temporary menu is deleted.
    RemoveMenu
    On Error GoTo 0
End Sub

Sub RemoveMenu()
    Dim cb As CommandBar, cpop As CommandBarPopup
    ' Get the menu bar (CommandBar).
    Set cb = Application.CommandBars("Worksheet Menu Bar")
    ' Get the top-level menu created by BuildMenu.
    Set cpop = cb.FindControl(msoControlPopup, , "Run2")
    ' Delete it.
    cpop.Delete
End Sub
```

The FindControl method uses the Tag property of the top-level menu to locate the control so it can be deleted. That is a better technique than locating the menu through its index, which might change if the user or other code adds a new menu.

Change an Existing Menu

You can also add or remove commands on existing menus in code. For example, you might want to add Contact Us and About commands to the Help menu for a workbook add-in. To do so:

1. Get a reference to the menu toolbar.
2. Use the FindControl method to get a reference to the existing Contact and About items.
3. Modify those menu items.
4. Add new Contact Us and About items.

The following code demonstrates the preceding steps by changing the caption of the Contact Us menu item to Contact Microsoft, then adds new Contact and About items to the Help menu:

```
Sub ChangeHelpMenu( )
    Dim cb As CommandBar, cpop As CommandBarPopup, cbtn As CommandBarButton
    Dim index As Integer
    ' Get the menu bar (CommandBar).
    Set cb = Application.CommandBars("Worksheet Menu Bar")
    ' Get the Help menu (control's ID is 30010)
    Set cpop = cb.FindControl(msoControlPopup, 30010)
    ' Get the Contact Us item (control's ID is 7903)
    Set cbtn = cb.FindControl(msoControlButton, 7903, , , True)
    ' Change the caption.
    cbtn.Caption = "&Contact Microsoft"
    index = cbtn.index
    ' Add a new Contact item.
    Set cbtn = cpop.Controls.Add(msoControlButton, , , index, True)
    cbtn.Caption = "Contact &Author"
    cbtn.OnAction = "ContactAuthor"
    ' Get the About item
    Set cbtn = cb.FindControl(msoControlButton, 927, , , True)
    index = cbtn.index
    cbtn.BeginGroup = False
    ' Add a new About item.
    Set cbtn = cpop.Controls.Add(msoControlButton, , , index, True)
    cbtn.Caption = "About &" & ThisWorkbook.Name
    cbtn.OnAction = "ShowAbout"
    cbtn.BeginGroup = True
End Sub

' Procedures for the preceding OnAction properties.
Sub ContactAuthor( )
    ThisWorkbook.FollowHyperlink "mailto:someone@yourcompany.com" & _
```

```
        "&Subject=Chapter 19 Samples"
    End Sub

    Sub ShowAbout( )
        MsgBox "Version 1.0. Copyright 2005 Wombat Technology.", _
            vbOKOnly, "Chapter 19 Samples"
    End Sub
```

The FindControl method in the preceding code uses the ID of the existing controls to find the Help CommandBarPopup control and Contact and About CommandBarButton controls. Those control IDs aren't listed anywhere that I know of, but you can find them by running the following code:

```
    ' Displays the structure of the worksheet and chart menu bars
    ' with captions and control IDs.
    Sub ShowMenuStructure( )
        Dim cb As CommandBar, cpop As CommandBarPopup, cbtn As CommandBarButton
        For Each cb In Application.CommandBars
            If cb.Type = msoBarTypeMenuBar Then
                Debug.Print cb.Name
                For Each cpop In cb.Controls
                    Debug.Print , cpop.Caption, cpop.id
                    On Error Resume Next
                    For Each cbtn In cpop.Controls
                        Debug.Print , , cbtn.Caption, cbtn.id
                    Next
                    On Error GoTo 0
                Next
            End If
        Next
    End Sub
```

The preceding code lists all of the menu items along with their control IDs in the Immediate window.

Reset an Existing Menu

If you change an existing menu, you may want to remove your changes without deleting the entire menu. To do that, use the Reset method as shown here:

```
    Sub RestoreHelpMenu( )
        Dim cb As CommandBar, cpop As CommandBarPopup
        Dim index As Integer
        ' Get the menu bar.
        Set cb = Application.CommandBars("Worksheet Menu Bar")
        ' Get the Help menu.
        Set cpop = cb.FindControl(msoControlPopup, 30010)
        ' Remove changes.
        cpop.Reset
    End Sub
```

The preceding code restores the default menu settings for the Help menu, removing the changes made by the ChangeHelpMenu procedure earlier.

You can also call Reset on the CommandBar object to restore the defaults for all menus:

```
Sub RestoreMenuBar()
    Dim cb As CommandBar
    ' Get the menu bar
    Set cb = Application.CommandBars("Worksheet Menu Bar")
    ' Remove changes.
    cb.Reset
End Sub
```

 Reset removes the user's changes as well as changes made in code.

Build Context Menus

You can't change Excel's context menus through the user interface. Instead, you must use code to add or remove items on a context menu. For example, the following code adds a Send Range item to the context menu displayed when you right-click a selected range of cells:

```
Sub AddCellMenuItem()
    Dim cb As CommandBar, cbtn As CommandBarButton
    Dim index As Integer
    ' Get the context menu by name.
    Set cb = Application.CommandBars("Cell")
    ' Add the new menu item.
    Set cbtn = cb.Controls.Add(msoControlButton, , , , True)
    ' Set the caption and action.
    cbtn.Caption = "&Send Range"
    cbtn.OnAction = "SendRange"
End Sub

' Procedure used by OnAction property.
Sub SendRange()
    ' Copy the range.
    Selection.Copy
    ' Display a mail message.
    ThisWorkbook.FollowHyperlink "mailto:someone@yourcompany.com" & _
      "&Subject=Selection from " & ActiveSheet.Name
    ' Wait two seconds for message to display.
    Application.Wait Now + TimeSerial(0, 0, 2)
    ' Paste range into message body.
    SendKeys "^v"
End Sub
```

To see how this works, run AddCellMenuItem to add the new menu item, select a range of cells, right-click, and choose Send Range. Excel creates a new mail message and pastes the range into the message body as shown in Figure 19-11.

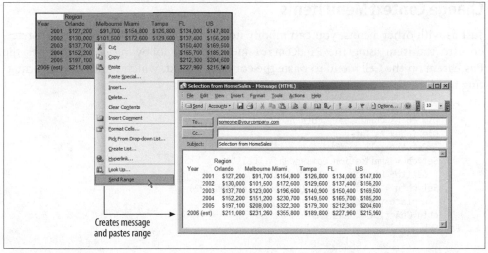

Creates message
and pastes range

Figure 19-11. New item on the cell context menu sends a range of cells

The context menus are CommandBar objects, just like the top-level menu bars, but they have a Type property set to msoBarTypePopup. You get a reference to a context menu from the Application object's CommandBars collection using one of the menu names, which are listed here:

ActiveX Control	Auto Sum	AutoCalculate
AutoFill	Built-in Menus	Button
Canvas Popup	Cell	Chart
Column	Connector	Curve
Curve Node	Curve Segment	Desktop
Diagram	Dialog	Document
Excel Control	Find Format	Floor and Walls
Format Axis	Format Data Series	Format Legend Entry
Formula Bar	Inactive Chart	Layout
List Range Layout Popup	List Range Popup	Nondefault Drag and Drop
Object/Plot	OLE Object	Organization Chart Popup
Paste Special Dropdown	Phonetic Information	Pictures Context Menu
Pivot Chart Popup	PivotChart Menu	PivotTable Context Menu
Plot Area	Ply	Query
Query Layout	Replace Format	Rotate Mode
Row	Script Anchor Popup	Select
Series	Shapes	Title Bar (Charting)
Trendline	WordArt Context Menu	Workbook tabs
XLM Cell	XML Range Popup	

Change Context Menu Items

Just as with other menus, you can modify items on context menus by getting a reference to the item using the FindControl method. The following code modifies the Paste item on the Cell menu to paste the contents as text, which removes any formatting from the source:

```
Sub ChangeCellMenuItem( )
    Dim cb As CommandBar, cbtn As CommandBarButton
    Dim index As Integer
    ' Get the cell context menu.
    Set cb = Application.CommandBars("Cell")
    ' Get the Paste menu item (ID is 22).
    Set cbtn = cb.FindControl(msoControlButton, 22)
    ' Replace the action.
    cbtn.OnAction = "PasteAsText"
End Sub

' Procedure used by OnAction property.
Sub PasteAsText( )
    ActiveSheet.PasteSpecial "Text"
End Sub
```

As I mentioned earlier, finding the control ID for menu items can be tricky. The following code displays a list of the context menu names, the items they contain, and the control IDs for each of the items:

```
Sub ListContextMenus( )
    Dim cb As CommandBar, cbtn As CommandBarButton
    Debug.Print "Context menus", ""
    For Each cb In Application.CommandBars
        If cb.Type = msoBarTypePopup Then
            Debug.Print cb.Name
            On Error Resume Next
            For Each cbtn In cb.Controls
                Debug.Print , cbtn.Caption, cbtn.id
            Next
            On Error GoTo 0
            ' Uncomment the following line to stop at a
            ' specific context menu:
            'If cb.Name = "Cell" Then Stop
        End If
    Next
End Sub
```

Restore Context Menus

To restore the default context menu after making changes, use the Reset method as you would for top-level menu bars. The following code resets the cell context menu back to its default settings:

```
Sub RetoreCellMenu( )
    Dim cb As CommandBar
    Dim index As Integer
    ' Get the cell context menu.
    Set cb = Application.CommandBars("Cell")
    ' Remove changes.
    cb.Reset
End Sub
```

Create New Context Menus

You can create custom context menus from scratch using the CommandBars collection's Add method. Once it is created, you control the display of the context menu using the ShowPopup method. The following code demonstrates how to create and display a new context menu similar to the menu in Figure 19-10:

```
' Module-level variable.
Dim m_cb As CommandBar

Sub CreateNewContextMenu( )
    ' Delete the menu bar if it already exists.
    On Error Resume Next
    Application.CommandBars("New").Delete
    On Error GoTo 0
    ' Create a new context menu bar.
    Set m_cb = Application.CommandBars.Add("New", msoBarPopup, False, True)
    ' Add some items to the menu bar.
    With m_cb.Controls.Add(msoControlButton, , , , True)
        .Caption = "Sample &1"
        .OnAction = "Sample1"
    End With
    With m_cb.Controls.Add(msoControlButton, , , , True)
        .Caption = "Sample &2"
        .OnAction = "Sample2"
    End With
    With m_cb.Controls.Add(msoControlButton, , , , True)
        .Caption = "Run &All"
        .OnAction = "TestMenus"
        .BeginGroup = True
    Fnd With
    ' Display the menu.
    m_cb.ShowPopup 100, 100
End Sub
```

 The CommandBar variable is defined at the module level so you can use it more easily from other parts of your project.

Build a Toolbar

To create a toolbar in Excel:

1. Choose Tools → Customize → Toolbars. Excel displays the Toolbars tab of the Customize dialog box.

2. Click New. Excel display the New Toolbar dialog.

3. Type a name for the toolbar and click OK. Excel creates a new, empty toolbar.

4. Click the Commands tab, select a category, and drag items from the Commands list to the toolbar as shown in Figure 19-12.

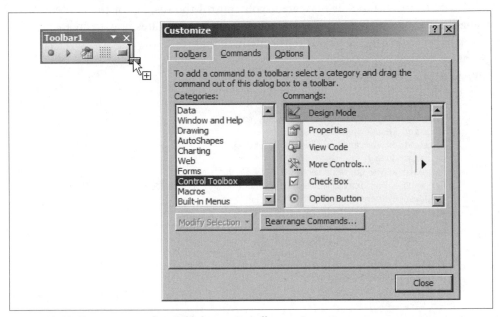

Figure 19-12. Drag commands to add them to a toolbar

5. Right-click any button on the new toolbar to rename the button, assign a macro, or change the button image, as shown in Figure 19-13.

Create Menus Using Toolbars

Toolbars and menu bars aren't very different. In fact, you can make a toolbar that looks just like a menu bar by following these steps:

1. Choose Tools → Customize → Toolbars. Excel displays the Toolbars tab of the Customize dialog box.

2. Click New. Excel display the New Toolbar dialog.

3. Name the toolbar Menu1 and click OK. Excel creates a new, empty toolbar.

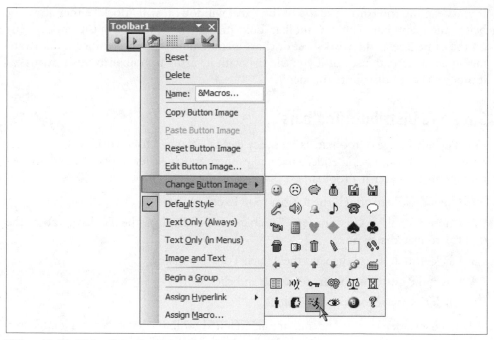

Figure 19-13. *Right-click a button to change its properties*

4. Click the Commands tab, select New Menu from the Category list, and drag New Menu from the Commands list onto the toolbar.

5. Select Macros from the Categories list and drag Custom Menu Item from the Commands list onto the menu you just added to the toolbar.

6. Repeat Step 5 two more times, then right-click each of the new menu items and set their name properties as shown in Figure 19-14.

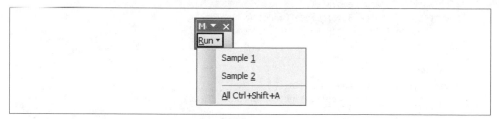

Figure 19-14. *Using a toolbar to create a menu*

7. Click OK to close the Customize dialog box.

 You can add existing menus to the toolbar by selecting Built-in Menus in the Categories list and then dragging the menu from the Commands list onto the toolbar.

If you drag the toolbar to the top of the Excel window, it will "dock" either above or below the menu bar. The new toolbar looks just like a menu bar, but it can't coexist on the same line as the worksheet or chart menu bars—that's a significant disadvantage in some situations, but if you can live with it, using a toolbar in this way makes it much easier to distribute the menu.

Save and Distribute Toolbars

One key advantage of toolbars is that they can be attached to a workbook, template, or add-in without writing code. That makes them much easier to distribute than custom menus. To attach a toolbar:

1. Open the file to attach the toolbar to in Excel.
2. Choose Tools → Customize → Toolbars. Excel displays the Toolbars tab of the Customize dialog box.
3. Click Attach. Excel displays the Attach Toolbars dialog.
4. Select the custom toolbars to attach and click Copy.
5. Click OK twice to close the dialogs.

When a user opens a file that contains an attached toolbar, that toolbar is loaded and will be saved in the user's *.xlb* file when she closes Excel. That makes the toolbar available to all workbooks on the user's machine.

If you want the toolbar to appear only when the containing workbook or template is loaded, delete the toolbar in the file's Workbook_BeforeClose event procedure. If the toolbar is attached to an add-in, use the Workbook_AddinUninstall event procedure instead. The following code handles either of those situations:

```
' ThisWorkbook class.

' For workbooks and templates.
Private Sub Workbook_BeforeClose(Cancel As Boolean)
    If Not Me.IsAddin Then Application.CommandBars("Menu1").Delete
End Sub

' For add-ins.
Private Sub Workbook_AddinUninstall()
    If Me.IsAddin Then Application.CommandBars("Menu1").Delete
End Sub
```

I delete the toolbar rather than making it invisible so the user can't try to display the toolbar after the file is uninstalled. Deleting the toolbar removes it from the toolbars list.

Create Toolbars in Code

Because custom toolbars are easier to distribute than custom menus, there is less reason to create them in code; however, you can if you like. Toolbars are `CommandBar` objects, just like menus, but they have a `Type` property set to `msoBarTypeNormal`. You get a reference to a toolbar from the `Application` object's `CommandBars` collection using the toolbar's name. The toolbars are:

3-D Settings	Align or Distribute	Annotation Pens
AutoShapes	Basic Shapes	Block Arrows
Borders	Callouts	Chart
Chart Type	Circular Reference	Clipboard
Compare Side by Side	Connectors	Control Toolbox
Diagram	Draw Border	Drawing
Drawing and Writing Pens	Drawing Canvas	Envelope
Exit Design Mode	External Data	Fill Color
Flowchart	Font Color	Formatting
Forms	Formula Auditing	Full Screen
Ink Annotations	Ink Drawing and Writing	Insert Shape
Line Color	Lines	List
Nudge	Online Meeting	Order
Organization Chart	Pattern	Picture
PivotTable	PivotTable Field List	Protection
Refresh	Reviewing	Rotate or Flip
Shadow Settings	Standard	Stars & Banners
Stop Recording	Task Pane	Text To Speech
Visual Basic	Watch Window	Web
WordArt		

Use the `CommandBar` object's `Show` method to display a toolbar. For example, the following code displays each of the toolbars in turn, pausing between each. This is useful for finding the name of a particular toolbar:

```
Sub ShowToolbars()
    Dim cb As CommandBar, show As Boolean
    For Each cb In Application.CommandBars
        If cb.Type = msoBarTypeNormal Then
            Debug.Print cb.Name
            ' Get visible state.
            show = cb.Visible
            ' Show the toolbar.
            If cb.Enabled Then
                cb.Visible = True
```

```
            VBA.DoEvents
            ' Wait.
            Application.Wait Now + 0.00001
            ' Restore the original state.
            cb.Visible = show
        End If
    End If
Next
End Sub
```

 Be sure to check the Enabled property before setting Visible to True; otherwise, you'll get an error.

Add Edit Controls to Toolbars

The best reason I can think of to create a toolbar in code is if you want to use edit controls, such as a drop-down list or combo box, within the toolbar. There's no way to drag one of those types of controls onto a toolbar manually; you can create them only through code.

To create an edit control on a toolbar:

1. Get a reference to the toolbar.
2. Use the Controls collection's Add method to create the control on the toolbar.
3. Set the control's properties and populate any lists it contains.

The Add method creates different types of controls on a toolbar based on the *Type* argument as described in Table 19-1.

Table 19-1. MsoControlType constants for creating command bar controls

Type argument	Creates	Object type of control is
msoControlButton	Toolbar button or menu item	CommandBarButton
msoControlComboBox	A combo list box (select an item or enter text)	CommandBarComboBox
msoControlDropdown	A drop-down list box (select an item)	CommandBarComboBox
msoControlEdit	An edit box (enter text)	CommandBarComboBox
msoControlPopup	A menu of other items	CommandBarPopup

The middle three control types in Table 19-1 are edit controls. You can get or set the values of those controls from code. For example, Figure 19-15 shows a toolbar that lists all the macros in the current workbook in a drop-down list. You can select an item from the list and click Run to run the macro. The toolbar also includes some built-in commands that I often use.

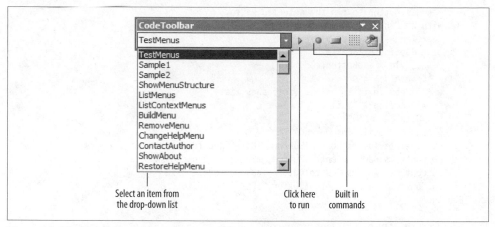

Figure 19-15. A toolbar with an edit control

The following code creates the toolbar in Figure 19-15. The code is a little complicated because it must populate the values in the drop-down list:

```
' Creates a CodeToolbar for running macros.
Sub BuildCodeToolbar( )
    Dim cb As CommandBar, obj As Object, str, list
    ' Delete the command bar if it exists.
    DeleteCodeToolbar
    ' Create a new toolbar.
    Set cb = Application.CommandBars.Add("CodeToolbar", , , True)
    cb.Left = Application.Width \ 2
    cb.Top = Application.Height \ 6
    ' Set command bar properties.
    cb.Visible = True
    cb.Position = msoBarFloating
    ' Add a drop-down list to the toolbar.
    With cb.Controls.Add(msoControlDropdown)
        .Caption = "&Macro"
        .Width = 200
        .Tag = "cboMacros"
        ' Use helper procedure to add macro names to the combo box.
        list = GetMacroList
        For Each str In list
            .AddItem str
        Next
    End With
    ' Add a button to run the selected macro.
    With cb.Controls.Add(msoControlButton)
        .Tag = "cmdRun"
        .Caption = "&Run"
        .Style = msoButtonIcon
        .FaceId = 186
        ' Set the procedure to run when button is clicked.
        .OnAction = "cmdRun_Click"
    End With
```

```
        ' Add a button to run the selected macro.
        With cb.Controls.Add(msoControlButton)
            .Tag = "cmdRefresh"
            .Caption = "&Refresh"
            .Style = msoButtonIcon
            .FaceId = 459
            ' Rebuild this toolbar (refreshes list).
            .OnAction = "BuildCodeToolbar"
        End With
        ' Add some built-in commands.
        cb.Controls.Add msoControlButton, 184  ' Record macro
        cb.Controls.Add msoControlButton, 282   ' Button control
        cb.Controls.Add msoControlButton, 485   ' Toggle grid
        cb.Controls.Add msoControlButton, 1695 ' VB Editor
End Sub

' Procedure used by OnAction property.
Sub cmdRun_Click( )
        Dim cb As CommandBar, cbc As CommandBarComboBox, _
          macro As String
        ' Get the command bar.
        Set cb = Application.CommandBars("CodeToolbar")
        ' Get the combo box.
        Set cbc = cb.FindControl(msoControlDropdown, , _
          "cboMacros", , True)
        ' Get the selected item in the combo box.
        macro = cbc.list(cbc.ListIndex)
        ' If an item is selected, then run the macro.
        On Error Resume Next
        If macro <> "" Then _
          Application.Run ActiveWorkbook.Name & "!" & macro
        If Err Then
            MsgBox "Error: " & Err.Number & ", " & Err.Description, , macro
        End If
        On Error GoTo 0
End Sub
```

The following helper function builds an array of macro names from using the VBE object model. Again, this code is a bit complicated, but it works and you can find it in the sample workbook for this chapter.

```
' Builds a list of the macros in the current workbook
' And returns it as an array.
Function GetMacroList() As String( )
        Dim obj As Object, str As String, list As String, _
          i As Long, j As Long, eol As Long
        For Each obj In ActiveWorkbook.VBProject.VBComponents
            If obj.Type = 1 Then
                ' Copy all of the code into a string.
                str = str & obj.codemodule.Lines(1, obj.codemodule.countoflines)
            End If
        Next
        i = 1
        ' Get the names of each Sub procedure.
```

```
        Do
            i = InStr(i, str, vbCrLf & "Sub ") + 6
            eol = InStr(i, str, vbCrLf)
            j = InStr(i, str, "()")
            If i = 6 Then Exit Do
            If eol > j Then _
                list = list & Mid(str, i, j - i) & ","
        Loop
        ' Return the list as an array.
        GetMacroList = Split(list, ",")
    End Function
```

Delete Toolbars

Before you create a custom toolbar, you should delete it. No, I'm not crazy: calling the CommandBars Add method fails if a toolbar with the same name already exists. The easiest way to make sure that name has not already been used is to delete it and ignore any errors as shown here:

```
    Sub DeleteCodeToolbar()
        ' Delete the toolbar if it already exists.
        On Error Resume Next
        Application.CommandBars("CodeToolbar").Delete
        On Error GoTo 0
    End Sub
```

This technique assumes you've used a fairly unique name for your toolbar. A common name like Toolbar1 might result in deleting one of the user's custom toolbars.

CommandBar and CommandBars Members

Use the CommandBars collection to add new menus and toolbars to Excel or to get existing menus or toolbars. Use the Application object's CommandBars property to get a reference to this collection. Use the CommandBar object to add controls to the menu or toolbar or to get existing controls to modify. The CommandBars collection and CommandBar object have the following members. Key members (shown in **bold**) are covered in the following reference section:

ActionControl[1]	**ActiveMenuBar**
AdaptiveMenus[2]	**Add**[1]
Application[2]	**BuiltIn**
Context	**Controls**
Count[1]	Creator[2]
Delete	**DisableAskAQuestionDropdown**[1]
DisableCustomize	**DisplayFonts**
DisplayKeysInTooltips	**DisplayTooltips**[1]
Enabled	**FindControl**[2]
FindControls[1]	Height
Id	Index

Item[1]	LargeButtons[1]
Left	MenuAnimationStyle[1]
Name	**NameLocal**
Parent[2]	**Position**
Protection	**ReleaseFocus[1]**
Reset	**RowIndex**
ShowPopup	Top
Type	Visible
Width	

[1] Collection only
[2] Object and collection

commandbars.ActionControl

Returns the CommandBarControl object that ran the current procedure. If the current procedure was not run by a CommandBarControl, returns Nothing. The following code displays a message in the Immediate window when Sample2 is called from a menu item or toolbar button:

```
Sub Sample2( )
    Dim cbc As CommandBarButton
    MsgBox "Sample2"
    Set cbc = Application.CommandBars.ActionControl
    If Not cbc Is Nothing Then _
      Debug.Print "Sample2 called by: " & cbc.Tag
End Sub
```

commandbars.ActiveMenuBar

Returns the worksheet menu bar object or the chart menu bar object, depending on which menu bar is currently displayed.

commandbars.AdaptiveMenus [= setting]

True causes Excel to display shortened top-level menus initially and then expand them after a brief period. False displays full menus.

commandbars.Add([Name], [Position], [MenuBar], [Temporary])

Creates a new menu or toolbar as a CommandBar object.

Argument	Settings
Name	The name of the menu or toolbar to create.
Position	An MsoBarPosition constant indicating the docking location of the command bar. Can be one of these settings: msoBarLeft, msoBarTop, msoBarRight, msoBarBottom, msoBarFloating, msoBarPopup, or msoBarMenuBar (Macintosh only). Default is msoBarTop.

Argument	Settings
MenuBar	True replaces the active menu bar with the menu bar created by Add. Default is False.
Temporary	True prevents the command bar from being saved when Excel closes. False saves the command bar in the user's *.xlb* file when Excel closes. Default is False.

When creating context menus, use the *Position* msoBarPopup. When creating floating toolbars, use the *Position* msoBarFloating. For example, the following code creates a context menu; then displays it at the coordinates (100, 200):

```
Sub CreateNewContextMenu( )
    Dim cb As CommandBar
    ' Create a new context menu bar.
    Set cb = Application.CommandBars.Add("ContextMenu1", _
        msoBarPopup, , True)
    ' Add some items to the menu bar.
    With cb.Controls.Add(msoControlButton, , , , True)
        .Caption = "Sample &1"
        .OnAction = "Sample1"
    End With
    With cb.Controls.Add(msoControlButton, , , , True)
        .Caption = "Sample &2"
        .OnAction = "Sample2"
    End With
    With cb.Controls.Add(msoControlButton, , , , True)
        .Caption = "Run &All"
        .OnAction = "TestMenus"
        .BeginGroup = True
    End With
    ' Display this context menu.
    cb.ShowPopup 100, 200
End Sub
```

The *MenuBar* argument lets you replace the top-level worksheet or chart menu bars with your own custom menu bar. For examples, the following code replaces the top-level menu bar with a blank menu bar:

```
Sub ReplaceTopLevelMenuBar( )
    Dim cb As CommandBar
    Set cb = Application.CommandBars.Add("BlankBar", , True, True)
    cb.Visible = True
End Sub
```

To restore the original menu bar, simply delete the menu bar you just created:

```
Sub RestoreTopLevelMenuBar( )
    Application.CommandBars("BlankBar").Delete
End Sub
```

*commandbar.*BuiltIn

Returns True if the command bar is built in to Excel, False if it is a custom command bar.

*commandbar.*Controls

Returns the `CommandBarControls` collection used to add controls to the command bar and to get controls from the command bar. For example, the following code displays worksheet menu bar controls three levels deep:

```
' List Worksheet menus three levels deep.
Sub ListWorksheetMenus( )
    Dim menu As CommandBarControl, item As CommandBarControl, _
      subitem As CommandBarControl
    Debug.Print "Worksheet Menu Bar"
    For Each menu In Application.CommandBars("Worksheet Menu Bar").Controls
        Debug.Print , menu.Caption
        For Each item In menu.Controls
                Debug.Print , , item.Caption, item.id, item.Tag
                If item.Type = msoControlPopup Then
                    For Each subitem In item.Controls
                            Debug.Print , , , subitem.Caption, _
                                subitem.id, subitem.Tag
                    Next
                End If
        Next
    Next
End Sub
```

*commandbar.*Delete( )

Deletes a command bar. You can't delete built-in command bars. Before creating a new command bar, it is a good idea to use `Delete` to make sure a command bar doesn't already exist, as shown here:

```
Sub DeleteContextMenu( )
    ' Ignore error if command bar doesn't already exist.
    On Error Resume Next
    Application.CommandBars("ContextMenu1").Delete
    On Error GoTo 0
End Sub
```

*commandbars.*DisableAskAQuestionDropdown [= *setting*]

True displays a question box (Figure 19-16) on the top-level menu bar; False hides the box. Default is True.

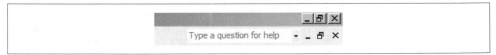

Figure 19-16. Excel question box

The following code turns the question box on and off:

```
' Switches question box on/off.
Sub QuestionBox( )
    Application.CommandBars.DisableAskAQuestionDropdown = Not _
        Application.CommandBars.DisableAskAQuestionDropdown
End Sub
```

commandbars.DisableCustomize [= *setting*]

True prevents users from changing menus and toolbars; False allows changes. Default is False. This property does not prevent changes made through code. The following code turns customization on and off:

```
' Switches customization on/off.
Sub CustomizationOnOff( )
    Application.CommandBars.DisableCustomize = Not _
        Application.CommandBars.DisableCustomize
End Sub
```

commandbars.DisplayFonts [= *setting*]

True displays font names in the Font box in their actual fonts; False uses the default font. Default is True.

commandbar.DisplayKeysInTooltips [= *setting*]

True displays shortcut keys in the tool tips for command bar controls; False hides shortcut keys. Default is False.

commandbars.DisplayTooltips [= *setting*]

True displays pop-up tool tips when the mouse pointer pauses over a command bar control; False does not display tool tips. Default is True.

commandbar.Enabled [= *setting*]

True includes the toolbar in the toolbars list; False removes the toolbar from the list. Default is True. To see a list of toolbars, right-click on a command bar.

Removing the toolbar from the toolbar list hides the toolbar and prevents the user from displaying it. The following code demonstrates the Enabled property by turning the Visual Basic toolbar off and on:

```
' Turn Visual Basic toolbar on/off.
Sub VBToolbarOnOff( )
    ' First, display the toolbar.
    CommandBars("Visual Basic").Visible = True
    ' Switch Enabled on/off.
```

```
            CommandBars("Visual Basic").Enabled = Not _
                CommandBars("Visual Basic").Enabled
        End Sub
```

commandbar.FindControl([*Type*], [*Id*], [*Tag*], [*Visible*], [*Recursive*])

Returns a CommandBarControl object from the command bar's Controls collection using the Id or Tag properties of the control. Returns Nothing if the control is not found.

Argument	Settings
Type	An msoControlType constant indicating the type of control to return.
Id	The internal ID for the control. Use this argument to find built-in controls.
Tag	The Tag property associated with the control when it was created. Use this argument to find custom controls.
Visible	True includes only visible controls in the search; False includes all controls. Default is False.
Recursive	True includes controls on submenus and subtoolbars in the search; False searches only for top-level controls on the command bar. Default is False.

Built-in controls have unique Id properties but do not have a Tag property setting, while custom controls don't have unique Id properties but may have unique Tag properties. See the Controls member topic for an example that lists the Id and Tag properties of controls on a command bar.

The *Type* argument allows you to specify the type of the control you want to find. Controls on a command bar can be referenced as the base CommandBarControl type or as a derived CommandBarButton, CommandBarComboBox, or CommandBarPopup type. Using those derived types rather than the base type lets you more easily use the full set of members provided by that type.

For example, the CopyFace method is available only on the derived CommandBarButton type; therefore, although both of the following procedures work, the second is preferable since it supports Auto Complete, is more precise, and less error-prone:

```
        Sub UseBaseControlType()
            Dim cb As CommandBar, cbc As CommandBarControl
            ' Get the command bar.
            Set cb = CommandBars("Worksheet Menu Bar")
            ' Use base type
            Set cbc = cb.FindControl(, 682, , , True)
            cbc.CopyFace        ' Note: no auto complete.
            ActiveSheet.Paste
        End Sub

        Sub UseDerivedControlType()
            Dim cb As CommandBar, cbb As CommandBarButton
            ' Get the command bar.
            Set cb = CommandBars("Worksheet Menu Bar")
            ' Use the derived type.
            Set cbb = cb.FindControl(msoControlButton, 682, , , True)
            cbb.CopyFace         ' Auto complete works now.
            ActiveSheet.Paste
        End Sub
```

See Table 19-1 earlier in this chapter for a list of the command bar msoControlType constants and the derived control types they return.

Finally, the *Recursive* argument is important when working with menu bars since they are often several levels deep. Setting *Recursive* to True searches down that hierarchy to find a control. *Recursive* is False by default, so I usually set it to True any time I use FindControl.

*commandbars.*FindControls([*Type*], [*Id*], [*Tag*], [*Visible*])

Returns a collection of command bar controls. The arguments are the same as for the FindControl method, except there is no *Recursive* argument (that argument is assumed to be True). The following code lists the captions and IDs of all of the pop-up menu controls:

```
Sub FindControlsDemo( )
    Dim cbcs As CommandBarControls, cpop As CommandBarPopup
    ' Get the collection of pop-up menus.
    Set cbcs = CommandBars.FindControls(msoControlPopup)
    ' Show the caption and ID of each control.
    For Each cpop In cbcs
        Debug.Print cpop.Caption, cpop.id
    Next
End Sub
```

*commandbar.*Id

Returns a numeric identifier for the command bar. The following code lists the names and IDs of all the command bars:

```
Sub ListCommandBars( )
    Dim cb As CommandBar
    For Each cb In CommandBars
        Debug.Print cb.Name, cb.id
    Next
End Sub
```

*commandbars.*LargeButtons [= *setting*]

True displays command bar buttons larger than normal; False displays normal-size buttons. Default is False.

*commandbars.*MenuAnimationStyle [= *msoMenuAnimation*]

Sets or returns how menus are animated. Can be one of these settings:

msoMenuAnimationNone (default)

msoMenuAnimationRandom

msoMenuAnimationSlide

msoMenuAnimationUnfold

commandbar.Name [= setting]

Sets or returns the name of the command bar. This property is read-only for built-in command bars.

commandbar.NameLocal [= setting]

Sets or returns the name of the command bar in the user's selected language. This property is read-only for built-in command bars.

commandbar.Position [= msoBarPosition]

Sets or returns the location where a command bar is docked. Can be one of these settings:

    msoBarBottom
    msoBarFloating
    msoBarLeft
    msoBarMenuBar
    msoBarPopup
    msoBarRight
    msoBarTop (default)

commandbar.Protection [= msoBarProtection]

Sets or returns the type of customizations allowed for a command bar. Can be one of these settings:

    msoBarNoChangeDock
    msoBarNoChangeVisible
    msoBarNoCustomize
    msoBarNoHorizontalDock
    msoBarNoMove
    msoBarNoProtection (default)
    msoBarNoResize
    msoBarNoVerticalDock

CommandBars.ReleaseFocus( )

Releases the focus from any of the command bar controls.

commandbar.Reset( )

Restores a built-in command bar to its default settings, removing any customizations that have been made.

commandbar.RowIndex [= *msoBarRow*]

Sets or returns the order of the command bar in its current docking area. Can be any integer greater than zero, msoBarRowFirst, or msoBarRowLast.

commandbar.ShowPopup([*x*], [*y*])

Displays a context menu bar at the specified coordinates. Causes an error if the command bar does not have a Type property of msoBarTypePopup.

Argument	Settings
x	The horizontal position of the menu in pixels
y	The vertical position of the menu in pixels

The following code pops up a context menu created earlier:

```
Sub ShowMenu( )
    CommandBars("ContextMenu1").ShowPopup 100, 200
End Sub
```

commandbar.Type

Returns an msoBarType constant identifying the type of the command bar. Can be one of these settings:

    msoBarTypeMenuBar (menu bar)

    msoBarTypeNormal (toolbar)

    msoBarTypePopup (context menu)

CommandBarControl and CommandBarControls Members

Use the CommandBarControls collection to add new controls to a command bar. Use the CommandBar object's Controls property to get a reference to this collection. Use the

CommandBarControl object to set the appearance, caption, and action of a command bar control. The CommandBarControls collection and CommandBarControl object have the following members. Key members (shown in **bold**) are covered in the following reference section:

Add[1]	Application[2]
BeginGroup	**BuiltIn**
Caption	**Copy**
Count[1]	Creator[2]
Delete	**DescriptionText**
Enabled	**Execute**
Height	**HelpContextId**
HelpFile	**Id**
Index	**IsPriorityDropped**
Item[1]	Left
Move	OLEUsage
OnAction	**Parameter**
Parent[2]	**Priority**
Reset	**SetFocus**
Tag	**TooltipText**
Top	**Type**
Visible	Width

[1] Collection only
[2] Object and collection

commandbarcontrols.Add([*Type*], [*Id*], [*Parameter*], [*Before*], [*Temporary*])

Adds a control to a command bar and returns a reference to the new object.

Argument	Settings
Type	An msoControlType constant for the type of control to create. Can be one of these settings: msoControlButton, msoControlComboBox, msoControlDropdown, msoControlEdit, or msoControlPopup.
Id	The Id property of an existing command to add to the command bar. Use this argument to add built-in commands rather than custom commands.
Parameter	A value to pass to the command via the Parameter property.
Before	The position of the control on the command bar. Default is to insert after the last control on the command bar.
Temporary	True prevents the control from being saved when Excel closes. False saves the control in the user's *.xlb* file when Excel closes. Default is False.

The following code adds a custom smiley button to the worksheet menu bar; fortunately it's only temporary:

```
Sub AddCommandBarControl( )
    Dim cb As CommandBar, cbc As CommandBarControl
```

```
        ' Get a command bar
        Set cb = CommandBars("Worksheet Menu Bar")
        Set cbc = cb.Controls.Add(msoControlButton, , , , True)
        cbc.Caption = "Smiley"
        cbc.FaceId = 1131
        cbc.OnAction = "DontWorry"
    End Sub

    Sub DontWorry( )
        MsgBox "Don't worry, be happy."
    End Sub
```

commandbarcontrol.BeginGroup [= setting]

True adds a separator bar before the control on menu bars; False removes the separator bar if it exists. Default is False.

commandbarcontrol.BuiltIn

Returns True if the control is a built-in command and its OnAction property has not been set; returns False if the control is a custom control.

commandbarcontrol.Caption [= setting]

Sets or returns the caption that appears for the control. Use the ampersand (&) to specify an accelerator key in the caption. For command bar buttons, the caption appears as the tool tip for the control.

commandbarcontrol.Copy([Bar], [Before])

Copies a control from a source command bar to a destination command bar.

Argument	Settings
Bar	The destination command bar object. Default is the source command bar.
Before	The position in the destination command bar for the copied control. Default is to copy the control to the end of the command bar.

commandbarcontrol.Delete([Temporary])

Deletes a control from a command bar.

Argument	Settings
Temporary	True prevents the change from being saved when Excel closes; False saves the change to the command bar in the user's .xlb file when Excel closes. Default is False.

*commandbarcontrol.*DescriptionText [= *setting*]

Sets or returns a description of the control. This description is not displayed to the user.

*commandbarcontrol.*Enabled [= *setting*]

True enables a control, allowing it to be selected; False disables a control.

 Setting a built-in control's Enabled property to True does not enable the control if Excel's state does not allow the control to be enabled.

*commandbarcontrol.*Execute( )

Executes the control's command. For example, the following code displays the About Excel dialog box:

```
Sub ShowAbout( )
    Dim cbc As CommandBarControl
    ' &About Microsoft Office Excel command is ID 927.
    Set cbc = CommandBars.FindControl(msoControlButton, 927)
    cbc.Execute
End Sub
```

*commandbarcontrol.*HelpContextId [= *setting*]

Sets or returns the context ID of the control in the help file for the workbook, template, or add-in.

*commandbarcontrol.*HelpFile [= *setting*]

Sets or returns the help file for the workbook, template, or add-in.

*commandbarcontrol.*Id

For built-in controls, returns the numeric identifier for the control. For custom controls, returns 1.

*commandbarcontrol.*IsPriorityDropped

If CommandBars.AdaptiveMenus is True, this property returns False if the control is not visible because it was not recently used or there is not enough space to display it and returns True if the control is visible.

commandbarcontrol.Move([Bar], [Before])

Moves a control from a source command bar to a destination command bar.

Argument	Settings
Bar	The destination command bar object. Default is the source command bar.
Before	The position in the destination command bar for the control.

 Move without arguments moves the control to the last position on the source command bar.

commandbarcontrol.OLEUsage [= msoControlOLEUsage]

Sets or returns how the control is merged with controls from another Office application when Excel is embedded within another application. Can be one of these settings:

    msoControlOLEUsageBoth
    msoControlOLEUsageClient
    msoControlOLEUsageNeither
    msoControlOLEUsageServer (default)

In OLE terminology, the server is the object provider (in this case Excel) and the client is the application that consumes the embedded object.

commandbarcontrol.OnAction [= setting]

Sets or returns the Visual Basic procedure to run when the control executes. Setting this property of a built-in control overrides the built-in behavior and replaces it with the Visual Basic code.

commandbarcontrol.Parameter [= setting]

Sets or returns a string variable that may be used from the control's code.

commandbarcontrol.Priority [= setting]

Sets or returns a priority number that helps determine whether or not the control is dropped from the toolbar if there is not enough room to display it within its docked position. Must be between 0 and 7; a setting of 1 prevents the control from being dropped. Default is 3.

commandbarcontrol.Reset( )

For built-in commands, Reset restores the default behavior and appearance of the control.

commandbarcontrol.SetFocus( )

Switches the keyboard focus to the control. Causes an error if the command is not enabled or is not visible.

commandbarcontrol.Tag [= setting]

For custom controls, sets or returns a string used to locate the control through the FindControl method.

commandbarcontrol.TooltipText [= setting]

Sets or returns the tool tip displayed for the control. The default tool tip is the control's Caption property.

commandbarcontrol.Type

Returns the type of the control as an msoControlType constant. Can be one of these settings:

```
msoControlButton
msoControlComboBox
msoControlDropdown
msoControlEdit
msoControlPopup
```

CommandBarButton Members

Use the CommandBarButton object to work with menu items and toolbar buttons. Use the CommandBar object's Controls collection or FindControl method to get a reference to this object. The CommandBarButton object is derived from the CommandBarControl object and has the following members. Members that are unique from CommandBarControl (shown in **bold**) are covered in the following reference section:

Application	BeginGroup	BuiltIn
BuiltInFace	Caption	Copy
CopyFace	Creator	Delete
DescriptionText	Enabled	Execute
FaceId	Height	HelpContextId

HelpFile	**HyperlinkType**	Id
Index	IsPriorityDropped	Left
Mask	Move	OLEUsage
OnAction	Parameter	Parent
PasteFace	**Picture**	Priority
Reset	SetFocus	**ShortcutText**
State	**Style**	Tag
TooltipText	Top	Type
Visible	Width	

commandbarbutton.CopyFace( )

Copies the button bitmap onto the clipboard.

commandbarbutton.FaceId [= *setting*]

Sets or returns the numeric ID of the button's bitmap from a list of built-in button faces. The following code builds a list of the built-in button faces on a new worksheet:

```
Sub ListButtonFaces( )
    Dim cbb As CommandBarButton
    ' Create a new worksheet.
    Worksheets.Add
    ' For each command bar button.
    For Each cbb In CommandBars.FindControls(msoControlButton)
        ' List FaceID.
        ActiveCell = cbb.FaceId
        ActiveCell.Next(, 1).Select
        ' Copy and paste face onto worksheet.
        cbb.CopyFace
        ActiveSheet.Paste
        ' Move to the next row.
        ActiveCell.Next(2, -1).Select
    Next
End Sub
```

commandbarbutton.HyperlinkType [= *msoCommandBarButtonHyperlinkType*]

Sets or returns a value that determines whether the button represents a normal button, a hyperlink, or a picture file to insert. Can be one of these settings:

msoCommandBarButtonHyperlinkNone (default)

msoCommandBarButtonHyperlinkInsertPicture

msoCommandBarButtonHyperlinkOpen

When *msoCommandBarButtonHyperlinkType* is set to msoCommandBarButtonHyperlinkInsertPicture or msoCommandBarButtonHyperlinkOpen, the TooltipText property contains the URL of the hyperlink. For example, the following code adds a button to the worksheet menu bar that opens a Google search page:

```
Sub AddHyperlink()
    Dim cb As CommandBar, cbb As CommandBarButton
    ' Get a command bar
    Set cb = CommandBars("Worksheet Menu Bar")
    Set cbb = cb.Controls.Add(msoControlButton, 7343, , , True)
    cbb.HyperlinkType = msoCommandBarButtonHyperlinkOpen
    cbb.TooltipText = "http:\\www.google.com\"
End Sub
```

Similarly, this code adds a button that inserts an image on the active sheet:

```
Sub AddInsertPictureButton()
    Dim cb As CommandBar, cbb As CommandBarButton
    ' Get a command bar
    Set cb = CommandBars("Worksheet Menu Bar")
    Set cbb = cb.Controls.Add(msoControlButton, 2619, , , True)
    cbb.HyperlinkType = msoCommandBarButtonHyperlinkInsertPicture
    cbb.TooltipText = ThisWorkbook.Path & "\logo.jpg"
End Sub
```

commandbarbutton.Mask

Returns an IPictureDisp object representing the mask image for the command bar button. The mask image determines what parts of the button image are transparent.

commandbarbutton.PasteFace()

Pastes a picture from the clipboard onto the command bar button.

commandbarbutton.Picture

Returns an IPictureDisp object representing the image for the command bar button.

commandbarbutton.ShortcutText [= setting]

Sets or returns the shortcut key text displayed next to the item when it appears on a menu.

commandbarbutton.State [= msoButtonState]

Sets or returns the interactive state of the control. This property is read-only for built-in commands. Can be one of these settings:

```
msoButtonDown
msoButtonMixed
msoButtonUp
```

For menu items, msoButton down places a check mark beside the item's caption; msoButtonUp removes the check mark. The following code toggles the selection of a menu item:

```
Sub ShowCodeHelper( )
    Dim cbc As CommandBarButton
    ' Get the menu item
    Set cbc = CommandBars("Worksheet Menu Bar").FindControl( _
        , , "mnuCodeHelper", , True)
    ' Toggle the state (adds or removes a check mark
    ' beside the menu item).
    cbc.State = Not cbc.State
End Sub
```

commandbarbutton.**Style** [= *msoButtonStyle*]

Sets or returns the display style of the command bar button. Can be one of these settings:

msoButtonAutomatic (default)

msoButtonCaption

msoButtonIcon

msoButtonIconAndCaption

msoButtonIconAndCaptionBelow

msoButtonIconAndWrapCaption

msoButtonIconAndWrapCaptionBelow

msoButtonWrapCaption

CommandBarComboBox Members

Use the CommandBarComboBox object to work with edit box, drop-down list, and combo box controls on toolbars. Use the CommandBar object's Controls collection or FindControl method to get a reference to this object. The CommandBarComboBox object is derived from the CommandBarControl object and has the following members. Members that are unique from CommandBarControl are shown in **bold**:

AddItem	Application	BeginGroup
BuiltIn	Caption	Change
Clear	Control	Copy
Creator	Delete	DescriptionText
DropDownLines	**DropDownWidth**	Enabled
Execute	Height	HelpContextId
HelpFile	Id	Index
IsPriorityDropped	Left	**List**
ListCount	**ListHeaderCount**	**ListIndex**
Move	OLEUsage	OnAction

Parameter	Parent	Priority
RemoveItem	Reset	SetFocus
Style	Tag	**Text**
TooltipText	Top	Type
Visible	Width	

commandbarcombobox.**AddItem**(*Text*, [*Index*])

Adds an item to the control's list.

Argument	Settings
Text	The item to add to the list.
Index	The position of the item in the list. The default is to insert the new item at the end of the list.

The following code creates a new drop-down list on the worksheet menu bar and adds three items to the list:

```
Sub AddDropDown( )
    Dim cb As CommandBar, cbo As CommandBarComboBox
    ' Get a command bar
    Set cb = CommandBars("Worksheet Menu Bar")
    ' Create the combo box.
    Set cbo = cb.Controls.Add(msoControlDropdown, , , , True)
    ' Add a Tag so this control can be found from other code.
    cbo.Tag = "cboSelectText"
    ' Add items.
    cbo.AddItem "This"
    cbo.AddItem "That"
    cbo.AddItem "the"
    cbo.AddItem "other"
    ' Set the procedure to run.
    cbo.OnAction = "ShowSelection"
End Sub
```

commandbarcombobox.**Clear**( )

Removes all the items from the list. The following code removes the items added in the preceding AddDropDown procedure:

```
Sub RemoveAll( )
    Dim cbo As CommandBarComboBox, i As Integer
    ' Get the control
    Set cbo = CommandBars("Worksheet Menu Bar").FindControl _
      (msoControlDropdown, , "cboSelectText", , True)
    ' Remove the items.
    cbo.Clear
End Sub
```

commandbarcombobox.DropDownLines [= setting]

Sets or returns the number of lines to display when the user clicks the drop-down arrow on the control. The default is 0, which causes Excel to calculate the number of lines to display.

commandbarcombobox.DropDownWidth [= setting]

Sets or returns the width of the drop-down list in pixels.

commandbarcombobox.List(Index)

Returns one or all of the items in the list. You can get the selected item by using the Text property or by using this method in combination with the ListIndex property as shown here:

```
Sub ShowSelection()
    Dim cbo As CommandBarComboBox, str As String
    ' Get the control
    Set cbo = CommandBars("Worksheet Menu Bar").FindControl _
      (msoControlDropdown, , "cboSelectText", , True)
    ' Get the selection.
    str = cbo.list(cbo.ListIndex)
    ' Display selection.
    MsgBox "You selected: " & str
End Sub
```

commandbarcombobox.ListCount

Returns the number of items in the list.

commandbarcombobox.ListHeaderCount [= setting]

Sets or returns the position of a separator bar in the drop-down list. For example, the following code adds a separator bar after the third item in the list created earlier:

```
Sub AddDropDownListSeparatorBar()
    Dim cbo As CommandBarComboBox
    ' Get the control
    Set cbo = CommandBars("Worksheet Menu Bar").FindControl _
      (msoControlDropdown, , "cboSelectText", , True)
    cbo.ListHeaderCount = 3
End Sub
```

commandbarcombobox.ListIndex [= setting]

Sets or returns the index of the currently selected item.

commandbarcombobox.RemoveItem(*Index*)

Removes a single item from the list.

commandbarcombobox.Style [= *msoComboStyle*]

Sets or returns how the control's caption is displayed. Can be one of these settings:

msoComboLabel (display caption)
msoComboNormal (default; don't display caption)

commandbarcombobox.Text [= *setting*]

Sets or returns the text in the edit portion of the control. The following code creates a combo box on the worksheet menu bar; if the user enters a value in the edit box, ShowText displays that value:

```
Sub AddTextBox( )
    Dim cb As CommandBar, cbo As CommandBarComboBox
    ' Get a command bar
    Set cb = CommandBars("Worksheet Menu Bar")
    ' Create the combo box.
    Set cbo = cb.Controls.Add(msoControlEdit, , , , True)
    ' Add a Tag so this control can be found from other code.
    cbo.Tag = "cboEditText"
    ' Display a label with the text box.
    cbo.Caption = "Enter some text"
    cbo.Style = msoComboLabel
    ' Set the procedure to run.
    cbo.OnAction = "ShowText"
End Sub

Sub ShowText( )
    Dim cbo As CommandBarComboBox
    ' Get the control
    Set cbo = CommandBars("Worksheet Menu Bar").FindControl _
      (msoControlEdit, , "cboEditText", , True)
    ' Display selection.
    MsgBox "You entered: " & cbo.Text
End Sub
```

CommandBarPopup Members

Use the CommandBarPopup object to work with menu controls. Use the CommandBar object's Controls collection or FindControl method to get a reference to this object. The CommandBarPopup object is derived from the CommandBarControl object and has the following members. Members that are unique from `CommandBarControl` (shown in **bold**) are covered in the following reference section:

Application	BeginGroup
BuiltIn	Caption
CommandBar	Control
Controls	Copy
Creator	Delete
DescriptionText	Enabled
Execute	Height
HelpContextId	HelpFile
Id	Index
IsPriorityDropped	Left
Move	**OLEMenuGroup**
OLEUsage	OnAction
Parameter	Parent
Priority	Reset
SetFocus	Tag
TooltipText	Top
Type	Visible
Width	

commandbarpopup.Controls

Returns the `CommandBarControls` collection for the pop-up menu. Use this collection to add or remove items from the menu. For example, the following code creates a menu on the worksheet menu bar and adds three menu items to it:

```
Sub AddPopupMenu( )
    Dim cb As CommandBar, cpop As CommandBarPopup
    ' Get a command bar
    Set cb = CommandBars("Worksheet Menu Bar")
    ' Create the combo box.
    Set cpop = cb.Controls.Add(msoControlPopup, , , , True)
    ' Add a Tag so this control can be found from other code.
    cpop.Tag = "cpopCustomMenu"
    cpop.Caption = "&Custom Menu"
    ' Add items.
    With cpop.Controls.Add(msoControlButton, , , , True)
        .Caption = "Item &1"
        .OnAction = "Item1_Click"
        .Tag = "cbbItem1"
    End With
    With cpop.Controls.Add(msoControlButton, , , , True)
        .Caption = "Item &2"
        .OnAction = "Item2_Click"
        .Tag = "cbbItem2"
    End With
    ' Built-in command.
    With cpop.Controls.Add(msoControlButton, 1695, , , True)
```

```
        ' Add separator bar.
        .BeginGroup = True
    End With
End Sub

Sub Item1_Click( )
    ' Add code to respond to menu item Click Here...
End Sub

Sub Item2_Click( )
    ' Add code to respond to menu item Click Here...
End Sub
```

commandbarpopup.OLEMenuGroup [= *msoOLEMenuGroup*]

Sets or returns the menu group that this menu is merged with when an Excel document is embedded in another Office application document. Can be one of these settings:

msoOLEMenuGroupContainer

msoOLEMenuGroupEdit

msoOLEMenuGroupFile

msoOLEMenuGroupHelp

msoOLEMenuGroupNone

msoOLEMenuGroupObject

msoOLEMenuGroupWindow

CHAPTER 20

Building Dialog Boxes

Chapter 7 showed you how to display the built-in Excel dialog boxes and how to use InputBox and the File dialogs to get information from the user. In this chapter, I show you how to create more complex data-entry forms, validate entries, and use the Visual Basic Forms Designer to create custom dialog boxes.

This chapter includes task-oriented reference information for Forms 2.0 user forms and controls: UserForm, CheckBox, ComboBox, CommandButton, Control, Font, Frame, Image, Label, ListBox, MultiPage, OptionButton, Page, RefEdit, ScrollBar, SpinButton, TabStrip, TextBox, ToggleButton. Those objects aren't part of the Excel object model and so aren't part of the Excel VBA Help. Instead, the help topics for those objects are found in *C:\Program Files\Common Files\Microsoft Shared\VBA\VBA6\1033\FM20.CHM*.

 Code used in this chapter and additional samples are available in *ch20.xls*.

Types of Dialogs

There are many different ways to display dialog boxes using Visual Basic in Excel, so it is helpful to organize those techniques by starting with the type of dialog box you want to display. The three main sorts of dialog boxes are informational displays, data-entry forms, and other tasks. Table 20-1 organizes the ways to display dialogs based on those types.

Table 20-1. Types of dialogs and how to display them

Type of dialog	Example	Use one of these	See
Informational display	Success message	MsgBox function	Chapter 3
	Help	Help or FollowHyperLink method	Chapter 6
Data-entry	Enter values in a list	ShowDataForm method	This chapter
	Advanced data entry	User form	This chapter

Table 20-1. *Types of dialogs and how to display them (continued)*

Type of dialog	Example	Use one of these	See
Task-specific	Get a value or range	`InputBox` method	Chapters 3, 7
	Get a file or folder name	`FileDialog`, `GetOpenFilename`, or `GetSaveAsFilename` method	Chapter 7
	Show a built-in Excel dialog box	`Dialogs` method	Chapter 7
	Set task options or custom properties	User form	This chapter
	Wizard	User form	This chapter

As you can see from Table 20-1, Excel handles the well-structured tasks for you, but as your needs become open-ended, you need to start creating your own user forms. The lesson from Table 20-1 is to not start with the Forms Designer—look around first to see if Excel already does the work for you!

Create Data-Entry Forms

Entering data in a worksheet is straightforward, but there's nothing preventing users from entering values in the wrong cells, entering invalid data, or leaving required fields blank. To address those problems, Excel provides data forms, validation tools, and lists. You can use those tools together to create a fairly sophisticated data-entry process.

To see how data forms work:

1. Create a new worksheet.
2. Enter three column headings—Item, Quantity, and Price—on the first row.
3. Select those cells.
4. Choose Data → Form. Excel displays a data form with fields for each of the column headings.
5. Enter data in each field, pressing Return after each. Excel adds a record to the list after you press Enter on the last field, as shown in Figure 20-1.

The data form doesn't check whether the data is valid; it merely displays a form with blank fields for each column in the list. To add validation rules:

1. Select the first cell (A2) and choose Data → Validation. Excel displays the Data Validation dialog box.
2. Enter the values shown in Figure 20-2. Click OK when done.
3. Repeat Steps 1 and 2 for the Quantity and Price columns using the settings in Table 20-2.

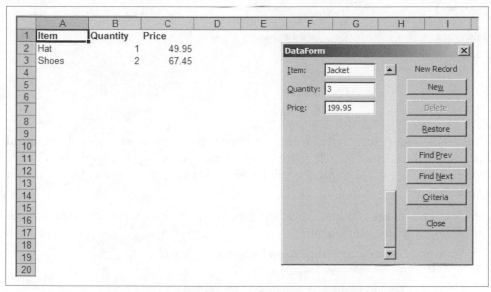

Figure 20-1. Using a data form to enter values

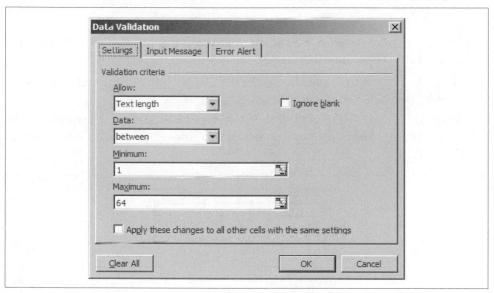

Figure 20-2. Entering validation rules

Table 20-2. Sample validation settings

List column	Validation property	Setting
Quantity	Allow	Whole number
	Data	Greater than
	Minimum	0
	Ignore blank	(Cleared)

Table 20-2. Sample validation settings (continued)

List column	Validation property	Setting
Price	Allow	Decimal
	Data	Greater than
	Minimum	0
	Ignore blank	(Cleared)

The validation settings in Table 20-2 designate the columns as required fields and specify the data type for each column, but those validation rules apply only to the first row of the list. To apply the validation rules to all of the rows, choose one of these options:

- Select the entire row and repeat the preceding procedure to apply the data validation rules to each column.
- Convert the data-entry range to an Excel list.

> The lists feature was introduced in Excel 2003.

Converting the range to a list extends the validation rules to each new row as it is added to the list. To see how that works:

1. Select the range A1:C2 and choose Data → List → Create List. Excel displays the Create List dialog.
2. Select My List Has Headers, and click OK. Excel indicates that the range is a list by adding a blue border and a new item row to the range, as shown in Figure 20-3.

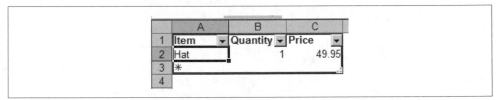

Figure 20-3. Converting the range to an Excel list

Now if you select any cell in the range and choose Data → Form, incorrect entries cause validation errors, as shown in Figure 20-4.

Blank fields are not flagged from the data form, but blank fields are flagged with a validation error that appears as a note on the blank cell. You can add more descriptive error messages and prompts for the cells from the Input Message and Error Alert tabs on the Data Validation dialog box. I won't show those here, since they are pretty self-explanatory.

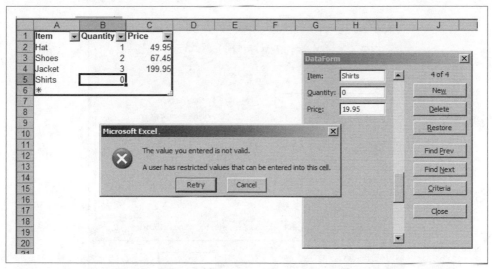

Figure 20-4. Invalid values are flagged during data entry

Advanced Validation

Validation can do more check the type and range of an entry. You can also look up a value from a range of possible entries. To see that in action, follow these steps:

1. Create a new worksheet and add the following values to a range of cells: Hat, Shoes, Jacket, Shirts, and Socks.
2. Select the range and name the range ItemSettings.
3. Return to the data-entry worksheet and select cell A2.
4. Choose Data → Validation and make the changes shown in Figure 20-5.
5. Click OK to apply the changes.

Now, entries in the Item column must match one of the values in the ItemSettings named range. Not only that, but Excel displays the possible settings in a drop-down list when you edit the worksheet, as shown in Figure 20-6.

Data Forms from Code

To display a data form from code, take these steps:

1. Get a reference to the worksheet containing the data-entry range.
2. Call the ShowDataForm method on that worksheet object.

The following code displays the data form for the DataForm worksheet:

```
Sub ShowDataForm( )
    Dim ws As Worksheet
    Set ws = Worksheets("DataForm")
    ws.ShowDataForm
End Sub
```

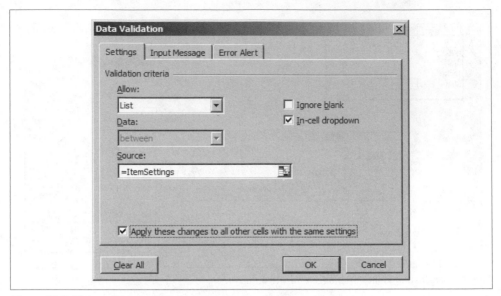

Figure 20-5. Using a list of values for validation

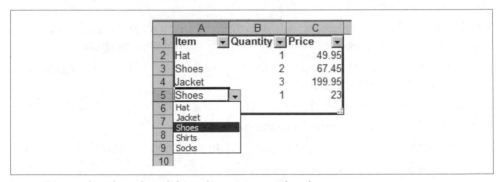

Figure 20-6. Values from the validation list appear in a dropdown

The data-entry range should be contiguous. Blank rows or columns within that range cause problems entering new records.

Design Your Own Forms

If the built-in forms don't meet your needs or if your task is more complex than the preceding data-entry sample, you can use the Visual Basic Forms Designer to create your own custom forms in Excel.

To create a custom dialog box using the Forms Designer:

1. Start the Visual Basic Editor and choose Insert → User Form. Visual Basic displays a new form and the Control Toolbox.

2. Drag controls from the Toolbox onto the form as shown in Figure 20-7.

---

3. Set the properties in the Properties window (Figure 20-8) as you position the controls on the form. Table 20-3 lists the controls and property settings used for the Stock History sample.

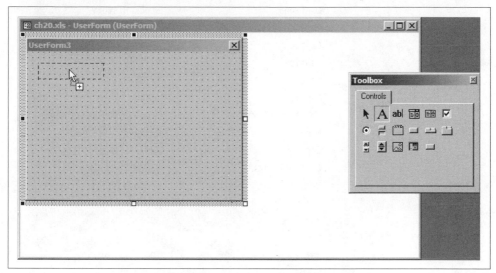

Figure 20-7. Drag controls from the Toolbox onto the user form

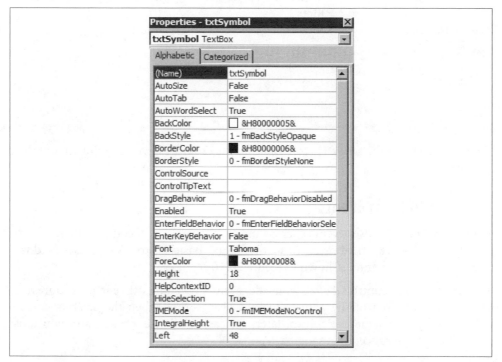

Figure 20-8. Set the controls' properties as you place them on the form

Table 20-3. Controls and property settings for the Stock History form

Control	Property	Set to
User form	Name	frmStockHistory
	Caption	Stock History
Label	Caption	Symbol
Label	Caption	#Days
Label	Caption	Preview
TextBox	Name	txtSymbol
	Caption	^IXIC
	ControlTipText	Stock symbol or index
TextBox	Name	txtDays
	Caption	100
	ControlTipText	Value from 1 to 300
SpinButton	Name	spnDays
	Delay	20
	Max	300
	Min	1
	Value	100
Image	Name	imgChart
	Height	150
	Width	180
CommandButton	Name	cmdGetHistory
	Accelerator	G
	Caption	Get History
CommandButton	Name	cmdViewChart
	Accelerator	V
	Caption	View Chart

Figure 20-9 shows the Stock History once all the controls have been drawn and their properties set.

Respond to Form Events

Controls respond to user events such as mouse clicks. To add code for these events, simply double-click on the control in the Visual Basic Editor. Visual Basic adds a procedure for the event, as shown in Figure 20-10.

Be sure to name controls *before* you add event procedures. Event procedures are associated with controls by name—spnDays_Change runs when the spnDays control changes. If you rename the control later, that association is broken and you must rename the event procedure to match.

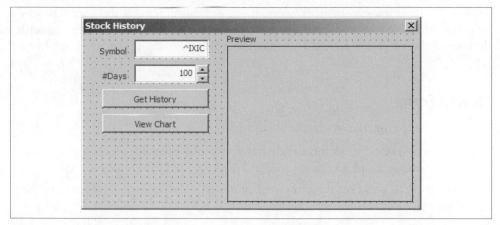

Figure 20-9. The Stock History form

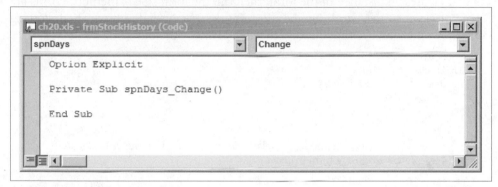

Figure 20-10. Adding event procedures to a form

The following code shows a simple event procedure that links values of the spnDays and txtDays controls:

```
Private Sub spnDays_Change()
    txtDays.Value = spnDays.Value
End Sub

Private Sub txtDays_Change()
    ' Ignore error if txtDays isn't between spnDays Min and Max.
    On Error Resume Next
    spnDays.Value = txtDays.Value
End Sub
```

Why set the values both places? Doing that ensures that the text box value doesn't change unexpectedly if you type a value in the text box then click up or down on the spin button. The two procedures don't cause an infinite loop since the Change event occurs only when a value actually changes; it doesn't occur if the new setting is equal to the existing setting.

Finally, the On Error statement is necessary to avoid problems if the user types 1000 or some other high value in the text box. The spin button's Max and Min properties determine the valid range, and I use the ControlTipText to inform the user of that range.

Show a Form

To test the form from the Visual Basic Editor:

1. Make sure the form or form code has focus and press F5 or click Run. Visual Basic switches to the Excel window and displays the form in Run mode.

2. Click the Close box on the form or click Reset in Visual Basic to return to Design mode.

To display the form from the Excel interface, you must create a procedure in a module that creates an instance of the form, then call the form's Show method. Forms are a type of class, so they can't just be run from the Macro dialog box. The following code shows a procedure that displays the Stock History dialog:

```
' StockHistoryModule
Sub StockHistoryDialog()
    Dim f As New frmStockHistory
    f.Show False
End Sub
```

 Use the Show method to display a form in code. Use the Unload statement to close a form in code.

In the preceding code, I called Show with the *Modal* argument set to False. That shows the form *nonmodally*, which means you can still select cells and do tasks in Excel while the form is displayed. *Modal* forms block user access to Excel while they are displayed.

It is usually easier to program with modal forms, since the user can't change the state of Excel while the form is running. However, modal forms are best suited for linear tasks. For nonlinear tasks, use nonmodal forms.

Once you've created a procedure in a module to show your form, you can display the form by assigning that macro to a menu item, toolbar button, or some other user action in Excel. See Chapter 19 for details on creating menus and toolbars.

Separate Work Code from UI Code

Whenever you work with forms, your code winds up in two places:

- The form's class contains the event procedures that initialize the form and respond to user actions.
- The form's work module displays the form and contains the procedures that perform tasks in Excel.

Can't you just put all the code in the form class? Not really: first, you can't show the form from there, and second, it's harder to debug procedures in a class since you must first instantiate the class before it can run. That's kind of a chicken-and-the-egg problem, and the best solution is to separate the two types of code in two different places.

For example, the following form class responds to the events on the Stock History form:

```
' frmStockHistory class
Option Explicit

Private Sub spnDays_Change()
    txtDays.Value = spnDays.Value
End Sub

Private Sub txtDays_Change()
    ' Ignore error if txtDays isn't between spnDays Min and Max.
    On Error Resume Next
    spnDays.Value = txtDays.Value
End Sub

Private Sub cmdGetHistory_Click()
    Dim fname As String
    ' Show the source worksheet.
    Worksheets("VBForm").Activate
    ' Make sure the user entered a symbol.
    If txtSymbol.Text <> "" Then
        ResetWorksheet
        CreateQuery txtSymbol.Text, spnDays.Value
        HideUnneededCells
        fname = CreateChart(imgChart.height, imgChart.width)
        ' Update the image control.
        Set imgChart.Picture = LoadPicture(fname)
    End If
End Sub

' Create a copy of the worksheet and a full-sized chart.
Private Sub cmdViewChart_Click()
    AddChartSheet (txtSymbol.Text)
    ' Close this dialog.
    Unload Me
End Sub
```

As you can see, the event procedures call work module procedures for all tasks that relate to the worksheet or charts. The form code merely organizes those steps and updates itself. That technique is called *isolating the interface from the business logic*.

The work module is more complex because it deals with the specific Excel objects. Much of this code is based on samples from earlier chapters, so I won't explain all of it here. However, I will point out that breaking the tasks into steps makes the procedures easier to debug and reuse:

```
' StockHistoryModule - work module.
Option Explicit

' Run dialog.
Sub StockHistoryDialog()
    Dim f As New frmStockHistory
    f.Show False
End Sub

' Clear worksheet and remove existing query table.
Sub ResetWorksheet()
    Dim qt As QueryTable
    Worksheets("VBForm").Activate
    ActiveSheet.Rows.Hidden = False
    ActiveSheet.Columns.Hidden = False
    ActiveSheet.UsedRange.Delete
    ActiveSheet.ChartObjects.Delete
    ' Remove query tables
    For Each qt In ActiveSheet.QueryTables
        qt.Delete
    Next
End Sub

' Get stock history from Yahoo as a query table.
Public Sub CreateQuery(symbol As String, days As Integer)
    Dim ws As Worksheet, qt As QueryTable, conn As String
    Set ws = Worksheets("VBForm")
    ws.Activate
    ' Build query string.
    conn = "URL;http://chart.yahoo.com/d?" & _
YahooDates(VBA.Date - days, VBA.Date) & symbol
    ' Get query
    Set qt = ws.QueryTables.Add(conn, [A1])
    qt.WebFormatting = xlNone
    qt.WebSelectionType = xlSpecifiedTables
    qt.WebTables = "3"
    ' Make sure background queries are off.
    qt.BackgroundQuery = False
    ' Get data.
    qt.Refresh
End Sub

' Converts start and end dates to Yahoo query string for
' stock history.
Function YahooDates(dtstart As Date, dtend As Date) As String
    ' Query sample string from Yahoo has this form:
    ' a=10&b=4&c=2003&d=1&e=5&f=2004&g=d&s=sndk
    Dim str As String
```

```
    str = "a=" & Month(dtstart) - 1 & "&b=" & Day(dtstart) & _
    "&c=" & Year(dtstart) & "&d=" & Month(dtend) - 1 & _
    "&e=" & Day(dtend) & "&f=" & Year(dtend) & "&g=d&s="
    YahooDates = str
End Function

' Cleans up query table prior to plotting chart.
Sub HideUnneededCells()
    Dim endRow As Long
    [b:b].EntireColumn.Hidden = True
    [g:l].EntireColumn.Hidden = True
    Range(Rows(1), Rows(5)).Hidden = True
    endRow = ActiveSheet.UsedRange.Rows.Count
    Range(Rows(endRow - 2), Rows(endRow)).Clear
End Sub

' Plot history as a High/Low/Close chart.
Function CreateChart(height As Integer, width As Integer) As String
    Dim rng As Range, ws As Worksheet, chrt As Chart
    Set ws = Worksheets("VBForm")
    ws.Activate
    ' Create the chart
    Set chrt = ws.ChartObjects.Add(500, 0, width, height).Chart
    ' Get the range to chart
    ' Plot the data in a named range.
    chrt.SetSourceData ws.UsedRange, xlColumns
    ' Set the chart type to Open, High, Low, Close.
    chrt.ChartType = xlStockOHLC
    chrt.ChartArea.Font.Size = 6
    chrt.Legend.Delete
    ' Dates are in descending order, so reverse the axis.
    chrt.Axes(xlCategory).ReversePlotOrder = True
    CreateChart = SaveChart(chrt)
End Function

' Saves a chart as a JPEG file.
Function SaveChart(chrt As Chart) As String
    Dim fname As String
    fname = ThisWorkbook.Path & "\temp.jpg"
    chrt.Export fname, "JPEG", False
    SaveChart = fname
End Function

' Create a chart sheet for chart.
Sub AddChartSheet(name As String)
    Dim ws As Worksheet, chrt As Chart
    Set ws = Worksheets("VBForm")
    ws.Activate
    ws.Copy , ws
    Set ws = ActiveSheet
    ws.name = GetSheetName(name & "_Data")
    ' Create the chart
    Set chrt = Charts.Add(, ws)
    ' Get the range to chart
```

```
        chrt.SetSourceData ws.UsedRange, xlColumns
        ' Set the chart type to Open, High, Low, Close.
        chrt.ChartType = xlStockOHLC
        ' Dates are in descending order, so reverse the axis.
        chrt.Axes(xlCategory).ReversePlotOrder = True
        chrt.name = GetSheetName(name & "_Chart")
    End Sub

    ' Generates a unique sheet name.
    Function GetSheetName(name As String) As String
        Dim i As Integer
        On Error Resume Next
        Do Until Err
            i = i + 1
            Debug.Print "Exists: " & Sheets(name & i).name
        Loop
        On Error GoTo 0
        GetSheetName = name & i
    End Function
```

To see the completed Stock History form in action:

1. Run StockHistoryDialog. Visual Basic displays the form.

2. Type the name of a stock symbol and click Get History. Excel queries Yahoo for the price history, plots the data, then displays the chart in the image control as shown in Figure 20-11.

3. Click View Chart to create a full-size chart with its own source worksheet and close the dialog.

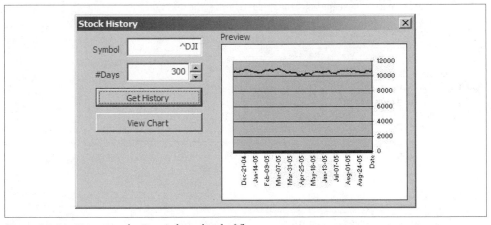

Figure 20-11. Hmmm…the Dow's been kind of flat

Why the 300-day limit?

The web query to Yahoo! returns a maximum of 200 trading days of price history. That translates to about 300 calendar days, so I imposed that limit on the sample to keep it simple. Well…somewhat simple.

Enable and Disable Controls

It is common practice to enable or disable controls based on what other options are selected. Controls are enabled by default. Use the control's Enabled property to disable or reenable the control after disabling.

For example, to make the View Chart button available only after the user has clicked Get History, set the View Chart button's Enabled property to False in the Properties window, and add this code to the cmdGetHistory_Click procedure:

```
Private Sub cmdGetHistory_Click()
    Dim fname As String
    ' Show the source worksheet.
    Worksheets("VBForm").Activate
    ' Make sure the user entered a symbol.
    If txtSymbol.Text <> "" Then
        ResetWorksheet
        CreateQuery txtSymbol.Text, spnDays.Value
        HideUnneededCells
        fname = CreateChart(imgChart.height, imgChart.width)
        ' Update the image control.
        Set imgChart.Picture = LoadPicture(fname)
    End If
    ' Add this to enable View Chart button.
    cmdViewChart.Enabled = True
End Sub
```

While disabled, the control appears grayed and cannot receive user actions. You can do something similar by setting the control's Visible property, but that is less common. Hiding and showing controls is usually reserved for complex or multistep tasks.

Create Tabbed Dialogs

Tabbed dialog boxes are common in Excel. They break complex dialogs into multiple pages that replace each other as the user clicks on the different tabs. The Options dialog is a good example of a tabbed dialog.

The Toolbox includes two tabbed controls: TabStrip and MultiPage. The main difference between the two controls is that the MultiPage control provides paged containers for other controls. When a user clicks one of the tabs, that page automatically replaces the current page. With the TabStrip control, you have to create your own containers (usually a Frame control) and set the Visible property of that container to show or hide pages. In short, use the MultiPage to quickly create a tabbed dialog; use the TabStrip when you want to control the contents of pages programmatically.

To see how tabbed dialogs work, follow these steps based on the earlier Stock History sample:

1. In the Visual Basic Editor, choose Insert → UserForm to create a new form.
2. Click and drag a MultiPage control onto the form.

3. Open the original Stock History form, select all the controls (Ctrl-A) and copy them (Ctrl-C). Select the MultiPage control and paste (Ctrl-V) the controls onto it.

4. Copy and paste the code from the frmStockHistory class to the frmStockHistory2 class.

5. Click the Page1 tab on the MultiPage control and set its Caption to History.

6. Click the Page2 tab on the MultiPage control and set its Caption to Options. Then add the controls shown in Figure 20-12 with the settings listed in Table 20-4.

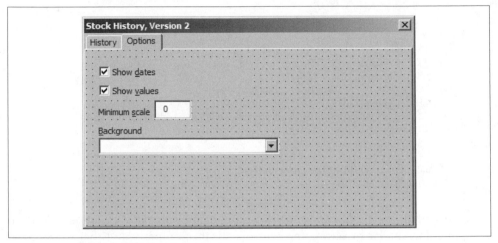

Figure 20-12. Tabbed dialog in Design mode

Table 20-4. Tabbed control property settings

Control	Property	Set to
User form	Name	frmStockHistory2
	Caption	Stock History, Version 2
CheckBox	Name	chkDates
	Accelerator	D
	Caption	Show dates
CheckBox	Name	chkValues
	Accelerator	V
	Caption	Show values
Label	Accelerator	S
	Caption	Minimum scale
TextBox	Name	txtScale
	Caption	0
Label	Accelerator	B
	Caption	Background
ComboBox	Name	drpBackground

If you save and run the dialog box at this point, you'll see that the controls on the History tab work exactly as they did on the original form, but that the controls on the Options tab are nonfunctional. We haven't implemented their code yet!

To implement the Options tab, add the following code to the frmStockHistory2 class:

```
' Add to frmStockHistory2.
Private Sub UserForm_Initialize()
    ' Add items to drop-down list.
    drpBackground.AddItem "Gray"
    drpBackground.AddItem "White"
    drpBackground.AddItem "Gradient"
    drpBackground.AddItem "Pattern"
    ' Get settings from the chart.
    GetChartOptions chkDates.Value, chkValues.Value, CInt(txtScale.Value), ""
End Sub

Private Sub MultiPage1_Change()
    Dim fname As String
    fname = SetChartOptions(chkDates.Value, chkValues.Value, _
        txtScale.Value, drpBackground.Text)
    ' Update the image control.
    Set imgChart.Picture = LoadPicture(fname)
End Sub
```

The preceding code uses two procedures from the StockHistoryModule to connect the controls on the Options tab to the properties of the chart. GetChartOptions uses the current chart properties to set the initial values of the controls, and SetChartOptions changes the chart properties using the control settings. These types of procedures are sometimes called *accessor functions* because they provide an interface between the user interface and the work procedures.

The following code shows the additions to the StockHistoryModule. There are two very important points I want you to notice: First, I didn't change any code in the module; I just added new code and reused everything else. Second, I added a new procedure to run the new dialog so that you can easily run either version. These two things are much easier to do because I separated the user interface code from the work code at the beginning:

```
'''''''''''''''''''''''''''''''''''''''''''''''''''''
' Added for version 2.
' Run dialog.
Sub StockHistoryDialog2()
    Dim f As New frmStockHistory2
    f.Show False
End Sub

' Gets the chart settings to show on the Options tab.
Sub GetChartOptions(xAxis As Boolean, yAxis As Boolean, _
    minScale As Long, background As String)
    Dim chrt As Chart, ax As Axis
    ' Get the chart
```

```
    Set chrt = Worksheets("VBForm").ChartObjects(1).Chart
    ' Does the chart have x- and y-axes?
    xAxis = chrt.HasAxis(xlCategory, xlPrimary)
    yAxis = chrt.HasAxis(xlValue, xlPrimary)
    ' Get the Minimum scale from the y-axis.
    If yAxis Then _
        minScale = chrt.Axes(xlValue, xlPrimary).MinimumScale
End Sub

' Updates the chart with changes from the Options tab.
Function SetChartOptions(xAxis As Boolean, yAxis As Boolean, _
    minScale As Long, background As String) As String
    Dim chrt As Chart, ax As Axis
    ' Get the chart.
    Set chrt = Worksheets("VBForm").ChartObjects(1).Chart
    ' Set the Minimum scale property
    chrt.HasAxis(xlValue, xlPrimary) = True
    chrt.Axes(xlValue, xlPrimary).MinimumScale = minScale
    ' Turn the axes on/off.
    chrt.HasAxis(xlCategory, xlPrimary) = xAxis
    chrt.HasAxis(xlValue, xlPrimary) = yAxis
    ' Set the background.
    Select Case background
        Case "White"
            chrt.ChartArea.Fill.Solid
            chrt.ChartArea.Fill.ForeColor.SchemeColor = 2
            chrt.PlotArea.Fill.Solid
            chrt.PlotArea.Fill.ForeColor.SchemeColor = 2
        Case "Gray"
            chrt.ChartArea.Fill.Solid
            chrt.ChartArea.Fill.ForeColor.SchemeColor = 15
            chrt.PlotArea.Fill.Solid
            chrt.PlotArea.Fill.ForeColor.SchemeColor = 15
        Case "Gradient"
            chrt.ChartArea.Fill.TwoColorGradient msoGradientDiagonalUp, 1
            chrt.PlotArea.Fill.TwoColorGradient msoGradientDiagonalUp, 1
        Case "Pattern"
            chrt.ChartArea.Fill.PresetTextured (msoTextureBlueTissuePaper)
            chrt.PlotArea.Fill.PresetTextured (msoTextureBlueTissuePaper)
        Case Else
            ' No change if not recognized.
    End Select
    ' Update the chart and return the exported filename.
    SetChartOptions = SaveChart(chrt)
End Function
```

To see the tabbed dialog box in action, run StockHistoryDialog2, select the Options tab, change settings, and click the History tab to see their effect (Figure 20-13).

I'm not really done yet. The preceding code doesn't preserve the options if you click View Chart. See the sample workbook for the completed dialog and code.

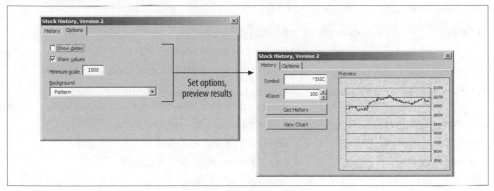

Figure 20-13. The tabbed Stock History dialog in action

Provide Keyboard Access to Controls

As on menus, controls on dialog boxes can have accelerator keys that allow you to move from control to control by typing rather than using the mouse. On dialogs however, accelerator keys are closely associated with tab order.

Tab order is the order in which controls receive focus as the user presses the Tab or Enter key. That order is determined by two control properties:

- `TabIndex` determines the location of the control in the tab order.
- `TabStop` determines whether or not the control is included in the tab order.

Accelerator keys are set by specifying a letter from a control's `Caption` in its `Accelerator` property. If a control doesn't have a `Caption` property, create a label with an accelerator key and set that label's `TabIndex` to be just before the target control's `TabIndex`, as shown in Figure 20-14.

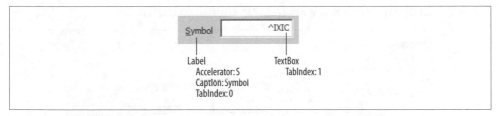

Figure 20-14. Using a label to provide an accelerator key for a text box

Choose the Right Control

The Toolbox includes 15 standard controls that you can draw on forms. Table 20-5 lists those controls and describes their use.

Table 20-5. Built-in form controls (Forms 2.0)

Control	Toolbox icon	Use to
Label	A	Display text the user can't change.
TextBox	abl	Display text the user can edit. Text boxes can display scrollable text.
ComboBox		Allow selections from a drop-down list of choices. Combo boxes can include a text box where the user can type a choice not in the list.
ListBox		Allow selections from a scrollable list of choices.
CheckBox	☑	Get or display yes/no choices.
OptionButton	⊙	Get or display a set of either/or choices.
ToggleButton		Get or display on/off options.
Frame		Group option buttons or other related controls.
CommandButton		Execute a command.
TabStrip		Show or hide frames used to organize complex dialog boxes.
MultiPage		Show or hide pages used to organize complex dialog boxes.
ScrollBar		Scroll controls or text up and down.
SpinButton		Scroll a value up or down.
Image		Display a picture.
RefEdit		Get a cell range from a worksheet.

In addition to these built-in controls, you can also add custom controls to the Toolbox. To add custom controls:

1. Right-click the Toolbox and select Additional Controls. Visual Basic displays a list of controls that are installed on your computer.

2. Select the controls you want to add to the Toolbox and click OK. The custom controls now appear on the Toolbox.

Figure 20-15 illustrates adding a ProgressBar control to the Toolbox.

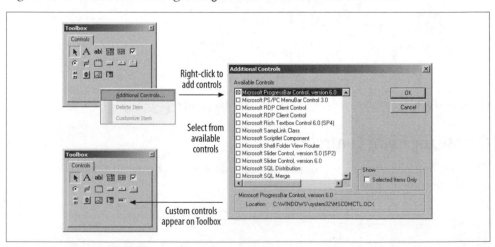

Figure 20-15. Adding custom controls to the Toolbox

The list of available custom controls is determined by what programming tools you have installed on your system. I have quite a few, so my list of custom controls is very long. Some controls, such as the progress bar, are part of the common control library (*MSCOMCTL.OCX*) which is distributed with Microsoft Office and other applications. However, other custom controls may require that you license and install their executable *.OCX* or *.DLL* file on your user's machines. Be sure you understand the licensing and distribution requirements of any custom control you plan on using.

Use Controls on Worksheets

How is the Excel team like my mom? They never throw anything away. That was handy when I needed copies of my high school humor column, but it meant Mom's house was a bit cluttered. In Excel's case, it means you've got two toolbars full of similar-looking controls that you can use on a worksheet (Figure 20-16).

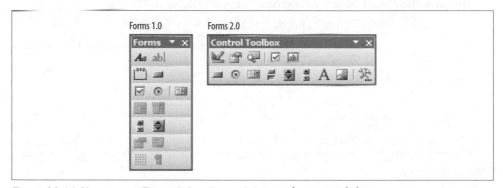

Figure 20-16. You can use Forms 1.0 or Forms 2.0 controls on a worksheet

The Forms 1.0 controls are included mostly for backward-compatibility with earlier versions of Excel. They lack events and the full set of properties you get with Forms 2.0 controls. However, there are two items on the Forms toolbar that are very handy, so I will tell you how to add them to the Control Toolbox here:

1. In Excel, choose View → Toolbars → Forms and View → Toolbars → Control Toolbox to display the two toolbars shown in Figure 20-16.

2. Choose Tools → Customize to display the Customize dialog box and enable changes to the toolbars.

3. Hold down the Ctrl key and click and drag the Toggle Grid from the Forms toolbar to the Control Toolbox. Excel copies the button onto the Control Toolbox.

4. Repeat for the Button control, copying it from the Forms toolbar to the Control Toolbox.

5. Close the Forms toolbar and never think of it again.

The Toggle Grid button turns a worksheet's gridlines on and off. That helps create a cleaner appearance when you are using controls on a worksheet.

The Button control runs a macro. That is often more convenient to use on a worksheet than a CommandButton because command buttons respond to Click events in the worksheet's class—which is overkill if you just want to run a single procedure.

Add a Simple Button

To see how the Button control is still useful, follow these steps to extend the Stock History sample:

1. Create a new, blank worksheet.
2. Click the Toggle Grid button to turn the worksheet gridlines off.
3. Click the Button control that you added to the Control Toolbox in the previous section and click and drag on the worksheet to draw the button control. Excel displays the Assign Macro dialog box (Figure 20-17).
4. Select StockHistoryDialog2 and click OK.
5. Type Get History in the button caption and then click the worksheet to deselect the button.
6. Click the Get History button to run the sample.

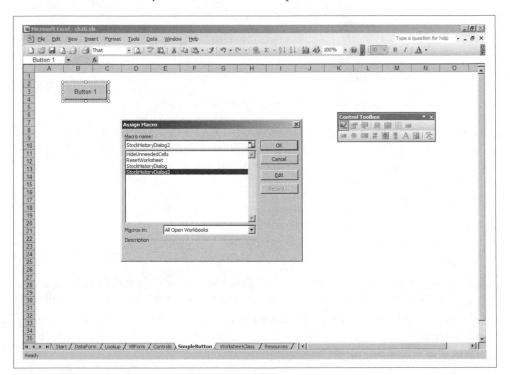

Figure 20-17. Use the Button control to run a macro

The Button control offers fewer properties than the CommandButton, and they are accessed differently as well. To change the macro assigned to the button, edit its caption, or change any other setting, right-click the button and choose the property to change from the context menu.

Use Controls from the Worksheet Class

A key advantage of the Forms 2.0 controls is that they can interact with the worksheet class. That's an abstract advantage best illustrated by a short example:

1. Create a new worksheet.
2. Click the SpinButton control on the Control Toolbox and draw the control at the edge of cell B2 on the worksheet, as shown in Figure 20-18.

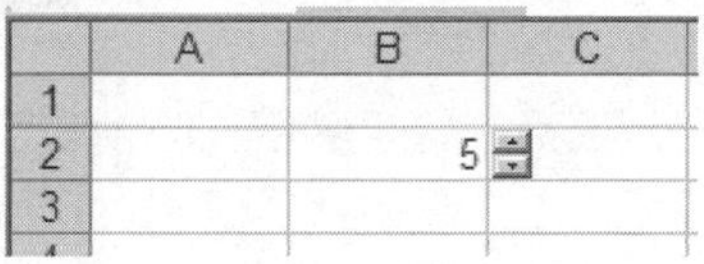

Figure 20-18. Using a SpinButton to set the value of a cell

3. Click View Code on the Control Toolbox. Excel displays the sheet's class in the Visual Basic Editor.
4. Enter the following code in the spin button's Change event procedure (shown in **bold**):

```
Private Sub SpinButton1_Change( )
    SpinButton1.BottomRightCell.Offset(-1, -1).Value = SpinButton1.Value
End Sub
```

5. Return to the worksheet and click Exit Design Mode on the Control Toolbox.

The cool thing about this sample is that if you move the SpinButton to another location, the effect of clicking up or down moves to the adjacent cell. That's possible because the control is a member of the sheet's class.

One thing you'll notice about this sample is that the SpinButton stops spinning at 0. That's because the control's Min property is 0 by default. To change that:

1. Click Design Mode on the Control Toolbox.
2. Select the SpinButton control on the worksheet.
3. Click Properties on the Control Toolbox. Excel displays the Properties dialog box (Figure 20-19).
4. Change the Min property to -100 and click Exit Design Mode.

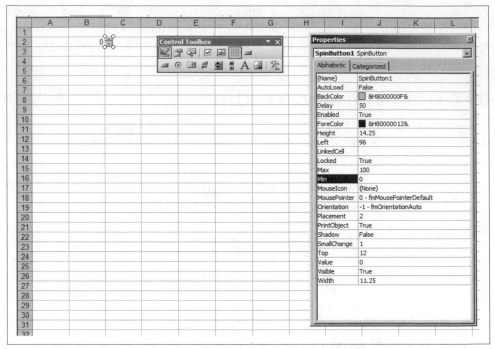

Figure 20-19. Setting control properties on a worksheet

Controls on a Worksheet Versus Controls on a Form

Using controls on a worksheet is a little different from using them on a form. For one thing, you don't need to create an instance of the worksheet since it already exists. Your code starts running as soon as you exit Design mode and click on the control.

Also, fewer controls are available in the worksheet Control Toolbox. If you want to use a control not found on the Control Toolbox, click the More Controls button, then choose the control from the list shown in Figure 20-20.

Another difference is that controls on a worksheet controls don't support all of their properties. Specifically, `ControlSource`, `ControlTipText`, `TabIndex`, and `TabStop` aren't available for controls on a worksheet.

Finally, you can't copy controls from a form in the Visual Basic Editor onto a worksheet. If you want to re-create a form as a worksheet, you must redraw the controls manually. In fact, Figure 20-21 shows the Stock History sample implemented as a worksheet rather than a form.

Since I used the same control names as the original sample, I could copy the code from the form class with only two changes:

- Deleted `Me.Unload` from `cmdViewChart_Click`
- Added `Me.Activate` to `cmdGetHistory_Click`

See the sample workbook for the full code.

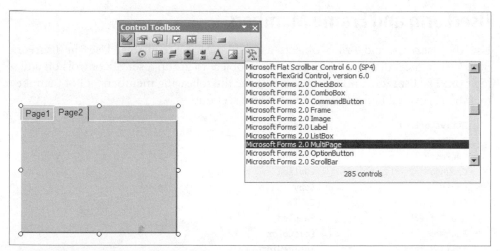

Figure 20-20. Using controls not found on the Control Toolbox

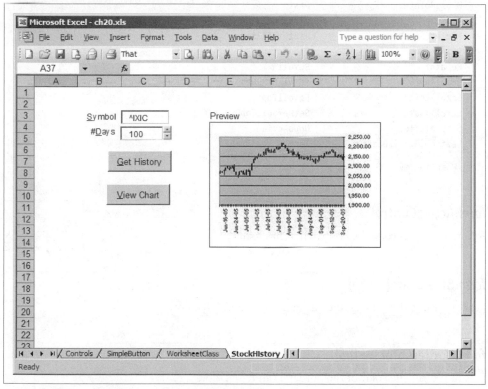

Figure 20-21. The Stock History sample as a worksheet

UserForm and Frame Members

Use the UserForm and Frame objects as containers for controls. Use the UserForm object to create a dialog box. Use the Frame object to group a set of controls on a dialog box. The UserForm and Frame objects have the following members, all of them key members, covered in the following reference section:

ActiveControl	BackColor
BorderColor	BorderStyle
CanPaste	CanRedo
CanUndo	Caption
Controls	Copy
Cut	Cycle
DrawBuffer[1]	Enabled
Font	ForeColor
InsideHeight	InsideWidth
KeepScrollBarsVisible	MouseIcon
MousePointer	Paste
Picture	PictureAlignment
PictureSizeMode	PictureTiling
PrintForm	RedoAction
Repaint	Scroll
ScrollBars	ScrollHeight
ScrollLeft	ScrollTop
ScrollWidth	SetDefaultTabOrder
SpecialEffect	UndoAction
VerticalScrollBarSide	Zoom

[1] UserForm only

---

form.ActiveControl

Returns a reference to the control that has focus.

---

form.BackColor [= *rgb*]

Sets or returns the color of the background as an RGB color.

---

form.BorderColor [= *rgb*]

Sets or returns the color of the border as an RGB color.

---

form.BorderStyle [= *fmBorderStyle*]

Sets or returns the style of the border. Can be either fmBorderStyleNone or fmBorderStyelSingle. Use the SpecialEffect property to create other border effects.

---

form.CanPaste

Returns True if the clipboard contains data that can be pasted to this object, False otherwise.

form.CanRedo

Returns True if the most recent action on the form can be redone; returns False if the action can't be redone. Actions such as typing in a text box may be redone.

form.CanUndo

Returns True if the most recent action on the form can be undone; returns False if the action can't be undone. Actions such as typing in a text box may be undone.

form.Caption [= *setting*]

Sets or returns the caption appearing on the object. On forms, the caption appears at the title of the dialog box; on frames, it appears at the top of the frame.

form.Controls

Returns the collection of controls on the form or frame.

form.Copy( )

Copies the active control onto the Clipboard.

form.Cut( )

If the active control was created at runtime, deletes the active control and places it on the Clipboard. If the active control was created at design time, cause an error.

form.Cycle [= *fmCycle*]

Sets or returns how pressing the Tab key cycles through controls when a form contains other containers such as frames or pages. Can be fmCycleAllForms (default) or fmCycleCurrentForm.

form.DrawBuffer [= *setting*]

Sets or returns the number of pixels drawn at one time when the form is rendered. Default is 32,000. This property can be set only at design time.

form.Enabled [= setting]

True enables the object to receive focus and respond to user actions; False prohibits focus. Default is True.

form.Font [= setting]

Sets or returns the Font object used by new controls added at runtime. To change the font of existing controls in code, use the Font property of the control. For example, the following code sets a large font size for both existing controls and runtime controls:

```
Private Sub UserForm_Initialize()
    Dim c As Control
    ' Set size of font for runtime controls.
    Me.Font.Size = 24
    ' Set size of font for design time controls
    For Each c In Me.Controls
        c.Font.Size = 24
    Next
End Sub
```

form.ForeColor [= rgb]

Sets or returns the color of the foreground as an RGB color.

form.InsideHeight

Returns the height of the usable area of the form or frame in points.

form.InsideWidth

Returns the width of the usable area of the form or frame in points.

form.KeepScrollBarsVisible [= fmScrollBars]

Sets or returns how scrollbars are displayed when they are no longer needed. Can be one of these settings:

    fmScrollBarsNone
    fmScrollBarsHorizontal
    fmScrollBarsVertical
    fmScrollBarsBoth (default)

form.MouseIcon [= *setting*]

Sets or returns a custom picture used as the mouse pointer. The following code displays a magnifying glass as the mouse pointer:

```
Private Sub UserForm_Initialize()
    ' Change mouse pointer.
    Me.MousePointer = fmMousePointerCustom
    Me.MouseIcon = LoadPicture(ThisWorkbook.Path & "\magnify.ico")
End Sub
```

form.MousePointer [= *fmMousePointer*]

Sets or returns the mouse pointer that is displayed. Can be one of these settings:

fmMousePointerAppStarting	fmMousePointerArrow
fmMousePointerCross	fmMousePointerCustom
fmMousePointerDefault (default)	fmMousePointerHelp
fmMousePointerHourglass	fmMousePointerIBeam
fmMousePointerNoDrop	fmMousePointerSizeAll
fmMousePointerSizeNESW	fmMousePointerSizeNS
fmMousePointerSizeNWSE	fmMousePointerSizeWE
fmMousePointerUpArrow	

form.Paste( )

Pastes a control from the Clipboard to the form or frame.

form.Picture [= *setting*]

Sets or returns the picture loaded as the background. The picture can be set at design time in the Properties window or at runtime using the LoadPicture function. For example, the following code displays a logo as the background of a form, centers the picture, and sizes it to fit the form while preserving the aspect ratio:

```
Private Sub UserForm_Initialize()
    Me.Picture = LoadPicture(ThisWorkbook.Path & "\logo.bmp")
    Me.PictureAlignment = fmPictureAlignmentCenter
    Me.PictureSizeMode = fmPictureSizeModeZoom
End Sub
```

form.PictureAlignment [= *fmPictureAlignment*]

Sets or returns how the background picture is placed. Can be one of these settings:

fmPictureAlignmentTopLeft
fmPictureAlignmentTopRight

fmPictureAlignmentCenter (default)
fmPictureAlignmentBottomLeft
fmPictureAlignmentBottomRight

form.PictureSizeMode [= fmPictureSizeMode]

Sets or returns how the background picture is sized. Can be one of these settings:

fmPictureSizeModeClip (default)
fmPictureSizeModeStretch (may change the aspect ratio of the picture)
fmPictureSizeModeZoom (preserves aspect ratio)

form.PictureTiling [= setting]

If the picture does not exactly fit the dimensions of the background and the PictureSizeMode is not fmPictureSizeModeStretch, True repeats the picture to fill the background and False displays the picture one time.

form.PrintForm

Prints the form on the default printer.

form.RedoAction( )

Reverses the effect of the most recent Undo action. Actions such as typing in a text box may be undone or redone. Check CanRedo to tell if there is an action available to be redone.

form.Repaint( )

Redraws the form or frame on screen.

form.Scroll([ActionX] [, ActionY])

Scrolls the form or frame one line or page at a time.

Argument	Settings
ActionX	An fmScrollAction constant indicating how much to scroll horizontally
ActionY	An fmScrollAction constant indicating how much to scroll horizontally

ActionX and ActionY can be one of these settings:

fmScrollActionNoChange (default)
fmScrollActionLineUp

```
fmScrollActionLineDown
fmScrollActionPageUp
fmScrollActionPageDown
fmScrollActionBegin
fmScrollActionEnd
```

The following code implements navigation buttons on a frame named fNav at the top of a form. The command buttons scroll the form, and the UserForm_Scroll event moves the frame to keep it visible as the form scrolls:

```
' Requires a frame (fNav) containing four command buttons.
Private Sub cmdHome_Click()
    Me.Scroll fmScrollActionBegin, fmScrollActionBegin
End Sub

Private Sub cmdEnd_Click()
    Me.Scroll fmScrollActionEnd, fmScrollActionEnd
End Sub

Private Sub cmdPageLeft_Click()
    Me.Scroll fmScrollActionPageDown, fmScrollActionNoChange
End Sub

Private Sub cmdPageDown_Click()
    Me.Scroll fmScrollActionNoChange, fmScrollActionPageDown
End Sub

Private Sub UserForm_Scroll(ByVal ActionX As MSForms.fmScrollAction, _
  ByVal ActionY As MSForms.fmScrollAction, _
  ByVal RequestDx As Single, ByVal RequestDy As Single, _
  ByVal ActualDx As MSForms.ReturnSingle, _
  ByVal ActualDy As MSForms.ReturnSingle)
    ' Move frame to keep buttons visible as form is scrolled.
    fNav.Left = fNav.Left + ActualDx
    fNav.Top = fNav.Top + ActualDy
End Sub
```

form.ScrollBars [= *fmScrollBars*]

Sets or returns how scrollbars are displayed. Can be one of these settings:

fmScrollBarsNone (default)

fmScrollBarsHorizontal

fmScrollBarsVertical

fmScrollBarsBoth

Depending on the setting of KeepScrollBarsVisible, scrollbars may or may not be visible on a form. The ScrollHeight and ScrollWidth properties determine whether the form is scrollable.

The following code shows how these properties interact by adding 100 lines of text to a label, then resizing the label so that it extends off the form. The UpdateScrollSize procedure calculates the required dimensions for the form and sets ScrollHeight and ScrollWidth so users can view the entire form area:

```
Private Sub UserForm_Initialize()
    ' Scrollbar settings
    Me.ScrollBars = fmScrollBarsBoth
    Me.KeepScrollBarsVisible = fmScrollBarsNone
    ' Initialize data
    FillLabel
    ' Update scrollbars.
    UpdateScrollSize
End Sub


' Adds 100 lines of text to a label, then
' resizes it to demo scrolling a form.
Private Sub FillLabel()
    Dim i As Integer
    Label1.Caption = ""
    For i = 1 To 100
        Label1.Caption = Label1.Caption & _
        "Line: " & i & String(90, "*") & vbCrLf
    Next
    Label1.AutoSize = True
End Sub


' Find the dimensions required to display all of the controls
' on the form and reset ScrollHeight and ScrollWidth to match.
Private Sub UpdateScrollSize()
    Dim c As Control, maxHeight As Double, maxWidth As Double
    For Each c In Me.Controls
        maxHeight = c.Top + c.height
        maxWidth = c.Left + c.width
        If maxHeight > Me.ScrollHeight Then _
          Me.ScrollHeight = maxHeight
        If maxWidth > Me.ScrollWidth Then _
          Me.ScrollWidth = maxWidth
    Next
End Sub
```

 UpdateScrollSize is written in a general way so you can reuse it.

form.ScrollHeight [= setting]

Sets or returns the height of the scrollable area in points.

form.ScrollLeft [= setting]

Sets or returns the position of the horizontal scrollbar in points. The following code scrolls left one page at a time:

```
Private Sub cmdPageLeft_Click()
    Me.ScrollLeft = Me.Left + Me.InsideWidth
    ' Reposition this control to keep it visible.
    cmdPageLeft.Left = cmdPageLeft.Left + Me.InsideWidth
End Sub
```

form.ScrollTop [= setting]

Sets or returns the position of the vertical scrollbar in points. The following code scrolls down one page at a time:

```
Private Sub cmdPageDown_Click()
    ' Scoll form
    Me.ScrollTop = Me.ScrollTop + Me.InsideHeight
    ' Reposition this control to keep it visible.
    cmdPageDown.Top = cmdPageDown.Top + Me.InsideHeight
End Sub
```

 It's usually easier to use the Scroll method than ScrollLeft and ScrollTop. See that topic for an example.

form.ScrollWidth [= setting]

Sets or returns the width of the scrollable area in points.

form.SetDefaultTabOrder( )

Sets the tab order of controls automatically using a top-to-bottom, left-to-right order.

form.SpecialEffect [= fmButtonEffect]

Sets or returns a special border appearance. Can be one of these settings:

    fmSpecialEffectFlat (default for forms)
    fmSpecialEffectRaised
    fmSpecialEffectSunken (default for frames)
    fmSpecialEffectEtched
    fmSpecialEffectBump

form.UndoAction( )

Undoes the last user action. Actions such as typing in a text box may be undone or redone. Check CanUndo to tell if there is an action available to be undone.

form.VerticalScrollBarSide [= fmVerticalScrollbarSide]

Sets or returns the side on which to display the vertical scrollbar. Can be set to fmVerticalScrollbarSideRight or fmVerticalScrollBarSideLeft.

form.Zoom [= setting]

Sets or returns the percentage to scale the contents of the form or frame by. Must be between 10 and 400. Zoom doesn't change the size of the form or frame. The following code zooms in or out on a background picture depending on which mouse button is pressed:

```
Private Sub UserForm_Initialize( )
    ' Load a background picture.
    Me.Picture = LoadPicture(ThisWorkbook.Path & "\turtle.jpg")
    ' Change mouse pointer.
    Me.MousePointer = fmMousePointerCustom
    Me.MouseIcon = LoadPicture(ThisWorkbook.Path & "\magnify.ico")
End Sub

Private Sub UserForm_MouseDown(ByVal Button As Integer, ByVal Shift_
 As Integer, ByVal X As Single, ByVal Y As Single)
    On Error Resume Next
    ' If left button, zoom in.
    If Button = 1 Then
        Me.Zoom = Me.Zoom * 1.1
    ' If right button, zoom out.
    ElseIf Button = 2 Then
        Me.Zoom = Me.Zoom * 0.9
    End If
    On Error GoTo 0
End Sub
```

Control and Controls Members

Use the Controls collection to add new controls dynamically at runtime and to perform general operations on all of the controls on a form. Use the UserForm object's Controls property to get a reference to this collection. Use the Control object to set the name, position, and other general properties of a control. Specific control types may have other properties that are available; the Control object contains the general members available for most controls. The Controls collection and Control object have the following members. Key members (shown in **bold**) are covered in the following reference section:

Add[1]	**Cancel**
Clear[1]	**ControlSource**
ControlTipText	Count[1]
Default	Height
HelpContextID	Item[1]
LayoutEffect	Left
Move[2]	Name
Object	**OldHeight**
OldLeft	**OldTop**
OldWidth	Parent
Remove[1]	**RowSource**
SetFocus	**TabIndex**
TabStop	**Tag**
Top	Visible
Width	**ZOrder**

[1] Collection only
[2] Object and collection

controls.Add(*ProgID* [, *Name*] [, *Visible*])

Adds a control to the form or frame and returns a reference to that control.

Argument	Settings
ProgID	A string identifying the class name and version of the control to add. See Table 20-6 for a list of the values for common controls.
Name	The name to assign the control.
Visible	True displays the control; False hides it. Default is True.

Table 20-6. ProgIDs for Forms 2.0 controls

Control	Class name and version (ProgID)
CheckBox	Forms.CheckBox.1
ComboBox	Forms.ComboBox.1
CommandButton	Forms.CommandButton.1
Frame	Forms.Frame.1
Image	Forms.Image.1
Label	Forms.Label.1
ListBox	Forms.ListBox.1
MultiPage	Forms.MultiPage.1
OptionButton	Forms.OptionButton.1
ScrollBar	Forms.ScrollBar.1
SpinButton	Forms.SpinButton.1

Table 20-6. ProgIDs for Forms 2.0 controls (continued)

Control	Class name and version (ProgID)
TabStrip	Forms.TabStrip.1
TextBox	Forms.TextBox.1
ToggleButton	Forms.ToggleButton.1

 Even though the version number in the ProgID is 1, these names refer to the Forms 2.0 controls.

The following code creates label and text box controls for each of the columns in a list created in the data form example created earlier:

```
Private Sub UserForm_Initialize()
    Dim ws As Worksheet, lc As ListColumn, _
      c As Control, tp As Single, lft As Single, wd As Single, _
      ht As Single
    Set ws = Worksheets("DataForm")
    ' Control's initial height and width values.
    wd = 60
    ht = 18
    ' Add a label and a text box for each list column.
    For Each lc In ws.ListObjects(1).ListColumns
        ' Add a label.
        Set c = Frame1.Controls.Add("Forms.Label.1", lc.name)
        ' Set label's properties.
        c.Caption = lc.name
        c.Top = tp
        c.Left = lft
        c.width = wd
        c.height = ht
        ' Increment the position for next control.
        lft = lft + c.width
        ' Add a text box.
        Set c = Frame1.Controls.Add("Forms.TextBox.1", lc.name)
        ' Set text box's properties.
        c.Top = tp
        c.Left = lft
        c.width = wd
        c.height = ht
        ' Set the position for the next control.
        tp = tp + c.height
        lft = 0
    Next
End Sub
```

control.Cancel [= *setting*]

For command button controls, True indicates that the control's Click event procedure is called when the user presses the Esc key. Default is False.

controls.Clear( )

Deletes all of the controls created at runtime. This method fails if the container has design-time controls, so you should put your runtime controls in a frame if you want to clear controls from a form with a mix of runtime and design-time controls. The following code clears controls from the frame used in the Add method example:

```
Private Sub cmdClear_Click( )
    Frame1.Controls.Clear
End Sub
```

control.ControlSource [= setting]

Sets or returns the address of a range to use as the source of the value for the control. For example, the following code links the value in a text box to cell A1 on the DataForm worksheet:

```
Private Sub UserForm_Initialize( )
    TextBox1.ControlSource = "DataForm!a1"
End Sub
```

control.ControlTipText [= setting]

Sets or returns the tool tip text to display for the control.

control.Default [= setting]

For command button controls, True indicates that the control's Click event procedure is called when the user presses the Enter key. Default is False.

control.LayoutEffect

In the form's Layout event, fmLayoutEffectInitiate indicates that the control was moved; fmLayoutEffectNone indicates that the control was not moved. This property is not available in other code.

controls.Move ([Left][, Top][, Width][, Height][, Layout])

Moves one or all of the controls on a form or frame. For individual control objects, Move can also resize the control.

Argument	Settings
Left	The new horizontal position of the control in points.
Top	The new vertical position of the control in points.
Width	The new control width in points (Control object only).

Argument	Settings
Height	The new control height in points.
Layout	True triggers the Layout event for the control's container; False does not trigger the Layout event. Default is False. (Control object only.)

control.Object

Returns a reference to the base class instance of the object. Use this property when a control implements a member that has the same name as one of the Control object members. In that case, the Control object's member shadows the control's member and you must add Object to the expression to use the control's member.

control.OldHeight

In the form object's Layout event, returns the height of the control before it was resized.

control.OldLeft

In the form object's Layout event, returns the horizontal position of the control before it was moved.

control.OldTop

In the form object's Layout event, returns the vertical position of the control before it was moved.

control.OldWidth

In the form object's Layout event, returns the width of the control before it was resized.

control.Remove(*Index*)

Removes a control created at runtime from the Controls collection. *Index* may be the name of the control or a number indicating the index of the control in the collection.

control.RowSource [= *setting*]

For ComboBox and ListBox controls, sets or returns the address of the range that provides values for the control. The following code adds items from A1:A5 on the Lookup worksheet as items in a listbox:

```
Private Sub UserForm_Initialize( )
    ListBox1.RowSource = "Lookup!A1:A5"
End Sub
```

control.SetFocus( )

Moves focus to the control.

control.TabIndex [= *setting*]

Sets or returns the position of the control in the tab order. Must be a positive whole number. The following code makes TextBox1 the first control in the tab order and gives that control focus when the form is first displayed:

```
Private Sub UserForm_Initialize( )
    TextBox1.TabIndex = 0
End Sub
```

control.TabStop [= *setting*]

True includes the control in the tab order; False removes it. Default is True.

control.Tag [= *setting*]

Set or returns additional information about the control.

control.ZOrder([*zPosition*])

Places the control in front of or behind any other controls layered on top of this control.

Argument	Settings
zPosition	fmTop displays the control on top of others; fmBottom displays the control beneath other controls. Default is fmTop.

Font Members

Use the Font object to change the appearance of text on a form, frame, or control. Use the Font property of the form or control to get a reference to this object. The Font object has the following members:

```
Bold
Italic
Size
StrikeThrough
Underline
Weight
```

The following code makes the text on a form's controls bold:

```
Private Sub UserForm_Initialize()
    Dim c As Control
    For Each c In Me.Controls
        c.Font.Bold = True
    Next
End Sub
```

CheckBox, OptionButton, ToggleButton Members

Use the CheckBox, OptionButton, and ToggleButton controls to get and display settings that are on, off, or Null. In addition to the members listed for the general Control object, these controls have the following members. Key members (shown in **bold**) are covered in the following reference section:

Accelerator	Alignment
AutoSize	BackColor
BackStyle	Caption
Enabled	Font
ForeColor	**GroupName**
Locked	MouseIcon
MousePointer	Picture
PicturePosition	SpecialEffect
TextAlign	**TripleState**
Value	WordWrap

---

control.AutoSize [= *setting*]

True automatically resizes the control to display its contents; False uses a fixed size determined by the Height and Width properties. Default is False.

---

control.BackStyle [= *fmBackStyle*]

Sets or returns whether the control's background is transparent or opaque. Can be fmBackStyleTransparent or fmBackStyleOpaque (default).

---

control.GroupName [= *setting*]

For option buttons, sets or returns a name used to identify an exclusive set of options. When an option button belongs to a group, only one of the OptionButton controls in that group can be True at any given time.

control.**Locked** [= *setting*]

True prevents the user from setting the control's value; False allows changes. Default is False. Locking a control is different from setting its Enabled property to False in that the control is not grayed and can still receive focus.

control.**TripleState** [= *setting*]

For CheckBox and ToggleButton controls, True allows the user to select a third state (Null); False allows only True/False settings. Default is False.

ComboBox Members

Use the ComboBox control to get and display settings from a list of choices. Combo boxes combine a listbox control with a text box control. In addition to the members listed for the general Control object, these controls have the following members. Key members (shown in **bold**) are covered in the following reference section:

AddItem	AutoSize	**AutoTab**
AutoWordSelect	BackColor	BackStyle
BorderColor	BorderStyle	**BoundColumn**
CanPaste	**Clear**	**Column**
ColumnCount	**ColumnHeads**	**ColumnWidths**
Copy	**CurTargetX**	**CurX**
Cut	**DragBehavior**	**DropButtonStyle**
DropDown	Enabled	**EnterFieldBehavior**
Font	ForeColor	**HideSelection**
IMEMode	**LineCount**	**List**
ListCount	**ListIndex**	**ListRows**
ListStyle	**ListWidth**	Locked
MatchEntry	**MatchFound**	**MatchRequired**
MaxLength	MouseIcon	MousePointer
Paste	**RemoveItem**	**SelectionMargin**
SelLength	**SelStart**	**SelText**
ShowDropButtonWhen	SpecialEffect	**Style**
Text	**TextAlign**	**TextColumn**
TextLength	**TopIndex**	Value

control.**AddItem**(*Item*[, *Index*])

Adds an item to the list.

Argument	Settings
Item	The item to add.
Index	The position of the item in the list. Default is to add the item to the end of the list.

The following code adds three items to a drop-down list and selects the first item:

```
Private Sub UserForm_Initialize()
    ComboBox1.AddItem "this"
    ComboBox1.AddItem "that"
    ComboBox1.AddItem "other"
    ComboBox1.Style = fmStyleDropDownList
    ComboBox1.ListIndex = 1
End Sub
```

control.AutoTab [= *setting*]

True causes focus to switch to the next control in the tab order when a user enters MaxLength characters in the text box portion of the control; False does not tab to the next control. Default is False.

control.AutoWordSelect [= *setting*]

True extends selected text one word at a time in the text box portion of the control; False extends the selection one character at a time. Default is True.

control.BoundColumn [= *setting*]

Sets or returns the index of the column that determines the Value property of the control. The following code loads three columns of data from the DataForm worksheet into a combo box and displays the value of the third column when the user selects an item from the list:

```
Private Sub UserForm_Initialize()
    Dim rng As Range
    ComboBox1.ColumnCount = 3
    Set rng = Worksheets("DataForm").UsedRange
    ComboBox1.RowSource = rng.Address
    ComboBox1.BoundColumn = 3
End Sub

Private Sub ComboBox1_Change()
    If ComboBox1.Value <> "" Then _
      MsgBox "Selected value is: " & ComboBox1.Value
End Sub
```

control.Clear( )

Removes all of the items from the list.

control.Column([Column][, Row])

Sets or returns the value of a list column or an item within a column of the list.

Argument	Settings
Column	The index of the column in the list
Row	The index of the item within the column

Use Column to get a value from items in a row of a multicolumn combo box. The BoundColumn topic shows how to create a combo box with three columns. You can get the value from any of those columns using the Column method as shown here:

```
Private Sub ComboBox1_Change()
    If ComboBox1.Value <> "" Then _
        MsgBox "Second column is: " & ComboBox1.Column(1, ComboBox1.ListIndex)
End Sub
```

Column and Row indexes start at 0, so 1 is the second column.

control.ColumnCount [= setting]

Sets or returns the number of columns to display in the list. Must be between -1 and 9. The setting -1 displays all columns.

control.ColumnHeads [= setting]

True converts the first row in the list to column headings; False does not create column headings. Default is False. Column headings are separated from the list items by a separator bar and can't be selected. The ColumnHeads property can't create column headings from items in a range set through the RowSource property.

control.ColumnWidths [= setting]

Sets or returns the width of list columns in points. Use a semicolon to specify different widths for each column, as shown here:

```
Private Sub UserForm_Initialize()
    Dim rng As Range
    ComboBox1.ColumnCount = 3
    Set rng = Worksheets("DataForm").UsedRange
    ComboBox1.RowSource = rng.Address
    ComboBox1.ColumnWidths = "30;20;40"
End Sub
```

control.CurTargetX

Returns the preferred horizontal position of the insertion point in a list in ten-thousandths of a meter. The control must have focus before you can access this property.

control.CurX [= setting]

Sets or returns the horizontal position of the insertion point in a list in ten-thousandths of a meter. The control must have focus before you can access this property.

control.DragBehavior [= fmDragBehavior]

Sets or returns whether selected text can be dragged from the control. Can be either fmDragBehaviorDisabled (default) or fmDragBehaviorEnabled.

control.DropButtonStyle [= fmDropButtonStyle]

Sets or returns the appearance of the drop-down button on the control. Can be one of these settings:

    fmDropButtonStylePlain
    fmDropButtonStyleArrow (default)
    fmDropButtonStyleEllipsis
    fmDropButtonStyleReduce

control.DropDown( )

Displays the list portion of the control.

control.EnterFieldBehavior [= fmEnterFieldBehavior]

Sets or returns how the contents of the control are selected when the user selects the control or tabs to it. Can be set to either fmEnterFieldBehaviorSelectAll (default) or fmEnterFieldBehaviorRecallSelection.

control.HideSelection [= setting]

True removes highlighting from selected text when the control loses focus; False preserves highlighting when the control loses focus. Default is True.

control.IMEMode [= *fmIMEMode*]

For forms created for the Far East, sets or returns the Input Method Editor (IME) for the control. Can be one of these settings:

fmIMEModeNoControl (default)	fmIMEModeOn
fmIMEModeOff	fmIMEModeDisable
fmIMEModeHiragana	fmIMEModeKatakana
fmIMEModeKatakanaHalf	fmIMEModeAlphaFull
fmIMEModeAlpha	fmIMEModeHangulFull
fmIMEModeHangul	

control.LineCount

Returns the number of lines in the edit portion of the control. This is always 1 for combo boxes.

control.List([*Row, Column*]) [= *setting*]

Sets or returns the value of one item within the list or all items in the list.

Argument	Settings
Row	The row of an item in the list
Column	The column of an item in the list

Omit *Row* and *Column* to get or set the array containing all items in the list. For example, the following code loads an array of strings into the control:

```
Private Sub UserForm_Initialize()
    ComboBox1.List = Split("This, that, other", ",")
    ' Select the first item.
    ComboBox1.ListIndex = 0
End Sub
```

control.ListCount

Returns the number of items in the list.

control.ListIndex [= *setting*]

Sets or returns the index of the currently selected item in the list. The List topic example selects the first item in the list.

control.ListRows [= *setting*]

Sets or returns the number of rows to display when in the drop-down list portion of the control.

control.ListStyle [= *fmListStyle*]

Sets or returns how list items are displayed. Can be `fmListStylePlain` (default) or `fmListStyleOption` (displays items with option buttons).

control.ListWidth [= *setting*]

Sets or returns the width of the list portion of the control in points.

control.MatchEntry [= *fmMatchEntry*]

Sets or returns how to search for matching list items as the user types in the edit portion of the control. Can be set to `fmMatchEntryFirstLetter`, `fmMatchEntryComplete` (default), or `fmMatchEntryNone`.

control.MatchFound

If `MatchEntry` is set to `fmMatchEntryNone`, returns True if the text typed in the edit portion of the control matched a list item, False if it did not.

control.MatchRequired [= *setting*]

True validates text entered in the text portion of the control against the list; False does not validate entries. Default is False.

control.MaxLength [= *setting*]

Sets or returns the maximum number of characters that can be entered in the control. The default is 0, which indicates no maximum.

control.RemoveItem(*Index*)

Removes an item from the list. This method causes an error if the control is bound to a range through the `RowSource` property.

control.SelectionMargin [= setting]

True allows the user to select an item by clicking the margin to the left of the item in the list; False doesn't select items when the margin is clicked. Default is True.

control.SelLength [= setting]

Sets or returns the number of characters selected in the edit portion of the control.

control.SelStart [= setting]

Sets or returns the starting position of the selected text in the edit portion of the control.

control.SelText [= setting]

Sets or returns the text that is selected in the edit portion of the control.

control.ShowDropButtonWhen [= fmShowDropButtonWhen]

Sets or returns how the drop-down button is displayed. Can be fmShowDropButtonWhenNever, fmShowDropButtonWhenFocus, or fmShowDropButtonWhenAlways (default).

control.Style [= fmStyle]

Sets or returns whether the control includes a text box. Can be fmStyleDropDownCombo (default) or fmStyleDropDownList (omits the text box).

control.Text [= setting]

Sets or returns the text in the edit portion of the control.

control.TextAlign [= fmTextAlign]

Sets or returns how text is aligned in the control. Can be fmTextAlignLeft (default), fmTextAlignCenter, or fmTextAlignRight.

control.TextColumn [= setting]

Sets or returns the index of the column displayed in the edit portion of the control when the user select an item from a multicolumn list. The setting -1 (the default) displays the first visible column; 1 displays the first column, 2 the second, and so on.

control.TextLength

Returns the number of characters in the edit portion of the control.

control.TopIndex [= setting]

Sets or returns the index of the item displayed at the top of the list.

CommandButton Members

Use the CommandButton control to execute or cancel actions. In addition to the members listed for the general Control object, the CommandButton control has the following members. Key members (shown in **bold**) are covered in the following reference section:

Accelerator	AutoSize
BackColor	BackStyle
Caption	Enabled
Font	ForeColor
Locked	MouseIcon
MousePointer	**Picture**
PicturePosition	**TakeFocusOnClick**
WordWrap	

control.Picture [= setting]

Sets or returns the picture loaded as the face of the command button. The picture can be set at design time in the Properties window or at runtime using the LoadPicture function. The following code displays a button with a picture on it:

```
Private Sub UserForm_Initialize()
    CommandButton1.Picture = LoadPicture(ThisWorkbook.Path & "\logo.jpg")
    CommandButton1.PicturePosition = fmPicturePositionCenter
    CommandButton1.Caption = "Wombat"
    CommandButton1.Font.Bold = True
End Sub
```

control.PicturePosition [= fmPicturePosition]

Sets or returns the location of the picture relative to the caption. Can be one of these settings:

fmPicturePositionLeftTop	fmPicturePositionLeftCenter
fmPicturePositionLeftBottom	fmPicturePositionRightTop
fmPicturePositionRightCenter	fmPicturePositionRightBottom

fmPicturePositionAboveLeft

fmPicturePositionAboveRight

fmPicturePositionBelowCenter

fmPicturePositionCenter

fmPicturePositionAboveCenter (default)

fmPicturePositionBelowLeft

fmPicturePositionBelowRight

control.TakeFocusOnClick [= setting]

True causes the control to receive focus when clicked; False does not change the current focus. Default is True.

Image Members

Use the Image control to display pictures. In addition to the members listed for the general Control object, the Image control has the following members. Key members (shown in **bold**) are covered in the following reference section:

AutoSize	BackColor
BackStyle	BorderColor
BorderStyle	Enabled
MouseIcon	MousePointer
Picture	**PictureAlignment**
PictureSizeMode	**PictureTiling**
SpecialEffect	

control.Picture [= setting]

Sets or returns the picture loaded in the control. The picture can be set at design time in the Properties window or at runtime using the LoadPicture function. The following code displays a picture using the image control:

```
Private Sub UserForm_Initialize( )
    Image1.Picture = LoadPicture(ThisWorkbook.Path & "\turtle.jpg")
    Image1.PictureSizeMode = fmPictureSizeModeZoom
End Sub
```

control.PictureAlignment [= fmPictureAlignment]

Sets or returns how the picture is placed. Can be one of these settings:

fmPictureAlignmentTopLeft

fmPictureAlignmentTopRight

fmPictureAlignmentCenter (default)

fmPictureAlignmentBottomLeft

fmPictureAlignmentBottomRight

control.PictureSizeMode [= *fmPictureSizeMode*]

Sets or returns how the picture is sized. Can be one of these settings:

fmPictureSizeModeClip (default)

fmPictureSizeModeStretch (may change the aspect ratio of the picture)

fmPictureSizeModeZoom (preserves aspect ratio)

control.PictureTiling [= *setting*]

If the picture does not exactly fit the dimensions of the control and the PictureSizeMode is not fmPictureSizeModeStretch, True repeats the picture to fill the background; False displays the picture one time.

Label Members

Use the Label control to display text that the user can't change. In addition to the members listed for the general Control object, the Label control has the following members:

Accelerator	AutoSize
BackColor	BackStyle
BorderColor	BorderStyle
Caption	Enabled
Font	ForeColor
MouseIcon	MousePointer
Picture	PicturePosition
SpecialEffect	TextAlign
WordWrap	

ListBox Members

Use the ListBox control to display scrollable lists of items. In addition to the members listed for the general Control object, the ListBox control has the following members. Key members (shown in **bold**) are covered in the following reference section:

AddItem	BackColor	BorderColor
BorderStyle	BoundColumn	Clear( )
Column	ColumnCount	ColumnHeads
ColumnWidths	Enabled	Font
ForeColor	IMEMode	**IntegralHeight**
List	ListCount	ListIndex
ListStyle	Locked	MatchEntry
MouseIcon	MousePointer	**MultiSelect**

RemoveItem	Selected	SpecialEffect
Text	TextAlign	TextColumn
TopIndex	Value	

The listbox control is similar to the combo box control, except the list is always displayed and it does not include an edit region. The ListBox members are nearly identical to the ComboBox members, so see "ComboBox Members," earlier in the chapter, for those topics. The two members that are unique to the ListBox control are covered here.

control.IntegralHeight [= *setting*]

True resizes the height of the control to display full lines of text; False allows partial lines to be displayed. Default is True.

control.MultiSelect [= *fmMultiSelect*]

Sets or returns a value indicating whether multiple items in the list can be selected at the same time. Can be fmMultiSelectSingle (default), fmMultiSelectMulti, or fmMultiSelectExtended. The following code loads a range of values into a three-column list that allows multiple selections; the list includes checkboxes to show the selected items:

```
Private Sub UserForm_Initialize( )
    ListBox1.ColumnCount = 3
    ListBox1.ColumnWidths = "30;20;40"
    ListBox1.RowSource = [DataForm!A2:D4].Address
    ListBox1.MultiSelect = fmMultiSelectExtended
    ListBox1.ListStyle = fmListStyleOption
End Sub
```

MultiPage Members

Use the MultiPage control to organize complex dialogs into multiple pages of controls. In addition to the members listed for the general Control object, the MultiPage control has the following members. Key members (shown in **bold**) are covered in the following reference section:

BackColor	Enabled
Font	ForeColor
MultiRow	**Pages**
SelectedItem	**Style**
TabFixedHeight	**TabFixedWidth**
TabOrientation	Value

control.MultiRow [= *setting*]

True displays tabs in multiple rows; False displays a single row of tabs. Default is False.

control.Pages

Returns a collection of Page controls contained in the MultiPage control. Use the Pages collection to add or delete pages. The following code searches the workbook's folder for bitmap files and then creates a new page to display each file:

```
Private Sub UserForm_Initialize()
    ' Requires reference to the Microsoft Scripting Runtime.
    Dim fo As New filesystemobject, fld As Folder, _
      f As File, pg As Page
    ' Get the workbook folder.
    Set fld = fo.GetFolder(ThisWorkbook.Path)
    ' Delete all the pages from the multipage control.
    MultiPage1.Pages.Clear
    ' For each file in the folder.
    For Each f In fld.Files
        ' If the file is a bitmap.
        If fo.GetExtensionName(f) = "bmp" Then
            ' Create a page for it.
            Set pg = MultiPage1.Pages.Add(, f.name)
            ' Load the picture in the page.
            pg.Picture = LoadPicture(f)
            pg.PictureSizeMode = fmPictureSizeModeZoom
        End If
    Next
End Sub
```

control.SelectedItem

Returns the currently selected Page control.

control.Style [= *fmTabStyle*]

Sets or returns the type of tabs displayed. Can be fmTabStyleTabs (default), fmTabStyleButtons, or fmTabStyleNone.

control.TabFixedHeight [= *setting*]

Sets or returns the height of the tabs in points. Default is 0, which sets the height automatically.

control.TabFixedWidth [= setting]

Sets or returns the width of the tabs in points. Default is 0, which sets the width automatically.

control.TabOrientation [= fmTabOrientation]

Sets or returns the placement of the tabs on the control. Can be one of these settings:

fmTabOrientationTop (default)
fmTabOrientationBottom
fmTabOrientationLeft
fmTabOrientationRight

Page Members

Use the Page control to organize other controls within a MultiPage control. In addition to the members listed for the general Control object, the MultiPage control has the following members. Key members (shown in **bold**) are covered in the following reference section:

Accelerator	ActiveControl	CanPaste
CanRedo	CanUndo	Caption
Controls	ControlTipText	Copy
Cut	Cycle	Enabled
Index	InsideHeight	InsideWidth
KeepScrollBarsVisible	Name	Parent
Paste	Picture	PictureAlignment
PictureSizeMode	PictureTiling	RedoAction
Repaint	Scroll	ScrollBars
ScrollHeight	ScrollLeft	ScrollTop
ScrollWidth	SetDefaultTabOrder	Tag
TransitionEffect	**TransitionPeriod**	UndoAction
VerticalScrollBarSide	Visible	Zoom

The Page control is similar to UserForm and Frame, except pages always appear as part of a MultiPage control. The Page members are nearly identical to the UserForm and Frame members, so see "UserForm and Frame Members," earlier in the chapter, for those topics. Two members unique to the Page control are covered here.

control.**TransitionEffect** [= *fmTransitionEffect*]

Sets or returns a visual transition between pages. Can be one of these settings:

fmTransitionEffectNone (default)   fmTransitionEffectCoverUp
fmTransitionEffectCoverRightUp   fmTransitionEffectCoverRight
fmTransitionEffectCoverRightDown   fmTransitionEffectCoverDown
fmTransitionEffectCoverLeftDown   fmTransitionEffectCoverLeft
fmTransitionEffectCoverLeftUp   fmTransitionEffectPushUp
fmTransitionEffectPushRight   fmTransitionEffectPushDown
fmTransitionEffectPushLeft

control.**TransitionPeriod** [= *setting*]

This property has no effect in Excel.

ScrollBar and SpinButton Members

Use the ScrollBar and SpinButton controls to scroll through items or values. In addition to the members listed for the general Control object, the ScrollBar and SpinButton controls have the following members. Key members (shown in **bold**) are covered in the following reference section:

BackColor	Delay
Enabled	ForeColor
LargeChange[1]	**Max**
Min	MouseIcon
MousePointer	**Orientation**
ProportionalThumb[1]	**SmallChange**
Value	

[1] ScrollBar only

control.**LargeChange** [= *setting*]

Sets or returns the increment to scroll when the user clicks the scrollbar above or below the scroll box. Must be between the Min and Max property settings.

control.**Max** [= *setting*]

Sets or returns the maximum value of the control. The default is 32,767 for scrollbars and 100 for spin buttons.

control.Min [= *setting*]

Sets or returns the minimum value of the control. The default is 0.

control.Orientation [= *fmOrientation*]

Sets or returns how the control is oriented. Can be fmOrientationAuto (default), fmOrientationVertical, or fmOrientationHorizontal.

control.ProportionalThumb [= *setting*]

True sizes the scrollbox proportional to the scrolling region; False uses a fixed size. Default is True.

control.SmallChange [= *setting*]

Sets or returns the increment to scroll when the user clicks the scroll arrow. Must be between the Min and Max property settings. Default is 1.

TabStrip Members

Use the TabStrip control to organize groups of settings for a similar set of controls. In addition to the members listed for the general Control object, the TabStrip control has the following members. Key members (shown in **bold**) are covered in the following reference section:

BackColor	**ClientHeight**
ClientLeft	**ClientTop**
ClientWidth	Enabled
Font	ForeColor
MouseIcon	MousePointer
MultiRow	SelectedItem
Style	TabFixedHeight
TabFixedWidth	TabOrientation
Tabs	Value

The TabStrip control doesn't automatically show or hide pages of controls the way that the MultiPage control does. Instead, use it to display groups of similar settings. The following code demonstrates that technique by using a tab strip control to display the attributes and contents of the XML files in the current workbook's folder:

```
' Create a tab for each .xml file.
Private Sub UserForm_Initialize()
    ' Requires reference to the Microsoft Scripting Runtime.
```

```
    Dim fo As New filesystemobject, fld As Folder, _
        f As File
    ' Get the workbook folder.
    Set fld = fo.GetFolder(ThisWorkbook.Path)
    ' Delete all the tabs from the TabStrip control.
    TabStrip1.Tabs.Clear
    ' For each file in the folder.
    For Each f In fld.Files
        ' If the file is XML.
        If fo.GetExtensionName(f) = "xml" Then
            ' Create a tab for it.
            TabStrip1.Tabs.Add , f.name
        End If
    Next
    ' TextBox properties
    txtFile.MultiLine = True
    txtFile.ScrollBars = fmScrollBarsBoth
    txtFile.TabKeyBehavior = True
End Sub

' Display the attributes for the file on the selected tab.
Private Sub TabStrip1_Change()
    Dim fo As New filesystemobject, _
        f As File, fname As String
    fname = TabStrip1.SelectedItem.Caption
    ' Get the file.
    Set f = fo.GetFile(ThisWorkbook.Path & "\" & fname)
    ' Display file attibutes in four label controls.
    lblCreated = "Created: " & f.DateCreated
    lblModified = "Modified: " & f.DateLastModified
    lblAccessed = "Accessed: " & f.DateLastAccessed
    lblSize = "File size: " & f.Size \ 1024 & "K"
    On Error Resume Next
    ' Read the file into the text box.
    txtFile.Text = f.OpenAsTextStream.ReadAll
    If Err Then txtFile.Text = "File too big."
    ' Close the file.
    f.OpenAsTextStream.Close
    On Error GoTo 0
End Sub
```

In the preceding code, the four label and text box controls always appear. Only their settings change as the user selects from among the tabs.

control.ClientHeight

Returns the height of the client area of the tab strip. The client area is the region of the control where other controls may be placed.

control.ClientLeft

Returns the horizontal coordinate of the client area.

control.ClientTop

Returns the vertical coordinate of the client area.

control.ClientWidth

Returns the width of the client area of the tab strip. The client area is the region of the control where other controls may be placed.

control.Tabs

Returns the collection of Tab objects on the tab strip. Use the Tabs collection to add or remove tabs at runtime.

TextBox and RefEdit Members

Use the TextBox control to get text entries from a user. Use the RefEdit control to get a selected range from the user. In addition to the members listed for the general Control object, the TextBox and RefEdit controls have the following members. Key members (shown in **bold**) are covered in the following reference section:

AutoSize	AutoTab	AutoWordSelect
BackColor	BackStyle	BorderColor
BorderStyle	CanPaste	Copy
CurLine	CurTargetX	CurX
Cut( )	DragBehavior	Enabled
EnterFieldBehavior	**EnterKeyBehavior**	Font
ForeColor	HideSelection	IMEMode
IntegralHeight	**LineCount**	Locked
MaxLength	MouseIcon	MousePointer
MultiLine	**PasswordChar**	Paste
ScrollBars	SelectionMargin	SelLength
SelStart	SelText	SpecialEffect
TabKeyBehavior	Text	TextAlign
TextLength	Value	**WordWrap**

The TextBox and RefEdit members are a subset of the ComboBox members, so see that object for those topics. See the previous section, "TabStrip Members," for an example of loading files into a text box and using the MultiLine and ScrollBar properties. Several TextBox and RefEdit members that are not found in the ComboBox control are covered here.

control.CurLine [= *setting*]

When the control has focus, sets or returns the index of the line that currently has the cursor.

control.EnterKeyBehavior [= *fmEnterFieldBehavior*]

Sets or returns how the contents of the control are selected when the control receives focus due to a user action. Can be set to fmEnterFieldBehaviorSelectAll (default) or fmEnterFieldBehaviorRecallSelection.

control.IntegralHeight [= *setting*]

True resizes the height of the control to display full lines of text; False allows partial lines to be displayed. Default is True.

control.LineCount

Returns the number of lines of text in the control.

control.MultiLine [= *setting*]

True allows multiple lines of text; False allows only a single line. Default is True.

control.PasswordChar [= *setting*]

Sets or returns a character to display in place of the actual text, usually *. Use PasswordChar when you want to hide what the user typed.

control.ScrollBars [= *fmScrollBars*]

Sets or returns how scrollbars appear on the control. Can be one of these settings:

    fmScrollBarsNone (default)
    fmScrollBarsHorizontal
    fmScrollBarsVertical
    fmScrollBarsBoth

control.TabKeyBehavior [= *setting*]

If MultiLine is True, setting TabKeyBehavior to True inserts a tab character when the user presses the Tab key and False moves focus to the next control when the user presses Tab. Default is False.

control.WordWrap [= *setting*]

If MultiLine is True, setting WordWrap to True wraps long lines of text to the next line of the control and False does not wrap long lines. Default is True.

CHAPTER 21

Sending and Receiving Workbooks

In Chapter 5, you learned how to send a simple email from Excel. In this chapter, you'll learn how to email workbooks, worksheets, and charts as well as how to route workbooks to multiple reviewers for comments or approval.

This chapter includes task-oriented reference information for the following objects: MsoEnvelope, MailItem, and RoutingSlip.

 Code used in this chapter and additional samples are available in *ch21.xls*.

Send Mail

Table 21-1 lists the different ways to send mail within Excel.

Table 21-1. Sending mail from Excel

To	Use	Notes
Compose a text email message	The FollowHyperLink method with the mailto: protocol	Doesn't support attachments.
Compose an email with an attached workbook	The Dialogs method to display the email dialog box	User must fill in addresses and subject on the message.
Send a workbook	The SendMail method	Doesn't display message before send; shows security warning.
Send a worksheet or chart	The MailEnvelope property	Unlike SendMail, this allows access to CC and BCC lines; avoids security warning. (Requires Outlook.)
Collect review comments	The SendForReview method	Allows you to link to a shared workbook for collecting comments.
Route for approval	The RoutingSlip object and Route method	Routes to addresses in sequence.

I've used `FollowHyperlink` technique a few times already in this book. In case you missed it, here's short sample:

```
Sub SendTextMail()
    ThisWorkbook.FollowHyperlink "mailto:someone@microsoft.com" & _
        "?Subject=Test message.&Body=The message goes here..."
End Sub
```

The `mailto:` protocol starts the user's default email client and creates a new message. It's up to the user to send the message, so there are no real security hurdles to this approach. You can't attach files using `mailto:` however. To create a quick email with the current workbook attached, use the `Dialogs` method as shown here:

```
Sub SendAsAttachment()
    Application.Dialogs(xlDialogSendMail).Show
End Sub
```

That approach creates a new, blank message with the file attached. The user must fill in the address and add the subject and body of the message before sending the message. The `SendMail` method also sends the workbook as an attachment, but it doesn't display the message before it is sent. That poses a risk because you don't want anyone sending mail from your system without your knowledge. To address that, Outlook displays a notice any time you use `SendMail`. For example, the following code displays the warning shown in Figure 21-1:

```
Sub SendWorkbook()
    ' Trap error in case user cancels send.
    On Error Resume Next
    ' Send this workbook (don't run this from VBE!
    ' It may cause a lockup.)
    ThisWorkbook.SendMail "someone@microsoft.com", "Please review"
    On Error GoTo 0
End Sub
```

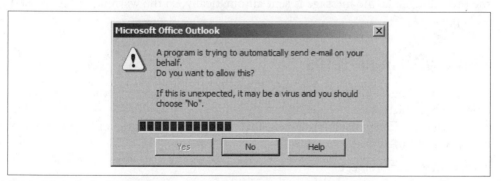

Figure 21-1. Outlook warns users when Excel sends automated mail

You'll notice the comments warn you not to run `SendMail` directly from the Visual Basic Editor (as when debugging). That can lock up Excel, and the only way to recover is to use the Task Manager to close the Outlook dialog box that appears with an Excel icon on the Windows task bar.

Sending mail this way isn't a great practice in my opinion. It's much better to be up front with users, show them the message, and let them choose whether to send. To do that, use the `MailEnvelope` property. The following code composes a message containing the active worksheet in Excel as shown in Figure 21-2:

```
Sub SendActiveSheet()
    Dim ws As Object, env As MsoEnvelope
    ' Get the active sheet.
    Set ws = ActiveSheet
    ' Show email header from Workbook object.
    ws.Parent.EnvelopeVisible = True
    ' Get the MsoEnvelope object
    Set env = ws.MailEnvelope
    ' Set the email header fields.
    env.Introduction = "Sales in first quarter:"
    With env.Item
        .to = "someone@yourcompany.com"
        .cc = "yourboss@yourcompany.com"
        .subject = ws.Name
        ' Uncomment this to send automatically.
        '.send
    End With
End Sub
```

With this approach, the user can choose to send the message or not, so there's no need to display a security warning. However, if you uncomment the `Send` method in the preceding code, the message is sent automatically, so the warning in Figure 21-1 will appear.

Work with Mail Items

In the preceding `SendActiveSheet` example, the `Item` property returns a `MailItem` object. That object is part of the Microsoft Outlook object library—not Excel's. The `MailItem` object is very useful in Excel, since it allows you to attach files and control all aspects of the message.

To use the `MailItem` object:

1. In the Visual Basic Editor, choose Tools → References. Visual Basic displays the References dialog box.

2. Select the Microsoft Outlook 11.0 Object Library and click OK.

3. Declare a variable using the `MailItem` type.

4. Get a reference to the `MailItem` object.

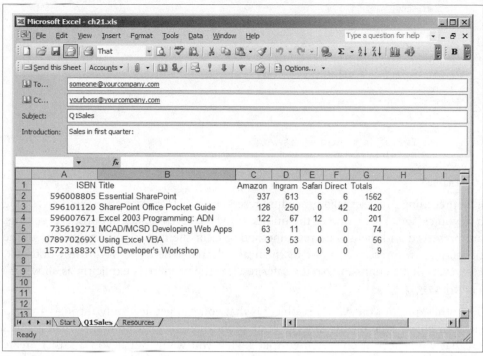

Figure 21-2. Composing an email in Excel

The following code creates a mail item and attaches the current workbook:

```
Sub SendAsMailItem( )
    ' Requires reference to Microsoft Outlook
    Dim ws As Worksheet, env As MsoEnvelope, mi As MailItem
    ' Get the active worksheet.
    Set ws = ActiveSheet
    ' Save the workbook before mailing as attachment.
    ws.Parent.Save
    ' Show email header.
    ws.Parent.EnvelopeVisible = True
    ' Get the MsoEnvelope object
    Set env = ws.MailEnvelope
    ' Set the email header fields.
    env.Introduction = "Please revew attached file."
    ' Get the MailItem object.
    Set mi = env.Item
    ' Clear the MailItem properties.
    ClearMessage mi
    ' Set MailItem properties.
    mi.Importance = olImportanceHigh
    mi.To = "someone@microsoft.com"
    mi.CC = "someoneelse@yourcompany.com"    mi.Subject = "Subject text."
    ' Attach this workbook.
    mi.Attachments.Add ThisWorkbook.FullName
    ' Uncomment this to send automatically.
```

```
            'mi.send
        End Sub

        Sub ClearMessage(mi As MailItem)
            Dim at As Attachment
            mi.Importance = olImportanceNormal
            mi.To = ""
            mi.CC = ""
            mi.BCC = ""
            mi.Subject = ""
            For Each at In mi.Attachments
                at.Delete
            Next
        End Sub
```

The preceding `ClearMessage` procedure resets the `MailItem` properties before creating a new message. That's one of the quirks of the `MailItem` object: its property settings are preserved and there is no reset method to clear them. Actually, only some of the properties are preserved; most of them are cleared when you save the workbook. However, that's confusing, so it's safer to clear the properties explicitly as shown by `ClearMessage`.

The other quirk of the `MailItem` object is that you can get at it only through a worksheet or chart. That means that the body of the mail message contains whatever was on that worksheet or chart. Often that's what you want, but if you'd rather create your own message body, close the message, then call the `Display` method as shown here:

```
        Sub SendWorkbookAsMailItem( )
            ' Requires reference to Microsoft Outlook
            Dim ws As Worksheet, env As MsoEnvelope, mi As MailItem
            ' Get the active worksheet.
            Set ws = ActiveSheet
            ' Save the workbook before mailing as attachment.
            ws.Parent.Save
            ' Show email header.
            ws.Parent.EnvelopeVisible = True
            ' Get the MsoEnvelope object
            Set env = ws.MailEnvelope
            ' Set the email header fields.
            env.Introduction = "Please revew attached file."
            ' Get the MailItem object.
            Set mi = env.Item
            ' Clear the MailItem properties.
            ClearMessage mi
            ' Set MailItem properties.
            mi.Importance = olImportanceHigh
            mi.To = "someone@microsoft.com"
            mi.CC = "someoneelse@yourcompany.com"    mi.Subject = ActiveWorkbook.Name
            mi.Body = "Please review the attached workbook."
            ' Attach this workbook.
            mi.Attachments.Add ThisWorkbook.FullName
```

```
            ' Close message composition header (gets rid of worksheet).
            mi.Close olDiscard
            ' Open in mail message window.
            mi.Display
        End Sub
```

The preceding Close/Display trick disposes of the content from the worksheet or chart and allows you to use the Body property to set the message body as shown by Figure 21-3.

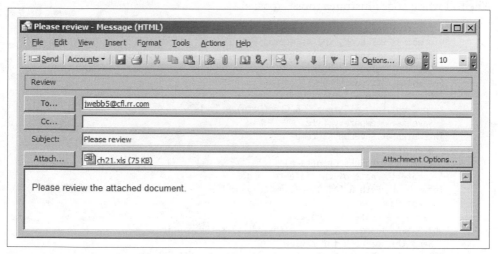

Figure 21-3. Sending a workbook as an attachment

 The MailItem object requires that you use Outlook as your email application. If you don't use Outlook, read the following section for an alternate approach.

Collect Review Comments

Another way to send the entire workbook as an attachment is to use SendForReview. That method composes an email message with the workbook as an attachment, plus it allows you to display the message and thus avoid the security warning. The following code sends the active workbook as a message identical to that shown in Figure 21-3:

```
        Sub SendForReview( )
            ThisWorkbook.SendForReview "someone@microsoft.com", _
                "Please review the attached workbook", True, False
        End Sub
```

Since SendForReview is intended for collecting review comments, the method displays a dialog asking if the file should be saved as a shared workbook before composing the message. There's no easy way around that. In fact, since saving workbooks as shared files is difficult from code, you've got to take these steps if you want to send a workbook out for review without any extra prompts:

1. Create a temporary copy of the workbook.

2. Open that copy and save it as a shared review copy.

3. Get a reference to the shared review copy and send that workbook for review.

4. Close the shared workbook and delete the temporary file.

The following code illustrates those steps:

```
Sub SendForReview( )
    Dim wb1 As Workbook, wb2 As Workbook, _
      fname As String, temp As String
    ' Get the active workbook.
    Set wb1 = ActiveWorkbook
    ' Create a unique temporary filename
    temp = wb1.Path & "\temp_" & CLng(Date) & ".xls"
    ' Save as a temporary file.
    ThisWorkbook.SaveCopyAs temp
    ' Open the review copy.
    Set wb2 = Workbooks.Open(temp)
    ' Create the name of the file to send.
    fname = wb1.Path & "\" & "Review Copy of " & _
        wb1.Name
    ' Save as a shared workbook.
    wb2.SaveAs fname, , , , , , xlShared, xlUserResolution
    ' Send the workbook for review.
    ThisWorkbook.SendForReview "someone@microsoft.com", _
      "Please review the attached workbook", True, False
    ' Close the review copy (returns to ActiveWorkbook).
    wb2.Close False
    ' Delete the temporary file.
    Kill temp
End Sub
```

That's complicated, but it has the advantage of creating a shared review copy separate from your work file. Reviewers can return changes, which you can merge into the review copy without replacing the original file, which helps protect against unwanted changes.

Shared workbooks come with some restrictions. For instance, you can't edit code in a shared workbook. Also, shared workbooks can't contain XML maps. Using a SharePoint workspace is a better solution for collaborating on a workbook. See Chapter 8 for information on sharing workspaces through SharePoint.

Route Workbooks

Routing a workbook is similar to sending it for review, except the workbook can be sent to the email addresses serially instead of all at once. To route a workbook from code:

1. Get a reference to the workbook's RoutingSlip object
2. Set the RoutingSlip properties.
3. Call the workbook's Route method.

The following code illustrates those steps:

```
' Don't run this from VBE!
Sub RouteWorkbook()
    Dim wb As Workbook, rs As RoutingSlip
    ' Trap error in case user cancels send.
    On Error Resume Next
    Set wb = ActiveWorkbook
    ' Get the routing slip.
    Set rs = wb.RoutingSlip
    ' Clear it.
    rs.Reset
    ' Set the routing properties.
    rs.Delivery = xlOneAfterAnother
    rs.Recipients = Array("someone@microsoft.com", _
        "someone@microsoft.com")
    rs.Subject = wb.Name
    rs.Message = "Please review and route on."
    rs.TrackStatus = True
    rs.ReturnWhenDone = True
    ' Send the message.
    wb.Route
    On Error GoTo 0
End Sub
```

Like the SendMail example, running the preceding code from the Visual Basic Editor can lock up Excel. You should run it only from the Macro dialog box or from an event while Excel is active. Also like SendMail, routing will display the security prompt (Figure 21-1).

Routing has the following differences from other ways of sending workbooks:

- The workbook is attached to the message as a read-only file. If the user wants to make changes, he must first save the file as read/write. The new file retains its routing slip, however, and can be sent on to the next recipient.
- The recipient list is sent as an array of email addresses. Outlook verifies those addresses against the user's address book and may prompt for corrections.
- When a recipient closes a workbook that has a routing slip, Excel asks if the workbook should be forwarded on to the next recipient, as shown in Figure 21-4.

Routing can also be used to send workbooks to all recipients simultaneously. To do that, set the Delivery property to xlAllAtOnce. Sending all at once still sends the workbook as a read-only copy, but the user is prompted to route the workbook only if ReturnWhenDone is set to True.

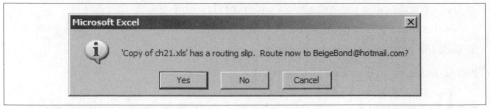

Figure 21-4. Excel routes a workbook on when recipients close the file

Read Mail

To read mail from Excel, use the `ActivateMicrosoftApp` method to start Outlook:

```
Sub ReadOutlookMail()
    Application.ActivateMicrosoftApp xlMicrosoftMail
End Sub
```

For HTML-based mail systems, use the `FollowHyperLink` method to open the mail system's account page:

```
Sub ReadGMail()
    ' Go to GMail.
    ThisWorkbook.FollowHyperlink "http://mail.google.com/"
End Sub
```

For other mail clients, use the `Shell` method to start the client application:

```
Sub ReadEudoraMail()
    Shell "C:\Program Files\Qualcomm\Eudora\Eudora.exe"
End Sub
```

MsoEnvelope Members

Use the `MsoEnvelope` object to send a worksheet or chart as an email. Use the `Worksheet` or `Chart` object's `MailEnvelope` property to get a reference to this object. The `MsoEnvelope` object has the following members. Key members (shown in **bold**) are covered in the following reference section:

```
CommandBars
```
Introduction
```
```
Item
```
Parent
```

---

mailenvelope.Introduction [= *setting*]

Sets or returns the text included at the top of the message body.

mailenvelope.Item

Returns a `MailItem` object used to set the recipients, priority, and other properties of the email.

MailItem Members

Use the `MailItem` object to set the attributes of the email sent using the `MsoEnvelope` object. Use the `MsoEnvelope` object's `Item` property to get a reference to this object. The `MailItem` object has the following members. `MailItem` is part of the Outlook object library and many of the members don't apply within Excel. Key members that are of use from within Excel (shown in **bold**) are covered in the following reference section:

 To declare a variable as a `MailItem` object, you must first add a reference to the Microsoft Outlook type library.

Actions	AlternateRecipientAllowed
Application	**Attachments**
AutoForwarded	AutoResolvedWinner
BCC	BillingInformation
Body	BodyFormat
Categories	**CC**
Class	ClearConversationIndex
Close	Companies
Conflicts	ConversationIndex
ConversationTopic	Copy
CreationTime	**DeferredDeliveryTime**
Delete	**DeleteAfterSubmit**
Display	DownloadState
EnableSharedAttachments	EntryID
ExpiryTime	FlagDueBy
FlagIcon	FlagRequest
FlagStatus	FormDescription
Forward	GetInspector
HasCoverSheet	**HTMLBody**
Importance	InternetCodepage
IsConflict	IsIPFax
ItemProperties	LastModificationTime
Links	MarkForDownload
MessageClass	Mileage

Move	NoAging
OriginatorDeliveryReportRequested	OutlookInternalVersion
OutlookVersion	Parent
Permission	PermissionService
PrintOut	**ReadReceiptRequested**
ReceivedByEntryID	ReceivedByName
ReceivedOnBehalfOfEntryID	ReceivedOnBehalfOfName
ReceivedTime	RecipientReassignmentProhibited
Recipients	ReminderOverrideDefault
ReminderPlaySound	ReminderSet
ReminderSoundFile	ReminderTime
RemoteStatus	Reply
ReplyAll	ReplyRecipientNames
ReplyRecipients	**Save**
SaveAs	Saved
SaveSentMessageFolder	**Send**
SenderEmailAddress	SenderEmailType
SenderName	**Sensitivity**
Sent	SentOn
SentOnBehalfOfName	Session
ShowCategoriesDialog	Size
Subject	Submitted
To	UnRead
UserProperties	VotingOptions
VotingResponse	

mailitem.Attachments

Returns an Outlook Attachments collection that you can use to add or remove files to send as attachments. The following code clears all of the attachments from a MailItem:

```
Sub RemoveAttachments(mi As MailItem)
    ' Requires reference to Microsoft Outlook.
    Dim at As Attachment
    For Each at In mi.Attachments
        at.Delete
    Next
End Sub
```

mailitem.BCC [= *setting*]

Sets or returns the addresses on the BCC field of the email. Separate multiple addresses with semicolons.

mailitem.Body [= *setting*]

Sets or returns the text of the email message. This property is ignored for email sent using the Excel mail composition header (Figure 21-2).

---

mailitem.CC [= *setting*]

Sets or returns the addresses on the CC field of the email. Separate multiple addresses with semicolons.

mailitem.Close(*SaveMode*)

Closes the mail item.

Argument	Settings
SaveMode	Determines whether the email is saved in the Drafts folder. Can be olDiscard, olPromptForSave, or olSave.

mailitem.DeferredDeliveryTime [= *setting*]

Sets or returns the date and time to send the message from the Outlook outbox.

mailitem.DeleteAfterSubmit [= *setting*]

True deletes the message from the Outlook Sent Items folder after it is sent.

mailitem.Display( )

Displays the email in a message window rather than using the Excel mail composition header. Combining Close and Display allows you to compose custom messages using the Body or HTMLBody properties, as shown here:

```
Sub SendHTMLEmail( )
    ' Requires reference to Microsoft Outlook
    Dim ws As Worksheet, env As MsoEnvelope, mi As MailItem
    ' Get the active worksheet.
    Set ws = ActiveSheet
    ' Show email header.
    ws.Parent.EnvelopeVisible = True
    ' Get the MsoEnvelope object
    Set env = ws.MailEnvelope
    ' Get the MailItem object.
    Set mi = env.Item
    ' Clear the MailItem properties.
    ClearMessage mi
    ' Set MailItem properties.
    mi.To = "someone@microsoft.com"
    mi.Subject = "Sending HTML emails from Excel"
    mi.HTMLBody = "<b>This text using <i>HTML</i> formatting.</b>"
    ' Close message composition header.
    mi.Close olDiscard
    ' Open in mail message window (gets rid of worksheet).
    mi.Display
End Sub
```

mailitem.**ExpiryTime** [= *setting*]

Sets or returns date value when the email expires and will be automatically deleted. The following code sends a message that expires in two days:

```
Sub SendMessageWithExpiration( )
    Dim ws As Worksheet, mi As MailItem
    ' Get the active worksheet.
    Set ws = ActiveSheet
    ' Show email header.
    ws.Parent.EnvelopeVisible = True
    ' Get the MailItem object.
    Set mi = ws.MailEnvelope.Item
    ' Set MailItem properties.
    mi.To = "someone@microsoft.com"
    mi.Subject = "Message will self-destruct " & Now + 2
    ' Expires in two days
    mi.ExpiryTime = Now + DateSerial(0, 0, 2)
End Sub
```

mailitem.**HTMLBody** [= *setting*]

Sets or returns the body of the message formatted using HTML tags. This property is ignored for email sent using the Excel mail composition header.

mailitem.**Importance** [= *setting*]

Sets or return the priority of the email. Can be `olImportanceHigh`, `olImportanceLow`, or `olImportanceNormal` (default).

mailitem.**PrintOut( )**

Sends the email to the default printer.

mailitem.**ReadReceiptRequested** [= *setting*]

True flags the message to request that an email be sent back to the sender when the original email is read; False does not request a return receipt. Default is False.

mailitem.**Recipients**

Returns an Outlook Recipients collection that you can use to add or remove addresses from the email's To field. Using the `Add` method of the `Recipients` collection displays a security warning. Setting the `To` property directly does not display a warning.

mailitem.Save( )

Saves the email in the Outlook Drafts folder.

mailitem.SaveAs(*Path, Type*)

Saves the email in the location specified by *Path* as the filetype specified in *Type*.

Argument	Settings
Path	The filename and path for the saved email.
Type	The format to use for the file. Can be one of the these olSaveAsType constants: olHTML, olMSG, olRTF, olTemplate, olDoc, olTXT, olVCal, olVCard, olICal, or olMSGUnicode.

mailitem.SaveSentMessageFolder [= *setting*]

Returns the Outlook MAPIFolder object representing the Outlook Sent Items folder.

mailitem.Send( )

Sends the email. Using the Send method displays a security warning.

mailitem.SenderEmailAddress

Returns the address of the user sending the email.

mailitem.SenderName

Returns the name of the user sending the email.

mailitem.Sensitivity [= *olSensitivity*]

Sets or returns the sensitivity of the email. Can be one of these settings:

    olConfidential
    olNormal
    olPersonal
    olPrivate

mailitem.Subject [= *setting*]

Sets or returns the text displayed in the Subject field of the email.

mailitem.To [= *setting*]

Sets or returns the addresses included in the To field of the email. Separate multiple addresses with semicolons.

RoutingSlip Members

Use the RoutingSlip object to control the distribution of a workbook through email. Use the Workbook object's RoutingSlip property to get a reference to this object, and use the Workbook object's Route method to send the workbook. The RoutingSlip object has the following members. Key members (shown in **bold**) are covered in the following reference section:

Application	Creator
Delivery	**Message**
Parent	**Recipients**
Reset	**ReturnWhenDone**
Status	**Subject**
TrackStatus	

routingslip.Delivery [= *xlRoutingSlipDelivery*]

Sets or returns the routing sequence for the workbook. Can be xlOneAfterAnother or xlAllAtOnce.

routingslip.Message [= *setting*]

Sets or returns the text to include in the body of the email.

routingslip.Recipients [= *setting*]

Sets or returns an array containing the addresses of the recipients to include in the To field of the email. The order of the items in the array determines the order of delivery.

 Setting this property displays an Outlook security warning. Don't run code to set this property from within the Visual Basic Editor (as when debugging) since it may cause Excel to lock up.

You can use the Split function to convert a string containing multiple addresses into an array, as shown here:

```
' Don't run this from VBE! Use Tools>Macros>Macro>Run instead.
Sub RouteActiveWorkbook( )
```

```
    Dim wb As Workbook, rs As RoutingSlip
    ' Trap error in case user cancels send.
    On Error Resume Next
    Set wb = ActiveWorkbook
    ' Get the routing slip.
    Set rs = wb.RoutingSlip
    ' Clear it.
    rs.Reset
    ' Set routing list. Use Split to convert address list to array.
    rs.Recipients = Strings.Split("someone@microsoft.com;" & _
        "someone@yourcompany.com;someoneelse@yourcompany.com", ";")
    rs.Subject = wb.Name
    rs.Message = "Please review and route on."
    ' Send the message.
    wb.Route
    On Error GoTo 0
End Sub
```

routingslip.Reset( )

Clears the routing slip.

routingslip.ReturnWhenDone [= setting]

True routes a copy of the workbook back to the original sender when the last recipient
closes the workbook. That recipient is prompted whether to send the email.

routingslip.Status

Returns the status of the workbook in the routing cycle. Can be one of these settings:

```
xlNotYetRouted
xlRoutingInProgress
xlRoutingComplete
```

routingslip.Subject [= setting]

Sets or returns the text in the Subject field of the email.

routingslip.TrackStatus [= setting]

True tracks the status of the workbook as it is routed between recipients. This property can
be set only if Status is xlNotYetRouted.

PART III

Extending Excel

These chapters teach you the advanced programming techniques used to create Excel add-ins, use external libraries, access data from the Web, use the next generation of programming tools, and secure your applications. These tasks extend Excel by building new components such as add-ins and by incorporating a wide range of existing components, from Windows DLLs to .NET assemblies. Since many of these topics are conceptual, these chapters feature more how-to and less reference than Part II.

CHAPTER 22

Building Add-ins

Creating an add-in in Excel is deceptively easy—just save the workbook as an add-in file (XLA). That's deceptive, because that's really not all there is to it. You need to combine many of the skills already covered in this book to create effective add-ins for others. This chapter brings those skills together and walks you through the best programming practices for creating add-ins.

This chapter includes task-oriented reference information for the AddIn object.

 Code used in this chapter and additional samples are available in *ch22.xls*.

Types of Add-ins

From a user's perspective, an add-in is a file that you load by selecting Tools → Add-ins from within Excel. Add-ins extend Excel in some way and usually display a toolbar or add menu items as a way to get at their features.

Table 22-1 lists the add-ins that ship with Excel. There also are many free sample add-ins available by searching *http://office.microsoft.com/* for "Excel add-ins."

Table 22-1. Add-ins installed with Excel

Add-in	Provides	Adds menu item
Analysis ToolPak	Advanced functions for financial and scientific data analysis	Tools → Data Analysis
Analysis ToolPak VBA	Support for using the Analysis Toolpak functions from Visual Basic	None
Conditional Sum Wizard	Formulas to sum data in lists	Tools → Conditional Sum
Euro Currency Tools	Conversion and formatting for the Euro currency	Tools → Euro Conversion
Internet Assistant VBA	Support for saving worksheets as HTML from Visual Basic	None
Lookup Wizard	Wizard to help create formulas to find value in a range	Tools → Lookup
Solver	What-if analysis of data	Tools → Solver

From a developer's perspective, add-ins are Excel applications without a worksheet interface. Instead, add-ins act on objects in the currently loaded workbook. There are two main types of add-ins:

- Code-only add-ins provide user-defined functions that can be used from Excel formulas or within Visual Basic.
- Visual add-ins provide wizards or toolbars to help users performs specific actions.

Some add-ins combine these two types. For example, the Analysis ToolPak VBA provides both the Data Analysis Wizard in Excel and provides access to those analysis functions from Visual Basic.

Code-Only Add-ins

Of the two add-in types, code-only add-ins are the simplest because they have no visual interface. To create a code-only add-in, follow these steps:

1. Create a new workbook, open the Visual Basic Editor, and write your user-defined functions.
2. Set project properties.
3. Optionally, delete unneeded worksheets.
4. Save file as a workbook.
5. Save file as an add-in.
6. Create help page or file for the add-in.
7. Close and test the add-in.

For example, I collected general-purpose procedures from earlier chapters in this book and organized them into several modules in a new workbook, as shown in Figure 22-1.

To set project properties, right-click the Project window and select Properties. I set the sample project properties as shown in Figure 22-2 and listed in Table 22-2.

Table 22-2. Sample add-in project property settings

Tab	Field	Setting
General	Project Name	Ch22
	Project Description	Numeric, text, and file functions
	Help File Name	http://www.excelworkshop.com/SampleHelp/Ch22.aspx
Protection	Lock Project for Viewing	Selected
	Password	Excel2003
	Confirm Password	Excel2003

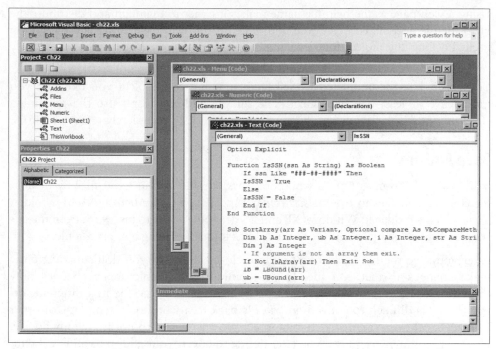

Figure 22-1. Write add-in code

Figure 22-2. Set add-in properties

Using a web page as the help file name makes it easier to maintain and distribute the Help for the add-in. You can even add links on the help page to update the add-in itself. Locking the project for viewing is very common for add-ins since you usually don't want others to alter your code. A simple password is usually sufficient protection.

You can delete the unneeded worksheets from the workbook if you like, but you must leave at least one worksheet. The sample add-in doesn't use the remaining sheet or workbook classes, but there is no way to hide or completely remove them.

Save Add-ins

Why save an add-in as both a workbook (*.xls*) and an add-in (*.xla*) file? By default, Excel saves *.xla* files to the *%UserProfile%\Application Data\Microsoft\AddIns* folder. That folder is hidden in Windows XP and it's generally easier to just work from the *.xls* source file and "compile" the file to the Addins folder by saving it as an *.xla* file.

After you save the file as an Excel add-in, close the file so you don't inadvertently make changes to that *.xla* file. In my opinion, you should make changes only through the *.xls* source file, because you can always save that file in a different format, but it is difficult to convert an *.xla* file back to a workbook, template, or other format. Excel doesn't enforce that approach, so you're free to not follow my advice. However, you may regret it if you later decide to covert your add-in to an Excel template (*.xlt*).

 Help files for add-ins can be created a number of ways. For this sample, I created a web page from the SharePoint document library. See Chapter 6 for more information on creating help files.

Create a Test Workbook

To test the add-in:

1. Close the *.xla* file you just saved.

2. Create a new workbook.

3. Select Tools → Add-Ins. Excel displays the Add-Ins dialog box. Your new add-in should appear in the list of Add-Ins, Available as shown in Figure 22-3.

4. Select the add-in you just created and click OK.

5. Choose Insert → Function and select User Defined from the category list. The functions from your add-in should appear as shown in Figure 22-4.

6. Use Insert Function to create formulas that use the add-in on the test worksheet. Click Help on This Function to see the help page.

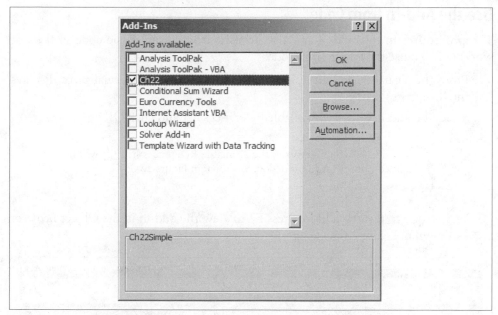

Figure 22-3. Load the add-in

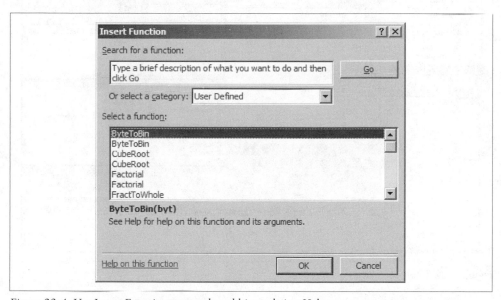

Figure 22-4. Use Insert Function to test the add-in and view Help

Use the Add-in from Code

The procedures in this add-in can also be used from Visual Basic code in the test workbook. To use the add-in from code:

1. From the Visual Basic Editor, choose Tools → References. Visual Basic displays the References dialog.

2. Select the add-in from the Available References list and click OK.

> The add-in won't appear in the Available References list if it was not loaded from the Add-Ins dialog, as shown in Figure 22-3.

3. Write code to test the add-in. Press F2 to view the add-in in the Object Browser as shown in Figure 22-5.

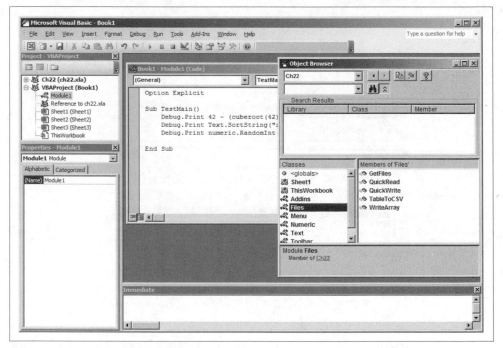

Figure 22-5. Using the add-in from code

Change the Add-in

You can't rebuild the add-in while it is loaded in Excel, and you can't unload the add-in if it is referenced from within Visual Basic. If you are creating the add-in from an *.xls* source file (as I recommend) you must take these steps before making changes:

1. Close any test workbook that contains code referencing the add-in. That removes the lock that prevents the add-in from unloading.
2. Deselect the add-in from the Add-Ins dialog box (Figure 22-3) to unload the file.
3. Open the *.xls* source file and make your changes.
4. Save the *.xls* file as an *.xla* file and then close it.
5. Reselect the add-in in the Add-Ins dialog box.

You don't need to remove the references made in Visual Basic. Just closing those workbooks removes the lock. When you reopen those workbooks, the reference will be updated.

Programming Tips

When creating add-ins, the following tips will help you avoid common pitfalls:

- Avoid referencing external libraries. Any reference that you include in your add-in must be present on the user's machine, and that makes deploying the add-in more difficult.
- Use modules to organize procedures. Module names group the add-in procedures in the Object Browser, as shown in Figure 22-5.
- Use module names that don't conflict with names from the VBA or Excel type libraries. Type libraries have priority, and if you use a module name like Math in your add-in, that module won't support the Auto Complete feature.
- Lock the project for viewing before saving it as an add-in. Otherwise, the Visual Basic Editor will display the add-in in code windows when the user goes to edit a macro. That is confusing for most users.

Visual Add-ins

Visual add-ins interact with the active sheet, selected range, or active workbook through menu items, dialog boxes, and toolbars that you create from within the add-in. By convention, visual add-ins add a menu item to the Tool menu in Excel (see Table 22-1).

Add-ins provide the following events that let you add and remove menu items and toolbars when the add-in is installed or uninstalled:

```
' ThisWorkbook class
Private Sub Workbook_AddinInstall( )
    ' Add menu items and toolbars here.
End Sub

Private Sub Workbook_AddinUninstall( )
    ' Remove menu items and toolbars.
End Sub
```

The `Workbook_Open` and `Workbook_BeforeClose` events aren't as useful from add-ins as the preceding events because they occur too often—whenever Excel opens or closes. The `Workbook_AddinInstall` and `Workbook_AddinUninstall` events occur only when the user selects or deselects the add-in from the Add-Ins dialog (Figure 22-3).

Add a Menu Item

To add a menu item for an add-in, follow these general steps:

1. Get a reference to the Tools pop-up menu on the worksheet's menu bar.
2. Find the location in that menu where you want to add the item. Usually, I add menu items just before the last separator bar (the next-to-last group).
3. Create a new command bar button control and add it to the menu.
4. Set the control's `Tag`, `OnAction`, and `Caption` properties.
5. Optionally repeat the task for the Chart menu bar.

The following code adds a menu item that displays the `CodeToolbar` created in Chapter 19; I've also included the code to remove the menu item since I'll use that next:

```
' Menu code module.
Sub AddMenuItem(Optional cb As String = "Worksheet Menu Bar")
    Dim cpop As CommandBarPopup, cbc As CommandBarControl, _
      loc As Integer
    ' Get the Tools menu.
    Set cpop = Application.CommandBars(cb).FindControl(, 30007)
    ' Find the last separator bar.
    For Each cbc In cpop.Controls
        If cbc.BeginGroup Then loc = cbc.index
    Next
    ' Insert the menu item before the last separator bar.
    Set cbc = cpop.Controls.Add(msoControlButton, , , loc, False)
    cbc.Caption = "&CodeToolbar"
    cbc.Tag = "mnuCodeToolbar"
    cbc.OnAction = "mnuCodeToolbar_Click"
End Sub

' Procedure for menu item's OnAction property.
Sub mnuCodeToolbar_Click()
    Dim cbc As CommandBarButton
    ' Get the menu item
    Set cbc = Application.CommandBars("Worksheet Menu Bar").FindControl( _
      , , "mnuCodeToolbar", , True)
    ' Exit if menu item not found.
    If cbc Is Nothing Then Exit Sub
    ' Toggle the state (adds or removes a check mark
    ' beside the menu item).
    cbc.State = Not cbc.State
    ' Display or hide the toolbar depending on state.
    If cbc.State Then
```

```
            BuildCodeToolbar
        Else
            DeleteCodeToolbar
        End If
    End Sub

    Sub RemoveMenuItem(Optional cb As String = "Worksheet Menu Bar")
        Dim cbc As CommandBarControl
        ' Find the menu item.
        Set cbc = Application.CommandBars(cb).FindControl( _
            , , "mnuCodeHelper", , True)
        ' If it's found, delete it.
        If Not (cbc Is Nothing) Then _
            cbc.Delete
    End Sub
```

The mnuCodeToolbar_Click procedure toggles a check mark on the menu item and displays the CodeToolbar when selected as shown in Figure 22-6.

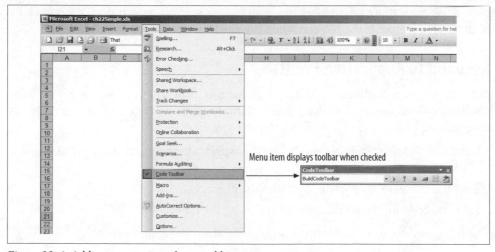

Figure 22-6. Adding a menu item for an add-in

To create the menu item when the add-in is installed, call the AddMenuItem procedure from the Workbook_AddinInstall event in the ThisWorkbook class. While you're there, add some code to remove the menu item when the add-in is uninstalled. The following code shows both procedures:

```
' ThisWorkbook class
Private Sub Workbook_AddinInstall()
    ' Add menu items and toolbars here.
    AddMenuItem "Worksheet Menu Bar"
    AddMenuItem "Chart Menu Bar"
End Sub

Private Sub Workbook_AddinUninstall()
    ' Remove menu items and toolbars.
```

```
        RemoveMenuItem "Worksheet Menu Bar"
        RemoveMenuItem "Chart Menu Bar"
    End Sub
```

The preceding code adds the menu item to both of the built-in Excel menu bars so it is available for both worksheets and charts.

Add a Toolbar

As I discussed in Chapter 19, toolbars can be attached to a file. If you attach a toolbar to an add-in, it will become available whenever the add-in is loaded. The only time you need to create a toolbar in code is when it contains dynamically created controls like those demonstrated by the CodeToolbar sample.

I created that sample for you in Chapter 19 using the BuildCodeToolbar procedure; and I showed how to delete the toolbar in Chapter 19 using the DeleteCodeToolbar procedure. See the sample workbook, or turn back to Chapter 19 to see those examples. I use both those procedures in the following section, which demonstrates how to dynamically update the toolbar when the user activates a new workbook.

Respond to Application Events

One of the key tricks to add-in programming is learning how to respond to application-level events. I showed you how to do that way back in Chapter 4, but in case that slipped by you, I'll spell out the steps again:

1. In the ThisWorkbook class, declare an Application object variable using the WithEvents keyword.
2. In the Workbook_Open event, initialize the object variable.
3. Write code for the application events using the object variable.

The following code illustrates those steps using the CodeToolbar example:

```
' ThisWorkbook class
' Declare an application object WithEvents.
Dim WithEvents m_app As Excel.Application

' Add-in level event.
Private Sub Workbook_Open( )
    ' Initialize the Application object variable so you
    ' can detect events.
    Set m_app = Application
End Sub

' Application-level events.
Private Sub m_app_WorkbookActivate(ByVal Wb As Workbook)
    ' When the active workbook changes, update toolbar.
    BuildCodeToolbar
End Sub
```

```
Private Sub m_app_WorkbookBeforeClose(ByVal Wb As Workbook, Cancel As Boolean)
    ' Remove the toolbar if the workbook closes.
    DeleteCodeToolbar
End Sub
```

 Don't confuse the add-in-level events (Workbook_Open) with the application-level events (m_app_WorkbookActivate and m_app_WorkbookBeforeClose).

You can respond to events on the currently active workbook using a similar technique with the passed-in Wb argument in m_app_WorkbookActivate procedure as shown by the following changes in **bold**:

```
' ThisWorkbook class
Dim WithEvents m_app As Excel.Application
Dim WithEvents m_wb As Workbook

Private Sub m_app_WorkbookBeforeClose(ByVal Wb As Workbook, Cancel As Boolean)
    ' Remove the toolbar if the workbook closes.
    DeleteCodeToolbar
    ' Initialize the workbook object variable
    Set m_wb = Wb
End Sub

' Workbook-level event.
Private Sub m_wb_SheetActivate(ByVal Sh As Object)
    Debug.Print Sh.Name & " is active."
End Sub
```

And you can navigate down the object model to respond to events on the active worksheet, chart, and so on using the same technique.

Set Add-in Properties

The document properties of the source workbook determine the title and description displayed in the Add-Ins dialog. To set the properties of an add-in:

1. Open the source workbook for the add-in.
2. Choose File → Properties. Excel displays the document Properties dialog box (Figure 22-7).
3. Set the properties and click OK.
4. Save the source workbook, then save the file again as an *.xla* file.

The Title property appears in the Add-Ins dialog in the list of available add-ins. The Comments property appears as the description at the bottom of the dialog when the add-in is selected. The other document properties are not displayed, but are available through the AddIn object.

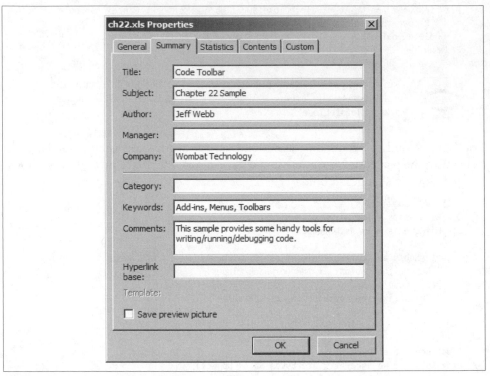

Figure 22-7. Setting add-in document properties

Sign the Add-in

Strictly speaking, add-ins don't have to be signed. By definition, add-ins contain code and the user must take affirmative action to install and load an add-in, so Excel doesn't display security warnings when a user loads an unsigned add-in in Excel.

However, you may want to sign an add-in anyway. There are three reasons for this:

- An unsigned file displays a security warning while you develop the add-in (which is annoying).
- Signing the add-in validates that the add-in is from you and hasn't been changed by someone else.
- Add-ins can potentially be loaded by an external reference from another workbook, which *does* display a security warning if the add-in is unsigned.

See Chapter 6 for instructions on getting a digital signature and signing code.

Distribute the Add-in

The easiest way to distribute an add-in is to copy it to the user's AddIns folder. That is the default location to which Excel saves add-ins, and any add-ins placed there are automatically displayed in the Add-Ins dialog box (Figure 22-3).

The following VBScript file installs an add-in in the user's AddIns folder and loads the add-in in Excel:

```
' InstallAddin.vbs
' Get the objects used by this script.
Dim oXL, oAddin, fso, wsh, srcPath, destPath, addin
addin = "\ch22.xla"
Set oXL = CreateObject("Excel.Application")
Set fso = CreateObject("Scripting.FileSystemObject")
Set wsh = WScript.CreateObject("WScript.Shell")
' Make Excel visible in case something goes wrong.
oXL.Visible = True
' Create a temporary workbook (required to access add-ins)
oXL.Workbooks.Add
' Get the current folder.
srcpath = fso.GetFolder(".")
destPath = wsh.Environment("PROCESS")("HOMEDRIVE") & _
  wsh.Environment("PROCESS")("HOMEPATH") & _
  "\Application Data\Microsoft\Addins"
' Copy the file to the template folder.
fso.CopyFile srcpath & addin, destpath & addin
' Add the add-in to Excel.
Set oAddin = oXL.AddIns.Add(destpath & addin, true)
' Mark the add-in as installed so Excel loads it.
oAddin.Installed = True
' Close Excel.
oXL.Quit
Set oXL = Nothing
```

To use the preceding VBScript installer with your own add-ins:

1. Change the `addin` variable to match your add-in filename.

2. Place the add-in and setup file in the same folder. That can be a public folder on your network, a folder on a CD, or some other media.

3. Instruct the user to run `InstallAddin`.

If you want to install the add-in at a custom location or provide an uninstall facility, you might consider using Visual Studio .NET to create a setup and deployment project:

1. Create a setup and deployment project.

2. Set the project's `Manufacturer` and `ProductName` properties.

3. Add the add-in to the Application Folder in the File System window.

4. Add the file to the `HKEY_CURRENT_USER\Software\Microsoft\Office\11.0\Excel\Add-in Manager` registry key.

5. Build the project.

Setup and deployment projects create Windows installation programs that walk the user through the setup and also provide an uninstall facility. See the Ch22AddinInstall sample project (*Ch22AddinInstall.sln*) for an example.

Work with Add-ins in Code

The previous VBScript sample in "Distribute the Add-in" demonstrates using Excel's `AddIn` object to load an add-in as part of the installation process. That's the primary use of the `AddIns` collection and `AddIn` object: loading, unloading, and enumerating add-ins.

For example, the following code lists the name and state of all the add-ins that are currently installed:

```
Sub ListAddins()
    Dim ad As AddIn
    Debug.Print "Title", "File name", "Loaded?"
    For Each ad In Application.Addins
        Debug.Print ad.Title, ad.FullName, ad.Installed
    Next
End Sub
```

The `Installed` property determines whether installed add-ins are loaded in Excel—not whether they are installed on the user's system as the name suggests. To load an add-in from code, set its `Installed` property to True. To unload it, set `Installed` to False. Use the `Add` method to install an add-in on the user's system.

AddIn and AddIns Members

Use the `AddIns` collection to copy add-ins onto the user's system. Use the `Application` object's `AddIns` property to get a reference to this collection. Use the `AddIn` object to load or unload the add-in in Excel. The `AddIns` collection and `AddIn` object have the following members. Key members (shown in **bold**) are covered in the following reference section:

Add[1]	Application[2]
Author	CLSID
Comments	Count[1]
Creator[2]	**FullName**
Installed	Item[1]
Keywords	Name

Parent[2]	Path
progID	Subject
Title	

[1] Collection only
[2] Object and collection

addins.Add(*Filename*, [*CopyFile*])

Installs an add-in and make it available from the Add-Ins dialog. Returns an add-in object.

Argument	Settings
Filename	The path and filename of the add-in to install.
CopyFile	True copies the file from removable media to the hard disk; False does not copy the file. Ignored if the file is already located on a fixed media.

Set the Installed property to True to load the add-in in Excel.

addin.Author

Returns the value from the Author property of the add-in's source workbook.

addin.Comments

Returns the value from the Comments property of the add-in's source workbook.

addin.FullName

Returns the full path and filename of the add-in.

addin.Installed [= *setting*]

True loads the add-in in Excel; False unloads the add-in.

addin.Keywords

Returns the value from the Keywords property of the add-in's source workbook.

addin.Path

Returns the path of the add-in file.

addin.Subject

Returns the value from the Subject property of the add-in's source workbook.

addin.Title

Returns the value from the Title property of the add-in's source workbook.

CHAPTER 23

Integrating DLLs and COM

VBA and Excel provide an extensive set of objects, properties, and methods that you can use to perform almost any imaginable task. However, in some areas those members don't do exactly what you need or don't do the task as simply as you might like. In those cases, you can extend your set of programming tools by bringing in functions from dynamic link libraries (DLLs) and objects from other Common Object Model (COM) applications.

 DLLs and COM are Windows-only features. They aren't present on the Macintosh.

DLLs grant you access to the low-level functions used by Windows itself. Just about any task that Windows performs can be accomplished in your Visual Basic code by accessing a system DLL.

COM is for higher-level tasks. Excel implements COM as the technology used to expose its objects, properties, and methods to Visual Basic. All of the other Office applications and many non-Microsoft applications implement COM, too. You can use any of those applications from Excel Visual Basic.

 Code used in this chapter and additional samples are available in *ch23.xls*.

Use DLLs

Dynamic link libraries (DLLs) are used everywhere in Windows. Many of the Visual Basic and Excel members merely encapsulate Windows DLL calls—for example, the `Shell` function is equivalent to the Windows `WinExec` function in *kernel32.dll* that is at the core of Windows.

There's little point in using `WinExec` instead of `Shell`; however, many other DLL functions aren't available from Visual Basic or Excel. In general, those functions give you access to low-level tasks that aren't the usual focus of Visual Basic or Excel.

To use a function from a DLL:

1. Find the function you want to use.
2. Declare the function at the module level.
3. Call the function within your code.

Find the Right Function

Windows is enormous, and finding the function for a specific task within its forest of DLLs can be daunting. The best guide through the Win32 API is *Programming Windows* by Charles Petzold (Microsoft Press). The second-best (and free) guide is the online Microsoft Developer's Network found at *http://msdn.microsoft.com*.

You should look to DLLs only when you have a specific task in mind and you've already exhausted possible solutions through the built-in members provided by Visual Basic and Excel. Often, programmers resort to DLL functions when the built-in features of Excel aren't specific enough. For example, the `Wait` method in Excel has a one-second resolution. If you want to pause for a fraction of a second, you need to resort to the `Sleep` DLL function.

One of the best tools for finding Win32 API functions is the API Viewer utility (*APILOAD.EXE*) that shipped with the Visual Basic Standard and Professional Editions, Versions 4.0 through 6.0. To use the API Viewer:

1. Run *APILOAD.EXE*.
2. Choose File → Load Text File and select *WIN32API.TXT*.
3. Choose Declares from the drop-down list and browse through the list of functions or type a few letters to find functions by name as shown in Figure 23-1.

 What if you don't have Visual Basic Professional or Standard Edition? The *WIN32API.TXT* file is freely distributable and you can find it with this book's samples. You can browse that file using Notepad or any other text editor.

Declare and Use DLL Functions

Use the API Viewer (Figure 23-1) or open *WIN32API.TXT* in Notepad to get the declarations of DLL functions you want to use in Visual Basic. The declaration tells Visual Basic how to find the function and what arguments the function expects. For example, the declaration for the `Sleep` function looks like this:

```
' Module level.
Public Declare Sub Sleep Lib "kernel32" _
  (ByVal dwMilliseconds As Long)
```

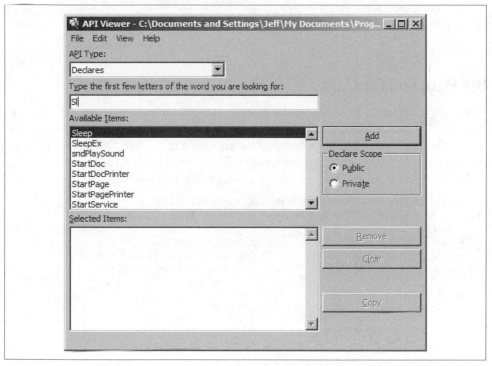

Figure 23-1. Use the API Viewer to hunt for DLL functions

That means the Sleep function is found in *kernel32.dll*, takes a single long-integer argument, and doesn't return a value. Once you declare the function, you can use it in code just like any other procedure:

```
Sub Pause()
    ' Pause 1/2 second.
    Sleep 500
End Sub
```

In Visual Basic terminology, Sleep is a Sub, not a function. However, most DLLs are written in C, which doesn't use that word. In C, all procedures are functions; functions that don't return values are called *void functions*.

However, most DLL functions do return a value, and that value usually indicates whether the function succeeded. If a function returns 0, the function failed. Any other value indicates success. For example, the following code plays *boing.wav*; if the sound can't play, the code displays a message in the Immediate window:

```
Public Declare Function sndPlaySound Lib "winmm.dll" Alias _
    "sndPlaySoundA" (ByVal lpszSoundName As String, ByVal uFlags As Long) _
    As Long

Sub Bounce()
    Dim res As Long
```

```
    res = sndPlaySound("boing", 0)
    If res = 0 Then _
        Debug.Print "Couldn't bounce."
End Sub
```

Use Flags and Constants

The uFlags argument in sndPlaySound is an example of another common C convention: you can often specify options using a long integer comprised of *bit flags*. I discussed those back in Chapter 3, but they haven't been much use up till now. Bit flags are numeric constants that can be combined into a single number. The following code demonstrates using bit flags to play a sound over and over again:

```
Public Declare Function sndPlaySound Lib "winmm.dll" Alias _
  "sndPlaySoundA" (ByVal lpszSoundName As String, ByVal uFlags As Long) _
  As Long
Public Const SND_ASYNC = &H1        ' play asynchronously
Public Const SND_LOOP = &H8         ' loop the sound until next sndPlaySound
Public Const SND_SYNC = &H0         ' play synchronously (default)

Sub BeginBouncing( )
    sndPlaySound "boing", SND_ASYNC Or SND_LOOP
End Sub

Sub StopBouncing( )
    sndPlaySound "boing", SND_SYNC
End Sub
```

I included StopBouncing because listening to *boing.wav* over and over again gets *really* annoying. You can find constants for each function by searching for the function by name at *http://msdn.microsoft.com*, then you can find the corresponding values for those constants using the API Viewer or by searching *WIN32API.TXT*.

Work with Strings

The quickest way to end your DLL programming experience is to pass a DLL an uninitialized string. For example, the following code will result in the error shown in Figure 23-2:

```
Public Declare Function GetTempFileName Lib "kernel32" Alias _
  "GetTempFileNameA" (ByVal lpszPath As String, _
  ByVal lpPrefixString As String, ByVal wUnique As Long, _
  ByVal lpTempFileName As String) As Long

Sub Crash( )
    Dim fil As String, res As Long
    res = GetTempFileName(ThisWorkbook.Path, "xl", 0, fil)
    Debug.Print fil
End Sub
```

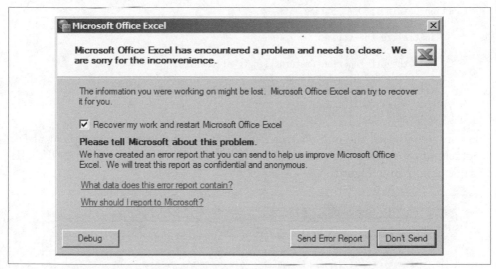

Figure 23-2. You'll crash if you don't initialize your strings

Don't send Microsoft this error report—it was your fault! To avoid this problem, fill a string with spaces before you pass it to a DLL. You need to make the string long enough to fit the passed-in data; 128 characters is usually sufficient:

```
Function CreateTempFile() As String
    Dim fil As String, res As Long
    ' Initialize the string!
    fil = Space(128)
    ' Pass the string to the DLL function.
    res = GetTempFileName(ThisWorkbook.Path, "xl", 0, fil)
    ' Return the string.
    CreateTempFile = fil
End Function
```

Figure 23-2 underscores the risks of working with DLLs—you are leaving the relatively safe world provided by Excel and are performing without a safety net. Mistakes can crash Excel and potentially shut down Windows. Save your work frequently when working with DLLs.

C strings end with a null character (ASCII 0). That's different than Visual Basic, which prepends each string with its length. In some cases, like the preceding example, the null character is ignored. However, in other cases, you need to trim off the excess characters when the DLL function returns. In those cases, the DLL function returns the length of the string argument; the GetWindowsDirectory function is a good example:

```
Public Declare Function GetWindowsDirectory Lib "kernel32" _
    Alias "GetWindowsDirectoryA" (ByVal lpBuffer As String, _
    ByVal nSize As Long) As Long
```

```
Function GetWinDir( ) As String
    Dim wdir As String, res As Integer
    ' Initialize the string.
    wdir = Space(128)
    ' Call the DLL function (returns length of result).
    res = GetWindowsDirectory(wdir, 128)
    ' Trim off excess before returning the result.
    WinDir = Left(wdir, res)
End Function
```

You can actually see the null character in the string if you set a breakpoint at End Function, run the preceding code, and then position the mouse pointer over the wdir variable as shown in Figure 23-3.

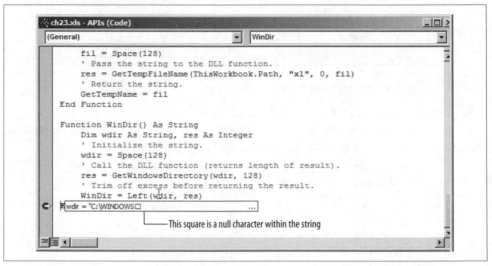

Figure 23-3. In some strings, you need to trim off nulls

The CreateTempFile and GetWinDir examples demonstrate how to create *wrappers* for DLL functions. Wrappers convert the DLL functions into Visual Basic functions that are much less confusing to use elsewhere in code. It is good programming practice to put all of your DLL declarations in a single module and include wrappers for each of those functions.

Handle Exceptions

Most DLL functions return a value indicating whether they succeeded. A return value of 0 indicates that the function did not complete its task. That type of exception is different from the error in Figure 23-2, which halts everything.

Just as with Visual Basic functions, you should anticipate and handle exceptions from DLL functions in your code, particularly when working with nonmemory resources like hard disks, printers, and other devices. To handle an exception from a DLL:

1. Call the DLL function.

2. Check the value returned by the function.

3. If the returned value is zero, handle the exception and optionally check `Err.LastDllError` to identify what went wrong.

The following changes to `CreateTempFile` demonstrate detecting and handling exceptions from a DLL function. If the caller tries to create a temporary file at an invalid path, `GetTempFileName` returns 0 and the code displays a message in the Immediate window. Optionally, you could uncomment the `Error` statement to raise a trappable Visual exception:

```
Function CreateTempFile(Optional path As String = "") As String
    Dim fil As String, res As Long
    ' Initialize the string!
    fil = Space(128)
    If path = "" Then path = ThisWorkbook.path
    ' Pass the string to the DLL function.
    res = GetTempFileName(path, "xl", 0, fil)
    ' If error, return empty string.
    If res = 0 Then
        Debug.Print "Error creating temp file: " & Err.LastDllError
        ' Optionally, raise can't Create temporary file error.
        ' Error 322
    End If
    ' Trim the excess off the string and return it.
    CreateTempFile = Left(fil, res)
End Function
```

The `Err` object's `LastDllError` property returns the error number from the DLL function. Those numbers are listed as `ERROR_xxx` constants in *WIN32API.TXT*, but it is almost impossible to know which error codes to expect from a DLL. The easiest way to solve this problem is to pass in values you know to be invalid and see what error code is returned. You can then search *WIN32API.TXT* to get the descriptive constant.

For example, typing the following line of code in the Immediate window displays error code 276:

```
?CreateTempFile("z:\")
```

A quick search of *WIN32API.TXT* for 267 yields this constant:

```
'   The directory name is invalid.
Const ERROR_DIRECTORY = 267&
```

I could use this constant to create a more descriptive message, but in reality there's not much I can do other than report the error and end the operation as gracefully as possible.

One of the side effects of returning 0 when an error occurs is that Left(fil, res) returns an empty string whenever there's an error. That's a good technique because it makes it easy to check if the function succeeded elsewhere in code, as shown here:

```
Sub TestCreateFile( )
    Dim tmp As String
    ' Get a temporary file.
    tmp = CreateTempFile
    If tmp <> "" Then
        ' Open the file and write some data
        QuickWrite "This is some data", tmp, True
        ' Display the file in Notepad.
        Shell "notepad.exe " & tmp
    Else
        Debug.Print "CreateTempFile failed."
    End If
End Sub
```

Use COM Applications

When Microsoft first developed COM, the company envisioned Office applications as building blocks that programmers could use to assemble customer-specific solutions. That vision has partly come true—it's not uncommon for a Word document to include data from Excel or for a PowerPoint presentation to use Word and Excel data—however, that reality is not nearly as grand as Microsoft's early marketing demos.

Meanwhile, Excel's feature set has grown to include its own spellchecker, drawing tools, mail, and Internet capabilities. In many ways, there is less reason to program across applications than there once was.

But here's the kicker: most of those new features were made possible because Microsoft implemented them as COM objects. That's the reason Excel's drawing tools look suspiciously like Visio objects. In fact, Microsoft's vision came true; it's just that Microsoft became the solution provider in the Office realm.

Is COM Modular?

While I was at Microsoft working on OLE 2.0 (later called COM), I complained to Brian Johnson about all the DLLs you had to install and register to get automation to work. "It's not modular," I whined. Brian looked at me and replied "It *is* modular; you just need all the modules!"

Program Other Office Applications

You can program any of the Office applications from Excel by following these steps:

1. In the Visual Basic Editor, choose Tools → References and select the Office application from the list of Available References (Figure 23-4) and click OK to close the dialog.

2. Declare an object variable using one of the Office application's objects.

3. Create an instance of that object.

4. Use the properties and methods of the object.

5. Close the object and set the object variable to Nothing when you are done.

Figure 23-4 shows establishing a reference to the Word object library. COM applications expose their object through type libraries (*.tlb*) or object libraries (*.olb*). Those two kinds of libraries are often used interchangeably and the words mean basically the same thing.

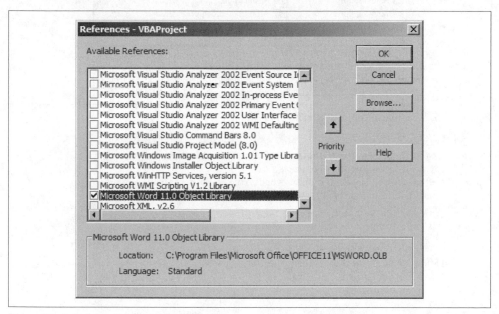

Figure 23-4. Referencing Word from Excel

Once you've created a reference to the application, you can view the objects the application provides in the Object Browser (Figure 23-5).

The following code demonstrates the programming steps for working with the Word application:

```
' Worksheet class
' Step 2: Declare object.
Dim WithEvents m_wd As Word.Application
```

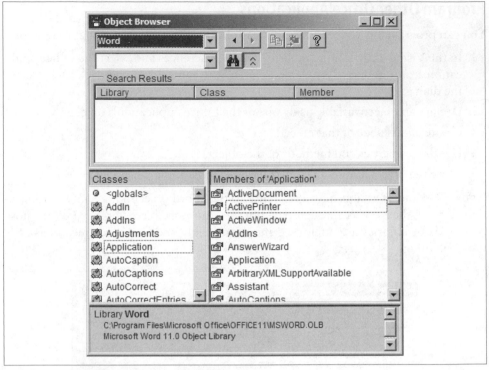

Figure 23-5. Browsing the objects from an application

```
Sub StartWord()
    ' Step 3: Create a new instance of the application.
    Set m_wd = New Word.Application
    ' Step 4: Use properties and methods (makes Word visible).
    m_wd.Visible = True
End Sub

Sub CloseWord()
    ' Step 5: Close Word.
    If Not (m_wd Is Nothing) Then m_wd.Quit
    ' Set the variable to Nothing.
    Set m_wd = Nothing
End Sub
```

There are a couple key things to point out in the preceding code:

- I wrote this code as part of a worksheet class so I could intercept events from Word by declaring the object variable WithEvents. You can't use WithEvents from a module.

- Not all objects are creatable. Within Word, you can create new instances of the Application and Document objects. To get other objects, you have to navigate down through the object model from one of those creatable objects.

Integrate Word

One of the challenges of integrating COM applications is that the organization and behavior of objects are inconsistent across applications. For example, the Excel and Word Application objects behave differently when their object variables are set to Nothing: Excel quits if the application is not visible and there are no open workbooks, but Word continues running.

For that reason, it is always a good idea to make objects visible when working across applications. That way, the user can easily close the application if she needs to. It is also a good idea to call Quit and set the object variable to Nothing.

Declare Application object variables at the class or module level so they are available to all of the procedures in the class or module. Using local variables for Application objects is impractical because it is difficult to get a reference to a specific instance of an application once it is running.

The following code demonstrates how to use the class-level Application object created earlier to copy a selected range from Excel into a new Word document:

```
Sub PasteRangeToWord( )
    Dim doc As Word.Document
    ' If a range of cells is selected.
    If TypeName(Selection) = "Range" Then
        ' Start word if it's not already running.
        If m_wd Is Nothing Then StartWord
        ' Copy the selected cells.
        Selection.Copy
        ' Create a new document
        Set doc = m_wd.Documents.Add
        ' Paste the range into the Word document.
        m_wd.Selection.Paste
    End If
End Sub
```

Since the Application object was declared WithEvents, you can respond to Word events from within your Excel code:

```
Dim WithEvents m_doc As Word.Document

' Runs when a new Word document is created.
Private Sub m_wd_NewDocument(ByVal doc As Word.Document)
    Debug.Print "Created Word document."
    ' Get the Document object to detect events.
    Set m_doc = doc
End Sub

' Runs when the Word document closes.
Private Sub m_doc_Close( )
    Debug.Print "Closed document."
End Sub
```

The preceding code uses the m_wd_NewDocument event to initialize the m_doc object variable so your Excel code can respond to events that occur on the new document.

Automate PowerPoint

You can use the same steps to automate PowerPoint that you used to automate Word from Excel. PowerPoint has two creatable objects: Application and Presentation, but only the Application object exposes events.

The following code demonstrates how to create a new slide in a presentation using a selected range of cells from Excel:

```
' Worksheet class.
Dim WithEvents m_ppt As PowerPoint.Application
Dim m_pres As PowerPoint.Presentation

Sub StartPPT()
    Set m_ppt = New PowerPoint.Application
    m_ppt.Visible = True
End Sub

Sub PasteRangeToPPT()
    Dim sld As PowerPoint.Slide, sh As PowerPoint.Shape
    ' If a range of cells is selected.
    If TypeName(Selection) = "Range" Then
        ' Start PowerPoint if it's not already running.
        If m_ppt Is Nothing Then StartPPT
        ' Copy the selected cells.
        Selection.Copy
        ' Create a new document
        If m_pres Is Nothing Then _
          Set m_pres = m_ppt.Presentations.Add
        ' Paste the range into the PowerPoint document.
        Set sld = m_pres.Slides.Add(1, ppLayoutClipartAndText)
        ' Add a title.
        Set sh = sld.Shapes(1)
        sh.TextFrame.TextRange.Text = ActiveSheet.Name
        ' Paste the range.
        Set sh = sld.Shapes(3)
        sh.TextFrame.TextRange.Paste
        ' Replace second shape with a logo.
        Set sh = sld.Shapes(2)
        sld.Shapes.AddPicture ThisWorkbook.path & "\logo.bmp", _
          False, True, sh.Left, sh.Top
        sh.Delete
    End If
End Sub

Sub ClosePPT()
    ' Step 5: Close PowerPoint.
    If Not (m_ppt Is Nothing) Then m_ppt.Quit
    ' Set the variable to Nothing.
```

```
    Set m_ppt = Nothing
End Sub

Private Sub m_ppt_NewPresentation(ByVal Pres As PowerPoint.Presentation)
    Debug.Print "Created presentation."
End Sub
```

The preceding code is similar to the Word example; however, PowerPoint uses Presentation, Slide, and Shape objects rather than Word's Document, Paragraph, and Range objects.

Handle Exceptions

When using COM applications, exceptions are handled as trappable errors. To start detecting exceptions, use the On Error Resume Next statement. To stop detecting exceptions, use the On Error Goto 0 statement.

There are other ways to detect exceptions in Visual Basic, but the preceding technique is the most useful one when working with COM applications because the error codes generated are not very specific. You really have to know what operation was just performed in order to anticipate the exceptions that can occur—the error code tells you almost nothing.

For example, the following additions (in **bold**) to previous code show how to anticipate exceptions working with Word from Excel:

```
Sub PasteRangeToWord()
    Dim doc As Word.Document
    ' If a range of cells is selected.
    If TypeName(Selection) = "Range" Then
        ' Start word if it's not already running.
        If m_wd Is Nothing Then StartWord
        ' Copy the selected cells.
        Selection.Copy
        ' Detect exceptions here.
        On Error Resume Next
        ' Create a new document
        Set doc = m_wd.Documents.Add
        ' Paste the range into the Word document.
        m_wd.Selection.Paste
        If Err Then
            ' Display message
            MsgBox "Could not paste. " & _
                "Make sure Word can run and try again.", vbExclamation And vbOKOnly
            CloseWord
        End If
        On Error GoTo 0
    End If
End Sub

Sub CloseWord()
    ' Step 5: Close Word.
```

```
    On Error Resume Next
    If Not (m_wd Is Nothing) Then m_wd.Quit
    ' Set the variable to Nothing.
    Set m_wd = Nothing
    Set m_doc = Nothing
    On Error GoTo 0
End Sub
```

In PasteRangeToWord are any number of different exceptions that might occur accessing the Word Document object at runtime. Since Word is visible, the user might close the document or quit Word itself. In those cases, you can't recover; you just notify the user and clean up so the procedure might work the next time. The situation is more straightforward in CloseWord. Quit fails only if that instance of Word has already closed, so it's safe to ignore the exception and reset the module-level variables.

If you like, you can add a line to display the error codes in the Immediate window to help during debugging:

```
    Debug.Print Err.Number, Err.Description
```

Not all COM applications are religious about raising exceptions. PowerPoint just waits if it can't overwrite a file. After a few seconds, it asks the user to try again. That's problematic for programmers because the application looks "hung" during the wait and the user is likely to start clicking on stuff and pressing keys at random. If the user cancels saving, PowerPoint does return an informative error message; however, the error code is a hexadecimal number, as shown by the following Immediate Windows statements:

```
?Err.Number, Err.Description
-2147467259   Method 'SaveAs' of object '_Presentation' failed
?hex(-2147467259)
80004005
```

 It's not unCOMmon to get unusual-looking error numbers. Use the Hex function to convert them to hexadecimal.

Get Help on Objects

If you're familiar with the Excel object model, you're likely to be confused by the object models of the other Office applications. I don't think that's an indictment of their design or a vindication of Excel's. It's just that the concept of a document and how to get at items with that document is different in each application.

There are several ways to address this problem:

- Use the Object Browser to search for common method names, like Select, Paste, Save, and Open. Often that task-oriented search will lead you to the object that you need to use to perform the task.

- Open the application's VBA help file directly rather than using context-sensitive Help. In Excel 2003, context-sensitive Help doesn't permit searching the file, which is a serious handicap. Microsoft copies the Office VBA help files to *C:\Program Files\Microsoft Office\OFFICE11\1033* by default. You can also get help from the Object Browser.

- Look for samples. Use Google to search for answers within newsgroups at *http://groups.google.com/* or check out Office online at *http://office.microsof.com/*.

For COM applications from other vendors, check the company's web site. Often help on programming objects is not part of the user documentation.

CHAPTER 24
Getting Data from the Web

Today it is hard to remember a time when the Web didn't matter, but it wasn't that long ago that it didn't even exist. Because Excel was created long before the Web existed, it has adapted as the Web evolved. There are now three main approaches to retrieving data from the Web:

Web queries

> Retrieve data directly from a web page and import that data into a query table on an Excel spreadsheet. Although this was one of the first web access features added to Excel (introduced in 1997), it is still very useful.

Web services

> Execute applications remotely over the Web to return results in XML format. The number of services available over the Web is growing quickly as this standard is becoming broadly adopted. Web services provide a standardized way of exchanging parameters and retrieving results over the Web—something that is missing from web queries.

Database access over the Web

> Is now available through most database software. Since the Internet is like any other computer network, this technique is much the same as database access over a local network and is not covered in this chapter.

This chapter describes how to use web queries and web services to retrieve data from the Web and import it into Excel. The samples in this chapter demonstrate a variety of programming tasks with these two approaches, including passing parameters, formatting results, getting data asynchronously, and displaying results through XML maps.

 Code used in this chapter and additional samples are available in *ch24.xls*.

Perform Web Queries

Web queries are a quick way to import data from a web page into a worksheet using a QueryTable object. To perform a web query:

1. From the Data menu, choose Import External Data, then choose New Web Query. Excel displays the Edit Web Query dialog shown in Figure 24-1.

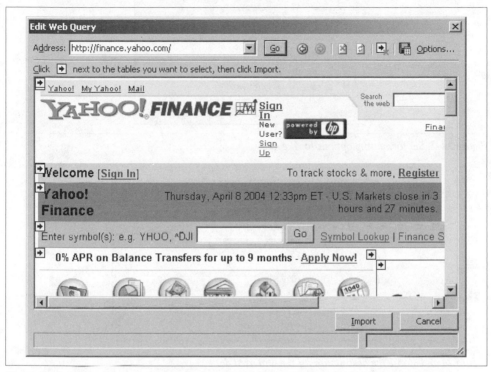

Figure 24-1. Use web queries to import data directly from a web page

2. Type the address of the web page you want to import data from in the Address bar and click Go to navigate to that page. It is usually easiest to find the page you want in your browser, then cut and paste that address into the Edit Web Query dialog box.

3. Excel places small yellow boxes next to the items you can import from the page. Click on the item or items you want to import and Excel changes the yellow box to a green check mark.

4. Click the Options button to set how Excel formats imported items. Formatting options are shown in Figure 24-2.

5. Close the Options dialog box and click Import. Excel displays the Import Data dialog box shown in Figure 24-3.

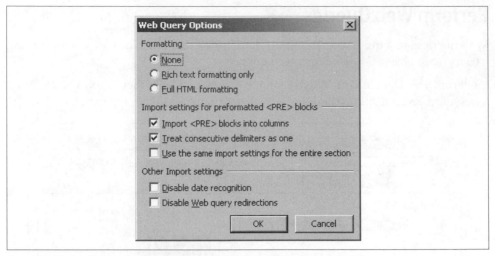

Figure 24-2. Set formatting options for the query

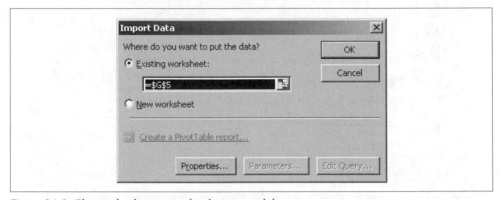

Figure 24-3. Choose the destination for the imported data

6. Click Properties to determine how the query is performed, such as how the data is refreshed. Figure 24-4 shows the query property settings.

7. Close the Properties dialog and click OK to import the data.

Figure 24-5 shows a real-time stock quote and quote history imported from the Yahoo! web site. Yahoo! is a good source for this type of web query because it is a free service and doesn't require you to register or sign in.

If you record the preceding web query, you'll get code that looks something like this:

```
With ActiveSheet.QueryTables.Add(Connection:= _
    "URL;http://finance.yahoo.com/q/ecn?s=SNDK", Destination:=Range("A2"))
    .Name = "Real-Time Quote"
    .FieldNames = True
    .RowNumbers = False
    .FillAdjacentFormulas = False
```

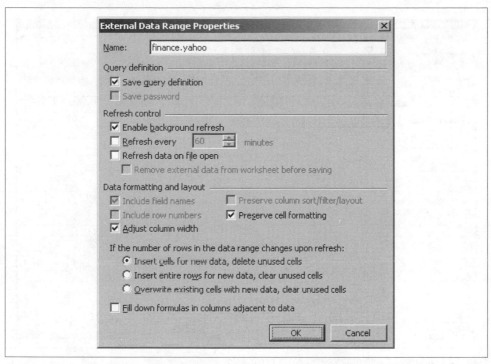

Figure 24-4. Use the Properties page to name the query, set how data is refreshed, and set how cells are inserted

```
    .PreserveFormatting = True
    .RefreshOnFileOpen = False
    .BackgroundQuery = True
    .RefreshStyle = xlOverwriteCells
    .SavePassword = False
    .SaveData = True
    .AdjustColumnWidth = True
    .RefreshPeriod = 0
    .WebSelectionType = xlSpecifiedTables
    .WebFormatting = xlWebFormattingNone
    .WebTables = "22"
    .WebPreFormattedTextToColumns = True
    .WebConsecutiveDelimitersAsOne = True
    .WebSingleBlockTextImport = False
    .WebDisableDateRecognition = False
    .WebDisableRedirections = False
    .Refresh BackgroundQuery:=False
    End With

With ActiveSheet.QueryTables.Add(Connection:= _
  "URL;http://finance.yahoo.com/q/hp?a=01&b=5&c=2003&d=01&e=5&f=2004&g=d&s=sndk" _
  , Destination:=Range("A9"))
    .Name = "Price History"
    .FieldNames = True
```

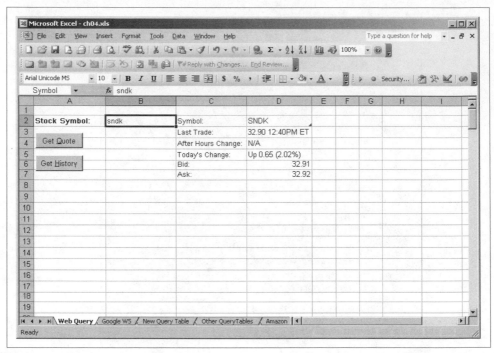

Figure 24-5. Using a web query to get stock price data

```
      .RowNumbers = False
      .FillAdjacentFormulas = False
      .PreserveFormatting = True
      .RefreshOnFileOpen = False
      .BackgroundQuery = True
      .RefreshStyle = xlOverwriteCells
      .SavePassword = False
      .SaveData = True
      .AdjustColumnWidth = True
      .RefreshPeriod = 0
      .WebSelectionType = xlSpecifiedTables
      .WebFormatting = xlWebFormattingNone
      .WebTables = "30"
      .WebPreFormattedTextToColumns = True
      .WebConsecutiveDelimitersAsOne = True
      .WebSingleBlockTextImport = False
      .WebDisableDateRecognition = False
      .WebDisableRedirections = False
      .Refresh BackgroundQuery:=False
   End With
```

Some key properties and methods shown in **bold** in the preceding sample bear mention here:

- The Add method creates the query and adds it to the worksheet.

- The RefreshStyle property tells Excel to overwrite existing data rather than to insert new cells each time the query is refreshed.

- The `WebTables` property identifies which item from the page to import. Excel assigns an index to each item on the page, and you can import one or more items or the entire page if `WebSelectionType` is set to `xlEntirePage`.
- The `Refresh` method imports the data onto the worksheet. Without this method, the query results are not displayed.

The query itself consists of the `Connection`, `WebTables`, and formatting properties. If you save the web query to a query file (*.iqy*), the data looks like this:

```
WEB
1
http://finance.yahoo.com/q/hp?a=01&b=5&c=2003&d=01&e=5&f=2004&g=d&s=sndk

Selection=30
Formatting=None
PreFormattedTextToColumns=True
ConsecutiveDelimitersAsOne=True
SingleBlockTextImport=False
DisableDateRecognition=False
DisableRedirections=False
```

When Excel updates a web query, a small, green globe is displayed in the status bar at the bottom of the screen, as shown in Figure 24-6. This symbol indicates that the query is being refreshed from the Internet.

Figure 24-6. Excel is refreshing the query from the Internet

Modify a Web Query

You can modify a web query by right-clicking on the query and selecting Edit Query. In many cases, however, you'll want a more automated approach. For example, you may want to let the user change the stock symbol in the previous sample. To do that, use code to:

1. Change the `Connection` property of the query.
2. Refresh the query.

For example, the following code allows the user to enter a stock symbol in a named range on the worksheet to get current and historical price data for that stock:

```
Dim ws As Worksheet, qt As QueryTable
Set ws = ThisWorkbook.Sheets("Web Query")
Set qt = ws.QueryTables("Real-Time Quote")
qt.Connection = "URL;http://finance.yahoo.com/q/ecn?s=" & _
   ws.Range("Symbol").Value
qt.Refresh
Set qt = ws.QueryTables("Price History")
qt.Connection =
```

```
"URL;http://finance.yahoo.com/q/hp?a=01&b=5&c=2003&d=01&e=5&f=2004&g=d&s="&_
_ws.[Symbol].Value
qt.Refresh
```

If you run the preceding code, you may notice that the query is not updated right away. By default, web queries are done in the background asynchronously. This avoids tying up Excel while the web site responds to the query, but it can cause an error if you refresh the query again before the first request has had a chance to respond. You can avoid this by not performing the query in the background. For example, the following code turns off asynchronous queries, waiting for a response before executing the next line:

```
qt.BackgroundQuery = False
qt.Refresh
```

or, more simply:

```
qt.Refresh False
```

This causes Excel to wait while the query completes. During this time, the user can't edit cells or perform other tasks. If this is too much of a burden, use the QueryTable object's Refreshing property to avoid asynchronous collisions:

```
Set qt = ws.QueryTables("Real-Time Quote")
If Not qt.Refreshing Then
    qt.Connection = "URL;http://finance.yahoo.com/q/ecn?s=" & _
        ws.[Symbol].Value
    qt.Refresh
Else
    MsgBox "Similar query is pending, please wait a second and try again."
End If
```

The preceding code checks whether the web query is already executing before calling Refresh. If a previous query is still executing, the user is told to try again later. Notice that this code checks the status of a query performed by a single query table. Other, different query tables may have pending results without causing a collision—you need to check the Refreshing property of only the target query table before attempting to change or refresh a query.

Perform Periodic Updates

If the data in a web query changes frequently, you may want to have Excel automatically update the information periodically. Since web queries already run asynchronously in the background, getting them to update periodically is a simple matter of setting a property:

```
Set qt = ws.QueryTables("Real-Time Quote")
qt.RefreshPeriod = 1
```

Now, the query will update every minute. To turn off the background query, set the RefreshPeriod to 0 as shown here:

```
qt.RefreshPeriod = 0
```

Interestingly, the BackgroundQuery property can be False and you can still perform periodic queries. In that case, the Excel user interface pauses periodically whenever the query is being refreshed.

Trap QueryTable Events

Performing web queries in the background can seem a little strange—particularly if they are set to refresh periodically. Most Excel actions are synchronous, and it might surprise a user to see Excel pause for a second, update some cells, and then continue on as if nothing happened. This can become a big problem if the source of the web query changes and causes the web query to fail—the user will see an error message periodically and may not know what to do or how to fix it (Figure 24-7).

Figure 24-7. Failed web queries may display errors asynchronously

To handle errors from asynchronous web queries, you must hook in to the QueryTable events. You have to declare a QueryTable object variable using the WithEvents keyword in order to trap its events. WithEvents can be used in only a class module or an Excel object module (such as the code module for a worksheet or workbook).

For example, to handle asynchronous events for a QueryTable in the wsWebQuery worksheet module, follow these steps:

1. Display the code window for the worksheet by double-clicking on wsWebQuery in the Visual Studio Project Explorer.

2. Add the following declaration to the worksheet's code module at the class level (outside of a procedure definition):

    ```
    Dim WithEvents qt As QueryTable
    ```

3. Select the qt object in the object list at the top of the code window, and then select AfterRefresh from the event list to create an empty event procedure.

4. Add the following code to disable/enable the command buttons and to get feedback from the user if an error occurs:

    ```
    Private Sub qt_BeforeRefresh(Cancel As Boolean)
        ' Disable command button.
        cmdQuote.Enabled = False
    End Sub

    Private Sub qt_AfterRefresh(ByVal Success As Boolean)
    ```

```
        ' If update failed, get feedback.
        If Not Success Then
            If MsgBox("An error occurred getting Web data. " & _
                "Cancel future updates?", vbYesNo, "Web Query") = vbYes Then _
                qt.RefreshPeriod = 0
        End If
        ' Reenable command button.
        cmdQuote.Enabled = True
    End Sub
```

5. Write code to initialize the QueryTable object and to begin updates. For example, the following procedure hooks an existing QueryTable up to the event handlers defined earlier and sets the stock symbol the query uses:

```
Private Sub cmdQuote_Click( )
    ' Get the QueryTable and hook it to the event handler object.
    Set qt = ActiveSheet.QueryTables("Real-Time Quote")
    ' Set the query.
    qt.Connection = "URL;http://finance.yahoo.com/q/ecn?s=" & [Symbol].Value
    ' Set the refresh period and make sure it's done asynchronously.
    qt.RefreshPeriod = 1
    qt.BackgroundQuery = True
    ' Refresh the data now.
    qt.Refresh
End Sub
```

Now, the user can stop the automatic updates if the query fails.

One of the really strange things that can occur while you are working with asynchronous events in Excel is that the event may run while you are editing it in Visual Basic. Often this will result in a runtime error because you haven't completed the code you were in the process of writing. It is a good idea to stop periodic updates while working on query table event code. You can do this by setting the query table's RefreshPeriod property to 0 in the Immediate window.

Anticipating potential asynchronous collisions can be a little tricky. One general way to deal with these is to lock out other operations in the BeforeRefresh event and reenable operations in the AfterRefresh event by enabling and disabling the command button as shown in Step 4. That prevents the user from changing a query while it is pending. Another way is to check the Refreshing property (shown earlier). A final solution is not to use asynchronous queries at all.

For example, the following code gets the price history for a stock. Since price history data isn't very volatile, the code performs the query synchronously and waits for the result:

```
' Displays one year of the current symbol's price history.
Private Sub cmdHistory_Click( )
    Dim ws As Worksheet, qt2 As QueryTable, conn As String
    Set ws = ThisWorkbook.ActiveSheet
    ' Build query string.
    conn = "URL;http://chart.yahoo.com/d?" & YahooDates(Date - 365, Date) & _
        ws.[Symbol].Value
```

```
      ' Get query
      Set qt2 = ws.QueryTables("Price History_1")
      ' Clear old history
      qt2.ResultRange.Clear
      ' Set connection property ·
      qt2.Connection = conn
      ' Make sure background queries are off.
      qt2.BackgroundQuery = False
      ' Refresh data
      qt2.Refresh
  End Sub

  ' Converts start and end dates to Yahoo! query string for
  ' stock history.
  Function YahooDates(dtstart As Date, dtend As Date) As String
      ' Query sample string from Yahoo! has this form:
      ' a=10&b=4&c=2003&d=1&e=5&f=2004&g=d&s=sndk
      Dim str As String
      str = "a=" & Month(dtstart) - 1 & "&b=" & Day(dtstart) & _
      "&c=" & Year(dtstart) & "&d=" & Month(dtend) - 1 & _
      "&e=" & Day(dtend) & "&f=" & Year(dtend) & "&g=d&s="
      Debug.Print str
      YahooDates = str
  End Function
```

When you run the preceding code, Excel changes the mouse pointer to the wait symbol and won't accept user actions till the query returns. This provides a much simpler logical path for programming.

Manage Web Queries

Most of the preceding samples get an existing QueryTable, modify its properties, and then call Refresh. I could have used the QueryTables collection's Add method to create these queries on the fly; however, you need to remember to delete previously created QueryTables.

For example, the following code creates three new query tables on the active worksheet:

```
Dim ws As Worksheet, qt As QueryTable, i As Integer
Set ws = ActiveSheet
For i = 1 To 3
    Set qt = ws.QueryTables.Add("URL;http://finance.yahoo.com/q/ecn?s=yhoo", [A12])
    qt.Name = "Temp Query"
    qt.WebTables = "22"
    qt.WebSelectionType = xlSpecifiedTables
    qt.WebFormatting = xlWebFormattingNone
    qt.BackgroundQuery = False
    qt.RefreshStyle = xlOverwriteCells
    qt.Refresh
Next
```

When this code runs, it creates three query tables on the worksheet named Temp_ Query, Temp_Query_1, and Temp_Query_2, respectively. There's no easy way to manage query tables through the Excel user interface; however, if you press Ctrl-G, you'll see the names for the new query tables listed in the Go To dialog box (Figure 24-8).

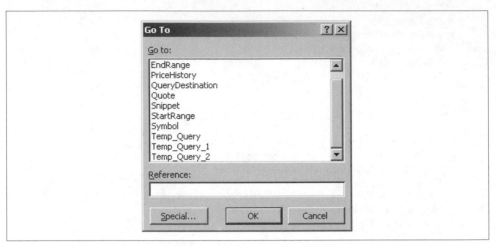

Figure 24-8. Excel automatically numbers query tables that have the same base name

It's possible to manually delete query tables by going to the named range and selecting Clear All, but that leaves the name in the worksheet, and subsequent names will be indexed _4, _5, and so on. The easiest way to clean up mistaken or trial query tables is to write some code to help you remove them. For example, the following procedure lists each query table on a worksheet and lets you remove or keep it:

```
Sub RemoveOldQueries( )
    Dim ws As Worksheet, qt As QueryTable, nm As Name
    Set ws = ActiveSheet
    For Each qt In ws.QueryTables
        If MsgBox("OK to delete " & qt5.Name & "?", vbYesNo, _
        "Web Queries") = vbYes Then
            qt.Delete
        End If
    Next
    For Each nm In ws.Names
        If MsgBox("OK to delete " & nm.Name & "?", vbYesNo, _
        "Names") = vbYes Then
            nm.Delete
        End If
    Next
End Sub
```

Getting rid of unneeded query tables on a worksheet can seem like an unimportant housekeeping chore, but it is very important to avoid having redundant or unneeded queries running in the background. Background queries degrade performance, spontaneously connect to the Internet, and can generate asynchronous errors as mentioned earlier. This can really confuse users!

Limitations of Web Queries

Web queries are great for the ad hoc import of data onto a worksheet, but they rely on the position of elements on the page. If the structure of the source web page changes, the query may break. This means that web queries aren't well-suited for deployed solutions, since you are likely to get a great number of support calls if the source web page changes or moves.

Also, you've got to compose complicated site-specific Connection properties (query strings) if you want to perform customized queries. The YahooDates helper function shown earlier is a good example of the type of work you have to do to get a web query to work correctly with variable data such as variable date ranges. Each web site has its own system of sending and receiving data through query strings and it can be difficult to reverse-engineer those query strings correctly.

These limitations are not present when using web services—that technique provides both a stable platform and a well-defined programming interface. However, web services are not available for all data on the Internet so, in many, many cases, web queries are still very useful.

QueryTable and QueryTables Web Query Members

Query tables are general-purpose objects that import data from a variety of sources including text files and databases. Many of the QueryTable object members apply only to those data sources, and not to web queries. Therefore, the members covered in this section (shown in **bold**) are specific to web queries:

Add[1]	AdjustColumnWidth
AfterRefresh	Application[2]
BackgroundQuery	BeforeRefresh
CancelRefresh	CommandText
CommandType	**Connection**
Count[1]	Creator[2]
Delete	**Destination**
EditWebPage	**EnableEditing**
EnableRefresh	**FetchedRowOverflow**
FieldNames	**FillAdjacentFormulas**
HasAutoFormat	ListObject
MaintainConnection	Name
Parameters	Parent[2]
PostText	PreserveColumnInfo
PreserveFormatting	**QueryType**
Recordset	**Refresh**
Refreshing	**RefreshOnFileOpen**
RefreshPeriod	**RefreshStyle**
ResetTimer	**ResultRange**

RobustConnect	RowNumbers
SaveAsODC	SaveData
SavePassword	SourceConnectionFile
SourceDataFile	Sql
TablesOnlyFromHTML	TextFileColumnDataTypes
TextFileCommaDelimiter	TextFileConsecutiveDelimiter
TextFileDecimalSeparator	TextFileFixedColumnWidths
TextFileOtherDelimiter	TextFileParseType
TextFilePlatform	TextFilePromptOnRefresh
TextFileSemicolonDelimiter	TextFileSpaceDelimiter
TextFileStartRow	TextFileTabDelimiter
TextFileTextQualifier	TextFileThousandsSeparator
TextFileTrailingMinusNumbers	TextFileVisualLayout
WebConsecutiveDelimitersAsOne	**WebDisableDateRecognition**
WebDisableRedirections	**WebFormatting**
WebPreFormattedTextToColumns	**WebSelectionType**
WebSingleBlockTextImport	**WebTables**

[1] Collection only
[2] Object and collection

querytables.Add(*Connection, Destination, [Sql]*)

Creates a new query table and adds it to the worksheet. Returns a QueryTable object.

Argument	Description
Connection	A string or object reference identifying the source of the data.
Destination	A Range object identifying the upper-lefthand corner of the destination of the query table.
Sql	If the *Connection* argument is an ODBC data source, this argument is a string containing the SQL query to perform. Otherwise, including this argument either causes an error or is ignored.

The *Connection* argument has different forms, depending on the type of data source being queried as described in the following table:

Data source	Use to	Sample connection argument
Web page	Perform a web query	"URL;http://finance.yahoo.com/q/ecn?s=yhoo"

The Add method's *Connection* argument uses the "URL;" prefix when performing a query on a web page. For example, the following code creates a new query table containing a real-time stock quote from Yahoo!:

```
Set ws = ThisWorkbook.Sheets("Other QueryTables")
strConn = "URL;http://finance.yahoo.com/q/ecn?s=dell"
Set qt = ws.QueryTables.Add(strConn, [QueryDestination])
qt.Refresh
```

*querytable.*AdjustColumnWidth [= *setting*]

True adjusts the widths of columns to fit the data in the query table; False preserves the current column width. Default is True.

*querytable.*BackgroundQuery [= *setting*]

True refreshes data in the query table asynchronously; False refreshes data synchronously. Default is True.

The BeforeRefresh and AfterRefresh events occur whether the query is refreshed synchronously or asynchronously. When synchronous, both events occur before the Refresh method completes. When asynchronous, only the BeforeRefresh event occurs before the Refresh method completes; then program flow continues.

BackgroundQuery has little discernible effect on text queries.

*querytable.*CancelRefresh

Cancels an asynchronous query. You can't refresh or delete a query while that query has refresh pending. When working with asynchronous queries, you should check the query table's Refreshing property and (possibly) cancel the pending refresh before deleting or refreshing that query again.

The following code cancels any pending refreshes before refreshing a query:

```
If qt.Refreshing Then qt.CancelRefresh
qt.Refresh
```

*querytable.*Connection [= *setting*]

Sets or returns the data source for the query table. For web queries, this is the *Connection* argument used to create the query. Getting or setting this property causes an error if the query table is created from a recordset (QueryType property is xlADORecordset or xlDAORecordset).

The following code displays the Connection property for each query table on the active worksheet:

```
Dim qt As QueryTable
For Each qt In ActiveSheet.QueryTables
    Select Case qt.QueryType
        Case xlADORecordset, xlDAORecordset
            Debug.Print qt.Name, qt.Recordset.Source
        Case Else ' Includes Web queries.
            Debug.Print qt.Name, qt.Connection
    End Select
Next
```

querytable.Delete

Deletes a query table. If the query table is refreshing asynchronously, Delete causes an error. Deleting a query table does not remove data from cells on a worksheet—it just removes the ability to refresh those cells from their data source.

The following code deletes all of the query tables on the active worksheet and clears all the data on the worksheet:

```
Dim qt As QueryTable
For Each qt In ActiveSheet.QueryTables
    If qt.Refreshing Then qt.CancelRefresh
    qt.Delete
Next
ActiveSheet.UsedRange.Clear
```

querytable.Destination

Returns a Range object containing the cell in the upper-lefthand corner of the query table.

The following code selects the first cell of a query table on the active worksheet and asks if the user wants to delete it:

```
For Each qt In ActiveSheet.QueryTables
    qt.Destination.Select
    If MsgBox("Delete query table?", vbYesNo) = vbYes Then
        If qt.Refreshing Then qt.CancelRefresh
        qt.ResultRange.Clear
        qt.Delete
    End If
Next
```

querytable.EditWebPage [= setting]

Sets or returns the address of the web page used by the Edit Web Query dialog box. EditWebPage is ignored for non-web queries (QueryType is not xlWebQuery).

For example, the following code performs a web query getting a quote for a specific stock, but displays the general financial page if the user decides to edit the web query:

```
Set ws = ActiveSheet
strConn = "URL;http://finance.yahoo.com/q/ecn?s=dell"
Set qt = ws.QueryTables.Add(strConn, [QueryDestination])
qt.EditWebPage = "http://finance.yahoo.com/"
qt.Refresh
```

querytable.EnableEditing [= setting]

True allows the user to change the query definition through the Data menu's Import External Data submenu; False disables the Import External Data menu items. Default is True.

querytable.**EnableRefresh** [= *setting*]

True allows the user to refresh the query through the Data menu's Refresh Data item; False disables the Refresh Data menu item. Default is True.

querytable.**FetchedRowOverflow**

Returns True if the number of records returned by the query exceeds the number of rows available on the worksheet.

querytable.**FillAdjacentFormulas** [= *setting*]

True causes calculated cells to the right of the query table to be repeated for each row when the query table is refreshed; False does not repeat adjacent formulas. Default is False.

Set FillAdjacentFormulas to True in order to create row totals, or other calculations, for each row in the query table automatically. To use this feature, create a query table, add a formula for the first row in the query table, set FillAdjacentFormulas to True, then refresh the data.

querytable.**PostText** [= *setting*]

For web queries, sets or returns a string posted to the server when the query table is refreshed. Most web queries are the result of HTTP GET actions; however, PostText allows you to pass data to a web address through HTTP POST.

querytable.**PreserveFormatting** [= *setting*]

True preserves the cell formatting of the query table when data is refreshed; False does not preserve formatting. Default is False.

If PreserveFormatting is True and a refresh imports new rows of data, formatting common to the first five rows of the query table is automatically applied to the new rows.

querytable.**QueryType** [= *xlQueryType*]

Returns a value identifying the type of data source used by the query table. Can be one of these settings:

```
xlTextImport
xlOLEDBQuery
xlWebQuery
xlADORecordset
xlDAORecordSet
xlODBCQuery
```

querytable.Refresh([*BackgroundQuery*])

Refreshes a query table from its data source. Returns True if the refresh was submitted successfully, False if the user canceled the refresh.

Argument	Description
BackgroundQuery	True refreshes the data asynchronously; False refreshes the data synchronously. Default is True.

Most types of query table store connection and data source information that is used by Refresh. The exception is recordset queries—you must set a new recordset before calling Refresh for query tables based on recordsets. See the Recordset property in Chapter 12 for an example.

When refreshing asynchronously, check the Refreshing property before calling Refresh. Otherwise, pending refreshes will cause an error. The following code cancels any pending asynchronous refresh before refreshing a query table:

```
If qt.Refreshing Then qt.CancelRefresh
qt.Refresh
```

querytable.Refreshing

Returns True if an asynchronous refresh is pending for this query table; False if no refresh is pending.

querytable.RefreshOnFileOpen [= *setting*]

True refreshes the query table when the workbook is opened; False does not refresh on open. Default is False.

querytable.RefreshPeriod [= *setting*]

Sets or returns the number of minutes between automatic refreshes. The default is 0, for no automatic refreshing. You can set automatic refreshing on synchronous or asynchronous queries. RefreshPeriod is ignored for query tables created from recordsets.

The following code creates a query table from an ODBC data source and sets the query table to refresh once a minute:

```
strConn = "ODBC;DRIVER=SQL Server;SERVER=.;UID=Jeff;APP=Microsoft Office " & _
"XP;WSID=WOMBAT2;DATABASE=pubs;Trusted_Connection=Yes"
strSQL = "SELECT titles.title, titles.price, titles.pubdate, titles.ytd_sales
FROM pubs.dbo.titles titles"
Set qt = ActiveWorksheet.QueryTables.Add(strConn, [QueryDestination], strSQL)
qt.RefreshPeriod = 1
qt.Refresh
```

*querytable.*RefreshStyle [= *xlCellInsertionMode*]

Determines how the query affects surrounding items on the worksheet when the query table is refreshed. Default is xlInsertDeleteCells.

Setting	Description
xlInsertDeleteCells	Inserts or deletes new rows and columns created by the query, moving surrounding items up or down and to the right or left as needed.
xlOverwriteCells	No new rows or columns are added to the worksheet. Surrounding items are overwritten as needed.
xlInsertEntireRows	Inserts a new row for each record returned by the query. Shifts existing items down as needed to accommodate the number of records returned.

The following code modifies an existing query table to insert new rows on the worksheet as needed, shifting existing items on the worksheet down:

```
Set qt = ActiveSheet.QueryTables(1)
' Query table records shift rows down.
qt.RefreshStyle = xlInsertEntireRows
qt.Refresh
```

If a subsequent query reduces the number of records returned, the contents of the query table are replaced, but the rows that were previously shifted down are not shifted back up again as they would be if RefreshStyle were set to xlInsertDeleteCells.

*querytable.*ResetTimer

Resets the timer used for periodic queries, in effect delaying when a query occurs. Use the RefreshPeriod property to automatically refresh a query periodically.

*querytable.*ResultRange

Returns the range containing the results of the query. For example, the following code clears the results from a query table on the active worksheet:

```
ActiveSheet.QueryTables(1).ResultRange.Clear
```

If a query table has been created but not yet refreshed, accessing ResultRange causes an error. There's no direct way to test whether a query table has been refreshed. One solution to this problem is to write a helper function similar to the following to check if a query table has a result before accessing ResultRange elsewhere in code:

```
Public Function HasResult(qt As QueryTable) As Boolean
    Dim ret As Boolean
    On Error Resume Next
    Debug.Print qt.ResultRange.Address
    If Err Then ret = False Else ret = True
    On Error GoTo 0
    HasResult = ret
End Function
```

Now, you can easily test if a query table has a result before clearing the result range or performing other tasks, as shown here:

```
Set qt = ActiveSheet.QueryTables(1)
If HasResult(qt) Then qt.ResultRange.Clear
```

*querytable.*TablesOnlyFromHTML [= *setting*]

This property is hidden and is provided for backward compatibility. It is replaced by the WebSelectionType and WebTables properties.

*querytable.*WebConsecutiveDelimitersAsOne [= *setting*]

For web queries, True interprets multiple consecutive delimiters as a single delimiter when importing data from a <PRE> (preformatted) section of a web page. Default is False.

*querytable.*WebDisableDateRecognition [= *setting*]

For web queries, True interprets strings that look like dates as text. Default is False.

*querytable.*WebDisableRedirections [= *setting*]

For web queries, True does not allow the query request to be redirected to another address; False allows redirection. Default is True.

*querytable.*WebFormatting [= *setting*]

For web queries, determines how much formatting is imported along with the data. Possible settings are:

```
xlWebFormattingNone (default)
xlWebFormattingAll
xlWebFormattingRTF
```

*querytable.*WebPreFormattedTextToColumns [= *setting*]

For web queries, True parses rows in <PRE> (preformatted) sections of a web page and places aligned items in separate cells. False parses each row in <PRE> sections as a single data item and places the entire row in one cell.

For example, the following code imports a sample web page and parses rows in <PRE> sections as multiple cells:

```
Set qt = ActiveSheet.QueryTables(1)
qt.Connection = "URL;file://" & ThisWorkbook.Path & "\preblocks.html"
```

```
qt.WebSelectionType = xlAllTables
qt.WebPreFormattedTextToColumns = True
qt.Refresh
```

The web page containing items parsed into cells looks like this:

```
<html>
<body>
<pre>
1    2    3    4
5    6    7    8
</pre>
</body>
</html>
```

*querytable.*WebSelectionType [*= xlWebSelectionType*]

For web queries, specifies how much of a web page to import. Can be one of these settings:

```
xlAllTables (default)
xlEntirePage
xlSpecifiedTables
```

Combine `WebSelectionType` with the `WebTables` property to import one or more specific tables from a web page. For example, the following code uses an existing query table to display a real-time quote, omitting unwanted items from the source web page:

```
Set qt = ActiveSheet.QueryTables(1)
qt.Connection = "URL;http://finance.yahoo.com/q/ecn?s=msft"
qt.Name = "Real-Time Quote"
qt.WebSelectionType = xlSpecifiedTables
qt.WebTables = "22"
qt.WebFormatting = xlWebFormattingNone
qt.BackgroundQuery = True
qt.Refresh
```

Interestingly, you must set `WebSelectionType` to `xlSpecifiedTables` before setting the `WebTables` property or an error occurs at runtime.

*querytable.*WebSingleBlockTextImport [*= setting*]

For web queries, True parses rows in <PRE> (preformatted) sections as a single block; False parses contiguous rows in <PRE> sections as blocks. Default is True.

This property is useful if a single <PRE> section contains multiple blocks of preformatted data that use different column alignment. For example, the following code imports a sample web page and parses contiguous rows within <PRE> blocks individually:

```
Set qt = ActiveSheet.QueryTables(1)
qt.Connection = "URL;file://" & ThisWorkbook.Path & "\preblocks.html"
qt.WebPreFormattedTextToColumns = True
qt.WebSingleBlockTextImport = False
qt.Refresh
```

The web page containing items parsed into cells looks like this:

```
<html>
<body>
<pre>
Col1    Col2    Col3    Col4
1       2       3       4
5       6       7       8

c1 c2 c3 c4
1  2  3  4
5  6  7  8
</pre>
</body>
</html>
```

The preceding code results in two blocks of data, each with four columns. If WebSingleBlockTextImport were set to True instead, the second table would contain only one column of data.

---

*querytable.*WebTables [= *setting*]

For web queries, specifies the index of the items to include from the source web page. To include multiple items from a web page, use a comma-delimited string.

For example, the following code includes the 3rd, 4th, and 10th items from a web page:

```
qt.WebSelectionType = xlSpecifiedTables
qt.WebTables = "3,4,10"
```

Note that you must set WebSelectionType to xlSpecifiedTables before you use the WebTables property.

The best way to find the index of an item on a web page is to record a macro performing the web query containing the items you want to import, then cut and paste the recorded WebTables setting.

Use Web Services

From an Excel perspective, web services are primarily useful for retrieving variable data over the Internet, but you can also use them to send data, to manipulate remote data, or to run other code on remote computers. Web services are designed to work just like procedure calls from code, so it is possible to use a web service without even knowing that it is running remote code.

That's possible, but it's not likely, since web service methods often rely heavily on their underlying foundation: XML. That means Excel programmers must become familiar with the Microsoft XML type library before they can effectively use web services. The good news is that, once you are comfortable working with XML, you can blast web service results directly into spreadsheet lists using Excel XML maps (which is *very* cool).

Web services, like many Internet-related things, are part of evolving standards. These standards have broad support by many companies, so web services are not likely to lose support in the future. However, since the standards are still evolving, there are different approaches to implementing, locating, and accessing web services. Of specific interest to Excel developers are the facts that:

- There are several ways to locate web services on the Internet. One way is through a directory service such as *http://uddi.microsoft.com/*, but a much more common way is just by browsing the business's own site or through a cross-listing site such as *http://www.xmethods.net/*.
- There are several ways to describe web services over the Internet. With Excel, you really need to worry about only one: WSDL.
- There are several ways to call web services. Some web services only support SOAP, while others such as Amazon also support access directly through their URL.

The samples in this chapter focus on two widely used web services provided by Google and Amazon, respectively. These services are nearly ideal for a chapter such as this because they are freely available, useful, well-documented, and demonstrate both SOAP and URL access. Before you continue, however, you should download the following toolkits:

Toolkit	Location
Microsoft Office Web Services Toolkit	*http://www.microsoft.com/downloads* and search for "Web Services Toolkit."
Google Web Service	*http://www.google.com/apis/*.
Amazon Web Service	Click on Web Services link at *http://www.amazon.com/*.

Both the Google and Amazon Web Services require you to register to get a developer ID to pass with method calls. I provide my developer ID with the code samples shown here, but you will want your own ID if you use these web services in your own code.

Use the Web Services Toolkit

Excel doesn't come with the Web Services Toolkit installed. In order to use web services from Visual Basic for Applications, you must first follow these steps:

1. Find the Microsoft Office Web Services Toolkit from Microsoft by searching for "Web Services Toolkit" at *www.microsoft.com/downloads*.
2. Download the Web Services Toolkit installation program (*setup.exe*).

3. Run the downloaded installation program and follow the steps provided by the Setup Wizard.

4. Start Excel and open the Visual Basic Editor.

5. In Visual Basic, select Web References from the Tools menu. Visual Basic displays the Microsoft Office Web Services Toolkit references dialog shown in Figure 24-9.

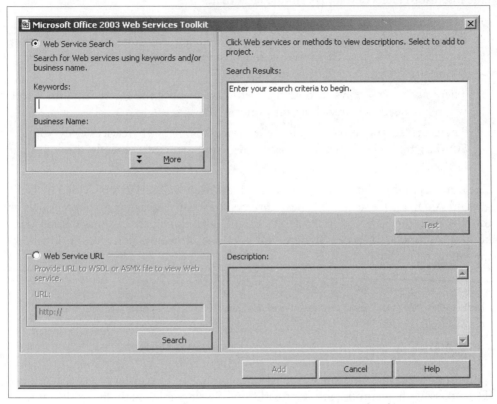

Figure 24-9. Use the Microsoft Office Web Services Toolkit to create a web reference

When you create a web reference, the Web Services Toolkit automatically adds references to the Microsoft Office SOAP type library and the Microsoft XML library. Then, the toolkit generates proxy classes for the web service. To see how this works, follow these steps:

1. From the Visual Basic Tools menu, select Web References.

2. Select Web Service URL and type the following line in the text box below that option:

```
http://api.google.com/GoogleSearch.wsdl
```

3. Click Search. The Web Services Toolkit displays the web services available from Google as shown in Figure 24-10.

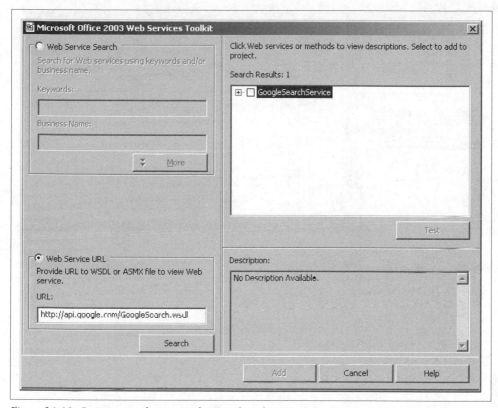

Figure 24-10. Creating a reference to the Google web service

4. Select GoogleSearchService and click Add. The Web Service Toolkit adds references to the SOAP and XML libraries and creates proxy classes for each of the services, as shown in Figure 24-11.

Proxy classes are modules of code that stand in for the code that runs on the server providing the web service. You have to have a local copy of this code so you can compile your application against something. These proxy classes provide the properties and methods you call on the web service—they package those calls, send them, and receive their responses.

The code in these proxy classes is not simple. Fortunately, you don't have to understand much of it; just create an instance of the main class (identified by the prefix clsws) and use its properties and methods. For example, the following code uses the generated classes to search Google for work I've done on Excel:

```
Dim i As Integer, wsGoogle As New clsws_GoogleSearchService
Dim wsResult As struct_GoogleSearchResult, wsElement As struct_ResultElement
```

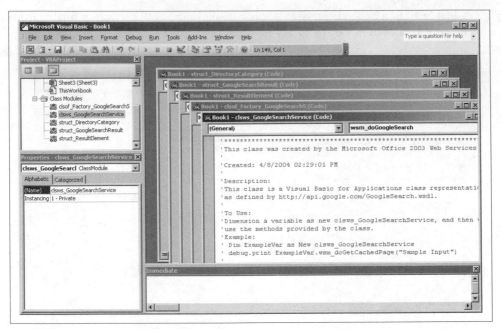

Figure 24-11. The Web Services Toolkit creates Google Web Service proxy classes

```
Dim devKey As String, searchStr As String
' This key is from Google, used to identify developer.
devKey = "ekN14fFQFHK7lXIW3Znm+VXrXI7Focrl"
' Items to search for.
searchStr = "Jeff Webb Excel"
' Call the search web service.
Set wsResult = wsGoogle.wsm_doGoogleSearch(devKey, _
    searchStr, 0, 10, False, "", False, "", "", "")
' For each of the results
For i = 0 To wsResult.endIndex - 1
    ' Get the individual result.
    Set wsElement = wsResult.resultElements(i)
    ' Display the result.
    Debug.Print wsElement.title, wsElement.URL
Next
```

OK, that's not simple either. Most of the complication here comes from the web service itself. Google requires a license key to use its service; I include my key in the devKey variable. Google allows 1000 search requests per day for this free license key, so you'll want to get your own key from Google.

Next, the wsm_doGoogleSearch method submits the search to Google. That method takes a lot of arguments and returns a structure, which is defined in another proxy class, so you need to use Set to perform the assignment. Similarly, you need to use Set to get elements from the result.

Use Web Services Through XML

Web services from different companies define their interfaces differently. For example, the Google Web Service provides methods that take simple string arguments, whereas the Amazon Web Service provides methods that take complex XMLNodeList arguments.

It's difficult to construct and debug XMLNodeList arguments for the Amazon Web Service. It's much easier to invoke this web service directly through its URL. For example, the following code performs a keyword search for books about wombats on Amazon:

```
Dim SearchUrl As String
' Create a new DOMDocument and set its options
Dim xdoc As New DOMDocument
xdoc.async = True
xdoc.preserveWhiteSpace = True
xdoc.validateOnParse = True
xdoc.resolveExternals = False

' Create the search request
SearchUrl = "http://xml.amazon.com/onca/xml2" & _
        "?t=" & "webservices-20" & _
        "&dev-t=" & "D1UCRO4XBIF4A6" & _
        "&page-1" & _
        "&f=xml" & _
        "&mode=books" & _
        "&type=lite" & _
        "&KeywordSearch=wombat"

' Issue the request and wait for it to be honored
Loaded = xdoc.Load(SearchUrl)
' Display the results
Debug.Print xdoc.XML
```

Because the results are returned as XML, you can create an XML map from the result and import the results into a list created from that XML map as shown here:

```
Set wb = ThisWorkbook
wb.XmlImportXml xdoc.XML, wb.XmlMaps("ProductInfo_Map"), True
```

Figure 24-12 displays the result of importing an Amazon search for wombats into a list on a worksheet.

The documentation for the Amazon Web Service is structured to show you how to call its methods using its URL rather than using proxy classes and SOAP. This means that you don't have to use the Web Services Toolkit to create proxies for the Amazon Web Service; just add a reference to the Microsoft XML type library.

This method of accessing a web service is sometimes called Representational State Transfer (REST). That acronym is useful as a search term when looking for this type of interface for a given web service. Type "REST Google API" in a Google search to see an active debate on the relative features of REST and SOAP.

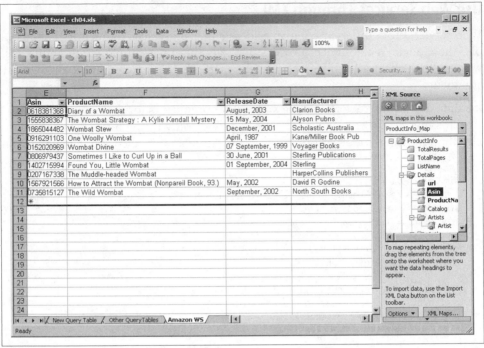

Figure 24-12. Displaying XML results from a web service through an XML map and list

The Google Web Service doesn't support direct access through its URL, but you can avoid the proxies and call it directly through SOAP. For example, the following code performs a search for wombats and imports the result through an XML map directly into a list:

```
Dim soap As New SoapClient30, xn As IXMLDOMNodeList, strXML As String
soap.MSSoapInit "http://api.google.com/GoogleSearch.wsdl"
Set xn = soap.doGoogleSearch("ekN14fFQFHK7lXIW3Znm+VXrXI7Focrl", _
   "wombats", 0, 10, False, "", False, "", "", "")
' Build a string containing the results from the search in XML.
strXML = "<GoogleSearchResults>"
For i = 1 To xn.Length - 1
    strXML = strXML & xn(i).XML
Next
strXML = strXML & "</GoogleSearchResults>"
' Import the results through an XML map into a list.
Set wb = ThisWorkbook
wb.XmlImportXml strXML, wb.XmlMaps("GoogleSearchResults_Map"), True
```

Call a Web Service Asynchronously

One advantage of calling a web service directly, rather than through proxies, is that it is very easy to handle the response asynchronously. The DOMDocument object provides an ondataavailable event that occurs when the object is finished loading XML from a source. This means that you can launch a web service request, release control to the user, and display results when a request is complete. Being able to handle a response asynchronously is especially important when the web service is returning a large amount of data.

To use the DOMDocument object to respond to a web service asynchronously, follow these steps:

1. Declare a DOMDocument object at the module of a class. The class can be a workbook, worksheet, or code class module. For example, the following variable is declared in the wsAmazon worksheet class:

   ```
   Dim WithEvents xdoc As DOMDocument
   ```

2. Select the xdoc object from the object list at the top of the code window, and then select ondataavailable from the event list to create an empty event procedure as shown here:

   ```
   Private Sub xdoc_ondataavailable()

   End Sub
   ```

3. In other code, initialize the xdoc object, set its async property to True, and then call the web service using the xdoc object's Load method. For example, the following event procedure searches *Amazon.com* for a keyword when the user clicks the Get Titles button on the wsAmazon worksheet:

   ```
   Sub cmdTitles_Click()
       Dim SearchUrl As String
       ' Create a new DOMDocument and set its options
       Set xdoc = New DOMDocument
       xdoc.async = True

       ' Create the search request
       SearchUrl = "http://xml.amazon.com/onca/xml2" & _
                   "?t=" & "webservices-20" & _
                   "&dev-t=" & "D1UCRO4XBIF4A6" & _
                   "&page=1" & _
                   "&f=xml" & _
                   "&mode=books" & _
                   "&type=lite" & _
                   "&KeywordSearch=" & txtSearch.Text

       ' Issue the request and wait for it to be honored
       Loaded = xdoc.Load(SearchUrl)
   End Sub
   ```

4. Add code to the ondataavailable event procedure to respond to the web service data once it is returned. For example, the following code imports the result through an XML map and displays it in a list:

   ```
   Private Sub xdoc_ondataavailable()
       Dim wb As Workbook
       ' Import the results through an XML map into a list.
   ```

```
        Set wb = ThisWorkbook
        wb.XmlImportXml xdoc.XML, wb.XmlMaps("ProductInfo_Map"), True
    End Sub
```

When the user clicks on the Get Titles button and the preceding code runs, Excel returns control to the user as soon as the click is done. The list is updated once the web service responds.

The Microsoft SOAP type library does not support asynchronous calls, so you can't use web services that provide only a SOAP interface asynchronously from Excel. The SOAP tools available with .NET do support asynchronous calls, however, so if you are programming with Visual Basic .NET outside of Excel, you can make asynchronous SOAP calls.

Reformat XML Results for Excel

One thing you may notice when you return web service results directly to Excel through an XML map is that mixed content is not automatically formatted. In other words, HTML formatting tags such as <b> and <i> appear as "<b>" and "<i>" rather than as bold and italic, as shown in Figure 24-13.

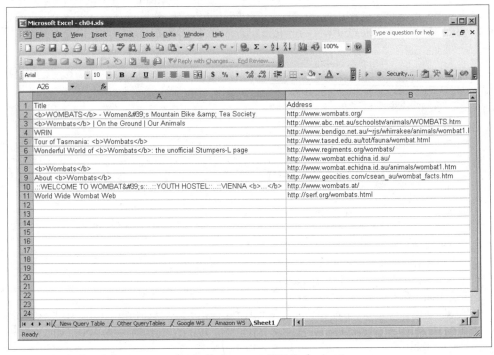

Figure 24-13. Excel does not automatically interpret HTML formatting

There's no simple way to prevent this problem, but you can fix it using the automatic text formatting features of Excel. Excel automatically reformats HTML text pasted from the clipboard, so all you have to do is place the data in the clipboard as HTML, then paste that data back into cells on the spreadsheet.

In Excel, you access the clipboard using the DataObject object, so the following code puts the data from each cell of a worksheet into the clipboard as HTML, then pastes that data back, causing Excel to correctly interpret HTML formatting:

```
Sub TestReformat()
    ' Call helper function to interpret HTML formatting codes.
    ReformatHTML ActiveSheet.UsedRange
End Sub

Sub ReformatHTML(rng As Range)
    Dim clip As New DataObject, cell As Range
    For Each cell In rng
        clip.SetText "<html>" & cell.Value & "<html>"
        clip.PutInClipboard
        cell.PasteSpecial
    Next
End Sub
```

After you run TestReformat on a worksheet, Excel interprets the HTML formatting codes as if you cut/pasted them from a web page, as shown in Figure 24-14.

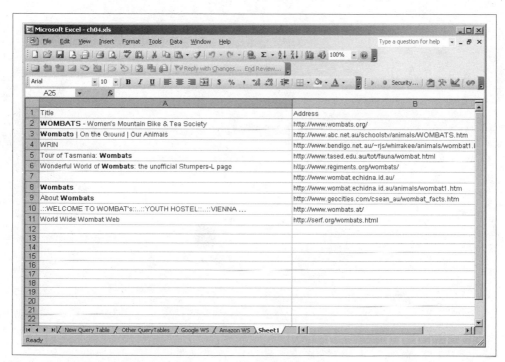

Figure 24-14. HTML formatting after running ReformatHTML

Resources

To learn about	Look here
Microsoft Office Web Services Toolkit	Search *http://www.microsoft.com/downloads* for "Web Services Toolkit."
MSXML 4.0 Documentation	*http://msdn.microsoft.com/library/en-us/xmlsdk/htm/sdk_intro_6g53.asp.*
DOMDocument	*http://msdn.microsoft.com/library/en-us/xmlsdk/htm/xml_obj_overview_20ab.asp.*
IXMLDOMNodeList	*http://msdn.microsoft.com/library/en-us/xmlsdk30/htm/xmobjxmldomnodelist.asp.*
Google Web Service	*http://www.google.com/apis/.*
Google Web Service description	*http://api.google.com/GoogleSearch.wsdl.*
Amazon Web Service	Click on Web Services link at *http://www.amazon.com/.*
Amazon Web Service description	*http://soap.amazon.com/schemas3/AmazonWebServices.wsdl.*
Representational State Transfer (REST)	*http://internet.conveyor.com/RESTwiki/moin.cgi/FrontPage.*

CHAPTER 25

Programming Excel with .NET

Visual Basic .NET is Microsoft's next generation of the Basic language. The name change marks another milestone in the evolution of Basic: BASICA, QuickBasic, Visual Basic, and Visual Basic .NET each mark distinct changes in underlying technology. This latest change marks the graduation from the Windows Common Object Model (COM) in Visual Basic to the .NET Framework in Visual Basic .NET.

.NET is a Windows technology. It is not supported on the Macintosh.

The .NET Framework solves a lot of the shortcomings in COM—it has a more complete security model; provides a well-organized library of objects for working with HTTP, XML, SOAP, encryption, and other things; is fundamentally object-oriented; protects against memory leaks and corruption; promotes self-describing code—gosh, I'm starting to sound like a commercial. In short, .NET is the future for programming Windows.

Now the bad news: Excel is (and probably always will be) a COM application. This means that you have to take special steps if you want to use .NET components from Excel or if you want to program Excel from Visual Basic .NET.

But back to the good news: Microsoft provides many tools for making the transition between COM and .NET as easy as possible. In this chapter, you will learn how to use those tools both to take advantage of .NET from Excel and vice versa.

Code used in this chapter and additional samples are available in *ch25.xls*.

Approaches to Working with .NET

There are three main approaches to using .NET with Excel. You can use .NET to create:

Components that can be used from Excel macros
> This approach works with all Excel versions and is much the same as creating COM components for use with Excel using earlier versions of Visual Basic. The .NET tools automatically generate the type libraries needed to use .NET objects from COM applications such as Excel.

Standalone applications that use Excel as a component
> This approach works best with Excel XP and 2003, since those versions provide the files needed to use Excel from .NET applications smoothly. In this scenario, the user starts a standalone application to create or modify Excel workbooks.

Workbook-based applications that run all of their code as .NET
> This approach works for Excel 2003 and later. In this scenario, the user opens the workbook, which automatically loads the .NET assembly containing the application code. The workbook contains a link to this assembly, so the workbook file (*.xls*) can be distributed to many different users and locations, while the assembly (*.dll*) resides in a single location (for example at a network address).

From the user's standpoint, the main differences between these approaches are how you start the application and what versions of Excel are supported. From a developer's standpoint, the differences affect how you develop, debug, and deploy the applications. Even the development tools you need vary somewhat between these approaches as described in Table 25-1.

Table 25-1. Software requirements for developing between Excel and .NET

To create	You need
.NET components for use in Excel	Visual Studio .NET Standard Edition or higher
Standalone .NET applications that use Excel	Visual Studio .NET Standard Edition or higher, Microsoft Office 2002 or later, and Primary Interop Assemblies (PIAs)
Excel .NET applications	Visual Studio .NET Tools for Office (includes project templates) and Microsoft Office 2003 or later

Create .NET Components for Excel

If you are an experienced VBA programmer, this is a great way to start learning .NET because you can take advantage of features built into the .NET Framework in small, incremental steps.

To create a .NET component for use in Excel:

1. From within Visual Studio .NET, create a new class library project using Visual Basic .NET or C#. Visual Studio creates a folder and template files for the project, as shown in Figure 25-1.

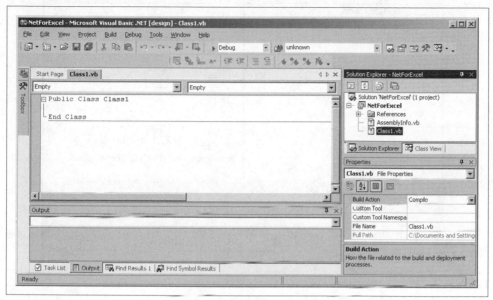

Figure 25-1. A new, empty .NET class library project

2. From the Project menu, choose Add Class. Visual Studio displays the Add New Item dialog box shown in Figure 25-2.

3. Give the new class a descriptive name and click OK. Visual Studio registers the project to interoperate with COM (the Register for COM Interop selection on the Project Options, Build dialog box) and creates a new, empty code template for your class as shown in Figure 25-3.

4. Add code to the class library for the objects, properties, and methods you want to use from Excel.

5. Compile the project by selecting Build Solution from the Build menu. Visual Studio builds the class library as a .NET assembly (*.dll*) and creates a type library file (*.tlb*) that allows Excel and other COM applications to use that assembly. Both of these files are placed in a *bin* folder within the project folder created in Step 1.

For example, the NetForExcel project (*NetForExcel.sln*) includes a simple class that provides a single method that displays a message passed in as an argument:

```
' .NET code.
Public Class NetObject
    Public Sub Test(ByVal arg As String)
        MsgBox(arg)
    End Sub
End Class
```

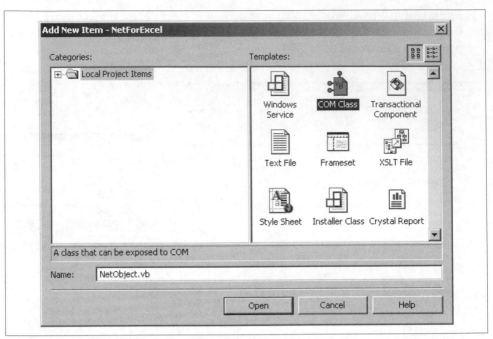

Figure 25-2. Create a new COM class to contain components for use from Excel

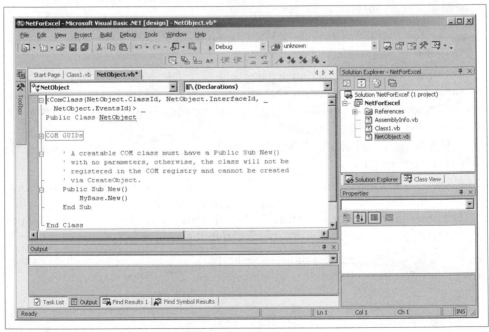

Figure 25-3. The COM class code template contains the basic elements you need for a component

The following section shows you how to use this sample .NET component from within Excel.

Use .NET Components in Excel

Once you compile a .NET component with Register for COM Interop enabled, using that component from Excel is simply a matter of following these steps:

1. From within the Excel VBA Editor, select References from the Tools menu. VBA displays the References dialog box.

2. Click Browse and navigate to the \bin folder for the .NET component you wish to use. Select the type library (.tlb) for the component, as shown in Figure 25-4, and click OK to add a reference to that component.

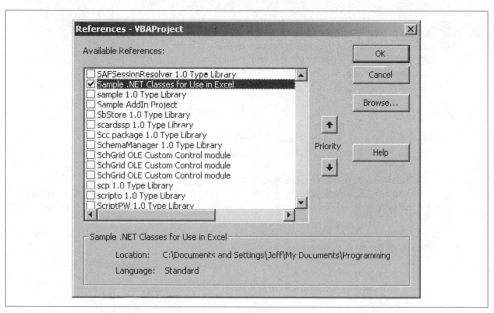

Figure 25-4. Use the .NET component's type library to create a reference to the component in Excel VBA

3. Click OK to close the References dialog box.

4. Declare an object variable for the .NET class using the New keyword, then call the members of the class.

The components you create using Visual Basic .NET are named using their project name (.NET calls that the *namespace* of the component), so you would use the following code to call the NetForExcel project's NetObject created in the preceding section:

```
' Excel code
Sub TestNetObj()
```

```
        Dim x As New NetForExcel.NetObject
        x.Test "I worked!"
    End Sub
```

Now, if you run the preceding code, Excel uses the type library to start the .NET assembly and invoke the Test method with a string argument. The .NET component, in turn, displays a message box saying "I worked!"

Though that demonstration isn't very impressive, what you can do with .NET components becomes exciting once you've learned more about the classes that come with the .NET Framework. For example, you can do some pretty useful things with even the basic .NET String and Array classes, as shown here:

```
' .NET code
Public Class NetString

    + COM GUIDS

    ' A creatable COM class must have a Public Sub New()
    ' with no parameters; otherwise, the class will not be
    ' registered in the COM registry and cannot be created
    ' via CreateObject.
    Public Sub New()
        MyBase.New()
    End Sub

    Public Function Split(ByVal arg As String, _
      Optional ByVal sep As String = " ") As String()
        If Len(sep) <> 1 Then _
          Throw New Exception("Separator must be one character long")
        Return arg.Split(CType(sep, Char))
    End Function

    Public Function Join(ByVal arg() As String, _
      Optional ByVal sep As String = " ") As String
        If IsArray(arg) Then
            If arg.Rank <> 1 Then _
                Throw New Exception("Array must have one dimension")
        Else
            Throw New Exception("First argument must be an array")
        End If
        Return String.Join(sep, arg)
    End Function

    Public Function Sort(ByVal arg As String, _
      Optional ByVal ascending As Boolean = True) As String
        ' Declare an array.
        Dim ar() As String
        ' Break the string up and put it in the array.
        ar = arg.Split(" "c)
        ' Sort the array.
```

```
        ar.Sort(ar)
        ' Reverse the order if requested.
        If Not ascending Then ar.Reverse(ar)
        ' Convert the array back to a string and return it.
        Return String.Join(" ", ar)
    End Function
End Class
```

To use the preceding .NET class in code, compile the project and establish a reference to that project in Excel's VBA Editor, then write code similar to the following:

```
' Excel code
Sub TestNetString( )
    Dim str As String, ar( ) As String, i As Integer
    Dim NetStr As New NetForExcel.NetString
    str = "Some random text that you'd want to sort."
    Debug.Print NetStr.Sort(str)
    ar = NetStr.Split(str)
    For i = 0 To UBound(ar)
        Debug.Print ar(i)
    Next
End Sub
```

The preceding code displays the sorted string in the Immediate window, then splits the string into an array and displays it one word at a time. Since Visual Studio .NET generates a type library for the component and registers it with your system, you automatically get Intellisense and Auto Complete features when you work with .NET objects in Excel VBA, as shown in Figure 25-5.

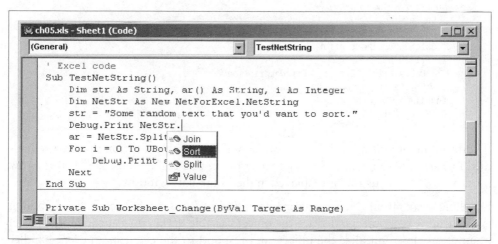

Figure 25-5. .NET objects registered for COM automatically get Intellisense and Auto Complete in VBA

Respond to Errors and Events from .NET Objects

The .NET code in the preceding section included a couple of lines that may be unfamiliar to you:

```
If Len(sep) <> 1 Then _
    Throw New Exception("Separator must be one character long")
```

and:

```
If IsArray(arg) Then
    If arg.Rank <> 1 Then Throw New Exception("Array must have one dimension")
Else
    Throw New Exception("First argument must be an array")
End If
```

These lines demonstrate Visual Basic .NET's new exception-handling constructs: Throw raises an exception, the error is created as a New Exception object, and it would be handled by a Try...Catch structure (not shown) if the method were called from .NET.

Since this code is called from Excel, however, you handle it using the VBA On Error statement. For example:

```
' Excel code.
Sub TestNetError()
    Dim ar(1, 1) As String
    Dim NetStr As New NetForExcel.NetString
    ar(0, 0) = "causes": ar(0, 1) = "an": ar(1, 0) = "error"
    On Error Resume Next
    ' Cause error.
    Debug.Print NetStr.Join(ar)
    ' Catch and report error
    If Err Then
        Debug.Print "Error:", Err.Description
        Err.Clear
    End If
    On Error GoTo 0
End Sub
```

If you run the preceding code, the Join method causes an exception that can be handled in Excel the same way as any other error. In this case, a message "Error: Array must have one dimension" is displayed in the Immediate window.

Handling events from .NET components in Excel VBA is much the same as handling events from Excel objects: declare the object variable WithEvents at the module level of an Excel class, initialize the object, and respond to the event in an event-handler procedure. For example, the following code defines and raises an event in the .NET NetString class:

```
' .NET code
Public Class NetString
    ' Declare event.
    Public Event Sorted As EventHandler
```

```
    Private m_value As String

    ' Other code omitted.

    Public Function Sort(ByVal arg As String, _
        Optional ByVal ascending As Boolean = True) As String
        ' Declare an array.
        Dim ar() As String, res As String
        ' Break the string up and put it in the array.
        ar = arg.Split(" "c)
        ' Sort the array.
        ar.Sort(ar)
        ' Reverse the order if requested.
        If Not ascending Then ar.Reverse(ar)
        ' Convert the array back to a string and set value property
        m_value = String.Join(" ", ar)
        ' Raise event.
        OnSorted()
        ' Return result
        Return m_value
    End Function

    ' By convention, events are raised from OnXxx procedures in .NET
    Friend Sub OnSorted()
        RaiseEvent Sorted(Me, System.EventArgs.Empty)
    End Sub

    ' Property that returns Sort result (added to illustrate event).
    Public ReadOnly Property Value() As String
        Get
            Return m_value
        End Get
    End Property
End Class
```

The preceding event occurs any time the Sort method completes a sort. This actually occurs very quickly, so this isn't the greatest use for an event, but it's clearer to
build on this previous example than to start a completely new one. To handle this
event in Excel, add the following code to the class for a worksheet:

```
' Excel code in a worksheet class.
Dim WithEvents NetStr As NetForExcel.NetString

Private Sub Worksheet_Change(ByVal Target As Range)
    If Target.Address = "$A$2" Then
        ' Create object if it hasn't been initialized.
        If TypeName(NetStr) = "Nothing" Then _
            Set NetStr = New NetForExcel.NetString
        ' Sort text in range A2.
        NetStr.Sort [a2].Text
    End If
End Sub

Private Sub NetStr_Sorted(ByVal sender As Variant, _
```

```
          ByVal e As mscorlib.EventArgs)
            ' When sort is complete, display result in range B2.
            [b2].Value = NetStr.Value
        End Sub
```

Now, you can change the text in cell A2 and the Sorted event displays the result in cell B2 once the sort is complete. A few points to note here:

- VBA can respond only to events from within classes—that includes workbook and worksheet classes, as well as custom classes (.NET calls these *instance classes*). You can't use events from modules (.NET calls these *static classes* or *code modules*).

- Once you declare a .NET object WithEvents, that component's events appear in the listbox at the top of the Excel VBA Editor Code window.

- You can't combine New and WithEvents, so you must initialize the object somewhere in a procedure (as shown in the earlier Worksheet_Change procedure).

Debug .NET Components

If you've been following along with the preceding example by writing code in Excel and Visual Studio .NET, you've probably noticed that you can't build the .NET project while Excel has a reference to that project's type library. You need to close Excel or remove the reference each time you make a change in the .NET project. That's because Visual Studio .NET can't overwrite the type library while another application is using it.

This makes debugging .NET components from Excel difficult. In fact, it's not a very good practice. It is a much better practice to add a second, test project to your .NET component solution and make that project the startup project. To add a test project to the NetForExcel sample, follow these steps:

1. From the File menu, choose Add Project, New Project. Visual Studio .NET display the Add New Project dialog box.

2. Select the Console Application template from the Visual Basic project types, give the project a descriptive name, and click OK. Visual Studio .NET creates a folder and template files for the new Windows console application.

3. Right-click on the new project title in the Solution Explorer and select Set as Startup Project from the pop-up menu as shown in Figure 25-6. Visual Studio .NET makes the project name bold, indicating it is the startup project.

4. Add code to the test project's Main procedure to test the .NET component.

For example, the following code tests the NetString class from the NetForExcel component created earlier:

```
' .NET test code
Module Module1
    Dim WithEvents NetStr As New NetForExcel.NetString
```

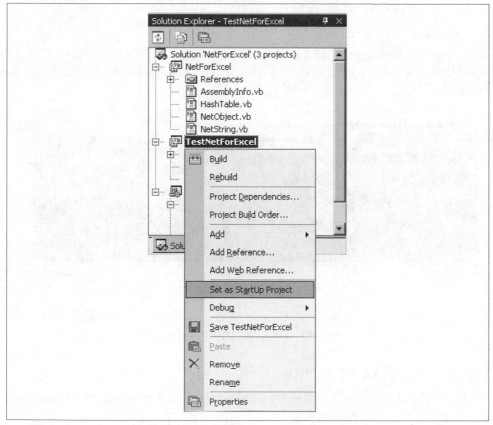

Figure 25-6. Make the test project the startup project for the solution

```
Sub Main( )
    Dim ar( ) As String = {"This", "That", "Other"}
    Dim ar2(1, 1) As String, str As String = "Some more text"
    ar2(0, 0) = "This" : ar2(0, 1) = "That" : ar2(1, 0) = "Other"
    Console.WriteLine(NetStr.Join(ar, ", "))
    Console.WriteLine(NetStr.Sort(str, False))
    ' Cause error.
    Try
        'NetStr.Join("Test, That, Other")
        'NetStr.Join(ar2)
        NetStr.Split(str, " r")
    Catch ex As Exception
        Console.WriteLine("Error: " & ex.Message)
    End Try
    ' Wait for Enter keypress to end.
    Console.Read( )
End Sub

Private Sub NetStr_Sorted(ByVal sender As Object, _
  ByVal e As System.EventArgs) Handles NetStr.Sorted
```

```
            Console.WriteLine("Sort event complete. Result: " & NetStr.Value)
        End Sub
    End Module
```

If you run the NetForExcel solution from Visual Studio .NET by pressing F5, Windows starts the test project and displays the results in a console window, as shown in Figure 25-7.

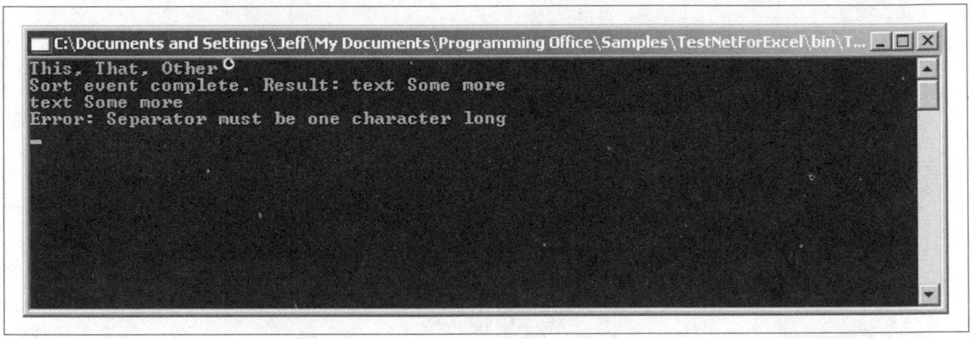

Figure 25-7. Using a console test project to debug a .NET component before using it from Excel

Now, you can use Visual Studio .NET's debugging tools to step in to procedures, set breakpoints and watches, and perform other typical debugging and testing tasks.

Distribute .NET Components

Visual Studio .NET uses setup and deployment projects to create the installation applications you use to distribute .NET components or any other type of application. These tools are greatly improved over the Visual Basic 6.0 setup wizards, and there are a number of paths you can take to create an installation program for your .NET components; the following steps outline one of the possible paths:

1. From the File menu, choose Add Project, New Project. Visual Studio .NET displays the Add New Project dialog box.

2. Select the Setup and Deployment project type, then select the Setup Wizard from the Templates list. Name the setup project descriptively and click OK. Visual Studio .NET starts the Setup Wizard to walk you through creating the project.

3. Follow the steps in the Setup Wizard to install a Windows application and select the Primary Output from NetForExcel project group in Step 3 of the wizard, as shown in Figure 25-8.

4. When you click Finish in the Setup Wizard, Visual Studio .NET creates a folder for the setup project, determines the dependencies for NetForExcel, and creates a setup project as shown in Figure 25-9.

Choose project outputs to include

You can include outputs from other projects in your solution.

Which project output groups do you want to include?

- ☑ Primary output from NetForExcel
- ☐ Localized resources from NetForExcel
- ☐ Debug Symbols from NetForExcel
- ☐ Content Files from NetForExcel
- ☐ Source Files from NetForExcel

Description:

Contains the DLL or EXE built by the project.

| Cancel | < Back | Next > | Finish |

Figure 25-8. Select the primary output for the project to install

Solution Explorer - SetupNetForExcel

- Solution 'NetForExcel' (3 projects)
  - NetForExcel
    - References
    - AssemblyInfo.vb
    - HashTable.vb
    - NetObject.vb
    - NetString.vb
  - **TestNetForExcel**
    - References
    - AssemblyInfo.vb
    - Module1.vb
  - SetupNetForExcel
    - Detected Dependencies
      - dotnetfxredist_x86.msm
      - NetForExcel.tlb
    - NetForExcel.dll

Solution Explorer   Class View

Figure 25-9. Setup project for the NetForExcel component

5. From the Build menu, select Build Solution or "Build setup project to package NetForExcel.dll and NetForExcel.tlb," and build an installation program to install and register those files on a client's machine.

6. The setup project creates *Setup.exe*, *Setup.msi*, and *Setup.ini* files in its *Debug* folder by default. Use those files to test deployment before changing the setup project's configuration to release and rebuilding.

The installation program created using the preceding steps installs the component in the *Program Files* folder on the user's machine and registers the component's type library in the system registry. Excel workbooks that reference this type library use the system registry to find the component by its GUID (which is part of the code generated automatically when you create the COM class in .NET).

The installation program also creates an entry in users' application lists so they can uninstall the application using the Windows Control Panel. In short, it does everything you need it to!

Use Excel as a Component in .NET

Another way for Excel to interact with the .NET world is to program with Excel objects directly in Visual Basic .NET. In this case, Excel becomes a component for use in a .NET application—the reverse of the case just shown.

Using Excel as a component in a .NET application is handy when you want to present application output using the Excel interface—as a spreadsheet or chart, for instance.

To create a .NET application that uses Excel as a component:

1. Create a new Windows application project in Visual Studio .NET.

2. From the Project menu, choose Add Reference. Visual Studio .NET displays the Add Reference dialog box. Click the COM tab. Visual Studio .NET displays the contents of your system's global assembly cache, as shown in Figure 25-10.

3. Select the Microsoft Excel 11.0 Object Library and click Select, then OK to add the reference to your project. Visual Studio .NET automatically references the PIA for the Excel object library if it is installed on your system.

4. If the PIA is not installed, Visual Studio .NET creates a new interop assembly and adds it to your project (this is not what you want—the PIA is much more reliable). To make sure you are using the PIA, check the Name and Path properties of the Excel reference. They should appear as shown in Figure 25-11.

5. In code, create an instance of the Excel Application object and use that object's member to perform tasks in Excel.

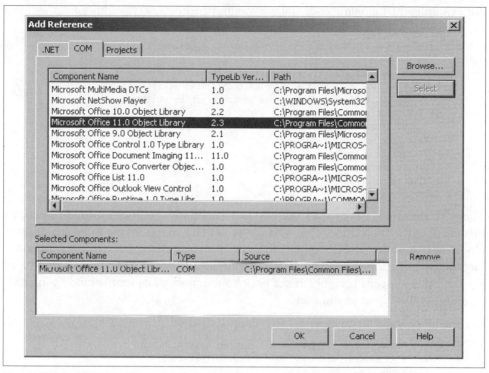

Figure 25-10. Adding a reference to the Microsoft Excel object library

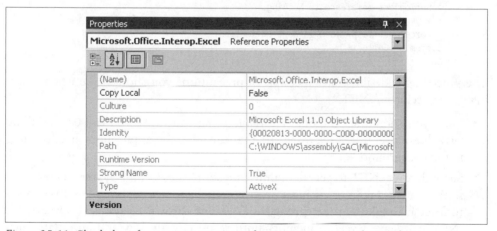

Figure 25-11. Check the reference properties to make sure you are using the Excel PIA

For example, the following code starts Excel and creates a new workbook:

```
' .NET Windows form code
Dim WithEvents m_xl As Microsoft.Office.Interop.Excel.Application

Private Sub cmdStartExcel_Click(ByVal sender As System.Object, _
    ByVal e As System.EventArgs) Handles cmdStartExcel.Click
    ' If not initialized, create a new instance of the object.
    If IsNothing(m_xl) Then _
        m_xl = New Microsoft.Office.Interop.Excel.Application
    ' Make Excel visible.
    m_xl.Visible = True
    ' Create a new workbook.
    m_xl.Workbooks.Add( )
End Sub
```

The m_xl variable is declared WithEvents so Visual Basic .NET can respond to events that occur in the application. The cmdStartExcel_Click initializes the Excel Application object if it was not already initialized and then calls the Workbook collection's Add method to create a new workbook. It is important to note that if Visible is not set to True, all this happens invisibly in the background, and while that is kind of interesting, it is not usually what you want.

Use the following code to close the Excel application when you are done:

```
Private Sub cmdQuitExcel_Click(ByVal sender As System.Object, _
    ByVal e As System.EventArgs) Handles cmdQuitExcel.Click
    ' Close the Excel application.
    m_xl.Quit( )
    ' Set object reference to Nothing.
    m_xl = Nothing
    ' Force .NET to perform garbage collection.
    System.GC.Collect( )
End Sub
```

The preceding code illustrates a couple of precautions you should take when working with Excel from .NET:

- First, you should set the object variable to Nothing after you call Quit. Calling Quit doesn't set m_xl to Nothing and that can keep the application alive, running in the background.

- Second, force .NET to get rid of unused resources by calling System.GC.Collect. .NET manages memory using a process called *garbage collection*, and you need to force it to take out the garbage after you've thrown away Excel. Otherwise, .NET will leave Excel in memory until resources run low and automatic garbage collection takes place (I think of this as waiting for my son to do the job, rather than doing it myself). You don't want to call GC.Collect frequently, because it is an expensive operation, but it is great when you want to free very large objects like Excel.

Work with Excel Objects in .NET

Once you've got an instance of the Excel `Application` object, you can use it to get at any of the other objects in the Excel object library. Visual Basic .NET provides an `Imports` declaration that you can use to create a shortcut for referring to objects from a particular library. For example, the following class-level declaration:

```
Imports Microsoft.Office.Interop
```

shortens the Excel application declaration to:

```
Dim WithEvents m_xl As Excel.Application
```

which is easier to type and read. Notice that you don't use `Set` to get object references in Visual Basic .NET. For example, the following code gets a reference to `Workbook` and `Range` objects to display powers of 2 on a worksheet:

```
' .NET code.
Dim wb As Excel.Workbook, rng As Excel.Range
' Create a new workbook.
wb = m_xl.Workbooks.Add( )
' Add some data
For i As Integer = 1 To 10
    rng = wb.Worksheets(1).Cells(1, i)
    rng.Value = 2 ^ i
Next
```

Visual Basic .NET could get rid of `Set` because it also got rid of default members. In Excel VBA, you can assign a value to a `Range` object because the `Value` property is the default member of the `Range` object. This is a clearer approach to a language—default members were never a very good idea.

This change can take some getting used to, especially if you don't explicitly declare a type for a variable. For example, the following .NET code gets a reference to a `Range` object, but then replaces that reference with an integer:

```
Dim obj
' Gets a reference to the A1 range object.
obj = wb.Worksheets(1).Cells(1, 1)
' Assigns a number to obj (does not set [A1].Value!)
obj = 42
```

Because of this, it is a good idea to declare variables with explicit datatypes when programming in Visual Basic .NET. Using explicit types also enables the Intellisense and Auto Complete features when working with variables—so there are a lot of good reasons to be explicit!

Respond to Excel Events in .NET

Responding to Excel events in .NET code is done much the same way as in Excel VBA, but with one difference: In .NET, event procedures are associated with objects using the `Handles` clause. Excel uses the procedure name to associate an event with an object. The .NET approach means that a single procedure can handle multiple events.

To respond to Excel events in .NET:

1. Declare a WithEvents variable for the Excel object, providing the events at the class level. For example, the following code declares a worksheet with events:

    ```
    Dim WithEvents m_ws As Excel.Workbook
    ```

2. Assign the variable an instance of the object for which to handle events. For example, the following code hooks up the events for the first worksheet in a workbook (created in earlier examples):

    ```
    m_ws = wb.Worksheets(1)
    ```

3. Select the m_ws object from the object list at the top of the Code window and then select an event from the event list. Visual Studio creates a new, empty event procedure.

4. Write code to respond to the event.

For example, the following code sorts any string entered in cell A2 and displays the result in B2. It may look familiar, since it uses the NetString class created earlier to perform the sort:

```
Private Sub m_wb_SheetChange(ByVal Sh As Object, _
  ByVal Target As Microsoft.Office.Interop.Excel.Range) _
  Handles m_wb.SheetChange
    If Target.Address = "$A$2" Then
        Dim NetStr As New NetForExcel.NetString
        m_wb.Worksheets(1).Range("B2").Value = NetStr.Sort(Target.Value)
    End If
End Sub
```

Respond to Excel Exceptions in .NET

In .NET, you handle exceptions using the Visual Basic .NET Try...Catch...End Try construct. When .NET receives an exception from a COM component, such as Excel, it checks the COM exception code (COM identifies exceptions as *HRESULTs* that are 32-bit numbers) and tries to map that code to one of the .NET exception classes, such as DivideByZeroException.

If .NET can't map an HRESULT to a .NET exception class, it reports that exception as a COMException. A COMException includes Source and Message properties that are filled in if they are available, plus it includes the HRESULT as an ErrorCode property.

When working with Excel from .NET, you will find that most errors are reported as COMExceptions and that the Source and Message properties are sometimes, but not always, helpful. For example, referring to a worksheet that doesn't exist causes an COMException with Source equal to "Microsoft.Office.Interop.Excel" and a Message property "Invalid index". But setting a cell to an invalid value is reported as a

COMException with an empty Source property and a Message property set to "Exception from HRESULT: 0x800A03EC".

The following code illustrates causing, catching, and reporting different types of Excel exceptions in .NET:

```
Private Sub cmdCauseErrors_Click(ByVal sender As System.Object, _
   ByVal e As System.EventArgs) Handles cmdCauseError.Click
      Try
         ' This worksheet (9) doesn't exist.
         m_xl.ActiveWorkbook.Sheets(9).Range("B2").value = 42
      Catch ex As System.Runtime.InteropServices.COMException
         Debug.WriteLine(ex.Source & " " & ex.Message & " " & Hex(ex.errorcode))
      End Try
      Try
         ' This is an invalid value for a cell.
         m_ws.Range("A3").Value = "=This won't work."
      Catch ex As System.Runtime.InteropServices.COMException
         Debug.WriteLine(ex.Source & " " & ex.Message & " " & Hex(ex.errorcode))
      End Try
      Try
         ' Set breakpoint here and edit a cell in Excel to see error.
         m_xl.ActiveWorkbook.Sheets(1).Range("B3").select()
         ' Can't change a cell while Excel is editing a range.
         m_xl.ActiveWorkbook.Sheets(1).Range("B2").value = 42
      Catch ex As System.Runtime.InteropServices.COMException
         Debug.WriteLine(ex.Source & " " & ex.Message & " " & Hex(ex.errorcode))
      End Try
   End Sub
```

The preceding code catches the COMException that occurs for each deliberately caused error. If you run the code, the following report will display in the Visual Studio .NET Output window:

```
Microsoft.Office.Interop.Excel Invalid index. 8002000B
 Exception from HRESULT: 0x800A03EC. 800A03EC
mscorlib Call was rejected by callee. 80010001
```

As you can see, the Source and Message properties are not always helpful (or even present). In many cases, it is better to use the ErrorCode that contains the original COM HRESULT.

HRESULTs consist of several parts, but the last 16 bits are the most useful when programming with Excel from .NET; those 16 bits contain the Excel error code for the error. The following helper function parses an HRESULT and returns the Excel error code:

```
' Returns the last 16 bits of HRESULT (which is Err code).
Function GetErrCode(ByVal hresult As Integer) As Integer
   Return hresult And &HFFFF
End Function
```

That said, Excel assigns the error code 1004 (application error) to most of the exceptions it returns. All of this means that it is pretty hard to find out what specific error occurred within Excel—usually you just know that the operation failed.

Therefore, the best strategy for handling Excel exceptions in .NET is to:

- *Unitize* Excel operations—that is, try to group operations that use Excel into a single procedure that performs some atomic operation, such as creating, populating, and saving a workbook.
- Call these unitized operations from within a Try...Catch structure.
- Notify user of a general problem if operation failed.
- Avoid user-interactive modes. Operations such as changing spreadsheet cell values can fail if the user is editing a cell when the programmatic operation occurs. Use the Excel Application object's Interactive property to turn user-interactive mode on and off.

The following code illustrates the preceding approaches in the context of making some changes to cells on a worksheet. The Excel operations are unitized in a single procedure, and those operations all run within a Try...Catch block. User interaction is turned off at the start of the procedure, then reenabled at the end:

```
Private Sub cmdChangeCells_Click(ByVal sender As System.Object, _
  ByVal e As System.EventArgs) Handles cmdChangeCells.Click
    If Not SquareCells() Then _
        MsgBox("Excel operation failed.")
End Sub

Private Function SquareCells() As Boolean
    Try
        ' Try to turn off interactive mode.
        m_xl.Interactive = False
        ' For each cell in the active sheet's used range...
        For Each cel As Excel.Range In m_xl.ActiveSheet.UsedRange
            ' Square the value.
            cel.Value = cel.Value ^ 2
        Next
    Catch ex As System.Runtime.InteropServices.COMException
        ' Something happened in Excel.
        Debug.Fail(ex.Source & " " & Hex(ex.errorcode), ex.Message)
        Return False
    Catch ex As Exception
        ' Something happened in .NET (display error while debugging)
        Debug.Fail(ex.Source, ex.Message)
        Return False
    Finally
        Try
            ' Try to turn interactive mode back on.
            m_xl.Interactive = True
        Catch ex As Exception
            ' No need to do anything here.
        End Try
```

```
        End Try
        ' Success.
        Return True
    End Function
```

There are a couple of important details to point out here. First, you must turn inter-activity back on inside its own Try...Catch block. This protects against an unhandled exception if m_xl is not a valid object (perhaps because the user has closed Excel). Second, if the worksheet contains cells with text, an error will occur, but it will be handled. This may or may not be what you want to occur—that decision is up to you.

 Be careful when using For...Each with the Excel UsedCells collection. Visual Basic .NET doesn't always recognize UsedCells as a proper collection—in those cases you will encounter a Member Not Found COM error. To avoid this problem, call UsedCells directly from the Application.ActiveSheet or Application.Worksheets(*index*) objects rather than from variables referencing those objects.

Distribute .NET Applications That Use Excel

Use the Visual Studio .NET setup and deployment project to create an installation program for applications that use Excel as a component. (See "Distribute .NET Components," earlier in this chapter, for a walk-through of using the Setup Wizard.)

The .NET setup tools detect the .NET Framework and Excel PIAs as dependencies of any application that uses Excel as a component and includes those files with the installation. However, the setup tools do not automatically check for the installation of Microsoft Excel, or any other Microsoft Office product. You can add required products as a launch condition in the setup project for your application.

PIAs are available for Excel 2002 and later. However, you can use Visual Studio .NET type library import tools to create interop assemblies for earlier versions of Excel (they won't work as well as the PIAs, but they *will* work). All interop assemblies are tied to a specific version of Excel, so you should check that the required version of Excel is installed on the user's computer before installing your application and each time your application starts. You can use the following code to detect which version of Excel is installed:

```
' Uses the following Imports statement for RegistryKey classes:
Imports Microsoft.Win32
Function GetExcelVer() As String
    ' Define the RegistryKey objects.
    Dim regRoot As RegistryKey, regExcel As RegistryKey, ver As String
    ' Get root registry entry.
    regRoot = Microsoft.Win32.Registry.ClassesRoot
    ' Get the Excel current version registry entry.
    regExcel = regRoot.OpenSubKey("Excel.Application\CurVer")
    ' If regExcel is Nothing, then Excel is not installed.
```

```
        If IsNothing(regExcel) Then
            ' Close Registry key.
            regExcel.Close()
            ' Return 0, no version is installed
            ver = "0"
        Else
            ver = regExcel.GetValue("")
        End If
        ' Close registry.
        regExcel.Close()
        ' Return the Excel version.
        Return ver
End Function
```

It is possible to have a .NET application work with multiple versions of Excel; however, you would have to install interop assemblies for each version, restrict the features you use based on the version of Excel that is installed, and expend considerable effort debugging and testing your application for each Excel version.

 According to Microsoft, you can distribute the Office PIAs and the .NET runtime as part of your application royalty free. Of course, you can't distribute Microsoft Excel or Microsoft Office royalty free. For answers to more subtle questions, you should consult the Microsoft licensing agreements.

Create Excel Applications in .NET

A third and final way for Excel and .NET to interact is through the Visual Studio .NET Tools for Office. This set of tools includes Visual Studio .NET project templates for Excel and Word. These project templates allow you to link a specific document to a .NET assembly that loads whenever the user opens that document. The .NET code in the assembly can control Excel and respond to Excel events as described in the preceding sections.

To create an Excel application in Visual Studio .NET:

1. From the Project menu, choose New, Project. Visual Studio .NET displays the New Project dialog box.

2. Select the Microsoft Office System Projects, Visual Basic Projects project type and Excel Workbook template. Give the project a descriptive name and click OK. Visual Studio .NET starts the Microsoft Office Project Wizard to walk you through.

3. Click Finish to create the project folder and empty workbook and code template files.

4. Visual Studio .NET doesn't automatically add the workbook to the project, so it is a good idea to add it at this point. From the Project menu, choose Add Existing Item and then select the *.xls* file found in the application folder.

5. Once the workbook is added to the project, select the workbook in the Solution Explorer and set its Build Action property to Content. This will ensure that the workbook is distributed with your application if you create an installation program.

When Visual Studio .NET creates an Excel project, it adds references to the Microsoft Office and Excel PIAs, adds Imports statements to provide shortcuts to the Office and Excel classes, and generates code to ThisApplication and ThisWorkbook objects, as shown in Figure 25-12.

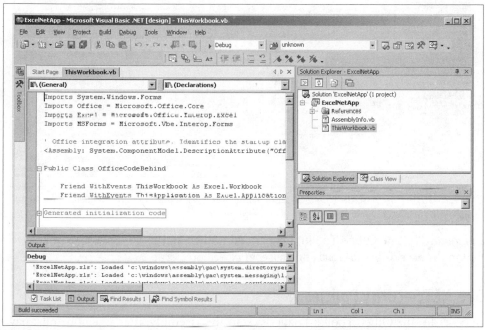

Figure 25-12. A newly created Excel project in Visual Studio .NET

Visual Studio .NET links the workbook to the project's assembly through two custom document properties: _AssemblyLocation0 and _AssemblyName0. The _AssemblyLocation0 property corresponds to the Visual Studio .NET project's Assembly Link Location property, as shown in Figure 25-13.

You might notice that an Excel project has both a \bin and a \projectname_bin folder. Excel projects write assembly output first to the \bin folder, then copy that file to the secondary folder. This allows the project to compile even if the Excel workbook has the assembly open in the secondary folder. Plus it allows the project to be automatically deployed to a public location every time you build it—a process Microsoft calls *no-touch deployment*.

When you open an Excel workbook that has _AssemblyLocation0 and _AssemblyName0 custom properties, Excel automatically starts the Office Toolkit Loader add-in

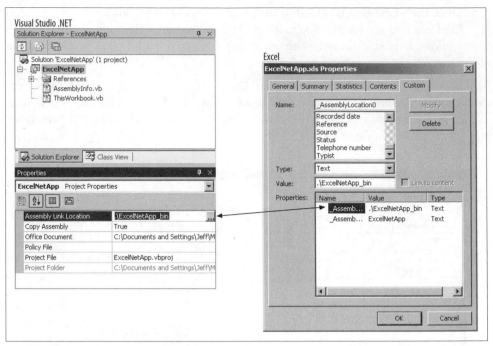

Figure 25-13. Setting Assembly Link Location changes the _AssemblyLocation0 custom document property in the Excel workbook

(*otkloadr.dll*). The Office Toolkit Loader add-in then starts the .NET assembly specified in the AssemblyLocation0 and _AssemblyName0 properties.

Set .NET Security Policies

In order for the Office Toolkit Loader to start the assembly, that assembly must have Full Trust permissions on the user's machine. The Microsoft Office Project Wizard automatically sets this permission on your machine, but if you move the project or deploy it, you will need to set the permission using the .NET Configuration Tool.

To set Full Trust permissions for the Excel project's assembly on your machine:

1. From the Control Panel, choose Administrative Tools and run the .NET Framework Wizard's utility for the most recent version of the .NET Framework installed on your machine.

2. Select Trust an Assembly Wizard. The Trust an Assembly Wizard starts and displays Step 1. Click Next.

3. Enter the address of the assembly (.*dll*), as shown in Figure 25-14, and click Next.

4. Set the level of trust to Full Trust, as shown in Figure 25-15, and click Next and then Finish to update your .NET security configuration.

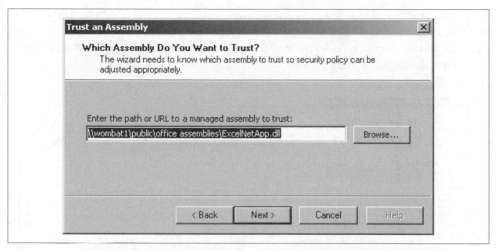

Figure 25-14. Set the location and name of the Excel application assembly

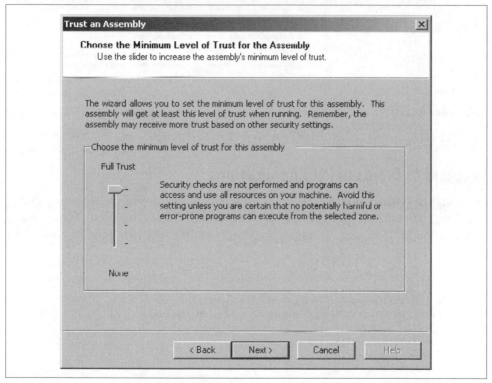

Figure 25-15. Set Full Trust for the Excel application assembly

You can view the .NET Framework security settings for .NET Office projects by starting the .NET Configuration Administrative Tool and expanding the My Computer, Runtime Security Policy, User, Code Groups, All_Code, Office_Projects tree-view item, as shown in Figure 25-16.

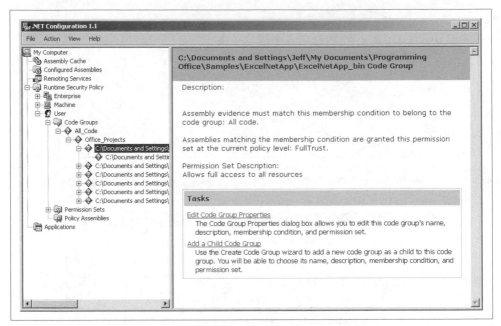

Figure 25-16. Viewing the .NET security policies for Excel .NET applications

Respond to Events in .NET Applications

The default Visual Studio .NET Excel project contains object declarations for the Excel `Application` and `Workbook` objects using the `WithEvents` keyword. That plus the initialization code in the `_Startup` procedure enable event handling for those two objects:

```
Public Class OfficeCodeBehind

    Friend WithEvents ThisWorkbook As Excel.Workbook
    Friend WithEvents ThisApplication As Excel.Application

#Region "Generated initialization code"
    ' Default constructor.
    Public Sub New()
    End Sub

    ' Required procedure. Do not modify.
    Public Sub _Startup(ByVal application As Object, ByVal workbook As Object)
        ThisApplication = CType(application, Excel.Application)
        ThisWorkbook = CType(workbook, Excel.Workbook)
```

```
        End Sub
' Remaining class definition omitted here...
```

You can use events that occur for the `Application` and `Workbook` objects by selecting the object and event from the listboxes at the top of the Visual Studio .NET Code window as you did in previous sections. If you want to add an Excel object to the objects and events lists, declare an object variable `WithEvents` and initialize the object somewhere in code. For example, the following additions (in **bold**) create an `ActiveWorksheet` object that responds to events:

```
Friend WithEvents ThisWorkbook As Excel.Workbook
Friend WithEvents ThisApplication As Excel.Application
Friend WithEvents ActiveWorksheet As Excel.Worksheet

' Called when the workbook is opened.
Private Sub ThisWorkbook_Open() Handles ThisWorkbook.Open
    ' Activate a worksheet.
    ThisApplication.Sheets("Sheet1").activate()
    ' Set the ActiveSheet object
    If ThisApplication.ActiveSheet.Type = Excel.XlSheetType.xlWorksheet Then _
        ActiveWorksheet = CType(ThisApplication.ActiveSheet, Excel.Worksheet)
End Sub

Private Sub ThisWorkbook_SheetActivate(ByVal Sh As Object) _
  Handles ThisWorkbook.SheetActivate
    ' Change active worksheet
    If Sh.Type = Excel.XlSheetType.xlWorksheet Then _
        ActiveWorksheet = CType(Sh, Excel.Worksheet)
End Sub
```

The preceding code creates an `ActiveWorksheet` object and hooks the active worksheet in Excel to that object's events. Whenever the active worksheet changes, the `SheetActivate` event updates the `ActiveWorksheet` object, ensuring that it is always current. If you add the following event procedure, any value entered in cell A1 is automatically squared and displayed in cell A2:

```
Private Sub ActiveWorksheet_Change(ByVal Target As Excel.Range) _
  Handles ActiveWorksheet.Change
    ' Square value entered in range A1 and displayed in A2.
    If Target.Address = "$A$1" Then
        ActiveWorksheet.Range("A2").Value = Target.Value ^ 2
    End If
End Sub
```

This approach works well for built-in Excel objects such as `Worksheets` and `Charts`, but when you add controls to a worksheet, you must use the code template's `FindControl` method to get the control so you can hook up its events. The `FindControl` method is *overloaded*—meaning it comes in two versions, as shown here:

```
' Returns the control with the specified name
' on ThisWorkbook's active worksheet.
Overloads Function FindControl(ByVal name As String) As Object
```

```
        Return FindControl(name, CType(ThisWorkbook.ActiveSheet, Excel.Worksheet))
    End Function

    ' Returns the control with the specified name on the specified worksheet.
    Overloads Function FindControl(ByVal name As String, _
       ByVal sheet As Excel.Worksheet) As Object
        Dim theObject As Excel.OLEObject
        Try
            theObject = CType(sheet.OLEObjects(name), Excel.OLEObject)
            Return theObject.Object
        Catch Ex As Exception
            ' Returns Nothing if the control is not found.
        End Try
        Return Nothing
    End Function
```

Because FindControl is overloaded, you can call the method with one or two arguments. If you provide only the object name, FindControl assumes that the control is
on the active worksheet. Overloading is Visual Basic .NET's way of dealing with
optional arguments. The following code (in **bold**) hooks up events for the cmdReformat
button found on Sheet1:

```
    Friend WithEvents cmdReformat As MSForms.CommandButton

    ' Called when the workbook is opened.
    Private Sub ThisWorkbook_Open() Handles ThisWorkbook.Open
        ' Activate the worksheet the control is found on.
        ThisApplication.Sheets("Sheet1").activate()
        ' Set the ActiveSheet object
        If ThisApplication.ActiveSheet.Type = Excel.XlSheetType.xlWorksheet Then _
           ActiveWorksheet = CType(ThisApplication.ActiveSheet, Excel.Worksheet)
        ' Find the control on the sheet and hook up its events.
        cmdReformat = CType(FindControl("cmdReformat"), _
           MSForms.CommandButton)
    End Sub
```

Notice that you need to convert the type of object returned by FindControl into a
CommandButton type. That is because the CommandButton class exposes a full set of
events (Click, MouseDown, DragOver, etc.) while the OLEObject class provides only
GotFocus and LostFocus events. Once you've hooked up the control's events, you can
write event procedures for that control, as shown here:

```
    Private Sub cmdReformat_Click() Handles cmdReformat.Click
        ReformatHTML(ActiveWorksheet)
    End Sub
```

Debug Excel .NET Applications

Excel projects do not report errors that occur in Excel the way you might expect.
Instead of halting execution when an error occurs, Excel projects just continue on as
if nothing happened. This can be very confusing since the code exits the procedure
where the error occurred and no warning is displayed. A good way to see this behavior is to try to activate a worksheet that doesn't exist. For example:

```
Private Sub ThisWorkbook_Open() Handles ThisWorkbook.Open
    ThisApplication.Sheets("doesn't exist").activate() ' Error! Code exits here.
    ' Set the ActiveSheet object
    If ThisApplication.ActiveSheet.Type = Excel.XlSheetType.xlWorksheet Then _
    ActiveWorksheet = CType(ThisApplication.ActiveSheet, Excel.Worksheet)
    ' Find the control on the sheet and hook up its events.
    cmdReformat = CType(FindControl("cmdReformat"), MSForms.CommandButton)
End Sub
```

In the preceding code, ActiveWorksheet and cmdReformat are never set because Excel can't find the worksheet to activate. The project keeps running, though, and you're just left to wonder why none of your event procedures are working.

You can prevent this by telling Visual Studio .NET to break into the debugger when exceptions are thrown, as described in the following steps:

1. From the Debug menu, choose Exceptions. Visual Studio .NET displays the Exceptions dialog box.

2. Select Common Language Runtime Exceptions and under "When the exception is thrown," select "Break into the debugger," as shown in Figure 25-17. Then click OK.

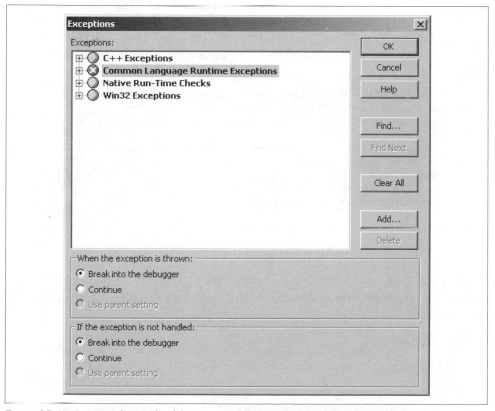

Figure 25-17. Set "Break into the debugger" to detect exceptions in Excel projects

Once you tell Visual Studio .NET to break on all runtime exceptions, you'll start seeing exceptions that are handled as well those that aren't. Two handled file-not-found exceptions occur every time an Excel project starts, as shown in Figure 25-18.

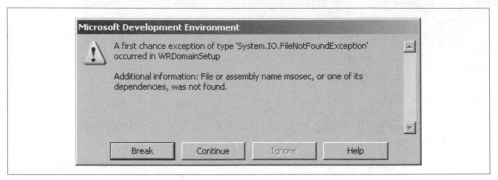

Figure 25-18. This (handled) exception occurs twice every time an Excel project starts

You can ignore these handled exceptions—clicking Continue a couple times each time you start is a little annoying, but at least you can catch code that doesn't work!

Another way to detect exceptions, without breaking for all of them, is to add Try... Catch blocks to your code. The FindControl method actually does this, but it omits a useful technique for reporting exceptions while debugging. It's a good idea to add a Debug.Fail statement to the code template's FindControl method, as shown here (in **bold**):

```
Overloads Function FindControl(ByVal name As String, _
   ByVal sheet As Excel.Worksheet) As Object
     Dim theObject As Excel.OLEObject
     Try
         theObject = CType(sheet.OLEObjects(name), Excel.OLEObject)
         Return theObject.Object
     Catch Ex As Exception
         ' Report the exception.
         Debug.Fail(Ex.Message, Ex.ToString)
     End Try
     Return Nothing
End Function
```

Now, FindControl displays an error message during debugging if a control is not found, rather than just continuing on. Debug.Fail is especially useful since it doesn't affect your released application—the .NET Framework disables the Debug class in code that is built for release.

Excel automatically loads the assembly associated with a workbook when you open that workbook. If the assembly has errors, or if you just want to bypass loading the assembly, hold the Shift key down while opening the workbook. That prevents Excel from running the startup code and loading the assembly.

Display Forms

Excel projects can use Windows forms to gather information and display results. To create a Windows form in Visual Studio .NET for use from Excel, follow these steps:

1. From the Project menu, choose Add Windows Form. Visual Studio .NET displays the Add New Item dialog box.

2. Enter a name for the form and click OK. Visual Studio .NET creates a new Windows form class and displays the class in the Designer.

3. Use the Designer to add controls to the form; then switch to the Code window. Unlike previous versions of Visual Basic, Visual Basic .NET describes the entire form in terms of code. The form and control properties are all maintained in the "Windows Form Designer generated code" region of the form's class.

4. In order to enable the form to interact with Excel, add the following lines to the generated code (shown in **bold**):

```
Imports Excel = Microsoft.Office.Interop.Excel

Public Class SimpleForm
    Inherits System.Windows.Forms.Form

    Dim xlCode As OfficeCodeBehind

#Region " Windows Form Designer generated code "

    Public Sub New(ByVal target As OfficeCodeBehind)
        MyBase.New()

        'This call is required by the Windows Form Designer.
        InitializeComponent()

        'Add any initialization after the InitializeComponent() call
        ' Get the OfficeCodeBehind class that created this form
        ' (used to return responses to Excel).
        xlCode = target
    End Sub
    ' Remainder of class omitted here...
```

5. Within the form's event procedures, use the xlCode object created in Step 4 to interact with Excel. For example, the following code squares each of the values in the active worksheet when the user clicks the Square Values button:

```
Private Sub cmdSquare_Click(ByVal sender As System.Object, _
  ByVal e As System.EventArgs) Handles cmdSquare.Click
    ' If SquareCells succeeds, then close this form.
    If SquareCells() Then Me.Close()
End Sub

Private Function SquareCells() As Boolean
    Try
        ' For each cell in the active sheet's used range...
        For Each cel As Excel.Range In _
```

```
         xlCode.ThisWorkbook.ActiveSheet.UsedRange
            ' Square the value.
            cel.Value = cel.Value ^ 2
      Next
   Catch ex As System.Runtime.InteropServices.COMException
      ' Something happened in Excel.
      Debug.Fail(ex.Source & " " & Hex(ex.errorcode), ex.Message)
      Return False
   Catch ex As Exception
      ' Something happened in .NET (display error while debugging)
      Debug.Fail(ex.Source, ex.Message)
      Return False
   End Try
   ' Success.
   Return True
End Function
```

6. Write code in the `OfficeCodeBehind` class to create the form and display it. For example, the following code creates a new form based on the `SimpleForm` class and displays it from Excel:

```
' In OfficeCodeBehind class.
Private Sub cmdSquare_Click() Handles cmdForm.Click
    ' Create a new form object.
    Dim frm As New SimpleForm(Me)
    frm.ShowDialog()
End Sub
```

The preceding procedure passes the `OfficeCodeBehind` class instance to the form's constructor in the code `New SimpleForm(Me)`. The form keeps that instance as the class-level `xlCode` variable defined in Step 4.

The .NET Framework provides two methods used to display forms: `ShowDialog` displays forms modally; the form stays on top and must be closed before the user returns to Excel. `Show` displays forms nonmodally; the form may appear in front of or behind the Excel window, depending on which window has focus.

When working with Excel, you'll usually want to display Windows forms modally (using `ShowDialog`). Exceptions to this rule might include cases in which you want to display some output that you want to keep around, such as a floating toolbar or a Help window. In these cases, you can use the `Show` method combined with the `TopMost` property to keep the nonmodal form displayed on top of Excel.

For example, the following code displays a new form based on the `SimpleForm` class nonmodally but keeps it on top of the other windows:

```
Private Sub cmdSquare_Click() Handles cmdForm.Click
    ' Create a new form object.
    Dim frm As New SimpleForm(Me)
    ' Show the form nonmodally but keep it on top.
    frm.TopMost = True
     frm.Show()
End Sub
```

Distribute Excel .NET Applications

One of the big advantages of Excel .NET applications is that they can be easily distributed through a network. Just set the project Assembly Link Location property to a network address and distribute the Excel workbook that uses the assembly. Whenever anyone uses the workbook, the assembly will then be loaded from that network location.

Before you can distribute applications in this way, however, you need to make sure your users meet the following requirements:

- They must be using Excel 2003 or later. Prior versions of Excel are not supported for Excel .NET applications.
- The Office PIAs must be installed on the user's machine.
- The .NET Framework Version 1.1 runtime must be installed.
- The user's .NET security policy must specify Full Trust for the network address from which the assembly is distributed.

The first two requirements are best handled using the Office Resource Kit's Custom Installation Wizard or Custom Maintenance Wizard. You can use those tools to create a chained installation that calls subsequent installation programs, such as the setup for Excel .NET application prerequisites and security policy settings.

The .NET setup and deployment projects detect the Office PIAs and .NET Framework as dependencies of the Excel application. According to the Visual Studio .NET Tools for Office documentation, you shouldn't distribute the PIAs through your setup program (instead, use the Office setup to do this as mentioned earlier). Special steps for creating an installation program for Excel .NET application prerequisites include:

1. Exclude the PIAs from the setup project. These are added as dependencies by default.

2. Optionally, exclude the Primary Output (*projectname.dll*) from the installation. Usually, you'll want to distribute the assembly from a network address, rather than installing it on client machines where it is harder to update.

3. Create a batch file, script, or Windows installer to set the client's .NET security policy to enable the assembly to load from its network address.

A simple way to set security policies on a client is to use a batch file that calls the .NET utility *caspole.exe*. The following batch file assigns Full Trust to the network location *wombat2\SharedDocs\bin*:

```
REM Adds FullTrust for \\wombat2\Sharedocs\bin location.
%WINDIR%\Microsoft.NET\Framework\v1.1.4322\caspol -pp off -m -ag
LocalIntranet_Zone -url \\wombat2\shareddocs\bin\* FullTrust -n
"Excel Project Assemblies" -d "Share point for .NET code running in
Office 2003 applications."
%WINDIR%\Microsoft.NET\Framework\v1.1.4322\caspol -pp on
```

You can also use *caspole.exe* to remove a security policy, as shown here:

```
REM Removes FullTrust for \\wombat2\Sharedocs\bin location.
%WINDIR%\Microsoft.NET\Framework\v1.1.4322\caspol -pp off -remgroup
"Excel Project Assemblies"
%WINDIR%\Microsoft.NET\Framework\v1.1.4322\caspol -pp on
```

Another way to distribute security policies is by using the .NET configuration utility to generate a Windows installer file (*.msi*) for a group policy. To do this, follow these steps:

1. Configure your machine with the security policies you want to deploy.

2. Start the .NET configuration utility for the current version of the .NET Framework.

3. Select the Runtime Security Policy item in the treeview and click Create Deployment Package as shown in Figure 25-19.

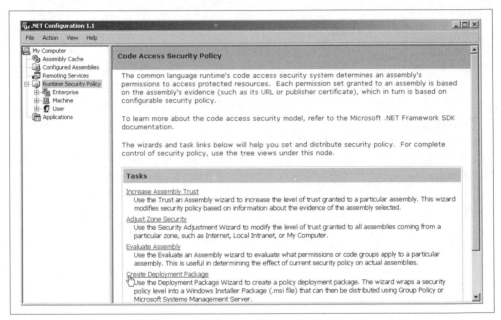

Figure 25-19. Creating a Windows installer for .NET security policies

4. Follow the steps in the wizard to create an *.msi* file containing the security policies to deploy (Figure 25-20).

5. Click Next, then Finish to create the Windows installer file (*.msi*).

Once you've created the *.msi* file, you can deploy that policy to your enterprise by using the Group Policy Editor snap-in from the Microsoft Management Console (*mmc.exe*) or by installing the *.msi* file individually on client computers.

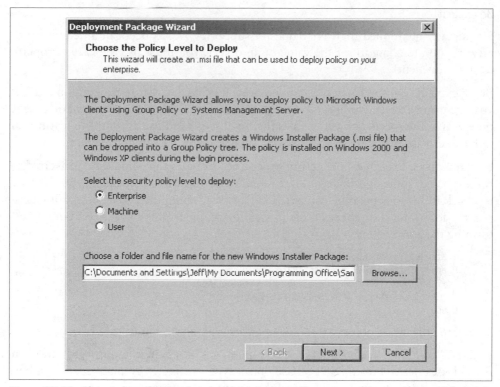

Figure 25-20. Choose the policy level to deploy and enter a filename to create

Migrate to .NET

If you are an experienced VBA programmer, you've got a good start on learning Visual Basic .NET; however, there are significant language differences, so be prepared for a learning curve and don't expect to be able to cut and paste code from an Excel VBA project into Visual Basic .NET and have the code run.

Existing Excel VBA code may provide a template for Visual Basic .NET code, but Visual Basic .NET is really a different language from Excel VBA. There are large as well as subtle differences. If you are new to Visual Basic .NET, you will save a great deal of time by buying and reading one of the many books on Visual Basic .NET. One of the best, in my opinion, is *Programming Microsoft Visual Basic 2005* by Francesco Balena (Microsoft Press).

The following sections list a few recommendations that may make your transition easier.

Be explicit

I've already mentioned that .NET doesn't support VBA's concept of a default property. If you are going to set the value of an object, you must use the Value property (or its equivalent).

Being explicit also applies to object references. It is much easier to program in .NET if you are using a specific object type, such as Worksheet, rather than the generic Object type. Using the specific object enables the Intellisense and Auto Complete features of .NET and helps detect inadvertent errors, such as incorrect variable assignments.

In many cases, Excel methods return generic object types that should be converted to the expected, more specific type. Use CType to perform this conversion, but be sure to check if the object can be converted before performing the conversion. For example, the following code checks if the passed-in argument Sh is a Worksheet before performing the conversion:

```
Private Sub ThisWorkbook_SheetActivate(ByVal Sh As Object) _
   Handles ThisWorkbook.SheetActivate
     If Sh.Type = Excel.XlSheetType.xlWorksheet Then _
        ActiveWorksheet = CType(Sh, Excel.Worksheet)
End Sub
```

Trying to convert an object to an incompatible type causes a runtime error.

In .NET, *everything* is an object. Even simple types like strings and integers are their own classes derived from .NET's base object type. At first, this might seem cumbersome, but the consistency and logic of this approach pay huge dividends.

Pass arguments by value

By default in VBA, procedures pass arguments by reference. The default in .NET is to pass arguments by value. If you cut and paste code from VBA, .NET will add ByVal to unqualified argument definitions, thus changing how the arguments are passed.

Collections start at zero

The index of the first element of any .NET collection is zero. For Excel objects, the first element of any collection is 1.

Data access is through ADO.NET

.NET provides access to databases, XML data, and in-memory data tables through ADO.NET, which is significantly different from prior data-access techniques. Backward-compatibility is provided for ADO data binding, but the best advice here is to pick up a good book on the subject and start learning.

Resources

Additional information about the topics in this section is available from the following online sources:

Topic	Source
Converting VBA code to .NET	Search *http://msdn.microsoft.com* for "Converting code from VBA to Visual Basic .NET."
Structure of COM HRESULTs	Search *http://msdn.microsoft.com* for "Structure of COM error codes."
Configuring .NET assembly security	Search *http://msdn.microsoft.com* for "How to: grant permissions to folders and assemblies."
Visual Studio .NET Tools for Office	Visit *http://msdn.microsoft.com/vstudio/office/* or *http://msdn.microsoft.com/vstudio/howtobuy/officetools/*.
Creating Excel .NET applications	Search *http://msdn.microsoft.com* for "Creating Office solutions."

CHAPTER 26

Exploring Security in Depth

In the physical world, *security* is the freedom from danger. There are myriad dangers in the physical world, but in the world of Excel, dangers relate to protecting data (absent an army of spreadsheet-driven killer robots). Specifically, Excel security is designed to protect you from:

- Unauthorized or accidental changes
- Malicious changes or destruction of data
- Theft or unauthorized distribution of restricted information
- Attack from viruses

This chapter explains approaches to protecting your data from these threats and explains how to implement those approaches within Excel.

 Code used in this chapter and additional samples are available in *ch26.xls*.

Security Layers

When it's cold you dress in layers, and security works the same way. The outer layer is a firewall, preventing attacks from the Internet. Next, virus detection software scans permitted attachments and other files from bringing in malicious code. Then, operating system security defines users and their permissions. Finally, Excel provides its own security layer.

Data most at risk is that which is shared outside of these layers, such as a workbook posted on a public server. In that case, Excel becomes the primary security layer. Of course not all data needs the same level (or type) of protection. Therefore, Excel itself provides layers through these security approaches:

- Password protection and encryption control read and write access to workbooks.

- Worksheet protection password-protects items within a workbook and alternately can authorize changes based on user lists.

- User-based permissions allow authors to limit the rights of others to read, change, print, copy, or distribute a document. Permissions can also set an expiration date for a document.

- Digital signatures identify the author of a document, ensuring that a document is the authentic original—not a modified or spoof copy. Signatures can also be applied to macros and ActiveX controls to ensure their code is from a trusted source.

- Macro security levels determine what level of trust is required before Excel will run code included in worksheets, templates, add-ins, or Smart documents.

- ActiveX control security levels similarly limit which controls Excel will trust.

- The Office Anti Virus API provides an interface for antivirus software to scan documents for malicious code before they are opened.

- The custom installation wizard permits administrators to configure which security options are enabled during installation on users' machines.

These security approaches can be combined to provide a high level of assurance while still allowing files to be shared, macros to be run, and (ultimately) work to be done. The rest of this chapter discusses each of these approaches, along with Windows file security, then provides a list of common security tasks and describes how you complete those tasks by combining Excel security features.

Understand Windows Security

Before we talk about Excel security, it is important to explain some general concepts related to the Windows operating system. This may seem basic to some of you, but Windows security features are somewhat hidden and it's a good idea to cover them somewhere.

Permissions are a set of capabilities that someone has or doesn't have. Permissions apply to files and locations, so someone may be able to open a specific folder, see files, but not write to that folder or edit the files it contains.

Users are identities that Windows uses to control access. When you sign on with a username and password, Windows authenticates that information and thereafter identifies you as *machinename\username* if your network uses workgroups or *domainname\username* if your network uses domains. Your identity is then used any time you request permission to use a resource, such as open a file or run an application. If your identity has permission to use that resource, you are granted access and the requested file opens or the application runs.

Groups are the security groups to which a username belongs. Windows comes with some groups already configured: Administrators, Users, Guests, Backup Operators, and Power Users. Groups provide an easy way to grant a set of permissions to a set of users rather than having to grant permissions to many individual users.

Certificates and *digital signatures* are small identifiers that can be attached to a data file or executable that identify the author of the file or executable. Certificates are issued by a third-party certificate authority (sometimes called a CA), such as Verisign, which provides the service that authenticates certificates. The idea here is that if a user knows who the author of a particular file is, he is more likely to trust that it will not harm his computer.

Set File Permissions in Windows XP

How you set permissions is not obvious from the default setup of Windows XP. First, you must disable the Use Simple File Sharing folder option in Windows Explorer, as shown in Figure 26-1.

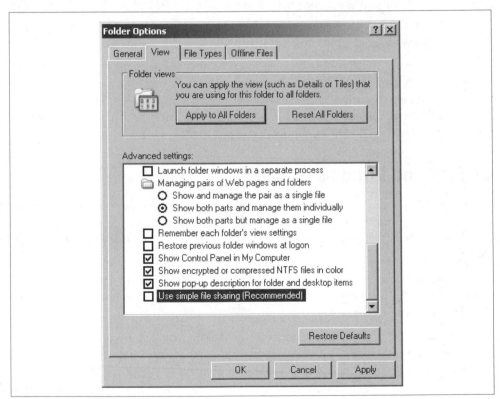

Figure 26-1. Disable simple file sharing in Windows XP to set permissions

To set permissions on a folder or file:

1. In Windows Explorer, select the file or folder to set permissions on and select Properties from the File menu.

2. Select the Security tab on the Properties dialog box (Figure 26-2). The top list displays user groups and individual users with permissions for the item. The bottom list shows the permissions assigned to each group or user.

3. Select a group or user, then assign or deny permissions by clicking on the boxes in the permissions list. Click OK when done.

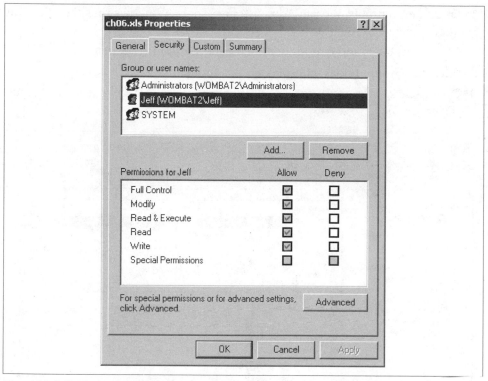

Figure 26-2. Setting permissions

If you're unfamiliar with how this works, it's a good idea to experiment with a file. For example, create an Excel workbook named *Book1.xls*, then deny Full Control for your username. OK, then try to open *Book1.xls* in Excel—you'll get an Access Denied error. Now change the file permissions to allow Read & Execute but deny Write access. You'll be able to open the file in Excel, but you can't save it as *Book1.xls*.

These permissions don't have much meaning in the preceding example because you can always change them back to allow writing or whatever. You own the file so you can do whatever you like. Permission settings are truly significant when a file is shared with other users, such as when the file is placed in a public network address.

For example, if you want to allow others to read workbooks but not to make changes, a simple solution is to create a shared folder that denies Write permission to everyone but you.

View Users and Groups in XP

When you set up user accounts from the Windows XP Control Panel, you have three types of accounts available: Computer Adminstrator, Limited, and Guest accounts. These accounts correspond to the Administrator, User, and Guest account groups within Windows. These aren't the only groups available, however. To view all the groups:

1. From the Control Panel, run Administrative Tools. Windows runs the Microsoft Management Console (MMC).

2. Click Local Users and Groups in the left pane to expand that item.

3. Select the Groups folder to display a list of Groups

4. Double-click on a group to view a list of the users that belong to that group (Figure 26-3).

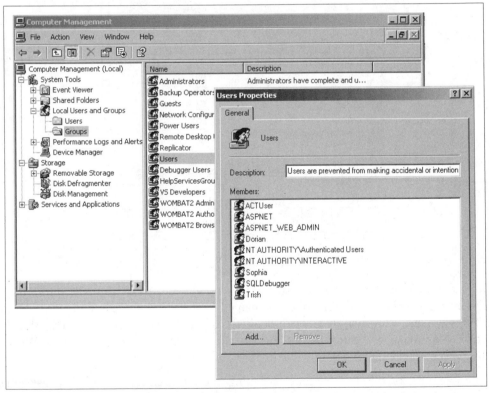

Figure 26-3. Viewing members of a group in MMC

Your list of groups may be different from the list shown in Figure 26-3 because applications often add groups and then add users as members of those groups. If you click around and explore a bit, you'll see that you can't set the permissions of groups or users through the MMC. That's because permissions are set on objects, not on identities.

For example, a folder in Windows may allow users that belong to the Administrators group to read and write files, but allow Users group member to only read those files, and prohibit Guest members from even reading files. In this case, the folder is the security object that defines the permissions for groups that have access.

Applications sometimes check whether a user belongs to a certain group before allowing her to perform a task. This is referred to as *role-based security*.

Password-Protect and Encrypt Workbooks

Passwords are a simple way to protect sensitive data in a workbook. You can use passwords to encrypt a workbook to provide added security. Encryption prevents hackers from being able to read your workbook by disassembling the file in some way.

To add a password to a workbook in Excel:

1. Choose Save As from the File menu. Excel displays the Save As dialog box.
2. On the Save As dialog box, click the Tools menu and select General Options. Excel displays the Save Options dialog box shown in Figure 26-4.

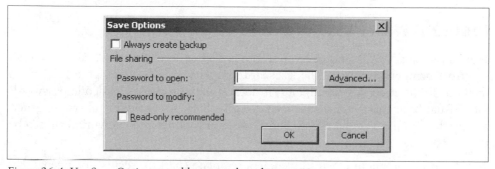

Figure 26-4. Use Save Options to add passwords and encryption

3. Enter passwords in the "Password to open" and/or "Password to modify" text boxes and click OK. To create a workbook that everyone can read but only password holders can edit, set "Password to modify" and leave "Password to open" blank.
4. Excel prompts you to confirm the passwords entered in the previous step.

To add encryption to a workbook:

1. Click the Advanced button after Step 2 in the preceding list. Excel displays the Encryption Type dialog box shown in Figure 26-5.
2. Select an encryption type from the listed encryption providers, choose an encryption key length, and click OK.
3. Proceed with setting the workbook password.

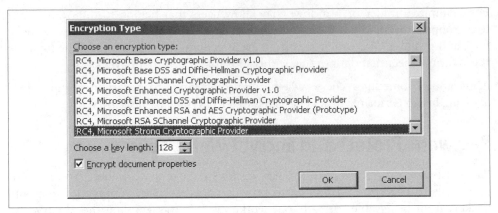

Figure 26-5. Choosing an encryption type

The encryption providers you have installed may vary depending on your location. Some encryption providers are not available outside of the United States, so you will want to take that into consideration if you are distributing encrypted files internationally. The longer the encryption key, the harder it is for a hacker to decrypt data. All software-based encryption is potentially reversible without the key.

Program with Passwords and Encryption

You can set passwords and encryption options in code using the `Workbook` object's security members, such as the `Password` property and `SetEncryptionProperties` method. From a security standpoint, it doesn't make sense to hardcode passwords into Visual Basic macros. Instead, the `Workbook` object's security members are generally used in conjunction with User Forms to set passwords and encryption chosen by the user through a customized interface.

For instance, you might create a document template (*.xlt*) for secure documents that can only be saved using a password and encryption. Such a template might include a user form to get the password, as shown in Figure 26-6.

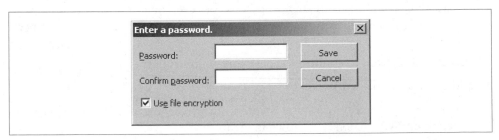

Figure 26-6. Password user form

The code for the user form confirms that the Password and Confirm Password text boxes match and allows the user to cancel the operation, as shown here:

```
' Public fields
Public Password As String, Encrypt As Boolean

Private Sub cmdCancel_Click()
    Me.Hide
    Password = ""
End Sub

Private Sub cmdSave_Click()
    If txtPassword.Text <> txtConfirm.Text Then
        MsgBox "Password and confirm password must match.", , "Confirm Error"
    Else
        Password = txtPassword.Text
        Encrypt = chkEncrypt.Value
        Me.Hide
    End If
End Sub
```

Then, the Secure template includes a workbook-level procedure to intercept the Save event. Whenever the user saves a document based on this template, the following code displays the password user form and sets the workbook password and encryption options (points of note are shown in **bold**):

```
Private Sub Workbook_BeforeSave(ByVal SaveAsUI As Boolean, Cancel As Boolean)
    Dim fname As String
    ' Exit if this is a template, not a workbook.
    If ThisWorkbook.FileFormat = xlTemplate Then Exit Sub ' (1)
    ' Cancel default operation.
    Cancel = True
    ' Get a password if one does not exist.
    If Not ThisWorkbook.HasPassword Then ' (2)
        frmPassword.Show
        ThisWorkbook.Password = frmPassword.Password ' (3)
        If frmPassword.Password = "" Then Exit Sub
        If frmPassword.Encrypt Then
            ThisWorkbook.SetPasswordEncryptionOptions _        ' (4)
                "Microsoft RSA SChannel Cryptographic Provider", _
                "RC4", 128, True
        End If
    End If
    ' Save the workbook by enabling the default action.
    Cancel = False    ' (5)
    ' Make sure the user form unloads.
    Unload frmPassword
End Sub
```

The key points are:

1. Exit the procedure if saving a template. This allows you to save the template without a password.

2. Use the `HasPassword` property to determine if a password has already been set. You can't use the `Password` property to test this, since it always returns asterisks whether or not a password is set (for security reasons).

3. You can set a password by assigning the workbook's `Password` property or by using the `SaveAs` method. Using `SaveAs` in this case would call the `Workbook_BeforeSave` event procedure again, resulting in an unwanted recursion.

4. Use the `SetEncryptionOptions` method to choose the type of encryption and the length of the encryption key. This is the only way to set encryption options, since the `PasswordEncryption` properties are all read-only.

5. Set Cancel to False to allow Excel to complete the save operation. As mentioned in Item 3, calling Save or SaveAs would result in unwanted recursion.

Workbook Password and Encryption Members

The Workbook object has more than 200 members. The following Workbook members deal with security; other Workbook members are described in Chapter 8:

HasPassword	Password
PasswordEncryptionAlgorithm	PasswordEncryptionFileProperties
PasswordEncryptionKeyLength	PasswordEncryptionProvider
SetPasswordEncryptionOptions	WritePassword
WriteReserved	WriteReservedBy

workbook.HasPassword

Returns True if a password is required to open the workbook. `HasPassword` does not detect whether or not a workbook has a write password. The following code removes a password if the workbook has one:

```
Dim wb As Workbook, pass As String
Set wb = ThisWorkbook
If wb.HasPassword Then
    wb.Password = ""
    MsgBox "Password removed.", , "Password"
Else
    MsgBox "No password found.", , "Password"
End If
```

workbook.Password [= setting]

Sets a password used to open the workbook. Returns "********" whether or not a password was previously set. The following code sets a password entered by the user in an InputBox:

```
Dim wb As Workbook, pass As String
Set wb = ThisWorkbook
pass = InputBox("Enter a password.", "Password")
If pass = "" Then Exit Sub
```

```
If pass = InputBox("Enter password again to confirm.", "Password") Then
    wb.Password = pass
    MsgBox "Password set.", , "Password."
Else
    MsgBox "Passwords don't match. No password set.", , "Password"
End If
```

The InputBox displays characters as they are typed. It is a better idea to use a user form with text boxes that display a password character to get passwords from users.

workbook.PasswordEncryptionAlgorithm

Returns a string indicating the type of encryption used for a workbook. The following code displays the encryption properties for a workbook in the Immediate window:

```
Set wb = ThisWorkbook
Debug.Print "Encrytpion algrorythm: " & wb.PasswordEncryptionAlgorithm, _
    "Encrypt properties? " & wb.PasswordEncryptionFileProperties, _
    "Key length:" & wb.PasswordEncryptionKeyLength, _
    "Provider: " & wb.PasswordFncryptionProvider
```

If a workbook is not encrypted, the PasswordEncryptionAlgorithm is OfficeStandard.

workbook.PasswordEncryptionFileProperties

Returns True if workbook file properties are encrypted, False if they are not.

workbook.PasswordEncryptionKeyLength

Returns the length of the encryption key.

workbook.PasswordEncryptionProvider

Returns the full name of the workbook's encryption provider. If the workbook is not encrypted, returns "Office".

workbook.SetPasswordEncryptionOptions(*PasswordEncryptionProvider, PasswordEncryptionAlgorithm, PasswordEncryptionKeyLength, PasswordEncryptionFileProperties*)

Sets the workbook's encryption properties.

Argument	Settings
PasswordEncryptionProvider	A string containing the full name of the encryption provider, such as "OfficeStandard" for no encryption or "Microsoft Base Cryptographic Provider v1.0".
PasswordEncryptionAlgorithm	A string containing the type of encryption to use. Use "Office" for no encryption, "RC4" for encryption.

Argument	Settings
PasswordEncryptionKeyLength	The length of the encryption key. Must be a valid value for the encryption provider.
PasswordEncryptionFileProperties	Set to True to encrypt the workbook's file properties, False to leave them unencrypted.

The following code sets strong encryption on a workbook:

```
Set wb = ThisWorkbook
wb.SetPasswordEncryptionOptions "Microsoft Strong Cryptographic Provider", _
    "RC4", 128, True
```

workbook.WritePassword [= *setting*]

Sets the workbook's Password to Modify setting in Excel. Always returns "********". The following code removes a workbook's Password to Open setting (read/write) and creates a read-only password:

```
Set wb = ThisWorkbook
wb.Password = ""
wb.WritePassword = "Excel2003"
```

workbook.WriteReserved

Returns True if the workbook has a WritePassword; otherwise, returns False. This property is similar to the HasPassword property, only it checks for a write password. The following code checks if the workbook has a write password and displays the name of the person who set the write password if it does:

```
Set wb = ThisWorkbook
If wb.WriteReserved Then _
    Debug.Print "Reserved by: " & wb.WriteReservedBy
```

workbook.WriteReservedBy

Returns the name of the author who set the write password. This is the same as the Last Author built-in document property of the workbook.

Excel Password Security

Encrypting a workbook makes it very difficult to extract passwords from a workbook by peeking inside the file in some way. However, Excel does leave passwords open to guessing attacks. In short, you can write a macro to call the Open method repeatedly with various passwords until you find one that works.

That's because Excel doesn't lock out attempts after a certain number of wrong passwords the way most networks do. Therefore, Excel passwords are only as good as their complexity.

For example, a four-character all-lowercase workbook password takes about 40 minutes to guess using brute-force techniques on a 2.0 GHz machine. By extrapolation, a mixed-case four-character password would take more than 10 hours, and a six-character password using any valid characters (letters, numbers, or symbols) would take 883 years.

That sounds pretty secure, but remember this is just using brute-force techniques—starting at Chr(33) and working through the valid character set. There are many ways to optimize guessing that would reduce these times. The controlling factors are how many attempts are made before guessing correctly and how long it takes Excel to run the Open method and return an error if the guess is wrong. For example, the Excel Key service on the Web promises password recovery in four to seven days regardless of password length.

These same guessing techniques can be applied to password-protected items within a workbook, such as worksheets. It is, in fact, much easier to guess the password for a protected worksheet since the Unprotect method returns an error five times faster than the Open method.

So what should you do? Here are some recommendations:

- Use strong passwords. Strong passwords are at least eight characters long and contain letters, numbers, and symbols.
- Encrypt password-protected files.
- Keep passwords secret. This is obvious, but it is also where most security breaches occur.
- Use third-party encryption tools for truly sensitive data. Buy a tool that is designed not to allow guessing attacks.
- Use Permissions to limit access to the file based on user identities rather than or in addition to passwords and encryption. See "Set Workbook Permissions," later in this chapter, for more information.

Permissions or other identity-based approaches are really much better at securing data than are password-based approaches.

Protect Items in a Workbook

Protecting prevents changes to parts of a workbook. You can apply protection to worksheets, charts, ranges, formatting, and window layout. Protection can use a password or it may omit the password if the protection is intended to prevent accidental changes rather than malicious ones.

You can protect multiple items within a workbook and you can use different passwords for each of those items, though that's generally a bad idea. The more passwords you use, the more likely you are to confuse them—especially within a single workbook. It's a good idea to use the same password when protecting multiple items.

To prevent changes to a worksheet:

1. Add data to your worksheet and adjust the formatting so that it appears the way you want it to.

2. From the Tools menu, choose Protection, then Protect a Sheet. Excel displays the Protect Sheet dialog box shown in Figure 26-7.

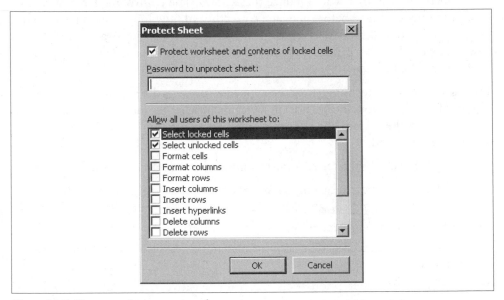

Figure 26-7. Use protection to prevent changes

3. Type a password and select the actions you want to permit on the worksheet from the list. Click OK. Excel prompts you to confirm the password.

After a worksheet is protected, you can't change it without unprotecting it first. To unprotect the worksheet, select Tools → Protection → Unprotect Sheet and enter the password.

Worksheet protection applies to all of the locked cells on a worksheet. To allow users to edit some cells on a worksheet while protecting most of the others, take the following steps *before* protecting the worksheet:

1. Select the cells you want to allow the user to edit.

2. From the Format menu, choose Cells. Excel displays the Format Cells dialog box shown in Figure 26-8.

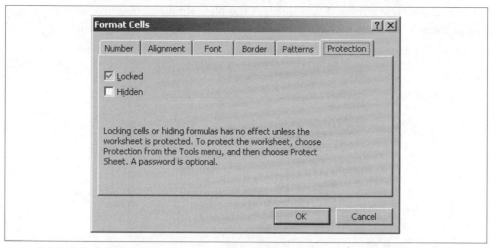

Figure 26-8. Unlock cells to allow changes on protected sheets

3. Select the Protection tab and clear the Locked check box. Click OK.

4. Protect the worksheet. Now, Excel allows changes in the unlocked cells.

You can also selectively protect ranges of cells by user. This lets some users but not others edit selected cells. To protect ranges by user, take the following steps *before* protecting the worksheet:

1. Select the range of cells to protect.

2. From the Tools menu, choose Protection, then choose Allow Users to Edit Ranges. Excel displays the dialog box shown in Figure 26-9.

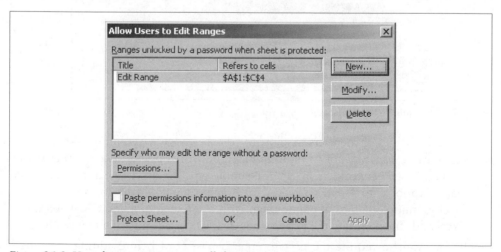

Figure 26-9. Use edit ranges to protect cells by user

3. Click the New button. Excel displays the New Range dialog box with the range of the selected cells listed in the Refers to Cells text box (Figure 26-10).

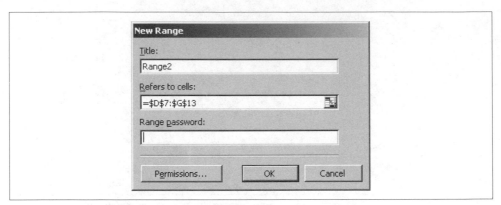

Figure 26-10. Setting the password for an edit range

4. Click on Permissions, then click Add on the Permissions dialog box. Excel displays the Select Users or Groups dialog box (Figure 26-11).

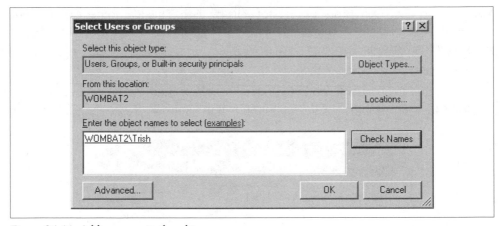

Figure 26-11. Adding users to the edit range

5. Type the names of the users to allow to edit the range. Usernames take the form *machinename\username* for workgroup-based networks or *domainname\username* for domain-based networks. You can also simply type the username and click Check Names to look up a user's machine or domain name if you don't know it. To specify multiple names, separate them with a semicolon. Click OK when done. Excel adds the names to the Permissions dialog box, as shown in Figure 26-12.

6. If you want to require the user to enter a password before editing the range, select the username and click the Deny check box. Click OK when done. Excel returns you to the New Range dialog box.

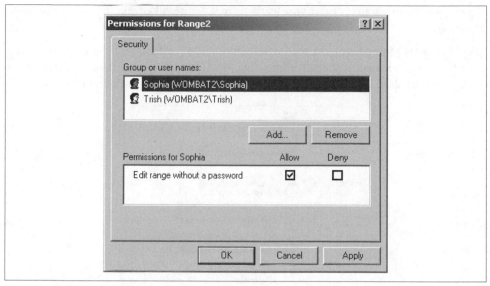

Figure 26-12. Viewing the users for an edit range

7. Enter a password for the range and click OK. Excel prompts you to confirm the password and then returns you to the worksheet.

8. Protect the worksheet using the steps at the beginning of this section. Protecting the worksheet activates the protection for the range—Excel does not enforce protections until the worksheet is protected.

In general, you use the preceding procedure to allow some users to edit ranges without the worksheet-level password. In this case, you would select the Allow check box in step 6, enter a password in Step 7, and probably specify the same password to protect the worksheet in Step 8. Then, all other users would have to enter a password before making changes to the range or to the rest of the worksheet.

If you don't enter a password for the range in Step 7, all users can edit the range. This is equivalent to unlocking the range as described in the previous procedure.

You can allow edits for a group of users. In that case, specify the group name in Step 5. For instance, WOMBAT1\Administrators allows members of the Administrators group on the machine *Wombat1* to edit a range.

In all cases, you must protect the worksheet in order for the range-level protections to take effect.

Program with Protection

Since protecting workbooks, worksheets, and ranges is a multistep process, it is sometimes convenient to automate protection—particularly if you frequently use the same types of protections or if you want to make sure all protections use the same password.

Excel provides methods for protecting Workbook, Chart, and Worksheet objects as well as subordinate objects for controlling various aspects of protection on Worksheet objects. Figure 26-13 illustrates the relationships among the protection objects.

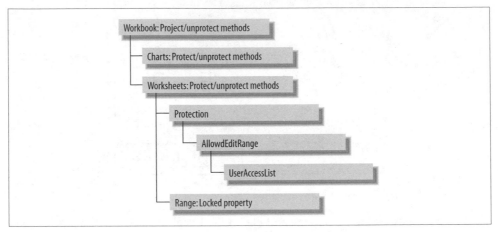

Figure 26-13. Protection object model

The protection objects are organized in a somewhat unusual way: First, the Workbook and Chart objects don't provide a Protection object since those objects allow only password protection. Second, the Worksheet object provides a Protection object that allows you to specify a list of users who can edit ranges on the worksheet. Finally, you set which cells on a worksheet are protected by setting the Range object's Locked property.

You can use the Worksheet object's Protect and Unprotect methods to work together with the Range object's Locked property to conditionally protect cells on a worksheet. For instance, the following code protects all worksheet cells that contain formulas:

```
Set ws = ThisWorkbook.Sheets("Protection")
' Make sure worksheet is not already protected.
ws.Unprotect
' Get each used cell in the worksheet.
For Each rng In ws.UsedRange
    ' If it contains a formula, lock the cell.
    If InStr(rng.Formula, "=") Then
        rng.Locked = True
    ' Otherwise unlock the cell.
    Else
        rng.Locked = False
    End If
Next
' Protect the worksheet.
ws.Protect
```

After you run the preceding code, users can edit data on the worksheet but not cells that contain calculations. The preceding Protect method doesn't specify a password, so no password is required to unprotect the cells. This isn't very secure, but it would prevent users from making accidental changes to formulas. An alternative is to hardcode a password into the macro or to prompt for a password as shown earlier in this chapter in "Program with Passwords and Encryption." For example, the following code gets a password using the password user form shown earlier:

```
frmPassword.Show
ws.Protect frmPassword.Password
Unload frmPassword
```

Now, the user will be prompted for a password if he attempts to edit a formula.

Password protection works well when there is one author for a workbook, but it is not very secure for multiple authors since the password must be shared with anyone who wants to make changes. The more people who know a password, the less secure it becomes.

To solve this problem, Excel provides Protection and UserAccessList objects so that you can apply user-based permissions for ranges on a worksheet. User-based permissions solve the multiple-author problem since users are authenticated by the network when they sign on.

Protection with user-based permissions still requires a password to protect the worksheet, but cells are automatically unlocked for certain users so those users aren't required to enter the password. For example, the following code password-protects a worksheet but allows members of the Power Users group to edit the range A1:C4:

```
Dim ws As Worksheet, aer As AllowEditRange
Set ws = ThisWorkbook.Sheets("Protection")
Set aer = ws.Protection.AllowEditRanges.Add("User Range", [A1:C4])
aer.Users.Add "Power Users", True
ws.Protect "Excel2003"
```

You have to get a reference to the AllowEditRange object in order to add users who are allowed to edit the range without a password. You can't use Excel's Record Macro feature to see how to add allowed users for a range—Excel only records the process of adding the named edit range, not adding the users or setting their permissions.

The names of edit ranges on a worksheet must be unique. You can remove previously created edit ranges, unprotecting the worksheet and using the Delete method as shown here:

```
ws.Unprotect
For Each aer In ws.Protection.AllowEditRanges
    aer.Delete
Next
```

Similarly, you can remove users added to an edit range using the Users collection DeleteAll method or the User object's Delete method as shown here:

```
ws.Unprotect
Set aer = ws.Protection.AllowEditRanges("User Range")
aer.Users("Power Users").Delete
```

Workbook Protection Members

The order of worksheets in a workbook can be protected from changes, as can the window and pane layout used to display the workbook. You can also use workbook protection to set passwords for shared workbooks.

The Workbook object has more than 200 members. The following Workbook members deal with protection; other Workbook members are described in Chapter 8:

```
Protect
ProtectSharing
ProtectStructure
ProtectWindows
Unprotect
UnprotectSharing
```

workbook.Protect([*Password*], [*Structure*], [*Windows*])

Protects a workbook, preventing changes to the order of sheets and/or the windows used to display the workbook.

Argument	Settings
Password	The password used to prevent changes.
Structure	True protects the order of sheets in the workbook; False does not protect. Default is False.
Windows	True protects the location and appearance of the Excel windows used to display the workbook; False does not protect. Default is False.

The following code password-protects the structure and windows of a workbook:

```
Set wb = ThisWorkbook
wb.Protect "Excel2003", True, True
```

workbook.ProtectSharing([*Filename*], [*Password*], [*WriteResPassword*], [*ReadOnlyRecommended*], [*CreateBackup*], [*SharingPassword*])

Saves a file for sharing and optionally sets protection, read-only, and read/write passwords.

Argument	Settings
Filename	The name to save the file as. When saving a workbook for sharing, it is common to save the file to a new (public) location.
Password	The password used to open the workbook.
WriteResPassword	The password used to open the workbook for read/write access.
ReadOnlyRecommended	True displays a prompt recommending that the workbook be opened for read-only access when the user opens the workbook in Excel; False does not prompt. Default is False.
CreateBackup	True automatically creates a backup version of the file before saving the file and sharing it; False does not create a backup. Default is False.
SharingPassword	The password used to remove sharing from the workbook.

The many password arguments for the ProtectSharing method can be confusing. The following code saves a workbook to a public location and sets three passwords for the file:

```
Set wb = ThisWorkbook
wb.ProtectSharing "\\wombat1\public\shared.xls", "pass1", "pass2", , , "pass3"
```

Once the preceding code runs, you use "pass1" to open the file, "pass2" to get read/write access to the file, and "pass3" to remove file sharing from the file.

workbook.ProtectStructure

Returns True if the order of the sheets in the workbook is protected, False if not. The following code displays the workbook's protection settings in the Immediate window:

```
Set wb = ThisWorkbook
Debug.Print "Structure protected? " & wb.ProtectStructure, _
  "Windows protected? " & wb.ProtectWindows
```

workbook.ProtectWindows

Returns True if the window display of the workbook is protected, False if not.

workbook.Unprotect([*Password*])

Removes protection from the workbook.

Argument	Settings
Password	The password used to protect the workbook. *Password* is required if the workbook was protected with a password.

The following code unprotects a workbook:

```
Set wb = ThisWorkbook
wb.Unprotect "Excel2003"
```

workbook.UnprotectSharing([*SharingPassword*])

Removes file sharing from a protected/shared workbook.

Argument	Settings
SharingPassword	The password used to share the workbook. Corresponds to the *SharingPassword* argument in the ProtectSharing method.

The following code removes sharing from a shared workbook stored in a public location:

```
Set wb = Application.Workbooks.Open("\\wombat1\public\shared.xls", , , , "pass1", _
    "pass2")
wb.UnprotectSharing pass3
```

Worksheet Protection Members

Protecting a worksheet can prevent changes to locked cells and other items on the worksheet. The Worksheet object has 135 members. The following Worksheet members deal with protection; other Worksheet members are described in Chapter 9:

```
Protect
ProtectContents
ProtectDrawingObjects
Protection
ProtectionMode
ProtectScenarios
Unprotect
```

worksheet.Protect([*Password*], [*DrawingObjects*], [*Contents*], [*Scenarios*], [*UserInterfaceOnly*], [*AllowFormattingCells*], [*AllowFormattingColumns*], [*AllowFormattingRows*], [*AllowInsertingColumns*], [*AllowInsertingRows*], [*AllowInsertingHyperlinks*], [*AllowDeletingColumns*], [*AllowDeletingRows*], [*AllowSorting*], [*AllowFiltering*], [*AllowUsingPivotTables*])

Protects a worksheet and sets options determining which items on the worksheet are protected. The arguments to this method correspond to the settings on the Protect Sheet dialog box shown in Figure 26-7.

Argument	Settings
Password	The password required to unprotect the worksheet.
DrawingObjects	True protects graphic objects such as command buttons and shapes on the worksheets; False does not protect. Default is True.
Contents	True protects the locked cells on the worksheet; False does not protect. Default is True.

Argument	Settings
Scenarios	True protects scenarios on the worksheets; False does not protect. Default is True.
UserInterfaceOnly	True protects the worksheet from changes made through the Excel interface, but allows macros to make changes to protected items; False applies the protection to both types of changes. Default is False.
AllowFormattingCells, AllowFormattingColumns, AllowFormattingRows, AllowInsertingColumns, AllowInsertingRows, AllowInsertingHyperlinks, AllowDeletingColumns, AllowDeletingRows, AllowSorting, AllowFiltering, AllowUsingPivotTables	If the contents are protected, then setting any of these arguments to True enables that task, such as formatting cells, sorting, etc. The default for each of these is False.

Use the Protect method arguments to selectively protect aspects of the workbook. For example, the following code protects only the drawing objects (which includes control objects like command buttons and text boxes) on a worksheet:

```
Set ws = ThisWorkbook.Sheets("Protection")
ws.Protect "Excel2003", True, False, False
```

The preceding code protects the controls on a worksheet. Don't confuse that with the *UserInterfaceOnly* argument, which permits macros to make changes to protected items. For example, the following code protects a worksheet, but allows macros to change cell values, insert rows, and make other changes:

```
ws.Protect "Excel2003", , True, , True
ws.Range("A1").Value = 42
```

Since *UserInterfaceOnly* is True in the preceding code, the macro can change the value of cell A1; however, the user can't change that cell.

worksheet.ProtectContents

Returns True if the worksheet's contents are protected; otherwise, returns False. The following code displays the types of protection applied to a worksheet in the Immediate window:

```
Set ws = ThisWorkbook.Sheets("Protection")
Debug.Print "Protections on workbook:"
Debug.Print "Contents?", "Controls?", "UI?", "Scenarios?"
Debug.Print ws.ProtectContents, ws.ProtectDrawingObjects, _
    ws.ProtectionMode, ws.ProtectScenarios
```

worksheet.ProtectDrawingObjects

Returns True if the worksheet's drawing objects are protected; otherwise, returns False.

worksheet.Protection

Returns a `Protection` object containing the protection property settings. See the section "Protection Members," later in this chapter, for a complete description.

worksheet.ProtectionMode

Returns True if the `UserInterfaceOnly` argument was set to True when the worksheet was protected; otherwise, returns False.

worksheet.ProtectScenarios

Returns True if the worksheet's scenarios are protected; otherwise, returns False.

worksheet.Unprotect([*Password*])

Removes protection from a worksheet.

Argument	Settings
Password	The password used to protect the worksheet

The following code removes the protection from a worksheet:

```
Set ws = ThisWorkbook.Sheets("Protection")
ws.Unprotect "Excel2003"
```

Chart Protection Members

Protecting a chart can prevent changes its appearance and data. The `Chart` object has 148 members. The following `Chart` members deal with protection; other `Chart` members are detailed by task in other sections and chapters. Members with differences from the `Worksheet` protection members (shown in **bold**) are covered in the following reference section:

Protect	ProtectContents
ProtectData	ProtectDrawingObjects
ProtectFormatting	**ProtectGoalSeek**
ProtectionMode	**ProtectSelection**
Unprotect	

chart.Protect([Password], [DrawingObjects], [Contents], [Scenarios], [UserInterfaceOnly])

The Protect method provides fewer arguments for the Chart object than for the Worksheet object.

Argument	Settings
Password	The password required to unprotect the chart.
DrawingObjects	True protects Shape objects drawn on the chart; False does not protect. Default is True.
Contents	True protects the chart. Default is True.
Scenarios	This argument is ignored for charts.
UserInterfaceOnly	True protects the chart from changes made through the Excel interface, but allows macros to make changes to protected items; False applies the protection to both types of changes. Default is False.

The following code protects a chart with a password:

```
Set chrt = ThisWorkbook.Sheets("Protected Chart")
chrt.Protect "Excel2003"
```

chart.ProtectData [= setting]

Sets or returns whether or not the user can change series formulas on the chart. Default is False. This setting operates independent of the other protection settings. The following code prevents changes to the way series are calculated on a chart:

```
Set chrt = ThisWorkbook.Sheets("Protected Chart")
chrt.ProtectData = True
```

chart.ProtectGoalSeek [= setting]

Sets or returns whether or not the user can change underlying charted values by clicking and dragging series data points on the chart. This setting operates independent of the other protection settings. The following code prevents the user from changing data by modifying the chart:

```
Set chrt = ThisWorkbook.Sheets("Protected Chart")
chrt.ProtectGoalSeek = True
```

chart.ProtectSelection [= setting]

Sets or returns whether or not the user can select items on the chart. This setting operates independent of the other protection settings. The following code prevents the user from selecting items on the chart and thus prevents changes:

```
Set chrt = ThisWorkbook.Sheets("Protected Chart")
chrt.ProtectSelection = True
```

chart.UnProtect([*Password*])

Removes protection from a chart. Does not affect the ProtectData, ProtectGoalSeek, or ProtectSelection settings of a chart. Those properties must be reset individually. The following code removes all protections from a chart:

```
Set chrt = ThisWorkbook.Sheets("Protected Chart")
chrt.Unprotect "Excel2003"
chrt.ProtectData = False
chrt.ProtectGoalSeek = False
chrt.ProtectSelection = False
```

Protection Members

Use the Worksheet objects Protection method to get a reference to the Protection object. The Protection object has the following members:

AllowDeletingColumns	AllowDeletingRows
AllowEditRanges	AllowFiltering
AllowFormattingCells	AllowFormattingColumns
AllowFormattingRows	AllowInsertingColumns
AllowInsertingHyperlinks	AllowInsertingRows
AllowSorting	AllowUsingPivotTables

The Protection object provides a set of read-only properties that describe the types of protection in effect on a worksheet. These settings correspond to the settings in the Protect Sheet dialog box and to the arguments used in the Worksheet object's Protect method. For example, the following code displays a report on the Protection property settings in the Immediate window:

```
Set ws = ThisWorkbook.Sheets("Protection")
Set prot = ws.Protection
Debug.Print "Can delete:", "Columns?", "Rows?"
Debug.Print , prot.AllowDeletingColumns, prot.AllowDeletingRows
Debug.Print "Can:", "Filter?", "Sort?", "Use Pivot Tables?"
Debug.Print , prot.AllowFiltering, prot.AllowSorting, prot.AllowUsingPivotTables
Debug.Print "Can format:", "Cells?", "Columns?", "Rows?"
Debug.Print , prot.AllowFormattingCells, prot.AllowFormattingColumns, _
    prot.AllowFormattingRows
Debug.Print "Can insert:", "Columns?", "Rows?", "Hyperlinks?"
Debug.Print , prot.AllowInsertingColumns, prot.AllowInsertingRows, _
    prot.AllowInsertingHyperlinks
```

You also use the Protection object to get a reference to the AllowEditRanges object, which lets you set user-level permissions on a worksheet.

protection.AllowDeletingColumns

True if the user can delete columns on the worksheet; otherwise, returns False.

protection.AllowDeletingRows

True if the user can delete rows on the worksheet; otherwise, returns False.

protection.AllowEditRanges

Returns an AllowEditRanges collection that lets you enable user-based permissions on a worksheet. See the next section, "AllowEditRange and AllowEditRanges Members," for more information.

protection.AllowFiltering

True if the user can filter columns on the worksheet; otherwise, returns False.

protection.AllowFormattingCells

True if the user can format individual cells on the worksheet; otherwise, returns False.

protection.AllowFormattingColumns

True if the user can format columns on the worksheet; otherwise, returns False.

protection.AllowFormattingRows

True if the user can format rows on the worksheet; otherwise, returns False.

protection.AllowInsertIngColumns

True if the user can insert columns on the worksheet; otherwise, returns False.

protection.AllowInsertingHyperlinks

True if the user can insert hyperlinks on the worksheet; otherwise, returns False.

protection.**AllowInsertingRows**

True if the user can insert rows on the worksheet; otherwise, returns False.

protection.**AllowSorting**

True if the user can sort rows on the worksheet; otherwise, returns False.

protection.**AllowUsingPivotTables**

True if the user can use pivot tables on the worksheet; otherwise, returns False.

AllowEditRange and AllowEditRanges Members

Use the `Protection` object's `AllowEditRanges` property to get a reference to the `AllowEditRanges` collection. The `AllowEditRanges` collection and `AllowEditRange` object provide the following members. Key members (shown in **bold**) are covered in the following reference section:

Add[1]
ChangePassword
Count[1]
Delete
Range
Title
Unprotect
Users

[1] Collection only

Use the `AllowEditRanges` collection to create ranges that allow edits by specific users. Excel prevents changes to ranges of cells that are protected and locked. The `AllowEditRanges` settings automatically unlock ranges of cells for the users included in the user-access list.

You must remove protection from a worksheet before you can add user-level permissions. For example, the following code unprotects a worksheet, creates a range that allows user-level permissions, and then restores protection:

```
Dim ws As Worksheet, ual As UserAccessList, aer As AllowEditRange, _
  usr As UserAccess
Set ws = ThisWorkbook.Sheets("Protection")
ws.Unprotect "Excel2003"
Set aer = ws.Protection.AllowEditRanges.Add("Edit Range", ws.[a1:c4])
Set usr = aer.Users.Add("Power Users", True)
ws.Protect "Excel2003"
```

alloweditranges.Add(*Title*, *Range*, [*Password*])

Creates and names a range that allows user-level permissions. Returns an `AllowEditRange` object.

Argument	Settings
`Title`	The name for the range. This name must be unique among the edit ranges in the worksheet.
`Range`	The Range object to allow edits on.
`Password`	The password the users not in the user-access list must enter before they can edit the range. Users that *are* in the range's user-access list are not prompted for the password.

alloweditrange.ChangePassword(*Password*)

Changes an existing password or sets a new password for an edit range.

Argument	Settings
`Password`	The new password that users must enter before they can edit the range

alloweditrange.Delete( )

Removes an edit range from a worksheet. For example, the following code deletes all the edit ranges in a worksheet:

```
Set ws = ThisWorkbook.Sheets("Protection")
For Each aer In ws.Protection.AllowEditRanges
    aer.Delete
Next
```

alloweditrange.Range

Returns the Range object that an edit range represents. For example, the following code displays the title and address for each edit range in a worksheet:

```
Set ws = ThisWorkbook.Sheets("Protection")
For Each aer In ws.Protection.AllowEditRanges
    Debug.Print aer.Title, aer.Range.Address
Next
```

alloweditrange.Title

Returns the name given to an edit range.

alloweditrange.Unprotect([*Password*])

Unlocks the range of cells specified by the edit range. After an edit range is unlocked, users can edit the range whether or not they are included in the range's user-access list and whether or not the worksheet is protected.

Argument	Settings
Password	The password used when creating the edit range.

alloweditrange.Users

Returns a reference to the UserAccessList collection for the edit range. Use this object to add users and groups of allowed users to the edit range. See "UserAccess and UserAccess-List Members," next, for more information.

UserAccess and UserAccessList Members

Use the AllowEditRange object's Users property to get a reference to the UserAccessList collection. The UserAccessList collection and UserAccess object provide the following members. Key members (shown in **bold**) are covered in the following reference section:

Add[1]
AllowEdit
Count[1]
Delete
DeleteAll[1]
Name

[1] Collection only

Use the UserAccessList collection to add users to the user-access list of an edit range on a protected worksheet. You can add individual users or groups to the user-access list, but the names must be valid user or group names for your system. For example, the following code adds the built-in Users group to the access list for an edit range:

```
Dim ws As Worksheet, ual As UserAccessList, aer As AllowEditRange, _
   usr As UserAccess
Set ws = ThisWorkbook.Sheets("Protection")
Set aer = ws.Protection.AllowEditRanges("Edit Range")
Set ual = aer.Users
Set usr = ual.Add("Users", True)
```

The UserAccessList collection does not support the For Each construct in Visual Basic. Instead, you must use a For statement with a counter to get each item in the collection as shown here:

```
For i = 1 To ual.Count
    Set usr = ual(i)
    Debug.Print usr.Name
Next
```

useraccesslist.**Add(***Name, AllowEdit***)**

Adds a user to the user-access list on an edit range.

Argument	Settings
Name	The name of the user or group to add.
AllowEdit	True allows this user or group to edit the range without supplying a password; False prohibits edits.

useraccess.**AllowEdit [=** *setting***]**

Sets or returns whether a user is required to enter the password specified in the Add method's AllowEdit argument before she can make changes.

useraccess.**Delete( )**

Removes a user from the edit range's user-access list.

useraccesslist.**DeleteAll( )**

Removes all the users from the edit range's user-access list.

Set Workbook Permissions

The problems with passwords are:

- They are susceptible to guessing attacks.
- There is no secure way to share them among a group.
- They tend to proliferate and become hard to remember. You can use the same password for all items, but that reduces security.

The solution to this problem is identity-based security. The preceding section showed how you could allow specific users to edit protected worksheets without the worksheet password. The larger solution is to define workbook permissions based on the user's identity.

Identity-based security solves the password problem because users maintain their own password—usually it's the one they use to sign on to the network—and then their identity travels with them wherever they go on a network. You don't have to set workbook passwords, share those with your workmates, and hope you don't lose or forget them.

Excel provides identity-based security through Microsoft Information Rights Management (IRM). This new feature comes at a cost, however. In order to use IRM, you must have a Windows 2003 server running Microsoft Windows Rights Management (RM) Services on your network. If you don't have that or if you want to share a workbook outside of your network, you can use Microsoft Passport identities instead of network identities.

 IRM and the workbook permissions are available only with the Windows editions of Office 2003 or later.

There are some huge advantages to IRM over other types of document protection:

- Identities are not susceptible to guessing attacks.
- You can control a wide variety of permissions, such as the ability to print, forward, edit, copy, save, and so on.
- Documents can have an expiration date.
- Changes to permissions are immediate and don't require the document to be redistributed.
- Users can request additional permissions from the author as needed.
- Users who don't have network accounts inside your organization can use Microsoft Passport accounts for authentication.

The disadvantages are significant, too:

- Using Passports for IRM is a trial service according to Microsoft and so might be discontinued. Microsoft pledges to give 90 days' notice before discontinuing support for this.
- The RM service for Windows 2003 requires a significant per-client license fee.
- All users need an identity—there's no mechanism for an anonymous user with limited rights.

The following procedures use the Microsoft Passport identities—hopefully that trial service will still be functioning when you read this! To set IRM permissions on a workbook for the first time:

1. From the File menu, select Permission, then select Do Not Distribute. Excel starts the Windows Rights Management Wizard, which walks you through creating Rights Management credentials and downloading them to your computer. When you are done, Excel displays the Permission dialog box shown in Figure 26-14.

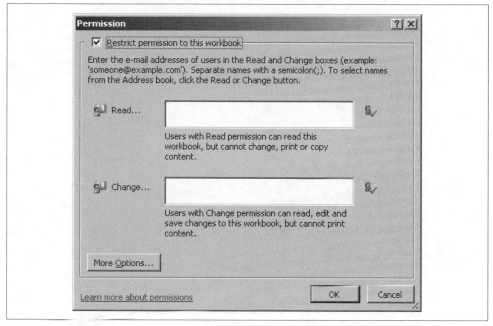

Figure 26-14. Restricting access through permissions

2. Select Restrict Permission to This Workbook to set permissions. Excel activates the dialog box so that you can enter data.

3. Enter a list of the users allowed to read and/or change the workbook. Users are identified by email address. Separate multiple addresses with semicolons.

4. To set an expiration date and restrict printing and other capabilities, click More Options. Excel displays the expanded Permissions dialog box shown in Figure 26-15.

5. Set the additional permissions by selecting the user and then changing the permission settings in the Permission dialog box. Click OK when done.

As the author of the workbook, you always have permission to open, edit, and distribute your document. The workbook will not expire for you since the author always has full control.

When someone other than the author opens a workbook with permissions enabled, several things may happen:

- If the user is included in the workbook's users list and has Office 2003 or later installed, the workbook opens in Excel and he may perform the actions specified by his permissions.

- If he is not included in the workbook's users list and has Office 2003 or later installed, he sees a description of where to send email to get permission to use the workbook (Figure 26-16).

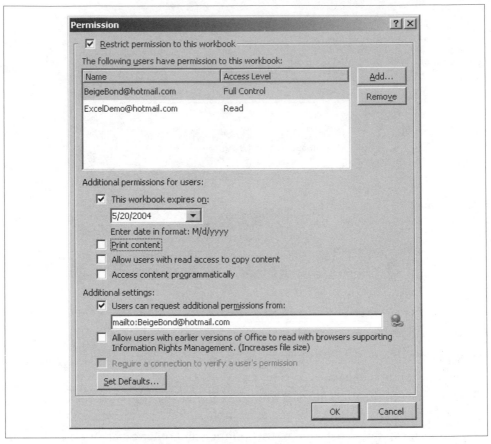

Figure 26-15. Advanced permission options

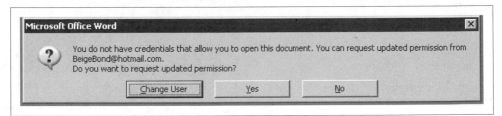

Figure 26-16. Users without permissions are told how to request access to an IRM-protected document

- If he does not have Office 2003 or later installed, he sees a description of how to get the IRM add-ins for Internet Explorer so he can view the workbook (Figure 26-17).

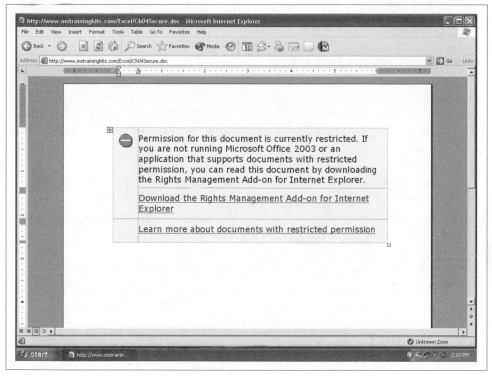

Figure 26-17. Users without Office 2003 are told how to get the IRM add-ins for Internet Explorer

Program with Permissions

Microsoft provides the permissions objects through the Office object library since permissions can be applied to Excel, Word, and PowerPoint documents. Figure 26-18 illustrates the hierarchy of the permission objects.

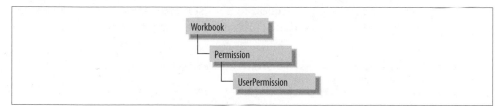

Figure 26-18. Office permission object model

You must have Rights Management credentials installed before you can set permissions on a document. Otherwise, most permission methods will cause runtime errors. See the preceding section for instructions on how to install credentials.

Once credentials are installed, you can restrict access to workbooks by setting the Permission collection's Enabled property to True, as shown here:

```
Dim irm As Office.Permission
Set irm = ThisWorkbook.Permission
irm.Enabled = True
```

The preceding code sets the workbook as Do Not Distribute. You are given full control, but no other users have permissions. Use the Add method to add permissions for other users. You must add each user individually, even if all have the same permissions, as shown here:

```
Set irm = ThisWorkbook.Permission
irm.Add "ExcelDemo@hotmail.com", MsoPermission.msoPermissionView
irm.Add "someone@microsoft.com", MsoPermission.msoPermissionView
```

Use Or to combine permissions for a user. For example, the following code allows *ExcelDemo@hotmail.com* to read, print, and copy a workbook:

```
irm.Add "someone@microsoft.com", MsoPermission.msoPermissionView Or & _
    MsoPermission.msoPermissionPrint Or MsoPermission.msoPermissionExtract
```

When you combine permissions, they may not display in the Excel Permission options dialog box. Instead, the user may appear as having Custom permissions in the Access Level list shown in the advanced Permission dialog (Figure 26-15).

You can set a date at which the user's permissions to the document expire using an argument in the Add method or by setting the Expiration property, as shown here:

```
Set irm = ThisWorkbook.Permission
Set usr = irm("ExcelDemo@hotmail.com")
usr.ExpirationDate = Date + 1
```

The preceding code sets the expiration date for the user one day from the current date. Expiration dates are always calendar dates—you can't set permissions to expire at a certain time.

You may also notice from the preceding code that there is no Users collection. Instead, you use the Permission collection to get UserPermission objects. For example, the following code displays the permissions for each user in the Immediate window:

```
Dim irm As Office.Permission, usr As Office.UserPermission
Set irm = ThisWorkbook.Permission
For Each usr In irm
    Debug.Print usr.UserId, usr.Permission, usr.ExpirationDate
Next
```

The simplest way to remove permissions from a workbook is to set the Permission collection's Enabled property to False:

```
ThisWorkbook.Permission.Enabled = False
```

Disabling the Permission collection removes all users and their permissions. Use the UserPermission object's Remove method to selectively remove users.

Permission and UserPermission Members

The `Permission` collection and `UserPermission` object are unusual in that they aren't directly related by name as are most collections and objects in Office products. (For example, the `Addins` collection contains `Addin` objects.) The `Permission` collection and `UserPermission` object have the following members. Key members (shown in **bold**) are covered in the following reference section:

Add[1]	Application[1]
ApplyPolicy[1]	Count[1]
Creator[2]	**DocumentAuthor**[1]
Enabled[1]	**EnableTrustedBrowser**[1]
ExpirationDate	Parent[2]
Permission	**PermissionFromPolicy**[1]
PolicyDescription[1]	**PolicyName**[1]
Remove	**RemoveAll**[1]
RequestPermissionURL[1]	**StoreLicenses**[1]
UserId	

[1] Collection only
[2] Object and collection

---

permission.**Add**(*UserId*, [*Permission*], [*ExpirationDate*])

Adds permission for a user to access a workbook. Returns a `UserPermission` object.

Argument	Description
UserId	The identity of the user for which to grant permissions
Permission	One or more of the `msoPermission` constants
ExpirationDate	The date after which the user no longer has permissions

The *Permission* argument can be one or more of the following constants. Join multiple permissions with the `Or` operator:

```
msoPermissionChange
msoPermissionEdit
msoPermissionExtract
msoPermissionFullControl
msoPermissionObjModel
msoPermissionPrint
msoPermissionRead
msoPermissionSave
msoPermissionView
```

For example, the following code grants a Passport account permission to view and copy a workbook:

```
Set irm = ThisWorkbook.Permission
Set usr = irm.Add("ExcelDemo@hotmail.com", MsoPermission.msoPermissionView _
    Or MsoPermission.msoPermissionExtract)
```

permission.ApplyPolicy(*FileName*)

Applies a set of externally defined usernames and permissions to a workbook.

permission.DocumentAuthor [= *setting*]

Sets or returns the identity of the author who set the workbook's permissions. If you are setting this property, the new identity must have Full Control permission to become the document author. The following code displays the author's identity and email address:

```
Set irm = ThisWorkbook.Permission
Debug.Print irm.DocumentAuthor, irm.RequestPermissionURL
```

permission.Enabled [= *setting*]

Sets or returns whether permissions are currently enforced. Setting Enabled to False sets the workbook's user count to zero, but does not remove those users from the permissions list. For example, the following code temporarily disables permissions:

```
Set irm = ThisWorkbook.Permission
irm.Enabled = False
```

and this code re-enables permissions as they were set before the preceding code ran:

```
irm.Enabled = True
```

permission.EnableTrustedBrowser [= *setting*]

Sets or returns whether to allow access by users who don't have Office 2003 or later installed. Setting this property to True is the equivalent of selecting "Allow users with earlier versions of Office to read with browsers supporting Information Rights Management" on the Permission dialog box.

userpermission.ExpirationDate [= *setting*]

Sets or returns the date after which a user's permission expires. For example, the following code displays the identities and expiration dates of users who have permissions on this workbook:

```
Set irm = ThisWorkbook.Permission
Debug.Print "User", , "Permission", "Permission Expires"
For Each usr In irm
    Debug.Print usr.UserId, usr.Permission, usr.ExpirationDate
Next
```

userpermission.Permission [= *setting*]

Sets or returns the permissions granted to a user. The Permission property can be one or more of the msoPermission constants. Join multiple permissions with the Or operator. For example, the following code grants a Passport account permission to change and print a workbook:

```
Set irm = ThisWorkbook.Permission
Set usr = irm("ExcelDemo@Hotmail.com")
usr.Permission = MsoPermission.msoPermissionChange Or _
    MsoPermission.msoPermissionPrint
```

permission.PermissionFromPolicy

Returns True if the permission was created from a policy file. Returns False if the permission was created from the user interface or from code.

permission.PolicyDescription

Returns the description from the policy description file used to create the permission.

permission.PolicyName

Returns the name from the policy description file used to create the permission.

userpermission.Remove( )

Revokes a user's permission to use a workbook. For example, the following code removes the ExcelDemo user:

```
Set irm = ThisWorkbook.Pcrmission
Set usr = irm("ExcelDemo@Hotmail.com")
usr.Remove
```

permission.RemoveAll( )

Revokes all users' permissions. Only the document's author remains in the list of permitted users. For example, the following code removes the users from the workbook's Permission object:

```
Set irm = ThisWorkbook.Permission
irm.RemoveAll
```

permission.RequestPermissionURL [= *setting*]

Sets or returns a string used to contact the author, so that nonauthorized users can request permission to read or edit the workbook. By default, this string takes the form *mailto:*

authoraddress, but you can change it to include subject lines or to display a web page. For example, the following code displays a web page when a user requests permission:

```
Set irm = ThisWorkbook.Permission
irm.RequestPermissionURL = "http://www.mstrainingkits.com/Excel/Permission.aspx"
```

permission.StoreLicenses [= *setting*]

When using Passport authentication, True caches the user's credentials after she is authenticated to allow the workbook to be viewed if a network connection is not available. False authenticates the user each time the workbook is opened. This property cannot be set to True if not using Passport authentication.

userpermission.UserId

Returns the identity of the user who has these permissions.

Add Digital Signatures

A digital signature identifies the author of the content or the macros contained in a workbook, template, or add-in. You add a digital signature as the last step before you distribute a file. When others open a signed file, they can see who the author is and therefore decide whether the information in the file is authentic and whether any macros it contains are safe to run.

The signature is overwritten any time a file is saved. Therefore, no one can open a signed file, make changes, save, then send the file on still bearing your signature. Workbooks and macros are signed separately even though they are contained in a single file. If you want to distribute a signed workbook containing macros, you must sign the macros first, then sign the workbook.

See Chapter 6 for instructions on how to get a digital certificate and how to use it to sign files.

Set Macro Security

Excel controls whether workbook macros are allowed to run through security settings. Users may choose to prohibit all macros, allow only signed macros from known sources, allow macros of the user's choosing, or allow all macros. These settings correspond to the Very High, High, Medium, and Low security settings on the Security dialog box (Figure 26-19). To set macro security, from the Tools menu, choose Macro, then choose Security.

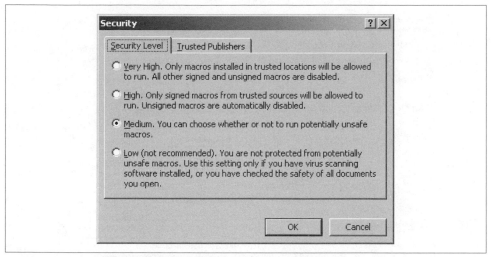

Figure 26-19. Choosing macro security settings

These settings are driven by trust—the user must choose whether to trust a publisher or a workbook. There is no way for the user to prohibit certain operations, such as reading or writing to the registry or erasing datafiles. Users discover if their trust is misplaced only after the damage is done.

For this reason, it is a good idea to encourage users to be suspicious of macros arriving in workbooks. It is a better idea to deploy macros as digitally signed templates or add-ins and to distribute those files from a secure network location.

The following scenario demonstrates how to distribute macros in a secure fashion:

1. Set up a public network share, for example, *Wombat1\Public\Templates*.

2. Set Windows security on the Templates folder to allow read-only access to all network users and read/write access to the Administrator (in this case, you).

3. Digitally sign templates and add-ins using a CA-issued digital certificate.

4. Copy the templates and add-ins to the public Templates folder.

5. Add the public Templates location to the alternate startup path for each Excel user.

6. For each user, open one of the signed templates in Excel and select "Always trust macros from this publisher" on the Security Warning.

7. Select the High or Very High macro security option for each Excel user.

To set the alternate startup path in Excel, set the "At startup, open all files in" text box in the Options dialog box as shown in Figure 26-20.

To set the alternate startup path in code, use the following line:

```
Application.AltStartupPath = "\\wombat1\public\templates"
```

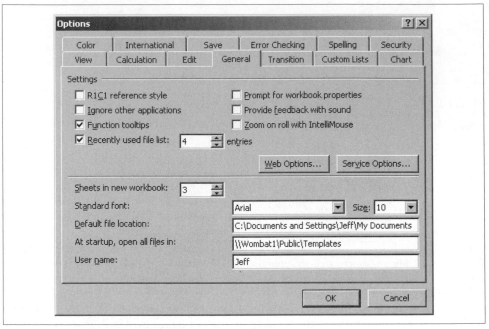

Figure 26-20. Setting the alternate startup path to a secure network location

Now, when users start Excel, templates and add-ins from *\\Wombat1\Public\ Templates* will be available automatically. If a file changes, the user will get the latest version. And since the files are digitally signed by a trusted publisher, users won't see the macro security warning every time they open a file.

 Smart tags are provided through a type of add-in, so macro security settings apply to them as well as the other types of files that can contain code (workbooks, templates, etc.).

Set ActiveX Control Security

Excel workbooks may contain ActiveX controls that execute code or respond to macros. ActiveX controls may be digitally signed and are marked by the publisher as to whether they are safe to initialize and safe to script. In this case, *safe* means that the control will not harm the user's system.

Whether Excel will download or run any new ActiveX control is determined security by settings in Internet Explorer. To see these settings in Internet Explorer:

1. From the Tools menu, select Internet Options and click on the Security tab.

2. Select the location that is the source of the ActiveX control and click Custom Level. Figure 26-21 shows the ActiveX security settings for the local intranet location.

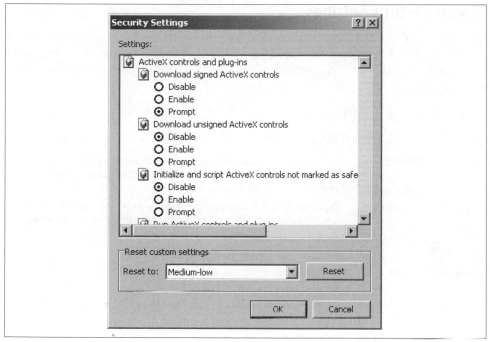

Figure 26-21. Changing ActiveX security settings

As a rule, you should never install unsigned ActiveX controls from any location. ActiveX controls are software, and you should always be careful when choosing which publishers to trust.

Distribute Security Settings

Changing macro security settings on individual computers is fine for personal use, but it doesn't work very well when trying to manage security for an organization. To solve that problem, Microsoft provides the following tools:

Microsoft Office Resource Kit
> Provides the Custom Installation Wizard (CIW), Custom Maintenance Wizard, and Profile Template Wizard that automate the installation and configuration of Microsoft Office across your organization

Certificate Manager (CertMgr.exe)
> Lets you export, distribute, and install certificates for trusted publishers on users' machines

Change Security Settings

The Microsoft Office Resource Kit is not included with the Microsoft Office product, but is available for free download from Microsoft (see "Resources" at the end of this chapter). Table 26-1 lists the four primary tools that come with the Office Resource Kit.

Table 26-1. Office Resource Kit tools

Tool	Use to
Custom Installation Wizard	Create customized installations for your organization. You can remove Office components, add your own components, set default installation paths, and determine Start menu and Desktop items created by Setup.
Custom Maintenance Wizard	Deploy changes to Office installations including new components and updates. This is similar to the Installation Wizard, but is designed for modifying existing installations rather than creating new ones.
Removal Wizard	Removes previous versions of Office applications.
Profile Template Wizard	Deploy Office user settings, such as macro security settings.

The basic steps for using the Custom Installation and Custom Maintenance Wizards are the same:

1. Set up an administrative installation point on your network. This is the location from which Setup will run and includes the Windows installer files (*.msi*) for Office.

2. Run the wizard to create a Windows installer transform (*.mst*) containing the modifications you wish to make to the Office installation. You can also add components (such as ActiveX controls or Smart tags) to the installation by including their *.msi* files to create chained installations.

3. Execute the installation from the client machines using remote administration, instructions to the user, or installation scripts. See *Setup.htm* on the Office installation CD for information on Setup command-line options and unattended installation.

The Custom Installation and Maintenance Wizards are important to security because they can remove components that might pose security risks for some users. For example, you may choose *not* to install Visual Basic for Applications and .NET Programmability Support (the Office .NET Primary Interop Assemblies or PIAs) to impede macros from running at all—that may be an appropriate setting for public workstations such as those available in libraries.

Use the Profile Template Wizard to create a file containing the Excel security settings you want to apply to client computers. For example, you may want to make sure all clients use the Very High macro security setting and disable trust access to VBA projects. To use the Policy Template Wizard, follow these steps:

1. Set up a computer with the user settings you want to export to all other clients.
2. Run the Profile Template Wizard on that computer and export the settings to copy to other clients. Figure 26-22 shows the Profile Template Wizard ready to export Excel security user settings.

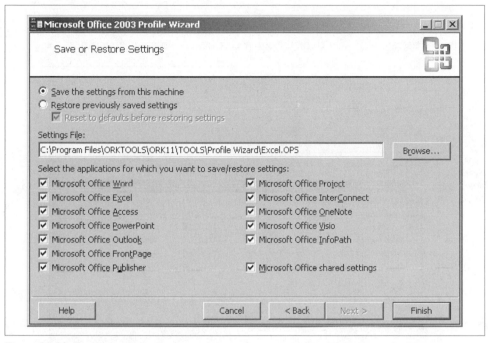

Figure 26-22. Exporting user security settings

Run the Profile Template Wizard on client machines using the template exported in Step 2. The wizard can be run from the command line; run `proflwz.exe /?` to see the command-line options.

Distribute Certificates

If you set macro security settings to Very High, Excel will not prompt the user to install certificates from new publishers. The only way the user can run those macros is to lower the security, reload the document, and select "Always trust macros from this publisher." If you are using the Very High security setting, you probably don't want users lowering it, installing certificates, then (maybe) raising it again.

To avoid this problem, you can distribute the certificates from trusted publishers beforehand using the Certificate Manager (*CertMgr.exe*). The Certificate Manager is available for download from Microsoft (see "Resources" at the end of this chapter) and comes with other certificate-related tools such as *SignCode.exe*.

To use the Certificate Manager to distribute certificates from trusted publishers:

1. Set up a computer with the certificates you want to distribute.

2. Run the Certificate Manager (Figure 26-23) and export the desired certificates *without* their private keys. The Certificate Manager provides a wizard to walk you through the export process.

3. Use the resulting certificate files (*.cer* or *.p7b*) with the command-line interface of the Certificate Manager to install those certificates on client machines.

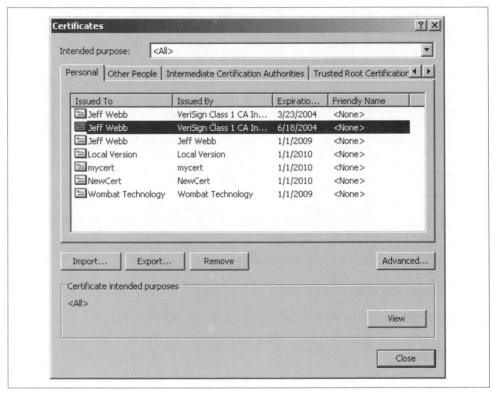

Figure 26-23. Use the Certificate Manager to export and import certificates from trusted publishers

Alternately, you can manage certificates using the Microsoft Management Console Certificates snap-in (*CertMgr.msc*). Figure 26-24 shows the snap-in administering certificates on a remote computer.

Using the Anti-Virus API

Microsoft provides an API for antivirus software developers so that they can write code to scan documents as they are opened in Excel. Since the scan is focused on the current file being opened, it can be more thorough than general scans of the user's

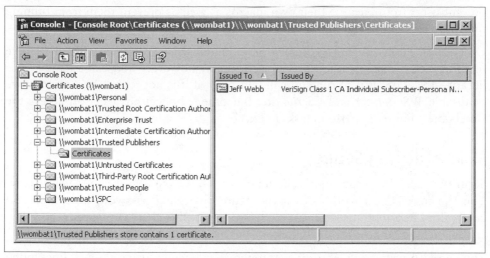

Figure 26-24. Use the certificates snap-in to administer certificates through the network

disk. Antivirus software that uses this API may display settings on the Macro Security Options dialog in Excel. See "Resources" at the end of this chapter for links to information on the Anti-Virus API.

Common Tasks

The following sections list quick answers to the most common security questions.

Get Rid of the Macro Security Warning

If you write macros for personal use and get tired of seeing the macro security warning every time you open personal workbooks, you can sign your macros with a personal digital certificate. To do so:

1. Choose Digital Certificate for VBA Projects from the Windows Office Tools menu to run *SelfCert.exe*.
2. Use *SelfCert.exe* to create a personal digital certificate.
3. From the Visual Basic Tools menu, choose Digital Signature.
4. Click Choose to add your digital certificate to the workbook's macros.
5. Repeat Step 4 each time you create a new workbook or template containing macros.

Prevent Someone from Running Any Macros

You can omit Visual Basic for Applications during installation or remove that component after installation by using Office Setup to perform maintenance. That will prevent users from creating their own macros as well as prevent them from running macros in existing workbooks.

Other applications, such as Windows Scripting Host (*WScript.exe*) will still be able to run macros that use the Excel object library, however. You can't remove this library—Excel needs it to run and will reinstall it if it is not found. You can remove or disable *WScript.exe* and *CScript.exe*, but other applications can still access the Excel object library to perform tasks in Excel.

Make a File Truly Secure

Security is a sliding scale, and I'd hesitate to say *anything* is ever completely secure. You can make Excel workbooks fairly secure by adding password protection and encryption. Be sure to use a strong password (eight-plus characters, upper- and lowercase, include numbers and symbols).

You can also protect access to files through Windows by using the NT Encrypting File System and using the Windows file security settings to prevent access by users other than yourself.

Finally, you can set permissions on a workbook using IRM to prevent any user other than yourself from reading or writing to the workbook in Excel. This last technique also provides a way to share workbooks in a secure way with restricted permissions.

Add a Trusted Publisher for a Group of Users

There are two ways to do this, depending upon your network setup and your distribution needs: you can create a command-line script that uses *CertMgr.exe* to install exported certificate files (*.cer*) on each user's machine, or you can use the Microsoft Management Console Certificates snap-in (*CertMgr.msc*) to install certificates on users' machines over a network—provided you have administrative privileges to their machines.

Resources

To learn about	Look here
Information Rights Management	*http://www.microsoft.com/windowsserver2003/technologies/rightsmgmt/default.mspx*
Anti-Virus API	*http://msdn.microsoft.com/workshop/security/antivirus/overview/overview.asp*
Excel Key	*http://www.lostpassword.com/excel.htm*
Microsoft Office 2000 Resource Kit	*http://www.microsoft.com/office/ork/2000/default.htm*
Microsoft Office 2003 Resource Kit	*http://www.microsoft.com/office/ork/2003/tools/default.htm*
Certificate management and code-signing tools	*http://office.microsoft.com/downloads/2000/pvkimprt.aspx*

PART IV

Appendixes

These appendixes feature reference tables that are too long and obtrusive to include in the regular chapters. These tables are important when working with specific aspects of Excel, such as displaying Excel's built-in dialogs or writing code that must work with earlier versions of Excel.

Appendix A, *Reference Tables*
Appendix B, *Version Compatibility*

Reference Tables

Dialogs Collection Constants

Use the Dialogs collection to display Excel's built-in dialog boxes. Each dialog box in Excel has a corresponding Dialogs constant as listed in Table A-1. To display the dialog box, use the Show method:

```
Application.Dialogs(xlDialogActiveCellFont).Show
```

The Show method takes a variable number of optional arguments, which are also listed in Table A-1. Those arguments set the initial property of the dialog box. For example, the following code displays the Font dialog box with Helvetica, Italic, 14 point selected:

```
Application.Dialogs(xlDialogActiveCellFont).Show "Helvetica", "Italic", "14"
```

The Show method returns True if the user clicks OK or False if the user cancels the operation. (Some dialog boxes don't have any options.)

Table A-1 lists some dialog box constants more than once. In those cases, the dialog box takes different arguments depending on what object currently has focus in Excel. For example, xlDialogPageSetup has three versions: the first is for printing worksheets, the second is for printing charts, and the third is for printing Excel 5.0 dialog sheets (which are obsolete).

Table A-1. Dialogs collection constants

Constant	Show arguments
xlDialogActivate	*window_text, pane_num*
xlDialogActiveCellFont	*font, font_style, size, strikethrough, superscript, subscript, outline, shadow, underline, color, normal, background, start_char, char_count*
xlDialogAddChartAutoformat	*name_text, desc_text*
xlDialogAddinManager	*operation_num, addinname_text, copy_logical*

Table A-1. Dialogs collection constants (continued)

Constant	Show arguments
xlDialogAlignment	*horiz_align, wrap, vert_align, orientation, add_ indent*
xlDialogApplyNames	*name_array, ignore, use_rowcol, omit_col, omit_row, order_num, append_last*
xlDialogApplyStyle	*style_text*
xlDialogAppMove	*x_num, y_num*
xlDialogAppSize	*x_num, y_num*
xlDialogArrangeAll	*arrange_num, active_doc, sync_horiz, sync_vert*
xlDialogAssignToObject	*macro_ref*
xlDialogAssignToTool	*bar_id, position, macro_ref*
xlDialogAttachText	*attach_to_num, series_num, point_num*
xlDialogAttachToolbars	
xlDialogAutoCorrect	*correct_initial_caps, capitalize_days*
xlDialogAxes	*x_primary, y_primary, x_secondary, y_secondary*
xlDialogAxes	*x_primary, y_primary, z_primary*
xlDialogBorder	*outline, left, right, top, bottom, shade, outline_ color, left_color, right_color, top_color, bottom_ color*
xlDialogCalculation	*type_num, iter, max_num, max_change, update, precision, date_1904, calc_save, save_values, alt_exp, alt_form*
xlDialogCellProtection	*locked, hidden*
xlDialogChangeLink	*old_text, new_text, type_of_link*
xlDialogChartAddData	*ref, rowcol, titles, categories, replace, series*
xlDialogChartLocation	
xlDialogChartOptionsDataLabels	
xlDialogChartOptionsDataTable	
xlDialogChartSourceData	
xlDialogChartTrend	*type, ord_per, forecast, backcast, intercept, equation, r_squared, name*
xlDialogChartType	
xlDialogChartWizard	*long, ref, gallery_num, type_num, plot_by, categories, ser_titles, legend, title, x_title, y_title, z_title, number_cats, number_titles*
xlDialogCheckboxProperties	*value, link, accel_text, accel2_text, 3d_shading*
xlDialogClear	*type_num*
xlDialogColorPalette	*file_text*
xlDialogColumnWidth	*width_num, reference, standard, type_num, standard_ num*
xlDialogCombination	*type_num*

Constant	Show arguments
xlDialogConditionalFormatting	
xlDialogConsolidate	*source_refs, function_num, top_row, left_col, create_links*
xlDialogCopyChart	*size_num*
xlDialogCopyPicture	*appearance_num, size_num, type_num*
xlDialogCreateNames	*top, left, bottom, right*
xlDialogCreatePublisher	*file_text, appearance, size, formats*
xlDialogCustomizeToolbar	*category*
xlDialogCustomViews	
xlDialogDataDelete	
xlDialogDataLabel	*show_option, auto_text, show_key*
xlDialogDataSeries	*rowcol, type_num, date_num, step_value, stop_value, trend*
xlDialogDataValidation	
xlDialogDefineName	*name_text, refers_to, macro_type, shortcut_text, hidden, category, local*
xlDialogDefineStyle	*style_text, number, font, alignment, border, pattern, protection*
xlDialogDefineStyle	*style_text, attribute_num, additional_def_args, ...*
xlDialogDeleteFormat	*format_text*
xlDialogDeleteName	*name_text*
xlDialogDemote	*row_col*
xlDialogDisplay	*formulas, gridlines, headings, zeros, color_num, reserved, outline, page_breaks, object_num*
xlDialogDisplay	*cell, formula, value, format, protection, names, precedents, dependents, note*
xlDialogEditboxProperties	*validation_num, multiline_logical, vscroll_logical, password_logical*
xlDialogEditColor	*color_num, red_value, green_value, blue_value*
xlDialogEditDelete	*shift_num*
xlDialogEditionOptions	*edition_type, edition_name, reference, option, appearance, size, formats*
xlDialogEditSeries	*series_num, name_ref, x_ref, y_ref, z_ref, plot_order*
xlDialogErrorbarX	*include, type, amount, minus*
xlDialogErrorbarY	*include, type, amount, minus*
xlDialogExternalDataProperties	
xlDialogExtract	*unique*
xlDialogFileDelete	*file_text*

Table A-1. Dialogs collection constants (continued)

Constant	Show arguments
xlDialogFileSharing	
xlDialogFillGroup	*type_num*
xlDialogFillWorkgroup	*type_num*
xlDialogFilter	
xlDialogFilterAdvanced	*operation, list_ref, criteria_ref, copy_ref, unique*
xlDialogFindFile	
xlDialogFont	*name_text, size_num*
xlDialogFontProperties	*font, font_style, size, strikethrough, superscript, subscript, outline, shadow, underline, color, normal, background, start_char, char_count*
xlDialogFormatAuto	*format_num, number, font, alignment, border, pattern, width*
xlDialogFormatChart	*layer_num, view, overlap, angle, gap_width, gap_depth, chart_depth, doughnut_size, axis_num, drop, hilo, up_down, series_line, labels, vary*
xlDialogFormatCharttype	*apply_to, group_num, dimension, type_num*
xlDialogFormatFont	*color, backgd, apply, name_text, size_num, bold, italic, underline, strike, outline, shadow, object_id, start_num, char_num*
xlDialogFormatFont	*name_text, size_num, bold, italic, underline, strike, color, outline, shadow*
xlDialogFormatFont	*name_text, size_num, bold, italic, underline, strike, color, outline, shadow, object_id_text, start_num, char_num*
xlDialogFormatLegend	*position_num*
xlDialogFormatMain	*type_num, view, overlap, gap_width, vary, drop, hilo, angle, gap_depth, chart_depth, up_down, series_line, labels, doughnut_size*
xlDialogFormatMove	*x_offset, y_offset, reference*
xlDialogFormatMove	*x_pos, y_pos*
xlDialogFormatMove	*explosion_num*
xlDialogFormatNumber	*format_text*
xlDialogFormatOverlay	*type_num, view, overlap, gap_width, vary, drop, hilo, angle, series_dist, series_num, up_down, series_line, labels, doughnut_size*
xlDialogFormatSize	*width, height*
xlDialogFormatSize	*x_off, y_off, reference*
xlDialogFormatText	*x_align, y_align, orient_num, auto_text, auto_size, show_key, show_value, add_indent*
xlDialogFormulaFind	*text, in_num, at_num, by_num, dir_num, match_case, match_byte*

Table A-1. *Dialogs collection constants (continued)*

Constant	Show arguments
xlDialogFormulaGoto	*reference, corner*
xlDialogFormulaReplace	*find_text, replace_text, look_at, look_by, active_cell, match_case, match_byte*
xlDialogFunctionWizard	
xlDialogGallery3dArea	*type_num*
xlDialogGallery3dBar	*type_num*
xlDialogGallery3dColumn	*type_num*
xlDialogGallery3dLine	*type_num*
xlDialogGallery3dPie	*type_num*
xlDialogGallery3dSurface	*type_num*
xlDialogGalleryArea	*type_num, delete_overlay*
xlDialogGalleryBar	*type_num, delete_overlay*
xlDialogGalleryColumn	*type_num, delete_overlay*
xlDialogGalleryCustom	*name_text*
xlDialogGalleryDoughnut	*type_num, delete_overlay*
xlDialogGalleryLine	*type_num, delete_overlay*
xlDialogGalleryPie	*type_num, delete_overlay*
xlDialogGalleryRadar	*type_num, delete_overlay*
xlDialogGalleryScatter	*type_num, delete_overlay*
xlDialogGoalSeek	*target_cell, target_value, variable_cell*
xlDialogGridlines	*x_major, x_minor, y_major, y_minor, z_major, z_minor, 2D_effect*
xlDialogImportTextFile	
xlDialogInsert	*shift_num*
xlDialogInsertHyperlink	
xlDialogInsertNameLabel	
xlDialogInsertObject	*object_class, file_name, link_logical, display_icon_logical, icon_file, icon_number, icon_label*
xlDialogInsertPicture	*file_name, filter_number*
xlDialogInsertTitle	*chart, y_primary, x_primary, y_secondary, x_secondary*
xlDialogLabelProperties	*accel_text, accel2_text, 3d_shading*
xlDialogListboxProperties	*range, link, drop_size, multi_select, 3d_shading*
xlDialogMacroOptions	*macro_name, description, menu_on, menu_text, shortcut_on, shortcut_key, function_category, status_bar_text, help_id, help_file*
xlDialogMailEditMailer	*to_recipients, cc_recipients, bcc_recipients, subject, enclosures, which_address*
xlDialogMailLogon	*name_text, password_text, download_logical*

Table A-1. Dialogs collection constants (continued)

Constant	Show arguments
xlDialogMailNextLetter	
xlDialogMainChart	*type_num, stack, 100, vary, overlap, drop, hilo, overlap%, cluster, angle*
xlDialogMainChartType	*type_num*
xlDialogMenuEditor	
xlDialogMove	*x_pos, y_pos, window_text*
xlDialogNew	*type_num, xy_series, add_logical*
xlDialogNewWebQuery	
xlDialogNote	*add_text, cell_ref, start_char, num_chars*
xlDialogObjectProperties	*placement_type, print_object*
xlDialogObjectProtection	*locked, lock_text*
xlDialogOpen	*file_text, update_links, read_only, format, prot_pwd, write_res_pwd, ignore_rorec, file_origin, custom_delimit, add_logical, editable, file_access, notify_logical, converter*
xlDialogOpenLinks	*document_text1, document_text2, ..., read_only, type_of_link*
xlDialogOpenMail	*subject, comments*
xlDialogOpenText	*file_name, file_origin, start_row, file_type, text_qualifier, consecutive_delim, tab, semicolon, comma, space, other, other_char, field_info*
xlDialogOptionsCalculation	*type_num, iter, max_num, max_change, update, precision, date_1904, calc_save, save_values*
xlDialogOptionsChart	*display_blanks, plot_visible, size_with_window*
xlDialogOptionsEdit	*incell_edit, drag_drop, alert, entermove, fixed, decimals, copy_objects, update_links, move_direction, autocomplete, animations*
xlDialogOptionsGeneral	*R1C1_mode, dde_on, sum_info, tips, recent_files, old_menus, user_info, font_name, font_size, default_location, alternate_location, sheet_num, enable_under*
xlDialogOptionsListsAdd	*string_array*
xlDialogOptionsListsAdd	*import_ref, by_row*
xlDialogOptionsME	*def_rtl_sheet, crsr_mvmt, show_ctrl_char, gui_lang*
xlDialogOptionsTransition	*menu_key, menu_key_action, nav_keys, trans_eval, trans_entry*
xlDialogOptionsView	*formula, status, notes, show_info, object_num, page_breaks, formulas, gridlines, color_num, headers, outline, zeros, hor_scroll, vert_scroll, sheet_tabs*
xlDialogOutline	*auto_styles, row_dir, col_dir, create_apply*
xlDialogOverlay	*type_num, stack, 100, vary, overlap, drop, hilo, overlap%, cluster, angle, series_num, auto*

Constant	Show arguments
xlDialogOverlayChartType	*type_num*
xlDialogPageSetup	*head, foot, left, right, top, bot, hdng, grid, h_cntr, v_cntr, orient, paper_size, scale, pg_num, pg_order, bw_cells, quality, head_margin, foot_margin, notes, draft*
xlDialogPageSetup	*head, foot, left, right, top, bot, size, h_cntr, v_cntr, orient, paper_size, scale, pg_num, bw_chart, quality, head_margin, foot_margin, draft*
xlDialogPageSetup	*head, foot, left, right, top, bot, orient, paper_size, scale, quality, head_margin, foot_margin, pg_num*
xlDialogParse	*parse_text, destination_ref*
xlDialogPasteNames	
xlDialogPasteSpecial	*paste_num, operation_num, skip_blanks, transpose*
xlDialogPasteSpecial	*rowcol, titles, categories, replace, series*
xlDialogPasteSpecial	*paste_num*
xlDialogPasteSpecial	*format_text, pastelink_logical, display_icon_logical, icon_file, icon_number, icon_label*
xlDialogPatterns	*apattern, afore, aback, newui*
xlDialogPatterns	*lauto, lstyle, lcolor, lwt, hwidth, hlength, htype*
xlDialogPatterns	*bauto, bstyle, bcolor, bwt, shadow, aauto, apattern, afore, aback, rounded, newui*
xlDialogPatterns	*bauto, bstyle, bcolor, bwt, shadow, aauto, apattern, afore, aback, invert, apply, newfill*
xlDialogPatterns	*lauto, lstyle, lcolor, lwt, tmajor, tminor, tlabel*
xlDialogPatterns	*lauto, lstyle, lcolor, lwt, apply, smooth*
xlDialogPatterns	*lauto, lstyle, lcolor, lwt, mauto, mstyle, mfore, mback, apply, smooth*
xlDialogPatterns	*type, picture_units, apply*
xlDialogPhonetic	
xlDialogPivotCalculatedField	
xlDialogPivotCalculatedItem	
xlDialogPivotClientServerSet	
xlDialogPivotFieldGroup	*start, end, by, periods*
xlDialogPivotFieldProperties	*name, pivot_field_name, new_name, orientation, function, formats*
xlDialogPivotFieldUngroup	
xlDialogPivotShowPages	*name, page_field*
xlDialogPivotSolveOrder	
xlDialogPivotTableOptions	

Table A-1. Dialogs collection constants (continued)

Constant	Show arguments
xlDialogPivotTableWizard	*type, source, destination, name, row_grand, col_grand, save_data, apply_auto_format, auto_page, reserved*
xlDialogPlacement	*placement_type*
xlDialogPrint	*range_num, from, to, copies, draft, preview, print_ what, color, feed, quality, y_resolution, selection, printer_text, print_to_file, collate*
xlDialogPrinterSetup	*printer_text*
xlDialogPrintPreview	
xlDialogPromote	*rowcol*
xlDialogProperties	*title, subject, author, keywords, comments*
xlDialogProtectDocument	*contents, windows, password, objects, scenarios*
xlDialogProtectSharing	
xlDialogPublishAsWebPage	
xlDialogPushbuttonProperties	*default_logical, cancel_logical, dismiss_logical, help_logical, accel_text, accel_text2*
xlDialogReplaceFont	*font_num, name_text, size_num, bold, italic, underline, strike, color, outline, shadow*
xlDialogRoutingSlip	*recipients, subject, message, route_num, return_ logical, status_logical*
xlDialogRowHeight	*height_num, reference, standard_height, type_num*
xlDialogRun	*reference, step*
xlDialogSaveAs	*document_text, type_num, prot_pwd, backup, write_res_ pwd, read_only_rec*
xlDialogSaveCopyAs	*document_text*
xlDialogSaveNewObject	
xlDialogSaveWorkbook	*document_text, type_num, prot_pwd, backup, write_res_ pwd, read_only_rec*
xlDialogSaveWorkspace	*name_text*
xlDialogScale	*cross, cat_labels, cat_marks, between, max, reverse*
xlDialogScale	*min_num, max_num, major, minor, cross, logarithmic, reverse, max*
xlDialogScale	*cat_labels, cat_marks, reverse, between*
xlDialogScale	*series_labels, series_marks, reverse*
xlDialogScale	*min_num, max_num, major, minor, cross, logarithmic, reverse, min*
xlDialogScenarioAdd	*scen_name, value_array, changing_ref, scen_comment, locked, hidden*
xlDialogScenarioCells	*changing_ref*

Table A-1. Dialogs collection constants (continued)

Constant	Show arguments
xlDialogScenarioEdit	*scen_name, new_scenname, value_array, changing_ref, scen_comment, locked, hidden*
xlDialogScenarioMerge	*source_file*
xlDialogScenarioSummary	*result_ref, report_type*
xlDialogScrollbarProperties	*value, min, max, inc, page, link, 3d_shading*
xlDialogSelectSpecial	*type_num, value_type, levels*
xlDialogSendMail	*recipients, subject, return_receipt*
xlDialogSeriesAxes	*axis_num*
xlDialogSeriesOptions	
xlDialogSeriesOrder	*chart_num, old_series_num, new_series_num*
xlDialogSeriesShape	
xlDialogSeriesX	*x_ref*
xlDialogSeriesY	*name_ref, y_ref*
xlDialogSetBackgroundPicture	
xlDialogSetPrintTitles	*titles_for_cols_ref, titles_for_rows_ref*
xlDialogSetUpdateStatus	*link_text, status, type_of_link*
xlDialogShowDetail	*rowcol, rowcol_num, expand, show_field*
xlDialogShowToolbar	*bar_id, visible, dock, x_pos, y_pos, width, protect, tool_tips, large_buttons, color_buttons*
xlDialogSize	*width, height, window_text*
xlDialogSort	*orientation, key1, order1, key2, order2, key3, order3, header, custom, case*
xlDialogSort	*orientation, key1, order1, type, custom*
xlDialogSortSpecial	*sort_by, method, key1, order1, key2, order2, key3, order3, header, order, case*
xlDialogSplit	*col_split, row_split*
xlDialogStandardFont	*name_text, size_num, bold, italic, underline, strike, color, outline, shadow*
xlDialogStandardWidth	*standard_num*
xlDialogStyle	*bold, italic*
xlDialogSubscribeTo	*file_text, format_num*
xlDialogSubtotalCreate	*at_change_in, function_num, total, replace, pagebreaks, summary_below*
xlDialogSummaryInfo	*title, subject, author, keywords, comments*
xlDialogTable	*row_ref, column_ref*
xlDialogTabOrder	

Table A-1. Dialogs collection constants (continued)

Constant	Show arguments
xlDialogTextToColumns	*destination_ref, data_type, text_delim, consecutive_delim, tab, semicolon, comma, space, other, other_char, field_info*
xlDialogUnhide	*window_text*
xlDialogUpdateLink	*link_text, type_of_link*
xlDialogVbaInsertFile	*filename_text*
xlDialogVbaMakeAddIn	
xlDialogVbaProcedureDefinition	
xlDialogView3d	*elevation, perspective, rotation, axes, height%, autoscale*
xlDialogWebOptionsEncoding	
xlDialogWebOptionsFiles	
xlDialogWebOptionsFonts	
xlDialogWebOptionsGeneral	
xlDialogWebOptionsPictures	
xlDialogWindowMove	*x_pos, y_pos, window_text*
xlDialogWindowSize	*width, height, window_text*
xlDialogWorkbookAdd	*name_array, dest_book, position_num*
xlDialogWorkbookCopy	*name_array, dest_book, position_num*
xlDialogWorkbookInsert	*type_num*
xlDialogWorkbookMove	*name_array, dest_book, position_num*
xlDialogWorkbookName	*oldname_text, newname_text*
xlDialogWorkbookNew	
xlDialogWorkbookOptions	*sheet_name, bound_logical, new_name*
xlDialogWorkbookProtect	*structure, windows, password*
xlDialogWorkbookTabSplit	*ratio_num*
xlDialogWorkbookUnhide	*sheet_text*
xlDialogWorkgroup	*name_array*
xlDialogWorkspace	*fixed, decimals, r1c1, scroll, status, formula, menu_key, remote, entermove, underlines, tools, notes, nav_keys, menu_key_action, drag_drop, show_info*
xlDialogZoom	*magnification*

Common Programmatic IDs

Programmatic IDs (progIDs) are used by several methods to create new instances of objects. For example, the following code creates a new checkbox on the active worksheet:

```
Sub AddCheckBox( )
    Dim ole As OLEObject
    ' Add new check box.
    Set ole = ActiveSheet.OLEObjects.Add("Forms.CheckBox.1", _
        , , , , , , 60, 60, 100, 20)
    ' Select the check box.
    ole.Object.Value = True
    ' Set its caption
    ole.Object.Caption = "New Check Box"
End Sub
```

Table A-2 lists common applications and the objects that they provide, along with the progIDs used to create those objects in code.

Table A-2. Common programmatic IDs

Application	Object	ProgID
ActiveX Controls	CheckBox	Forms.CheckBox.1
	ComboBox	Forms.ComboBox.1
	CommandButton	Forms.CommandButton.1
	Frame	Forms.Frame.1
	Image	Forms.Image.1
	Label	Forms.Label.1
	ListBox	Forms.ListBox.1
	MultiPage	Forms.MultiPage.1
	OptionButton	Forms.OptionButton.1
	ScrollBar	Forms.ScrollBar.1
	SpinButton	Forms.SpinButton.1
	TabStrip	Forms.TabStrip.1
	TextBox	Forms.TextBox.1
	ToggleButton	Forms.ToggleButton.1
	Calendar	MSCal.Calendar
Microsoft Access	Application	Access.Application
	CurrentData	Access.CodeData
		Access.CurrentData
	CurrentProject	Access.CodeProject
		Access.CurrentProject
	DefaultWebOptions	Access.DefaultWebOptions
Microsoft Excel	Application	Excel.Application
	Workbook	Excel.AddIn
	Workbook	Excel.Chart
	Workbook	Excel.Sheet
Microsoft Graph	Application	MSGraph.Application

Table A-2. Common programmatic IDs (continued)

Application	Object	ProgID
	Chart	MSGraph.Chart
Microsoft Office Web Components	ChartSpace	OWC.Chart
	DataSourceControl	OWC.DataSourceControl
	ExpandControl	OWC.ExpandControl
	PivotTable	OWC.PivotTable
	RecordNavigationControl	OWC.RecordNavigationControl
	Spreadsheet	OWC.Spreadsheet
Microsoft Outlook	Application	Outlook.Application
Microsoft PowerPoint	Application	PowerPoint.Application
Microsoft Word	Application	Word.Application
	Document	Word.Document
	Template	Word.Template
	Global	Word.Global

Version Compatibility

See Chapter 6 for instructions on how to check the Excel version at runtime and recommendations on how to handle version differences. Table B-1 lists the Excel objects by year introduced. The sections that follow the table summarize the changes for each version. In this table, X=available, H=hidden or obsolete, and M=Macintosh only.

Table B-1. Excel objects listed by product version

| Object | Excel year (version) | | | | |
	1995 (7)	1997 (8)	2000 (9)	2002 (10)	2003 (11)
AddIn	X	X	X	X	X
Adjustments		X	X	X	X
AllowEditRange				X	X
Application	X	X	X	X	X
Arc	X	H	H	H	H
Areas	X	X	X	X	X
AutoCorrect	X	X	X	X	X
AutoFilter	X	X	X	X	X
AutoRecover				X	X
Axis	X	X	X	X	X
AxisTitle	X	X	X	X	X
Border	X	X	X	X	X
Button	X	H	H	H	H
CalculatedFields		X	X	X	X
CalculatedItems		X	X	X	X
CalculatedMember				X	X
CalloutFormat		X	X	X	X
CellFormat				X	X

Table B-1. Excel objects listed by product version (continued)

| Object | Excel year (version) | | | | |
	1995 (7)	1997 (8)	2000 (9)	2002 (10)	2003 (11)
Characters	X	X	X	X	X
Chart	X	X	X	X	X
ChartArea	X	X	X	X	X
ChartColorFormat		X	X	X	X
ChartFillFormat		X	X	X	X
ChartGroup	X	X	X	X	X
ChartObject	X	X	X	X	X
ChartTitle	X	X	X	X	X
CheckBox	X	H	H	H	H
ColorFormat		X	X	X	X
Comment		X	X	X	X
ConnectorFormat	X	X	X	X	X
ControlFormat		X	X	X	X
Corners	X	X	X	X	X
CubeField			X	X	X
CustomProperty				X	X
CustomView		X	X	X	X
DataLabel	X	X	X	X	X
DataTable		X	X	X	X
DefaultWebOptions			X	X	X
Diagram				X	X
DiagramNode				X	X
DiagramNodeChildren				X	X
Dialog	X	X	X	X	X
DialogFrame	X	H	H	H	H
DialogSheet	X	H	H	H	H
DisplayUnitLabel			X	X	X
DownBars	X	X	X	X	X
Drawing	X	H	H	H	H
DrawingObjects	X	H	H	H	H
DropDown	X	H	H	H	H
DropLines	X	X	X	X	X
EditBox	X	H	H	H	H
Error				X	X
ErrorBars	X	X	X	X	X

Object	Excel year (version)				
	1995 (7)	1997 (8)	2000 (9)	2002 (10)	2003 (11)
ErrorCheckingOptions				X	X
FillFormat		X	X	X	X
Filter			X	X	X
Floor			X	X	X
Font			X	X	X
FormatCondition		X	X	X	X
FreeformBuilder		X	X	X	X
Global	X	X	X	X	X
Graphic				X	X
Gridlines	X	X	X	X	X
GroupBox	X	H	H	H	H
GroupObject	X	H	H	H	H
GroupShapes		X	X	X	X
HiLoLines	X	X	X	X	X
HPageBreak		X	X	X	X
Hyperlink		X	X	X	X
Interior	X	X	X	X	X
Label	X	X	X	X	X
LeaderLines		X	X	X	X
Legend	X	X	X	X	X
LegendEntry	X	X	X	X	X
LegendKey	X	X	X	X	X
Line	X	H	H	H	H
LineFormat		X	X	X	X
LinkFormat	X	X	X	X	X
ListBox	X	H	H	II	II
ListColumn					X
ListDataFormat					X
ListObject					X
ListRow					X
Mailer	M	M	M	M	M
Menu	X	H	H	H	H
MenuBar	X	H	H	H	H
MenuItem	X	H	H	H	H
Menus	X	H	H	H	H

Table B-1. *Excel objects listed by product version (continued)*

Object	Excel year (version)				
	1995 (7)	1997 (8)	2000 (9)	2002 (10)	2003 (11)
Module	X	H	H	H	H
Name	X	X	X	X	X
ODBCError		X	X	X	X
OLEDBError			X	X	X
OLEFormat		X	X	X	X
OLEObject	X	X	X	X	X
OptionButton	X	H	H	H	H
Outline	X	X	X	X	X
Oval	X	H	H	H	H
PageSetup	X	X	X	X	X
Pane	X	X	X	X	X
Parameter		X	X	X	X
Phonetic			X	X	X
Picture	X	H	H	H	H
PictureFormat		X	X	X	X
PivotCache		X	X	X	X
PivotCell				X	X
PivotField		X	X	X	X
PivotFormula		X	X	X	X
PivotItem	X	X	X	X	X
PivotItemList				X	X
PivotLayout			X	X	X
PivotTable	X	X	X	X	X
PlotArea	X	X	X	X	X
Point	X	X	X	X	X
Protection				X	X
PublishObject			X	X	X
QueryTable		X	X	X	X
Range	X	X	X	X	X
RecentFile		X	X	X	X
Rectangle	X	H	H	H	H
RoutingSlip	X	X	X	X	X
RTD				X	X
Scenario	X	X	X	X	X
Scenarios	X	X	X	X	X

Table B-1. Excel objects listed by product version (continued)

Object	Excel year (version)				
	1995 (7)	1997 (8)	2000 (9)	2002 (10)	2003 (11)
ScrollBar	X	H	H	H	H
Series	X	X	X	X	X
SeriesLines	X	X	X	X	X
ShadowFormat		X	X	X	X
Shape		X	X	X	X
ShapeNode		X	X	X	X
ShapeRange		X	X	X	X
Sheets	X	X	X	X	X
SmartTag				X	X
SmartTagAction				X	X
SmartTagOptions				X	X
SmartTagRecognizer				X	X
SoundNote	X				
Speech				X	X
SpellingOptions				X	X
Spinner	X	H	H	H	H
Style	X	X	X	X	X
Tab				X	X
TextBox	X	H	H	H	H
TextEffectFormat		X	X	X	X
TextFrame		X	X	X	X
ThreeDFormat		X	X	X	X
TickLabels	X	X	X	X	X
Toolbar	X	H	H	H	H
ToolbarButton	X	H	H	H	H
Trendline	X	X	X	X	X
UpBars	X	X	X	X	X
UsedObjects				X	X
UserAccess				X	X
Validation		X	X	X	X
VPageBreak		X	X	X	X
Walls	X	X	X	X	X
Watch				X	X
WebOptions			X	X	X
Window	X	X	X	X	X

	Excel year (version)				
Object	1995 (7)	1997 (8)	2000 (9)	2002 (10)	2003 (11)
Workbook	X	X	X	X	X
Worksheet	X	X	X	X	X
WorksheetFunction	X	X	X	X	X
XmlDataBinding					X
XmlMap					X
XmlNamespace					X
XmlSchema					X
XPath					X

Summary of Version Changes

In 1997, Excel Version 8.0 introduced object-oriented programming features including events and classes. User forms replaced dialog sheets, and pivot table objects were expanded. Forms 2.0 controls and the following objects were introduced:

Adjustments	CalculatedFields	CalculatedItems
CalloutFormat	ChartColorFormat	ChartFillFormat
ColorFormat	Comment	ControlFormat
CustomView	DataTable	FillFormat
FormatCondition	FreeformBuilder	GroupShapes
HPageBreak	Hyperlink	LeaderLines
LineFormat	ODBCError	OLEFormat
Parameter	PictureFormat	PivotCache
PivotField	PivotFormula	QueryTable
RecentFile	ShadowFormat	Shape
ShapeNode	ShapeRange	TextEffectFormat
TextFrame	ThreeDFormat	Validation
VPageBreak		

In 2000, Excel Version 9.0 introduced Visual Basic Version 6.0 and made minor additions to the object model. Mainly, Version 9.0 added OLAP to pivot tables and enabled publishing to the Web. The following objects were introduced:

CubeField	DefaultWebOptions
DisplayUnitLabel	Filter
Floor	Font
OLEDBError	Phonetic
PivotLayout	PublishObject
WebOptions	

In 2002, Excel Version 10.0 added smart tags, worksheet errors and watches, speech, and edit ranges. The following objects were introduced:

AllowEditRange	AutoRecover
CalculatedMember	CellFormat
CustomProperty	Diagram
DiagramNodeChildren	Error
ErrorCheckingOptions	Graphic
PivotCell	PivotItemList
Protection	RTD
SmartTag	SmartTagAction
SmartTagOptions	SmartTagRecognizer
Speech	SpellingOptions
Tab	UsedObjects
UserAccess	Watch

In 2003, Excel Version 11.0 introduced lists, XML, SharePoint, and Integrated Rights Management (IRM) features. Version 11.0 included these new objects:

ListColumn	ListDataFormat
ListObject	ListRow
XmlDataBinding	XmlMap
XmlNamespace	XmlSchema
XPath	

Macintosh Compatibility

The Macintosh versions of Excel generally support a subset of the Excel 2002 features. Notably, Excel 2004 for the Macintosh does not support the XML features introduced in Excel 2003 for Windows.

Excel for the Macintosh uses Visual Basic Version 5.0, and the Macintosh platform does not support ActiveX, COM, or any Excel features that require those technologies. Specifically, the Forms 2.0 controls are not available. Use the Forms 1.0 controls from the Forms toolbar when working on the Macintosh or creating workbooks that will be shared with Macintosh users.

Index

We'd like to hear your suggestions for improving our indexes. Send email to *index@oreilly.com*.

D

DAO (Data Access Objects), 421
  creating a recordset, 422
  objects and members, 450–457
    Database and Databases, 450
    DbEngine object, 452
    Document and Documents, 453
    QueryDef and QueryDefs, 453
    Recordset and Recordsets, 455–457
  tasks for, 126
  working with, 437
data cubes (OLAP), 470, 475
data lists, 133
data types
  arrays, 60
  constants, 58
  conversions, 53
    Visual Basic functions for, 54
  Excel lists, 521
  keywords for working with, 54
  objects in a collection, 71
  reference types, 53
  size of, 53
  testing, functions for, 100
  user-defined, 63
  value types, 53
  Visual Basic variables, 52
Database object (DAO), 450
database objects, 133
database queries, 422, 468
  creating in code, 422
  ODBC, 497
  optimization with OLAP, 470, 475
  pivot caches based on, 493
database query (.iqy), 192
database query file (.dqy), 468
Databases collection (DAO), 450
DatabaseSort property (PivotField), 505
DataBinding method (XmlMap), 587
DataBodyRange (ListObject), 531
DataBodyRange (PivotTable), 480
data-entry dialog boxes, 793
data-entry forms, 794–798
  adding validation rules, 794
  designing your own, 798–813
    adding a button, 814
    choosing controls, 811–813
    controls and property settings, 800
    creating tabbed dialogs, 807–810
    enabling/disabling controls, 807
    keyboard access to controls, 811
    responding to form events, 800

    separating work and UI
      code, 802–806
    showing a form, 802
    using controls on
      worksheets, 813–816
  displaying from code, 797
  how they work, 794
  validation settings, 795
  validation, advanced, 797
DataEntryMode (Application), 218
DataFields method (PivotTable), 480
DataLabel object, 666–671
DataLabel property (Trendline), 692
DataLabelRange (PivotTable), 480
DataLabels collection, 666–671
DataLabels method (Series), 648
DataObject object, 931
DataPivotField (PivotTable), 480
DataRange method (PivotField), 505
DataTable method (Chart), 621
DataTable object, 643
DataType, 435
  PivotField object, 505
Date function, 91
date/time formats, not supported by
    lists, 522
dates and times
  minutes between saving of automatic
    recovery files, 252
  setting procedure to run at specific
    time, 238
  Visual Basic functions for, 90
DateSerial function, 91
DateValue function, 91
Day function, 91
DbEngine object (DAO), 452
DDE link, updates, 321
Debug.Print statement, displaying code
    results, 24
debugging Excel .NET
    applications, 960–962
decimal separators
  operator system settings, 248
  text file imported into query table, 431
DecimalPlaces property
    (ListDataFormat), 539
decimals, fixed decimal places for data
    entries, 227
DecimalSeparator (Application), 219
declarations
  constants, 58
  DLL functions, 888

HasTitle property (Chart), 624
HasUpDownBars property
    (ChartGroup), 632
HeaderMargin method (PageSetup), 408
headers and footers, adding graphic
    to, 412–414
headings (column), displaying, 258
Height property, 140
    Application object, 229
height, default row height in points, 339
HeightPercent property (Chart), 624
Help
    adding Contact Us and About
        commands, 758
    Excel objects, 122
    Visual Basic Help for Excel, 32–34
    WorksheetFunction members, 154
help, 185–188
    compiled help files, 188, 196
    HTML documentation for
        application, 185
    linking items to HTML help pages, 185
    links to Help from menu items, 186
    macros and user-defined functions, 234
    objects in COM applications, 900
    on user-defined functions, 188
Help method (Application), 185, 229
HelpContextId (CommandBarControl), 782
HelpFile property
    (CommandBarControl), 782
Hidden property, 141
    Range collection, 357
    Scenario object, 368
HiddenFields (PivotTable), 484
HiddenItems method (PivotField), 506
HiddenItemsList (PivotField), 507
HiddenLevels property (CubeField), 518
HideSelection property (ComboBox), 836
hierarchy, object, creating using
    collections, 168
HighlightChangesOnScreen
    (Workbook), 305
HighlightChangesOptions (Workbook), 305
HiLoLines method (ChartGroup), 632
HiLoLines object, 682
Hinstance method (Application), 230
history of workbook changes, 298
    keeping, 306
    purging, 315
horizontal scrollbar, displaying, 258
HorizontalAlignment method (Range), 357

HorizontalAlignment property
    (TextFrame), 743
HorizontalAlignment property (Title), 666
HorizontalFlip property (Shape), 723
Hour function, 91
HPageBreak object
    Delete method, 393
    members, 405
HPageBreaks collection, 392
    members, 405
HRESULT, mapping to .NET exception
    class, 950
HTML document, workbook based on, 316
HTML Help Workshop (Microsoft), 188
HTMLBody property (MailItem), 864
HTMLProject method (Workbook), 306
HtmlType property (PublishObject), 415
Hwnd method (Application), 230
Hyperlink object
    Delete method, 372
    members, 380–383
Hyperlink property (Shape), 723
hyperlinks, 370
    adding to list on SharePoint server, 526
    allowing insertion in worksheet, 995
    automatically reformatting protocols
        as, 211
    creating in code, 371
    creating in Excel, 370
    Excel menu items to Help, 186
    linking to location on worksheet, 371
    in workbooks, 304
    (see also linking)
Hyperlinks collection
    Add method, 371, 381
    Delete method, 372
    members, 380–383
Hyperlinks method
    Chart object, 380
    Range collection, 357
    Worksheet object, 335, 380
HyperlinkType (CommandBarButton), 785

I

Id property
    CommandBar object, 777
    CommandBarControl object, 782
ID property (Shape), 723
#If...Then...#End If compiler directive, 112
If statements, 65
Image object, 841

MailSystem method (Application), 235
mailto: protocol, 853
MaintainConnection (PivotCache), 495
MaintainConnection property
         (QueryTable), 427
MajorGridlines method (Axis), 639
MajorTickMark property (Axis), 640
MajorUnit property (Axis), 640
MajorUnitIsAuto property (Axis), 640
MajorUnitScale property (Axis), 640
MakeConnection method (PivotCache), 495
manual page breaks, 393, 405
manual testing, 181
ManualUpdate (PivotTable), 484
Map method (XPath), 595
MAPI mail sessions
    creating new, 235
    ending, 235
MapPaperSize (Application), 236
MarginBottom property (TextFrame), 744
MarginLeft property (TextFrame), 744
MarginRight property (TextFrame), 744
MarginTop property (TextFrame), 744
MarkerBackgroundColor (Series), 651
MarkerBackgroundColorIndex (Series), 651
MarkerForegroundColor (Series), 652
MarkerForegroundColorIndex (Series), 652
MarkerSize property (Series), 652
MarkerStyle property (Series), 652
Mask property (CommandBarButton), 786
MatchEntry property (ComboBox), 838
MatchFound property (ComboBox), 838
matching patterns of characters, 83
MatchRequired property (ComboBox), 838
math, 79–81
    functions derived from intrinsic Visual
         Basic functions, 80
    Visual Basic functions, 79
Max property (ScrollBar, SpinButton), 846
MaxChange (Application), 236
MaxCharacters property
         (ListDataFormat), 540
Maximum method (RecentFiles), 329
MaximumScale property (Axis), 640
MaximumScaleIsAuto property (Axis), 641
MaxIterations (Application), 236
MaxLength property (ComboBox), 838
MaxNumber property
         (ListDataFormat), 540
MaxRecords property (QueryDef), 454
MDX method (PivotTable), 484

Me keyword (Visual Basic), active object
         and, 123–126
members, object, 114–117
    Application, 207–208
    common, 136–142
       Activate method, 137
       adding/deleting objects through
            collections, 139
       Application, 136
       Creator, 136
       listed by category, 136
       names and values, 137
       PrintOut and PrintPreview
            methods, 141
       size and position, changing, 140
    common to most collections, 123
    events, 117
    global, 116
    Global object, 147
    grouping of related members, 115
    WorksheetFunction object, 148–154
memory leaks, 173
MemoryUsed method (PivotCache), 495
menu items (Excel), links to Help, 186
MenuAnimationStyle (CommandBars), 777
menus, 749–763
    adding item for add-in, 878–880
    adding, objects used for, 127
    changes to, 750
    context menus, building, 760–763
       changing context menus, 762
       creating new menus, 763
       restoring context menus, 762
    creating using toolbars, 764
    Excel 4.0, displaying, 221
    right-clicking to display properties, 751
    top-level, 750–756
       assigning accelerator and shortcut
            keys, 754–755
       changing existing menus, 753–754
       creating on Excel menu bar, 751
       saving and distributing, 756
    top-level, creating in code, 756–760
       changing existing menus, 758
       removing on close, 757
       resetting existing menus, 759
    types in Excel, 749
Merge method, Range object, 358
MergeArea method (Range), 358
MergeCells property (Range), 358
MergeLabels (PivotTable), 484
MergeWorkbook method (Workbook), 308

RefreshPeriod property
   PivotCache object, 497
   QueryTable, 908
   QueryTable object, 429, 918
RefreshStyle property, 906
RefreshStyle property (QueryTable), 429, 919
RefreshTable method (PivotTable), 488
RegisteredFunctions method
         (Application), 241
RegisterXLL method (Application), 241
regression tests, 182
Regroup method (ShapeRange), 726
RejectAllChanges method (Workbook), 281,
         294, 315
relative references
   conversions, 217
   using when recording, 241
ReleaseFocus method (CommandBars), 778
ReloadAs method (Workbook), 316
RelyOnCSS (WebOptions), 419
RelyOnVML (WebOptions), 419
Remove method
   collections, 168
   Control object, 830
   UserPermission object, 1007
RemoveAll method (Permission), 1007
RemoveDocument method, 288
RemoveItem method
   ComboBox object, 838
   CommandBarComboBox object, 790
RemovePersonalInformation
         (Workbook), 316
RemoveUser method (Workbook), 316
Repaint method (UserForm), 822
Repeat item, Edit menu, 238
Repeat method (Application), 242
Repeating property (XPath), 596
Replace function, 82
Replace method, 89
   Range collection, 345, 361
ReplaceFormat method (Application), 242
ReplacementList method (AutoCorrect), 252
Reply method (Workbook), 317
ReplyAll method (Workbook), 317
ReplyWithChanges method
         (Workbook), 317
Representational State Transfer (REST), 927
   online information about, 932
RequestPermissionURL (Permission), 1007
Require Variable Declaration (Visual
         Basic), 18
Required property (ListDataFormat), 540

requirements for an application, 179
   design versus, 179
   hardware issues, 185
   questions answered by, 179
RerouteConnections method (Shape), 704, 726
reserved words, 115
Reset function, 92
Reset method, 759
   CommandBar object, 779
   CommandBarControl object, 784
   restoring context menus, 762
   RoutingSlip object, 867
ResetColors method (Workbook), 317
ResetPositionsSideBySide method
         (Window), 261
ResetTimer method
   PivotCache object, 497
   QueryTable object, 430, 919
Resize method (Range), 361
resizing windows, 259
resolving conflicts
   changes in linked files, 286
   lists, 522, 527
ResultRange property (QueryTable), 430, 919
results
   checking in Visual Basic, 100–102
   viewing, 21–25
return values, 40
   procedures, 41
ReturnWhenDone property
         (RoutingSlip), 867
ReversePlotOrder property (Axis), 642
review of a workbook, ending, 303
RevisionNumber (Workbook), 317
Right function, 82
RightAngleAxes property (Chart), 626
RightFooter method (PageSetup), 411
RightFooterPicture (PageSetup), 412
RightHeader property (PageSetup), 412
RightHeaderPicture method
         (PageSetup), 412
RightMargin property (PageSetup), 412
right-to-left display of Excel, 259
right-to-left languages, 217
RmDir function, 93, 98
Rnd function, 80
RobustConnect (PivotCache), 497
role-based security, 975
RollbackTrans method (Connection), 441
RootElementName (XmlMap), 589
RootElementNamespace
   XmlDataBinding object, 591
   XmlMap, 589

SourceURI (XmlDataBinding), 591
Space function, 82, 90
Spc function, 93
Speak method (Speech), 67, 389
SpeakCellOnEnter (Speech), 389
SpecialCells method (Range), 364
SpecialEffect property (UserForm), 825
Speech method (Application), 245
Speech object, 68, 378
    members, 388
spelling errors in Visual Basic, 15
spelling, checking, 214, 334, 352
SpellingOptions method (Application), 245
SpellingOptions object, members, 253
SpinButton control, using to get value of a
    cell, 815
SpinButton object, 846
Split function, 82, 866
Split property (Window), 262
    closing panes, 265
SplitColumn method (Window), 263
SplitHorizontal method (Window), 263
SplitRow method (Window), 263
SplitType property (ChartGroup), 633
SplitValue property (ChartGroup), 634
SplitVertical method (Window), 263
Sql property (PivotCache), 498
SQL property (QueryDef), 455
SQL Server database, creating pivot table
    from, 475
ss namespace prefix, 559
stack, 53
StandardFont method (Application), 246
StandardFontSize (Application), 246
StandardFormula property (PivotField), 509
StandardHeight method (Worksheet), 339
StandardWidth method (Worksheet), 339
starting and stopping code in Excel, 20
startup
    AltStartupPath (Application), 210
    setting startup paths, 204
StartupPath (Application), 246
StartupPath property (Application), 205
State property
    CommandBarButton object, 786
    Record object, 445
statements, 7
    conditional, 65
        in Visual Basic programs, 36
    failure to terminate, 15
    listing of completing items and arguments
        in Visual Basic, 13
    loops, 67–71

static classes or code modules (.NET), 942
Static procedures, 58
Static variables, 57
    destroying, 64
status bar, displaying, 222
Status property (RoutingSlip), 867
StatusBar (Application), 246
Step keyword, 70
StoreLicenses (Permission), 1008
StrComp function, 81, 83
StrConv function, 82, 85
String class (.NET), 938
String function, 82, 90
String type, length of, 53
strings, 81–90
    changing, 89
    comparing, 82–85
    converting, 85–89
    repeating characters, 90
    Visual Basic string functions, 81
    Visual Basic string operators, 81
    Visual Basic String variables, 53
    working with, using DLL
        functions, 890–892
structures, 63
Style property
    ComboBox object, 839
    CommandBarButton object, 787
    CommandBarComboBox object, 790
    MultiPage object, 844
    Range object, 364
Styles property (Workbook), 323
stylesheets, XML transformation, 554
Sub procedures, 40
    results, 41
SubAddress method (Hyperlink), 383
Subject property
    AddIn object, 886
    MailItem Object, 865
    RoutingSlip object, 867
    Workbook object, 323
SubtotalHiddenPageItems (PivotTable), 490
SubtotalName property (PivotField), 509
Subtotals property (PivotField), 509
SummaryColumn method (Outline), 343
SummaryRow method (Outline), 343
SurfaceGroup method (Chart), 628
Switch statements, 67
SyncScrollingSideBySide property
    (Windows), 263
syntax errors, 11
    fixing, 12–14

About the Author

Jeff Webb is one of the original Visual Basic team members. He was intensely involved with Excel VBA and conceived the first Office Developer's Kit. Jeff also wrote the first book on Excel VBA, *Using Excel Visual Basic for Applications* (Que), which has remained in print for an amazing 12 years.

Steve Saunders is also one of the original Visual Basic team members, as well as the lead designer of the original Microsoft Access online documentation system. He has been an active Access developer for over 10 years and has been a technical editor and reviewer for numerous books on Access, Word, and Excel programming. He is a frequent programmer writer consultant for Microsoft, lending his expertise to a variety of Office products and technologies.

Colophon

The animal on the cover of *Programming Excel with VBA and .NET* is a shoveler duck (*Anas clypeata*). Native to North America and much of the northern terrain of Europe and Asia, shovelers are easily distinguished from other breeds of duck by their oblong, spoon-shaped bills. Shoveler ducks are also characterized by their sexual dimorphism; the male of the species has more ostentatious coloring, with a lustrous green head, neck, and speculum, whereas the shoveler female is tinted in a more subdued palette of browns, grays, and blacks. Both genders have light-blue forewing feathers, visible only when the birds are in flight.

Shoveler ducks subsist in the open wetlands on a diet that consists largely of particles of plant and animal matter, including seeds, leaves, stems, mollusks, and insects. They feed by drawing water into their large spatulate bills, which are covered by approximately 110 teethlike projections called lamellae that filter out food for consumption.

Breeding season for shovelers typically runs from April to June. The female builds her nest on dry land, twirling her body on the ground to dig out a cup-shaped hole, which she lines with grass and feathers. She lays anywhere from 8 to 12 olive-colored eggs, which incubate for up to 25 days. During this time, the shoveler female is extremely protective of her offspring; if forced off her nest, she will frequently defecate on her eggs, a maneuver believed to discourage predation.

The cover image is from the Dover Pictorial Archive. The cover font is Adobe ITC Garamond. The text font is Linotype Birka; the heading font is Adobe Myriad Condensed; and the code font is LucasFont's TheSans Mono Condensed.

Related Titles from O'Reilly

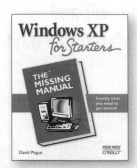

Windows Users

Access Cookbook,
  2nd Edition

Access 2003 Personal Trainer

Access 2003 for Starters:
  The Missing Manual

Access Database Design &
  Programming, *3rd Edition*

Analyzing Business Data
  with Excel

Excel Annoyances

Excel Hacks

Excel Pocket Guide

Excel 2003 Personal Trainer

Excel: The Missing Manual

Excel for Starters:
  The Missing Manual

Excel Scientific and Engineering
  Cookbook

Fixing Access Annoyances

Fixing PowerPoint Annoyances

FrontPage 2003:
  The Missing Manual

Outlook 2000 in a Nutshell

Outlook Pocket Guide

PC Annoyances,
  2nd Edition

PCs: The Missing Manual

Photoshop Elements 4:
  The Missing Manual

PowerPoint 2003 Personal Trainer

QuickBooks 2006:
  The Missing Manual

Quicken 2006 for Starters:
  The Missing Manual

Windows XP Annoyances
  For Geeks

Windows XP Cookbook

Windows XP Hacks,
  2nd Edition

Windows XP Home
  Edition: The Missing Manual,
  2nd Edition

Windows XP in a Nutshell,
  2nd Edition

Windows XP Personal Trainer

Windows XP Pocket Guide

Windows XP Power Hound

Windows XP Pro:
  The Missing Manual,
  2nd Edition

Windows XP for Starters:
  The Missing Manual

Windows XP Unwired

Word Annoyances

Word Hacks

Word Pocket Guide,
  2nd Edition

Word 2003 Personal Trainer

O'REILLY®

Our books are available at most retail and online bookstores.

To order direct: 1-800-998-9938 • *order@oreilly.com* • *www.oreilly.com*

Online editions of most O'Reilly titles are available by subscription at *safari.oreilly.com*